THE
BARONETAGE
OF
ENGLAND,
OR THE
HISTORY
OF THE
ENGLISH BARONETS,
AND SUCH
BARONETS OF SCOTLAND,
AS ARE OF ENGLISH FAMILIES;
WITH
GENEALOGICAL TABLES,
AND ENGRAVINGS OF THEIR
ARMORIAL BEARINGS;
COLLECTED FROM THE PRESENT BARONETAGES—APPROVED HISTORIANS—PUBLIC RECORDS—
AUTHENTIC MANUSCRIPTS—WELL ATTESTED PEDIGREES—AND PERSONAL INFORMATION.

BY THE REV. WILLIAM BETHAM,
EDITOR OF THE GENEALOGICAL TABLES OF THE SOVEREIGNS OF THE WORLD.

It is hardly necessary to observe, that Genealogy is so intimately connected with Historical Knowledge, that it is impossible to arrive at any proficiency in the one, without being minutely versed in the other.
RICHARDSON, on the Languages, &c. of the Eastern Nations, p. 74.

VOL. I.

IPSWICH:
PRINTED BY BURRELL AND BRANSBY,
FOR WILLIAM MILLER, OLD BOND-STREET, LONDON.

1801.

TO THE MOST NOBLE

JAMES CECIL, MARQUIS OF SALISBURY,

VISCOUNT CRANBORN,

LORD CHAMBERLAIN OF HIS MAJESTY'S HOUSEHOLD,

LORD LIEUTENANT, CUSTOS ROTULORUM,

AND COLONEL OF THE MILITIA OF THE COUNTY OF HERTS,

AND HIGH STEWARD OF HERTFORD;

VICE PRESIDENT OF ST. GEORGE'S HOSPITAL,

AND OF THE PHILANTHROPIC SOCIETY;

K.G. L.L.D. AND F.R.S.

THE FIRST VOLUME OF THE

BARONETAGE OF ENGLAND,

IS MOST HUMBLY INSCRIBED,

BY

HIS LORDSHIP'S

MOST OBLIGED, AND MOST OBEDIENT

SERVANT,

WILLIAM BETHAM.

Windham Press is committed to bringing the lost cultural heritage of ages past into the 21st century through high-quality reproductions of original, classic printed works at affordable prices.

This book has been carefully crafted to utilize the original images of antique books rather than error-prone OCR text. This also preserves the work of the original typesetters of these classics, unknown craftsmen who laid out the text, often by hand, of each and every page you will read. Their subtle art involving judgment and interaction with the text is in many ways superior and more human than the mechanical methods utilized today, and gave each book a unique, hand-crafted feel in its text that connected the reader organically to the art of bindery and book-making.

We think these benefits are worth the occasional imperfection resulting from the age of these books at the time of scanning, and their vintage feel provides a connection to the past that goes beyond the mere words of the text.

As bibliophiles, we are always seeking perfection in our work, so please notify us of any errors in this book by emailing us at corrections@windhampress.com. Our team is motivated to correct errors quickly so future customers are better served. Our mission is to raise the bar of quality for reprinted works by a focus on detail and quality over mass production. To peruse our catalog of carefully curated classic works, please visit our online store at www.windhampress.com.

PREFACE

TO THE

FIRST VOLUME.

FIVE years are now elapsed, since I first announced to the public, my wish, if suitable encouragement should be afforded me, to prepare a NEW AND CORRECT BARONETAGE OF ENGLAND; and I have, from that time, been diligently employed in collecting materials for that purpose. The first volume I now present to my subscribers, trusting, that the large additions I have made to every preceding publication of this nature, will both plead my excuse for the delay, which has unavoidably taken place, and prove a sufficient apology to every gentleman to whom I have applied for the importunity with which I have solicited information from their respective families.

The propriety of handing down to posterity, the history of an order of men, so highly favoured by their sovereign as the Baronets of England, whose distinction is hereditary, and from among whom the Peerage has been always, in so great a measure formed, that they have been emphatically called the stem of nobility, will, I trust, not be questioned.

" The genius, the virtues, and atchievements of eminent men, ought to be remembered; and even those, who although not prominent in public affairs, or engaged in pursuits interesting to strangers, had in their private spheres demeaned themselves with propriety, and supported the line of an eminent family with respectability, ought not to be forgotten: the line of a family may fail, but such a publication as this will preserve it in the recollection of the public."*

But, that I may not seem to arrogate to myself the merit of an original work, or to depreciate the labours of my predecessors in this line of history, it may perhaps be expected of me, to render some account of them, and the aid I have derived from their productions.

The first attempt, that I know of, to accomplish a history of the Baronets of England, was made in the year 1720, by Arthur Collins, Esq. whose long life was principally devoted to genealogical enquiries, with advantages few persons ever before possessed. His book, indeed, abounded with mistakes, as all such works must necessarily do, till revised and improved by new editions: for there will be always found in them many things to be corrected and added. Indeed, they ought to have a kind of *floating title* affixed to them, expressive of their imperfect state, similar to what Pliny tells us was practised by the greatest painters and statuaries of antiquity, such as *Apelles faciebat aut Polycletus*, but not *fecit;* claiming an indulgence to the artist, as if he was employed to his last moments in correcting the faults of his composition, but acknowledges that he had not been able to give it ultimate perfection.

In 1741, a complete history of the English Baronets, in 5 vols. 8vo. was given to the world by Mr. Wotton, sometimes attributed to the above-mentioned Arthur Collins, Esq. who was indeed a great encourager of the work, and to whom Wotton acknowledges himself considerably indebted. It contains a great deal of information; the indexes are copious and correct; and, upon the whole, it is not only a laborious, but useful performance.

The next work on this subject was published by Almon, in three small pocket volumes, in 1769, which gives the baronets an alphabetical order, but on a very contracted plan.

The great alterations that took place from 1741 to 1771, induced Kimber and Johnson to undertake a new account of the Baronetage, in three vols. 8vo. which

* Baronetage of Scotland, pref. fo. ii.

is principally an abridgement of Wotton, with the addition of a short history of 74 new-created baronets. Much historical matter, relating to families, which ought to have been preserved; many of the collateral branches, and all the monumental inscriptions, are omitted.

Of all these works, therefore, Wotton's is unquestionably the best, as far as it goes, viz. to the year 1741. But there is one imperfection incident to this, and indeed to every genealogical account I have seen, of the hereditary dignities of England, which is, that for the want of a systematic mode of bringing down the descent, and arranging the collateral lines, it becomes extremely difficult to disjoin the one from the other; and this inconvenience is very much increased, by the frequent recurrence of the same christian names, generally found in the contemporary members of the same family.

This defect I have endeavoured to remove: first, by marking numerically the several stages of descent in the principal branch, from the person who may be considered as the first known individual of that stock; which will instantly shew the presumed antiquity of each family: secondly, by marking, in a similar manner, the different successions of the BARONETS; but with Roman instead of Arabic numerals: thirdly, by throwing into a note, at the bottom of the page, the monumental inscriptions, and sometimes the collateral branches, with other incidental matter, which might otherwise perplex the context, and interrupt the easy deduction of the pedigree: and fourthly, by subjoining to the account of each family a complete GENEALOGICAL TABLE, containing the names, alliances and collateral branches, with numbers corresponding to those of the historical part; the principal descent being always marked out by blacker lines, in the mode I have adopted in my GENEALOGICAL TABLES, in folio, dedicated to his Majesty, which have already been distinguished by the public favour.

With the same view I have in many places altered the phraseology of my predecessors, where I have thought a less quaint and antiquated style than that employed by them, might prove more agreeable to my readers, or might conduce to a greater degree of correctness, and better elucidation of the subject.

When it is considered, that all the above-mentioned Baronetages are extremely scarce—that numerous changes have taken place since the last was published—that several creations have been absorbed, in higher titles,—several extinct—and that since the time of Wotton's writing, to the end of the year 1800, no less than 262 baronets have been added to the list; that of these many are the representatives of ancient families, who have held an important place in the community; many the descendants by collateral or female lines, of those, in whom titles have become extinct; and many who have been raised to the dignity, by the favour of their sovereign, as a reward for the honourable discharge of civil employment; or important duties performed in the naval or military service of the country; I shall not be deemed presumptious in saying, that a *new* and *correct English Baronetage*, is an undertaking highly expedient at the present moment, and if duly executed, worthy the public consideration and favour.

To enable myself to execute this work with tolerable success, I have had recourse to general and provincial history, to the Biographia Britannica, the printed narratives of parliamentary, judicial, naval, and military transactions, to a variety of original papers, and to scattered intimations or enquiries in the Gentleman's Magazine, the learned editor of which is entitled to the thanks of every traveller in the road of genealogical information. These various repositories have elucidated many dubious points which remained obscure, and brought forth much information which was unattainable at an earlier period.

But had even these, extensive as they are, been the only materials I needed, to give that ultimate fullness and correctness to my work, which I wished it to possess, I might certainly have given much greater dispatch to my undertaking, by digesting them under their proper heads, as my work proceeded, a labour requiring far less time and exertion than I had prescribed to myself. In future, there is reason to hope, much greater expedition will be practicable. Sensible, however, that I must have incurred the imputation of neglect, and that my history must have been imperfect, if I had confined myself to dead authorities; I have unceasingly endeavoured to obtain communication from the Baronets themselves, and their families, by repeated solicitations; in consequence of which, I now feel it my duty to offer my sincere acknowledgements, for the encouragement I have received, and for the use obligingly allowed me, of the papers and authenticated pedigrees of a considerable number of this honourable body. I have also had the assistance of two interleaved baronetages, formerly belonging to that industrious compiler, the late

Mr. Longmate, and the manuscript notes of other persons: and have to return my best thanks, for the flattering countenance and aid of the gentlemen of the Heralds' College.

* To determine how far my efforts have succeeded, now lies in the candid judgment of my subscribers and that of the public at large. To myself I feel conscious, that I have not entered upon the undertaking without zeal, nor pursued it without industry: so that I trust I am not carried away, by an expectation entirely unfounded, in looking for their favourable decision. I also presume to flatter myself, that the production of my present volume, will induce some gentlemen to send me their commuications, who may hitherto, perhaps, have witheld them, from a doubt, whether the work was actually in a progressive state. They may rest assured that every due attention shall be given to them, and all books or papers carefully returned, as soon as the necessary extracts shall have been made from them. In addition to this, it is with confidence that I solicit of the candid reader, that the errors and imperfections which will unavoidably escape the utmost caution and vigilance of a compiler, will be forgiven. Such works as this cannot be correct at first; repeated examinations by the families themselves, are absolutely necessary to bring them to perfection. The remarks, therefore, of any judicious reader, will be thankfully attended to, and noticed, in a supplement to the second volume.

The arms have been executed by Mr. Mutlow, an artist eminent in that stile of engraving, upon plates to be annexed to each volume respectively, or finally bound up in a detached one, when the whole shall be completed. I doubt not, that the specimens now produced will, by their elegance and correctness, reflect credit upon him and me. They are numbered to correspond with the series of the text, according to the dates of the creation of each baronetage respectively; and those coats of arms, upon separate sheets, the plates of which have been presented to this work by subscribers, will also, when ready, be delivered to other purchasers: the proof impressions in each case, being selected for subscribers.

With them, I could wish to adhere to my original proposals of Four Guineas, for the common; and six for the fine paper; but I fear I shall be compelled to impose some further advance, on account of the excessive rise of paper, and all the charges attending printing. To non-subscribers, at present, the price of the former will be 1*l*. 6*s*. and for the latter 1*l*. 16*s*. each volume; as the only means of my obtaining any pecuniary compensation for the continual pursuit and labour of a valuable part of my life.

Having now stated every thing, that seemed incumbent upon me to submit to the public consideration, concerning the plan and execution of the work, I will beg leave to close this preface with a few general observations.

The love of Biography, and spirit of Genealogical inquiry, are principles naturally incident to the human mind. They have discovered themselves in every period of the world; in every progressive stage of ignorance, or knowledge; barbarism, or refinement: their exertions secure its due honour to departed virtue, and stimulate the living to honourable action, as the only sure road to future fame. Nothing will more promote a spirit of emulation, than the countenancing family repute: it was this, in a considerable degree, that heightened the valour of the ancient English. They well knew that the estimation of merit was not confined to the short period of their own lives; but that their good or evil actions, would transmit some degree of honour, or infamy, to their descendants.

It was then family vied with family, which should produce the greatest number of heroes, and other worthies. This was their incentive to magnanimity, hospitality, and many other virtues they possessed. This thirst after family renown, it was, together with the reflection on the example of their ancestors, that animated them in their bitterest conflict, and occasioned them to meet death rather with transport than reluctance. The histories of many noble families, will sufficiently verify this assertion, such as Percy, Howard, Vere, Neville, &c. &c.

When persons have been observed, to be filled with a just and due veneration of the virtues of their ancestors, I believe they have seldom been known very glaringly to deviate therefrom; but to imitate, if not improve upon them. I am persuaded, that next to religion, nothing has so strongly actuated mankind, nor indeed produced so many good and brave men, as their being inspired with a desire of keeping up to the examples of their forefathers.

Such a spirit, therefore (however visionary its basis) is nationally requisite, and should be cherished, particularly amongst a military people. We love to trace the events and characters of preceding ages; generally feeling a more lively interest in the characters, than in the events: and we are fond of comparing the persons and manners of the present period, enlightened by science, with those, which the diligence of the antiquarian, or the speculations of the philosopher, may delineate for our instruction and amusement. The labours of the biographer and the genealogist promote also the interests of virtue and honour, while they gratify the ingenuous thirst of knowledge. Who can read the life of any great and good man, without wishing to be like him? Or can number him amongst his own ancestors, without feeling a constant solicitude, to be thought worthy of his descent; and an ambition to claim a share in his posthumous reputation? The examples of infamy likewise, recorded in such memorials, have a strong natural tendency, to impress a perpetual attention upon us to avert the shame, which our own misconduct might throw upon those who are to come after us.

These reflections seem to apply, with great propriety, to the order of BARONETS of ENGLAND, who were, at their original institution,* carefully selected from the distinguished families of the gentry; with the indispensible requisite of an honourable descent: holding the next degree to Peerage, and secured by royal covenant of his majesty, James I. that neither he, nor his successors, should ever create any hereditary honour, between them and the peers of the realm. They have generally become a consequential part in the concerns of their respective counties; and, like them, they are a part of the aristocracy of the country; but without being marked, by the cautious jealousy of our constitution, as unfit to interfere in parliamentary elections.

During the century now just concluded, the number of Baronets has been greatly augmented; and although landed property has been much regarded in those promotions, yet they have been confined, less than formerly, to the description of men, for whom the title was first intended. The enlargement of empire, the extension of commerce, the advance of wealth and the polite arts, the frequent recurrence and wide operations of war, have perhaps induced a necessity for some new, but honourable descriptions of men to this titular distinction; and the successes of the

* Sir Oliver Lambert, having reduced the province of Ulster, in Ireland, the king, in order to preserve it in subjection, and encourage a plantation therein by the English, instituted the hereditary dignity of Baronet, May 11, 1611. They engaged singly to maintain 30 foot soldiers in Ireland, for three years, at the rate of 8d. English by the day; and to pay the first year's wages into the Exchequer, at one payment, upon passing their patents, which, with fees of honour, amounted to near 1200l.

war we are now unhappily engaged in, have added to the list of Baronets the names of many, whose gallantry has promoted the glory of the British name.

The wisdom of all ages has decided, that both personal and hereditary distinctions are expedient, for the prosperous maintenance of a great and flourishing nation. The extravagant demolition of all honours in France, has not yet invalidated the truth of that position, or brought any conviction of its absurdity to a well-thinking mind. At the beginning of the century, when titles were in estimation, they were pious to their God, and polite to their neighbours; at the end of it, when they were abolished, impiety and insolence were their boast and their pride! But whilst we admit the solidity of this opinion, we must also feel the urgent propriety, of preserving every source of honour free from the contamination of unworthy members,* or the depreciation arising from a great increase of their numbers, without adequate reason; so that personal distinction may imply personal virtue, either in the possessor, or his ancestors. Then every good subject, who admires the mixed and balanced constitution of his country, and feels that the beautiful fabric of civilized society, must be held together by a discrimination of ranks, restrained by an equality of civil rights, will see, without repining or envy, the distinctions conferred upon a fellow subject, by the favour of his sovereign, or the elevation of his family, to hereditary honour and precedency.

---

* Dec. 6, 1782, it was ordered, that no Baronet in future, shall have his name and title inserted in any deed or other instrument, until he shall have proved his right to such title in the Heralds' Office; and, I believe, until he had entered his pedigree there.

BARONETS

CREATED BY

KING JAMES I.

1. BACON of REDGRAVE, Suffolk.

Created Baronet of England May 22, 1611.

THE learned Cambden, in his Britannia, says, that Buckinghamshire and Bucknam in Norfolk, were so called from the buchen or beechen trees there growing, *Regio enim fagifera in Germania Buchonia vocatur;* and from thence it may be the surname of this family, being anciently written de Bachone or Bacchone, as Trithemius; or Baucan or Baccoun, as Matthew Westminster, and some old records call them; as well as the word bacon, both in Latin and English, for swines' flesh, which Cambden, Verstegan, and Minshew, say, came from the same word, because the best of that kind was made upon their feeding upon beechen mast; nor is this opinion more strained or absurd than from what some of the best families in the kingdom pretend and derive theirs, as *De Querceto, Fraxineto,* and *Saliceto,* for the names of Oakely, Ashley, and Willoughby, places where their ancestors first inhabited; or that of Plantagenet, the name of our former kings, taken from a broom branch usually worn by Henry II. or his ancestors. And true it is, that upon the monument of Thomas Bacon, in Brome church, in Suffolk, there is a tree engraven in brass, and a man resting under it; and so likewise I have been informed, that the first lord keeper, Sir Nicholas Bacon, with his two wives, is so pourtrayed in Culford House.*

The Bacons of Hesset were, from the first, men of the shade, not camp, and therefore, in those ages, more affected to hierogliphical devices and rebuses than armorial escutcheons: so Baldock, bishop of London, and lord chancellor of England in the time of Edward II. in our ladies' chapel at St. Paul's, to which he was

* MSS. by Rev. F. Blomefield.

a great benefactor, had the device of *bald-oaks* to perpetuate his name: and of later times, bishop Islip, in his great buildings, of one *falling from a tree*, to denote and continue his.*

Cambden further says, that Anverton in the county of Suffolk, was the seat of the ancient family of Bacon, who held the manor of Thornage, and that of Broma, by conducting all the footmen of Suffolk and Norfolk to the wars in Wales.†

An extract of the grant, &c. in the custody of Sir Edmund Bacon, Bart.

" To all and singular, as well nobles and gentils as others, to whom these presentes shall come, be seen, read, heard, or understande, we, Sir Gilbert Dethick, Kt. alias Garter Principall King at Arms; Robert Cook, Esq. alias Clarencieux King of Arms, of the south partes of Englonde; and William Flower, Esq. alias Norroy King of Arms, of the north partes of Englonde, beyond the river of Trent, send greeting, &c. Forasmuch as aunciently, &c. (in common form) emongest the number whereof, Sir NICHOLAS BACON, Kt. lord keeper of the great seal of Englonde, being one of the bearers of these tokens of honour, to witte, of arms with heaulme, mantells, force, and crest, and yet not mind to bear, use, or shew forth any other than such as he lawfully may, hath required us, the said kings of arms, to make search for the aunciend arms belonging unto him from his auncestors, and to that name and family whereof he is descended, at whose suit and request we have not only diligently sought in the registers and recordes of our office remaining in the College of Heraultes, kept and holden at Derbie Place within the city of London, but also examined his old writings, and certain books sometimes appertaining to the Abbey of Bury St. Edmund's, in the countie of Suffolk; together with diverse coppies of records remaining in the Tower of London, shewed unto us in our said office, by John Hunte of Little Bradley, in the countie of Suffolk, one of the gentlemen ushers to the said lord keeper, and by exact trial thereof we do find the said Sir NICHOLAS BACON, Kt. is the second son of Robert Bacon, late of Drinkston, in the said countie of Suffolk, Gent. which Robert was son and heir of John Bacon, son and heir of John Bacon, son and heir of Walter Bacon of Drinkstone aforesaid, son and heir of Robert Bacon, who lived in the times of King Henry IV. and King Henry V. and was high sheriffe of Norfolk and Suffolk in the fift year of the reign of King Henry IV. aforesaid, which Robert Bacon was son and heir of Henry Bacon, son and heir of Adam Bacon, son and heir of John Bacon, Kt. second son of Sir Edmund Bacon, Kt. and heir to dame Margery, the second wife of the said Sir Edmund Bacon, daughter and heir of Robert Quapladde, Esq. which Sir Edmund was son and heir of William Bacon, Esq. who lived in the time of the reign of King Edward II. and so finding, by disentes, the antiquities of his ancestors, we could not, without the great prejudice of him and his posterity, but accordingly assign unto him and them, all those arms descended unto him and them, for his and their ancestors, as doth and may appear by the descent and declaration before specified, that is to say, that he and they may bear two several coates of arms quarterly, as followeth:—The first for Bacon, gules on a chief silver, two mullets sables. The second for Quapladde Barrey, of six pieces, gold and azure, a bend gules. And for as much as there can be no certain proof made of any creast or cognisance belonging or appertaining to the said armes (as to very many ancient coat of armes there is none) we, the said Kings of Armes, by power and authoritie to us committed, and also with the consent of the high and mighty Prince Thomas, Duke of Norfolk, Erle Marechall of Englonde, have assigned, given and granted unto the aforesaid Sir NICHOLAS BACON, Kt. lord keeper of the great seal of England, to these his ancient armes, a creast due and lawful to be borne, that is to say, on a force silver, and gueles a bore passant, ermine mantely'd asure doubled gold, as more pleynly appeareth depicted in the margent; which armes and creast, and every part and parcell thereof, we, the said Kings of Armes do by these presentes ratifye, confirm, give and grant unto the said Sir NICHOLAS BACON, Kt. and to his posterity, for ever, &c. &c.

In witness, &c. Feb. 22, 1568.

G. DETHICK, alias Garter Principall King of Armes,
ROBERT COOKE, alias Clarencieux Roy D'Armes,
P. MOY WYLLAM FLOWER, alias Norroy Roy D'Armes."

See the pedigree as brought down in the second table. ‡

---

* MSS. by Rev. F. Blomefield. † Britan. p. 352, edit. 1594. ‡ Dethick's Grants, No. 157.

BACON OF REDGRAVE.

This descent from Grimbald, of his two sons, Radulphus unto Peter de Letheringset, and of Ranulphus unto Reginald de Bacon, with the history of the foundation and presentation unto the church of Letheringset, was transcribed out of a book belonging unto Binham Priory, by the Rev. Francis Blomefield, then (1735) in the custody of Sir Thomas Witherington, late one of the commissioners for the great seal, and is at large inserted in the book of evidences concerning this family; and in the said book, at large, a deed is, from Reginald Bacon (a) the son of Robert of Letheringset, unto the church of St. Mary of Binham, of eight-pence a year rent, issuing out of his lands in Letheringset; and another deed of the said Reginald, to Simon the son of Simon, of all the lands of Richard (b) at the church of Letheringset, his brother; and for farther proof of this, a fine was levied *Term Trin.* 1261, between Robert de Beverley, demandant, and Richard, prior of Binham, deforciant, of the moiety of the advowson of the church of Letheringset, which the said Robert had of the gift of Reginald Bacon (a) to be the right of the said Robert and his heirs. And in the plea roll, 1298, John de Cave is demandant against Henry Bacon (c) of Letheringset, tenent, of the moiety of one acre of land, to which the advowson of the moiety of the church of Letheringset belonged, whereof Robert de Beverley was seized in the time of Henry III. who dying without issue, it descended to William, his cousin and heir, which William gave the same to Hugh Cave, ancestor to the demandant.

Richard Bacon (d) of Lodne in Suffolk, who married Alice, daughter of Conan, son of Elias de Moulton, was a great benefactor to Bungay Abbey,* and he or another Richard de Bacon was founder of the Abbey of Roucestree, which was confirmed by Ranulph, earl of Chester, his uncle; and the witnesses thereunto were Hugh Wace, William Bacoun, and Robert Baccoun (d).

In the Red Book of the Exchequer, Essex p. 104, of the fee of William de Montefychet, Robert Bacon (d), William Bacon (e), and Alexander Kerding, held of him 4 Kts. fees: this was in the time of Henry II.

In a Ledger Book belonging to the abbot of St. Edmund's Bury, and now at Redgrave, styled *Album Registrum* (fo. 27) there is a deed mentioned of William Bacon (e), of a tenement in Bradfield, which Eddicus Schute held in Bradfield: and in a little book of the said abbot's, there also (fo. 229) is a deed between abbot Sampson and William Bacon (e), of arable land in Bradfield. Abbot Sampson lived in the time of Richard I. and King John.

In the Register of John Lakenhithe, there also (fo. 131 & 132) Wido Bacon (f), holds, in Monks Bradfield, of the convent of St. Edmund's Bury, one messuage, &c.

And there also (p. 152) Robert (g) holds in Hegesset, one messuage of St. Edmund's fee. This was taken by inquisition, 14 Edward I.

Assisa apud Norwich, 10 John, Philip of Dawling claims the presentation to the church of Dawling, against Roger Bacon (h).

In a Charter of Simon, bishop of Norwich, to the monks of Castleacre, dated 1265, among other manors and lands, he grants unto them two parts of all the tithes in field Dawling, of the demeans anciently of Roger (h) and Richard Buchun (d).

* Monast. p. 514.

Sir Stephen (*i*), Sir Roger (*h*), and Sir Edmund (*k*), were generals in the wars in the time of Henry II. Henry III. Edward II. Edward III.

Sir Bartholomew (*l*), Sir Henry (*c*), John (*l*), were judges and justices itinerant in the times of Henry II. Henry III. Edward II. Edward III.

(*m*) ROGER BACON—Somersetshire gave birth to this illustrious person. He was born near Ilchester, in the year of our Lord, 1214. We have no farther information concerning him till we find him at Oxford, where he probably received the very tincture of science. Having gone through his grammatical and logical studies, he afforded such proofs of an uncommon capacity as excited the favour and patronage of the greatest lovers of learning in that period, and still more by being the brightest luminaries of the age.

Under their protection he acquired as much instruction as could be gained at Oxford, and then removed to Paris, whither it was customary for every one to resort who was desirous of making an extraordinary improvement in literature, the university of Paris being, at that time, in the highest reputation. In this city he pursued his inquiries with a zeal proportioned to his ardent thirst after science, and exceeded the hopes and wishes of his friends. His proficiency and diligence were so great, that he was considered as the glory of the university, and honour of his country. He did not confine his studies to any particular branch of learning, but extended his views to every object in which he could gain information; his exalted mind being content with nothing less than universal knowledge.

At Paris he staid till he was 26 years of age, and returned from thence to Oxford, having first taken his doctor's degree. About the same time he assumed the habit of the Franciscan order; but whether in England or France is not absolutely certain: be this as it may, when he was settled at Oxford, his reputation was so far from diminishing, that it continually increased; and the eminent men of the age regarded him as one of the most indefatigable inquirers after nature that the world had ever seen. Accordingly they did not only encourage him by their approbation, but assisted him with their purses, which indeed was essentially necessary to the execution of his schemes; for he had the sagacity and the fortitude to depart' from the idle and absurd method of the schools, and to build philosophy upon the solid basis of facts and experiments.

The same plan of inquiry was adopted by him that was afterwards so nobly proposed and pursued by the Lord Chancellor Bacon, and which has been attended with such amazing success in enlightening, adorning, and improving modern ages. It is true our learned friar was not, like his great namesake, fortunate enough to introduce a general reformation of science; but this was not his fault: he did all that lay in his power to promote a rational way of cultivating knowledge, and was himself a glorious instance of the excellence of the rules he had laid down, as will amply appear when we come to mention his particular inventions and discoveries. In the course of 20 years he expended no less than 2000*l*. in collecting authors, making trials of various sorts, and constructing different instruments. It has indeed been disputed, whether the money here specified consisted of French livres, which were then worth 6*s.* 8*d.* each, or of pounds sterling, though the latter is most probable; and it was a prodigious sum in those days.

While the progress of Roger Bacon increased his reputation, and procured him the friendship of the virtuous and understanding few, it raised the envy and malice of the ignorant and bigoted. In so dark a period, when scarcely ten persons had the least glimpse of philosophic science, his experiments must necessarily occasion much noise, and be liable to all the misconstructions of folly and superstition. The clergy in particular were willing to disguise their own idleness and stupidity, by throwing aspersions on his character, and by representing his operations as the result of more than human power. Accordingly they imputed them to magic, and stirred up a persecution against him, in consequence of which he was closely confined, and almost starved; was prohibited from sending his writings beyond the limits of his convent, excepting to the pope; and was restrained from giving lectures to youth. This last circumstance would, in an especial manner, be extremely afflictive to a soul like his, which had the noblest and most benevolent intentions. His aim was to form the youth to better principles than had heretofore been cultivated; and by a proper method of education, to introduce a reformation both in human and divine knowledge, between which he believed there was a close and inseparable connection. He was persuaded that the perfection of natural philosophy was the surest way of destroying superstition, heresies, and antichrist; and that moral philosophy would be highly effectual to establish true piety in the heart.

But though the avowed cause of the severity manifested against Bacon was, that he applied himself to the occult sciences, there is reason to apprehend that the real one was, the enlargement of his sentiments with respect to religion. He had treated the clergy with freedom; he had even been so daring as to write to the pope concerning the necessity of correcting some of the errors of the church. These were sufficient motives for exposing him to persecution; and his old patrons being dead, he was left a prey to the malice of his enemies.

Notwithstanding the hard usage he met with, he did not intermit the vigour of his studies; nor was it in the power of his adversaries to obstruct the progress of his reputation. His fame spread so wide, that it not only reached Rome, but induced Clement IV. to desire that he would send him all his works. The pontiff was one of the worthiest men who had filled the papal chair for a long time: he was a person of distinguished virtue, and possessed of a liberal mind: he had before his advancement entertained a peculiar admiration of, and respect for, Bacon; and had expressed a solicitude to be favoured with his writings.

No sooner did our friar receive the letter from the pope, than he set himself to comply with his request, and immediately began to revise, enlarge, and complete his compositions, and to put them into proper order. Having done this, he transmitted them by his favourite disciple, John of Paris, who was well qualified to explain the sentiments of his master. This collection of Bacon's performances, which were digested by him into one treatise, to be sent to the Roman bishop, is called *Opus Majus*, and contains a complete body of science for that age. In this work the excellent author builds on the most rational principles, points out extremely well the hindrances of knowledge, shews that the perfection of wisdom is to be found in the scriptures, and proves that philosophy is not inconsistent with divinity. He makes admirable remarks on the usefulness of the languages, mathematics, perspective, astronomy, chymistry, and other subjects; and gives us the result of his own inquiries with respect to these different parts of study. He evinces at large the importance and necessity of proceeding by experiments in order to come at truth; and in short, exhibits a detail of his numerous improvements and curious discoveries.

His writings obtained for him the favour of the pope, and some farther assistance and patronage in the prosecution of his noble schemes: but alas! the sunshine of his prosperity was a transient gleam, which was quickly overcast. The good pontiff died in a very little time, and then Bacon was exposed to fresh difficulties. These were occasioned by Jerome de Escuto, the general of the Franciscans, who ordered him to be imprisoned; and to prevent his making an appeal, took care to get from Rome an immediate confirmation of the sentence. Others tell us, it was Raymundus Golfredus, who was head of the order at this period, and who procured the condemnation of our philosopher; though the former account is by far the most probable. However that may be, he languished in confinement ten years, being shut up in his monastery, deprived of conversation, and obliged to a severe abstinence. The pretences for persecuting him were the same as heretofore, and are said in particular to have taken their rise from his Treatises *de Necromanticis, de Prognosticis ex Stellis*, and *de Astronomia vera*. But not even the continued hardships he endured could damp his zeal in the prosecution of his studies. Ill treated as he was by his cotemporaries, he was animated by a laudable thirst of fame, and fired with an ardent concern for the welfare of mankind. He laboured for future ages, and consigned his reputation and character to posterity; which has, though late, done justice to his merit.

After he had remained in imprisonment the time we have mentioned, his old enemy, Jerome de Escuto, was raised to the papal throne, and assumed the name of Nicholas IV. Notwithstanding the severity with which he had treated our worthy monk, he was, upon the whole, a man of virtue and science; and therefore Bacon hoped he might be able to pacify him, and conciliate his favours. With this view he wrote, and dedicated to him, a Treatise on the Means of avoiding the Infirmities of Age. This work is well spoken of by the best judges, and has been extremely admired by many eminent physicians. The author however was obliged, in compliance with the weakness of the age, and to avoid the dangers he might otherwise incur, to express his sentiments in several places with a studied obscurity, a thing by no means agreeable to his natural inclination; for it was always his desire to hold forth truth in her native simplicity.

We do not find that his application to the pope produced any considerable effect; but at length he was released from his confinement by the interposition of some noblemen, and returned to Oxford, where he composed his last performance, intitled, a Compendium of Theology. He spent the remainder of his days in peace, died in the college of his order on the 11th of June, in 1292, or as Dr. Jebb thinks, in 1294; and was buried in the church of the Franciscans.

These are all the particulars the most indefatigable inquirers have been able to collect concerning the life of Roger Bacon; and we must be contented with them, though curiosity and gratitude would wish for a fuller information; but the life of a sedentary is to be found in his works. To the compositions therefore of our ingenious friar must we have recourse, if we desire to know what he was, and to have a proper conception of his literary character. We may take notice that, notwithstanding Bacon existed in a dark period, he had all the benefits of education which the age could possibly afford. We do not here mean his being brought up at Oxford and Paris, which was a common thing in those days, and was the case of thousands who never made a figure in the republic of letters. What we have in view is, his peculiar felicity in enjoying the early patronage of Sherwood, Grostest, and their friends, who were almost the only persons among whom any traces of true knowledge were to be met with. But whatever might be his happiness in this respect, his advantages bore no proportion to his improvements. The progress he made in science can be accounted for on no other supposition, than that of his being endowed with a genius altogether surprising; and which, if he had been confined in the obscurest village, would have broken forth with a splendour that could not be resisted. His powers rose quite above the opportunities he had been favoured with, and pushed him to discoveries in the attainment of which he could receive no help from the period wherein he lived. His exalted mind saw at once through the errors of preceding times, and fixed immediately upon the only principle that can lead to solid truth. In his *Opus Majus* he shews, that too great a dependance on authority, the allowing an undue weight to custom, the fear of offending the vulgar, and the affectation of concealing ignorance under a specious display of wisdom, are the four grand impediments to the advancement of knowledge; and points out, in various instances, the mistakes they occasion. He proves that we are not under an obligation of adhering implicitly to what we hear and read; but have a right of examining into the sentiments of those who have gone before us; of adding to their opinions when defective, and of correcting them when wrong, provided we do it with modesty and decency. Besides laying open the sources of erroneous notions, he proposes the clearest and most judicious methods of arriving at real science; and, as we have already hinted, insists largely on the necessity of making experience our guide.

A perusal of Roger Bacon's works will convince us of the extent as well as brightness of his genius. Though his inquiries reached to almost every branch of literature, he did not perform them in a superficial, or even in a general way, but entered deeply into each subject; so that one would imagine it had been his sole pursuit. The accuracy and fullness with which he has expressed himself concerning the different parts of study, and such as he might be expected to have the least acquaintance with, form a high addition to his character.

A particular tribute of honour is due to him on account of the just sentiments he entertained with regard to moral philosophy and the scriptures. He saw in its full light the connection between natural and revealed religion: he perceived that they mutually support each other, and that the latter must be erected on the former, in order to stand on a solid and immoveable foundation. A noble principle this! which, by being properly attended to, has produced some of the best books the present enlightened age has seen; and has afforded the more rational and unanswerable vindications of christianity. In short, Roger Bacon was born to rise, in almost every respect, above the prejudices of his day. He was born to collect in himself, as in one focus, all the rays of knowledge that were scattered abroad in world; and not only to do so, but to make amazing additions to every separate branch of science, as will abundantly be manifested by our proceeding to give a more particular detail of his admirable improvements and discoveries.

The view we have already given of the life and literary character of Roger Bacon must have been sufficient to convince us, that, considering the period in which he flourished, he was a most extraordinary person; and that the enlargement of his mind, and the extent of his knowledge were extremely great: but were we to stop here we should be far from doing justice to his merits; far from representing him as he really was, with regard to his abilities and attainments. If we would have an adequate conception of the man we must pursue him more distinctly through the different branches of science, and examine the progress and discoveries which he made in every separate part of study.

Let us then begin with grammatical learning, which is the usual foundation of other improvements. No one had a higher sense of its value than our worthy friar, as appears from his *Opus Majus*, in which he points out at large the many advantages that flow from a skill in the languages, and shews the vast importance of being able to peruse the best authors in their originals. Accordingly his own proficiency was proportionably eminent; for he was perfectly acquainted with the Latin, the Greek, the Hebrew, and the Chaldee tongues. He was even capable of composing grammars in them; and has left indubitable marks that he understood them with a critical exactness. This was very surprising for that age, when few persons had any considerable knowledge in the languages, and when it was extremely difficult to get access to them, and obtain proper instructions concerning them. Nor were his philological inquiries pursued in a pedantic manner, but conducted with some degree of taste. He was fond of the Roman poets, and makes several quotations from them in his writings. His regard for Virgil induced him to compose observations upon the works of that divine genius; and his judicious reading of the ancients in general, is evident from his style, which, if it has not the classic purity and elegance of the Augustan period, has however a clearness, a precision, a neatness, and a strength greatly superior to his day. He had certainly a happy way of expressing his ideas, there being nothing awkward, obscure, or redundant in his diction. Nor was he meanly versed in other branches of the *belles lettres*. He wrote, for instance, upon chronology, and was well acquainted with it; as he was also with history, and especially the four grand empires of the world, of which he has given an accurate account. It is apparent likewise, that he had a complete knowledge of geography, so far as it could then be understood. He had even a fuller and more correct comprehension of the situation, extent, and inhabitants of many countries than some who have devoted their principal attention to the subject. His skill, in this respect, was so eminent, that it reached to the remotest places; for he had very just notions of Tartary, China, and the rest of the kingdoms in that part of the globe. The geographical observations he has left us in his *Opus Majus*, are allowed to have uncommon merit.

But though Roger Bacon's acquaintance with the several kinds of learning already mentioned, would have been sufficient to have gained him a high character, even if he had applied to nothing else, yet the reputation he hence deserved has been lost amidst the blaze of his other excellencies. While he shone with unparallelled splendour as a philosopher, persons scarcely thought it worth their while to take notice of and record his progress in grammatical and polite literature. Indeed it is as a philosopher that he is intitled to our principal admiration and praise. He has demonstrated in his *Opus Majus* the prodigious importance and use of the mathematics, and he exhibited in his own improvements a striking instance of the truth of his remarks. He has written upon all the parts of that sublime science in a manner that has excited the applause and esteem of the best judges. He composed likewise a number of pieces upon natural philosophy in general, and cultivated the particular branches of it with amazing success.

With regard to mechanics Dr. Freind has declared, that not a superior genius has sprung up since the days of Archimedes; and of this we have the clearest evidence in his performance on the secret works of art and nature, and the non-existence of magic, wherein he explained how nature may be wrought upon and heightened by art; and mentions a variety of machines, which might be invented and brought to perfection. He informs us, that a boat may be so constructed, and the oars so disposed in it, as to make more way with a single person, than another vessel would though fully manned. Some attempts of this sort have been made in later times, and not entirely without effect, in Flanders and Holland. It is possible too, he says, to contrive a chariot, which, without the assistance of animals, shall move with the utmost force and swiftness. He thinks also that flying instruments might be formed, in the middle of which a man might sit, and direct them by a kind of rudder. The reader may perhaps be disposed to smile at these instances of our learned monk's ingenuity; but they are decisive proofs of his extraordinary mechanical skill: and if the schemes seem a little whimsical, they have notwithstanding engaged the attention of other eminent philosophers besides Roger Bacon. He tells us moreover, that a machine may be made, which shall raise or sink, with ease, the greatest weights; whence it is apparent, that he understood the perpetual screw. He speaks likewise of many more instruments, and assures us, that he had seen and experienced all of them, except the apparatus for flying. Such was the surprising acquaintance of our friar with the secret powers of nature; and to this it was principally owing that he was treated as a magician; though he proposed his discoveries as having nothing extraordinary in them, but as being merely the result of a knowledge not difficult to be attained, and which he was ready to communicate to every honest inquirer.

Another part of science wherein his proficiency was equally amazing, was optics; in the theory and practice of which he took indefatigable pains. He was at much expence as well as labour to bring it to perfection; and though, at that time, an almost total ignorance prevailed with regard to it, was only studied by few persons; yet so successful were his researches, that he appears to have hit upon most of the grand inventions which, in modern ages, have reflected the highest lustre on individuals, and even on nations themselves. He has described the method of making reading glasses, and pointed out the use of them with a clearness and precision that do not admit of the least doubt. He has informed us also, that himself and his friend Peter de Maham, had constructed a number of burning glasses; and he has given us an account of the *Camera Obscura*. What perhaps will be esteemed still more surprising, it is evident that the important discovery of the telescope was made by him. That he understood this admirable instrument is indubitable from several passages in his works; nor had he merely an idea of it, as a possible thing, but put his idea into execution. Accordingly we have sufficient reason to believe, that he actually used telescopes in his astronomical observations. His apparatus indeed was neither so elegant nor so perfect as modern times have produced; nevertheless it was extremely serviceable to him in the acquisition of knowledge, and was applied by him to the most valuable purposes.

From this subject the transition is very natural to the consideration of Roger Bacon's proficiency with regard to astronomy, in which his skill was proportioned to the rest of his improvements. So extensive, so accurate was his acquaintance with this sublime science, that he saw clearly through the errors of the calendar, and was capable of specifying the proper method of correcting them. This knowledge he acquired without any assistance but from his own sagacity and diligence, and earnestly pressed Pope Clement IV. to undertake the alteration of the style. It is remarkable, that the scheme laid down by him was more exact and complete than the plan afterwards adopted by Gregory XIII. Our monk was for having the reformation begin from the birth of our Saviour, and not from the council of Nice. The calendar framed by him for this purpose is still extant; and it is with good reason supposed, that from him were borrowed the ideas which gave rise to the Gregorian correction; while, at the same time, the persons who carried it into execution had not the wisdom to render the design so perfect as Roger Bacon had proposed.

But let us view him as a chymist, where we shall find his character as extraordinary as in other respects. He may be almost considered as the introducer of chymistry into this kingdom; and it was pursued by him with such uncommon success, that he understood, and has spoken of many of the operations now in use. His comparatively accurate and extensive acquaintance with this science is acknowledged by all who are conversant with the subject; and he made several very capital discoveries. Among the rest gunpowder was known to him, both with regard to its ingredients and its application. He mentions clearly and distinctly the materials necessary to a composition of that sort, and the great effects it might produce. It is worthy of a particular notice, that he believes it was some preparation of this nature which enabled Gideon, with his 300 pitchers and lamps, to obtain a complete victory over the Midianites.

Another thing observable in our friar was, his skill in the transmutation of metals. Whatever be thought of his attempts to find out the philosopher's stone, as it has been called, or the art of converting baser substances into gold, it is certain he went as far that way as any man; and in the prosecution of his main subject, struck out a multitude of important truths. Several of his principles and positions have been since approved and confirmed by the most intelligent and curious philosophers: and Boerhave speaks of him with peculiar honour.

When we reflect upon the course of his chymical studies, we cannot wonder that he applied to medicine in general. To this we are indebted for his admirable treatise in avoiding the infirmities of age, of which an account has already been given. He wrote likewise other pieces in the same science.

While Roger Bacon employed himself in the most abstruse and sublime speculations and pursuits, while he cultivated several kinds, in which he was without a rival, one would imagine that he could have had no time to attend to the common literature of the age. This chiefly included logic and metaphysics, and consisted of a thousand subtle questions and distinctions which the schoolmen had lately introduced. However, if the fashionable learning was entitled to the least degree of praise, our friar understood it in all its extent, as is evident from his works; and his reputation in it was equal to that of the best of his contemporaries. With regard to ethics, as we have formerly observed, his merit was very distinguished; for so just and enlarged were his sentiments of moral philosophy, that he considered it as the end and perfection of human wisdom, as the same with divinity, and the foundation of revealed religion.

To crown the whole, he was so far from neglecting the peculiar business of his profession, that he rendered all his inquiries subservient to it, and seems to have had nothing in view but the honour of the supreme being, and the welfare of mankind. He entertained the utmost veneration for the scriptures, urged the study of them in their original languages, and thought that all other parts of literature would contribute to make them better understood. To evince this was the grand purpose of his writings, and particularly of his last performance, the Compendium of Theology, the publication of which would probably be extremely useful, and through much light on a variety of subjects. Nay, extraordinary and surprising as his character appears, there is reason to believe it would be deemed still more amazing, if all his manuscripts were collected from the dust of libraries, where some of them have long lain forgotten, and were brought into open day.

Such was friar Roger Bacon; and therefore it is no wonder that he was called *Doctor Mirabilis*, a title he well deserved, while the other authors of his time had no just pretensions to the pompous appellations which were bestowed upon them. His works have been read with astonishment by the best modern writers, and will ever be admired so long as the least love of science and learning remains in Britain.

We hope that none of our readers will be disposed to think less honourably of him because he did not, in all respects, discard the errors of the times. This is so far from affording cause of blame, that the matter of surprise is how, in so dark a period, and under such prodigious disadvantages, he was capable of striking out the light he did. As to his sentiments concerning Aristotle, though he looked upon his performances as the foundation of knowledge, let it be remembered, that this was the prevailing, the indisputable opinion of the age. Let it also be remembered, that our monk did not take that philosopher in the wretched translation then received, did not confine himself to his discoveries, but dared to differ from him where he saw reason; for no one had a higher sense of the possibility and importance of transcending the limits of ancient wisdom. With regard likewise to his favourable notion of judicial astrology, an attachment to it was the general mistake of the day, a mistake which continued in much more enlightened times. Besides, he did not imagine that the disposition of the stars absolutely controuled the course of events, or broke in upon moral agency and human liberty. We need not say, that the charge of his being addicted to magic was founded on the grossest ignorance;

or attempt to refute the ridiculous story of the brazen head, which has been applied to several other eminent men.

The more we consider the attainments of Roger Bacon, amidst the greatest obstructions, and under a long and severe persecution, the more we shall admire the vigour of his mind, the steadiness of his application, and the progress he made. Nor can we too much revere the virtues of his heart, his zeal for the public good, the freedom with which he communicated his inventions, and his rendering them all subservient to the best purposes. That such a man should be so harshly and injuriously treated, fills us with the highest indignation: but thus has the ungrateful world often used its noblest benefactors. The injustice shewn to the person of our friar extended also to his works. The odium cast upon his character, together with other concurring circumstances, had the unhappy influence of occasioning his writings to be so much neglected, that there was a danger of their being wholly lost; and Leland complains, that it would be easier to collect the sibyl's leaves than the titles of the books he composed. If they had not been almost entirely unknown mankind could not have continued so long ignorant of the valuable discoveries they contain. Late, very late it was, before his merit was set in a full light; and we are under great obligations to those who have rescued his name and productions from oblivion. Our acknowledgements are particularly due to Dr. Jebb, and the authors of the Biographia Britannica, whose excellent labours have enabled us to see, that Roger Bacon, all things considered, was perhaps the brightest genius which Britain, or the world, has produced.*

(*n*) JOHN BACON, or Baconthorp, or Bacondorp, surnamed the *Resolute Doctor*, was one of the most learned men of his time, was born towards the end of the 13th century, at Baconthorp, an obscure village in Norfolk, from which he took his name. In his youth he was a monk in the convent of Blackney, a small town in Norfolk, about five miles from Walsingham. After some years dedicated to learning and piety he removed to Oxford, and from thence to Paris, where he was honoured with the degrees in divinity and law, and acquired a great reputation for learning. Upon his return to England he was unanimously chosen the 12th provincial of the English Carmelites, in a general assembly of that order, held at London in the year 1329. Four years after he was invited by letters to Rome, where, in several disputations on the subject of marriage, he gave no little offence, by carrying the papal authority too high in the case of divorces; but he thought fit afterwards to retract his opinion, and was held in great esteem at Rome and other parts of Italy. He was small of stature, but of a great and lofty genius. He died 1346.†

From the united testimonies concerning him it appears, that considering the age in which he lived, he was an extraordinary man. Were we to give full credit to the encomiums past upon him,‡ we might almost be ready to rank him with Roger Bacon, to regret that his printed works should be so little attended to, and that his other tracts should either be lost, or buried in the dust of some old libraries.

*. New Ann. Reg. vol. IV. p. 21. † See more of him in the Biog. Brit. ‡ See Biog. Brit.

Dr. Fuller has, with his usual good humour, taken notice of the common custom of confounding several learned men of the name of Bacon with each other: the passage is curious, and deserves to be read. It is in his church history, wherein, having given a concise account of Roger Bacon, and the ill treatment he met with from the monks, he proceeds thus:—" For my own part I behold the BACON in Oxford, not as of an individual man, but of a corporation of men; no single cord, but a twisted cable of many together: and as all the acts of strong men of that nature are attributed to an Hercules; all the predictions of prophesying women to a sibyl, so I conceive all the atchievements of the Oxonian Bacons, in their liberal studies, are exhibited to one, as chief of the name: and this is in effect confessed by the most learned and ingenious orator of that university."*

(o) JOHN BACON, Chamberlain of the Exchequer, Secretary to the King, Master of the Rolls, and Dean of St. Martin's le Grand, from the 1st to the 7th of Richard II.

(p) Sir NICHOLAS BACON, Lord Keeper of the Great Seal in the reign of Queen Elizabeth. He was born in the year 1510, at Chislehurst in Kent. After having received the first rudiments of learning, either in the house of his father, or at some little school in the neighbourhood, he was sent, when very young, to Corpus Christi (vulgarly) Bennet college, in Cambridge, where, having improved himself in all branches of useful knowledge, he travelled into France, and made some stay at Paris, in order to give the last polish to his education.

On his return he settled in Gray's Inn, and applied himself with such assiduity to the study of the law, that he quickly distinguished himself in that learned profession; so that on the dissolution of the monastery of St. Edmund's Bury, in Suffolk, he had a grant from Henry VIII. in the 36th year of his reign, of the manors of Redgrave, Botesdale, and Gillingham, with the park of Redgrave, and six acres of land in Wortham, as also the tithes of Redgrave to hold *in capete*, by Knights service, which shews that he stood high at that time in the favour of his prince, who was one that never gave or preferred but where great abilities invited.

In the 38th of the same king he was promoted to the office of attorney in the court of wards, which was a place both of honour and profit. In 1552 he was elected treasurer of Gray's Inn. His great moderation and consummate prudence preserved him through the dangerous reign of Queen Mary. In the very dawn of that of Elizabeth he was knighted, and the great seal of England being taken from Nicholas Heath, archbishop of York, was delivered to him on Dec. 22, 1558, with the title of lord keeper.† He was also of the privy council of her majesty, who had much regard to his advice. The main business of the first session was the settlement of religion, in which no man had a greater share than the keeper, though he acted with such prudence as never to incur the hatred of any party. On this account he was made choice of, together with the archbishop of York, to be mode-

* Sir Isaac Wake in his Rex Platonicus, p. 209, 210. † Pat. 1 Eliz. p. 3, m. xxi.

14 BACON OF REDGRAVE.

TABLE I.

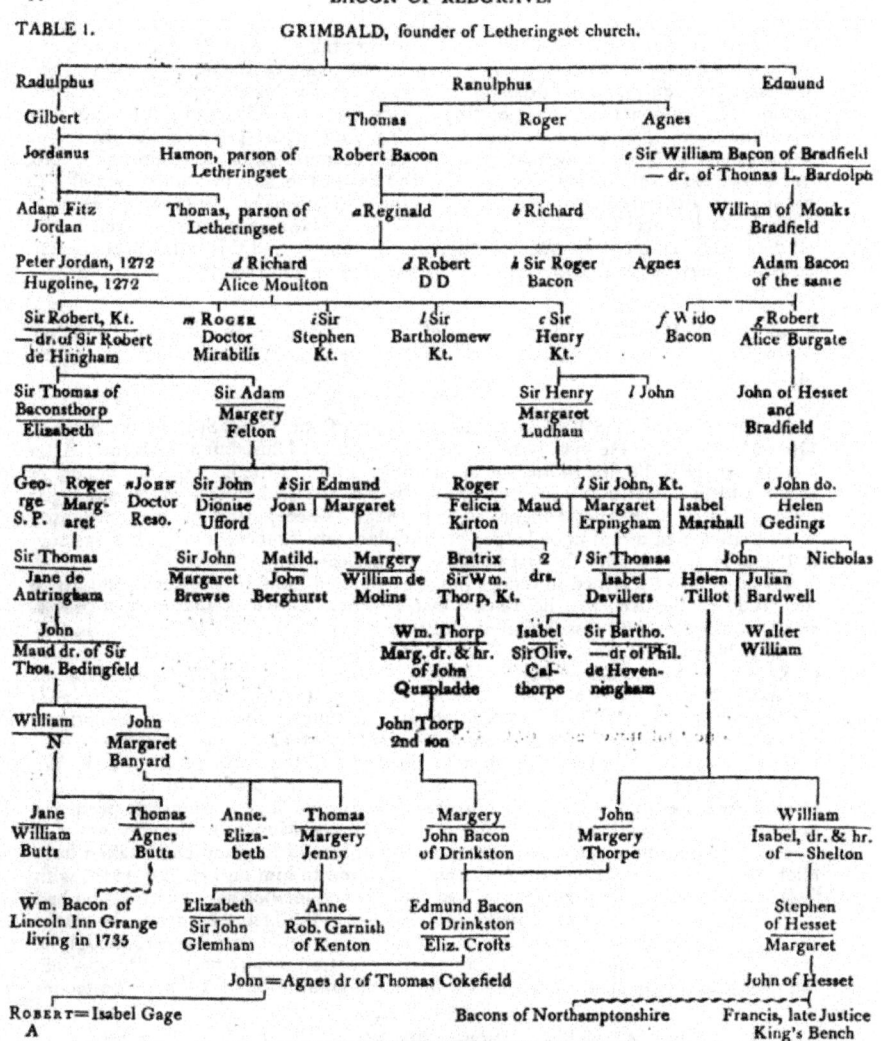

This table is taken from that drawn up by John Whiting of Lincoln's Inn, Esq. temp. Car. II. and since followed by Wotton and others; and though it does not perfectly agree with that mentioned in the grant to Sir Nicholas Bacon, it deserves considerable credit, as many quotations might be made from our most ancient writers, and particularly from Weever's Monuments, wherein there is mention made of many of the family.

rator in a dispute between eight protestant divines and eight popish bishops; and the latter behaving very unfairly in the opinion of both the moderators, and desiring, to avoid a fair disputation, to go away, the lord keeper put that question to each of them; and when all, except one, insisted on going, his lordship dismissed them with this memorandum:—*For that ye would not that we should hear you, perhaps you may shortly hear of us;* and accordingly, for this contempt, the bishops of Winchester and Lincoln were committed to the Tower, and the rest were bound to appear before the council, and not to quit the cities of London and Westminster without leave. The whole business of the session, than which there was none of greater importance throughout that reign, was chiefly managed by his lordship, who pursued therein his wise maxim:—*Let us stay a little, that we have done the sooner;* and thereby brought all to a good conclusion, ending the session as he began it, with a most excellent speech. Thenceforward he continued the head of her majesty's councils.

As a statesman he was remarkable for a clear head, and deep counsels; and while it was thought of some other great men, that they seemed wiser than they were, yet the common voice of the nation agreed in this, that Sir Nicholas Bacon was wiser than he seemed.

His great skill lay in balancing factions, and it is thought he taught the queen that secret, the more necessary to her because the last of her family, and consequently without many of those supports incident to princes. In the chancery he distinguished himself by a very moderate use of his power, and shewing great respect to the common law. He made use, on proper occasions, of set speeches, in which he was happier than most men, pleasing the people by their sound, and charming the wisest men of that age with their sense, whence he attained the reputation of uniting two opposite characters, viz. of a witty and a weighty speaker.

His great parts and great preferment were far from raising him in his own opinion, as appears from the modest answer he gave Queen Elizabeth when she told him his house at Redgrave was too little for him:—" *Not so* (returned he) *but your majesty has made me too great for my house.*" Yet to shew his respect for her majesty's judgment, he afterwards added wings to it. Towards the latter end of his life he became very corpulent, which made Queen Elizabeth say, merrily, that " *Sir Nicholas's soul lodged well.*" To himself however his bulk was very cumbersome, insomuch that after walking from Westminster Hall to the Star Chamber, which was but a very little way, he was usually so much out of breath that the lawyers forbore speaking at the bar till he recovered himself, and gave them notice of it by knocking with his staff.

After having held the great seal more than 20 years, this able statesman and faithful counsellor was suddenly removed from this life, as a certain writer informs us, by the following accident:—" He was under the hands of his barber, and the weather being sultry, had ordered a window before him to be thrown open: as he was become very corpulent he presently fell asleep, in the current of fresh air that was blowing in upon him, and awaked, after some time, distempered all over. Why (said he to the servant) did you suffer me to sleep thus exposed? The fellow replied, that he durst not presume to disturb him. Then said the lord keeper, by your civility I lose my life; and so removed into his bed-chamber, where he died a few days after." I have transcribed this story exactly, though I think there is some reason to doubt the circumstances of it; for all our writers agree, that he paid his last debt to nature on the 20th of Feb. 1579, and one would imagine that the weather could not then be very sultry.

Camden's character of him is just and plain:—" *Vir præpinguis, ingenio acerrimo singulari prudentia, summa eloquentia, tenaci memoria, et sacris consiliis alterum columen;*" i. e. A man of gross body, but most quick wit; singular prudence, happy memory, and for judgment, the other pillar of the state. His felicity was not greater in his fortune than his family.

His first wife, Jane, daughter of William Fernley, of West Creting, in the county of Suffolk, Esq. by whom he had issue three sons and three daughters. The sons were, 1. Sir Nicholas, 2. Sir Nathaniel Bacon, of Stiffkey, in Norfolk, K. B. who attained the perfection of a master in painting. He travelled into Italy, and studied in that country: but his manner and colouring approach nearer to the style of the Flemish school. Some of his works are preserved at Culford, where he lived; and at Gorhambury, which was the seat of his father, is a large picture in oil, done by him, which is admirably painted.* He married two wives, 1. Anne, daughter of Sir Thomas Gresham, of London, Kt. by whom he had three daughters, his co-heirs; 1. Anne, who being married to Sir Roger Townshend, of Rainham, in Norfolk, ancestor to Marquis Townshend, brought the Stiffkey estate into that family; 2. Elizabeth, the wife of Sir Thomas Knyvet, of Ashwelthorp, in Norfolk; and 3. Winifred, of Sir Robert Gawdy, of Claxton, in Norfolk, Kt. Sir Nathaniel's second wife was Dorothy, daughter of Sir George Hopton, of Suffolk, Kt. by whom he had no issue. 3. Edward Bacon, of Shrubland-Hall, in Suffolk, Esq. in right of his wife, Helen, daughter and heir of Thomas Littel, of the same place, Esq. and of Bray, in the county of Berks, by Elizabeth, his wife, daughter and co-heir of Sir Robert Litton, of Knetworth, in the county of Hertford, Kt. from whom was lineally descended the late Rev. Nicholas Bacon, of Coddenham, in Suffolk; and from younger sons of the said Edward, are the Bacons of Ipswich, in Suffolk, and Earlham, in Norfolk, descended.

The daughters were, 1. Anne, the wife of Sir Henry Wodehouse, of Waxham, in the county of Norfolk, Kt. 2. Jane, of Sir Francis Windham, Kt. one of the justices of the common pleas; and 2ly. of Sir Robert Mansfield, Kt. 3. Elizabeth, of Sir Robert D'Oyley, of Chislehampton, in Oxfordshire, Kt. 2ly. of Sir Henry Nevil, Kt. and 3ly. of Sir William Periam, Kt. lord chief baron of the Exchequer. After her decease he married Anne, daughter of Sir Anthony Cooke, of Giddy-Hall, in the county of Essex, Kt. a woman equally distinguished by her learning and piety, and as such highly commended by the writers of those times,† by whom he had two sons, Anthony and Francis.

* N. Ann. Reg. vol. xiii. p. 38.
† It was no unusual thing in those days for ladies to apply themselves to the same studies, with the same strictness, and consequently with the same success that the other sex did. The lady Jane Grey was excellently learned in Greek, and Queen Elizabeth translated several pieces both from that language and from the Latin. The most remarkable instance however of the spirit of learning which prevailed in that age was in the family to which this lady belonged; (*Lloyd's State Worthies, p.* 386) for all the four daughters of Sir Anthony Cooke were perfectly skilled in the learned languages, and this, his second

(p) ANTHONY, the elder son, from a variety of circumstances, appears to have been several years older than his brother Francis. He received an excellent education at home, and giving evident signs of pregnant parts, his father thought pro-

daughter Anne, made both a florid and exact translation of Bishop Jewell's Apology for the Church of England, from Latin into English, which was esteemed so useful in its nature, as well as correct in its manner, that in the year 1564 it was published for common use, by the special order of Archbishop Parker, with some additions of his own at the end *(Strypes Annals, vol. II. p.* 469). There have been ladies remarkable for their learning and their writings, but very few whose works, like the lady Bacon's were published by authority, and recommended to public reading.

It was to the great abilities and tender care of so accomplished a parent, that her two sons, Anthony and Francis owed the early part of their education; and without doing any injustice to the genius of either of these great men, we may affirm, that they were not a little indebted for the reputation they acquired, to the pains taken with them by this excellent woman in their tender years, when the mind is most susceptible of learning, and thereby rendered more capable of retaining the principles of science, than when they are instilled in an age farther advanced. It was in gratitude to her memory, and from a just sense of the advantages received from her in this way, that her son, the Viscount St. Albans, directed by his will, that his body should be laid near her's, in the church of St. Michael, within the precincts of Old Verulam *(Chauncey's Hertfordshire, p.* 464).

Though Lady Anne Bacon was a woman of great piety and virtue, as well as of distinguished abilities, yet her temper seems to have been very disagreeable. Her admonitions to her sons, which were often wise, and undoubtedly proceeded from her sincere regard for their welfare, were so harsh, that they could not submit to them with patience. Indeed her expressions were sometimes unreasonably severe. She was so full of resentment at Mr. Anthony Bacon's continuing longer abroad than appeared to her to be adviseable, that she called him a traitor to God and his country; and alledged, that he had undone her, and sought her death; but that when he should gain that which he sought for, he would have but a hundred pounds more than he had then. She was resolved, she said, to procure the Queen's letter to force him to return home, and that upon his coming back, if her majesty gave him his right, she would commit him to prison. She added, that she would not bear to hear of him, and that he was hated of all the chiefest in France, and cursed of God in all his actions, since Mr. Lawson's being with him. This Lawson was a servant of her son's, whom she had conceived an unconquerable aversion to, which circumstance, together with some other connections her son had formed, and her fears lest his religious principles should be corrupted, gave additional strength to the asperity of her language. Her continual reproaches, addressed to both her sons, at length extorted from her son Anthony the following letter:

"*Madam,*

"*For answer on my part to your Ladyship's letter to us both, having asked counsel and leave of him who only knoweth and guideth the heart, I found myself emboldened with warrant of a good conscience, and by the force of truth, to remonstrate unto your Ladyship with a most dutiful mind, and tender care of your Ladyship's soul and reputation, that howsoever your Ladyship doth pretend and alledge for reason towards us in your motherly affection, in that which concerneth Lawson; yet any man of judgment and indifferency must needs take it for a mere passion, springing either from presumption, that your Ladyship can only judge and see that in the man, which never any man yet has seen; or from a sovereign desire to over-rule your sons in all things, how little soever you may understand either the ground or the circumstances of their proceedings; or else from want of civility, abandoning your mind continually to strange and wrongly suspicions, notwithstanding all most humble submissions and endeavours possible on his part to procure your Ladyship's satisfaction and contentment. This my remonstrance, as I have just cause to fear, that it will at the first sight be offensive to your Ladyship, yet have I no less reason to hope, that almighty God, who knoweth with how dutiful intent, and to what end I have made the same, will in his mercy dispose your Ladyship's heart not to yield to your ∗∗∗∗∗∗∗∗∗∗∗∗∗, which you ∗∗∗∗∗∗∗∗ as it were so heinous an offence, but to truth and charity. Whereupon, entirely reposing myself as infallible grounds, I remain more ready to receive and endure your blame, for performing with free filial respect this my bounden duty, than your thanks or liking, for soothing or allowing by silence so dangerous humours and uncharitable misconceits: and so I most humbly take my leave.*" *(Birch's Memoirs of the Reign of Queen Elizabeth, vol. I p.* 56, 173, 174).

Mr. Anthony Bacon's expostulation with his mother did not produce the desired effect. By continuing to write to him in her usual splenetic manner, she drew from him a second complaint. In this he told her, that from a mother sickly and in years, he was content to take in good part any misconceit,

per to send him early abroad, to improve his abilities. He spent some years with profit to himself, though his father did not live to see the fruits of his great improvements.* In the course of his travels he was resident for some time at Venice, and having visited other parts of Italy, received the news of his father's death at Geneva, which very probably hastened him home.

The two brothers were alike prodigies of parts, but of very different kinds; for whereas the younger spoke eloquently, and wrote admirably, the elder was reserved in conversation, had a deep reach in politics, aud was the best versed in foreign affairs of any man of his time. He had the misfortune to be very lame, so that he was able to stir little abroad, and indeed would not so much as move about his room, for which reason the Earl of Essex, who relied much upon his advices, and made use of him in all his affairs; and even in those of the greatest secrecy, thought proper to take him into his house, and to make him a handsome allowance for his service.

As he laid the foundation of his brother, the Chancellor's fortunes, in one sense, so he was very useful to them in another likewise, I mean that of favour, since the first marks which Sir Francis Bacon received of King James's kindness and good will, are in the very grant expressed to be in consideration of the many good services rendered him before his accession to the throne of England, by his brother, Mr. Anthony Bacon, as well as by himself.†

---

misinterpretation, or causeless humourous threats whatsoever; "*Only this* (he says) *I may with reason, and must for once, upon the warrant of a good conscience, remonstrate unto your Ladyship, that your son's poor credit dependeth upon judgment, and not upon humour; and that your Ladyship cannot utter any thing in your passion to your son's lack, so long as God gives him the grace to be more careful in duty to please and reverence your Ladyship as his mother, than your Ladyship seemeth many times to be towards me as your son.*"—*Ibid, vol. II. page 24.*

The age and bad health of Lady Bacon here mentioned, form the best apology for her pevishness; to which it may be added, that notwithstanding the severity of her temper, she appears to have had the most ardent affection for her sons, and to have exerted herself, with great generosity and zeal, to promote their interest. She was the second daughter of Sir Anthony Cooke, and was born in 1528. She had the same liberal education which was bestowed upon her elder sister, and perhaps under the same tutor. Having added much acquired knowledge to great natural endowments, she made an illustrious figure among the *literati* of that period; and hence acquired so extraordinary a reputation, that she is said to have been constituted governess of King Edward IV. (*Ballard's Memoirs of British Ladies*, 2nd. edit. *p*. 132). If this be a fact, it is a very surprising one; since she could not be much more than 25 years of age at the death of that monarch, and only 19 when he began to reign. However that matter may stand, it is certain that she early became eminent for piety, virtue, and learning; and that she was skilled in the Greek, Latin, and Italian tongues.

At what time she married to Sir Nicholas Bacon has not exactly been ascertained. Her eldest son, Anthony, was born in 1558 (*Birch's Memoirs of Queen Elizabeth, vol. I. p. 2*), and her younger son, Francis, on Jan. 22, 1560-1. It was a great honour to her to be the parent of two gentlemen of such distinguished abilities, and especially of the younger of these, whose intellectual powers and attainments are so well known to have been above all praise. There can be no doubt, but that they were much indebted to their mother for the early cultivation of their understandings; and we may be assured, from her acknowledged character, that she was equally assiduous, if not equally successful, in forming their minds to the principles of piety and virtue. *See more of her, and her learned sisters, under the article of Sir Anthony Cooke, in the Biog. Brit.*

* Lloyd's State Worthies.   † Rymer's Fæd. tom. XV. p. 597.

(*q*) Sir FRANCIS, the younger son, was born at York-House in the Strand, on Jan. 22, 1560-1.* His infancy being past, his noble genius cultivated and encouraged by his excellent parents, gave early proofs of its surprising strength and pregnancy, inasmuch that we may justly say, his fame commenced with his childhood, as it accompanied him to his grave: for so remarkably conspicuous were his parts, even in his tender years, that persons of the highest dignity delighted to converse with him while a boy: and Queen Elizabeth herself, whose peculiar felicity it was to make a right judgment of merit, was so charmed with the solidity of his sense, and the gravity of his behaviour, that she would often call him *her young Lord Keeper*,† a happy presage, which in the succeeding reign was fully accomplished.

When he had acquired the necessary rudiments of learning to qualify him for academical studies, he was sent to the university of Cambridge; where, on the 10th of June, 1573, he was entered of Trinity college, under Dr. John Whitgift, in the 13th year of his age.‡ The quickness of his natural parts, assisted by an uncommon diligence and application, enabled our young scholar to make a most astonishing progress in his studies; so that before he was full 16, he had not only run through the whole circle of the liberal arts, as they were then taught, but began to perceive those imperfections in the reigning philosophy, which he afterwards so effectually exposed, and thereby not only overturned that tyranny which prevented the progress of true knowledge, but laid the foundation of that free and useful philosophy, which has since opened a way to so many great and glorious discoveries.§

His father, discovering in him such a ripeness of judgment as seemed to warrant his taking an extraordinary step in his education, resolved to send him, young as he was, to France, that he might improve himself in the knowledge of the world, under a minister, as capable and as honest as that age produced, Sir Amias Powlet. His behaviour while in the house of that able statesman was so well conducted, that he gained the esteem and confidence of Sir Amias to such a degree, as to be entrusted with a commission of importance to the Queen, which required both secrecy and dispatch, which he performed in such a manner as gained both himself and the ambassador credit. He afterwards returned to Paris; but while he was improving his talents abroad, his fortune received a very untoward check at home: by the sudden death of his father, who having provided amply for his eldest son by his second venter, had laid by a considerable sum of money for the settlement of the younger; but dying before he could find a proper purchase, Mr. Francis Bacon had no more than the fifth part of this money for his whole fortune, which obliged him to return to England; on which he applied himself to the study of common law, and for that purpose entered himself of the honourable society of Gray's Inn, where his superior talents rendered him the ornament of the house, as the affability of his deportment procured him the affection of all its members.

In 1558, and in the 28th year of his age, the Queen, who never overvalued any man's abilities, thought fit to call him to her services, by appointing him her counsel learned in law extraordinary. He seemed to come into the world with as great advantages, and with as high pretensions to preferment as any man of his time:

---

* Dr. Rowley's Life of Lord Bacon, prefixed to his *Resuscitatio*, p. 1.   † Lloyd's State Worthies, p. 829.
‡ Birch's Memoirs of Queen Elizabeth, vol. I. p. 11.   § Dr. Rowley's Life of Lord Bacon.

for besides being the son of a lord keeper of the great seal, and one of the ablest statesmen of the age, he was nephew to William Lord Burleigh, who married his mother's sister, and first cousin to Sir Robert Cecil, his son, who was principal secretary of state; so that one would have thought Mr. Bacon's abilities, supported by such powerful mediators, might easily have made their way at court.* But it was his misfortune to have too much merit, and too extensive interest. The former rendered him suspicious to his court patrons, and the latter engaging both parties in his favour, produced him much credit, but contributed more than any thing to spoil his fortune.

In the 40th year of his age he was chose double reader, which office he discharged with remarkable sufficiency, as appears by his learned reading on the statute of uses, being one of the first who argued Chudleigh's case, largely reported by Lord Coke.† He distinguished himself likewise during the latter part of the Queen's reign, in the House of Commons, where he spoke often, and yet with such weight and wisdom, that his sentiments were generally approved; and though he usually spoke on the side of the court, yet he was ever looked upon as a friend to the people.

After the death of the Queen, Mr. Bacon applied very early to her successor, King James VI. He had many reasons to hope, that this tender of his services would be well received by that prince, as he was known to be learned himself, and a great encourager of learning, as he was well acquainted with the general characters of all persons of note in England, and as he had a singular esteem for, on account of the signal services rendered him by his brother Anthony Bacon.‡

On the 23d of July, 1603, he received the honour of knighthood, as a mark of his majesty's gracious acceptance of past services, and of the tender he had made of the continuance of them for the future.§

On the 25th of Aug. 1604, he was constituted by patent, one of the king's counsel learned in the law, with a fee of 40*l.* a year, which is said to have been the first act of royal power of that nature.‖ On the same day he had granted, by another patent, a pension of 60*l.* a year, for special services received from his brother Anthony and himself, which I the rather take notice of, because it has not hitherto been mentioned by any of the authors who have undertaken to write his life.¶

In the year 1607 he married Alice, daughter of Benedict Barnham, Esq. alderman of London, a lady who brought him an ample fortune, but by whom he had no children. A little after this marriage there happened a promotion in the law which induced him to renew his application for the solicitorship, which was then likely to be vacant; in which, with some difficulty, he prevailed; and upon Sir John Dodridge's being advanced from that post to be the king's serjeant, he was appointed solicitor, with the consent at least of his cousin the Earl of Salisbury.

He had now the king's ear so entirely, that he obtained a promise of succeeding Sir Henry Hobart, then attorney-general, in case either of his death or removal. In the beginning of the year 1612, that worthy man had a very severe fit of illness,

---

* See article of Cecil (William) Lord Burleigh, in Biog. Brit. † Coke's Reports, Book I. fol. 113.
‡ See the king's own testimony, Rymer's Fæd. vol. XV. p. 597. § Dugdale's Baronage, vol. II. p. 438.
‖ Rymer, vol. XV. p. 596. ¶ Ibid, p. 587.

which induced Sir Francis to put the king in mind of his promise: and it seems, by another letter of his, that he was now on very good terms with the Earl of Salisbury, lord treasurer, who supported his pretensions.* However the attorney recovered, and he did not succeed him till the year following, when Sir Henry Hobart was made chief justice of the common pleas, upon the removal of Sir Edward Coke from that office, who was made chief justice of the king's bench. Sir Francis Bacon took possession of his new office on the 27th of Oct. 1613, in which he made as great a figure as any of his predecessors, and had some particular honours done him, which few or none of them had received; as for instance, he was allowed to take his seat in parliament, though it was adjudged, that by reason of his office he had no right to it, as being an attendant on the house of lords. But this favour was granted him purely out of respect to his person, and the services he had formerly rendered his country in that house.†

He was now trusted and employed by the king, not only in the business of his profession, but in so many affairs of another nature, and of superior consequence to the state, that he judged it would be for his own honour, and at the same time advantageous to the king's service, that he should be sworn of the privy council, which though unusual for a man in his situation, was by the interposition of his friend, Sir George Villiers, brought about; and he accordingly took his place at the board on the 9th of June, 1616.

He held the post of attorney-general for upwards of three years, and behaved himself with such prudence and moderation, and went through so many difficulties and perplexed affairs, with such evenness and integrity, that for any thing appears, his conduct was never called in question, nor has malice itself dared to utter of him the least reproach.‡ When this is considered, we need the less wonder at his so confidently expecting the high employment to which he was raised. It was a very natural elevation from the post he was then in. The good old lord chancellor desired to have him for his successor, and indeed there was no man of the profession so fit for it at that time as himself.

Upon the 7th of March, 1616-17 the king delivered him the great seal, then in the 57th year of his age, with the title of lord keeper, giving him at the same time these three cautions: first, *that he should not seal any thing but after mature deliberation;* secondly, *that he should give righteous judgments between parties;* and lastly, *that he should not extend the royal prerogative too far.* These wise and grave admonitions were highly worthy of a good prince; and happy had it been for the new lord keeper if they had been constantly remembered, as they were graciously given, and submissively received.§

On the 4th of Jan. 1618, Sir Francis Bacon had the title given him of lord high chancellor of England.‖ As the new year entered with an act of advancement, so the spring afforded frequent opportunities to the chancellor to ingratiate himself with his master, by free and honourable counsels, which inclined his majesty to confer still higher marks of his favour; and accordingly, by letters patent, dated

---

* Bacon's Works, vol. IV. p. 586. † Petyt's Placit. Parliament, p. 174. ‡ Mallet's Life of Lord Bacon.
§ Sanderson's Hist. of King James, p. 437. Camden's Annals, March 7, 1617. Wilson's Hist. of Great Britain, p. 705. ‖ Patent King James I. p. 4.

the 11th of July, 1618, Sir Francis Bacon was created Baron Verulam, in the county of Hertford; and in the preamble it is recited, that his majesty was moved thereto by the grateful sense of the many and faithful services rendered him by this worthy person, as well in the court of chancery as in the privy council, and elsewhere: and Jan. 27, 1627, he was advanced to the dignity of a viscount, by the style and title of Viscount St. Alban's, in the county of Hertford. In the preamble to this patent the king sets forth, that as he thought nothing could adorn his government more, than raising worthy persons to honour, or afford greater encouragement to virtue and public spirit, he, after mature deliberation, had thought fit to advance his dearly beloved and faithful counsellor, descended from an ancient and honourable family, so much the more illustrious by his succeeding his most worthy and prudent father in the office of keeper of the great seal, to which, through various offices of inferior dignity, from a just experience of his capacity and fidelity, he had by his majesty been led, and reflecting finally on the acceptable and faithful services which, as well by his assiduity and integrity in the administration of justice, as by his care and prudence in the discharge of his duty as a privy counsellor, and in the management of his revenue, without respect either of private advantage or vain breath of popularity, to a higher degree of nobility.* At the same time this new dignity was granted to him and his heirs male, there was annexed to it a small pension out of the customs. He was likewise solemnly invested in this new dignity, the Lord Crewe carrying the robe of state before him, which robe was held up by the Marquis of Buckingham; and the new viscount gave the king solemn thanks for the favours he had bestowed upon him, which he particularly recapitulated.†

But he was soon after surprised with a melancholy reverse of fortune; for about the 12th of March following, a committee was appointed of some members of the house of commons, to inspect the abuses of the courts of justices, whereof Sir Robert Philips was appointed chairman. The first thing they fell upon was bribery and corruption, of which the lord chancellor Bacon was accused by Awbery and Egerton, who affirmed, that they had procured money to be given to him, to promote their causes depending before him. This being corroborated by some circumstances, a report was made from the committee to the house upon the 15th of that month, yet with all imaginable tenderness and respect to his lordship, *in regard,* as the chairman declared, *it touched the honour of a great man, so endued with all parts both of nature and art, as that he would say no more of him, being not able to say enough.* Upon this a conference was had with the lords, and afterwards Baron Denham and the attorney-general were sent by the lords with a copy of the charge against him, and after several messages,‡ on Monday, April 29, he sent his confession and submission to the house of lords, in which he confessed some facts, denied others, and endeavoured to answer or explain the rest in such a manner, as to take off the malignity of the offence. But the lords taking this for a full and ingenuous confession, sent several of the members to see if the chancellor would own it, which he did in these words: *"My lords, it is my act, my hand, my heart,*

---

* In continuation of Rymer's Fœd. tom. XVII. p. 279. † Camden's Annals, Jan. 27, 1621.
‡ See the whole proceedings against him in State Trials, vol. I. p. 353.

I beseech your lordships to be merciful to a broken reed." This answer being reported to the house, the lords agreed to move the king to sequester the seal; and on Wednesday, May 2, it was resolved to give sentence against him next morning, and accordingly he was summoned to attend; but he answered, *" that he was sick, and protested that he did not feign this for an excuse, for if he had been well he would willingly have come."* On May 3, 1621, the lord chief justice pronounced the following judgment:—

" *That the Lord Viscount St. Alban's, lord chancellor of England, shall undergo a fine and ransom of 40,000l. and that he shall be imprisoned in the Tower during the king's pleasure.—That he shall be incapable of any office, place, or employment in the state or commonwealth, and never sit in parliament, or come within the verge of the court.*"

The prince of wales and some others endeavoured to have mitigated the severity of this sentence; and many of the lords, by way of excuse for the rigour of it, told him afterwards, that they knew they left him in good hands, and it might be presumed, that the king, who, as his lordship writes, *" had shed tears upon the news of his being accused,"* would be indulgent and beneficent to him upon his sentence.

There is a variety of opinions concerning his guilt in the points charged against him; Mr. Rushworth says* his decrees were generally made with so much equity, that though gifts rendered him suspected for injustice, yet never any decree made by him was reversed as unjust.

After the judgment given against him, and a short imprisonment in the Tower, he retired from the engagements of an active life, to the shade of a contemplative one, which he had always loved. The first, or at least the greatest act of kindness which the king extended to him, was the remitting the parliamentary fine, and granting it to some of his lordship's friends. In a letter to the king, dated July 30, 1624, wherein he uses the most pathetic speeches, he implores his majesty to grant him a total remission of his sentence, *" to the end that the blot of ignominy might be removed from him, and from his memory with posterity.* This request very probably was granted him; for we find that he was summoned to parliament in the first year of King Charles I. However it appears from the works, which he composed and designed during his retirement, that his thoughts were still free, vigorous, and noble; and as Dr. Tenison (afterwards archbishop of Canterbury) observes,† it did not appear by any thing during all the time of his eclipse of fortune, that there was any abjectness of spirit in him: his writings shew a mind in him, not distracted with anxiety, nor depressed with shame, nor slow for want of encouragement, nor broken with discontent; such vigour of conceit, such a masculine style, such quickness in composition, appeared in his learned labours. The last five years of his life he devoted entirely to his studies, a thing which he would often speak of during the active part of his life, as if he affected to die in the shade, and not in the light: in this recess he composed the greatest part of his Latin and English works.‡

* Historical Collections, vol. I. p. 51.   † In his Baconiana, p. 255.   ‡ A fine edition of which was published in the year 1740, in 4 vols. fol. with his life.

His lordship had happily escaped the plague, which infested the summer of the year 1625, and with some difficulty, being of a weak and tender constitution, passed the severe winter which followed; but going in the spring to make some experiment in natural philosophy, he was taken so ill, that he was obliged to stay at the Earl of Arundel's house, at Highgate, about a week, and there expired on Easter-day, the 9th of April, 1626, in the 66th year of his age, of a gentle fever, attended with a great cold, which occasioned such a defluxion of rheum, that he was suffocated with it. He married Alice, daughter and co-heir of Benedict Barnham, Esq. alderman of London: she lies buried at Eyeworth, in Bedfordshire, with her sister Dorothy, wife of Sir John Constable, of Dromonby in the county of York, Kt. having this inscription:*

Here lieth interred the body of
Dame Alice, Baroness Verulame, Viscountess St. Alban's,
one of the daughters of
Bennedickt Barnham, Alderman of London.
She departed this life the 29th of June,
Anno Dom. 1650.

He died without issue, and was buried near his mother in St. Michael's church, in St. Alban's, according to the direction of his last will, and had a monument of white marble erected to him by Sir Thomas Meautys, who had formerly been his secretary. This monument represented his full portraiture in a contemplative posture, with the following inscription, written by Sir Henry Wotton:

Franciscus Bacon, Baro de Verulam, S. Albani Vicecomes;
seu notioribus titulis, scientiarum lumen, facundiæ Lex, sic sedebat.
Qui postquam omnia Naturalis
sapientiæ & Civilis arcana evolvisset, Naturæ decretum explevit.
Composita solvantur, anno Dom. MDCXXVI. Ætatis LXVI.
Tanti veri Memoriæ
Thomas Meautus, superstitis Cultor, defuncti Admirator. H. P.

The learned Bayle says he was one of the greatest genius's of his age. M. Voltaire styles him the father of experimental philosophy; and the greatest writers of our nation, as well as those of other countries, conspire in giving him the noblest character imaginable; and the late Duke of Buckingham (Sheffield) in particular assures us,† "*that all his works are, for expression as well as thought, the glory of our nation, and of all latter ages.*" Dr. Rawley, who was his chaplain, observes, that he was eminent for the sharpness of his wit, his memory, judgment, and elocution, so that Sir Walter Raleigh once said before the doctor, that the Earl of Salisbury was an excellent speaker, but no good penman; the Earl of Northampton, and the Lord Henry Howard, excellent penmen, but no good speakers; but that Sir Francis Bacon was eminent in both. He read much, and with great judgement; and after a moderate relaxation of his mind from study, returned to it with fresh vigour, and would not suffer any moment to escape him without improvement.

* From the monument at Eyeworth church.   † In his works, oct. edit. vol. I. p. 288.

His conversation was extremely delightful and instructive. When his office called him, as he was one of the king's council, to charge any offenders, he did it with the greatest lenity; and in civil affairs, as counsellor of state, he never engaged his master in any severe or precipitate courses. Neither was he less in favour with the subject than with his sovereign, for he was always acceptable to the house of commons when he was a member thereof. He was generous to his servants, which was the cause (says Dr. Rawley) "*that so many young gentlemen of blood and quality sought to list themselves in his retinue; and if he were abused by any of them in places, it was only the error of the goodness of his nature, but the badges of their indiscretions and intemperances.*" He was religious, free from malice, "*which* (as he said himself) *he never bred nor fed.*" No revenger of injuries. He never endeavoured to remove others from their places, or accused any man to his prince. In his will he has this remarkable passage, "*for my name and memory, I leave it to mens' charitable speeches, and to foreign nations, and the next ages.*" *

* Though we have enlarged so much on Lord Bacon's personal character, we cannot avoid taking notice of what has been said concerning it by two or three late historians. Mr. Guthrie is very moderate and candid in his censures. "Bacon (says he) was generous, easy, good-natured, and naturally just: but he had the misfortune to be beset by domestic harpies, who in a manner farmed out his office; and he had given way to intolerable impositions upon the subject among the masters in chancery. Even in the charges against him in the house of commons it appears as if some of the presents that had been made to influence his justice, had neither come into his own pocket, nor been made with his knowledge. For some decrees had been given against the corrupters, and resentment for this, had brought them to accuse him in the committee of the commons."—*Brit. Biog. vol. IV. p.* 147.

Mr. Hume's account of his conduct, though written with much candour, is somewhat more pointed. He observes, that Bacon was "a man universally admired for the greatness of his genius, and beloved for the courteousness and humanity of his behaviour. He was the greatest ornament of his age and nation, and naught was wanting to render him the ornament of human nature itself, but that strength of mind which might check his intemperate desire of preferment, that could add nothing to his dignity, and restrain his profuse inclination to expence, that could be requisite neither for his honour nor entertainment. His want of œconomy, and his indulgence to servants, had involved him in necessities; and in order to supply his prodigality he had been tempted to take bribes, and that in a very open manner, from suitors in chancery. It is *pretended*, that notwithstanding this enormous abuse, he had still, in the seat of justices, preserved the integrity of a judge, and had given just decrees against those very persons from whom he had received the wages of iniquity. Complaints rose the louder on that account, and at last reached the house of commons, who sent up an impeachment against him to the peers. The Chancellor, conscious of guilt, deprecated the vengeance of his judges, and endeavoured, by a general avowal, to escape the confusion of a stricter inquiry. The lords insisted on a particular confession of all his corruptions. He acknowledged 28 articles."—*Hume's Hist. of Great Britain, vol. VI. p.* 52, 8vo. edit. 1763.

Mrs. Macauley, who does not suffer herself to be seduced by the shining qualities, and even private virtues of characters, into a palliation of the delinquency of their public principles and conduct, speaks of him with great severity. "Thus ignominious (says this ingenious lady) was the fall of the famous Bacon, despicable in all the active parts of life, and only glorious in the contemplative. Him the rays of knowledge served but to embellish, not enlighten; and philosophy itself was degraded by a conjunction with his mean soul. We are told, that he often lamented that ambition and false glory had diverted him from spending his whole time in the manner worthy his extensive genius: but there is too much reason to believe from his conduct, that these sentiments arose from the weight of his mortifications, and not from the conviction of his judgment. He preferred mean applications to James, and continued to flatter him so far, as to paint his grandfather, Henry VII. in an amiable light." The same writer adds, with regard to the letters written by Buckingham, in favour of different people who had causes depending in chancery, "that there is great reason to believe, that every one of their mandates were implicitly obeyed by the obedient Chancellor."—*Macauley's Hist. of England, Vol. I. p.* 163, 164, 4to.

Sir NICHOLAS BACON, eldest son of the lord keeper, was possessed of a very large estate upon the death of his father, holding of the crown, 22 Eliz. by

> When however we recollect the assertion of Rushworth, "that his decrees were generally made with so much equity, that though gifts rendered him suspected for injustice, yet never any decree made by him was reversed as unjust," we could hope that his obedience was not entirely so implicit as Mrs. Macauley supposes.
>
> Upon the whole, notwithstanding the softenings which Lord Bacon's character may in some respects admit of, from the spirit of the times, from his own peculiar circumstances, and from other considerations, yet when we call to mind his slavish submission in general to the will of the crown, and especially his ingratitude to Essex, and his corruption as a judge, we are obliged, though with the greatest regret, to join with Mr. Pope in styling him "*The wisest, brightest, meanest of mankind.*"
>
> We shall conclude this note with the just and fine estimate of his merit, which has been made by an author now living, of distinguished eminence in the philosophical and literary world, M. D'Alembert.—"On considering attentively the sound, intelligent, and extensive views of this great man, the multiplicity of objects his piercing wit had comprehended within its sphere, the elevation of his style, that every where makes the boldest images to coalesce with the most rigorous precission, we should be tempted to esteem him the greatest, the most universal, and the most eloquent of philosophers. His works are justly valued, perhaps more valued than known, and therefore more deserving of our study than elogiums. Bacon, born amid the obscurity of the most profound night, perceived that philosophy did not yet exist, though many had undoubtedly flattered themselves for having excelled in it: for the more an age is gross and ignorant, the more it believes itself informed of all that can be possibly known. He began by taking a general view of the various objects of all natural sciences: he divided those sciences into different branches, of which he made the most exact enumeration; he examined into what was already known as to each of those objects, and he drew up an immense catalogue of what remained to be discovered. This was the aim and subject of his admirable work, on the dignity and augmentation of natural knowledge. In this new organ of sciences he perfects the views he had pointed out in the first work; he carries them farther, and shews the necessity of experimental physics, which was not yet thought of. An enemy to systems, he beholds philosophy as only that part of our knowledge which ought to contribute to make us better or more happy. He seems to limit it to the science of useful things, and every where recommends the study of nature. His other writings are formed on the same plan. Every thing in them, even their titles are expressive of the man of genius, of the mind that sees in great. He there collects facts; he there compares experiments, and indicates a great number to be made. He invites the learned to study, and perfect the arts, which he deems as the most illustrious and most essential part of human knowledge. He exposes, with a noble simplicity, his conjectures and thoughts on different objects worthy of interesting men; and he might have said, as the old gentleman of Terence, '*that nothing affecting to humanity was foreign to him.*' Science of nature, morality, politics, œconomics, all seemed to be within the stretch of that profound wit; and we know not which most to admire, the richness he diffuses over all the subjects he treats of, or the dignity with which he speaks of them. His writings cannot be better compared than to those of Hippocrates on Medicine; and they would be neither less admired nor less read, if the culture of the mind was as dear to mankind as the preservation of their health. But there are none but the chiefs of sects of all kinds whose works can have a certain splendour. Bacon was not of the number, and the form of his philosophy was against it. It was too good to fill any one with astonishment. The scholastic philosophy, which had gained the ascendant in his time, could not be overthrown, but by bold and new opinions; and there is no probability that a philosopher who only intimates to men, '*this is the little you have learned; this is what remains for your inquiry,*' is calculated for making much noise among his cotemporaries. We might even presume to hazard some degree of reproach against the lord chancellor Bacon, for having been perhaps too timid, if we were not sensible with what reserve, and as it were with what supersition, judgment ought to be passed on so sublime a genius. Though he confesses that the scholastic philosophers had enervated the sciences by the minutiæ of their questions, and that sound intellects ought to have made a sacrifice of the study of general beings to that of particular objects, he seems notwithstanding, by the frequent use he makes of school terms, and sometimes also by the adopting of scholastic principles, and by the divisions and sub-divisions then much in vogue, to have showed too much deference for the predominant taste of his age. This great man, after breaking the shackles of so many irons, was still entangled by some chains, which he either could not or dared not to break asunder."— *See Biog. Bri. art. Bacon.*

BACON OF REDGRAVE.

TABLE II. according to Dethick's Grant.

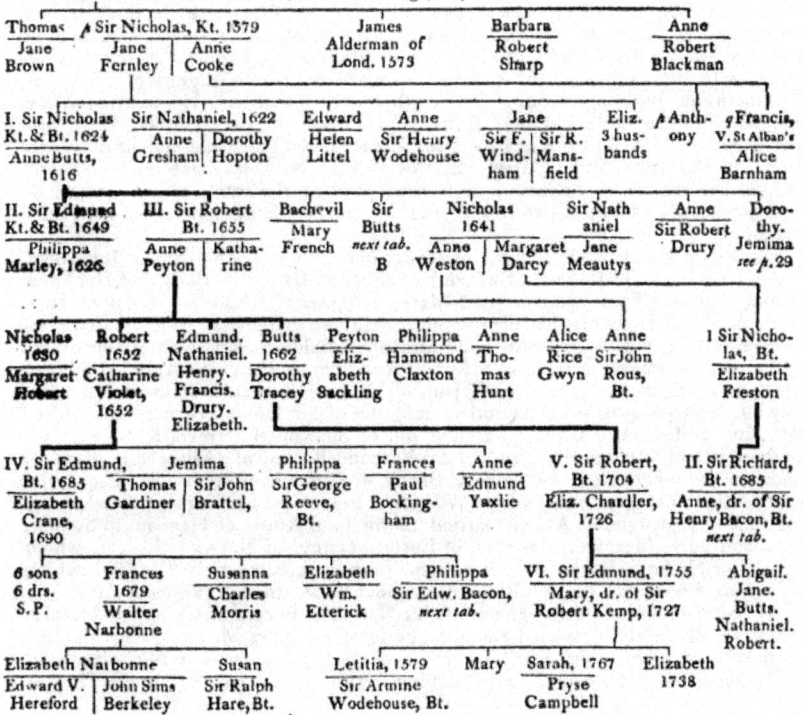

William Bacon, Esq. temp. Edward II.

Sir Edmund Bacon, Kt. = Margery, dr. of Robert Quapladde, Esq.

Sir John Bacon, Kt.

Adam Bacon

Henry Bacon

Robert Bacon, temp. Henry IV. and V.

Walter of Drinkston

John Bacon

John Bacon

A Robert of Drinkston = Isabella, dr. of John Gage, Esq.

several tenures of knights service, the manors and advowsons of Redgrave, Hinderly alias Hyldersley, and Wortham, Ricklinghall alias Westhall, and Wynerston; also the hundred of Blackborne, with the rent of 57 quarters of oats, with annual suit and service of the inhabitants within the parishes of Stow-Langtoft, Hunston, Langham, Walsham, Ashfilde, Barnham parva, Lyvermere, Culforde, Thorpe, Fakenham magna, Fakenham parva, Ixworth, Westhowe, Wordwell, Ryseworth, Watsfile, Rykenhall, Hynderly, Weston, Bardwell, and Stawnton; likewise the manor of Ashfield magna, and 40 messuages there, and in Little Ashfield and Ixworth: also the manors of Mettingham, Illetshall, and Sheap-Meadow, with 60 messuages; 60 tofts in Mettingham, Bungaye, and the rectory of Mettingham; the manor of Bromfield, and 70 messuages in Bromfield, Wenerston alias Waynston; the manors of Inham alias Ingham-hall, Tymworth, Barnham near Thetford, and Playford in Barnham, and 30 messuages, &c. in Ingham, with the advowsons of Ingham and Tymworth; the rectory and manor of Walsham; the liberties and franchises of St. Edmund's-bury; the manor and rectory of Tymworth, held of the manor of Ingham; also the manor and advowson of Burgat. He was knighted by Queen Elizabeth at Norwich, in her progress thither, Aug. 22, 1578, and had afterwards the honour to be the first person advanced to the dignity of a baronet, then instituted by King James I. in the 9th year of his reign. He married Anne, sole daughter and heir of Edmund Butts, of Thornage in com. Norfolk, Esq. (brother to Sir William Butts, Knt.) by Anne his wife, daughter and co-heir of Henry Buers, of Barrow in Suffolk, Esq. By this lady Sir Nicholas came possessed *inter alia*, of the manor of Foxhead, and three parts of the estate of Sir Andrew de Buers, who lived temp. Edward III. and by her had issue nine sons and three daughters.

The sons were, 1. Sir Edmund, his successor; 2. Henry, who died at Jerusalem, without issue; 3. Sir Robert, of whom hereafter; 4. Bachevell Bacon, of Hockham in com. Norfolk, Esq. (who married Mary, daughter of Thomas French in com. Essex, and left two sons that died young, and three daughters, who were co-heirs to their brother, viz. Mary, married to Sir Robert Baldock, Knt. one of the judges of the common-pleas; Philippa, to Robert Keddington, Esq. and Anne, to Nicholas Rookwood, Esq.) 5. Sir Butts Bacon, of Mildenhall in Suffolk, created baronet July 29. 1627 (who married Dorothy, daughter of Sir Henry Warner, of Mildenhall, Knt. and relict of William, second son of Sir Robert Jermyn, Knt.) ancestor to those late of Heringfleete, and to Sir Edmund Bacon, of Gillingham, Bart. of whom in its proper place: 6. Nicholas Bacon, of Gillingham in Norfolk, Esq. (who married 1st. a daughter of Sir James Weston, baron of the Exchequer, by whom he had only one daughter, Anne, married to Sir John Rous, of Henham in Suffolk, Bart. and 2dly. Margaret, daughter of Eustace Darcy, of Norwich, Esq. by whom he had Sir Nicholas Bacon, of Gillingham, Bart. so created Feb. 7, 1661, which title expired with his son Sir Richard, without issue, though the estate is in the present Sir Edmund, of Gillingham.) 7. Sir Nathaniel Bacon, of Culford in Suffolk, Knt. of the Bath, who married Jane, daughter of Hercules Meautys, Esq. (widow of Sir William Cornwallis, Knt.) by whom he had issue one son Nicholas, who died without issue male, and two daughters, Anne (married 1st. to Sir Thomas

Meautys, Knt. 2dly. to Sir Harbottle Grimston, Bart.) and Jane, who died unmarried. Sir Nicholas had two other sons that died young. The three daughters of Sir Nicholas the first baronet were, 1. Anne, married to Sir Robert Drury, of Hawsted in Suffolk, Knt. 2. Dorothy, married 1st. to Sir Bassingbourn Gawdey, of Harling in Norfolk, Knt. and 2dly. to Philip Colby, Esq. 3. Jemima, to Sir William Waldegrave, of Smallbridge, Knt.

Sir Nicholas and his lady lived 52 years together in wedlock. He died in 1624, she in 1616. They both lie buried in Redgrave church, under a most magnificent altar tomb, with both their effigies curiously carved in full proportion, out of the finest white marble, with the following inscriptions:—

The body of
Sir Nicholas Bacon, Knight and Baronet,
lieth here:
He took to wyfe Anne Butts, sole heyre to Butts, and half heyre to Bures.
They lived together 52 yeares,
when death makinge the separation on hir part,
he erected this monument to them both,
anno Domini 1616.

The lady Anne Bacon,
wife to the same Nicholas Bacon,
lyeth buryed in this place,
by whom he had 9 sonnes and 3 daughters:
She died in the 68 year of her age, the 19 day of September,
Anno Domini 1616.

II. Sir EDMUND, the eldest, succeeded his father in the title and estate, and married Philippa, one of the daughters and coheirs of the Right Hon. Edward Lord Wotton, Baron of Marley; but dying without issue, April 10, 1649, lies buried at Redgrave aforesaid, under a handsome mural monument, with this inscription:—

Within this vault was laid the body of
Sir Edmond Bacon, Knight and Baronet, the eldest son of
Sir Nicholas Bacon, Bart.
And the husband of that lady Philip Bacon, mentioned in the other table,
April the 10th, 1649.

This grave stone was layd over the bodye of the
Lady Philip Bacon,
daughter to the L. Edward Wotton, Baron of Marley,
and wife to
Sir Edmond Bacon, Knight, Barronet,
The 1st. of October, 1626.

III. He was succeeded by Sir ROBERT, his next surviving brother, known before by the denomination of Robert Bacon, of Riborough in Norfolk, Esq. (an estate now in the family) where he mostly resided, and in that parish church was buried with the following inscription:—

Robert Bacon,
of Redgrave in the County of Suffolk, Bart.
was buried the 16th of Dec. 1655.
And Dame Anne Bacon,
his wife,
was buried the 27th of Sep. 1640.

He married Anne, daughter of Sir John Peyton, of Isleham in com. Camb. Knt. and Baronet, and had issue by her, nine sons and three daughters, viz. Edmund, Nathaniel, Henry, Francis, and Drury, who all died young; Nicholas, who married Margaret, daughter and co-heir of —— Hobart, of Thwayte in Norfolk, Esq. but died without issue. The other sons were, Robert the eldest, who married Catherine, daughter to Grave Violet, of Pynkney-house, near Taterford in Norfolk, Esq. and dying in his father's life-time, Aug. 25, 1652, was buried at Redgrave, leaving issue one son, Edmund, successor to his grandfather, and four daughters: 1. Jemima, married to Thomas Gardiner, of Essex, Esq. and after to Sir John Brattel, Knt. assay-master of the Tower of London; 2. Philippa, married to Sir George Reeve, of Thwaite, Knt. and Bart. 3. Francis, to Paul Bockenham, of Great-Thornham, Esq. 4. Anne, to Edmund Yaxlee, of Yaxlee, Esq. all in the county of Suffolk.

Butts Bacon, Esq. another son of Sir Robert, married Dorothy, daughter and co-heir of Sir John Tracey, of Stanhow in Norfolk, Knt. and was father of Sir Robert, hereafter mentioned.

Peyton Bacon, Esq. another son, married Elizabeth, daughter of Charles Suckling, of Wotton in Norfolk, Esq. Sir Robert's daughters were, 1. Philippa, married Hamond Claxton, of Levermore; 2. Anne, to Thomas Hunt, of Sharington; and 3. Alice, to Richard Gwyn, of Fakenham-market, Esqrs.

IV. Sir EDMUND, only surviving son of Robert, aforesaid, succeeding his grandfather in title and estate, and married Elizabeth, one of the daughters and co-heirs of Sir Robert Crane, of Chilton in Suffolk, Knt. and Bart. by whom he had issue, six sons and ten daughters, all of which, except four daughters, died unmarried before him. The sons were, 1. Robert, 2. Nicholas, 3. Edmund, 4. Edmund, 5. Philip, 6. Francis. The daughters were, 1. Susan, 2. Elizabeth, 3. Catharine, 4. Jemima, 5. Jane, 6. Sarah. Those that married were, 1. Frances, to Walter Norborne, of Calne in the county of Wilts, Esq. (by whom he had issue only two daughters, Elizabeth, married to Edward Viscount Hereford, and Susan to Sir Ralph Hare, Bart.) 2. Susanna, to Charles Morris, of Loddington in com. Leicestershire, Esq. 3. Elizabeth, to William Ettrick, of the Middle-Temple, Esq. and 4. Philippa, to Sir Edmund Bacon, of Gillingham, Bart. grandfather of the present Sir Edmund of that place.

Sir Edmund Bacon, of Redgrave aforesaid, died Sep. 12, 1685, aged 52, and lies buried in that church, under a noble mural monument for him and his lady, with the following inscription:—

In the vault under this marble lyeth the body of
Sir Edmund Bacon, of Redgrave, Baronet, who married
Elizabeth, daughter of Sir Robert Crane, of Chilton-hall in Suffolk, Knt. and Bart.
and lived with her in marriage 35 years:
Had issue by her Six sons and Ten daughters.

He lived in the love and honorable esteem of his country: loyal to his king,
constant to the government in church and state:
A generous colonel, a good magistrate, and a just man:
A learned and most accomplisht gentleman;
and dyed a pious christian, on the 12th day of September, 1685,
in the year of his age 52.

In the vault of this marble lyeth the body of
Elizabeth, relict of Sir Edmund Bacon, mentioned in the other table;
by whom she had 6 sons and 10 daughters,
four of which only, and no sons, lived to the state of marriage; and of these
Frances was married to Walter Norborne, in the county of Wilts, Esq.
who are dead, and left issue
Elizabeth, Vicountess Hereford, and Susan:
Elizabeth to Wm. Ettricke, of the Midd. Temple, Esq.
Susan to Charles Morris, of Loddington in Lestr. Sh. Esq.
Philippe to Sir Edmd. Bacon, of Suff. Bart.

She was a lady of most exemplary piety and vertue;
a faithful wife,
a most tender and affectionate mother; a prudent governess of her family;
a most true and constant friend:
most eminently charitable to the poor, generous and great in her beneficence;
and having endured long sickness,
in satisfyed hopes of a blessed immortality, she committed her soul to God,
and departed this life
Dec. 6, 1690, in the year of her age 57.

After Sir Edmund's decease without issue male, the title and part of the estate descended to

V. Sir ROBERT BACON, his cousin, son and heir to Butts Bacon, Esq. which Sir Robert was before seated at Egmore in Norfolk; and after the death of his cousin, Sir Edmund, was possessed of the estate at Redgrave; which descending to him under some incumbrances, he thought convenient to sell that estate to the lord chief-justice Holt, and afterwards purchased at Garboldisham in Norfolk, where he built a handsome seat for the future residence of his family. He died Jan. 31, 1704, and lies buried in the chancel of All-Saints church in Garboldisham, under a handsome monument, with this inscription:—

Under this marble is buried the body of
Sir Robert Bacon, Baronet,
who departed this life on the 31st of Jan. in the year of our Lord 1704,
and of his age 52.

He left issue by the said Elizabeth his wife, daughter to Daniel Chandler, of London, Esq. two sons, Sir Edmund, his successor, and Butts, who died unmarried 1725-6, Nathaniel and Robert, his two other sons having died young before him; and two daughters, Abigal and Jane, who died unmarried.

VI. Sir EDMUND BACON, of Garboldisham in Norfolk, represented the borough of Thetford in parliament the ninth of Queen Anne, and the county of Norfolk in three parliaments. He married in Nov. 1712, Mary, daughter of Sir Robert Kemp, of Ubbeston in Suffolk, Bart. (and sole heir to her mother, Letitia, daughter of Robert King, of Great Thurlow, in the county of Suffolk, Esq.) which lady died Sep. 14, 1727, leaving only four daughters, Letitia, the wife of Sir Armine Wodehouse, Bart. but died March 30, 1759; Mary; Sarah, the wife of Pryse Campbell, jun. and died May 20, 1767; and Elizabeth, who died unmarried, May, 1738. Sir Edmund died in June, 1755. We now return to

1. Sir BUTTS BACON, the fourth son of the first baronet: he was created a baronet on the 29th of July, 1627, and married Dorothy, daughter of Sir Henry Warner, of Parham in Suffolk, Knt. widow of William, second son of Sir Henry Jermyn, Knt. by whom he had three sons, Charles and Clement, who both died without issue, and Sir Henry, his successor. He had also two daughters, Anne, the wife of Henry Kitchingman, of Bluntesdon-hall in Suffolk, and Dorothy, of William Peck, of Cove in the same county, Esqrs. He was succeeded by

2. Sir HENRY, his son, who removed to Herringfleet in Suffolk, where his father had built a seat. He married a daughter of William Gooch, of Mettingham in Suffolk, Esq. and had his successor; and Anne, the wife of Sir Richard Bacon, of Gillingham in Norfolk, Bart. but died without issue.

3. Sir HENRY BACON, successor to the title and estate, was of Herringfleet and Gillingham, and executor to his sister's husband, Sir Richard. He married Sarah, daughter of Sir John Castleton, of Sturston in Suffolk, Bart. by whom he had Sir Edmund, his successor; Henry and Nicholas, who died unmarried, and Richard, who married Elizabeth, daughter of Thomas Palgrave, of Norfolk, Esq.

4. Sir EDMUND BACON, Bart. the eldest son, married Philippa, daughter of Sir Edmund Bacon, of Redgrave in Suffolk, and died July 10, 1721, leaving issue, Sir Edmund, the succeeding baronet, Henry, Richard, Devereux, made surveyor-general of his majesty's dominions in North America, but died in his passage thither, July, 1731, unmarried; John, Ralph, and Elizabeth, who died unmarried, Sep. 1738; and Philippa. He married to his second wife, Mary, daughter of John Castell, of Raveningham, by whom he had Mary, the wife of Philip Bedingfield, Esq. Anne died in 1785. Robert, who died in 1716, and Castell, who married Elizabeth, daughter of Richard Dashwood, of Cockley Cley in Norfolk, Esq. who died in 1777, by whom he had two sons, Sir Edmund, the present baronet, and Dashwood, who was born in 1752, and married Anne Barbara, daughter of —— Ogilvie, of St. Christopher, by whom he has issue.

BACON OF REDGRAVE.

5. Sir EDMUND BACON, the eldest son, succeeded his father in title and estate. He represented the borough of Thetford in Norfolk the 6th, 7th and 8th parliaments of Great Britain. He married Susan, daughter of Sir Isaac Rebow, of Colchester in Essex, Knt. and died at Bath, Oct. 2, 1738. His issue was, Sir Edmund, his successor, and a second son, born Nov. 1726, who died in his infancy; and Susan, who was married in 1765, to Francis Schutz, Esq.

6. Sir EDMUND, his son and heir, succeeded him; and on the death of Sir Edmund Bacon, of Garboldisham, before mentioned, succeeded to that title likewise; so that his family enjoys the title of baronet, not only by virtue of the patent granted in 1627, to Sir Butts Bacon, of Mildenhall, aforesaid, fifth son of Sir Nicholas Bacon, of Redgrave, Bart. but likewise by that of 1611; by which means the present Sir Edmund stands first on the honourable list of baronets. Sir Edmund died unmarried in 1750, and was succeeded by his uncle,

7. Sir HENRY BACON, Bart. who died unmarried in 1753, and was succeeded by his brother,

8. Sir RICHARD BACON, Bt. of Colchester, who married 1st. Bridget, daughter of ———— Mahew, of Colchester, who died in 1726; 2ly, Lucy Gardiner, who died in 1765. He died in 1773, and was succeeded by the present baronet, who is the son of Castell Bacon before mentioned.

9. Sir EDMUND BACON, Bart. was born in 1749. He married Anne, daughter of Sir William Beauchamp Proctor, Bart. and K. B. by whom he has issue. *See tab.*

TABLE 3.

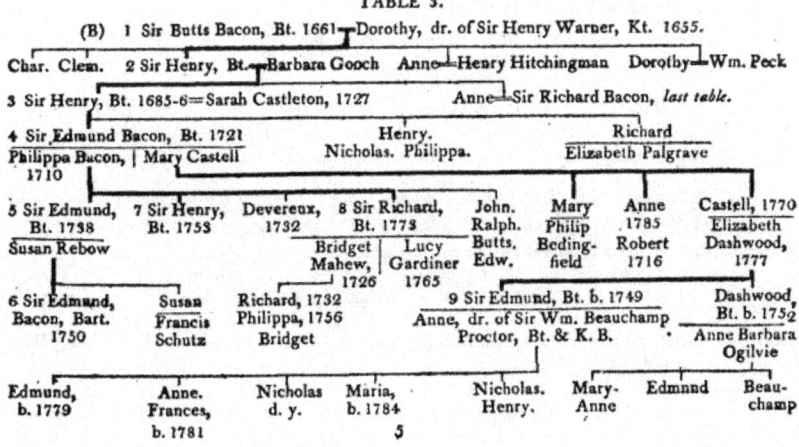

ARMS—Quarterly, first and fourth gules, on a chief argent, two mullets, sable, for Bacon. Second and third, Barry of Six, or and azure, over all a bend gules, for Quapladde.

CREST—On a wreath argent and gules, a boar passant ermine.

MOTTO—*Mediocra Firma.*

SEAT—Raveningham, Norfolk.

☞ *See more of the Barons in Biog. Brit. Blomefield's Hist. of Norfolk, vol. I. p. 89, 95, 180. Vol. II. p. 493, 554, 583, 681-2-3-4-7, 719, 854-5-6. Salmon's Essex, p. 251, 288. Brit. Mag. 1760, p. 673 and seq.*

---

2. HOGHTON of HOGHTON-TOWER, LANCASHIRE.

Created Baronet May 22, 1611.

THIS family, anciently written de Hocton and Hoghton, have been of great eminency in the county of Lancaster, in former ages, and were so denominated from Hoghton-Tower, a stately and large stone edifice, built upon a high and very steep hill, in the middle of a park, in the hundred of Leyland. The first mentioned is

1. ADAM de HOCTON,* who had one carucat of land in Hocton, temp. Henry II. whose great grand-son was

2. Sir ADAM de HOGHTON, written Knt. 50 Henry III. He is mentioned among the witnesses to a charter of Henry duke of Lancaster,† to the abbey of Whaley, in Lancashire, 34 Edwward I. He had two sons.

3. RICHARD, stiled *Filius dom. Adæ*, 2 Edward I. and Adam de Hoghton, stiled also in deeds, *Filius dom. Adæ*, 20 Edward I. and afterwards, *Frater magistri Richardi;* which Richard was sheriff of the county of Lancaster, 29 Edward I. an office in those days of great trust and authority. He had a son Richard, who dying without issue, the estate came to his cousin and heir, another

4. RICHARD de HOGHTON, son of Adam de Hoghton; which Richard was a Knt. and in 16 Edward II. with Sir Gilbert de Singilton, Knt. were returned knights of the shire for the county of Lancaster, in the parliament held at York, and had their wages allowed for attendance, &c. In the same year he and Edmund de Nevyle served as knights of the shire for the afore-mentioned county, as also in the 11th of that king's reign, and had their wages allowed. He died 14 Edw. III. 1340, having not a little increased the estate, by means of his wife Sibyll, daughter

* Ex Collect. Rog. Dodsworth. † Monast. Ang. vol. I. Rot. Pipe 29, E. 1.

and heir to Henry de Lea, who had great possessions, and were owners of the manor of Molington Banaster, in Chestershire, in right of Clementia, daughter of Robert Banaster, baron of Manaton, and wife of William de Lea, who received the same from her father in frank marriage; and although these Leas sometimes sealed with five mascles in bend for arms, and differed in the writing their names; yet were they nevertheless cadets of the first dynasty of the Lancasters, primitively barons of Kendal, in Westmorland, and lineal descendants from Ivo Talbois, earl of Anjou in France, and barons of Kendal, temp. Wm. Conq. Their usual arms were argent, three bars, sable: the reverse of which colours the family of Hoghton now bears. The said Richard, by his wife Sibyll before-mentioned, had issue Adam de Hoghton, and a daughter named Sibyll, the wife of William, son of Richard de Bold.

5. ADAM, last mentioned, is stiled a knight in deeds, 22 Edw. III. in which year he and John Cockaine served in parliament, as knights of the shire for the county of Lancaster, and had for their expences 15*l.* 4*s.* for 30 days. In the 37th of that king's reign he served again, as knight for that shire; as also in the 39th, and had, with the other knight, 17*l.* 4*s.* for 43 days attendance. He died 10 Rich. II. 1386, leaving issue by Ellen his wife, who survived her husband, two sons, Richard and Henry, and as many daughters. Agnes, the eldest, was wife to Sir Thomas, son of Sir Adam Banaster, Kt. and Sibyll, to William, brother of that Sir Thomas. Sir Henry de Hoghton, the younger son, was one of the knights of the shire for the county of Lancaster, 9 Henry IV. and was progenitor to the Houghtons of Pendleton, in that county, which, in aftertimes, went off in two daughters: Catharine, married to a younger son of Hoghton of Hoghton, as hereafter mentioned; and Mary, first married to George Singleton of Stayning, and secondly to Livesey Coner.

6. RICHARD de HOGHTON, eldest brother to the last Henry, was returned with Robert de Clifton, as knights of the shire for Lancaster, 6 Richard II. as also 4 Henry IV. with Sir Nicholas de Haverington, Kt. in which year the sheriffs were directed to levy 27*l.* for their coming, attendance, and returning, computing 69 days. 38 Edward III. he had licence to inclose and impark at Hoghton. He was a knight, founded a chantry in the church of Riblechester 7 Henry IV. and died 10 Henry V. leaving a daughter, Catharine, married to Hugh Venables, baron of Kinderton, and his grandson Richard, son of

7. ADAM de HOGHTON, heir to the estate. He had also another son Edward, who held lands at Preston and Writtington, and is supposed to be the ancestor to the Hoghtons in Sussex, who are said to be derived from Edward, a third son of this family.

8. RICHARD, grandson and heir of Sir Richard, did his homage, and had livery of his lands in Hoghton and Lea, 4 Henry VI. 1425, was a Knt. 22 Henry VI. and died 19 Edward IV. He had five sons, Lawrence, Alexander, William, Thomas, who married Anne, daughter of Oliver Culcheth, and Edward: the two last died without issue.

9. LAWRENCE succeeded in the estate, and dying the same year,

10. ALEXANDER, his brother and next heir, is found to be possessed of the inheritance, and was aged 26 years, 19 Edward IV. 1479, when the office was taken. In the 22d of that king's reign, having valiantly behaved himself under the Duke of Gloucester, in Scotland, he was made knight banneret, with several others on St. James's eve. He died 15 Henry VII. 1499, leaving a sole daughter and heir, aged 11 years at the time of the inquisition; and 17 Henry VII. her mother Elizabeth, daughter of William Troutbeck, had assignation of dower. The greatest part of the estate descended to his next brother and heir,

11. WILLIAM HOGHTON, Esq. third son of Richard, who was in the expedition into Scotland, under the duke of Gloucester, and received from him the honour of knighthood, at the same time his brother, Sir Alexander, was made a banneret. He purchased lands in Ingolhead, 11 Henry VII. and died in the 17th of that king's reign, 1501, leaving issue by Mary his wife, daughter of Sir John Southworth of Samlesbury, Knt.

12. RICHARD, his son and heir, aged 30 years: he was afterwards knighted, and served with Thomas Butler, as knights of the shire for the county of Lancaster, 1 Edward VI. 1547. He married four wives, first Alice, daughter and co-heir of Sir Thomas Assheton of Assheton Underline, in Lancashire, Knt. and cousin and heir of Sir James Harrington of Wolphage, in Northamptonshire, Knt. by whom he left issue Thomas, his son and heir, aged 40 years at the death of his father. Alexander and Isabella, married to —— Holden of Duxbury. His second wife was Alice, daughter of —— Morley, by whom he had Thomas, Rowland, and Richard; Agnes, wife of Richard Butler of Rawcliffe, Alice and Anne. His third wife was Elizabeth, daughter of John Grigson, and the fourth Anne, daughter of Roger Browne of Whitney. By the two last he left no issue.

13. THOMAS, the eldest son and heir, married Catharine, daughter of Sir Thomas Gerard of Bryne, in Lancashire, Knt. and died 22 Eliz. 1579, leaving Jane, his daughter and heir, 26 years old at his death, and at that time wife to James, son and heir of Roger Bradshaigh of Haigh, in Lancashire, Esq. who had a great contest about the estate, which was at length decided for Alexander, second brother, and next heir male to Thomas, father of Jane before mentioned; which

14. ALEXANDER HOGHTON, Esq. married twice, first to Dorothy, only daughter of Richard Assheton of Middleton, in Lancashire, Esq. by Catharine, his second wife, daughter of Sir Robert Bellingham, Knt. and afterwards to Elizabeth sister of Thomas and Bartholomew Hesketh, Esqrs. and widow of George Warburton, Esq. but he left no issue by either of them; whereupon the estate descended to Thomas, his half brother, viz. eldest son to Sir Richard Hoghton, last mentioned, by his second wife Alice, daughter of —— Morley; which

15. THOMAS was sheriff of Lancashire 6 Eliz. and was killed in the 49th year of his age, at Lea-Hall, an estate now in the family, by —— Langton of Newton, commonly called baron of Walton and Newton, 21 Nov. 32 Eliz. 1589. His wife Anne, daughter of Henry Kighley of Kighley, in Lancashire, Esq. son and heir of Sir Henry Kightley alias Kighley, Knt. became afterwards second wife to Sir Richard Sherburn of Stonyhurst, Knt. She died at Lea, Oct. 30, 1609, aged 60

HOGHTON OF HOGHTON-TOWER, LANCASHIRE.

years; having issue by her first husband, 1. Sir Richard, Kt. and Bart. 2. William of Grimsargh, who died 1642, and left posterity, which became extinct, and the estate devolved to the head branch of the family. 3. Thomas, who married Catharine, one of the daughters and co-heirs of John Hoghton of Pendleton, Esq. and left four daughters, his co-heirs. 4. Adam of Lea-Moor, who left posterity: and 5. Henry, who married Anne, daughter of Lawrence Townley, Esq. also two daughters, Mary, second wife to Thomas Walmsley of Dunkenhalgh, in Lancashire, Esq. and Catharine, wife of Thomas Middleton of Leighton, Esq.

I. Sir RICHARD HOGHTON of Hoghton, Kt. and Bart. eldest son of Thomas, was under age at his father's death, and in ward to Sir Gilbert Gerard: he succeeded to a very great estate, was knighted by Queen Elizabeth, and sheriff of Lancashire the 41st year of her reign, and made a baronet with the first advanced to that dignity. He served in several parliaments as knight of the shire for the county of Lancaster, entertained King James I. at Hoghton-Tower, for several days, when that king called there in his progress into Scotland 1617, and died Nov. 12, 1630, aged 60 years, 6 weeks, and 2 days. He married Catharine, daughter of Sir Gilbert Gerard of Gerard's Bromley in Staffordshire, Kt. master of the rolls, who died Nov. 17, 1617, aged 48 years and 6 months: he had by her 5 sons and 8 daughters, 1. Gilbert, 2. Thomas, 3. Richard, 4. Ratcliff, and 5. Roger, slain in Germany. The last three left no issue. Of the daughters, Anne married first Sir John Cotton of Landwade in Cambridgeshire, Kt. and afterwards Sir John Carleton of Brightwell in Oxfordshire, Kt. and Bart. Catharine was wife to James Stewart, Lord Galloway; Elizabeth to Nicholas Girling, Esq. Gilibert was married to Sir George Muscamp, of the county of Northumberland, Kt. Frances, Alice, Margaret, and Eleanor all died unmarried.

II. Sir GILBERT HOGHTON, Bart. his successor, was 39 years old at the death of his father, and was knighted at Whitehall, July 21, 1606. He was in great favour with King James I. whom he served at court several years; and after his death honourably distinguished his loyalty to King Charles I. Hoghton-Tower, in those unhappy times, served as a garrison, and part of it was blown up by accident, which is since rebuilt. Sir Gilbert served also several years in parliament as knight of the shire for the county of Lancaster; was an accomplished gentleman, and, by a prudent management, made acquisitions to the estate that descended to him. He died in April 1647, having married Margaret, the eldest of the four daughters and co-heirs of Sir Roger Aston of Cranford, in Middlesex, Kt. gentlemen of the bed-chamber, and master of the great wardrobe to King James I. to which Sir Roger, the said king, by writ under the privy seal, in the 9th year of his reign, granted to his coat-armour, an augmentation out of the two national badges of England and Scotland, viz. the rose of England, and the thistle of Scotland impaled, in a canton or, in regard of the marriage of the said Sir Roger with Mary, daughter of Andrew Stewart, who died during the life of his father Andrew Stewart, Lord Avingdale, in Scotland, descended from the blood royal: Sir Gilbert's descendants therefore bear the same in right of his lady, who died Dec. 23, 1657, and bore him six sons and four daughters:—1. George, the eldest son, died young; 2. Richard, succeeded to the title and estate; 3. Roger, who was killed in the battle at

Hessam-Moor, 1643; 4. Gilbert, major in the regiment of Sir Gilbert Gerard, Kt. governor of Worcester; married Lettice, daughter and co-heir of Sir Francis Gamull of Chester, Knt. and died 1661; 5. Thomas, died young; and 6. Henry, captain of horse under the Earl of Derby, who took to wife Mary, daughter of Peter Egerton of Shaw, in Lancashire, Esq. and relict of Sir Thomas Stanley of Bickerstaff, in Lancashire, Bart. Of the daughters, Catharine, married to Thomas Preston of Holker, in Lancashire, Esq. Mary, to Sir Hugh Calverly of Lee, in Cheshire, Knt. Margaret, to Alexander Rigby of Middleton, in Lancashire, Esq. and Anne died young.

III. Sir RICHARD HOGHTON, Bart. who succeeded his father in the title and estate, was elected knight of the shire for the county of Lancaster, in the reign of King Charles II. and departed this life Feb. 1677-8. One who knew him well gives this character of him:—"It has pleased Almighty God, by a sudden stroke, to make a sad breach in a worthy family, in taking away the chief head thereof; a person of great worth and honour, of an honourable extraction, of a generous disposition, and of a courteous, kind, and affable temper, whose high degree was so seasoned with an humble carriage towards all inferiors, as laid upon them a just obligation for true honour and service: he was free and hospitable in the entertainment of his friends, and most pleased with their kind and cheerful visits. His comportments at home and abroad were like himself, ever bespeaking a generous and worthy mind; and suitable to that eminency of interest and repute, which upon just accounts he held in this country. 'Twas his great and deserved commendation, that he was free from those vices which are the grand stains of true honour; I mean intemperance, debaucheries, revelling, dissolute practices, profligate courses, and the like; in a word, I may truly say, that the country has lost a good patriot, the gentry an eminent person in their number, the poor neighbourhood a constant and charitable supporter, his friends an hospitable receiver, kindred an honourable and respective relation, servants have lost a good master, children an indulgent father, an honourable and virtuous lady a dear consort." He married lady Sarah, daughter to the right honourable Philip Stanhope, earl of Chesterfield, and had issue several sons and daughters: of the sons, those arrived to maturity were, Sir Charles, his successor, and Benjamin, who died unmarried.

IV. Sir CHARLES HOGHTON, Bart. who succeeded to the title and estate, married Mary, eldest daughter of John Skeffington, lord viscount Massarene, in the kingdom of Ireland, by whom he had issue five sons and six daughters: of the sons, John, the eldest, died at the age of 21 years, whilst he was pursuing his studies in the Temple, and is interred in the church there. Sir Henry succeeded to the title and estate; Philip married the eldest daughter of Thomas Sclater of Denham, Esq. by whom he has one son, Henry, and one daughter: Skeffington was unmarried, and James died young. Of the daughters, Mary, the eldest, died at Chester 1710. Cordelia married to Robert Davie of York, Esq. and had two daughters, who are both dead. Anna married to Samuel Crooke of Coppul, Esq. who was killed by Mr. Buckley, in the road between Hoghton-Tower and Preston, and left one son. Margaret married to Samuel Watson of Hull, Esq. by whom she had one son and one daughter. Elizabeth married Thomas Fenton of Hounslett, near

Leeds, Esq. and left eight sons and two daughters. Lucy married Thomas Lutwidge of Whitehaven, Esq. and had seven sons and one daughter.

Sir Charles Hoghton, Bart. was three times elected knight of the shire for the county of Lancaster, in the reigns of King Charles II. King James II. and King William III. He died at Hoghton-Tower June 10, 1710, and was buried at Walton, amongst his ancestors, with the following inscription over them:

> Near this place is interred the remains of
> Sir Charles Hoghton, Bart.
> who was very exemplary for his piety and usefulness to his family and others.
> He died the 10th of June 1710, much lamented,
> in the 67th year of his age.

He was succeeded in honour and estate by his second son,

V. Sir HENRY HOGHTON, Bart. who married three wives, first in October 1710, Mary, eldest daughter of Sir William Boughton of Lawford in Warwickshire, Bart. who died at Dover 1720. After her decease (April 14, 1721) he married Lady Russel, relict of Lord James Russel, fifth son of William, the late Duke of Bedford: she died Sep. 1736, by neither of whom he had any issue. And after her death he married Susanna, eldest daughter of Thomas Butterworth of Manchester, Esq. but he left no issue. He served in parliament for the borough of Preston in Lancashire, in 9 Queen Anne; and also again for the same corporation in 1 George I. and 8 George I. he served in parliament for Eastlow, in Cornwall; and was afterwards twice elected for Preston. For his signal services in opposing the rebellion at Preston in the year 1715, he was chosen in parliament one of the commissioners for the forfeited estates, and after that commission determined, his majesty appointed him by patent, advocate-general, or judge-martial of his land forces: he is the fifth that has born this title of baronet, and the 19th generation of the surname on record. In 1740 he resigned his seat in parliament, after having represented the borough of Preston near 30 years. From that time he resided at Walton-Hall, and continued to serve his country, as a magistrate, with vigilance and activity, almost to the last period of his life, which ended on Feb. 23, 1768, being then 89 years of age. His lady died Oct. 11, 1772: leaving no issue, he was succeeded by his nephew,

VI. Sir HENRY HOGHTON, Bart. son of Philip, third son of Sir Charles, who was born on Oct. 22, 1728: in 1761 he married Elizabeth, only daughter and heiress of William Ashurst of Hedingham Castle, in the county of Essex, Esq. by which marriage he became possessed of the beautiful seat and estate of Hedingham Castle. She died the year following in child-bed, leaving a daughter, Elizabeth, who, on July 15, 1798, was married to Lewis Majendie, Esq. captain in the king's regiment of light dragoons.

Sir Henry Houghton married July 8, 1766, his second wife, Fanny, the eldest of the two daughters and co-heiresses of Daniel Booth, Esq. a director of the Bank. By this lady, who survives him, he left two sons, Henry Philip, his successor, born June 12, 1768, and Daniel, born August 28, 1770, a major in the army. Sir Henry was educated a dissenter from the established church, and continued invariably in communion with that body. He was however of that description termed moderate dissenters, both with regard to religious and political opinions. When it was proposed in the house of commons to obtain a repeal of the test and corporation acts, consistently with his sentiments, he lent his weight of countenance and argument to the proposal, by seconding the motion. The uniform tenour of his conduct as a member of parliament for near 30 years, during which he represented the borough of Preston, was highly respectable and exemplary. His attention to his duty was unremitted: in the agitation of great political questions he did not suffer his judgment to be controuled by party spirit, but conscientiously decided as appeared to him most for the welfare of the state. To the local interests of the town he represented, and indeed to the spirit of improvement, which has of late so much distinguished the whole manufacturing county of Lancaster, he proved himself at all times a zealous friend. This may suffice as a faint outline of the worth of his public character: concerning his many virtues in private life, the testimonies are as numerous and unanimous as his acquaintance was extensive: a marked gentleness and sweetness of disposition distinguished his whole social conduct; but these were especially conspicuous in the domestic relations of husband, father, and master: he was a warm and active friend, and to the poor a most humane and liberal benefactor. Happy is it for society when eminence of station is rendered still more attractive and respectable by the most virtuous principles, the most amiable manners, and the most beneficent conduct.* He died at Walton-Hall, March 9, 1795, aged 67; and was succeeded by his son,

VII. Sir HENRY PHILIP HOGHTON, the present baronet, member of parliament for the borough of Preston, who married —— the widow of Thomas Townley Parker, of Cuerden, Esq.

ARMS—Sable, three bars argent; with the augmentation of the rose of England and the thistle of Scotland, impaled, in a canton or.

CREST—On a wreath, a bull passant argent. They bore anciently a bull's head argent, collared with three bars sable.

SUPPORTERS—Over the gates of Hoghton-Tower, put up the beginning of the reign of Queen Elizabeth, two bulls argent.

MOTTO—*Malgre le tort.*

SEATS—Hoghton-Tower, and Walton-Hall, both in Lancashire; and Hedingham Castle in Essex.

* Gent. Mag. 1795, p. 260

HOGHTON OF HOGHTON-TOWER, LANCASHIRE.

TABLE 4.

1 ADAM de HOCTON, temp. Hen. II.   Ivo Talbois, E. of Anjou

2 Sir Adam de Hoghton, Kt.

3 Richard, Sheriff of Lanc. in 1301.   Adam   Henry de Lea

  Richard de Hoghton   4 Sir Richard, 1340 — Sibyll de Lea

5 Sir Adam, Kt. 1386 — Ellen   Sibyll = William de Bold

6 Sir Richard de   Anne   Sibyll   Sir Henry de
  Hoghton, Kt. 1422 Sir Thos. Banaster, Kt. Sir Wm. Banaster   Hoghton

7 Adam de Hoghton   Catharine = Hugh B. of Kinderton   Edward de Hoghton

8 Richard de Hoghton, 1479   Hoghtons' in Sussex

9 Law-   10 Alexander,   11 Sir William, 1501   Thomas   Edward   KINGS
  rence   Kt. Ban. 1499   Mary Southworth   Anne Culcheth   of
  1479   Eliz. Troutbeck   SCOTLAND

  a dr.   12 Sir Richard Hoghton, 1558   Andrew
              Alice   Alice   Elizabeth   Anne   L
              Assheton Morley   Grigson   Browne   Avingdale

13 Thomas, 1579   14 Alexander   Isabella 15 Sir Thomas, Rowland. Agnes   John   Andrew
   Catharine   Dorothy   Elizabeth — Hol- Kt. 1589 Richard. Richard. of   Stewart
   Gerard   Assheton   Hesketh   den   Anne Kighley, Alice. Butler. Pendle-
                                                   1609   Anne.   ton

I. Sir Richard, William,   Thomas   Henry   Mary   Catharine Catharine Mary
   Kt. & Bt. 1630 1642   Catharine Anne   Thomas   Thomas   Thomas   Sir
   Catharine   Adam   Hoghton   Townley Walmsley Middleton Hoghton   Roger
   Gerard, 1617   Aston

II. Sir Gilbert, Thomas.   Anne   Catharine Elizabeth Gilbert   4 drs. Margaret
    Bt. 1647   Richard.   Sir John Sir John James   Nicholas   Sir George   Sir Gilbert
    Margaret   Ratcliffe. Colle-   Carle-   L   Gir-   Muscamp,   Hoghton
    Aston   Roger.   ton   ton   Galloway ling   Kt.

III. Sir Richard, George.   Gilbert   Henry   Catharine Mary   Margaret
     Bt. 1678   Roger.   1661   Mary   Thomas   Sir Hugh   Alexander
     Sarah, dr. of Philip, Thomas.   Lettice   Egerton   Preston   Calverly. Rigby
     E. Chesterfield   Anne.   Gamull   Kt.

IV. Sir Charles, Bart. 1710 — Mary, dr. of John V. Massarine   More Children

John   V. Sir Henry, Bart. 1768   Philip, 1748   Skef-   Cordelia, Anne   Marg. Eliz. Lucy
d. V. P.   Mary   — wid. of Sus. But- — dr. of fington. 1768   1760   Sam.   Thos. Thos.
          Broughton, Sir Js. Rus- terworth, Thomas   James.   Robert Sam.   Wat-   Fen-   Lut-
          1720   sel, 1736   1772   Sclater   Mary.   Davie   Crooke son   ton   widge

VI. Sir Henry Hoghton, Bart. 1795   Mary   Anne
    Eliz. Ashurst, 1761 | Fanny Booth

Eliz. — L Majendie   VII. Sir Henry Philip Hoghton, Bart. — wid. of T. Townley Parker   Daniel
1 son 2 drs.

3. PEYTON of ISLEHAM, CAMBRIDGESHIRE.

Created Baronet May 22, 1611.

THE Peytons, as Mr. Camden observes, are of the same family as the Uffords, earls of Suffolk, who descended from William Malet, a Norman baron, who was sheriff of Yorkshire in 3 Wm. I. and from him received the grants of many lordships and manors; and among others he possessed those of Sibton and Peyton-Hall, in Suffolk, at the time of the general survey. "Isleham (says this author) formerly belonged to the Bernards, which came to the family of the Peytons by marriage. Which knightly family of Peyton, flowered out of the same stock whence the Uffords, earls of Suffolk, descended; albeit they assumed the surname of Peyton, according to the use of that age, from their manor of Peyton-Hall in Boxford, in the county of Suffolk."

The first of this family whom we find by the name of Peyton, is REGINALD de PEYTON, second son to Walter, lord of Sibton, in Suffolk, younger brother to Mallet, sheriff of Yorkshire, and lord of the manor of Eye, in Suffolk. This Reginald held the lordships of Peyton-Hall in Ramshold and Boxford, in Suffolk, of Hugh de Bigod; and had two sons, William and John.

2. JOHN had issue four sons, John the elder, Robert, Peter, and John the younger. Robert was lord justice of Ireland in the time of Henry III. and Edw. I. and being lord of Ufford, assumed his surname from that place: whose son, Robert de Ufford, was created earl of Suffolk 11 Edw. III. 1336, and made knight of the garter. He was at the battle of Cagn, and behaved so well, that the king rewarded him with the honour of Eye, formerly belonging to his family. Brothers to the earl were, Thomas de Ufford, knight of the garter, "and John Ufford, who was brought up at Cambridge, and made doctor of law; promoted first to the deanery of Lincoln, then to the chancellorship of England, and lastly to the archbishoprick of Canterbury, which he never enjoyed, being cut off by the plague, (which consumed nine parts of the men in England) before he received either his pall or consecration, June 7, 1348, and lieth obscurely buried in that cathedral church."* Peter de Peyton, lord of Peyton-Hall, who held lands in Ramshot and Peyton, in the time of King John; and took to wife Helena —— of whom he had issue Robert de Peyton, father to Sir John de Peyton, Knt. of the same places; whose male issue seemed to fail temp. Edw. III. The fourth son was John de Peyton, jun. who sold to John, his eldest brother, all the lands which he had in Boxford, of the fee of the abbey of St. Edmund's and Stoke Neyland, which their father John de Peyton, and William their uncle, formerly possessed.

3. Sir JOHN, the eldest son, succeeded, and was lord of Peyton-Hall in Boxford, and possessed lands at Stoke Neyland, in Suffolk. He had three sons and one

* Weever's Fun. Mon. p. 222.

daughter, Agnes, mentioned in the last will and testament of her brother: William, and James de Peyton, who was witness to a dateless charter of his father, and to another of his eldest brother, who was

4. Sir JOHN de PEYTON, Knt. successor to his father; to whom, and Clementia his wife, 27 Henry III. John, son of William de Effington, gave two acres of land, &c. Sir John served in the parliament held at Westminster, as one of the knights of the shire for the county of Suffolk, having reasonable allowance for his expence; as also in another parliament 29 Edw. I. soon after which he died. He had three wives, Agnes, Agnes, and Clementia.

5. Sir ROBERT, the eldest son, succeeded, who in many of his evidences is stiled Chevalier and Monsieur. He died 25 Edw. III. and was buried near his father. He had two wives, first the lady Christiana de Apleton, widow of William de Apleton, who died 19 Edw. II. leaving no children, and was buried at Stoke Neyland, with great pomp. Her funeral expences are thus set down:—50 quarters of wheat 4*l.* 10*s.* one hogshead of wine 53*l.* 4*s.* 4 muttons 5*s.* 8 barrow hogs 24*s.* 10 calves, &c. His second wife was Joan de Marney, of the noble family of the Marneys of Layer-Marney, in Essex, by whom there was issue Sir John, the next heir, and William, who lies buried at Wicken.

6. Sir JOHN succeeded, and married Margaret, the daughter and co-heir of Sir John Gernon of Lees, in Essex, Knt. lord of Wicken in Cambridgeshire, and Bankwell in Derbyshire. She died, and was buried at Wicken in 1414. Sir John died 17 Richard II. and was succeeded by his son,

7. JOHN de PEYTON, Esq. who took to wife Joan, daughter and heir of Sir Hammon Sutton of Wickesho, in Suffolk, Knt. by whom Wickesho came to this family. He died about the 5th of Henry IV. leaving issue by his said wife (afterwards married to Sir Roger Drury, Knt.) Margery, wife of Thomas Daubeny of Sharrington, in Norfolk, Esq. and three sons, John, Thomas, and Robert. Joan, in her widowhood, gave the manor of Wickesho, by deed dated 13 Henry IV.

8. JOHN, the eldest, was left a minor, being 15 years old, 8 Henry IV. at which time an agreement was made between the lady Margaret, his grandmother, Joan, his mother, of the one part, and John Burgoyne of Drayton, in Cambridgeshire, of the other, for an intermarriage with Grace, daughter of the said Burgoyne: which marriage took place; and from thence proceeded two sons, John and Thomas, and a daughter Anne, married to Jeffry Lockton, Esq. He died in the flower of his age, the 6th of Oct. 4 Henry V.

9. His son JOHN, aged 2½ years at his father's death, died in his minority, the 29th of Oct. 11 Henry VI. whereupon Thomas, then aged 17 years, and seized of the manor of Esthorp, was the next heir; and his mother Grace dying the 6th of May, he was found her heir to the manor of Messing, which was held of the crown, as of the honour of Keynes, by the service of one knight's fee; also of the manor of Binchall, and the castle. This Thomas was high-sheriff of Cambridge and Huntingdon 21 and 31 Henry VI. and about 17 Edw. IV. he began to re-build the church at Isleham, agreeing then with John Waltham, alias Sudbury, free-mason,

for the same; in the chancel of which church he lies interred, having a monument erected there to his memory, viz. his effigy cast in brass, with the following inscription:—

Orate pro animabus Thomæ Peyton, Armigeri,
& Margaretæ ac Margaretæ uxoribus ejus.
Qui quidem Thomas obiit 30die mensis Julii, A.D. 1484.
Quorum animabus proprietur Deus. Amen.

He married first Margaret, daughter and co-heir of Sir John Bernard of Isleham, Knt. by which match Isleham descended to this family; and he had issue by her, Thomas, hereafter-mentioned, Margaret, and Grace. His second wife was Margaret, daughter and co-heir of Sir Hugh Francis of Giffords, in the parish of Wickhambrook, in Suffolk (widow of Thomas Garnish of Kenton, in Suffolk, Esq.) Of this match proceeded two sons, Christopher and Francis. 1. Christopher Peyton, Esq. who had great possessions in Wickhambrook and Bury. In the 12th of Henry VII. he was sheriff of the counties of Cambridge and Huntingdon; and having married Elizabeth, daughter of Leonard Hide of Hide-Hall, in Hertfordshire, Esq. left no issue. He died 15 Henry VII. and, with his wife, was buried in Isleham church, on the roof whereof are these words cut in wood:

Pray for the good prosperity of Christopher Peyton, and Elizabeth his wife; and for the soul of Thomas Peyton, Esq. and Margaret his wife; father and mother of the said Christopher Peyton:
And for the souls of all the posterity of the said Christopher Peyton.

Francis Peyton of St. Edmund's Bury, Esq. second son, heir to his mother, was of Coggeshall, in Essex. He married Elizabeth, daughter of Reginald Brook of Aspall-Stonham, in Suffolk, Esq. by whom he had Christopher and Edmund, customer of Calais, who married, but left no male issue. Christopher Peyton of St. Edmund's Bury, married Jane, daughter of Thomas Mildmay, Esq. and sister to Sir Thomas Mildmay of Chelmsford, in Essex, Knt. and was father of three sons, Thomas, Christopher, and Henry of London. 1. Thomas Peyton of St. Edmund's Bury, customer of Plymouth, who by Cicely, daughter of John Bourchier, earl of Bath (and Eleanor Manors, his wife, daughter of Henry, earl of Rutland) was father of Sir Henry Peyton, knighted by King James I. who followed long the wars in the Low-Countries, and married Mary, daughter of Edward Seymour, duke of Somerset, and widow of Andrew Rogers of Brianson in Dorsetshire, Esq. eldest son to Sir Richard Rogers, Knt. 2. Christopher Peyton of St. Edmund's Bury, who was knighted by King James I. and auditor in Ireland. He married Anne, daughter of William Palmer of Warwickshire, Esq. and left three daughters, his co-heiresses: 1. Elizabeth, married first to Sir Richard Cooke, Knt. secretary of state in Ireland; and 2dly, to Sir Henry Cowley, Knt. ancestor by this lady to the present Richard Cowley Wellesley, earl of Mornington in Ireland, and Baron Wellesley in Great Britain. 2. Ciceley, married to Henry Rookwood of Ewsham; and 3. Thomazin, married first to Capt. Baptist, castillion of the bed-chamber to Queen Elizabeth, and secondly to Robert Pigot, of the Desart in Ireland, Esq. 3. Henry Peyton of London, who married Mary, daughter of William Pickering of London, and left posterity.

PEYTON OF ISLEHAM, CAMBRIDGESHIRE.

10. THOMAS PEYTON, the only son of Thomas, by the first venter, died before his father; and by his wife Joan, the daughter of —— Calthorp of Norfolk, he had issue Thomas (who died issueless) Robert, John, and Edward; and four daughters, Elizabeth married to Edward Langley of Knowlton, in Kent, Esq. Jane to John Langley of Lowleworth in Cambridgeshire, Esq. Anne to John Asheby of Harefield, in Middlesex, Esq. (ancestor to those now of that place) and Dorothy. Joan, surviving her husband, married secondly William Mauleverer, Esq.

11 The eldest son, Sir ROBERT, inherited, who was sheriff of Cambridge and Huntingdon 14 Henry VII. and died March 18, 9 Henry VIII. He left issue by Elizabeth, daughter of Sir Robert Cleer of Ormsby, in Norfolk, 1. Sir Robert, 2. John, who married Dorothy, daughter of Sir Robert Tyndall of Hockwould, in Norfolk, Kt. of whom descended the Peytons of Knowlton and Doddington, Barts. the former of which titles is extinct, and the latter will hereafter be mentioned in its proper place; and 3. Edward, who died without issue. Also two daughters, Margaret, the wife of Francis Jenney of Knotshall in Suffolk, Esq. from whom descend the Jenneys of that place; and Elizabeth, the wife of Sir Wm. Wigston of Wolston, in Warwickshire, Kt.

12. Sir ROBERT was the next heir, who was sheriff of the two aforesaid counties 17 and 27 Henry VIII. and accompanied that king to the seige of Bullen; and was again sheriff 1 Q. Mary. He married Frances, daughter and heir of Francis Hassylden of Little Chesterford, in Essex, Esq. and of Steeple-Morden, in Cambridgeshire, by whose right he became possessed of those places; besides lands in Rutlandshire. This lady founded the famous hospital at Isleham, and was buried by her husband in that church, where their memories are still preserved on a monument. They had six sons and two daughters, 1. Robert, 2. William, 3. Richard of Little Chesterford, in Essex, who married Mary, daughter of Leonard Hyde of Hyde-Hall, in Hertfordshire, Esq. She, after his decease, married Sir John Cary, lord Hunsdon. The three other sons were Christopher, Edward, and John. The daughters, Catharine, wife of —— Williams of Oxfordshire, Esq. and Elizabeth, wife of Thomas Wrenne of Hinton, in Hadenham, in the Isle of Ely, Esq.

13. ROBERT, the eldest, lord of Isleham, was knight of the shire for Cambridge 4th and 5th of Queen Mary, and high sheriff of the united counties of Cambridge and Huntingdon 9 Eliz. and received the honour of knighthood from King James I. at Royston, Novem. 1608. He married the lady Elizabeth Rich, daughter of Richard, baron Rich of Leez, lord high-chancellor of England; by whom he had issue three sons; Robert, who died unmarried during his father's life; Sir John, the baronet; and Richard, who died without issue: and as many daughters; Mary, first the wife of Robert Balam of Wolsoken, in Norfolk, Esq. and secondly of Sir Richard Cox of Braham, in the Isle of Ely, Knt. Frances, wife of John Hagar of Bourn-Castle, in Cambridgeshire, Esq. and Winnifred, married first to —— Osborne, Esq. counsellor at law, and afterwards to John Hornbye of Lincolnshire, Esq.

I. Sir JOHN PEYTON of Isleham, knighted by King James I. succeeded his father, Sir Robert, and was lord of Peyton-Hall in Boxford, Wicken, and Wickesho, &c. He was sheriff of the counties of Cambridge and Huntingdon 35 Eliz.

and knight of the shire for the last-mentioned county, as also 1 James I. and the next year sheriff again; and in the 9th of that reign received the new order of baronet. By his wife Alice, daughter to Sir Edward Osborn, who was lord-mayor of London 25 Eliz. 1583, and progenitor to the duke of Leeds, he had five sons and six daughters; Sir Edward, the next baronet; John, who died without issue; Robert, fellow of Queen's College, in Cambridge; Roger, William of Worlingworth, in Suffolk (who married Tabitha, daughter of Henry Payne of Walthamstow, in Essex, and left two sons, John and William) and Thomas, who was slain at the Burse in Holland. The daughters were, Anne, married to Sir Robert Bacon of Riborough, in Norfolk, Bart. third son of Sir Nicholas Bacon of Redgrave, Bart. Alice, wife of Sir John, son and heir of Sir John Peyton of Doddington, Knt. Elizabeth, of Sir Anthony Irby of Boston, in Lincolnshire, Knt. Mary, of Sir Roger Meers of Hoghton, in Lincolnshire, Knt. Frances and Susan Peyton both died unmarried. He was succeeded in estate and honour by his eldest son,

II. Sir EDWARD, who was bred at St. Edmund's Bury school, and afterward educated at Cambridge. He was knighted at Whitehall, Feb. 4, 1610, and during his father's life was denominated of Great Bradley, in Suffolk; and served in parliament from 8 James I. to 3 Charles I. as one of the knights of the shire for the county of Cambridge; and was *custos rotulorum* thereof, which office he was deprived of by the endeavours of the great favourite of James I. the duke of Buckingham; whereat he was so much disgusted, that he first drew his pen against the court, and writ several pamphlets with great acrimony of stile against King Charles I, and the royalists; and at length, siding with the presbyterians in the times of the great rebellion, had his share of sufferings for that cause, while the war lasted; which so impoverished him, that he sold Isleham (which had continued in the family so many years) and ruined the whole estate, drawing in his eldest son to join with him in the sale thereof, only reserving annuities for both their lives. This Sir Edward married three wives, first Matilda, daughter of Robert Livesay of Tooting, in Surrey, Esq. by whom he had issue John, Edward (who was a clergyman, and had three sons, Edward, Robert, and Henry) and Robert: also a daughter Anne, married to Henry Lawrence of St. Ives, in Huntingdonshire, and of St. Margaret's in Hertfordshire, Esq. Sir Edward married to his second lady, Jane, daughter of Sir James Calthorp of Cockthorp, in Norfolk, Knt. and widow of Sir Henry Thymelthorp of Norfolk, Knt. by whom he had issue one son, Thomas Peyton of Rougham, in Norfolk, Esq. who married Elizabeth, daughter of Sir William Yelverton of Rougham, Bart. by whom he had four sons; 1. William Peyton of Dublin, who died 1686. He married Frances, daughter and co-heir of Sir Herbert Lunsford, Knt. by whom he had no male issue; 2. Robert of Virginia, who left no male issue; 3. Charles Peyton of Grimston, in Norfolk, Esq. who married Elizabeth, daughter of William Bladwell of Swanington, in Norfolk, Esq. they both lie buried at Swanington, having had six sons; 1. Sir Yelverton, hereafter mentioned; 2. Bladwell, who married Mary, daughter of William Probart of Court-Evangwenge, in Radnorshire, Gent. by whom he has issue one son Charles, and two daughters, Mary and Elizabeth, all young: 3. William of Grimston, in Norfolk, who married Alice, daughter of William Robotham of Grimston, Gent. and died at Leverington, in the Isle of Ely, without issue: 4. Charles, who died at sea, without issue; 5. Colby, drowned at Lynn, without issue; 6. John Peyton, citizen of London, who married first Dorothy, daughter of James Altham of Marks-Hall, in Essex, Esq. by whom he had one son, John; and by his second wife Susan, daughter of Peter Calvert of Hunsdon, in Hertfordshire, Esq. (and sister to Peter Calvert of Hunsdon, Esq.) he had another son named Yelverton. The fourth son of Thomas Peyton of Rougham, Esq. was Yelverton, who married a daughter of Mr. Roberts, a merchant in Bristol, niece of Sir John Roberts of Bromley, in Middlesex, Bart. Thomas Peyton, Esq. the father of these sons, died in 1683.

Sir Edward married to his third lady, Dorothy, daughter of Mr. Edward Ball of Stockwell, in Surrey, by whom he had two sons; 1. Edward Peyton of Surinam, merchant, who died in 1675. He married Mary, daughter of Mr. Mulfin, an Italian merchant, and left one daughter, his sole heir, named Signora Angiola, married to Francis Ceffis of Peesroneer, in Venice: 2. Joseph Peyton, who, by Mary, daughter and co-heir of Marmaduke Vincent of Great Smeaton, in Yorkshire, had issue Vincent Peyton, only child living, 3 years old 1688. He died at Wicken in Cambridgeshire, in 1657; and was succeeded by his eldest son by the first marriage,

III. Sir JOHN PEYTON, Bart. who had two wives, 1. ―― daughter of Sir Edward Bellingham, who left no issue: but by his second wife ―― daughter of ―― Hobart, he had three sons; Edward, who died young; Sir John Peyton, Bart. who succeeded him; and Thomas, who was first an ensign, and afterwards captain in the guards; a gentleman of bright parts, and great accomplishments, which recommended him to the notice and favour of King Charles II. he died a batchelor. Sir John had also one daughter, Martha, married to George Duncombe of Shalford, near Guilford in Surrey, Esq. Sir John died in 1666, and was buried in St. Giles's in the Fields, London; and was succeeded by his only son,

IV. Sir JOHN PEYTON, Bart. who served his king and country in several military stations; for presently after the restoration he went with the earl of Rutherford to Tangier, under whom he served there till the death of the earl, when, returning to England, he rode in the guards, in the lord of Oxford's regiment; from whence, by the interest of the late duke of Leeds, his near relation, he was preferred to be a lieutenant in Sir John Hanmer's company, in the duke of Buckingham's regiment, in which he served at sea in the Dutch war; and when that was ended, went into Ireland with the regiment, 1674. The next year the Earl of Essex gave him a company, which he exchanged for a commission of lieutenant of horse: and, in King James's reign, when the lord Tyrconnel turned out the protestants, he agreed with his secretary to surrender to him his post, upon the payment of the yearly value of 100*l. per annum* for his life. He was attainted by an act of parliament in the time of King James II. and restored by King William's parliament. During the administration of the Earl of Rochester her majesty, Queen Anne, made him governor of Ross-Castle, in Kerry; but his choice determining him to reside at Dublin, he quitted that post. He first married the daughter of Mr. Newman, and widow of Mr. Kana O Hara. His second wife was the daughter of ―― Lloyd of Morton-Hall, in Wales, Esq. and widow of Richard Barry. His third wife was Mrs. Rebecca Williams of Liverpool, widow of the

PEYTON OF ISLEHAM, CAMBRIDGESHIRE.

TABLE 5.

Walter, L. of Sibton in Suffolk — 1 Reginald de Peyton
William Malet
    William de Peyton   2 John de Peyton

3 Sir John, Knt.—Matilda de Bueris   Robert   Peter—Helena   John, jun.

4 Sir John de Peyton, Kt.   Wm.   Agnes   Robert, E. of   Thomas de   John,   Robert de Peyton
Agnes | Agnes | Clementia   James.   Suffolk   Ufford, K.G.   abp. of Canterbury, 1348

5 Sir Rob. de Peyton, 1331=Chris. Apleton & Joan Marney   John   Gelian   Robert de Peyton

6 Sir John, 1394—Margaret Gernon, 1414   William   Sir John de Peyton

7 John d. about 1406—Joan, dr. of Sir Hammon Sutton, Knt.

8 John, 1406—Grace Burgoyne   Margery—T. Daubeny   Thomas   Robert

9 John, 1433   Marg. dr. of Sir J. Bernard, Knt.—Thomas, 1484—Marg. dr. of Sir Hugh Francis, Knt.

10 Thomas—J. Calthorpe   Margaret   Grace   Chris. 1501—Eliz. Hyde   Francis of Bury—Eliz. Brook

Thomas   11 Sir Robert, 1518   John.   Elizabeth   Jane   Anne, 1503   Doro-   Christopher   Edmund
d. V.P.   Eliz. Cleer, 1510   Edw.   E. Langley   J. Langley   J. Asheby   thy   J. Mildmay   Peyton

12 Sir Robert, Knt. 1550   John   Edw.   Marg.   Eliz.   Thomas   Sir Christ.   Henry
Frances Hassylden,   Dorothy   Francis   Sir Wm.   Cicely, dr.   Anne   Mary
1580   Tyndall   Jenney   Wigston, Kt.   of John   Palmer   Pickering
                                                     E. of Bath

13 Sir Rob.   Rich.   Wm.   Cath.   Eliz.   Peytons   Sir Henry,   Elizabeth   Cicely   Thomazin
Kt.   1574   Chris.   —Wil-   Thos.   of   Knt.   Sir R.   Sir H.   Hen.   Capt. | Rob.
Eliz. dr. of   Mary   Edw.   liams   Wrenne   Dod-   Mary   Cooke,   Cowley,   Rook-   Bap- | Pigot
Rich. B. Rich   Hyde   John.   dington   Seymour   Kt.   Kt.   wood   tist

Robert   I, Sir John, Bt.   Richard   Mary   Frances   Winifred
       Alice Osborn   Robert | Richard   John   Counsel.   —Hare- | John
                     Balam | Cox   Hagar   Osborne   fleet | Hornbey

II. Sir Edw. Kt. & Bt. 1657   John.   William   Anne   Alice   Elizabeth   Mary   Thomas.
Matilda | Jane | Dorothy   Robert.   Tabitha   Sir Rob.   Sir John   Sir Anth.   Sir R.   Frances.
Livesay | Calthorpe | Ball   Roger.   Payne   Bacon, Bt.   Peyton   Irby   Meers   Susan.

III. Sir John, Bt.   Edward   Robert   Anne   Thomas, 1683   Edw. 1675   Joseph   John
1666   N.   Henry   Eliz. | —wid. of   Mary   Mary   William
—Beling- | —Ho-   Law-   Yelverton | —Hacon   Mulfin   Marmaduke
ham   bart   rence

Edw.   IV. Sir John, Bt. 1721   Thomas   Martha   Edw.   Wm. 1686   Robert   Charles   Yelverton
d. y.   —New- | Miss | Rebecca   George   Robert.   Frances   Eliz.   —Roberts
man | Lloyd | Tomlinson   Duncombe   Henry   Lunsford   Bladwell

V. Sir Yelv. Peyton, Bt.   Bladwell   William   Charles.   John Peyton, 1741
   Flora Tracy   Mary Probart   Alice Robotham   Colby.   Dorothy Altham | Susan Calvert
Yelv. & Bladw. d. y.   Charles.   VI. Sir John Peyton, Bt.   VII. Sir Yelv. Peyton,
                            Mary. Eliz.   1772   —wid. of Felix Calvert, Esq.

Rev. Daniel Tomlinson. He died in Dublin, March 23, 1721, without issue, and was succeeded by his cousin,

V. Sir YELVERTON PEYTON, Bart. eldest son of Charles Peyton of Grimston, in Norfolk, Esq. who was the third son of Thomas Peyton of Rougham, Esq. only son of Sir Edward Peyton, Bart. by his second marriage, before mentioned. He married Flora, daughter of Sir Philip Tracy, but died without issue, and was succeeded by his nephew,

VI. Sir JOHN PEYTON, Bart. who died 1772, without issue, and was succeeded by his half brother,

VII. Sir YELVERTON PEYTON, the present baronet, who, March 19, 1773, married —— widow of Felix Calvert, Esq.

ARMS—Sable, a cross engrailed, or.
CREST—On a wreath, a griffin sejant, or.
MOTTO—*Patior potior.*

4. CLIFTON of CLIFTON, NOTTINGHAMSHIRE.

Created Baronet May 22, 1611.

THIS family took their surname from Clifton, a ville about two miles from Nottingham; which, in its Saxon etymon, signifies a ville upon a rock, or shelving ground, as Sir W. Dugdale observes, "here the Cliftons have a noble seat, from which, ascending by many steps, we rest upon the top on a fair bowling-green, that affords a most pleasant prospect, overlooking the Trent, the town of Nottingham, the vale of Belvoir, and part of the forest of Sherwood."

They derive themselves from Alvaredus de Clifton, a knight, said to be living in the time of William Peverell, the conqueror's bastard; and for proof of this, Alvaredus, and two others of his lineal posterity is cited in an authority amongst the collections of Mr. St. Lo. Kniveton, wherein it is said, Alveredus was warden of Nottingham-Castle in the time of William Peverell; and in which office he was succeeded by his son and grandson, Robert and Gervase.*

* Thoroton, in his Antiquities of Nottinghamshire, treating of Clifton, says, "This worthy family therefore, which held lands here, and had their name from their residence at this place, and sometimes at Wilford, must not, till this time (9 Edw. 1.) pretend to be lords of it, notwithstanding the received tradition and old parchment-writing, importing that Sir Alvered de Clifton, Knt. was lord of the manor

It is believed however, that his son and grandson were both named Gervase; for 20 Henry III. there was a fine levied between Gervase de Clifton (supposed to be the son) and Hugh de Bel, concerning two oxgangs of land in Wilford. Anno 52 Henry III. Gervase, son of Gervase de Clifton (the grandson) gives one mark for a writ in the county of Nottinghamshire.

3. GERVASE de CLIFTON, I find mentioned in the time of Henry II. had a daughter Cicely, the wife of Roger de Cressi, and a son,

4. Sir GERVASE, who married the daughter of Robert de Alvedelog, and was succeeded by his son,

5. Sir GERVASE, who must be accounted a principal advancer of this family; for he purchased the manor of Clifton and Wilford, and the manor of Broughton Sulney, of John de Soleni. He was constituted high sheriff of the counties of Nottingham and Derby in 1279, and continued for seven years; and in 1286 he was appointed high sheriff of Yorkshire, and continued for six years. In his shrivalty of the 18th year, upon complaint of John de Carleton, he was committed to goal, for making a false return of a writ. In the 20th of Edw. I. a mandate was issued out to the sheriff of Nottingham and Derby, that he should attach the said Gervase, to compel him to give his accounts for the time wherein he was sheriff of Yorkshire, at a certain time appointed; at which day he came, and accounted accordingly; and the same year had allowance for several sums of money, which in the 19th, while he was sheriff of Yorkshire, he had expended by the king's command. Robert de Tiptot, the constable, 12 Edw. I. demised Nottingham-Castle, with the apurtenances, to him, for 68*l. per ann.* which, if there were no other reason, might occasion the story of the guardianship.* He married Amflicia, the daughter of Sir William Sampson of Eperston, in Nottinghamshire, and died in 1324. His son,

6. GERVASE, who was sometimes called of Glapton, where he lived, died before his father, in 1316, having married Alice, daughter and co-heir of Robert, son of Gervase de Rabacy. His son,

7. Sir ROBERT de CLIFTON, 1324, was found heir to his grandfather, and above 26 years of age: he married Emma, daughter of Sir William Moton, by whom he had a son,

8. Sir GERVASE, who was high sheriff of the counties of Nottingham and Derby, in 1344; and the next year escheator of the same counties. We meet with no account of his death; nor is any thing to be found concerning him after the year 1388.† His son,

9. ROBERT very probably died before his father, as no account of him after is any where mentioned. It is supposed that Isabel, the first wife of this Robert de

---

of Wilford, and guardian of the castle at Nottingham in the time of William Peverell, and his son Sir Robert de Clifton, after him in like manner. There is no manor of Wilford in Domesday-book, and King William, or William Peverell, built the castle of Nottingham himself, and dwelt in it, and his son after him; yet tis not unlike but that they might have some considerable trust or employment under the Peverells." *Thoroton's Nott.* p. 52.

* Thoroton's Nott. p. 54.   † Ibid.

Clifton, was the daughter of —— Neville of Rolleston, in Nottinghamshire; for he married secondly (1361) Agnes de Grey, by whom he had

10. Sir JOHN CLIFTON,* who, in 1403, served in parliament, with Sir Richard Stanhope, for Nottingham, and had their wages allowed for 65 days. He was that year slain at the battle of Shrewsbury, fighting on the king's side against the Percies; having (as Hollenshed tells us) received from the king that morning the order of knighthood, which, if true, must be the dignity of a banneret; for he was a knight before. He brought a great increase of estate into the family, by his wife Catharine, daughter of Sir John de Cressey of Hodsack, in the county of Nottingham, Knt. and sister and co-heir of Sir Hugh de Cressey, who died in the 9th year of the same king: the other sister and co-heir, Elizabeth, was the wife of Sir John Markham, the elder judge; between which families of Clifton and Markham, the inheritance of Cressey was divided. After her husband's death she married Ralph Makarell. He was succeeded by his son,

11. Sir GERVASE CLIFTON, as appears from a grave-stone in Clifton church, which has, in the north aisle, this inscription:

Hic jacet Isabella, filia Rob. Fraunceis de Formarke militis, uxor Gervasii Clifton militis, filii dom. Johannis Clifton militis, cujus anima propitietur Deus quæ obiit 13 Junii, 1457.

He died in 1454, and was succeeded by

12. Sir GERVASE CLIFTON, but whether son or brother to the last is not clear; for the records here are intricate. He was lieutenant to Humphrey duke of Gloucester, constable of Dover Castle. In the 30th of Henry VI. the king granted to him the custody of all the temporals of the archbishoprick of Canterbury. In the same year he was also treasurer of the town of Calais, which office was given him (in recompence of his good service) May 24, in the 29th of that king, upon the resignation of Sir Richard Vernon, his predecessor in that office, he having delivered up his letters patent to be cancelled. He was twice sheriff of Kent; and once treasurer of the king's houshold; for there is a warrant in an uncertain year of that king, directed to the keeper of the privy seal, commanding him to direct his letters to the chamberlains of the exchequer, to pay to certain persons the sum of 460*l*. due to them while Sir Gervase Clifton stood treasurer of the houshold.

---

* "About this time (Dr. Thoroton says) there was a famous Sir Gervase Clifton of this family, who has been thought to be the son of this Sir John Clifton: but whether he was son, brother, or cousin, I cannot yet discover. He married Isabel, daughter of —— Harbare, alias Finch, of Bradbourn in Kent, the widow of William Scot; and was several times in the reign of Henry VI. sheriff of Kent. He was (1445) lieutenant of Dover Castle, under Humphrey Duke of Gloucester. The king (1451) upon the resignation of Sir Richard Vernon, made him, for his good service, treasurer of Calais, and the marches of the same; and the next year following committed the temporalities of the archbishoprick of Canterbury unto his hands, upon the death of John the archbishop. He was a commander at several places in France. After Robert Lord Willoughby of Eresby, and Thomas Nevil, he was third husband to Maud, neice and co-heir of Ralph Lord Cromwell, by Maud, his sister, second wife of Richard Stanhope. In a pardon he had 9 Edw. IV. he was stiled Gervas Clifton, Knt. late of Bradbourn, alias of Eresby, in the county of Lincoln: but continuing his zeal to his old master's interest, he was (1470) dispatched at Tewkesbury, and (1471) among the rest, proclaimed rebel and traitor. He left issue by his first wife two daughters, Joan married to John Digges, and Isabell to John Jerningham. He bore the same arms with this family, as appears by his seal."

In 1465 he, with Maud his wife, daughter of Sir Richard Stanhope, relict of Robert Lord Willoughby of Eresby, and also of Sir Thomas Nevil, and neice and coheir of Ralph Lord Cromwell, granted to Anthony Widevile Lord Scales, divers manors in the counties of Lincoln, Nottingham, Derby, and Warwick, which were lately the inheritance of Ralph Lord Cromwell: and the chronicles tell us, that Richard Duke of York, in 1440, made Sir Gervase Clifton captain of Pontoise near Paris (having been commander at several places in France) when the French king besieged, and took the town by assault, but lost above 3000 men before it: and that in 1471, the Monday after the battle at Tewksbury, Sir Gervase Clifton (who was then taken prisoner) was beheaded in the market-place there, together with Edmund Duke of Somerset, and others.

It is plain there was a Sir Gervase Clifton of Clifton, temp. Henry VI. and that Robert Clifton was his son and heir, who was high sheriff of Nottingham and Derby 29 and 38 Henry VI. and after, in 7 Edw. IV. Robert Clifton, Knt.[*] is mentioned then as late sheriff of Nottingham and Derby.[†] He had another son Robert Clifton, who was archdeacon of the East Riding in Yorkshire. Sir Robert began to found the College of the Holy Trinity at Clifton, but died in 1478, before he had accomplished his design, yet his son Sir Gervase religiously performed it.

13. GERVASE CLIFTON, his son and heir, was high sheriff of Nottingham and Derby 11 and 17 Edw. IV. 22 Edw. IV. that king ordains the said Gervase sheriff of the counties of Nottingham and Derby, and assigns him 100l. out of the Exchequer, for the better sustaining of his charge in that office. Anno 1 Richard III. he was made one of the knights of the bath at the coronation.

Sir John Beaumont (in his poem of Bosworth-Field) says, he was slain there, fighting on Richard's side, against the Earl of Richmond (after King Henry VII.) and that Biron, being his friend (but of the other party) procured the conqueror to restore his lands to his son. But it is plain he was not slain there, and probably did not serve there; or if he did, it was on the other side, repenting that he had adhered to the usurper; for not long after the beginning of King Henry the Seventh's reign, we find him not only entrusted, but rewarded by him, being in his third year made sheriff of the counties of Nottingham and Derby; and the same year having granted him the custody of the manors of Carleton in Lindrike, and Kinston in Carleton, being then in the king's hands, by reason of the minority of George Lord Fitz-

---

[*] Le Neve makes Sir Robert Clifton, Knt. to be son and heir of Sir Gervase, by Isabella, daughter of Sir Robert Frauncis, Knt. which is also agreeable to the pedigree in Thoroton's Nott. p. 53.

[†] To this Sir Robert Clifton, and Gervase Clifton, his son and heir, King Edward IV. in the 16th year of his reign, granted licence to found a college in the chapel of the Trinity, within the parish church of St. Mary of Clifton, to the honour of God and the blessed Virgin, *pro uno custode & duobus capellanis*, to celebrate divine service every day, for the good estate of the said king, and Elizabeth his queen, while they lived, and for their souls after their decease; and for the good estate of the said Sir Robert Clifton, and Gervase, &c. and for the soul of William Booth, late archbishop of York; and for the souls of dame Alice Clifton, late wife of the said Robert, and of Seth Worsley, Esq. &c. dated at Nottingham Castle, July 22. This Alice, wife of the said Sir Robert, was daughter of John Booth of Barton, in Lancashire, Esq. and sister of William, the archbishop, as appears by the following inscription upon her monument in Clifton church.

Hic jacet Dom. Alicia Clifton, filia Johannis Bothe, Armig. soror bonæ memoriæ Dom. Will. Bothe, quond. Ebor. Archiep. & uxor Dom. Rob. Clifton mil. Quæ obiit 9 die Septemb. Anno Dom. 1470, *cujus*, &c.

CLIFTON OF CLIFTON, NOTTINGHAMSHIRE,

Hugh; and that he married first Alice, daughter of Thomas Nevil of Rolleston, Esq. relict of Richard Thurland: secondly, Agnes, daughter of Sir Robert Constable of Flamborough, in Yorkshire, Knt. relict of Sir Walter Griffith, Knt. and died in 1491, in the house of the Fryers Predicants in London, and was buried in Clifton church.

The inquisition, after his death, taken at Blithe, October 30, anno 7 Henry VII. says, that he died the 12th day of May last past (which was in the 6th year of that king) and Robert Clifton, clerk, was his son and heir, and above 30 years old at the death of his father. This Robert Clifton became a secular priest, and died unmarried; and gave his estate to his younger brother,

14. GERVASE CLIFTON, afterwards knighted; for he was made a knight of the bath by King Henry the VIIth. in the 10th year of his reign, at the time he created his second son, Henry Duke of York. He married first Agnes, daughter of Sir Walter Griffith above-mentioned; secondly, Joan, daughter of John Bussy, widow of Sir Nicholas Byron, Knt. by the last he had no issue. In the 17th of Henry VII. he was made sheriff of the counties of Nottingham and Derby: he died June 5, 23 Henry VII. It appears by the inquisition taken after his son's death, 1518, that Robert Clifton was his son and heir; and that he had a younger son, Hugh Clifton, and though not mentioned in the inquisition, he had another son, Gervase Clifton, who was of the Custom-house of the port of London, and was father of Sir Gervase Clifton, summoned to parliament as a baron of the realm, the 6th of James I. by the title of Lord Clifton of Leighton-Bromswold.

15. ROBERT, his eldest son, married first Alice, daughter of Simon Digby, Esq. lieutenant of the Tower of London, by whom he had no issue; and by his second wife he added the greatest lustre to his family; for he married Agnes, daughter to Henry Lord Clifford, and sister to Henry, the first earl of Cumberland, who through the lines of Clifford, Percy, and Mortimer, was lineally descended from Lionel Plantagenet, duke of Clarence, third son of King Edward III. She was married after his death to Robert Melford. This Robert died a young man, Sep. 3, 1518, and was succeeded by his son,

16. GERVASE CLIFTON, not then two years old. He was justice of the peace and quorum the greatest part of his life; and sheriff of Nottingham and Derby in the last year of Henry VIII. and again the first of the reign of Queen Mary; and after, of Nottingham alone, in 13 Q. Eliz. He had likewise several military employments; for he served under Henry VIII. at the seige of Bulloigne, and was knighted (says Hollinshed in his chronicles) at Muscleburgh, by the duke of Somerset, in the reign of Edw. VI. It is likely he was there, but it is manifest he was knighted in the days of Henry VIII. In 1560 he served at the seige of Leith in Scotland, under the Lord Grey; and upon notice of the peace concluded, Sir Gervase Clifton was sent into the trenches, on the west side of Leith, to command the soldiers to forbear hostility; and the next day (June 7) he was sent into the town, with Sir Francis Leke, to cause the peace to be proclaimed, where he was feasted by Mons. Doysel, the governor.

He was a person of great authority both in peace and war, yet notwithstanding this martial inclination, he was a gentleman of so courteous and affable a disposition, that he was usually stiled Sir Gervase the gentle, which character, Queen Elizabeth gave him (if this distich was her's, which tradition affirms) of four of her Nottinghamshire knights:—

   'Gervase the gentle, Stanhop the stout,
   Marcham the lion, and Sutton the lout.

He was twice married, first to Mary, daughter of Sir John Nevil of Cheet, in Yorkshire, Knt. by whom he had five children, viz. Elizabeth, the first wife of Sir Peter Frechevile of Staveley, in Derbyshire, Knt. Frances, Robert, Gervase, and Anthony, which four last died young unmarried. The second wife of Sir Gervase was Winifred, daughter and heir of William Thwaites of Owlton, in Suffolk, Esq. relict of Sir George Pierpont of Holme, Knt. by whom he had

17. GEORGE, his son and heir,* who married Winifred, daughter of Sir Anthony Thorold of Marston, in Lincolnshire, Knt. (by Anne, his wife, daughter and co-heir of Sir John Constable of Kinalton, Knt.) and died during the life of his father, Aug. 1, 1587, leaving his wife with child of Sir Gervase Clifton, Bart. being, at the time of his death, but 20 years and 7 months old. His lady surviving him, married first Henry Kervile of Wigenhale, in Norfolk, Esq. and secondly, Sir Edward Gawsell of Watlington, in Norfolk, Knt.

Sir Gervase Clifton, his father, died in the same year, 1587, on the 20th of Jan. and lies buried under a stately monument in Clifton church; and was succeeded by his grandson,

I. Sir GERVASE CLIFTON, but four months old. He was made knight of the bath at the coronation of King James I. and afterwards advanced to the dignity of baronet. He served in eight parliaments, he was knight of the shire, temp. James I. and Charles II. and served for Retford, temp. Charles I. and was commissioner at Oxford and Newark, for King Charles I. and for one thing he was more remarkable (having in that gone beyond any of our nation as yet heard of) he had six wives, and married a seventh when he was near 70 years old. His first lady was Penelope, daughter of Robert Rich, earl of Warwick; she died October 26, 1613, aged 23. He had by her Sir Gervase, his eldest son and successor. By his second, lady Frances, daughter of Francis Clifford, earl of Cumberland, he had issue Sir Clifford Clifton, and four daughters: Margaret, married first to Sir John South of Kelstern, in Lincolnshire, Knt. secondly, to William Whichcote of Dunston, in Lincolnshire, Esq. thirdly, to Robert, lord Hunsdon. Frances was wife, first of Richard Tempest of Bracewell, in Yorkshire, Esq. and secondly to Anthony Eyre of Rampton, in Nottinghamshire, Esq. Anne, to Sir Francis Rodes of Barlbro, in Derbyshire, Bart. and Lettice, to Clifton Rodes, Esq. brother to Sir Francis: this lady died Nov. 22, 1627, aged 33 years. The third was Mary, daughter of John Egiock of Egiock, in Worcestershire, Esq. widow of Sir Francis Leke of Sutton, in Derbyshire, Knt. by her he had no issue: she died January 19, 1630. His fourth lady was Isabel, daughter of —— Meek of Wolverhampton, Esq. relict of John Hodges, Esq. alderman of London: she died also without issue, and was buried at

* The descent from this George, to Sir Clifford Clifton, Knt. was from a pedigree in the hand-writing of Sir William Dugdale, and was in the possession of T. Wotton.

Clifton (as were also his two first ladies) July 10, 1637. The fifth was Anne, daughter of Sir Francis South of Kelsterne, in Lincolnshire, Knt. buried at Clifton (having no issue) June 1, 1639. The sixth was Jane, daughter of Anthony Eyre of Rampton, Esq. (by whom he was father of Robert Clifton, who married Sarah, daughter of Nathaniel Parkhurst of Woodford, in Essex, Esq. by whom he had Sir Gervase Clifton hereafter-mentioned, and Robert Clifton of Carleton, Esq. who married —— daughter of —— Packe, and died 1715; by whom he had Robert Clifton of Walthamstow, in Essex, who married Anne, daughter of —— Marshall, and widow of John Rowe of Essex, by whom he had James, Anne, and Catharine, the wife of Charles Packe of Prestwold, in Leicestershire; James was surgeon of marines at Chatham, and married Sarah, daughter of William Martin of Chatham, who died March 26, 1793: he died March 24, 1796, leaving one son Charles James Clifton, captain in the 28th regiment of light dragoons, and Frances. Charles, who died unmarried; Jane, wife of Christopher Pack of Coates, in Leicestershire, Esq. Elizabeth and Mary, who died young) she died at London, and was buried at Clifton March 17, 1655. The seventh wife of Sir Gervase was Alice, daughter of Henry earl of Huntingdon, by whom he had no issue: she survived her husband, but died the same year, and was buried in St. Giles's church, London (1666) as was his third lady. He* was succeeded in the dignity and estate by his eldest son by his first lady,

II. Sir GERVASE CLIFTON, Bart. who married Sarah, daughter of Timothy Pusey of Selston, in Nottinghamshire, Esq. of the ancient family of the Puseys in Berkshire: she died Jan. 22, 1652; and he dying without issue, Jan. 14, 1675, was succeeded by his nephew,

III. Sir WILLIAM CLIFTON, Bt. only surviving son of Sir Clifford Clifton, Kt. and Frances his wife, daughter of Sir Heneage Finch, Kt. recorder of London; which Sir Clifford was the only son of Sir Gervase by his second marriage: this Sir William died unmarried, leaving two sisters, his co-heirs; Catharine married to Sir John

---

* Dr. Thoroton, in his Antiquities of Nottinghamshire, says, "This Sir Gervase was of a sound body, and a cheerful and facetious spirit; yet in his latter time timorous, so that his last part was miracle enough to convert an atheist, to see his christianity so far prevail over his nature, that without the least shadow of fear, unwearied with grief or sickness, he left the choicest things of this world with as great pleasure as others enjoy them. He received from me the certain notice of his near approaching death, as he was wont to do an invitation of good friends to his own bowling-green (one of the most pleasant imaginable) and thereupon immediately called for his old chaplain, Mr. Robert Thirleby, to do the office of his confessor, as if it had been to attend him to that recreation he often used and loved; and when he had done with him, for his children, whom, patriarch like, he particularly blessed and admonished, with the smartness and ingenuity of an excellent and well-studied orator. The day following he received visits from divers friends, sitting in the old dining-room near his bed-chamber, who were not so sensible of his danger, because he entertained them after his usual manner: yet, that night (as I easily foretold him) his sleepiness began, which could never be taken away, by reason that both his ureters were so petrified (as things are by the dropping-well, near Knaresburgh in Yorkshire) that no urine could descend into his bladder, as at the opening of his body did manifestly appear; as also, that one of his kidneys had, of long time before been totally stopped with a wonderful great stone, as is reported of the pious and learned Dr. Hammond, whose hair was also red, like that of this worthy Sir Gervase, who died June 28, 1666, and was buried Aug. 2 following, with great solemnity; Mr. Dugdale Norroy, Mr. Ashmole Windsor, and Mr. Ryley Lancaster, heralds; the choir of Southwell, and many mourners attending his funeral."

CLIFTON OF CLIFTON, NOTTINGHAMSHIRE.

TABLE 6.

1 ALVEREDUS de Clifton
2 Robert de Clifton
3 Gervase=Ysmenia
4 Gervase=dr. of Rob. de Alvedeley   Cicely=R. de Cressi   GERVASE
5 Sir Gervase, 1324=Amflicia Sampson   Robert de Rabacy
6 Gervase, 1316=Alice   Margaret=Richard Martell

EDWARD III.
7 Sir Robert, Knt. 1327=Emma, dr. of Sir Wm. Moton
Lionel D. of Clarence
8 Sir Gervase Clifton, Knt.=Margaret Pierpont
Philippa=Edm. E. of March   Isabel Neville=9 Robert=Agnes de Grey   Sir J. de CRESSEY
Eliz.=Henry Hotspur
10 Sir John, 1403=Catharine=Ralph Makarell
Eliz.=John L. Clifford
11 Sir Gervase, Knt. 1454=Elizabeth Francis, 1457 —— BOOTH
Thomas L. Clifford
12 Sir Robert, 1478=Alice Booth, 1470   Wm. Archbp. York
John L. Clifford, 1461
13 Sir Gervase Clifton, K. B. 1491   Robert   Margaret
   Alice Neville | Agnes Constable   Archd. of York Sir E.   Sir E.
                                                    Hastings Wentham
Henry L. Clifford, 1523   Robert, *a priest* 14 Sir Gervase Clifton, K. B. 1509
                                              Agnes Griffith | Joan Hussey
Anne, or Agnes (2d wife)=15 Sir Robert=Alice Digby (1st)   .Hugh   Gervase
     Mary Neville, 1564=16 Sir Gervase, 1587=Winifred Thwaytes
        Elizabeth   Frances,   Gervase.   17 George Clifton, 1587
        Sir P. Frechvile, Robert, Anthony.   Winifred Thorold

I. Sir Gervase Clifton, K. B. & Bart. 1666

| Penelope, dr. of Rob. E. of Warwick, 1615 | Frances, dr. of Fran. E. of Cumland, 1627 | Mary, dr. of John Egioke, 1650 | Isabel Meck 1637 | Anne, dr. of Sir Fr. South, 1659 | Jane, dr. of Anth. Eyre, 1655 | Alice, dr. of Hen. E. of Huntingdon, 1666 |

II. Sir Gervase, Sir Clifford, Margaret   Frances   Anne Letitia Robert Jane Chas.
   Bart. 1675   Kt. 1669   Sir J. Wm. Rob. L. Rich. Anth. Sir   1627   Sarah Christ. Eliz.
   Sarah Pusey, Frances South Which- Hunx- Tem- Eyre Fran. Clifton Park- Pack Mary.
   1652   Finch   Kt. cote   don pest   Rodes Rodes hurst

III. Sir Wm.   Catharine   Arabella   IV. Sir Gerv. Clifton, Bt. 1731   Robert
    Clifton, Bt. Sir J. Parsons, Bt. Sir F. Wheler, Kt. Anne, dr. of Dudley Bagnell —— dr. of —— Packe

V. Sir Robert Clifton, Bt. & K. B. William Alfred. George   Jane.   Robert, 1764
Fran. dr. of Nathan —— dr. of Sir Mrs.   Dudley.   Anne   10 sons.   Anne
Coot, E. of Bellamont Tho. Lombe, Kt. Wharton   Sacheverell   Marshall
                    | 1748
        Frances   VI. Sir Gervase Clifton, Bt. b. 1744   James   Anne   Catharine
  —— Tyrconnel   —— dr. of —— and heiress of ——Lloyd, 1799 S. Martin   C. Packe

Robert, b. 1767   Gervase   James Julius   N. b. 1773   Charles James   Frances
                  1779   Margaret Delancy Rev. R. Markham

Parsons, Bart. (mother of Sir William) and Arabella, married to Sir Francis Wheeler, Knt. one of the admirals under King William, who was unfortunately cast away near Cadiz. He was succeeded in title and estate by his cousin,

IV. Sir GERVASE CLIFTON, Bart. eldest son of Robert Clifton, Esq. son of Sir Gervase, by Jane his sixth wife; which Sir Gervase married Anne, daughter of Dudley Bagnell of Newry, in Ireland, Esq. (which family is now the only remaining branch of those two famous brothers, Sir Samuel and Sir Henry Bagnall, who were sent into Ireland by Queen Elizabeth, the first with the title of Marshal of that kingdom, and the latter distinguished himself very eminently at the taking of Cadiz, where he received eight wounds, and covered with blood, was then knighted) by whom he had fifteen sons and one daughter; ten of the sons died unmarried; the others were, 1, Sir Robert, his successor; 2, William, who married Mrs. Wharton, by whom he had no issue; 3, Alfred, first an officer in the French service, after in the Russian; 4, Dudley, who embraced a religious life; 5, George, who married Anne, only daughter and heir of Robert Sacheverell of Barton, in Nottinghamshire, Esq. by whom he has two daughters· Jane, only daughter of Sir Gervase, was a nun of the order of St. Clare, at Graveline. Sir Gervase died in March 1730-1, and his lady surviving him, married William Blackburne of High Ongar, in Essex, Esq. She died in 1734.

V. Sir ROBERT CLIFTON, his eldest son, succeeded his father in title and estate, and married lady Frances, daughter of the right honourable Nanfan Coote, earl of Bellamont, of the kingdom of Ireland (by lady Frances his wife, youngest daughter of the right honourable Henry de Nassau, earl of Grantham): she died, leaving him only one daughter, Frances. He had the honour, in the year 1725, to be made one of the knights of the honourable order of the bath; and was elected in several parliaments, one of the representatives for East Retford, in Nottinghamshire. He married secondly, in June 1740, ———, eldest daughter and co-heir of the late Sir Thomas Lombe, Knt. alderman of London, who died in 1748, by whom he had issue, and was succeeded by

VI. Sir GERVASE CLIFTON, Bart. who married ———, daughter and heiress of the ancient family of the Lloyds in Pembrokeshire, who died of a putrid fever, caught by constantly attending two of her sons in that disorder; the second of whom, Gervase, died Aug. 9; she in Sep. 1779: by which lady he has two sons and one daughter, who in 1797 was married to the Rev. Robert Markham, archdeacon of York. His second son, James Julius, in 1794, married Margaret, daughter of James Delancy, Esq. of Bath.

ARMS—Sable, seme of cinquefoils, and a lion rampant, argent.
CREST—Out of a ducal coronet a demi peacock, *per pale*, argent and sable, his wings expanded, counter changed.
MOTTO—*Tenez le droit.*
SEAT—At Clifton, near Nottingham.

5. GERARD of Bryn, Lancashire.

Created Baronet May 22, 1611.

1. THIS family derives its origin from Otho, or (as the earl of Plymouth's pedigree has it) Other, a rich and powerful lord in the time of king Alfred, descended from the dukes of Tuscany, whom from Florence or Norway passed to Hetruria in Normandy, and thence to England, where, and in Wales, they flourished, until Richard Strongbow, earl of Pembroke, their kinsman, engaged them to partake in his expedition to Ireland, in which Maurice Fitzgerald embarked, and was one of the conquerors of the kingdom.* Sir William Dugdale tells us, that the aforesaid Otho,† was a baron of England in the 16th of King Edward the Confessor, and was father of

2. WALTER FITZOTHO, or Fitzother, who, at the general survey of that kingdom, in 1078, was castellan of Windsor, and appointed, by William the Conqueror, warden of the forests in Berkshire, being then possessed of two lordships in that county, three in Surrey, three in Bucks, three in Dorsetshire, four in Middlesex, nine in Wiltshire, one in Somersetshire, and ten in the county of Southampton; all which Otho, his father, held in the time of King Edward the Confessor. He married Gladys, the daughter of Rywall ap Conyn, by whom he had three sons, Gerald, Robert, and William.‡ Robert was baron of Eston or Estaines in Essex: he was succeeded by his son William, who left a daughter, the wife of Robert de Hastings, and their daughter Delicia, was the wife of Henry de Cornhill, whose only child Jane, being married to Sir Godfrey de Lovaine, lord of Lovaine, was mother of Sir Matthew, who held the manor of Eston by barony; and his heir general being matched into the family of Bourchier, they possessed the said barony un-

---

* Lodge's Peerage of Ireland.   † Baronage, vol. 1, p. 411, 509.

‡ The seniority of these sons is disputed by those who have drawn the pedigrees of this family: Gerald, the eldest, in the earl of Kildare's pedigree, being made the youngest in *that* of the earl of Kerry, drawn in the year 1615, and attested by Sir William Seager, garter king of arms, who is followed by his successors, Dugdale and Anstis, for which they assign this reason, viz. *That the appellation of Fitz Walter was given to this* Gerald, *because he was the younger son.* To controvert this is to encounter great authority; but we think it deserves an inquiry, how the consequence of his being a younger son can be drawn from his having the appellation of Fitz Walter? The custom of that age warrants us to affirm the contrary, and to assert, that the eldest son *especially* assumed for his surname the christian name of his father, with the addition of Fitz, &c. of which many instances occur in this family: and this continued in use until surnames began to be fixed about the time of Edw. I. and among the elder branches of many families till long after that time, younger sons not being so frequently known, or called by their father's christian name, as by *that* of his office, employment, &c. for which reason the two brothers of this Gerald are not called *Fitz Walter*, but *De Windsor*. Wherefore, waving farther arguments, we shall depend on the authority of a pedigree communicated by the earl of Kildare, carefully drawn up in 1662, by the ingenious Robert Saunderson, Esq. Lancaster herald, and fix upon Gerald for the eldest son, and William the youngest. *Lodge's Irish Peerage.*

GERARD OF BRYN, LANCASHIRE.

til it was purchased in Queen Elizabeth's reign by Sir Henry Maynard, and now gives title to his descendant, Lord Maynard of Estaines. William was ancestor to the lords Windsor, barons of Stanwell, from whom descended the Earl of Plymouth, and the Lord Viscount Windsor, whose family is extinct.

3. GERALD, or Gerard, the eldest son, was generally surnamed Fitz Walter, by which name Camden styles him, when he mentions the grant made to him by King Henry I. of Molesford in Berkshire: the Carews, as well of England as Ireland, descended from him. He was constable of Pembroke Castle, which he fortified and defended with great courage against the Welch; and having slain Owen, son of Cadugan ap Blethyn, chief lord of Cardiganshire, was made president of the county of Pembroke. He had by Nesta, his wife, daughter of Rees, son of Theodore the Great, prince of South Wales, three sons; William, Maurice, and David; the last was bishop of St. David's, in 1148, and died 1176; of whom Giraldus Cambrensis has written. Maurice Fitz Gerald, the second son, was one of the adventurers with Richard Strongbow, earl of Pembroke, in the conquest of Ireland, in 1170; as he had been with Robert Fitz Stephen, when he landed two years before, and took Weishford; and here was the first colony of the English settled in Ireland; and by their valour opened a way for subjecting that dominion to the crown of England: the said Maurice, settling there, became the ancestor to several great and noble families which flourished in that kingdom, particularly to the earls of Kildare, premier earls of that realm.

4. WILLIAM FITZ GERALD, eldest son of Gerald, was possessed of the castle of Kerriu, or Carrio, in Carmarthenshire, the inheritance of his mother. He died in 1173, and left issue; 1. Odo, from whom the numerous family of the Carews descend; 2. Raymond Crassus, a principal sharer in the conquest of Ireland, who had a natural son named Maurice, from whom the lords Fitz Maurice of Kerry, in Ireland, derive themselves. The other sons of William were Silvester, Henry and

5. WILLIAM, who was the direct ancestor to this family of Gerard. He was justice in Eyre, in Chestershire, and was father of

6. WILLIAM, who married Emme, eldest daughter and co-heir to Sir Richard Kingsley of Kingsley, in Chestershire, Knt. and of Joan, his wife, daughter and co-heir of Alex. de Stanton; whose mother, Annabella, was daughter and heir of Randolph Silvester, 18 Edw. I. The said William Gerard, 16 Edw. I. was one of the jury on the death of Sir Hamon Massy of Dunham-Massy. He left two sons William and John.

7. WILLIAM, the eldest, married Matilda, daughter of Henry de Glasehouse, and did homage to Edward, earl of Chester, afterwards King Edw. II. for his lands in Cheshire, and died at Eaton-Hall 26 Edw. III. He left two sons, William and Thomas. From Thomas the Gerards of Crew in Cheshire descended, that ended in an heiress, married to Edward Norris of Speake, in Lancashire, Esq.

8. WILLIAM, the eldest brother, married ―― daughter and heir of Peter de Bryn, or Brynhill, in Lancashire, and was succeeded by his son,

GERARD OF BRYN, LANCASHIRE.

9. Sir PETER GERARD de BRYN, who died 1381, leaving issue three sons, Thomas, Peter, and John, who married Helen, only daughter and heiress of Richard de Ince, from whom the late earls of Macclesfield and other branches are descended; and from a younger son of the Gerards of Ince was Sir William Gerard, Knt. descended; who was recorder of Chester, master of the requests, and lord chancellor of Ireland, &c. temp. Eliz. Thomas Gerard of Bryn, the eldest son and heir of Peter, before-mentioned, was knighted in the Scottish wars, having valiantly behaved himself, and brought considerable succours to that service, 17 Rich. II. being then a knight, he served in parliament for Lancashire,* and left issue, Sir Thomas Gerard, Knt. who left issue a son of his own name, and John Gerard. The last Sir Thomas Gerard, Knt. left issue, Sir Thomas Gerard, Knt. 13 Henry VI. who was in the wars against France; of whom Piere Daniel says, "*Anno* 1437, at the siege of Montereau, where the king of France attended in person, the garrison behaved with great valour, having at their head an English knight, named Thomas Guerard."† But he dying without issue, Sir Thomas Gerard of Kingsley became his heir, who was great grandson to

10. PETER GERARD of Kingsley, before-mentioned, who was living temp. Hen. IV. and marrying Isabel, daughter of Thomas Strangeways, Esq. had issue

11. JOHN, who died in 1432, father to

12. PETER, who died in 1490, father to

13. Sir THOMAS GERARD, last named, aged 14 years, 18 Henry VII. which Sir Thomas marrying Dowse, daughter of Sir Thomas Assheton of Assheton-Underline, in Lancashire, Knt. had issue by her,

14. PETER, who married Margaret, daughter of Sir William Stanley of Hooton, Knt. and heir to her mother, Margaret, daughter and heir to Sir John Bromley of Bromley, in Staffordshire, Knt. but died before his father, 1492. The said Peter left issue, Sir Thomas Gerard, and four daughters; Joan, wife to Richard Done of Utkington, in Cheshire; Isabel married Richard Langton, styled baron of Walton and Newton, in Lancashire; the third daughter married William Ratcliff of Wimbersly, and the fourth John Southworth of Samlesbury, Esqrs.

15. Sir THOMAS GERARD succeeded his grandfather, Sir Thomas, in the estates at Bryn and Kingsley; he brought considerable succours of his tenants and archers, to the assistance of Thomas, earl of Surrey, against the Scots, who in 1513, entered Northumberland, whilst King Henry VIII. was busy in his wars in France. At Flodden Field, both armies engaging, Sir Thomas behaved himself with great valour; and to the Lancashire Archers the fame of that great victory is generally owned, wherein the king of Scotland was slain, and the principal of his nobility and gentry had the same fate, or were taken prisoners. This Sir Thomas, by Margaret his wife, daughter of Sir Edmund Trafford of Trafford, in Lancashire, Knt, widow first to —— Longford, secondly to Sir John Port of Etwall, in Derbyshire.

* Prynn's Regist. vol. IV. p. 423.   † Daniel's Hist. de France, 4to. vol. VI. p. 147.

Knt. had issue by her Thomas, and four daughters; Margaret, wife to Peter Legh of Lyme, in Chestershire; Catharine, wife to Thomas Hoghton of Hoghton-Tower; Elizabeth, wife of Richard Bold of Bold; and —— wife to Richard Assheton of Middleton in Lancashire, Esqrs.

16. THOMAS, son and heir of the last Sir Thomas, received also the honour of knighthood; was knight of the shire for Lancashire 8 and 9 Q. Eliz. He married Jane, daughter of Sir Peter Legh of Lyme, and was high sheriff in 1548. They left issue Catharine, married to William Tarbock, Esq. and

17. Sir THOMAS GERARD, Knt. who was high sheriff of Lancashire 1553 and 1558. He married Elizabeth, eldest daughter of Sir John Port of Etwall, in Derbyshire, Knt. (and Elizabeth his wife, daughter and heir to her mother's inheritance, being daughter of Sir Thomas Gifford of Chillington, in Staffordshire, Knt. and Dorothy his wife, daughter and co-heir of Sir John Montgomery, Knt.) which Sir John Port, was son of John Port, Esq. and Jane his wife, daughter of John Fitzherbert of Etwall, in Derbyshire, Esq. and relict of John Pole of Radburn, in the same county, Esq.* George, earl of Huntingdon, married Dorothy, the second daughter, and Sir Thomas Stanhope, ancestor to the present earl of Chesterfield, Margaret, the third daughter, co-heiresses to the said Sir John Port, who was founder of the hospital of Etwall, and the free school of Repton in the said county; of which said hospital and school, worth above 500*l. per ann.* the said three families are governors, by the last will and testament of the said Sir John Port, and by letters patent, granted by King James I. The said Sir Thomas Gerard was sent to the Tower twice, being accused of a design to deliver the Queen of Scots out of her confinement; and was forced, to procure his own liberty, to give the noble estate of the Bromleys, descended to him by his great grandmother, to his kinsman, then attorney-general, Sir Gilbert Gerard, afterwards master of the rolls, and to dispose of and mortgage several lordships in Leicestershire, Derbyshire, Cheshire, and Yorkshire, besides Brindall, Scormensdale, and half Kirkby, in Lancashire. The said Sir Thomas Gerard left issue three daughters; Mary, wife to John Jennison of Walworth, in Durham, Esq. Dorothy married to Edmund Peckham, Esq. son of Sir George; and Martha married to Michael Jennison, Esq. brother to John: also two sons, Sir Thomas Gerard, Knt. and John Gerard, who was several times tortured in the Tower, out of which he made his escape, and was chiefly instrumental in building the college at Liege, where he died.

I. Sir THOMAS GERARD, Knt. the eldest son, was created a baronet at the first institution of that honour, in 1611, 9 James I. The 1000*l.* which he was to have given for it, was returned, in consideration of his father's great sufferings upon the Queen of Scots' account, mother to the said king: a grant for perpetuating the sheriffdom of Lancashire in his family, and some other beneficial grants were promised him, but not performed, being alledged to be against the liberty of the subject. He married three wives; 1. Cecily, daughter of Sir Walter Maney of Staplehurst, in Kent, Knt. 2. Mary, daughter of James Hawes of London, and

* Le Neve's MSS. of the Baronets, vol. I. p. 11.

widow of Sir Robert Lee of London, Knt. and 3. Mary, daughter of William Dormer, Esq: and widow of —— Browne, Esq. By the two last he had no issue; but by the first he had Sir Thomas, his successor, and a daughter Frances, married to Ralph Standish of Standish, in Lancashire, Esq. but died without issue.

II. Sir THOMAS, successor to the title and estate, married during his father's life Frances, daughter of Sir Richard Molineux of Sefton, in Lancashire, Bart. and had issue six sons; 1. Sir William, 2. Richard, 3. Gilbert, 4. Peter, 5. Thomas, and 6. John. The four last died unmarried: also a daughter Frances, who took a religious habit at Graveline in Flanders. Richard Gerard, the second son of Sir Thomas, born in Oct. 1613, at the age of 21 was one of those that went first into Maryland with Mr. Calvert, the Lord Baltimore's uncle, lord proprietor thereof, where he continued till the latter end of the year 1635, at which time he raised a company of foot, with which he went into the service of the king of Spain in the Low Countries, and continued in that service till the breaking out of the civil wars in England, when the then queen of England, coming over into Holland, to her son-in-law the prince of Orange, to obtain some succours from him, he then quitted the Spanish service, and came to the queen at the Hague, where her majesty was pleased to order him to raise a regiment of foot-guards, whereof he was to be lieutenant-colonel. Coming over into England with her majesty, and landing at Burlington Bay, he immediately repaired to the earl of Newcastle, from whom he received his commission as lieutenant-colonel of the said regiment, dated March 16, 1642. Then marching with her majesty to Oxford, in his way was ordered to attack the town of Burton upon Trent, then garrisoned by the parliament; and being joined by a party of horse, under the command of Sir Thomas Tyldesly, the town was attacked by the horse over the bridge, and by the foot through the river, in which he received a shot through his thigh, notwithstanding the town was carried. After which he continued his march to Oxford, where he lay ill a long time of his wound, so that he was not able to take the field again till the second Newbery battle, where he then commanded the reserve, consisting of the regiment of guards and Hawkins's; and upon the surrender of Oxford he had the benefit of those articles. Waiting upon his majesty when he was prisoner at Hurst Castle, he was the last person sent by his majesty to the queen, then in France. Upon the restoration of King Charles II. he was sworn cup-bearer in ordinary, and waiter to the then queen-mother, in which office he continued till her majesty's death. He died the 5th of Sep. 1686, at Ince. He married two wives; first Frances, daughter of Sir Ralph Hansly of Tickhill Castle, in the county of York, Knt. by whom he had a son, who died in his infancy; secondly, Judith, daughter to Sir Nicholas Steward of Pateshall, in the county of Northampton, Knt. by whom he had six sons; Thomas, Richard, William, Nicholas, John, and Charles, which four last all died unmarried before him: and three daughters; Frances died abbess of Ghent in Flanders; Anne, a nun at Liege; and Juliana, died in her infancy. 1. Thomas Gerard of Ince, and Aspul, his eldest son, left five daughters (two of which were nuns at Brabant) and four sons; 1. Richard, 2. William, 3. Thomas, and 4. Carryl, who embraced religious lives. 2. Richard Gerard, who left issue one son Richard, who had three children, William, Mary, and Elizabeth.

III. Sir WILLIAM GERARD, Bart. who succeeded his father in title and estate, married Elizabeth, daughter of Sir Cuthbert Clifton of Lytham, Knt. and just before the unfortunate breaking out of the civil wars, he sold Etwall in Derbyshire, the only remaining part of his great grandmother Elizabeth Port's large and fair estate, for an intended purchase of the whole manor of Newton in Lancashire; but the sum designed for that end, being 10,000*l.* was spent in the king's service; the greatest part of which was given to the marquis of Worcester and the earl of Derby for that use: the said Sir William Gerard was governor of Denbigh Castle, one of the last in the kingdom which held out for the king: his estate was sequestered, which he was forced to purchase from the parliament. Sir William had issue four sons, Sir William, his successor, Thomas, who was first a captain, and afterward took to a religious life; Cuthbert, and John Gerard, who married the heiress of Ince (the three last died without issue) and one daughter Frances, wife of Francis Howard of Corby, in Cumberland, Esq.

IV. Sir WILLIAM GERARD, Bart. the eldest son, married first Anne, daughter of Sir John Preston, Bart, by Jane his wife, daughter and co-heir of Thomas Morgan of Weston, in Warwickshire, Esq. and eldest sister of Sir Thomas Preston of the manor in Furness, in Lancashire, Bart. (whose eldest daughter and co-heir, Mary, married to William, marquis of Powis; and Anne, the second daughter, was wife to Hugh, lord Clifford) and by her had issue Sir William Gerard, Thomas, John, and Francis, which three last died without issue; and six daughters, Mary, Elizabeth, Anne (who married Charles Waterton of Walton, in the county of York, Esq.) Bridget, Frances, and Winifred, who all died unmarried, except Anne. The second wife to Sir William Gerard was Mary, sister to Sir Edward Mostyn of Talacre, in Flintshire, Bart. and widow of James Pool of Poole, in Cheshire, Esq. by her he had no issue.

V. Sir WILLIAM GERARD, Bart. his eldest son and successor, married Mary, second daughter of John Cansfield of Cansfield, Esq. and Elizabeth his wife: she, by the death of her elder sister, Anne, widow and relict of Richard Sherburn of Stonyhurst, Esq.) became sole heiress to her father's estate, as also to her mother's, who was daughter to James Anderton of Birchley, Esq. Her grandfather, Sir John Cansfield, behaved himself with great courage and bravery in the civil wars; and King Charles I. owed the preservation of his own life, and that of his son the prince of Wales, at the second Newberry battle, in a great measure to his valour, as appears from a testimonial in Latin, under the hand of that king, in the custody of Sir William Gerard. Sir William had issue, first three daughters, Anne, Mary, and Elizabeth, who all died unmarried; and afterward three sons, Sir William, his successor; John, and Thomas, who died an infant.

VI. Sir WILLIAM GERARD, Bart. who succeeded his father in title and estate, married Elizabeth, fourth daughter of Thomas Clifton of Lytham, in Lancashire, Esq. by whom he had three sons and one daughter, Sir William, his successor, Thomas, Robert, and Mary.

VII. Sir WILLIAM GERARD, Bart. the eldest son, was the next baronet; but dying unmarried he was succeeded by his brother,

GERARD OF BRYN, LANCASHIRE.

TABLE 7.

1 OTHO, a Baron of England
2 Walter Fitz Otho=Gladys, dr. of Rywall ap Conyn
3 Gerald=Nesta of Wales, 1136 — Robert, B. of Eston — William
4 William Fitzgerald, 1173 — Maurice Fitzgerald, 1177 — David, bp. of St. David's — William, B. of Eston — Earls of Plymouth
Odo Fitzgerald — Raymond Crassus — Silvester — 5 Wm. Henry — Dukes of Leinster — N — R. de Hastings
Carews — Maurice — 6 William=Emme Kingsley — Delicia=Henry de Cornhill
Earls of Kerry, &c. — 7 William=Matilda Glasehouse — John — Jane=Sir God. de Lovaine
8 William — dr. of Peter de Bryn — Thomas — Sir Mat. de Lovaine
9 Sir Peter Gerard de Bryn, 1381
Geralds of Crew
Sir T. Gerald of Bryn — 10 Pet. Gerald=Isa. Strangeways — John=Helen de Ince
Sir Thomas, Knt. — 11 Sir John Gerard, Knt. 1432 — Earls of Macclesfield, &c.
Sir Thomas, Knt. — John — 12 Peter Gerald, 1490
Sir Thomas, Knt. — 13 Sir Thomas Gerard=Dowse, dr. of Sir Thomas Assheton
J. FITZHERBERT — Sir J. MONTGOMERY, Knt. 1544 — 14 Pet. Gerald of Kingsley=Marg. Stanley
Jane — Dorothy — 15 Sir Thomas — Joan — Isabel — N — N
John Port — Sir T. Gifford, Knt. — Marg. Trafford — R. Done — R. Langton — W. Ratcliff — J. Southworth
Sir John Port, 1557 — Elizabeth — 16 Thomas — Margaret — Catharine — Elizabeth — N
Elizabeth — Sir John Port — Jane Legh — Peter Legh — T. Hoghton — R. Bold — R. Assheton
Elizabeth — Dorothy — Marg. — 17 Sir Thomas Gerard, Knt. — Katharine
Sir Tho. Gerard — Geo. E. of Huntingdon — Sir T. Stanhope — Elizabeth Port — Wm. Tarbock

I. Sir John Gerard, Knt. & Bart. — Mary — Dorothy — Martha — John Gerard
C. Marney | M. Hawes | M. Dormer — J. Jennison — Edm. Peckham — M. Jennison

II. Sir Thomas, Bart.=Frances Molineux — Frances=Ralph Standish

III. Sir William B.rt. — Richard Gerard, 1686 — Gilbert. — Thomas.
Elizabeth Clifton — Fran. Hansley | Judith Steward — Peter. — John, & Frances

IV. Sir William, Bart. — Thomas. — John — Frances — Thomas — Richard — William. — Frances.
A. Preston | M. Mostyn — Cuthbert — Heiress of Ince — Francis Howard — Nicholas. John & Charles — Anne. Juliana

V. Sir William, Bart. — Thomas. — Mary. — Anne — Bridget — Richard
Mary Cransfield — John. Frances — Eliz. Waterson — Charles Winifred — Frances. — Richard. Wm. — Thomas. Carryl

VI. Sir William, Bart. — Anne. — John — William — Mary — Elizabeth
Eliz. Clifton — Mary. Elizabeth — Thomas

VII. Sir William Gerard, Bart. — VIII. Sir Thomas Gerard, Bart.=Tasborough — Robert — Mary
— a dr. — Claré, 1798

VIII. Sir THOMAS GERARD, who married ——, daughter of —— Tasborough, by whom he had two daughters: Clare, the younger died April 5, 1798, and gave three-fourths of her ample fortune to the poor. Sir Thomas died June 25, 1780, and his lady Aug. 20, 1783. He was succeeded by

IX. Sir FRANCIS GERARD, Bart. who died Sep. 14, 1791, and was succeeded by

X. Sir WILLIAM GERARD, the present baronet.

ARMS—Argent, a saltire, gules.
CREST—On a wreath, a lion rampant, ermine, crowned, or.
MOTTO—*En dieu est mon esperance.*
SEAT—At Bryn in Lancashire.

---

6. SHELLEY of Michelgrove, Sussex.

Created Baronet May 22, 1611.

THIS family is undoubtedly of great antiquity, and came out of France with William the Conqueror.[*]

Sir Richard Shelley, Knt. was knight of the shire for Huntingdon, and allowed 37 marks for his attendance in parliament. *temp.* Wm. Ruf. several of his descendants had summons to parliament among the barons. Sir Thomas Shelley, Knt. was sent ambassador into Spain in 1205; and Sir William Shelley was sent ambassador to the emperor of Germany, *temp.* Hen VII. and in great esteem with Philip II. king of Spain, who employed him in several embassies to the see of Rome and Germany. Of this family, though a younger branch,[†] was judge Shelley, who was sent by King Henry VIII. to cardinal Woolsey, to demand the surrender of York-Place, near Westminster (now Whitehall) belonging to the archbishoprick of York, into the king's hands. After some altercation between the judge and the cardinal, the latter was obliged to submit; but charged the judge to request his majesty to call to his most gracious remembrance, *that there was a heaven and a hell.*[‡]

---

[*] Ex Inform. Dom. Jo. Shelley, Bar.

[†] Though several pedigrees make this judge Shelley to be Sir William Shelley, the immediate ancestor of Sir John; and to marry Alice, daughter of Sir Henry Belknap, hereafter mentioned.

[‡] He told the cardinal, "That his highness had sent for all the judges, and all his learned council, to know their opinions thereupon; whose opinions were, that your grace must make a recognizance, and before a judge to acknowledge and confess the right thereof to belong to the king and his successors, wherefore the king hath appointed and sent me hither to take of you the same recognizance, having in your grace such affiance, as that ye will not refuse so to do;

Of this family also was Sir Thomas Shelley, one of the first gentlemens' families of distinction that became protestants, *temp.* Eliz. as were also Richard Shelley and Henry Shelley.

Sir Richard Shelley was the last English grand prior of the order of St. John of Jerusalem, in the reigns of Mary and Elizabeth. This honour was conferred on him by the former queen, through the interest of Cardinal Pole. It entitled him to a seat in the upper house of parliament, next to the lord abbot of Westminster, and above all lay barons. Finding it prudent to decline both the style and privileges of his office in the reign of her successor, he retired to Spain on her accession, and there resided 17 years under that of *turcopolier*, one of the first great offices of the order, equivalent to that of general of the cavalry, and one of those dignities necessary to arrive at, previous to that of being elected grand master. It was always annexed to the grand priory of England; but the English knights being deprived of their benefices by Henry VIII. they consequently lost the rank and consideration they had enjoyed at Malta, and at the death of Shelley's predecessor the grand master thought proper to resume the title, and keep it to himself, till the state of the Roman Catholic interest in England was determined. Finding the friendship between the courts of England and Spain was abating Sir Richard, in 1561, obtained the king of Spain's licence to go and assist at the relief of Malta, then besieged by the Turks; but he was scarcely arrived at Genoa when he received letters of recall, and others from the grand master, requiring him to take up the title of his priory, which he could not omit to do without prejudice to the order. Thus he came to be called *prior of England*, and again set out for Malta, where he was well received by the grand master, John de Valetta, and continued with him as long as he lived, and till his successor the prior of Capua almost forced him away. He then retired to Venice, from whence he solicited her majesty's permission to return to England, pleading,

and I desire to know your grace's pleasure therein." "Master Shelley (quoth my lord) I know that the king of his own nature is of a royal stomach, not willing more than justice shall lead him unto by the law; and therefore I counsel you, and all other judges and learned men of his council, to put no more into his head than law that may stand with conscience; for when ye tell him this is the law, ye should tell him also, that although this be the law, yet this is conscience; for law without conscience is not meet to be given to a king by his council: for every counsellor to a king ought to have a respect to conscience before the rigour of the law. The king ought, for his royal dignity and prerogative, to mitigate the rigour of the law, where conscience hath no more force. Therefore I say to you, that in this case, although you, and other of your profession, perceive by the orders of the law, that the king may lawfully do that thing which ye require of me: how say you, Master Shelley, may I do it with conscience, to give that away which is none of mine, from me and my successors? If this be the law and conscience, I pray you shew me your opinion." "Forsooth, my lord (quoth he) there is a great conscience: but having regard to the king's higher power, and to a better purpose, it may the better stand with conscience, who is sufficient to recompence the church of York with double the value." "That I know well; but here is no such condition (quoth my lord) but only a bare and simple departure with another's right: for if every bishop that may should do so, then might every prelate give away the patrimony of their dignities, which should be but smally to the king's honour. Well, I will not stand with you long in this matter, let me see your commission." To whom M. Shelley shewed the same, and that seen, "Master Shelley (quoth he) ye shall shew the king's highness, that I am his most faithful subject, obediencer, and beadman, whose royal commandment and request I will in no wise disobey, but fulfil his pleasure in all such things, wherein the fathers of the law say, that I may lawfully do; therefore I charge your conscience to discharge me: howbeit, shew his highness from me, that I most humbly desire his majesty to call to his most gracious remembrance, that there is both a heaven and hell." And therewithall the clerk wrote the recognizance, and after some secret talk they departed. *Stow's Chron. p. 550.*

that though he could not renounce his religious opinions, and had met with great losses in his fortune by the failure of foreign merchants, he had refused a pension offered by the king of Spain, rather than disoblige his rightful sovereign, whose father, Henry VIII. had been so good a friend to his father, as to compel him, in the beginning of his reign, to become his serjeant and judge, and who had the honour to entertain his majesty highly to his satisfaction at his family seat, at Michelgrove in Sussex. While he continued at Venice he was however employed to negotiate the revocation of certain new imposts to be levied on the Levant traders; which, though it did not succeed to his satisfaction, yet in the year 1584, seems to have been brought to a desirable issue. Sir Richard was born in 1514, for in one of his letters, dated Venice, Aug. 24, 1582, he describes himself as a man of threescore years and eight. He was a son of judge Shelley's.*

This family removed from Huntingdonshire near 500 years ago, and have ever since continued at Beckley, and Michelgrove in Sussex. The first mentioned in their pedigree is John Shelley, who had two sons, John, and Thomas Shelley, whose daughter and heir, Alice, married Sir William Brampton. Knt.

2. John Shelley, the eldest son, by Margaret his wife, daughter and heir of John Rolph, had three sons, who were all great men in their time, and received the honour of knighthood. 1. Sir John, who for eminent services done on the coast of France, in the beginning of Richard II. altered the family coat to sable, a fess ingrailed, between three periwincles, or. 2. Sir Thomas, who served as knight of the shire for Bucks, 21 Rich. II. and had 11*l.* 12*s.* allowed for 24 days expences, for himself and Sir Thomas Ailesbury, who served with him. He was attainted with his brother Sir John Shelley, for endeavouring to rethrone King Richard II. whereby they lost great estates, part of which was enjoyed by the heirs of the earl of Conningsby. Sir Thomas performed also considerable services on the coast of France with his brother, under that eminent commander Sir Robert Knowles. 3. Sir William Shelley, lord of Offerdary, Chelsey, and Applesham, in Sussex, who had two sons; Richard, the eldest, died without issue; Robert the second son married Elizabeth, daughter and co-heir of John Pettit, by whom he left issue two sons, John and Thomas; which last was of Hunsdon; who, for distinction from the Michelgrove family, altered their coat to argent, a chevron between three escallops, sable: but this line terminated in an heir female, Alice, married to Thomas Randall, Esq.

3. John, the eldest son was a burgess in parliament for the town of Rye in Sussex, 5, 8, and 9 Henry V. He married Beatrix, daughter and heir of Sir John Hawkwood, Knt. by whom he had one son,

4. John, who married Elizabeth, daughter and heir to John Michelgrove, Esq. (by Mary his wife, daughter of Sir Wm. Sydney of Penshurst, Kent) by whom he had three

---

* The compilers of our former baronetages seem not aware of this connection, for they only say, that Sir Richard was a descendant of the same lineage. They add, he was *dominus natus*; therefore, when in Spain refused to be called *prior d'Inglaterra*, and styled himself *turcopolier* for the English nation; whereas the truth is, he took this latter title as a less obnoxious one to his protestant countrymen.

Gent. Mag. 1785, *p.* 713.

SHELLEY OF MICHELGROVE, SUSSEX.

sons;* 1, Richard of Patcham, in Sussex, who by Mary, daughter of Sir Richard Urdeswick, Knt. was ancestor to the Shelley's of Patcham; 2, Sir William, who continued the line; 3, Edward, who was of Warminghurst Park, in Sussex, and father of Henry Shelley of Warminghurst, Esq. who married Anne, daughter and heir to Richard Sackvile of Buckhurst, Esq. and was ancestor to those of that place. He died January 3, 1526.

5. Sir William Shelley married Alice, eldest daughter of Sir Henry Belknap, Knt. (and Margaret his wife, daughter of Sir Richard Knowles, Knt.) sister and co-heir to Sir Edward Belknap, Knt.† by whom he became possessed of a considerable estate in Warwickshire; and had issue by her five sons; 1, John; 2, Sir Richard; 3, Sir James, who were both knights of Malta;‡ 4, Edward, slain at Muscleburgh Field, in Scotland; 5, Thomas of Maple-Durham, who by Mary, daughter of Sir Roger Copley, Knt. was father of Henry Shelley of Maple-Durham, Esq. who married Mary, daughter and co-heir of Sir John Lutterell, Knt. and was ancestor to those of that place. Sir William had also three daughters, of which Elizabeth was wife of Sir Roger Copley, Knt. and Catharine, married to Henry Browne, Esq. son of Sir Matthew Browne of Beechworth Castle in Surrey, Knt.

6. John Shelley of Michelgrove, Esq. the eldest son, married Mary, daughter of Sir William Fitz-Williams, Knt. and Maud his wife, daughter of Sir Richard Sackvile of Buckhurst, Knt. (who surviving him, married Sir Robert Guldeford, Knt.) by whom he had two sons and six daughters; 1, William, who married to his first wife, Jane, daughter and heir of —— Lingen of Sutton, in Herefordshire, Esq. and secondly Mary, daughter of Thomas Wriothesley, earl of Southampton, relict of —— Lister, Esq. son and heir of Sir Martin Lister, Knt. but left no issue. He was attainted for treason, committed Dec. 15, 25 Eliz. whereby his estate was forfeited to the crown during his life, for he did not die till April 15, 39 Eliz. when, by virtue of an entail, the estates both in Sussex and Warwickshire descended to his brother John, of whom hereafter. Of the daughters, 1, Elizabeth was married to Sir

---

* Some pedigrees make four sons, and that the youngest was Sir John Shelley, Knt. slain at the winning of Rhodes.

† This Sir William Shelley, in several pedigrees, is said to be one of the justices of the common pleas. —— Philpot, in his *Villare Cantium*, p. 259, says, Sir Henry Belknap had three daughters and co-heirs; Alice married to Sir William Shelley; Anne matched to Sir Robert Wotton, and Elizabeth first wedded to Sir Philip Cook of Giddy-Hall, in Essex, and after to Leonard Dannett of the county of Worcester, who divided his patrimony. In Sir Wm. Dugdale's Antiquities of Warwickshire, vol. I. p. 523, Sir Edward Belknap is said to have four sisters and co-heirs; Alice married to Sir William Shelley, Anne to Sir Robert Wotton, Elizabeth to John Coke, and Mary to Gerard Danet, squire of the body to King Henry VIII. It is thougt a barony is now in the descendants from the daughters and co-heirs of Sir Henry Belknap, he being descended lineally from Joan, sister and heir of John lord Sudley, who marrying William lord Boteler, by him had two sons, Thomas and Ralph, successively lord Botelers of Sudley; who both dying without issue, their sisters Joan and Elizabeth became their co-heirs: Elizabeth married Sir John Montgomery, Knt. and dying without issue, the claim to the barony of Sudley was vested in Joan, the sole surviving sister and heir; which Joan married Hamon Belknap, lord of Oston, and had issue Sir Henry Belknap, lord of Oston, who married Margaret, daughter of Sir Richard Knowles, by whom he had the daughters and co-heirs before-mentioned. *Ex Inform. Dom. Joh. Shelley, Bar.* When a barony in fee is merged in daughters and co-heirs, the king may give it to which of them he pleases.

‡ These knights were first called knights hospitallers of St. John of Jerusalem, afterwards the knights of Rhodes, and at this time the knights of Malta. *Vertot's Hist. of the Knights of Malta, vol. I. p. 1.*

Thomas Gifford, Knt. 2, Eleanor, to Thomas Norton, Esq. son and heir to Sir John Norton of Norwood, in Kent, Knt. 3, Margaret to Edward Gage, Esq. 4, Mary to Sir George Cotton of Warblington, in Southamptonshire, Knt. 5, Bridget married to Sir Anth. Hungerford of Downampney, in Wilts, Knt. and 6, Anne, wife to Sir Richard Shirley of Wiston, in Sussex, Knt. This Sir John Shelley, Esq. the father of these children, died Dec. 16, 1550.

7. John Shelley, Esq. second son, heir to his mother, married Eleanor, daughter of Sir Thomas Lovell of East-Harling, in Norfolk, Knt. (son of Sir Francis Lovell of Barton, Knt. and Anne his wife, daughter of George Ashby of —— in Middlesex, Esq.) by whom he had two sons, John and Henry, who died unmarried; also one daughter Elizabeth, married to Sir Thomas Timperleigh of Suffolk, Knt.

I. JOHN SHELLEY of Michelgrove, Esq. the eldest son and heir, was advanced to the degree of a baronet at the first erection of that dignity, 9 James I. He sold the estate in Warwickshire, and purchased in Sussex, where he lived in great honour and esteem. He married Jane, daughter of Sir Thomas Reresby of Thribergh, in Yorkshire, Knt. by whom he had two sons, Sir William and John Shelley, Esq. who married Mary, daughter and heir of George Bayley, Esq. and died without issue. Sir William Shelley, Knt. his eldest son, married Christiana, daughter of Sir James Vantelet, Knt. and died in 1635, during his father's life, leaving only one son,

II. Sir CHARLES SHELLEY, Bart. successor to his grandfather, who, by Elizabeth, daughter of Benjamin Weston of Walton upon Thames, in Surrey, Esq. (and Elizabeth his wife, daughter of Sir William Sheldon of Honby, in Leicestershire, Esq. and relict of Christopher Villers, earl of Anglesea) the fourth son of Richard Weston, earl of Portland. He had four sons, Benjamin and Charles, who died young; Sir John, his successor, and William, who died without issue; also two daughters, Elizabeth and Christiana, who both died unmarried. His second wife was Mary, daughter of Thomas Gifford of Dunton Walcot in Essex, Esq. and relict of George lord Abergavenny, by whom he had no issue. He died about 1681, and was buried at Roan in France; and his lady, who survived him, died in 1695. He was succeeded in dignity and estate by his eldest surviving son,

III. Sir JOHN SHELLEY, Bart. who married to his first wife, Bridget, only daughter of George lord Abergavenny, by whom he had only one daughter, Frances, married to Richard lord viscount Fitz-Williams of Mount-Merion, in the kingdom of Ireland, by whom she had several children; of which Mary, the eldest was married to Henry earl of Pembroke. Sir John's second wife was Mary, daughter and co-heir of Sir John Gage of Firle in Sussex, Bart. co-heir with the lady viscountess Fauconberg.) He died April 25, 1703, leaving issue by his second lady, two sons, Sir John, his successor, and Richard, who married Mrs. Fleetwood, by whom he had issue; also three daughters, Mary married to Sir John Lawson of Brough, in Yorkshire, Bart. Elizabeth to Edward Sheldon of Weston, in Warwickshire, Esq. and Catharine to —— Matthews of Ireland, Esq. He was succeeded by his son,

IV. Sir JOHN SHELLEY, Bart. who abjured the errors of popery, Feb. 26, 1716; and on May 21, 1717 he married Catharine, daughter of Sir Thomas Scawen,

SHELLEY OF MICHELGROVE, SUSSEX.

TABLE 8.

1 JOHN SHELLEY
2 John Shelley—Margaret, dr. of J. Rolph   Thomas Shelley
3 Sir John Shelley, Knt.   Sir Thomas Shelley, Knt.   Sir William, Knt.   Alice
  Beatrix Hawkwood   N   Sir Wm. Brampton
4 John—Eliz. Michelgrove   Richard   Robert—Eliz. Pettit
Richard—Mary Urdeswick   5 Sir Wm. Kt.—Alice Belknap   Edward, 1526   John & Thos.

Shelleys of   6 John, 1550   Sir Richard.   Thomas   Elizabeth   Catharine   Henry
Patcham   Mary Fitz-   Sir James.   M. Copley   Sir R. Copley, Kt.   H. Browne   Anne Sack-
            Williams   Edward   ville

William, 1597   7 John   Elizabeth   Eleanor   Margaret   Mary   Bridget   Anne   Henry
Jane | Mary   Eleanor   Sir T.   Thomas   Edward   Sir G.   Sir A.   Sir R.   Mary
Lin- | Wrio-   Lovett   Gifford   Norton   Gage   Cotton   Hunger-   Shir-   Luttrell
gen | thesley   ford   ley   Shelleys of Buckhurst

I. Sir John Shelley, Bt.—Jane Reresby   Henry   Elizabeth=Sir T. Timperley, Kt.

Sir William Shelley, Knt. 1635—Christiana Vantelet   John Shelley=Mary Bayley   Shelleys of Maple-Durham

II. Sir Charles Shelley, Bart. died about 1681
Eliz. dr. of B. Weston | Mary, dr. of T. Gifford, 1695

Benjamin & Charles   III. Sir John Shelley, Bart. 1703   William d. S. P.
   both d. y.   Bridget, dr. of Geo. L. | Mary, dr. of Sir John   Elizabeth
                         Abbergavenny   Gage, Bart.   Christiana

Frances   IV. Sir John Shelley, Bart. 1771   Richard   Mary   Elizabeth   Catharine
Richard V. Fitz-   Catharine, dr. of Sir | Marg. sister to   Mrs.   Sir John   Edward   ———
  Williams   T. Scawen, Kt.   Thomas D. of   Fleetwood   Lawson, Bt.   Sheldon   Matthews
                 1726   Newcastle

Catharine.   V. Sir John Shelley, Bart. 1783   Henrietta   Elizabeth   Triphena   N   N
Mary   W. Newnham | — Woodcock   George   John   Charles   Sir Cha.   James
                                   L. Onslow   Cannon   Polhill   Whitworth   Best

VI. Sir J. Shelley, Bart. b. 1771   3 daughters

Knt. alderman of London, by whom he had issue two daughters, Catharine and Mary: this lady dying in 1726, he married secondly Margaret, sister to Thomas duke of Newcastle, who died Nov. 13, 1768. In 1771 he, joined with his son, the right honourable John Shelley, in obtaining an act of parliament for selling the manor of Hurst among others of his settled estates, and died Sep. 6, 1771, having issue, by his second wife, one son John, and three daughters; Henrietta, who in June 26, 1753 was married to the right honourable George, now lord Onslow; Elizabeth, the wife of James Cannon, Esq. Tryphena, of Charles Polhill of Chepstead, in Kent, Esq. He was succeeded by his son,

V. The right honourable Sir JOHN SHELLEY, Bart. who was keeper of the records in the Tower, and clerk of the pipe for life; and for some time treasurer of the king's houshold: he served in parliament for Shoreham, and in 1766 was sworn of the privy council. He married first Wilhelmina, daughter of ―― Newnham, in Sussex, by whom he left one son, the present baronet; she died in 1772: and secondly ――, daughter of Edward Woodcock, Esq. (who in 1790 became the wife of Dr. Stewart of Southampton) by whom he left three daughters. He died Sep. 11, 1783, and was succeeded by his only son,

VI. Sir JOHN SHELLEY, Bart. who was born in 1771.

ARMS—Sable, a fess ingrailed, between three periwincles (whelks) or.
CREST—On a wreath, or and sable, a griffin's head erased, argent beaked, and ducally gorged, or.
SEAT—At Beckley, and Michelgrove in Sussex.

7. BARRINGTON of Barrington-Hall, Essex.

Created Baronet June 29, 1611.

Mr. CAMDEN in his Britannia says, " Barrington-Hall (heretofore) the seat of that eminent family of the Barringtons, who in the time of King Stephen were greatly enriched with the estate of the lords Montfitchet; and in the memory of our fathers a match with the daughter and co-heir of Henry Pole lord Montacute, son and heir to Margaret countess of Salisbury, rendered them more illustrious, by an alliance with the royal blood."

The first we find mentioned in the pedigree, in Chauncy's Hertfordshire is, Sir Odynell Barrington, or Barentone, as the name was anciently written, descended from Barrington, that served Queen Emme, wife of King Etheldred, father of Edward the Confessor; he was baron of Wegon, and incurred the common fate of his country, becoming subject to the Normans, which may be the reason that none of the name, either as chief lords or sub-tenants, in Essex, are mentioned in Doomsday Book; yet Selden finds Radulfus de Barentona, to be sworn among others in the hundred of Trepeslau in Cambridgeshire, to take the conqueror's survey; and the town and parish of Barrington, near Cambridge, is said to take name from him.

Mr. Le Neve (Norroy king at arms) says the Barringtons are descended from Barentone, a Saxon, who had the custody of the forest of Hatfield-Regis, *temp.* Wm. I. as may be gathered out of the old writings of the family, and that

2. Eustachius de Barentona (son of Barentone the Saxon) was servant to King Henry I. and had granted him by that king lands, and the custody of the forest; and that he died in the time of King Stephen.

3. Humphrey, his son and heir, married Grisilde, sister to Sir Ralph Marcy. Their son,

4. Humphrey de Barenton, was under age at his father's decease, and in ward to King Henry II. He lived in the reigns of Henry II. Rich. I. and King John,[*] and was high sheriff of Essex and Hertfordshire, 9 Rich. I. By his wife Amicia, the only daughter of Sir William, third son of Sir Jeffery de Mandeville, earl of Essex, founder of the abbey of Walden, he had a son

5. Nicholas, who was knighted; which Sir Nicholas de Barenton, custos of the forest, by deed styled *Dnus Nic de Barenton*, lived in the reigns of King John, and Henry III. He first took to wife Mary, daughter of John Bovile; secondly, Maud, daughter of Sir Ralph Mortoft, Knt. He had no issue by the first, but by the latter a daughter, Margaret, married to Sir James Umfreville, and several sons, whereof

6. Nicholas, the eldest, succeeded to the inheritance, was knighted, and living *temp.* Henry III. and Edward I. by Agnes his wife, daughter and heir to Sir William Chetwynde, was father of another Sir Nicholas, John, and Philip; and four daughters, of which Margaret married Sir Martin Suchemer, Knt.

7. Sir Nicholas, the eldest son, living *temp.* Edward II. and Edward III. was knight of the shire for Essex in 1308 and 1313.[†] He married Alice, daughter and heir of Sir Richard Belhouse, Knt. by whom he had four sons, Nicholas, Thomas, Roger, and Sir Philip, who married Margaret, daughter of Sir William Tey of Essex, Knt. and was father of Nicholas Barrington of Raleigh-Park, in Essex, Esq. Sister and heir to John was Thomazine, living *temp.* Henry VI. who first married William Lunsford, Esq. (from Lunsford of Lunsford, in Sussex) secondly, William Sydney of Penshurst, in Kent, Esq. (from whom the earls of Leicester descended) and thirdly she married John Hopton, Esq.

8. Nicholas Barenton, eldest son of the last Sir Nicholas, and brother to Sir Philip, was living *temp.* Edw. II. and Edw. III. having to his wife, Emme,

---

[*] Chauncy, in his Hertfordshire, p. 366, says, "There was about this time Sir Warren of Barrington; I know not whose son he was. He is buried at Therhale-Priory, in the forest of Hatfield."
[†] Muilman's Essex, vol. IV. p. 115.

daughter and co-heir to Sir Robert Baard, Knt. by whom he had four sons, Sir John, Humphrey, Thomas, and Philip; and a daughter Lettice, who died unmarried. He was succeeded by his eldest son,

9. John, who was knighted, and married Margaret, daughter and heir of Sir John Blomvile, Knt. by whom he had two sons, John and Edward. He was member of Parliament for Essex in 1330.*

10. John Barenton, the eldest son, was styled Barrington, and the first that was so called: he was living *temp*. Henry IV. and V. and by his wife Alice, one of the daughters and heirs of Thomas Battle, younger son of Sir John Battle, of Ongar Park in Essex, Knt. by Elizabeth his wife, daughter and heir of Sir Richard Ennefield, Knt. had issue Thomas, Humphrey, and Elizabeth, married to John Sulyard.

11. Thomas, the eldest son, was the inheritor of his father's lands in Hatfield, Writtle, &c. and after the death of his uncle, Edward Barrington, was seized of the manors of Chevesfield, Graveley, Lecheford, and lands in Weston; at the first of which places he held a court, 16 Henry VI. 1438; was high sheriff of Essex and Hertford, 30 Henry VI. He married first Margaret ———, secondly Anne, the second daughter, and one of the heirs of Sir John Holbeach, Knt. and of his wife, the daughter and co-heir of Sir John Rochford, of Lincolnshire, Knt. He lies buried with his wife Anne, in the church of Hatfield Broad-Oak. She dying the day after him this distich was made on them:

He first deceas'd; she for a few hours tried
To live without him, lik'd it not, and died.†

12. Humphrey Barrington,‡ son and heir to the said Thomas, married Margaret, daughter of ——— Bretton of Essex, and had issue,

13. Nicholas, who took to wife Anne, daughter of Thomas Darcy, of Tolshunt-Darcy, in Essex; and left two sons, Richard and Sir Nicholas; which Richard was aged 20 years at his father's death, Sep. 27, 21 Henry VII. but died without issue. The said Nicholas had a wife named Elizabeth, that survived him, but whether she, and not Anne, was the daughter of Thomas Darcy is uncertain.

14. Sir Nicholas, son to Nicholas aforesaid, died about the year 1521; for in October that year his will was proved, which bore date, July 22, 1515, wherein he disposed of all his lands and manors in trust for his heir apparent, John, then about eight years old, when he came to the age of 21 years. Elizabeth, his wife, survived him; she was daughter of Sir John Brocket of Brocket-Hall, in Hertfordshire, and afterwards married William Boughton of Lawford, in Warwickshire, Esq.

15. The said John Barrington, succeeding to the inheritance, was in ward to Thomas Bonham, and living 25 Henry VIII. he married Elizabeth, daughter of Thomas Bonham, by Catharine his wife, sister and heir to the lord Marney, knight of the garter: he had by her a son Thomas, whom he left under age; and had two wives; 1, Alice, daughter of Henry Parker, lord Morley, by whom he had.

---

* Muilman's Essex, vol. IV. p. 115.   † Fuller in Essex, p. 240.   ‡ Muilman says was brother to Thomas, who died v. p.

only one daughter, Elizabeth; and 2, Winifred, youngest daughter and co-heir of Henry Pole, lord Montagu, and relict of Sir Thomas Hastings, Knt. Catharine, the eldest daughter and co-heir of the said Henry lord Montagu, was married to Francis earl of Huntingdon, eldest brother to Sir Thomas Hastings; which Henry was son to Sir Richard Pole, knight of the gartor, by Margaret Plantagenet his wife, countess of Salisbury, sister and sole heir to Edward earl of Warwick, and daughter to George duke of Clarence, younger brother to King Edward IV. and of this illustrious marriage descended two sons, Sir Francis Barrington, Bart. and Henry, a gentleman pensioner, who died without issue: as also a daughter Catharine, wife of William, son and heir to Sir Ralph Bourchier of Beningborough, in Yorkshire, Knt.

I. FRANCIS, son and heir, served as knight of the shire for Essex, in the parliament held at Westminster, 43 Eliz. and on the accession of King James I. to the English crown, was knighted at Theobalds, May 7, 1603; and by the said prince farther advanced to the degree of a baronet at the first institution of that dignity, 1611. He married Joan, daughter to Sir Henry Cromwell, alias Williams, of Hinchingbrook, in Huntingdon, Knt. sister of Sir Oliver Cromwell, Knt. and had issue four sons, and five daughters; 1, Sir Thomas; 2, Robert, of Hatfield Broad-Oak, who married Dorothy, daughter of Sir Thomas Eden of Sudbury, in Suffolk, Knt. the widow of ―― Barret, Esq. brother to Sir Edward; by whom he left posterity, which ended in a daughter Joan, married to Mr. Gyles, of the six clerks office in Chancery; 3, Francis Barrington of London, who, by a daughter of Mr. Richard Doucet, had a son Francis; and 4, John, a captain, who died in Germany. The daughters were, Elizabeth, married to Sir James Altham of Marks-Hall, in Essex, Knt. and afterwards to Sir William Masham of High-Laver, in Essex, Bart. 2, Mary, to Sir Gilbert Gerard of Flamberds, Harrow on the Hill, Bart. 3, Winifred, wife of Sir William Meux of Kingston, in the Isle of Wight, Knt. 4, Ruth, wife of Sir George Lamplugh of Cumberland, Knt. and 5, Joan, married to Sir Richard Everard of Much-Waltham, in Essex, Bart. Sir Francis died in 1628, and was succeeded by his eldest son,

II. Sir THOMAS, who received the honour of knighthood during his father's life. He married first Frances, daughter and co-heir of John Gobert of Coventry, Esq. by whom he had a daughter Lucy, first married to William Cheyney of Chesham-Boys, in Bucks, Esq. and secondly to Sir Toby Tyrrel of Thornton, in Bucks, Bart. and two sons, Sir John, who succeeded him, and Sir Gobert Barrington of Tofts, in Little Baddow in Essex, Knt. who married first Lucy, daughter of Sir William[*] Wiseman of Torrel's-Hall, in Essex, Knt. by whom he had six sons, Thomas, Francis, Richard, Robert, John, and Theophilus: the four last died young. Thomas Barrington, the eldest son, a colonel in the army, died without issue, having previously made over the estate to his brother, Francis Barrington of Tofts, Esq. He married Elizabeth, daughter and co-heir of Samuel Shute Esq. of London, who was sheriff of that city in 1681, by whom he had no issue, and left his estate to his wife's cousin german, John Shute, Esq. of Becket-Park, Berks, who, by an act of par-

---

* Antiquities of Essex, p. 175.

liament changed his name to Barrington, and was created lord Barrington of Newcastle, in the county of Dublin, and Viscount Barringron of Ardglass, in the county of Down in Ireland, 7 George I. and died in Dec. 1734, leaving issue William viscount Barrington, many years secretary at war; John, a major-general in the army, father to William, now Viscount Barrington; Daines, one of the judges for Wales; Samuel, admiral of the white; and Shute, bishop of Durham; besides two daughters, married respectively to Robert Price of Foxley, Esq. and Thomas Clarges, son and heir of Sir Thomas Clarges, Bart. Sir Gobert married to his second lady, Elizabeth, relict of Hugh Lawton, Esq. by whom he had no issue. He died about 1695, and was buried at Hatfield: she departed this life in 1702-3, aged 84, and lies buried at St. Saviour's, Southwark. Sir Thomas had to his second lady, Judith, daughter of Sir Rowland Lytton of Knebworth, in Hertfordshire, Knt. and widow of Sir George Smith of Annables, in the same county, Knt. which Judith died without issue in 1657, aged 65 years, and Sir Thomas in 1644. He was succeeded by his eldest son,

III. Sir JOHN BARRINGTON, Knt. and Bart. who married Dorothy, daughter of Sir William Lytton of Knebworth, in Hertfordshire, Knt. (she survived him, and died Oct. 27, 1703) by whom he had five sons; 1, Thomas; 2, Francis, who died unmarried; 3, John, who married Elizabeth, daughter to Edward Hawkins of Bishop-Stortford, Gent. and had issue Sir John, his son and heir; 4, Francis, who died unmarried; and 5, William, who married Sarah, daughter and heir of Richard Young of London, merchant, but died without issue: she, surviving him, afterwards married ——— Wynne, Esq. Also nine daughters; of which Winifred was wife to Richard Wiseman, Esq. son to Sir Richard Wiseman of Torrel's-Hall, in Essex, Knt. and Lucy, wife to John Walter of Chepstow, in Monmouthshire, Esq.

Thomas Barrington, Esq. eldest son of Sir John, married the lady Anne, daughter and co-heir to Robert Rich, earl of Warwick; and had by her three sons, Sir John, Sir Charles, and Richard, who died unmarried: and two daughters; Mary, who died unmarried in Oct. 1727, and Anne, wife to Mr. Charles Shales, goldsmith to Queen Anne and King George I. and II. she died Nov. 17, 1729, and he Oct. 5, 1734, leaving two sons; Richard, who died S. P. and John Shales Barrington of Hatfield Broad-Oak, Esq. The said Thomas, dying during his father's life, Jan. 1681, his relict afterwards married Sir Richard Francklyn of Ryslip, in Middlesex, Bart. whereupon the dignity and estate descended to his eldest son, John, as heir to his grandfather, which

IV. Sir JOHN dying unmarried (of the small-pox in 1691) was succeeded by his brother,

V. Sir CHARLES BARRINGTON, Bart. who was several times elected in parliament, against powerful opposers, one of the knights of the shire for the county of Essex, and was made by Queen Anne vice-admiral of the said county. He died Jan. 29, 1714-15. His first wife was Bridget, sole daughter of Sir John Monson of Broxburn, in Hertfordshire, Bart. (by Judith his wife, daughter of Sir Thomas Pelham, Bart. great grandfather to Thomas duke of Newcastle) and after her decease married Anna-Maria, daughter to William earl Fitz-William, of the kingdom of Ireland (who was seated at Milton near Peterborough, and dying July 1717, was buried at Marham near Peterborough) but by neither of them had any issue. The

BARRINGTON OF BARRINGTON-HALL, ESSEX.

1 BARENTONE, *temp.* Wm. I.
2 Eustachius de Barentona, *temp.* King Stephen
3 Humphrey=Grisilde Marcy   TABLE 9.
4 Humphrey=Amicia, dr. of Sir William Mandeville

Mary Bovile=5 Sir Nicholas, Knt.=Maud Mortoft

6 Sir Nicholas=Agnes Chetwynde   Margaret=Sir James Umfreville
7 Sir Nicholas de Barenton, Kt.=Alice Belhouse   John & Philip   Margaret=Sir M. Suchemer, Kt.
8 Nicholas=Emme Board   Thomas   Roger   Sir Philip=Margerey Tey
9 Sir John=M. Blomvile Humph. Thomas Philip Lettice Nicholas   Edw. III. K. Eng.
10 John=Alice Battle   Edward   John of Gaunt   Edmund of York
11 Thomas, 1472   Elizabeth   Humphrey   Joan   Richard,
Marg. | A. Holbeach. J. Sulyard   Ralph, E. of Westmoreland   E. of Cambridge
12 Humphrey=Marg. Bretton   Ralph, E. of Salisbury   Rich. D. of York
Anne Darcy=13 Nicholas, 1507=Elizabeth   Rich. E. of Warwick   Geo. D. of Clarence, 1471
                                                                   Isa. dr. of Rich. E. Warw.
Richard   14 Sir Nicholas, Kt. about 1521   Isabel   Anne
           Elizabeth Brocket   Geo. D. Clarence   Rich. III.

15 John=Eliz. Bonham   Margaret, Countess of Salisbury=Sir Rich. Pole, K. G.

                                Henry L. Montagu, 1558=Jane, dr. of Geo. L. Abergavenny

Alice Morley=Thomas=Winifred   Catharine=Francis, E. of Huntingdon

Eliz. I. Sir Francis, Kt. & Bt. 1628=Joan Cromwell   Henry   Cath.=W. Bourchier   Baroness of Hun-
                                                                                    ford
II. Sir Tho. Kt. & Bt. 1644 Rob. Francis John Elizabeth   Mary Winifred Ruth   Joan
Frances | Judith   Dorothy   —   Sir J. Sir W.   Sir G.   Sir Wm. Sir G. Sir Rich.
Gobert | Lytton, Eden   Doucet Altham Masham Gerard Meux   Lamplugh Everard
         1567
                                                               Francis   Francis Shute
          Lucy   III. Sir John, Kt. & Bt. 1682   Sir Gobert, Kt.
W. Cheyney|Sir T. Tyrrel   Dorothy Lytton, 1703   L. Wiseman | E. Lawton   Sam.   Benj.

Thomas John   William Winifred   Lucy 2 sons Thos. 4 sons, Francis=E. Shute
Anne   Eliz. Sarah   Richard   John 7 drs.   & 6 drs.
Rich   Hawkins Young   Wiseman   Walter   John, V. Bar-   Mary
                                                                    rington   S. Offley

IV. Sir John, Bt. V. Sir Charles, Bt. 1715   Richard.   Anne   VI. Sir John, Bt. 1717
    1691   B. Munson | A. M. Fitzwilliams Mary, 1727 Charles   Susan Draper

VII. Sir John, Bt. 1776   Charles   VIII. Sir Fitzwilliam, 1792   Susan   Sarah
     Mary Roberts, 1752   — Mead | Jane Hall   Barrington Flack

IX. Sir John Barrington, Bart.   Fitzwilliam   Anne   Winifred   Jane
                                 —, dr. of S. Marshal   R. Pope   W. Browne

greatest part of his estate he left by will to his sister Shales, and after her decease to his nephew, Richard Shales Barrington, Esq. her eldest son, who dying unmarried, it came to his youngest brother, John Shales Barrington, Esq. of Hatfield-Broad-Oak, in Essex; but the title descended to

VI. Sir JOHN, son and heir of John Barrington, Esq. third son of Sir John Barrington, Bart. grandfather to Sir Charles; which Sir John Barrington, Bart. married Susan, daughter of George Draper of Hitchin, in Hertfordshire, Gent. and left issue three sons, Sir John, Charles, and Fitzwilliam, who married, June 1741, to the sole daughter and heir of Capt. Thomas Mead; and two daughters: Susan married to Barrington Flacke of Linton, in Cambridgeshire, Esq. and Sarah. Sir John dying Aug. 1717, was succeeded in dignity and estate by his eldest son,

VII. Sir JOHN BARRINGTON, Bart, who was a member of parliament for Newton, in the Isle of Wight. He married Mary, daughter of Patricius Roberts, Esq. (by Elizabeth, eldest daughter of John Weston of Ockham, in Surrey, Esq.) by whom he had no issue. His lady died June 11, 1752, and he May 4, 1776; and was succeeded by his brother,

VIII. Sir FITZWILLIAM BARRINGTON, Bart, who died Sep. 24, 1792, in the 85th year of his age, having been afflicted with the palsy for the last ten years of his life. By his second wife he had issue; 1, Sir John; 2, Fitzwilliam, who in 1789 married ——, daughter of Capt. Samuel Marshall, of the navy; 3, Anne; 4, Winifred, the wife of Robert Pope of Blackford, in the Isle of Wight, Esq. in 1778; and Jane, one of his daughters, was the wife of the Rev. William Browne of Canfield-Place, Hatfield. He was succeeded in title and estate by his son,

IX. Sir JOHN BARRINGTON, the present baronet, member for Newton before-mentioned, in the two last parliaments.

ARMS—Argent, three chevronells, gules; a label of as many points, azure.
CREST—On a wreath, an hermit's bust, with a cowl, vested paly, argent and gules.
MOTTO—*Ung durant ma vie.*
SEAT—At Swagnston in the Isle of Wight, Hampshire.

8. MUSGRAVE of Eden-Hall, Cumberland.

Created Baronet June 29, 1611.

THIS family is of great antiquity and reputation, and came into England with the Conqueror, and settled at Musgrave* in Westmoreland.

* We adopt the etymology of the name, as given by our predecessors, with such additional observations of our own as our more extended researches enable us to suggest. Musgrave, like most other

The first of the name we have met with was Peter Musgrave, who lived about the time of King Stephen; for in the next reign, Henry II. we find a dispute between

2. Robert, son of Peter Musgrave, and the monks of Byland, concerning the boundaries of their respective manors: which dispute was settled in the county court at Appleby, William Fitz-hugh being then sheriff.* The next we meet with is

3. Sir Adam de Musgrave, in the reign of King John, who, among other persons of note, was witness to a grant of wood and turbary at Sandford, by William de Sandford, to the first Robert de Veteripont. He was in great favour with the said Robert, unto whom the king gave the barony of Appleby, and the perpetual sheriffdom; and held Musgrave of him in cornage,† as part of the barony. In the next reign was

4. Sir Thomas de Musgrave; for in 1252, to a grant of the last Robert de Veteripont, of lands to Richard Clerke of Appleby, one of the witnesses was Thomas de Musgrave, the sheriff of Westmoreland, who was afterwards executor to the will of the said Robert. The next that occurs was

5. Richard de Musgrave. In 1286, in the partition of the Veteripont inheritance between the two daughters and co-heirs of the last Robert de Veteripont, the homage and service of Richard de Musgrave was assigned to Idonea, the younger daughter.

6. Thomas de Musgrave, his son and heir, was returned to serve in parliament for the county of Westmorland 14, 15, 17, 18 Edw. III. and in 1341, upon the invasion in the North, made by David Bruce, king of Scotland, he joined with the barons in those parts, was one of the commanders in the van of that army, which gave him battle near Durham, utterly routing his forces, and taking the king prisoner. The same year he was associated with the bishop of Carlisle and others, in guarding the marches; and in 1342 was made governor of Berwick, and sole justicier throughout all the king's lands in Scotland, and afterwards accompanied Ralph

---

names, was, no doubt, originally a name of office. *Grave*, or *graff*, is the Teutonic or German title of a prefect, keeper, or governor. Thus *burg-graff*, *plas-graff*, *land-graff*, and *mar-graff* denote respectively the superintendant of the *city*, *palace*, *land*, *marches*, or *boundaries*. We have softened the word down into *reeve*, in our own *shire-reeve* or *sheriff*. Graff or grave appears to us not to be derived, as lexicographers in general imagine, from the Saxon *geref*, *exigere*, *rapere*, but from the Teutonic *grou*, which implies *hoary*, *venerable*; and hence the title seems to be something like senator. Neither is Musgrave equivalent to Margrave: its obvious derivation, we think, is from the old Saxon word *mew*, which originally denoted the place in which the hawks were kept, and now denotes stables; perhaps for no better reason, than that the king's stables, near Charing-Cross, are built on the site of the ancient *Mews*. Hence *Mews-grave* or *Musgrave* is clearly *the keeper of the hawks*, or perhaps the king's equerry, or master of the horse.

In the reign of Edward III. they became purchasers of Hartley-Castle, where they chiefly resided, till Eden-Hall came into the family, in the time of Henry VI. by a marriage with Joan, one of the coheiresses of Sir William de Stapleton of Eden-Hall, Knt. since which it has been the principal seat of the Musgrave family, until Sir Peter, the late baronet, removed to Kempton Park in Middlesex, a fine estate presented to him by his maternal uncle, the late Sir John Charden, Bart. in 1746.

* Burn's Hist. Westmoreland, p. 590. *Hutchinson's Cumberland.*

† A kind of grand serjeanty; the service of which tenure is to blow a horn when any invasion of the Northern enemy is perceived; and by this many hold their land northward about the Picts wall. *Cowell's Interp. and Camden's Brit.* p. 1049.

lord Nevil in the Scotch wars, 1356. He received command to reside upon his lands in the marches towards Scotland, for the defence of the country against any incursion. In 1358 he obtained a charter for free warren in all his demesne lands at Musgrave and Souleby, in Westmoreland, with power to impark his woods, called Hevenings, containing 200 acres. He, in 1359, was made governor of York-Castle, and sheriff of Yorkshire. 42 Edw. III. he was constituted Escheator for the counties of York, Northumberland, Cumberland, and Westmoreland; and for his good service had a grant of 100 marks *per annum* out of the Exchequer. In 1372 he was associated with the bishop of Carlisle and others in the office of warden of the west marches. At length, after many signal services, and continual trusts, he had the fate to be taken prisoner by the Scots, 1379, with Thomas his son; but procuring John lord Nevil, of Raby, and others, to be sureties for 10,000 marks, they were set at liberty. This Thomas purchased Harcla-Castle from Ranulph, baron of Raby. He was also, for his signal knowledge in national affairs, summoned by writ, among the barons of this kingdom, from 24 to 47 Edw. III. inclusive. He married three wives; 1, Margaret, daughter and co-heir of William Roos of Yotton; 2, Mary, daughter of John Vaux, relict of Thomas Holland, earl of Huntingdon; 3, Isabel, widow of Robert, son of Robert lord Clifford, and daughter to Thomas lord Berkley, by whom he had a daughter, married to Henry Wharton; and two sons: Thomas, taken prisoner with his father, and William. He died in 1384, and was succeeded by his son,

7. Sir Thomas de Musgrave, Knt. who married Elizabeth, daughter and co-heir of Sir William Fitzwilliam of Sprotsburgh, in Yorkshire. He was sheriff of Cumberland in 1393, and knight of the shire for Westmoreland in 1400. He died in the year 1409, and was succeeded by his son,

8. Sir Richard de Musgrave, Knt. who, by Elizabeth ———, left

9. Thomas, his son and heir, who married Joan, daughter of William lord Dacre. He died in 1447, leaving Richard, his heir, and Elizabeth, the wife of Henry Wharton.

10. Sir Richard Musgrave, Knt. who married Elizabeth, daughter of Sir Thomas Betham of Betham-Castle, in Westmoreland, Knt. and sister of Sir Edward Betham, Knt. He died in 1464, and left issue; 1, Elizabeth, the wife of Thomas Gayt; 2, Isabel, of Thomas Middleton of Middleton-Hall, Esq. 3, Thomas; 4, Margaret, the wife of Thomas Elderton; 5, Eleanor, of Rowland Thornborough; 6, Mary, of Thomalin Warcop; 7, Richard, who married one of the daughters and co-heirs of Sir William Stapleton, and widow of Sir William Hilton; 8, William, to whom William lord Dacre, warden of the west marches, in 1447, paid 100*l.* for the repairs of Bew-Castle; 9, Agnes, the wife of Robert Warcop; 10, John, who died S. P.

11. Thomas de Musgrave, son and heir of Sir Richard, married Joan, the other daughter and co-heir of Sir William Stapleton, by Margaret his wife; and with her he had Eden-Hall. He died in 1469, and had issue Richard, John, Nicholas, and William; from whom descended the four families of Eden-Hall, Musgrave-Hall, or Fairbank; Hayton, and Crookdake: and four daughters, Margaret, the wife of John Sandford; Eleanor, of Christopher Lancaster; Mary, of Nicholas Ridley; and Isabella, of John Crackenthorp of Newbiggin, Esq.

MUSGRAVE OF EDEN-HALL, CUMBERLAND.

Sir John Musgrave, second son, was knighted at the battle of Newark upon Trent, by King Henry VII. and was sheriff of Cumberland, 7 Henry VII. He seated himself at Fairbank in Cumberland, and married twice; first, Joan, daughter of John Crackenthorp; and secondly, Margaret, sister to the lord Dudley; and had posterity by both wives. The third son, Nicholas Musgrave, was of Hayton-Castle,* who married Margaret, daughter and co-heir of William Filiol: and William Musgrave, the fourth son, was of Crookdake in Cumberland: he married first, Felix, daughter and co-heir of William Filiol; and secondly, Margaret, daughter of Thornton and relict of Middleton, and was progenitor to the Musgraves of that place.

12. Sir Richard Musgrave, eldest son and heir to Sir Thomas, took to wife Joan, daughter to Thomas lord Clifford, and had issue three daughters; Margaret, wife to John Heron of Chipchase, Esq. Mary, to John Martindale, Esq. and Jane, who died unmarried. He had also as many sons; Edward, Thomas, and John.

13. Sir Edward Musgrave of Harcla, Knt. son and heir of Richard, during his father's life was styled of Caterlin. In 1514 he was sheriff of Cumberland with John Crackenthorp, Esq. and again in that post alone in 1520. His first wife was Alice, daughter of Thomas Radcliffe, Esq. by whom he had Mary, the wife of John Martindale; and Margaret, of John Heron of Chipchase, Esqrs. His second wife was Joan, daughter and co-heir of Sir Sir Christopher Ward of Gryndall, in Yorkshire, Knt. standard-bearer to Henry VIII. at the seige of Bologne; by whom the Musgraves had Gryndall. (The arms of Ward are, azure, a cross moline, or). By her he had 1, William; 2, Edward, who died without issue; 3, Simon; 4, Elizabeth, the wife of John Nevill, lord Latimer; 5, Magdalene, the wife of Thomas Blenkinsop of Helbeck, Esq. and 6, Joan.

14. Sir William Musgrave of Harcla, Knt. son and heir of Edward, married Jane, daughter of Sir Thomas Curwen, Knt. In 1533 and 1542 he was sheriff of Cumberland. In 1543 he was charged by the king's letter to send 60 horse and 40 foot; and assisted Sir Thomas Wharton in that memorable defeat of the Scots at Sollom Moss. He had issue an only child,

15. Sir Richard Musgrave, Knt. who married Anne, daughter of Lord Wharton, and died in 1555. (his widow afterwards became the wife of Humphrey Musgrave of Hayton, Esq. The said Sir Richard had issue,

16, Thomas, who died in the 13th year of his age, 1565; 2, Eleanor, the wife of Robert Bowes of Aske, in Yorkshire, Esq. who died without issue. And here the direct line failing, we go back to Simon, third son of Edward; which

17. Sir Simon Musgrave, Knt. in 1569, was sheriff of Cumberland. He married Julian, daughter of William Elleker of Yorkshire, and by her had issue; 1, Christopher; 2, Thomas Musgrave,† captain of Bew-Castle, who married to his first wife,

* The Musgrave's of Hayton-Castle deny they are descended from this Nicholas, and say, that the Musgraves of Hayton-Castle and Eden-Hall, are two distinct families.
† Concerning this Thomas we have met with an anecdote, which is curious, as it exhibits the form and manner of proceeding to the ancient trial of battle, viz. "It is agreed between Thomas Musgrave and Lancelot Carleton, for the true trial of such controversies as are betwixt them, to have it openly

Ursula, daughter and co-heir of Sir Richard Carnaby, and widow of Edward Witherington: to his second wife he married a Scotch woman. 3, Richard Musgrave of Norton Conyers, who married Jane, daughter of Sir John Dalston, Kt. 4, John, who married Isabel, daughter of Thomas Musgrave of Hayton, Esq. 5, Anne, married to Sir Nicholas Curwen of Workington.

18. Christopher Musgrave, Esq. eldest son of Simon, married Jane, daughter of Sir Henry Curwen of Workington, and sister to Sir Nicholas. He died before his father, and left issue; 1, Richard; 2, Julian, the wife of Thomas Skelton of Armathwaite, Esq. 3, Mary, who died unmarried; 4, Margaret, the wife of Francis Whitfield of Whitfield, Esq.

I. RICHARD MUSGRAVE, Esq. son and heir, represented the county of Westmoreland in parliament 1 James I. and at the coronation of that king was made knight of the bath; and in the 9th year of that reign was created a baronet. At the age of 14 he married Frances, daughter of Philip lord Wharton. He died at Naples, and lies interred in the cathedral church therein, 1615. He left issue by his said wife; 1, Mary, who died unmarried, and a son.

II. Sir PHILIP MUSGRAVE, Bart. his heir, aged then 7 years. He was committed to the tuition of his uncle Philip lord Wharton; and married Julian, youngest daughter of Sir Richard Hutton of Goldsbro, in Yorkshire, Knt. one of the judges of the common pleas. He was returned one of the knights of the shire for

tried by way of combat, before God and the face of the world, to try it in Canonby Holme, before England and Scotland, upon Thursday in Easter week, being the 8th day of April next ensuing, A. D. 1602, betwixt nine of the clock and one of the same day; to fight on foot; to be armed with jack, steel cap, plaite sleeves, plaite breeches, plaite socks, two swords, the blades to be one yard and half a quarter of length; two Scotch daggers, or dirks, at their girdles: and either of them to provide armour and weapons for themselves, according to this indenture. Two gentlemen to be appointed in the field, to view both the parties, to see that they both be equal in arms and weapons, according to this indenture; and being so viewed, the gentlemen to ride to the rest of the company, and to leave them but two boys, viewed by the gentlemen, to be under 16 years of age, to hold their horses. In testimony of this our agreement, we have both set our hands to this indenture, of intent all matters shall be made so plain, as there shall be no question to stick upon that day: which indenture, as a witness, shall be delivered to two gentlemen. And for that it is convenient the world should be privy to every particular of the grounds of the quarrel, we have agreed to set it down in this indenture betwixt us, that, knowing the quarrel, their dyes may be witness of the trial.

The Grounds of the Quarrel.

1. Lancelot Carleton did charge Thomas Musgrave before the lords of her majesty's privy council, that Lancelot Carleton was told by a gentleman, one of her majesty's sworn servants, that Thomas Musgrave had offered to deliver her majesty's castle of Bewcastle to the king of Scots; and to which the same Lancelot Carleton had a letter under the gentleman's own hand for his discharge.

2. He chargeth him, that whereas her majesty doth yearly bestow a great fee upon him as captain of Bewcastle, to aid and defend her majesty's subjects, therein Thomas Musgrave hath neglected his duty; for that her majesty's castle of Bewcastle was, by him, made a den of thieves, and an harbour and receipt for murderers, felons, and all sorts of misdemeanors, &c.

Thomas Musgrave doth deny all this charge, and saith, that he will prove, that Lancelot Carleton doth falsely belie him, and will prove the same by way of combat, according to the indenture. Lancelot Carleton hath entertained the challenge, and, by God's permission, will prove it true, as before; and hath set his hand to the same.

What the event of the combat was we have not found.

THOMAS MUSGRAVE.
LANCELOT CARLETON.

the county of Westmoreland, in the parliament which met April 3, 1640; and again for the same place in that which met the November following. In April 1642, disliking the violent proceedings of that parliament, he withdrew from the house of commons, and returned to it no more till after the restoration. In 1644 he was made commander in chief of the counties of Cumberland and Westmoreland, by a commission from the marquis of Newcastle. He asserted the royal cause with all courage and dutiful allegiance; and was made governor of the city and citadel of Carlisle. When the king was at York he waited on his majesty there, and afterwards at Oxford. To the marquis of York he sent first 600 soldiers, then 1800, and afterwards, to prince Rupert, 1000 more, whom he raised in the counties of Cumberland and Westmoreland. After the battle at Marston Moor, he, with Sir Thomas Glenham, retired to Carlisle; upon the surrender of which garrison (the last that yielded to the rebels) he attended the king at Cardiff in Wales. At the desire of some loyal gentlemen, a new regiment of foot being raised in Cumberland, he was appointed colonel of it; but in September following, 1645, they were all defeated at Rowton Moor, near Chester,* by Pointz, a rebel officer, and either killed or taken prisoners. Sir Philip was among them, and was sent to York; but had some favour shewn to him by means of his uncle, the lord Wharton, engaged on the other side. Upon his enlargement after being taken at Rowton Moor, in April 1648, he received, from Sir Marmaduke Langdale, a new commission, to be commander in chief of the counties of Cumberland and Westmoreland; and having taken Carlisle from the rebels by surprise, was appointed governor. After the battle of Worcester, Sir Philip attended on his majesty King Charles II. both in France and Holland, and from the latter, waited on him in Scotland, where all the king's servants being enjoined to depart that kingdom within eight days, he retired to the Isle of Man, where he was honourably entertained by the earl of Derby, until that earl received from the king an order to meet him in England, with such forces as he could raise in the island; and that he should send Sir Philip Musgrave to him with all speed. Upon the receipt of this order Sir Philip sailed for Scotland; but being so long detained at sea, by contrary winds, that the king's army had marched before his arrival, and not being able to escape the vigilance of the rebels, he was forced to desist from his design of following the king, and to stay in Scotland until the Countess of Derby sent a ship on purpose to fetch him back to the Isle of Man, and appointed him governor; which place he bravely defended under the countess, of Derby, until it was reduced to the last extremity; and then, that lady having surrendered upon honourable terms, he had leave to retire to any part of England. At the restoration of King Charles II. 1660, he was made governor of Carlisle, and had some other reparation made him by the crown, for the sufferings of his family.†

* Lord Clarendon says thus of him:—At the battle of Chester there were many persons of quality taken prisoners, among the rest Sir Philip Musgrave, a gentleman of a noble extraction and ample fortune in Cumberland and Westmoreland, who lived to engage himself again in the same service, and with the same affection; and after very great sufferings, to see the king's restoration. Vol. II. p. 2, p. 713, 8vo. edit.
† March 14, 1648-9. Resolved (by Cromwell's parliament) that Charles Stewart, eldest son of the late king; James, second son of the late king; John earl of Bristol, William earl of Newcastle, Sir William Widdrington, George lord Digby, Sir Philip Musgrave, Sir Marmaduke Langdale, Sir Richard Gren-

He had a warrant for creating him Baron Musgrave of Hartley Castle, but never took out the patent. He departed this life at his seat at Eden-Hall, Feb. 7, 1677-8, aged 70 years, in great honour and esteem, for a wise, loyal, and brave man. He lies interred under a monument of white marble in the chancel of the parish church of St. Cuthbert, Eden-Hall, the burial-place of the family. He married Julian, youngest daughter of Sir Richard Hutton of Goldsbro, in Yorkshire, Knt. one of the judges of the common pleas, who died in 1659, aged 53; by whom he had six sons; Sir Richard, Philip, who died at Charenton in France; Sir Christopher, William, Simon, who was unfortunately drowned; and Thomas, dean of Carlisle and prebendary of Durham, who married first Mary, daughter of Sir Thomas Harrison of Allerthorp in the county of York, Knt. (by Margaret, daughter of the lord Darcy of Hornby Castle, in Yorkshire) by whom he had one daughter Margaret.— His second wife was Anne, daughter of Sir John Craddock of Richmond, in the same county, Knt. by whom he left no issue. He died March 28, 1686, aged 47, and lies buried in Durham cathedral. Sir Philip's only daughter Frances, was married to Edward Hutchinson of Wickham-Abbey, in Yorkshire, Esq.

III. Sir RICHARD MUSGRAVE, Bart. eldest son and heir to Sir Philip, succeeded him in title and estate: he was of an infirm constitution, and did not concern himself in any public affairs; and having married Margaret, daughter of Sir Thomas Harrison of Allerthorp, in Yorkshire, Knt. left only one daughter, Mary, the wife of Thomas Davison of Blackston, in Durham, Esq. whereupon

IV. Sir CHRISTOPHER MUSGRAVE, Knt. third son to Sir Philip, succeeded in the dignity and estate. While he was young he was very active in the royal cause, and suffered much by imprisonment and otherwise, towards the end of the usurpation, being found to be concerned in Sir George Booth's rising. After the restoration he had a commission, as captain of the guards, and was knighted; made governor of Carlisle, and lieutenant-general of the ordnance; and in the first year of her majesty Queen Anne, made one of the four tellers of the exchequer. He was twice married; his first lady was Mary, daughter and co-heir of Sir Andrew Cogan of Greenwich, Bart. by whom he had two sons and one daughter, viz. Philip Musgrave, Esq. hereafter-mentioned, Mary, and Christopher. This lady died in childbed at Carlisle Castle, July 1664, in the 28th year of her age. His second lady was Elizabeth, daughter of Sir John Franklyn of Willesden, in Middlesex, Knt. by whom he had six sons, John, Richard, who died young; Joseph, who served as a representative in parliament for Cockermouth in 1713, and died unmarried in 1757. Simon, who died in the East Indies in 1756, and George in 1751: he was storekeeper of the dock at Chatham, and married Sarah, youngest daughter of Mr. Benjamin Rosell, relict of lieutenant Young; by whom he had three sons, Joseph, Thomas, and George. Sir Christopher had also six daughters, Elizabeth, married to John Wyneve of Brettenham, in Suffolk, Esq. Dorothy, married to James Hawley of Brentford, in Middlesex, Esq. Mary, Frances, Anne, and Barbary. Sir Christopher

ville, Sir Francis Doddington, the earl of Worcester, Sir John Winter, Sir John Colepeper, Sir John Byron, and George duke of Buckingham, shall be proscribed as enemies and traitors to the commonwealth, and shall die without mercy, wherever they shall be found within the limits of this nation; their estates confiscated, and forthwith employed for the use of the commonwealth. *Parl. Hist. vol. XIX. p. 58.*

represented the city of Carlisle in parliament, and on all occasions demonstrated himself a loyal subject and an able statesman. He died at London, of an apoplexy, July 29, 1704, and lies buried at St Trinity, in the Minories, near his eldest son, Philip, having a handsome monument erected for him at Eden-Hall, with the inscription below.* Philip, eldest son of Sir Christopher, was a gentleman of great hopes, and had all the advantages of education, both at home and abroad. He married Nov. 12, 1685, Mary, eldest daughter of George Legg, lord Dartmouth, master-general of the ordnance. He was clerk of the council in the reign of King James II. and clerk of the deliveries in the ordnance; and dying July 2, 1689, was buried in the chapel of Trinity Minories (where his father-in-law, Lord Dartmouth, was afterwards buried' 1691) having a handsome monument erected to his memory, at Eden-Hall.* He left a son Christopher, and a daughter Barbara, the wife of Thomas Howard of Corby-Castle, in Cumberland, Esq. Christopher Musgrave, Esq. youngest son of Sir Christopher, by his first lady, was born at Carlisle, and bred to the law; and upon the death of his elder brother, succeeded him as clerk of the council. He served the city of Carlisle as their representative in parliament, in the reign of Queen Anne, and was principal officer of the ordnance. He died a bachelor, Sept. 1718, and lies buried in Westminster Abbey.

V. Sir CHRISTOPHER MUSGRAVE, Bart. succeeded his grandfather, Sir Christopher. He was born in London in 1688; had his education at Eaton School, and at Christ Church College in Oxford. He succeeded his uncle, Christopher Musgrave, Esq. as clerk of the council, in 1710. He represented the city of Carlisle in the last parliament of Queen Anne, and the county of Westmoreland in 1722. He married Julia, daughter of Sir John Chardin, Knt. and from her brother, Sir John Chardin, Bart. who died without issue, her son, Sir Philip Musgrave, Bart. became possessed of Kempton-Park, in Middlesex, in the year 1746. He died in 1735, at the house of his friend and kinsman, Henry Fleetwood of Penwortham, in the county of Lancaster, Esq. and was interred (according to his own

---

* Christopher Musgrave, Esq. consecrates this monument to the memory of his father, Sir Christopher Musgrave, Knt. and Bart. who died of an apoplexy, in London, the 29th of July, A. D. 1704, in the 73d year of his age, and was buried in the chapel of Trinity Minories, near the Tower of London. He was married to his first wife, Mary, on the 31st day of May, 1660, who was daughter of Sir Andrew Cogan; she died the 11th of July, 1664, and lies here buried. By her he had two sons, and one daughter; Philip, Christopher, and Mary. His second wife was daughter of Sir John Franklyn, Bart. who died the 11th of April, 1701, and lies here buried by her. He had six sons and six daughters, viz. John, Richard, Joseph, Simon, Thomas, and George: Elizabeth, Dorothy, Frances, Mary, Anne, and Barbara.

In the reigns of King Charles II. King James II. and Queen Anne, he enjoyed very considerable and honourable employments; and it is worthy to be remembered, that in his youth, during our civil dissentions, when loyalty was criminal, he was active and faithful to the crown: in his riper years, when faction and sedition prevailed, he gave constant and useful proofs of his affection and fidelity to his prince; when the laws, liberty, and religion of his country were insulted and invaded, he chose to sacrifice his fortune and employments to his integrity, whose service, for the space of forty years in parliament, the sphere wherein his abilities shined with greatest lustre, affords such, and so many instances of sublime virtue, as are as hard to praise as imitate.

* To the memory of Philip Musgrave, Esq. eldest son of Sir Christopher Musgrave, of Eden-Hall, in the county of Cumberland, Knt. and Bart. by Mary, his first wife, daughter of Sir Andrew Cogan of Greenwich, in the county of Kent, Bart. who having had all the advantages of education at home, and travel abroad, was qualified at the age of 25 years, to serve his majesty King Charles II. as clerk of the council, and one of the principal officers of the ordnance; and his country also in parliament.

MUSGRAVE OF EDEN-HALL, CUMBERLAND.

desire) in the chancel of the parish church there, where his son, Sir Philip Musgrave, caused a monument to be erected to his memory. By her he had issue, 1, Philip; 2, Christopher, fellow of All Soul's college, Oxford, and rector of Barking, in Essex; he married Dec. 23, 1775, Mrs. Perfect of Hatton-Garden. 3, Hans, lieutenant-colonel in his majesty's forces; 4, Chardin, provost of Oriel college, Oxford; 5, Mary, first the wife of Hugh Lumley, Esq. of the kingdom of Ireland, and secondly of John Pigot, Esq. of the same kingdom; 6, Julia, the wife of Edward Hasel of Dalemain, Esq. 7, Barbara, first the wife of John Hogg, Esq. of Scotland, and secondly of the lord chief baron Idle; 8, Anne, of Henry Aglionby of Nunnery, Esq. 9, Elizabeth, first of Edward Spragge of Greenwich, in Kent, Esq. and secondly of John Johnstone, of the city of London, Esq. 10, Charlotte, who died unmarried; and 11, Dorothy, wife of the Rev. William Wroughton, rector of Welburn in Lincolnshire. Sir Christopher died Jan. 3, 1736, and was succeeded in title and estate by his son,

VI. Sir PHILIP MUSGRAVE, Bart. who married Jane, daughter of John Turton of Orgreave in the county of Stafford, Esq. and by her had issue; 1, Jane, who married in 1761 to Joseph Musgrave of Kypier, in the county of Durham, Esq. before-mentioned, and died Nov. 29, 1762, leaving a daughter, who did not long survive her; 2, Elizabeth, was married in 1768, to Heneage Legge of Idlicote, in the county of Warwick, Esq. now of Aston-Hall, in the same county; 3, Charlotte, in 1794, to the Rev. Charles Mordaunt of Massingham, in the county of Norfolk, brother to Sir John Mordaunt, Bart. 4, Henrietta, in 1794, to John Morris of Clermont, in the county of Glamorgan, Esq. 5, John Chardin, the present baronet, born Jan. 5, 1757; 6, Christopher, born May 29, 1759, who married in 1790 Elizabeth Anne, second daughter of the late Lord Archer, by whom he has two daughters. Sir Philip died July 5, 1795, at Kempton-Park, aged 84, and was interred in the parish church of Sunbury. No monument is placed there to his memory, one having been, by his own desire, erected in the parish church of Eden-Hall; and was succeeded in title and estate by his son,

VII. Sir JOHN CHARDIN MUSGRAVE, Bart. who married July 13, 1791, Mary, daughter of the Rev. Edmund Filmer of Crandale, in Kent, brother of Sir John Filmer of East Sutton Place, in the same county, Bart. by whom he has two sons, Philip Christopher, John, and one daughter, Julia.

ARMS—Azure, six annulets, or, 3, 2, and 1.
CREST—Two arms in armour, proper, gauntled, and grasping an annulet, or.
MOTTO—*Sans changer.*
SEATS—Eden-Hall, Cumberland, and Kempton-Park, Middlesex.

MUSGRAVE OF EDEN-HALL, CUMBERLAND.

1 PETER DE MUSGRAVE, *temp.* K. Steph. 6 Sir Thomas, 1334 — M. Ross = M. Vaux = J. Clifford

2 Robert de Musgrave, *temp.* Henry II. 7 Sir Thomas, 1409 — E. Fitzwilliam N = H. Wharton

3 Adam de Musgrave, *temp.* K. John 8 Sir Richard, Kt. = Elizabeth

4 Sir Thomas de Musgrave 9 Thomas, 1447 = Joan Dacre Sir T. BETHAM, Kt.

5 Richard de Musgrave 10 Sir Richard, 1464 = Elizabeth Betham

11 Sir Thos. 1469	Richard	Wm.	Elizabeth	Isabel	Margaret	Eleanor	Mary	Agnes
Joan Stapleton	M. Stapleton	John.	T. Gayt	T. Middleton	T. Elderton	Rowland Thornborough	T. Warcop	Robert Warcop

12 Sir Rich.	Sir John, Kt,	Nicholas	William	Mary	Eleanor	Marg.	Isabel
Joan Clifford	J. Crackenthorp	Marg. Dudley	*Mar P. Colville ville M. Thornton	J. Sandford	C. Lancaster	Nich. Ridley	J. Crackenthorp

Murgo

Oliver.
Lancelot Richard. Musgraves
Anne. of Cuthbert

13 Sir Edward, Knt.	Thomas.	Margaret	Mary		Margaret.	Hayton
A. Radcliffe	J. Ward	John.	John Heron	J. Martindale		

Mary	Marg.	14 Sir William	Edward.	17 Sir Simon	Elizabeth	Magdalen	
J. Martindale	J. Heron	Joan Curwen	Joan.	Jul. Ellerker	John, L. Latimer	J. Blenkinsop	Cuthbert

15 Sir Richard	18 Christopher	Thomas	Richard	John	Anne	
Anne Wharton	Jane Curwen	Ursula Carnaby	Jane Dalston	I. Musgrave	Sir N. Curwen	Cuthbert — Bowman

| 16 Thomas, 1565 | Eleanor Sir Robert Bowes, Kt. | I. Sir Richard Bt. & K.B. 1615 F. Wharton | Julian Thos. Skelton | Margaret Fran. Whitfield | Musgraves of Bewcastle | Musgraves of Caterlane | Sir Wm. |

II. Sir Philip, Bart. 1686 = Julian Hutton, 1659   Mary   Thomas of Crookdake

III. Sir Richard	Philip	IV. Sir Christopher, 1704	Wm.	Thomas, S.T.P.	Frances	
Marg. Harrison	M. Cogan	E. Franklyn	Simon.	M. Harrison	A. Cradock	E. Hutchinson

Marg.	Mary	Philip, 1689	Chris.	John	Elizabeth	Dorothy	George	Frances.
Sir F. Davison	Mary, dr. of Geo. L. Dartmouth	Mary	Richard. Joseph, Simon, Thomas.	J. Wyneve	J. Hawley	Sarah Rosell	Mary. Anne. Barbara.

V. Sir Christopher, Bart. 1736   Barbary   Joseph   Thomas   George
Julia, dr. of J. Chardin, Knt.   T. Howard   Jane Musgrave

VI. Sir Philip 1795	Chris. Hans.	Dr. Chardin — Tipping	Mary H. Lumley	Julia J. Pigot	Barbary Edw. Hasel	Anne John Hogg	Elizabeth J. Idle	Dorothy Hen. Aglionby	Edw. Spragge	J. Johnstone	Wm. Wroughton
Jane Turton											

VII. Sir John Chardin Musgrave, Bt.	Christopher	Jane	Julia.	Eliz.	Charles	Henrietta
Mary Filmer	Miss Archer	Joseph Musgrave	Mary. Dorothy	H. Legge	C. Mordaunt	J. Morris

Philip, b. 1794   Christopher   John, b. 1797   Julia

* Called daughters and co-heirs of Wm. Filiol.

9. COPE of HANWELL, OXFORDSHIRE.

Created Baronet June 29, 1611.

THIS ancient family descends from John Cope, Esq. a very eminent person in the reigns of King Richard II. and Henry IV. He was elected one of the knights of the shire for Northampton, in all the parliaments from the first to the ninth year of King Henry IV. and dying, was succeeded by

2. John Cope, Esq. his son and heir, who was the father of

3. Alexander Cope of Dishanger, Esq. who was the father of

4. William Cope, Esq. who was in great esteem and favour with Henry VII. He died in April 1513. He married two wives; by the first he had one son, Stephen Cope, Esq. serjeant of the poultry to the houshold of Henry VIII. who married Anne, daughter and co-heir of William Saunders of Oxfordshire, from whom the family at Bedhampton in Hampshire descended, that extinguished in daughters, and by his wife Jane, daughter of John Spencer of Hodnell, in Warwickshire, Esq. sister and heir of Thomas Spencer of Hodnell, Esq. (and heir to her mother Anne, sister and co-heir to Sir Richard Empson, Knt.) he had three sons; Anthony, hereafter-mentioned; William, who died unmarried, and John, who was knighted and seated at Copes Ashby, in Northamptonshire, before called Canons Ashby. Sir John Cope, Knt. married three wives; 1, Bridget, daughter of Edward Raleigh of Farnborough, in Warwickshire, Esq. 2, Margery, daughter of —— Mallory; 3, Margaret, daughter and co-heir of Sir Edmund Tame, Knt. by the two last he had no issue, but by the first three sons, and two daughters; 1, Erasmus, who married Mary, daughter of John Heneage of Towse, in Lincolnshire, Esq. by whom he had one son, Edward who died during the life of his father; 2, George, who married Dorothy, daughter and co-heir of Thomas Spencer of Everden, in Northamptonshire, Esq.* she surviving him, married secondly Gabriel Pulteney of Misterton, in Leicestershire, Esq. and 3, Anthony.† The daughters were, Elizabeth, married to John Dryden, Esq. and Joan, married to Stephen Boyle of Kentish Town, in Middlesex, but died without issue. Sir John died seized of all the monks possessions in Canons, or Copes Ashby, in 1558; and Edward, his grand-son, succeeded to part of the estate, and the rest devolved upon Mr. Dryden, in right of Elizabeth, his wife. Edward, grand-son of Sir John, having received the honour of knighthood, died in 1620. He married first Elizabeth, eldest daughter of Sir Christopher Yelverton of Easton Mauduit, in Northamptonshire, Knt. one of the

---

* Bridges's Northamptonshire, p. 56.
† Mr. Bridges, in his History of Northamptonshire, p. 146, says, that George and Anthony, the two youngest, died without children, though other pedigrees make George to die in 1572, and to leave three sons; George, who died S. P. John, and Erasmus; and a daughter, Dorothy, married to — Kenton of Northamptonshire.

COPE OF HANWELL, OXFORDSHIRE.

judges of the king's bench, and secondly Catharine, daughter of Sir Edward Aston of Tixhall, in Staffordshire, Knt. relict first of Stephen Slaney of London, Esq. and secondly of Sir William Chetwynd of Ingestree, in Staffordshire, Knt. who died in 1646, and was interred in the church of St. Giles's in the Fields, in Middlesex, to which she was a benefactress, and her arms impaled with those of her three husbands, were in the windows of that church, before it was rebuilt. Sir Edward left the manor of Eydon to Erasmus, his son and heir; of whom we find no more, only that from the family of Cope, the manor passed to John Browne, Esq. clerk of the parliament in the reign of King Charles II. who having issue only one daughter, Martha, the wife of Sir Roger Cave of Stanford, Bart. upon his decease it descended to her and her heirs.

5. Anthony, eldest son and heir of William Cope, Esq. the cofferer, by his second wife, was bred in Oriel college, and having excellent parts, improved and cultivated by a learned education, was soon distinguished among his neighbours, and esteemed by the most learned men of that age, both at home and abroad. His appetite after knowledge was not confined to his own country only, but by travelling into France, Germany, Italy, and other parts of Europe, visiting the universities, he sought the acquaintance of the most considerable persons abroad famed for learning, contracted an intimacy with many of them, and wrote several things while beyond the seas, as well as at home. He had the honour of being made one of the knights of the carpet, in 1 Edw. VI. was high sheriff of Oxfordshire and Berks 2 Edw. VI. and was buried in the chancel of the church of Hanwell four years after, 1551; leaving, by Jane, his wife, daughter of Matthew Crew of Pynne, a son named Edward, heir to his estate; and a daughter Anne, wife to Sir Kenelm Digby of Stoke Dry, in Rutlandshire, Knt. which

6. Edward, marrying Elizabeth, daughter and heir of Walter Mohun of Wollaston, in Northamptonshire, Esq. who survived him, and afterwards married George Carleton of Walton upon Thames, in Surrey, Esq. second son of John Carleton of Baldwin Brightwell, in Oxfordshire, Esq. had issue, besides daughters, two sons, Anthony and Walter, who was of Kensington, and knighted; and was master of the court of wards in the reign of King James I. and one of the chamberlains of the Exchequer by patent, dated July 1, 1608. He left a great estate to his sole daughter and heir, Isabel, married to Henry Rich, earl of Holland.

Lord Clarendon, speaking of this earl of Holland, says, he was a great favourite of the duke of Buckingham's; he first preferred him to a wife, the daughter and heir of Cope, by whom he had a good fortune; and among other things the manor and seat of Kensington, of which he was shortly after made baron.

I. ANTHONY COPE, Esq. eldest brother to this Sir Walter, succeeded his father in the estate at Hanwell; was high sheriff of Oxfordshire in the 24th and 33d years of Queen Elizabeth: received from her the honour of knighthood; and served for the borough of Banbury in five several parliaments during her reign. He had, by many worthy acts, acquired much reputation, and the esteem of all that knew him; and no doubt his character and interest in the country induced King James to appoint him his first high sheriff of Oxfordshire, after his accession to the crown. That prince likewise knighted his eldest son, William, among the first he conferred that honour upon; and when he erected the degree of baronets, advanced this Sir Anthony to that dignity (by letters patent, bearing date June 29, 1611.) He kept an hospitable house in the old English way, and integrity and virtue shined in all he did. Desiring retirement in the latter part of his life, he recommended to his countrymen his eldest son, Sir William Cope, for their knight of the shire in parliament, and they manifested their love, by chusing him in the three last parliaments of King James I. He died, full of honour, in the 66th year of his age, 1615, and was buried in the chancel of the church of Hanwell.

This Sir Anthony Cope, Bart. by Frances his first wife, daughter of Sir Rowland Lytton of Knebworth, in Hertfordshire, Knt. (by Anne his second wife, daughter of George Carleton of Brightwell, in Oxfordshire, Esq.) had three daughters; Anne, the wife of Sir John Leigh, Knt. Elizabeth, of Sir Richard Cecil, Knt. from whom the earls of Exeter descended; and Mary, of Henry Champernown of Dartington, in Devonshire, Esq. also seven sons, four of which lived to mens estate; Sir William, Anthony, Richard, and John. Anthony and Richard went into Ireland, and left families in that kingdom: the former had three sons, Henry, Anthony, and John; Richard, the second son, who was of Wicklow (and by Anne, his wife, sister to Sir William Walter of Wimbleton, in Surrey) had issue, among others, 1, Walter Cope of Wicklow, Esq. (who married two wives, ———, daughter of the bishop of Kilmore, and ———, daughter of Henry lord Blany, baron of Monaghan, and left issue, Walter Cope, Esq. his son and heir); 2, Richard, who married Elizabeth, daughter of John Pate of Leicestershire; 3, Anthony; 4, William Cope of Icombe, in Gloucestershire, Esq. who married lady Elizabeth, daughter of Francis earl of Westmoreland, relict of Sir John Cope, Bart. hereafter-mentioned, and had issue two sons, Henry and William, and two daughters: Elizabeth, the wife of Thomas Whitney, Esq. son and heir of Sir Robert Whitney of Herefordshire, Knt. and Rachael, who died unmarried.

Sir Anthony Cope, Bart. married to his second lady, Anne, daughter of Sir William Paston of Paston, in Norfolk, Knt. relict first of Sir George Chaworth of Wiverton, in Nottinghamshire, Knt. and afterwards of Sir Nicholas L'Estrange of Hunstanton in Norfolk, Knt.

II. Sir WILLIAM COPE, Knt. and Bart. eldest son and heir of Sir Anthony) was elected in the first parliament called by King James I. a burgess for Banbury, and for the county of Oxford one of the knights of the shire in three other parliaments, viz. 12, 18, and 21 of that reign, and was high sheriff of Oxfordshire in 1619. He died Aug. 2, 1637, and was buried the 22d of the same month, in the chancel of the church of Hanwell. By Elizabeth, his wife, daughter and heiress of Sir George Chaworth of Wiverton, in Nottinghamshire, Knt. and Anne, his wife, daughter of Sir William Paston, Knt. he became possessed of Marneham, in the county of Nottingham, the most ancient inheritance of the Chaworths, and left issue, two sons, Sir John, his successor, and Jonathan; and three daughters, Frances, the wife of Robert, son and heir of Sir Robert Lee of Billeslee, in Warwickshire, Knt. Mary, and Ursula, who died unmarried. Jonathan, second son, married Anna, daughter of Sir Hatton Fermor of Easton, in Northamptonshire, Knt. was seated at Rawton Abbey, in Staffordshire, and left issue, Jonathan, his son and heir, ancestor to Sir Jonathan Cope, Bart. of Norton, in Huntingdonshire.

III. Sir JOHN COPE, Bart. eldest son of Sir William, married first Mary, daughter of Sir John Walter, Knt. lord chief baron of the exchequer, who died, leaving him an only daughter, Anne. He afterwards married lady Elizabeth, daughter of Francis earl of Westmoreland, and had issue, three sons; Sir Anthony, William, who died young, and Sir John: and two daghters, Mary, who died an infant, and Elizabeth, married to Thomas Estcourt of Shipton-Estcourt, in Gloucestershire, Esq. Lady Elizabeth, surviving her husband, Sir John, afterwards married William Cope of Icomb, in Gloucestershire, Esq. before-mentioned.

IV. Sir ANTHONY COPE, Bart. eldest son of Sir John, married Mary, daughter of Dutton lord Gerard of Gerard's Bromley, in Staffordshire, and had issue a daughter, Mary, and three sons; John, Anthony, and Henry, who all died young. This Sir Anthony was bred in Oriel college, Oxford, and served for Banbury at the restoration of King Charles II. and the next year in the first parliament called by that prince, was chosen knight of the shire for the county of Oxford; in which parliament he sat till he died, *anno* 1675, when, for want of issue male the title and estate devolved on his brother,

V. Sir JOHN COPE, Bart. who was bred up at Queen's college, Oxford, and having travelled into France, Italy, and Germany, at his return, had an honourable command in Dunkirk; when that fortress was delivered to the French; and on the death of his brother was chosen in his room, knight of the shire for the county of Oxford, and was likewise elected for the same county in two other parliaments, in the reign of King Charles II. and also in the first year of King William and Queen Mary, and in the 10th of William III. for Banbury. He took to wife Anne, daughter of Mr. Philip Booth, by whom he had issue a daughter, Elizabeth, who died young; and after her, seven sons successively, viz. 1, Sir John, his successor; 2, Anthony, who married Anne, daughter of the Rev. Nathaniel Spinkes, formerly rector of Peakirk, in Northamptonshire, and prebendary of Sarum (author of the Sick Man visited, and several other pieces) and sister to the late William Spinkes, Esq. by whom he has no issue; 3, Charles; 4, Galen, who was first a captain of horse, but afterwards quitted the army, and lived retired some time; then took orders, and was rector of Eversley in Hampshire: he married Jane, the daughter of Richard Onslow of Drunswick, in Sussex, by whom he had two sons, Sir Richard, the present baronet, and William; 5, Daniel; 6, Albian, and 7, William, who was a lieutenant in the foot guards, and died June 7, 1706. The three last died unmarried. Sir John died Jan 11, 1721.

VI. Sir JOHN COPE, his eldest son, had his education in Oriel college, Oxford, and about the year 1691, he and his brother Anthony both travelled abroad, and spent about two years in the academy of Wolfenbuttle, from whence they went to most of the courts in Germany and Italy; and at their return home John, the eldest, was knighted by King William, at Kensington, Jan. 1695-6. In the fourth of Queen Anne he served in parliament for the borough of Plympton, and was elected in several parliaments for the borough of Tavistock in Devonshire; and for the counties of Southampton and Limington.

Sir John married in 1696, Alice, daughter of Sir Humphrey Monnoux of Wotton, in Bedfordshire, Bart. by whom he had issue, two sons; Monnoux, his successor,

COPE OF HANWELL, OXFORDSHIRE.

TABLE 11.

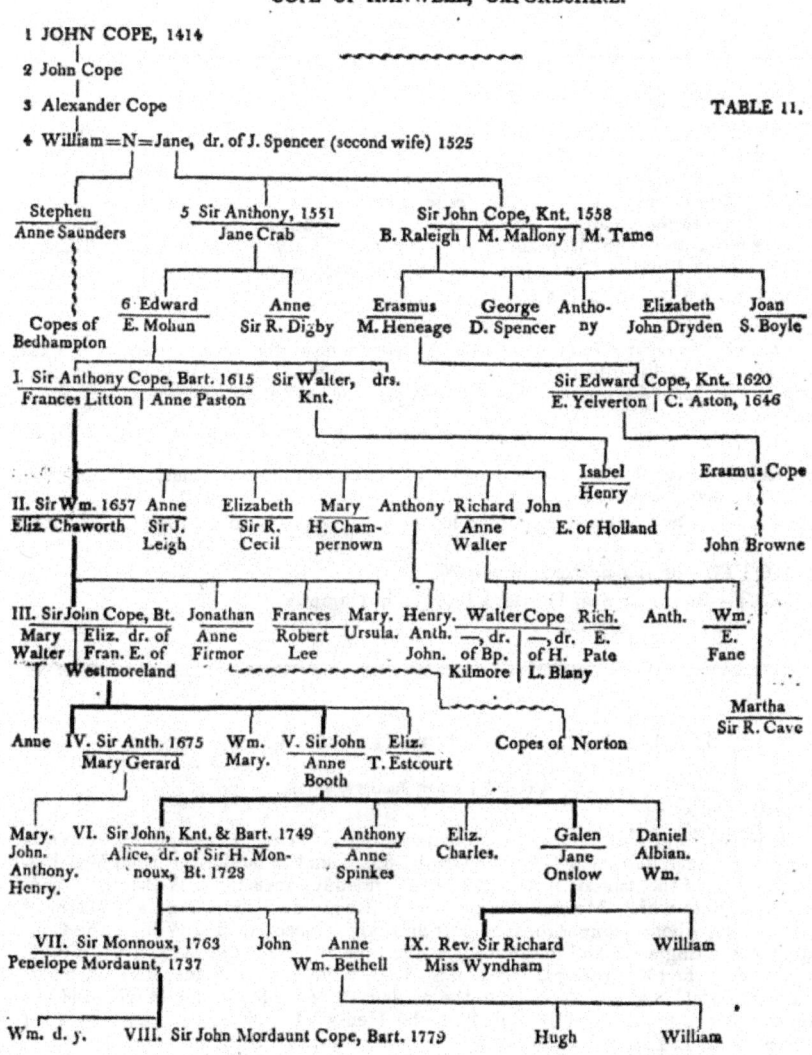

and John, who was gentleman-usher to George II. also a daughter Anne, wife of William Bethell of Rise, in the county of York, Esq. by whom he had two sons, Hugh and William. This lady died in Feb. 1728, and Sir John Dec. 8, 1749. He was succeeded by his eldest son,

VI. Sir MONNOUX COPE, Bart. who was member in several parliaments for Banbury in Oxfordshire. He married Penelope, only daughter of the Hon. Henry Mordaunt, Esq. lieutenant-general of his majesty's forces (next brother to Charles earl of Peterborough) by his second wife, Penelope, only child of William Tipping of Ewelen, in the county of Oxford, Esq. by whom he had two sons, William, who died young, and John Mordaunt, his successor. His lady died in Dec. 1737, and Sir Monnoux June 24, 1763, aged 67; and was succeeded by his son,

VII. Sir JOHN MORDAUNT COPE, Bart. who died March 7, 1779, and was succeeded by

IX. The Rev. Sir RICHARD COPE, Bart. who is the son of Galen, the sixth son of Sir John, the fifth baronet: he is rector of Eversley, and prebendary of Durham. He married ——, sister of R. H. Wyndham of Yately, in Hampshire, Esq.

ARMS—Argent, on a cheveron azure, between three roses gules, slipt proper; as many fleur de lis, or.
CREST—On a wreath, a fleur de lis, or; a dragon's head issuing from the top thereof, gules.
MOTTO—*Æquo adeste Animo.*
SEAT—Bramsell, near Hertford Bridge, in Hampshire.

10. GRESLEY of Drakelow, Derbyshire.

Created Baronet June 29, 1617.

THE origin of this family (denominated from Greseley in Derbyshire) anciently written Gresele, Greselei, Greslea, Gresly, &c. I find to be derived from Malahulcius, uncle to the famous Rollo, duke of Normandy, ancestor to William the conqueror; from which Malahulcius descended Roger de Toeny, standard-bearer of Normandy, whose younger sons, Robert and Nigel, accompanied William the Conqueror into England: and the former, at the time of the general survey, 14 Wm. I. possessed near 150 lordships, whereof Stafford, being his residence, he thence surnamed himself, and was ancestor to the noble race of the Staffords; of whom Humphrey was created duke of Buckingham, by Henry VI. with precedency before all dukes, both in England and France, the blood-royal excepted.

1. Nigel, the younger son, held Drachelawe, Thorpe, Kingesley, Morton, and other lordships, in Derbyshire and Staffordshire, as appears by Doomsday Book, and is the direct ancestor of this family.

2. William Greisley, the son of Nigel, was founder of the monastry of Grescley, in honour of St. George, now in ruins; but the estate and manor still remains with the family.

3. Robert de Greslei, his son and heir, in 1134 founded an abbey of Cistertian monks, at Swineshed in Lincolnshire. Robert de Greslea and Henry, his brother, are likewise mentioned in Sir Wm. Dugdale's *Monasticon*, as witnesses to a deed of Robert Abbot of Burton upon Trent; and in a charter of King John, confirming grants to the knights hospitalers of St. John of Jerusalem; for therein Ralph de Greslea, by the concession of his brethren, Robert, Nigel, Henry, and William; and of William earl of Ferrars, their lord, gives to those knights all their fee and tenement in Hedria, and in Kaveston, with all the apurtenances. From this Robert, by a younger branch, descended the Gresleys, that had summons to parliament among the barons of the realm, whereof Thomas de Greslei, having summons to parliament from 1 till 4 Edw. II. inclusive, died without issue; and Joan, his sister, became his heir, who was the wife of John, son of Roger de la Warre, and brought a fair inheritance to that noble family, from whom the present earl de la Warre is descended.

4. William de Greslei, his eldest son and heir had issue,

5. Sir Geoffery de Gresley, lord of Morton, who was returned with Robert de Frechville, knights of the shire for Derby, at the parliament held in London 28 Edw. I. and in the same year and following, returned for the same county with Ralph de Frechville, in the parliament held at Lincoln. This Sir Geoffery married Margaret, daughter of Maud de Somerville of Cosington, in Leicestershire.

6. Sir William, his son and heir, by Elizabeth his wife, daughter of John Bakepuiz, lord of Burton, left issue,

7. Geoffery de Gresley, who by Agnes his wife, was father of

8. Peter, who married Joan, daughter of Robert lord Stafford of Egginton, in Derbyshire; and was succeeded in his estate by

9. Geoffery, his son and heir, who married Margaret, daughter of Sir Gernon of Lavington, by whom he had two sons, Sir John, who was high sheriff of Staffordshire 46 Edw. III. He married Alice, daughter of Sir Roger Swynerton of Swynerton, Knt. but died without issue male; and was succeeded by his second son,

10. Sir Nicholas, who was living in 1300, and having married Thomazine, daughter and heir of Sir Thomas Gwasteness or Wasteneys, Knt. lord of Colton in Staffordshire, and the heir of that ancient family, a great addition was made to his estate, which descended to Thomas, his son and heir, though he had another son, Roger, of Church Gresley, who left a daughter and heir, Margaret, the wife of William Babthorp of Elston, in Leicestershire, Esq. He was succeeded by

11. Sir Thomas de Gresley, his son and heir, who was returned one of the knights for Derbyshire, in the parliament held 2 Henry IV. and before that time had re-

ceived the honour of knighthood: he was likewise elected for the said shire in the parliament held 2 and 5 Henry V. served high sheriff of Staffordshire 1 Henry VI. and was returned among the knights of the said counties 12 Henry VI. He married Margaret, daughter of Sir Thomas Walsh of Wanlip, in Leicestershire, Knt. and left issue,

12. John, his son and heir, who married Margaret, daughter of Sir Thomas Clavel, or Clarell, of Yorkshire, Knt. by Matilda, daughter of Sir Nicholas Montgomery, Knt. and had by her a daughter Catharine, the wife of Sir William de Peto, Knt. He was elected one of the knights for Staffordshire, in the parliaments held in 31 Henry VI. and one of the knights for Derbyshire in 39 Henry VI. and was succeeded by his son,

13. Sir John Gresley, who likewise served in parliament in 17 Edw. IV. for Derbyshire. He left issue, by Anne his wife, daughter of Sir Thomas Stanley of Elford, in Staffordshire, Knt. three daughters; the eldest was wife of John Egerton of Wrinehill, the second of Thomas Darell of Croteney, and the third of Simon Mountford of Coleshill, Esqrs. He was succeeded by his son,

14. Sir Thomas Gresley, Knt. who married Anne, daughter of Sir Thomas Ferrers of Tamworth Castle, in Warwickshire, Knt. and had issue five sons; William, John, a priest; George, Robert, and James. He was succeeded by his eldest son,

15. Sir William, who served King Henry VIII. in his wars in France, and was with him at the siege of Teroven, and the battle of Spurs; and received from him the honour of knighthood, October 14, at Lisle. He married Benedict, daughter of Henry Vernon of Haddon, in Derbyshire, Esq. but died without issue; so that George, his brother, became heir to the estate, which

16. George Gresley was made knight of the bath, at the coronation of Queen Anne Bullen, 1538; and having married first Margaret, daughter of John Mulsho of Findon, in Northamptonshire, Esq. and secondly Catharine, daughter of Edward lord Dudley, knight of the garter, had by the former only one son, William, and a daughter Catharine, the wife of Edward Winter of ———, in Leicestershire, Esq. and by the latter two sons, Edward and Thomas, and a daughter Elizabeth, the wife of Charles Somerset, Esq.

17. William, the eldest son and heir, was high sheriff of Staffordshire in 4 Eliz. and afterwards received from that queen the honour of knighthood. He had issue, by Catharine his wife, daughter of Sir Edward Aston of Tixall, in Staffordshire, Knt. three sons; Thomas, his successor in the estate, Hastings, and Simon: and four daughters; Jane, Mary, Elizabeth, and Grace, the wife of Sir Thomas Cookley, Knt. which

18. Thomas Gresley was high sheriff of Staffordshire in 25 Eliz. and in 33 and 45 of that queen's reign high sheriff of Derbyshire. He was knighted at Worsop in Nottinghamshire April 20, 1603, having met King James in his journey from Scotland, to take possession of the English crown. He married first Catharine, daughter of Sir Thomas Walsingham of Scadbury, in Kent, Knt. (and Dorothy his wife, daughter of Sir John Guldeford, Knt. and Barbara his wife, daughter of Thomas West, lord de la Warre) and had issue, five sons and three daughters. Henry, the

eldest son died in 1583, aged 4 years; 2, George; 3, John, who married Joan, daughter of Jasper More of Lardner, in Salop; 4, William; 5, Walsingham, who appears to have been a considerable traveller, and it is imagined was in some public employ abroad; for we find him a correspondent with James Howell, Esq. one of clerks of the council, *temp*. Charles I. The daughters were 1, Catharine, the wife of Francis Dethick of Newhall, Esq. secondly, of Sir Bartholomew Hales of Somerfield, Knt. and thirdly, of Henry Gibbs, Esq. 2, Catharine, the wife of Sir Richard Harpur of Swerkston, in Derbyshire, Knt. and 3, Dorothy, of Sir Alexander Barlow of Barley Moor, in Salop, Knt. This Sir Thomas had a second wife, Mary, daughter of Sir Richard Southwell of Woodrising, in Norfolk, Knt. by whom he had no issue.

I. GEORGE GRESLEY, Esq. eldest surviving son, resided at Drakelow, in Derbyshire, the possession of his ancestors, from the conquest; he was advanced to the dignity of a baronet June 29, 1611. He was a gentleman of good understanding, and an encourager of learning. It is said, that Sir William Dugdale owed, in some measure, his rise to him; for Sir George being well known to Thomas earl of Arundel, earl marshal of England, introduced him to his acquaintance on his first coming to London. He served in parliament 3 Charles I. for Newcastle Underline, in Staffordshire; and having married Susan, daughter of Sir Humphrey Ferrers of Tamworth Castle, in Warwickshire, Knt. had issue two daughters; Elizabeth, who died unmarried, and Dorothy, first the wife of Robert Milward of Bradley-Ash, Esq. and secondly, of Edward Wilmot, D D. also one son, Thomas Gresley, Esq. who married Bridget, daughter of Sir Thomas Burdet of Bramcot, in Warwickshire, and Formark in Derbyshire, Bart. and died during the life of his father, having had ten children; 1, Jane; 2, Henry; 3, George, who died infants; 4, Sir Thomas, successor to his grandfather; 5, Frances, the wife of John Whitehall of Pipe Ridware, in Staffordshire, Esq. 6, Bridget, the wife of Thomas Brome of Fisherwick, in Staffordshire, Esq. 7, George, who married Jane, daughter of Thomas Nelson of Northampton, and died without issue; 8, Catharine, the wife of Richard Dyot of the city of Litchfield, Esq. 9, Elizabeth, of Philip Trafford of Swithamly, in Staffordshire; 10, Mary, of John Harpur, rector of Morley in Derbyshire, grand-son of Sir Richard Harpur of Littleover, in Derbyshire, Knt.

II. Sir THOMAS GRESLEY, Bart. who succeeded his grandfather in the estate and title, married Frances, daughter and co-heir of Gilbert Morewood of London, and afterwards of Nether Sele, in Leicestershire, Esq. and had issue three sons and eleven daughters; 1, Frances, wife of William Inge of Thorp Constantine, in Staffordshire, Esq. 2, Bridget; 3, Elizabeth, who died infants; 4, Dorothy, the wife of Thomas Ward; 5, Mary, of Daniel Watson of Burton, in Staffordshire, Esq. 6, Grace, of Robert Roby of Donnington Castle, in Leicestershire; 7, Sir William, his successor; 8, Anne; 9, Catharine; 10, Letitia; 11, Thomas, who married Elizabeth, daughter of John Lee of Ladyhole, in Derbyshire, Gent. and heir to her brother; and had issue, Lee, William, John, and Elizabeth; 12, Isabel, who died unmarried; 13, Charles, of Dunstall in Staffordshire, Esq. who by Anne his wife, daughter and co-heir of John Bott of Dunstall aforesaid, Gent. left only three daughters, his co-heirs, Elizabeth, Frances, and Anne; Elizabeth, the wife of

Thomas Bott of Coventry, Gent. nephew to John before-mentioned, who bought the shares of Frances and Anne Gresley, and thereby became sole possessor of the estate at Dunstall: 14, Sarah, the wife of Paul Balladon of Stapenhill, in Derbyshire, Esq. He died June 15, 1699, aged 70; and was buried at Gresley church. His second son, his executor, erected to his memory a noble monument, with a figure as large as life kneeling in an arch, with all the matches of the family, in proper shields, round it, and his offspring with their matches underneath it; also the proper atchievements of the family, with this motto—*Meliore fide quam fortuna.*

III. Sir WILLIAM GRESLEY, Bart. son and heir of Sir Thomas, married Barbara, daughter of John Walcot of Walcot, in Salop, Esq. and relict of Richard Okeley of Okeley, in the said county, Esq. and had issue two sons, Sir Thomas and William, who died an infant; also, a daughter Bridget, the wife of Adam Ottley of Pitchford, in Salop, Esq. and dying Oct. 17, 1711, in the 48th year of his age, was succeeded in dignity and estate by his only surviving son,

IV. Sir THOMAS GRESLEY, Bart. who married in 1719, first Dorothy, daughter and co-heir of Sir William Bowyer, Bart. by whom he had issue seven sons and three daughters, who all died young except Sir Thomas and Sir Nigel;* secondly, lady Gertrude, daughter and co-heir of John Grammar, Esq. of Pledwick in Yorkshire, by whom he had two children, Geoffery and Gertrude, who died in her infancy. Geoffery died in America, leaving a son Thomas, who died in 1798, and a daughter, married to the Rev. ——Willowby, of Clift in Warwickshire.

V. Sir THOMAS GRESLEY, Bart. who was member of parliament for Litchfield, succeeded his father in 1746, and married Wilmot, daughter of Mr. Hood of Leicester, by whom he had only one daughter, who after her father's death became possessed of the Drakelow estate. Sir Thomas died of the small pox in 1753, and was succeeded by his brother,

VI. Sir NIGEL GRESLEY, Bart. who became possessed of the Knippersley estate, which was his mother's: he was high sheriff of Staffordshire in 1759. He married in 1753 Elizabeth, daughter of the Rev. Mr. Wynn of Cheshire, by whom he had one son Nigel Bowyer, and six daughters; 1, Anne, the wife of Sir John Hethcote of Lington in Staffordshire, Knt. by whom she has five sons and six daughters: she died May 13, 1795; 2, Elizabeth; 3, Frances; 4, Louisa, the wife of the Rev. William Gresley of Nether Seal, in Leicestershire, her cousin; 5, Harriet, the wife of John Jelly of the city of Bath, Gent. by whom he has issue, two sons and four daughters; 6, Mary, the wife of the Rev. Baptist John Proby,

---

* In the body of the church of Gresley, on the south side, a very neat monument, of various sorts of marble, is erected by Sir Thomas Gresley, to the memory of this lady, with the following inscription:

Near this place lieth the body of Dame Dorothy Gresley,
Wife of Sir Thomas Gresley, Bart. of Drakelow, in this parish, and one of the daughters
and co-heirs of Sir William Bowyer of Knippersley, in the county of Stafford, Bart.
She was a good wife, a tender mother, and a sincere friend;
And departed this life the 31st day of July, 1736.

Near this place lie also the remains of several of the children of the said Dame Dorothy Gresley.

GRESLEY OF DRAKELOW, DERBYSHIRE.

eldest son of the dean of Litchfield, by whom he has three sons and two daughters. Sir Nigel was, in his early days, in the British navy, and after the title and estate devolved on him he was one of those hospitable, generous, friendly country gentleman of which this nation (alas in those days) can boast of few remaining.* He died April 7, 1787, aged 60, and was succeeded by his son,

VII. Sir NIGEL BOWYER GRESLEY, the present baronet, who married to his first wife, Wilmot Gresley, only daughter of Sir Thomas Gresley, who left him three daughters, Wilmot-Maria, Emma-Sophia, and Elizabeth-Augusta; and died Dec. 4, 1790. He married secondly Eliza-Maria Garway, by whom he has one daughter, Louisa-Maria.

ARMS—Vaire, ermine and gules.
CREST—On a wreath, a lion passant ermine, armed, langued and collared, gules.
MOTTO—*Meliore fide quam fortuna.*
SEATS—At Drakelow in Derbyshire, and Knipersley in Staffordshire.

---

* Sir Nigel Gresley possessed a character, that ought not to be passed by without one eulogium however just. He was brave without boasting, and was just such a man as Sterne describes his uncle Toby, to whose kindness the weak would fly for protection. His manners were simple and unaffected, not such as are formed by the dancing master, or acquired in foreign tour; they were far better, and had a nobler source, for they sprung from an excellent heart. His form indeed was robust beyond common appearance, but his disposition was mild, generous, and unsuspecting; it was rather a difficult matter to make him think ill, and it was very easy to persuade him to think well of others. These and other associate virtues had, in some part of his life, involved him in difficulty and inconvenience. While his family laments, and his friends regret his loss, a distant and forgotten admirer of his character lays a humble tribute of regard upon his grave. *A Correspondent, Gent. Mag.* 1787.

In Memory of Sir Nigel Gresley, Bart. who died at Bath,
April 7, 1787, aged 60.

Those generous hearts that manly worth can charm,
Which friendship and domestic virtues warm,
Will here their sympathetic offerings leave,
Indulging sorrow at their brother's grave;
For such was Gresley, as in far better days,
Were dauntless England's pride, support, and praise;
Brave, artless, upright, hospitable, kind,
The fairest copy of the ancient mind;
A life rever'd in bounteous goodness pass'd,
O'er his high-trac'd descent congenial lustre cast.

GRESLEY OF DRAKELOW, DERBYSHIRE.

[TABLE 12.

1 Nigel de Stafford   6 Sir William=Eliz. Bakepuiz

2 William Greslei   7 Geoffery de Gresley=Agnes

3 Robert. Henry. Nigel. Wm. Ralph   8 Peter de Gresley=Joan, dr. of Robert L. Stafford

4 William de Greslei   9 Geoffery de Gresley=Marg. Gernon

5 Sir Geoffery=Maud de Somerville   Sir John=A. Swynerton   10 Sir Nicholas=T. Gwasteness

11 Sir Thomas=Marg. Walsh   Matilda=Sir T. Clavell

12 Sir John=Marg. Clavell   Marg.=Sir John Gresley

13 Sir John=Anne Stanley   Catharine=Sir Wm. de Peto   K. EDWARD I.

14 Sir Thomas, Knt.   N   N   N
Anne Ferrers | J. Egerton | T. Darell | S. Mountford   T. West, L. Delawar

15 Sir William, Knt. | John, | 16 Sir George Gresley, Knt.   Robert.   Barbara
Benedict Vernon | a priest | Marg. Mulso | Cath. Dudley   James.   Sir J. Guildford

17 Sir William, Knt. | Catharine | Edward. | Elizabeth   Dorothy
Cath. Aston | Edw. Winter | Thomas. | C. Somerset   Sir T. Walsingham

18 Sir Thomas Gresley, Knt. | Hastings. | Jane. | Grace   Catharine
C. Walsingham | M. Southwell | Simon. | Mary & Eliz. | Sir T. Wolseley   Sir T. Gresley

Henry, | I. Sir George, Bart. | John | William. | Catharine | Catharine | Dorothy
1583 | Susan Ferrers | Joan More | Walsing. | F. De- | Sir B. | Henry | Sir R. | Sir Alex.
                                   thick | Hales | Gibbs | Harpur | Barlow

Thomas Gresley | Elizabeth   Dorothy
Bridget Burdet   R. Milward | E. Wilmott, D.D.

Jane. | II. Sir Thomas, 1699 | Frances | Bridget | George | Catharine | Elizabeth | Mary
Henry. | Frances Morewood | John | Thomas | Jane | Richard | Philip | Rev. J.
George.   Whitehall | Brome | Nelson | Dyot | Trafford | Harpur

III. Sir Wm. 1711 | Frances | Bridget. | Dorothy | Mary | Grace | Anne | Thomas | Charles | Sarah
Barbara | Wm. | Eliz. | Thomas | Daniel | Robert | Cath. | Eliz. | Anne | Paul
Walcot | Inge   Ward | Watson | Roby | Let. & Isa. | Lee | Pott | Balladon

IV. Sir Thomas, Bart. 1746 | Wm. | Bridget | Lee. | Elizabeth | Elizabeth   Frances.
D. Bowyer, | G. Grammer   Adam Ottley | Wm. | John | Thomas Bott   Anne.
1736

V. Sir Thomas, Bart. 1753 | VI. Sir Nigel, Bart. 1787 | 5 sons | Geoffrey | Gertrude
Wilmot Hood, 1797   Eliz. Wynn   3 drs.

Wilmot=VII. Sir Nig. Bowyer Gresley | Anne | Elizabeth | Frances | Louisa | Harriet | Mary-Susanna
          E. M. Garway   Sir John | 1797   Rev. Wm. | John | Rev. B.
                         Hethcote   Gresley | Jelly | Roby

Wilmot- | Emma- | Elizabeth- | Louisa-
Maria. | Sophia. | Augusta. | Maria   5 sons & 5 drs.   2 sons & 4 drs.   3 sons & 2 drs.

11. MOLINEUX of Teversal, Nottinghamshire.

Created Baronet June 29, 1611.

WHEN William the Conqueror entered this kingdom, 1066, he was attended by many noble Normans, among whom was William des Molines, no less famous for his virtue than for his noble extraction, as appears from the roll of Battle-Abbey, in which list his name is the 18th; and in the most ancient chronicles of the dutchy of Normandy remaining, it is to be seen, that this William des Molines is set down as chief man in nearness and singular credit with William the Conqueror. To this William des Moulines or Molins, Roger de Poytiers, who was then possessed of all that tract of land in Lancashire, between the rivers of Ribble and Mersey, by the gift of William the Conqueror, gave, among other lands, by consent of the conqueror, the manors of Sephton, Thorneton, Kerdon or Kuerdon, ten carucates and a half of land, at the service of half a knight's fee, whereof he made Sephton his chief seat, wherein he was succeeded by

2. Vivian,* his son and heir, who by his wife Siwarda, had issue,

3. Adam, *dominus* de Sefton in Lancashire, who married Annota, sole daughter and heir of Benedict de Garnett, lord of Speke in Lancashire, and had issue three sons; 1, Robert; 2, Gilbert; 3, Henry; and a daughter Siwarda, the wife of —— Fitzannot.

4. Robert, the eldest son, married Beatrice, daughter and heir of Robert de Villers, lord of Little Crosby, son of Alan, son of Pagan de Villers, who entered England with William the Conqueror, and was first lord of Crosby after the conquest. He was succeeded by his son.

5. Richard, who married Edith, daughter of Aumary Pincerna (*i. e.* Butler) of Warrington; he had issue, Adam and Robert, from which Robert proceeded Richard, father to another Robert, of Thorneton, progenitor to those of Mellingwood.

6. Adam, the eldest son of Robert, succeeded at Sephton, being styled *dominus* Adam de Molineus. He is supposed to be the knight who was portrayed in the

---

* Other accounts differ from this, and say, that William and Vivian de Moulines, his brother, were in the first expedition of the army sent by William the Conqueror, under the conduct of Roger de Poytiers; and that the said Roger gave the lordship of Sephton, Thorneton, and Kerdon to Vivian de Molines, and to his posterity, shortly after the entrance of the Normans, which is also agreeable to other authorities. Mr. Camden, in his Britannia, speaking of Lirpole (Liverpool) observes, "The name is not to be met with in old writings; but only that Roger de Poictiers, who was lord of the honour of Lancaster (according to the language of those days) built a castle there, the government whereof was enjoyed for a long time by the noble family of the Molineaux, Knts. and now lords Molineaux, whose chief seat is hard by, at Sefton, which the said Roger de Poictiers bestowed upon Vivian de Molineaux, a little after the coming in of the Normans; for all the land between the Ribell and the Mersey belonged to the said Roger, as appears by Doomsday.

glass of three windows, in the upper part of Bridgnorth church, in Salop, in antique mail, cloathed with a surcoat and girt, with his sword and spurs; over which is an equilateral triangular shield, on which the arms of Molineux are depicted. Roger, the youngest son, bore for his arms, the cross argent, quarter-pieced; and had issue, William, father to James, who having married Margaret, the daughter and heir of William de Aula de Brentworth, left his estate to his two daughters, his co-heirs; Julian the wife of Richard de Windsor, lord of Stanwell in Middlesex, from whom are descended the earl of Plymouth, and lord Windsor; and Agnes of Sir Robert Markham, Knt.

7. Sir William de Molineus of Sefton, Knt. eldest son of Adam, was called to receive the degree of knighthood by Philip de Ulnesby, sheriff of that county, 1256. He gave to William, son of his brother Roger, lands in Netherton, near Sefton, to hold by knights service, and the yearly rent of a halfpenny, by a deed without date; and by Margaret his wife, daughter of Sir Alan de Thornton, Knt. had three sons, Sir Richard, William, and Simon: to the two latter their father gave lands in Letherland. He was succeeded by

8. Sir Richard, who gave to Thomas his son the Edge (others call it the Hegg) within his demesne of Sefton, to hold at the rent of one penny yearly; by Emme his wife, daughter of —— Done, he had three sons; 1, Sir William; 2, Thomas, who bore for arms, azure a cheveron, between three cross Molines, or. He released all his right of common of pasture in the marsh of Richard of Hawkley, from whom are descended the Molineuxes of that place; 3, Peter; also a daughter Joan, a nun at Leicester.

9. Sir William Molyneux, the eldest son, was dubbed knight banneret in Gascoigny, by Edmund earl of Lancaster, second son to Henry III. 1286. He married Isabel, daughter of —— Scarisbrick, and had issue a son Richard, and a daughter Jane, wife of Robert de Erneys.

10. Sir Richard his son, aged 17 at the death of his father, and in the wardship and custody of John duke of Lancaster, married Agatha, daughter and heir of Sir Roger Hlerton, Knt. and had issue; 1, Sir William; 2, Richard of Larbeck, Wynnersley, &c. whose son Richard died S. P. 3, John, to whom his father gave lands in Netherton; 4, Thomas of Kennerdal, who was slain in battle, *temp*. Rich. II. he married the daughter and heir of Alexander de Kennerdall, and left issue a daughter and heir, married to Osbaldeston of Osbaldeston; 5, Roger of Raynhull, whose grand-daughter and heir was married to —— Lancaster.

11. Sir William de Molineux, the eldest son and heir, had two wives; the first was Joan, the daughter and heir of Jordan Ellhall, forester of Wyresdale, by Alice his wife, one of the daughters and co-heirs of Thomas de Twenge. The second was lady Margaret, widow and relict of Sir Robert Holland of Enkeston, Knt. (brother to Sir Thomas Holland, knight of the garter) and daughter and heir of Sir Alan Heyton of Bushell, Knt. By the former he had several sons; 1, Sir William; 2, Sir Thomas of Kuerdale, who added a fleur de lis argent, in the dexter canton of his arms. This Sir Thomas Molvneux was constable of Chester, a man of great power, authority, and special credit. in Cheshire and Lancashire, to whom the king expressly writ and sent, commanding him to conduct Robert de Vere, duke of Ire-

land, his dear and most familiar friend, to his presence, and not to respect any charges, travel, or pain whatsoever; and for the special love he bore to his country, raised 5000 men, and brought the said duke as far as Radcot Bridge, four miles distant from Chipping Norton, where he was beset on every side by the duke of Gloucester, and the earls of Derby, Warwick, and Nottingham, and forced, for his better safety, to take the water, hoping, as the duke before him did, to have escaped the force of his enemies: however he was slain by Sir Thomas Mortymer, 1388; 3, Sir John Molineux of Crosby, who left three daughters, his heirs; one married to —— Blundell of Crosby, another to Robert Erneys, and the other to —— Charnock of Aston; 4, Richard, parson of the church of Sefton; also Robert, Peter, and Simon.

12. William, the eldest son of the last Sir William, was likewise a knight. He distinguished himself at the battle of Navarre in Spain, under Edward the Black Prince, and was there made a knight banneret, 1367. Under his command he served in all those wars,[*] as he did in those of France; and in his return homewards died at Canterbury, 1372, and was there buried, with the epitaph below.[†] He left an heir to his estate, by Jane his wife, daughter and co-heir to Sir Robert Holland, Knt. (by Margaret, daughter of Sir Alan Heyton, Knt.) viz.

13. Sir Richard Molineux, Knt. who, 1 Henry IV. was found cousin and next heir of Thomas Chatterton of Ellhall, viz. son of Sir William Molineux, Knt. son of William, son of Joan, daughter of Alice, sister of Laderina, mother to Alan, father of Alan, father of William, who was father to the aforesaid Thomas Chatterton. This Sir Richard was high sheriff of the county of Lancaster, and with Sir Robert de Ursewill, served as knights of that shire in the parliament held at Westminster 20 Rich. II. and had for their expences for 34 days attendance, 13l. 12s. He married Ellen, daughter of Sir Thomas Ursewick, Knt. who was afterwards the wife of Sir Thomas Savage, Knt. By her first husband she had two daughters; Agnes, wife of Thomas Clifton, Esq. and Anne of Richard Nevil of Leversedge: and three sons; 1, Richard; 2, Adam, LL.D. who was elected dean of Salisbury Oct. 24, 1441, and some time clerk of the council: he was consecrated bishop of Chicester in 1445, and presently after had the keeping of the privy seal committed to him by Henry VI. He was murdered at Portsmouth June 9, 1449, by mariners procured by Richard duke of York; he gave to the high altar certain rich clothes of crimson velvet: and 3, Robert, who was found heir to his brother Adam, by the *Inquisit. post mortem* He married Margaret, daughter of Sir Baldwin L'Estrange, Kt. and left only a daughter, wife of Sir William Troutbeck, Kt. whose daughter and heir, Ellen, was the wife of Gilbert Talbot of Grafton, Esq.

14. Sir Richard, son and heir of the last Sir Richard, eminently distinguished himself in the wars of France, at the battle of Agincourt; and received the honour of

---

[*] Fuller's Worthies, p. 115.

[†] Miles honorificus Molyneus subjacet intus:
Tertius Edvardus dilexit hunc ut Amicus.
Fortia qui gessit, Gallos, Navarrosq; repressit,
Hinc cum recessit, morte feriente decessit.
Anno milleno trecento septuageno,
Atque his junge duo; sic perit omnis homo.

knighthood in the reign of Henry V. He was in favour also with Henry VI. who, by letters patent, gave to him, his sons, and their heirs, the chief forestership of the royal forests and parks in west Derbyshire; the stewardship in Salfordshire, and the office of constable of Liverpool. He was slain at Blore Heath in Staffordshire, together with Lord Audley, 1460.

He had two wives, first Joan, daughter and heir of Sir Gilbert Haydock, Knt. relict of Sir Peter Leigh of Lyme, in Chestershire, Knt. and by her had several sons; 1, Richard, ancestor to lord viscount Molineux; 2, Thomas of Haughton, in Nottinghamshire, whose posterity we are now to treat of; 3, John, rector of Sefton; 4, Henry; 5, Gilbert, who married the lady of Cheneys, in Bucks; 6, Edward; 7, Robert; 8, William. The daughters were Catharine, wife of Sir Robert Ratcliff, Knt. and afterwards of John Stanhope, Esq. Elizabeth, the wife of Sir Richard Southworth, Knt. and Joan of Robert Preston, Esq. By a second wife, Helen, daughter of —— Radcliff of the Tower, and relict of Sir William Harrington, he had two daughters, Anne, wife of Richard Nevil of Leversedge, and Margaret of Sir Peter Leigh of Bradley, Knt.

15. Sir Thomas Molineux, Knt. second son of Sir Richard Molineux, Knt. was one of the privy-council to King Edw. IV. and behaving himself valiantly in the expedition into Scotland, 1482, was made a knight banneret, by Richard duke of Gloucester, at Berwick; in the same year he built the church and a fair house at Hawton, and died in 1492. He married two wives, first Elizabeth, daughter of Sir Robert Markham of Cotham, in Nottinghamshire, Knt. by whom he had a son Robert, of whom hereafter, and a daughter Elizabeth, first the wife of John Becard, and secondly of Stephen Hatfield of Willoughby, Esq. secondly Catharine, daughter of John Cotton of Ridware, in Staffordshire, Esq. (by his second wife, a daughter of Nicholas Fitzherbert of Norbury, in Staffordshire, Esq.) and relict of Thomas Poutrell of Hallam in Derbyshire, Esq. by whom he had two sons, Sir Edmund, one of the justices of the common pleas, 4 Edw. VI. and Anthony, D D. rector of Sefton and Walton in Lancashire, and Tring in Hertfordshire, a man of great integrity, and liberal to the poor. He departed this life in 1558; leaving two daughters, Ellen, wife of John Bond of Coventry, and afterwards of Laurence Ireland of Lidiat; and Margaret of Sir Hugh Willoughby of Risley, in Derbyshire, Knt.

Sir Edmund Molineux, knight of the bath, eldest son by the second venter, was was made one of the justices of the common pleas in 1550, and died in 1552. His lady was Jane, daughter of John Cheyney of Chesham-boys, in the county of Buks, Esq. by whom he had several children, 1, John; 2, Thomas, who married Jane, daughter of Sir Richard Molineux of Sefton, Knt. 3, Edmund; 4, Anthony, and 5, Christopher; also two daughters, Margaret, wife of Francis Fletcher, Esq. (whose son Francis, married Frances, daughter of Francis Molineux, Esq.) and Dorothy, wife to Robert Purslow. John Molineux of Thorp, the eldest son, married Anne, daughter of George Lascells of Gatford, in Nottinghamshire, Esq. and had issue, Edmund Molineux of Thorp, Esq. and Rutland Molineux of Woodcotes, Esq. who married Mary, daughter and heir of Cuthbert Bevercotes, of Bevercotes, in Nottinghamshire, Esq. Edmund married first —— the daughter of John Hearle, Esq. and had a daughter Anne, who it is presumed died unmarried: his second wife was Bridget, daughter and co-heir of Robert Sapcotes, Esq. by whom he had Sir John Molineux of Thorp, Knt. Edmund, and Richard.

16. Robert, only son of Sir Thomas by his first wife, succeeded to the inheritance at Hawton: he had, by Dorothy his wife, daughter of Thomas Poutrell of West Hallam, in Derbyshire, Esq. several sons; Thomas, who died without issue; Richard, William (who left a daughter and heir, Dorothy, first wife of George Cartwright of Ossington, in Nottinghamshire, Esq. and secondly of William Dabridgecourt) Robert, and Edmund: and four daughters; Anna, the wife of —— Veale, Elizabeth, Catharine, and Mary. He died April 13, 1539; and William, his brother, the last day of Oct. 1541.*

17. Richard, the eldest surviving son, married Margaret, daughter of Edmund Bussy of Hather, in Lincolnshire, Esq. by whom he had Francis and Mary, the wife of Daniel Disney.

18. Francis, married Elizabeth, eldest daughter and co-heir of Thomas, son of Roger Greenhalgh of Teversal, in Nottinghamshire, Esq. by whom he came possessed of the manor of Teversal. He was high sheriff of the county of Nottingham 24 Eliz. and had issue five sons, Thomas, Gervase, John, Robert, and Richard; and two daughters, Jane the wife of Francis Linley of Skegby, in Nottinghamshire, Esq. and Frances wife of Francis Fletcher of Stockbald, Esq.

19. Thomas, the eldest son, by his wife Alice, daughter and co-heir of Thomas Cranmer of Aslacton, in Nottinghamshire, Esq. (great nephew to the famous archbishop Cranmer) had issue two sons, John and Thomas; and a daughter the wife of Sir Anthony Thorold of Marston, in Lincolnshire, Knt. the said Alice had for her second husband Sir John Thorold of Cawnton, in Nottinghamshire, Knt. This Thomas dying in 1507, was succeeded by his eldest son,

I. JOHN, who had a grant from Queen Elizabeth of the lordships of Carleton, Kingston, and Carleton-baron; and all singular messuages, lands, &c. which were the possessions of Thomas lord Dacre, and which his descendants afterward sold to Sir Gervase Clifton, Bart. he was sheriff of Nottinghamshire† 7 and 9 James I. by whom he was knighted, and advanced to the degree of a baronet. He lived in great splendour, beyond the income of his estate, and mortgaged his manor of Hawton to Sir John Leek, which afterwards became the inheritance of the Earl of Scarsdale. He married two wives, first Isabel, daughter of John Markham of Sedgbrook, in Lincolnshire, Esq. by whom he had Sir Francis and Thomas, who died without issue; Mary, the wife of Michael Fawkes of Farnley; Elizabeth of Gilbert Gregory of Barnby Dun, both in Yorkshire, Esqrs. Anne, and Elizabeth: secondly Anne, daughter of Sir James Harrington of Ridlington, in Rutlandshire, Knt. widow of Sir Thomas Foljamb of Walton, in Derbyshire, Knt. by whom he had a son, colonel Roger Molineux, who married Jane, the eldest daughter and co-heir of Sir Robert Monson of Carleton, in Lincolnshire, Knt.

* Thoroton's Nott. p. 182.   † Fuller's Worthies in Nott.

MOLINEUX OF TEVERSAL, NOTTINGHAMSHIRE.

II. Sir FRANCIS MOLINEUX, Bart. son and heir of Sir John, married Theodosia, daughter of Sir Edward Heron of Cressey-Hall, in Lincolnshire, K. B. by whom he had issue, Sir John, his successor, and Francis of Mansfield, in Nottinghamshire, who married Grace, daughter of Conyers lord Darcy of Hornby Castle, in Yorkshire (relict of John Best of Middleton, in Yorkshire, Esq. and afterwards of Moses Janes, Esq.) by whom he had issue two sons; Darcy Molineux, Esq. the eldest, married Elizabeth, daughter of Mr. Basset of Doncaster, in Yorkshire, and left issue two sons, William and John: Francis, second son, married Mary, daughter of Charles Tanckred of Whixsley, in Yorkshire, Esq. and had four daughters; Dorothy the wife of Lucius Henry, lord viscount Falkland. The daughters of Sir Francis were, Elizabeth, wife of Hugh Cartwright of Hexgrave, in Nottinghamshire, Esq. Theodosia of Edward Bunney of Newland, in Yorkshire, Esq. Anne, and Isabel. Sir Francis died Oct. 12, 1674.

III Sir JOHN MOLINEUX, Bart. his successor, was born in 1623. He married Lucy, daughter of Alexander Rigby of Middleton, in Lancashire, Esq. one of the barons of the exchequer, and widow of Robert Hesketh of Rufford, in the said county, Esq. by whom he had issue three sons, Sir Francis, John, who died unmarried, and Thomas, a Turkey merchant, but afterwards of Preston in Lancashire, who married Mary, daughter of Gilbert Mundy of Allestree, in Derbyshire, Esq. and dying May 25, 1727, left issue one son, Rigby Molineux, Esq. who married a daughter of Oliver Martin of Lancaster, Esq. and one daughter, Mary, the wife of John Bushell, M. D. and secondly of captain Griffiths. Sir John had likewise several daughters, of whom Mary married the honourable Richard Leek, Esq. father of the earl of Scarsdale; and Elizabeth, Edmund Jodrell of Erdsley, in Cheshire, Esq.

IV. Sir FRANCIS MOLINEUX of Teversal, Bart. succeeded his father in 1691: he served as one of the knights of the shire for the county of Nottingham, in the reign of Queen Anne; and having married Diana, daughter of John How of Langar Castle, in Nottinghamshire, Esq. and sister to the late Scroop, lord viscount How, had issue seven sons; 1, John; 3, Scroop; 4, Charles; and 6, William. Francis, second son, was one of the verdurers of Sherwood Forest: he married Mary, daughter and co-heir of —— Brewer, near Bristol, Esq. and died at Winchester Oct. 1733, leaving only two daughters, Diana and Mary. Sir Francis had three daughters, Annabella, the wife of John Plumptre, Esq. Lucy of Charles Croke Lisle of Moyle's Court, Esq. and Diana. He died March 1742, aged 87; and was succeeded by his fifth, but eldest surviving son,

V. Sir CHARLES MOLINEUX, Bart. He served high sheriff for the county of Nottingham, and died unmarried July 28, 1764; and was succeeded in title and estate by his only surviving brother,

VI. Sir WILLIAM, the late baronet, who was one of the verdurers of Sherwood Forest. He married the only daughter and heir of William Challand of Welhaw, in Nottinghamshire, Esq. by whom he had one son, Francis, and two daughters, Anne and Juliana, the wife of Henry Howard, Esq. of Glossop, in Derbyshire, son and heir of Bernard Howard (by Anne his wife, daughter of Christopher, fourth lord Teynham) son of Bernard, eighth son of Henry earl of Arundel, Surrey,

MOLINEUX OF TEVERSAL, NOTTINGHAMSHIRE.

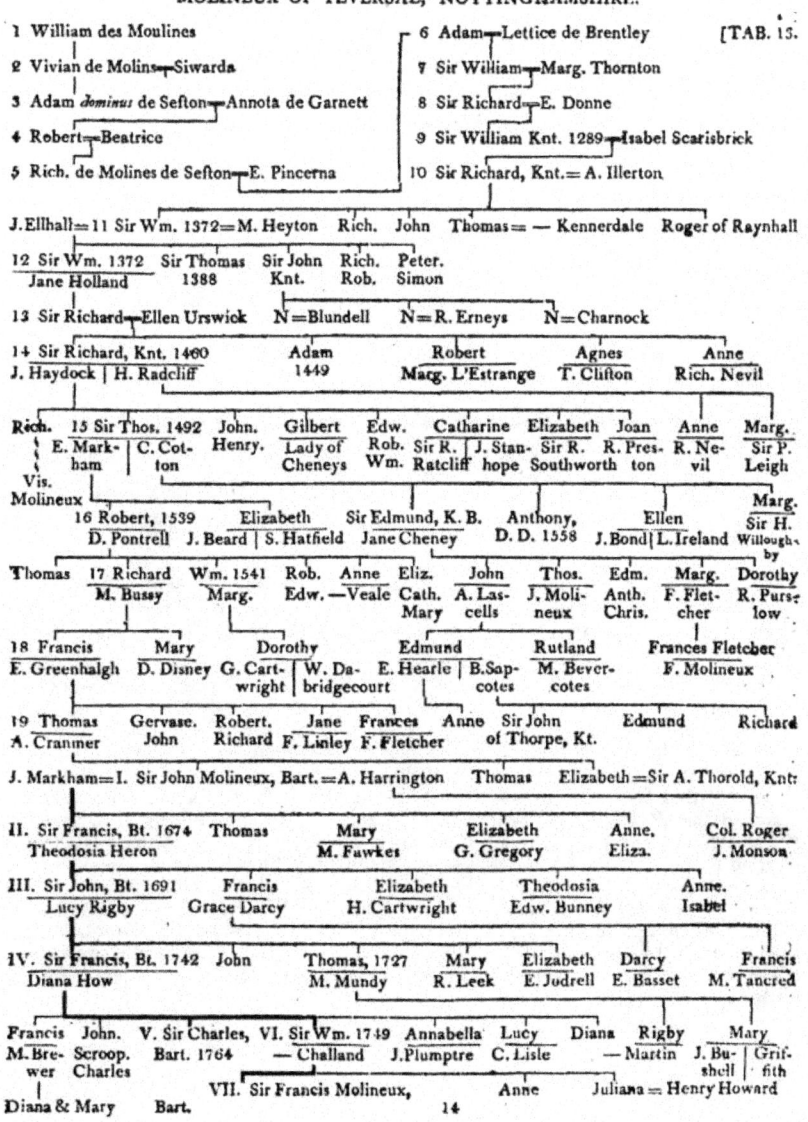

[TAB. 15.

and Norfolk, and brother of Henry, sixth duke of Norfolk. By her he has left three sons, Bernard-Edward, heir to the duke of Norfolk; Thomas of Thornborough Castle, in Gloucestershire, and Edward-Charles; and two daughters, Mary-Bridget, wife of the honourable Robert-Edward, eldest son of Lord Petre; and Juliana-Barbara, the wife of Lord Petre. Sir William died March or April 1781, and was succeeded in title and estate by his son,

VII. Sir FRANCIS MOLINEUX, Bart. He was knighted and made gentleman-usher of the black rod in 1765.

ARMS—Azure, a cross moline quarter-pierced, or.
CREST—Out of a hat, gules, turned up in front, argent; between the hat and the turned-up front, a plume of peacock's feathers, proper.
SEAT—At Teversal in Nottinghamshire.

---

12. HARRINGTON of REDLINGTON, RUTLANDSHIRE.

Created Baronet June 29, 1611.

THIS family, which was anciently written Haverington, is denominated from their possession, a lordship of that name in Cumberland; though their chief place of residence was, from Edw. I. at Adlingham in Lancashire, a manor given to

1. Robert de Haverington or Harrington, on his marriage with Agnes, sister and heir of William de Cancefield, son and heir of Richard de Cancefield, by Alice his wife, sister and heir of Michael, son of William, son of Michael Flameng, all lords of that manor. By this marriage were John, of whom hereafter, and Robert, who married ——, daughter and heir of —— Banister, by whom he had Sir Nicholas, who had three sons; 1, Sir William of Hornby, knight of the garter, and founder of that line which opposed the house of York; 2, Sir James, who was ancestor to the Wolfage race, whose heir females, sisters and co-heirs of Urswick, Bradshaw, and Verden, being ten in number, about the reign of Henry VIII. were married to —— Stanley of Hoton, —— Ashton of Ashton Underline, —— Tresham, —— Myrfield, —— Norris, —— Standish, —— Hilton, afterwards to Pilkington, —— Ashton of Challerton, —— Leicester of Toft, and —— Lumley of Clipsam, dividing a considerable inheritance among them; and 3, Sir Nicholas Harrington of Heyton, in Lancashire, whose posterity resided there in the beginning of the last century, enriched by two intermarriages with the daughters and heirs of Latham and Twyford.

2. John, the eldest son of Robert and Agnes before-mentioned, attended Edw. I. in 1306, in his expedition into Scotland, and was made knight of the bath with

Prince Edward, afterwards Edw. II. In 1311 he had summons to appear at Carlisle, and march against the Scots; and in 1340 he had a charter for free warren at Wytherslack in Westmoreland, with licence to impark 600 acres within the precincts of his lordship of Aldingham. He was summoned among the barons of the realm from 1325 to 1347, in which year he died.* By Margaret, his wife, daughter of Sir Richard Barlingham, Knt. he had a son,

3. Robert, who died before his father; but left issue by his wife Elizabeth, daughter and co-heir of John de Multon, baron of Egremond, John, Robert, and Simon. John, the eldest, succeeded to the barony of Harrington, on the death of his grandfather, and died in 1363: from him descended the barons Harrington, which terminated in an heiress, Elizabeth, the wife of William Bonvile, jun. whose son William, commonly called Lord Harrington, was slain at the battle of Wakefield, in 1461. His daughter Cicely was the wife of Thomas Grey, marquis of Dorset, and conveyed the title of Lord Harrington, with that of Bonvile, to the Greys, both of which are extinct. Simon, the third son, married Alice, daughter and heiress of John Bishton of Bishton, in Salop; and was ancestor to the Harringtons of Bishton.

4. Robert Harrington, the second brother of John, was a knight; and died in 1399, leaving a son,

5. Sir John Harrington, Knt. who married Agnes, daughter and heir of Sir Richard Fleet of Fleet, in Lincolnshire, Knt. and was possessed of that inheritance which he left to his son,

6. John de Harrington, who married ———, daughter of Sir John de Launde, who was succeeded by his son,

7. John, who married Catharine, daughter of Sir Thomas Colepeper.

8. Robert, his son and heir, was sheriff of Rutlandshire in 1493 and 1499: he died in 1502.

9. John, his son, was sheriff of that county in 1522, and having devised all his lands and tenements in Cotesmere and Gretham to Robert, his youngest son, he died in 1524. By Alice, the daughter of Henry Southell of Lincolnshire, he had two sons, Sir John and Robert, the ancestors of the Harringtons of South Witham.

10. Sir John, the eldest son, was high sheriff of Rutland 12, 25, and 32 Henry VIII. and again in 6 Edw. VI. and died in 1552. By Mary his wife, daughter and heir of Robert Moton of Peckleton in Leicestershire, he had four sons, James, Edmund, Robert, and John.

11. Sir James, his eldest son, was sheriff of Rutlandshire in the latter part of 1552, his father dying in that office, and again in 3, 8, and 28 of Eliz; and died in 1591, leaving issue, by Lucy, daughter of Sir William Sidney, Knt. three sons and several daughters: ——— was the wife of Bonitto duke of Frantasquo in Spain; by her he had one daughter, who is said to have been the wife of ———, duke of Feria, and by him to have had one daughter, who was married to a king of Portugal;† and that, from the above Sir James Harrington and his lady have

* Dugdale's Bar. vol. I. p. 99. † Toland's Life of Harrington, affixed to Oceana, &c. p. 41.

been, and are descended, or nearly allied to their descendants by collaterals, no less than 8 dukes, 3 marquisses, 70 earls, 9 counts, 27 viscounts, and 36 barons, of which number 16 were knights of the garter.*

12. Sir John, the eldest son was high sheriff of Rutland 36, 40, and 44 Eliz. and was created a baron by the title of Lord Harrington of Exton, 1 James I. The same year he had the tuition of Elizabeth, the king's daughter, till her marriage with Frederick Count Palatine of the Rhine: he attended her into that country; but died on his return, at Worms in Germany, 1613, leaving issue by Anne his wife, daughter of Robert Kelway, Esq. John lord Harrington, who dying without issue in 1615, the title was extinct. His sister Lucy was the wife of Edward earl of Bedford, and Frances of Sir Robert Chichester of Ralegh in Devonshire, knight of the bath.

Sir Henry, the second son of Sir James, married Cecily, daughter and heir of Francis Agar, Esq. of the king's privy council in Ireland, and of Elmsthorpe in Leicestershire; and had two sons; Sir John, who left an only daughter, Sarah, the wife of John lord Fetchvile, and Jacob.

I. JAMES HARRINGTON, the third son of the before-mentioned Sir James, was of Redland in Rutlandshire, and high sheriff of the county, 35 Eliz. He was created a baronet June 29, 1611: and married Frances, daughter and co-heir of John Sapcoat of Elton, in Bedfordshire, Esq. by whom he had three sons; 1, Sir Edward, 2, Sir Sapcoat, Knt. who married first Jane, daughter of Sir William Samwell of Upton, in Northamptonshire, Knt. by whom he had the famous James Harrington, groom of the bed-chamber to King Charles II. and author of the *Oceana*, a work which Mr. Hume says was well adapted to that age, when the plans of imaginary republics were the daily subjects of debate and conversation; and even in our time it is justly admired as a work of genius and invention. The idea however of a perfect and immortal common-wealth will always be found as chimerical as that of a perfect and immortal man. The style of this author wants ease and fluency; but the good matter which his work contains makes compensation. He died, without issue, in 1677, aged 66. Sir Sapcoat's second wife was Jane, daughter of Sir John Woodward, Knt. by whom he had several children: 3, John, who died without issue.

II. Sir EDWARD, eldest son and heir of Sir James, received the honour of knighthood during his father's life; he was likewise high sheriff for Rutlandshire 19 James I. and 12 Charles I. married Margaret, daughter and heir of John D'Oyley of Merton, in Oxfordshire, Esq. by whom he had that seat and estate. He had issue James and Bridget, the wife of Sir Edward Gore of New Place, in Hertfordshire, Knt. He was succeeded by his son,

III. Sir JAMES HARRINGTON, Bart.† who married Catharine, daughter and co-heir of Sir Edmund Wright, Knt. lord mayor of London; by whom he had a numerous issue; and was succeeded by his eldest son,

* MSS. Tillson.

† Collin says, that for abetting the unjust sentence against King Charles I. he was, after the restoration of the royal family, degraded of his dignity and estate by act of parliament; and that the title expired.

HARRINGTON OF REDLINGTON, RUTLANDSHIRE.

TABLE 14.

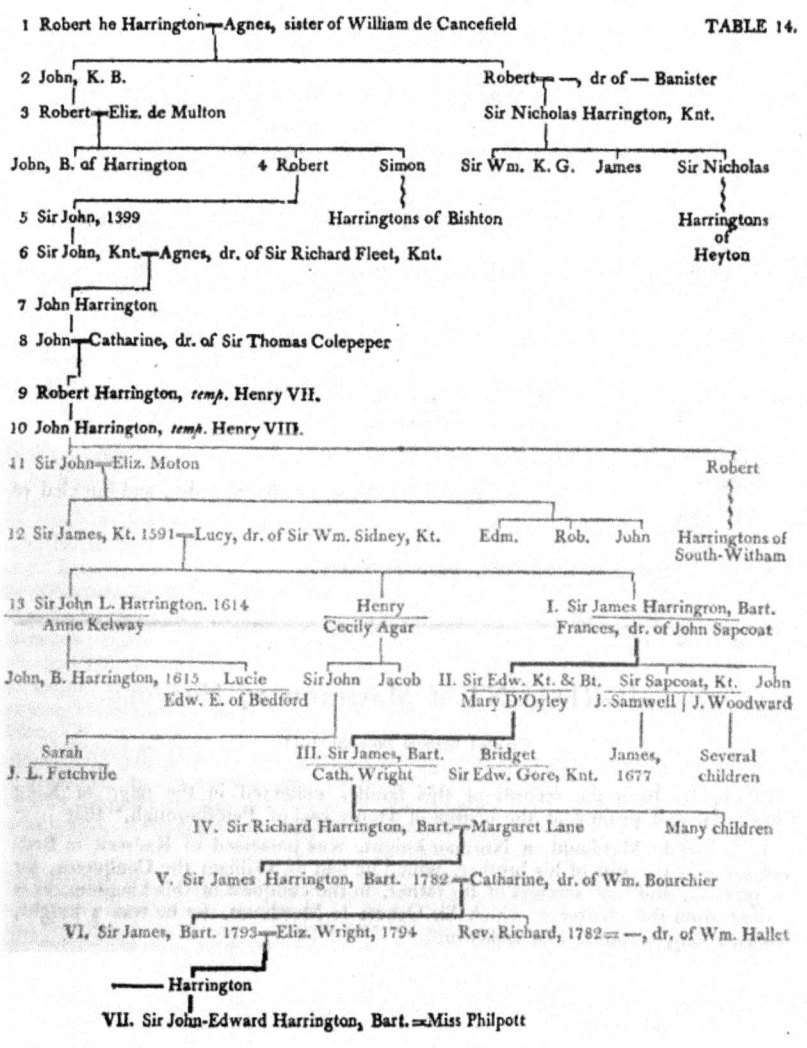

1 Robert he Harrington = Agnes, sister of William de Cancefield

2 John, K. B.
3 Robert = Eliz. de Multon
John, B. of Harrington 4 Robert Simon
5 Sir John, 1399
6 Sir John, Knt. = Agnes, dr. of Sir Richard Fleet, Knt.
7 John Harrington
8 John = Catharine, dr. of Sir Thomas Colepeper
9 Robert Harrington, *temp*. Henry VII.
10 John Harrington, *temp*. Henry VIII.
11 Sir John = Eliz. Moton
12 Sir James, Kt. 1591 = Lucy, dr. of Sir Wm. Sidney, Kt.   Edm. Rob. John
13 Sir John L. Harrington. 1614   Henry
    Anne Kelway   Cecily Agar
John, B. Harrington, 1615 Lucie Sir John Jacob
                           Edw. E. of Bedford
Sarah   III. Sir James, Bart.   Bridget   James,
J. L. Fetchvile   Cath. Wright   Sir Edw. Gore, Knt. 1677

Robert
Harringtons of South-Witham

I. Sir James Harringron, Bart.
Frances, dr. of John Sapcoat
II. Sir Edw. Kt. & Bt.   Sir Sapcoat, Kt. John
    Mary D'Oyley   J. Samwell   J. Woodward

Harringtons of Bishton

Sir Wm. K. G. James Sir Nicholas
Harringtons of Heyton

Robert = —, dr of — Banister
Sir Nicholas Harrington, Knt.

Several children

IV. Sir Richard Harrington, Bart. = Margaret Lane   Many children
V. Sir James Harrington, Bart. 1782 = Catharine, dr. of Wm. Bourchier
VI. Sir James, Bart. 1793 = Eliz. Wright, 1794   Rev. Richard, 1782 = —, dr. of Wm. Hallet
——— Harrington
VII. Sir John-Edward Harrington, Bart. = Miss Philpott

IV. Sir RICHARD HARRINGTON, Bart. who married Margaret, daughter of William Lane of Cowley, in Middlesex, Esq. and was succeeded by his son,

V. Sir JAMES HARRINGTON, Bart. who married Catharine, daughter of William Bourchier of the Middle Temple, Esq. by whom he had James, and the Rev. Richard Harrington of Penny Pound, in Monmouthshire, who married ——, the relict of William Hallet, Esq. late of Soho Square (only son of the late William Hallet, Esq. of Farringdon, in Berks) who died Nov. 21, 1783. Sir James died Jan. 1782, and was succeeded by his eldest son,

VI. Sir JAMES HARRINGTON, Bart. who was the only surviving issue of Sir James Harrington, by Lucy, daughter of Sir William Sidney, and Aunt to the great Sir Philip. He married Elizabeth, daughter of Henry Wight of Blakesly Hall, in Northamptonshire (and perhaps the widow of William Moore of Newton, in Somersetshire in 1776). She died in 1794: he in 1793, and was succeeded by his grand-son,

VII. Sir JOHN EDWARD, who is in the East India Company's service in India. He married ——, daughter of —— Philpot, of Northumberland, in 1788.

ARMS—Sable, a fret, argent.
CREST—On a wreath a lion's head erased, or; collared gules, and buckled of the first.
MOTTO—*Nodo Firmo*.
SEAT—Bourton on the Water, Gloucestershire.

13. MORDAUNT of Massingham, Norfolk.

Created Baronet June 29, 1611.

IT appears from the records of this family, collected in the reign of King Charles II. and printed at the charge of Henry earl of Peterborough,* that

1. Osbert le Mordaunt, a Norman knight, was possessed of Radwell in Bedfordshire, by the gift of his brother, which he had of William the Conqueror, for his services, and the services of his father, in the conquest of this kingdom, as is evident from the charter;† which Sir Osbert le Mordaunt, for he was a knight, had two sons, Osmond and Baldwin.

* Halsted's Geneal. and Rec. de Fam. Mordaunt, &c.
† "Eustachius de Sancto Ægidio, omnibus hominibus & Amicis suis tam Francigenis, quam Anglicis, salutem. Sciatis me dedisse, & hac præsenti Charta confirmasse, Osberto dicto le Mordaunt, fratri

2. Osmond was the father of Eustach and Robert.

3. Eustach le Mordaunt married Alicia, eldest daughter and co-heir of William de Alneto, or Alno, modernly called Dauney, by whom he had

4. William Mordaunt, his son and heir, who was lord of Turvey, Radwel, Asthul, and other lands. He married Amicia, daughter of William Olney of Olney, in Bucks; and was succeeded therein by a son,

5. William, who was likewise possessed of Chicheley, and had licence from King Edw. I. in 1291, to enclose his pasture of Wolesey, his field called Turvey Lees, his pasture of Manselgrove, and other his lands in Turvey, to form a park. He had issue, by Rose his wife, daughter of Sir Ralph Wake, Knt.

6. Robert, his son and heir, mentioned in charters, in 16 Edw. II. and 7 and 29 Edw. III. was knight of the shire for the county of Bedford in 1341. He married Joan, daughter of Thomas Frowick, and had issue,

7 Edmund le Mordaunt, who added to the possessions of his ancestors, Clifton, and Shephall. He married Helen, daughter and co-heir of Ralph Brook (from whose other daughter and co-heir, Agnes, the Duke of Montague is descended: and the said Ralph Brook was the son of Laurence Brook, who married Elizabeth, daughter and heir of Ralph Perrot and Cassandra his wife, daughter and heir of Gyles de Argenten). From which match proceeded

8. Robert le Mordaunt, his son and heir, who is mentioned in deeds in 49 Edw. III. and 14 Rich. II. and having married Agnes, daughter and heir of John Strange, of Ampton-Tynworth in Suffolk, by Elizabeth his wife, daughter and heir of William Butler of Walden, in Essex, had issue, a son,

9. Robert, who in 1421 was one of the knights for the county of Bedford; and by Elizabeth his wife, daughter of John Holdenby of Holdenby, in Northamptonshire (who re-married to Thomas Tanfield of Geyton, in the same county, Esq.) was father of

10. William Mordaunt, Esq. who married Margaret, daughter of John Pecke of Cople, in Bedfordshire, by whom he had, among other children, John, serjeant at law, chancellor of the dutchy of Lancaster, and one of the privy council *temp.* Hen. VII. ancestor to the Earl of Peterborough; and William: also a daughter Joan, wife of Sir Giles Strangeways of Melbury, in Dorsetshire, Knt.

11. William, the second son, covenanted 14 Feb. 10 Henry VII. to marry Anne, second daughter and co-heir of Thomas Huntingdon of Hempsted, in Essex, Esq. which was consummated on the 5th of June following.* His sons Christopher and

---

meo, pro Homagio & Servitio suo, Terram meam de Radwell, cum omnibus pertinentiis, & Libertatibus suis, sibi & Hæredibus ejus, tenendum de me & Hæredibus meis liberè & quietè, honorificè & hæreditariè, sicut illium ego inter alia recepi ac tenui de Donatione & Munificentia Willielmi illustrissimi Regis Angliæ, pro Servitiis quæ Pater meus in Conquestu, & ego sibi fecimus, per Servitium dimidiæ Partis Feodi unius Militis pro omni Servitio seculari. Ego vero prædictus Eustachius de Sancto Ægidio, & Hæredes mei prædictam Terram prædicto Osberto, & Hæredibus ejus contra omnes Homines & Fœminas warrantizabimus. His Testibus, Ranulpho Filio Thomæ Harveo, &c."

* His brother, John Mordaunt, settling on her, as a jointure, the manor of Woodend, with the appurtenances, and several lands and tenements in Rocksden, Bereford, Chalnestre, Colmouth, and Collesden, in Bedfordshire; and all his lands in Tychmersh and Clopton, in Northamptonshire; and the

George died June following, without issue. Edmund was seated at Thundersley in Essex, and married Agnes, daughter of Richard the first Lord Rich.

12. Robert Mordaunt, the eldest son, married Barbara, daughter and heiress of John Strange of Little Massingham, in Norfolk, Esq. by whom he had

13. Philip, who married Mary, daughter of —— Calthorp, Esq. and died during his father's life, leaving issue, John, James, Robert, Henry, and Edward.

14. John succeeded his grandfather, and died in 1574.

15. James, his brother, was his heir, who dying without issue, the estate came to

16. Robert, who also dying without issue, the estate came to

17. Henry, who married Anne, daughter of —— Poley, by whom he had

I. L'ESTRANGE MORDAUNT, who was born about the year 1572: he was bred to arms in his youth, and signalized himself in the Low Country wars, between the Spaniards and the States of Holland, in the reign of Queen Eliz. and during his stay there married Margaret, daughter of —— Charles, of Antwerp. He was afterwards called into the service of the said queen, against the rebels in Ireland, where he remained several years, till he succeeded to the estate of his ancestors at Massingham, &c. by the death of his father and his uncles; when he returned into England, and was created a baronet June 29, 1611. He departed this life in the year 1627, and was buried at Massingham, leaving two sons; Sir Robert, his successor; and Henry of Congham, in Norfolk, who married Barbara, daughter of James Calthorp of Cockthorp, in Norfolk, Esq. and was father to L'Estrange Mordaunt, Esq. who married Barbara, daughter of Richard, and sister of Sir Nevil Catlin of Kirby-Cane, in Norfolk, Knt. by whom he had issue, Henry Mordaunt of Congham, in Norfolk, Esq. and Barbara, the wife of captain John Brown of Scarning, in the same county.

said Thomas Huntingdon, her father, settled on them, after his death, and on John Paris of Linton, in Cambridgeshire, Esq. (who had married his other daughter) all his manors and lands in Cambridgeshire and Essex. This William Mordaunt, writing himself of Hempsted in Essex, makes his will 22d Dec. 19 Henry VIII. the probate whereof bears date June 22, 1513; and orders his body to be buried by his wife, in the church of Hempsted, if he died at London, or as near to Hempsted as London; and that, as soon as may be after his decease, there be five masses said for his soul of the five wounds, and five trentals for his soul, and for the soul of Anne his wife, whereof one to be at the Friers of Bedford, and the other four to be at the four orders at Cambridge. He bequeathed to the church of Hempsted a suit of vestments, and a cope of black velvet, of the price of 20l. with the arms of him and his wife on the cope and vestments: and that a stone of marble be provided by his executors, to be laid upon him and his wife, with their images, and this inscription graven on the stone: "Hic jacet Willielmus Mordaunt, de Hempsted, nuper capitalis Prothonotariis Cur. Domini Regis de Com. Banco, Filius Willielmi Mordaunt, de Turvey, in Com. Bedford, Armiger; & Anna Uxor ejusdem Willielmi Filii, quæ Anna obiit die Sabbati, 12 Die Decembris, Anno Domini Millesimo Quingentesimo XVII." And that his executors cause the day and year of his decease to be put on the same stone, with Quorum Animabus propitietur Deus, Amen. He moreover wills, that his Bible, and all his other books, as well of the law as of entries, English books and Latin books, remain to the heirs male of his body, lawfully begotten, from one to the other, without selling or putting away any of them. He bequeathes to Christopher Mordaunt, his son, his manor of Weldberne, and lands in Depden: to Edmund Mordaunt, his son, his manor of Burghall, and lands and tenements in Swaffham Bulbeck, Swaffham Prior, and Roche and elsewhere in the county of Cambridge; to George Mordaunt, his son, his manor of Dales in Thundersley, and all his lands in Wymbish

II. Sir ROBERT was knighted during his father's life, and succeeded him in the title and estate. He died Aug. 23, 1638, leaving by Amy, his wife, daughter of Sir Austin Southerton,* in Norfolk, Knt. three sons; 1, Sir Charles, his successor; 2, Robert of Hesperton, in Warwickshire, who by Elizabeth, daughter of Mr. Rouse of Utrecht, in Holland, had a daughter Elizabeth, the wife of Robert, son of Clement Throckmorton of Hasely, in Warwickshire, Esq. and a son, John-Lewis Mordaunt, who married the daughter of —— Harrington of Lincolnshire, Esq. relict of Sir William Thorold of Haugh, in Lincolnshire, Bart. 3, William of Scovis Town, in Pembrokeshire, who married the daughter and heir of —— Butler of Scovis Town, and left issue. Of Sir Robert's daughters, Amy was the wife of —— Estcourt, and Anne of —— Pickering, Esqrs.

III. Sir CHARLES succeeded to the title and estate, resided at Massingham, and during the civil wars testified his loyalty to King Charles I. had his estate sequestered, and was one of those shut up in Lynn when it was besieged by the rebels. He married Catharine,† daughter of Sir Lionel Tollemache of Helmingham, in Suffolk, Bt. by whom he had four sons; Sir Charles, his successor; Tollemache, who died before his father; Sir John, and Henry, who died young: also three daughters, Catharine, Elizabeth, and Amy, who died unmarried. Sir Charles died at London July 10, 1648. His widow afterwards was the wife of Sir Charles Lee of Billeslee, in Warwickshire, Knt.

IV. Sir CHARLES, his eldest son and successor, married Elizabeth, daughter and co-heir of Mr. Nicholas Johnson of London, and neice to Sir William Turner, Knt. lord-mayor of London. He died without issue; and his widow was re-married to Francis Godolphin of Colston, in Wilts, Esq. Tollemache died before his father; he was therefore succeeded by his brother,

V. Sir JOHN MORDAUNT, Bart. who residing at Walton in Warwickshire, was chosen one of the knights of the shire for that county in several parliaments in the reigns of King William and Queen Anne. He married first Anne, daughter of William Risley, of the Friery in Bedford, Esq. by whom he had only one daughter, Penelope, who died young. She died in 1692, in the 30th year of her age.

Sir John afterwards married Penelope, daughter of Sir George Warburton of Arley, in Cheshire, Bart. and left issue two sons, Sir Charles and John; and two daughters, Penelope, the wife of Joseph Herne, Esq. and Catharine of Dr. Dobson, warden of Winchester College. He died Sept. 6, 1721, and was succeeded in dignity and estate by his eldest son,

VI. Sir CHARLES MORDAUNT, who was one of the knights of the shire for the county of Warwick. He married Dec. 1, 1720 ———, daughter of John Conyers of Walthamstow, in Essex, Esq. who died March 1726, by whom he had issue Penelope, who died unmarried, and Dorothy, now living. He married to his second lady, 1730, Sophia, only daughter of Sir John Wodehouse of Kimberley, in Norfolk, Bart. who died in April, 1738; by whom he had two daughters, Sophia and Mary, who both died unmarried; and two sons, John, the present baronet, and Charles, rector of Massingham in Norfolk, who in 1774 married Char-

---

* Dugdale's Warw. vol. I. p. 577.   † Ibid.

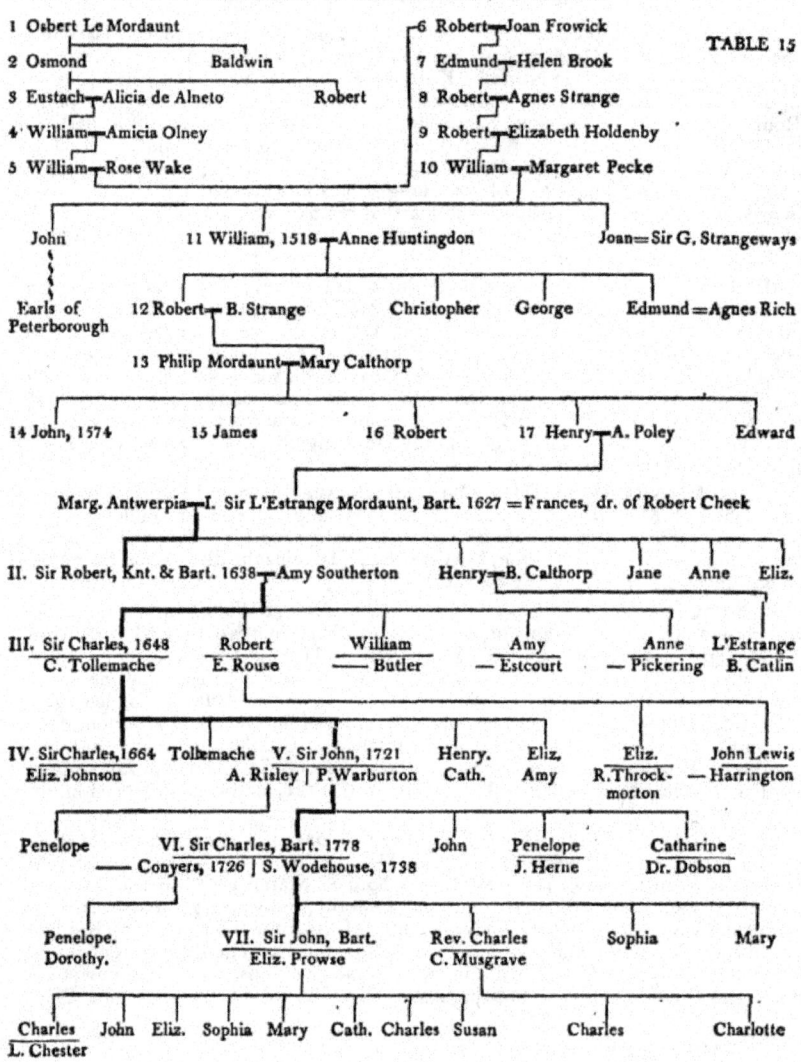

MORDAUNT OF MASSINGHAM, NORFOLK.

TABLE 15

lotte, daughter of Sir Philip Musgrave of Kempton Park, Bart. by whom he has one son Charles, and a daughter Charlotte. Sir Charles died March 11, 1778, and was succeeded by his son,

VII. Sir JOHN MORDAUNT, L L D. Bart. who married Elizabeth, daughter and co-heir of Thomas Prowse of Axbridge, in Somersetshire, by whom he has two sons and six daughters; Charles, who Nov. 16, 1793, married Louisa, daughter of the late Charles Chester, Esq. John, Elizabeth, Sophia, Mary, Catharine, Charlotte, and Susan.

ARMS—Argent, a cheveron, between three estoiles, sable.
CREST—On a wreath, a negroe's head couped at the shoulders, proper; wreathed about the temples with ribbands, and terminating in a double beau-knot, or and azure.
SEATS—At Walton D'Eivile in Warwickshire, and Massingham in Norfolk.

14. WORSELEY of Apuldercombe, Hampshire.

Created Baronet June 29, 1611.

1. SIR Elias de Workesley, or Workedeley, took his name from his lordship of the same name in Lancashire. He is mentioned in the chronicles of the holy wars, to have made an expedition to Palestine, where he fought many battles for the love of Christians, and died at Rhodes. He left

2. Richard, his son and heir, who dying *temp.* Henry I. left

3. Roger de Workedeley, lord of Workedeley. This Roger dying *temp.* Henry II. left

4. Richard, his heir, who left

5. Geoffrey, lord of Workesley, father of

6. Richard, *temp.* Henry III. who dying 1299, left

7. Henry, his heir, father of

8. Richard, lord of Workesley, which Richard was father to

9. Jordan de Workesley: which Jordan was the elder brother by a first wife, and Henry was from a second wife, who yet obtained the manor of Workesley, which might be the reason that Jordan, in despight, left his paternal coat, and gave for his coat, argent, a cheveron, between three choughs, sable. This Jordan lived in the beginning of the reign of Edw. III. From Henry are descended the family of Worseley, who are now seated at Hovingham in Yorkshire. Jordan left

10. Geoffrey, his son and heir, who was made a knight, and was retained by John duke of Lancaster, to accompany him in his expedition into France, 1374, where he, with several other knights, was made prisoner.* The parliament petitioned the king,† that in consideration of their great services he would please to redeem and set them at liberty; the ransom set on them being so high, as was past their ability to pay. This Sir Geoffrey is said, in the Glastonbury Chronicle,‡ together with Sir John Harleston, captain of Cherburgh in France, to have obtained a glorious victory over the French. He was also *locum-tenens* of the county of Kent, and keeper of the castle and town of Cherburgh in France.§ He left

11. Ralph, his son and heir, who married the daughter and heiress of —— Pemberton, near Wigan in Lancashire. He left

12. Hugh, his son and heir, who married Anne, daughter of Ralph Standish of Standish, in Lancashire, Esq. and left William, his eldest son, and

13. Sir James, his second son, who was a page of the chamber to King Henry VII. and on King Henry the VIII.th's accession to the crown was first made yeoman of the king's wardrobe; 1513, keeper of the lions in the Tower, in which office he succeeded John earl of Orford; 1514 he had a grant of the office of constable of the castle of Caresbrook in the Isle of Wight, in reversion for life; and was governor of the Isle of Wight, steward of the crown lands, and warden of the chase. He married Anne, the only surviving daughter and sole heir of Sir John Lye of Leigh, in Dorsetshire, Knt. by Agnes, one of the daughters and co-heirs of John Hacket of Knighton, in the Isle of Wight, Esq. and had with her the manor of Apuldercombe, and divers other manors and lands He had issue, two sons, Richard and John, hereafter-mentioned; and dying in 1538,‖ was succeeded by the then favourite Lord Cromwell, in the office of constable of Caresbrook Castle; and in the government of the said Isle, by his son

14. Richard, who married Ursula, daughter of John St. Barb, Esq. by whom he had two sons,

15. John and George, who were both unfortunately blown up by gunpowder at Apuldercombe, in the porter's lodge, 1567; their mother being then newly remarried to the famous Sir Francis Walsingham, Knt. whereupon

16. John, younger son of Sir James, succeeded: he built and endowed a free school at Godshill, as he had been directed by the will of Lady Worsley, his mo-

* Hist. Ed. III, per J. Barnes. † Rot. Par. 50 Ed. III. ‡ Bib. Cotton Cleopatra, D. IV. Chron. Glastonb.
§ We find in the pedigree of this family another Sir Geoffrey Workesley; but as he lived 19 Henry VI. about 60 years after these things said of Geoffrey, 48 Edw. III. and also, that Sir Robert de Workesley, ancestor to the younger Sir Geoffrey, was knight of the shire for the county of Lancaster, about the time when the first Sir Geoffrey is spoken of: it appears from hence, that we are right in this account.

‖ By his will, after many pious and charitable bequests, he gave to the king his best gold chain; to Lord Cromwell, then lord privy seal, his largest standing cup, and to eight other of his friends, each a silver cup. Richard Worsley, on the attainder of Lord Cromwell, succeeded him in the office of constable of Caresbrook, in 1540 *(Godwin's Annals, 1545, and Stow's Ann.)* The French being much superior to us at sea, attempted our fleet, then in Portsmouth harbour, but not being able to succeed, they turned to St. Helen's in the Isle of Wight, which they intended to take, and to build forts there; but they were, by the people of the Isle, and the conduct of their captain, Richard Worsley, soon drove

ther. He married Jane, daughter of Richard Meaux of Kingston, in the Isle of Wight, Esq. and dying in 1580, left two sons under age; John, the younger, died in his minority, and the wardship of

17. Thomas was committed to Sir Francis Walsingham, under whose tuition he was so well educated, that he became an honour to his country. He married Barbara, daughter of William St. John of Farley, in Southamptonshire, Esq. and dying in 1604, left Richard, his heir, and John, his second son, to whom he bequeathed the manor of Gatecomb in the said Isle; which John, by Cecily, daughter of Sir Edward Richards of Yaverland, Knt. was father to Sir Edward Worseley, Knt. who loyally, and with great hazard of his life, attempted the delivering of King Charles I. from his imprisonment in the Isle of Wight; and from him descend the Worseleys of Gatecomb.

I. RICHARD, son and heir of Thomas, was created a baronet June 29, 1611: he married Frances, daughter of Sir Henry Nevill of Billingbare, in Berkshire, Knt and dying in 1622, left issue by her four sons and three daughters; 1, Sir Henry, his successor; 2, Richard; 3, Thomas; 4, John: Richard and John both died unmarried. Thomas married Sarah, daughter of —— Roe of Salop, from whom the Worseleys of Pitford are descended. Anne, the wife of Sir John Leigh of Bury, in Suffolk, Knt. died without issue. Elizabeth of Sir John Meaux of Kingston, Bart. Dorothy died unmarried. He was succeeded by his son,

II. Sir HENRY WORSELEY, Bart. who married Bridget, daughter of Sir Henry Wallop of Fairley-Wallop, in Southamptonshire, Knt. and died Sept. 11, 1666: he had three sons and six daughters; 1, Henry, who died young; 2, Sir Robert, knighted at Whitehall, Dec. 29, 1664,* who succeeded his father; 3, Sir James Worseley of Pilewell, knighted April 19, 1669,† who married Mary, daughter of Sir Nicholas Stuart of Harsley-Maudit, in Southamptonshire, Bart. left issue two sons and one daughter; 1, James Worseley of Pilewell, Esq. of whom hereafter; 2, Charles was a bencher of the Middle Temple, and died unmarried Aug. 1739; 3, Stuart also died without issue. Sandys was the wife of Peter Bottesworth of Brockenhurst, in Southamptonshire, Esq. by whom he had two sons, Peter and James, who both died without issue. Of the daughters of Sir Henry, Bridget was the wife of John Williams of Luel, in Dorsetshire, Esq. and Jane of Sir George Brown of Woolverton, in Southamptonshire, Knt. the rest died unmarried.

III. Sir ROBERT WORSELEY, Knt. and Bart. succeeded his father, Sir Henry, and married Mary, daughter of James Herbert of Kingsey, in Bucks, Esq. second son of Philip earl of Pembroke; and dying in 1675, left issue Sir Robert, his successor, and Henry, who was sent envoy to the court of Portugal in 1714, and was continued in the same character by King George I. by whom he was made pleni-

---

back to their ships, with the loss of their general. The said Richard held his commands till the death of King Edward VI. when he was displaced by Queen Mary, for having been active in promoting the reformation. On the accession of Queen Elizabeth he was restored to all his commands, and being well skilled in military affairs, was joined in commission with Lord Chidiock Paulet, to fortify Portsmouth. (*Strype's Ann. of Eliz.*) He was after this sent to fortify the isles of Guernsey and Jersey, which were then threatened by the French. (*Ibid, 2 Eliz.*)

* Le Neeve's MSS. vol. I. p. 57.   † Ibid.

potentiary at the same court, and was appointed governor of Barbadoes in 1721: he served, in several parliaments, for the borough of Newton in the Isle of Wight, and died unmarried March 1739-40. Sir Robert had also a daughter Jane, the wife of Sir Nathaniel Napier of Critchell, in Dorsetshire, Bart. and died without issue. He was succeeded by his son,

IV. Sir ROBERT WORSELEY, Bart. who married Frances, only daughter of Thomas viscount Weymouth, by whom he had issue four sons* and five daughters: Frances was the wife of John lord Carteret, afterwards Earl of Granville; by whom she had one son, Robert earl of Granville, and four daughters: Grace the wife of Lionel earl of Dysart; Louisa, the second wife of Thomas, second Viscount Weymouth; Georgiana-Caroline was first the wife of the honourable John Spencer, father to the present Earl Spencer, and secondly of William earl Cowper; Frances, of John marquis of Tweedale, who died in 1762. Thynne Worseley, Esq. son of Sir Robert, married Henrietta, daughter of Charles Withers, Esq. of Moneydown Hall, in Southamptonshire, and died in 1742, without issue. The other sons and daughters of Sir Robert died young and unmarried. Sir Robert died at his house in New-Burlington Street, July 29, 1747; on which a good estate devolved on his grand-son, Robert lord Carteret, son of John earl of Granville. He was succeeded in title by his cousin,

V. Sir JAMES WORSELEY of Pilewell, Bart. son of Sir James, his uncle: he was one of the representatives for the borough of Newton in the Isle of Wight, in nine parliaments; and married Rachael, daughter of Thomas Merrick, Esq. by whom he had several children. He died in 1756, and was succeeded by his son,

VI. Sir THOMAS WORSELEY, Bart. who married Elizabeth, daughter of John earl of Cork and Orrery, and Baron Boyle of Marston, in Somersetshire (by his first wife, Lady Harriot Hamilton) by whom he had one son, Richard, the present baronet, born Feb. 13, 1751; and one daughter, Henrietta, who died single. Sir Thomas died in 1768, and was succeeded by his only son,

VII. Sir RICHARD WORSELEY, Bart.† who, Sept. 20, 1775, married Seymour, daughter of the late Sir William Fleming of Rydal, Bart. by whom he had one son and one daughter, both dead.

---

* In St. John's College Chapel, Cambridge, is the following inscription for his eldest son:—Robertus Worsley, Ar. Filius & Hæres apparens Roberti Worsley, de Apuldercomb, in insulâ Vecte, in com. Southton. Baronetti, ex Franciscâ Conjuge filia præhonorabilis Thomæ Thynn, Vice-Comitis de Weymouth, unica susceptus: illustrissimâque adeo Principe hujus Collegii fundatrice prognatus.

Obiit 2do Die Martii, Anno Dom. 1714. Ætatis 19.

Si qualis fuerit rogas, ex subscriptis disce;
Cui mens labe vacans, legi cui consona Vita,
Pectora perfidiæ nescia, Lingua doli.

On a grave-stone on the floor:—Depositum Roberti Worsley, Ar. 1714.

† Sir Richard represented the borough of Newport in two parliaments, 14 George III. 1774, and 20 George III. 1780. In 1798 he stood a contested election for the county of Hampshire, which he lost by a small majority. He has since represented the borough of Newton in the two last parliaments, which is the joint property of Sir Richard and Sir John Barrington, Bart. In 1777 he was appointed one of the clerks comptrollers of the board of green cloth; in Nov. 1779 sworn of his majesty's privy

WORSELEY OF APULDERCOMBE, HAMPSHIRE.

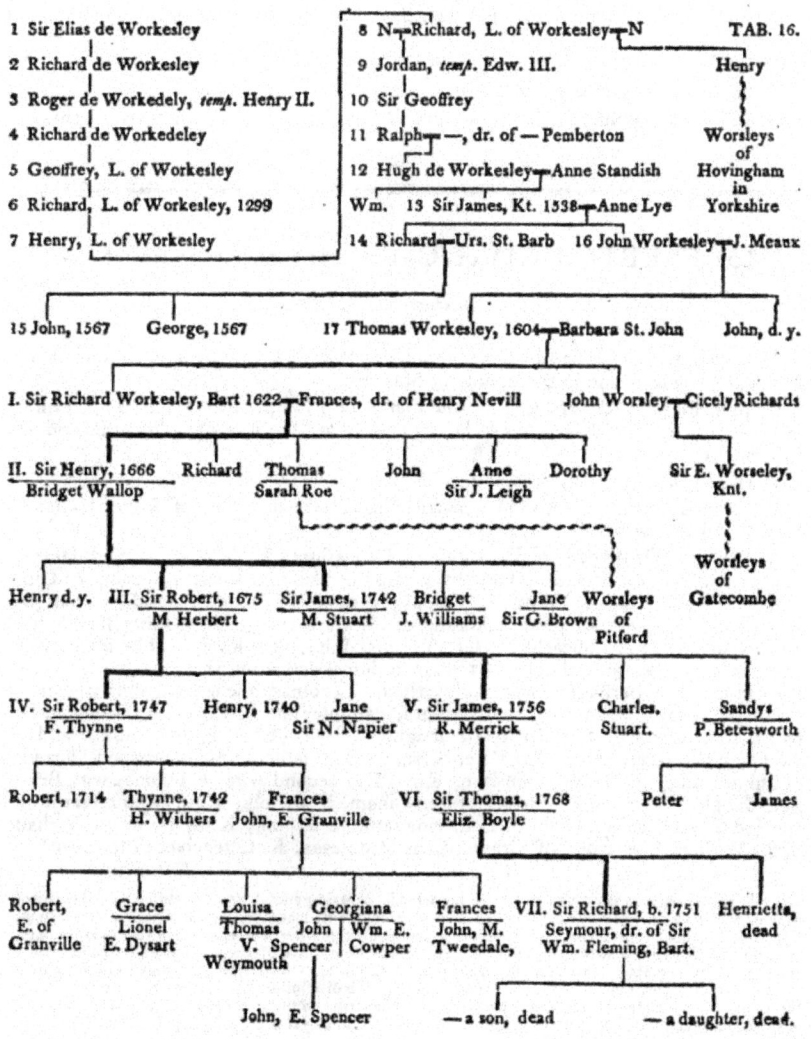

FLEETWOOD OF CALWICHE, STAFFORDSHIRE.

ARMS—Argent, a cheveron between three hawks, sable; beaked, belled, and jessed, or.
CREST—A wolf's head erased, or.
MOTTO—*Ut sursum de super.*
SEATS—At Apuldercombe Park, and the Sea Cottage, in the Isle of Wight.

---

15. FLEETWOOD of CALWICHE, STAFFORDSHIRE.

Created Baronet June 29, 1611.

THIS family, which had been seated in Lancashire for many ages, came about the year 1600 to reside in the county of Stafford.

1. John Fleetwood was lord of the manor of Plumpton Parva, in Lancashire, *temp.* Edw. III. He was father of Henry and Anne, the wife of John Ethalston of Ribleston.

2. Henry, the only son, was living 3 Henry VI. whose son

3. Edward, living 13 Edw. IV. married Elizabeth, daughter of Roger Holland, Esq. by whom he had

4. William Fleetwood of Heskith, in Lancashire, Esq. who married Helen, daughter of Robert Standish, Esq. by whom he had four sons; 1, John; 2, Thomas; 3, Robert; and 4. Edmund, a monk, at Sion in Middlesex: and two daughters, Agnes, the wife of John Jellibrand of Chorley, and Janet of John Blackledge of Leyland, both in Lancashire. Of the sons, John, the eldest, will be mentioned hereafter; and as several considerable men descended from the younger sons, we shall insert some particulars concerning them. Thomas, the second son, was master of the Mint: he married first Barbara, daughter and heir of ——, by whom he had a son, Everard, who by Joan, daughter of —— Cheney, left issue; and a daughter Margaret, married to Peter Dormer, Esq. father of Sir Fleetwood Dormer of Shipton Lee, in Buckinghamshire, Knt. The second wife of Thomas was Bridget, daughter of Sir John Spring of Lavenham, in Suffolk, Knt. (who afterwards married Sir Robert Wingfield of Letheringham, in Suffolk, Knt.) by whom he had 1, Sir William Fleetwood of Cranford, in Middlesex, Knt. receiver of the court of

council, and appointed comptroller of the household, captain-general and vice-admiral of the Isle of Wight, which he resigned in April, 1782; soon after which he made the tour of Greece, Asia Minor, Egypt, &c. &c. which induced him to publish a work called *Museum Worsleyanum*, in two folio volumes, most beautifully printed at the Shakespear press, chiefly descriptive of the curiosities he collected at Athens and other places in his tour through the Levant. In 1793 his majesty appointed him his minister to the republic of Venice, where he continued until the dissolution of that ancient government, by the entry of 15,000 French troops, commanded by Buonaparte, on the 15th of May 1797. He is colonel of the South Hampshire regiment of militia, and fellow of the Royal and Antiquary Societies.

wards, of whom hereafter; 2, Edward; 3, Michael; 4, Henry; 5, Sir George Fleetwood, of the Vache, in Chalfunt St. Giles's, in Bucks, Knt. who by Catharine, daughter of Henry Denny of Cheshunt, in Hertfordshire, Esq. (and Honora his wife, daughter of William lord Grey of Wilton) and sister to Sir Edward Denny, earl of Norwich, had a numerous issue. James, his seventh son, was bishop of Worcester.*

Of the daughters of Thomas, master of the mint, Bridget was the wife of Laurence Ashburnham, Esq. father of Sir Denny Ashburnham of Bromham, in Sussex, Bart. and Joyce was wife first of Sir Hewit Osborne, Knt.† (ancestor to the duke of Leeds) and secondly to Sir Peter Frechville, of Stavely, in Derbyshire, Knt.

Sir William Fleetwood of Cranford, Knt. eldest son of Thomas, master of the Mint, married Joan, sister to Lord Clifton, by whom he had Miles Fleetwood, Esq. receiver of the court of wards; and Sir William Fleetwood, cup-bearer to King James I. and King Charles I. and comptroller of Woodstock Park, who married two wives: by his first he had Sir Miles Fleetwood of Aldwinkle, in Northamptonshire, Knt. and Col. William Fleetwood; and by his second wife, the daughter of —— Harvey, he had several sons, of which Charles Fleetwood was the eldest, and commonly called Lord Fleetwood: he was general and commander in chief to Richard Cromwell, the protector, and married to his first wife, Bridget, daughter of Oliver Cromwell, the protector, and widow of General Ireton, by whom he had no issue.‡ He married to his second wife Frances, daughter of Solomon Smith of Norfolk, Esq.‖ and left issue Smith Fleetwood of Feltwell in Norfolk, Esq. who

---

* He was admitted a scholar of King's college, Cambridge, 1622 *(Wood's Athenæ Oxon. vol. II. Fasti, p. 30)* afterwards he became chaplain to Dr. Wright, bishop of Litchfield, by whom he was preferred to the vicarage of Prees in Shropshire, and soon after collated to the prebendship of Eccleshall, belonging to the church of Litchfield; but before he was admitted or installed, the rebellion broke out. Afterwards, being forced for his loyalty to forsake his preferment, he betook himself to the wars, and became chaplain to the regiment of John earl of Rivers, and in the quality of a chaplain he continued to the end of the wars. In 1642 he was, by the kings special command, honoured with the degree of doctor of divinity, for the service he did him at Edge-Hill fight, and soon after, was made chaplain to Charles, prince of Wales, and rector of Sutton-Colfield, in Warwickshire. After the wars were ceased he became tutor to the Earl of Litchfield, Earl of Kildare, and Earl of Sterling: afterwards, to Esme duke of Richmond and Lenox, and to Charles, who succeeded him in his dukedoms. After the restoration of King Charles II. he was the first that was sworn chaplain in ordinary; was made provost of King's college, Cambridge, in June 1660, and about that time rector of Anstey in Hertfordshire, and of Denham in Bucks. In July, 1765, he was appointed bishop of Worcester; and died July 17, 1683, æt. 81, and was buried in Worcester Cathedral; over whose grave is a marble monument.

† Collins's Peerage of England, vol. I. p. 96.

‡ "This General Fleetwood," Lord Clarendon's says *(Hist. Rebellion, 8vo. edit. vol. VI. p. 692)* " was a weak man, but very popular with all the praying part of the army; a man whom the parliament would have trusted, if they had not resolved to have no general, being as confident of his fidelity to them, as of any man's; and Lambert knew well he could govern him, as Cromwell had done Fairfax; and then, in the like manner, lay him aside. When he received intelligence of any murmurs among the soldiers, he would prostrate himself in prayer, and could hardly be prevailed with to join the troops. Even when among them he would, in the midst of any discourse, invite them all to prayer, and put himself on his knees. If any of his friends exhorted him to more vigour, they could get no other answer than, that God had spitten in his face, and would not hear him. Men now ceased to wonder why Lambert had promoted him to the office of general, and had contented himself with the second command in the army. *(Hume's Hist. vol. VII. p. 513.)*

‖ Blomefield's Norfolk, vol. I. p. 500.

married Mary, daughter of Sir John Hartopp, Bart. and had two sons, Smith Fleetwood and Charles Fleetwood, Esqrs. George, another son of Sir William, was one of those who signed the death warrant of the king.*

George Fleetwood, another son of Sir William, receiver of the court of wards, and brother to Sir William the cup-bearer, went into Sweden, was a famous general there, and was created a baron; and was father of Gustavus lord Fleetwood, in Sweden. Robert, the third son of William, by the daughter of —— Standish, was father of Sir William Fleetwood, Knt. an eminent lawyer of the Middle Temple, recorder of London, and serjeant at law, *temp.* Eliz.† He was a great antiquary; and dying in 1593, left two sons, Sir William and Sir Thomas, who was attorney-general to Prince Henry, eldest son of King James I. also two daughters, Cordelia, the wife of Sir David Foulis of Ingleby, Bart. and Elizabeth of Sir Thomas Chaloner, Knt. tutor to Prince Henry. But to return from this digression to the eldest branch,

5. John Fleetwood, Esq. the eldest son of William, by the daughter of —— Standish, was seated at Penwortham,‡ near Preston in Lancashire; and married Jane, daughter and co-heir of Thomas Langton, baron of Walton, and lord of the manor of Newton, became possessed of that lordship, and had issue three sons, and several daughters.

6. Thomas, the eldest son by Mary, daughter of Sir Richard Shirburne of Shirburne, in Lancashire, Knt (and Maud his wife, daughter of Sir Richard Bold of Bold, Knt. and Margery his wife, daughter of Sir Thomas Butler of Beausey, both in the county of Lancaster, Knts.) left issue Richard, his son and heir, and William, who married Dorothy, daughter of Sir Edward Cokaine of Ashborne, in Derbyshire, Knt. and Anne, the wife of Richard Kippax, Gent. who died Sept. 14, 1625;|| which

I. RICHARD, the eldest son, was the first that resided in Staffordshire, and was seated at Calwiche: he was advanced to the dignity of a baronet 9 James I.

---

* Never was a family more divided than the Fleetwood's at this time: the eldest branch, the baronets, were strict Roman Catholics; Many kept true to the church of England, whilst Charles, and his brother George became the wildest enthusiasts. George was devoted to the parliament: at the commencement of the civil war he slided to the interest of the army, and was entirely under the interest of the chief leaders in it, especially Cromwell. He was named one of the commissioners to try his sovereign, accepted the infamous office, and signed the death warrant of the king, who had so eminently patronised his family. At the restoration he was one of those excepted out of the act of indemnity, though he had surrendered himself in obedience to the proclamation of the convention parliament. He was at this time a lieutenant-general in the army; but he was arraigned only as George Fleetwood, Esq. When he was asked, whether he was guilty or not guilty, he prudently replied, "My Lord, I came in upon his majesty's proclamation;" and when directed to answer in the affirmative or negative, he replied, "I am guilty," and then delivered a petition to the court, which was directed to his majesty and the parliament. When he was found guilty, and asked what he had to say, why sentence should not pass? he said, "My Lord, I have already confessed the fact; I wish I could express my sorrow," and wept. Through the interest of his venerable father, and other friends, his majesty not only respited the sentence, but permitted him to go at large. He retired to America. *Noble on the Regicides, vol. I. p. 245.*

† Wood's Athenæ, vol. I. p. 261.

‡ There is a family of the Fleetwoods, who have resided at Penwortham many years in great reputation, and enjoy a very considerable estate.

|| Ashmole's Berkshire, vol. II. p. 419.

FLEETWOOD OF CALWICHE, STAFFORDSHIRE.

and married Anne, daughter of Sir John Peshall of Horsley, in that county, Bart. by whom he had five sons; 1, Sir Thomas, his successor; 2, Richard, who died without issue; 3, William; 4, Robert, who married a daughter of Mr. Colman of Cank, in Staffordshire; and 5, Henry, who married Agatha, daughter of Thomas Gifford of Plardick, in Staffordshire; and died in 1689, and his wife in 1692. The daughters of Sir Richard were, Mary, who died S. P. Elizabeth, the wife of —— Broughton; and Dorothy of —— Barnesfield.

II. Sir THOMAS FLEETWOOD, Bart. succeeded his father in title and estate, and marrying Gertrude, daughter of Rowland Eyre of Hassop, in Derbyshire, Esq. had issue; 1, Sir Richard; 2, Thomas (who had two wives; by the first, Elizabeth, daughter of —— Coyney, Esq. he had Sir Thomas, hereafter-mentioned; and by his second two other sons; William, who died a batchelor, and Sir John, hereafter-mentioned); 3, Rowland of Prestwood, in Ellaston parish, in Staffordshire, who died S. P. and left his estate to his nephew, Sir John, hereafter-mentioned; 4, William, who married a daughter of the baron of Kinderton, and relict of —— Pigot of Salop, Esq. also one daughter Anne, the wife of Edward Tildesley, of the Lodge in Lancashire, Esq.

III. Sir RICHARD, the eldest son, succeeded to the title and estate, and by Anne, daughter of Sir Edward Golding of Colston Basset, in Nottinghamshire, Bart. had three sons; 1, Thomas, who died before his father, and by the daughter and heir of Christopher Bannister of Bank, in Lancashire, Esq. was father of one daughter, the wife of Thomas Leigh, Esq. younger brother to Peter Legh of Lyme, in Cheshire, Esq. 2, Rowland; and 3, Edward, who both died unmarried: also five daughters. Sir Richard Fleetwood leaving no issue male, the title devolved on his nephew,

IV. Sir THOMAS FLEETWOOD, Bart. son of his brother Thomas, by Elizabeth, daughter of —— Coyney, Esq. his first wife, who married Magdalen, daughter of Thomas Berrington of Mott-Hall, in Salop, Esq. and dying without issue, Dec. 1739, was interred at New Church in Cheshire; and was succeeded by his half brother,

V. Sir JOHN FLEETWOOD, who married Philippa, daughter of William Berrington of Shrewsbury, niece to his brother's lady, and died in 1741: she died June 4, 1786, aged 70; by whom he had

VI. Sir THOMAS FLEETWOOD, Bart. who died a batchelor Jan. 1780.

ARMS—Party per pale, nebule, or and azure, six martlets counterchanged.
CREST—A wolf passant, regardant, argent, wounded in the breast, gules.
SEAT—At Martin Sands in Cheshire.

FLEETWOOD OF CALWICHE, STAFFORDSHIRE.

TABLE 17.

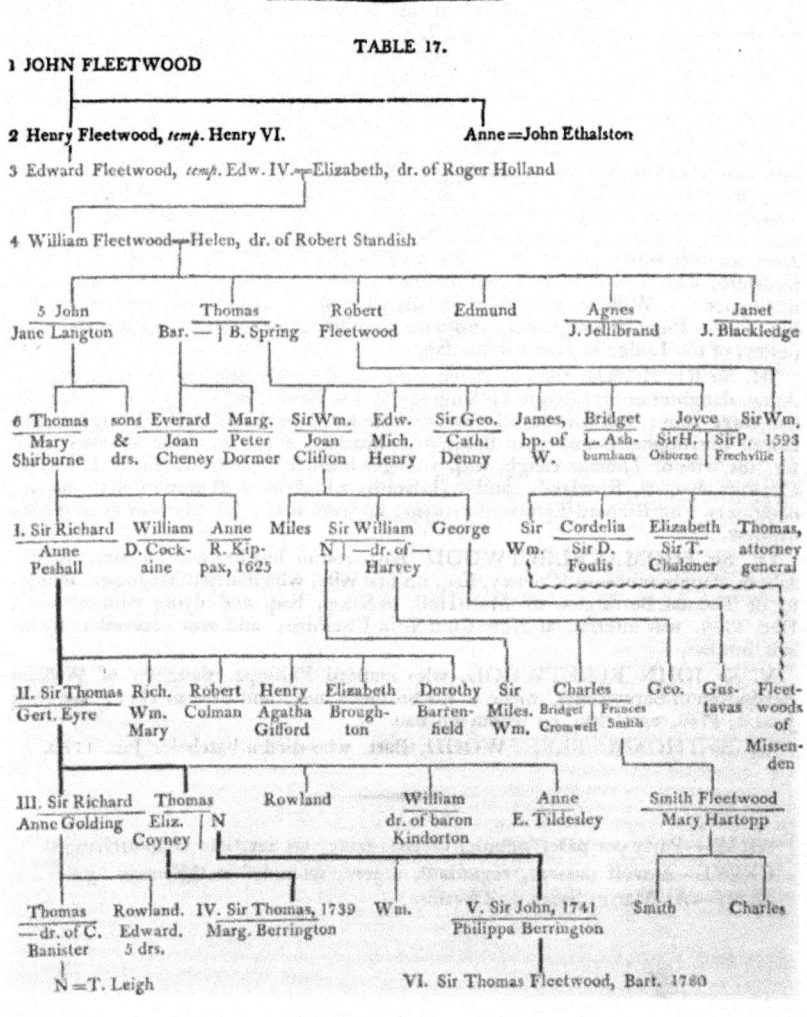

16. TWYSDEN of ROYDON HALL, EAST-PECKHAM, KENT.

Created Baronet, June 29, 1611.

TWYSDEN-borough, anciently Twysenden, now usually called Burrs Farm, in the hundred of West Barnefield in Kent, was the ancient inheritance of this family, and from which they took their name. Philipot, in his survey in the county aforesaid, speaking of Sandhurst, says, "Here is a place in this parish which however it be now under a cloudy and obscure character, was, in ages of higher gradation, the inheritance of the noble family of Twysden, when they writ *De Denna Fracta*, and from them it hath borrowed the title of Twysden street or borough, which it retains to this day."

1. Adam de Twysden possessed this estate in the reign of Edw. I. and dying without issue, as well as his brother Gregory, was succeeded by

2. John, his brother, who by Christiana his wife, had issue

3. Thomas de Twysden, who is mentioned in deeds in the reigns of Edw. II. and Edw. III. he was father of

4. John de Twysden, who married Christiana, daughter of —— Rogers, and had issue,

5. Roger, who in the reign of Rich. II. was steward of the abbey of St. Augustine, a place of great trust in those days.* He married Elizabeth, daughter and heiress of Thomas Chelmington of Chelmington, in Great Chart in Kent, Esq. who bore for his arms, argent, 3 cheverons azure, 9 cross crosslets sable; by whom he had

6. Roger Twysden, who was born in 1390, as appears by an inquisition 18 Henry VI. He married first Alice; secondly Anne, or Agnes, daughter and co-heiress of John Baker of Caldham, in Folkeson in Kent, by whom he had issue Thomas and Margaret.

7. Thomas Twysden was of Chelmington, and married Bennetta, daughter of Richard Lewkenor of Sussex, Esq. (relict of William Barnes, and afterwards wife of Vincent Finch) by whom he had William and Roger. He died Dec. 8, 1500.

8. William married Margaret, daughter of —— Colepeper of Wakehurst, in Sussex, Esq. and died without issue, leaving his brother,

9. Roger, his heir, who was likewise of Chelmington, Esq. He married Jane, daughter of Christopher Cooper of Stone, and widow of —— Sharpe of

---

* In the 5th year of Henry IV. he sealed with an impression of a cockatrice, as appears by a deed in the possession of the present baronet; a singular thing in those days, when crests were very unusual, and only began to be customary when those eminent families, who took part in the factions of the houses of York and Lancaster, assumed them as marks of distinction of the parties they sided with. This crest is still borne by the different branches of the family. *Hasted's Kent, vol. III. p.* 37.

Chart, in Kent. and had issue by her four sons; William, his heir; Thomas, who died in 1590; Christopher, and George, who died without issue: and one daughter, Catharine, the wife of —— Bringborne, and afterwards of —— Swan. He was succeeded by his eldest son,

10. William Twysden, Esq. who married Elizabeth, daughter and co-heiress of Thomas Roydon of Roydon Hall, in East-Peckham in Kent, Esq. by Margaret his wife, daughter of William Whettenhall. His wife surviving him, was afterwards the wife of Cuthbert Vaughan, Esq. and lastly of Sir Thomas Golding, Knt. She died Aug. 19, 1595, aged 73, leaving two children; Margaret, the wife of Richard Dering of Pluckley, in Kent, Esq. and a son

11. Roger Twysden of Roydon Hall, Esq. who was captain of a troop of Kentish gentlemen, at the camp formed at Tilbury,* to oppose the hostile eruptions of the Spaniards, in the year 1588, and high sheriff of Kent 41 Q. Eliz. He married Anne, eldest daughter of Sir Thomas Wyat of Allington Castle, in Kent, Knt. who was beheaded in Queen Mary's time, 1553; and had four daughters; Elizabeth, the wife of Adam Ashburnham of Bromham, in Sussex, Margaret, of Henry Fane of Hadlome, in Kent, and Bennetta, of —— Bathurst of the same county, Esq. also two sons, William and Thomas, who married Anne, the daughter of Thomas Paget. The said Roger died in Nov. 1603, aged 61: his lady June 4, 1592. He was succeeded by his eldest son,

I. WILLIAM TWYSDEN, Esq. who was knighted by King James, at the Charter House, the 11th of May, 1603, being one of those that conducted him to London when he came first from Scotland, to take possession of the English crown; and afterwards advanced him to the dignity of a baronet. He had a learned education, and was well read in the Hebrew and Greek languages, which induced him to purchase many valuable books and manuscripts. The collections he made were useful to the public, both in defence of the protestant religion, and the ancient constitutions of the kingdom. He lived to the 63d year of his age, and died much lamented Jan. 8, 1627-8: his lady, who survived him, died Nov. 14, 1638, aged 64. She was Anne, daughter of Sir Moyle Finch of Eastwell, in Kent, Knt. and Bart. her mother was the sole daughter of Sir Thomas Heneage, Knt. (treasurer of the chamber, vice-chamberlain of the household, chancellor of the dutchy of Lancaster, and one of the privy counsellors to Queen Elizabeth) was a lady of such excellent endowments, that King James I. advanced her to the dignity of viscountess of Maidstone; and King Charles I. to that of the countess of Winchelsea; which honours were limited to the heirs of her body: and the earls of Winchelsea and Nottingham, and Aylesford descend from her.

Sir William Twysden had issue by her five sons and two daughters that lived to maturity; 1, Sir Roger, his successor; 2, Sir Thomas, who was one of the justices of the King's Bench, and advanced to the dignity of a baronet; of whom mention will be made in the proper place: 3, William, who died unmarried July 30, 1641, aged 36; and lies buried at Bath: 4, John, who was a fellow of the College of Physicians, at London, and M. D. he was a person of general

---

* Philipot's Kent, p. 176.

learning, as his works both in physic and mathematics, testify. He wrote a Disquisition touching the Sybills and Sybilline Writings, &c. He died unmarried Sep. 13, 1688, aged 84, and was buried in St. Margaret's church, Westminster. 5, Francis died unmarried, aged 63, and was buried, 1675, in East-Malling church in Kent, in a vault where his brother, judge Twysden, was afterwards laid. Elizabeth, eldest daughter, was the wife of Sir Hugh Cholmley of Whitby, in Yorkshire, Bart. and Anne, of Sir Christopher Yelverton of Easton-Mauduit, in Northamptonshire, Bart. ancestor to the earl of Sussex. He was succeeded by his eldest son,

II. Sir ROGER TWYSDEN, Bart. who was 31 years old at his father's death.* He married Isabella, youngest daughter and co-heiress of Sir Nicholas Saunders of Ewell, in Surrey, Knt. (a lady of singular patience and prudence; she struggled through many troubles and hardships, in assisting her husband in his long imprisonment) and died in 1655, aged 52: he died June 7, 1672, in the 75th year of his age, leaving issue three sons and three daughters; 1, Sir William, who succeeded to the title and estate; 2, Roger, educated in the profession of the law, who died unmarried Feb. 20, 1676, aged 35; 3, Charles, who travelled to Turkey, the Holy Land, Egypt, and several courts of Europe; was esteemed an ingenious person, and took the degree of doctor of physic: he died unmarried, in the 49th year of his age, 1690. Anne, eldest daughter, was the wife of John Porter of Lamberhurst, in Kent. Esq. who died without issue soon after his marriage. Isabella died unmarried, in 1726. Frances was the wife of Sir Peter Killigrew of Arnewick, in Cornwall, Knt. and Bart. and died in 1711.

III. Sir WILLIAM TWYSDEN, Bart. eldest son of Roger, was born in the year 1635: he served in several parliaments, and in the first year of King James II. was elected one of the knights of the shire for Kent. Understanding several languages, he employed his vacant hours in the noble library his father and grandfather had furnished. He died at London on November the 27th, 1697, and was buried at Peckham, with his ancestors. His lady, Frances, daughter and heiress of Josias Cross, Esq. survived him, and was a worthy example of love to her husband, tenderness for her children, and christian resignation, in patiently bearing the loss of several of them, taken off in the flower of their age, in the

* He obtained from King Charles I. a charter of free-warren, to make the park at East-Peckham. He assisted Mr. Philipot in his survey of Kent, who returns him acknowledgments, as a person to whom, for his learned conduct of those his imperfect labours, through the gloomy and perplexed paths of antiquity, and the many difficulties that assaulted him, he was signally obliged. He was indeed a person every way accomplished, well versed in the learned languages, and exemplary in his devotion to the church of England. He was loyal to his prince, and detesting the undutiful behaviour of many of his subjects, was not content to sit still, but was one of the first to oppose their arbitrary proceedings, which drew on him a severe persecution: he was confined seven years a prisoner, his estate sequestered, his timber cut down, and paid a fine of 1300*l.* when he was restored to his estate: for the usurpers permitted him to compound, after they had brought all things to their own desire. When he came again to his seat he lived retired, and his greatest comfort was, the conversing with the learned fathers of the primitive church, and the ancient laws and constitutions of his country, hoping for a time when both might be vindicated; which he afterwards saw accomplished, having the satisfaction of seeing the restoration: and the *Decem Scriptores* appearing in the world, with several other collections, were owing to his endeavours, and he wrote a learned preface before them; and was the author of The Historical Defence of the Church of England. *Philipot's Villare Cant.* p. 105.

defence of their country. They had nine sons and three daughters, of whom those that lived to maturity were, Roger, their eldest son, born in 1666, but died in the year 1685; Sir Thomas succeeded to the title and estate; Sir William, his succesor; Charles, who died in 1698, aged 20; Heneage, a captain of foot in Sir Richard Temple's regiment, and being aid-de-camp to the Duke of Argyle, was mortally wounded in the battle of Blaregnies, in 1709, in the 29th year of his age; to whose memory a handsome monument of black and white marble is erected in the north aisle of Westminster Abbey. John, eighth son, was a lieutenant in Sir Cloudsley Shovel's ship, and was cast away with him, in the 24th year of his age, 1707. Josias, youngest son, was a captain of foot, and received a mortal wound by a musquet shot, in Flanders, 1708, aged 23. They are both commemorated by inscriptions on two neat tables on each side the aforesaid monument, in Westminster Abbey. Anne, eldest daughter of Sir William, died unmarried; Frances, and Isabella, wife of Richard Lybbe of Hardwicke, in Oxfordshire, Esq.

IV. Sir THOMAS TWYSDEN, Bart. (second, but eldest surviving son of Sir William) was 21 years of age at his father's death, and soon after travelled into France, during the short interval of the peace of Reswick. He married, in the year 1710, Catharine, daughter and sole heiress of Sir Frances Withens, Knt. one of the judges of the King's Bench; and departing this life the 10th of Oct. 1712, left only two daughters; Frances, the wife of George Ogle, Esq. nephew to the late Sir George Markham, Bart. and Catharine, of George Cooke, Esq. one of the prothonotaries of the court of common pleas, son and heir of Sir George Cooke, Knt. (His widow afterwards was the wife of brigadier-general Jocelyn, youngest son of Sir Robert Jocelyn of Hyde Hall, in Hertfordshire, Bart. and died in April 1730) whereupon the title and estate descended to his brother,

V. Sir WILLIAM TWYSDEN, Bart. who married Jane, daughter of Francis, youngest son of Sir Thomas Twisden of Bradburn, in Kent. Bart. one of the justices of the King's Bench before-mentioned, by whom he had three sons; Sir William, his successor; Thomas; Philip, bishop of Raphoe in Ireland:* and three daughters, Jenny, Harriot, and Elizabeth. He died Aug. 20, 1751, and was succeeded by his eldest son,

VI. Sir WILLIAM TWYSDEN, Bart. who married Jane, daughter of ―― Jervis, Esq. by whom he had three sons; Sir William Jervis, his successor, Henry, and Thomas; and one daughter, Frances. He died in 1767, and was succeeded by his eldest son,

---

* Mr. Beckford, in his Thoughts upon Hunting, has enlivened his book with several laughable stories; but seems not to have been acquainted with an anecdote respecting Bishop Twysden, which I think is more diverting than any he has advanced. When that gentleman, who was never very clerical, became bishop of Raphoe, he used, in the autumn, to come over to England, to take the diversion of hunting; and in particular with Mr. Sheldon, a Roman Catholic, who lived in the county of Gloucester. With this gentleman the bishop used to hunt much in the north part of that county, where the divisions of the fields consist of dry stone walls, a sort of fences very incommodious to sportsmen. However, our good Lord of Raphoe, who was a light agile man, and an excellent horseman, surmounted all difficulties with the greatest ease, and often left the boldest rider behind him. Mr. Sheldon's huntsman and whipper-in were astonished at the abilities of the prelate; and, with a mixture of envy and admiration, exclaimed, " they never saw such a son of a b―h of a bishop to ride in all their lives."

Gent. Mag. 1784, *b*, 781.

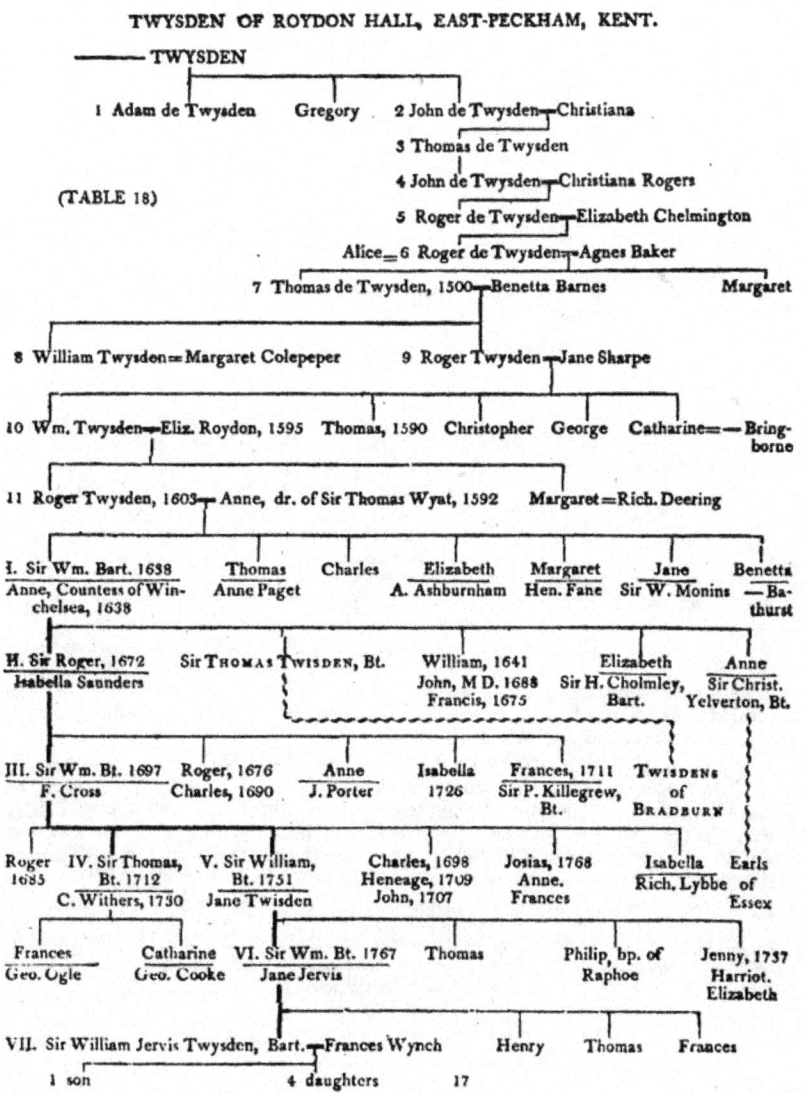

VII. Sir WILLIAM JERVIS TWYSDEN, Bart. who married Frances, daughter of Alexander Wynch, late governor of Madras, by whom he had four sons and one daughter.

ARMS—Gyrony of four, argent and gules; a saltire between four cross crosslets, all counterchanged.
CREST—On a wreath a cockatrice sejeant, gules, winged, &c. or.
SEAT—At Roydon Hall, at East-Peckham in Kent.

17. HALES of Woodchurch, Kent.

Created Baronet June 29, 1611.

THE town of Hales in the county of Norfolk, in all likelihood gave name to this ancient family; for Roger de Hales (19 Henry II.) gave a tenement which he was possessed of in the said town, to the abbey of Bungay,* in that county; and another Roger de Hales (18 Edw. I.) was returned by the sheriff of Norfolk,† as a knight, or freeman on the jury, in a cause between the king, the bishop of Norwich, &c. whom I take to be the same person, whose daughter Alice was so beautiful, as to captivate Thomas de Brotherton, earl of Norfolk, one of the sons of King Edw. I. from which marriage proceeded Margaret, who was created duchess of Norfolk 21 Richard II. from whom the illustrious house of Howard descends.

By what means this family came into Kent doth not appear; but that they gave name to their habitation in Halden, called from them Hales Place, Mr. Philipot voucheth in his survey of Kent. "From whence (says he) as from their fountain, the several streams of the Hales's, that in divided rivulets have spread themselves over the whole county, did originally break forth.‡

1. Nicholas Hales of Hales Place, had issue Sir Robert Hales, who was knight-prior of the hospital of St. John of Jerusalem, and admiral of the north parts of England, in the reign of Edw. III. and was constituted treasurer of England Feb. 1, 1381;§ but in the same year had the hard fate in the beginning of the insurrection under Wat Tyler, to have his head struck off on Tower Hill; and his house at Hybury, built like another paradise, was utterly destroyed.

2. Sir Nicholas de Hales, Knt. brother and heir to this Sir Robert, left issue,

3. Thomas de Hales of Hales Place, who had three sons; 1, John; 2, Thomas (from whom descended the Hales of Warwickshire) 3, Henry, whose son George was of Ledenham in Kent, and was father to Edward Hales of Rumford, in Essex.

* Mon. Ang. vol. I.   † Ryley's Placit. Parl. p. 48.   ‡ Philipot's Vill. Cant. p. 176.
§ Dugdale's Orig. Jurid.

HALES OF WOODCHURCH, KENT.

4. John, the eldest son, was possessed of Hales Place, and was succeeded by

5. Henry, his son, who married Julian, daughter and heiress of Richard Capel of Tenterden, Esq. and had issue two sons; John, hereafter mentioned, and Thomas, who was father of Sir Christopher Hales, Knt. attorney-general, and master of the rolls, in the reign of Henry VIII.*

6. John, the eldest son, had issue a son,

7. John Hales, who was baron of the Exchequer, and seated at the Dungeon, near Canterbury: he married Isabel, daughter and co-heiress of Stephen Harris,† and had issue four sons and a daughter, Mildred, the wife of John Honywood of Seen, near Hithe in Kent, Esq. Of the sons, James, the eldest, will be mentioned hereafter; 2, Thomas of Thanington, in Kent, ancestor to the Hales of Beaksbourne, of whom in its proper place; 3, Edward, ancestor to the branch we are now treating of; and 4, William of Nackington.

8. Sir James, the eldest son, in 1549, was constituted one of the justices of the common pleas, and was the only judge that refused (the rest being intimidated by the frowns of the duke of Northumberland) to subscribe the king's will for disinheriting the ladies Mary and Elizabeth, as against both law and conscience; yet in the next reign, by the influence of Stephen Gardner, bishop of Winchester and lord chancellor, he was committed to prison, and hardly used, for urging the observation of some laws of King Edward VI. and so threatened by his keeper, that he endeavoured to have killed himself; and though the queen, in consideration of his fidelity to her interests, ordered his release, yet he afterwards grew melancholy, and in that change drowned himself,‡ near his house in Kent, 1555. He left isssue by his wife, ——, daughter and heiress of Thomas Hales of Henley upon Thames, in Oxfordshire, Esq. two sons and a daughter.

9. Humphrey, his eldest son, had the seat and estate of the Dungeon, near Canterbury, and was father to Sir James Hales, knighted by Queen Elizabeth at Cobham Hall, Sep. 1573: but this line is extinct.

8. Edward, third son of Baron Hales, was seated at Tenterden; and by Margaret his wife, daughter of John Honywood of Seen, in Kent, Esq. had issue two daughters; Anne, the wife of Sir Thomas Honywood of Elmsted, in Kent. Knt. and Elizabeth, of William Austin of Tenterden, Esq. likewise three sons, John and Edward, who left no issue, and

9. William, who was successor, both to his father and brothers, in the estate at Tenterden; and having married Elizabeth, daughter to Paul Johnson

---

* He died in 1542, leaving issue by Elizabeth his wife, daughter of John Caunton, alderman of London, three daughters; Elizabeth, the wife of Sir George Sydenham, Knt. Margaret, first of —— West, secondly of —— Dodman, and thirdly of William Horden of Kent: and Mary, first of —— Culpeper, and secondly of —— Arundel.

† Hasted calls her Harvey.

‡ Strype, in his Memorials under Queen Mary, says, the family of Beaksbourne, deny that he drowned himself, and say, that retiring to his seat at Thanington near Canterbury, he amused himself with the pleasures of a country life, and crossing the river over a narrow bridge, as he was walking in his meadows, fell in accidentally, and was drowned; aged 85." See Hale's of Beaksbourne's account, postea.

of Fordwich, in Kent, Esq. had two daughters, Mary was the wife of Simon Smith of Boughton-Monchelsey, in Kent; and Elizabeth, of Robert Kenrick of King's-Sutton, in Northamptonshire, Esqrs. and one son, Edward.

I. Which EDWARD became possessed of a good estate, by marriage with Deborah, daughter and heiress of Martin Harlackenden of Woodchurch, in Kent, Esq. and having received the honour of knighthood, was advanced to the dignity of a baronet in 1611. He served in several parliaments; took part with those that raised the rebellion against King Charles I. and died in Sep. 1654, aged 78, and had issue, by the aforesaid Deborah, four sons; 1, John; 2, Edward of Chilson, in Kent (whose son Edward, by the daughter of John Evelyn of Deptford, in Kent, Esq. left issue) 3, Samuel; and 4, Thomas, who died S. P. Sir Edward having buried his first wife, married secondly Martha, daughter of Sir Matthew Carew, Knt. and relict of Sir James Cromer of Tunstall, in Kent. Knt. whereby he added a fine estate to his family. John, his eldest son, having married Christian, one of the daughters and co-heirs of the aforesaid Sir James Cromer of Tunstall, Knt. died in 1639, and left issue,

II. Sir EDWARD HALES, Bart. who in his younger years risqued his person and fortune, in endeavouring the rescue of King Charles I. from his imprisonment in the Isle of Wight.* He died in France some years after the restoration, and left issue by his lady, one of the daughters and co-heirs of Thomas lord Wotton of Boughton Malherbe, in Kent, Sir Edward, his successor; John, of the Inner Temple, who died unmarried; Charles, and Thomas, who also died unmarried.

* Of which enterprize lord Clarendon gives the following relation:—"Mr. L'Estrange (the famous Sir Roger) says he, had a great friendship with a young gentleman, Mr. Hales, who lived in Kent, and was married to a lady of noble birth and fortune, he being heir to one of the greatest fortunes in that country, but was to expect the inheritance from the favour of an old severe grandfather, who, for the present, kept the young couple from running into any excess: the mother of the lady being of as sour and strict a nature as the grandfather, and both of them so much of the parliament party, that they were not willing any part of their estates should be hazarded for the king. At the house of this Mr. Hales, Mr. L'Estrange was, when, by the communication which that part of Kent always hath with the ships which lie in the Downs, the report first did arise, that the fleet would presently declare for the king: and those seamen who came on shore, talked as if the City of London would join with them. This drew many gentlemen of the country, who wished well, to visit the ships, and they returned more confirmed of the truth of what they had heard. Good fellowship was a vice spread every where; and this young great heir, who had been always bred among his neighbours, affected that which they were best pleased with; and so his house was a rendezvous for those who delighted in that exercise, and who every day brought him the news of the good inclinations of the fleet for the king; and all men's mouths were full of the general hatred the whole kingdom had against the parliament as well as the army."

In this posture of affairs Mr. L'Estrange easily induced Mr. Hales to put himself at the head of those young gentlemen who were resolved to do somewhat for his majesty's service, at a juncture when the Scots were ready to march into England, and most parts of the kingdom ready to rise; but not being enough conversant in the affairs of the world, he referred himself and the whole business to be governed by Mr. L'Estrange, who was believed, by his discourse, to be an able soldier. Accordingly letters were dispatched to particular gentlemen, and warrants to constables of hundreds, requiring, in his majesty's name, all persons to appear at a time and place appointed, to advise together, and lay hold on such opportunities as should be offered for relieving the king, and delivering him out of prison. Mr. Hales was their general, and accordingly, a body of horse and foot were drawn together at Maidstone, Mr. Hales having taken up, on his own security, near 80,000l. to defray the expence; and they were so strong, that the commander of the parliament forces, sent to suppress them, durst not advance. Soon after this he retired, with his friend Mr. L'Estrange, to Holland, and lived beyond the seas, on account of the great debts he had contracted for the king's service.

III. Sir EDWARD HALES, Bart. son and heir of Sir Edward, was in much favour with King James II. under which king he had a regiment of foot, was one of his privy council, and one of the lords of the admiralty, deputy governor of the cinque ports, and lieutenant governor of the Tower of London. He had an action brought against him by Arthur Godden, his coachman, for the penalty of 500*l.* for neglecting to take the oaths of supremacy and allegiance, within three months after he had his regiment, grounded upon the act of 25 Charles II. and was convicted at Rochester assizes for the same; but moving it into the king's bench, pleaded the king's dispensing power, and had judgment given for him;* eleven of the judges being of opinion, that the king might dispense in that case. At the revolution he was confined for a year and half in the Tower: on his release went to France, and in consideration of his services was created earl of Tenterden in Kent,† by the late

---

* This memorable affair was argued by Sir Edward Northey for the plaintiff, and Sir Thomas Powis for the defendant; and the lord chief justice Herbert delivered the opinions of the twelve judges. See the whole proceedings at large in State Trials, fo. vol. VII. p. 612.

† Abstracted from his patent of creation. — "James the Second, by the grace of God, &c.

"To our archbishops, dukes, marquisses, earls, &c. Whereas it is a kingly act and a singular testimony of our benevolence, to enoble those persons we find worthy of our favour, as well that others may see how grateful the faithful duty of our subjects is to Us, as that they themselves may be encouraged to endeavour at greater matters. Whereas therefore the fidelity of our well-beloved and most faithful counsellor, Sir Edward Hales of Hackington, otherwise St. Stephen's, in our county of Kent, baronet, has been by various changes abundantly known to us, and likewise bring to our minds the ancient nobility of his family, as well on the father as mother's side; and especially the great merit of Robert Hales, formerly lord high treasurer of our kingdom of England, and the prior of the hospital, who upon account of a most prudent advice which he gave to our predecessor, King Richard the Second, had on a popular sedition by the fury of the mob, his head struck off; and his father's great grand-father, who in a rebellion, by reason of their fidelity towards the most serene kings, our father and brother, of happy memory; besides what they otherwise suffered by the loss of liberties and large possessions: and his great grand-father, Sir Edward Hales of Tunstall, in the county of Kent, baronet, suffered five years imprisonment in the Tower of London; and his father, Sir Edward Hales of Tunstall aforesaid, baronet, suffered banishment and confiscation of goods. His mother sprung from the ancient Earls of Hereford, and from the sister of St. Edward the Confessor; and finally, the said Sir Edward Hales, by his wise administration of many offices, and for his fidelity to us and the catholic church, has with great fortitude suffered by the present rebellion, &c. &c.

His eldest son Edward in the mean time, a youth, by the brightness of his wit, the politeness of his manners, the greatness of his mind, very dear to us, was killed in Ireland, at the battle of the Boyne, as he was courageously fighting against the enemy, &c. &c.

Know ye therefore, that we, out of a special grace, &c. &c. have raised, preferred, created, and established the said Sir Edward Hales, Bart. to the state, degree, style, dignity, title, and honour of Baron Hales of Elmley, and Viscount Tunstall, in our county of Kent, &c. &c. and to the heirs male of his body issuing, and for want of such issue to his brother, John Hales, Esq. and the heirs male of his body issuing, and for want of such issue to his brother, Charles Hales, Esq. and the heirs male of his body, &c. &c. &c.

And moreover of our more plentiful special grace, &c. have made, preferred, and created the said Sir Edward Hales, Bart. Earl of Tenterden, in our county of Kent, &c. &c. by girding on him a sword, a cap of honour, and putting on his head a golden coronet, and delivering to him a golden rod, to have and to hold the same name, state, title, degree, style, honour and dignity of Earl Tenterden aforesaid, with all and singular the preeminences and the rest of the honours to such name, state, degree, dignity, &c. (*With limitations to his brothers John and Charles, as before, with* 20£. *a-year better to support the said dignity*), &c. &c.

We also will and by these presents do grant unto the said Sir Edward Hales, Bart. that he shall have these our letters patent made, and sealed under our great seal of England, without any fine or fee, great or small, to be rendered, paid, or made into our hanaper, or elsewhere, to our use for the same,

King James, while he was in that kingdom; and died there in 1695. He married Frances, daughter of Sir Frances Windibank of Oxfordshire, Knt. who died in 1693, and had issue five sons and seven daughters. Sir John only survived him: Edward, the eldest, was killed at the battle of the Boyne, fighting for King James II. Charles, Robert, and James lived to men's estate, and died unmarried.

Anne died unmarried; Mary was the wife of —— Bauwens, Esq. judge of the admiralty at Ostend; Frances, of the right honourable Peter earl of Fingall, in Ireland; Jane, Elizabeth, and Catharine died unmarried: and Clare was the wife of Mr. Hussey of the kingdom of Ireland.

IV. Sir JOHN HALES, Bart. married first Helen, daughter of Sir Richard Bealing of Ireland, secretary to the queen dowager of King Charles II. by whom he had two sons; 1, John, who died in his infancy; 2, Edward, who married Mrs. Parker, grand-daughter of Sir Richard Bulstrode, Knt. who died at St. Germain's in France, Oct. 1711, aged 102; by whom he had two sons; John, who died in his infancy, and Edward, his heir; and a daughter, Frances the wife of George Henry, earl of Litchfield. He married secondly Helen, daughter of Dudley Bagnell of Newry, in the kingdom of Ireland, Esq. by whom he had three sons; James, who was an officer in the Emperor's service, and was killed in Italy in 1735; Alexander, and Philip. This lady Hales died at Luckly near Oakingham, Berks, Nov. 1737. Sir John died in 1744, and was succeeded by his grand-son,

V. Sir EDWARD HALES, Bart. who married first Barbara, daughter of Sir Thomas Webb, Bart. by whom he had several children who died in their infancy: the surviving ones are Edward Hales, Esq. who in 1789 married Lucy, the second daughter of Henry Darell of Colehill, Esq. by whom he has yet no issue: Anne, the eldest, became a nun; and the two youngest were both married to officers in the French service. His lady died Sep. 26, 1770, and he married secondly, in 1790, the relict of Mr. Palmer, of the kingdom of Ireland, by whom he has yet no issue.

ARMS—Gules, three arrows or, feathered and bearded, argent.*

CREST—On a wreath a dexter arm, bended at the elbow and armed, proper, garnished or, and bound about with a ribband gules, holding an arrow, as in the arms.

SEATS—At St. Stephen's near Canterbury; at Tunstall, and Woodchurch, all in Kent.

in witness whereof we have caused these our letters to be made patent; witness myself at Tionville, the third day of May, in the 8th year of our reign,

By the King himself.

The same king gave to the present Sir Edward's mother the blue ribband which he had wore himself, to be given to her son, the present Sir Edward Hales (and still remains in his possession) and which he might claim if the said king, or any of his descendants should be upon the throne of England.

Lewis, king of France, caused a servant of Lord Hales to be arrayed like a herald, with trumpets and banners, and sent him into King Edward the Fourth's camp, where he had audience.

Speed's Chron. p. 872.

* It appears by Sir Robert Cotton's House of Antiquities, that the three broad arrows are quartered with the royal arms of England.

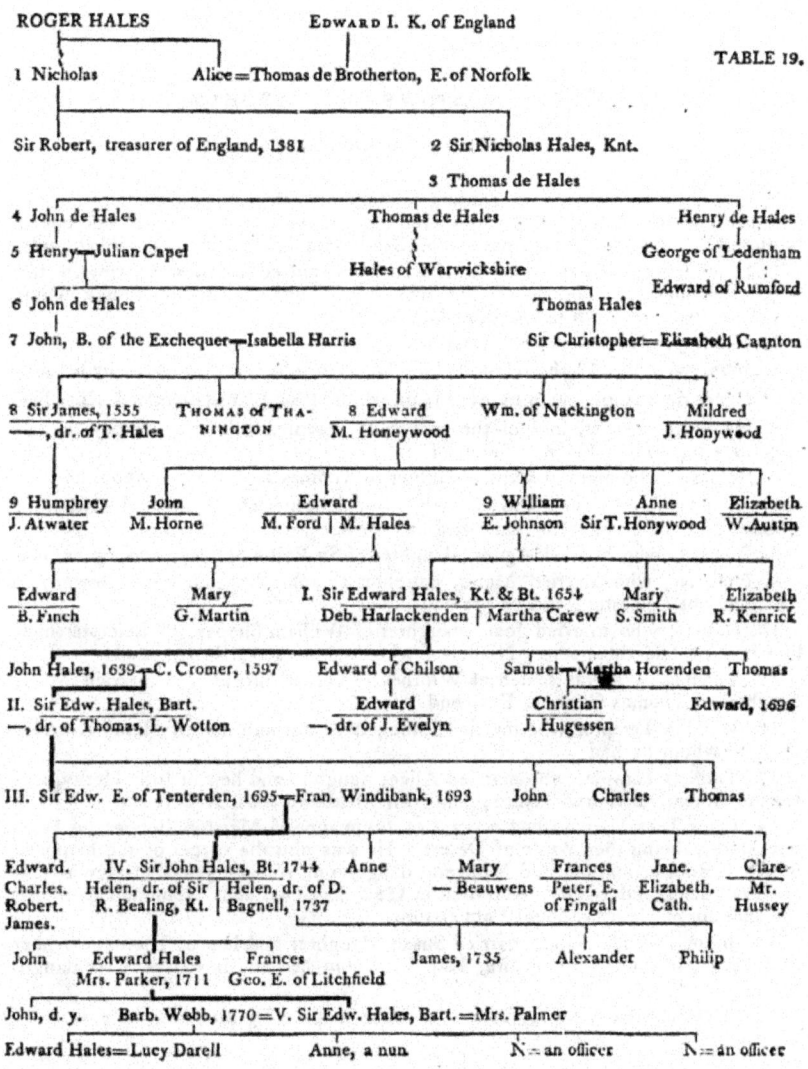

18. TEMPLE of Stowe, Buckinghamshire.

Created Baronet Nov. 25, 1612.

THIS family of Temple is, according to many genealogists, descended from Leofric, earl of Mercia, and the famous Godiva, who is reported to have rode naked through Coventry, to obtain from her husband some immunities to the inhabitants.

1. Henry, the younger son of Leofric, by his said countess, was living in the reign of William the Conqueror; and was wrote Henry del Temple, from a manor so called, near Bosworth in Leicestershire.

2. Geoffrey, his son and heir, was the father of

3. John, who lived in the reign of King Henry I. who was succeeded by his son,

4. Henry de Temple, who by Maud, daughter of Sir John Ribbesford, Knt. had

5. Henry de Temple, lord of the manor of Temple, and Little Shepey, in the reign of King John. He was father of

6. Richard, who married Cath. daughter of Thomas Langley, by whom he had

7. Nicholas de Temple, who married ——, daughter of Sir Richard Corbet of Sibbeston, in Leicestershire, Knt. and had by her

8. Richard, who married Agnes, daughter of Sir Ralph Stanley, and by her had

9. Nicholas, who married Maud, daughter of John Burguillon of Newton, in the county of Leicester; and by her had

10. Robert, who married Joan, daughter of William Shepey, of Leicestershire, by whom he had three sons; Nicholas, who died in 1506; Robert, and

11. Thomas, who was seated at Whitney in Oxfordshire:* He married Mary, daughter of Thomas Gedney, Esq. and left

12. William Temple, who married Isabel, daughter and heir of Henry Everton, Esq. by whom he had

13. Thomas Temple, who married Alice, daughter and heir of John Heritage of Burton Dorset, in Warwickshire; and by her had two sons, Robert and

14. Peter Temple, who had a grant of the manor of Merston Boteler, in Warwickshire,† being then wrote of Desert. He was also the owner of the manor of Stowe in Bucks; and married Millicent, daughter of William Jekyll of Newington, in Middlesex; and by her, who died in 1582, had two sons, John and Anthony, the ancestor of Henry viscount Palmerston.

15. John, the eldest son, married Susan, daughter and heir of Thomas Spencer of Everton, in Northamptonshire, Esq. by whom he had six sons and six daugh-

---

* Vincent's Bucks, No. 131, 55 b. 56 a, in Offic. Ann.   † Pat. 7 Edw. VI. p. 4.

ters, as appears by an English inscription on a monument in the church of Dorset, where the said John and Susan lie interred; under which inscription* are these lines:—

> *Cur liberos hic plurimos,*
> *Cur hic amicos plurimos,*
> *Et plurimas pecunias,*
> *Vis scire cur reliquerit?*
> *Tempellus ad plures abiit.*

His sons were, Sir Thomas, George, who died an infant; John of Franckton, in Warwickshire; Sir Alexander of Longhouse, in the parish of Chadwell in Essex; William, who married Jane, daughter of Sir Thomas Beaumont of Stoughton, Knt. and Peter, who married ——, daughter of —— Kendall.

I. Sir THOMAS, the eldest son, succeeded his father at Stowe: he was knighted by King James I. 1603, and in 1612 was created a baronet. He married Esther, daughter of Miles Sandys of Latimers, in Bucks, Esq. by whom he had four sons and nine daughters, who so exceedingly multiplied, that his lady lived to see 700 descendants. This is affirmed by Dr. Fuller, in his Worthies of England, who relates that he bought the truth thereof by a wager lost on the subject.†

II. Sir PETER TEMPLE, the eldest son and successor, served for the town of Buckingham in the two last parliaments of Charles I. and married first Anne, daughter and co-heir of Sir Arthur Throgmorton of Paulerspury, in Northamptonshire, Knt. and secondly, Christian, sister and co-heir of Sir Richard Leveson of Trentham, in Staffordshire, K. B. By the first of these ladies, who was buried at Stowe in 1619: he had two daughters, Anne, the wife of Thomas Roper, viscount Baltinglass; and Martha, of Weston Ridgeway, earl of Londonderry; and by the latter, who died in 1655, he had Sir Richard and two daughters, Frances and Hester. Sir Peter died in 1653.

III. Sir RICHARD TEMPLE was born in 1634: he was lord lieutenant for the county of Bucks in 1660. In 1661 he was one of the 68 persons created K. B. to attend Charles II. at his coronation. He was a leading member in the house of commons during the reign of Charles II. and distinguished himself in the prosecution of the Popish plot, and in promoting the bill for excluding James duke of York succeeding to the crown. He married Mary, daughter of —— Knap of Weston, in Oxfordshire, Esq. and heir to her brother; and by her had four sons, who all died without issue, except the eldest, Sir Richard. He had also, by the said lady, six daughters, whereof two died young. Hester, the second, was the wife of Richard Grenville of Wotton, Esq. grandfather to the Marquis of Buckingham: Christian of Sir Thomas Lyttleton, Bart. Maria, first of Dr. West, prebendary of Winchester, and secondly of Sir J. Langham of Cottesbroke, in Northamptonshire,

* Dugdale's Warwickshire.
† This Esther lady Temple (of whom there is an original picture at Stowe) far surpassed Mrs. Honeywood of Mark's Hall, in Essex, who lived to see 367 descendants of her own body; for Lady Temple saw many more, the last of whom, ——, daughter of Sir Henry Gibbs of Hunnington in Warwickshire, died in Dec. 1737, in extreme old age.

TEMPLE OF STOWE, BUCKINGHAMSHIRE.

TABLE 20.

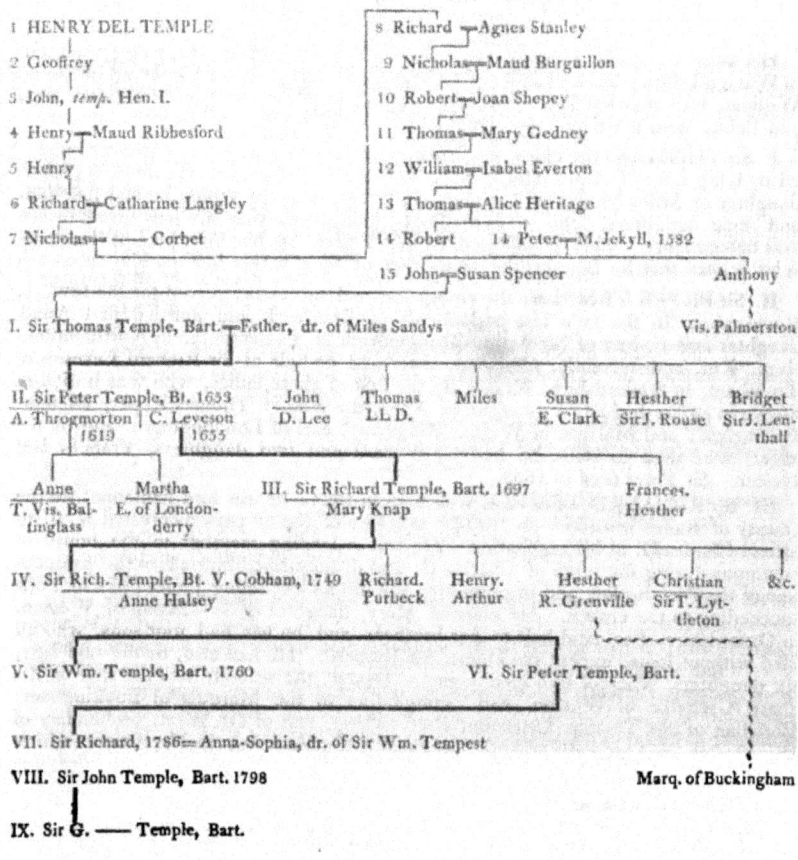

Bart. and Penelope of Moses Berenger, of the city of London, Esq. Sir Richard was buried at Stowe, May 15, 1697; and was succeeded by his son,

IV. Sir RICHARD TEMPLE, Bart. who was chosen, on his father's death, for the town of Buckingham; and 4 Queen Anne, was one of the knights of the shire. He gained great honour by his bravery and conduct in the wars in Flanders, where, on Jan. 11, 1709-10, he was made a lieutenant-general; and by King George I. created baron and viscount Cobham of Cobham, in Kent. He was also one of his majesty's privy council, ambassador extraordinary to the Emperor, and colonel of his own royal regiment. He married Anne, daughter of Edmund Halsey, Esq. but died, in 1749, without issue, when the peerage in him became extinct; but the title of baronet descended to

V. Sir WILLIAM TEMPLE, the next male heir; but whose son he was, I have not been able to learn. He died April 10, 1760, and was succeeded by his brother,

VI. Sir PETER, who died in Feb. 1761, and was succeeded by his son

VII. Sir RICHARD, who married Anna-Sophia, daughter of Sir William Tempest, Bart. In 1761 he was appointed one of the commissioners of the navy, and in 1764, one of the commissioners of the revenue at New York. He died Nov. 15, 1786, without issue, and was succeeded by

VIII. Sir JOHN TEMPLE, Bart. but as this branch of the family have resided at New England in America, for more than a century, I have not been able to procure information what relation he was to his predecessor. He was agent and consul-general in the United States of America; died Oct. 12, 1798, and was succeeded by his son,

IX. Sir G. —— TEMPLE, Bart.

ARMS—Argent, on two bars gules, six martlets or.
CREST—On a mount, vert, a talbot, sejant, sable.
MOTTO—*Templa quam dilecta.*
RESIDENCE—New England in America.

20. WRAY of GLENTWORTH, LINCOLNSHIRE.

Created Baronet Nov. 25, 1612.

SIR Christopher Wray, Knt. lord chief justice of England, father of Sir William, was the first of this family that resided at Glentworth; but his ancestors were anciently seated in the bishoprick of Durham, and afterwards possessed estates in the county of York.

1. John Wray of Richmond, by Alice his wife, daughter of Thomas Clyburn, had issue

2. Richard, who by his first wife, ———, daughter of John Udall, had issue,

3, Humphrey Wray, who married a daughter of ——— Warcop, and was succeeded in his estate by

4. Robert, his son and heir, who by his wife, a daughter of John Danby, had issue four sons, William, Thomas, John, and Christopher.

5. William, the eldest son, had to wife ———, daughter and heir of ——— Jackson of Snydall, in Yorkshire, and had issue several sons and daughters: four of the sons, Christopher, Richard, Thomas, and Leonard lived to men's estate, and had posterity.

6. Christopher, the eldest, was of Magdalen college, Cambridge, and was by Queen Elizabeth, who well knew the deserts of her ministers and servants, promoted to the high station of chief justice of England. He had served for Burrowbridge in Yorkshire in all the parliaments of Queen Mary; and being an eminent lawyer, and well versed in parliamentary proceedings, was chosen speaker of the house of commons in the next reign. 4 Eliz. he was elected autumn reader to the society of Lincoln's Inn, to which persons of great learning were always chosen. The year following quad reader of the same society; and was again autumn reader 9 Eliz. in which year, on the 18th of June, he was called to the degree of queen's serjeant at law, and soon after knighted: and on the 14th of May, 14 Eliz.* promoted to be one of the justices of the common pleas, and two years after, viz. the 18th of Nov. 16 Eliz.† was constituted lord chief justice of the queen's bench. He was an upright judge, for though he respected every man in his proper station when he was off the bench, when he was upon it, he had no such regard for the greatest of men, so as to bias his judgment. ‡ He died May 8, 1592, after having sat on the bench 17 years, and filled it with great credit. Her majesty, Queen Elizabeth, had so just a sense of his merits, that she gave him the profits of her coinage, till he had built that noble house now remaining at Glentworth.§

* Pat. 14 Eliz. p. 10.   † Pat. 16 Eliz. p. 9.

‡ He sat as lord privy seal, and chief in the court, when secretary Davison was sentenced in the starchamber: he, collecting the censures of all the commissioners, and concurred to fine him; but with this comfortable conclusion:—That it was in the queen's power to have punished him, so her highness might be prevailed with for mitigating or remitting of the fine: and this, our judge, may be presumed no ill instrument in the procuring thereof. Five particulars, I have heard old men say, he was choice in: 1, his friend, which was always wise and equal; 2, his wife; 3, his book; 4, his secrets; 5, his expression and garb. By four things, he would say, an estate was kept; 1, by understanding it; 2, by spending not until it comes; 3, by keeping old servants; 4, by a quarterly audit. He was mindful of what is past, observant of things present, and provident for things to come.

§ He was indulgent to his servants, and charitable to the poor, as appears from his last will and testament, made July 30, 1589, wherein he gives to the former several annuities and legacies; and orders several sums of money to be distributed to the latter, and enjoins his son William, his heirs and assigns for ever, owners of his manor and lands of Glentworth, to find and maintain six poor persons, of honest conversation and religion, in the alms-house at Glentworth, with 10d. per week, a gown yearly, and three loads of ash-wood, and three loads of turf; and that the said poor people should have their dinner every Sunday, in Glentworth Hall, if able to come thither, and a house kept, else every one a penny loaf of bread. And if his son, his heirs, or assigns, make default of payment in form aforesaid, he empowers the dean and chapter of Lincoln to destrain yearly on the tenants for the money, wood, &c. and also for three pounds every month after such default of payment. He lived to a great age: his son was his sole executor, and the lord-treasurer Burleigh, and solicitor-general Egerton (after lord-chancellor) su-

He left issue, by Anne his wife, daughter of Nicholas Girlington of Normanby, in Yorkshire, Esq. one son, William, and two daughters, Isabel, the wife of Godfrey Foljamb, Esq. secondly of Sir William Bowes, Knt. thirdly of John lord Darcy; and Frances, first the wife of Sir George St. Paul of Snarford, Bart. and afterwards of Robert Rich, earl of Warwick.*

I. WILLIAM, his only son served in parliament for Grimsby, was knighted by Queen Elizabeth, and elected knight of the shire for the county of Lincoln, in the last parliament she called; and by King James I. was created a baronet in 1612. He had issue by his first wife, Lucy, eldest daughter of Sir Edward Montague of Boughton, in Northamptonshire, Knt. (ancestor to the dukes of Montague and Manchester, the earls of Sandwich and Halifax) ten sons and five daughters. She died March 1, 1599.

Sir William had by his second wife, Frances, relict of Sir Nicholas Clifford, and daughter of Sir William Drury of Hawsted, in Suffolk, Knt. lord-deputy of Ireland, and co-heir to her brother, Sir Robert Drury of the same place, Knt. two sons, Sir Christopher, hereafter mentioned, and Charles, who died in Spain; also a daughter Frances, wife of Sir Anthony Irby of Boston, in Lincolnshire, Knt. Of the sons of the first marriage, only Sir John and Edward lived to men's estate; the latter was groom of the bed-chamber to King Charles I. and married Elizabeth, daughter and sole heir of Francis earl of Berkshire, and baron Norris of Rycot, in Oxfordshire; but had only one daughter, Bridget, first the wife of Edward Sackvil, Esq. secondly of Edward earl of Dorset, by whom she had no issue; and thirdly, Montague Bertie, earl of Lindsey: James Bertie, Esq. (eldest son by the said marriage) had the title of baron Norris allowed him, by descent from his mother, at the restoration of King Charles II. and was afterwards created earl of Abingdon, and ancestor to the present earl. He died Aug. 13, 1617, and was succeeded by his eldest son by his first lady.

II. Sir JOHN WRAY, Bart. who was knighted during his father's life, and served as knight of the shire for Lincoln, in three several parliaments. He had by Grissil, daughter and heiress of Sir Hugh Bethell of Ellerton, in Yorkshire, Knt. five sons and three daughters; Sir John, Christopher, Theophilus, William, and Bethell: Frances the wife of John Hotham of Scorburgh, in Yorkshire, Bart. Gris-

pervisors, and left both of them legacies. He lies buried in the chancel of the church of Glentworth under a noble monument, whereon is the effigies, in full proportion, of a judge in his robes, with his lady by him.

* In Magnia Britannia in Lincolnshire, vol. II. p. 1453, the author, speaking of Glentworth, says, " The native place of that pious and charitable gentlewoman, Mrs. Frances Wray, daughter of Sir Christopher, lord chief justice of the king's bench: she was first married to Sir George St. Paul of this county, and then to Robert Rich, first earl of Warwick of that surname. She was a person of a shining conversation, and eminent bounty, of which, though we have not a particular account, yet we cannot but name one instead of all, which is, that she was a great benefactress to Magdalen college in Cambridge, which her father had before her much improved, by not only completing the buildings, but adding three fellowships and six scholarships. She died in the beginning of King Charles the Second's reign." In vol. VI. p. 608, he says, " She founded, in Magdalen college, one fellowship and a scholarship, and intended to have laid out 300£. in enlarging the buildings of that college, had not one Hammerton, an old servant, deceived her: she was also a great benefactress to the parish of Bedall, but in what particulars we are not informed."

sil, of Anthony Thorold of Marston, in Lincolnshire, Esq. and Theodosia of Sir Richard Barker, Knt. He was succeeded by his eldest son,

III. Sir JOHN WRAY, Bart. who married first Elizabeth, daughter of Sir Henry Willoughby of Risley, in Derbyshire, Bart. and widow of Sir Simon D'Ewes of Stow Hall, in Suffolk, Bart. and she dying without issue, he took to his second wife Sarah, daughter of Sir John Evelyn of West Dean, in Wiltshire, Knt. (who surviving him, remarried to Thomas viscount Fanshaw, and afterwards to George viscount Castleton) by whom he had an only daughter, Elizabeth, who was the wife of the honourable Nicholas Saunderson, Esq. eldest son of George lord viscount Castleton, of the kingdom of Ireland, by whom she had issue Wray Saunderson, who married Mary, eldest daughter of the earl of Rockingham, and died without issue. Elizabeth, his mother, surviving, was possessed of the Glentworth estate on the death of her father, Sir John Wray, Bart. and all his brothers dying without issue, the male line of the first marriage of Sir William, the first baronet, being extinct, the dignity descended to his heirs by the second wife, Frances, daughter of Sir William Drury, Knt. and Sir Christopher, the only surviving son of the said marriage, received the honour of knighthood from King James I.. and served in several parliaments. By his wife Albina, second daughter and co-heir to Edward Cecil, viscount Wimbleton, third son of the earl of Exeter, had issue four sons; Sir William, Edward, Sir Drury, and Cecil, who married Susanna, daughter of —— Cressey of Bigsley, in Lincolnshire, Esq. by whom he had one son, William, and one daughter, who died unmarried. William, his son, married Isabella, one of the daughters and co-heirs of John Ullithorn of Slemingford, in the county of York, Esq. by whom he had three sons; Sir John, hereafter mentioned; William, who died without issue; and Cecil, who married Frances, the daughter of —— Holmes (by whom he had one son William Ullithorn Wray, who married Frances Bromley, by whom he had two sons; Cecil, who died without issue, William-James; and five daughters, Lucy, Mary-Anne, Frances, Isabella, and Eliza.

1. Sir William Wray of Ashby, the eldest son, born about the year 1625, was advanced to the dignity of a baronet June 27, 1660, at which time he served in parliament for Grimsby, and departing this life in 1670, had issue by his wife, Olympia, daughter of Sir Humphrey Tufton, Knt. and Bart. (a younger son of John earl of Thanet) six daughters that became his co-heirs; 1, Margaret, the wife of the Rev. Dr. Jeffries, prebendary of Canterbury, brother to the lord chancellor Jeffries; 2, Tufton, of Sir James Montague, Knt. lord chief baron of the Exchequer, and brother to Charles earl of Halifax) 3, Drury, of Sir William Sanderson of Combe, in Greenwich, Bart. usher of the black rod; 4, ——, of —— Lewis, and two that died unmarried: and four sons; Sir Christopher, Edward, William, and Drury, who all died without issue.

2 and IV. Sir CHRISTOPHER, the eldest son, succeeded his father in the title and estate; and on the death of his cousin, Sir John Wray of Glentworth, succeeded in that baronetship; but dying without issue, the patent his father received from King Charles II. became extinct; and the title by the first patent, descended to his cousin,

WRAY OF GLENTWORTH, LINCOLNSHIRE.

V. Sir BAPTIST-EDWARD WRAY, son of Edward (second son of Sir Christopher Wray, Knt.) by his wife Dorothy, daughter and heiress of Hannibal Horsley, of the Isle of Wight, Esq. and widow of the honourable —— Fane, Esq. which Sir Baptist-Edward Wray dying likewise without issue, the title came to his uncle,

VI. Sir DRURY WRAY, third son of Sir Christopher, eldest son by the second venter, of the first Sir William Wray, Bart. before-mentioned; which Sir Drury Wray, Bart. was born in Lincolnshire, July 29, 1633, and became possessed of a fair estate of inheritance in Ireland, by marriage with Anne, daughter and heir of Thomas Casey, of Rathcannon, in the county of Limerick, Esq. by his wife Bridget, daughter and co-heir of Sir John Dowdall, Knt. He had issue by her three sons; Sir Christopher, William, who died during his father's life, and Sir Cecil, with several daughters. Sir Drury died the 30th of Oct. 1710.

VII. Sir CHRISTOPHER, his eldest son, succeeded to the title and estate: he was in arms for his majesty King William, at the battle of the Boyne; and afterwards in Flanders, Spain, and Portugal, in the reign of Queen Anne, being lieutenant-colonel in General Farrington's regiment, and eminently distinguished himself at the attack of Ostend. In the year 1710 he was preparing to go again for Spain, and being at Portsmouth to embark with the fleet, died there unmarried, Nov. 21, 1710. Upon his death the title and estate devolved on his only brother,

VIII. Sir CECIL WRAY, Bart. who was a captain in the same regiment with his brother, and served in Flanders, Spain, and Portugal, and high sheriff of Lincolnshire in 1720. He married Mary, daughter of Edward Harrison of Morely, in the county of Antrim in Ireland, Esq. (by Johanna his wife, daughter of the right reverend Dr. Jeremiah Taylor, bishop of Dromore, Downe, and Connor, in that kingdom) by whom he had no issue; and dying, May 1736, was succeeded in the title, and part of the estate by his cousin,

IX. Sir JOHN WRAY, Bart. eldest son of William, the only son of Cecil, the fourth son of Sir Christopher Wray, Bart. by Albina, daughter and coheir of Edward lord viscount Wimbleton, before-mentioned. He married Frances, daughter of Fairfax Norcliff of Langton, in the East Riding of Yorkshire, Esq. who died the 7th of July 1770, by whom he had issue, Sir Cecil, his successor; John, who died without issue; Mary, the wife of Sir James Innes, Bart. Isabella, of Captain John Dalton; and Frances, of Thomas Arthington, of Arthington in Yorkshire. Sir John died Jan. 26, 1752, and was succeeded in the title and estate by his eldest son,

X. Sir CECIL WRAY, Bart. who married Esther Summers.

ARMS—Azure, on a chief or, three martlets, gules.
CREST—On a wreath, an ostrich, or.
MOTTO—*Et juste et vray.*
SEAT—At Summer Castle, Lincolnshire.

WRAY OF GLENTWORTH, LINCOLNSHIRE.

TABLE 21.

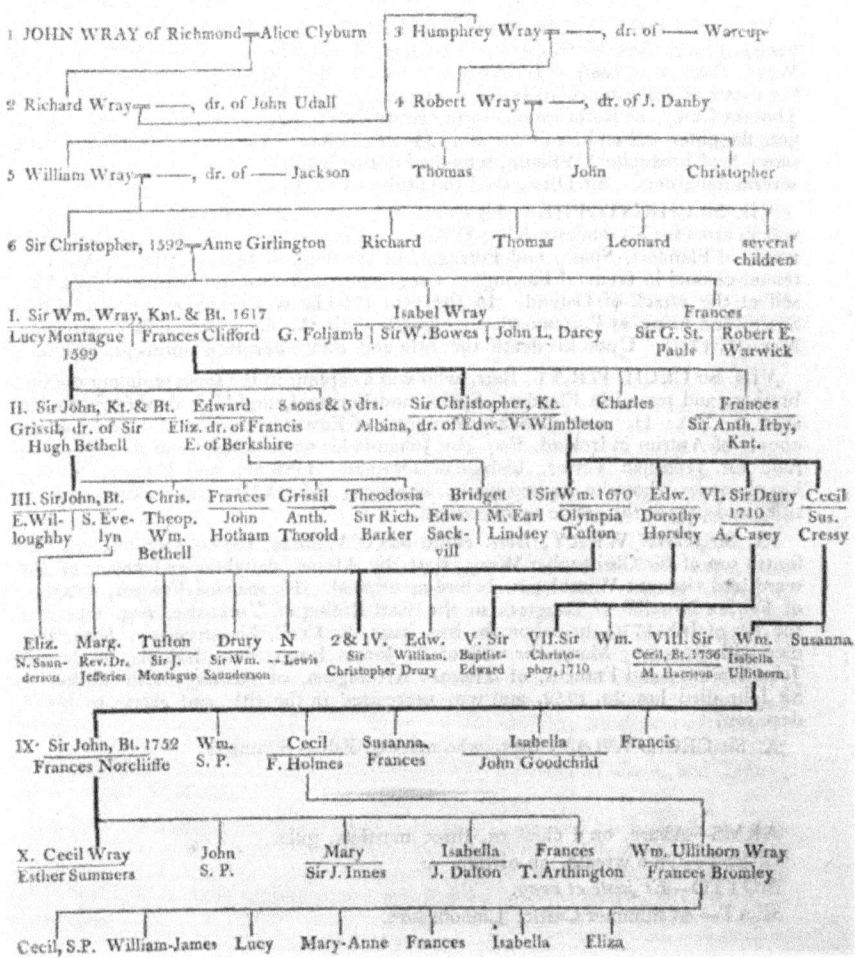

21. ENGLEFIELD of Wotton-Basset, Wiltshire.

Created Baronet Nov. 25, 1612.

THIS very ancient family, according to Camden, surnamed from the town of Englefield, or Englesfeld, in Berkshire, are said to be possessed thereof in the second year of the reign of King Egbert, 264 years before the Norman conquest, in the year 803; at which time was an oratory, as appears by a terrier of the land belonging to the same, where it is called *Cantaria de Englefeld*. This family has always been reputed of Saxon extraction, as indeed the ancient writing of the name, de Engelfelt, and their being fixed at Englefeld aforesaid, in the time of the Saxons, seem to indicate: the writing thereof has varied, according to the variations in our spellings, and is found in the ancient records of the family, Englefelt, Inglefeld, Englefyeld, Englefield, &c.

1. In several pedigrees Hasculfus de Englefyld is first mentioned as lord of Englefyld, about the time of King Canutus; and also in the fourth year of Harold I. and in the reign of Hardicnute, and died in the time of Edward the Confessor.

2. Guy, son and heir of Hasculf, lived *temp.* Wm. I. and was father of,

3. Hely de Englefeld, *temp.* Wm. II. who had issue two sons, William and Peter; the former gave the parsonage of Englefeld to the abbey of Reading, as appears by his deed without date.

4. This William had three sons; Sir William, who died without issue;

5. Sir Alan Englefeld, and Thomas.

6. William, son and heir of Sir Alan, *temp.* Rich. I. was father of

7. John Englefeld of Englefeld, who had issue,

8. Sir William Englefeld, who was one of the justices itinerant for the counties of Sussex, Southampton, and Wilts in 1255; for Norfolk and Suffolk in 1257; for Bedford, Essex, Hertford, and Kent in 1262; and for Southampton and Wilts in 1263.

9. Sir John de Englefeld was his son and heir, and died in 1276: he was also lord of Shiplake, Ascot, &c. whose son,

10. Sir William, died in France, in the reign of King Edw. I. having had issue, Sir Roger Englefeld, Andrew, and William.

11. Sir Roger was returned one of the knights for Berkshire in 1313, and dying in 1362, left, by Joan his wife, a daughter Alice, the wife of ———— Mortely, and two sons, Sir Philip and William.

12. Sir Philip, eldest son, died in 1380, and by Joan his wife, had three sons; 1, Sir John; 2, Philip, of whom hereafter; and 3, Nicholas Englefeld of Ricot,

in Oxfordshire, Esq. comptroller of the houshold to King Richard II. He married Jane, daughter and heir of John Clark of Lanynton-Gernon, and died April 1, 1415, as appears by his epitaph in Ashdon church, in Essex. He left two daughters; Cicely, the wife of William Fowler, and Sibil, of Richard Quatermains, with whom the estate of Ricot aforesaid passed to the Quatermains, and with them to the Berties, now earls of Abingdon. Sir John Englefield, the eldest son of Sir Philip, was knight of the shire for Berks, 21 Rich. II. He had posterity to the third generation; but the line expiring without issue male, the estate came to the descendants of his brother,

13. Philip, who by Alice, daughter and heir of Walter Rossale, sister and heir to Sir John Rossale, Knt.* had the Isle of Rossel, Udlington, Eton, and Yeagden, in Salop; and had issue a daughter, Philippe, the wife of Edward Brudenel of Ayno, in Northamptonshire, Esq. ancestor to the earls of Cardigan; and two sons, Philip Englefeld, Esq. and Robert, of whom hereafter. Philip, the eldest son, was high sheriff of Berkshire in 1430, and died in 1439: he lies buried in the south aisle, near the entrance into Englefield church. It is presumed he died unmarried, or without issue; for his brother

14. Robert succeeded him in the lordship of Englefeld, and died in 1473.

15. John, his eldest son, died before his father, leaving issue by Joan, daughter of John Milborn of London, one son, Thomas, heir to his grandfather. This John died Feb. 26, 1464.

16. Thomas received the honour of knighthood on the marriage of prince Arthur, son of Henry VII. In 1496 he was elected speaker of the house of commons, and in 1505 was made judge or justice of Chester, which he held till his death; and was speaker of the first parliament called by King Henry VIII. He married Margery, daughter of Sir Richard Danvers, Knt. by whom he had two sons; Richard, who died without issue, and Thomas, his heir; and four daughters, Elizabeth, the wife of Robert White; Joan, of Henry Lenham; Anne, of William Delabere, and Margaret, of John Lyngen, Esq.

17. Thomas Englefeld, eldest surviving son and heir, was high sheriff of Berkshire and Oxfordshire in 1520, and having been educated at the Middle Temple, was the next year autumnal reader; and the year after called to the dignity of the coif, by the king's letters patent, dated Dec. 3, 1524. He had 100*l. per ann.* granted him for life, and three years after was constituted one of the justices of the common pleas. He was knighted, and departed this life 1537: he married Elizabeth, daughter of Sir Robert Throckmorton of Coughton, in Warwickshire, Knt. by whom he had three sons; Sir Francis; John, hereafter-mentioned; and Thomas; and nine daughters, Anne, the wife of Humphrey Coningsby, Esq. ancestor to the earls of Coningsby; Susan, of Humphrey Burdet, Esq. Margaret, first of George Carew, Esq. and secondly of Sir Edward Saunders, Knt. lord chief baron of the Exchequer, *temp.* Eliz.

* See the partition of Sir John Rossale's lands, between Eleanor, the wife of Sir Nicholas Dagworth, and Alice, the wife of Philip de Englefeld, Dors. Claus. 4 Hen. V. N. 19, and Claus. 9 Hen. IV. M. 11. Le Neve's MSS. vol. I. p. 17.

18. Sir Francis, the eldest son, succeeded, and was high sheriff of the counties of Berkshire and Oxfordshire at the death of Henry VIII. and the first year of Edward VI. and was knighted Feb. 22, 1547. He was one of the chief officers in the princess Mary's family; and was one of those sent for by the protector and council, to forbid them hearing or saying mass in the princess's house;* but refusing to deliver such orders, and submitting rather to any punishment, he, together with Sir Robert Rochester, Sir —— Walgrave, and Dr. Francis Mallet, her chaplain, were committed to prison for many months. Upon Queen Mary's accession to the crown he was, in consideration of his faithful services, made one of her privy council, and master of the wards; and had the manor and park of Fulbrook,† in the county of Warwick, granted to him, to hold *in capite*, being part of the lands forfeited by the attainder of John Dudley, duke of Northumberland: he was likewise knight of the shire for the county of Berks in every parliament held by Queen Mary; but on Queen Elizabeth's accession to the throne, he being extremely attached to his religion, and the interest of Mary Queen of Scots, was with lord Morley, Sir Thomas Gage, Sir Thomas Shelley, and others, obliged to leave the kingdom. In 6 Eliz. he was indicted and convicted of high treason, at the parliament 29 Oct. 28 Eliz. and all his manors, lands, and vast possessions were declared forfeited to the Queen;‡ but the said Sir Francis, having by indenture of the 18th of Eliz. settled his manor and estate of Englefield on Francis, his nephew, with power notwithstanding of revoking his grant, if he, during his life, should deliver or tender to his nephew a gold ring, with intent to make void the uses of his said settlement, various disputes and points of law arose, whether the said manor and estate of Englefield were forfeited to the Queen: after various arguings, the case not being clear, the Queen, in the next parliament, scil. 35 Eliz. had a special act of parliament to confirm the attainder, and establish the forfeiture of his manors, lands, &c. By this act of power the manor and estate of Englefield, which had now been upwards of 780 years in the family, were taken from them, and forfeited to the crown. Sir Francis retired to Valladolid in Spain, where he was a bountiful benefactor to the English college;§ and being worn out with persecution and years, died, and was buried there about 1592; where his grave is shewn with respect to English travellers going thither. He married Catharine, daughter and heir of Sir Thomas Fettiplace of Compton-Beauchamp, in the vale of Berks, but dying without issue, he was succeeded by his brother,

19. John Englefield, lord of Wotton-Basset, who married Margaret, daughter of Sir Edward Fitton of Gawsworth, in Cheshire, Knt. lord president at Connaught in Ireland, and Mary his wife, daughter of Sir Guiscard Harbottle of Horton, Knt. and Jane his wife, daughter of Sir Henry Willoughby of Risley, in Derbyshire, Knt. He died April 1, 1567: his lady Aug. 29, 1612. He was succeeded by his only son,

I. FRANCIS ENGLEFIELD, Esq. of Wotton-Basset in Wilts (of which place his father was also nominated) as well as Englefield in Berkshire. In 1612 he was

* See the princess Mary's letter, in Fox, Strype's Animadversions, Goodwin's Ann. Heylin's Reformation, &c.   † Dugdale's Warwickshire, vol. II. p. 670.   ‡ See Englefield's case at large, in Coke's Reports, p. vii. fo. 11.   § Fuller's Worthies and Church History.

advanced to the dignity of a baronet. He married Jane, daughter of Anthony Browne, Esq. eldest son of Anthony lord viscount Montague, by whom he had ten children, seven sons and three daughters; 1, Thomas, who married Mary, daughter of William Wollascot of Shenfield, in Berks, Esq. but died before his father, without issue; 2, Sir Francis, his successor; 3 Sir Thomas, successor to his nephew; 4, John, who died before his father, unmarried; 5, Anthony, of White-Knights near Reading, who married Susan, daughter of —— Ryley of Oxford, Esq. She died June 2, 1664, in the 60th year of her age: her husband died about 1665, leaving issue Anthony, his son and heir, ancestor to the present baronet, of whom hereafter. The sixth son of Sir Francis Englefield, Bart. was William, who left a daughter and heir, the wife of —— Fettiplace, Esq. and died April 27, 1662; and 7, Henry, who had three wives; first Elizabeth, daughter of —— Pickford of Cornwall, by whom he had no issue; secondly, Elizabeth, daughter to Sir Walter Blount of Sodington, in Worcestershire, Bart. by whom he had Henry, who died unmarried, and three daughters; Elizabeth, the wife of Sir William Kennedy of Ireland; Mary, of Thomas Havers of Thelton, in Norfolk, Esq. and Catharine: and to his third wife he married Anne, daughter to John Huband of Ipsley, in Warwickshire, Esq. by whom he had no issue. Of the three daughters of Sir Francis, Dorothy was the wife of Sir Edward Morgan of Llanternam, in Monmouthshire, Bart. Mary, of Christopher lord Teynham; and Margaret, who had two husbands, first Hatton Berners of Whittlebury, in Northamptonshire, Esq. and secondly, Sir William Bradshaigh, Knt. a younger son of the family of Bradshaigh of Haigh, in Lancashire. Sir Francis died Oct. 26, 1631, aged 69 years; and was succeeded by his eldest surviving son,

II. Sir FRANCIS ENGLEFIELD, Bart. who received the honour of knighthood from King James I. at East Hamsted, Aug. 10, 1622. In his behalf we meet with this* indemnifying letter of King Charles I. He married Winifred, daughter and co-heir of William Brooksby of Sholeby, in Leicestershire, Esq. by whom he had one son, Sir Francis, his successor, and three daughters; Helen, the wife of Sir Charles Waldgrave, Bart. father of the first Lord Waldgrave; Mary, of Sir George Browne, K. B. and Catharine, of William Turvile of Aston-Flamvile, in Leicestershire, Esq. He died in May 1665.

III. Sir FRANCIS, his son and successor, married Honora, daughter of Henry O Bryan, earl of Thomond, by whom he had no issue: his lady surviving him became the wife of Sir Robert Howard, Knt. sixth son of Thomas, the first earl of Berkshire; whereupon the title and estate went to his uncle,

IV. Sir THOMAS ENGLEFIELD, Bart. second surviving son of Sir Francis Englefield, the first baronet; who married two wives, first Mary, daughter of Sir Henry Winchcomb of Bucklebury, in Berks, Bart. by whom he had no issue; se-

* CHARLES REX. Whereas our trusty and well-beloved Sir Francis Englefield, knight and baronet, being a recusant, is thereby subject to our laws and statutes in that case provided: these are to signify our royal will and pleasure, that no person shall at any time hereafter sue, prosecute, or implead, either by way of indictment, information, or otherwise, against the said Sir Francis, for being a recusant, or convicted by virtue of any of our laws or statutes against popish recusants, till we shall signify our pleasure to the contrary. Given under our signet, at our palace of Westminster, Dec. 6, in the 10th year of our reign.

ENGLEFIELD OF WOTTON-BASSET, WILTSHIRE.

TABLE 22.

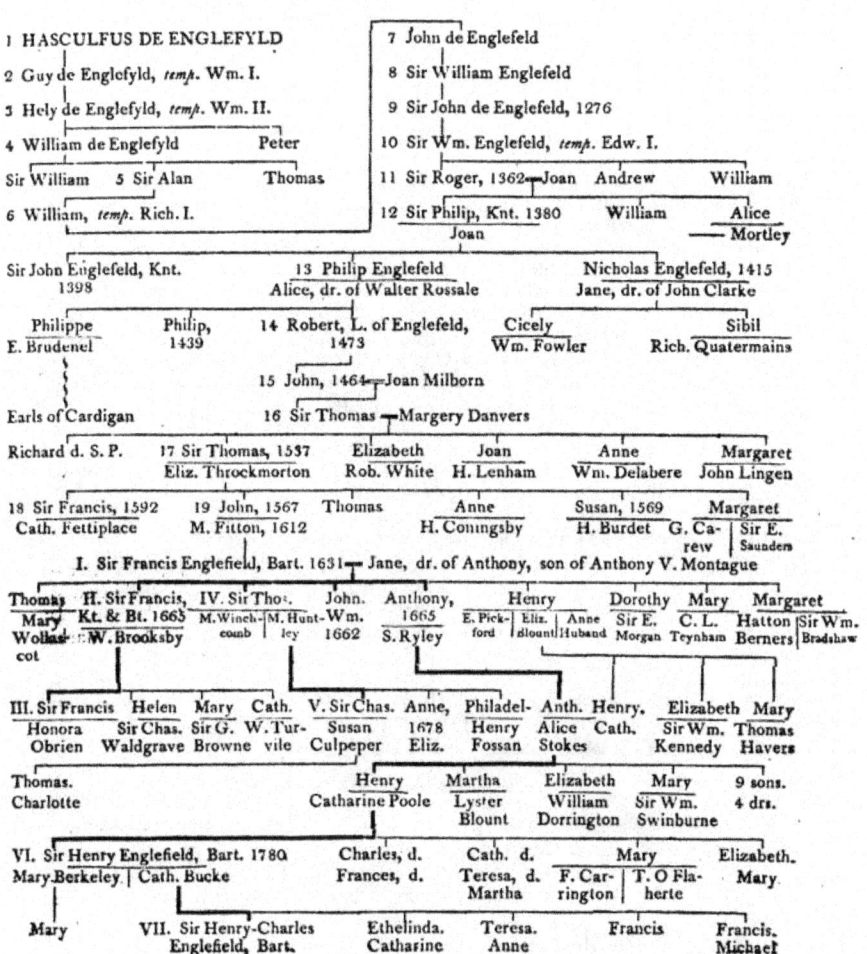

condly, Mary, daughter of George Huntley of ———, in Gloucestershire, Esq. by whom he had one son, Sir Charles, his successor, and three daughters; 1, Anne, who died unmarried in 1678; 2, Philadelphia, the wife of Henry Fossan, Gent. died S. P. and 3, Elizabeth.

V. Sir CHARLES ENGLEFIELD, Bart. succeeded his father, and married Susan, natural daughter of John lord Culpeper, by Mrs. Susan Willis (and owned by lord Culpeper, as one of his children) by whom he had a son, Thomas, and a daughter, Charlotte, which both died young. Sir Charles dying in April, 1728, was succeeded in dignity and estate by his cousin,

VI. Sir HENRY ENGLEFIELD, Bart. eldest son of Henry Englefield of White Knights, Esq. son of Anthony, who was son of Anthony, fifth son of Sir Francis Englefield, the first baronet, and Jane, his wife, daughter of Anthony Browne, viscount Montague, before-mentioned; which Anthony Englefield, Esq. (son and heir of Anthony, fifth son of Sir Francis) by Alice his wife, daughter of Thomas Stokes of London, Esq. had issue 17 children, viz. ten sons and seven daughters; of which Martha was the wife of Lyster Blount of Maple-Durham, in the county of Oxon, Esq. Elizabeth, of William Dorrington, son of Sir John Dorrington of Sussex, Knt. and Mary, of Sir William Swinburne of Capheaton, in Northumberland, Bart. the others were either nuns, or died unmarried. The ten sons died all unmarried, except Henry, the fourth son, who succeeded to his father's estate, and was of White-Knights aforesaid, and married Catharine, daughter of Benjamin Poole of London, Esq. (who surviving him, was the wife of Edward Webb of Gray's Inn, Esq.) by whom he had three sons and six daughters, Sir Henry, of whom hereafter; Charles, and Francis, who died without issue: Catharine, Teresa (both dead) Martha, first the wife of Francis Smith Carrington of Wotton Hall, in Warwickshire, Esq. and secondly of Thadee O Flaherty of the kingdom of Ireland, Esq.

VI. Sir HENRY ENGLEFIELD, Bart. in 1742, married Mary, daughter of Thomas Berkeley of Spetchley, in Worcestershire, Esq. she died in child-bed of his first child, named Mary, who likewise died in the eighth year of her age. In 1751 Sir Henry married to his second wife, Catharine, daughter of Sir Charles Bucke of Hanby Grange, in Lincolnshire, Bart. and Anne his wife, daughter of Sir Thomas Sebright of Beechwood, in Hertfordshire, Bart. by whom he had five children, viz. Henry-Charles, Ethelinda-Catharine, Teresa-Anne, Francis, and Francis-Michael. Sir Henry died May 25, 1780, and was succeeded by his son,

VII. Sir HENRY-CHARLES ENGLEFIELD, Bart.

ARMS—Barry of six, gules and argent, on a chief or, a lion passant, azure.

CREST—On a wreath, an arm couped at the elbow, vested per pale, azure and gules, holding a branch, proper. The other crest of the family is a spread eagle per pale, azure and gules, which latter is likewise on the tomb-stones in Englefield church.

SEAT—At White-Knights near Reading, in Berkshire.

22. CLARKE of Salford, Warwickshire.

Created Baronet May 1, 1617.

THIS family, about the time of William the Conqueror, being possessed of Woodchurch in Kent, were thence denominated.

Raphe, son of Anchitel de Woodchurch, is said to be custos* of the castle of London in the time of William Rufus: he was father of

3. Roger, who married Isabel, daughter of Richard Wakehurst, by whom he had

4. Thomas Woodchurch, who married Anne, daughter of Sir Walter Harvy, Kt. lord mayor of London, in the reign of King John, by whom he had

5. Sir Simon Woodchurch, Knt. who by Susan, daughter and heir of Henry Clarke, had issue two sons; 1, Simon, who married Isabel, daughter of Sir Robert Rockesly of Horton-Kirkby, near Dartford in Kent. and left only a daughter and heir, Isabel, the wife of Adrian Fortescue.

6. Clarke Woodchurch, heir to his mother's lands, married Benet, daughter and co-heir of Robert Shert of Woodchurch, and was father of

7. Peter Clarke, alias Woodchurch, who married Eleanor, daughter of Peter Rowling, and had two sons, John and Henry, batchelor in divinity, who died S. P.

8. Sir John Clarke, Knt. eldest son, was at the battle of Poitiers, and winning of Calais: he married Mildred, daughter and heir of —— Delahay, and had a son,

9. Henry Clarke, alias Woodchurch, who by Maud, daughter of — Ichingham of Ichingham, had issue,

10. Robert Clarke de Woodchurch, who married Catharine, daughter of Richard Edingham of Edingham, in Kent, by whom he had,

* Mr. Philipot, in his discourse on Woodchurch, gives an account, That Woodchurch, in the hundred of Blackburn in Kent, was the habitation of a family of as deep root in antiquity, as any in this track; who extracted their surname, as well as borrowed their first original from this place. Roger de Woodchurch is the first who does occur; who in the ancient evidences, and deeds of this place, which are not cloistered within any date, finds a frequent mention; and from him (as appears from an old pedigree of this family) did it revolve to his grand-child, Sir Simon de Woodchurch, who is in the register of those eminent persons who accompanied Edw. I. in his victorious and triumphant expedition into Scotland, where his victories entailed upon his memory the character of *Malleus Scotorum*; but in this Sir Simon, the name though not the male line, determined; for he, by matching with Susan, heir of Henry le Clerke of Munfidde, brought a large inheritance to own the signiory of Woodchurch; and his successors, in gratitude to a family which had added so much of splendour, and annexed so plentiful a revenue to his name, altered their paternal appellation from Woodchurch to Clerke; and so in all their deeds subsequent to this match have written Clerke, alias Woodchurch ever since. But as all families have their descent and period, as well as gradation and ascent, so had this; for after this manor had for so many hundred years continued in this family, which had been productive of men which had been planted in places of the greatest eminence, by which they were obliged to perform their service to their country, it came down at last to Humphrey Clerke, Esq. who about the year 1594 passed it away by sale, to Walter Harlackenden, Esq. whose daughter and heir, Debora, married Sir Edw. Hales, Bart.

11. William Clarke of Woodchurch, who had three wives; 1, Julian, daughter of —— Roberts of Glassenbury in Kent; 2, Benet, daughter of —— Ashburnham, Esqrs. by neither of which had he any issue; 3, Elizabeth, daughter and heir of William Winterborne of Sandhurst, in Kent, Esq. by whom he had two sons;

12. 1, Robert, who married the daughter of —— Hales of Halden, in Kent; but his issue failed; 2, John, who married Rabege, daughter and co-heir of Thomas Godfrey of Allington, Esq. by whom he became possessed of Fauconhurst. This William built the south aisle at Woodchurch, and was there buried in 1473.

13. Humphrey Clarke, son of John Clarke of Woodchurch, was afterwards of King's-North in Kent; and by Margaret his wife, daughter of John Many of Biddenden in Kent, Esq. had issue four daughters; Margaret, the wife of William Brockman of Newington; Elizabeth of Richard Tucke of Aldington; Joan, first of Reginald Knight, secondly of Thomas Graunt, and thirdly of Sir Walter Ascough, Knt. and Lettice, first the wife of Martyn Culpeper, M. D. and secondly of Robert Purslow: and two sons; 1, Humphrey Clarke of Buckford, in Great-Chart, who sold the Woodchurch estate;

14. 2, Walter Clarke of Ratcliffe, in Bucks, Esq. who married Elizabeth, daughter of Simon Edolph of St. Radigan's, in Kent, Esq. and had issue four sons; Simon, Martin, who died S. P. John, who married Mary, daughter of —— Randall of Dunkirk; and Humphrey, who married Cicely, daughter of —— Nicholls; and a daughter Anne, the wife of Abel Barnard.

I. SIMON CLARKE, Esq. the eldest son, was created a baronet May 1, 1617. He was a great encourager of Sir William Dugdale, in his Antiquities of Warwickshire: and paid 800*l.* to the sequestrators for his estate, *temp.* Charles I. on account of his loyalty. By Margaret, daughter and co-heir of John Alderford of Abbots-Salford in Warwickshire, Esq. (by Elizabeth, daughter of Peter Dormer of Newbottel, Esq.) He had issue five sons; Sir John, Walter, Thomas, Peter, a captain in the low countries, and Woodchurch (who married the daughter of Thomas D'Abitot of Ridmarsley, in Worcestershire, and left issue Simon) also a daughter Elizabeth. His second lady was Dorothy, daughter of Thomas Hobson of Cambridge, Gent. by whom he had no issue. She died in 1699, aged 84.

II. Sir JOHN CLARKE, eldest son and successor to Sir Simon, married Anne, daughter of John Williams of Marnhevill, Esq. and dying without issue was succeeded by his nephew,

* In Salford-Priors church, in Warwickshire, in the chancel, on the north wall, between two pillars, are several shields, with coats of arms depicted thereon, and inscriptions under them: in the midst, in a nich of the wall there is a little statue of a lady lying along, and leaning her head upon her hand, and under it—Here lyeth Walter Clarke, who died the 3 of May, 1607; and Thomas Clarke, who died the 27 of May, 1616, being second and third sonnes of Sir Simon Clarke, Knt. and Bart. by Dame Margaret, his first wife, who died the 2 of May, 1617, and is here interred, being daughter and co-heir of John Alderford of Abbots-Salford, Esq. by Elizab. Dormer, his wife. He died the 27 of Decemb. 1606, and is heere buried.

This monument was erected according to the lineal descents from father to sonne, of the Clarke's, alias Woodchurch, of Woodchurch in Kent, with their wives and cotes of armes, by Sir Simon Clarke, lord of this manor, anno 1631, in memory of his first wife, and his two sons by her, and the lady Dorothy, daughter to Thomas Hobson, his second wife. *Dugdale's Warw. vol. II. p.* 864, 865.

CLARKE OF SALFORD, WARWICKSHIRE.

III. Sir SIMON CLARKE, son of Peter Clarke, Esq. (who was killed in 1639 by lord Morley) by Elizabeth his wife, daughter of —— Corbyson of Warwickshire: he married Mercy, daughter of Philip Brace of Doverdale, in Worcestershire, Esq. by whom he had two sons, Sir Simon, his successor, and Philip (who left two sons, Sir Simon, hereafter-mentioned, and Philip) and two daughters, Elizabeth and Mary.* Sir Simon died Nov. 10, 1687, and was succeeded by his eldest son,

IV. Sir SIMON CLARKE, Bart. who married ——, daughter of the Rev. Mr. Castle, by whom he had

V. Sir SIMON PETER CLARKE, Bart. who first went to sea with the king's letter, on board the Assistance man of war, and afterwards served in several different capacities at sea; but dying without issue, was succeeded by his cousin,

VI. Sir SIMON CLARKE, Bart. eldest son of Philip, second son of Sir Simon, by Mercy, daughter of Philip Brace, Esq. before-mentioned. In May 1770, an express arrived in London from Jamaica, with an account of his death. He left two sons, Sir Simon and George, who lived in London, as a factor for many of the Jamaica planters: whether he is alive or not I have not been able to learn.

VII. Sir SIMON CLARKE, Bart. married ——, daughter of —— Houghton of the island of Jamaica, with a fortune of 100,000*l.* He resided in Jamaica, and left (I believe) two sons, Philip Houghton and Simon Houghton. He was succeeded by his eldest son,

VIII. Sir PHILIP HOUGHTON CLARKE, Bart. who died in May 1798, and was succeeded by his brother,

IX. Sir SIMON HOUGHTON CLARKE, Bart.

ARMS—Gules, three swords erected in pale, argent; hilts or.
CREST—A hand couped at the wrist, proper, holding a sword, as in the arms.
RESIDENCE—Jamaica.

---

* He was buried at Salford-Priors in Warwickshire, where, on a flat stone is this inscription:—Here lies interred the body of Sir Simon Clarke, Baronet, the only son of Peter Clarke, Esq. 2d son to Sir Simon Clarke, Knt. and Bart. who was born at Dunkirk, in Flanders, his father being then a chief commander in the wars between the Spaniards and the United Netherlands; from whence he was brought an infant to this realm, where he soon appeared to be the true heir of his father's courage and virtues; and was accordingly chosen to serve his king and country in the quality of military employment, by the right hon. Earl of Northampton, which he performed with great loyalty and integrity. He had four children by dame Mercy, the daughter of Philip Brace, Esq. of Doverdale, in the county of Worcester, viz. Sir Simon Clarke, Bart. Philip, Elizabeth, and Mercy, now living. He was brought up in the faith, constantly continued, and at last died in the communion of the church of England, Die Nov. 10, Anno Dom. 1687, Ætatis 52.

Here lies interred the body of dame Mercy Clarke, relict of Sir Simon Clarke, Bart. she departed this life the 22d day of December, Anno Domini 1698, Annoq. Ætatis 56. She was the best of wives, best of mothers, and best of friends.

CLARKE OF SALFORD, WARWICKSHIRE.

TABLE 23.

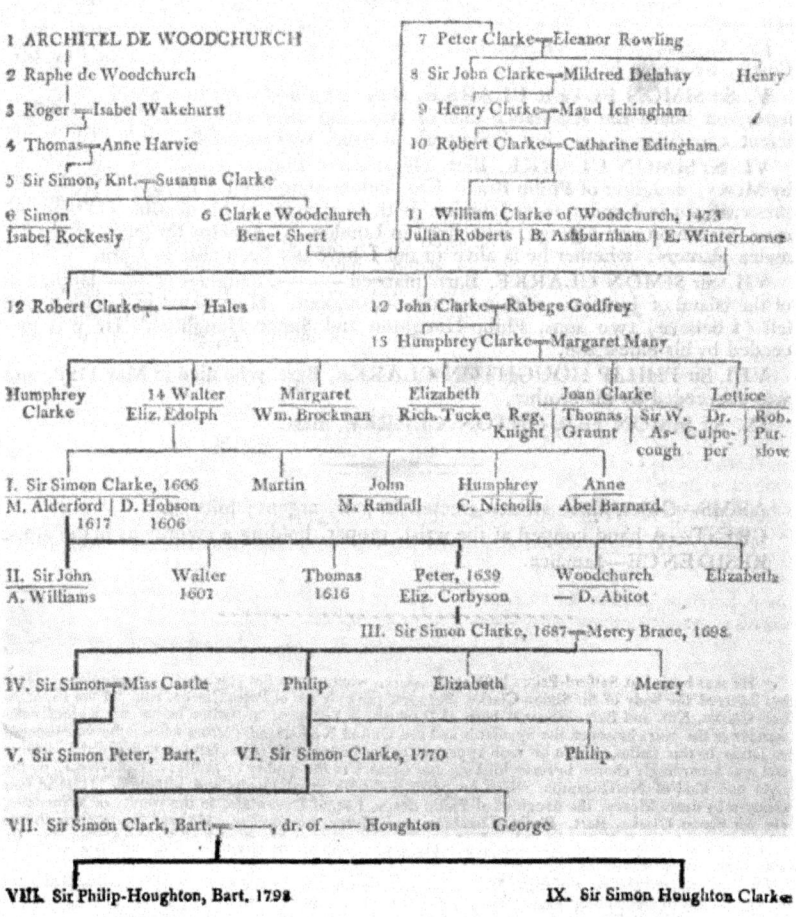

1 ARCHITEL DE WOODCHURCH
2 Raphe de Woodchurch
3 Roger — Isabel Wakehurst
4 Thomas — Anne Harvie
5 Sir Simon, Knt. — Susanna Clarke
6 Simon / Isabel Rockesly   6 Clarke Woodchurch / Benet Shert

7 Peter Clarke — Eleanor Rowling
8 Sir John Clarke — Mildred Delahay   Henry
9 Henry Clarke — Maud Ichingham
10 Robert Clarke — Catharine Edingham
11 William Clarke of Woodchurch, 1473
Julian Roberts | B. Ashburnham | E. Winterborne

12 Robert Clarke — Hales   12 John Clarke — Rabege Godfrey
13 Humphrey Clarke — Margaret Many

Humphrey Clarke | 14 Walter / Eliz. Edolph | Margaret / Wm. Brockman | Elizabeth / Rich. Tucke / Reg. Knight | Joan Clarke / Thomas Graunt | Sir W. Ascough | Dr. Culpeper | Lettice / Rob. Purslow

I. Sir Simon Clarke, 1606 / M. Alderford | D. Hobson 1617 | 1606   Martin   John / M. Randall   Humphrey / C. Nicholls   Anne / Abel Barnard

II. Sir John / A. Williams   Walter 1607   Thomas 1616   Peter, 1639 / Eliz. Corbyson   Woodchurch — D. Abitot   Elizabeth

III. Sir Simon Clarke, 1687 — Mercy Brace, 1698.

IV. Sir Simon — Miss Castle   Philip   Elizabeth   Mercy

V. Sir Simon Peter, Bart.   VI. Sir Simon Clarke, 1770   Philip

VII. Sir Simon Clark, Bart. — ——, dr. of —— Houghton   George

VIII. Sir Philip-Houghton, Bart. 1798.   IX. Sir Simon Houghton Clarke

23. BOYNTON of BARMSTON, YORKSHIRE.

Created Baronet May 25, 1618.

THIS is a family of very great antiquity, and the first mentioned in the pedigree is Bartholomew de Boynton, who was seized of the manor of Boynton, from whence the family were denominated: he lived in 1067, and was succeeded in his estate by his son Walter, who lived in the time of William Rufus, 1091. Some time after we meet with

1. Bruis de Boynton, a witness with the prior of Tinmouth, and others to a donation in frank Almoigne, made by Ranulf de Merley, in 1129, confirming to the monks of Durham, Morvic, with the appurtenances, that his father William de Merley had before granted them. He was succeeded by

2. Sir Ingram de Boynton, Knt. who had issue,

3. Sir William, his son and heir, living in the reign of Edw. I. father to another

4. Ingram de Boynton, who left issue, by Margaret his wife, daughter of Sir Walter Grindal, Knt.

5. Walter, his son and heir, who was knighted in 1356, being in the service of Edward prince of Wales, in Britanny, had the king's letters of protection, dated the 8th of Feb. the same year. He had issue,

6. Sir Thomas Boynton of Aclam, who married Catharine, daughter and coheir of Sir Gifford Rossels of Newton under Gundsbrough, in Cleveland, and is the same person who, jointly with Thomas de Ingelby, had a grant from King Edw. III. in the 39th year of his reign, for free warren, in Aclam in Cleveland, Aresome, Rouseby, Neuton, Swaynton, and Boynton, in Yorkshire. He was succeeded by his son,

7. Thomas de Boynton,* who was likewise a knight, and by Margaret his wife, daughter of —— Sawcock, left a son,

8. Henry de Boynton, son and heir of Sir Thomas, was suspected to be in the interest of Henry Percy, earl of Northumberland, and his son, who had taken arms against King Henry IV. for in the fourth year of the reign of that prince, when the battle of Shrewsbury was fought, John Wokerington, Gerald Heron, and John Mitford, were commissioned to tender an oath to this Henry de Boynton and others, to be true to the king, and renounce Henry earl of Northumberland and his adherents; yet three years after this he was concerned with the said earl, Thomas Mow-

---

* Contemporary with the said Sir Thomas was Robert de Boynton, governor of Berwick Castle; and in 1 Rich. II. a commissioner, among others, for receiving at Berwick 4000 marks from Robert king of Scots (in part of 56,000 marks) which he had orders to pay to William de Melton, chevalier, mayor of the city of York.

bray, earl marshal, Richard Scroope, archbishop of York, and others, who had taken arms in 7 Henry IV. and flying to Berwick, was apprehended, on the surrender thereof to the king, and with seven others executed, being then a knight. He had issue, by Elizabeth his wife (afterwards the wife of John Felton) two daughters; Elizabeth, the wife of Thomas Marton of Marton, in Cleveland; and Jennet, of John Wydisworth: likewise two sons, Thomas de Boynton, who died without issue, and

9. Walter; other pedigrees say, William, temp. Henry VI. who by his wife Jane, daughter of Simon Harding, left issue,

10. Sir Thomas Boynton, Knt. his son and heir; who by marriage with Isabel, daughter to Sir William Normanvile of Kilnwick, in Yorkshire, Knt. had issue two sons; Henry, hereafter-mentioned, and Sir Christopher, progenitor to the Boyntons of Sadbury, in the liberty of Richmond in Yorkshire, the eldest line whereof expired in one daughter and sole heir, Isabel, the wife of Henry, second son to Sir William Gascoigne of Gawthrop, Knt. and from a second son of this branch descended the Boyntons, who were settled at Willerby, and afterwards at Rawcliff; which likewise expired in heirs females, one of whom was mother to Boynton Appleyard, Esq. who bears the name of Boynton-Boynton, by right of substitution and adoption.

11. Henry Boynton, Esq. son and heir of Sir Thomas, beforementioned, and elder brother to Sir Christopher, increased his fortune very considerably, by marrying Margaret; daughter and co-heir of Sir Martin del See, lord of Barmston in Yorkshire, by Margaret his wife, daughter and co-heir of Christopher Spencer; for thereby he enjoyed a large estate of her inheritance, and principally the manor of Barmston, anciently possessed by John Mounceux; whose daughter and heir, Margaret, married to Bryan at See, brought it to Sir Martin del See, son of the said Bryan; and from the aforesaid marriage with Boynton, it accrued to this family, and has been their principal seat ever since. The said Henry Boynton had a daughter Isabel, the wife of Bryan Tonstall; and four sons, Thomas, Martyn, Cuthbert, and Henry.

12. Thomas Boynton, Esq. the eldest, succeeded at Barmston and Aclam, and married Cicely, daughter to Sir James Strangeways of Smeton, in Yorkshire, Knt. had issue two daughters; Anne, the wife of Robert Haldenby of Haldenby; Jane, of Thomas Goldsborough of Goldsborough, Esqrs. and a son,

13. Matthew Boynton, Esq. who had a grant for life from King Henry VIII. in the 29th year of his reign, of the office of steward of all his lordships, &c. in the counties of Lincoln and York, that were forfeited by the attainder of William Wood, late prior of Bridlington. He married Anne, daughter of Sir John Bulmer, Knt. and had issue a son Thomas, and three daughters; Margaret, the wife of William Frobysher; Anne, of William, fourth son of Richard Norton of Norton, in Yorkshire, and Cecily, maid of honour to Queen Elizabeth, and afterwards the wife of Edmund Norton, third son of Richard.

14. Thomas Boynton, Esq. son and heir of Matthew, was sheriff of Yorkshire in 18 Eliz. and afterwards had the honour of knighthood from the queen, at Hampton Court, in Jan. 1577. He had two wives, Frances, daughter of Francis Frobysher of

Doncaster, by whom he had his son and heir, Francis, and Anne, the wife of Francis Vaughan of Sutton-Darwent, in Yorkshire. By his second lady, Alice, daughter of Nicholas Tempest of Holmeside, in the bishoprick of Durham, Esq. he had no issue; and she, afterwards marrying Sir Christopher Place of Halnaby, in Yorkshire, Knt. had, among other issue, Dorothy (at length sole heir of that family) who was the wife of the aforesaid Francis Boynton, Esq. eldest son and heir of Sir Thomas, which

15. Sir Francis was sheriff of Yorkshire in 28 Eliz. and received the honour of knighthood at York the 17th of April, 1603, when King James passed through that city in his way from Scotland. He left issue by the said Dorothy, daughter and co-heir of Sir Christopher Place, Knt. and Alice his wife, relict of Nicholas Tempest of Holmeside, and Anne his wife, daughter of John Marley, Esqrs. a daughter Dorothy, the wife of Sir Henry Bellingham of Levinz, Knt. and a son,

I. Sir MATTHEW BOYNTON, who was knighted by King James I. at Whitehall, May 9, 1618; and on the 25th of May following was advanced to the dignity of a baronet. He served in parliament for the borough of Heydon in the reign of King Charles I. and was one of those the rebels chiefly entrusted in Yorkshire; for when Sir John Hotham and his son, captain Hotham, were contriving the surrender of Hull to the king, this Sir Matthew Boynton had orders from the parliament, to have an eye on them, and endeavour to preserve the town if he perceived it in danger; pursuant to which he contrived the seizing him; and colonel Boynton, his son, actually took Sir John prisoner. He died in the year 1646, and by Frances his wife, daughter of Sir Henry Griffith of Agnes-Burton, Knt. and Bart. (and heir to her brother, Sir Henry) had seven sons and four daughters; Mary died unmarried; Dorothy was wife to John Anlaby of Etton, in Yorkshire; Elizabeth, of John Heron, son of Richard Heron of Bockenfield, in Northumberland; and Margaret, of John Robinson of Rither, in Yorkshire, Esqrs. Sir Francis, successor to the title and estate; Matthew married Isabel, daughter of Robert Stapleton of Wighill, Esq. and was slain at Wigan, in the advance of the army of King Charles II. out of Scotland, towards Worcester. He left issue two daughters, one of them was the wife of the nominal duke of Tirconnel, when colonel Talbot, and the other to the celebrated earl of Roscommon; Marmaduke; 4, John; 5, Gustavus; 6, Cornelius, and 7, Charles, all died unmarried.

II. Sir FRANCIS BOYNTON, Bart. son and heir of Sir Matthew, aged 47 years, 1665, married Constance, daughter of William viscount Say and Seal, who bore him a daughter Frances, the wife of George Whitchote of Harpswell, in Lincolnshire, Esq. and three sons; 1, William; 2, Nathaniel, who died unmarried; 3, Henry, rector of Barmston, who married first Dorothy, daughter of Alexander Amcotts, of the bishoprick of Durham, Esq. and had issue Sir Francis Boynton of Beverley, of whom hereafter; and Elizabeth, who died young. He married secondly Margaret, daughter of —— Robinson of Newton-Garth, in the east riding of Yorkshire, Esq. who died without issue. William Boynton, Esq. eldest son and heir apparent to Sir Francis, died before his father, about the year 1689; and by Elizabeth his wife, daughter and co-heir of John Bernard of Kingston upon Hull, Esq. left issue Sir Griffith Boynton, Bart. successor to his grandfather, and a daughter Constance, the wife of Richard Kirshaw, D. D. rector of Ripley in Yorkshire.

III. Sir GRIFFITH BOYNTON of Burton-Agnes, Bart. married first Adriana, daughter of Mr. John Sykes, merchant at Dort: she died in 1725, but had no issue. He married in Nov. 1728, to his second lady, a daughter of John White of Wallingwells, in Northamptonshire, Esq. He died Dec. 22, 1731, without issue; and his lady Oct. 8, 1732; and was succeeded in dignity and estate by his cousin, Sir Francis Boynton, Bart. only son of Henry, rector of Barmston, who was third son of Sir Francis Boynton, Bart. beforementioned; which

IV. Sir FRANCIS BOYNTON, Bart. was elected member of parliament for Headon in Yorkshire, and one of the members of the house of commons who, by order of the house in April 1736, was appointed to congratulate her late majesty Queen Caroline, on the nuptials of the prince of Wales with the princess of Sax-Gotha: he was also appointed by the house of commons, to congratulate their royal highnesses the prince and princess of Wales upon the birth of prince Edward; and was recorder of Beverley. He married Frances, daughter of James Heblethwayte of Norton, in the east riding of Yorkshire, Esq. (by Bridget his wife, daughter of Sir William Cobb of Beverley, in Yorkshire, Knt.) by whom he had issue three sons and three daughters; Sir Griffith, his successor, Francis, and William: Constance, Adriana, and Dorothy. This Sir Francis died Sep. 16, 1739, and was succeeded in dignity and estate by his eldest son

V. Sir GRIFFITH BOYNTON, who married Anne, second daughter of Thomas White of Wallingwells, in the county of Nottingham, Esq. which lady died in childbed of their only issue, Sir Griffith, Feb. 22, 1745. Sir Griffith died at Agnes-Burton in Yorkshire, Oct. 22, 1761; and was succeeded in dignity and estate by

VI. Sir GRIFFITH BOYNTON, who married May 9, 1762, Charlotte, eldest daughter of Dr. Topham: she died in childbed Sep. 9, 1767, and the child soon after. Sir Griffith married to his second lady Aug. 8, 1768, Mary, daughter of Sir James Heblethwayte; and died Jan. 12, 1778. He was succeeded by his son,

VII. Sir GRIFFITH BOYNTON, Bart. who married Aug. 7, 1790, Anna-Maria, daughter of Robert Parkhurst of Cotesby, in Northamptonshire, Esq.

ARMS—Or, a fess between three crescents, gules; though the fess was formerly charged with a lion passant, or.

CREST—On a wreath, a goat passant, sable, guttee d'argent, beard, horns, and hoofs, or.

MOTTO—*Il tempo passa.*

SEAT—At Burton-Agnes in the east riding of Yorkshire.

BOYNTON OF BARMSTON, YORKSHIRE.

TABLE 24.

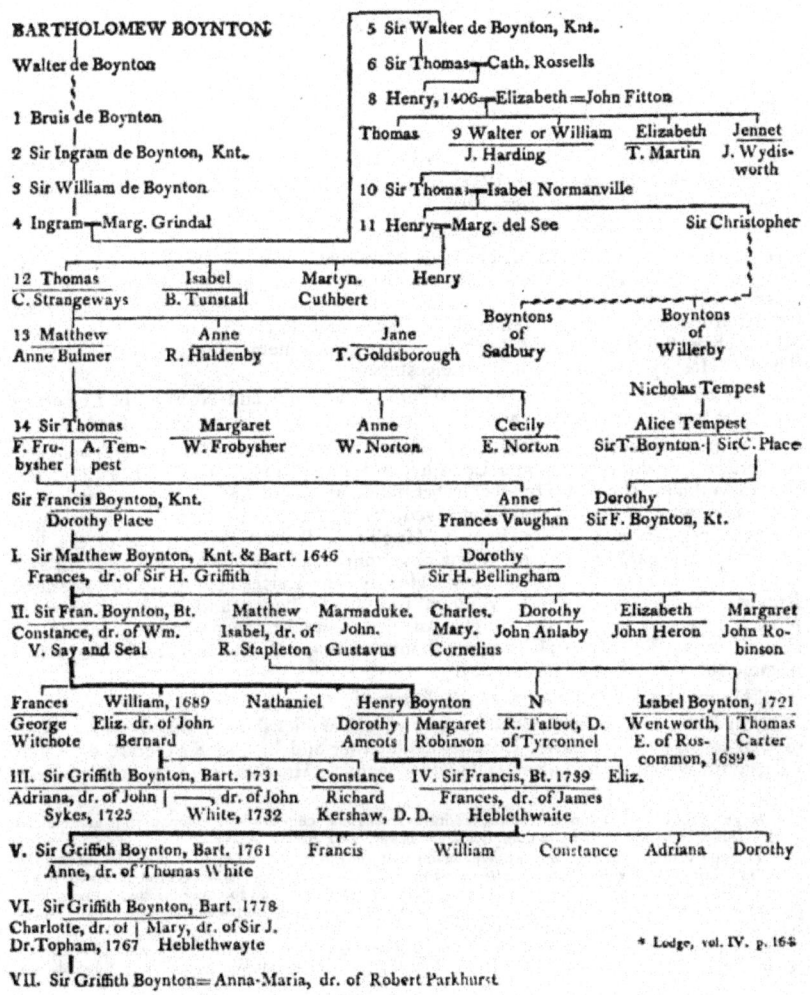

* Lodge, vol. IV. p. 164.

24. BURDET of BRAMCOTE, WARWICKSHIRE.

Created Baronet Feb. 25, 1618.

HUGH de Burdet came into England with William the Conqueror in 1066:* he left issue,

2. William Burdet, lord of Louseby in Leicestershire, who founded the priory at Aucote near Seckingdon, in Warwickshire, temp. Henry II. to expiate the murder of his wife.† He was succeeded by his son,

3. Hugh, who married Matilda de Sumeri, by whom he had

4. Sir William, who with Richard de Mandeville and the sheriff of the county, were in 36 Henry III. commissioners for assessing a tollage upon all the king's demesnes within the county of Warwick and Leicester. By Alice ———, his wife, he left three sons; Hugh, father of William; Sir Richard, and William; from whom came the Burdets of Allington, whose heir general, Jane, was the wife of Thomas Harvey of Elmsthorpe, in Leicestershire.

5. Sir Richard, the second son, was lord of Louseby and Newton in Leicestershire: he was living in 1226, and left four sons; James, John, Sir Richard, and

6. William Burdet of Louseby, who was living in 1258: he had four sons; 1, Richard, of Newton-Burdet and Louseby, in Leicestershire, who died in 1278, (father to William, slain at Dundee in Scotland, in 1283; father to John, father to Elizabeth, who as heir general conveyed, by marriage, the manor of Louseby to her husband, Thomas Ashby, Esq. 2, Hugh; 3, Robert Burdet, one of the justices for the gaol-delivery at Warwick, from 1283 to 1292: he died without issue in 1303, and left his manor of Huncote in Leicestershire to his nephew, Robert, hereafter named; 4, William Burdet of Shepey and Cosby, in Leicestershire: he was one of the knights of that shire in the parliament held in 25 Edw. I. whose heir general, Agnes, about the reign of Richard II. or Henry IV. became the wife of William Shepey.

7. Hugh, the second son, was the father of

8. Sir Robert, who first settled at Arrow in Warwickshire, a manor which came to him in right of his wife, Elizabeth, daughter and heir to Sir Gerard de Camville, with whom he had also divers other lands.‡ He died in 1333, and left issue

---

* Hugo de Burdet nobilissimus Normannus intravit Angliam cum Gulielmo Conquestori anno salutis 1066. Dus Manorii de Louseby in com. Leic. *R. Brooke, York Herald, p.* 211.

† The said William, being a devout man, made a journey to the Holy Land, in order to subdue the infidels: his steward, in his absence, attempted the chastity of his lady, who resisted him with scorn. On his master's arrival in England the steward went to meet him, and to cover his own crimes complained of her looseness with others, which so enraged her husband, that when she approached to receive him with joyful embraces, he mortally stabbed her.

‡ In 14 Edw. II. he served in parliament as one of the knights of the shire for the county of Warwick, and in 17 Edw. II. was one of the commissioners for the gaol-delivery at Warwick; in 18 Edw. II. one

Gerard and Robert Burdet, both knights; which Sir Robert was of Burton, super Dunsmore, in Warwickshire, in right of his wife, Elizabeth, daughter and co-heir to Robert Garshale of Ibstoke and Huncote both in Leicestershire, by gift of his father, whose posterity continued lords thereof, in the male line, till Henry IV.th's time, that the heir-general, Elizabeth, marrying Sir Humphrey Stafford of Grafton, in Worcestershire, Knt, brought them to that family.

9. Gerard had his principal seat at Arrow, so called from the adjacent river, (probably from its swiftness, as the Tigris of the ancients). In 20 Edw. III. he served in the wars of France, being then of the retinue to Maurice de Berkeley, an English baron, and departed this life about 1259, leaving by Eleanor his wife (sister and heir to John Veale of Compton-Scorfin, in Warwickshire).

10. John, his son and heir, under age, the custody of whose lands, together with his marriage, was granted in 1359, by Sir Richard Stafford, Knt. to Richard de Clodshale of Saltby, in Warwickshire. By the death of John de Veale, his uncle, without issue, in 1360, he was found to be one of his cousins and next heirs; and in 1 Richard II. being then a knight, served in parliament for Warwickshire. In 2 Richard II. he was constituted one of the commissioners of the said county, for taxing a subsidy, at that time granted the king; and married Margaret, daughter of Thomas Fitton of Gausworth, in Cheshire, Esq. was succeeded by his son,

11. Sir Thomas Burdet, Knt. a person honoured with divers great employments.* He left issue by Anne his wife, daughter and co-heir of John Waldief,

12. Nicholas, his son and heir, who had summons to attend the king in person, 7 Henry V. for defence of the realm, and received of John Salvaine, treasurer at war to the duke of Bedford, for himself, two men at arms, and seven archers, 29*l*. 11*s*. 6*d*. for one quarter's wages. In 1425 he was one that defended the town of St. James de Beveron in Normandy, upon the frontiers of Britanny, on the siege thereof, by Arthur earl of Richmond and Yverie, constable of France; and making a couragious sally, seven or eight hundred of the enemy were slain, fifty taken prisoners, with eighteen standards and one banner. In 15 Henry VI. he was a knight, and was slain at the battle of Pontoise, 1440. He was chief butler of Normandy, and governor of Eurieux: by his wife Joan, cousin and heir of Henry Bruin (with whom he had the manor of Bramcote in Warwickshire) he had

of the knights for Leicestershire: in 19 Edw. II. again knight for Warwickshire; as likewise in 1, 2, and 4 Edw. III. for Leicestershire; in the former of which years he had free warren granted to him and his heirs in all his demesne lands at Arrow and Sekingdon in Warwickshire, as also for those at Huncote and Mithe in Leicestershire, by charter bearing date at Worcester, Dec. 25. He was, before the end of the following year of the last-mentioned king, constituted sheriff for both counties; being also a commissioner for the goal delivery at Warwick. In 7 Edw. III. he was again commissioner for the goal-delivery: also by a special patent, bearing date at York, Feb. 4. the same year, had licence to impark his woods at Arrow, and so to hold them to himself and his heirs for ever.

* He was constituted one of the commissioners for the array in 5 Rich. II. served in parliament as one of the knights of the shire for the county of Warwick, in 16 Rich. II. as also in 2 and 8 Henry IV. In 3 Henry V. he was made sheriff for the counties of Warwick and Leicestershire. In 6 Henry V. he was again one of the commissioners of array in Warwickshire; and the year following jointly entrusted with the sheriff and others, to treat with the people for a loan of money to the king; and was in commission for assessing and collecting a subsidy in 9 Henry V.

13. Thomas Burdet, Esq. his son and heir, who in 1450 was employed in his country about levying the subsidy then granted to the king: he was a person of great note and figure there, and from the 7th to the 14th of Edw. IV. was in commission for conserving the peace; but in 1477 he incurred the king's displeasure, for his affection to the duke of Clarence: so strict were the eyes and ears of his enemies, that an advantage was soon taken to take away his life; for hearing that the king had killed a white buck in his park at Arrow, which he set much store by, he passionately wished the horns in his belly that moved the king so to do; for which words he was arraigned and convicted of high treason, upon inference of a mischievous meaning to the king himself, and was beheaded in 1477. After his death there was a great contest for his manor of Arrow and other lands, between Richard Burdet, his son, by Agnes, daughter of John Waldeif, a former wife, that had been, for nearness of kindred, divorced from him in 1464, and John Burdet, his son, by Margaret, daughter of John Rodney: for the said Thomas (by licence obtained from the crown) had alienated his lands to his younger son, of which he became afterwards so sensible, that as he was drawn from the Tower to the place of his execution, espying his eldest son in Westcheap, over against St. Thomas Becket's hospital (now Mercers chapel) he caused himself to be staid, and there asked his said son forgiveness, and acknowledging the wrong he had done him, concluded that to be the cause of God's vengeance then against him. But in the suit afore-mentioned John, the younger son prevailed; for Margaret, his mother, held her estate therein for life, and became the wife of Thomas Woodhill: notwithstanding which the said Richard Burdet prevailed with his brother John, and also with the said Margaret and her husband, to levy a fine of the manor of Arrow, Compton-Scorfin, with other lands, and give him possession thereof; with the remainder to Thomas, his son; and for want of issue by him, to Robert, his other son, and the heirs of his body; and for his want of such issue, to the right heirs of the said Richard for ever. Which two sons died young, during their father's life, and Richard himself, by Joyse, daughter of Sir Simon Montfort, Knt. (who survived him, and afterwards was the wife of Sir Hugh Conway, treasurer of Ireland) left no heir male.*

* By this circumstance the manor of Arrow, and the rest of the entailed estate, was likely to be transferred into another family, by Anne, the daughter and heir of Richard. The said John exhibited a petition in parliament to King Henry VIII. wherein, the better to ingratiate himself, he set forth his adherence to Henry duke of Bucks, in the behalf of Henry earl of Richmond (afterwards King Henry VII.) against King Richard III. alledging, that upon the miscarriage of that duke, in his said attempts, he himself was taken at Gloucester, and there kept prisoner; and moved, that the said fine should be made void, so that himself and his heirs might enjoy that estate in such sort, as he and they should and ought to have done had it not been levied. This John Burdet was one of the retinue to Sir Edward Howard, admiral, in 4 Henry VIII. for scouring the seas on the southern coast of England, and in no small favour at court; for his petition took such an effect, that he pursued his claims to the said lordship, and all other the lands whereof his father was seized, against Edward Conway, and Anne his wife, daughter and heir to the aforesaid Richard Burdet, as if there had been no such entail as before specified; which suits continued many years, to a very great expence, and ended not in the said Sir John's days, who died in 1529; for Thomas, his son, and Edward Conway and Anne, his wife, submitted to the arbitration of Clement, then abbot of Evesham; William, prior of Worcester; Roger Winter, and John Russel, Esqrs. whose award did not give satisfaction; for about two years after they made choice of Sir Anthony Fitzherbert, and Sir William Shelley, Knts. then justices of the common pleas, to determine the business; who decided, that the said Thomas Burdet and his heirs should have the manors of Bramcote, Seking-

BURDET OF BRAMCOTE, WARWICKSHIRE.

The said Thomas, by his last wife had five sons; Sir John, Nicholas, Robert, George, and Edward; and two daughters, Joan, and Isabel.

14. John, the eldest son, married Anne, daughter of William Harewell, in Warwickshire, by whom he had four sons; Thomas, John, William, and George; and four daughters, Joan, Osburna, wife of George Dalston, in Gloucestershire; Elizabeth, of John Copeland; and Anne, of John Hull. He died in 1529, and was succeeded by his eldest son,

15. Thomas Burdet, who died about the 31st of Henry VIII. leaving, by Mary his wife, daughter of Sir Robert Throckmorton, Knt. Robert Burdet, Esq. his son and heir; Clement, a clergyman; Humphrey, William, and Ethelbert; also three daughters, Blanche, the wife of —— Samborne; Catharine, of —— Ludlow; and Eleanor, of —— Willenscote; which

16. Robert was elected one of the knights of the shire for the county of Warwick, and died in 1548: by Elizabeth his wife, daughter to Sir Thomas Cockaine of Ashburne, in Derbyshire, Knt. he had issue; Thomas Burdet, his heir, Francis, George, William, student in the Middle Temple, and John.

17. Thomas died July 15, 1591, and having married Bridget, daughter of Thomas Curson of Croxhall, in Derbyshire, Esq. had issue Robert, Thomas, Lawrence, and John; also three daughters, Dorothy, the wife of John Barwell of Sekingdon, Gent. Anne, of —— Sheffield, Gent. and Mary; and was succeeded by

18. Robert Burdet, Esq. his son and heir, who married Mary, daughter of Dr. Thomas Wilson, dean of Durham, one of the principal secretaries of state to Queen Elizabeth; and died March 27, 1603.* They had issue Thomas, and six daughters; Bridget, the wife of William Whelpdale; Anne, of John Bowes of Elford, in Staffordshire, Esq. Mary, of Richard Frampton, Esq. Elizabeth, of Anthony Hutton of Penrith, in Cumberland, Esq. son of Sir William Hutton, Knt. Lettice, of Richard Skelton of Armenthwaite, in Cumberland, Gent. and Lucretia, who died unmarried.

don, Compton-Scorfin, and Welmecote, in the county of Warwick; Longdon-Travers, Little Longdon, Arminscote, and Newbold in Worcestershire, with Larkstoke, Myculton, Pebworth, Quinton, and Kyrmscote, in Gloucestershire; as also 200 marks in money: and the said Edward Conway, and Anne his wife, and their heirs, the manor of Arrow, with those of Lodington, Kingley, Alymore, and Camylhill, in Warwickshire; Belne, Hoblench, Clodshall, Upton Warryn, Upton upon Severn, with Beeley and Elmbrigge, in Worcestershire.

* A fine mural monument was erected to his memory, representing (under a canopy supported by two pillars) the figures of a gentleman in armour, and his lady in the dress of the times, kneeling on cushions, with a table between them; behind him three sons, habited like their father, in armour; behind her the figures of as many daughters, in praying postures, habited in the dress of the times; and underneath a latin inscription in Roman capitals, importing that he was in the commission of the peace, and a gentleman of piety and probity, a faithful patriot to his country, a friend to the poor; and that his wife, surviving him, raised the said monument. She lies buried in St. Andrew's choir, adjoining to the parochial church of Penrith in Cumberland, having this incription:—Here lyeth Mary, daughter of Thomas Wilson, secretary of state to Queen Elizabeth, who was first married to Robert Burdet of Bramcourt, in the county of Warwick, Esq. by whom she had Sir Thomas Burdet, Bart. and several sons and daughters: and was afterwards married to Sir Christopher Lowther, of Lowther in the county of Westmoreland, Knt. Her daughter, Elizabeth Burdet, married Anthony Hutton, of Penrith in the county of Cumberland, Esq. with whom she lived and died the last day of May, A. D. 1622.

I. THOMAS BURDET, son of the said Robert, born Aug. 3, 1585, was advanced to the dignity of a baronet. He married Jane, daughter and heir of William Frauncys, Esq. nephew and heir to John Frauncys of Formark, Esq. which seat has, since that time, been the chief residence of the family. He was esteemed a very charitable and good man: his lady was a correspondent with some of the most eminent divines, particularly the famous archbishop Sheldon, who found an agreeable sanctuary at Bramcote, during the exile of King Charles II. She survived her husband: they had three sons; 1, Sir Frauncis, his successor; 2, Robert, a merchant and alderman of the city of London (who, by Mary his wife, daughter of alderman Wright, left issue) 3, Leicester, who died at Aleppo, unmarried. Likewise seven daughters; Catharine, the wife of Sebright Repington of Amington in Warwickshire, Esq. Isabel, of Francis Merick, merchant, of London; Lettice, of William Houncel, merchant, of London; Mary, of George Bowes of Elford, in Staffordshire, Esq. Jane, betrothed to Gilbert Thacker of Repton, in Derbyshire, Esq. Dorothy died unmarried, and Bridget was the wife of Thomas, son and heir of Sir George Gresley of Drakelow, Bart. He was succeeded by his son,

II. Sir FRAUNCIS BURDET, Bart. who was born Sep. 10, 1608, and married Elizabeth, daughter of Sir John Walter, Knt. lord chief baron of the Exchequer, a lady of exemplary prudence and behaviour. The building and endowing the church of Formark is a lasting monument of their piety and regard for religion: it was consecrated in the year 1662. She died April 17, 1701, in the 88th year of her age; and his death and sepulture is commemorated by the following inscription on a plain stone upon the ground in the aforesaid church:—

> The body of Sir Frauncis Burdet, baronet, founder of this chapel, is here interred; who dy'd the 30th of Decemb. MDCXCVI. in the 89th year of his age. Was 61 years husband to Elizabeth, daughter of Sir John Walter, lord chief baron; by whom he had nine children, all surviving him.

These were, 1, Sir Robert, his successor; 2, Francis, who died unmarried, the 18th of April, 1709; 3, Walter, who was of the Inner Temple, London, and afterwards of Knowl-hill in Derbyshire, who died unmarried; and during the pregnancy of Elizabeth, wife of his nephew, Robert Burdet, Esq. (as shewn hereafter) took upon himself the title of baronet: 4, John, late of Donisthorpe, in the counties of Derby and Leicester, who married Anna, the daughter of Mr. Muggleston, but died without issue; 5, Thomas, who died unmarried, Aug. 12, 1698: and four daughters; Dorothy, who died unmarried Sep. 4, 1718; Mary, born Jan. 23, 1643, and died April 15, 1701; Elizabeth, the wife of Edmund Jodrell of Eardsley and Twamlow in Cheshire, Esq. and Jane, of Edward Hopegood, Esq.

III. Sir ROBERT BURDET, Bart. born Jan. 11, 1640, was before his father's death, elected knight of the shire for the county of Warwick in two parliaments, in the reign of Charles II. Likewise for the city of Litchfield in 1 & 2 W. M. and 7 W. III. He died the 13th of Jan. 1715-6, in the 76th year of his age, having had three wives; 1, Mary, only daughter of Gervase Pigot of Thrumpton, in Nottinghamshire, Esq. and co-heir of John St. Andrew of Goteham, in the same county, Esq. who died in the 27th year of her age, Aug. 31, 1688 (leaving an only daughter, Elizabeth, the wife of Charles Jenens of the Middle Temple, and of Gospall in Leicestershire, Esq.) 2, Magdalen, daughter of Sir Thomas Aston of Aston, in Cheshire, Bart. and lastly Mary, daughter to Mr. Thomas Brome of Croxhall, in Derbyshire, who survived him without issue; but by Magdalen, his second wife, he had four sons and four daughters; Magdalen, Lettice, and Dorothy died infants, and Jane was the wife of John Cotton of Gedding, in Huntingdonshire, son and heir of Sir Robert Cotton, Bart. and died his widow, March 17, 1767. Frauncis, the eldest son, was born Sep. 3, 1666, and died the 25th of May, 1667; John, the third son, died an infant; and Henry, the youngest, was unfortunately drowned at Oxon. Robert, second son, was born June 25, 1680, and died eleven days before his father, leaving Elizabeth his wife, daughter of William lord viscount Tracy, with child, who was delivered the 28th of May 1716, of a son, Sir Robert, Bart. she likewise had by him six daughters; Elizabeth, who died unmarried, Feb. 1762; Jane, who also died unmarried; Mary, relict of colonel Richard Pyott, son of Richard Pyott of Streetway, in the county of Stafford, Esq. by whom she had one son: Frances; Anne, the wife of Wrightson Mundy of Osbaston, in Leicestershire, Esq. and Dorothy, the wife of the Rev. John Rolleston, rector of Aston upon Trent, in Derbyshire: Elizabeth, surviving her said husband, Robert Burdet, Esq. became the wife of Robert Holden of Aston, in Derbyshire, Esq.

IV. Sir ROBERT BURDET, Bart. successor to his grandfather in title and estate, married in Nov. 1739, Elizabeth, the only daughter of Sir Charles Sedley of Nuthall, in the county of Nottingham, Bart. who died Aug. 28, 1747; by whom he had three sons and two daughters; Robert-Thomas-Sedley, who died when four years old; Elizabeth, the wife of Francis Mundy of Formark, near Derby, Esq. Francis, born in April, 1743, and married Eleanor, daughter and co-heir of William Jones of Ramsbury manor, Wilts; by whom he had Robert, born in 1768, Sedley, drowned in the Rhine,* and Sir Francis, the present baronet. He married, Aug. 5, 1793, to his second lady, ———, daughter of Thomas Couts, banker in London; and died Feb. 3, 1794. 3, John, died at the age of 20; and Frances. Sir Robert married to his second wife, June 18, 1753, the right honourable lady

* Sedley Burdet, Esq. second son of Francis Burdet, Esq. and grandson of Robert Burdet, Esq. who inherited considerable property from the late Sir Charles Sedley, Bart. was unfortunately drowned at one of the falls of Schauffhausen in the Rhine, with George-Samuel, 8th viscount Montague. The unfortunate fate of these two travellers was owing to a very rash attempt, from which no remonstrances could divert them. His lordship, accompanied by Mr. Burdet, was uncommonly anxious to pass the famous water-falls of Schauffhausen in Switzerland, which had hitherto been unattempted by any visitant. The magistrates of the district, having heard of the resolution of these travellers, and knowing that inevitable destruction would be the consequence of such an attempt, had ordered guards to be placed for the purpose of preventing the execution of it. Such however was the force of their curiosity, that they found means to elude every precaution. Having provided themselves with a small flat-bottomed punt, as they were about to step into it, Lord Montague's servant stopped short, and as it were instinctively seized his master by the collar, declaring, that for the moment he should forget the respect of the servant in the duty of the man. His lordship however extricated himself at the expence of part of his collar and neckcloth, and pushed off immediately with his companion. They got over the first fall in safety, and began to shout and wave their handkerchiefs, in token of success. They then pushed down the second fall, by far more dangerous than the first; from which time they have not since been heard of. It is supposed that the boat, hurried by the violence of the cataract, jammed them between two rocks.

The servant remained three weeks near the place, bewailing the fate of his beloved master, who in the prime of life, had thus fallen a victim to his curiosity, while he was hourly expected at Midhurst, which owed so much to his ancestors.

BURDET OF BRAMCOTE, WARWICKSHIRE.

TABLE 25.

1 HUGH BURDET, temp. Wm. I.   3 Hugh Burdet = Matilda de Sumeri

2 William Burdet   4 Sir William Burdet, living in 1252 = Alice

Hugh		5 Sir Richard Burdet				William
William	James	John	Sir Richard	6 William		
						Burdets of Allington
Richard, 1278	7 Hugh		Robert, 1303	William, 1297		
William, 1283	8 Sir Robert, 1333 = Eliz. de Camville					Nicholas
John	9 Sir Gerard, 1259 = Eleanor Veale		Sir Robert = Eliz. Garshale			Richard
Elizab. = T. Ashby	10 Sir John, Knt. = Margaret Fitton					John
	11 Sir Thomas = Anne Waldeif				Wm. Shepey = Agnes	

12 Sir Nicholas Burdet, Knt. 1440 = Joan, cousin of Henry Bruyn

Agnes Waldeif = 13 Thomas, 1477 = Marg. Rodney = Thomas Woodvill

Richard, 1493 Joyce Montfort	14 Sir John, 1529 Anne Harewell		Nicholas. Robert	George. Edward	Joan. Isabel
Thomas. Robert	Anne E. Conway, 1546	15 Thomas, 1540 M. Throckmorton	John. Wm.	George. Joan	Osburna G. Dalston	Elizabeth J. Copland	Anne J. Hall
16 Robert, 1548 E. Cockaine	Clement. Humphrey	William. Ethelbert	Blanch — Samborne	Catharine — Ludlow	Eleanor — Wellencote
17 Thomas, 1591 = B. Curzon	Frances	George	William	John	
18 Robert, 1603 Mary Wilson, 1622	Thomas. Lawrence	Dorothy J. Barwell	Anne — Sheffield	John. Mary	
I. Sir Thomas, Bart. Jane Frounceys	Bridget W. Whelpdale	Anne J. Bowes	Mary R. Frampton	Elizabeth A. Hutton	Lettice R. Skelton	Lucretia
II. Sir Frauncis, 1696 Eliz. Walter, 1701	Robert M. Wright	Catharine S. Repington	Isabel F. Merick	Lettice W. Houncel	Mary G. Bowes	Jane G. Thacker	Leicester. Doro.	Bridget T. Gresley
III. Sir Rob. Burdet, Bt. 1716 M. Pigot | M. Aston | M. Brome 1668	Francis. Walter	John A. Muggleston	Thomas, 1698 Dorot. 1718	Mary, 1710	Elizabeth E. Jodrell	Jane E. Hopegood
Elizabeth C. Jenens	Magdalen. Lettice	Jane J. Cotton	Dorothy. Frauncis	Robert, 1716 E. Tracy	John, d. y. Henry	
IV. Sir Robert Burdet, 1797 E. Sedley | C. Manners 1747 1769	Eliz. 1762 Jane	Mary Col. Pyott	Francis	Anne W. Mundy	Dorothy Rev. J. Rolles
Rob. T. Sedley	Elizabeth = F. Mundy	E. Jones = Francis = — Couts		John	Frances
Robert	Sedley	V. Sir Francis			

Caroline Manners, widow of Sir Henry Harpur, Bart. and daughter of John duke of Rutland, by lady Lucy, sister to Bennet Sherrard, earl of Harborough; by which marriage he had no issue. This lady died Nov. 10, 1769.

Sir Robert was member for the borough of Tamworth in several parliaments; and had the degree of L. L. D. conferred upon him by the university of Oxford, at the opening of the Radcliffe library, April 14, 1749 He died Feb. 22, 1797, and was succeeded by his grandson,

V. Sir FRANCIS BURDET, Bart.

ARMS—Azure, two bars, or.
CREST—On a wreath, a lion's head erased, sable, langued, gules.
SEATS—At Bramcote in Warwickshire, and Formark in Derbyshire.

---

25. MACKWORTH of Normanton, Rutlandshire.

Created Baronet June 4, 1619.

MACKWORTH in Derbyshire, gave name to this ancient family, seated there for many generations; one of which was of the retinue to the famous James lord Audley,* K. G. who was very instrumental in obtaining the glorious victory at Poictiers, under the Black Prince, in 20 Edw. III. where the French, though much superior, received an overthrow; the king and dauphin of France, many of his nobles, and innumerable common soldiers being taken prisoners. A descendant of

---

* This lord Audley, acquainted the prince, that he had vowed to be the first in the battle; to which the prince said, *Sir James, God give you this day that grace to be the best knight of all others*; and thereupon departing with his four esquires (Mackworth being one of them) went to the front of the battle: and Walsingham adds this farther of him, that by his extraordinary valour he broke through the French army, and caused much slaughter. His conduct so pleased the brave prince, that as a testimony thereof, he gave him land worth 500 marks a-year (a considerable estate in those days) which this lord settled on his four esquires. The prince being immediately acquainted therewith, demanded *whether he liked not his bounty, or thought the gift beneath his acceptance*; to which he answered, *that they deserved as much as himself, for without their assistance he, a single man, could have done but little*; the prince thereupon thanked him for so doing, and gave him 600 marks per ann. more. The posterity of all the four esquires have, in memory of this victory, added the said lord's coat armour to their own, as plainly appears by the cheveron gules, frettè, or, bore by this family of Mackworth, Delves, Haukeston, &c.

John Touchet, lord Audley, son-in-law, and at length heir of the aforesaid James, in consideration that John and Thomas Mackworth were valiant men, and of the good services done by them and their ancestors, to the said lord Audley's family; and for their farther honour, grants part of their arms to be borne by them and their heirs, with due difference, viz. party per pale, indented, sable and ermine, a cheveron, gules, frettè, or. In testimony to which grant (whereof this is an abstract) he puts his seal of arms. Dated at his manor of Marketon, Aug. 1, 1404.

this family was John Mackworth, L. L. D. he succeeded John de Shepey, as dean of Lincoln, in 1412, and died in 1451. But the chief of this line, who first settled in the county of Rutland, was

1. Thomas Mackworth of Mackworth, in Derbyshire, Esq. who served in parliament for the county of Derby in 3 and 4 Henry VI. and marrying Alice,* sister and heir to Sir John de Basings, who died without issue in 1446, became possessed of the towns and manors of Normanton, Empingham, and Hardwick, in Rutlandshire, which first place from thenceforth became their capital mansion. He was succeeded by

2. Henry, his son and heir, who fixing in the county of Rutland, was sheriff thereof in 18 Edw. IV. and (John, his son and heir, dying during his life) was succeeded by his grandson,

3. George Mackworth, sheriff of the county of Rutland, in 12 Henry VII. and 14, 22, and 26 Henry VIII. He died in 1536, leaving by Anne his wife, a daughter Lucy, the wife of Francis Browne of Stamford, Esq. and one son;

4. Francis Mackworth† of Normanton, Esq. who married Ellen, one of the eight daughters of Humphrey Hercy of Grove, in Nottinghamshire, Esq. by Elizabeth his wife, daughter of Sir John Digby of Kettleby, Knt. sister and co-heir of Sir John Hercy, Knt. who died S. P. He was sheriff of Rutlandshire in 30 and 35 Henry VIII. also 3 Queen Mary; and died in 1559, leaving

V. George, his son and heir, who was thrice sheriff in the reign of Queen Eliz. and by Grace his wife, daughter of Ralph Rokebey, Esq. serjeant at law, had issue,

I. THOMAS MACKWORTH of Normanton, Esq. sheriff of Rutland in 41 Eliz. and 7 James I. was advanced to the dignity of a baronet June 4, 1619. He married Margaret, daughter and heir of —— Hall of Gretford, in Lincolnshire, (sole heir to her mother, daughter and co-heir of Francis Neale of Tugby, in Lincolnshire, Esq.) by whom he had four sons and a daughter, who died young. The sons were 1, Sir Henry; 2, Sir Francis, who died unmarried; 3, Peregrine, who married ——, widow of —— Moor of Grantham, in Lincolnshire, Esq. barrister at law, but had no issue; and 4, Neale Mackworth, who died unmarried.

II. Sir HENRY MACKWORTH, Bart. successor to his father in title and estate, rebuilt the manor house at Normanton, and married Mary, daughter of Ro-

* This Alice, sister to Sir John, son of Thomas, son of William de Basings, by Margaret his wife, daughter and heir of Thomas de Normanville, son of Ralph, son of Thomas de Normanville, who died temp. Henry III. whose ancestors, soon after the conquest, were lords of Normanton, and were also seated at Kenerton, in the hundred of Blackborne in Kent, till their male issue failing, both that estate and this in Rutland, went by match, to the Basings, a family of great account and antiquity, descended from Adam de Basing, lord mayor of London in 1251, whose habitation was where Blackwell-hall now stands, and from whom the street and ward thereunto adjoining had the denomination of Basing's-hall-street, and Basing's-hall ward.

† It was found by office, in 3 Eliz. that Francis Mackworth, Esq. held certain lands in Empingham and Hardwicke, of the yearly value of 43l. of Lord Barkley, by knight's service, and that George Mackworth is his son and heir; which George was the great grandfather of Sir Thomas Mackworth, Bart. lord of Empingham, which he enjoys, by inheritance, from the beforementioned Ralph de Normanville, who died 43 Henry III. this estate having now continued in the same blood, though not in the same name, above 400 years. *Wright's Rutland*, p. 46.

bert Hopton of Wittam, in Somersetshire, Esq. second sister and co-heir of Ralph lord Hopton, of Stratton in Cornwall, had issue by her two daughters and five sons; 1, Sir Thomas; 2, Robert, who married first Elizabeth, daughter of John Hatcher of Empingham, Esq. and secondly Martha, daughter of Edward Corbet, D. D. of the Edgemond line, in Salop, by both which he had issue; but none survived him by the last: he died Feb. 1, 1717-8, aged 95. Robert, by his first wife, had two sons (1, Thomas, who married Mrs. Parker of Stamford, by whom he left no issue; and 2, Robert of Huntingdon, who married Mary, daughter of William Dowse of Huntingdon, merchant, and left issue Thomas, and Elizabeth, the wife of Lewis Smith of Great Gedding; Thomas married Elizabeth, daughter of John Maule of Ecton, in Northamptonshire, Gent. and had one daughter, Mary) 3, Henry, who married Mrs. Dorothy Hall of Gretford, in Lincolnshire, and had issue two sons; Henry, who married Mrs. Kate Roberts of Empingham, by whom he had issue three sons; 1, Sir Henry; 2, Thomas, killed in a duel; 3, Thomas; and a daughter: 4, Edmund, a merchant, who died at Aleppo, S. P. 5, Gustavus, who married Dorothy, widow to Thomas lord Grey of Groby, eldest son and heir apparent to Henry earl of Stamford, and daughter and co-heiress of Edward Bouchier, earl of Bath, by whom he left only one daughter, Mary, married to a gentleman in Lincolnshire. Sir Henry's two daughters were Margaret, the wife of Philip Young of Keniton, in Salop, Esq. and Jane, first the wife of Hugh Underwood of Wittlesea, in the Isle of Ely, Esq.

III. Sir THOMAS MACKWORTH, Bart. eldest son and heir of Sir Henry, had all the advantages of education, and was highly valued in his country. He was one of the knights for the county of Rutland, in all parliaments, from 31 Charles II. to the time of his death, 1694; and having married two wives, first Dorothy, daughter of Capt. George Darrel of Cale-hill, in Kent, had issue by her one son, Thomas, who died during the life of his father, and two daughters; Dorothy, the wife of John Wingfield of Tickencote, in Rutlandshire, Esq. and Utrechia, who died unmarried: but by Anne, his second lady, daughter of Humphrey Mackworth of Betton, in Salop, Esq. (a cadet of this ancient family) he had issue four daughters; Mary and Anne both died unmarried; Jane was the wife of Abraham Rys of Lincolnshire, Gent. who left her a widow, but no issue; and Elizabeth: likewise three sons; Humphrey and Hopton both died unmarried, and Sir Thomas, who succeeded to the title and estate; which

IV. Sir THOMAS MACKWORTH was one of the knights in parliament for the county of Rutland, in the room of his father, and was likewise elected for the said county in the first and fourth of Queen Anne, and in the two last parliaments of King George I. He died unmarried in Feb. 1744-5, and was succeeded by

V. Sir THOMAS MACKWORTH, Bart. who was an apothecary at Huntingdon (only son of Robert, who was the second son of Robert, the second son of Sir Henry Mackworth, Bart.) who first married Elizabeth, daughter of John Maule, Esq. and had issue four daughters; 1, Mary, the wife of the Rev. Charles Nailour of New Ross, in the county of Wexford in Ireland, and had Oliver, Charles, Sarah, and Mary, who all died young: 2, Elizabeth; 3, Sally; and 4, Sukey. Sir Thomas married secondly Mary, relict of the late Rev. Mr. Waller of Great Stough-

MACKWORTH OF NORMANTON, RUTLANDSHIRE.

ton, in Huntingdonshire, and daughter of the Rev. Leonard Reresby of Thriberg, in Yorkshire, by whom he had no issue. He died Oct. 17, 1769, and was succeeded in title by his second cousin,*

VI. Sir HENRY MACKWORTH, Bart. (the eldest son of Henry, who was the eldest son of Henry, the third son of Sir Henry Mackworth, the second baronet) who married Elizabeth, daughter of the Rev. Edward Lamb, rector of Acle in Norfolk, and died Oct. 23, 1773; by whom he had one son,

VI. Sir HENRY MACKWORTH, who (I believe) is the present baronet.

ARMS—Party per pale indented, sable and ermine, a cheveron gules, frettè or.
CREST—On a wreath a wing, per pale, indented as the shield.

TABLE 26.

```
1 THOMAS MACRWORTH=Alice Basings          3 George, 1736=Anne
2 Henry Mackworth, 1478                   4 Francis, 1559=Ellen Hercy    Lucy=F. Brown
         John, d. V. P.                   5 George Mackworth=Grace, dr. of Ralph Rokeby
1. Sir Thomas Mackworth=Margaret Hall
II. Sir Henry=M. Hopton      Sir Francis          Peregrine=Wid. Moor         Neale
III. Sir Thomas, 1694   Robert, 1718   Henry  Edmund  Gustavus   Marg.      Jane
     D.Darell | A.Mackworth  E.Hatcher | M.Corbet  D. Hall  D. Bouchier  P. Young  H.Underwood

Tho-  Dorothy  Utre-  Mary.  Jane    Eliz.  IV. Sir Tho-  Thomas   Robert    Henry     Thomas
mas   J.Wing   chita  Anne   A. Rys  Humph. mas, 1745     Mrs.     Mary      Kate Roberts
      field                         Hopton               Parker   Dowse
V. Sir Thomas, 1769              Elizabeth              VI. Sir Henry, Bart.              Thomas.
E. Maule | M.Walker, 1755        L. Smith                   E. Lamb                       Robert
Mary=C. Nailour    Elizabeth    Sally    Sukey     VII. Sir Henry Mackworth, Bart.
Oliver    Charles    Sarah       Mary
```

---

* Mr. Longmate says he was succeeded by his son, who is now (1787) one of the alms-men in the Charter House, London; but not having received any information from this family, I am not able to say which is right.

26. HICKS of BEVERSTON, GLOUCESTERSHIRE.

Created Baronet July 21, 1619.

THE family of the Hicks's has been very anciently seated in Gloucestershire.

1. John Hicks of Tortworth, in Gloucestershire, died 2 Henry VII.

2. Robert Hicks, son and heir of the said John, was a citizen of London, and raised a very great estate: he married Julian, daughter of Arthur Chapham of the county of Somerset, Esq. and had issue two sons, Michael and Baptist. Baptist, the youngest, taking to his father's business, acquired a large fortune, and came afterwards to great honours: he was knighted by King James I. and was created a peer 4 Charles I. by the title of Baron Hicks of Ilmington, in Warwickshire, and Viscount Campden of Campden, in Gloucestershire; which honours are now enjoyed by the present Earl of Gainsborough, Edward viscount Noel, having married Julian, daughter of the said Baptist, obtained a grant of them, to himself and his heirs male. Mary, the youngest daughter of the said Sir Baptist, was the wife of Sir Charles Morison of Cashiobury, in Hertfordshire, Knt. and from an heiress of that family the estate is now in the Earl of Essex.*

3. Michael Hicks, eldest son and heir of the said Robert Hicks, was secretary to lord treasurer Burleigh: he was knighted, and purchased the castle and manor of Beverston and Witcombe, both in the county of Gloucester. In 1604 he married Elizabeth, daughter of Mr. Colston of Lowlayton, in Essex, and died in 1612, aged 65. He left two sons, William and Michael, who died young, and a daughter, Elizabeth (so named from Elizabeth countess of Derby, one of her god-mothers, the other being the countess of Warwick) the wife of Sir William Armine of Osgodly, in Lincolnshire, Bart.

I. WILLIAM, the eldest, was created a baronet July 21, 1619: he married Margaret, daughter of William lord Paget, and died Oct. 22, 1680, aged 84; by whom he had issue Baptist, Elizabeth, Sir William, Letitia, the wife of Arthur earl of Donnegal, in the kingdom of Ireland; Catharine, Francis, Sir Michael, and Elizabeth, whereof only three survived. The sons were both knighted in their infancy, by King Charles, at Ruckholt. Sir Michael married Susan, youngest daughter of Sir Richard How, Knt, some time sheriff and alderman of London, and widow of Samuel Beaumont-Everard, of the Middle Temple, Esq. by whom he had ten children; but two only survived, How Hicks, Esq. and Alice, the wife of William Somerford, in Wiltshire, Esq.

II. Sir WILLIAM HICKS, Knt. and Bart. was sheriff of the county of Essex: he married Marthagnes, daughter of Sir Henry Coningsby, Knt. and dying in 1703,

---

* Stow, in his Survey of London, says, it was reported that these two heiresses were worth 100,000l. each. His large charities and good deeds to the town of Campden in Gloucestershire, &c. are set down at large in Stow, vol. I. p. 288.

left issue two sons, Henry and Charles, who married the daughter of —— Coningsby, Esq. and died in 1760, leaving one son, Jophn-Baptist, who upon failure of the elder branch became baronet; and two daughters, Mary, the wife of James Darcy, and Margaret of Anthony Wharton.

III. Sir HENRY, eldest son and heir of Sir William Hicks, succeeded his father, and married to his first wife Margaret, daughter of Sir John Holmes, Knt. by whom he had one son Henry, who died unmarried. He married to his second wife Barbara, daughter of Joseph Johnson, Esq. and dying in 1754, left issue by her two sons, Robert and Michael: the latter died unmarried in 1764.

IV. Sir ROBERT succeeded his father, but dying without issue in 1768, the title of baronet devolved on

V. Sir JOHN-BAPTIST HICKS, before-mentioned, who died Nov. 23, 1791. I now return to Sir Michael Hicks, Knt. second son of Sir William Hicks, Bart. he was lord of the manor of Great Witcombe in Gloucestershire, and married Susanna, daughter of Sir Richard Howe; and dying in 1710 left one son, Howe Hicks, Esq. who married Mary, daughter of Jeffery Watts, Esq. of Essex, and died in 1728: he left issue one son, now the present baronet.

VI. Sir HOWE HICKS of Witcombe Park, in Gloucestershire: he married Martha, daughter of the Rev. John Browne, and has two sons, William, who in Aug. 1793, married ————, daughter of the late Thomas Lobb Chute of the Vine, Hants, Esq. and Michael.

ARMS—Gules, a fesse wavy, between three fleurs-de-lis, or.
CREST—On a wreath a buck's head, couped at the shoulder, or; gorged with a chaplet of roses, gules.
SEAT—Witcombe Park near Gloucester.

---

1 JOHN HICKS, 1488　　　　　　　　　　　　　　　　　　　　　　　TABLE 27.

2 Robert Hicks═Julian, dr. of Arthur Chapham

3 Sir Michael, 1612═Eliz. Colston, 1634　　　　　　　　Sir Francis, V. Campden, 1629

I. Sir William, Bart. 1680　　　　Elizabeth　　　　Julian　　　　Mary
Marg. dr. of Wm. L. Paget　　Sir W. Armine, Bart.　Edw. V. Noel, 1643　Sir C. Morison

II. Sir William, Bart. 1703　　　Letitia　　　Sir Michael, 1710　　Earls of Gainsborough
Martha Agnes Coningsby　　Arthur, E. of Donnegal　Susanna Howe

III. Sir Henry Hicks, Bart. 1754　Margaret　　Charles, 1760　　How Hicks, 1728
M. Holmes | B. Johnson　　　A. Wharton　　— Coningsby　　Mary Watts

Henry, d.　IV. Sir Rob. Hicks,　Michael, 1764　V. Sir John-Baptist　VI. Sir How Hicks, Bt.
　　　　　Bart. 1768　　　　　　　　　　Hicks, Bt. 1791　　Martha Browne

William═Miss Lobb　　Michael

27. MILL of Camois Court, Sussex.

Created Baronet Dec. 31, 1619.

THE family of Mill is of considerable antiquity, and has flourished for many generations in Sussex. It was anciently written Atte Mill, Atte Mull, Mull, Mille, but for a considerable time Mill.

1. John Atte Mille, was lord of Gretham in Sussex 39 Edw. III. he had issue two sons, Robert Atte Mull, or Mille, of Guildford in Surrey, who lived temp. Rich. II. as appears by several deeds:* he was sheriff of Sussex and Surrey 13 Rich. II. and died without issue.

2. Richard Mille, his brother, had a son,

3. John Atte Mull of Neetborne, living 1420 and 1424: he had issue,

4. Robert Mull, alias Mille: he had issue two sons, Richard Mille of Gretham, who died in 1504, and Edmund of Pulborough, in Essex; which line terminated in a daughter, the wife of Nicholas Anstie.

5. Richard, the elder son, married Agnes, daughter of Thomas Lewknor, relict of Andrew Sackville (she was thirdly the wife of — Kighley) and had issue two sons,

6. William Mull of Gretham, in Sussex, living in 1499 and 1531; from whom Thomas Mill of Gretham aforesaid, Esq. that was living in 1634, and married Dorothy, daughter of Ralph Cooper of Slingford, in Sussex, Esq. was lineally descended; and from him descended William Mill of Gretham, Esq. who died in June, 1729, whereupon this branch terminated in daughters and co-heirs.

7. John Mill of Hampton, and also of Gretham (second son of Richard) by Alice, his wife, living in 1547, had issue,

8. John Mill of Gretham aforesaid, who married Catharine, daughter and co-heir of Sir Roger Lewknor of Trotton, and also of Camois Court in Sussex, Knt. (by Ellen, his third wife, daughter of Thomas Mefant; lineally descended from Roger Lewknor, high sheriff of Sussex and Surrey 20 Edw. III. son of Thomas, son of Roger de Lewknor, high sheriff of Surrey 12 Edw. I. by which match the family of Mill became allied to the noble families of Bardolph, D'Oily, Carew of Mulford, Dalingrigg, Lord Camois, and Pelham) by whom he had issue,

9. Lewknor Mill of Camois Court, in Sussex, who married Cicely, daughter of John Crook of Southampton, Esq. by whom he had issue four sons and four daughters; 1, John Mill of Camois Court, in Sussex, and Newton Berry in Southamptonshire, was advanced to the dignity of a baronet; 2, Lewknor, who died Dec. 5, 1567,† 3, John, and 4, Thomas; which three last died without issue: Dowsabella, Catharine, and Mary.

---

* Le Neeve's MSS. of the Baronets.   † See church notes in visit. of Hants, by Sir H. St. George, p. 16.

I. Sir JOHN MILL, Bart. was elected a member for the town of Southampton in 21 James I. as also in several succeeding parliaments in the reign of King Charles I. He married to his first wife, Elizabeth, daughter of Sir George More of Losley, in the county of Surrey, Knt. who died without issue; and afterwards Anne, daughter of Sir Thomas Fleming, Knt. lord chief justice of England, by whom he had issue eight sons, viz. 1, Sir John Mill of Newton Berry, in Southamptonshire, Knt. who was made a knight banneret by King Charles I. and killed by one Slatford, near Oxford, during his father's life; 2, Thomas, of Nutshelling in Southamptonshire, Esq. who married Catharine, daughter and sole heiress of Andrew Mundy of Nutshelling aforesaid, Esq. 3, Anthony, who died young; 4, Richard, who died unmarried; 5, Lewknor Mill of Plaitford, in Wilts, died unmarried; 6, Edward, of Eling in Southamptonshire, who married Jane, daughter of Thomas Burgess of Byton, in the said county, by whom he had two daughters; 7, George; and 8, William, both died young.

The last-mentioned Sir John Mill, Knt. (who died *vitâ patris*) married Philadelphia, daughter of Sir Henry Knollys of Grove Place, in the parish of Nutshelling, in Southamptonshire, Knt. comptroller of the houshold to King Charles I. (she surviving him, married Christopher Roper, lord Teynham, from whom the present lord Teynham descended) by whom he had issue,

II. Sir JOHN MILL of Newton Berry, Bart. successor to his grandfather, who died in the 28th year of his age, 1670. He married Margaret, daughter of colonel Henry Sandys of Montisfont, in Southamptonshire (who was mortally wounded, on the king's part, in the fight of Bramdene near Alsford, in the said county, March 29, 1644, and died April 6 following) by Jane his wife, daughter of Sir William Sandys of Muserden, in the county of Gloucester, Knt. The said colonel Henry Sandys was son of Sir Edwin Sandys of Latimers, in Bucks, Knt. by Elizabeth his wife, daughter and heir of William lord Sandys of the Vine, lineally descended from Sir William Sandys, K. G. lord chamberlain of the houshold to King Henry VIII. first Lord Sandys of the Vine, by Margaret, daughter and sole heiress of John Bray, Esq. (son of Sir Richard Bray, Knt. one of the council to King Henry VI.) and niece to Sir Reginald Bray, one of the knight's-companions of the most noble order of the garter. The aforesaid Margaret, wife of Sir John Mill, was sister of Edwin, last lord Sandys of the Vine, and at length one of his co-heirs, who dying unmarried, gave to his nephew, Sir John Mill (the son of the said Margaret) his estate.

III. Sir JOHN MILL, Bart. (the nephew of Edwin lord Sandys) was high sheriff for the county of Southampton in 1685: he married Margaret, daughter and heir of Thomas Grey of Woolbeding, in Sussex, Esq. by whom he had issue two sons and four daughters; 1, Sir John, his successor; 2, Sir Richard, of whom hereafter: the daughters were; 1, Margaret, the wife of Robert Knollys, younger brother of Henry, and son of Robert Knollys of Grove Place, in Southamptonshire, Esq. 2, Mary, died unmarried; 3, Elizabeth, the wife of Sir Thomas Hobby of Somerley, in Southamptonshire, Bart. and 4, Philadelphia.

IV. Sir JOHN MILL, Bart. succeeded his father in title and estate; but dying unmarried was succeeded by his brother,

V. Sir RICHARD MILL, Bart. who served the office of high sheriff for the county of Southampton in 1723, was member of parliament for Midhurst in Sussex, and afterwards for Penryn in Cornwall: he married Margaret, eldest daughter of Robert Knollys of Grove Place, in Southamptonshire, Esq. who died in 1744; by whom he had four sons and five daughters; Richard, John, Henry, Charles, Margaret, Philadelphia, Elizabeth, Mary, and Martha. He died May 16, 1760, and was succeeded by his eldest son,

VI. The Rev. Sir RICHARD MILL, Bart. who married, in August, 1760, Dorothy, daughter and heir of Richard Warren of Redcliff, in Somersetshire; by whom he had issue two daughters; the youngest born 1766. Sir Richard was knight of the shire for the county of Southampton, and died March 17, 1770. He was succeeded by his brother,

VII. The Rev. Sir CHARLES MILL, Bart. L. L. B. who was of Clare Hall, Cambridge: he died July 19, 1792, in the 72d year of his age.

VIII. Sir CHARLES MILL, the present baronet, is (perhaps) the son of the last baronet; but I am not certain.*

ARMS—Party per fesse, argent and sable, a pale counterchanged, and three bears, saliant, 2 and 1, counterchanged, muzzled and chained, or.

CREST—On a wreath, a demi bear, as in the arms.

MOTTO—*Aides Dieu.*

SEATS—At Mottisfont and Newton Berry, both in Southamptonshire; and Woodbeding in Sussex.

---

* Henry Mill, many years principal engineer to the New-River Company *(Gent. Mag. 1779, p. 537)* a man to whom the city of London and its environs have had many and great obligations, was of this family: he was born in London soon after the year 1700. He had a liberal education. Genius, we know, blazes forth at different ages, and often in a manner altogether unexpected. He displayed his skill in mechanics at an early period, and though we are unable to fix his age, or the time, yet it is certain, that he was very young when the New-River Company engaged him as their principal engineer; in which station he continued, with the highest esteem, till his death. His general knowledge, the fruit of constant study, was great; but in hydraulics he was probably unequalled. The Company placed implicit confidence in him, and with the utmost reason; for through his skill and labours their credit, their power, and their capital, were constantly increasing. A share in their property, which was originally 100*l.* is now worth between 7 and 8000. Mr. Mill supplied also the town of Northampton with water, for which he was presented with the freedom of that corporation. His skill also carried an ample supply of water to the seat of Sir Robert Walpole, at Houghton in Norfolk, which was before so deficient in this respect, that Cibber one day, being in the gardens, exclaimed, "Sir Robert, Sir Robert, here is a crow will drink up all your canal!"

He was a man of great simplicity of life and manners; in a word, it seemed to be his care to have a conscience void of offence; and as far as we can see another's heart, his was wholly free from guile.— On Christmas Day, 1770, he was suddenly seized with a fit, and died the next morning. His surviving sister, Mrs. Hubert, erected a monument to his memory, in the church of Breemore, near Salisbury. *Biog. Dic.*

MILL OF CAMOIS COURT, SUSSEX

TABLE 28.

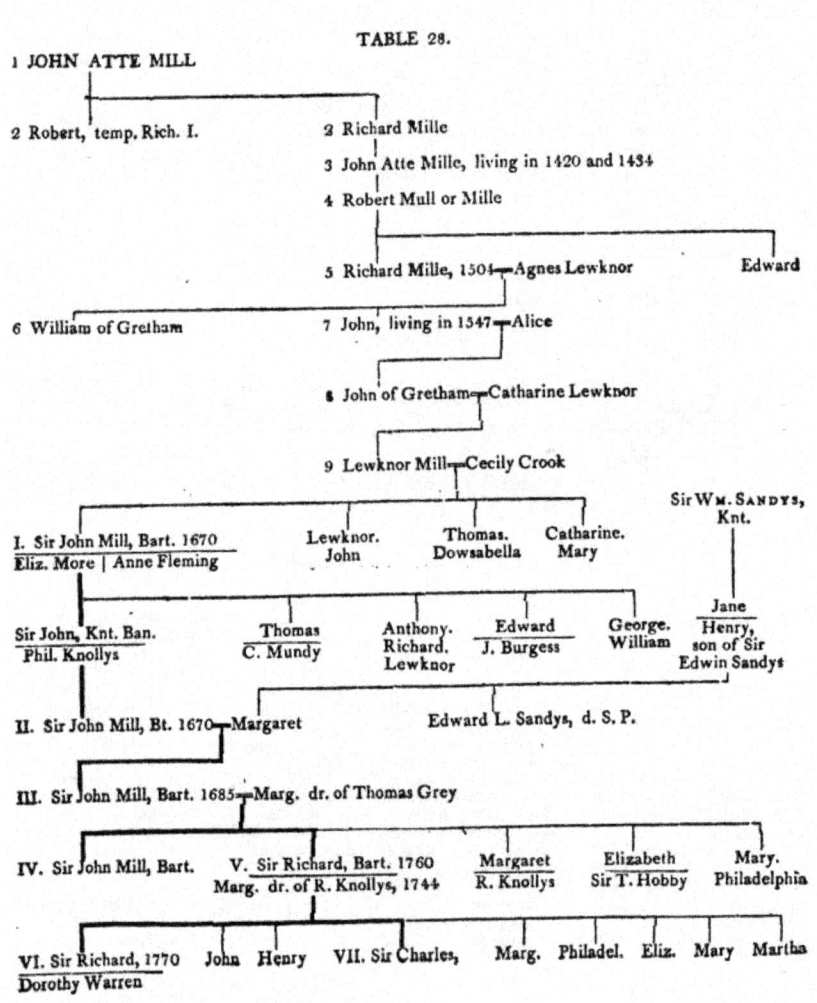

28. FOULIS of Ingleby, Yorkshire.

Created Baronet Feb. 6, 1619.

THIS surname is of French extraction, and is derived from the word *feuilles*, which signifies leaves, and to which their arms allude, being three bay leaves, &c.

Taylor, in his history of Gavelkind, tells us, that one of this name was a considerable man in Kent before the Norman invasion, and that being treated with much severity by William I. he fled into Scotland. The family appears to have been numerous, and considerable proprietors of land there in very early times; for there are several baronies and fine seats in the counties of Perth, Angus, Ross, &c. which bear the name of Foulis, and probably have been the property of people of that surname. Reginaldus de Foulis is witness in the first charter to the lord high steward of Scotland, in the reign of Alexander II. but the immediate ancestor of this family was

1. William de Foulis, who lived in the reigns of Robert II. and III. and left two sons, James, his heir, and William de Foulis, who being bred to the church, and a man of learning, was archdean of St. Andrews, secretary to James I. of Scotland, and keeper of the privy seal in 1424. He was often employed to negotiate affairs of state with the court of England, and always acquitted himself with honour. He acquired a considerable fortune, which he left to his nephew, William, son of his elder brother.[*]

2. James de Foulis, who succeeded his father, lived in the reigns of James I. and II. and was succeeded by his son,

3. William de Foulis, who succeeded also to his uncle, as before observed, and got thereby a considerable accession to his estate. In the reign of James III. he married Elizabeth, daughter of Sir Walter Ogilvie, by whom he had two sons, William,[†] who died without issue, and

4. James de Foulis, who married Margaret, daughter of Sir James Henderson of Fordel, in the county of Fife; by whom he had two sons, James, his heir, and William, who got a charter under the great seal, dated April 18, 1541.[‡] He was succeeded by his son,

5. James Foulis, who acquired from William, master of Glencairn, the lands and barony of Colington, in the shire of Edinburgh, 1519; which has ever since been the chief seat and title of the eldest branch of this family. He was a man of extraordinary accomplishments and merit, and was appointed king's advocate in 1528; clerk register in 1531, by James V. and had his commission renewed by Queen Mary in 1543: in short, he was concerned in all the public transactions of his time, and always acted with fidelity and honour. He married Catharine, daugh-

[*] Fordun, vol. II. p. 509   Nisbet, vol. I. p. 402.   [†] Nisbet's App. p. 18.   [‡] Hart. in Pub. Arch.

ter of —— Brown of Hartrie : he was one of the commissioners employed by the estates of the nation to negotiate a marriage between Mary Queen of Scotland and Prince Edward of England, which did not take effect.* He was succeeded by his son,

6. Henry Foulis, who married ——, daughter of —— Haldane of Gleneagles. He was a faithful subject to Queen Mary, and obtained a letter from her to be one of the senators of the college of justice, upon the first vacancy; but the troubles of that reign prevented its taking place.† He was succeeded by his son,

7. James Foulis of Colinton, who married Agnes Heriot, heiress of Lumphoy, by whom he had five sons; 1, James, ancestor to Sir James Foulis of Colinton, in Scotland, Bart. 2, George, progenitor of the Foulis's of Ravelstone, Ratho, Woodhall, &c. 3, David; 4, ——; 5, John, whose grand-daughter, Anne, was the wife of Sir James Hope of Hopeton; from whom the present earl of Hopetoun is descended.

I. DAVID, the third son, being in great favour with King James VI. accompanied him into England, and was knighted by his royal master, at the Tower of London, May 13, 1603, before his coronation, two years after which, waiting on his majesty to Oxford, he was created master of arts in that university, and had the dignity of a baronet conferred upon him: he was cofferer to Prince Henry, eldest son of the said King James, and after his decease he bore the same office under Prince Charles (afterwards King Charles I.) he purchased the manor and seat of Ingleby in Cleaveland, in Yorkshire, of lord Eure, where he resided, and was made one of his majesty's council for the northern parts, and custos rotulorum and deputy lieutenant for the north riding of that county: but as he appeared with some zeal in 1632, against the commission which was issued to compel gentlemen to compound for not having taken the honour of knighthood, to which they were obliged, by an old obsolete law, and had let fall some expressions reflecting upon Thomas lord viscount Wentworth, lord president of the council in the north, for his proceedings therein; he and his eldest son, Henry, were censured for it in the court of star-chamber, in 1633;‡ Sir David was declared incapable of all the offices and places which he held, was committed prisoner to the Fleet during his majesty's pleasure, fined 5000l. to the king, and 3000 to Lord Wentworth; for the payment of which fines, he was forced to sell part of his estate. His son and heir, Henry, was also committed prisoner to the Fleet during his majesty's pleasure, and fined 500l. This Sir David married Cordelia, the daughter of William Fleetwood of Great Missenden, in Bucks, Esq. serjeant at law, and recorder of London, in the reign of Queen Elizabeth; by whom he had issue two daughters; 1, Anne, the wife of George Purvis, doctor in physic; 2, Elizabeth, who died unmarried, and five sons; 1, Sir Henry, his successor; 2, Robert; 3, John; 4, Edward; and 5, William, who all died without issue. Sir David died in 1642, and was succeeded by his eldest son,

II. Sir HENRY FOULIS, Bart. who married Mary, the eldest daughter of Sir Thomas Clayton of Sexho, in Yorkshire, Knt. by whom he had issue four sons and four daughters; 1, Sir David, his successor; 2, Henry, who was fellow of Lincoln college, Oxford, and wrote with some reputation both against the papists and

* Rymer. tom. XV. p. 4.   † In the advocate's library.   ‡ Rushworth's Coll. p. ii. p. 215.

presbyterians: he was the author of the History of the wicked Plots and Conspiracies of the Presbyterians, in fol. 1674; and the History of Romish Treasons, in fol. 1681.* He died Dec. 24, 1669, aged 33. 3, Edward; 4, Thomas, who was captain of a man of war, and lost his life in the Dutch wars, in the reign of King Charles II. he left two sons and a daughter, who all died without issue. The daughters of Sir Henry were 1, Cordelia; 2, Mary, the wife of Robert Shafto of Benwell, in Northumberland, Esq. 3, Catharine, of Sir Ralph Cole of Brancepeth, in Durham, Bart. 4, Elizabeth, who died unmarried.

III. Sir DAVID FOULIS, Bart. succeeded his father, and married Catharine, the eldest daughter of Sir David Watkins, of Middlesex, Knt. and had issue six sons and five daughters; 1, David; 2, Henry; 3, Sir William; 4, Thomas; 5, Charles; and 6, John, who all died without issue, except Sir William, his third son. The daughters were, 1, Honor, the wife of William, eldest son of Sir Edward Chaloner of Gisborough, in Yorkshire, Knt. 2, Mary, of William, second son of John Turner of Kirkleatham, in Yorkshire, Esq. serjeant at law, kinsman and heir of Sir William Turner, Knt. lord-mayor of London; 3, Catharine, of John Rudd of Durham, Esq. 4, Anne, of Sir Reginald Graham of Norton-Conyers, in Yorkshire, Bart. and 5, Jane. This Sir David served in parliament for the borough of North Allerton, in the first year of King James II. and died March 13, 1694, in the 62d year of his age: he was succeeded in title and estate by

IV. Sir WILLIAM FOULIS, Bart. his third, but eldest surviving son, who married Anne, daughter of John Lawrence of the city of Westminster, Esq. widow of Sir Lumley Robinson of Kentwell Hall, in Suffolk, Bart. by whom he left issue only one son, Sir William, and died in Oct. 1741, aged 83.

V. Sir WILLIAM FOULIS, only son and successor to his father in dignity and estate, married in 1721, Mildred, the eldest daughter of Henry lord viscount Downe; in the kingdom of Ireland, and of Cowick near Snaith, in the west riding of Yorkshire; by whom he had issue one son, William, and four daughters, Mildred, Anne, the wife of William Preston of Moreby, in Yorkshire, Esq. Catharine, of Robert Jubb; and Mary, of Boynton Langley of Wykeham Abbey, in Yorkshire, Esq. Sir William died in 1756, and was succeeded in title and estate by his only son,

VI. Sir WILLIAM FOULIS, Bart. who in 1758 married Hannah, the only daughter of John Robinson of Bucton, in the east riding of Yorkshire, by whom he had two sons, William, his successor, and John Robinson, who married Beatrice Decima, eldest daughter of Sir Christopher Sykes, Bart. by whom he has one son, John Robinson. He died in Feb. 1780, and was succeeded by his son,

VII. Sir WILLIAM FOULIS, Bart. who in 1789 married Mary Anne, second daughter of Edmund Turner of Ponton, in Lincolnshire, Esq. by whom he has one son, William, and three daughters, Hannah, Mary, and Catharine.

* Anthony Wood says, "The product of his writings shew him to have been a true son of the church of England, a hater of popery, presbytery, and sectarism. He was endowed with a happy memory, understood books, and the ordering of them so well, that with a little industry he might have gone beyond the great Philobiblos Jamesius. He had also in him a most generous and noble spirit, a carelessness of the world and things thereof (as most bookish men have) a most becoming honesty in his dealings, a just observance of collegiate discipline, and a hatred to fangles, and the French fooleries of his time."

FOULIS OF INGLEBY, YORKSHIRE.

ARMS—Argent, three laurel or bay leaves, erect, proper.
CREST—On a wreath, out of a crescent, argent, a cross formé fiché, sable; also, a demi unicorn, winged, has been sometimes borne.
SEAT—At Ingleby manor near Stokesley, in Cleaveland, in the north riding of Yorkshire.

TABLE 29.

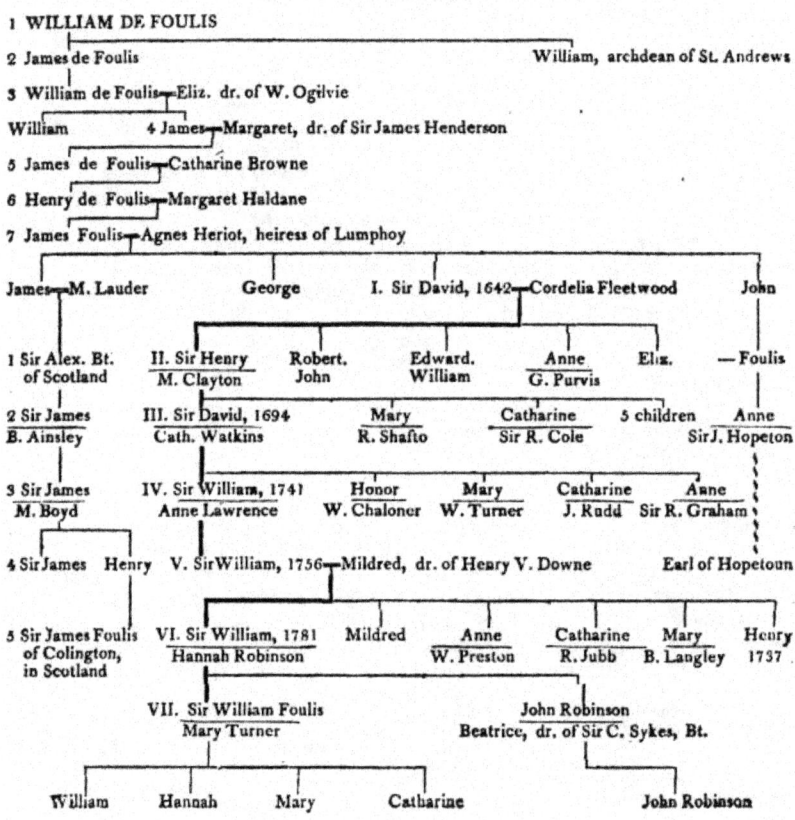

29. BERNEY, of PARKHALL in REEDHAM, NORFOLK.

Created Baronet May 5, 1620.

THIS family took their name from the town of Berney, near Walsingham, in Norfolk, where they were seated at the time of the conquest. In some very ancient writings which belonged to the priory of Bynham,

1. Roger de Berney is mentioned as lord of Berney; as also his son,
2. Sir Henry de Berney, Knt. whose son,
3. Richard de Berney, by Catharine, daughter of Roger Gynney, Esq. had issue
4. Henry de Berney, who lived in 1268, and was father of
5. John de Berney, who resided chiefly in the city of Norwich, and married Joan, daughter of Bartholomew de Witchingham, by whom he had
6. John de Berney, who resided at Witchingham: he was one of the citizens of Norwich in the parliament at York, 9 Edw. III. also he, with Robert Clare, Esq. were the king's commissioners, before whom an inquest upon a writ of *ad quod damnum*, concerning the fee of the castle of Norwich was taken, 19 Edw. III. The year following he was elected one of the knights in parliament for the said county, as he was again 22 Edw. III. together with Robert Clare, Esq. and were allowed 14l. 10s. for 34 days attendance: he also served in parliament 31 Edw. III. and for attending 32 days had 6l. 8s. allowed for his expences. He married Sarah, daughter of Bartholomew Bateman; and secondly Catharine, daughter of Peter Bedingfield, Esq. and left two sons, Robert and Thomas (the eldest Sir Robert Berney) who was knight batchelor of the duke of Guyen and Lancaster, and from whom were descended the two branches of the family, viz. the Witchingham and Gunton, which continued several descents, but are now extinct. This Sir Robert married Margaret, daughter and co-heir of Walter de Walcot, who was a lineal descendant of two very ancient families united in him; one derived from Sir Clement Clopton, Knt. who lived in 1122: Margery, another sister, was a nun at Currow Abbey. By this marriage he had the manor of Gunton, where four generations afterwards, a Sir Robert Berney, his descendant, who was sheriff of Norfolk and Suffolk 7 and 11 Henry IV. built a very capital house.

7. Sir Thomas de Berney, the second son, married Margaret, daughter and heiress of William de Reedham, Esq. by Margaret, daughter and heiress of Sir Robert Caston, Knt. of a very ancient family, seated at Reedham in Norfolk at the time of the Conqueror's survey. By this marriage, besides several other estates and lordships, he had the manor of Reedham, whither he removed in the reign of Edw. III. from Witchingham, which continued the seat of his elder brother, Sir Robert, and his descendants. He left issue,

8. John Berney of Reedham, his son and heir, who married Isabel, daughter and heiress of Sir John Heveningham, Knt. and died in 1440; by whom he had three sons; 1, Thomas; 2 Robert; and 3, John, who died issueless in 1461.*

9. Thomas Berney, the eldest son, by Eva, daughter of John Clipsby of Clipsby, Esq. left issue,

10. John Berney, who married Catharine, daughter of Asbert Munford of Hockwold, whose son and heir,

11. John Berney, married ——, daughter of Richard Southwell, Esq. and secondly ——, daughter of John Wentworth of Suffolk, by whom he had

12. John Berney, who first married Margaret, daughter of William Reade of Beccles, in Suffolk; and secondly, Alice, daughter of Richard Joyner, and relict of Paul Sydnor of Kent, Esq. He died in 1557, having issue Thomasine, the wife of Thomas Osborne of Kirby Bedon, Esq. another, the wife of —— Sydnor of Blundeston, Esq. Mary, of Robert Jenney of Herringfleet; and the youngest of —— Cuddon of Shadingfield, all in Suffolk; and one son,

13. Henry Berney, Esq. who removed the old seat of the family, which stood near Reedham church, into the park in Reedham, where he built a magnificent house, and made very large gardens to it, calling it Parkhall in Reedham. He died in 1584, having had a numerous issue, by Alice his first wife, daughter of Roger Apleton of Comb, in Essex: his second wife was Agnes, daughter of Walter Clarke of Hadleigh, in Suffolk, Esq. and heiress of her brother Edward.

14. Sir Thomas Berney, Knt. the eldest son, was high sheriff of Norfolk 7 James I. and died in 1616, leaving issue by Juliana, daughter of Sir Thomas Gaudy of Redenhall, in Norfolk, Knt. one of the justices of the common pleas, several children; 1, William, married ——, daughter of the lord chief justice Coke, but had no issue; 2, John, died unmarried; 3, Richard, became his heir. Thomas, the youngest, was high sheriff of Norfolk in 1647, and married Dorothy, daughter of John Smith of Arminghall, from whom is descended John Berney of Bracon, Esq. who was high sheriff of Norfolk in 1760.

I. Sir RICHARD BERNEY, the third son of Sir Thomas, by his two elder brothers dying without issue, became heir, and was created a baronet May 5, 1620: he was high sheriff of Norfolk in 1622, and died in 1668. By Anne, daughter of Michael Smallpage of Chichester, in Sussex, Esq. besides four daughters he had 1, Sir Thomas; 2, Richard; 3, John; 4, William; and 5, Henry. He left all his estates at Reedham and elsewhere, belonging to the family, to his second son, Richard Berney de Reedham, Esq. who was twice high sheriff of Norfolk, in 1662

---

* He willed "his body to be buried in the porch of the north part of the church of Reedham; and bequeaths, for finding lights before the blessed virgin Mary, St. Peter, and St. Nicholas, the bishop, 3s. 4d. each. Also to the brotherhood of St. John Baptist, of the town of Reedham, 6s. 8d. and to the brotherhood of St. Thomas, of the said town, 6s. 8d. Likewise one great cypress chest, for the safe keeping the ornaments of the said church. He settles on John Berney, his nephew (son of Thomas Berney, his brother) his manor of Caston; as also the manor of Shipdon, and the manor of Turteviles, in Witchingham Parva; ordering the said John, and his executors, to maintain one chaplain after his decease, to pray for his soul, and the souls of John Berney, his father, and Isabel, his mother, in the church of Reedham, for four years, with a competent salary."

and 1670. He married ——, daughter of Sir Jacob Gerrard of Langford, in Norfolk, Bart. and by her had one son, Richard Berney, Esq. who was high sheriff of Norfolk in 1692; and died the same year unmarried.

John Berney of Westwick, third son of Sir Richard, married Susan, daughter of John Stains, and left two sons, John and Richard: the eldest, John Berney, married first Bridget, daughter of William Branthwaite of Hethel, Esq. and had two daughters; Julian, the wife of Thomas Brograve of Essex, Esq. and Elizabeth of John Petre of Westwick: to his second wife he married Elizabeth, daughter of Maurice Kendall of Northwalsham, Esq. but by her he had no issue. Richard Berney, late of Langley in Norfolk, second son of John Berney of Westwick, was recorder of Norwich; for which city he was returned member in the two last parliaments of Queen Anne. By Mary, daughter of Augustine Briggs of the same city, Esq. he left only one daughter, Elizabeth, the wife of Thomas Bramston of Skreens, in Essex, Esq. formerly one of the knights for that county. William, the fourth son of Sir Richard, married a daughter of Thomas Browne of Elsinghall, in Norfolk, Esq. and had issue. Henry, the fifth son died a bachelor.

II. Sir THOMAS BERNEY of Norwich, Bart. eldest son of Sir Richard, by Sarah his second wife, daughter of Thomas Tyrell of Essex, Esq. governor of Languard Fort on the restoration of Charles II. had several children. John Berney of Wesenham, Esq. the third son, married Philippa, daughter of Thomas Browne of Elsing, Esq. and, besides other children, left Thomas Berney, Esq. recorder of Lynn Regis in Norfolk, who married Julian, daughter of Sir Richard Berney of Kirby, Bart. hereafter-mentioned, by whom he had issue two sons, Thomas and Richard, both of Lynn. William Berney, fourth son of Sir Thomas, was rector of Stokesby and Westwick; and by Mary, daughter of Henry Harcock, had one son, William Berney, rector of Newton Flotman in Norfolk, who married Dorothy, another daughter of the said Sir Richard Berney, Bart. by whom he had several children, of which Richard Berney, his eldest son and heir, was rector of Westwich. Sir Thomas Berney died in 1693, and was succeeded by

III. Sir RICHARD BERNEY of Kirby Bedon, Bart. his eldest son and heir, who married Dorothy, daughter of William Branthwayte of Hethel, Esq. and had a numerous issue; of which, besides the two daughters married as above-mentioned, and Sir Richard and Sir Thomas, Robert, the third son, resided several years, and died in Barbadoes. John, his eighth son, doctor of divinity, was one of his majesty's chaplains in ordinary, archdeacon of Norwich, and rector of Saxlingham and Hetherset: he married the eldest daughter, and one of the co-heiresses of John Barns, D. D. dean of Norwich, by whom he had no issue. Sir Richard died in 1706, and was succeeded in title and estate by his eldest son,

IV. Sir RICHARD BERNEY, Bart. who died unmarried in 1710, aged 22; and was succeeded by his brother,

V. Sir THOMAS BERNEY, Bart. who married Elizabeth, only daughter and heiress of Simon Folkes of Suffolk, Esq. by Elizabeth his wife, who was daughter and one of the co-heiresses of Samuel Hanson of the island of Barbadoes, Esq. by whom a plantation, called Hanson's, in that island, came to the family. He died in 1742, and left only two sons, Sir Hanson and the Rev. Richard, who died Dec.

184   BERNEY, OF PARKHALL IN REEDHAM, NORFOLK.

1794, aged 70. He was rector of Stokesby and Bramston, in that county. Sir Thomas was succeeded by his son,

VI. Sir HANSON BERNEY, Bart. who was sheriff of Norwich in 1762: he married Catharine, daughter and heiress of William Woolball of Walthamstow, in Essex, Esq. who died in 1792, by whom he had one son, John, and two daughters, Elizabeth and Catharine; and died in 1762. He was succeeded by his son,

VII. Sir JOHN BERNEY, Bart. who in 1770 married the honourable Miss Nevill, daughter of the Earl of Abergavenny.

ARMS—Quarterly, gules and azure, over all a cross, engrailed, ermine.
CREST—On a wreath, ermine and gules, a plume of ostrich feathers, per pale, azure and gules.
MOTTO—*Nil temere, neque timore.* SEAT—At Kirby Bedon in Norfolk.

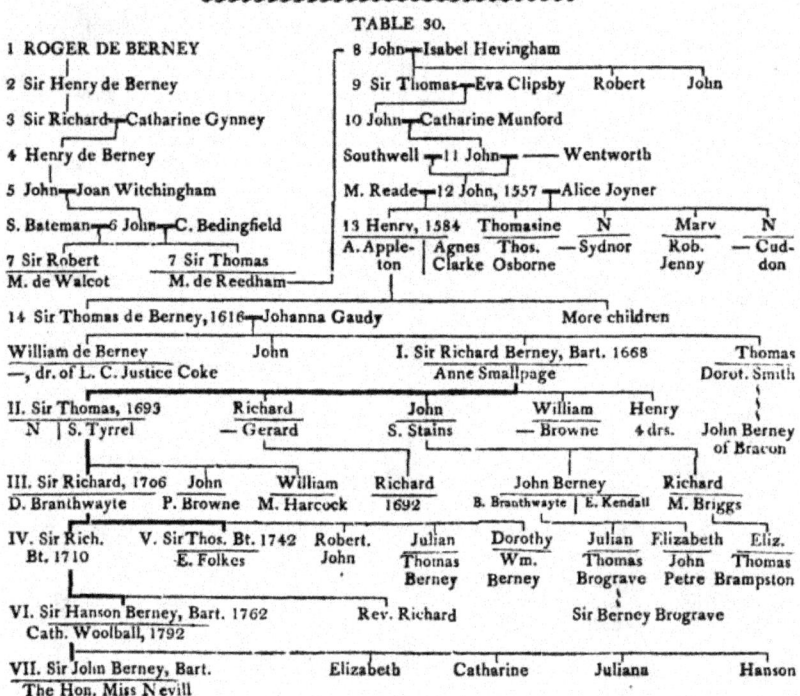

30. PAKINGTON of AILSBURY, BUCKINGHAMSHIRE.

Created Baronet June 22, 1620.

THE antiquity of this family is unquestionable: it is manifest from the foundation of the monastery of Kenelworth, that they flourished in the reign of Henry I. neither is it to be doubted but they were so called from the place of their abode, from one of the Pakingtons of Staffordshire, Warwickshire, or Leicestershire; for in each of those counties we meet with lordships of that name, whose owners anciently wrote themselves de Pakington.*

1. Robert Pakington lived in the reign of Henry IV. and was father of

2. John Pakington, Esq. recited in an office found before Robert Russel, escheator of the county of Worcester 14 Henry VI. He had issue a son,

3. John Pakington, Esq. who by Elizabeth his wife, daughter and heir of Thomas Washbourne of Stanford, in Worcestershire, Esq. had issue three sons, John, Robert, and Humphrey. John, the eldest, was of the society of the Inner Temple, and in 24 Henry VII. constituted chirographer of the court of common pleas; and in 1520 elected lent reader: also, in 1529, treasurer of the society of the Inner Temple; in which year he had a memorable grant from the king.† In 1532 he

---

* Richard de Pakington *(Dugdale's Warwick. vol. II. p. 1118, edit. 1730)* married one of the sisters and co-heirs of Robert de Kaily, lord of Freseley in Warwickshire, who lived in the time of Henry II. and there are now in the possession of Sir John Pakington, Bart. two ancient deeds, without date, one of Robert Wittington, clerk, signed and sealed in the presence of Peter Wyke, Hugh Pakington, and Alexander Abbetot, Knts. the other attested by Richard Spechell and Hugh Pakington, Knts. the latest of which deeds is judged to be above 400 years old.

Pagington *(Erdeswick's Survey of Staffordshire, MS.)* in Staffordshire, was held of the bishop, temp. Henry III. *(In Mr. Le Neeve's MSS. of the Baronets, vol. I. p. 131, is this entry: Robtus de Pakenton tenuit quartam partem feodi unius militis in Pakington, in com. Staff.)* by Robert de Pakington; and in 24 Edw. I. by David de Pakington. Thomas de Pakington *(Monast. Angl. vol. I. p. 273)* was prior of Burton Abbey in Staffordshire, and presided in the same 36 years: he died in 1305, and was buried there. Another Thomas de Pakington *(Ibid. p. 428)* named of Brailsford, founded a chantery in the chapel of Chelmscote, in 1322. Henry, abbot of Lilleshull, grants lands to Roger de Pakington, and Agnes his wife, in Blackfordby, in 1339. William de Pakington was treasurer of the king's houshold, keeper of the wardrobe, chancellor of the exchequer, rector of East Wrotham in Northamptonshire, prebendary of Tamworth, Lincoln, and York, archdeacon of Canterbury, dean of the royal chapel of St. Mary, Stafford, St. Martin le Grand, and Litchfield. He died about 1392. Leland quotes largely in English from his Chronicle, which began at 9 John, and was continued to his own time; but does not appear to be now extant. He wrote, in French, the Victorious Atchievements of the Black Prince. *Pitt's, p. 530. Nicholson's Hist. Lib. p. 66. Tanner Bib. Brit. p. 569.*

† That he, the said John Pakington *(Patent 28 Henry VIII. part 2, in the chapel of the rolls)* for the time to come, shall have full liberty, during his life, to wear his hat in his presence, and his successors, or of any other persons whatsoever, and not be uncovered on any occasion or cause whatsoever, against his will and good liking: also, that he shall not be appointed, called, or compelled, to take the order of knighthood, or degree, state, or order, of a baron of the exchequer, serjeant at law, or any office or incumbrance thereto relating. And farther, out of his abundant grace, grants, that if he be chosen to any offices, incumbrances, or honours aforesaid, and those shall refuse to take, that he shall neither in-

was called to be serjeant at law, for which the king gave him a special discharge for taking the said degree; and having been appointed a justice of North Wales, was, in 1535, commissioned to conclude and compound all forfeitures, offences, fines and sums of money due to the king, or his father, Henry VII. In 1542 he had a patent for justice of Brecknock, Glamorgan, and Radnor, in South Wales, during life. The many other honours conferred on him are too numerous here to be repeated, and at the time of his death, 1560, was seized of 31 manors, and of other lands that he had purchased of 70 different persons, as appears from a large book concerning his estate, now among the evidences of the family, at Westwood.

His lady was Anne, widow of ——— Tychbourne, and of the family of Rolle, who dying August 22, 1563, was buried in the east end of the chancel of St. Buttolph's, Aldersgate-street, London. The great estate this Sir John Pakington left, was divided between his daughters, and his two younger brothers, Robert and Humphrey. Ursula, his eldest daughter, was the wife of Sir John Scudamore, Knt. from whom descended the late lord viscount Scudamore, whose daughter and sole heir was the dutchess of Beaufort; and Bridget, of Sir John Lyttleton of Frankley in Worcestershire, Knt. Humphrey Pakington, youngest brother of Sir John, was a merchant of London, and left an only son, John, who was of Harvington in Worcestershire; which line expired in two daughters, great heiresses; one of them was the wife of Sir John Yate, Bart. the other of Sir Henry Audley, Knt.

4. Robert Pakington, the second brother of Sir John before-mentioned, was member of parliament for the city of London, and was barbarously murdered in the streets of London in 1537, by the papists, whom he had opposed.* It appears that he forsook the errors of the church of Rome, in those times when many suffered on account of their religion. The murderer was never discovered, but by his own confession, made when he came to the gallows at Banbury, to be hanged for felony.

He had issue by Catharine, one of the co-heirs of Sir John Baldwin, Knt. lord chief justice of the common-pleas and ——— his wife, daughter of William Dormer of Wycombe in Bucks, Esq. (by this match came the manor of Ailsbury in Bucks, with other considerable lands) an only son, Thomas, and three daughters, viz. Elizabeth the wife of John Lane, Esq. and afterwards of Sir Richard Mallory, Knt. alderman of London; Anne, of Richard Cupper of Glympton, in Oxfordshire; Esq. and Margaret of Benedict Lee of Burston, in Bucks, and afterwards of Thomas Scot of the county of York, Esqrs.

cur, forfeit, or lose, for such contempt, any loss, pain, forfeiture, or other issues, fines, amercements, or redemptions whatsoever, on occasion of omission, refusal of taking, or non-omission; likewise, that this charter of exemption, sole produced before any of the justices, treasurer, or barons of the exchequer, of the king, or his successors, or in any place or court of record throughout the whole kingdom, shall be sufficient, without any other writ, precept, mandate or any other proclamation made. Whereof all justices, judges, barons of the exchequer, sheriffs, escheators, coroners, mayors, provosts, bailiffs, and all other officers and ministers; and his leige and faithful people are commanded to take notice, and not to disturb, molest, or grieve the said John Pakington, against the tenour of this grant, or effect of these presents; any statute, act, ordinance, or proviso, made or published to the contrary, or any other cause or matter whatsoever. Signed by the king himself, at Westminster, the 5th of April, the year aforesaid.

* Stow, vol. I. p. 29.

5. Thomas, son and heir to the said Robert, was in ward to the lord privy-seal in 1546, when Catharine his mother, then 23 years of age, was found one of the co-heirs to Sir John Baldwin (who died Dec. 22, in the same year:) he received the honour of knighthood from Queen Mary; and on the death of his uncle, Sir John, succeeded to a great estate: he was sheriff of the county of Worcester in 3 Eliz. and died June 2, 1571. His lady, who survived him, was the daughter of Sir Thomas Kitson of Hengrave, in Suffolk, Knt. (and afterwards the wife of Thomas Tasmagh, Esq.) she died in the 65th year of her age, 1575. This Sir Thomas had five sons, of which only John, the eldest, survived his father; and three daughters, Mary, the wife of Sir Walter Long of Draycot, in Wilts, Knt. Catharine of John Davis of the same county, Esq. secondly of Sir Jasper Moor, and lastly of —— Mompesson of Teddington, in Wilts, Knts. and Margaret of Thomas Litchfield, Esq. gentleman of the privy chamber to Queen Elizabeth.

6. Sir John Pakington was a great favourite of Queen Elizabeth's, and one of her privy council: she invited him to attend her court, where he lived at his own expence, in splendour and reputation, with an equipage not inferior to some of her greatest officers, though he had no other honour besides that of knight of the bath. He was remarkable for his stature and comely personage, and had distinguished himself so much by his manly exercises, that he was called the lusty Pakington: he entered into articles to swim against three noble courtiers, for 3000*l*. from the bridge at Westminster to the bridge at Greenwich; but the queen prevented it.

Having, by his expensive life, contracted great debts, he took the wise resolution of retiring into the country, and said he *would feed on bread and verjuice till he had made up his extravagancies;* in consequence of which the queen gave him a grant of a gentleman's estate in Suffolk, of 8 or 900*l*. per ann. besides goods and chattels, which had escheated to the crown; but after he had been there to take possession, he could not behold the miseries of that distressed family without regard and compassion; and the melancholy spectacle of the distressed lady and her children so effectually wrought upon him, that he repaired immediately to court, and humbly beseeched her majesty to excuse him from enriching himself by the calamities of a gentleman who fell by a combination of his enemies; and would not leave the queen till he had obtained his request.

After his settlement in the country her majesty granted him for 60 years,[*] for his faithful services heretofore done (stiling him her trusty and well-beloved servant) several lordships, &c. that were come to the crown by forfeiture, &c. in Devonshire, Gloucestershire, Leicestershire, Lancaster, and Cornwall; Somersetshire, Hertfordshire, Yorkshire, Surrey, Cambridgeshire, Carmarthenshire, Middlesex, London, Wiltshire, Monmouthshire, Essex, and Buckinghamshire: he was also lieutenant and custos rotulorum for Worcestershire. He was generally the first named in all commissions of importance, and was the principal director in the government of his county. By his affability and obliging behaviour he acquired the good opinion of his equals and inferiors, and by his courage and resolution he had rendered himself awful to those above him; a memorable proof of which he gave when he executed the office of sheriff; for the lord chief baron Periam, having committed a gen-

[*] Pat. 25 Eliz. p. 5.

tleman at the assizes, Sir John, sitting in his sheriff's seat, called to him to stay, telling the judge he would answer for his forth-coming; neither could he be dissuaded by all the menaces of the bench from adhering to this resolution, boldly alledging that the gentleman was his prisoner, and he, as sheriff, was accountable for him. His prudence did not only extricate him out of his former difficulties, but in a short time enabled him to become what he intended to be, a great builder.

He married the daughter of Mr. Humphrey Smith of Cheapside, Queen Elizabeth's silk-man, of an ancient family in Leicestershire: she was the widow of Benedict Barnham, Esq. one of the aldermen of London, and very rich; which consideration, together with her youth and beauty, made it impossible for her to escape the addresses, even of the greatest persons about the court. She had, by her first husband (the alderman) four daughters, which were very young when they lost their father, and therefore needed a faithful friend to manage and improve their fortunes; in which trust Sir John acquitted himself so honourably, that they had 10,000*l*. each for their portion, an immense sum in those days. One of these ladies was the wife of lord Audley; another of Sir Francis Bacon, lord viscount St. Albans; a third of Sir William Soames, and the fourth of Sir William Constable. The design of this work obliging me to brevity, I cannot therefore transcribe all the memorable passages of his life, which Mr. Tomkins has recorded; but it appears that he had a spirit truly great and noble, which discovered itself upon every proper occasion: his designs were always such as became a man of honour; he had a regard to his reputation in every thing he did, which had this inseparable effect, that the whole scene of his life was nothing but a continued series of bright and laudable actions. His sense of injuries was somewhat too nice; he knew not how to bear a neglect from his superiors with that submission which was usually expected:—upon the death of the earl of Pembroke, King James appointed lord Zouch his successor in the presidentship of the marches of Wales, &c. as soon as he had obtained his commission, he sent his letters of deputation to the gentlemen of Worcestershire, and among the rest to Sir John Pakington, to be one of the lieutenants of that county; but as he did not shew him the same respect as his predecessor had done (for he had the honour to be particularly named a lieutenant in the same patent the earl of Pembroke had) refused to take the letter of deputation from the messenger, telling him, *that he had an estate as well as his master, and did not mean to venture it in mustering the king's subjects with no better a warrant than that which was only signed by his lord's hand.* After he had finished his stately structure at Westwood, he invited the earl of Northampton, lord president, and his lady, to a house warming; and as his lordship was an honourable and jovial companion, a train of above 100 knights and gentlemen accompanied him, who staid there some time, and at their going away, acknowledged they had met with so kind a reception, *that they did not know whether they had possessed the place, or the place them.* The delightful situation of his habitation was what they had never before seen; the house standing in the middle of a wood that is cut into twelve large ridings, and at a good distance one ring-riding through all of them, and the whole encompassed with a park of six or seven miles, at the farther end whereof, facing the house, is a canal of 122 acres, which gives a noble lustre, the trees gracing the water, and the water the woods.

His most magnificent entertainment was that which he gave King James and his Queen (with the greatest train that ever accompanied them) at Ailsbury, when his majesty honoured him with a visit, after his arrival from Scotland, before his coronation: upon this occasion he set no bounds to his expence, thinking it a disparagement to be outdone by any fellow subject, when such an opportunity offered; and the king and the whole court acknowledged they never met with a more noble reception.

At length this great man having lived to see his children's children, departed this life at his house at Westwood, in the 77th year of his age, in Jan. 1625.* His lady survived him, and became the wife first of Lord Kilmurry, who lived about two years, and then of Thomas, earl of Kerry. By Sir John Pakington she had one son, John, and two daughters, Anne, the wife of Sir Humphrey Ferrers of Tamworth, Knt.† and surviving him was the second wife of Philip, earl of Chesterfield; Mary, of Sir Robert Brook of Nacton, in Suffolk, Knt. master of the ceremonies to James I. whose son, Robert Brook, was created a baronet in 1661.

I. JOHN, his son, was created baronet June 22, 1620: he was member for Ailsbury 21 James I. and died Oct. 29, 1624, in the 24th year of his age, leaving issue by Frances his wife,‡ daughter of Sir John Ferrers of Tamworth, Knt. John, and a daughter, the wife first of colonel Washington, and secondly of Samuel Sandys of Ombersley, in Worcestershire, Esq. but died S. P. 1698. Frances, their mother, was, by a second marriage, the wife of that noted general, Alexander Lesley, earl of Leven.

II. Sir JOHN PAKINGTON, Bart. only son, succeeded, and resided at Westwood after his grandfather's death, who left him in his minority (at the age of four years, four months, and six days) under the guardianship of Thomas lord Coventry, keeper of the great seal of England. He was elected one of the knights for Worcestershire in 15 Charles I. and when the rebellion broke out was a member in parliament for the town of Ailsbury; and having on all occasions given proofs both of his fidelity to the crown, and the rights of the subject, was entrusted by the king, in 1642, with a commission for arraying men for his service in Worcestershire; on

---

* Mr. Lloyd, in the Lives of the Statesmen and Favourites of England since the Reformation, says, *(Fragmenta Regalia, p. 432)* "His handsome features took the most, and his neat parts, the wisest at court. He could smile ladies to his service, and argue statesmen to his design, with equal ease. His reason was powerful, his beauty more. Never was a brave soul more bravely seated: nature bestowed great parts on him, education polished him to an admirable frame of prudence and virtue. Queen Elizabeth called him her Temperance, and Leicester his Modesty. It is a question to this day, whether his resolution took the soldiers, his prudence the politicians, his compliance the favourites, his complaisance the courtiers, his piety the clergy, his integrity and condescension the people, or his knowledge the learned, most? This new court star was a nine-days wonder, engaging all eyes, until it set satisfied with its own glory. He came to court, he said, as Solomon did, to see its vanity; and retired, as he did, to repent it. It was he who said first what bishop Sanderson urged afterwards, *That a sound faith was the best divinity, a good conscience the best law, and temperance the best physic.* Sir John Pakington, in Queen Elizabeth's time, was virtuous and modest, and Sir John Pakington, in King Charles's time, loyal and valiant; the one did well, the other suffered so: Greenham was his favourite, Hammond his; the one had a competent estate and was contented, the other hath a large one, and is noble: this suppresseth factions in the kingdom, the other composed them in the court, and was called by courtiers Moderation. Westmoreland tempted his fidelity, and Norfolk his stedfastness; but he died in his bed, on honest and an happy man."

† Dugdale's Warw. vol. II. p. 1136. ‡ Ibid.

account of which he was taken prisoner, committed to the Tower, and fined 5000*l*. had his estate sequestred, his house in Buckinghamshire (one of the best of that county) levelled with the ground, and such great wastes committed in his woods, that an estimate of the loss, now remaining in the hand-writing of his lady, amounts to 20,348*l*. Notwithstanding he had suffered so much for his loyalty, he had the courage to go with a troop of horse to Charles II. at the battle of Worcester, and was taken prisoner there;* but when the rebels tried him for his life (upon an indictment of his raising and heading a troop at the battle of Worcester†) they could not procure one witness to swear against him, he was therefore acquitted, and set at liberty, but was afterwards fined 7670*l*. and forced (on petition of Thomas Scot, and others, of the town of Ailsbury, to have the fine granted them for their services to the then pretended parliament) for the said fine, to convey the market house, the tolls, court-leet, and certain grounds called Heydon-hill, parcel of his estate at Ailsbury, to the said Scot (who was one of the king's judges) and other trustees, for the use of the town, which they kept till after the restoration, when, by a special act of parliament, the said conveyances were made void.

His lady was one of the daughters of Thomas lord Coventry, keeper of the great seal of England, the most accomplished person of her sex for learning, and the brightest example of her age for wisdom and piety. Her letters and other discourses remaining in the family, and the hands of her friends, are an admirable proof of her excellent genius and vast capacity; and as she has the reputation of being thought the author of the Whole Duty of Man, so none that knew her well, and were competent judges of her abilities, could in the least doubt of her being equal to such an undertaking, though her modesty would not suffer her to claim the honour of it; but as the manuscript, under her own hand, now remains with the family, there is hardly room to doubt it.‡ By her great virtues and eminent attainments in knowledge, she acquired the esteem of all our learned divines, particularly Dr. Hammond, Bishop Morley, Bishop Fell, Bishop Pearson, Bishop Henchman, and Bishop Gunning, who were ever ready to confess they were always edified by her conversation, and instructed by her writings. She was buried May 13, 1679; and Sir John Jan. 3 following. He left issue a son, John, and two daughters; ——, the wife of Anthony Eyre of Rampton, in Nottinghamshire, Esq. and ——, of William Godfrey of Lincolnshire, Esq. and was succeeded by his son,

III. Sir JOHN PAKINGTON, Bart. who served in parliament in the reigns of Charles II. and James II. as one of the knights for Worcestershire, and was steady

---

* Echard's Hist. of Eng. vol. II. p. 712.   † Dr. Hicks's prefaratory Epist. before his Saxon Gram.

‡ Upon the whole it still remains uncertain, and it is much easier to prove who was not the author, than to assert who was: however, lady Pakington seems to have as good or better claim than Abraham Woodhead, Obadiah Walker, Bishop Fell, Bishop Chapple, Dr. Allistree, Dr. Henchman, or Mr. Fulman.
See Gent. Mag. for 1754, *p*: 26, *and Dr. Atterbury's Sermon on* 1 *Tim.* vi. 1.

Dr. Hicks, in his preface to the Anglo. Saxon Grammar, says, she was deservedly supposed to be the author. Lady Pakington died in 1679; and dean Hicks was made prebendary of Worcester in 1680, and soon after dean. After all it may be supposed, that the Whole Duty of Man, and the Decay of Christian Piety were both written by lady Pakington, though very amply and materially corrected by Bishop Fell, between whom there subsisted a long and uninterrupted correspondence.

Nash's Worces. 4. 352.

to the establishment in church and state, as his answers in writing, to the three queries proposed to him by Lord Carrington, lord lieutenant of the county of Worcester in those trying times, sufficiently shew.* He was buried the 28th of March, 1688; and by Margaret, daughter of Sir John Keyt of Ebrington, in Gloucestershire, Bart. left issue his only son and heir,

IV. Sir JOHN PAKINGTON, Bart. who was a strenuous asserter of the rights and liberties of his country; and in the year 1702 made a complaint to the house of commons against William lord bishop of Worcester, and Mr. Lloyd, his son, for interfering in the election for the county of Worcester, and by sending threatening letters to the clergy and freeholders, and aspersing his behaviour in parliament.†

---

* Quer. I. *If he was elected a member of parliament, whether he would consent to the taking off the test and penal laws?*
  Answ. The intent of the test and penal laws, being to serve the church of England, amongst which the act of uniformity seems to be the most important, till I am either convinced it is in less danger than when those laws were enacted, or some better security proposed than they afford, I humbly conceive they cannot be taken off without imminent hazard, if not ruin of the church of England; of which, I professing myself a member, can neither in honour or conscience consent to the repealing a tittle that relates to its protection, which consequently includes my answer to the second query, viz.
  Quer. II. *Whether he would contribute to the electing of such as would repeal the test and penal laws?*
  Answ. For what is not justifiable when done in one's own person, can never become so by proxy; for which reason I cannot contribute to the electing such members as shall abrogate the test and penal laws; that being in effect, to promote an action in another which I myself disapprove.
  Quer. III. *Whether you will live peaceably and quietly with neighbours of all persuasions?*
  Answ. Living peaceably and quietly with neighbours of all persuasions is a doctrine so suitable to my inclination and constant practice, that by growing mutinous I must offer all violence imaginable, both to nature and custom, which makes it superfluous to tell your lordship how readily I concur in that proposal, with which, if in any circumstance my future behaviour should not perfectly agree, your lordship must reckon it my misfortune, not my fault.
  In fine, my lord, I esteem it my greatest misfortune, that it should be in his majesty's power to ask that of me, which is not in mine, at the same instant to comply with; but I comfort myself with this assurance, that so nice a critic as his majesty is in points of honour and conscience, will never condemn me for acting by those very principles to which his great example has given so much vigour and encouragement.

† The house of commons, after hearing the evidence, and mature consideration,
  Resolved, *Nemine contradicente*,
  That Sir John Pakington has, by evidence, fully made out the charge which he exhibited against the lord bishop of Worcester.
  Resolved *Nemine contradicente*,
  That Sir John Pakington has, by evidence, fully made out the charge against Mr. Lloyd, the said lord bishop's son.
  Resolved,
  That it appears to this house, that the proceedings of William lord bishop of Worcester, his son and his agents, in order to the hindering of the election of a member for the county of Worcester, has been malicious, unchristian, and arbitrary, in high violation of the liberties and privileges of the commons of England.
  Resolved,
  That an humble address be presented to her majesty, that she will be graciously pleased to remove William lord bishop of Worcester from being lord-almoner to her majesty.
  Ordered,
  That Mr. Attorney-general do prosecute Mr. Lloyd, the lord bishop of Worcester's son, for his said offence, after his privilege, as a member of the lower house of convocation, is out.
  Veneris 20 die Novembris, 1702.
  Mr. Comptroller reported to the house, that their resolution and address to her majesty, for removing William lord bishop of Worcester from being lord-almoner to her majesty, had been presented to her ma-

Sir John was constantly elected one of the knights for Worcestershire, in every parliament from his first being chosen, at 19 years of age (except one, when he voluntarily declined it) to his death, notwithstanding the powerful opposition which was generally made against him; and was sworn recorder for the city of Worcester in the room of the earl of Plymouth: he died Feb. 21, 1725-6. By his first lady, Frances, eldest daughter of Sir Henry Parker of Hunnington, in Warwickshire, Bart. he had two sons, John, who died at Oxford, in the 19th year of his age, 1712, and Thomas, who died on his travels, at Rome in 1724, unmarried; also three daughters, Margaret, Frances, the wife of Thomas-Charles lord viscount Tracy, of the kingdom of Ireland, and Dorothy, who died in her infancy. By his second, Hester, daughter and sole heiress of Sir Herbert Perrot of Haroldstone, in the county of Pembroke, Knt. (who died in 1715) he had one son, Sir Herbert-Perrot, his successor, and died Aug. 13, 1727.

V. Sir HERBERT-PERROT PAKINGTON, Bart. succeeded his father, not only in the title and estate, but his seat in parliament, and was elected one of the knights of the shire for the county of Worcester. He married, in 1721, Elizabeth, daughter of John Conyers of Walthamstow in Essex, Esq. by whom he had two sons, John and Perrot, and two daughters, Hester and Cecilia. Sir Herbert-Perrot dying Sep. 24, 1748, at Leyden in Holland, was buried at the College church there, in the 47th year of his age; and was succeeded in title and estate by his eldest son,

VI. Sir JOHN PAKINGTON, Bart. who in 1761 married Mary, daughter of Henry Bray of Bromyard, in Herefordshire, Gent. and dying without issue, Nov. 30, 1762, in the 40th year of his age, was succeeded in title and estate by his only surviving brother,

VII. Sir HERBERT-PERROT PAKINGTON, Bart. who in 1759 married Elizabeth, widow of Herbert Wylde of Ludlow, in Shropshire, Gent. by whom he had issue Sir John, Thomas, Elizabeth, Dorothy, Anne, and Herbert-Perrot; and died at Bath in 1795, and was succeeded by his son,

VIII. Sir JOHN PAKINGTON, the present baronet.

ARMS—Party per cheveron, sable and argent, in chief, three mullets, or; in base, as many garbs, gules.
CREST—On a wreath, an elephant passant or, armed gules.
SEAT—At Westwood in Worcestershire.

jesty, and that her majesty was pleased to give this most gracious answer:—" I am very sorry that there is occasion for this address against the bishop of Worcester; I shall order and direct, that he shall no longer continue to supply the place of almoner, but I will put another in his room to perform that office."

PAKINGTON OF AILSBURY, BUCKINGHAMSHIRE.

TABLE 31.

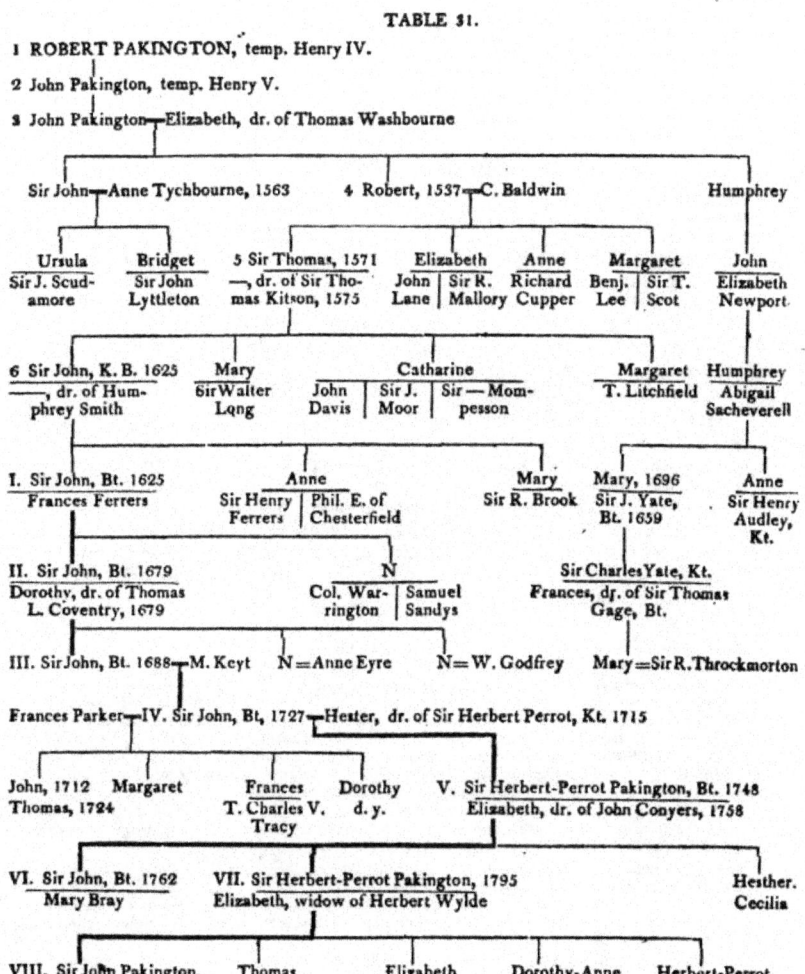

25

31. BISHOPP of PARHAM, SUSSEX.

Created Baronet July 24, 1620.

OF this family was Benedict Biscopp or Bishopp, a Saxon, who was a soldier in his youth, but afterwards a monk: he died of the palsy Jan. 12, 690, and was buried in the church of Weremouth.*

An ancient MS. deducing the descent of this family from Sibella, the sister of Benedict, existed some years ago in the north of England. Walter went into France and settled in Gascony, and his descendant, Walter, returned to England with Henry II. Thomas Bishopp, the 13th in descent from the said Walter *(see table)* married Elizabeth, relict of William.Scot of the county of Essex, Esq. and only daughter of Sir Edward Belknap, Knt. privy counsellor to Henry VII. and VIII. by Alice, daughter of —— Barton, Esq. became thereby possessed of a good estate in the county of Sussex. She died in 1569; by whom he had,

I. THOMAS BISHOPP, Esq. born in 1549: he served in parliament for Gatton in Surrey, in the 27th of Queen Eliz. and the year following for Steyning in Sussex; he was afterwards knighted, and by James I. created a baronet. He married first Anne, daughter of William Cromer of Tunstall, in Kent, Esq. by whom he had no issue; secondly, Jane, daughter of Sir Richard Weston of Sutton, in Surrey, Knt. by whom he had three sons; Thomas, who died a batchelor; Sir Edward, his successor, and Henry, who died unmarried; also two daughters, Elizabeth, the wife of Sir John Gresham of Titsey, in Surrey, Knt. and Frances, of John Aldford of Offington, in Sussex, Esq.

---

* Bede styles him Biscopus cognomento Benedictus: he was descended of a noble family of the Anglis, and having been rewarded with lands for his military services, by Oswy, king of Northumberland, he betook himself to a religious life. He made several voyages to Rome, to visit the holy see, and to purchase sacred books; and was once to have been accompanied by Alkfrid, the king's son; but was prevented by the king. He was deputed by Pope Vitallian, with two others, missionaries into Britain; Theodore was made archbishop of Canterbury, and Benedict abbot of St. Peter and St. Paul, in that city. On his return the fourth time he proposed to put himself under the protection of Cenowalch, king of the West Saxons; but finding him dead on his arrival, he returned to Northumberland, and with the assistance of Egfrid, founded the monastery of Weremouth and Janow.

In 675 he brought with him skilful masons and artists, to build the church of the abbey, after the manner of the Roman architecture; and added to the monastery an ample library, which he stored with Greek and Latin MSS. brought from Italy. *Bede's Hist. of the Abbey at Weremouth.*

In one of his expeditions to Rome he brought over John, archchanter of St. Peter's church, who introduced the Roman method of singing mass. He also brought from Rome two silken palls of exquisite wormanship, with which he afterwards purchased of King Alfred, successor to Elfrid, two pieces of land for his monastery. Bale censures him for being the first who introduced painters, glaziers, &c. into England. *Bale's Lives of the Abbots.*

John Bisshopp, as appeared by his will, dated 1465, was possessed of premises at Lenham in Kent. *(Hasted's Kent, vol. II. p. 443).* In 1496 William Bisshopp was prior of the cathedral church of Rochester. *Ibid. p. 443.*

BISHOPP OF PARHAM, SUSSEX.

II. Sir EDWARD BISHOPP, Bart. son and heir of Sir Thomas, was knighted by King Charles I. at Hampton Court, on the 18th of Dec. 1625; and was returned for Steyning to the first parliament called by that prince; and taking part with his sovereign against his rebellious subjects, was made a prisoner in Arundel Castle, and had his inheritance sequestered. He married Mary, fourth daughter of Nicholas Tufton, earl of Thanet, by whom he had issue four daughters; Frances, the wife of Sir George Warburton of Arley, in Chestershire, Bart. Diana, of Sir Henry Goring of Highden, in Sussex, Bart. Mary, who died an infant; and Christian, the wife of Sir Thomas Cobb of Adderbury, in Oxfordshire, Bart. also three sons, Thomas, who died unmarried; Edward, who died an infant; and

III. Sir CECIL BISHOPP, who succeeded to the estate and title, and married Anne, daughter and heir of George Berry of Cullum, in Oxfordshire, Esq. and died June 3, 1705; by whom he had two sons and three daughters; Edward, who died before his father, in the 21st year of his age, and Sir Cecil, his successor; Sarah, the wife of Sir Richard Newdigate of Harfield, in Middlesex, Bart. Christian, of Sir Robert Fagg of Wiston, in Sussex, Bart. and Mary, of Thomas Mannock, of Great Bromley Hall in Essex, Esq. younger son of Sir Frances Mannock of Gifford's Hall, in Suffolk, Bart.

IV. Sir CECIL BISHOPP, Bart. the only surviving son, and successor to his father, married Elizabeth, daughter and heir of Henry Dunch of Newington, in Oxfordshire, Esq. and had issue Sir Cecil, his successor, Henry, Charles, who died at Prague of a fever, March 29, 1739, unmarried; James, and John: also Mary, the wife of the hon. Mr. Dormer, son to Lord Dormer: she died Nov. 2, 1739. Sir Cecil dying Oct. 1725, was succeeded in dignity and estate by his eldest son,

V. Sir CECIL BISHOPP, Bart. who was representative for Penryn in Cornwall, and afterwards for Boroughbridge, in Yorkshire. In Aug. 1755 he was appointed superintendant of his majesty's founderies. He married, in 1726, Anne, second daughter of Hugh Boscawen, viscount Falmouth, by which lady, who died in May, 1741, he had four sons and eight daughters; Cecil, who succeeded him; Thomas, a colonel in the army, now living, and unmarried; Edward, one of the chief clerks in the Treasury, and afterwards a commissioner of the Salt Office, who died in 1792, leaving one legitimate son, Henry, now living at Stonington in Sussex, a colonel in the Cheshire fencibles. 1, Anne, the wife of Robert Brudenell, son of the late earl of Cardigan: she has two children, Robert and Augusta. 2, Charlotte, of Sir William Maynard, Bart. by whom she had the present Viscount Maynard, and another son and daughter: Lady Maynard died in 1762. 3, Frances, appointed in 1761 maid of honour to her present majesty; and married, in 1764, to Sir George Warren, K.B. 4, Harriot, the wife first of Thomas Drummer, Esq. of Cranbury in Hampshire, and secondly to Nathaniel Dance, Esq. member in the last and present parliament for East Grinsted. 5, Catharine; the wife first of Sir Charles Cope, Bart. by whom he had a son, who survived his father, but is since dead; and two daughters, one married to the Duke of Dorset, and the other to the Earl of Aboyne: Lady Cope married secondly, in 1782, the right hon. Charles Jenkinson, since created Baron Hawkesbury, and Earl of Liverpool; by him she has one daughter, Charlotte, and a son, Cecil: the other three daughters died young, and unmarried. Sir Cecil died in 1778, and was succeeded by his eldest son,

VI. Sir CECIL BISHOPP, Bart. who married Susan, eldest daughter of John Hedges of Finchley, in Middlesex, who died in 1791; by whom he had two sons and a daughter: Hugh, the second son, married in 1784 Elizabeth-Rebecca, the only daughter of John Swain, Esq. of Stonington in Sussex, and has one son, Hugh. He died in Sep. 1779, and was succeeded by his eldest son,

VII. Sir CECIL BISHOPP, Bart. who married in July, 1782, Harriot-Anne, daughter of William Southwell, Esq. of Frampton in Gloucestershire, uncle to Lord de Clifford, and has two sons and two daughters; Cecil, Charles-Cecil, Harriot-Anne, Catharine-Annabella. Sir Cecil is member in the present parliament, as he was in the two former, for the borough of Shoreham and of Bramber, and is fellow of the Royal Society.

ARMS—On a bend, cottized gules, three bezants.
CREST—On a ducal coronet or, a griffin sejant argent, resting his dexter claw on an escutcheon, argent.
MOTTO—*Pro Deo et Ecclesia.*   SEAT—At Parham in Sussex.

The barony of Zouche of Harringworth is an ancient barony, created by writ of summons to William la Zouche, in the reign of King Edw. II. and continued in that family, by an uninterrupted chain of descent, for upwards of 300 years, till upon the death of Edward, the last Lord Zouche, in 1625, without issue male, it fell into abeyance between his two daughters; the eldest was the wife of Sir William Tate, and the youngest of Thomas Leighton, Esq. The line of the youngest is believed to be extinct, but the eldest was continued for several generations in the family of Tate, and the late Bartholomew Tate, Esq. The last heir male of that family was advised to assert his claim, but having no child left to inherit after him he declined it, and died in 1776, without issue; and the title fell again into, and now remains, in abeyance between the issue of his two sisters: Catharine, the elder, became the wife of Charles Hedges, Esq. and Mary of Samuel Long, Esq. There is issue from both these sisters; but Sir Cecil Bishopp, by the recent death of his uncle, John Hedges, Esq. in August last, without issue, finding himself in the situation of grandson and heir of the eldest of those sisters, and so heir-general of the body of the eldest co-heir to the barony of Zouche, proposes to submit his case to his majesty's royal consideration, in the hope, that if he should be able, as he trusts he is, to prove the descent as herein stated, his majesty may be graciously pleased to terminate the abeyance of the said barony in his favour. See also *Gent. Mag. for* 1799, *p.* 1013.

BISHOPP OF PARHAM, SUSSEX.

WALTER BISHOPP came into England with Henry II.=—, dr. and beiress of John Pocklington, Kt. of the Saxon race

Robert Bishopp of Pocklington=—, dr. of —Metham

- John=—, dr. of Sir J. Grimston
- William, chancellor of York
- Thomas, abbot of Beverley

John Bishopp=—, dr. of —— Hedworth of Harrington

William Bishopp=—, dr. of —— Coyner of Horton

Thomas=—, dr. of Sir Wm. Gascoigne, Knt.

TABLE 32.

Robert=—, dr. of —— Hawsworth of Norton

William=—, dr. of —— Fenwick of Wallington

- Thomas=—, dr. of —— Talboys
- Robert, dean of Norwich

- William=—, dr. of —— Fairfax
- John, prior of Brackley

- Thomas=—, dr. of John Brampston
- Robert went into Oxfordshire

- Thomas=—, dr. of —— Arthington
- John, bishop of Brailes=—Bloomer

- Robert=—, dr. of —— Donstable
- Wm. town-clerk of Chichester
- Wm. of Brailes=—Willington

John Bishopp | THOMAS=Eliz. Belknap, 1569 | EDWARD L. ZOUCHE, 1625

| Anne —Benyon | Elizabeth H. Towers | I. Sir Thomas Bishopp, Bt. Anne Cromer | Jane Weston | * Elizabeth Sir Wm. Tate, 1617 | N T. Leighton |

Thomas | II. Sir Edw. Kt. & Bt. Mary Tufton | Henry | Elizabeth Sir J. Gresham | Frances J. Aldford | Zouche Tate 1650

| Thomas. Edward. Mary | Frances Sir G. Warburton | Diana Sir Henry Goring | Christiana Sir Thomas Cobb, Bt. | III. Sir Cecil Bishopp 1705 Anne Berry | Wm. Tate 1695 |

Edward | IV. Sir Cecil Bishopp, 1725 Eliz. Dunch, 1739 | Sarah Sir R. Newdigate | Christian Sir R. Fagg | Mary T. Mannock | Bartholomew Tate 1703

V. Sir Cecil Bishopp, Bt. 1778 Anne Boscawen, 1741 | Henry. Charles | James. John | Mary —Dormer | Bartholomew S.P. 1776 | Catharine C. Hedges | † Mary S. Long

| VI. Sir Cecil Bt. 1779 S. Hedges 1791 | Thos. Edw. 1792 | Anne Rob. son of the E. of Cardigan | Charlotte 1762 Sir Wm. Maynard K.B. | Frances Sir George Warren | Harriot Thos. Drummond | Catharine Nath. Dance | Susan Sir C. Cope Bt. | Anna-Maria Chas. E. of Liverpool | Rob. Sir C. Bishopp | Hon. W. Bateman | Long, 1772 |

VII. Sir Cecil Bishopp, Bt.=Harriot Southwell | Hugh=E. R. Swain

Cecil | Charles-Cecil | Harriot-Anne | Catharine-Annabella

Jane Mary Lucy all married, and have issue.

* Elizabeth, eldest daughter and co-heir, and the only child from whom there is any known issue, married Sir Wm. Tate, Knt.
† The share which Mary Long, the second sister of Mr. Tate, had in the original abeyance of the barony, is fallen into a second abeyance among her three grand-daughters, the children of her eldest son: it is presumed therefore, that no direct claim can be made from that line, as those ladies are only co-heirs of a co-heir; whereas Sir Cecil is the grandson and sole heir of the eldest co-heir.
‡ Anna-Maria married Feb. 1753 to the Hon. Wm. Bateman, second son of the first Viscount Bateman, by Lady Anne Spencer, only daughter of Charles earl of Sunderland, and grand-daughter to the great Duke of Marlborough, who died in June 1783. Mrs. Bateman is now living, a widow in 1799.

31. VINCENT of Stoke-D'abernon, Surrey.

Created Baronet July 26, 1620.

THIS family, on the marriage of Thomas Vincent, Esq. in the reign of Queen Elizabeth, with Jane, only daughter and heir to Thomas Lyfield of Stoke D'abernon, Esq. became possessed of that inheritance; which seat has ever since been their principal residence, though they were for ages before eminent in the county of Northampton. Some of the family were also at Swinford* in Leicestershire; for in 10 Edw. II.

1. Miles Vincent was owner of many lands there, in the hundred of Guthlackston, upon the banks of the river Avon, which divides that county from Northamptonshire. By Jane his wife he had two sons, John and Robert Vincent of Rothwell, living 49 Edw. III. father to John Vincent of the same place.

2. John, the eldest son, in 6 Edw. III. was, by the king's letters patent, made receiver of his rents and profits in the county of Pontive, in France,† Oct. 15, in the fourth year of his reign; about which he suffered imprisonment in the Tower of London, 8 Edw. III. until he had settled his accounts: he was the father of

3. Sir Thomas Vincent of Swinford, Knt. living in 1409, who added to his estate the lordship of Bernake, by marriage with Joan, daughter and heir to Sir John Bernake of Bernake, in Northamptonshire, Knt. son and heir to Geoffery Bernake of the same place, by Isolda his wife, daughter and heir to Henry Paas of Bernake; and was succeeded by his son,

4. John Vincent of Bernake and Swinford, who by Margaret his wife, daughter of Sir Baldwin Drayton of Cranford, had issue

5. Richard Vincent, lord of the said manors, who was slain by Henry Killigrew, in 1434, having had, by Elizabeth his wife, four sons; 1, John; 2, Robert, who had the lands in Swinford, from whom the Vincents of Thingdon in Northamptonshire descended; 3, Richard, and 4, William, a monk in the abbey of Crowland, who died March 1437. Richard was succeeded by his eldest son,

6. John Vincent of Bernake, who married Margaret, daughter to John Jordaine of the county of Stafford, and had two sons, Robert and Richard; from which Richard those of the name at Messingham in Lincolnshire, and of Peckleton in the said county, and of Smeton in Yorkshire, and those of Horpole in Northamptonshire are derived.

7. Robert Vincent, the eldest son, married Catharine, daughter and co-heir of Thomas Semark, and was father of

8. Thomas Vincent, who was seated at Bernake in 1461; and having married twice, had issue only by his last wife, Cicely, daughter of Sir John de Causton, Knt.

* Burton's Leicest. p. 278.   † Pat. 4, Edw. III. m. 1.

9. John Vincent of Bernake, temp. Henry VII. who married Anne, daughter to Charles Hill; and was succeeded by his son and heir,

10. David Vincent, Esq. who in 1531 had a grant for life of the office of keeper of the king's wardrobe, within his manor of Richmond; and the next year of keeper of the wardrobe at Greenwich: also in 1536 a grant for life of the office of warden of the mint within the Tower, after the death or surrender of John Pate. In 1539 the king demises to him the lordship of Pyrrybar, in Suffolk; and the year after constitutes him keeper of his wardrobe at Hampton Court, during life. In 1542 he had a grant (with Robert Bocher, Gent.) of the scite of the house of the Grey Friars in Grantham, and the scite of the priory called Black Friars in Stamford in Lincolnshire, and was in such favour with his prince, that he was called to be one of the witnesses to his last will and testament, and therein had a legacy left him of 100*l*. In the reign of Edw. IV. he was one of the gentlemen of the bed-chamber, and had a grant of the manor and rectory of Long Ditton in Surrey, as also of a messuage at Richmond in the same county, in which he resided at the time of his death, 1565.* His first wife was Elizabeth, daughter of —— Spencer, of the county of Northampton, Esq. by whom he had Thomas, Henry, and Anne, the wife of Sir Edward Heron, Knt. one of the barons of the Exchequer. His other wife was Jane, daughter to William Rotsey, Esq. of Worcestershire, who had issue by him three daughters, Elizabeth, Mary, who died unmarried, and Jane, the wife of John Chaworth of Crophill-Butler, in Nottinghamshire, Esq. and was mother to Sir George Chaworth, Knt. viscount Chaworth, of the kingdom of Ireland: he was succeeded by his eldest son,

11. Thomas Vincent, Esq. who married Jane, daughter and sole heir of Thomas Lyfield of Stoke-D'abernon, Esq. by Frances his wife, daughter and co-heir of Edmund lord Bray; and in her right was possessed of that estate which lies upon the river Mole, and for distinction is called D'abernon, from the Dabernons, ancient lords of that place, as the inscription in the church thereof farther shews;† which

---

* By his last testament, bearing date Aug. 20, 1565, he gives several sums of money to the reparations of the churches of Bernack, Long Ditton, Hampton, and Richmond; ordering likewise 20s. to be distributed to the poor in every of the said parishes. He leaves to Anne, his daughter, 200*l*. at the day of her marriage, beside one gold ring, with a diamond, and a chain of gold; also a tablet, with the picture of St. Michael, graven on an agate, set in gold, which his first wife was wont to wear; likewise her mother's wedding ring; and to his other daughters, Elizabeth, Mary, and Jane, 100*l*. each, and a gold ring at their marriage. He farther bequeaths to Henry, his youngest son 100*l*. at the age of 21 years, and a lease of Tenhall Grange; also, that his executors allow him 20 nobles yearly, till he comes to 26 years of age, for his better maintenance and learning at Oxford, Cambridge, or the inns of the court of chancery. He constitutes his son Thomas, and two others, and one of his servants executors, desiring the earl of Bedford, and Sir William Cecil, Knt. principal secretary of state, to see his will performed.

† Here lyeth buried the body of Frances, the wife of Thomas Lyfield, Esq. owner of the manor of Stoke-D'abernon, in the county of Surrey: the which Frances was the youngest daughter of Sir Edmund Bray, Knt. Lord Bray, and of the Lady Jane, his wife; which Jane was sole daughter and heir of Richard Haleighwell, Esq. and Anne, his wife; which Richard was son and heir to Sir John Haleighwell, Knt. and the said Anne was sole daughter and heir of Sir John Norbury, Knt.* which Sir John was son and heir of Sir Henry Norbury, Knt. and Anne his wife; the which Anne was daughter and heir to William

* Sir John Norbury lies buried in the chancel in Stoke church, belonging to the Vincent family, which chancel he built, and has a little marble monument there erected to his memory, whereon he is represented kneeling, in complete armour. Ex infor. Dom. Hen. Vincent, Bar.

said Thomas Vincent, Esq. fixing his residence at Stoke, as before-mentioned, exchanged his manor of Bernake with Thomas Cecil, earl of Exeter, for lands in the county of Surrey, that his estate might lie more contiguous. He lived in great reputation and esteem, and Queen Elizabeth, as a mark of her favour, gave him the honour of a visit at Stoke, on Sep. 25, 1601, at which time her majesty conferred on him the honour of knighthood. He died Dec. 14, 1613, aged 70. she, Jan. 23, 1619. They had issue two sons, Francis and Bray, who died unmarried; also a daughter, the wife of Sir Matthew Brown, of Beechworth Castle in Surrey, Knt.

I. Sir FRANCIS, the eldest son, was knighted in his father's life-time; was afterwards created a baronet, by letters patent, July 26, 1620; and in the first year of the reign of King Charles I. served in parliament for the county of Surrey. He had three wives; 1. Sarah, daughter of Sir Amias Paulet, Knt. governor of Guernsey and Jersey, and of the privy-council to Queen Elizabeth; 2, Mary, daughter of Sir Henry Archer of Essex, Knt. and 3, Eleanor, daughter and sole heir of Robert Mallet of Welley, Esq. and widow to Sir Arthur Ackland, Knt. By Sarah, his first wife, he had several sons, who died without issue, and two daughters, Elizabeth, the wife of John Ackland of Devonshire, Esq. and Margaret of Sir Francis Gabell of Cobham, in Surrey, Knt. but of the sons, only Anthony, the youngest, survived his father; which

II. Sir ANTHONY VINCENT, Bart. born in 1594, was sheriff of the county of Surrey, in the 12th year of the reign of King Charles I. which county, before that year, was united with Sussex, and one sheriff served both. He behaved himself with all dutiful allegiance to his prince during the great rebellion in 1641, and suffered with other loyalists on that account. He married Elizabeth, daughter of Sir Arthur Ackland of Killerton, in Devonshire, Knt. and was succeeded in title and estate by his son and heir,

III. Sir FRANCIS VINCENT, Bart. who was a member for the port of Dover, in the long parliament in the reign of King Charles II. and married, 1, Catharine, daughter of George Pitt of Harrow on the Hill, in Middlesex, Esq. serjeant at law, by whom he had three sons, Sir Anthony, Sir Francis, and Arthur, who died with-

Crosier, Esq. the which William was son and heir to Sir William Crosier, Knt. and Elizabeth his wife; the which Elizabeth was daughter and heir to Sir William D'Awbernon, Knt. who descended from D'Awbernon, the Norman,* who came into England with William the Conqueror, and from whom this manor did descend lineally to the same Sir William. And the aforesaid Sir Henry Norbury was son and heir to Sir John Norbury, Knt. and Elizabeth his wife; the which Sir John Norbury was treasurer of England in the time of King Henry IV. and the said Elizabeth, his wife, was eldest sister to Sir Ralph Butler, lord Sudley, and lord steward of the household to King Henry VI. the which Sir Ralph was son and heir to Thomas Butler, lord Sudley; and the said Thomas was son and heir to Sir William Butler, who married the daughter and heir of John, lord Sudley, lineally descended from King Harold, whom William the Conqueror slew in the field: which said Frances Lyfield died 27 Maii, A. D. 1592, in the 70th year of her age; leaving issue, by the said Thomas Lyfield, Jane, now the wife of Thomas Vincent, Esq. *Aubrey's Surrey, vol. III. p. 146, 147.*

* Sir John D'Abernon, the Norman, lies buried, as does also Sir William D'Abernon, in the chancel of Stoke church, before the communion table: the stones which cover them are inlaid with brass, with two figures of armed knights, bearing the arms of D'Abernon on their shields. The said arms see well painted, on glass, in the window over the communion table; as also in several compartments are, the arms of Crosier, Norbury, Haleighwell, Bray, Lyfield, Vincent, with their intermarriages placed there, by Sir Francis Vincent, the first baronet. Ex infor. Dom. Hen. Vincent, Bar.

out issue; and two daughters, Catharine and Elizabeth, who both died unmarried: and by his second wife, Elizabeth, daughter of Sir Henry Vane, of Hadlow in Kent, Knt. had two sons; 1, Thomas of Fetcham, in Surrey, who married twice, first Margaret, daughter and heir of William Bluck of Hadley, in Middlesex; secondly Mary, daughter of Sir Arthur Onslow of West Clandon, in Surrey, Bart. relict of Sir Robert Reeve of Thwaite, in Suffolk, Bart. by whom he had no issue: Henry, second son of Sir Francis, died in the late wars in Spain, S. P. Sir Francis had likewise two daughters; Elizabeth, the wife of Philip Hildyard of East Horsley, in Surrey, Esq. and Frances, who died unmarried. This Sir Francis was succeeded by his eldest son,

IV. Sir ANTHONY VINCENT, Bart. who married Anne, daughter of Sir James Austen of Southwark, Knt. and left only a daughter, Catharine, the wife of the Rev. Dr. Warren of Marden, in Hertfordshire, whereupon the title and estate devolved on his brother,

V. Sir FRANCIS VINCENT, Bart.* who was elected one of the knights for the county of Surrey, in two parliaments, the one in the second year of the reign of King William and Queen Mary, and the other in the 9th year of the reign of Queen Anne: he married Rebecca, daughter of Mr. Jonathan Ashe of London, merchant, by whom he had six sons, Anthony, Francis, Thomas, Henry, Richard, and William; as also four daughters, Catharine, Frances, Elizabeth, and Anne. Anthony, the eldest son, died young; Francis at the age of 28, and Thomas, unmarried. Sir Henry, the eldest surviving son, was his successor; Richard, William, married the daughter of the Rev. Dr. Warren of Marden, in Hertfordshire, by whom he had two sons and two daughters, William, Arthur, Diana, and Catharine.

Of the four daughters of Sir Francis, Catharine, the eldest, was the wife of George Phipps of Oxford, Esq. Frances, of William Ward of London, merchant; Elizabeth, of the Rev. John Butterfield, rector of Stoke D'Abernon; Anne died young; Sir Francis died Feb. 10, 1736, aged 90, and was succeeded in dignity and estate by his eldest surviving son,

VI. Sir HENRY VINCENT, who in 1727-8, was elected member of parliament for Guildford: he married Elizabeth, daughter of Bezaliel Sherman of London, Esq. Turkey merchant, and had issue two sons, Francis, and the Rev. Thomas, who died at Oxford in 1740, unmarried; and five daughters; the two eldest, named Anne, both died young: Elizabeth, who died May 25, 1759, unmarried; Hester, the wife of John Smyth, earl of Clanrickard, of the kingdom of Ireland; and Sarah. Sir Henry died Jan. 20, 1757, aged 70, and was succeeded in title and estate by his only son,

VII. Sir FRANCIS VINCENT, Bart. who married 1, Elizabeth, daughter and heir of Mr. David Kilmaine of London, banker, who had 30,000*l.* to her fortune: she died Nov. 22, 1744, without issue. 2, Mary, daughter of Lieut. Gen. Thomas Howard, by whom he had four sons, Francis, Henry-Dormer; George, and Thomas both died young; and Mary, the wife of Niel Primrose, earl of Roseberry, K. T. This second lady died Aug. 16, 1757. 3, Mary, daughter and co-heir of Sir John Astley of Patteshall, Bart. and sister of the countess Dowager of Tankerville:

* Salmon's Hertfordshire, p. 278.

VINCENT OF STOKE-D'ABERNON, SURREY.

TABLE 33.

```
1 MILES VINCENT=Jane                    KING HAROLD              D'Awbernon, the Norman
        |                                    |                            |
2 John Vincent              Robert      John L. Sudley           Sir Wm. D'Awbernon
3 Sir Thomas=J. Bernake      John       N =Sir Wm. Butler        Eliz.=Sir Wm. Crosier
4 John=Marg. Drayton                    Thomas L. Sudley         Wm. Crosier
5 Richard, 1434=Elizabeth        John   Elizabeth=Sir J. Norbury
6 John=M. Jordaine   Robert   Richard   Wm.   Sir Henry Norbury = Anne Crosier
7 Robert    Richard   Vincents  Vincents                         Sir John Norbury
  C. Semark  Vincent    of       of
                     Thingdon  Shepey                                  Anne
8 Thomas                                                         Rich. Haleighwell
  N | C. Cawston           Vincents of Messingham, &c.
                                                                 Jane=Edw. L. Bray
9 John Vincent=Anne Hill                                         Frances, 1592=T. Lyfield
E. Spencer =10 David Vincent, 1565 =Jane Rotsey
                                                                 Jane Lyfield
11 Sir Thomas, 1613   Henry    Anne     Elizabeth.   Jane        Sir Thos. Vincent, 1613
   Jane Lyfield, 1619         Sir E. Heron   Mary    J. Chaworth
                                                                        N
I. Sir Francis Vincent, Knt. & Bart. 1613        Bray            Sir M. Browne
   Sarah Pawlet, 1608 | M. Archer | Eleanor Mallet

II. Sir Anthony, Bart.           Many sons    Elizabeth          Margaret
    Eliz. Ackland                             John Acland        Sir Francis Gabell

Cath. Pitt=III. Sir Francis Vincent, Bart.=Eliz. dr. of Sir Henry Vane, Knt.

IV. Sir Anthony    V. Sir Francis, 1736   Arthur.    Thomas Vincent   Henry    Elizabeth
    Anne Austen      Rebecca Ashe    Cath. Eliz.    M. Black | M. Onslow   Frances   P. Hildy

Catharine, 1702  Anthony.  VI. Sir Henry, 1757   Rich.   William    Catharine   Frances   Eliz.
Rev. Dr. Rich.   Francis.      Eliz. Sherman             — Warren   G. Phipps   W. Ward   J. But-
Warren           Thomas                                                                   terfield
       VII. Sir Francis Vincent, Bart. 1775   Thomas.   Anne     Hesther     Sarah
E. Kilmaine | M. Howard, 1757 | M. Astley     Anne      Eliz.    J. E. of Clanricard
1744
       VIII. Sir Francis, 1791    Henry.    George    Thomas    Mary
       Miss Muilman         Dormer, living in 1765  d. y.    d. y.

IX. Sir Richard Vincent, Bart.
```

she was the relict of Anthony Langley Swymmer, Esq. by whom he had no issue: she died June 29, 1795. Sir Francis, in 1741, was chosen representative for the town of Guildford, and afterwards for the county of Surrey: he died in May, 1775, and was succeeded by his son,

VIII. Sir FRANCIS VINCENT, Bart. who was resident at Venice: he married Miss Muilman, daughter of Richard Muilman French Chiswell, Esq. M.P. for the borough of Aldborough in Yorkshire, by whom he had one son, Richard, born July 23, 1780, and a daughter, ——, born in 1789: he died in 1791, and was succeeded by his son,

IX. Sir RICHARD VINCENT, Bart.

ARMS—Azure, three quatuor foiles, argent.
CREST—Out of a ducal crown, proper, a bear's head, argent.
MOTTO—*Vincenti dabitur.*
SEAT—At Stoke D'abernon, near Cobham, in Surrey.

---

33. TICHBORNE of Tichborne, Hampshire.

Created Baronet March 8, 1620.

THIS family, variously written Titchebourn, Tichbourne, and Tichborne, is presumed to be of Saxon origin, deduced from Ticceburn.* But to come to what is certain, it is found in ancient deeds, records, &c.

1. Sir Roger de Ticheburne, a valiant and daring knight, was possessed of the lordship of Tichburne, in the county of Southampton, temp. Henry II. and by marriage with Mabell,† sole heir of the family of Lymerston in the Isle of Wight, had

---

* Mon. Ang. vol. I. p. 37.

† A MS. I understand is now in the possession of the present baronet, which speaks of the alliances of the Tichbornes with most of the noble families in this kingdom, and with the Guises in France; and also of this dame Mabell, who being bed-ridden, and extremely ill, petitioned her husband for the means of instituting a dole of bread, to be given to all poor persons who might ask for it, on every succeeding Lady Day. In return he promised her as much ground as she could walk round in the neighbourhood of the house, should be appropriated to the aforesaid purpose; on which she caused herself to be taken out of bed, and carried to a choice piece of ground of several acres extent, on the north-east side the mansion house, and there, on her hands and knees, contrived to *crawl* round it, from which circumstance it has retained the name of *Crawls* to the present day.

This, I believe, has been continued almost without any exception, till within these three years. Sir Henry has in his possession the original weight of the dole bread; on one side of which is engraved *Fundatum Henrico regnante secundo*; on the other, *Tichborne dole weight*, 1lb. 10oz. avoir. It was generally the custom to bake about 1200 of these loaves, and if any people remained after the distribution of this

also possession of that estate, and left issue by her two sons and a daughter, Sir Walter de Tichbourne, Knt. Geffery, and Phelippe.

2. Sir Walter succeeded, and left issue, Sir Roger de Tichborne, Knt. and a son named John.

3. Sir Roger,* by his wife Alicia Hake, or Hacket, had no issue; so that

4. John de Tichbourne, his brother, succeeded :† he married Margaret, daughter and heir of Roger Sipherwast, the chief of a noted family, that had large possessions in Dorsetshire, and the western parts of England, which by this marriage devolved on the Tichbournes. He had issue by her two daughters, Catharine and Margaret; and two sons, Sir Roger and John Tichbourne: his wife surviving afterwards married Thomas Durant.

5. Roger Tichebourne, eldest son of Sir John, married Catharine, daughter of Roger Loveday, sister and heir of Richard Loveday, as appears by inquisition, taken in 1319, upon the death of the said Richard, who then died seized of the manor of Brisset in Sussex, and of divers lands in the county of Cambridge, and elsewhere: his sisters, Margaret, aged 30 years; Anne, wife of Richard Hackum, aged 28; Eleanor, aged 26; and Catharine, wife of Roger Ticheborne, aged 24 years, being heirs thereto.

6. This Roger de Tichborne died before his father; for in 1337 his son, Roger Ticheborne was found to be 23 years of age, and cousin and heir to his grand-mother, Margaret, late wife of Thomas Durant.

7. John, his son and heir, who was knighted, and by his wife Cecily, daughter and heir of Sir Adam de Rake, had issue a daughter, Olivia, and a son,

bread, each one received two-pence. One year, when Lady Day happened on a Sunday, 1225 loaves were distributed, and 8*l.* in two-pences. For a week or two before, the dole vagabonds from all quarters use to assemble in the neighbourhood, and many people came who did not stand in need of such charity. It was generally a scene of riot and confusion, fighting and quarrelling; and for these reasons Sir Henry has discontinued it. The bread was thrown at one another, wasted, and spoiled. Some old women indeed preserved it with great care, as a specific for the use of *agues*, and most other disorders. There is a tradition, that the dole was once discontinued, and a part of the house sunk. This is accounted for by an old woman's prophecy, that if the dole be discontinued, the family will soon be extinct, and the house fall to ruins.

Michael Blount, Esq. of Maple Durham, Oxon, near Reading, great grand-son of Sir Henry-Joseph, who died in 1743, among other curiosities belonging to the family, is in possession of a large painted picture of the manner of distributing the dole, containing the family, the chaplain, the neighbours, with many poor persons (all portraits) and the old house, &c. which from the dresses is judged to have been painted either in the reign of James I. or Charles I. It is esteemed a real curiosity.

* He released and quit claimed for himself and heirs, to the chapel of St. ———— of Lymmerston, and to the chaplains there serving, all his right and title in the land at Langred, which Geffery de Titchbourne, his uncle, had given them, witnessed by Sir William de Insula, or Lisle, Sir Jordan de Insula, Jordan de Kingston, and others. The charter bears no date, but the seal annexed is the graphical description of a knight, cloathed in antique mail, under an upper robe or garment; his right hand brandishing a sword, and his left obscured by an oblong target of arms, covering his breast, mounted on a war horse in full course, and circumscribed in the characters of the age, *S. Rogeri de Tichbourne.*

† This Sir John Tichbourne was a person of great eminence, serving in the parliaments of the ninth and tenth of Edw. II. as one of the knights of the shire for the county of Southampton: he had (as usual in those days) his expences allowed. He was sheriff of the same county in 14 Edw. II. and at the same time (with Adam Walrand) was sheriff of Wiltshire and Dorsetshire. On the 8th of Oct. 1322 he was

8. John,* who married Margaret, daughter to John Moking of London, of a family surnamed from Moking, their capital residence, situate in Middlesex; and had issue by her, John, William, and Eleanor.

9. John Tichborne, Esq. the eldest, married Joan, daughter of Thomas Wandesford, alderman of London, sister and co-heir to William Wandesford, Esq. and had issue,

10. John Tichborne, Esq. who was sheriff of Hampshire in 3 Henry VII. He married Margaret, daughter and heir to Richard Martin of Eden Bridge. in Kent; by Margaret his wife, daughter and heir of Walter Wallis of Cowden, in Sussex, and had by her four sons; 1, William, who died without issue; 2, Nicholas; 3, Thomas, who had his mother's inheritance at Eden Bridge, and was progenitor to a family, from whom, as heirs general, were descended Calthrop and Potter, and as heir male, John Tichborne, D. D. The fourth son was Henry Tichborne, who married Anne, daughter of ——. Marvin, and had a numerous issue.

11. Nicholas enjoyed the ancient patrimony, was sheriff of the county of Southampton in 1 Edw. VI. but dying soon after, left issue by his wife Anne, daughter of Robert White of Southwarnborough in Southamptonshire, Dorothy, the wife of John Sambourne of Berkshire; Margaret, of John Bruin, from whom the Bruins of Farnham descended; and Dorothy, of Thomas Leigh of Cheshire. He had also four sons, Nicholas, Bartholomew, Roger, and William.

12. Nicholas succeeded, and in 1 Queen Mary was sheriff of the county of Southampton; as also elected for the same county one of the knights of the shire in the parliament that queen called to meet at Oxford. By his first wife, Juliana, daughter and heir of Robert Fenrother, alderman of London, he had only a daughter, Juliana, the wife of Thomas Cresswell of Odiam, in Southamptonshire, Esq. but by his second wife, Elizabeth Rythe of Rythe (sole heir of her brothers Thomas, William, and James) he had five sons and three daughters; Constance, the wife of Robert Knight of Lyford, in Berks; Anne, of John Beronsam; and another of —— Bend of Sussex. The five sons were, Benjamin, Gilbert, Ambrose, Martin, and Jeremy; and was succeeded by his son,

I. BENJAMIN TICHBORNE of Tichborne, Esq. sheriff of the county of Southampton in 21 Eliz. as also in the last year of the reign of that queen, and distinguished himself in a very particular manner; for as soon as he had notice of her death, he, without any order from the administration, immediately proclaimed at

---

constituted castellan and warden of the king's castle of Old Sarum. He was also one of the king's justices itinerant; and died about 1334: by Amicia his wife, he had a daughter Catharine, a nun at Whorwell, as also four sons; 1, Roger; 2, Richard, who married Alice, daughter and co-heir of John de la Hode of Tisted, and had issue Richard, who assumed the name of Tisted from the inheritance that came by his mother, and was ancestor to the Tisteds of Tisted, that in the fourth generation terminated in heirs female; 3, Walter de Tichborne, who married Agatha, the other daughter and co-heir of John la Hode; 4, Thomas.

* The same arms, crest, and supporters, that his descendants now bear, are appendant to a deed, wherein he is stiled John Tichborne, son and heir of John Tichborne, Knt. granting to William Warner, his servant, for his good service performed, all his lands, tenements, woods, meadows, rents, and services, with a water-mill in Dorsetshire, which his father, Sir John Tycheborne, Knt. purchased of John Gille, the son of William Gille, at Mulle in the parish of Morden, in the said county. Given at Tichebourne upon the feast of St. Mark the Evangelist, 10 Henry IV. after the conquest.

Winchester, and through the whole county of Southampton, the accession of King James I. to the crown of England; which was so acceptable to his majesty, who was informed of the interest he had in his country, that he conferred the honour of knighthood on him and his four sons; and for other his faithful services granted the castle of Winchester, in fee farm, to him and his heirs for ever, as also a pension of 100l. per ann. during his own life, and the life of his son, Sir Richard: he likewise honoured him with several visits, at his seat at Tichborne, and advanced him to the title of baronet. He married Amphilis, daughter of Richard Weston, Esq. one of the justices of the common pleas, and had four sons; Sir Richard, his successor, Sir Walter, Sir Benjamin, and Sir Henry, all three knights; and three daughters: and departed this life in 1621.

He was a gentleman of great honour, and of considerable interest in his county; and on all occasions shewed himself a true patriot, both as a magistrate, and in the parliament, being elected thereto in 35 Eliz. as one of the knights of the shire for the county of Southampton. He was a tender husband, indulgent father, and a kind master. His eldest son erected a noble monument to his memory, with the effigies of himself and his lady in full proportion; and on the side of the tomb are four sons in armour, and three daughters in the dress of the times, kneeling, with the the inscription below.*

Of his daughters, Elizabeth was the wife of Robert Garth, and after his decease of William Owen, Esqrs. Anne, first of William Brock, Esq. and secondly of Sir William Timperly, Knt. and Amphilis, of William Gratwick, Esq. Sir Walter, his second son, knighted at Whitehall Nov. 16, 1604, acquired an estate at Aldershot in Southampton, in right of Mary his wife, daughter and co-heir of Robert White of Aldershot, in Hants, Esq. (by the daughter of —— Foster, the heir of Bradley, of the county of Derby) son of Sir John White, lord-mayor of London: and from this Sir Walter descended James Tichborne of Frimley, in Surrey, and of Aldershot aforesaid, Esq. likewise, by a second son of the said Sir Walter descended Sir Benjamin Tichborne of Rickmonsworth, in Hertfordshire, Knt. Sir Benjamin, his third son, knighted at Tichborne Aug. 29, 1618, and elected for Petersfield in two parliaments in the reign of Charles I. died without issue. Sir Henry Tichborne, his fourth son, distinguished himself by many brave actions, and an unshaken love to his country, in which respect I shall distinctly treat of him and his descendants in a note.†

* Anno Dom. 1621: erected and dedicated to the memory of Sir Benjamin Tichborne, Knt. and Bart. and of dame Amphilis, his wife, daughter of Richard Weston of Roxwell, in the county of Essex, Esq. one of the justices of the honourable court of common pleas; who having lived together with inviolate affection, by the space of 49 years, had issue four sons, Richard, Walter, Benjamin, Knts. and Henry, Captine of the Lifforde, in Ireland; and three daughters, Elizabeth, Anne, and Amphilis. After he had fulfilled the number of his days, in the favour and grace of his prince; being a gentleman of the privy chamber to the most illustrious monarch James, king of Great Britain, France, and Ireland: and having, with loyalty to his sovereign, and integrity to his country, bourne and performed all the offices of dignity in this country, hath here chosen, together with his beloved wife, to sleep with his fathers in this chapel, founded by his auncestor, Sir Roger Tichborne, Knt. in the time of Henry I. where they expect the blessed resurrection of their bodies; and in the merits and mercy of Jesus Christ, our alone Saviour, to be partaker of that comfortable invitation, *Come, ye blessed, and receive the kingdom prepared for you*, Eccles, chap. xii. ver. 13. A good life hath the days numbered, but a good name endureth for ever.

† He was born in 1681, and being trained up from his youth in military discipline in Ireland and the Low Countries, he acquired the reputation of an experienced officer, and was by King James I. pre-

TICHBORNE OF TICHBORNE, HAMPSHIRE.

II. Sir RICHARD TICHBORNE, Bart. eldest son and heir of Sir Benjamin, had the honour of knighthood conferred on him at the Charter House, May 11,

ferred to the command of an independant company of foot, in Ireland, and made governor of the castle of Lifford; after which his majesty conferred on him the honour of knighthood at Tichborne, Aug. 29, 1623. He was a colonel of a regiment of foot at the breaking out of the horrid rebellion and cruel massacre of the protestants in Ireland, in 1641, and being esteemed the best officer in that kingdom, was appointed, with his own regiment of 1000 men, Sir Thomas Lucas's, and Sir Adam Loftus's troops of horse, to secure the town of Drogheda, and to be governor thereof: which town, situate on both sides the river Boyn, about three miles distant from the sea, was become the rebels' chief aim, and of such importance, that next to Dublin it was the chief care of the state to preserve; and with Cork and Carrickfergus were the only places the protestants could then keep in that kingdom. Sir Henry Tichborne arrived at Drogheda with his forces Nov. 4, 1641; but was so coldly received by the popish inhabitants, that he waited in the streets from two o'clock till nine, before he could get a lodging, and then was forced to take one by his own authority. The town was without bulwark, or any other fortification than an ordinary ditch, and an old wall; yet, by a diligent application in repairing those defects, he sustained a siege of three months, against the whole power of the rebels (who, with 14,000 men, sat down before the place in three weeks after he came) notwithstanding he had many traitors within the town who plotted to deliver it up: his garrison was also pinched with the hardships of famine, to the degree of eating horses, dogs, and cats. He shewed in these extremities a peculiar constancy of mind, an uncommon intrepidity, and excellent conduct.

His successful sallies so dispirited the enemy, that at length they drew off with great loss, before the earl of Ormond (who intended the raising the siege) marched out of Dublin. In consideration of which services he was sworn of the privy council; and on May 12, 1642, one of the lord's justices of Ireland, in the room of Sir William Parsons; for which alteration no reproach could be fastened on the king, as Lord Clarendon asserts, " Sir Harry Tichborne, being a man of so excellent a fame, that though the parliament was heartily angry at the removal of the other, and knew this would never be brought to serve their turn, yet they had nothing to object against him." He continued one of the two lord's justices till the marquis of Ormond was sworn lord lieutenant; and during his administration (which was two years) endeavoured, by all ways, to support and relieve the distressed protestants with such zeal and disinterestedness, that he preserved the good opinions both of the king and parliament; for when the royal cause was quite ruined, and the marquis of Ormond had surrendered Dublin to the parliament forces, and their commissioners had reduced some regiments, they yet kept Sir Henry Tichborne in pay, as also continued him in his government of Drogheda; and he, joining their general, Jones, was a means of gaining the great victory at Dungan Hill (that happened on Aug. 18, 1647) 6000 of the rebels being killed on the spot: but after the murder of King Charles I. he forsook the service, and retired till such time as the confusions among those who had usurped the government had given opportunity to the well-wishers of the royal family to shew themselves.

King Charles II. had so just a sense of his services, that he constituted him field-marshal of his forces in the kingdom of Ireland; which post Sir Henry held till his death, 1667, when he was in the 86th year of his age. He lies buried at Drogheda, with Jane his wife, daughter of Sir Robert Newcomen, of Ireland, Bart. who lived with him many years, and died about the year 1664. They had five sons and three daughters: Benjamin, their eldest son, a captain of horse in the service of King Charles I. was killed by the rebels at Belruddery, in the county of Dublin, in the 21st year of his age, unmarried; William, second son, succeeded to the estate of his father; Richard, third son, was major of the horse-guards in Ireland, and died unmarried; as did likewise Henry, fourth son; and Samuel, fifth son, died young. Of the daughters, Dorcas was the wife of William Toxteth of Drogheda, Esq. a native of Lancashire; Amphilis, of Richard Broughton, Esq. major of the foot-guards in Ireland, in the reign of King Charles II. younger brother of Sir Edward Broughton; and Elizabeth, of Roger West, of the Rock, in the county of Wicklow, Esq. William Tichborne, eldest surviving son and heir, resided at Beaulieu in the county of Louth; was knighted by King Charles II. and by Judith his wife, daughter and one of the co-heirs of John Bysse, Esq. lord chief-baron of the Exchequer, in Ireland (a branch of the family of Bysse of Somersetshire) had six sons and one daughter; Margaret, the wife of Stephen Stanley of Grange Gorman, in the county of Dublin, Esq. father of Sir John Stanley, Bart. The said Sir William Tichborne, died in the 58th year of his age, March 12, 1693: he was a major of horse.

His six sons were 1, Henry lord Tichborne, of Ireland; 2, Benjamin, who was killed in the 39th year of his age, at the battle of Hoekstet in Germany, 1704, and by Elizabeth his wife, daughter of major

1603, succeeded to the title of a baronet. He was sent by King Charles I. ambassador to the queen of Bohemia; and when that prince was oppressed by his rebellious subjects he assisted him to the utmost of his power. He had two wives, first Ellen, daughter and co-heir of the before-mentioned Robert White of Aldershot, Esq. by whom he had a daughter, Amphilis, the wife of Sir Laurence Hyde, Knt. serjeant at law: by Susan, his second lady, daughter and co-heir of William Waller of Oldstoke, Esq. he had three sons and three daughters; Anne, the wife of Charles, son and heir of Sir John Tasborough of Flixton Hall, in Suffolk, Knt. Susan, who died unmarried; and Elizabeth, the wife of Sir James Philips of Stoke Charity, in Southamptonshire, Bart. His two eldest sons, Richard and John died infants; and he was succeeded by his only surviving son,

III. Sir HENRY TICHBORNE, Bart. who in defence of Charles I. hazarded his life in several enterprises. He was in the battle of Cheridown in Hampshire, and with Lord Ogle in Winchester castle, wherein he behaved with great bravery, which drew on him the malignity of the usurpers, who sequestered his estate, and forced him to live in an obscure condition till the restoration. King Charles made him lieutenant of New Forest in Hampshire, and King James II. constituted him lieutenant of the ordnance. He died in 1689, and by Mary his wife, daughter of William Arundel, Esq. brother to Thomas lord Arundel of Wardour, had issue three sons, Sir Henry-Joseph, his successor, John, and Charles, who died young: and three daughters; Winifred, who died an infant; Lettice, the wife of Henry Whettenhall of Peckham, in Kent, Esq. and Mary, a nun.*

Edward Gibbs of the city of Gloucester, left only three daughters, whereof Judith was first the wife of Charles earl of Sunderland; secondly, of Sir Robert Sutton, K. B. William, third son, a captain in the sea service, was cast away off Plymouth in 1692, in the 23d year of his age, unmarried; John Tichborne, fourth son was a colonel of his majesty's forces, and governor of Athlone in Ireland; Richard, fifth son, was master of arts of Trinity college, Dublin, and some time of Magdalen college, Oxford, and died unmarried in 1692, aged 21; Bysse, youngest son, was a captain of foot, and lost his life in the defence of Gibraltar, 1704. Henry Tichborne, Esq. eldest son, born in 1663, succeeded his father at Beaulieu, and in consideration of his services in the revolution was knighted by his majesty King William, 1694, and created a baronet of England July 29, 1694; also on the accession of King George I. was advanced to the dignity of a peer of the kingdom of Ireland, by the title of Baron Farrard.

He married in 1683 Arabella, sixth daughter of Sir Robert Cotton of Cumbermere, Knt. and Bart. by whom he had three sons, Henry, William, and Cotton, died young; also three daughters, whereof only Salisbury lived to maturity, and was the wife of William Aston of the county of Louth, Esq. Henry, eldest son and heir, born April 20, 1684, married Mary, daughter and sole heir of John Fowke of Atherdee, Esq. and coming to England in the year 1709 was unfortunately cast away in the bay of Liverpool, leaving his wife with child, who was delivered of a daughter, named Elizabeth, who died young; William, second son, married Charlotte-Amelia, second daughter of Robert, late lord viscount Molesworth of the kingdom of Ireland, by whom he left no issue; so that upon Lord Farrard's death the peerage in this family became extinct.

* A MS. now in being, which seems to be that of Sir Henry to his son and successor, Sir Henry-Joseph, it appears, that having spent three years in his travels through France and Italy, he returned with his lady and family to England, in the autumn of 1768, says, "On Nov. 21, 1768, by warrant from the lord chief Justice Scraggs, I was committed for high treason to the prison at Winchester; a crime so very horrid to my thoughts, that I stood amazed at it; where I remained till the 13th day of Dec. and then, by order of the house of lords, was removed to the Tower of London, where, for a year and half I was kept close prisoner; and in all that time, nor never before, ever knowing what I had done, nor ever examined, nor brought to appear before the lord chief justice, the house of lords, the council, or any committee, or other person whatever." He then proceeds to state, that his house was ransacked,

IV. Sir HENRY-JOSEPH TICHBORNE, Bart. succeeded his father in title and estate, and married in 1689 Mary, daughter of Anthony Kemp of Slyndon, in the county of Sussex, Esq. and by her had three sons, Henry, Henry-John, and John, who are all deceased; and three daughters, Mary-Agnes, wife of Michael Blount of Maple-Durham, in Oxfordshire, Esq. grand-father to the present Michael Blount, Esq. of that place: she died May 20, 1777. Frances-Cicely, the wife of George Brownlowe Doughty of Snarford Hall, in the county of Lincoln: she died August 20, 1765, aged 72. And Mabella, the wife of John Webb of Hathrop, in Gloucestershire, Bart. and died Sep. 1727. Sir Henry-Joseph died in July, 1743, and was succeeded by

V. Sir HENRY TICHBORNE, Bart. son of James Tichborne, Esq. of Trimley in the county of Surrey, who descended from Sir Walter, second son of Sir Benjamin, the first baronet: he married Mary, daughter of Michael Blount of Maple-Durham, in Oxfordshire, Esq. by Mary, the daughter of the late Sir Henry-Joseph Tichborne, Bart. by whom he had issue Henry, who died young; Mary-Agatha, who died about the age of 21; and another son, after-mentioned, born Sep. 6, 1756. Sir Henry dying on the 16th of July, 1785, was succeeded by his only surviving son,

VI. Sir HENRY TICHBORNE, the present baronet, who in the year 1777 married Elizabeth, daughter of —— Plowden of Plowden, in Shropshire, and has had issue by her ten children, nine of whom are now living, viz. Henry-Joseph, born Jan. 5, 1779; Benjamin-Edmund, Sep. 2, 1780; Edward, March 27, 1782; James-Francis, Oct. 3, 1784; John-Michael, Feb. 22, 1788; George, April 15, 1789; Mary-Barbara, Aug. 24, 1790, who died in June, 1792; Roger-Robert, Feb. 15, 1792; Elizabeth-Charlotte, June 14, 1798; and Lucy-Mary, March 22, 1800.

ARMS—Vaire, a chief, or.
CREST—On a wreath, a hind's head couped, proper, between a pair of wings, gules; but Thomas lord Tichborne's crest is thus blazoned—on a wreath, a cap of maintenance, on which is a wing erect, parti per fess, as in the arms, that is, the upper part or, and the lower vaire.
SUPPORTERS—Two lions guardant, gules.
MOTTO—*Pugna pro patria.*
SEAT—At Tichborne in Hampshire.

---

the very cielings and wainscots pulled down in search after arms, letters, and commissions; that Bedloe was his accuser: that after a year and a half in the Tower, by a writ of habeas corpus, he was brought before the judges of the King's Bench, and there bailed to farther liberty; and that it was another year and a half before he was totally discharged.

TICHBORNE OF TICHBORNE, HAMPSHIRE.

TABLE 34.

1 Sir ROGER de TICHBORNE, Knt. temp. Henry II.=Mabell Lymerston

2 Sir Walter de Tichborne, Knt.   Geffery   Philippe

3 Sir Roger=Alicia Hake   4 Sir John=Marg. Sipherwast

5 Sir Roger=C. Loveday   John=Amicia   Catharine   Margaret

6 Roger Cath. Roger   Richard=Alice de la Hode   Walter=Agatha de la Hode   Thomas

7 Sir John=Cecily de Rake   Richard Tisted

8 John=Marg. Moking   Olivia   Walter Wallis
                                  Tisted of Tisted
9 John=Joan Wandesford   William Eleanor   Marg.=Rich. Martin

10 John Tichborne=Marg. Martin

William   11 Nicholas=Anne White   Henry=Anne Marven

12 Nicholas Tichborne   Bartholomew,   Dorothy   Margaret   Dorothy
J. Fenrother | E. Rythe Roger, William J. Sambourne J. Bruin   T. Leigh

Juliana I. Sir Benj. 1621 Gilbert, Martin, Constance Anne   N   Bruins of Farnham
T. Cres- A. Weston   Ambrose Jenny   R. Knight J. Beron- Bond
well   sam

II. Sir Richard Sir Walter Sir Benj. Sir Henry, 1667   Elizabeth   Anne   Amphilis
E. White | S. Waller M. White   J. Newcomen   R. Garth | W. Owen W. Brook | Sir W. W. Grat-
                                                                              Timperley   wick

Amphilis III. Sir Hen. 1689 Anne &c.   N   Benj. Sir Wm. 1693 Rich.   Dorcas   Samuel,
Sir. L. Hyde M. Arundel C. Tasborough   J. Bysse   Henry W. Foxteth   &c.

IV. Sir H. Joseph, 1743 John   Lettice   Henry L. Farrand   Benjamin   Marg.
Mary Kemp   Charles, H. Whet-   Arabella Cotton   E. Gibbs.   S. Stanley
             Winif.   Mary tenhall

M. Agnes   F. Cecily, 1765 Mabella James   Henry   William &c.   Judith
M. Blount G. Doughty   J. Webb Tichborne M. Fowke   C. Molesworth   E. Sun- | Sir R.
                                                                             derland Sutton
——— Blount   Mary Blount=V. Sir Henry Tichborne, Bart. 1785   More children

Michael Henry- Benj-   Edward, James-   John-   George, Mary-   Roger- Eliz-   Lucy-
Blount, Joseph, Edm.   b. 1782 Francis, Mich.   b. 1789 Barbara, Rob.   Charlotte, Mary
Esq.   b. 1779 b. 1780   b. 1784 b. 1788   b. 1790 b. 1792 b. 1798   b. 1800
                                                            d. 1792

34. PALMER of WINGHAM, KENT.

Created Baronet, June 29, 1621.

THE Palmers of Wingham are descended from a very ancient family at Angmerin in the county of Sussex. The surname of Palmer owes its rise to that zeal for the Holy Land, which for some ages was very warm in Christendom, and drew many persons of distinction to embark in the crusades for carrying on the Holy war. The soldiers who returned home frequently brought a branch of palm of the growth of Palestine, and wore it as a sacred badge and token that they had performed their vows of fighting against the Infidels; and from this they were called Palmers, as Sir Henry Spelman tells us. In the number of these warriors were some of the ancestors of this ancient family.*

1. Ralph Palmer was possessor of a great estate in the county of Sussex, in 1307, whose son,

2. John Palmer, married a daughter of Sir John Pelham, K. B. sheriff of Sussex and Surrey, by whom he had,

3. Adam Palmer, who married one of the co-heirs of John Sedinghouse, and by her left a son,

4. Robert Palmer of Steyning, in Sussex, Esq. he married Isabel, daughter and co-heir of William Stopham of Stopham, Esq. in that county,† by whom he had

5. Robert Palmer of Angmerin, Esq. who was his son and heir,

6. John Palmer, Esq. who by Joan, daughter of —— Julian, Esq. was the father of another

7. John Palmer, Esq. who considerably augmented the estate by marrying Isabel, sole heiress of Edward Bilton, Esq. and by her had three sons, Edward, Robert, and Sir Thomas Palmer of Calais, in France, who died without issue.‡

---

* Several of the Palmers lie buried in the church of Snodland in Kent, particularly Thomas, who married ——, daughter of Fitzsumond; and died 1407. Weaver recites his epitaph, now obliterated:

Palmers all our faders were;	On the blest assention day,
I, a Palmer, livyd here,	In the cherful month of May,
And travylled till worn wythe age,	A thousand wyth fowre hundred seven,
I endy'd this world's pylgramage,	And took my journey hense to heaven.

† By indenture he divided his father-in-law's estate with John Bartlet, Esq. who had married the other daughter. By this partition all the lands in Angmerin, Beringham, Polyng, Ruston, and Preston, with part of the lands in Terring and Goring, fell to the share of Robert Palmer, which he left to his son.

‡ Robert, the second son, married Beatrix, sole heiress of John Wesse, and became the head of a younger branch of the family, seated at Parham in Sussex, whose second son, Robert, married Mary, daughter of James Audley, Esq. younger brother of Lord Audley; but his eldest son was Sir Thomas Palmer of Parham, Knt. that had two wives; first Bridget, daughter of —— Caryll, Esq. serjeant at law; by whom he had only three daughters, Elizabeth, the wife of John Leeds of Steyning; Mary, of Thomas Palmer of Angmerin; and Dorothy of Henry Roberts, Esqrs. and by his second wife, Catharine, daugh-

PALMER OF WINGHAM, KENT.

8. Sir Edward Palmer, Knt. the eldest son, married one of the sisters and co-heirs of Sir Richard Clement, of the Moat in Ightam, in Kent, Knt. and by her had three sons, born on three Sundays successively, who all lived to be eminent men: John, the eldest, was twice sheriff of Sussex and Surrey, 25 and 35 Henry VIII. and marrying Mary, daughter of William lord Sandys, left Sir Thomas Palmer, Knt. who married Mary, daughter of Sir Thomas Palmer of Parham, Knt. was the father of another Sir Thomas Palmer, Knt. that first married Margaret, daughter of Sir John Parker, Knt. son of archbishop Parker, and after her death, ——, daughter of Sir Miles Sonds, Knt. but left no issue. Thomas, the youngest of the three brothers, made his fortune at court, under Henry VIII. and Edward VI. and being knighted, began to build a spacious house in the Strand (which was afterwards enlarged and beautified by Sir William Cecil, lord Burleigh, lord high treasurer of England) but unfortunately taking part with John Dudley, duke of Northumberland, in favour of Lady Jane's title to the crown, by virtue of King Edward's will, he was, upon Queen Mary's accession to the throne, beheaded, with the duke, upon Tower Hill, where he had the christian courage and constancy upon the scaffold, to own his religion to be protestant.*

9. Sir Henry Palmer, Knt. the second son, became possessed of Wingham in Kent soon after the suppression of the monasteries,† where his family continued for many years: he was master of the ordnance, and supervisor and warden of the forest, and bailiff or steward of the county of Guisnes during life. In 36 Henry VIII. he‡ was at the taking of Bologne; had his arm broke when he was old, in a rencounter with the French; and when their forces, under the conduct of the duke of Guise, first made themselves masters of the fortress of Calais, at the latter end of the reign of Philip and Mary, and then with their victorious army sat down before Guisnes, this brave man (whose motto was *Vie pour mon prince*) in the noble defence thereof lost his life, at above 70 years age; and that castle quickly followed the fate of Calais, both which places had been above 200 years in the possession of the English. He‖ married Jane, daughter of Sir Richard Windebank of Guisnes, Knt. and by her left three sons, Thomas, Arnold, and Edward.

I. Sir THOMAS PALMER of Wingham, eldest son and heir, was§ knighted by the Earl of Essex, for his valour at the taking of Cadiz, and advanced to the dignity of a baronet. He married Margaret, daughter of Edmund Poley of Badley, in Suffolk, Esq. and by her had six sons, three of which were knighted (Sir Thomas, Sir Roger, and Sir James) and five daughters; three sons and three daughters died

---

ter of Sir Edward Stradling of St. Donats, in Glamorganshire, Knt. left a son John, and he by Elizabeth, daughter of Hugh Verney of Fairfield, in Somersetshire, Esq. left another Sir Thomas Palmer, Knt. that died in Spain, leaving by a daughter of John Mallet, Esq. a son William Palmer, Esq. who settled at Fairfield in Somersetshire.

* This Sir Thomas Palmer was imprisoned with Edward duke of Somerset, lord protector, 5 Edw. VI. as an accomplice, yet he ruined the duke, his evidence being the chief against him; for Sir Thomas being brought by the Duke of Northumberland, privately, to King Edw. VI. related the whole conspiracy. *See the Duke of Somerset's trial, in State Trials, fo. vol. VII. p. 15.*

† Philpot says, King Edw. VI. in the seventh year of his reign, granted the college in Wingham to Sir Henry Palmer. *See his second Errata.*

‡ Rymer's Fœd. tom. XV. p. 54.   ‖ M S. a Wood's in Musæo Ashmol. Not. F. 3.   § Camden's Annals of Queen Elizabeth, in anno 1596.

young: Margaret, the youngest of the surviving daughters, was the wife of Richard Amhurst of Bayhall, in Kent, Esq. serjeant at law; and Jane, the elder, was first the wife of Sir William Meredith, Knt. treasurer and paymaster, in the reigns of Queen Elizabeth and King James I. of their majesties armies and cautionary towns, Brill and Flushing, with all other their garrisons in the Low Countries; and after his death she was the wife of John lord Vaughan, earl of Carbury, who had no issue by her: to her first husband she brought Sir William Meredith, Bart. ancestor to the late Sir Roger Meredith of Leeds Abbey, in Kent, Bart. and two daughters; Anne, the wife of Francis lord Cottington, chancellor of the exchequer, and master of the court of wards under King Charles I. and commissioned by King Charles II. in his exile, to be lord high treasurer of England; and Jane, the wife of Sir Peter Wyche, ambassador to the grand signior, to whom she brought Sir Peter and Sir Cecil Wyche, and a daughter Jane, the wife of Sir John Greenvill, created Earl of Bath. Of the sons, Sir Roger Palmer, the second, was knight of the bath, and having been cup-bearer to the two Princes of Wales, Henry and Charles, was first made master of the houshold and cofferer to King Charles I. He married Catharine, daughter of Sir Thomas Porter of Gloucestershire, Knt. relict of Sir Ralph Welsh, Knt. but died without issue, leaving his estate to the descendants of his two brothers; the youngest of which was Sir James Palmer, knight of the bed-chamber to James I. and gentleman of the privy chamber to Charles I. and chancellor of the most noble order of the garter; who had two wives; by his first wife, Martha, daughter of Sir William Garrard of Dorney, in Bucks, Knt. he left Sir Philip Palmer of Dorney aforesaid, Kt. cup-bearer to Charles II. who married Phebe, daughter of Sir Henry Palmer of Howleech, in Kent, Knt. vice-admiral of the narrow seas, under King Charles I. and had by her four sons, Roger, Henry, Philip, and Charles. Roger Palmer of Dorney, Esq. the eldest son, married Anne, daughter and heir of Henry Ferrers, Esq. by whom he had two sons that died infants: Henry, the second son, died unmarried: Philip, the third son, married Catharine, daughter of Sir George Southcote, Bart. relict of James Palmer, Esq. brother to Roger earl of Castlemain, and died without issue: 4, Charles Palmer of Dorney Court, Esq. heir to his brothers, who married Jane, daughter of John Jenyngs of Hayes, in Middlesex, Esq. and died Aug. 8, 1714, leaving issue two sons; 1, Sir Charles Palmer, Bart. hereafter mentioned; and 2, Philip, who married Jane, daughter of Mr. Thompson of Ludgate-hill, mercer; and one daughter, Phebe, the wife of Richard Harcourt of Wigsell, in Sussex, Esq. Sir James Palmer, Knt. before-mentioned, married to his second lady, Catharine, relict of Sir Robert Vaughan of Lloydwrd, in Montgomeryshire, Knt. and daughter of Sir William Herbert, knight of the bath, created earl of Powis (and lady Eleanor Piercy, his wife, daughter of Henry earl of Northumberland) and was father of Roger Palmer, earl of Castlemain, in Ireland, who was sent by King James II. ambassador extraordinary to Rome, who married Barbara Villiers, sole daughter and heir of the lord viscount Grandison: she was created by King Charles II. baroness of Nonsuch, countess of Southampton, and dutchess of Cleaveland: a woman prodigal, rapacious, dissolute, violent, revengeful; she failed not to attempt and undermine Clarendon's credit with his master, and her success was for a time made apparent to the whole world.* She died at

* Hume's Hist. Eng.

Chelsea in Middlesex, Oct. 9, 1709; and he in North Wales, 1705, without issue.* The eldest son of Sir Thomas Palmer of Wingham, Knt. and Bart. was Sir Thomas Palmer, Knt. who married Margaret, daughter of Herbert Pelham of Sussex, Esq. and died during his father's life, leaving two sons; Herbert, the younger, was president of Queen's college in Cambridge, but died unmarried.

II. Sir THOMAS PALMER of Wingham, Bart. the eldest son succeeded his grandfather in dignity and estate, 1625: he suffered much for his loyalty to King Charles, and zeal to the church, by sequestrations and imprisonments; and died under confinement. He married Elizabeth, daughter and co-heir of Sir John Shirley of Isfield, in Sussex, Knt. by whom he had six sons, Sir Henry, Roger, Herbert, James, Thomas, and John; and six daughters; Margaret, the second wife of Sir Arnold Bream of Bredg, in Kent, Knt. Sybilla, of John Everard of Seabrights, in Essex, Esq. and after his death of William Mildmay, Esq. (who bore arms in defence of King Charles I.) Elizabeth, of Samuel Argol, doctor of physic; Mary, first of Francis Sommers, Esq. and secondly of —— Sainthill, Esq. Anne died young; and Esther was the wife of George Clayton of London, Esq. Of the sons, Roger and James, fellow of Trinity college in Cambridge, with John, who travelled into France with Lord Hollis, when he went ambassador from King Charles II. to the French king, died batchelors. Herbert, the third son, married Dorothy, daughter and co-heir of John Pincheon of Writtel, in Essex, Esq. and dying in 1700, left by her two sons, Sir Thomas, hereafter mentioned, and Henry, who died a batchelor in 1710, in the 26th year of his age; and two daughters, Anne, the wife of Robert Whitfield of Chartham, in Kent, Gent. and Elizabeth, who died unmarried. The fifth son was Thomas Palmer of London, Esq. an eminent member of the company of merchants trading to the Levant, who fined for sheriff of the city. He married Lucy, daughter of James Young of London, merchant, descended from an ancient family of the Youngs of Axminster, in Devonshire, and died without issue.

III. Sir HENRY PALMER, Bart. the eldest son, succeeded his father, 1666: he was always loyal to the crown, faithful to the church, and respected by the county, of which he was sheriff in the year 1691. He married Anne, daughter of Sir William Luckin of Waltham, in Essex, Bart. but died without issue, 1706, in a good old age, leaving his estate and dignity to his nephew,

---

* Sir Thomas Palmer, Bart. lies buried in Wingham church, where, on a handsome monument, is the following inscription:—"To the memory of Sir Thomas Palmer of Wingham, Knt. and Bart. and of Dame Margaret, his wife, daughter of John Poley of Badley, Esq. of that ancient family in the county of Suffolk. This place was the seat of his inheritance, but not of his descent, being lineally extracted from the house of Angmering, in the county of Sussex. God crowned him with the blessing of a long and prosperous life, and augmented it with the comfort of a virtuous and pious wife, with whose beloved society he was enriched 62 years. The threads of their lives were evenly spun: they lived in concord, died in peace; his period was 85, her's of 83 years. They were beloved of their neighbours, lamented by their friends, honoured by their children, and missed by the poor, for whose sakes they never brake up house in this place for 60 years. Thus lived they happily, and died christianly: he the 7th of January, she the August following, anno 1625. They had issue six sons and five daughters, whereof John, Mabell, Henry, Mary, John, Frances, died young. Sir Thomas Palmer, Knt. (father to Sir Thomas Palmer, Bart. now living) died before his father, and lies here also interred. Sir Roger Palmer, knight of the bath, was cup-bearer to the princes Henry and Charles, and now master of the household to King Charles. James Palmer, of the bed-chamber to King James, of blessed memory. Jane first married to Sir William Meredith, Knt. and after to the Lord Vaughan. Margaret married to Richard Amhurst, Esq. serjeant at law: these last four are yet living, anno 1627."

IV. Sir THOMAS, son of his brother Herbert, who was elected to serve his country, as knight of the shire for Kent, in the parliament summoned 8 Queen Anne, and in the first parliament called by King George I. was chosen for Rochester, and was one of the commissioners for stating the debts of the army. He married first Elizabeth, one of the daughters of Sir Robert Marsham, of the Moat near Maidstone, in Kent. Knt. and Bart. and sister to the first Lord Romney, by whom he had three sons, Henry, Thomas, and Robert, who all died young; and four daughters; 1, Margaret, who died unmarried; 2, Anne, first the wife of Sir Brooke Bridges of Godnestone, in Kent, Bart. and secondly, of the honourable Charles Fielding, Esq. brother to the earl of Denbigh; 3, Elizabeth, the wife of the honourable Edward Finch, who afterwards took the name of Hatton, pursuant to the will of Anne, his aunt, who died in 1764, and was the youngest daughter of Christopher viscount Hatton, by Elizabeth his third wife, daughter of Peter Hazlewood, of the county of Northampton, Esq. and heir to her brother, William viscount Hatton, who died unmarried. He was envoy extraordinary and plenipotentiary to Sweden, minister plenipotentiary to the diet of Ratisbon, and envoy and plenipotentiary to the states general, and afterwards to Muscovy; by whom he had George Finch Hatton, and four other sons and three daughters, Anne, Henrietta, and Mary; and 4, Mary, the wife of Daniel earl of Winchelsea. Sir Thomas married to his second lady, Mrs. Cox; and to his third, Mrs. Markham; but dying in 1723, without issue male,* the title descended to

V. Sir CHARLES PALMER of Dorney Court, in Bucks, Bart. eldest son of Charles Palmer, Esq. grandson of Sir James Palmer, Knt. chancellor of the garter, who was the youngest son of Sir Thomas Palmer of Wingham, in Kent. the first baronet of the family. He married, June 1729, Anne, daughter of Richard Harcourt, of the Inner Temple, Esq. (by Elizabeth his wife, daughter of Sir Philip Harcourt, Knt. half sister to the right honourable Simon, the first lord viscount Harcourt) by whom he had seven children, three sons and four daughters; Charles, Harriot, and Dorothy; Thomas and Harcourt, twins, and two Annes. Charles was an ensign in the second regiment of foot-guards, and afterwards a captain in the East India service, under Lord Clive; and died in 1764, in the island of Sumatra: by his wife, Sarah, daughter of Mr. Clack, and sister of the Viscountess Courtenay, he had one son Charles. Harriot, the wife of Dottin Battyn, Esq. of the island of Barbadoes, and afterwards a merchant in London. Dorothy, of Goussé Bonnin, Esq. of the island of Antigua. Sir Charles's brother, Philip Palmer, married Jane, daughter of Mr. Thompson of Ludgate Hill, mercer, by whom he had three sons, Philip, John, Charles; and two daughters, Jane and Anne. Sir Charles died Nov. 8, 1773: his lady in 1774; and was succeeded by his grandson,

VI. Sir CHARLES-HARCOURT PALMER, Bart. who has been in the commission of the peace for Bucks since the year 1784, and acts as a magistrate.

* At his death he, by his will, gave his seat at Wingham *inter alia*, after his widow's decease, intail to his natural son, Herbert Palmer, Esq. who married Bethia, fourth daughter of Sir Thomas DA'eth, of Knolton, Bart. He died in 1760, without issue, and having, by recovery, barred the intail, by his will devised his estate in the reversion of this seat, with the parsonage, to his wife Bethia, for her life, and afterwards to his sister Frances intail. But he never had possession of it; for Lady Palmer survived him, on whose death, in 1763, Mrs. Bethia Palmer, his widow, became entitled to it; and afterwards became the wife of John Cosnan, Esq. who died in 1778, without issue. *Hasted's Kent, vol. III. p.* 700.

PALMER OF WINGHAM, KENT.

ARMS—Or, two bars, gules, each charged with three trefoils of the field, in chief, a greyhound currant, sable.

CREST—A demi panther, rampant, issuing flames out of his mouth and ears, holding a palm branch, all proper.

MOTTO—*Palma virtuti.*

SEAT—At Dorney Court near Windsor, in Bucks.

TABLE 35.

1 RALPH PALMER, living in 1307

2 John = ——— Pelham

3 Adam = ——— Sedinghouse

4 Robert = Isabel Stopham

5 Robert Palmer

6 John Palmer = Joan Julian

7 John Palmer = Isabel Bilton

8 Sir Edward — Clement | Robert = Beatrix Wasse | Sir Thomas Palmer

John M. Sandys | 9 Sir Henry = J. Windebank | Sir Thomas Palmer

Sir Thomas = M. Palmer

Sir Thomas Palmer

M. Parker | — Sands | Sir Thomas M. Pelham | Sir Roger | Sir James Palmer M. Garrard | C. Vaughan | Jane Palmer Sir W. Meredith | J. earl of Cardigan | Margaret R. Amhurst

I. Sir Thomas, Bart. 1625
Margaret, dr. of Edw. Poley

Arnold. Edward

II. Sir Thomas, Bt. 1656 Eliz. Shirley | Herbert | Sir Philip Phebe Palmer | Roger E. of Castlemain Barb. Villiers

III. Sir Henry Bt. 1706 A. Luckin | Roger D. Pincheon | Herbert | James, Thos. & John | 6 drs. | Roger Anne Ferrers | Henry C. Southcote | Philip | Charles, 1714 J. Jennings

IV. Sir Thomas, 1723 Eliz. Marsham | Mrs. Cox | Mrs. Markham | Henry 1710 | Anne Robert Whitfield | Elizabeth | V. Sir Charles, 1773 Anne Harcourt 1774 | Philip J. Thompson | Phebe R. Harcourt

Henry, Thos. Rob. & Marg. | Anne Sir B. Bridges | Elizabeth Chas. Fielding | Mary Edw. Hatton | — E. of Winchelsea | Herbert 1760 Bethia D'Aeth | Charles 1764 Sarah Clarke | Harriot Dottin Battyn | Dorothy Gousse Bonnin | &c. 3 sons 2 drs.

VI. Sir Charles Palmer, Bart.

35. RIVERS GAY of Chafford, Kent.

Created Baronet July 19, 1621.

OF this name of Rivers, anciently written Ripariis and Riveries, have been many eminent persons in former ages.

Richard de Ripariis, by his wife Maud, daughter of Sir Richard Lucy, had a son Richard, a noble baron, in the reign of King John (and by descent from his mother was lord of Angue in Essex) whose grandson and heir, John de Rivers, was summoned among the barons from 25 Edw. I. 1298 to 9 Edw. II. Nicholas de la Rivers was summoned in 22 Edw. I. A.D. 1295, to appear with horse and arms.

From this Nicholas it is probable this family is descended.*

1. Sir Bartholomew Rivers, Knt. lived in the reign of Edw. IV. to whom he was firmly attached: his son,

2. William Rivers, had a command in the reigns of Edw. IV. and Henry VII. and by his will, dated March 22, 1506, ordered his body to be buried in the cathedral church of Rochester. He left, by Alice, his wife,

3. Richard, his son and heir, who was father of

4. Richard Rivers of Penshurst, steward of the lands of Edward duke of Buckingham, who had one daughter, ———, the wife of Robert Streatfield, ancestors to the Streatfields of Chedingston, &c. in Kent.† and one son.

5. Sir John Rivers, Knt. was of Chafford, and served the office of lord-mayor in the 15th year of the reign of Queen Eliz. He married Elizabeth, daughter of Sir George Barnes, Knt. lord-mayor of London,‡ by whom he had several children.§

6. Sir George Rivers, Knt. his eldest son, was member of parliament for East Grinsted in Sussex, 39 Eliz. and married Frances, daughter and co-heir of William Bower, Esq. of Sussex, by whom he had three sons; 1, John; 2, George,

---

* Mr. Philipot, Somerset herald, p. 57, derives them from the Rivers of River's Hill, in Hampshire, who bore for their arms *Quarterly, 1st and 4th azure, 2 bars dancette or, in chief 3 bezants, by the name of Rivers; 2d and 3d azure, a fesse engrailed argent, surmounted by another, not engrailed, gules, charged with 3 roses argent, between as many swans, proper;* which last was an augmentation of honour given to Sir Bartholomew Rivers, Knt. by King Edw. IV. for his good and faithful services to the house of York. This coat of arms, together with the crest of Rivers, viz. *a bull at gaze,* was carved on the gate-way of Chafford house, built by one of the family. Peacham says, the grant of this coat was in the hands of Sir George Rivers of Chafford, Knt. and might be seen in *Claus,* anno 5 King Edw. IV. 4 M. 12 *intus,* in the Tower of London. *Complete Gent. p. 236. Hasted's Kent, vol. I. p. 417.*

† Stem. Fam. de Streatfield.

‡ She afterwards was the wife of Thomas Potter, of Well-street in Westerham, Esq. whose daughter Dorothy, by his first wife, Mary, daughter of Richard Tichbourne, Esq. was the wife of Sir John Rivers, Bart. grandson of this lady Elizabeth Rivers.

§ *Peacham's Complete Gent. p. 237. Monum. in Westerham church, Kent.*

who was of Hadlow in the county of Kent, who had issue Edward Rivers of Fishhall in Hadlow, Esq. who died Dec. 21, 1660, aged 33; and a daughter Frances, the wife of Edward Sadlow of London: she died Oct. 23, 1656. 3, William, who was of London, and married Elizabeth, daughter of Thomas Cobbet, of London, clerk, by whom he left issue: and a daughter Elizabeth, the wife of Nicholas Rowe of Muswell Hill, in Middlesex, Esq.*

I. JOHN RIVERS, Esq. the eldest son, succeeded his father, and was created a baronet July 19, 1621; and married Dorothy, only daughter and heir of Thomas Potter, of Well-street in Westerham;† by whom he had four sons; 1, James; 2, John, who died without issue; 3, George, who married the daughter of ―― Barrington, but had no issue; 4, Nizell, of Oakham near Lewes, in Sussex, who married the widow of ―― Culpepper, Esq. and died without issue. He had also three daughters; Elizabeth, the wife of John Baker of Mayfield; Dorothy, of William Newton, Esq. of Southover, both in Sussex; and Cecily,‡ of Sir Robert Goodwin, of Fairleigh near East Grinstead, in the same county, Knt.

James Rivers, Esq. the eldest son, was of Comb in Sussex, and died during his father's life, June 8, 1641; and was buried in the church of St. Bartholomew the Great, in Smithfield.§ He married Charity, daughter of Sir John Shirley of Isfield, in Sussex, Knt.‖ by whom he had issue four sons and eight daughters, viz.

II. Sir THOMAS, successor to his grandfather, Sir John, who succeeded his brother James, who died without issue; and another son, who died young. Of the daughters, Elizabeth was the wife of ―― Bodenham; Charity, of John Eldred of Saxham in Suffolk; another the wife of ―― Bridger of Well-street in Westerham; another to ―― Hamden. On Sir Thomas Rivers's death, unmarried, in 1657, his next brother, John, succeeded him in title and estate; which

III. Sir JOHN RIVERS, Bart. married Anne, daughter of Sir Thomas Hewet of Pishiobury, in Hertford, Bart. by whom he had four sons; 1, Sir George, his successor; 2, John, who died without issue; 3, Thomas, L L D. prebendary of Winchester, who married Mary, daughter of Richard Holbrooke of the Isle of Wight, Gent. and died Sep. 8, 1731, leaving issue three sons, John and Peter, successively baronets; James and a daughter Anne, who died young. The fourth son was James, who was a colonel in the army, and died without issue, at the siege of Barcelona; and also two daughters, Margaret and Anne.

IV. Sir GEORGE RIVERS, Bart. eldest son and successor to his father, married Dorothea, daughter of Sir William Beversham [of Holbrook Hall, in Suffolk, Knt. by whom he had four sons and seven daughters; of whom Beversham died

---

* MSS. pedigree of Rowe.

† He procured an act of parliament in the 21st of that reign, to alter the tenure and custom of his lands, those of Sir George Rivers, Knt. his father, as well as those of Thomas Potter, Esq. above-mentioned, being then of the nature of gavelkind; and to make them descendable, according to the course of common law, and to settle the inheritance of them upon the said Sir John Rivers, and his heirs, by dame Dorothy, abovementioned, his wife. *Robinson's Gavelkind, p.* 306.

‡ In Aubrey's Hist. Surrey, vol. I. p. 213, called Mary.

§ Strype's Stowe's Survey, Book III. p. 237.

‖ She was of consanguinity to archbishop Chichester. See Stem. Chich. No. 10.

unmarried, aged 23; George married Isabella, daughter of Philip Packer of Groombridge, Esq. by whom he left no issue; Thomas and William both died infants: Dorothy was the wife of Thomas Goodall of St. James's, London, Esq. Anne died unmarried; Philadelphia was the wife of George Baker of Mayfield Place, in Sussex, Esq. Henrietta-Maria, of Joseph Webb, surgeon, and died in 1756; Charlotte died, aged 12; Margaret was the wife of John Groombridge of Tunbridge, Gent. and Elizabeth died young.

Sir George Rivers dying without issue male, by his will devised his seat and estate to his surviving daughters; and was succeeded by his nephew,

V. Sir JOHN RIVERS, Bart. eldest son of his brother, Dr. Thomas Rivers, on whose death, in 1743, he was succeeded by his brother,

VI. The Rev. Sir PETER RIVERS, Bart. prebendary of Winchester, who took the name of Gay, and married, in 1768, ——, daughter of —— Coxe, Esq. and died July 20, 1790: he was succeeded by

VII. Sir THOMAS RIVERS GAY, Bart. who (I believe) is his son.

ARMS—Azure, two bars dancette, or; in chief three bezants.
CREST—On a mount, vert, a bull passant, argent; collared, ringed, lined, and armed, or. *Granted in* 1583.

TABLE 36.

1 Sir BARTHOLOMEW RIVERS
2 William Rivers = Alice
3 Richard Rivers
4 Richard Rivers   Sir George Barnes
5 Sir John Rivers = Elizabeth = Thomas Potter = M. Tichborne
6 Sir George Rivers, Knt. = Frances Bowyer   Dorothy = Sir J. Rivers

I. Sir John = D. Potter   George   William = E. Cobbet   Frances = E. Sadlow   Eliz. = N. Rowe

James, 1641   John   George   Nizell   Elizabeth   Dorothy   Cecily
C. Shirley   — Barrington   — Culpeper   J. Baker   W. Newton   Sir R. Goodwin

II. Sir Thos. Rivers   III. Sir John   James   Elizabeth   Charity   N   N
Bart. 1657   A. Hewet   — Bodenham   J. Eldred   — Bridger   — Hamden

IV. Sir George   John   Thomas, 1734   Col. James   Margaret   Anne
D. Beversham   M. Holbrooke

Beversham   George   Thos.   Dorothy   Philadel.   Henrietta   Marg.   V. Sir John   VI. Sir Peter, 1790   Jas
    Isa. Packer   Wm.   T. Goodall   G. Baker   J. Webb   J. Groombridge   Rivers 1743   —, dr. of — Coxe   & Anne
                                    VII. Sir Thomas Rivers Gay, Bart.

36. HEWET of HEADLEY-HALL, YORKSHIRE.

Created Baronet Oct. 11, 1621.

THE family of Hewet is of ancient extraction,* of which was Robert Hewet, Esq. who possessed a considerable estate at Killamarch in Derbyshire, in the reign of Henry VIII.† He left two sons; Robert, who died without issue, and William, who succeeded his father, and died in 1599, aged 77.‡ He left four sons; John, Solomon, Thomas, and William: from the three last are descended the families of Hewet of Pishiobury, in Hertfordshire (of which was Sir Thomas Hewet, created a baronet July 19, 1660, and afterwards an Irish viscount) the Hewets of Shire-Oaks, in Nottinghamshire, both now extinct, and the Hewets of Stretton, in Leicestershire.

John, the eldest son, survived his father but three years, dying in 1602. He left issue by his wife Elizabeth, daughter of Sir Robert Hampson, Knt. alderman of London (who was afterwards the wife of Sir Gilbert Wakering, and Sir Robert Bevile, of Chesterton in Huntingdonshire, K. B. successively) one son, John, and a daughter Catharine, who in 1617 was given in marriage, with an ample dowry, to George Byng of Wrotham, in Kent, Esq. great grandfather to Pattee lord viscount Torrington.

I. JOHN, who succeeded his father, was created a baronet, and married Catharine, daughter of Sir Robert Bevile, sen. K. B. who died in 1636, and sister and co-heir of Sir Robert Bevile of Chesterton, in Huntingdonshire, K. B. in the reign

---

* There was a Sir Walter Hewet, who made a considerable figure in the wars of Edw. III. in France; vide Barnes's Edw. III. p. 652.

† Of this family was Sir William Hewet, lord-mayor, 1559, but whether brother to this Robert, is not certain: of this Sir William, we find the following remarkable story in Stowe's Survey of London, vol. II. book 5, p. 133. " Sir William Hewet, cloth-worker, mayor, 1559, son to Edmund Hewet of Wales, in Yorkshire. He died the 6th of Feb. 1566. His wife was the daughter of Leveson of Kent.

"This mayor was a merchant possessed of a great estate, valued at 6000l. per ann. and was said to have had three sons and one daughter; to which daughter this mischance happened (the father then living upon London Bridge). The maid playing with her, out of a window over the river Thames, by chance dropped her in, almost beyond expectation of being saved. A young gentleman, named Osborne, then apprentice to Sir William, the father (which Osborne was one of the ancestors of the duke of Leeds in a direct line) at this calamitous accident, immediately leaped in bravely, and saved the child. In memory of which deliverance, and in gratitude, her father afterwards bestowed her in marriage on the said Mr. Osborne, with a very great dowry. Whereof the late estate of Sir Thomas Fanshaw, in the parish of Barking in Essex, was a part, as the late duke of Leeds himself told the Rev. Mr. John Hewyt, from whom I have this relation; and together with that estate in Essex, several other lands in the parishes of Harthill and Wales, in Yorkshire, now in the possession of the said most noble family. All this from the old duke's own mouth to the said Mr. Hewyt.

"Also, that several persons of quality courted the said young lady, and particularly the earl of Shrewsbury; but Sir William was pleased to say, Osborne saved her, and Osborne should enjoy her. The late duke of Leeds, and the present family, preserve the picture of the said Sir William, in his habit of lord-mayor, at Kiveton House, in Yorkshire, to this day, valuing it at 200l."

‡ Stowe's Survey of London, vol. I. book 3, p. 162."

of James I. who died in 1640: by her he had two sons, Sir John and Robert, and five daughters; Elizabeth, Catharine, the wife of Robert Cheek of Purgo, in Essex, Esq. Frances, Anne, and Grace, wife of Sir Thomas Brograve of Hamels, in Hertfordshire, Bart. Sir John died in 1657, after he had seated his family at Waresly, in Huntingdonshire: he was persecuted greatly for his loyalty.

II. Sir JOHN, his eldest son, succeeded him, and married Frances, daughter of Sir Toby Tyrrell of Thornton, in Bucks, Bart. (surviving him she afterwards was the wife of Philip Cotton of Connington, in Cambridgeshire, Esq. grandson of Sir Robert Cotton, founder of the library) by whom he had eleven sons; 1, Sir John, his successor; 2, Tyrrell, rector of Scotter in Lincolnshire, who married, but died without issue; 3, Robert, who died unmarried; 4, Thomas, who died young; 5, Benjamin, who died unmarried; 6, Charles; 7, William, of St. Neots, who left issue three sons, Sir William, hereafter mentioned, Tyrrell, who married a daughter of Mr. Robert Gedding, of the Post-office, and had one daughter and a son Thomas; 8, James, blown up at sea, being a lieutenant in the Carlisle man of war; 9, Thomas, M.D. who married Mrs. Pinkney, and left a son Thomas of Clare Hall, and a daughter Anne; 10, Toby, and 11, Benjamin: also seven daughters; 1, Hester, the wife of Ulysses Blount, Esq. seventh son of Sir Henry Blount of Titenhanger, in Hertfordshire, Knt. 2, Frances, of Henry Scrope of St. Neot's, in Huntingdonshire, Esq. but had no issue; 3, Theodora; 4, Edith, the wife of William Dove of Upton, in Northamptonshire, Esq. 5, Catharine; 6, Arabella, and 7, Elizabeth, the wife of ―――― Broke of Nacton, in Suffolk, Esq. Sir John dying Sep. 30, 1684, was succeeded in honour and estate by

III. Sir JOHN HEWET, Bart. his eldest son, high sheriff of Cambridge and Huntingdonshires 2 James II. who first married Anne, daughter of Francis Stokes of Tiderton, in Wilts, Esq. (son of Christopher Stokes of Tiderton, Esq. whose wife was sister to lord chancellor Hyde, earl of Clarendon) by whom he had two sons, who died without issue, and two daughters; Anne, the eldest, was the wife of John Hagar of Bourne, in Cambridgeshire, Esq. and left one son, Hewet Hagar, Esq. Sir John married to his second wife, Eleanor, eldest daughter to the late Sir John Osborne of Chicksands, in Bedfordshire, Bart. by whom he had no issue; and dying without issue male, 1737, was succeeded in the title by his nephew,

IV. Sir WILLIAM, son of his brother William, of St. Neots; who was captain of the Colchester man of war, and married Elizabeth, daughter of Mr. Levemore, of Gosport in Hampshire; and had three sons, William, Levemore, and Herbert; and one daughter, Elizabeth. Sir William died in 1749, and was succeeded by his eldest son,

V. Sir WILLIAM HEWET, captain of his majesty's ship the Duc d'Acquitain, which was lost before Pondicherry, Jan. 1, 1761. With Sir William perished his brother Levemore, who was a lieutenant on board the said ship. Herbert, the youngest son, being dead some years before, the title descended to his uncle,

VI. Sir TYRREL HEWET, Bart. who married ――――, daughter of ―――― Gedding, by whom he had two sons, Bing and Thomas. He died Feb. 17, 1770, and was succeeded by his son,

HEWET OF HEADLEY-HALL, YORKSHIRE.

VII. Sir BING HEWET, Bart. who went to India in the East India company's service, in the year 1768. He died and was succeeded by

VIII. The Rev. Sir THOMAS HEWET, Bart. who (I believe) is his brother.

ARMS—Gules, a cheveron engrailed, between three owls, argent.
CREST—On a wreath, on a stump of a tree, proper, a faulcon standing, or.
MOTTO—*Ne te quæsiveris extra.*
SEAT—At Potton in Bedfordshire.

TABLE 37.

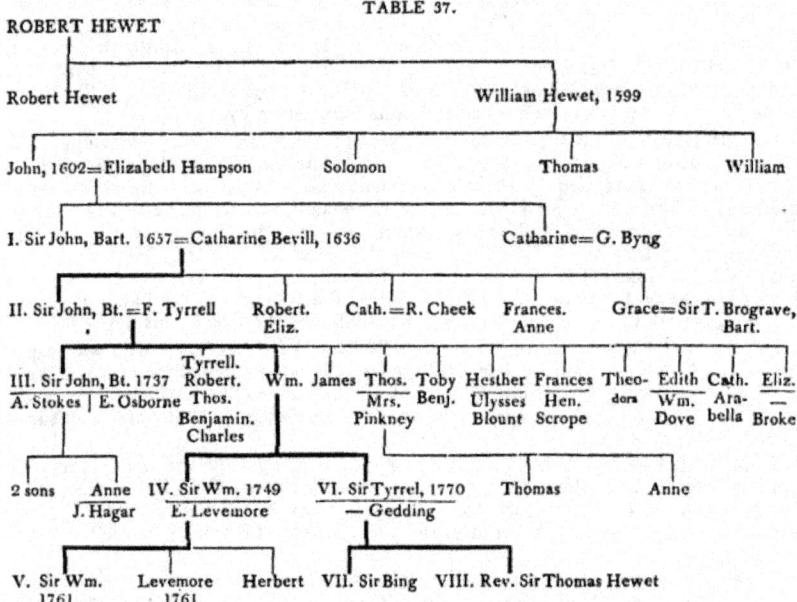

37. JERNINGHAM or JERNEGAN of Cossey, Norfolk.

Created Baronet October 16, 1621.

THIS family is said to be of Danish extraction.* The first I meet with upon record is Jernegan,† who is mentioned in the Castle Acre Register, fo. 63, b. as a witness to a deed without date, by which Bryan, son of Scolland, confirmed the church of Melsombi to the monks of Castle Acre, and died about the year 1182. He married Sibilla, who in 1183 paid 100*l.* of her gift into the Exchequer. His son was called

2. Hugh or Hubert Fitz Jernegan: he gave a large sum of money to King Henry II. and paid it into the Exchequer anno 1182.‡ He was witness to a deed in 1195, by which divers lands were granted to Byland Abbey in Yorkshire.§ He married Maud, daughter and co-heir of Thorpine, son of Robert de Watheby, and died anno 1203: ‖ he was succeeded by his son,

3, Sir Hubert Jernegan or Jerningham of Horham, in Suffolk, Knt. who had been engaged in the insurrection of the barons against King John; but on the accession of Henry III. in 1216, he submitted himself, and obtained his pardon.¶ But it seems that he had not recovered all his estates in 1219; for in that year Gilbert de Gant gave to Robert Marnison, jun. the wardship of the land late Hugh Jernegan's, in Hundemaneby;* and in the year 1240 Margery late wife of Hubert

---

* Weever, fo. 770, tells us, that "the name of Jerningham has been of exemplary note from before the conquest, and adds the following account, as extracted out of the pedigree of the family, anno MXXX. Canute, king of Denmarke and of England, after his return from Rome, brought with him diverse captains and souldiers from Denmarke, whereof the greater part were christened here in England, and began to settle themselves here, of whom Jernegan or Jerningham, and Jenihingo, now Jennings, were of most esteem with Canute, who gave unto the sayde Jerningham certaine royalties; and at a parliament held at Oxford, the sayde King Canute did give unto the sayde Jerningham certaine manors in Norfolke; and to Jennings certaine manors, lying upon the sea side, neere Harwich in Suffolke, in regard of their former services done to his father, Swenus, king of Denmark."
I have not been able to discover from whence the above note was taken by Weever; the pedigree however of this family can be traced up to a period little subsequent to the conquest.
† Vide Blomefield's Norfolk, from which this account is chiefly taken.
‡ Mag. Rot. 29 Henry II. Madox's Hist. Excheq. p. 190. § Regr. Abbatiæ Byland, fo. 102.
‖ By her the manor of Wathe, in North Cove in Suffolk, came into the family. He is mentioned by the name of Hubert de Jernegan, in the Black Book of the Exchequer, as published by Herne (vol. I. p. 301) among the Suffolk knights, who held of the honour of Eye. In the third year of King John, in the account of the sheriff of Yorkshire, under the title of Scutages, and fines of knights, among others, Hugh, son of Jernegan, paid 20*l.* fine for three knights fees and an half, which he held of the honour of Brittain *(Rot. pip. pasch. 3 John. Rot. 16. Talley-Court Excheq).* The king granted the wardship of all his large possessions, and the marriage of his wife and children, to Robert de Veteri Ponti, or Vipount; so that he married them without disparagement to their fortunes. *Blomefield, fo. 659.*
¶ Claus. 1, Henry III. part. 2, M. 1. * Coiar. in Sciio. 4 Henry III.

Jernegan, sued Hugh Jernegan, her son, for lands in Stonham-Jernegan in Suffolk;* so that he died about the year 1239. He married Margery, daughter and heir of Sir —— de Herling, of East Herling in Norfolk, Knt.† and by her had issue four sons, Godfrey, William, Robert, and Hugh ‡ He was succeeded by his second son,

4. Sir William Jernegan, Knt. who married Julian, daughter and co-heir of Sir —— Gymingham of Burnham, Knt.§ He died without issue, and was succeeded by his youngest brother,

5. Sir Hugh Jernegan, Knt. who in the year 1243 entered into an agreement with his mother Margery, and settled upon her, in lieu of the dower of Sir Hubert, her late husband, the capital messuage and manor of Horham in Suffolk, with the park, wind-mill, and demean lands, and the services and rents of Horham manor, with house-bote, hey-bote, and pannage; and in consideration of this settlement Margery released all her right in Dower, in two carucates of land, and a messuage in Stonham-Jernegan in Suffolk, and in all his other estates in Norfolk and Suffolk.‖ Sir Hugh died about the last year of the reign of King Henry III. and was succeeded by his son,

6. Sir Walter Jernegan of Horham, and of Stonham-Jernegan, Knt.¶ who married Isabella, daughter and at length heir of Sir Peter Fitz-Osbert of Somerley Town in Suffolk, Knt. This lady was the widow of Sir Henry de Walpole, Knt. ancester to the late earls of Orford, and was endowed with a third part of the manor of Houghton, in the same county, as appears by a charter,* wherein she is styled " the lady Isabella Jernegan, late wife of Sir Henry de Walpole, father of Sir Henry de Walpole," then living. She afterwards became co-heir to her brother, Roger Fitz-Osbert, summoned among the barons to parliament 22 Edw. I.† Sir Walter must have died before the 34th of Edw. I. his wife Isabella being described that same year as a widow, 40 years of age. He was succeeded by his son,

7. Sir Peter Jernegan of Somerley-Town, Knt. who on the death of his mother succeeded to the large possessions of the Fitz-Osbert family; for his maternal un-

---

* Rot. 16 de Talley-Court, Plitæ Juris & assis. coram Willo. de Ebor. apud Bucks, 25 Hen. III. Rot. 9.
† Heralds' Books.   ‡ Assize Rolls, 34 Henry III.
§ Hugh de Polsted married Hawise, the other co-heir, and levied a fine of all the Gymingham estate in Burnham. *Fines Norf.* 10 *John.*
‖ In 1224 he was witness to the deed of Henry duke of Lovaine, made to the monks of Eye *(Regr. Eye, fo.* 52). Elizabeth, his wife, is mentioned in the Assize Rolls. In the year 1249 he had lands in Hillington and Congham, in Norfolk *(Fines* 52 *Hen. III. No.* 65) and he appears to have lived to a great age; for in 1269 he held of Roger, son of Peter Fitz-Osbert, divers lands in Stovene and Bugges, for which he did homage to Roger, son of the said Peter, in the presence of Sir Walter de Redisham, Knt. Sir William Rector, of Hillington, Knt. &c. His second wife was Ellen, daughter and co-heir of Sir Thomas Ingaldesthorpe, Knt. who survived him. *Plita. Juris. & assis. apud Chelmesford,* 57 *Hen. III. Rot.* 3.
¶ On Walter's marriage his father settled on him the ancient seat at Horham, residing himself at Stonham-Jernegan, which he made the principal seat of the family *(Blomefield, fo.* 659). He likewise settled upon his daughter Jane, on her marriage with John Leyston, Esq. several manors, lands, and tenements, situate in Heythyl in Norfolk, and in Fressingfield and Hurdenhall in Suffolk. *Blomefield MSS. inter Eviden. Baron Wodehouse de Kimberley.*
* 4 Edw. II. No. 13, in Jurri. Lond.   † Dugdale's Summons.

cle, Roger baron Fitz Osbert, dying without issue,* the estates devolved to Isabella, his mother, and to the issue of Alice, her sister and co-heir, married to Sir John Noyoun, Knt. on a division made between the two sisters, the manor of Somerley Town and Uggeshall, in Suffolk, and Hadeston and Wittingham in Norfolk, were settled upon Isabella.† From this period until the reign of King James I. Somerley became the chief seat of the Jerningham family. It appears from the Eye Register, fo. 986, that Sir Peter's first wife was Alice, daughter of Hugh Germayne, and Basil his wife: his second is stated to have been Matilda, daughter and heir of Sir Roger Herling, and also of Sir Peter Fitzmortimer; and that his third was Ellen, daughter of Sir Roger de Huntingfield, of Huntingfield in Suffolk, Knt.‡ He appears to have died, at an advanced age, towards the middle of the reign of King Edw. III. and was succeeded by his son,

8. Sir John Jernegan of Somerley, Knt. he married Agatha, daughter of Sir Robert Shelton of Shelton, in Norfolk,§ and was succeeded by his son,

9. Sir John Jernegan, sen. of Somerley, Knt ‖ This Sir John inherited the other moiety of the Fitzosbert estates, at the death of his cousin, Sir John Noyoun, Knt. He married Joan, daughter and co-heir of Sir William de Kelvedon, relict of Sir John Lowdham of Frense, in Norfolk: she was jointly seized of all his manors of Somerley-Town, Wathe, Horham, &c. at the time of his death, anno 1375; and was succeeded by his son,

10. Sir John Jernegan, jun. of Somerley, Knt. who in 1374¶ married Margaret, daughter of Sir Thomas Vise de Lou, Knt. of an ancient Norman family; and his father then settled the manor and advowson of Stonham-Jernegan, and Horham, upon them and their heirs. They had issue two sons and two daughters; Sir Thomas, their successor, Humphrey, who died in 1446;* Alice, the wife of John Cleresby; and Elizabeth, of John Gonvile, Esq.

11. Sir Thomas Jernegan of Somerley, Knt. in 1406 had a charter of free warren in Somerley, Flixton, Ilketishall, and Wathe, in Suffolk; and Hadeston, Bunwell, &c. in Norfolk. He married Joan, daughter of John Appleyard of Dunston, in Norfolk, Esq.† and was succeeded by his son,

12. John Jernegan of Somerley, Esq. who married Joan, daughter of Sir John Darell of Cale Hill, in Kent, Knt. ancestor of the present —— Darell, Esq. of the same place. She died before him,‡ and was buried in St. Mary's Chapel, in the

---

* Inquis. post. mort. Rogeri. filii Petri Fitz Osbert, 34 Edw. I. † Blomefield, fo. 660. ‡ Ibid.
§ This descent is omitted in Blomefield.   ‖ Esch. 50 Edw. III. No. 26.
¶ Fines Suff. 49 Edw. III. between John, son of John Jernegan, and Margaret, daughter of Sir Thomas Vise de Lou. John Jernegan and Joan, his wife, desforceants of the manor of Stonham-Jernegan.
* Weever's Fun. Mon. fo. 784.   † Pat. 8 Henry IV. part A. Mem. 16.
This Sir Thomas and his lady lie buried under an altar tomb now standing at the north-east corner of Somerley church chancel: the arms of Jerningham still remain at the west end; and on the south side, impaling Appleyard, azure, a cheveron or, between three owls, argent. They glazed the chancel, and their arms were still seen on the windows when Blomefield wrote his history.
‡ In 1473 he made his will, which was proved Dec. 9, 1474, by the name of John Jernegan, sen. of Little Wirlingham in Suffolk, Esq. in which he ordered his body to be buried by his wife in the aforesaid.

priory of St. Olave', at Herringfleet in Suffolk, now called St. Tooley's Bridge. He was succeeded by his son,

13. John Jernegan of Somerley, jun. Esq. upon whom, on his marriage in 1459 with Isabella, daughter and heir of Sir Gervase Clifton, Knt.* his father had settled the manor of Horham, and had also given up to him the family seat at Somerley, and retired himself to Cove near Beccles, where he was living in 1465. John Jernegan, jun. died in 1503.† He left issue two sons, Sir Edward and Sir Richard, and several daughters; Mary was the wife of Thomas Stanhope, Esq. ancestor of the present earl of that name. His second son, Sir Richard, was with King Henry VIII. in his wars in Flanders, and there received the honour of knighthood.‡ He was sent by him in 1523, as his ambassador to the Emperor Charles, then in Spain.§ Several letters of his correspondence with Cardinal Wolsey at that time, extant are among the Harlean manuscripts in the British Museum.‖

14. Sir Edward Jernegan of Somerley, Knt. eldest son and heir of John Jernegan, jun. had two wives: his first was Margaret, the only daughter of Sir Edmund Bedingfield of Oxburgh, in Norfolk, Knt. (ancestor of the present Sir Richard Bedingfield, Bart.) who died March 24, 1504.¶ From this marriage came the Jernegans of Somerley-Town, now extinct.

---

chapel, where his ancestors were entombed. He gave Little Wirlingham manor, which he had lately purchased of William Cove, to his son Osbert for life; and also his manor of Wattle; or Wathe Hall, in North Cove: and to John, his eldest son, he bequeathed the manors and advowsons of Somerley-Town, Stonham-Jernegan, Horham, and Bradwell; and the foundation of the house of St. Olave's: besides gifts to his three daughters, who were nuns, viz. Anne Jernegan, at Brusyerd in Suffolk; Thomasine, at Denny in Cambridgeshire; and Barbara, at Champsey in Suffolk.

* Proved by fine levied 38 Henry VI. and Petitions in Chancery anno 2 Rich. III.

† Regr. Gilbert, fo. 34, a.

‡ Stow, in his Annals, relates that "certain gentlemen of the privie chamber, which through the king's lenitie in bearing with their lewdness, forgetting themselves and their duty towards his grace, in being too familiar with him, not having due respect to his estate and degree, were removed by order taken from the councel, unto whom the king had given authoritie to use their discretions in that behalf; and then were four sad and auncient knights put into the king's privie chamber, whose names were Sir Richard Wingfield, Sir Richard Jernegan, Sir Richard Weston, and Sir William Kingston."

Lord Herbert, in describing the splendid tilts and tournaments given at the champ du Drap D'or, in presence of the two kings of France and England, tells us that the "aiders on the English side were the Duke of Suffolk, the Marquis of Dorset, Sir William Kingston, Sir Richard Jernegan, Sir Giles Capel, Mr. Nicholas Carew, and Mr. Anthony Knevit. The aiders on the French party were M. le Duc de Vendosme, M. de St. Pol, M. de Montmorency, M. de Bryon, M. de Mesme, Master de Boucall, and Master Tabani." Vide Hall, 77, b.

§ Litteræ patentæ inter Eviden. Cossey, dated May 17, 1523. ‖ No. 297, 17, 18, 19, 20, 21, 23.

¶ Weever's Mon. fo. 784.

By her he had issue six sons, viz. John, Thomas, Olyff, Robert, Nicholas, and Edward; and two daughters: Anne, who had five husbands; 1, Edward lord Grey; 2, —— Berkeley, Esq. 3, Edward Barley; 4, Sir Robert Drury; and 5, Sir Edmund Walsingham. Margaret, his second daughter, was the wife first of John Blenerhasset, Esq. and secondly of Richard Holdich, Esq.

Sir Robert Jernegan, Sir Edward's 4th son, was much famed for his valour, and was knighted by the Duke of Suffolk at the taking of Montdidier in France (Hall, fo. 120) 15 Henry VIII. He also greatly distinguished himself in the wars in Italy, under the French general Lautrech, who, as Lord Herbert says, "was commanded to proceed with his army, in which Sir Robert Jernegan, gentleman of the bedchamber both to King Henry and Francis, had the command of 200 horse paid by our king, whereupon the Imperialists, knowing how much it concerned them to defend the kingdom of Naples, retired thi-

JERNINGHAM OF COSSEY, NORFOLK.

His second wife was Mary, daughter and co-heir of Richard Scroope, second son of Henry lord Scroope, of Boulton, re-married to Sir William Kingston, knight of the garter: she died in 1548, and lies buried in the church of Leyton, with an inscription on a brass tablet against the wall.* By this lady Sir Edward had issue, 1, Sir Henry Jernegan of Huntingfield, &c. 2, Ferdinand; 3, Edmund, gentleman of the bed-chamber to King Henry VIII. and died Feb. 9, 1546; 4, Edward, born after his father's death; and 5, Elizabeth, maid of honour to Queen Mary.

15. Sir Henry Jerningham of Huntingfield and Wingfield, in Suffolk, and founder of the Cossey family, was one of the first, with the earls of Sussex, Bath, and

---

ther with a small remnant of their army. The siege of Naples, after a blockade of above four months, was raised by the French army, having lost by sickness the greater part of their troops. Lautrech himself fell a victim to the contagion, and Sir Robert Jernegan died there April 25, 1528, and was honourably interred, his company being afterwards given to Master John Carew, his lieutenant." This Sir Robert is frequently mentioned in our old chronicles, for his valourous achievements in Henry the Eighth's wars in Flanders, particularly by Hall.

Sir Edward obtained a grant from King Henry VIII. of the manors of Lowestoft and Mutford, and others in Suffolk (*quæ fuerunt Edmundi de la Pole.* Originalia 1 *Henry VIII.* Rot. 63) and died Jan. 6, 1515, seized of the manors of Horham, Newton, Corton, Stonham-Jernegan, Somerley-Town, Wathe, Lowestoft, East, West, North, and South Lete, in Gorleston; Mutford, Astreby, &c. and is said to be buried in Somerley church chancel, by his wife. (*Blomefield, fo.* 661) He was succeeded by his eldest son,

15. Sir John Jernegan of Somerley, Knt. He married Bridget, daughter of Sir Robert Drury of Halsted, Knt. of a very ancient family, who took their name from a village in Normandy, from whence their ancestor came over with the Conqueror. By her he had three sons, George, Robert, and John; and two daughters; Anne, the wife of Sir Thomas Cornwallis, Knt. ancestor of the present Marquis of that name; and Elizabeth, the wife of John Sulyard of Wetherden, in Suffolk, Esq. ancestor to the late Edward Sulyard, Esq. of Haughley, in the same county: she died Jan. 19, 1518, and was buried in the church of Wetherden. (*Weever's Mon. fo.* 779) Sir John was succeeded by his eldest son,

16. George Jernegan of Somerley, Esq. representative in parliament for the borough of Orford in Suffolk in 1553. He married Eleanor, third daughter of Sir John Spelman of Harburgh, in Norfolk, second justice of the king's Bench; and by her had six sons and four daughters. His fourth son, Thomas, who represented in parliament the county of Suffolk in 1553, married Elizabeth, daughter of Edward Thompson of Bishop's Stortford, by whom he had three sons, George, Thomas, and Francis; and seven daughters, Mary, Susanna, Elizabeth, Jane, Anne, Eleanor, and Penelope. George Jernegan was succeeded by his eldest son,

17. John Jernegan of Somerley, Esq. who married Catharine, daughter of George Brook, Lord Cobham, leaving four daughters, his co-heirs, viz. Elizabeth, Catharine, the wife of Wymond Carew of Norfolk; Frances, of Thomas Bedingfield, Esq. of Oxburgh, by whom she had two sons, and secondly of her cousin, Henry Jerningham of Cossey, in Norfolk (of whom hereafter); and his fourth daughter was Margaret, the wife of —— Ford, Esq. of Butley in Suffolk.

* Lyson's Environs of London, vol. IV. p. 166.

"If you wyll the truythe have, | Was buryed honorably 4th day of September,
Here lyethe in this grave, | The yere of our lord reckyned truely,
Dyrectly under this stone, | M D. fourty and eight surely;
Good lady Marie Kyngstone; | At the costs of her son, Sir Henry Jernyngham truely,
Who departyd this world, the truth to say, | Who was at this makyng * * * * *
In the month of August, the XV day; | Of the queen's garde cheffe capteyn, 1557."
And as I do well remember,

Sir William Kingston, the second husband of this lady, in his will, proved in 1541 (*Regr. Alynger in cur Prerog. Cant. fo.* 33) bequeathed to his son, Anthony Kingston, six great bowls of silver, &c. and to his son-in-law, Sir Henry Jernegan, 20*l.* and a gown of black sattin, furred with sables, which the king gave him: to his son-in-law, Edmund Jernegan, 20*l.* to his brother, George Kingston, towards the marriage of his daughters, 40*l.* to his son Anthony, his manors of Clopton and Rushe, in Berks, &c.

Oxford, Lord Wentworth, Sir Thomas Cornwallis, Sir Henry Bedingfield, Sir William Waldegrave, and several others of the Norfolk and Suffolk gentry, who came forward in support of Queen Mary, at the death of Edw. VI. and proclaimed her in Norwich July 12, 1553. The interest of the Jerninghams at that time being very considerable in and about the town of Yarmouth, Sir Henry was enabled to get possession of six large ships, which proved of signal service to the queen's party.* He was afterwards commander of the forces under the Duke of Norfolk, when sent to suppress the insurrection of Sir Thomas Wyat, and routed the rebels near Charing Cross, after their failure at Whitehall, and in their attempt to follow their leader into the city.† He was immediately, on the queen's accession, made privy councellor, vice chamberlain, captain of her guard, and lord-lieutenant of the county of Kent.‡ She also made him a grant, by letters patent, of several large manors in Norfolk, Suffolk, Herefordshire, and Gloucestershire;§ and particularly of the manor of Cossey.‖

Sir Henry pulled down the old hall at Cossey, which stood under the hill, on the south side of the water, and erected the present mansion house, which he finished in 1564, as appears by the date over the porch. He resided during the building of it at the royal palace at Eltham in Kent, of which he was keeper ¶ He married Frances, daughter of Sir George Baynham of Cloriwell, in Gloucestershire, Knt. and heir to her maternal uncle, Sir Anthony Kingston. This lady brought into the family the manor of Painswick in Gloucestershire. She survived her husband, and had the estate at Cossey settled upon her for life.

---

* Hollingshead, in his Chronicle, relates the matter thus: — "About this time six ships, well manned, that were appointed to lie before Yarmouth, and to have kept the ladie Marie, if she had fled that way, were, by force of weather, driven into the haven, where Maister Jerningham was raising power on the ladie Mary's behalfe, who hearing there f, came thither; whereupon the captains took a boat and went to their ships; but the sailors and souldiers asked Maister Jerningham what he would have, and whether he would have their captains or no? and he said yea. Marrie, said they, ye shall have them, or we throw them into the bottome of the sea. But the captains said forthwith, that they would serve Queen Marie willinglie, and so brought forth their men, and conveyed with them their great ordinance. Of the coming of these ships the ladie Marie was wonderfully joyous, and afterwards doubted little the duke's puissance; but when news thereof was brought to the Tower, each man there began to draw backward, and over that, word of a great mischief was brought to the Tower, that is to say, that the noblemen's tenants refused to serve their lords against Queen Marie."

† Speed's Chron. fo. 1115.   ‡ Cossey Evid.

§ Manerium de Cossey, co. Norf. 3 pars originalia. Manerium de Jaynton, co. Hereford, originalia, Rot. 51, 64, 106. Manerium de Wingfield, co. Suff. origin. Rot. 112. Maneriæ de Vealis & Sylham, co. Suff. 2 pars. origin. Rot. 62.

‖ This manor is reckoned one of the largest in the county of Norfolk, extending itself into upwards of twenty of the adjacent parishes, over which it has the superiority in as ample a manner as the lord of the hundred has over the rest. It belonged to Guest in the Confessor's time, and after the conquest fell to the share of Alan earl of Richmond. In the year 1384 it was granted by patent to Michael de la Pole, earl of Suffolk; but upon the attainder of Edmund de la Pole, in 1513, it escheated to the crown. King Henry VIII. made a grant of it to the lady Anne of Cleves, after whose death it continued in the crown, until Queen Mary granted it to Sir Henry Jerningham, with the whole park and deer therein, with all its rights, members, privileges, and appurtenances in Cossey, Earlham, Baberough, Bowthorpe, Easton, Colton, Marlingford, Barford, Wramplingham, Melton, Netherset, Honningham, East Tuddenham, Brandon, Runhall, Weston, Morton, Ryngland, Felthorpe, Faverham, Carlton, Sawle, and Yaxham, to be held by him and his heirs in capite, by knights service." She also granted the castle and manor of Wingfield in Suffolk, which had likewise been part of the extensive property of the de la Pole family.   ¶ Cossey Eviden.

Sir Henry entertained Queen Elizabeth in her progress into Norfolk, at his house at Cossey:* but on account of the attachment which he shewed to the ancient religion of his ancestors, and to which his posterity have inviolably adhered, he was in no favour with the court. He had issue by his lady (who survived him and died in 1583) three sons and two daughters, viz. Henry, his successor, William, Francis, Mary, the wife of Sir Thomas Southwell of Rising, in Norfolk; and Jeronyma, of Charles Waldegrave (ancestor of the present Earl Waldegrave) and dying in 1626, was buried on the 5th of Feb. in the church at Cossey, as appears by the register of that parish. Sir Henry died Sep. 7, 1572, aged 63;† and was succeeded by his eldest son,

16. Henry Jerningham, sen. of Cossey, Esq. His first wife was Eleanor, daughter of William lord Dacres of Gillesland (by Elizabeth, daughter of George Talbot, Earl of Shrewsbury, and Anne his wife, daughter of Lord Hastings, chamberlain to Edward IV.) by whom he had issue, 1 Henry, his successor; 2, Thomas, who married the widow of a Norwich citizen; 3, William, who died unmarried; 4, George, who married Eleanor, daughter of Sir George Philpot of Hampshire, Knt. by whom he had a son George; 5, Edward; 6, Anne, the wife of John, son and heir of Sir John Arundel of Lanherne, in Cornwall, Knt. His second wife was Frances, daughter and co-heir of John Jerningham of Somerley-Town, by his wife, Catharine, daughter of George Brook, Lord Cobham; and by her (who was the relict, as before-mentioned of Edmund Bedingfield, Esq.) he had issue a son Francis, and a daughter Anne; besides two other daughters buried at Cossey, Feb. 24, 1615.‡ He had an act passed to sell certain lands in Norfolk and Suffolk, 2 James I. and died June 15, 1619; and was buried in St. Margaret's church, Westminster.§ He was succeeded by his eldest son,

I. Sir HENRY JERNINGHAM of Cossey, Bart. He married Eleanor, daughter of Thomas Throckmorton of Coughton, in Warwickshire, Esq. by Margaret, daughter and co-heir of William Whorwood, attorney-general to King Henry VIII. and sister to the countess of Warwick. This Thomas Throckmorton was ancestor to the present baronet of that name.‖

Sir Henry was created a baronet Oct. 16, 1621. He had issue by his lady three sons and two daughters; 1, John, who died V.P. 2, William, who married Mary, eldest daughter of Francis Bernard of Margeretting, in Essex, Esq. relict of Hugh Lee of Twyford, in Middlesex, and also of John Yonge, Esq. secretary to Lord Bacon; 3, Thomas, who was knighted for his gallant behaviour at the Isle of Rhè, under the command of Villiers duke of Buckingham, in 1627, being then about 19 years of age. Sir Henry's two daughters were 1, Elizabeth, who died single; 2, Catharine, married in 1624, to Francis Saunders of Shankston, in Leicestershire. He died at Cossey in 1646, and was buried Sep. 1, in the church of

---

* Q. Eliz. Progress. † Vinc. No. 429, for funer. Certif. ‡ Blomefield. § Fun. Cert. Herald's Coll.
‖ By the settlement made upon Sir Henry on his marriage, dated Jan. 31, 34th Eliz. *(Inter Evid. Cossey)* Henry Jerningham, the father, appears to have been seized of the manors, lordships, &c. of Paynswick, Morton, Valence, Haresfield, and Messerdyne, in the county of Gloucester; and Cossey, Dages in Ramingham, Heringflete, alias St. Olave's, Lothingland, Mutford, Wingfield, Frumbalds, Old Wingfield Hall, Syleham Comites, Veales in Fresingfield, and Storars, in Norfolk and Suffolk.

that parish: his eldest son was John Jerningham, Esq. who died in 1636, aged 38. He married in 1619 Mary, daughter of Sir Francis Moore of Fawley, in Berkshire, Bar*t*. by whom he had issue Henry, successor to his grandfather; Frances, the wife of Philip Crambleton of Newtham, in Yorkshire; and Dorothy, the wife of Thomas Pegge of Yeldersley, in the county of Derby, Esq.*

II. Sir HENRY JERNINGHAM of Cossey, Bart. succeeded his grandfather in 1646: he married Mary, daughter of Benedict Hall of High Meadow, in Gloucestershire, Esq. by whom he had Benedict, who died at Paris, unmarried, 1668; Francis, his successor, and one daughter. His lady died April 30, 1653, and was buried in Bookham church, Surrey.† Sir Henry died Oct. 6, 1680, and was succeeded by his son,

III. Sir FRANCIS JERNINGHAM of Cossey, Bart. who married Anne, daughter of Sir George Blount of Toolington, in Worcestershire, Bart. by whom he had ven sons; 1, John, his successor, baptized at Cossey Sep. 6, 1678; 2, George, baptized June 2, 1680; 3, Charles, professor of physic, who married 1st, Elizabeth, daughter of Christopher lord Teynham; and this lady dying without issue, Nov. 14, 1736, he married secondly Frances, daughter of Rowland Belasyse, brother of Lord Viscount Fauconberg, and departed this life at Cossey April 28, 1760, in the 73d year of his age; and lies buried in the chancel of the church, leaving no issue by his second lady, who survived him some years: 4, Henry Jerningham, who married Mary, daughter of Nicholas Jonquet L'epine, and had issue by her five sons and three daughters, viz.‡ 5, Edward, who married Elizabeth, daughter of John Keighley of Gray's Inn, Esq. and had issue George, who died 17—, S. P. and Henrietta, a nun, now living at Pontoise in France; 6, Francis, of the order of the Jesuits, who died in 1739; and 7, Richard Jerningham, who died young. Sir Francis had also two daughters, who were nuns at Bruges; and he died August 26, 1730, aged 80 years, and was buried in Cossey church. Anne, his lady, survived him, and was buried near her husband, Feb. 17, 1735.

* It appears by the papers and evidences at Cossey, that during the life of his father, Sir Henry, the family property was much involved; that the manor and castle of Wingfield in Suffolk, with other estates, were sold; and that the park at Cossey was let down, and the deer destroyed; the manor house, with the domaine let to a farmer during the civil wars, and part of the building taken down. John Jerningham chiefly resided at the house of his father-in-law, in Berkshire.

† Le Neve's Mon. vol. II. p. 19.

‡ 1, Francis; 2, Henry, who married and settled in America, where he departed this life Nov. 20, 1772, in the province of Maryland, leaving issue two sons and five daughters; 1, Charles-Edward Jerningham, born in 1749, and died in 1777, S. P. 2, Henry-Tobias, born in 1765; 3, Frances-Henrietta, bo n 1745, a nun at Hengrave, in Suffolk; 4, Mary, born in 1754, and died in 1777; 5, Helosyia, born in 1757, and married in 1779, to John Lancaster, Esq. of Charles County, Maryland, by whom she has living four sons and two daughters; 6, Anne-Edwardina, born in 1761, and married in 1787 Joseph Queen, Esq. by whom she has three sons and two daughters; 7, Olivia, born in 1763, married in 1785 Henry Hammersley, Esq. and died in 1793, having issue one son. The third son of Henry Jerningham, and his wife, Mary L'Epine, was Charles, a general in the Imperial service, now residing at Vienna; and married to his second wife a German lady, by whom he has issue; his first was ——, daughter of —— Dickenson of Wrightling on, in Lancashire, Esq. The fourth son was Nicholas, who married the widow of the late Mr. Carte, and died in 1785. The fifth, Hugh, a religious, in the convent of English Franciscans, at Douay in Flanders; and died at Dover in 1793. His three daughters were Mary, Elizabeth, and Edwardina, nuns at Bruges, but came over to England in 1794, with the rest of the community, and settled at Hengrave near Bury. The two eldest are since dead.

JERNINGHAM, OF COSSEY, NORFOLK.

IV. Sir JOHN JERNINGHAM, of Cossey, Bart. eldest son, married in 1704, Margaret, daughter of Sir Henry Bedingfield, of Oxburgh, Bart. but by her had no issue. He resided chiefly during the life of his father, at Painswick, in Gloucestershire, and died at Bath, June 14, 1737, and is buried in the cathedral of that city. His widow retired, after his death, to Winchester, where she departed this life in 17—. He was succeeded by his brother,

V. Sir GEORGE JERNINGHAM, of Cossey, Bart. who had passed the greater part of his youth upon the continent, and was in his 54th year when he married, in 1733, Mary, eldest daughter, and at length heiress of Francis Plowden, Esq. by Mary, daughter of the hon. John Stafford Howard, younger son of William, lord viscount Stafford, beheaded in 1680. Sir George had issue four sons; John, who died, aged 22, of the small pox, at Stonor, in Oxfordshire; William, his successor; Edward (the author of many elegant publications in verse) and Charles, a general officer in the service of the late King of France, and knight of Malta and St. Lewis. Sir George had also a daughter Mary, who died an infant. He departed this life at his seat in Norfolk, Jan. 21, 1774, in the 94th year of his age, and lies buried in the church at Cossey. Mary lady Jerningham, his widow, survived him, and died in London, in 1785.

VI. Sir WILLIAM JERNINGHAM, the present baronet, son and heir of Sir George, married in June 1767, Frances, eldest daughter of Henry, 11th Viscount Dillon, of the kingdom of Ireland; by whom he has had issue three sons and two daughters, viz. George-William, who married Dec. 26, 1799, Frances, youngest daughter and co-heiress of the late Edward Sulyard, of Haughley, in Suffolk, Esq. William-Charles, now an officer in the English army, and lately in the Austrian service; where, during the hard and perilous campaigns, from 1792 to the treaty of Campo Formio, he signalized himself by distinguished bravery and judgment: Edward, of Lincoln's Inn; Mary, who died an infant; and Charlotte-Georgina, married in June 1795, to Sir Richard Bedingfield, of Oxburgh, Bart. by whom she has issue. Sir William Jerningham has inherited, through his mother, maternally descended from the noble family of Stafford, the baronial castle of that name, with several other considerable estates in the counties of Salop and Stafford, formerly a part of the vast possessions of Edward Stafford, duke of Buckingham, beheaded 13 Henry VIII. and which were afterwards restored, with the barony, to his son, Henry, lord de Stafford. Sir William will also, at the death of lady Anastatia Stafford, neice to the last earl of that name, become sole heir to the remaining honours of that noble family.

ARMS—Argent, three arming buckles, gules.
CREST—A faulcon, issuing from an imperial crown, proper.
MOTTO—*Virtus basis vitæ*.
SEATS—At Cossey, or Costessey Hall, Norfolk,* and Shiffnal manor, Shropshire.

---

* The Park at Cossey, one of the most ancient in the county of Norfolk, has been much beautified by its present possessor, who has restored its former limits, and greatly improved the surrounding country, by extensive plantations, &c.

JERNINGHAM, OF COSSEY, NORFOLK.

TABLE 33.

1 JERNEGAN, 1182=Sibilla

2 Hubert Fitz-Jernegan, 1203=Maud de Watheby   Amice=Robert Marmjon

3 Sir Hubert Jernegan, cir. 1239=Margery, dr. and heiress of Sir — de Herling

Godfrey   4 Sir William=J. Gimmingham   Robert   5 Sir Hugh=Ellen Inglethorpe

6 Sir Walter Jernegan=Isabel Fitz-Osbert   Jane=John Leyston

7 Sir Peter Jernegan   1 RALPH, 1st E. of STAFFORD, K.G. 1372
A. Germayne | Matilda de Herling | Ellen Huntingfield   Margaret, dr. and heiress of Hugh de Audley, L. of Gloucester, by Isabella, dr. and co-heiress of Gilbert de Clare, E. of Gloucester

8 Sir John Jernegan=A. Shelton   2 Hugh, E. of Stafford, K.G.=Philippa, dr. of T. Beauchamp, E. of Warwick

9 Sir John Jernegan, 1375   3 Thomas, E. of Stafford, 1393   4 Wm. E. of Staff. 1395   5 Edmund, E. of Stafford, 1405
Joan de Kelvedon   Anne, dr. of Thos. son of K. Edw. III.

10 Sir John Jernegan   Jane   6 Humphrey, E. of Stafford & D. of Buckingham, 1460
Margaret, dr. of Sir Thomas Vise de Loo   Sir G. Debenham   Anne, dr. of Ralph, 1st E. of Westmoreland, by Joan, dr. of John of Gaunt, D. of Lancaster

11 Sir Thomas | Alice | Elizabeth | Humph. 1446   7 Humph. E. of Staff. 1455   John Stafford, K.G. E. of Wiltshire
J. Appleyard | J. Cleresby | J. Gonvile   Marg. dr. & co-heiress of Edm. D. of Somerset   C. Greene

12 John Jernegan   Margaret   8 Henry, second D. of Buck. K.G.
Jane Darell | Agnes ——   Catharine, sister & co-heiress of Rich. E. of Rivers

13 John Jernegan, 1503   Osbert, Thomasine, Barbara   Edw. third & last D. of Buck. 1522   Henry, E. of Wiltshire K.G. 1523
Isabel, dr. of Sir Gervase Clifton   Eleanor, dr. of Henry, 4th E. of Northumberland   Muriel, sister of John Grey, V. Lisle

14 Sir Edw. Jernegan, 1515   more children   Henry, L. Stafford, 1558*
M. Bedingfield | M. Scroope   Ursula, dr. of Sir Richard Pole, Knt. by Margaret, daughter of George, D. of Clarence, brother to King Edw. IV.

Jernegans of Somerley Town, extinct   15 Sir Henry, 1572   Ferdinand, Edm. Edw. Eliz.   Edw. L. Stafford
        Frances Beynham   Mary, dr. of Edw. E. of Derby

16 HENRY JERNINGHAM, 1619   William, Francis   Mary T. Southwell   Jeronima C. Waldegrave   Edw. L. Stafford, 1625
Eleanor Dacres | Fran. Jernegan   Isabella Foster

1. Sir Hen. Bt. 1646   Thomas   Wm.   Anne J. Arundel   George E. Philpot   Frances, Anne, &c.   Edw. Stafford
E. Throckmorton   —, of Norwich   Anne Wilsford

John, 1636   William   Sir Thomas Jerningham   Henry L. Stafford, 1639   Mary, C. of Stafford, &c.
M. Moore   F. Bernard   S. P.   Sir Wm. K.B. son of Thomas Howard E. of Arundel, 1680.†

* The ancient fee barony of de Stafford was restored to him, by act of restitution, 1 Edw. VI.

† Sir Wm. Howard was created Baron and Viscount Stafford, by King Charles I. and was attainted and beheaded in 1680; a victim to perjury, and to the credulity of the times. His widow, Mary, Baroness de Stafford in her own right, was created a Countess for life, 1 James II.

George Radcliffe Jerningham (p. 229, line 15) married Eleanora, daughter of Sir George Philpot, of Hampshire, and had issue, one son George, and five daughters; Anne, Mary, Elizabeth, Frances, and Catharine: the four eldest were nuns in Flanders; Mary and Elizabeth established an English monastery at Paris, in 1658, which remained till overturned by the revolution, in 1799.

a				b	
II. Sir Henry, 1680	Frances	Dorothy	Henry, E. of Stafford	John Stafford	Howard, 1714
Mary Hall, 1655	P. Cramble-ton	T. Pegge	1719	M. Southcote	T. Strickland

| Benedict, 1668 | III. Sir Francis, 1730 Anne, dr. of Sir G. Blount | Wm. 2d E. of Stafford, 1734 A. Holman, 1754 | John Paul, 4th E. of Stafford, 1762 | Xaveria & Louisa | Mary F. Plowden |

| IV. Sir John, 1737 Marg. dr. of Sir H. Bedingfeld | V. Sir Geo. M. Plowden 1735 | Wm. Matthias 3d E. of Stafford, 1750 | Mary Appol-lonia | Anastasia b. 1722 | Anne b. 1725 d. 1792 S. P. | Francis Plowden d. S. P. | Mary, 1785 Sir Geo. Jerningham | Lou-isa |

| Mary d. y. | John d. aged 22 | VI. Sir Wm. Jerningham, Bart. The Hon. Frances Dillon | | Edward | Charles |

| Mary, d. y. | Charlotte=Sir R. Bedingfield | George=F. Sulyard | William | Edward |

---

38. STEPNEY of PRENDERGAST, PEMBROKESHIRE.

Created Baronet Nov. 24, 1621.

THE origin of this family is deduced by genealogists from

1. Henry Stepney, Esq. of Aldenham in Hertfordshire,* who was succeeded by his son,

2. Ralph Stepney, Esq. who was interred in Aldenham church, in 1544.† He married ——, daughter and heir of —— Cressey, by whom he had

3. William Stepney, lord of Aldenham, the father of

4. Thomas Stepney, Esq.‡ He married —— the daughter of John Wynde or Wyld, of Ramsey in Huntingdonshire, Esq. by whom he had two sons; Robert, the first, married, and had issue Pool Stepney, and

5. Alban Stepney, Esq. second son, was register of the diocese of St. David's. He married first Margaret, daughter and co-heir of Thomas Catharn of Prendergast, Esq. by whom he had no issue: he married secondly Mary, daughter and co-heir of William Philipps of Picton Castle, Esq. by which matches he became possessed of a very plentiful estate. By the latter he had issue three sons; John, Philip, a barrister at law, who died S. P. and Sir Thomas Stepney, Knt. who was a great courtier, and travelled into France and other countries: he married first

---

* Chauncy, in his Antiquities of Hertfordshire, says, the manor of Aldenham coming to the crown upon the dissolution, King Henry VIII. granted it, with the advowson, to Henry Stepney, who died, leaving issue Ralph Stepney, who held it of King Edw. VI. in *capite*.

† Here lyeth Ralph Stepney, esquyre, the first lord of the lordship of this towne of Aldenham, and patron of this church, who dyed Dec. 3, 1544, on whose sowl Jesu have mercy. Amen. *Weever's Fun. Mon.* p. 592.   ‡ Vincent's Wales, p. 548.

the daughter of —— Fisher of Hants, Esq. relict of —— Wallop, of the same county, Esq. by whom he had no issue; secondly, Mary, eldest daughter and co-heir of Sir Bernard Whetstone of Woodford, in Essex, Knt. by whom he had Bernard, and other children:* the said Alban had also two daughters; Dorothy, the wife of Sir Francis Mansell of Muddlescombe, Bart. and Joan, of John Philipps of Nash, in Pembrokeshire, Esq.

I. JOHN STEPNEY, Esq. son and heir, was created a baronet in 1621: he married Catharine, daughter of Sir Francis Mansell of Muddlescombe, in Carmarthen, Bart. by whom he had four sons; 1, Sir John, his successor; 2, Alban, who died, aged 21; 3, Thomas, who married Price, daughter and co-heir of Sir Henry Jones of Albermarles, in Carmarthen, Bart. by whom he had Sir John, hereafter-mentioned; 4, Charles, who married ——, daughter of Sir Richard Pryse of Gogarthan, in Cardigan, Bart. relict of —— Vaughan of Lhanelthy, Esq. by whom he had three sons; Richard, who married the daughter of —— Tancred, and died S. P. Charles, who was paymaster to Waller's marine regiment, and died of his wounds received at Cork, 1690, S. P. and Alban, who died at sea, S. P. and one daughter, Jane, the wife of Mr. Bloysdon, of Dresden in Germany. Sir John had also four daughters; Jane, the wife of Thomas Vaughan of Penteparke, in Carmarthen, Esq. Dorothy, of Richard Bloome of Aberguilly, in Carmarthen, Esq. Martha, of William Bladwell of Swannington, in Norfolk, Esq. and Frances. Sir John died in Aug. 1634,† and was succeeded by his son,

II. Sir JOHN STEPNEY, Bart. he married Magdalen, daughter and co-heir of Sir Henry Jones of Albermarles, in Carmarthen, Bart. by whom he had issue only one daughter, Frances, the wife of Henry Mansell of Lhanelthy, Esq. Sir John Stepney dying without issue male, the dignity and great part of the estate devolved to

---

* George Stepney, Esq. an English poet and statesman, who was born in London in 1663, is supposed to be a son of this Sir Thomas Stepney, Knt. He received his education at Westminster school, and was removed thence to Trinity college, Cambridge, in 1682, where, being of the same standing with Charles Montague, Esq. afterwards Earl of Halifax, a strict friendship grew up between them. To this fortunate incident was owing all the preferment Stepney ever enjoyed, who is supposed not to have had parts sufficient to have risen to any distinction, without the immediate patronage of so great a man as Halifax. When Stepney first set out in life, he seems to have been attached to the Tory interest; for one of the first poems he wrote was an Address to James II. upon his Accession to the Throne.

Upon the revolution he was nominated to several foreign embassies, and was very successful in his negotiations, which occasioned his constant employment in the most weighty affairs. He died at Chelsea in 1708, and was buried at Westminster Abbey, where a fine monument was erected over him, with a pompous inscription. *See Le Neve's Monumen. Anglica. vol. IV. p. 228.*

"It is reported (says Dr. Johnson) that the juvenile compositions of Stepney *made grey authors blush*. I know not whether his poems will appear such wonders to the present age. One cannot always easily find the reason for which the world has sometimes conspired to squander praise. It is not very unlikely that he wrote very early as well as he ever wrote; and the performances of youth have many favourers, because the authors yet lay no claim to public honours, and are therefore not considered as rivals by the distributors of fame. He professed himself a poet, and added his name to those of the other wits in the version of juvenal; but he is a very licentious translator, and does not recompence his neglect of the author by beauties of his own. In his original poems now and then a happy line may perhaps be found, and now and then a short composition may give pleasure; but there is in the whole, little either of the grace or wit, or the vigour of nature."

† Goff's Notes, 146.

III. Sir JOHN STEPNEY, Bart. (son of his brother Thomas, who married Price, another daughter and co-heir of Sir Henry Jones, Bart.) He married Justina, daughter and heir to Sir Anthony Vandyke, Knt.* the celebrated limner, by whom he had issue one son, Thomas, and two daughters, who were nuns at a monastery at Brussels: they became abbesses, and lived to so great an age, that the late Sir Thomas went to see them. Sir John was succeeded by his son,

IV. Sir THOMAS STEPNEY, who married Margaret,† sister and co-heir of Walter Vaughan of Llanelthy, in Carmarthenshire, Esq. who died Nov. 1, 1733, aged 73 years. Sir Thomas represented the county of Carmarthen in several parliaments, and dying in Feb. 1744,‡ was succeeded by his son,

V. Sir JOHN STEPNEY, who married Eleanor,§ daughter and heir of John Lloyd of Buckleethwen, in Carmarthenshire, Esq. who died in 1733; by whom he had one son, Thomas, and three daughters; Margaret, who died unmarried; Mary, the wife of John Allen, Esq. of Dale, in Pembrokeshire; and Justina, the

---

* Burnet, in the History of his own Times, speaking of Gowry's conspiracy, says, p. 18, 19. "One thing, which none of the historians have taken any notice of, and might have induced the Earl of Gowry to have wished to put King James out of the way; for upon the king's death he stood next to the succession to the crown of England: for King Henry the Seventh's daughter, that was married to King James IV. did, after his death, marry Dowglass earl of Angus; but they could not agree, so a pre-contract was proved against him, upon which, by a sentence from Rome, the marriage was voided, with a clause in favour of the issue, since born under a marriage, *de facto*, and *bona fide*. Lady Margaret Dowglas was the child so provided for. I did peruse the original bull, confirming the divorce: after that the queen dowager married one Francis Steward, and had by him a son, called Lord Methuen, by King James V. In the patent he is called *frater noster uterinus*. He had an only daughter, who was mother or grand-mother to the Earl of Gowry; so that by this he might be glad to put the king out of the way, that so he might stand next to the succession of the crown of England. He had a brother, then a child, who when he grew up, and found he could not carry the name of Ruthen, which by an act of parliament, made after this conspiracy, none might carry, he went and lived beyond sea; and it was given out, that he had found the philosopher's stone. He had two sons, who died without issue, and one daughter, married to Sir Anthony Vandyke, the famous picture drawer." *For the Trial of the Earl of Gowry and the Conspirators, see State Trials, fo. vol. VII.*

† Here lie the remains of Lady Margaret Stepney, wife of Sir Thomas Stepney, Bart. In all relations of life she was amiable and endearing; courteous, affable, humane: in deportment graceful, in friendship sincere, in affection tender. Every virtue she sweetened with kindness, and every excellency she heightened with humility: her piety was exemplary, her charity universal. Enriched with these happy accomplishments, she was the very treasure of goodness; a treasure never more valuable, or more to be desired, than now, when hidden. She died Nov. 1, 1733, aged 73 years. In honour to her memory, this monument was erected by her loving and equally beloved husband.

‡ In memory of Sir Thomas Stepney, Bart. a person less distinguished by his illustrious descent from Henry VII. of England, than by his many excellent virtues. In him were seen, admired, and revered, the wisdom of the senator, the public spirit of the patriot, the polite address of the courtier, the sincerity of friend, the more private virtues of the good husband, parent, and master; and to crown all the unaffected piety of the christian, qualities too rarely united in the same character, *Vix ea nostra voco*, he died A. D. 1744, aged 76.

§ Near this place resteth the body of Mrs. Eleanor Stepney, wife of John Stepney, Esq. and daughter of John Lloyd of Llangeneck, Esq. She was a most obliging, endearing wife; a most tender, but prudent mother: happy in all valuable endowments, religious and moral; constant in her devotions to God, ever sincere to her friend, charitable to the poor, just and benevolent to all; a pattern truly worthy the imitation of her sex. In her husband's affectionate esteem she still lives; and as an instance of that esteem this monument is erected to her memory. She died Jan. 3, 1733, aged 32 years.

wife of Thomas Popkin, Esq. of Forest in Glamorganshire. He died in 1748,* and was succeeded by his son,

VI. Sir THOMAS STEPNEY, who married Eleanor,† only daughter and heir of Thomas Lloyd of Danyralt, in the county of Carmarthen, Esq. who died in June 1795, and was buried at Bath; by whom he had Margaretta-Eleanor, who died in 1794, unmarried; Sir John, the present baronet; Elizabeth-Bridgetta, born in 1749, the wife of Joseph Gulston, Esq. of Ealing Grove, in the county of Middlesex: she died in 1779. Justina-Maria, the wife first of Francis Head, Esq. of St. Andrew's Hall in Norfolk; secondly of Col. Cowel, of the Coldstream guards: and Thomas Stepney, Esq. unmarried. Sir Thomas died Oct. 7, 1772, and was succeeded by his son,

VII. Sir JOHN STEPNEY, Bart. who was envoy extraordinary, in 1775, at the court of Dresden, and at Berlin in 1782.

ARMS—Gules, a fess checky, or and azure, between three owls, argent.

CREST—On a wreath, or and azure, a talbot's head erased, gules eared, and holding in his chaps a hart's horn, or; about his neck a collar, checky, or and azure.

---

* In memory of Sir John Stepney, Bart. who, preferring the innocent repose of a rural retirement to the noise and hurry of a more busy, active scene of life, chose to confine himself to a narrower sphere of action, although his talents were equal to the greatest; and being less studious of applause than of deserving it, his ambition and his happiness was, to fill up the several relations of private life with grace and dignity suitable to his rank.—*Prodesse quam videri.* He died A. D. 1748, aged 56. This monument was erected by his son, Sir Thomas Stepney, Bart. A. D. 1751, whom providence has blessed with a promising issue.—*Non deficit alter.*

† In Llandybea church, Carmarthenshire.—Sacred to the memory of Elizabeth, eldest daughter of John Vaughan of Court Derllys, in the county of Carmarthen, Esq. and one of the co-heiresses of her uncle (her father's brother) Richard Vaughan of Derwydd, Esq. barrister at law, chief justice of the several counties of Carmarthen, Pembroke, and Cardigan; and representative in parliament of the borough of Carmarthen in seven successive parliaments: whose father was John Vaughan, son of the hon. Richard Vaughan of Court Derllys, Esq. one of the sons of John lord Vaughan, baron of Mullenger, Emlyn, and earl of Carbery. She was twice married, first to Thomas Lloyd of Danyralt, Esq. by whom she had one daughter, who married Sir Thomas Stepney of Llanelly, Bart. she was afterwards married to John Vaughan of Golden Grove, Esq. by whom she had no issue.

In the exercise of religious duties she was sincere and exemplary, without affectation; fervent, without enthusiasm; devout, without superstition; and in an uniform practice of every social virtue, free from the avarice of praise, but careful to deserve it. She reflected a lustre on the several relations of life: in her disposition sweet and engaging; her heart enlarged with sentiments of humanity and benevolence; and how diffusive her charity, the undissembled grief of the poor, fatherless, and widows, best testify their loss, and her liberality. In a word every quality that constitutes and adorns the faithful beneficent friend, the obedient wife, the affectionate parent; and to sum up all, the good christian, were happily blended and united in her.

To perpetuate the example, and a testimony of her dutiful affection, Lady Stepney has erected this monument of her mother's piety and virtue, who died the 20th of July, in the 57th year of her age, and in the year of our redemption 1754.

STEPNEY OF PRENDERGAST, PEMBROKESHIRE.

MOTTO—*Fide et vigilantia.* **SUPPORTERS**—two foxes, proper.
SEAT—At Prendergast, near Haverford-West, Pembrokeshire.

Quarterings of Sir John Stepney, Bart. as certified by Mr. Townshend, at the Herald's College, March 21, 1796.

1. Stepney—Gules, a fess checky, or and azure, between three owls, argent.
2. Cressy—Argent, a lion rampant, queue fourcheé, sable.
3. Wynde—not found.
4. Phillips—Argent, a lion rampant, sable, collared and chained, or.
5. Kadivor-vaur—Argent, a lion rampant, gardant, sable.
6. Bledry, lord of Kelsant—Argent, three bulls' head caboshed, sable; armed, or.
7. Sir Aaron ap Rhys—Argent, a lion rampant, gardant, gules.
8. Donne, of Picton—Azure, a fox rampant, argent.
9. Wogan—Or, a chief, sable; three martlets of the field.
10. Blethin ap Maynarch—Sable, a chevron argent, between three spears'-heads of the last embrued.
11. Philip Gwis—Gules, a chevron, ermine.
12. Jones of Albermarles—Argent, a chevron, azure, between three ravens, proper, within a bordure
13. Griffith ap Kydrick—Sable, a lion rampant, regardant, argent. [sable bezanteé
14. Vandyke }
15. Ruthven } not found, which prevents Ruthven being introduced.
16. Vaughan }
17. Lloyd } not ascertained in the Herald's College, but Lloyd (the late Lady Stepney) was, ar-
18. Lloyd } gent, a lion rampant, sable.

TABLE 39.

HENRY VII. 1 HENRY STEPNEY

Margaret 2 Ralph Stepney of St. Alban's, 1548=dr. and heir of —— Cressey
F. Steward

  3 William Stepney

L. Methuen 4 Thomas=——, dr. and heir of John Wynde

N 5 Robert Stepney=Marg. Cathain   5 Albany=Mary Philipps

N. br. to the   Pool   I. Sir John Stepney, 1684   Philip   Sir Thomas   Dorothy   Joan
E. of   Stepney   Cath. Mansell   Stepney —Wal-|M.Whis- Sir F.   J. Phi-
Gowry   lop   ton   Mansell   lips

  N   II. Sir John   Alban   Thomas   Charles   Jane   Dorothy   Martha   Francis   chil-   Richard, E.
SirA.Van- M.Jones   P.Jones —Pryce T.   R. Bloome Wm.   dren   of Carbery
 dyke   Vaughan   Bludwell

Justina   Frances   III. Sir John Stepney   Richard   Charles, 1690   Jane   John Vaughan
SirJ.Stepney H. Mansel Justina Vandyke   —Tancred   Alban   —Bloydson

            IV. Sir Thomas, 1744=Marg. Vaughan, 1733.   John   Richard
            V. Sir John, 1748= Eleanor Lloyd, 1733.   T. Lloyd=Eliz. 1754=J.Vaughan

VI. Sir Thomas, 1772   Margaret   Mary   Justina   Eleanor
Eleanor Lloyd, 1795   J. Allen   T. Popkin   Sir T. Stepney

VII. Sir John Stepney,   Margaretta-   Eliz.-Bridg. 1779   Just.-Maria   Thomas
     Bart.   Eleanor, 1794 Joseph Gulson   F. Head | Col. Cowel Stepney

39. WAKE of Clevedon, Somersetshire.

Created Baronet Dec. 5, 1621.

THE Wakes are mentioned by Brompton, among the nobles and others who came over with William the Conqueror: but it is the opinion of antiquaries, that the Wake recorded in the roll of Battle-Abbey, was one of those who being weary of Harold's usurpation, fled over into Normandy to invite the Conqueror.

Dr. Stukeley* deduces their genealogy from

1. Oslac, who was general and butler to King Athelwulf in 849; and that his son,

2. Morcar, in 870, was lord of Brun.

3. Ediva, great grand-daughter of Oslac, † was the wife of Leofric, son of Ralf, earl of Hereford, surnamed Scalre. Dr. Patrick observes, that their son

4. Hereward or Herewaldus, the outlaw, was the greatest hero of his age; and that his actions are celebrated by Ingulphus. He was nephew to Brando, abbot of Peterborough,‡ and married Thurfrida, by whom he had an only daughter,

5. Thurfrida, the wife of Hugh Evermue, lord of Deping and Brun, by whom she had an only daughter, the wife of

6. Richard de Rulos;§ and had issue one daughter,

7. Adheldis, the wife of Baldwin Fitz-Gilbert, earl of Glomery, and founder of Deping Priory, who died in 1171;∥ by whom she had one son, Roger, and a daughter

8. Emma, who was their heir,¶ and wife of Hugh de Wac, by whom she had

9. Baldwin lord Wake, founder of the abbey of Brun. He gave the priory of Deping to Thorney Abbey, and died in 1156;* and was the father of

10. Baldwin lord Wake, and Lydel in Cumberland: he died July 20, 1224, and was buried at Harombel, a castle in Gascoign, by his wife Alicia, who after his death was remarried to Joselyn, lord of Great Styvecle in Huntingdonshire.† He had one son,

11. Baldwin lord Wake, who died in 1213.‡ He married first Isabella, daughter and heir of William Bruer, lord of Torbay; secondly, Beatrix de Vanne, mistress of Reginald earl of Cornwall. By the former he had one son,

12. Hugh Wake, lord of Wake, Lydel, and Brun; and died in 1233. By his wife, Johanna, heiress of Nicholas d'Estoteville, lord of Cottingham;§ (after his death she was the wife of Hugh Bigod, lord justice of England, and died on St. Ambrose's day, 1260) he had two sons, Baldwin and Hugh.∥

---

* Itinerarium Curiosum, fo. 9. † Ingulph. p. 67. ‡ Dugdale's Imbanking. § Ingulph. An. 1114.
∥ Monas. Ang. vol. I. p. 469. vol. II. p. 23. York's Herldry, p. 191. ¶ Do. vol. I. p. 462. vol. II. p. 236. * Dugdale's Baron. † Inqui. 38 Henry III. 2 Vincent. A. B. C. No. 43, p. 891. ‡ Dugdale's Baron. § Mon. Ang. vol. II. p. 348. ∥ Rymer's Fœd. I. p. 493.

13. Baldwin, the elder, was lord of Wake, Brun, Lydel, and Cottingham; and died in 1281.* He married Eleanor, daughter of Sir John Montgomery, by whom he had two sons, John and Hugh.†

14. Sir Hugh, younger son of Baldwyn, the last baron of that name, and brother of John baron Wake, before-mentioned, had by gift of his said father, the lordship of Deping in Lincolnshire, and Blyseworth in Northamptonshire. He was one of the knights of the shire for the county of Northampton, in 30 Edw. I. and 2, 3, 4, 5, and 6 Edw. II. and in 34 Edw. I. one of the knights in parliament for Wilts. The same year he was in the Scottish wars; as also in 4 Edw. II. and died in 1346. leaving issue by Joan, daughter and co-heir of John de Wolverton, one daughter, Mirabella, first the wife of John lord St. John, and secondly of Thomas Aspal; and had issue by both of them: and one son,

15. Thomas, his son, who was among the knights of the county of Northampton that were returned into chancery in 1343. He died in 1345, and was buried at Deping. This Sir Thomas was the valiant seneschal of Rovergne, who gallantly distinguished himself with the Black Prince at the battle of Najara: he also maintained the city of Millaud, and another fortress, for about a year and a half; and when he capitulated he marched out with colours flying, and all the honours of war. He was likewise sheriff of Northamptonshire 11, 12, 13, 14, and 15 Edw. III. By Alice, his wife, daughter and co-heir to Sir John Pateshull of Blethso, in Bedfordshire, Knt. one of the barons of the realm. He was father of

16. Sir Thomas, who married Maud, daughter of Sir Thomas Pigot, Knt. and whose son,

17. Sir Thomas, died in 1385. In 2 Rich. II. he was sheriff of Northamptonshire. His wife was Margaret, daughter and co-heir of Sir John Philpot, of Kent, Knt. by whom he was father of

18. Sir Thomas Wake, Knt. gentleman of the privy-chamber, and of the council to king Edw. IV. He possessed divers manors in the county of Somerset, Northamptonshire, Kent, and Wales; and was called the Great Wake. He was one of

---

* Rymer's Fæd. p. 777.

† John, the elder, was in the wars of Gascoigne, 26 Edw. I. and afterwards in those of Scotland, being in commission with the archbishop of York, for securing the marches. He had summons to parliament, as Lord Wake of Lydell in Northamptonshire, from 23 to 28 Edw. I. His son Thomas was appointed constable of the Tower of London, and justice in Eyre of the forests south of Trent, by Queen Isabell, in opposition to her husband, King Edw. II. after whose deposal he also had Hertford Castle committed to his government: but in the succeeding reign had his lands seized, on suspicion of his adherence to Edmund earl of Kent; but acquitting himself thereof, was restored, and made governor of Guernsey, Jersey, Sark, and Alderney, and guardian of the Lincolnshire coast. He had summons among the barons to parliament, from 22 Edw. II. to 22 Edw. III. and died soon after, without issue by his wife, lady Blanch Plantagenet, sister to Henry duke of Lancaster; whereupon the inheritance passed with his sister and heir, Margaret, by marriage to Edmund of Woodstock, earl of Kent (youngest son of King Edw. I.) by whom she had issue, Joan (after the death of her two brothers) countess of Kent, and for her beauty called the fair maid of Kent; who marrying Sir Thomas Holland, second son of Sir Robert Holland of Lancashire, one of the first founders of the garter, he thereupon had the titles of earl of Kent, and Baron Wake of Lydel, allowed him. This Joan afterwards, by marriage with Edward the black prince, became mother of King Richard II.

the knights in parliament for Northamptonshire in 1, 5, and 8 Henry V. and sheriff thereof 2 Henry V. as also 13, 25, and 29 Henry VI. likewise in 27 Henry VI. was one of the knights for Somersetshire. He married Agnes, daughter and heir of Sir Thomas Lovell, Knt. by whom he had

19. Roger Wake of Blyseworth, who founded a free-school at Blyseworth, and was sheriff of Northampton in 2 Rich. III. and siding with that prince at the battle of Bosworth, against Henry earl of Richmond (afterwards King Henry VII.) was attainted in parliament Nov. 7, 1487, but afterwards obtained his pardon and restitution of lands. He died in 1505, leaving issue by Elizabeth, daughter of Sir William Catesby of Ashby-legers, in Northamptonshire, Knt. four sons; 1, Thomas, who married Isabel, sister and co-heir of Sir Edward Sapcotes of Burleigh, in Rutlandshire, Knt. but his issue failed; 2, Richard, who continued the line; 3, William, who had lands in Carynton in Bedfordshire; and 4, John Wake of Milton in Somersetshire, Esq. who left an only daughter.

20. Richard, second son of Roger, married Dorothy, daughter of Sir John Dive of Bromham in Bedfordshire, Knt. to his first wife; and Margaret, daughter of Thomas Grey, marquis of Dorset, to his second. He had issue six sons; 1, John Wake of Clyffedon, also of Hartwell; 2, William; 3, Richard; 4, Thomas of Fenny Stratford, in Bucks; 5, Robert of London; and 6, Francis.

21. John, son and heir of Richard, married Elizabeth, daughter and co-heir of Sir Edward Gorges, Knt. and had issue five sons; 1, John; 2, Edward; 3, Arthur; 4, Robert; and 5, William Wake, from whom was descended William Wake, archbishop of Canterbury.

22. John Wake, Esq. eldest son of John aforesaid, married Margaret, daughter and heir of Robert Goodwin of Portbury, in Somersetshire, Esq. and had issue,

I. BALDWIN WAKE of Clevedon, in Somersetshire, Esq. whom King James I. thought fit to fix somewhat nearer to the station of his ancestors, by creating him a baronet. He married Abigail, daughter of Sir George Digby of Coleshill, in Warwickshire, Knt. (ancestor to the Digbys, barons of Geashill, created earl of Bristol) by whom he had issue three sons; Sir John, his successor, George, and Baldwin; also a daughter Abigail, the wife of William Pitt of Hartley-Westpool, in Southamptonshire, Esq. (who left a daughter, the wife of Lord Stawell).

II. Sir JOHN WAKE of Clevedon, Bart. raised a troop of horse for King Charles I. and mortgaged his estate to serve him. He married to his first wife Bridget, daughter and co-heir of Henry Sandys of Blunpton, in Northamptonshire, Esq. by whom he had issue Sir William, and George Wake, chancellor of the diocese of Peterborough, who left no issue. His second lady was Anne, daughter and co-heir of Gregory Brokesby of Frithby, in Leicestershire, Esq. by whom he had one son, Charles, who died without issue.

The manor of Deping in Lincolnshire came to the crown by the Black Prince's marrying Joan, the fair maid of Kent, who was daughter to Edmund of Woodstock, earl of Kent, and of Margaret, sister and heiress to Thomas Wake, the last of that line. It is very remarkable, that she had been twice married before, and twice divorced. *Camden's Britannia, vol. I. p. 557.*

In one of the church windows at Chesterfield in Derbyshire are the arms of Edmund Plantagenet, and Margaret Wake, abovementioned, impaled together.

III. Sir WILLIAM WAKE, Bart. successor to his father, married Diana, daughter to Sir Drue Drury of Riddlesworth Hall, in Norfolk, Bart. by whom he had eight sons; 1, Sir John, his successor; 2, William, who died unmarried; 3, Sir Baldwin, successor to his brother; 4, Robert; 5, Samuel Wake Jones, who was possessed of Waltham Abbey in Essex, by the gift of Sir Samuel Jones; and left it to his nephew, Charles Wake Jones, Esq. hereafter-mentioned; 6, Isaac; 7, Drury; and 8, George, who died unmarried.

IV. Sir JOHN WAKE, Bart. the eldest son, succeeded his father in Jan. 1697-8, and died without issue in 1714, whereupon the dignity fell to his brother,

V. Sir BALDWIN WAKE, Bart. who married Mary, daughter of Mr. Hart, of Burford, in Oxfordshire, and had issue two sons and two daughters. Baldwin, the eldest son, married Mary, daughter and co-heir of Edward Lane of Hanslope, in Buckinghamshire, Esq. and died March 14, 1734-5; and his wife Feb. 19, 1736-7, leaving one son, Charles, heir to his grandfather, which

VI. Sir CHARLES WAKE, on the death of his uncle, Charles Wake Jones, took upon him the name of Jones, and became entitled to the manors of Waltham Holy Cross and Nazeing, in the county of Essex, and Courteen Hall in Northamptonshire, of very considerable value; and died without issue in Jan. 1755.

Charles, his uncle, who had taken the name of Jones pursuant to the will of his uncle, Samuel Jones, Esq. married Elizabeth, daughter of Sir Samuel Sambrooke, Bart. and died in 1739, without issue.

The daughters were, Diana, the wife of the Rev. Mr. Tinsley of Chipping Norton, in Wilts; and Mary, of Henry Jones, Esq. and died March 17, 1728-9.

Robert Wake, the fourth son of Sir William, was rector of Buxtead in Sussex, and dean of Bocking in Essex: he married Elizabeth daughter of William Greenfield of Marlborough, in Wilts, Esq. and by her had three sons; Robert, who died unmarried; Thomas, who died an infant; and

VII. Sir WILLIAM, who on the death of Sir Charles Wake Jones, in 1755, succeeded to the title. He married Sarah Walker of Weston in Yorkshire, and by her left four sons; William, Charles, Drury, and Baldwin, who married —— of the West Indies; and a daughter Mary, the wife of Mr. Clark of Broom, in Suffolk. Sir William died in Sep. 1765, and was succeeded by his eldest son,

VIII. Sir WILLIAM WAKE, Bart. who married Mary, daughter and only child of Richard Fenton of Bank Top in Yorkshire, Esq. by whom he has left a son, William, the present baronet, born April 5, 1768; ——, a daughter, born March 22, 1770; ——, another daughter, born in 1773; and Richard, July 16, 1775, who married Nov. 17, 1798, ——, daughter of Sir William Dunkin, one of the judges of the supreme court of Calcutta, in the East Indies. Sir William[*] died at Waltham Abbey of the gout in his head, after an illness of seven days, and was buried in the parish church of Courteen Hall, Nov. 6, 1785. He was succeeded by his eldest son,

---

[*] He represented the town of Bedford. In public life his name stands high in the list of those very few, who unbiassed by party prejudice or private interest, made the good of their country the sole aim of all their actions. *Gent. Mag.* 1785.

WAKE OF CLEVEDON, SOMERSETSHIRE.

TABLE 40.

```
1 OSLAC                                      7 Adeldis=Baldwin, E. of Glomery
     |                                       |
2 Morcar          Ralf, E. of Hereford       8 Emma=Hugh de Wac                    Rogerus
     |                                       |
3 Ediva=Leofric                              9 Baldwin lord Wake
     |                                       |
4 Hereward=Thurfrida                        10 Baldwin lord Wake=Alicia
     |                                       |
5 Thurfrida=Hugh Evermue            Isabella Bruer=11 Baldwin, 1213=Beatrix de Vanne
     |                                       |
6 N, a dr.=Richard de Rulos                 12 Hugh=Johanna=Hugh Bigod
                                             |
                                            13 Baldwin, 1281=E. Montgomery         Hugh
John, 1304=Johanna                           |
                                            14 Sir Hugh, 1316=Joan de Wolverton
Thomas de Wake, 1343      Margaret          15 Sir Thomas Wake, 1345              Mirabella
Blanch Plantagenet    Edm. 3d son of Edw. I.    Alice Pateshail          John,  | Thomas
                                                                      L. St.John  Aspal
Joan, the fair maid of Kent                 16 Sir Thos. Wake=Maud Pigot
Wm. E. of | Sir T. | Edw. the
Salisbury  Holland  Black Prince            17 Sir Thomas Wake=Margaret Philpot

                                            18 Sir Thomas Wake=Agnes Lovell

                                            19 Roger de Wake, 1405=Eliz. Catesby

        Thomas=Isabella Sapcoats     D. Dive=20 Richard=Marg. Grey    William      John
  21 John=Eliz. Gorges      William       Richard      Thomas        Robert     Francis
  22 John=Marg. Goodwin     Edward        Arthur       Robert                   William
   I. Sir Baldwyn=Abigail Digby
                                                                                William,
   B. Sandys=II. Sir John=Anne Brokesby   George   Baldwin   Abigail=Wm. Pitt  abp. of Cant.
  III. Sir Wm. 1698=D. Drury      George      Charles       Lord Stawell
  IV. Sir John, 1714    William   V. Sir Baldwin   Robert   Samuel  Isaac  George
                                  Martha Hart   E. Greenfield WakeJones Drury
Baldwin, 1435    Charles Jones, 1734    2 drs.    Robert.    VII. Sir Wm. 1765   Anne.
Mary Lane, 1737  Eliz. Sambrooke                  Thomas     Sarah Walker        Eliz.
VI. Sir C. Wake  VIII. Sir Wm. Wake, 1785  Charles   Drury   Baldwin             Mary
Jones, 1755            Mary Fenton                           —, of the West      —Clark
                                                             Indies
IX. Sir Wm. Wake      N, a dr.    N, a dr.     Richard                           Rev. Mr.
Miss Sitwell | —Gambier                        —Dunkin                           Clark
     |
N, a son
```

IX. Sir WILLIAM WAKE, Bart. who in 1790 married ——, daughter of Francis Sitwell of Renshaw Hall, in Derbyshire, Esq. who after being safely delivered of a son and heir, died Nov. 22, 1791. Her death was occasioned by an incurable disorder in her stomach, supposed of long duration. Sir William married April 22, 1793, to his second lady, ——, daughter of the late Admiral Gambier.

ARMS—Or, two barrs gules, in chief, three torteauxes.
CREST—On a wreath, a knot (commonly called Wake's knot).
MOTTO—*Vigila & ora.*
SEATS—Waltham Abbey in Essex, Courteen Hall in Northamptonshire, and Riddlesworth Hall in Norfolk.

40. HOTHAM of Scorbrough, Yorkshire.

Created Baronet Jan. 4, 1621.

THIS family is descended from John de Trehouse, lord of Kilkenny in Ireland, who, for his good services at the battle of Hastings, had a grant of the castle and manors of Colley Weston in Northamptonshire, and Hotham in Yorkshire. The fourth, in a direct descent from this Sir John de Trehouse, was

1. Peter de Trehouse, who, from his residence at Hotham, assumed that surname, which his descendants ever after retained: he was living in 1188, and his son,

2. Sir John Hothum (as the name was anciently wrote) by a daughter of Baldwin lord Wake, was grandfather to

3. Sir Peter de Hothum, and to John de Hothum, one of the most eminent men of his age.*

4. Sir John Hothum, knight of the bath, son and heir of Sir Peter de Hothum, elder brother of the bishop, was summoned to parliament, as a baron of the realm,

---

* John Hothum, S. T. P. provost of Queen's College, Oxford, chancellor of the university, and also chancellor and treasurer of England, was bishop of Ely in 1316. In his time the steeple of the cathedral falling down, he re-edified it; and also finished the presbytery, begun by Bishop Norwold, and built, in a great measure, the episcopal palace in Holborn, London; and gave abundance of vestments, plate, &c. to his cathedral.

The inscription on his tomb.
Johannes Hotham, Episcopus Eliens. Angliæ Cancellarius, deinde Regni hujus Summus Thesaurius, hic situs est. Vir prudens, justus & munificus: qui Lanternam a ruina, sumptu 2406*l*. 16*s* 11*d*. in hanc admirandam structure formam restituit. & in perficiendo presbyterio supra 2034*l*. 12*s*. 8*d*. expendit. cum annos 20 sedisset par ilisi per biennium correptus, tandem decessit Januarii 25, 1336.
Willis's Cathedrals, vol. II. p. 352.

in 8 Edw. II. as is evident from Sir William Dugdale's baronage, and other authorities.* By Agnes his wife, daughter and heir of Sir John Hasleton of Hasleton, in Yorkshire, Knt. he had issue,

5. Sir John Hothum, his son and heir, and Thomas Hothum, second son, who by the failure of issue male of his brother, inherited the manors of Scorbrough, Wyathorp, and other lands.†

6. Thomas succeeded his brother, and had three sons, Sir Robert, Nicholas, and Thomas.

7. Sir Robert Hotham, Knt. married ——, daughter and heir of Sir Hugh Beeston of Driffield, Knt.

8. Sir John Hotham, Knt. his son and heir, married Margaret, daughter of Sir William Ingleberd, Knt. by whom he had Sir John and Richard.

9. Sir John Hotham, Knt. married Oswald, daughter and heir of —— Fitz-Archer, by whom he had a son and a daughter Eleanor, wife of Thomas Leeds, Esq.

10. Sir Robert Hotham, Knt. his son, married ——, daughter and heir of Sir William Daniel, Knt. and left issue,

11. Sir John Hotham, Knt. married ——, daughter of Sir William Nesonne, and left issue in 1412.

12. Sir John Hotham, Knt. married Winifred, daughter of Sir William Bruce of Pickering, Knt. and left a son,

13. Sir John Hotham, Knt. who married ——, daughter of John Pilkington, Esq. and had one son, John, and four daughters.

14. John Hotham, Esq. married ——, daughter of Sir William Eure of Witton, Knt. and had one son, Sir John, and a daughter Maud, wife of Sir Thomas Metham, Knt. by whom she left issue.

15. Sir John Hotham, Knt. married Elizabeth, daughter of Sir Robert Hildyard of Wensted Knt. (by Elizabeth, daughter of Sir John Hastings of Fenwick, Knt. and sister of Sir Pierce) by whom he had one son,

16. Sir John Hotham, Knt. who was chief gentleman of the privy chamber to Henry VIII. from whom, in a direct descent from several knights, who had that honour conferred on them for their services in the wars, was

17. Sir John Hotham of Scorbrough, Knt. who, by Lora, daughter of Ralph Constable of Halsham, Esq. had issue,

* Edw. III. in the first year of his reign, granted the manors of Trogford and Stony-Dunham, in com. Cest. to John, son of Peter de Hotham, cousin and heir to John, bishop of Ely, cart. 1, E. 3. m. 7. Le Neve's MSS. vol. II. p. 17, where are these entries:—Gulielmus Hotham, archiep. Dublyn, obiit 1298. See Sir James Ware's catalogue.—Jo. Hotham had free warren in Hotham & Bursay, com. Ebor. & Bondeby in com. Linc. cart. 9, E. 2, n. 14.

† From this Thomas lineally descended another Sir John Hothum, who was found one of the cousins and co-heirs to Thomas de Thweng, baron of Thweng and Kilton Castle, a barony in fee, which lies dormant betwixt the present earl of Scarborough, and the present Sir Charles Hotham, Bart. See the descent of the barony of Thwenge in Yorkshire, and how it came between Scarborough and Hotham, in the Precedents and Arguments concerning Baronies by Writ, and other Honours, fo. 395.

18. John, his son and heir, who married Elizabeth, daughter of ——— Metham of Yorkshire, Esq. (who was re-married to ——— Constable, Esq.) and had issue,

19. Sir Francis Hotham of Scorbrough, Knt. who married Mary, daughter of Humphrey Hercy of Grove, in Nottinghamshire, Esq. (and Elizabeth his wife, daughter of Sir John Digby of Kettilby, Knt. and ——— his wife, daughter of Sir John Griffin, Knt.) and sister and co-heir to Sir John Hercy, Knt. her brother, by whom he had

20. Sir John Hotham, Knt. who had three wives; 1, Julian, daughter of Sir Michael Stanhope of Shelford, in Nottinghamshire, Knt. by whom he had several children, who all died S. P. 2, Mary, daughter of Sir George Goring of Burton, in Sussex, Knt. by whom he had no issue; 3, Jane, daughter of Richard Lydyard (quere Legard) of Rysome, in Holderness, Esq. by whom he had Mary, the wife of Richard Remington of Lund, in Yorkshire, Esq. Elizabeth, and Faith, who both died unmarried; also,

I. Sir JOHN HOTHAM, Knt. his son and heir, created baronet 19 James I. who had five wives; 1, Catharine, daughter of Sir John Rodes of Barlbrough, in Derbyshire, Knt. by whom he had two sons, Sir John Hotham, Knt. and Richard, who had a son that died S. P. also two daughters, Margaret, that died an infant, and Frances, the wife of John Gee of Beverley, Esq. and secondly of Sir Philip Stapleton of Wartre; in Yorkshire, Knt. his second wife was Anne, daughter of Ralph Rokesby of York, Esq. secretary to the council at York, by whom he had Charles Hotham, rector of Wigan in Lancashire, who married Elizabeth, daughter of Stephen Thompson of Humbleton, in Yorkshire, Esq. and had a daughter Mary, the wife of Michael Burton of Holmesfield, in Dronfield parish in Derbyshire, Esq. and one son, Sir Charles, hereafter mentioned; William, and Durant Hotham of Lockington, in Yorkshire, Esq. who married Frances, daughter of Richard Remington of Lund, Esq. by whom he had several children that died young. Sir John's third lady was Frances, daughter of John Legard of Ganton, in Yorkshire, Esq. by whom he had several children that died young: his fourth lady was Catharine, daughter of Sir William Bamborough of Housam, in Yorkshire, Knt. by whom he had Francis and Jane, that died young. Sir John's fifth lady was Sarah, daughter of Thomas Anlaby of Etton, in Yorkshire, Esq. by whom he had Dorothy and Alathea, that died young; Catharine, the wife of Sir William Cholmley of Whitby, in Yorkshire, Bart. and Sarah.*

---

* This Sir John Hotham, Bart. was governor of Hull in 1643: he and his son were discovered to hold correspondence with the royal party; in consequence of which Sir John was taken prisoner, and brought before a court martial at Guildhall, Nov. 30, 1644, where upon the proof of thirty witnesses, whose evidence tended to accuse him of many capital crimes against the parliament; and after leave being given him to make a full defence, on the 7th of Dec. he received this sentence:—That he should suffer death, by having his head cut off, on Monday, the 16th day of Dec. but on his lady's petition for time to settle his estates, the execution was deferred.

His son, Capt. John Hotham, came to his trial before the same court, charged with crimes of much the same nature as his father's; and being convicted thereof, received sentence to be beheaded on the 24th of December.

These two unfortunate gentlemen, who seem, in the opinion of different authors, to have embarked too hastily in a cause which proved their ruin, suffered death on Tower Hill, pursuant to their sentence. Lord Clarendon says, Sir John was master of a noble fortune, rich in money, of very ancient fa-

Sir John Hotham, Knt. the eldest son (who was beheaded just before his father) married three wives; 1, Frances, daughter of Sir John Wray of Glentworth, in Lincolnshire, Knt. and Bart. by whom he had one son, Sir John, successor to his grandfather, and two daughters; Elizabeth, the wife first of Peter le Gay of London, merchant; and secondly of —— Hay, Esq. alderman of London; and Frances, of John Daniel, Esq. son of Sir Ingleby Daniel of Beswick, in Yorkshire, Knt. Sir John's second lady was Margaret, daughter of Thomas lord Fairfax, viscount Emlyn, by whom he had no issue; and his third was Isabel, daughter of Sir Henry Anderson of Long Cauton, in Yorkshire, Knt. by whom he had one son, Henry, who died young.

II. Sir JOHN HOTHAM, Bart. who succeeded his grandfather in title and estate, married Elizabeth, daughter of Sapcoat, lord viscount Beaumont of Swords, in the kingdom of Ireland, by whom he had two sons; Sir John, his successor, and Robert, who died S. P. and two daughters, Elizabeth, the wife of William Gee of Bishops Burton, in Yorkshire, Esq. and Bridget; and dying in the year 1689, was succeeded by his eldest son,

III. Sir JOHN HOTHAM, Bart. who departed this life without issue male, in 1691, whereupon the title and estate devolved on Sir Charles Hotham, Bart. eldest son and heir of Charles Hotham, rector of Wigan (by Elizabeth his wife, daughter of Stephen Thompson of Humbleton, in Yorkshire, Esq. before-mentioned) third son of Sir John Hotham, the first baronet of this family; which

IV. Sir CHARLES HOTHAM of Scorbrough, Bart. was colonel of the king's own royal regiment of dragoons, and representative in parliament for Beverley in Yorkshire most part of the reign of Queen Anne, and all King George I till his death: he married two wives; first Bridget, daughter of William Gee of Bishops Burton, in Yorkshire, by whom he had issue two sons, Sir Charles, and Sir Beaumont; and three daughters; Elizabeth, the wife of Sir Thomas Style of Wateringbury, in Kent, Bart. Philippa, of William Gee of Bishops Burton, in Yorkshire; and Charlotta, of Warton Warton of Beverley, in Yorkshire, Esq. His second wife, Mildred, youngest daughter of James Cecil, earl of Salisbury, and widow of Sir Uvedale Corbet of Longmore, in Salop, Bart. by whom he had one son, Richard, who died young. He died Jan. 8, 1722-3, and was succeeded by his eldest son,

V. Sir CHARLES HOTHAM, Bart. who was elected, on the death of his father, representative in parliament for Beverley, and served in the following parliaments till his death: he was colonel of the first troop of horse grenadier guards, and groom of the bed chamber to his late majesty; and married, in the year 1724, Gertrude, eldest daughter of Philip Stanhope, earl of Chesterfield, and died Jan. 15, 1757, leaving one son, Charles, and three daughters; Caroline, Melusina, and Gertrude: the two former died unmarried. He was succeeded by his son,

mily, and well allied: his affections to the government very good, and that no man less desired to see the nation involved in a civil war than he, not imagining when he accepted the employment from the parliament, it would engage him in a rebellion.

HOTHAM OF SCORBROUGH, YORKSHIRE.

TABLE 41.

SIR JOHN DE TREHOUSE

1 Peter de Trehouse
2 Sir John Hotham = —, dr. of Baldwin L. Wake
3 Sir Peter de Hotham — John bp. of Ely
4 Sir John Hotham = Agnes Haselton — Thomas
5 Sir John — 6 Thomas
7 Sir Rob. = — Beeston — Nicholas — Thomas

8 Sir John = Marg. Ingleberd
9 Sir John = Oswald Fitz-Archer — Richard
10 Sir Rob. = — Daniel — Eleanor = T. Leeds
11 Sir John, 1412 = — Nesonne
12 Sir John Hotham = Winifred Bruce
13 Sir John = — Pilkington
14 John = — Eure — 4 drs.

15 Sir John = Eliz. Hildyard — Maud = Sir Thomas Metham — Sir John Constable, Knt.
16 Sir John Hotham, temp. Henry VIII. — N = Sir John Digby
17 Sir John = Lora Constable — Elizabeth = Humphrey Hercy
18 John Hotham = Elizabeth Metham
19 Sir Francis = Mary Hercy

20 Sir John Hotham of Scorbrough, Knt.
Julian Stanhope | Mary Goring | Jane Lydyard

Several children | I. Sir John Hotham, Knt. & Bart. governor of Hull, 1645 | Mary | Eliz.
| C. Rodes | A. Rokesby | F. Legard | C. Bamborough | S. Anlaby | R. Rennington | Faith |

Sir John, 1645 | Rich. | Frances | Charles | Wm. | Durant | Frances. | Dorothy. | Cath. | Sarah
F. Wray | M. Fair- | J. An- | Marg. | J. Gee | Sir P. | E. Thompson | F. Rennington | Jane | Alathea | Sir Wm. | C. Cooper
fax | derson | | | Stapleton | | | | Cholmley |

II. Sir John, 1689 | Eliz. | Frances | Henry | IV. Sir Chas. Bt. 1723 | Mary | many
E. Beaumont | P. Gay | — ay | J. Daniel | d. y. | B. Gee | M. Cecil | M. Burton | children

III. Sir John, | Rob. | Eliz. | Bridg. | V. Sir Chas. 1758 | VII. Sir Beau. 1771 | Eliz. | Philippa | Charlotte
Bt. 1691 | | W. Gee | | G. Stanhope | F. Thompson | Sir T. Style | W. Gee | W. Warton

VI. Sir Charles, 1767 | Caroline. | VIII. Sir Charles, 1794 | John | Wm. | Sir Beau. | George
C. A. Clutterbuck | Melusina. | D. Hobart | J. Mack- | B. Ho- | T. Hankey | D. Wharton
| Gertrude | | worth | tham | Beaumont | —, a dr. b. 1775

Henrietta | IX. Sir Charles Hotham, Bart.

VI. Sir CHARLES HOTHAM, Bart. who was groom of the bed chamber to his present majesty: he married Clara-Anne, daughter and heiress of Thomas Clutterbuck of Mill Green, in Essex, who died in June, 1759, and he in October, 1767, without issue; and was succeeded by his uncle,

VII. Sir BEAUMONT HOTHAM, Bart. who was a commissioner of his majesty's customs, and married Frances, sister of William Thompson of Humbleton in Yorkshire, Esq. had issue five sons; 1, Sir Charles; 2, John, late bishop of Clogher, in Ireland, who by his wife Sarah, daughter of Herbert Mackworth of Knoll, in Glamorganshire, Esq. had issue one son, Charles, the present baronet; 3, William,* admiral of the blue; 4, Sir Beaumont Hotham, Knt. baron of the court of Exchequer, who by Susan, daughter of Sir Thomas Hankey of Clapham, Knt. has one son, Beaumont; 5, George, who married Dinah Wharton. Sir Beaumont died Aug. 29, 1771, and was succeeded by his son,

VIII. Col. Sir CHARLES HOTHAM, Bart. of the 15th regiment, and one of the grooms of the bed chamber to his majesty, who married Dorothy, sister to the Earl of Buckinghamshire, who died Oct. 14, 1771: he died Jan. 25, 1794, and left one daughter, Henrietta, born 1758, and was succeeded by his nephew,

IX. Sir CHARLES HOTHAM, Bart. son of his brother John, the bishop of Clogher.

ARMS—Barry of ten, argent and azure, on a canton or, a cornish chough, proper,
CREST—A demi seaman issuing out of water, proper, holding in his right hand a flaming sword, and in the left a shield of the Hotham's arms.
MOTTO—*Certum pete Finem.*
SEATS—At Scorbrough and South Dalton, in the East Riding of Yorkshire, and Chislehurst in Kent.

* He was created, March 7, 1797, a baron of the kingdom of Ireland, by the name, style, and title of Baron Hotham of South Dalton, with remainder (in default of issue male) to Sir Charles Hotham, Bart. of Scorbrough, the nephew of the said William, and the grandson and heir male of Sir Beaumont Hotham, Bart. of Scorbrough aforesaid, deceased, the father of the said William Hotham; and to the heirs male of the body of the said Sir Charles Hotham, Bart. and in default of such issue, to the heirs of the body of the said Sir Beaumont Hotham, deceased.

41. MANSEL of MUDDLESCOMBE, CARMARTHENSHIRE.

Created Baronet Jan 14, 1621.

THIS ancient and honourable family is descended from Philip Mansel, who came into England with William the Conqueror, and was nephew to Sir Henry Harley, Knt. who out of the large possessions he held in South Wales, gave to the said Philip the manor of Oswick or Oxmuche, in the county of Glamorgan, where he built a very fine mansion-house, which became the residence of his family for many generations. This Philip married ——, daughter of —— Mountsorrell, and had issue by her,

2. Henry, Andrew, Robert, Michael, and Philip. From Henry, the eldest son, descended

3. Sir John Mansel, Knt.* who was chancellor of London, and provost of Beverley: he was appointed, with others, to go to the King of Castile, to make a league between him and the King of England. In 38 Henry III. he was sent, with others, to the King of Scotland, with power to take into their protection such of the Scots as were inclinable to adhere to them; and the next year was appointed to take possession of the kingdom of Apulia, which the pope had granted to him, and Edmund his son. In 40 Henry III. being at that time a knight, and in Wales, he sent advice to the king of the rebellion of Lewellin, prince of Wales, and that on the approach of Sir John de Grey and others, they dispersed and fled to the mountains. In 40 Henry III. he was sent into the marches of Scotland, to take care of the king's affairs; and the next year was, with others, by Edmund king of Sicily, on an embassy to the pope, to procure better terms, in the relation to the grant of that kingdom, with power, if they thought fit, to give up the same kingdom: and was also one of the twelve who were appointed to reform the state of the kingdom. In 42 Henry III. being at the same time treasurer of York, he was appointed, with others, to treat of a peace in Scotland. In 46 Henry III. there being some apprehension of his stirring up strife between the king and his peers, the king wrote to the pope and cardinals, that he was innocent. He was lord-chan-

---

* Sir John Mansel was in great esteem with King Henry III. and loaded with dignities and preferments, ecclesiastical and temporal. According to Matt. Paris and Mr. Newcourt he was the king's special councellor, and by him preferred to the following dignities, viz. in 1242, two prebends in the church of St. Paul's; 1243, the chancellorship of St. Paul's, and a prebend in the church of Wells; 1244, a prebend in the church of Chichester; 1247, the deanery of the cathedral church of Winburne in Dorsetshire: 1248 he was made provost of Beverley; in 1256 the king granted him the treasureship of the church of York; in 1258 presented him to the church of Sawbridgeworth, in the diocese of London; in 1262 to that of Hocton, in the diocese of Durham; and committed to him the custody of the Tower of London. Weever adds, that he was parson of Maidstone in Kent, and of Wigan in Lancashire; to whom King Henry III. did grant, that his town of Wigan should be a borough. He was chief justice of England; the king's ambassador into Spain; a great soldier, who with his own hands, in a battle between the English and French, near to Tailbourge in France, took prisoner one Peter Orige, a gentleman of eminent place and quality: he was crossed to go to Jerusalem; he feasted at his house in Tolehill Field, at one time, two kings and two queens, with their dependencies: 700 messes of meat scarce serving for the first dinner; of which a more particular account is given by John Stow, p. 283. Alexander, king of Scots, with Margaret his wife, came into England about the beginning of Aug. 1256, who found the king of England, and his queen, at his manor of Woodstock. On the feast of the decollation of St. John, the two kings and queens came to London, where they were honourably received, and conveyed to Westminster. John Mansel, the king's chaplain, besought the two kings, and other states, to dine with him, whereto they granted; where they were entertained with marvellous chear. There were 700 dishes served up; but the multitude of guests were such, that the house could not receive them, so that tents were set up abroad. The like dinner had not been made by any chaplain before.

About the 31st of King Henry III. at the instance of the said king, he was first made keeper of the great seal, as vice chancellor; for, saith Matt. Paris, yet for all this glorious pomp and great promotions, I find his end to be poor, wretched, and miserable, beyond seas: but I find no place of his death nor burial, only it appears he died some time before Feb. 7, 1264.

From Newton's Hist. Maidstone, p. 56, 57, 58.

cellor to that king, and is said, by the pedigrees of this family, to have issue, by Joan his wife, daughter of Simon Beauchamp, baron of Bedford.

4. Sir Thomas Mansel, knight banneret, who was (as Hollinshed writes) taken prisoner in the barons' wars, in 48 Henry III. at Northampton. This Sir Thomas had issue,

5. Henry Mansel, who in the reign of King Edw. I. settled in Glamorganshire, and was father of

6. Sir Walter Mansel, Knt. who held of King Edw. I. the manor of Missenden in Bucks, in capite. He was buried in St. Botolph's church in London, and was succeeded by

7. Sir Robert Mansel, Knt. his son and heir, father of

8. Robert Mansel, Esq. who had issue,

9. Richard, his son and heir, who married Lucy, daughter and heir of Philip Scurlage, lord of Scurlage Castle, in the county of Glamorgan, by whom he had

10. Sir Hugh Mansel, Knt. whose wife was Elizabeth, daughter and heir to Sir John Penrys, Knt. lord of Oxwick, and other large territories in Glamorganshire, which accrued to him by the said marriage, and by her he was father of

11. Richard Mansel of Oxwick, who by Elizabeth his wife, daughter to Hamon Turbervile of Penlyne, in Glamorganshire, had issue,

12. John Mansel of Oxwick, who by Maud, daughter of William ap Llewellin, ap Howel ap Poclin, Esq. was father of

13. Philip Mansel, Esq. who was slain in the wars between the houses of York and Lancaster, and attainted: he married Mary, daughter to Griffith ap Nicholas of Newton, in the county of Carmarthen, Esq. by whom he had

14. Jenkin Mansel, his son and heir, who procured a repeal of his father's attainder, and a restoration in blood and estate: he married Edith, daughter and co-heir of Sir George Kyme (or Keene) of the county of Kent, Knt. and had issue three sons; 1, Rice; 2, Hugh, who married Jane, daughter and co-heir of Richard Owgan of Kent (and left issue Robert Mansel, Esq. groom of the bed chamber to King Henry VIII.) and Philip, who married Anne, daughter of William Dabridgecourt: also, four daughters; Alice, the wife of John Drew of Bristol; Anne, of David ap Rees Wynn of St. Cothens; Jane, of John Wynn ap Jenkin ap Richard; and Elizabeth, of Christopher Flemyng.

15. Rice, the eldest son, received the honour of knighthood before the 27th of Henry VIII. in which year he was sent with a supply of soldiers into Ireland, to assist the lord-deputy in suppressing a rebellion raised in that kingdom by the earl of Kildare. In 28 Henry VIII. he had a grant for life of the office of chamberlain of the county palatine of Chester; and in 32 Henry VIII. a grant of the scite of the monastery of Margam in Glamorganshire, and the royalty of Avon Water, to him and his heirs.* He married three wives; by his first, Eleanor, daughter and sole

---

* His last will and testament bears date on the 10th of Dec. 1588, and the probate thereof the 10th of May, 1589. He bequeaths to Mary Foskew, late the wife of his son, Philip Mansel, Esq. deceased, his manor of Penrys in Glamorganshire, for her life, and after, to his son, Edward Mansel, and his

heir of James Basset of Beaupre, in Glamorganshire, Esq. he had no issue that survived to maturity: by his second, Anne, daughter of Sir Giles Bruges of Coberley, in Gloucestershire, Knt. ancestor to the duke of Chandos, he had three sons, who all died in his life-time, and three daughters, whereof only two survived, viz. Catharine, the wife of William Basset of Beaupre, Esq. and Elizabeth, of William Morgan of Llanternam, in Monmouthshire, Esq. By his third, Cicely, daughter of William Dabridgecourt, Esq. he had Edward, who succeeded him in his estate; Anthony, who married Elizabeth, daughter of John Basset of Lanthrithed, Esq. and Mary, wife of Sir Thomas Southwell of Uprising, in Norfolk, Knt.*

16. Edward, his eldest surviving son and heir, received the honour of knighthood in the year 1572; was chamberlain of Chester, and a man of great honour, integrity, and courage, distinguishing himself in many services during the reign of Queen Elizabeth. He married Jane Somerset, youngest daughter of Henry earl of Worcester; by whom he had 1, Sir Thomas, ancestor to Lord Mansel of Margam; 2, Sir Francis, and 3, Sir Robert Mansel, who was knighted by the earl of Essex, for his valour, in the taking of the town of Cales, in 1596; and after having signalized himself in several encounters, was made vice-admiral of the fleet by King James I. in which station he was continued by King Charles, and lived to a very old age, much esteemed for his great integrity, personal courage, and experience in maritime affairs.†

assigns. To his son Anthony, all his lands in the lordship of Falway in Glamorganshire, with other lands in Gloucestershire. To his daughter Mary, 600 marks, for her marriage portion. To lady Jane Mansel, wife of his son Edward, an upper abiliment of goldsmith's work, a gown of purple cloth of silver, a gown of green velvet, and a gown of black velvet. To his daughter, Catharine Basset, a gown of black damask, and an ale-cup, with a cover of silver, gilt. To his daughter, Elizabeth Morgan, a gown of damask, with a like cup. To his daughter Mary, a crimson velvet gown, the second black velvet gown, and a sattin gown, that were his wife's; a bed of purple damask, with curtains paned with yellow damask and crimson, and a diamond pointed, which Queen Mary gave to his wife, as also his wife's wedding and other jewels. To his son Anthony, a bed of tawney velvet, and a bed of russet and yellow sattin; also a cup, with a cover of silver, gilt, and his wife's signet ring. He desires his son Edward, to give his children a learned education, whom he constitutes sole executor.

It further appears by his will, that he was an inhabitant of Clerkenwell parish in London; and that he was bountiful to his servants, charitable to the poor, as the several sums he left to poor householders of many parishes, shew.

* In a chapel, on the south side of Margam church, in the county of Glamorgan in South Wales, is a handsome monument of white marble erected to his memory, with the effigies of him and his lady, lying at full length; on the sides their children, and over their heads their matches. At the head are three children in full proportion, Sir Edward, Mary, and Anthony; and at the foot of the monument is this inscription:—Here lyeth the portraitures of Sir Rice Mansel, Knt. and Dame Cicill, his wife, being descended of the noble family of Dabridgecourt, of Hampshire: both are buried in Little St. Bartholomew's, near Smithfield, London. This monument is here made for his remembrance, because he was the first purchaser of this seat, and had issue, Sir Edward Mansel of Margam, Knt. Anthony Mansel of Lanthrithed, Esq. and Mary Mansel, married to Thomas Southwell, of Uprising in Norfolk.

The said Sir Rice was twice formerly married, first to Eleanor Basset, the heir of Beaupre, and by her had issue, but all died young: secondly he married a sister of Sir John Bridges, afterwards Lord Chandos, and had issue by her three sons and three daughters, whereof only two daughters survived him; Catharine, married to William Basset of Beaupre, Esq. at whose marriage, Sir Rice Mansel, assured back again Beaupre. Elizabeth married William Morgan of Lanternam, in the county of Monmouth, Esq.

† He lies buried in the chapel, on the South side of Margam church, where a fair monument of white marble is erected to his memory, whereon is the effigies of him and his lady, lying at full length, and at the head, the figures of four sons in armour, kneeling, representing Sir Thomas Mansel, Knt.

MANSEL OF MUDDLESCOMBE, CARMARTHENSHIRE.

I. FRANCIS MANSEL, Esq. second son of Sir Edward, before-mentioned, being advanced to the dignity of a baronet, 19 James I. married two wives; first Catharine, daughter and heir of Henry Morgan of Muddlescombe, in Carmarthenshire, Esq. by whom he had four sons; 1, Walter, who left no issue; 2, Sir Anthony Mansel, Knt. slain at Newby in Yorkshire, temp. Charles I. who by Jane, daughter of William Price of Britton Ferry, Esq. left issue Sir Edward, successor to his grandfather; 3, Francis, S. T. P. principal of Jesus' College, Oxford, and in 1648 deprived, and his temporal estate put under sequestration, and suffered greatly for his loyalty: in the year 1659 he was thought of for a bishoprick, as appears by a passage in Dr. Barwick's letter to the lord chancellor.* The fourth son of Sir Edward was Richard, who by Catharine, daughter and heir of Rees Morgan of Ischoed, in Carmarthenshire, Esq. left issue Sir Richard, hereafter-mentioned Sir Francis's second lady was Dorothy, daughter of Alban Stepney of Prendergast, in Pembrokeshire, Esq. by whom he had three sons; 1, John, who married Mary, daughter of Sir Henry Vaughan of Derwith, in Carmarthenshire, Knt. 2, Edward, a captain; 3, Rawleigh; and two daughters, Catharine, the wife of Sir John Stepney of Prendergast, in Pembrokeshire, Bart. and Cicely, the wife of George Jones of Abercothy in Carmarthenshire, Esq.

II. Sir EDWARD MANSEL of Muddlescombe, Bart. eldest son of Sir Anthony, succeeded his grandfather in title and estate, but dying without issue male, the title and estate descended to his cousin,

III. Sir RICHARD, eldest son of Richard Mansel, Esq. (youngest son of Sir Francis) by Catharine, daughter and heir of Rees Morgan of Ischoed, Esq. before-

and Bart. Sir Francis Mansel, Bart. Sir Robert Mansel, Knt. and Philip Mansel, Esq. also on the south side are two daughters, kneeling, and on the north, two more in the same posture; and at the foot of the monument the following inscription:—Heere lyeth Syr Edward Mansel, Knight, and Dame Jane, his lady, who was the daughter to Henry earl of Worcester: he died the 5th of August, 1595, about the — yeere of his age: she died the xvi October, 1597, about the age of lxvii yeeres, having borne xv sons and iiii daughters, whereof x of the younger sons died without issue male. Sir Thomas Mansel, Knight and Baronet, Sir Francis Mansel, Baronet, now living, have many issues male and female, and Sir Robert Mansel, Knt. liveth; Philip Mansel died, and left Thomas Mansel, his son. Elizabeth, eldest daughter of the said Sir Edward, was married to Sir Walter Rice of Newton, in the county of Carmarthen, Knt. and had issue Henry Rice, Esq. &c. Cicill married Rowland Williams of Llangiby, in the county of Monmouth, Esq. and had issue Sir Charles Williams, Knight, &c. Mary married Christopher Turbervile of Pennlyne, Esquire, and hath issue, Anthony Turbervile, &c. Anne married Edward Carne of Nashe, Esquire, and hath issue William Carne, &c. both of the county of Glamorgan.

* "There is another whom I also much reverence, Dr. M.* whose years and modesty are so great, as it is thought by those that know him better than I, he will rather chuse a private life; and it were great pity to cast a load upon him against his will, now when he is come to that condition as to need a coadjutor, if he were already in the office. His sight is almost quite gone, and his infirmities otherwise so great, as he can hardly come up hither to receive consecration, which is but the preface to his work." Aug. 1, 1660, he was restored to his college by the king's commissioners, and died May 1, 1665, almost 80, having been a very great benefactor to his college,† both in its buildings and revenues; and lies buried in Jesus' College Chapel.

* Dr. Barwick's Life, p. 439, where, in a reference to Dr. M. is this: Dr. Francis Mansel, principal of Jesus college, Oxford, his obstinate refusal of the episcopal dignity, more than once, is mentioned on his epitaph, in that college, where he was interred. Infulas episcopales---non semel oblatas, serio tremuit, obstinatus refugit.
† Walker's Sufferings of the Clergy, p. 120.

MANSEL OF MUDDLESCOMBE, CARMARTHENSHIRE.

TABLE 42.

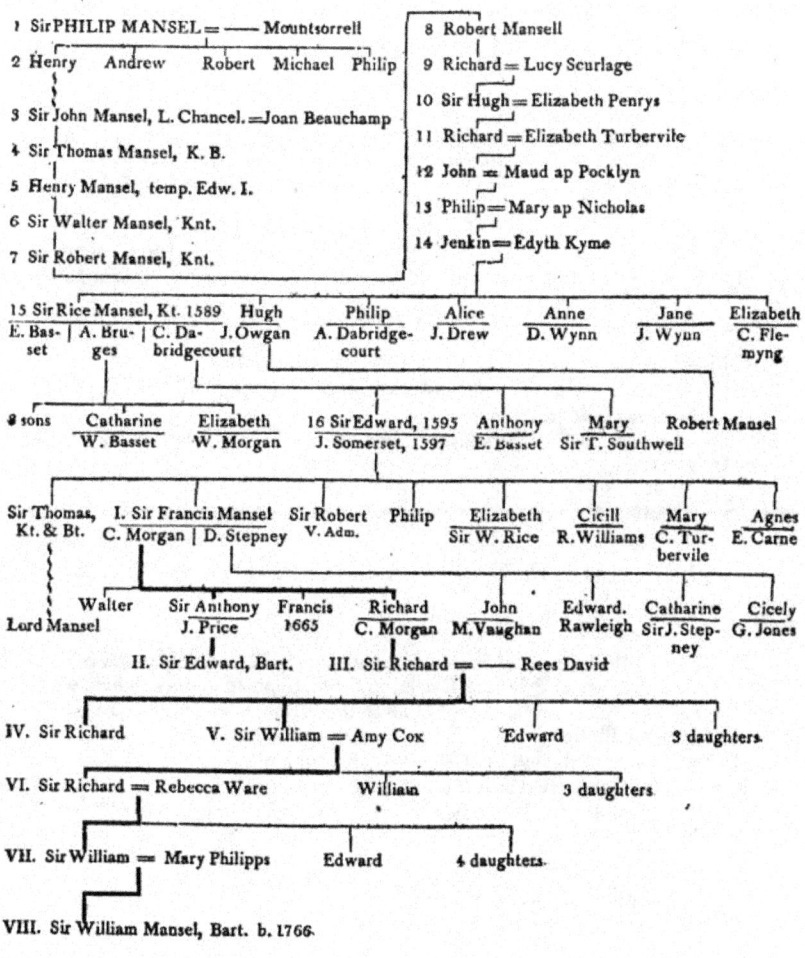

mentioned; which Sir Richard Mansel, Bart. married a daughter and heir of Rees David of Pentry-Estill, in Glamorganshire, Esq. by whom he had three sons, Sir Richard, Sir William, and Edward; and three daughters.

IV. Sir RICHARD MANSEL, Bart. the eldest son, succeeded his father in the title, and lordship of Ischoed and Pentry-Esthill, and died in London, unmarried, whereupon the dignity and estate devolved upon his next brother,

V. Sir WILLIAM MANSEL, Bart. who married Amy, eldest daughter of Sir Richard Cox, lord chancellor of Ireland, by whom he had issue two sons, Sir Richard and William, and three daughters.

VI. Sir RICHARD MANSEL, the eldest son, who succeeded his father in dignity and estate, married Rebecca, eldest daughter of William Ware of Farranalough, in the county of Cork in Ireland, Esq. by whom he had two sons, William and Edward, deceased: likewise four daughters. He was succeeded by his only son,

VII. Sir WILLIAM MANSEL, Bart. who married Mary, only daughter of John Philipps of Coedgain, in Carmarthenshire, Esq. by whom he had issue one son,

VIII. WILLIAM, born April 29, 1766, who (I suppose) is the present baronet.

ARMS—Argent, a chevron between three manches, sable.
CREST—A cap of maintenance enflamed on the top, proper.
MOTTO—*Quod vult, valde vult.*
SEATS—Ischoed in Carmarthenshire, and Woodstone, in the county of Cork, in Ireland.

42. PRIDEAUX of NETHERTON, DEVONSHIRE.

Created Baronet July 17, 1622.

THE name of Prideaux is of undoubted antiquity in Cornwall and Devonshire; their first residence was at Prideaux Castle, in the first-named county, where we find

1. Peganus de Prideaux was seized of it at the Norman conquest: he had two sons, Richard and Philip.
2. Richard succeeded, and died in 1122: his son,
3. Baldwin Prideaux, died in 1165: his son,
4. Nicholas, lord of Prideaux, died in 1169, and left twins, Richard* and

* 5. Richard, whose son,
6. Richard, was lord of Prideaux, and died in 1250: his son,
7. Baldwin, was lord of Prideaux, and was succeeded by his son,

PRIDEAUX OF NETHERTON, DEVONSHIRE.

5. Herden, who married ———, daughter and heir of Ralph Orcharton, in the parish of Modbury in Devonshire, by whom he had one son,

6. Sir Jeffery Prideaux of Orcharton, Knt. who was succeeded by

7. Ralph, his son, who married the daughter of Sir William Bigberry of Bigberry, in Devonshire, Knt. and left issue

8. Roger, who married Catharine, daughter and heir of Hugh, son and heir of Sir Walter Treverbian, Knt. and had issue

9. Roger, who married Elizabeth, daughter and heir of Sir John Clifford, Knt. and was chosen one of the knights of the shire for the county of Devon, temp. Edw. III. by her he had

10. John Prideaux of Orcharton, created knight banneret, and was several times chosen knight of the shire for Devon: he married ——— the daughter of Roger Mortimer, earl of March, by whom he had

11. Piercy Prideaux of Orcharton, also made knight banneret, who married Isabella, daughter of William Montacute, earl of Salisbury, and king of the Isle of Man, and had issue Roger and Sir John, of whom hereafter.

12. Roger succeeded his father, and had one son,

13. Sir John Prideaux, who killed his relation, Sir William Bigberry,* in a duel, and was obliged to part with several considerable manors to save his life,† being of the party against Henry IV.‡

12. Sir John Prideaux, Knt. second son of Sir Percy Prideaux of Orcharton, knight banneret, married Joan, daughter and sole heir of Gilbert Adeston of Adeston, in Devonshire, Esq. by whom he had

13. Giles Prideaux of Adeston, who married the daughter and heir of ——— Gunstone, and was succeeded by

---

8. Thomas, lord of Prideaux, who married ———, daughter of Sir Philip Bodrigan, Knt. He was succeeded by his son,

9. Robert, lord of Prideaux Castle, who left a son,

10. Jeffery Prideaux, who was succeeded by his son,

11. Roger, who married Alicia, daughter of Sir Richard Bodyford, Knt. by whom he had

12. Richard Prideaux, who married Cecilia, daughter of Oates de Rupe, alias Roch or Rock; and dying in 1329, was succeeded by his son,

13. Richard, who married Agnes or Agrietta, daughter or aunt of Ralph Revill, lord of Treverbiam or Treverkin; and died in 1345, leaving another

14. Richard, who married Jane ———: he died in 1374, and was succeeded by his son,

15. Richard, who married Margery, daughter of John Collen, lord of Collen: he died in 1388, leaving a daughter

16. Jane, his heir: she was the wife of Philip Arvas, by whom she had

Richard Arvas, lord of Prideaux Castle, who married Joan, daughter of Richard Metheron, and left a daughter Joan, his heir, who was the wife of Thomas Herle of West Herle, in Northumberland, Esq. by which marriage he became possessed of Prideaux Castle.

* Prince's Worthies of Devon. p. 507.

† Sir John Prideaux, who killed his kinsman, Sir William Bigberry, at the five crosses, near Modbury, parted with the manors of Colm-John, Coningham-head, Stoking-head, Godford, Halcomb-Dean, Newton, and Poplesford, and their demesnes, to obtain his pardon. *Leland's Itin. vol. III. p. 28. and Risdon's Devon. vol. II. p. 243.*

‡ There are several monuments belonging to the Prideaux family, in Modbury church, of stone and marble, which were sadly defaced in the last civil war.

14. Sir John Prideaux of Adeston, Knt. who had three wives; 1, Joan, daughter and heir of Nicholas Bromford of Bromford, in Devonshire; 2, ——, daughter of —— French (by whom he had three daughters; 1, ——, the wife of —— Somester; 2, ——; and 3, ——, of John Fortescue) and 3, ——, daughter of John Shepton; and was succeeded by his son by his first wife,

15. William Prideaux, who had three wives; the first was a daughter of Hugh Mighelstone, by whom he had no issue; his second was a daughter of John Fortescue, Esq. by whom he had some daughters; his third was Alice, daughter and heir of Stephen Gifford of Thewborough, in Devonshire, by whom he had issue,

19. Sir Fowke Prideaux, who married first Joan, daughter of Sir Richard Edgecombe, Knt. by whom he had no issue; secondly, Catharine, daughter of Sir Humphrey Poynts of Langley, in Devonshire, Knt. by whom he had Humphrey, and eight other sons, who died without issue, and four daughters; Elizabeth, the wife of Robert Yeo of Shebber; Alice, of Thomas —— of Cornwall; Margaretta, of John Williams, and secondly of Leonard Kernayn; Jane, of Thomas Hussey of Shipwicke, in Dorsetshire. He was succeeded by his son,

17. Humphrey Prideaux of Thewborough and Adeston, who married first Jane, daughter of Richard Fowell of Fowelscombe, in Devonshire, Esq. secondly, Edith, daughter of William Hutch of Aller, in Devonshire. By his first wife, he left three sons; 1, Sir Richard Prideaux, Knt.* 2, William; and 3,

18. Roger Prideaux of Soldon, Esq. who was in considerable employments, and high sheriff of Devonshire the beginning of Queen Elizabeth's reign: he married Philippa, daughter of Sir Richard York, Knt. serjeant at law, and had issue two sons, Sir Nicholas† and

---

* Sir Richard married first Joan, daughter of Thomas Gilbert, by whom he had no issue; secondly, Catharine, daughter of Sir John Arundel of Terrice, Knt. by whom he had issue hereafter-mentioned; thirdly, Mary, daughter of John Bovill of Garnack, who died without issue. By his second wife he had four sons and two daughters; Richard, Humphrey, John, and Robert; Jane and Charity. Richard, the eldest son, married Grace, daughter and heir of Nicholas Carminor of Nespine, in Cornwall, by whom he had five sons and five daughters; Jonathan, Charles, Hugh, Francis, and Benjamin; Elizabeth, Philippa, Prudence, Jane, and Susan. Jonathan, the eldest son and successor, married Winifred, daughter and co-heiress of Tristram Gorges of Batshead, in Devonshire, by whom he had one son, Richard, aged 14 (1620) and four daughters; Grace, Anne, Zenobia, and Margaret. Here this line ended, at least in the male descent.

† Sir Nicholas Prideaux of Soldon, married first Thomasin, daughter and co-heir of John Henscott, of the parish of Bradford, near Holdsworthy in Devonshire; secondly, Cheston, daughter and co-heir of William Violl of St. Breock, in Cornwall, by whom he had a son John, who married Anne, daughter of Robert Moyle, and dying without issue, left his estate to Edmund, the third son of his half brother, Humphrey; thirdly, Mary,* daughter of John Castle of Ashbury, in Devonshire, and relict of John Morice, chancellor of Exeter; but by her he had no issue. By his first wife he (Nicholas) had one son, Humphrey, who married Honora, daughter of Sir Edmund Fortescue of Fallow-pit, in Devonshire, Knt. by whom he had four sons and two daughters; 1, Nicholas, from whom the family of Soldon is descended: he married Anne, daughter of William Coryton, Esq. 2, John, who died without issue; 3, Edmund of Padshaw, father of the learned Humphrey, dean of Norwich, who died Nov. 1, 1724.;† 4, Humphrey, who married Elizabeth, the relict of —— Specot: 1, Thomasin, the wife of John Fortescue of Buckland Felligh; and Elizabeth, of Sir William Morrice, Knt. secretary to King Charles II.

* She gave 100l. to the chamber of the city of Exeter, for placing poor young children into the hospital there, anno 1630. Izack's List of Benefactors to the County of Devon and City of Exeter, p. 128. Edmund Prideaux, Esq. gave 100l. towards the promoting and advancing of Hele's Hospital, in the said city. Ibid. p. 129.   † For particulars, see Blomefield's Norfolk, vol. II. p. 453.

PRIDEAUX OF NETHERTON, DEVONSHIRE.

I. EDMUND, who studied the law in the Inner Temple, where he contented not himself with the formalities of a student, that is, with gown, cap, and commons in the hall, but so diligently applied his business, that he became very eminent for his skill and learning in that profession, so that in 40 Eliz. he was autumn-reader of his house, and 6 James I. he became treasurer of the same, and in the 13th of the same reign, he was double reader: he made a great figure in the law, and raised a large estate in the counties of Devon and Cornwall; and was, by King James I. advanced to the dignity of a baronet. He married first Bridget, daughter of Sir John Chichester of Raleigh, in Devonshire, Knt. by whom he had three daughters; Tabitha, the wife of Thomas Aylworth of Cornwall, Esq. Sarah, of John Fortescue of Fallow-pit, in Devonshire, Esq. and Admonition to John Moyle of Bake, in Cornwall, Esq. He married secondly Catharine, daughter of Piers Edgecombe of Mount Edgecombe, Esq. by whom he had two sons, Sir Peter, his successor, and Edmund Prideaux of Ford Abbey, Esq.* Sir Edmund married to his third lady, Mary, daughter of Richard Reynell of East Ogwell, and relict of Arthur Fowell of Fowelscombe, both in Devonshire, Esqrs. by whom he left no issue. Sir Edmund died at Netherton on the 28th of March, 1628, aged 74.

II. Sir PETER PRIDEAUX, Bart. his eldest son and successor, married Susanna, daughter of Sir Anthony Poulet, Knt. sister of John, the first Lord Poulet, of Hinton St. George, by whom he had three sons, Edmund and John, who both died unmarried before their father; and Sir Peter, his successor: and two daughters, Margaret, the wife of Thomas Drew of the Grange, in Devonshire, Esq. and Mary; and dying in the year 1682, was succeeded in dignity and estate by his youngest son,

III. Sir PETER PRIDEAUX, Bart. who married lady Elizabeth, daughter of the immortal Sir Bevil Granville of Stow, in Cornwall, Knt. and sister to John earl of Bath,† by whom he had issue four sons, Sir Edmund, his successor; Peter,

---

* This gentleman was bred to the law, and of so great reputation, as well for zeal to religion as skill in the law, it is not strange he was chosen a member of that which was called the long parliament, wherein he became a very leading man; for striking in with the prevailing party of those times (though he never joined with them in setting upon the life of his sovereign) he grew up to great wealth and dignity: he was made commissioner of the great seal, worth 1500l. per ann. and by ordinance of parliament, practised within the bar, as one of the king's council, worth 5000l. per ann. After that he was attorney-general, worth what he pleased to make it, and then postmaster-general for all the inland letters, which at 6d. the letter, as they went in those days, was worth 15,000l. per ann. from all which rich employments he acquired a great estate, and among other things purchased the abbey of Ford, lying in the parish of Thorncombe, in Devonshire, where he built a noble new house, out of the ruins of the old, which he left unto Edmund Prideaux, Esq. his only son by his second wife, the daughter and co-heir of William Ivory of Cothay, in Somersetshire, Esq. (for his first wife, the daughter of —— Collins of Ottery St. Mary, in Devonshire, died without issue) which Edmund, by Amy his wife, daughter and co-heir of John Fraunces of Combeflory, in Somersetshire, Esq. and had issue Elizabeth, married to John Speke of White Lackington, in Somersetshire, Esq. who died without issue, and Margaret, his only surviving daughter, married in 1690 to Francis Gwyn of Lansanor, in Glamorganshire, Esq. member in several parliaments for the city of Wells; by whom she had several children, whose eldest surviving son and heir, Francis Gwyn of Ford Abbey, Esq. married ——, a sister of Thomas Pitt of Boconnock, in Cornwall, Esq. *Prince's Worthies of Devon.* p. 509.

† All the children of Sir Bevil were ennobled, and to take place and precedency as earls daughters, by the patent to John earl of Bath.

fellow of All Souls College, Oxford; John, who married Anne, daughter and heir of Humphrey Prideaux of Soldon, in Devonshire, Esq. and Roger, who died S. P. also several daughters; ——, the wife of Sir William Drake of Ash, in Devonshire, Bart. and another of the Rev. Mr. Harwood. Sir Peter dying in Nov. 1705, was succeeded in dignity and estate by his eldest son,

IV. Sir EDMUND PRIDEAUX, Bart. who represented the borough of Tregony in Cornwall in the last parliament of Queen Anne, and first of King George I. He married three wives; first Susanna, daughter of James Winstanley of Branston, in Leicestershire, Esq. relict of —— Austin of Durhams, in Middlesex, Esq. by whom he had two sons and a daughter, viz. Sir Edmund, his successor, and Peter, who married first Susanna, widow of Richard Coffin, Esq. and daughter of —— Kellond, Esq. by whom he had a daughter and heir, Susanna, the wife of Charles Evelyn, Esq. second son of Sir John Evelyn, Bart. secondly, Dorothea, eldest daughter of Clement Pettit of Dentyleon, in the Isle of Thanet in Kent, Esq. by whom he had no issue, and died before his elder brother, Sir Edmund: Susanna, the daughter was the first wife of Phineas Cheek, Esq. Sir Edmund's second lady was Elizabeth, daughter and co-heir of George Saunderson of Thoresby, in Lincolnshire, Esq. and grand-daughter of Nicholas Saunderson, lord viscount Castleton, by whom he had only one child, Sir John, successor to his brother: his third wife was Mary, daughter of Spencer Vincent, Esq. alderman of London, relict of Sir John Rogers of Wisdom, in Devonshire, Bart. by whom he had no issue; and dying Feb. 1719, was succeeded in dignity and estate by his eldest son by the first marriage,

V. Sir EDMUND PRIDEAUX, Bart. who married two wives; first, Mary, daughter of Samuel Reynardson of Hillingdon, in Middlesex, Esq. by whom he had only one daughter, Mary, the wife of James Winstanley of Branston, near Leicester, Esq. his second was Anne, daughter of Philip Hawkins of Pennans, in Cornwall, Esq. by whom he left only one daughter, Anne, the wife of John Pendarves Basset of Tihiddy, in Cornwall, Esq. who died Sep. 25, 1739, leaving her with child of a son and heir, John Prideaux Basset, whose son and heir, Francis, was created a baronet by patent, Oct. 1, 1779; Lord Dunstanville in 1796, and Lord Basset in 1797; a vice-president of the Westminster Dispensary. Sir Edmund dying Feb. 26, 1728-9, without issue male, was succeeded in honour and estate by his half brother,

VI. Sir JOHN PRIDEAUX of Netherton, who married Anne, eldest daughter of John lord viscount Lisburne (by Lady Mallet Wilmot, his wife, daughter of John Wilmot, earl of Rochester) by whom he had three sons and two daughters; 1, Saunderson, who was killed at Carthagena in April, 1741; 2, John, who was a brigadier-general, and killed at Niagara in 1759: he married Elizabeth, daughter of Thomas Rolt of Saycombe, in Hertfordshire, Esq. and sister of Sir Edward Baynton Rolt of Wiltshire: they had issue Sir John Wilmot Prideaux, the present baronet; Edward-Baynton, Edmund, and one daughter, Elizabeth. 3, Peter. Elizabeth, the wife of Edward Chichester of Northover, in Somersetshire, Esq. and Anne. Sir John died in Aug. 1766, and was succeeded by his grandson,

VII. Sir JOHN WILMOT PRIDEAUX, Bart.

TABLE 45.

```
1 PAGANUS DE PRIDEAUX                          10 Sir John = ――― Mortimer
  |                                               |
2 Richard, 1122          Philip                 11 Sir Percy = Isabella Montacute
  |                                               |
3 Baldwin, 1165                                 12 Roger         12 Sir John = Joan Adeston
  |                                                                 |
4 Nicholas, 1169                                13 Sir John     13 Giles = ――― Gunston
  |                                               |
5 Richard         5 Herden = ――― Orcharton      14 Sir John Prideaux, Knt
  |                                               J. Bromford | ― French | ― Shepton
6 Sir Jeffery of Orcharton                      
  |                                             15 William Prideaux
7 Ralph = ――― Bigberry                            ― Mighelston | ― Fortescue | A. Gifford
  |
8 Roger = Cath. Treverbian                      16 Sir Fowke Prideaux, Knt.
  |                                               J. Edgcombe | Cath. Poyntz
9 Roger = Eliz. Clifford
```

```
17 Humphrey         8 sons        Elizabeth        Alicia          Margaretta              Jane
   J. Fowell | E. Hutch            R. Yeo          Thomas      J. Williams | L. Kernayn    T.
                                                                                           Hussey
18 Sir Richard Prideaux, Knt.      William      18 Roger Prideaux, temp. Eliz.
   J. Gilbert | C. Arundel | M. Bevill             Philippa, dr. of Richard York

   Richard     Humphrey.    Jane.       Sir Nich. Prideaux         I. Sir Edm. Prideaux, Bart. 1628
   G. Carminor  John. Rob.  Charity     T. Hens- | C. Violl | M. Cas-   B. Chi- | C. Edge- | M. Reynall
   |                                    cott                tle        chester   combe
   Jonathan      4 sons                                                 
   W. Gorges     4 drs.     Humphrey    Tabitha   Sarah    Admonition  II. Sir Peter, 1682   Edmund
   |                        H. Fortescue T. Ayl-  J. For-  J. Moyle        S. Paulet       ― Col- | ― Eve-
 1 son & 4 drs.                           worth   tescue                                     lins       ry

   Nicholas  Edmund      Humphrey                        III. Sir Peter, 1705   Marg.      Mary    Edmund
   A. Coryton  |         ― Specot                             E. Granville     T. Drus              A. Frances
             Edmund,
             dean of    IV. Sir Edm. 1719     Peter.    John    N          N    Eliz.       Marg.
             Norwich    S. Win- | E. Saun- | Mary  Rog.  A. Prideaux  Sir   ― Har-  John   Francis
   Prideaux of          stanley  derson    Vincent                   W. Drake wood  Spoke   Gwyn
   Soldon

   V. Sir Edmund, 1729     Peter Prideaux          Susan      VI. Sir John, Bart. 1766    Francis
   M. Reynard- | A. Haw-   S. Killond | D. Pettit  P. Cheek   A. dr. of John V. Lisburne, 1767   ― Pitt
      son         kins
   |
   Mary           Anne        Susanna       Saunderson    John, 1759    Peter      Eliz.         Anne.
   J. Winstanley  J. P. Basset  C. Eve-       1741         E. Rolt                  E. Chichester
                                 lyn

   VII. Sir John Wilmot Prideaux, Bart.     Edward-Baynton     Edmund        Elizabeth
```

ARMS—Argent, a chevron sable, in chief a label of three points, gules.
CREST—An eagle volant, argent, beaked and legged, gules.
SEAT—At Netherton in Devonshire.

43. HESILRIGE of Nosely, Leicestershire.

Created Baronet July 21, 1622.

THIS family is descended from Roger de Hesilrige, who came with William the Conqueror from a place of that name in Normandy: he settled in Cumberland, and the place took his name. From him descended

2. Simon de Hesilrige, lord of Wettissade and West Brunton, in Northumberland,* to whom King Edward I. gave the manors of Yetham Corbet and Yetham Maine, in the county of Roxburgh, 9 Edw. I. His son,

3. Simon de Hesilrige was father of

4. William de Hesilrige of Fawdon, in Northumberland, 36 Edw. III. and 10 Richard II. and by Joan his wife, had issue

5. Thomas, 20 Richard II. who married Isabel, daughter and co-heir of Sir Roger Heron, Knt.† by Margaret, daughter of Sir Ralph Hastings, Knt. which Margaret was sole heir to her mother, Isabel, daughter of Sir Robert de Sadington, Knt. by this match the Nosely estate came into the family.

6. Thomas Hesilrige of Nosely, Esq. son and heir, was high sheriff of Leicestershire 16 Hen. VII. he married Elizabeth, daughter of — Brocket, and died in 1467.

7. William Hesilrige, Esq. his son and heir, married Elizabeth, daughter and co-heir of Thomas Staunton of Staunton Harold, in Leicestershire, Esq. and dying in 1473, was buried at Nosely.

8. Thomas Hesilrige, Esq. his son and heir, was squire of the body to Henry VIII. he married Lucia, daughter and heir of Thomas Entwissel, Esq. and lies buried at Nosely.‡

9. Bertin Hesilrige of Nosely, Esq. his son and heir, in 1563 married Anne, daughter of John Southill of Stockerston, in Leicestershire, Esq. and was father of

10. Miles Hesilrige, Esq. who by Bridget, daughter of Sir Thomas Griffin of Braybrooke, in Northamptonshire, Knt. (who was remarried to William Lane of Cottesbrooke, Esq.) had issue

* Burton's Leicest. p. 213.   † Ibid.
‡ Hic jacent Thomas Hasilrig, Armiger, pro Corpore excellentissimi Domini Henrici octavi, & Lucia, Uxor ejus, quæ quidem Lucia obiit octavo Die Mensis Octobris, A°. 1525, & dictus Thomas, obiit —— Die —— quorum Animabus propitietur Deus. Amen.
By which monument it appears, that they had 18 children, viz. ten sons and eight daughters.

11. **Thomas**, his son and heir, who married Ursula, daughter of Sir Thomas Andrews of Charwelton, in Northamptonshire, Knt. (by Catharine, his first wife, daughter of Edward Cave of Newbold Revel, in Warwickshire, Esq. and had issue

I. Sir THOMAS HESILRIGE of Nosely, Knt. high sheriff of the county of Leicester 10 James I. and advanced to the dignity of a baronet 20 James I. He married Frances, daughter and heir of Sir William Gorges of Alderton, in Northamptonshire, Knt. and had issue eight sons and six daughters. He died Jan. 11, 1629, aged 66,* and his lady in 1638; and was succeeded in dignity and estate by his eldest surviving son,

II. Sir ARTHUR HESILRIGE, Bart. who represented the county of Leicester in parliament in 1640, and thinking that the constitution was in danger, he opposed the measures of the court, and preferred to the house of commons† a bill for the attainder of the Earl of Stafford, of high treason; but growing obnoxious to the court, he was one of the six members‡ that had articles of high treason exhibited against him, by Herbert, the attorney-general; he afterwards joined in opposing the king's measures, and was colonel of a regiment of cuirassiers, called the lobsters, which did great mischief to the king's affairs: he was governor of Newcastle, and in great favour with the protector, and indeed one of the most considerable and active of his friends, in all circumstances that required exertion and dispatch.§ Sir Arthur married 1, Frances, daughter of Thomas Elmes of Lilford, in Northamptonshire, Esq. by whom he had two sons, Sir Thomas, his successor, and another that died before him; and two daughters. This lady dying in 1632, he married to his second wife Dorothy, sister to Robert Grevile, lord Broke, baron of Beauchamp Court, by whom he had three sons and five daughters. Sir Arthur died in 1660, and his second lady Jan. 28, 1650.

---

* " He was entrusted with offices of great trust and power in the country. He was prudent, and of impartial justice; of great temperance and sobriety." Eight boys and six girls are in the act of prayer on his monument, below the figures of himself and wife. *Thoresby's Leicest. vol. I. p.* 300.

† Clarendon, vol. I. p. 226.   ‡ See Hume, vol. VI. p. 1642.

§ Sir Arthur Hesilrige, in 1650, received the following letter the day before the fight at Dunbar.

"*Deere Sir, wee are upon an engagement very difficult; the enemie hath blocked up our way att the passe at Copperspeth, through which wee cannot gett without almost a miracle. He lieth so upon the hills, that wee knowe not how to come that way without great difficulty; and our lying here dayly consumeth our men, who fall sicke beyond immagination. I perceive your forces are not in a capacitye for present reliefe, wherefore (whatever becomes of us) itt will be well for you to get what forces you can together in the South, to helpe what they can; the businesse neerly concerneth all good people. If your forces had been in readenesse to have fallen upon the back of Copperspeth, itt might have occasioned supplies to have come to us, but the only wise God knowes what is best; all shall work for good; our spirits are comfortable (praised be the Lord, of whose mercy wee have had large experience). Indeed, doe you gett together what forces you can against them; send to frendes in the South, to help with more. Lett H. Vane knowe what I write: I would not make it publick least danger should accrue thereby. You know what use to make hereof. Let me hear from you. I rest your servant,*

"*It is difficult for me to send to you; lett me heare from you after. Sep.* 3, 1650." OLIVER.

" *For the Hon. Sir Ar. Haselrige, at Newcastle or elsewhere, Thease. Haste.*

In the year 1647, 1649, and 1650 he and his son made the following purchases:—In 1647, at the sale of the lands of the see of Durham, Sir Arthur Hesilrige bought Bishop's Aukland manor, March 8, for 6102*l.* 8*s.* 11*d.* Nov. 9, 1649, Thomas Hesilrige, Esq. bought Middleham manor, in Northumberland, for 3306*l.* 6*s.* 6*d.* April 5, 1650, Sir Arthur bought Easing Wood borough for 5833*l.* 9*s.* 9*d.* June 1, Wolsingham manor for 6764*l.* 14*s.* 4*d.*

HESILRIGE OF NOSELY, LEICESTERSHIRE.

III. Sir THOMAS HESILRIGE, Bart. his only surviving son by the first marriage, succeeded him in dignity and estate, and married Elizabeth,* daughter and co-heir of George Fenwick of Brunton Hall, in Northumberland, Esq. and had issue one son, Sir Thomas, his successor, and three daughters; Mary, the wife of Francis Blith of Allesly, in Warwickshire, Esq. and Arabella of Rawson Hart, Esq. Sir Thomas died Feb. 24, 1680, aged 55, and his lady May 30, 1673.

IV. Sir THOMAS HESILRIGE, Bart. his only son and successor, served in parliament for the county of Leicester in 1660, and died unmarried, July 11, 1700, aged 36; whereupon the dignity and estate devolved upon his uncle, Sir Robert, the only surviving son of Sir Arthur, by the second venter, which

V. Sir ROBERT HESILRIGE, Bart. married Bridget, daughter of Sir Samuel Rolle of Heanton, in Devonshire, Knt. by whom he had four sons, who all died unmarried, in his life-time, but one, Sir Robert; and four daughters, who all died unmarried, before him, except one, who died June 10, 1721. Sir Robert died May 22, 1713, and his lady July 26, 1697. He was succeeded in dignity and estate by his only surviving son,

VI. Sir ROBERT HESILRIGE, Bart. who married Dorothy, second daughter of Banaster lord Maynard, and died May 19, 1721, aged 55, leaving one son, Sir Arthur, and a daughter Dorothy, the wife of the Rev. Mr. Battle of Hertfordshire.

VII. Sir ARTHUR HESILRIGE, only son and successor, married June 1725, Hannah, daughter of Mr. Sturges, by whom he had several sons and daughters; 1, Sir Robert; 2, Arthur, who was in the commission of the peace, and a captain in the Leicestershire militia, and died April 11, 1791; 3, Thomas-Maynard of Hoxne Hall, in Suffolk, Esq. who married Mary, daughter of Edmund Tyrrell of Gipping Hall, Esq. 4, Elizabeth, the wife of the Rev. Richard Buckley, rector of Segore in Ireland; 5, Charles,† who married Sarah, daughter of —— Wall; 6, Grey, who is a major in the army, and married Bridget, the daughter of the Rev. Mr. Buckley; 7, Bridget, &c. Sir Arthur died in 1763, and was succeeded in title by his eldest son,

VIII. Sir ROBERT HESILRIGE, Bart. who married Sarah, daughter of Nathaniel Waller of Roxburgh, in New England, by whom he had one son Arthur, who is judge and collector of the department of Jesson, and married Elizabeth Charnaud of Smyrna, who died in 1797, at Calcutta, without issue; Sarah, the wife of David Henly, a colonel of the provincial regiment; Hannah, of the Rev. Thomas Abbot of Roxburgh.

---

* A long inscription of her virtues is summed up in these words:—" She was the phœnix of her sex." *Thoresby's Leicest. vol. I. p. 300.*

† He succeeded to the estate by the will of his father, and served high sheriff for the county in 1770. At the assize he made an extraordinary appearance; his carriage was drawn by six fine blood chesnut horses, which it was said cost 500l. He had in his suite, 30 javelin men, clothed in green, and buff breeches: he gave them stockings, hats, and gloves. The procession was conducted by a marshal, two trumpeters, with silk flags, finely emblazoned thereon the arms of the family. There were also two french-horn-men, who preceded the cavalcade; two servants out of livery, several footmen, and two pages, in light handsome dresses, on each side of the carriage. *Ibid.*

HESILRIGE OF NOSELY, LEICESTERSHIRE.

TABLE 44.

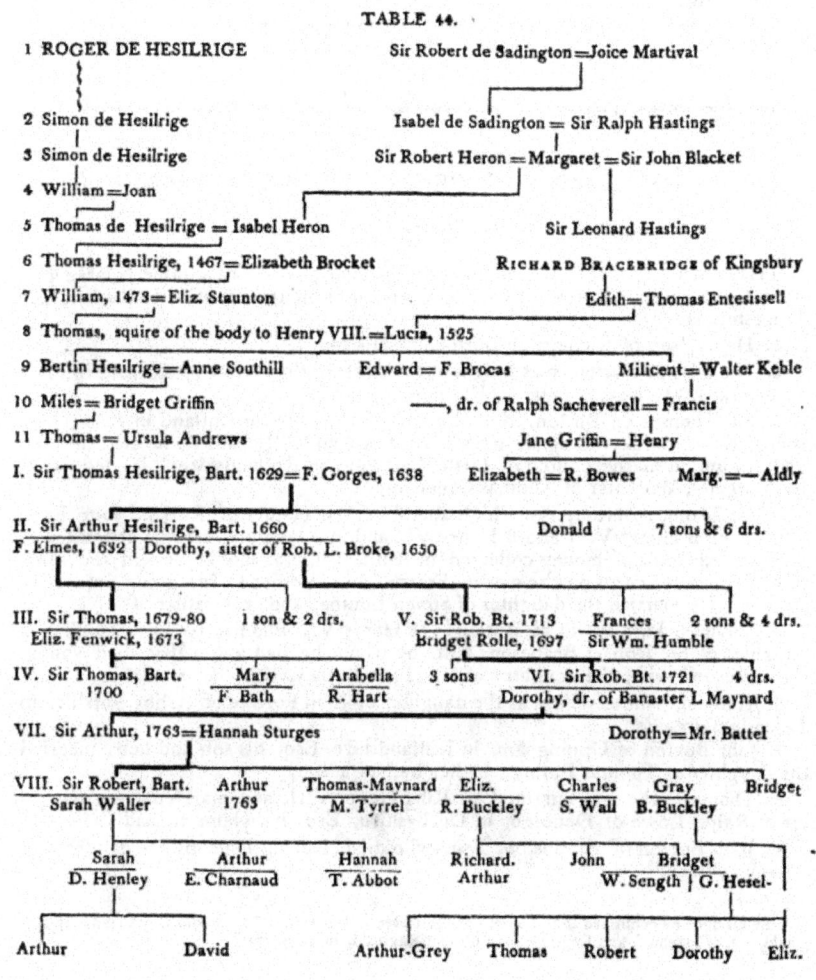

BURTON OF STOCKERSTON, LEICESTERSHIRE.

ARMS—Argent, a chevron between three hasel leaves, vert.
CREST—On a chapeau, gules, lined, ermine, a scot's head, proper.
SUPPORTERS—On the dexter side a stag, proper; on the sinister a talbot, argent, pied sable, and gorged with a plain collar, gules.
MOTTO—*Pro aris et focis.*

44. BURTON of Stockerston, Leicestershire.

Created Baronet July 22, 1622.

THE first I find mentioned of this ancient family, which had formerly large possessions, and were of great esteem and reputation in the counties of Rutland and Leicester, is

1. Henry, son of Richard de Burtone.* His son,

2. Nicholas de Burton, was knight of the shire for the county of Rutland in 1316: he died in 1375, leaving issue by Eleanor, his wife,

3. Sir Thomas de Burton, Knt. knight of the shire for Rutland in 1377; high sheriff 1379, and served again in parliament in 3 and 5 Richard II. he died in 1384, and lies buried in the church of Little Casterton in Rutlandshire. He left issue, by Margaret, daughter of Thomas Grenham,

4. Sir Thomas Burton, Knt. high sheriff of the county of Rutland four times, viz. 4 and 8 Henry V. 1 and 6 Henry VI. and in 9 Henry V. he was appointed to receive such sums of money collected in Rutlandshire as should be lent the king, to enable him to carry on the war in France, and in order to his going into Normandy. He married the daughter of Simon Louthe, and was father of

5. Thomas, high sheriff of Rutland, 18 Henry VI. who had two wives; first, a daughter of Sir Robert Brabeson, Knt. by whom he had a son that died young. By his second wife, the daughter of Sir Hugh Bushey, Knt. he was father of

6. William, whose wife was the daughter of John Folville of Ashby Folville, in Leicestershire, Esq.

7. John Burton of Uppingham, in Rutlandshire, Esq. his son and heir, married the daughter of Thomas Basing: by her he had a son,

8. Thomas, who was knighted by King Henry VIII. and married ———, daughter of Ralph Lowe of Denbigh, in Derbyshire, Esq. by whom he had

9. John Burton of Braunston, Esq. who died, leaving issue by the daughter of ——— Blackwell,

* By his deed he confirmed to the monks of Geronden in Leicestershire, the donations made by Reginald, son of Ingehulf, and Reginald, son of that Reginald, in Ybestoke.

BURTON OF STOCKERSTON, LEICESTERSHIRE.

10. William, his son, of the same place, who married Alice, daughter of Richard Peck of Ridlington, in Rutlandshire, by whom he had three sons; 1, John Burton, of whom hereafter; 2, Bartin Burton of Okeham, Esq. ancestor to those of that place, and of Exton; 3, Simon Burton of Braunston, Esq. ancestor of that line.

11. John Burton, eldest son and heir, was of Stockerston: he married Anne, daughter and heir of Thomas Digby of Coats, Esq. (son of Lybeus Digby of Coats, and Luffenham, Esq. a fourth brother of Sir Simon Digby of Coleshill) by which marriage a good estate accrued to them, and had issue,

I. THOMAS BURTON, Esq. who having been knighted was afterwards (20 James I.) advanced to the title of baronet: he had two wives, first Philippa, daughter of Henry Cobham, alias Brook, Esq. grand-daughter of George lord Cobham, and relict of Walter Calverley of Calverley in Yorkshire, Esq. by whom he had three daughters, Anne, first wife of Sir Abel Barker of Hambleton, in Rutlandshire, Bart. Elizabeth and Frances, who died unmarried. By his second lady, Anne, daughter of Robert Reynolds of London, Gent. he left his only son and successor,

II. Sir THOMAS BURTON of Stockerston, Bart. who eminently distinguished himself in behalf of King Charles I. and was in the first commission of array with Sir George Villiers, Sir Henry Skipwith, and others,* in the county of Leicester, upon the breaking out of the rebellion in 1641, and suffered sequestration and imprisonment for the royal cause: and by Elizabeth, daughter of Sir John Prettyman of Lodington, in Leicestershire, Bart. of Nova Scotia (who was remarried to Sir William Halford of Welham, in Leicestershire, Knt.) he had Sir Thomas, his successor, and John, who died S. P.

III. Sir THOMAS BURTON, Bart. married Anne, eldest daughter of Sir Thomas Clutterbuck of London, and of Blakesware in Hertfordshire, Knt. and dying in 1735, was buried at Newark in Nottinghamshire. This Sir Thomas sold the Stockerston estate to Sir Charles Duncomb, Knt. He left two sons, Charles and Thomas, and was succeeded by his son,

IV. Sir CHARLES BURTON, Bart.

ARMS—Sable, a chevron between three owls, argent; crowned, or.
CREST—On a torce an owl, as in the arms.

* Rushworth's Collection, vol. IV. p. 655.

TABLE 45.

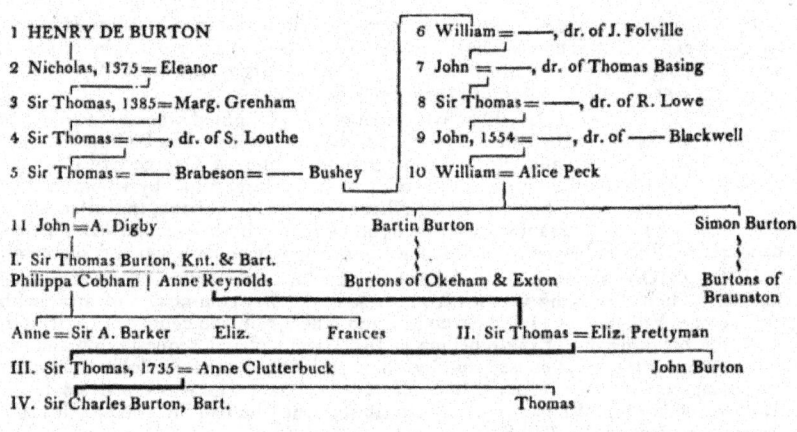

45. DRAKE of Buckland, Devonshire.

Created Baronet Aug. 2, 1622.

THE first person of any note of this family is Sir Francis Drake, one of our most distinguished naval heroes, in the reign of Elizabeth: he was the son of Edmund Drake, a sailor, and born near Tavistock in Devonshire, in 1544. He was brought up at the expence, and under the care of Sir John Hawkins, who was his kinsman; and at the age of 18 was purser of a ship trading to Biscay: at 20 he made a voyage to Guinea, and at 22 had the honour to be made captain of the Judith. In that capacity he was in the harbour of St. John de Ulloa, in the Gulph of Mexico, where he behaved most gallantly in the glorious actions under Sir John Hawkins, and returned with him to England with great reputation, though not worth a groat. Upon this he projected a design against the Spaniards in the West Indies, which he no sooner published than he had volunteers enough ready to accompany him. In 1570 he made his first expedition with two ships, and the next year with one only, in which he returned safe, if not with such advantages as he expected. He made another expedition in 1572, wherein he did the Spaniards some mischief, and gained considerable booties. In these expeditions he was much assisted by a nation of Indians, who then were, and have been ever since, engaged in wars with the Spaniards. The prince of these people was named Pedro, to whom Drake presented a fine cutlass from his side, which he saw the Indian greatly admired. Pedro, in return, gave him four large wedges of gold, which Drake threw into the common stock, with this remarkable expression, that *" he thought it but just, that such as bore the charge of so uncertain a voyage on his credit, should share the utmost advantages that voyage produced."* Then embarking his men, with all the wealth he had obtained, which was very considerable, he bore away for England, where he arrived in Aug. 1573.

His success in this expedition, joined to his honourable behaviour towards his owners, gained him a high reputation, and the use he made of his riches still greater; for fitting out three stout frigates at his own expence, he sailed with them into Ireland, where, under Walter earl of Essex, the father of the famous unfortunate earl, he served as a volunteer, and did many glorious actions. After the death of his patron he returned to England, where Sir Christopher Hatton, vice-chamberlain to Queen Elizabeth, introduced him to her majesty, and procured him countenance and protection at court. By this means he acquired a capacity of undertaking that grand expedition, which will render his name immortal. The first thing he proposed was a voyage into the South Seas, through the Straits of Magellan, which was what hitherto no Englishman had ever ettempted. The project was well received at court: the queen furnished him with means, and his own fame quickly drew together a force sufficient. The fleet with which he sailed on this extraordinary undertaking consisted only of five small vessels, compared with modern ships, and no more than 164 able men. He sailed from England Dec. 13, 1577; on the 25th he fell in with the coast of Barbary, and on the 29th with Cape Verd. March 13 he passed the equinoctial; made the coast of Brazil April 5, 1578, and entered the river De la Plata, where he lost the company of two of his ships; but meeting them again, and taking out their provisions, he turned them adrift. May 29 he entered the port of St. Julian, wherein he continued two months. Aug. 20 he entered the Straits of Magellan, and Sep. 25 passed them, having then only his own ship. Nov. 25 he came to Macao, which he had appointed for a place of rendezvous, in case his ships separated; but Capt. Winter, his vice-admiral, having re-passed the Straits, was returned to England: thence he continued his voyage along the coasts of Chili and Peru, taking all opportunities of seizing Spanish ships, and attacking them on shore, till his crew were sated with plunder; and then, coasting North America, to the height of 48 degrees, he endeavoured to find a passage back into our seas on that side, but could not. However he landed, and called the country new Albion, taking possession of it in the name, and for the use of Queen Elizabeth; and having careened his ship, set sail from thence Sep. 29, 1579, for the Moluccas. He is supposed to have chosen this passage round, partly to avoid being attacked by the Spaniards at a disadvantage, and partly from the lateness of the season, whence dangerous storms and hurricanes were to be apprehended. Oct. 4 he had sight of the Moluccas, and coming to Ternate, was extremely well received by the king thereof, who appears, from the most authentic relations of this voyage, to have been a wise and politic prince. Dec. 10 he made Clebes, where his ship unfortunately run upon a rock. Jan. 9 following, from which, beyond all expectation, and in a manner miraculously, they got off, and continued their course. March 16 he arrived at Java Major, and from thence intended to have directed his course to Molucca, but found himself obliged to alter his purpose, and to think of returning home. March 25, 1580, he put this design into execution, and June 15 doubled the Cape of Good Hope, having then on board 57 men, and but three casks of water. July 12 he passed the Line, reached the coast of Guinea on the 16th, and there watered. Sep. 11, he made the island of Tercera, and Nov. 3 entered the harbour of Plymouth. This voyage round the globe was performed in two years and about ten months.*

In 1585 he sailed with a fleet to the West Indies, and took the cities of St. Jago, St. Domingo, Carthagena, and St. Augustin. In 1587 he went to Lisbon with a fleet of 30 sail, and having intelligence of a great fleet assembled in the Bay of Cadiz, which was to have made part of the armada, he with great courage entered that port, and burnt there upwards of 10,000 tons of shipping, which he afterwards merrily called "*burning the King of Spain's beard.*" In 1588, when the armada from Spain was approaching our coasts, he was appointed vice-admiral, under Charles lord Howard of Effingham, high-admiral of England, where fortune favoured him as remarkably as ever; for he made prize of a very large galleon, commanded by Don Pedro de Valdez, who was reputed the projector of this invasion. This lucky affair happened in the following manner:—July 22, Sir Francis observing a great Spanish ship floating at a distance from both fleets, sent his pinnace to summon the commander to yield: Valdez replied, with much Spanish solemnity, that they were 450 strong, that he himself was Don Pedro, and stood much upon his honour, and thereupon propounded several conditions, upon which he was willing

---

* His success, and the immense mass of wealth he brought home, raised much discourse throughout the kingdom; some highly commending, and some as loudly decrying him: the former alledged, that his exploit was not only honourable to himself, but to his country; that it would establish our reputation for maritime skill in foreign nations, and raise an useful spirit of emulation at home; and that, as to the money, our merchants having suffered much from the faithless practices of the Spaniards, there was nothing more just than that the nation should receive the benefit of Drake's reprisals. The other party alledged, that in fact he was no better than a pirate; that of all others it least became a trading nation to encourage such practices; that it was not only a direct breach of all our late treaties with Spain, but likewise of our old leagues with the house of Burgundy; and that the consequences would be much more fatal than the benefits reaped from it could be advantageous. Things continued in this uncertainty during the remainder of 1580, and the spring of the succeeding year. At length they took a turn in favour of Drake; for April 4, 1581, her majesty going to Deptford, went on board his ship, where after dinner she conferred on him the honour of knighthood, and declared her absolute approbation of all he had done. She likewise gave directions for the preservation of his ship, that it might remain a monument of his own and his country's glory.

Camden, in his Britannia, has taken notice of an extraordinary circumstance relating to this ship of Drake's, where, speaking of the shire of Buchan in Scotland, he says, "It is hardly worth while to mention the clayks, a sort of geese, which are believed by some, with great admiration, to grow upon trees on this coast, and in other places, and when they are ripe they fall down into the sea, because neither their nest nor eggs can any where be found: but they who saw the ship in which Sir Francis Drake sailed round the world, when it was laid up in the river Thames, could testify, that little birds breed in the old rotten keels of ships, since a great number of such, without life and feathers, stuck close to the outside of the keel of that ship."

This celebrated ship, which had been contemplated many years at Deptford, at length decaying, it was broke up, and a chair, made out of the planks, was presented to the university of Oxford.

to yield; but the vice-admiral replied, that he had no leisure to parly, but if he thought fit instantly to yield he might, if not he should soon find that Drake was no coward. Pedro, hearing the name of Drake, immediately yielded, and with 46 of his attendants, came on board Drake's ship. This Don Pedro remained about two years in England, and when he was released, paid him for his own and his captains' liberties, a ransom of 3500*l.* Drake's soldiers were well recompensed with the plunder of this ship; for they found in it 55,000 ducats of gold, which was divided among them.*

In 1589 he commanded, as admiral, the fleet sent to restore Don Antonio, king of Portugal, the command of the land forces being given to Sir John Norris; but they were hardly got to sea before the commanders differed, and so the attempt proved abortive. The war with Spain continuing, a more effectual expedition was undertaken by Sir John Hawkins and Drake, against the settlements in the West Indies, than had hitherto been made during the whole course of it; but the commanders here again not agreeing about the plan, this also did not turn out so successfully as was expected. All difficulties, before these two last expeditions had given way to the skill and fortune of Drake, which probably was the reason why he did not bear these disappointments so well as he otherwise would have done. A strong sense of them is supposed to have thrown him into a melancholy, which occasioned a bloody flux, and of this he died on board his own ship, near the town of Nombre de Dios in the West Indies, Jan. 28, 1596. He was succeeded in his estate by his nephew and god-son,†

* It may be proper to observe, that a little before this formidable Spanish armament put to sea, the ambassador of his Catholic Majesty had the confidence to propound to Queen Elizabeth, in latin verse, the terms upon which she might hope for peace; which, with an English translation by Dr. Fuller, we will insert in this place, because Drake's expedition to the West Indies makes a part of this message. The verses are these:—

Te veto ne pergas bello defendere Belgas:
Quæ Dracus eripuit nunc restituantur oportet:
Quas pater evertit jubeo te condere cellas:
Religio Papæ fac restituatur ad unguem.

These to you are our commands:	And those abbies build anew,
Send no help to the Netherlands:	Which your father overthrew:
Of the treasure took by Drake,	If for any peace you hope,
Restitution you must make;	In all points restore the pope.

The Queen's extempore return:——Ad Græcas, bone rex, fient mandata calendas.
Worthy king, know this your will,
At Latter-Lammas will fulfill.

† His death was lamented by the whole nation, but more especially by his countrymen, who had great reasons to love him for the circumstances of his private life, as well as to esteem him in his public character. He was elected burgess for the town of Bossiny, alias Tintagal, in the county of Cornwall, in the 27th parliament of Elizabeth; and for the town of Plymouth in Devonshire, in the 35th.* He married Elizabeth, daughter and sole heiress of Sir George Sydenham of Combe-Sydenham, in the county of Devon, Knt. who afterwards married William Courtenay, Esq. of Powderham Castle in the same county. As all men have enemies, and all eminent men abundance of them, we need not wonder that Sir Francis Drake, who performed so many great things, should have as much ill spoken of him as any man of the age in which he lived. His voyage round the world however remains an incontestible proof of his courage, capacity, patience, quick-sightedness, and public spirit; since therein he did every thing that could be expected from a man who preferred the honour and profit of his country to his own

* Willis's Notitia Parl. vol. II p. 122, 295.

DRAKE OF BUCKLAND, DEVONSHIRE.

I. FRANCIS DRAKE, who was created a baronet Aug. 2, 1622, and in the beginning of the next reign was returned one of the knights of the shire for the county of Devon. He married first Jane, daughter of Sir Amias Bamfylde of Poltimore, in the same county, Knt. by whom he had a daughter Dorothy, who died an infant; secondly Joan, daughter of William Strode of Newnham, Knt. by whom he had four sons; Sir Francis, his successor; Thomas, who married ——, daughter of —— Grimes, Esq. and was father of Sir Francis, hereafter-mentioned; 3, —— of Joybridge; and 4, Joseph.

II. Sir FRANCIS DRAKE, Bart. eldest son and heir, succeeded his father in title and estate: he served in parliament for Newport in Cornwall, and Beer-Alston in Devonshire, temp. Charles II. and married Dorothy, daughter of —— Pym of Brymore, in Somersetshire, Esq. but dying without issue, was succeeded in dignity and estate by his nephew,

III. Sir FRANCIS DRAKE, Bart. who served in parliament for Tavistock, temp. Charles II. and again temp. Wm. and Mary. He married first Dorothy, daughter of Sir John Bamfylde of Poltimore, Bart. secondly Anne, daughter and co-heir of Thomas Boon of Mount Boon, in Devonshire, Esq. and had no issue by either of them; and thirdly ——, daughter of Sir Henry Pollexfen, Knt. lord chief justice of the common pleas, by whom he had a daughter, the wife of Thomas Martin, Esq. one of the judges of the counties of Carnarvon, Merioneth, and Anglesea; also his son and successor,

IV. Sir FRANCIS HENRY DRAKE, Bart. who represented the borough of Tavistock in the two parliaments of King George I. and served again for the same borough in the first parliament of George II. and was afterwards elected for Beer-Alston in Devonshire. He married Anne, daughter of Samuel Heathcote of Hurseley, in Hampshire, Esq. sister to Sir William Heathcote, Bart. by whom he had three sons and two daughters; 1, Sir Francis-Henry; 2, Francis-William, who married first Grace-America, daughter of Col. Samuel Glidhill, governor of Placentia, in Newfoundland (of the Richmond family, High-head Castle, Cumberland,)* by whom he had Frances-Augusta-Caroline, Francis-Thomas, Francis-Richmond, all dead, and Francis-Henry, born in Aug. 1756, the present baronet. He married secondly Elizabeth, sister of the late Sir Thomas Heathcote, Bart. by whom he had two daughters, Mariana and Sophia. 3, Sir Francis-Samuel, rear-admiral in Rodney's fleet, in the West Indies, was created a baronet in consequence of the glorious victory on the 12th of April, 1782. He married first Elizabeth Hayman of Kent, secondly ——, daughter of George Onslow, Esq. many years M. P. for Guildford; and died in 1789, but left no issue.

reputation or private gain. He had the happiness to live under the reign of a princess who never failed to distinguish merit, and what was more, to reward it. He was always her favourite, and she gave an uncommon proof of it in respect to a quarrel he had with his countryman, Sir Bernard Drake, whose arms Sir Francis assuming, the other was so provoked, that he gave him a box on the ear; upon this the queen took up the quarrel, and gave Sir Francis a new coat, which is thus blazoned:—*Sable, a fesse wavy, between two pole stars, argent*; and for his crest, *a ship on a globe under ruff, held by a cable, with a hand out of the clouds*; over it this motto, *Auxilio divino*; underneath, *Sic parvis magna*; in the rigging whereof is hung up by the heels a *wivern, gules*, which was the arms of Sir Bernard Drake.

* Hutchinson's Cumberland, vol. II. p. 429. *Prince's Worthies of Devon. p. 245.*

DRAKE OF BUCKLAND, DEVONSHIRE.

His two daughters were Anne, and Sophia, the wife of the Rev. John Pugh. He died Jan. 26, 1740, aged 47, and was succeeded by his son,

V. Sir FRANCIS-HENRY DRAKE, Bart. wl.o in June, 1751, was appointed ranger and master of his majesty's forest of Dartmouth in Devonshire, and in 1752 was made clerk-comptroller of the board of green cloth, died single Feb. 22, 1794, and was succeeded by his nephew (the sole surviving child of his brother Francis-William.

VI. Sir FRANCIS-HENRY DRAKE, Bart. who in 1795 married Anne-Frances, daughter of Thomas Maltby, Esq.

ARMS—Sable, a fesse wavy, between the two pole stars, argent.

CREST—On a helmet a ship under ruff, drawn round a globe with a cable-rope, by a hand out of the clouds: over it this

MOTTO—*Auxilio divino*, and under it *Sic parvis magna*.

SEAT—At Buckland-Monachorum, near Tavistock in Devonshire.

TABLE 46.

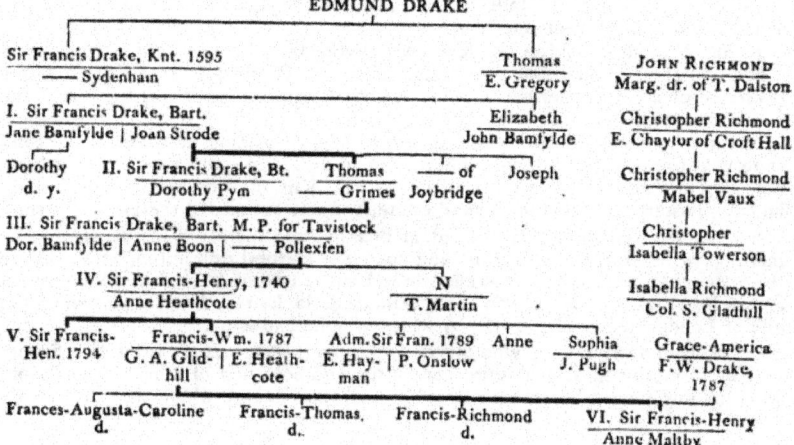

46. SKIPWITH of PRESTWOULD, LEICESTERSHIRE.

Created Baronet Dec 20, 1622.

THIS family, denominated from the town and lordship of Skipwith, in the east riding of Yorkshire, is descended from

1. Robert de Estotevill, baron of Cottingham, in the reign of William the Conqueror.*

2. Robert, his son, became possessed of a great inheritance, by marriage with Eneburga, daughter and heir of Hugh, son of Baldrick, a great Saxon thane, and among other lands had the lordship of Skipwith or Skipwic (as anciently written): he left three sons; from Robert, the eldest, descended the barons of Cottingham, whose male line terminated 17 Henry III. From Osmund, second son, who died at Joppa in Palestine, the Estotevills of Gressinghall descended.

3. Patrick, the youngest son, being possessed of the lordship of Skipwith, by gift of his father, his descendants assumed their name from that town, according to the custom of the age. By Beatrix, his wife, daughter and heir of Sir Pagan de Langtun, he had a son,

4. Jeffery, who succeeded, and who, by Mariana, his wife, daughter and heir of William de Menithorp, had two sons, Reginald and Gerard; which

5. Reginald was an hostage to the king, for the Lord Scales, in the barons' wars, 9 John, and his son and heir,

6. Sir William de Skipwith, Knt. was living temp. Henry III. and marrying Alice, daughter of Sir John, cousin and heir of Sir William Thorp, Knts. became possessed of a great inheritance in the county of Lincoln, and was the last of the family that resided at Skipwith.

7. Sir John de Skipwith, Knt. his son and heir, residing at Thorp in Lincolnshire, was from his habitation, sometimes stiled de Thorp; and having married Isabel, daughter and heir of Sir Robert de Arches, Knt. of Wranby, in Lincolnshire, had also possession of that manor and estate, and was succeeded therein by his son,

8. John de Skipwith, who resided at Beakby, and increased his patrimony, by marriage with Margaret, daughter and co-heir of Herbert de Flinton, in Yorkshire (by a daughter and co-heir of Walter de la Lynde, lord of Laseby in Lincolnshire, and of Bulbrook in Sussex, son of Sir William de la Lynde, Knt. seneschal of the city of London temp. Henry III.) by which wife he had issue,

9. William de Skipwith, who married Margaret, daughter of Ralph Fitz-Simon, lord of Ormesby in Lincolnshire, and sister and sole heir of Simon Fitz-Ralph, whereby this family became possessed of that inheritance, which was the posses-

* Dugdale's Baronage of England.

sion of Sir Ralph Eitz-Simon, Knt. temp. Henry III. who in several charters was termed *Nobilis,* and had obtained that manor by his wife, the daughter and heir of —— Ormesby of Ormesby; by whom he had three sons; viz.

10. John Skipwith, who, with his father, died in 1336; 2, Sir William Skipwith; 3, Sir Ralph, from whom descended the Skipwiths of Heburgh in Lincolnshire.

11. Sir William Skipwith succeeded his brother in his estate: he was one of the judges of the king's bench, and sworn in trinity term 36 Edw. III. lord chief baron of the exchequer, continuing therein till the 40th year of that king's reign, at which time he died. He married Alice, sole daughter and heir of Sir William de Hiltoft, lord of Ingoldmells, by Alice his wife, sister and sole heir to Ralph de Muer, lord of Calthrop and Covenham in Lincolnshire,* by whom he had four sons; William, John, Patrick, and Stephen; and two daughters, Alice, wife of Robert lord Willoughby, and Margaret of William Vavasor, Esq.

12. William, the eldest son, was one of the justices of the king's bench 50 Edw. III. and his patent was renewed 1 Richard II. when he was senior judge of that court, and acted therein with that candour and integrity, that his name is transmitted to posterity by all our historians with great honour. He left only one daughter, the wife of George lord Monboucher, whereupon the bulk of his estate descended to his brother,†

13. John Skipwith of Ormesby, Esq. high sheriff of Lincolnshire 18 Richard II. and one of the knights of the shire for the county, in parliament temp. Henry V. had issue by Alice his wife, daughter of Frederick Tilney of Tilney, in Norfolk, Knt. three sons; William, who died without issue, Thomas, and Patrick: the Skipwiths of Utterby in Lincolnshire descended from the latter, and by a younger son of that line those of the name of Snore in Norfolk.

---

* Which Sir William de Hiltoft was son of another Sir William, by Agnes his wife, daughter of Thomas, and one of the sisters and co-heirs of William de Munby, a family extracted from the house of Willoughby; for Sir William Willoughby having two sons, Robert and Thomas, by his wife, the heir of Baron Beke of Eresby, Robert, the eldest, had the barony, and Thomas, his brother, having married Margaret, sister and co-heir to Alan de Munby, William, his son, took the name of Munby, and dying without issue, Sir William Hiltoft, before-mentioned, by marrying his sister became his heir.

† In the same year his patent was renewed, he obtained free warren in all his demesnes,* at Ormesby, Ingoldmells, Carleton, Covenham, and Bekeby; and in the 11th of that reign, had at his own request, a quietus from his office of justice.† Knighton, in his Chronicle, says, that notwithstanding the threats of the duke of Ireland he did not appear at the council at Nottingham, when the judges were summoned to meet there, in order to subscribe to several questions, whereby they might take occasion to work the death of the duke of Gloucester; he wisely foreseeing the event, got his quietus. His brethren were afterwards arrested on the bench, by the desire of the parliament, being charged with over-ruling the determinations of the lords, and were all of them (except Sir William Skipwith) condemned ‡ to be drawn and hanged as traitors, their heirs disinherited, and their lands, &c. forfeited; but this sentence, as to their lives, was respited.

The collar of Esses, now worn by the judges, first introduced from the initial letters of *Sanctus Simon Simplicius,* an uncorrupted justicier in the primitive times, well suited this Sir William Skipwith, who died full of honour, without issue male.

* Cart. R. II. n. H.   † Lib. 11. R. II. m. 6.   ‡ Rot. Parl. 11. R. II.

14. Thomas, second son, succeeded his father in 1421: he distinguished himself in the French wars, and was knighted by King Henry V. in France.* He died before the 19th of Henry VI. for in that year

15. William, his son and heir, was possessed of his estate: he was knighted in France temp. Henry VI. and was high sheriff of Lincolnshire in 1459, and departing this life in 1487, lies buried in the church of Ormesby. He married first Joan, daughter of Sir Robert Mortimer, Knt. by whom he had no issue: secondly, Agnes, daughter of Sir John Constable of Burton-Constable, in Yorkshire, Knt. widow of Sir —— St. Quintyn, by whom he had issue John, and a daughter Alice, wife of Sir John Markham, Knt. which

16. John, defeating Perkin Warbeck, for his service had the honour of knight banneret conferred on him. He married Catharine, daughter of Richard Fitz-Williams of Wadsworth, Esq. by whom he had issue William, and four daughters; 1, Catharine, the wife of Sir Thomas Heneage of Hampton, in Lincolnshire, Knt. 2, Mary, of George Fitz-Williams of Mablethorp; 3, Elizabeth, of Anthony Riggs, afterwards of Matthew Thimelby, Esq. 4, Margaret, of Richard Yarborough, Esq.

17. William succeeded to the estate, and was high sheriff of Lincolnshire 18 Henry VIII. before which time he had received the honour of knighthood. He married first Elizabeth, daughter of Sir William Tyrwit of Kettleby, in Lincolnshire, Knt. by whom he had four sons and four daughters; 1, William; 2, Lionel, from whom the Skipwiths of Calthorp descended; 3, John of Walmsgare, whose son Lionel died without issue; 4, George Skipwith of Cotes or Cotenham: the daughters were 1, Elizabeth, the wife of Thomas Clifford of Brakenburgh, in Lincolnshire, Esq. 2, Anne, of William Hatcliffe of Hatcliffe; 3, Bridget, one of the maids of honour and bed-fellow to Queen Elizabeth, and afterwards the wife of —— Cave of Leicestershire, Esq. and 4, Eleanor, of Richard Bolles, Esq. William, the eldest son, was ancestor to the Skipwiths of Newbold Hall, now extinct.

The said Sir William, by Alice his second wife, daughter and heir of Sir Lionel Dymock of Scrivelsby, in Lincolnshire, Knt. (with whom he had a great estate) left

18. Henry Skipwith, Esq. who married Jane, daughter of Francis Hall of Grantham, in Lincolnshire, Esq. by whom he had four sons; 1, Sir William, of whom hereafter; 2, George, slain at Bomwell in Hollandia, without issue; 3, Francis, who died without issue; and 4, Henry of Knighthorp, in Leicestershire, who by Jane, daughter of Leonard Aston of Longdon, in Staffordshire, Esq. left issue.

Sir William had also eight daughters; 1, Jane, the wife of William Samwell of Upton, in Northamptonshire; 2, Ursula, of Edward Ascough of Cotham, in Lincolnshire; 3, Margaret, of Matthew Saunders of Shankton, in Leicestershire, Esqrs. 4, Catharine, of Sir Walter Ascough of Blithburgh, in Lincolnshire, Knt. 5, Dorothy, of John Woodward of Botelers-Marston, in Warwickshire; 6, Bridget, of Walter Ascough of Washingburgh in Lincolnshire; 7, Anne, of Henry Smith of Withcock, in Leicestershire; and 8, Elizabeth, of Thomas Harrington of South Witham, in Lincolnshire, Esqrs.

* It may be presumed he lived some time at Hampsted near London; the arms and portraitures of him and Margaret, his wife, daughter of John lord Willoughby of Eresby, being finely painted in glass in an ancient house in that town.

SKIPWITH OF PRESTWOULD, LEICESTERSHIRE.

19. Sir William Skipwith, Knt. his eldest son, *Dominus de Cotes*, in Leicestershire, married Margaret, daughter of Roger Cave of Stanford, in Northamptonshire, Esq. by whom he had three sons; 1, Sir Henry; 2, George, who died without issue; 3, Thomas, who married ——, daughter of John Bluet of Halaston, in Lincolnshire, and left issue: also three daughters; 1, Jane, the wife of George, son and heir of George Throckmorton of Fulbrooke, in Oxfordshire, Esq. 2, Anne, of Edward, son and heir of Henry Pate of Eve-Kettleby, in Leicestershire, Esq. and 3, Elizabeth, of Sir John Pate of Sisonby, in Leicestershire, Bart.

I. Sir HENRY SKIPWITH, Knt. the eldest son, was seated at Prestwould in Leicestershire, and was advanced to the dignity of a baronet by King James I. he married the third daughter and co-heir of Sir Thomas Kempe of Kent, Knt. by whom he had four sons and two daughters; 1, William, who died V. P. without issue; 2, Sir Henry, successor to his father; 3, Thomas, who died without issue; 4, Sir Grey, of whom hereafter: also Elizabeth and Diana.

II. Sir HENRY SKIPWITH, Bart. eldest surviving son and successor to his father, died unmarried soon after him, whereupon the title and estate went to his next surviving brother,

III. Sir GREY SKIPWITH, Bart. who in the time of the rebellion in England, after the death of King Charles I. went with several other gentlemen over to Virginia, to avoid the usurper Cromwell, and there married, and left only one son,

IV. Sir WILLIAM SKIPWITH, Bart. who also married in Virginia, and in the year 1730 was about 60 years of age, and had eight children; and dying —— was succeeded in the title by his eldest son,

V. Sir GREY SKIPWITH, Bart. who also resided in Virginia.

VI. Sir WILLIAM SKIPWITH, Bart. his successor, died in Virginia in 1764, and was succeeded by

VII. Sir PEYTON SKIPWITH, Bart. who (I suppose) is the present baronet.

ARMS—Argent, three barrs, gules; in chief a greyhound currant, sable; collared, or.
CREST—On a wreath, a reel, proper.
SEAT—In Virginia.

SKIPWITH OF PRESTWOULD, LEICESTERSHIRE.

TABLE 47

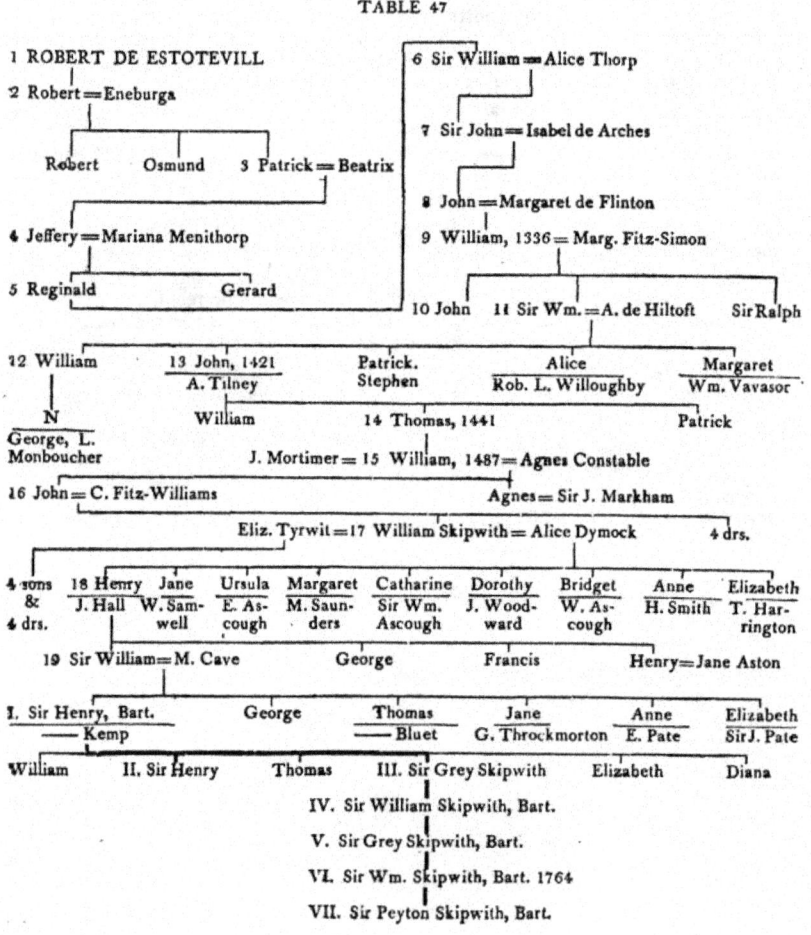

47. HARPUR of CALKE, DERBYSHIRE.

Created Baronet Sep. 8, 1626.

THIS family was originally seated at Chesterton in Warwickshire, of which place was Gilbert le Harpur, son of Roger, son of Hugh, son of Hugh, son of Richard; which last Hugh lived in the reign of Henry I. the above-named

5. Gilbert married Hawise, daughter and heir to Walter de Elmedon, and cousin and heir to Robert de Brock of Chesterton; by whom he had

6. Gilbert le Harpur, who lived in the time of Edw. I. he married Isolda, daughter of Henry Moton of Peckleton, in Leicestershire, by whom he had

7. Sir Robert le Harpur, Knt. who married Isabel, daughter of John Hercy, lord of Pillerton Hercy, in Warwickshire, by whom he had

8. John le Harpur, who was living 6 Edw. II. he married Elizabeth, daughter of —— Lisle of Moxhull, in the county of Warwick, by whom he had issue John and Richard.

9. John le Harpur married Joan, daughter of Richard Vernon of Harleston, in Staffordshire, Esq. he died without issue.

10. Richard le Harpur, his brother, was his heir, which Richard, by Alice his wife, daughter of Roger de Culy, had issue,

11. John le Harpur, who married Isabel, daughter of Sir Robert Appleby, Knt. from whom descended the Harpurs of Rushall in Staffordshire. The first of this family mentioned there was

12. Sir John Harpur of Rushall, who married Eleanor, daughter and heir of William Grober of Rushall,* by whom he had issue 1, William; 2, Richard, who was father of Sir George Harpur, Knt. who married Mildred, the daughter and heir of Nicholas Clifford; and 3, Henry, of whom hereafter.

13. William, the eldest son, was lord of Rushall, and married Margaret, daughter and heir of Henry Cook of Catthorp, in Leicestershire, Gent.† They left issue, 1, Sir John Harpur, Knt. 2, Humphrey, who married Elizabeth, daughter of —— Stokes, by whom he had issue Walter Harpur of Chinnor, in Oxfordshire, who by Mary his wife, daughter of Henry Blunt, left issue Thomas; which Thomas, by Cicely his wife, daughter of Robert Coleir of Darlaston, in Staffordshire, Esq. had is-

---

* He was son of Robert, who married Catharine, daughter and heir of William Bowles, son of William, who married Agnes, sister and heir of Sir Henry Hanbury, Knt. which William was son of William, son of Hugh, by Alice his wife, daughter and heir of Richard de Rushall of Rushall, in Staffordshire, Esq.

† In one of the windows of that church was painted in glass, argent, a lion rampant, within a bordure ingrailed, sable (Harpur) impaling, argent, a bend, and an annulet in the sinister point, azure (Cook) and under written, *Orate pro bono statu Willielmi Harpur et Margaretæ Uxoris Ejus.*

sue Edward Harpur, who married Dorothy, daughter of Thomas Parker of Kent, Esq. also a daughter Mary, who was the wife of Sir Thomas Shirley, Knt. Nicholas, third son of William, married Margaret, daughter and co-heir of Thomas Hadde of Sutton Valence, Esq. the widow of William Wright, and left issue a son John, who was of Cobham, in the reign of Queen Elizabeth, and left several children. The said William had also four daughters,‡ 1, Dorothy, the wife of Sir John Ferrers of Tamworth, in Staffordshire, Knt. 2, Anna, of John Whirley of Honesworth, in the same county, Esq. 3, ——, of Thomas Newham, Gent. and the youngest to William Cokaine, Esq.

14. Sir John Harpur aforesaid, the eldest son, left issue by Margaret his wife, daughter and one of the co-heirs of Sir John Bromley, Knt.

15. Robert, who had issue one daughter, ——, the wife of Sir Anthony Kingston, Knt. afterwards of Sir Richard Egerton, Knt. she died without issue, so that his two sisters became his heirs. Dorothy was the wife of Thomas Hord of Hord Park, Esq. who had one daughter, Frances, the wife of Thomas Farmour, but died without issue, by which Elizabeth, her aunt, became sole heir; which Elizabeth was the wife of William Leigh of Wellington, in Shropshire, Esq gentleman usher to King Henry VIII.

I now return to Henry Harpur, third son of Sir John, by Eleanor, daughter and heir of William Grober; which Henry was father or grandfather of Richard Harpur, Esq. one of the justices of the common pleas, temp. Eliz. who seated himself at Swerkston in the county of Derby:* he married Jane, daughter of George Findern of Findern, in Derbyshire, Esq. and heir to Thomas, her brother; and left issue two sons, Sir John and Sir Richard.†

‡ Hasted calls them the daughters of Nicholas.

* A monument in Swerkston church has this inscription:—Here under were buried the bodyes of Richard Harpur, one of the justices of the common bench at Westminster, and Jane his wife, sister and heir of and unto Thomas Fynderne of Fynderne, Esq. He died Jan. 29, anno 1573.

† 16 Sir Richard Harpur of Littleover, in Derbyshire, Knt. by Mary his wife, daughter of Thomas Reresby of Thribergh, in Yorkshire, Esq. had issue George and Francis, who died unmarried; also three daughters; Jane, the wife of Godfrey Thacker of Rapton, in Derbyshire, Esq. Elizabeth, of Jacinth Sacheverel of Morley, in the same county, Esq. and Mary.

17. Richard Harpur, eldest son of Sir Richard, married Elizabeth, daughter of John Hacker of Bridgford, in Nottinghamshire, Esq. by whom he had issue Richard, who died unmarried, and

18. John Harpur, rector of Morley, who married Mary, daughter of Paul Ballidon of Derby, Esq. by whom he had issue Richard, who died young; Elizabeth, the wife of Sir Samuel Sleigh of Etwal, in the county of Derby, Knt. Mary, and Joyce, who died unmarried; and by Mary, his second wife, daughter of Thomas, and sister of Sir Thomas Greseley of Drakelow, Bart. John Harpur of Littleover, Esq. and a daughter Dorothy; which

19. John married Mary, daughter of Edward Walker of Derby, by whom he had issue Richard Harpur of Littleover, Esq. and several other sons and daughters. Henry, third son of Richard, eldest son of Sir Richard Harpur of Littleover, as above, died unmarried; Joseph, of Eveley in Derbyshire, fourth son, married Dorothy, daughter of —— Pegg of Rodesley, in Derbyshire, Gent. had issue John and William, who died unmarried; also Dorothy, wife of Thomas Goodwin of Derby, Esq. William, fifth son, was a merchant in Plymouth; he died without issue. The above Richard, eldest son of Sir Richard, had also three daughters; Elizabeth, the wife of Robert Draper of Coland, in Derbyshire, Gent. Mary, who died unmarried, and Catharine, the wife of Henry Arden of Longcroft, in Staffordshire, Esq. George Harpur second son of Sir Richard Harpur of Littleover, before-mentioned, seated himself at Twyford in Derbyshire. He married ——, daughter of —— Vernon of Sudbury, and died Nov. 16, 1658, aged 64. He had issue George, Edward, John, and Richard, who died without issue, and two daughters;

HARPUR OF CALKE, DERBYSHIRE.

16. Sir John Harpur of Swerkston, Knt. eldest son of the judge, married Isabel, daughter of Sir George Pierpont of Holme, in Nottinghamshire, Knt. by whom he had issue Sir Richard, John Harpur of Bredsall, Esq. and Sir Henry Harpur of Calke, in Derbyshire, Bart. also five daughters; 1, Winifred, who died young; 2, Jane, the wife of Patrick Low of Denby, in Derbyshire, Esq. 3, Dorothy, of Sir John White of Tuxford, in Nottinghamshire, Knt. 4, Winifred, of John Brown of Stretton in the Fields, in Derbyshire, Esq. 5, Isabel, of Sir Philip Sherrard of Stapleford, in Leicestershire, Knt. he had four more sons; Francis, William, Thomas and George, who died unmarried. Sir John married to his second wife, Elizabeth, daughter of Sir Andrew Noel of Dalby, Knt. by whom he left no issue. He died Oct. 7, 1622.

17. Sir Richard Harpur of Swerkston, Knt. eldest son of Sir John, married Catharine, daughter of Sir Thomas Greseley of Drakelow, in Derbyshire, Knt. by whom he had issue Sir John Harpur of Swerkston, Knt.* who married Barbara, daughter and heir of Sir Henry Beaumont of Gracedieu, in Leicestershire; but died without issue. She re-married to Sir W. Dixie of Bosworth in Leicestershire, Bart. Dorothy, eldest daughter of Sir Richard, was the wife of Henry Gilbert of Locko, in Derbyshire. Catharine, second daughter, of Sir John Cooper of Thurgarton, in Nottinghamshire, Knt. John Harpur of Bredsall, second son of Sir John, eldest son of the judge, as before-mentioned, married Dorothy, daughter and sole heir to John Dethick of Bredsall, Esq. by whom he left issue Sir John Harpur of Swerkston, Knt. and Dorothy, wife of Sir John Fitzherbert of Norbury, in Derbyshire, Knt. She re-married to Sir John Shore of Derby, Knt. doctor in physic, and died March 16, 1666; but left no issue by either of her husbands.

Sir John Harpur first married Catharine, daughter and heir of Henry Howard, Esq.† third son of Thomas earl of Suffolk, by Elizabeth his wife, daughter and sole heir to William Basset of Blore, in Staffordshire, Esq. (who surviving Mr. Howard, was re-married to William duke of Newcastle). Sir John had issue by her Henry, who married Frances, daughter of Sir Jeffery Palmer, Bart. attorney-general to his Majesty King Charles II. and died without issue: in the life-time of his father, Frances, his widow, re-married to John, son of Sir Erasmus de la Fountain of Kirkby Bellere, in Leicestershire, Knt. Sir John married for his second wife Frances, daughter of William lord Willoughby of Parham. He died in 1677, leaving no issue: Frances, his second lady, re-married to Henry Kirkhouen, Baron Wotton and Earl of Bellamont, in the kingdom of Ireland, whom she survived; and thirdly,

---

Mary, the wife of John Alleyn of Greseley, Esq. Elizabeth, of John Dalton of Derby, Esq. George Harpur, eldest son of George, married Catharine, daughter of Edward Wardour of Nether Haven, in Wiltshire, Esq. She died in 1669, aged 28; he in 1672, aged 32. They had issue John Harpur, doctor in physic; Catharine, the wife of George Alleyne of Greseley, and Frances.

* In the books belonging to the commissioners for compositions with delinquents is the following entry:—Jan. 10, 1645, Sir John Harpur of Swarkston, in the county of Derby, Knt. to settle 110l. per ann. viz. 20l. upon the vicar of Barrow, 40l. per ann. upon the church of Tycknall, and 50l. per ann. upon the church of Repton, for which he is to be allowed 583l. and so his fine of 4583l. is reduced to 4000l.

This (in part) shews how this family suffered for their loyalty in those times: it also appears, by the catalogue of the lords and knights that compounded for their estates, that Sir John Harpur of Calke, Bt. paid also 578l. 18s for his composition.

† Dugdale's Baron. p. 280, 422.

to Henry Heveningham of Heveningham, in Suffolk, Esq. She died May 25, 1714, aged 71.* I now come to

I. Sir HENRY HARPUR of Calke, in Derbyshire, Bart. (so created anno 2 King Charles I.) third son of Sir John Harpur of Swerkston, Knt. aforesaid, which Sir Henry married Barbara, daughter of Sir Anthony Faunt of Foston, in Leicestershire, Esq. and widow of Sir Henry Beaumont of Gracedieu, in the same county, Bart. She died July 2, 1649, aged 68. He had issue by the said Barbara three sons; Sir John, Henry, a merchant in London, who died without issue, and William Harpur of Bilston, in Leicestershire: also six daughters; Elizabeth, the wife of Richard, younger son of Sir John Manley, clerk of the green cloth to King Charles I. 2, Jane, of Thomas Twyford, citizen of London; 3, Dorothy, of Sir Nicholas Wilmot of Osmaston, in Derbyshire, Knt. 4, Isabel, of Nicholas Hurt of Castern, in Staffordshire, Esq. 5, Barbara, of John Manley, youngest son to the before-named Sir John; and Catharine, who died unmarried.

William Harpur of Bilston aforesaid married Alice, daughter of William, son and heir of Sir Francis Coke of Trusley, in Derbyshire, Knt. by whom he had issue John Harpur of Bilston, and of Twyford, in Derbyshire, Esq. Wolston Harpur, citizen of London, who by Bathsuah his wife, daughter of William Bradford of Stoke Golden, in Leicestershire, had issue John, rector of Stanton, *juxta pontem*, in Derbyshire. Henry, third son of the above William, married Catharine, daughter of ———— Barbour of Tamworth, by whom he had issue William and John, who died without issue, and Henry: also three daughters; Mary, Catharine, and Dorothy. John Harpur of Bilston and Twyford, Esq. as before-mentioned, married Dorothy, youngest daughter of Sir John Harpur of Calke, Bart. by whom he had issue John, who died young; Dorothy, the wife of Richard Guile of Stoke Golden, in Leicestershire; Alice, Barbara, Elizabeth, and Mary, who all died young: Anne, sixth daughter, was the wife of Henry Franceys of Derby, Gent. and Frances, of Robert Revil of Carnfield, in Derbyshire, Esq.

II. Sir JOHN HARPUR of Calke, Bart. son and heir of Sir Henry, married Susan, daughter to ———— West, citizen of London, by whom he had issue five sons, Sir John, Henry, Richard, Charles, and Edward, who all (excepting the eldest) died unmarried: also five daughters; Barbara and Elizabeth died unmarried; Jane was the wife of Henry Dyson of Seagrave, in Leicestershire, Esq. Susannah, of James Dean, rector of Halloughton in Leicestershire, and Dorothy, of John Harpur of Twyford aforesaid, Esq. He died in 1669, aged 53, and was succeeded in dignity and estate by

III. Sir JOHN, his eldest son (to whom Sir John Harpur of Swerkston, Knt. before-mentioned, who died in 1667, and leaving no issue, gave his large estate). He married Anne, second daughter of William lord Willoughby of Parham, by whom he had issue Sir John and a daughter Anne, the wife of Borlace Warren of Stapleford, in Nottinghamshire, Esq. He died in 1681, and was succeeded by his son and heir,

* Mon. inscrip. in Swerkston church.

HARPUR OF CALKE, DERBYSHIRE.

TABLE 48.

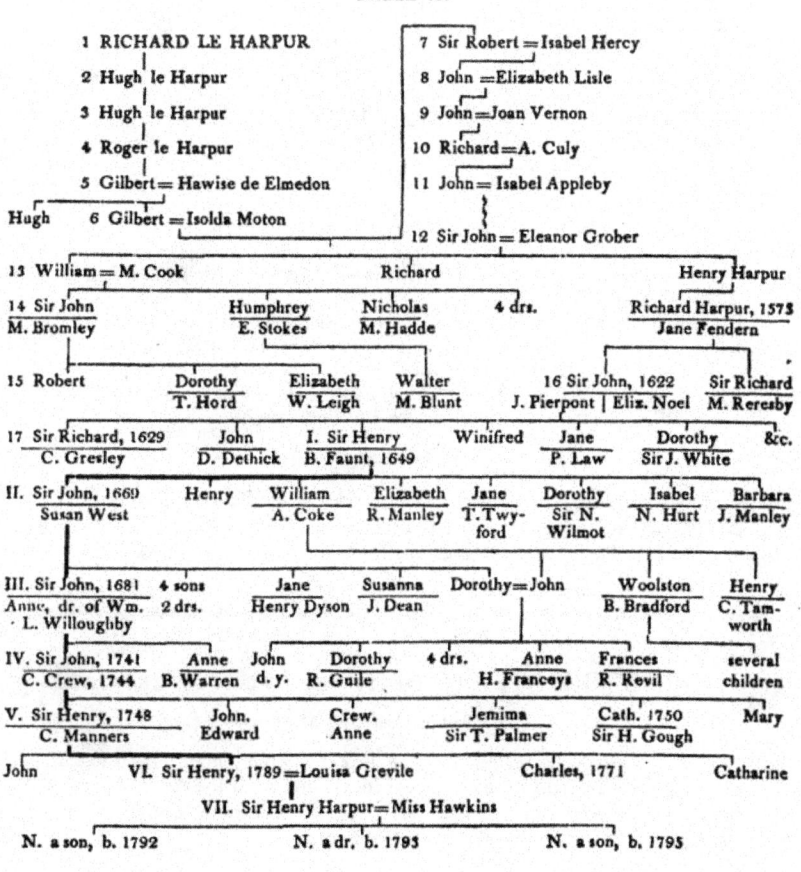

IV. Sir JOHN HARPUR of Calke, Bart. born March 23, 1679, who married Catharine, youngest daughter and co-heir of Thomas lord Crew of Stene, by his second wife, Anne, daughter and co-heir of Sir William Airmin of Osgodby, in Lincolnshire, Bart. and widow of Sir Thomas Wodehouse of Kimberley, in Norfolk, Bart. by whom he had issue Sir Henry, John, Edward, who died in 1761, and Crew, who died in 1724-5: also four daughters; Anne, who died an infant; Jemima, the wife of Sir Thomas Palmer of Carlton, in Northamptonshire, Bart. Catharine, of Sir Henry Gough of Edgbaston, in Warwickshire, Bart. she died in 1740; and Mary. Sir John died suddenly at Calke in Derbyshire, June 24, 1741, leaving behind him a most extraordinary character for charity, religion, honour, and integrity: he was succeeded in dignity and estate by his eldest son,

V. Sir HENRY HARPUR, Bart. who married Caroline, daughter of John duke of Rutland (by Lucy, sister of Bennet earl of Harborough) by whom he hath three sons and one daughter, Caroline, the wife of Adam Hay, Esq. (she had 30,000*l.*) 1, John, who died young; 2, Sir Henry, his successor; 3, Charles, who was a major in the 38th regiment of foot, and died in 1770. Sir Henry was elected for Worcester in 1744, and for Tamworth in the next parliament; and died June 7, 1748: his widow, who is since dead, became the wife of Sir Robert Burdett, Bart. He was succeeded by his son,

VI. Sir HENRY HARPUR, Bart. who was member of parliament for the county of Derby, and married Louisa-Augusta Grevile, eldest daughter of Francis earl Brooke and Warwick, by whom he had one son,

VII. Sir HENRY HARPUR, Bart. born May 13, 1763, and married Miss Hawkins in 1792, by whom he has two sons and one daughter.

ARMS—Argent, a lion rampant, and border engrailed, sable.
CREST—On a wreath a boar passant, or; collared with a ducal crown, gules.
SEATS—At Calke, and Swerkston, both in Derbyshire.

---

48. SEBRIGHT of Besford, Worcestershire.

Created Baronet Dec. 20, 1626.

THE Sebrights were originally of Sebright Hall in Much Baddow, in Essex, where they were seated in the time of Hen. II. and until the reign of Hen. VIII.*

1. William Sebright of Sebright Hall, married Elizabeth, daughter and heir of Sir Henry de Ashe, Knt. by whom he had

---

* Morant's Essex, vol. II. p. 19.

2. Stephen Sebright, the father of

3. Walter Sebright, whose son,

4. Peter Sebright, lived in 1294, and had two sons; Giles of Sebright Hall, and

5. Mabell Sebright, who had an estate called Brooke's Place in Much Baddow, 22 Edw. I. as appears by deed: he married Catharine, daughter and heir of Ralph Cowper of Blackshall in the parish of Wolverley, which seems to have brought the family into the county of Warwickshire. From Mabell descended

6. John Sebright* of Blackshall, who lived in 6 Henry VII. This John sold 30 acres of land, called Brookes, lying in Much Baddow in Essex, to Robert Arthure of Stepley, in Essex, 1492: his son

7. Humphrey of Blackshall, in Wolverestone or Wolverley, married Catharine, daughter of —— Ridge of Ridge, in Staffordshire, and was father of

8. Edward, who married Joyce, daughter of William Grosvenor of Bubington, in Staffordshire, Esq. by whom he had a daughter Eleanor, the wife of Thomas Austin of Oxley, in Staffordshire, Esq. and two sons, John and William, who was town clerk of London 16 Eliz.† Habington calls him the loving father of the poor of Wolvereslow‡ and the neighbouring parishes, whose large gifts are recorded in Wolverley church. § He married ——, daughter of —— Goldston of London;

---

* In Mr. Habington's MS. survey of Worcestershire, wrote about 1630, he mentions the Sebrights in Wolverley as of long standing in the county of Worcester, and names, out of an old register of the priory of Worcester, John Sebright, as possessed of lands in Wolverley 6 Edw. I.

† Stow's Survey of London, vol. II. B. 5, p. 163.   ‡ Habington's MS. survey of Worcestershire.

§ In the north aisle of Wolverley church is a table with these arms and inscription:—1, Argent three cinquefoils, sable; 2, Azure, ten besants; 3, Or, a saltire, gules, debruised with a fesse, sable; the fourth as the first.

Psalm cxii. verse 6. *The righteous shall be had in an eternal remembrance.*

A briefe memoriall of the charitable actes and deedes of that worshipfull deceased christian William Sebright of London, Esquyre, a patern of religious pietie to incite and move the mindes of others in the blissinges of God uppon theyre substance to bee good to the poore; who by assurance of lawe hath conveyghed over in his lyfe-time to the paryshe of Wolverley, in almes of 14 pennyes weekely for eaver for the provision and buying of fourteene penny fyne wheaten loafes, the which said wheaten breade uppon eavery sabath daie duringe the tyme of divine service or sermon to bee placed on the communion table, and after the end thearof to bee distributed and delivered to fowreteene of the most meanest and neediest inhabitantes of the sayde paryshe of Wolverley, and the lyke almes of breade aforesayd, and in manner before-mentioned is accordingly assured and conveyghed over unto thease severall neere adjoyninge parishes, viz. Kyderminster, Kinuard, Ould Swinford, Chartesley, Corbet, Alveley and Bewdley, to the same use to continue for eaver; and to this parysh clearke for the tyme beeinge for bringinge the said breadye and placinge the same on the communion table, and deliveringe the same to the poore 10s. for eaver: and further, in this paryshe of Wolverley, beeing the paryshe whearein hee was borne, the sayd worthy gentellman hathe caused a free gramar schoole to bee erected, and made of stone, and hathe gyven to the mayntenance of a schoole master theare 20l. per annum for eaver.

The sayd worthy gentlellman by hys last will and testament hathe also assured to and with the sayde three poundes and eight shillings for the providinge of the aforesayde breade so heeretofore to be bestowed severally upon each and eavery the aforesayde seavne severall paryshes, unto the paryshe of Wolverley, a certaine overplus of mony yee.ly, accrewinge and arisinge out of the particular landes by hym assured and conveyghed to be imployed by certaine feffees by his said will nominated and appointed, and theyre successors, as by them shall be thought fit to bee equally imployed and distributed to good and charitable uses within the saide parishe of Wolverley, as the repayringe of Wolverley church and the foure bridges in that parishe, or the increase of the scholmaster's wages yf theare shal bee good cause,

secondly, Elizabeth, daughter of James Morley of London, relict of Thomas Bourcher (by whom she had Sir James Bourcher, father of Elizabeth, wife of Oliver Cromwell); but dying without issue, in Lombard Street, Oct. 27, 1620, he left a considerable estate to his nephew, son of his brother John, who was created a baronet.*

9. John Sebright of Blackshall, Esq. son and heir of Edward, married Anne, daughter of Richard Bullingham, Esq. by whom he had William, who died without issue, and Edward; and several daughters, Judith, the wife of Edward Broad of Dunelme parish, in Worcestershire, Esq. Sarah,† wife of Thomas lord Coventry, keeper of the great seal; and Anne, of John Burnell of London, Esq. After the decease of this John Sebright, Esq. his relict re-married ‡ to Thomas Walshe of Stockton, in Worcestershire, Esq.

I. EDWARD SEBRIGHT of Besford, Esq. son and heir, was§ sheriff of the county of Worcester 19 James I. and advanced to the dignity of a baronet 2 Charles I. He was looked upon as a great royalist, for which he was obliged to pay 1809*l*. composition for his estate to the sequestrators.‖ He married first Theodocia, daughter of Gerard Whorwood of Compton, in Staffordshire, Esq. by whom he had William, who died S. P. John, aged 16, 1627; Elizabeth,¶ wife of Sir John Repington of Amington, in Warwickshire, Knt. and others. Sir Edward married secondly Elizabeth, eldest daughter of the first Earl of Manchester, relict of Sir Lewis Mansel of Margam, in Glamorganshire, Bart.

II. Sir EDWARD SEBRIGHT, Bart. his son and successor, married Elizabeth,* daughter of Sir Richard Knightly of Fawesley, in Northamptonshire, K. B. (by Anne, his second wife, daughter of Sir William Courteen, Knt.) by whom he had two sons, Sir Edward, and Richard of Croxton, in Norfolk, who died without issue, 1722, and left his estate to his nephew, Edward, hereafter-mentioned.

III. Sir EDWARD SEBRIGHT, Bart. who succeeded his father in title and estate, married Anne, daughter and heir of Thomas Saunders of Beechwood, in Hertfordshire, Esq. and Ellen his wife, daughter and heir of Robert Sadleir of Sopwell, in that county, Esq. by whom he had two sons and two daughters; 1, Sir Thomas Saunders, his successor, and 2, Edward of Croxton, in Norfolk, to whom his uncle left his estate, who was barbarously murdered Sep. 20, 1723, near Calais, as he was travelling with some English gentlemen; to whose memory a monument was erected on the spot where this villainy was committed.† Anne, the el-

---

and hee will deserve itt, as by the sayd feffees for the tyme beeinge, or the more part of them shal bee thought fitt. Item, hee hathe lastly, at his deceese, given tenne pounds to the poore of thys parishe, and as much to many other of the aforesayd, which by a generall consent of theause parishes is set forthe to the best profitt, and the benefitt yeerely bestowed on the poore.

This guift aforesaid of bread began to take effect the first Sundaye after the feast daye of All Saintes, beeinge in hys lyfe tyme in each and eavery of the parishes abovesayd. Anno 1618.

* Habington's Worcest. MS.   † Collins's Peerage, vol. III. p. 503.   ‡ Visit. of Worcest. 1683, fo. 89.
§ Fuller's Worthies in Worcest.   ‖ See list of those that compounded in letter S.   ¶ Dugdale's Warw. vol. I. p. 1143.   * St. George's Visit. of Northtun. p. 127, and Bridge's Northamptonshire, p. 65.

† ✢ Ad Annum MDCCXXIII Sept. xx° et quarta circiter post meridiem hora dum fatali peregrinandi studio adductus ad Lutetias usque Parisiorum proficisceretur Edvardus Seabright Armiger illus-

dest was the wife of Sir Charles Buck of Hanby Grange, in Lincolnshire, Bart. and the other of John Coke of White Parish, in Wilts, Esq. This Sir Edward died in the 36th year of his age, Dec. 1702, and was buried in the chancel at Besford, near Parshore, in Worcestershire. His lady surviving him married secondly Charles Lyttleton, Esq. elder brother to Sir Thomas Lyttleton of Hagley, in Worcestershire. Bart.

IV. Sir THOMAS-SAUNDERS SEBRIGHT, Bart. who succeeded his father in title and estate, was of Jesus College, Oxford; and in Aug. 1732,* was created doctor of laws, with the Earl of Litchfield, Lord Gower, and Watkin Williams Wynne, Esq. by the university in full convocation: he represented the county of Hertford in parliament from 1 George I. till his death. He married ———, daughter of Sir Francis Dashwood of Wicomb, in Oxfordshire, Bart. who died in Charles Street, Berkeley Square in 1771 or 1772. He died April 12. 1736, leaving two sons, Sir Thomas, his successor, and John.

V. Sir THOMAS SEBRIGHT, the eldest son, succeeded his father in title and estate, and dying unmarried Oct. 25, 1765, was succeeded by his only brother,

VI. Sir JOHN SEBRIGHT of Beechwood, Bart. a lieutenant-general of his majesty's forces, colonel of the royal Irish regiment of foot, and M. P. for the city of Bath. He married in June 1766, Sarah, daughter of Edward Knight of Wolverley, in the county of Worcester, Esq. by whom he had Sir John Saunders Sebright, the present baronet; 2, Thomas, a lieutenant-colonel, who died in 1795; 3, Harriot, the wife of the Hon. Henry Lascelles, M. P. for Yorkshire; 4, Edward-Amherst-Saunders, captain in the army; 5, Mary. Sir John died in March 1794, and was succeeded by his eldest son,

VII. Sir JOHN-SAUNDERS SEBRIGHT, Bart. who in Aug. 1793 married Harriet, daughter of Richard Crofts of Harling, in Norfolk, Esq. by whom he has three daughters; 1, Frederica-Anne-Saunders; 2, Emily, and 3, Caroline.

ARMS—Argent, three cinquefoils, sable.
CREST—On a wreath a tyger, seiant, argent; maned and crowned, or.
SEATS—At Besford Court in Worcestershire, and Beechwood in Hertfordshire.

---

trissimi Thomæ Seabright apud Anglos Barti. Frater unicus septem hoc in Loco inermemet imparatum Adolescentem Adorti Latrones privatum Pecuniis Vulneribus Perfossum Corpore Vita tandem Spoliavere Occubuerunt una longo et pio avorum stemmate præclarus Henricus Mompessen Armig. Johannes Davis et Johs. Lock, generosi orti sanguine et inferioris subsellii duo Anglus alter et alter Gallus in honesto nimium fato correpti omnes.

* Peerage of England by Collins, vol. IV. p. 368.

SEBRIGHT OF BESFORD, WORCESTERSHIRE.

TABLE 49.

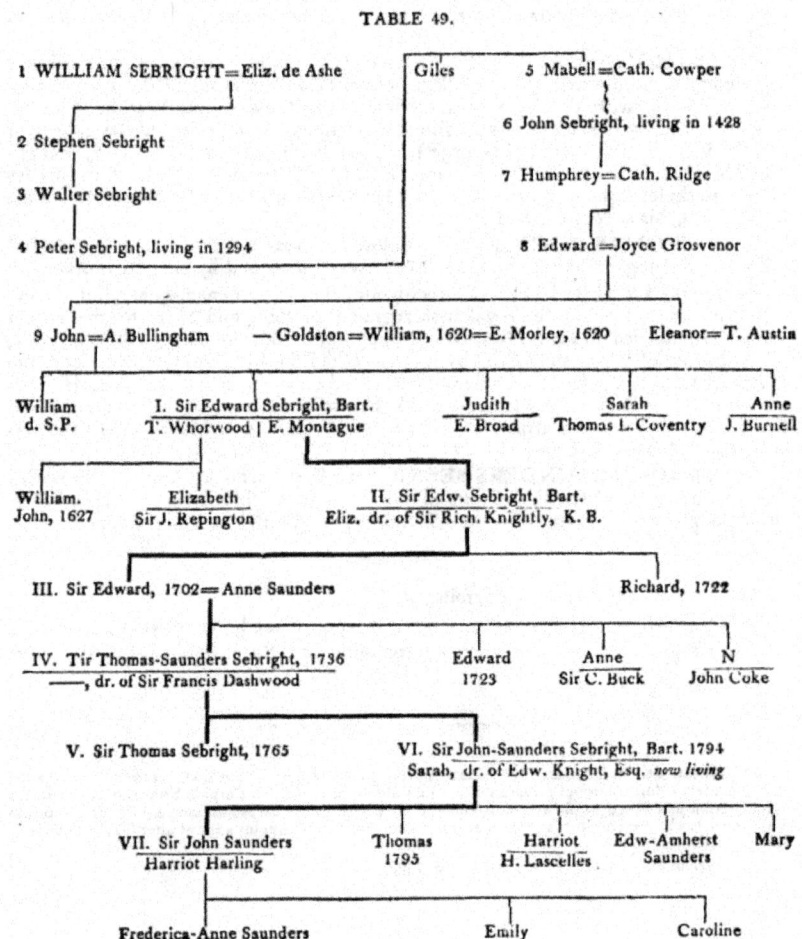

49. DERING of Surenden-Dering, Kent.

Created Baronet Feb. 1, 1626.

WOTTON, in his Baronetage, vol. II. p. 13, gives the origin of this family from an account which was sent by themselves to the editor of the former edition of it in 1727, as follows:—Dering is a Saxon word, and signifies terror; and the horse, which is the crest of the family, was the arms of the chief Saxons, and particularly of Hengist himself, and of all the Kings of Kent successively. In the *Textus Roffensis* we find, that Diering Miles was a witness to a deed, by which King Etheluff gave certain lands in Cucolastone to the church of Rochester in 880: and he is said to be descended in a direct line from Ethelward king of Diera, whose father, Oswald, was slain by Penda the Mercian in 642; and Ethelward, being then an infant not four years old, was deprived of his kingdom by Osway, his bastard uncle, and forced to fly into Kent, where his posterity were called the Dierans, as coming from that country. From this Diering Miles to the Norman invasion, are reckoned seven generations, the last of which was called *Dering filius Syredi*, who was slain with King Harold at Battle in Sussex. He was father of Syred de Ferningham, who was the father of Leofget, who upon the death of William the Norman, took up arms with Odo, bishop of Baieux, in behalf of Duke Robert; but being over-powered, he retired with his family into Normandy, where he had two sons, Normanus Dering, so called from the place of his birth, and Robert, so called from Robert duke of Normandy. This Normanus Fitz-Dering married Matilda, only sister and heir of William de Ipres, earl of Kent, and King Stephen's general; and was himself vice-comes Cantii, a place of the highest trust and honour in those times.

At the battle of Lincoln, where King Stephen was taken prisoner, this gentleman was slain near the king's person, endeavouring to rescue his majesty; and being found after the battle with his shield covered with blood, his posterity were allowed to add to their paternal coat of arms three torteauxes in chief, in memory of his loyalty and bravery.

Hasted, in his History of Kent, says, vol. III. p. 228, What authorities the family may have had for many of the above circumstances I cannot learn, the only account I have been able to gather from the family papers and manuscripts, in the Dering library, and from other evidence, is as follows:—that the family of Dering is descended from *Norman de Morinis*, whose ancestor, *Vitalis Fitz-Osbert*, lived in the reign of King Henry II. He died in the reign of King Richard I. having married Keneburga, daughter of Deringus, descended from Norman Fitz-Dering, sheriff of this county in King Stephen's reign, who married Matilda, sister and heir of William de Ipre, earl of Kent, and held lands in several places in it; and was a descendant of that Dering who is mentioned in the book of Doomsday, as holding lands in Farningham, in the time of the Saxons, before the conquest. They had issue

1. Deringus de Morinis, who married Elveva, sister and heiress of Alanus de Hayton; and their son,

2. Deringus Fitz-Deringus was the first who deserted the name of Morinis. His son,

3. Wymund Fitz-Dering, was possessed of lands in Farningham, and, as well as his father, was a benefactor to the abbey of Boxley, wherein they were both buried.* His son,

4. Richard Fitz-Dering, *filius Deringi*, was of Heyton, and died in the latter end of the reign of King Henry III. leaving issue by Claricia Shillinghelde, his wife,

5. Peter Dering, who held lands in the counties of Kent, Essex, and Leicester. He married Agnes, daughter and heiress of Ralph de Badlesmere, by whom he had

6. Richard Dering, whose son,

7. Sir John Dering of Westbrooke, Knt. died in 1364.† He was father of

8. Sir Richard Dering of Heyton, Knt. lieutenant of Dover Castle in the reign of King Richard II. who married Joan, sister of Sir Arnold St. Leger, Knt. and lies buried in Lyd church;‡ whose son,

9. John Dering of Westbrooke, Esq. married Christian, eldest daughter and co-heir of John Haut, Esq. and died in 1425.§ He had two sons, of whom

10. Richard Dering, the eldest, was of Surenden, and was twice married; first to the daughter and heir of —— Bertyn, and secondly to Agnes, daughter of —— Eyton of Eyton, in the county of Salop. He died in 1481, and was buried the chapel of the Virgin Mary, which he had re-built, as appears by his arms at the

---

* He bore for his arms, Or, *a fesse sable, in chief three torteauxes,* as his descendants did for some time afterwards; the family of Morinis bearing Or, *a saltire, sable.*

† His arms being *a fesse, in chief three roundells,* being carved in stone on the roof of the cloysters at Canterbury.   ‡ Weever, p. 294.

§ He lies buried in the south chancel of Pluckley church, being the chapel of the blessed Virgin Mary, rebuilt by his son. His grave-stone has his figure in brass, clad in armour, with sword and spurs; his head resting on his crest, mantled, being a horse; and his feet on a horse couchant, with his epitaph round it.

Philpot, in Pluckley, p. 276, says, John Dering, Esq. married Christian, daughter and co-heir of James Haut of Pluckley, in Kent, Esq. (by Joan, daughter and heir of John Surrenden, Esq. and Agnes his wife, daughter and heir of William de Pluckley) and so became possessor of Pluckley. Now, if you will enquire where lay the ancient land of Dering, if my assertion might be credited, I should affirm, that it was at Stamford by Hithe, where they were lords of some part of the little manor of Heyton; for by an old roll I find, that Normanus de Morinis married Kineburga, daughter and heir of Deringus; and his son, as was customary in those times, called himself Deringus de Morinis, and matched with Elveva, sister and heir of Alanus de Heyton, and so was invested in the propriety of the manor of Heyton, from whom it successively came down to Richard Fitz-Dering, who was son of Dering, and great-grand-child to this man, who was the first who deserted the sirname de Morinis, and assumed that of Dering; and died possessed of the manor of Heyton 42 Henry III. and from this Richard Fitz-Dering is Sir Edward Dering, Bart. now lineally extracted, who is the present Lord of Pluckley and Surrenden-Dering, where Sir Edward Dering, Knt. and Bart. not many years since deceased, raised that elegant structure, as eminent for its magnificence and beauty, as it is for its contrivance and curiosity.

bottom of the arches.* He left issue by his second wife four sons; John of Surenden; Richard, monk and cellarer of Christ Church, Canterbury;† James, and William, who was of Petworth in Sussex, and ancestor of the Derings of that place, and of the county of Hants.

11. John Dering, the eldest son, was of Surenden, which in his time, from their long possessions of it, acquired the name of Surenden-Dering. He died in 1517, having married Julian, sister of Sir John Darrell of Colehill, Knt. who lies buried with him in the south aisle of this church.‡ They had issue two sons, Nicholas and Richard Dering, who was lieutenant of Dover Castle, and the five ports under five lord wardens, and died in 1556;§ also two daughters: which

12. Nicholas Dering succeeded his father at Surenden, and died possessed of it in 1518, having married Alicia, daughter and heir of William Betenham of Cranbrook, Esq.‖ by whom he had four daughters and one son,

13. John Dering, who was of Surenden, where he resided in the reign of King Henry VIII. and died in 1550. He married Margaret, daughter of John Brent, Esq. by whom he had five sons and four daughters.¶

---

* His grave-stone had the portraitures of himself and his two wives on it, in brass, both which were remaining in Weever's time.

† He gave the hangings of rich arras, which for many years afterwards adorned the choir of Canterbury cathedral, on which was, in many parts, the device of his name, a *deer* and a *ring*; and this legend, *Richardus Dering hujus ecclesiæ commonachus & celerarius me fieri fecit, Anno Dom. milesimo quingentissimo undecimo*: and there are likewise six embroidered cushions given for the priors' seat; and afterwards for the stalls of the dean and prebendaries, on which were worked the arms of Dering, impaling both Bertyn and Eyton; by which it should seem, that they were given by the cellarer's father, John Dering of Surenden, Esq.

‡ He was taken out of his house at Lyd, in this county, and carried prisoner into France, whence he ransomed himself. In 1490 he was admitted into the society of Modenden in Kent.
In the Surenden library is the following deed, which shews the tenor of those pardons and indulgenties. It is as follows:—Brother Richard, of the house of Motynden, of the order of the holy trinity, and of the redemption of captives, who are imprisoned for the faith of Jesus Christ, by the Pagans, sendeth greeting: We certify, that whereas many of the Roman pontiffs have endowed all and singular the co-brethren and co-sisters of our aforesaid order with many privileges, especially in that our co-brethren and co-sisters may make choice for themselves of a fit priest for a confessor, who may absolve them from all matters not reserved to the apostolic see; and once in their lives, even from all matters whatsoever so reserved, and concerning which the see itself is of course to be consulted; and that each confrere shall have a certificate of the said fraternity, and shall not be denied ecclesiastical sepulture, of whatever death he may die, as well in the time of an enterdict as otherwise, unless he shall be excommunicated by name, &c. And whereas John Dering of Surenden-Dering, Esq. has taken his fraternity in the manner of a confrere, and has become a benefactor to comply with the tenor of the apostolic letters; therefore we associate him in his life, as well as in death, together with all our friends alive and dead, in all masses and prayers, and suffrages of our religion aforesaid. Dated under the seal of our confraternity aforesaid, Anno Dom. 1494. *Hasted's Hist. Kent, vol. II. p.* 391.
The brass of his grave-stone is gone, but that on her's remains. The inscription—Julian Deryng, gentlewoman, obt. Feb. 4, 1626.

§ He married Benedicta, daughter of —— Brockhall of Thumham, who lies buried with him, under an arch in the above aisle, having had his portraiture in brass on his stone, now gone.

‖ They lie buried in the south chancel. The brass of their portraitures, with those of their five children, as well as his shield of arms remains.

¶ The inscription of John Dering, and Margaret his wife, in brass, is on his grave-stone, with his effigy, kneeling on a cushion, in his surcoat of arms, bare-headed, in his own hair, having had once an

14. Richard Dering, Esq. the eldest, succeeded him at Surenden, and dying in 1612, aged 82, was buried in the chancel there,* as was his wife Margaret, daughter of William Twysden of East Peckham, Esq. by whom he had five sons and three daughters; of whom

15. Sir Anthony Dering, Knt. the eldest son, succeeded to Surenden, and dying in 1636, aged 78, was buried in the same chancel here, having been twice married; first to Mary, daughter of Sir Henry Goring, Knt. who died in 1588, and was buried near him, her inscription in brass remaining on her grave-stone, as does that of her only child, Jane, who died unmarried in 1617; secondly, Frances, daughter of Sir Robert Bell, Knt. chief baron of the exchequer, by whom he had six sons and two daughters.

I. EDWARD, the eldest, was knighted Jan. 22, 1618; made lieutenant of Dover Castle, and created a baronet on Feb. 1, 1626, and in the 16th of that reign one of the knights in parliament for this county: he was a man of parts and learning, his vanity to shew which induced him to present to the house of commons a bill for extirpating bishops, deans, and chapters, which he did from the gallery, with the two verses of Ovid, the application of which was said to be his greatest motive:

Cuncta prius tentanda sed immedicabile vulnus
Ense recidendum est, ne pars sincera trahatur.

His repentance and apology for this conduct offended the republicans so much, that he was declared a delinquent by the common-wealth; but escaping to the king, he had the command of a regiment of horse, which post illness made him relinquish, and retiring with his wife and children to one of his farm-houses, he there died on June 22, 1644, and was buried in the family chancel. During his continuance with the king his whole estate was confiscated, his newly-furnished house was four several times plundered by the parliament's soldiers, his goods and stock were all seized and took away, his farm-houses and fences ruined and destroyed, his woods and timbers felled; so that few suffered more than he did for his inconsistent conduct.

He published a volume of his speeches in parliament, a manuscript copy of which is in the British Museum, among the Harleian MSS.

He was the founder of the library at Surenden, for which he collected a great number of books, charters, and curious manuscripts; and caused others to be transcribed with no small labour and expence, and deposited in it, among which were the registers and chartularies of several of the dissolved monasteries in this coun-

---

altar tomb here, long since removed. She was sister and heiress of Thomas, and cousin and heiress of Robert Brent of Wellsborough, Esq. She was secondly the wife of John Moore of Benenden, Esq. by whom she had children, and died in 1562, and was buried near her first husband. Of the sons by John Dering, Anthony, the second, was of Charing; Edward, the third, died without issue; John, the fourth son, was of Egerton, where his descendants continued many years; Christopher, the fifth, was a posthumous child. He was of Wickens in Charing, which remains in his posterity at this time.

* The figures of himself and wife, kneeling at an altar, in brass, remain on their grave-stone. Their sons were Anthony, Thomas, Twysden, George, and Edward.

ty, and a series of deeds and muniments relating not only to the family of Dering, but to others connected with it: but most of these valuable manuscripts have been unwarily, not many years since, dispersed into other hands. The different characters given of him may be seen in Wotton's Baron. vol. II. p. 17, and in Peck's. Desid. Curios. vol. II. b. 14, 19, 20.

He married three wives; first Elizabeth, daughter of Sir Nicholas Tufton, afterwards Earl of Thanet: she died in 1622, having had by him an only son, Anthony, who died in 1620, aged 14. Secondly, Anne, third daughter of Sir John Ashburnham of Sussex, Knt. who died in 1628, aged 23: by her he had one son, Edward, his successor, and a daughter Elizabeth, the wife of Sir John Darell of Calehill, Knt. Thirdly, Unton, daughter of Sir Ralph Gibbes of Warwickshire, Knt. who died in 1676, by whom he left two sons; Henry, to whom he gave Pevington; and Edward and two daughters.* He was succeeded in title and estate by his eldest son by his second wife,

II. Sir EDWARD, then a minor, who afterwards represented the county of Kent in parliament in the 12th year of Charles II. and was one of the commissioners of the Treasury: he died in 1684, aged 59, having married Mary, daughter of Daniel Harvey of Combe, in Surrey, Esq. who died in 1704, aged 75 (one of the brothers of the famous Dr. Harvey);† by whom he had five sons and five daughters.‡ He was succeeded in title and estate by his eldest son,

III. Sir EDWARD DERING, Bart. who represented the county of Kent in parliament in 31 and 32 Charles II. and dying in 1689, aged 39, was buried in the south chancel, as was his wife, Elizabeth, eldest daughter of Sir William Cholmeley of Whitby, in Yorkshire, Bart. who died in 1704, aged 47, leaving issue three sons and one daughter.*

---

* William, the second son, died in 1735; Daniel, the third, died without issue; and Cecilia, the daughter, was the wife of George Scott of Scott's Hall.

* Edward, the second son, commonly called *Red Ned*, was knighted, and was a merchant in London; and married Dorcas, daughter of Sir Robert Barkham. He died without male issue. Of the daughters, Dorothy was the wife of Thomas English of Buckland, in Maidstone; and Frances, of Thomas Cowper.

† There is a monument erected to their memories in the south chancel. Of her I had the following anecdote from a respectable clergyman in this county:—That Daniel Harvey, her father, was an eminent citizen of London, and a great loyalist at the death of Charles I. and had this Mary, his only daughter, and heir of all his wealth. At the same time he had an apprentice in the house, his first cousin, who found an opportunity of marrying the daughter clandestinely, and had bedded with her twelve months before the marriage was discovered, which was occasioned by her father's intention of marrying her to Sir Edward Dering: on which he found means to get the marriage dissolved, and obtained testimonials for it, not only from Bishop Juxton, but from the most eminent civilians of that time. Two of their opinions were—one, that the young man's father was great uncle to her, and he being dead, his son represented him, and consequently was great uncle to her: the other, that it was so notorious a breach of honesty in him, that no state should suffer so bad an example to be countenanced.

Some years ago the late Mr. Eliab Harvey, king's council, found this relation, with the above-mentioned opinions, in a black box, among his mother's papers. *Hasted's Kent, vol. III.*

‡ Viz. Sir Edward, his successor; Charles, auditor of Ireland, who married ——, daughter of —— and relict of the Lord Blaney; Daniel, a colonel in Ireland, who married Helen, daughter of Sir John Percival of Burton, in Yorkshire; John, and Robert: Elizabeth, the wife of Sir Robert Southwell; Mary, of Sir Thomas Knatchbull, Bart. Anne, of Wortley Whorwood of Dentons; Catharine, first of Sir John Percival, and secondly of Col. Butler; and Jane died unmarried.

IV. Sir CHOLMELEY DERING, Bart. the eldest son, succeeded his father, and represented the county in parliament in the 4th and 9th of Queen Anne: he was killed in a duel, May 19, 1711, aged 32,† having married Mary, daughter and sole heir of Edward Fisher, Esq. who died in 1707, aged 20. By her he had two sons, Edward and Cholmeley, who died in 1768, unmarried.

V. Sir EDWARD DERING, Bart. the eldest son, represented the county of Kent in the four first parliaments of George II. He inherited Surenden-Dering, the mansion of which he much improved, inclosing the park with a brick-wall, and resided there with much hospitality; and died in London, greatly lamented by the county in general, for his many amiable and good qualities, on April 15, 1762.

He married first in 1728, Elizabeth, daughter and co-heir of Edward Henshaw of Eltham, Esq. who died in 1735, leaving issue two sons; Edward, born in 1732, and Daniel, who died in 1760: secondly in 1735, Mary, daughter of Charles Fotherly of Barham, Esq. and widow of Henry Mompesson, Esq. (a young widow with 30,000*l.*) who died in 1775; by whom he had issue Charles Dering of Barham, Esq. who married Eliz. daughter of Sir Thomas Farnaby, Bt. Thomas Dering of London, Esq. and Mary, the wife of Robert D'Arcy, now Sir Rob. Hildyard, Bart. He died in 1762, and was succeeded by his eldest son by his first wife,

VI. Sir EDWARD DERING, late Bart. who was elected in five successive parliaments for New Romney in Kent: he married first in 1755 Selina, daughter and co-heiress of Sir Robert Farnese of Waldershare, in Kent, Bart. who died in 1757; by whom he had a son Edward, born in 1757, and a daughter Selina, the wife of Dr. Dealtry, in Ireland. Sir Edward married secondly, in 1765, Deborah, only daughter of John Winchester of Nethersole, in Kent. Esq. by whom he had four sons and three daughters; 1, Cholmeley, now colonel of a regiment of light dragoons, called the New Romney fencibles, the two first troops of which were raised by Sir Edward Dering, and the corporation of New Romney, in April 1794; and which, in April 1795, were, by its present commander, who is a member of the corporation of New Romney (with the approbation and assistance of government) completed to a regiment of six troops, and received the honour of the additional title of his royal highness the Duke of York's name (then commander in chief in Great Britain) and was called the New Romney (or Duke of York's own) Fencible Light Dragoons. Col. Dering married Charlotte-Elizabeth, daughter of Sir Joseph Yates, Knt. late one of the judges of the court of common pleas, by whom he has one son, Cholmly-Edward-John. 2, Robert-Charles, who died in May 1795, first lieutenant on board his majesty's frigate Iphigena, in the West Indies; 3, George, who married his cousin Elizabeth, daughter of Charles Dering; 4, Harry, who died an infant: 1, Elizabeth, the wife of Daniel Byam Mathew, late of Felix Hall in Essex, Esq. by whom she has a son Daniel Dering, and a daughter Elizabeth; 2, Charlotte; 3, Harriot, who died at Paris in 1760. Sir Edward died Dec. 8, 1798, and was succeeded in title and estate by his son,

† This duel was fought with Richard, son of Major Richard Thornhill of this county, within swords' length, with pistols, both of which were fired, and Sir Cholmeley was shot through the body, and died the same afternoon. Mr. Thornhill immediately surrendered himself, and on the 11th of May was tried for the above fact, at the Old Bailey, and found guilty of *man-slaughter*. An appeal was entered, but was not prosecuted.

DERING OF SURENDEN-DERING, KENT.

TABLE 50.

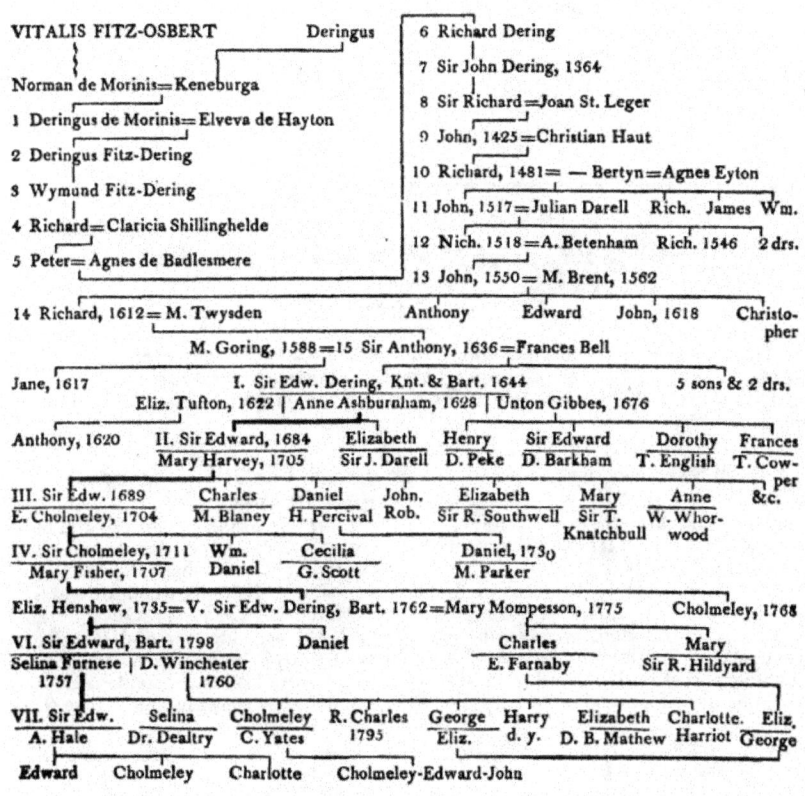

VITALIS FITZ-OSBERT — Deringus

Norman de Morinis=Keneburga

1 Deringus de Morinis=Elveva de Hayton

2 Deringus Fitz-Dering

3 Wymund Fitz-Dering

4 Richard=Claricia Shillinghelde

5 Peter=Agnes de Badlesmere

6 Richard Dering

7 Sir John Dering, 1364

8 Sir Richard=Joan St. Leger

9 John, 1425=Christian Haut

10 Richard, 1481= — Bertyn=Agnes Eyton

11 John, 1517=Julian Darell Rich. James Wm.

12 Nich. 1518=A. Betenham Rich. 1546 2 drs.

13 John, 1550= M. Brent, 1562

14 Richard, 1612=M. Twysden   Anthony   Edward   John, 1618   Christopher

M. Goring, 1588=15 Sir Anthony, 1636=Frances Bell

Jane, 1617   I. Sir Edw. Dering, Knt. & Bart. 1644   5 sons & 2 drs.

Eliz. Tufton, 1622 | Anne Ashburnham, 1628 | Unton Gibbes, 1676

Anthony, 1620 II. Sir Edward, 1684 Elizabeth Henry Sir Edward Dorothy Frances
               Mary Harvey, 1705   Sir J. Darell D. Peke D. Barkham T. English T. Cowper

III. Sir Edw. 1689 Charles   Daniel   John.   Elizabeth   Mary   Anne   &c.
E. Cholmeley, 1704 M. Blaney H. Percival Rob.   Sir R. Southwell   Sir T.   W. Whorwood
                                                                     Knatchbull

IV. Sir Cholmeley, 1711 Wm.   Cecilia   Daniel, 1730
Mary Fisher, 1707   Daniel G. Scott   M. Parker

Eliz. Henshaw, 1735=V. Sir Edw. Dering, Bart. 1762=Mary Mompesson, 1775   Cholmeley, 1768

VI. Sir Edward, Bart. 1798   Daniel   Charles   Mary
Selina Furnese | D. Winchester   E. Farnaby   Sir R. Hildyard
1757   1760

VII. Sir Edw. Selina   Cholmeley R. Charles George Harry Elizabeth   Charlotte. Eliz.
A. Hale   Dr. Dealtry C. Yates   1795   Eliz.   d. y. D. B. Mathew Harriot   George

Edward   Cholmeley   Charlotte   Cholmeley-Edward-John

VII. Sir EDWARD DERING, Bart. who was born in 1757; and in 1782 he married Anne, daughter of William Hale of King's Wolden, in Hertfordshire, by whom he has two sons, Edward and Cholmeley, and one daughter, Charlotte.

ARMS—Quarterly, first and fourth, argent, a fesse, azure; in chief three torteauxes (as the augmentation); second and third, or, a saltire, sable.
CREST—On a ducal coronet, or, a horse passant, sable; maned, or.
SUPPORTERS—Two horses, sable; maned, or.
MOTTO—ꝧeꞃinᵹ onꝺpæꞇaꝺ no ꞇeꞃinᵹ; and sometimes ——— *Terrere nolo timere nescio.*
SEAT—Surenden-Dering in Kent.

50. STYLE of WATERINGBURY, KENT.

Created Baronet April 21, 1627.

THIS pedigree is taken chiefly from one authenticated by the several books remaining upon record in the College of Arms, examined and testified by John Philipot, Somerset, and others, 1640. This family was originally seated in Suffolk, and is descended from

1. William Style of Ipswich, the father of

2. John Style, alderman of London, who married Elizabeth, daughter and co-heir of Sir Guy Wolston of London, Knt. by whom he had

3. Sir Humphrey Style of Langley, Knt. who was one of the esquires of the body to King Henry VIII. and sheriff of the county of Kent in the 35th year of the same reign:* he died April 9, 1557, and was buried at Beckenham church. He married first Bridget, daughter of Sir Thomas Baldrey, Knt. by whom he had issue three sons; 1, Edmund, born at Langley, March 27, 1538; 2, Oliver, who was sheriff of London, of whom hereafter; 3, Nicholas, alderman and sheriff of London, and knighted in the 5th of King James I. 1607: he died Nov. 16, 1615, and was buried in the church of St. Margaret, Lothbury, London, leaving issue by Gertrude his wife, daughter of Edw. Bright of London, one son, Humphry, who was

---

* He procured a grant from Sir Thomas Wriothesley, garter principal king at arms, reciting, that not being willing to bear arms in prejudice to the other branches of his family, he had petitioned for a coat with a proper difference, which the said king at arms, March 28, 1529, granted, and under his hand and seal, as follows, viz. *Sable, a fesse ingrailed between three fleurs de lis, within a border, or; the fesse fretted of the field*; to him and his posterity. He procured, with others, an act of parliament in the second and third years of King Edw. VI. for the disgavelling of his lands in the county of Kent.

STYLE OF WATERINGBURY, KENT.

of Westerham, and a daughter Mary, the wife of Simon Lawrence of London, merchant.† Sir Humphrey Style, Knt. married secondly Elizabeth, daughter of George Penent of the county of Hertford, Esq. (who after his death was the wife of Christopher Mead of the county of Warwick) by whom he had a daughter Mary, and a son Edward, who died an infant.

4. Edmund Style of Langley, Esq. eldest son of Sir Humphrey, by his first wife, married Mary, daughter of John Berney of Reedham, in Norfolk, by whom he had William Style of Langley, Esq. and Edmund, who married Catharine, daughter of John Scot of Halden, by whom he had a son John, and a daughter Mary.

5. William, the eldest son of Edmund, had two wives; first Anne, daughter of John Eversfield of Den, in Sussex, Esq. by whom he had one son, Humphrey, and a daughter Anne, the wife of Sir Nicholas Miller of Oxenheath, Knt.‡ His second wife was Mary, daughter of Sir Robert Clarke, Knt. one of the barons of the exchequer, by whom he had eight sons and three daughters; Mary, Elizabeth, and Margaret. Of the sons; 1, William; 2, George; 3, Richard; 4, Robert; 5, Edmund; 6, Michael; 7, Thomas, L L D. who died July 3, 1677; and 8, Francis.*

6 Sir Humphrey Style of Langley, Knt. eldest son of William, by his first wife, Anne, was gentleman of the privy chamber to King James, and cup bearer to King Charles I. and was created a baronet (in his epitaph he is said to have been created knight and baronet of England and Ireland) by privy seal, dated May 20, 1627.† He married Elizabeth, daughter and heiress of Robert Pershall of Lincoln's Inn, and widow of Sir Robert Bosvill of Eynsford, Knt. and leaving no issue, his title became extinct,‡ and he was succeeded in the estate of Langley by his half brother, William, the eldest son of William Style, by his second wife before-mentioned.§ We now return to

4. Oliver, the second son of Sir Humphrey Style of Langley, Knt. who was born in 1542: he served the office of high sheriff of London, and on purchasing the manor of Wateringbury in Kent, retired to the mansion of it, called Wateringbury Place, where he died March 4, 1622. He was twice married; first to Susan, daughter of John Bull of London, Esq. by whom he had three sons; 1, John; 2, Oliver;

---

† The several charities of these Styles to the city of London may be seen in Strype's Stow's Survey, book. I. p. 268, book II. p. 40, 81, 168, book III. p. 52, book V. p. 57.   ‡ See Reg. Rott. p. 879.

* William Style of Langley, Esq. was a barrister at law, and was of the society of the Inner Temple. He married Elizabeth, daughter and heiress of William, son of John Duleing, one of the alderman of the city of Rochester; by whom he had issue two sons and two daughters, Mary and Esther; and died in Dec. 1699, aged 80. Of the sons, William Style, the eldest, died without issue in his father's life-time; *(I imagine him to be the Col. William Style who lies buried in Bunhill Fields burying ground: he died March 2, 1670. See Strype's Stow's Survey, book IV. p. 55.)* and Humphrey succeeded his father in his seat at Langley; but dying without issue male, his daughter and heir, Elizabeth, carried it in marriage to Sir John Eltwell, Bart. who died in 1727, without issue by her. She was afterwards the wife of Mr. Henry Bartlett, and died June 16, 1731.

† Rym. Fæd. vol. XVIII. p. 986. Though this branch was the elder to those of Wateringbury, yet these last were the senior baronets, being created April 21, 1627.

‡ By an inscription in the neighbouring church of Hayes, it appears, that dame Hester Style, widow of Sir Humphrey Style, Bart. was the wife of John Scott, Esq. eldest son and heir of Sir Stephen Scott, Knt. of the county of Kent.   § Hasted's Hist. Kent, vol. I. p. 86, &c.

3, Thomas; and three daughters, 1, Elizabeth; 2, Susan; and 3, Margaret; of whom only Thomas survived him. His second wife was Juliana, daughter of Charles Barnes of London, and widow of Sir Thomas Cutler, Knt. by whom he had no issue. He was succeeded by

I. THOMAS, his only surviving child, who was created a baronet April 21, 1627: he died Oct. 18, 1637, leaving issue by Elizabeth his wife, daughter and heiress of Robert Foulkes of Mountnesing, in Essex, Esq. who died May 20, 1750; by whom he had Sir Thomas, his successor, and three daughters; Elizabeth, the wife of John Monins, Esq. Susan, of Sir John Read of the county of Hertford, Bart. and Anne, of Sir John Buck of the county of Lincoln, Bart. He was succeeded by his son,

II. Sir THOMAS STYLE, Bart. who was twice married; first to Elizabeth, daughter of Sir William Armine of Osgodby, in the county of Lincoln, Bart. who died Dec. 10, 1679; by whom he had issue six sons; Thomas, the eldest, married Mary, only daughter of Sir Stephen Langham, Knt. by whom he had issue a son Thomas, who died an infant in 1674. He died Aug. 30, 1672. His widow was afterwards the wife of Sir Thomas Midleton of Stansted-Mount-Fitchet, in Essex, Knt. 2, William; 3, Michael; 4, Sir Oliver; 5, Armine. Sir Thomas's daughters were 1, Elizabeth, the wife of William Carter of Kinmall, in Denbighshire, Esq. 2, Mary, of Sir Felix Ward of Maling, in Kent, Bart. 3, Susan, of Thomas Dalyson of Namptons, in Kent, Esq. and 4, Anne, of John Marriot of Sturston Hall, in Suffolk, Esq.* Sir Thomas married to his second wife Margaret, daughter of Sir Thomas Twisden of Bradbourne, Bart. who survived him, and died Dec. 5, 1718, aged 71, by whom he had issue Thomas, who died in his life-time, without issue, another Thomas, who survived him; and Humphrey and Roger, who died without issue: and Margaret, the wife of Robert Vyner of Swakley, in Middlesex, Esq. one of the knights of the shire for the county of Middlesex. Sir Thomas died Nov. 19, 1702, aged 78: he was succeeded in title and estate by his only surviving son by the first marriage,

III. Sir OLIVER STYLE, Bart. who died on the 12th of Feb. following, without issue; and lies buried under a handsome monument in the south part of Wateringbury church yard; on which the title and estate descended to his half brother,

IV. Sir THOMAS STYLE, Bart. who in 1707 pulled down the mansion of Wateringbury Place, a very ancient building, moated round, and erected the present seat more to the westward, in which he kept his shrievalty in 1710. He married Elizabeth, eldest daughter of Sir Charles Hotham, Bart. who died Oct. 25, 1737, by whom he had issue four sons; 1, Thomas, who died in 1741, and was buried at Ormskirk, in the county of Lancaster; 2, Charles, the present baronet; 3, Robert, now vicar of Wateringbury and rector of Mereworth, who married Priscilla, daughter of the Rev. John Davis, late rector of Mereworth, by whom he has issue; 4, William, colonel of the third regiment of foot, who married Catharine, sister and co-heir of John Long Bateman of the kingdom of Ireland, Esq. and died with-

* Visit. county Kent, 1619. Mon. inscrip. in Wateringbury church.

STYLE OF WATERINGBURY, KENT.

out issue in 1786: and also two daughters; Elizabeth died in 1795, and Charlotte in 1786, both unmarried. Sir Thomas died in 1769, and was succeeded in title and estate by

V. Sir CHARLES STYLE, Bart. who March 7, 1770, married Isabella Wingfield, sister to Lord Viscount Powerscourt, of the kingdom of Ireland, by whom he had one son, Charles, and a daughter Dorothy, the wife of John Larking of Clare House, in Kent, Esq. He died in 1774, and was succeeded by his only son,

VI. Sir CHARLES STYLE, the present baronet, who married Camilla, eldest daughter of James Whatman of Vinters, in Kent, Esq. by whom he has two sons, Thomas and Thomas-Charles; and one daughter, Isabella-Anne.

ARMS—Sable a fesse, or, fretted of the field, between three fleur de lis, and within a border of the second.

CREST—On a wreath a wolf's head couped, proper; the lower part of the neck fretté, as in the arms.

SEAT—At Wateringbury Place, near Maidstone, in Kent.

TABLE 51.

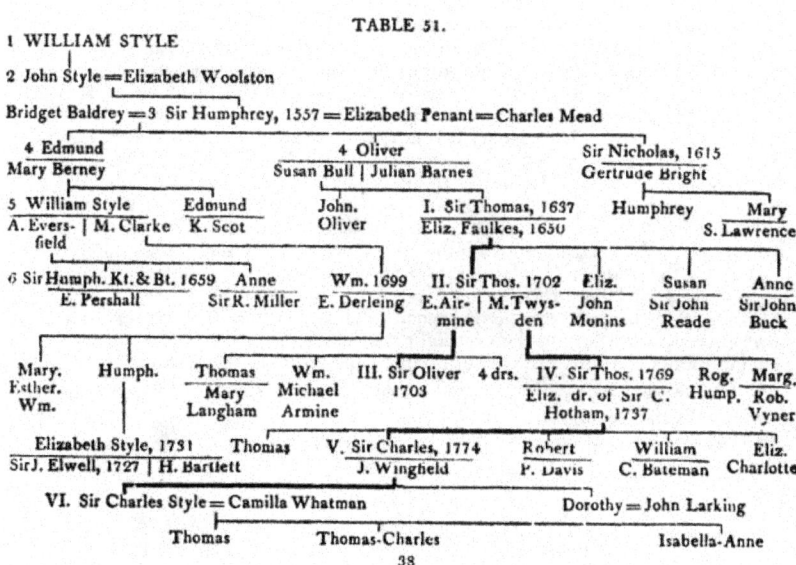

51. ISHAM of LAMPORT, NORTHAMPTONSHIRE.

Created Baronet May 30, 1627.

NOT tradition alone, but a concurrent testimony of authentic records sufficiently prove, that this family has, for many ages, been seated in Northamptonshire, and likewise seem to evince a certainty of their being denominated from Isham, a town of the said county, in the hundred of Orlingbury. Such authority, supported by a variety of corroborating circumstances, gives us encouragement to begin at the Norman epocha, from which æra we shall attempt to deduce them to our days, in as uninterrupted a series as this distance of time, and the many casualties incident to it will admit.

1. Either Azor or Azo, who lived when William the Conqueror made his general survey, if they were different men, which the small variation of a letter would incline one to think they were not, was probably the person who is recorded to be father of

2. Roger de Isham, one of the first benefactors to the priory of St. Andrew, in Northampton, founded by Simon de St. Liz, in the 18th year of the Conqueror; giving thereto two parts of the tithe of all his demesnes in Isham.

3. Henry de Isham, next occurs in the records of the said priory, as a witness to the grant of Henry de Harwedon, son of Simon de Harwedon, of all the tithes of his fee in Isham: very likely Roger was father of this Henry, to whom are attributed two sons, Henry and Thomas; from which last the existing branch of the family derive their descent. That Henry had a son who bore his name is very clear; for Henry, son of Henry de Isham, presented Master Hervey de Fackham,* to one mediety of the church of Isham, in the year 1237. It is certain, that this last Henry was likewise succeeded by a son after his own name, a minor. We also meet with William de Isham, whose daughter and heir, Elizabeth, was the wife of William Bernake of Bernake; which William leaving an heir female, the estate in Isham passed into the house of Luffewick of Luffewick, and from thence was conveyed the same way into that of Pickering.

Having thus brought the eldest branch to a period in an heir general, we shall now proceed, according to the best light we have at present, in the account of the younger branch; in order to which it will be necessary to re-ascend to

4. Thomas de Isham, second son of the first Henry, which Thomas was father of

5. Robert de Isham, living in 1261; and he of

6. Henry de Isham, who was impleaded by William, son of John le Wylies, 3 Edw. III.

---

* Reg. Rob. Grosthead, Ep. Linc. A. 2, Pont. 1237. 21 Henry III.

ISHAM OF LAMPORT, NORTHAMPTONSHIRE.

7. Robert de Isham we take to be the son of Henry, and find him frequently mentioned towards the latter end of Edw. III. He is supposed to be father of

8. Robert Isham, the first we observe to have *de* left out before his name. Contemporary with Robert, perhaps his brother, was John Isham, prior of Wymondham in Norfolk: he was admitted July 18, 1416, and governed that house four years.* This Robert died March 13, 1424, leaving a son named

9. Robert, of the age of 22 years: he married Elizabeth, daughter and co-heir of —— Aston of Knoston, alias Nuston, near Irchester, in Northamptonshire. He died about the 14th of Edward IV. leaving 1. William, his eldest son, of whom hereafter; 2, Robert, who was prebendary of Lincoln† from 1467 to 1501-3; 3, Richard, who died before the 16th of May, 1491, as appears from the probate of his will; and by Alice his wife, he left issue Richard, who died Nov. 24, 1493; Robert, heir to his brother, and a daughter named Dorothy: 4, John, who was of Broughton, and married Jane, daughter of Robert Kynnesman of Loddington. Richard, his son and heir, married Isabella, daughter of Drugo Brudenel, Esq.

10. William Isham, the eldest son of Robert before-mentioned, was one of those gentlemen of Northamptonshire to whom Rich. III. sent a letter, requiring a loan of 40*l*. his name likewise occurs upon other accounts on the lists of the nobility and gentry of the county. He married Elizabeth, daughter of ——, widow of Thomas Braunspath, who died in 1478, and he in 1510, leaving

11. Thomas Isham of Picheley, Esq. their son, who was about 54 years of age at his father's death: he married Elena, daughter of Richard Vere of Addington, Esq. (by Isabella his wife, daughter and at length heir of John Green of Drayton, Esq.) and sister to Sir Henry Vere, sheriff of Northamptonshire, 1 Henry VII. who being the last heir male of that antient and martial family, descended from Sir Robert de Vere, second son of Aubrey de Vere, chief justiciary of England, and brother to Aubrey de Vere, first of the name, Earl of Oxford; his eldest daughter and co-heir, Elizabeth, became the wife of John, the first Lord Mordaunt, ancestor to the present Earl of Peterborough.

The issue of this match is Euseby, John, and Henry, who was in that unfortunate expedition of the Emperor Charles V. to Algiers in 1541.‡ He married Anne, relict of William Scot, daughter and co-heir of Thomas Fogge, serjeant porter of Calais, by whom he had Edward Isham, whose daughter and heir, Mary, was the wife of Sir George Parkins of Bunny, in Nottinghamshire, Knt.

12. Euseby Isham, the eldest son of Thomas, married Anne, eldest daughter of Giles Pulton of Desborough, Esq. and Catharine his wife, daughter of Thomas Lovet, sen. of Astwell, Esq. by whom, in one and twenty years, he had twenty children; the names of ten, the rest dying young and unmarried, are transmitted down to us, viz. 1, Giles; 2, Robert; 3, Gregory; 4, John, ancestor of the Lamport line; and 5, Henry: 6, Catharine, the wife of Richard Pagitt of Cranford, student

---

* Hist. of Abbies, by Br. Willis, Esq. p. 155, and Blomefield's Hist. of Norf. vol. I. p. 732.
† Willis's Survey of the Cathedrals of Lincoln, &c. p. 220.
‡ Will. Malim's Dedicat. to Sir Thomas Chaloner's book, de republica Anglorum instauranda.

of the law (from whom descended, by the eldest son, James Pagitt, one of the barons of the Exchequer, in the reign of Charles I. and by Euseby, a clergyman, old Father Ephraim Pagitt, above 40 years rector of St. Edmund, Lombard Street, which it is said, upon the breaking out of the civil war, he was forced to quit merely for quietness sake); 7, Elena, first the wife of Thomas Hoyse, secondly of Thomas Boseworth of Great Oakley; 8, Ely, the wife of Henry Bellamy, citizen and mercer, of London, afterwards of Hadley, near Barnet in Middlesex; 9, Edith, of Richard Slatier of Braunston; and 10, Isabella, of Thomas Barker, merchant, whose sister, Elizabeth, was the wife of John Isham, his wife's brother.*

---

* Giles Isham, Esq. the eldest son, was brought up to the study of the law, wherein he made great proficiency; and settling at Picheley, upon the death of his grandmother, was put into the commission of the peace. In the first year of the reign of Queen Mary he was elected* for the city of Peterborough, to the parliament summoned to meet at Oxford; and again to that held at Westminster 4th and 5th of Philip and Mary. He died in Aug. 1559, leaving by Mary his wife, who survived him not a year, three daughters, all married to gentlemen of good families: Anne, to Edward Thorne, of Syresham; Jane, to Leonard Barker, and after him to Nicholas D'arcy of Kew, in Surry, Esq; and Margery, to Edmund D'Ayrell, of Langport, alias Lamport, in Buckinghamshire.

Robert Isham, second son, was of Christ College in Cambridge, where he proceeded master of arts, after which he was promoted to be one of Queen Mary's chaplains; and died unmarried, May 5, 1564.

Gregory Isham, third son, merchant, purchased a good estate at Braunston, and elsewhere, but did not live long to enjoy it, dying under 40 years of age, Sept. 4, 1558. He married Elizabeth, daughter of Matthew Dale, of Bristol, who after his decease, had to her second husband William Roswell, Esq. sollicitor-general to Queen Elizabeth. By her he was father of Sir Euseby, Thomas, Mary, the second wife of Thomas Andrews, of Charwelton, Esq. who seems to be the sheriff of Northamptonshire, according to Camden, that attended on Mary Queen of Scots to her execution, at Fotheringhay Castle; and Elizabeth, of Henry Cave of Ingarsby, in the county of Leicester, Esq.

Sir Euseby Isham of Picheley, and Braunston, Knt. was five years old at the time of his father's death, 36 Eliz. he was sheriff of Northamptonshire; and May 11, 1603 received the honour of knighthood from King James I. at the Charter-house. He was once possessed of a very large estate, built a fair house at Picheley, which is now standing, where he walled in a park, and inclosed the lordship; but after living to a considerable age, he died June 11, 1626; and, as tradition delivers it, in no very good circumstances, though in all appearance his children were well provided for, of whom he had a good number, by his Lady, Anne†, the daughter of John Borlase of Marlow, in Bucks, Esq. The sons were, 1, John Isham, Esq. who married first Anne, daughter of Sir William Fitz-Williams of Milton, Knt. by whom he had Anne the wife first of William Lane of Horton and Glendon, Esq. and after his decease, of Pierce Walsh, Esq. secondly Elizabeth, daughter of Edmond Dunch of Wittenham, in the county of Berks, Esq. who brought him no issue: he died Dec. 9, 1626. and this last wife Aug. 6, 1657. 2, Euseby, who married Susanna, relict of Daniel Kechen; 3, William, who by Mary his wife, had issue, Euseby and Anne; 4, Gregory; 5, Thomas, who married Elizabeth, daughter of Sir Thomas Denton of Hillersdon, in Bucks, Knt. by whom he had Thomas Isham of the Middle Temple, who died a bachelor, July 17, 1676, aged 30, besides a son and daughter that died young.‡ 6, Anthony. Sir Euseby's daughters were, Anne, who died an infant; another Anne, the wife of Edward Glover of Baxterley, in Warwickshire, Esq. Mary, first the wife of Edward Reede of Cottesbrooke, Esq. and afterwards of Sir Fleetwood Dormer of Lee-grange, in Buckinghamshire, Knt. Sarah, of Henry Turvile of Thurleston, in the county of Leicester, Esq. Susanna, of John Faldo of Goldington-Green, in the county of Bedford, Esq. and Elizabeth.

Henry, fifth and youngest surviving son of Euseby Isham, comptroller of the customs, temp. Eliz. and married Jane, daughter of Mr. Breesley, who belonged to the queen's wardrobe, and by her had issue, 1, Gregory; 2, Nathaniel; 3, Zaccheus; and 4, Matthias.

Gregory Isham of Barby, Esq. had by his wife, Elizabeth, daughter of Robert Catelyne of Raundes, Gent. a numerous progeny, viz. Robert of Barby, Henry, another Henry, living at Laguna in the Ca-

* MS. List of Memb. of Parl. for county of Northton, by Browne Willis, Esq. † Vincent's Visitat. of North. MS. Harl. vol. II. p. 52. ‡ Br. Willis's Hist. Bucks, p. 200, 201.

ISHAM OF LAMPORT, NOTTINGHAMSHIRE.

13. John Isham of Lamport, Esq. their fourth son, was born in Aug. 1525: he was, 5 Edw. VI. made free of the city of London, and of the mercers' company, to which he was often warden. In the year 1576 he was in the commission of the peace, and in 1581 underwent the office of sheriff: he departed this life March 17, 1595, aged 71, leaving behind him the character of a wise, just, and good man.* He married Elizabeth, the daughter of Nicholas Barker of the house of Sunning, in Berkshire, and relict of Leonard Barker, citizen of London, by whom he had Anne, the wife of Richard Saunders of Agmondesham, in Bucks, and Elizabeth, of George Pulton of Desborough, Esqrs. 1, Thomas, of whom hereafter; 2, Robert, who died young; 3, Henry, who married Eliz. Caunton, by whom he had Euseby, Edward, who left posterity; Thomas, Richard, John, Henry, Barbara, Mary, the wife of George Neale, mercer; and Anne, of Thomas Bunning, rector of Lamport: 4, Richard married Barbara Webster, by whom he had Thomas, Augustine, Richard, Anne, Elizabeth, the wife of William Tresham of Old; Susanna, and Mary.

14. Thomas Isham, Esq. succeeded his father, and had the misfortune to lose his sight when very young, by a fit of sickness, notwithstanding which, by the help of an excellent memory, he became well versed in divinity and history. He died Dec. 3, 1605, aged 50, leaving by his wife Elizabeth, daughter of Christopher Nicholson of Cambridge, Gent. who survived him till Aug. 9, 1621, one son, John,

---

naries in 1624; Richard, James, Gregory, John, William, Edward, Arthur; Anne, the wife of John Pey, who had a place at court; Eliza, Eleanora, who died unmarried, aged 80; Penelope, Catharine, Elizabeth, the wife of Thomas Burrard of Lymington, in Southampton, Esq. Jane, of —— Lodge, one of which was the second wife of Sir Sidney Mountague, father to the first Earl of Sandwich.

Zaccheus, the third but second surviving son, married Jane, daughter of Francis Sturtivant of Carlton upon Trent, in Nottinghamshire, and by her had Edward of Willey, in the county of Warwick; Mary, the wife of —— Wren; Jane, of —— Ducket; and Elizabeth. Thomas, batchelor of divinity, rector of Barby, father of that learned and eminent divine, Zaccheus Isham, D. D. rector of St. Botolph's, Bishopsgate, in London, which he resigned upon being presented to the living of Solyhull in Warwickshire, prebendary of Canterbury and St. Paul's, and several times proctor in convocation for the city of London, who died at Solyhull, July 5, 1705, leaving issue by Elizabeth, his wife, daughter of Thomas Pittis, D. D. chaplain to King Charles II. (who was his predecessor, as rector of St. Botolph's, Bishopsgate aforesaid) by Elizabeth his wife, sister of Sir William Stephens of Barton, in the Isle of Wight, Knt. Thomas, Justinian, Henry, Francis, and Elizabeth, who all died young or unmarried; Mary, the wife of Arthur Brooke, Gent. (who had issue two daughters, Mary and Dorothy); and Jane. The aforesaid Thomas was likewise father of Francis Isham of Sudborow, who was older than the doctor, and died without issue. Matthias, the third surviving son of Henry, by his wife Meril Tisdale, had issue Gregory, Elizabeth, and Jane. Besides these sons, Henry Isham had the following daughters, Susanna, the wife of Edmund Borlase, and mother of Sir John Borlase, Bart. one of the lords justices of Ireland in the years 1640 and 1643; Apollonia, the wife of Rowland Leigh, and Mary, of Giles Parslo, both of the city of London.

* This John Isham, Esq. is the first that lies buried at Lamport, having this inscription over him, upon a brass plate, in black letters:—John Isham, one of the twenty children of Euseby Isham of Picheley, and of Anne his wief, daughter of Giles Pulton of Desburgh, Esquier, maryed Elizabeth, daughter of Nicholas Barker, citizen of London, and was once governor of the Englishe marchant adventurers in Flaunders, and thrice warden of the mercers of London: purchased the mannor and patronage of this parishe of Lamport; and was twenty-two yeares justice of peace, and once sheriff of this shyre of Northton; and died the seventeeth day of March, anno domini one thousand, five hundred, ninety five, aged seventy years, six monthes: and the said Elizabeth died the .... daye of January, An^o D^{ni} 1594, leaving III sonnes, Thomas, Henry, and Richard. God make us thancfull for them.

and three daughters; Elizabeth, first the wife of Sir Anthony Denton of Tunbridge, in Kent: secondly, of Sir Paul D'Ewes of Stow Hall, in Suffolk, Knts. Susanna, the wife of Sir Martin Stutvile of Dalham, in Suffolk, Knt. and Jane, of John Ardys of Rouhall, in Bedford, Esq.*

I. JOHN ISHAM, Esq. afterwards Knt. and Bart. the only son, was 23 years of age at the time of his fathers decease: he was knighted by King James I. March 29, 1608, and the 9th of the said king made sheriff of Northamptonshire, where acting as justice of the peace, he bore a great sway until the unhappy troubles, being esteemed an eminent and upright magistrate. King Charles I. advanced him to the dignity of a baronet May 30, 1627. He married Oct. 19, 1607, Judith, daughter of the learned William Lewyn of Ottringden, in Kent, doctor of laws, some time official principal of the arches, and judge of the prerogative court of Canterbury, &c.† who died June 25, 1625, aged 34; by whom he had one son and two daughters, Elizabeth and Judith, who both died unmarried: he died July 8, 1651, and was buried at Lamport, with his lady. He was succeeded in honour and estate by his son,

II. Sir JUSTINIAN ISHAM, Bart. who was born January 20, 1610, was esteemed one of the most accomplished persons of his time, being a gentleman not only of fine learning, but famed for his piety and exemplary life. During the time of the grand rebellion he adhered firmly to the royal cause, for which he suffered both in person and estate; for the latter he was obliged to compound at no less than 1106l.‡ notwithstanding which he was remarkably liberal to the orthodox clergy, which he generously assisted in their necessities. Thus distinguished, his country, upon the happy restoration of the church and monarchy, elected him one of their knights to the parliament, which met May 8, 1661. He married first Jane, daughter of Sir John Garrard of Lamer, in Hertfordshire, Knt. and Bart. and Elizabeth his wife, daughter of Sir Edward Barkham, Knt. by whom he had four daughters; Jane, Elizabeth, and Judith, twins, and Susanna; the first and third died unmarried; Elizabeth was the second wife of Sir Nicholas L'Estrange of Hunstanton, in Norfolk, Bart. and Susanna, of Sir Nicholas Carew of Bedington, in Surrey, Knt. besides these he had one son, John, who lived only a few days; his mother also dying in childbed of him, March 3, 1638, lies buried at Lamport, with an inscription. Sir Justinian married in 1653 to his second wife, Vere, daughter of Thomas lord Leigh of Stonely, by Mary his wife, daughter and co-heir of Sir Thomas Egerton, eldest son of Thomas lord Elsemere, viscount Brackley, high chancellor of

---

* This Thomas Isham, Esq. lies buried in Lamport church, having the following inscription upon his monument: Here lyeth the body of Tho. Isham, Esquire (son and heire of John Isham, Esquire, and Elizabeth his wife) who married Elizabeth, daughter of Christopher Nicholson, Gent. He died the third day of Dec. A° Dⁿⁱ 1605, being of the age of fifty yeares, leaving behind him his wife and son John, of the age of 23 yeares, and three daughters, Elizabeth, Susan, and Jane.

† She was sister to Sir Justinian Lewyn, of the same place, Knt. upon the demise, without issue of whose grand-daughter, Elizabeth, first the wife of Charles Cavendish, lord Mansfield, eldest son of William marquis of Newcastle; and after his decease, of Charles Steward, duke of Richmond and Lenox. Sir Justinian Isham, son of Sir John, in right of his mother Judith, became heir to the said dutchess, jointly with Elizabeth, first lady of Robert earl Ferrers, and Justinian Pagitt of Gray's Inn, Esq. who were descended from the other sisters of the said Sir Justinian Lewyn.

‡ See list of those who compounded for their estates.

England. This lady, who died October 29, 1704, brought him six sons and two daughters; 1, Thomas; 2, Justinian; and 3, John, who died in Oct. 1746, aged 47: he was under secretary each time the Earl of Nottingham was one of the principal secretaries of state, and in the latter end of King William's reign, a commissioner for the forfeited estates in Ireland. He married Frances, daughter and coheir of Sir Richard Ashfeild, Bart. who died in April 1755, aged 72; by her he had two sons and a daughter: Justinian, who died in April 1743, aged 36, married Mary, daughter of Sir Stephen Anderson of Eyworth, in Bedfordshire, Bart. John, and Frances, dead. 4, Charles, who died in the 11th year of his age; 5, Ferdinando, and 6, Henry, both died very young men. Mary, the first wife of Sir Marmaduke D'Ayrell, Knt. late of Castle Camps, in Cambridgeshire: she died June 5, 1679, aged 23; and Vere, young ladies that were learned beyond their sex and years, the first in the latin tongue, the latter in mathematics and algebra. Sir Justinian, being at Oxford to place one of his sons in Christ Church, was seized with a fit of the stone, and died March 2, 1674, in the 65th year of his age. He was sucseeded by his son,

III. Sir THOMAS ISHAM, Bart. a gentleman of polished manners and great attainments, who died July 26, 1681, aged 24, upon which the title and estate descended to his next brother,

IV. Sir JUSTINIAN ISHAM, Bart. who met with the news of his brother's death as he was returning to England from France. In 1685 he was elected a burgess for the town of Northampton, and upon the landing of the Prince of Orange he appeared in arms at Nottingham, where several lords and gentlemen formed themselves into a troop, as a guard to the Princess Anne, the command of which he modestly declining, the choice fell on the Right Rev. Dr. Compton, bishop of London, whom he proposed, and he contented himself with being their cornet, the standard he bore having this motto, in letters of gold, *Nolumus leges Angliæ mutari*. In 1689 he was elected by the almost unanimous voice of the county of Northampton, one of their knights of the shire, and continued to represent the said county to the day of his death. He married July 16, 1683, Elizabeth, the only daughter of Sir Edmund Turnor of Stoke Rochford, in the county of Lincoln, Knt. by Margaret his wife, daughter of Sir John Harrison of Balls, in Hertfordshire, Knt. Sir Justinian died May 13, 1730, aged 72. By her he had 14 children, 8 sons and 6 daughters; 1, Sir Justinian, who succeeded him; 2, John, fellow of All Souls, Oxon, who died there Nov. 17, 1716; 3, Edmund, who died in his infancy; Sir Edmund, successor to his brother, of whom hereafter; 5, Thomas, brought up to the sea: he married in 1734 Mary, daughter of Thomas Kenton, rector of Bugbrook in Northampton, by whom he had one daughter: this Thomas died in April 1743, aged 51. 6, Henry, died an infant; 7, Euseby, who was rector of Lamport and Haselbeach, and rector of Lincoln College, Oxon; and in May 1739 married Mary, daughter of Matthew Panting, D. D. master of Pembroke College, Oxon: he died June 17, 1755, aged 57, leaving three sons; 1, Sir Justinian, born July 18, 1740, of whom hereafter; 2, the Rev. Euseby, born July 17, 1742, now rector of Lamport, &c. who married Diana, daughter of Edward Baber, Esq. of Berkshire, and has issue one son, Charles-Euseby, born February 24, 1770, and four daughters; Julia-

Charlotte, Charlotte, Diana, and Matilda. 3, the Rev. Edmund Isham, D.D. born Feb. 17, 1743-4, warden of All Souls College, Oxon; and 4, one daughter, Philippa, born April 3, 1753: the two latter are unmarried, but they are all at present living, as is their mother, Mrs. Elizabeth Isham, daughter of the said Dr. Panting. 8. Charles, who in 1744 married Elizabeth, daughter and co-heir of Edward Cuthbert, Esq. counsellor at law, and deputy recorder of Northampton, by whom he has no issue. Of the daughters, two Elizabeths died in their infancy; Vere died June 30, 1760, aged 74; Edmunda died April 28, 1766, aged 67; Susanna died at Bath June 5, 1726, unmarried; and Hester, widow of Francis Raynsford of Brixworth, Esq. died Nov. 14, 1763, aged 68.

V. Sir JUSTINIAN ISHAM, Bart. succeeded not only to the title and estate of his father, but to his seat in parliament. Some of his younger years he spent abroad: in 1711 he was constituted one of the commissioners of the then new erected office of the duty on hides, &c. as also commissioner for the affairs of the land tax and windows; but his commission being superseded the first of King George I. some time after he took a tour into the Netherlands, France, and Italy; and after his return married Mary, only surviving child of the late L'Isle Hacket of Moxhull, in the county of Warwick, Esq. and of his second wife, Dorothy, daughter of Sir John Bridgeman of Castle Bromwich, in the said county, Bart. which L'Isle Hacket, Esq. was eldest son to Sir Andrew Hacket, by Mary his wife, first daughter and co-heir of John L'Isle of Moxhull, Esq. descended of a family that had been owners of the said place upwards of 500 years, and in those days esteemed of the superior rank in Warwickshire. Sir Justinian was a man of letters, had considerable knowledge in heraldry and antiquity, and was well versed in several languages: he made great improvements at his seat at Lamport, and particularly in building a fair and costly library. He died without issue March 5, 1736-7, in the 50th year of his age, as he was attending his duty in parliament, being much lamented by all who had the pleasure of his acquaintance. He was succeeded in honour and estate, and also in his seat in parliament by his next surviving brother,

VI. Sir EDMUND ISHAM, Bart. who was fellow of St. Mary Magdalen College, Oxford; and taking the degree of doctor of laws in 1723, removed to the college of Civilians, in London, and was there admitted into the number of advocates. After this he was appointed advocate for the Admiralty, which he resigned in 1742. He was many years knight of the shire for Northampton, and married first Elizabeth, eldest daughter of Edward Wood of Littleton, in Middlesex, Esq. who died July 19, 1748, aged 48; secondly, in May 1759, Philippa, only daughter of Richard Gee of Orpington, in Kent, Esq. and died Dec. 15, 1772, at the advanced age of 82; and was succeeded by his nephew,

VII. Sir JUSTINIAN ISHAM, the present baronet, who in 1766 married Susanna, daughter of —— Barret, Esq. and has issue four sons; 1, Justinian, born April 24, 1773, now a captain in the Northamptonshire militia; 2, Vere, born Sep. 13, 1774, who married —— Chambers, niece to Sir William Chambers; 3, Edmund, born Dec. 14, 1775, bred to the sea service in the royal navy; 4, Henry, born Feb. 14, 1777: also seven daughters; 1, Susanna; 2, Harriot; 3, Sophia, married to Thomas, son and heir of Sir John Palmer, Bart. 4, Louisa; 5, Maria; 6, Anne-Philippa; and 7, Eliza.

ISHAM OF LAMPORT, NOTTINGHAMSHIRE.

TABLE 52.

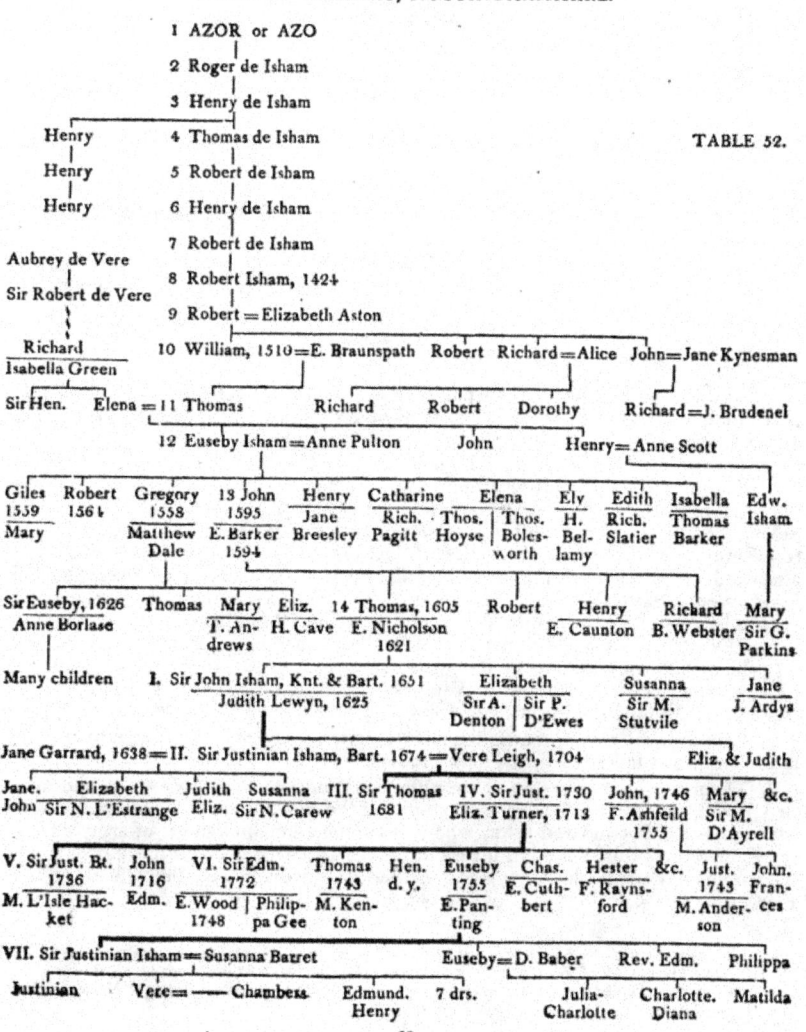

39

ARMS—Gules, a fesse, and in chief three piles, wavy, argent.

CREST—Upon a torce of the colours, a swan's neck and breast, with wings displayed, proper.

MOTTOS—Over the crest, *Ostendo non Ostento*. To the arms, *On things transitory resteth no glory*.

SEAT—Lamport in Northamptonshire.

52. LITTLETON of PILETON-HALL, STAFFORDSHIRE.

Created Baronet June 28, 1627.

IT is evident, from an ancient pedigree in the Heralds' Office,[*] that the family of Littleton was settled at Frankley in Worcestershire, about 1235; whereby it appears, that

1. Thomas de Lyttleton married Emma de Frankley, a sole heiress, and lady of the manor of Frankley; but whether he was a stranger in the county, or resided in the town of South Lyttleton, in the vale of Evesham, as there is reason to think he did, is a matter of doubt by the heralds and antiquaries. They had an only daughter, Emma, the wife of — Tatlington of Tredington, in Worcestershire, Esq. and afterwards of Nicholas Whetamstede: she was a benefactress to the abbey of Halesowen in Shropshire, and died in 1298. He married secondly Asselm, daughter and heiress of William Fitz-Warin of Upton, in Worcestershire, Esq. (second son of Fulk Fitz-Warin, lord marcher of Wales, a man of great note temp. Henry I.[†] which William was one of the justices itinerant, and judge of the common pleas 12 Henry III. and sheriff of Worcestershire the next year, by whom he had three sons; Edmund, Thomas, and John.

2. Edmund, the eldest, married Lucia de Bois, or Atwood, by whom he had no issue, and was succeeded by his next brother,

3. Thomas, who was knight of the shire for Worcestershire 9 Edw. II. and married Julian, daughter of Robert de Somery, of the great house of Dudley, and had issue two sons, Thomas and John, who was appointed commissioner of array 1 Henry IV. on a rumour of a foreign invasion. He married Beatrix Freschevil, of a noble family in Warwickshire, by whom he had an only daughter, the wife of Jeffery Frere, Esq.[‡]

---

[*] Visit. Salop. C. 20. In this visitation is a faithful transcript of a book, said to be drawn up by one Mr. Lyttleton, town-clerk of Worcester temp. James I. (the original is in the hands of Sir Edward Littleton) wherein are copied the ancient evidences of the Littletons of Frankley, Pileton, Henligh, &c.

[†] Dugdale's Baron. vol. I. p. 449.   [‡] MSS. Lyttleton.

4. Thomas, the elder, was esquire of the body to Henry IV. and V. and had annual pensions granted him by both kings, out of the fee-farm rents of Worcester, *pro bono & gratuito servicio*, as expressed in the grants.* He married Maud, daughter and heir of Richard Quatermain of Ricote and North Weston, in Oxfordshire, by Joan his wife, daughter and co-heir of Grey of Rotherfield, in that county. He was probably a benefactor to Frankley chapel, for his portrait, with that of his wife, with their arms, was finely painted in a north window of the said chapel, but was destroyed in the last civil wars; together with the portraits of his son and daughter Wescote, in the opposite window, and of many of his posterity. By her he had an only daughter, Elizabeth, the wife of Thomas Westcote, Esq.

He died about 1421, and Maud became the wife of John Massing, Esq. The said heiress,

5. Elizabeth, having large possessions from her ancestors, De Lyttleton, and from her mother, the daughter and heir of — Quatermain, resolved to continue the honour of her name, and therefore provided, by Westcote's assent, before marriage, that her issue should be called by the name of De Lyttleton.† Wescote was escheator of Worcestershire 29 Henry VI. and died in that reign: his widow remarried Thomas Hewster of Litchfield, Esq. She left issue by Westcote four sons, and as many daughters; 1, Thomas, of whom hereafter; 2, Nicholas;‡ who married Agnes, daughter and heir of Edmund Vernon of Staffordshire, Esq. by Joan, the daughter and heir of —— Handsacre of Handsacre, from whom the Westcotes of that county are descended; 3, Guy, who married — Greenevill of Gloucestershire, from whom the present Westcotes of Devon and Somerset are descended; 4, Edmund, who died unmarried. Of the daughters we find but one married, viz. Anne, the wife of Thomas Porter of Barston, in Warwickshire.

6. Thomas Westcote, alias Littleton, the eldest son, was born about the beginning of the 15th century; and after receiving a liberal education was entered in the Inner Temple. His abilities as a lawyer procured him, from Henry VI. the place of Steward of the court; and in 1455 he went the northern circuit as a judge. Edward IV. continued him in his posts, and also appointed him one of the judges of the court of common pleas. In 1475 he was created knight of the bath. He died in 1481. By Joan his wife, one of the daughters and co-heirs of William Burley of Bromscroft Castle, in Salop, Esq. and relict of Sir Philip Chetwynd of Staffordshire, Knt. he had three sons; 1, Sir William, ancestor to the late Sir Thomas Littleton of Frankley in Worcestershire, Bart. 2, Richard, to whom his father de-

---

* He spelt his name Luttleton, and sealed with the cheveron between three escallops (*MSS. Lyttleton*) as now used by his posterity, but bore a different crest, viz. a greyhound's head, collared. About the close of the reign of Henry V. he served the office of high sheriff of Worcestershire, under Beauchamp earl of Warwick, titular and hereditary high sheriff of that county.

† Coke's Proemium to first Institute.

‡ With his brother Guy, Nicholas retained the name of Westcote, though often solicited by their mother to call themselves Lyttleton. She, once expostulating with them, whether they thought better of themselves than their eldest brother, they answered, that he had a fair estate to alter his name, and if they might share with him, they would do the like.

dicated his book of Tenures,§ ancestor to the branch we are now to treat of; and 3, Thomas of Speechley in Worcestershire.*

§ Which was commented upon by Sir Edward Coke, and which is so much studied by gentlemen of the profession. The celebrity and usefulness of this work have subsisted to our own time; and notwithstanding the prodigious accession of statutes and reports, the large alterations both in the knowledge and practice of the law, and the accumulation of publications, Littleton, with Coke's Commentary, will ever continue to demand the attention and applause of our ablest advocates. *N. An. Reg. p.* xii.

* Thomas, the third son, by Anne, daughter of John Botreaux of Abbots Salford, in Warwickshire, Esq. had several children: John, his second son, and heir to his elder brother Thomas, was parson of Mounslow in Salop. He married Alice, daughter of Richard Thornes, of Cundover in the same county, Esq. by whom he had several sons. This John-Littleton made his will, dated Aug. 12, 1560. Thomas, his eldest son, was of Stoke Milburgh in Salop, and married Frances, daughter of Adam Lutley of Broomscroft Castle, in Salop, Esq. died in 1621, leaving five sons; first Sir Adam of Stoke Milburgh, created baronet Oct. 14, 1642, who by Etheldred, daughter and co-heir of Thomas Poyntz of North Okenden, in Essex, Esq. had several children. His eldest son was Sir Thomas Littleton, Bart. who married Anne, daughter and sole heir of Edward lord Littleton, the lord keeper, and was father of Sir Thomas Littleton of Stoke Milburgh and North Okenden, Bart. one of the lords of the treasury, treasurer of the navy, and speaker of the house of commons in the reign of King Wm. III. who died in 1709, which title is now extinct. Richard, the second son, died unmarried; 3, Thomas, vicar of Hales Owen in Shropshire, father of Dr. Adam Littleton, one of the prebendaries of Westminster, and sub-dean of that church, who was the author of the Latin and English Dictionary, and other works. He died June 30, 1694 *(Stow's Survey, vol. II. app. p.* 71) and lies buried in Chelsea church. 4, John; and 5, George, vicar of Long Stanton in Salop.

Sir Edward Littleton of Henley, in Salop, Knt. second son of John, parson of Mounslow, was chief justice of North Wales *(MS. Littleton, p.* 20) and dying Sep. 1621, left issue by Mary, daughter of Edmund Walter of Ludlow, in Salop, Esq. chief justice of South Wales, eight sons; 1, Edward, of whom hereafter; 2, William, serjeant at law; 3, James, fellow of All Souls College, Oxford, who, as well as his brother William, died unmarried; 4, William, who married, but left no male issue; 5, John, fellow of All Souls College, Oxford, and elected master of the temple in 1638, from whence he was ejected in 1644 *(Walker's Sufferings of the Clergy, p.* 173) for being in the king's army; 6, Nathaniel, a gentleman in the Earl of Southampton's company, in the Low Countries; 7, Sir Timothy Littleton, Knt. one of the barons of the Exchequer, who died in 1679 *(Stow's Survey, vol. I. B.* 3, *p.* 275) and lies buried in the Temple church; 8, Samuel: the three last died unmarried.

Edward Littleton, the eldest son, was lord keeper of the great seal of England in the reign of King Charles I. was born in Shropshire in 1589, admitted a gentleman commoner of Christ Church, Oxford, in 1606, and there took the degree of A. B. in 1609; after which, being designed for the law by his father, he removed to the Inner Temple, and soon became eminent in his profession. In 1628 we find him in parliament; and on the 6th of May he was appointed, together with Sir Edward Coke and Sir Dudley Digges, to carry up the petition of right to the house of lords. He had also the management of the charge of the high presumption made against the Duke of Buckingham about King James's death; on which occasion he behaved himself with universal applause, between the jealousy of the people and the honour of the court *(Clarendon's Hist. Rebell. &c. vol. II. and Lives of the Lord Chancell. &c. vol. I.)*

His first preferment in the law was the appointment to succeed his father as a Welch judge; after which he was elected recorder of London, being about the same time counsel for the university of Oxford; and in 1632 he was chosen summer reader of the Inner Temple. In 1634 he was made solicitor-general, and knighted in 1635. In 1639 he was constituted lord chief justice of the common pleas, and in 1640, on the flight of lord keeper Finch from the resentment of the parliament, the great seal was put into his custody, with the same title. In February following he was created a peer of England, by the title of Lord Littleton, baron of Mounslow in Shropshire.

In this station he preserved the esteem of both parties for some time, both houses agreeing to return their thanks by him, for passing the triennial bill, and that of the subsidies; but as he concurred in the votes for raising an army, and seizing the militia, in March the following year, the king sent an order from York to Lord Falkland, to demand the seal from him; and with Sir John Colepeper, to consult about his successor in the post with Hyde, afterwards Earl of Clarendon; which last step prevented the order from being put into execution. Hyde having always entertained a great regard for the keeper,

7. Richard, the second son of Sir Thomas, the judge, married Alice, daughter and heir of William Winesbury of Pileton-Hall, in Staffordshire, Esq. by whom he had two sons; Richard, who died S. P. and Edward, of whom hereafter; also four daughters; Ellen, the wife of John Cotes of Woodcote, in Salop, Esq. and afterwards of William Basset of Blore, in Staffordshire, Esq. Margaret, first the wife of Humphrey Pigot of Shropshire, and afterwards of —— Clifton of Derbyshire, Esqrs. Lucy, of Robert Swinnerton of Eccleshall, in Staffordshire; and Anne, of Thomas Middlemore of Edgbaston, in Warwickshire, Esqrs. He died in 1518, and his wife in 1529.

8. Sir Edward Littleton, the eldest son, was a knight, and had a grant from Henry VIII. of the office of constable and keeper of the castle of Stafford, and keeper of his parks, and bailiff of his manor of Farebriggs in Staffordshire, &c. for his life. He was sheriff of Staffordshire 15 and 31 Henry VIII.* and 4 Edw. VI. He married two wives; first Helen, daughter of Humphrey Swynnerton of Swynnerton, in Staffordshire, Esq. and secondly, Isabel, relict of —— Wood, and daughter of Richard Hill, sister and heir of Robert Hill of Hounhill, in Staffordshire, Esq. She

had, upon his late behaviour, paid him a visit at Exeter House, when the keeper freely opened himself, bewailing his condition, in that he had been advanced from the common pleas, where he was acquainted with the business, and the persons with whom he was to deal, to an higher office, which required him to deal with another sort of men, and in affairs in which he was a stranger; nor had he one friend among them with whom he could confer upon any difficulty that occurred to him. He proceeded to speak of the unhappy state of the king's affairs, and said *they would never have done what they had already, unless they had been determined to do more; that he foresaw it would not be long before a war would break out, and of what importance it was, in that season, that the great seal should be with his majesty; that the prospect of this necessity had made him comply so much with that party, that there had lately been a consultation, whether, in case the king might send for him, or the great seal be taken from him, it were adviseable to keep it in some secure place, where the keeper should receive it upon occasion, they having no mind to disoblige him; that the knowledge of this had induced him to vote as he did in the late debates; and by that compliance, which he knew would give the king very ill impressions of him, he had gained so much credit with them, that he should be able to preserve the seal in his own hands till his majesty should demand it, and then he would be ready to wait on the king with it, declaring, that no man should be more willing to perish with, and for his majesty, than himself.*

Mr. Hyde acquainted Lord Falkland with this conference, and being very positive that the lord keeper would keep his promise, procured the advising of his majesty to write a kind invitation to the keeper to come to York, and bring the seal with him, rather than think of giving it to any other person. The advice was embraced by the king, who, though he still continued doubtful of the man, was moved by the reasons assigned; and accordingly the seal was sent to York on the 22d, and followed by the keeper on the 23d of May, 1642.

There is a tradition in the family, that Elliot forced it from him with a pistol; that the lord keeper, foreseeing the bad consequence such an outrage would be to the credit of the king and Elliott, prudently followed Elliott to York, in order to prevent it, by giving it the appearance of being his own voluntary act. But notwithstanding this piece of service, and eminent proof of his loyalty, at the risk of his life, he could never totally regain the king's confidence, or the esteem of the court party. He continued however to enjoy his post, in which he attended his majesty to Oxford; was there created doctor of laws *(Wood's Fasti. vol. II. col. 26)* and made one of the king's privy counsel, and colonel of a regiment of foot in the same service, some time before his death, which happened Aug. 27, 1645, at Oxford.

He was twice married; first to Anne, daughter of John Lyttleton, by whom he had a boy and two girls, who all died infants. His second wife was ——, relict of Sir George Calverley, and daughter of Sir William Jones, judge of the king's bench, by whom he had an only daughter, whose son Edward died in 1664, and lies interred in the Temple church. In the south window of the Inner Temple Hall is a fine shield of the keeper's arms, with 15 quarterings, distinguished by a crescent within a mullet, which shews him to have been of the third house.

* Fuller's Worthies in Staffordshire.

afterwards was the wife of Ralph Egerton of Wrinehill, in the same county, Esq. By the last wife he had no issue, but by the first seven sons; the six eldest died without issue; 7, Sir Edward, of whom hereafter: also two daughters; Barbara, the wife of Henry Gower of Worcestershire, Esq. and afterwards of John Folliott of Pirton, in the same county, Esq. and Constance, the wife of Sir James Fuljambe, Knt.*

9. Sir Edward Littleton, Knt. the only surviving son, was sheriff of Staffordshire† 5 Eliz. and married Alice, daughter of Francis Cockayne of Ashburne, in Derbyshire, Esq. by whom he had eight sons and several daughters; 1, John, who died S. P. 2, Sir Edward; 3, Thomas, who by Cassandra, daughter of Thomas Lane of Bentley, in Staffordshire, Esq. left issue; 4, Francis of Melsho, in Salop, who by Gertrude, daughter of Thomas Sutton of Overhaddon, in Yorkshire, Esq. left issue; 5, Walter of Eccleshall, in Staffordshire, who married Alice, daughter of John Comberford of Staffordshire, Esq. and left issue; 6, John, who died S. P. 7, James, whose wife was Mercy, daughter of John Stone of London, Esq. relict of William Bowyer, Esq. by whom he left issue; and 8, Devereux, who by Jane, daughter of George Allen of Woodhouse, in Derbyshire, left issue. The daughters of Sir Edward that married were 1, Jane, the wife of John, son of Thomas Lane of Bentley; 2, Constance, of Thomas Holt of Gristlehurst, in Lancashire; 3, Mary, of Walter Vernon of Hounhill, in Staffordshire; 4, Grace, first of Francis Harnage of Belzardine, in Salop, and afterwards of Silvanus Lacon, of the same county, Esqrs. 5, Margaret, of Sir John Repington of Amington, in Warwickshire, Knt.‡

10. Sir Edward Littleton, Knt. eldest surviving son, was sheriff of Staffordshire 25 and 35 Eliz. He was provost marshal in 1588, and deputy lieutenant to George earl of Shrewsbury, lord lieutenant of the county of Stafford, and one of the knights of the shire for the county of Stafford 39 Eliz. He married Margaret, daughter and co-heir of Sir William Devereux, Knt. youngest son of Walter lord viscount Hereford, by whom he had six sons and eight daughters; 1, Edward, of whom hereafter; 2, Thomas, who married Elizabeth, daughter and heir of Adam Morton of Wilbrighton, in Staffordshire, Esq. and left issue; 3, William; 4, George; 5, Gilbert; and 6, John, who died young. Of the daughters, 1, Mary, was the wife of Richard Fowler of King's Harnage, in Salop; 2, Anne, of Humphrey Salway of Stanford, in Worcestershire; 3, Dorothy, who died young; 4, Jane, of Richard Knightley of Fawesley, in Northamptonshire; 5, Ellen, of William Babington of

---

* In Penkrich church is an altar tomb of marble, with the effigies of a knight in armour lying between his two wives, and round the edge this inscription in Saxon characters:—Hic jacent corpora Edwardi Littleton, Militis & Helenæ Swynnerton & Isabellæ Wood uxorum ejus: qui quidem Edwardus obiit Decimo Die Octobris Anno Dni. MCCCCCLVIII. quorum animabus propitietur Deus, Amen.

† Fuller's Worthies.

‡ Sir Edward Littleton, Knt. lies buried in Penkrich church, where is an altar tomb of white marble; on the top are the effigies of a knight, about his neck a collar of SSS, at his feet a dog, collared, and on his left hand the effigies of his lady and several of their children; and about the edge this circumscription in Saxon characters:—Here lieth the bodies of Sir Edward Littleton, Knt. the seventh son of Sir Edward Littleton of Pileton-Hall, Knt. and dame Alice his wife, daughter of Francis Cockayne of Ashburne, in the county of Derby, Esq. which Sir Edward departed the 19th day of July, in the year of our Lord God, 1574.

Curborough, in Staffordshire, Esqrs. 6, Margaret, of John Skinner of Cofton, in Worcestershire, Gent. 7, Lettice, of John Fulnetby, archdeacon of Stafford; and 8, Constance, of Richard Hill of London, Gent.

11. Sir Edward Littleton, Knt. his eldest son, was knight of the shire in parliament 21 James I. and sheriff of the county the 24th of that reign. He married Mary, daughter of Sir Clement Fisher of Packington, in Warwickshire, Knt. by whom he had four sons and four daughters; 1, Edward; 2, Fisher, who married Anne, daughter of James Baynton, of Wilts, Esq. 3, Sir Walter Littleton, Knt. chancellor of the diocese of Litchfield and Coventry. He married Priscilla, daughter of Sir Lewis Pemberton of Rushden, in Northamptonshire, Knt. by whom he had four sons; 1, Walter of Lichfield, who married a daughter of William Talbot of Sturton Castle, in Staffordshire, Esq. and left issue; 2, Edward, who married a daughter of ———— Mulins, but left no issue; 3, Fisher, doctor of laws, who married Elizabeth, daughter of ———— Pincebeck of London, and relict of ———— Skegnes; and died March 1696-7, without issue, and was buried at St. Andrews, Holborn: 4, Henry, a merchant in London, who left no issue. The fourth son of Sir Edward was William, who married the daughter and heir of John Webster of Amsterdam, merchant. The daughters of Sir Edward were Lettice, first the wife of William Washbourne of Washbourne, in Worcestershire, and afterwards of John Clent of Knightwick, in the same county, Esqrs. 2, Mary, of Euseby Shuckburgh of Naseby, in Northamptonshire, Esq. 3, Margaret, first of Sir George Browne of Radford, in Warwickshire, Knt. and secondly of Francis, third son of Sir Robert Fisher of Packington, Bart. and 4, Anne, the wife of Sir Thomas Holte of Aston, in the county of Warwick, Bart.* Sir Edward died in July, 1629.

I. EDWARD LITTLETON, Esq. son and heir of Sir Edward, by Mary, daughter of Sir Clement Fisher, Knt. was sheriff and deputy lieutenant for Staffordshire. He was likewise advanced to the dignity of a baronet 3 Charles I. He was rated by the sequestrators at 1347*l*. 6*s*. 8*d*. for composition for his estate, on account of his loyalty. He married Hester, daughter of Sir William Courteen of London, Knt. by whom he had three sons; 1, William, who died in his father's life-time, without issue; 2, Sir Edward, his successor; 3, James, who died without issue. Also two daughters; Anne, the wife of — Cole of Shrewsbury, Gent. and Margaret, of Robert Napier of Luton Hoo in Bedfordshire, Bart. by whom she had issue one son, Robert. After the death of Sir Edward Littleton, Bart. the same dame Hester became the wife of Thomas Thorne of Shelvock, in Salop, Esq. and was buried in Ryton church Dec. 12, 1674.

II. Sir EDWARD LITTLETON, Bart. eldest surviving son and successor to the title and estate, was also high sheriff and deputy lieutenant for Staffordshire; and married Mary, daughter of Sir Walter Wrotesley of Wrotesley, in Staffordshire, Bart. by whom he had two sons and three daughters; 1, Edward, of whom here-

---

* In the chancel of Penkrich church, against the wall is a very noble monument of variegated marble, whereon are the effigies of two knights, and their ladies, under two arches, one above the other, the arms in great measure broken off; the names of the children, with their effigies, were about the tomb; but the latter are entirely defaced.

after; 2, Walter, a major in Lord Oxford's regiment, who married Lady Anne Knowles, daughter of Nicholas earl of Banbury, by whom he had one daughter, Anne, who died unmarried, at the age of 18. This Walter Littleton was killed in a duel, and after his death Lady Anne was the wife of Capt. Philip, a younger son Sir John Lawson of Brough, in Yorkshire, Bart. and thirdly, of Col. Harvey of Leicestershire: also a third son, James, who died without issue. Of the daughters, Mary was the wife of Henry Gough of Perry Hall, in Staffordshire, Knt. and left issue Elizabeth; 2, Elizabeth, of Walter Chetwynd of Ingestree, in Staffordshire, Esq. and had issue; 3, Hester, of Humphrey Persehouse of Reynolds Hall, in Staffordshire, Esq. and had issue.

Sir Edward married secondly Joyce, daughter of —— Littleton, Esq. of Teddesley-Hay, his cousin, by whom he had six sons and two daughters; 1, Devereux, who died unmarried, at his seat at Tamworth in Staffordshire, June 7, 1747, aged 73; 2, Walter, who died unmarried; 3, Henry, deputy governor of Cork in Ireland, who married, but died without issue; 4, Fisher, a barrister at law, who succeeded to the estates of his brother Devereux, and died unmarried; 5, William, a captain in the navy, who married and left one son, Edward, who succeeded to the estates of — Fisher, his uncle, and married Joyce, his cousin, the eldest daughter of Humphrey Wofferstan of Statfold, in Staffordshire; and died without issue: 6, Adean, who was killed in a duel. Of the daughters, the eldest was the wife of — Delke of Maxloke Castle, in Warwickshire, and had issue; and Sarah, of Stanford Wolferston of Statfold, in Staffordshire, Esq.

Edward Littleton, Esq. the eldest son by the first wife, died in the life-time of his father. He was sheriff for the county of Stafford, and deputy lieutenant. He married Susanna, daughter of Sir Theophilus Biddulph of Elmhurst, in Staffordshire, Bart. by whom he had three sons and six daughters; 1, Sir Edward; 2, Fisher, who left issue by Frances, the eldest daughter and co-heiress of James Whitehall of Pipe Ridware, in Staffordshire, Esq.* 3, Theophilus, who was of Baliol College in Oxford, and died there in Nov. 1704. 1, Susanna, was the wife of Sir John Coryton of Newton, in Cornwall, Bart. 2, Mary, of Edmund Arblaster of Longdon, in Staffordshire, Esq. 3, Elizabeth, of Humphrey Hodgetts of the same county, Esq. 4, Catharine, of John Floyer of Litchfield, Knt. M. D. 5, Jane, of John Egington of Rodbarton, in Staffordshire, Esq. 6, Anne, who died unmarried.

This Edward Littleton died Jan. 24. 1704, and Susanna his wife Aug. 27, 1722. They both lye buried near the west end of the south aisle of Penkrich church.

III. Sir EDWARD LITTLETON, Bart. son of Edward before-mentioned, was sheriff and deputy lieutenant for the county of Stafford. He succeeded his grand-father in title and estate, and married Mary, the only daughter of Sir Richard Hoare, Knt. formerly lord-mayor of London, and one of the representatives in parliament for the said city, in the reign of Queen Anne, by whom he had no issue. He died at Pileton-Hall Jan. 2, 1741-2. Dame Mary Littleton, his lady, April 18, 1761.

* The other daughter and co-heiress was the wife of the right hon. Sir Thomas Parker, Knt. lord chief baron of the court of Exchequer, by whom he had issue Thomas and George.

Fisher Littleton, Esq. brother to Sir Edward last-mentioned, left by Frances his wife, the eldest daughter and co-heiress of James Whitehall of Pipe-Ridware, in the county of Stafford, Esq. two sons and two daughters. He died in May 1740, and lies buried at Pipe-Ridware; together with Frances his wife, who died March 25, 1768. Their issue were, 1, Edward; 2, Fisher, a barrister, who married Mary, only daughter and heiress of Thomas Seace of Northreps, in Norfolk, by whom he had no issue; 3, Frances, the wife of Moreton Wallhouse, of Hatherton, in the county of Stafford, Esq. by whom she has issue; 4, Anne, who died an infant.

The said Fisher dying in the life-time of his brother, Sir Edward, the title and estate descended to his eldest son,

IV. Sir EDWARD LITTLETON, Bart. who died in 1752, married Frances, eldest daughter of Christopher Horton of Catton, in the county of Derby, Esq. by Frances, sole daughter and heiress of Sir Eusebius Baswell of Cadeby, in the county of Leicester, Bart. and whose eldest son, Christopher, married Anne, second daughter of the Earl of Carhampton, by whom she had one son, who died an infant, and was buried at the same time with his father, at Croxall in the county of Derby: and on the death of her first husband, Christopher Horton, Esq. she married his royal highness the late Duke of Cumberland. Elizabeth, the third daughter, married Lord Carbery, of the kingdom of Ireland, and is mother of the present Lord Carbery. Eusebius, the fourth son, married Phœbe, daughter of Davies Davenport of Capesthorn, in the county of Chester, Esq. by whom he has two daughters. None of the other children were married.

Frances, wife of Sir Edward Littleton, died Aug. 29, 1781, S. P. and was buried at Penkrich in Staffordshire.

The present Sir Edward Littleton, Bart. raised a company in the rebellion, in 1745-6, in the regiment commanded by Lord Gower, in which he was a captain, and was elected member in parliament for the county of Stafford in the present and two former parliaments.

ARMS—Argent, a cheveron between three escallops, sable, with due difference.

CREST—On a wreath, argent and sable, a stag's head caboshed, sable; attired, or: between the attires a bugle horn of the second, hanging, and fastened by a bend, gules.

MOTTO—*Ung Dieu & ung Roy.*

SEAT—At Tedesley-Hay in Staffordshire.

LITTLETON OF PILETON-HALL, STAFFORDSHIRE.

TABLE 53.

E. de Frankley = 1. THOMAS DE LITTLETON = Asselm

Tatlington = Emma, 1298 = N. Whetamstede 2 Edmund = L. de Bois 3 Thomas = J. de Somery John

4 Thomas, 1421 = M. Quatermain   John = Beatrix Freschevil

5 Elizabeth = Thomas Wescote   N = Jeffery Frere

6 Thomas = J. Chetwynd Nicholas = A. Vernon Guy = — Greenvile Edm. Anne = T. Porter

Sir Wm. Littleton, Knt. 1506   7 Richard, 1518 = Alice Winesbury, 1529   Thomas = Anne Botreaux

Richard   8 Sir Edward, 1558   Ellen   Margaret   Lucy   Anne
           H. Swinnerton | J. Wood J. Cotes | W. Bas- H. Pi- | —— R Swinnerton T. Middle-
                                              set   got Clifton   more

6 sons.   9 Sir Edward, 1574 = A. Cockayne   H. Gower = Barbara = J. Folliol

John 10 Sir Edw. Thomas Francis Walter John James Devereux Jane Constantia Mary &c.
      M. Devereux Cassand. Gertr. A. Cum-   Mercy Jane John Thomas Walter
                  Lane   Sutton berford   Stone Allin Lane Holt Vernon

11 Sir Edw. 1629 Thomas Wm.   Mary   Anne   Doro- Jane Ellen Marg. Lettice &c
Mary Fisher   Eliz. Mor- Geo. Richard Humph. thy R. Knight- W. John J. Fulneby
                  ton   Gilb. Fowler Sulway   ley Babing- Skinner
                         John   ton

I. Sir Edward Fisher   Sir Walter William   Lettice   Mary   Margaret   Anne
Helen Courteen Anne   Priscilla —, dr. of W. Wash- John E. Shuck- Sir G. Fran. Sir T.
               Baynton   Pemberton J. Webster bourne Clent burgh   Browne Fisher Holt

Wm.   II. Sir Edward James   Anne   Marg.   Walter   Edward Fisher   Henry
      M. Wrio- | J. Littleton   — Cole Robert — Talbot — Mu- Eliz. Pinch-
      thesley   Napier   lins   beck

Edw. 1704 Walter   Mary   Elizabeth Hester   Devereux. Wm.   Adam   N   Sarah
S. Bid-   A. Knowles Sir H. W. Chet- H. Perse- Walter.   — Dilke H. Wol-
dulph   Gough wynd   house   Fisher   ferstan

III. Sir Edw. 1742 Fisher   Theophilus Susanna   Mary   Elizabeth Catharine Jane   Anne
M. Hoare, 1761   F. Whitehall 1704   Sir J. Co- E. Arblas- H. Hod-   Sir J.   J. Eging-
                                         ryton   ter   getts   Floyer   ton

IV. Sir Edw. Bart. = F. Horton, 1781   Fisher = M. Scace   Frances = M. Walhouse Anne
                                                                                     d. y.

53. GORING of Highden, Sussex,
As BOWYER of Leighthorn, Sussex.
Created Baronet, July 23, 1627.

Whose grand-son and heir, Sir James Bowyer, Bart. by another patent, dated May 18, 1678, had the honour intailed, after his decease, upon Henry Goring of Highden, in the same county, Esq. with precedence according to his grand-father's patent, and was accordingly succeeded therein by the said Henry.

THE family of Goring is of considerable antiquity in this county, being surnamed from Goring, in the rape of Arundel; of which was

1. John Goring of Burton, who married Margaret, daughter and co-heir of Sir Ralph Radmill of Radmill, in Sussex. Their great grand-son,

2. Sir William Goring, Knt. was one of the gentlemen of the privy chamber to Edw. IV. and married Elizabeth, daughter and co-heir of John Covert of Slaugham, in Sussex, Esq. and had issue two sons, Sir Henry and George of Hurst-Pierpont, in Sussex, whose son, George, was (by Anne, sister to Edward Denny, earl of Norwich) father of George Goring, Esq. who was created Baron Goring of Hurst-Pierpont 14 Charles I. and the 20th of that reign Earl of Norwich, who was general of horse to King Charles I.

3. Sir Henry, the eldest son, married Dorothy, daughter and co-heir of William Everard of Sussex, Esq. and had Sir William Goring of Burton, Knt. (ancestor to Sir William Goring of Burton, who was created a baronet by King James I. May 14, 1622, which title became extinct on the death of the late Sir William, in 1725) and Edward, from whom those of Highden are descended; which

4. Edward, by Elizabeth, daughter and co-heir of —— Wiseman of Essex, Esq. was father of

5. Henry Goring of Highden, Esq. who married Mary, daughter of Sir Thomas Eversfield of Den, in Sussex, Knt. whose son,

I. Sir HENRY, on the decease of Sir James Bowyer, Bart. succeeded him in his honour, as before mentioned; and married Diana, daughter of Sir Edward Bishopp of Parham, Bart. (by Mary his wife, fourth daughter of Nicholas Tufton, earl of Thanet) had issue two sons; 1, Capt. Henry Goring, and Charles Goring, doctor of laws, who married a daughter of —— Bridger of Oakham, near Lewes in Sussex, Esq. and died without issue.

Capt. Henry Goring died in his father's life-time: he had two wives; first ——, by whom he had Sir Charles, the succeeding baronet; and by his second wife, the daughter of Sir John Covert of Slaugham, in Sussex, Bart. he had Sir Harry, hereafter-mentioned.

GORING OF HIGHDEN, SUSSEX.

II. Sir CHARLES GORING, successor to his grand-father, married a daughter of —— Bridger of Oakham, near Lewes in Sussex, Esq. and dying without issue, was succeeded by his half brother,

III. Sir HARRY GORING, Bart. who served in several parliaments in the reign of Queen Anne, for Steyning in Sussex, and married one of the daughters and co-heirs of Sir George Matthews of Southwark, Knt. who died March 27, 1741, by whom he had nine sons and two daughters: Frances was the wife of Dr. Ballard, rector of Langford Magna in Wiltshire. Sir Harry died in Nov. 1731, at Horsham in Sussex, and was succeeded in dignity and estate by his eldest son,

IV. Sir CHARLES MATTHEWS GORING, who married in July 1731, Mary, youngest daughter of William Blackburne of High Ongar, in Essex, Esq. high sheriff of that county 1 George I. by whom he had one son, Harry, the present baronet, and two daughters; Elizabeth, the wife of Timothy Burrell of Cuckfield, in Sussex, Esq. who died without issue; and ——, the wife of Colvill Bridger, Esq.

Sir Charles Matthews Goring married secondly, in 1743, Betty, sister of Sir Robert Fagg, Bart. with a portion of 3000*l*. per annum; and was succeeded in dignity and estate by his son,

V. Sir HARRY GORING, Bart. who married Sep. 9, 1767, Miss Anne Foster, who died in June 1774: he married secondly, in 1777, Miss Fisher of Barbadoes, who died in July 1780.

ARMS—Argent, a cheveron, between three annulets, gules.
SEAT—At Highden in Sussex.

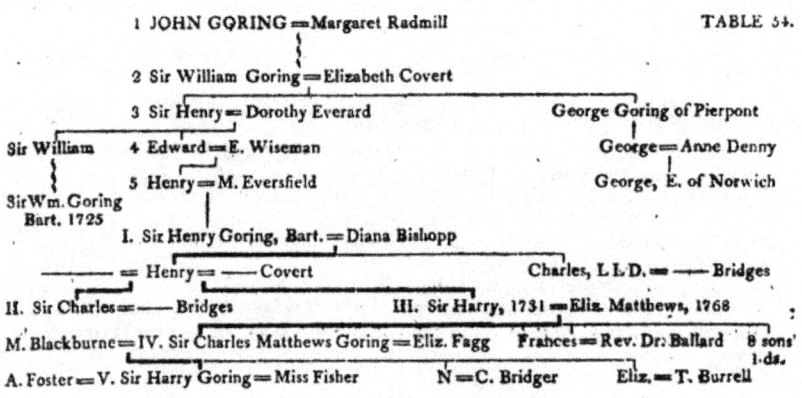

54. STONHOUSE of Radley, Berkshire.

Created Baronet May 7, 1628.

WHETHER this family took their surname from Stonhouse in Gloucestershire, which was the habitation of the Mildmays temp. Richard II. is a point not easy to be determined; but they were gentilitial in Surrey near a century before Henry Stonhouse was returned for Guildford, temp. Edw. II. to the parliament held at Rippon in Yorkshire.

1. Robert Stonhouse of Barsted, in Kent, married Rose, daughter of —— Royden of Essex, by whom he had

2. George Stonhouse of Little Peckham, in Kent, Esq. who was one of the clerks of the green cloth to Queen Elizabeth, and purchased the estate at Radley, in Berks. He died in 1575, having had two wives; 1, Elizabeth, daughter of Nicholas Gibson of Kent, Esq. 2, Elizabeth, daughter of Davy Woodcroft, alderman of London, relict of Walter Lawson, Esq. By this last he left a daughter Dionysia, the wife of Sir Edward Hexto of Somersetshire, Knt. and four sons; William, Nicholas, Walter, and James, who was of Amerden Hall, and created a baronet; but his male issue failing, that title became extinct.

I. WILLIAM, the eldest, was created a baronet 4 Charles I. he married Elizabeth, sole daughter and heir of John Powell of Wales, Esq. and had by her several children, four of which died infants; but three sons, Sir John, Sir George, and William of Cockthorp, in Oxfordshire, married, and had issue: also five daughters; Elizabeth, the wife of Edward Perrot of Hinky, in Berks, Esq. Mary, of William Langton, D.D. Ursula, of John Denton of North Aston, in Oxfordshire; Anne, of George Windsor of Bentley, in Hants, Esqrs. and Dionysia, of Sir Cornelius Fairmeadow, Knt. Sir William died Feb. 5, 1631, aged 76, and lies buried in Radley church in Berkshire; where, against the south wall of the chancel is a very fair arched monument raised, whereon lies the portraiture of Sir William Stonhouse, in armour, with his lady, in the same posture near him. At the head of the monument is the figure of a man in armour, and on the sides are sons in long mourning cloaks; four young children in their swadling clothes, and five daughters.

II. Sir JOHN, the eldest son, succeeded to the title and estate, having been knighted in Aug. 1629; but died unmarried in about four months after the death of his father, June 14, 1632, aged 31.

III. Sir GEORGE, his next brother, succeeded him in title and estate: he was fined for his loyalty to King Charles I. and paid 1460*l*. composition for his estate to the sequestrators.* He married Margaret, daughter of Richard lord Lovelace,† and

---

* See list of those that compounded for their estates, in letter S.   † Peerage of Eng. vol. IV. p. 218.

STONHOUSE OF RADLEY, BERKSHIRE.

by her was father of three sons, Sir George, Sir John, and James; and one daughter, Elizabeth, the wife of Lord Byron, and afterwards of Sir Richard Stidolph of Norbury, in Surrey, Bart.* This Sir George surrendered his father's patent of creation, and had a new one granted him, dated May 5, 22 Charles II. 1670, of the title to himself for life, with remainder to his second son, John, and his heirs male; and in default thereof to James, his third son, and his heirs male, and his heirs male, with precedence, according to the former patent, intending to exclude thereby his first son.

IV. Sir GEORGE, his eldest son however claimed and enjoyed the title, according to the first patent, and married Mrs. Anne Scarlett, of an ancient family, but no fortune; by whom he had issue two daughters, Susanna and Anne, and one son,

V. Sir GEORGE STONHOUSE, Bart. his successor, who married Anne, daughter of James Ashton, Esq. of an ancient family in Lancashire, by whom he had 16 children; whereof George, the eldest, lived to be a captain of foot; but all that survived him were only one son, Sir John, and a daughter, Margaret. Sir George died in Fetter Lane, London, Feb. 24, 1736-7; and was succeeded in the title by his only son,

VI. Sir JOHN STONHOUSE, Bart. who died unmarried in July 1740, whereupon the title was extinct, and an end put to an unfortunate branch of a good family.

4. Sir JOHN, the second son of Sir George (the eldest Sir George above named being disinherited) succeeded him in the estate and title granted by the latter patent: he married Martha, daughter and sole heiress of Robert Brigges of Derbyshire, Esq. brother of Sir Humphrey Brigges of Haughton, in Salop, Bart. and relict of Richard Spencer of London, Turkey merchant; and was succeeded by his son,

5. Sir JOHN STONHOUSE of Radley, Bart. who served as knight of the shire in several parliaments for the county of Berks; and married first Mary, daughter, and at length sole heiress of Henry Mellish of Sandersteed, in Surrey, Esq. by whom he had two daughters, Martha, the wife of Arthur Vansittart of Shottesbrooke, in Berks, Esq. and Mary. His second lady was Penelope, daughter of Sir Robert Dashwood of Northbrooke, in Oxfordshire, Bart. by whom he had nine children; Penelope, the wife of Sir Henry Atkins of Clapham, in Surrey, Bart. and surviving him, afterwards of the right hon. Lord Gower, and died at Trentham in Staffordshire, in Aug. 1734; Catharine was married in May 1745, to the hon. Robert Lee, afterwards Earl of Litchfield: she died his widow, March 8, 1784. Anne was the wife of Sir William Bowyer of Denham, in Bucks, Bart. Sir John, his successor; Margaret, who died June 30, 1746; William; Dionysia, the wife of the Rev. Mr. Benet; James; and Susanna, the wife of Peter Serle, Esq. of Testwood near Southampton; by whom she had a daughter, the wife of Sir William Oglander of Nunwell, in the Isle of Wight. Sir John died Oct. 10, 1733, and was succeeded by his eldest son,

6. Sir JOHN STONHOUSE, who died unmarried, and was succeeded by his brother,

* Aubrey's Antiquities of Surrey, vol. II. p. 295, 296.

7. Sir WILLIAM, who was succeeded by his brother,

8. Sir JAMES STONHOUSE, Bart. who died in 1792, and was succeeded by

9. Sir JAMES STONHOUSE, the late baronet: he was a native of Berkshire, and educated at St. John's College, Oxford, where he took his degree of M.D. and afterwards settled at Northampton: here he contracted an intimacy with Mr. Harvey, Dr. Doddridge, and other eminent divines. About 1762 he entered into orders, and died in 1795, aged 80. He was an admirable preacher, and a most exemplary man.* He was succeeded by his son,

10. Sir THOMAS STONHOUSE, the present baronet.

ARMS—Argent, on a fesse sable, between three hawks volant, azure, a leopard's face between two mullets, or.

CREST—On a wreath, a talbot's head, coup'd, argent; collared sable, lined or; catching a dove volant, argent.   SEAT—At Radley in Berks.

---

* Through a long course of years he there successfully discharged the urgent claims of his professional duties, with equal care and equal fidelity, to the poor and to the rich. With affectionate sympathy and regard, he administered his assistance to the humblest victims of poverty and disease; nor did he neglect the opportunities that were afforded him of offering the balm of consolation to afflicted minds, whilst he exercised the powers of medicine for the relief of corporeal infirmities. To him alone is owing the institution of the Infirmary at Northampton, in the year 1743, an institution originally promoted by his benevolence, forwarded by his activity, and for many years regulated by his judgment. The admirable book of Statutes and Orders, which he compiled for its government, and which, on account of its superior excellence, has been admitted into other establishments of the like nature, will remain an everlasting monument of his vigilance and attention; and his Friendly Advice to a Patient, a work both in its design and execution worthy of its author, clearly proves that he was not unambitious of being a physician of the soul.

From principle and not from prejudice, from candid enquiry and not from blind zeal, from the certainty of conviction, and not from the prevalence of custom, was Dr. Stonhouse strongly attached to the tenets of the established church; and from the desire of enlarging the sphere of his exertions in making *wise unto salvation*, was he induced to relinquish the practice of physic, for the more important engagements of the clerical function. This circumstance of his life cannot possibly be attributed to any undue spirit of self-interest and accommodation, since the advantages arising to him from his former profession were much more considerable, and the difficulties attending it (to a mind like his) much less arduous than those which awaited him in the discharge of his parochial duties. Soon after he entered into holy orders, he was presented by Lord Radnor to the rectories of Great and Little Cheverel, in Wiltshire, where he continued zealously to enforce the saving truths of the gospel, till bodily infirmities rendered it necessary for him to spend a great part of his time at Bristol, for the benefit of the medicinal waters.

Yet even when thus separated from his flock, he still preserved a most anxious concern for their welfare, which was continually manifested by the wise and liberal provision which he made for their temporal as well as spiritual necessities: but though these claimed his special regard, yet his zeal rested not here; that benevolence which is the true offspring of vital religion, pointed out an ample range for the exertion of his talents. His leisure hours he employed in preparing exhortations and devotional tracts, of which he published a considerable number. Some of them have been very widely disseminated by the Society for the promoting Christian Knowledge; and a more judicious choice could not have been made, since they pourtray, in the clearest manner, the tendency of virtue to happiness, and of vice to misery; and are remarkably calculated to enliven our faith, to confirm our hopes, and to invigorate our charity.

Such are the rude outlines of the life of the Rev. Sir James Stonhouse, and of such a life who would not rejoice to hear, that the conclusion was characterized by calm resignation and serene devotion? He died at his house at the Hot Wells, Bristol.

STONHOUSE OF RADLEY, BERKSHIRE.

TABLE 55.

```
1 ROBERT STONHOUSE = Rose Roydon
         |
   E. Gibson = 2 George, 1575 = Eliz. Woodcroft
         |
I. Sir William, 1631 = E. Powell   Dionysia = Sir E. Hexto   Nicholas   Walter   Sir James
II. Sir John   III. Sir George   Wm.        Elizabeth   Mary          Ursula      Dionysia
    1632       M. Lovelace                  E. Perrot   W. Langton    J. Denton   Sir C. Fair-
                                                                                  meadow
IV. Sir George   4 Sir John Stonhouse   James        Elizabeth
    A. Scarlett    Martha Briggs                     Sir R. Stidolph | —, L. Byron
V. Sir George, 1737   Susanna.          5 Sir John Stonhouse, 1733
   Anne Ashton        Anne              Mary Mellish | Penelope Dashwood
George.   Marg.   VI. Sir John, 1740   Martha = A. Vansittart   Mary
6 Sir John   7 Sir Wm.   8. Sir James   Penelope   Catharine   Anne       Marg.   Dionysia   Susanna
                          1792          Sir H.   —, L.    Robert   Sir Wm.   1746   Rev. —   Peter Serle.
                                        Atkins   Gower    Lee     Bowyer            Benet
                                                                                  N = Sir Wm. Oglander
```

---

55. WREY of TREBITCH, CORNWALL.

Created Baronet July 30, 1628.

WOTTON, from an old pedigree, deduces this family from Robert le Wrey, who lived in the time of King Stephen, and thinks they were denominated from some office; but others suppose they took their name from their habitation and possession of Wrey in Devonshire. This Robert married Sibil, daughter of Ralph Abbot, and had issue

2. William le Wrey of Wrey, who by his wife Alice, daughter of John Kelley of Brodewood, was father of

3. Elias, and he of another of the same name; which last

4. Elias or Elye, married Joan, daughter and heir of Nicholas Holwaye, and left issue,

5. Richard, who married Joan, sister and heiress of John Norris, and was father of

6. Stephen le Wrey, who was father of

7. Thomas le Wrey, who married Elizabeth, daughter of Robert Yeo, and had issue John and Walter, and Alice, the wife of John Glanvile.*

8. John, by his wife Constance, the daughter of —— Hatch, left issue only a daughter, Constance, the wife of William Shylston; so that he was succeeded by his brother,

9. Walter, who married Constance, daughter of John Shylton, by whom he had

10. William Wrey of North Russel, who had two sons, Walter and Thomas.

11. Walter succeeded his father, and had a son,

12. Robert Wrey, who had three sons, Walter, Thomas, and William.

13. Walter succeeded his father, and married Bridget, daughter of Robert Shylston, by whom he had a daughter, Jane, first the wife of John Wikes of Cocktree; secondly, of Thomas Welcote; and thirdly, of Robert Fry; also a son,

14. John Wrey, Esq. who married Blanch, daughter and heir of Henry Killigrew of Wolston, in Cornwall, Esq. with whom he had large possessions, and the lordship of Trebitch, in the parish of St. Ives, in that county, which became thenceforward their capital mansion. He was high sheriff of the county of Cornwall 28 Eliz. and had two daughters, Philippa and Jane, the wife of Peter Coryton, Esq. and six sons; 1, William; 2, John, who married Eleanor, daughter and heir of Bernard Smith of Totness, Esq. relict of Sir John Fulford of Fulford, in Devonshire, Knt. and died without issue; 3, Edward, who married Jane, daughter of Price ap Howel; 4, Arthur, who married Joyce, daughter and heir to Tristram Harris of Hayne; also Robert and George, who died without issue.

15. William, the eldest son succeeded his father at Trebitch, and was high sheriff of Cornwall 41 Eliz. Mr. Carew, in his survey of that county,† characterises him as a man of hospitality, and a general welcomer of his friends and neighbours. He was knighted at Whitehall July 27, 1603, before the coronation of King James I. and died in June 1636. By Elizabeth his wife, daughter of Sir William Courtenay of Powerham, in Devonshire, Knt. he had one son,

I. WILLIAM, who was 20 years of age in 1620: he married Elizabeth, daughter of Sir Edward Chichester (then of Eggesford in Devonshire, Knt.) earl of Donegall in the kingdom of Ireland, by whom he had three daughters; 1, ——, the wife of —— Bluet, Esq. 2, ——, of —— Erisey, in Cornwall; and 3, ——, of —— Nichols, Esq. and having received the honour of knighthood, was advanced to the dignity of a baronet in the fourth year of King Charles I. He died in Aug. 1645, and was succeeded by his only son and heir,

II. Sir CHICHESTER WREY of Trebitch, Bart. was born in 1628: he faithfully adhered to his majesty, King Charles I. and took up arms in his cause, wherein he behaved with much bravery. About the year 1652 he married Anne, countess, do wager of Middlesex, relict of James earl of Middlesex, third daughter and coheir of Edward Bourchier, earl of Bath, by whom he became entitled to a joint

* About which time, or not long before, was Roger Wrey, who held a fourth part of a knight's fee in Wyke Chalveligh, in Devonshire, of the barony of Okehampton, 19 Edw. III. which Walter le Wrey formerly held. *Pole's MSS. Cart. de Com. Devon. p.* 492. † P. 117.

claim to the barony of Fitzwarine, and also possessed of a great estate in the county of Devon, and the noble seat of Tawstock, where the family now resides. After the restoration of the royal family he was made colonel of the Duke of York's regiment, and governor of Sheerness; and served in parliament for Lestwithiel in Cornwall, 13 Charles II. and died in May, 1668, having issue a daughter Anne, the wife of Sir Francis Northcote of Nimpton, in Devonshire, Bart. and four sons; 1, Sir Bourchier; 2, Chichester, a colonel in his majesty's armies, who was killed in the defence of Fort Montjouic, near Barcelona, in 1706; 3, Edward, and 4, John, who was killed before Tangier, at 19 years of age.

III. Sir BOURCHIER WREY, the eldest son, succeeded his father in title and estate: he was created one of the knights of the bath at the coronation of King Charles II. and soon after was a captain in the Duke of York's regiment, of which his father was colonel. He served under the Duke of Monmouth at the seige of Maestricht, and other places in the Netherlands. After the revolution he commanded a regiment of horse; and in 1690 was with that regiment in Torbay, where he was very instrumental in preventing the landing of the French, who then appeared with their fleet on the western coasts. He served as member of parliament for Leskard in Cornwall all the latter end of his life, and died July 28, 1696, leaving issue by Florence, his lady, daughter of Sir John Rolle of Stevonstone, in Devonshire, knight of the bath, a daughter Florence, the wife of John Cole, Esq. son of Sir Michael Cole of Inniskillin, in the county of Fermanaugh, in the kingdom of Ireland: also two sons, Sir Bourchier and, Chichester, rector of Tawstock.

IV. Sir BOURCHIER WREY of Tawstock, in Devonshire, Bart. successor to the title and estate, represented the borough of Camelford in Cornwall, in parliament 10 and 12 Queen Anne, and married Diana, daughter of John Rolle of Stevenstone, Esq. eldest son of the said Sir John Rolle, by Christian, daughter of the Earl of Aylesbury, sister to John Rolle of Stevenstone, Esq. and widow and relict of John Sparkes of the Friery, in Plymouth, Esq. Sir Bourchier died in 1726, and left five sons and four daughters; 1, Sir Bourchier, his successor; 2, John; 3, Chichester; 4, Robert, now a general in the Queen of Portugal's army; 5, Charles, since dead; 6, Diana, the wife of John Stafford of Roborough, in Devonshire, Esq. 7, Florence, of Edward I'Ans, Esq. collector of the customs at Biddesford in Devonshire; 8, Christian; and 9, Catharine. He was succeeded in dignity and estate by his eldest son,

V. Sir BOURCHIER WREY, Bart. who in 1749 married Mary, daughter of John Edwards of Highgate, Esq. who died in 1751, aged 27, on which account an elegant copy of Latin verses was composed, not designed as a monumental inscription, but to preserve to posterity the character of so excellent a lady. Sir Bourchier married secondly, May 1, 1755; ——, daughter of —— Thresher, Esq. In 1748 Sir Bourchier was elected representative for Barnstaple in Devonshire, and in 1759 was appointed colonel of the Devonshire militia; and died April 13, 1784, leaving two sons; 1, Bourchier, the present baronet; 2, William Bourchier, rector of Combintinhead; and four daughters, all married; Dionysia, the wife of Robert Harding of Upcott, Esq. Florentia, of Richard Long, jun. Esq. Anna-Maria, of Roundell Toke of Godington in Kent, Esq. Sir Bourchier died April 23, 1784, and was succeeded by his eldest son,

WREY OF TREBITCH, CORNWALL.

TABLE 56.

```
1 ROBERT LE WREY = Sibyl Abbot
2 William = Alice Kelley
3 Elias le Wrey
4 Eliasor Elye = Joan Holwaye
5 Richard = Joan Norris
6 Stephen le Wrey
7 Thomas le Wrey = E. Yeo
```

8 John = C. Hatch	9 Walter = C. Shylston				Alice = J. Glanvile
Constance = W. Shylston	10 William Wrey of North Russel				
	11 Walter Wrey			Thomas Wrey	
	12 Robert Wrey				
	13 Walter = B. Shylston		Thomas		William
	Jane = J. Wikes = T. Welcote = R. Fry				

14 John, 1586 = B. Killegrew						Henry, 1st E. of Stamford
15 Sir Wm. 1636	John	Edward	Arthur	Robert.	Philippa Jane	
E. Courtenay	E. Smith	J. ap Howel	J. Harris	Geo.	P. Coryton	
I. Sir Wm. Knt. & Bart. 1645		EDW. BOURCHIER,				Diana
Eliz. Chichester		E. of Bath				Rob. E. of Aylesbury
II. Sir Chichester Wrey, 1668 = Anne = James, E. of Middlesex						John Rolle = Christian
III. Sir Bourchier, 1696	Chichester	Edward,	Anne		Florence	John Rolle
Florence Rolle	1706	John	Sir F. North- cote		Sir B. Wrey	
IV. Sir Bourchier, 1784	Florence	Chichester				Diana
Diana Rolle	John Cole					Sir B. Wrey
V. Sir Bourchier, 1784	John,	Robert,	Diana	Florence	Christian,	
M. Edwards | —Thresher 1751	Chichester	Charles	J. Stafford	Edw. I'Ans	Catharine	
VI. Sir Bourchier Wrey	William	Dionysia	Florentia	Anna-Maria		
Anne Palk | Anne Osborne		R. Harding	Richard Long	R. Toke		

Anna-Eleonora   Bourchier   Robert-Bourchier   Eleonora-Elizabeth   Henry-Bourchier

TRELAWNY OF TRELAWNY, CORNWALL.

VI. Sir BOURCHIER WREY, the present baronet, who in 1786 married Anne, daughter of Sir Robert Palk of Haddon House, in the same county, Bart. by whom he has issue, 1, Anna-Eleanora; 2, Bourchier; 3, Robert-Bourchier. He married secondly in 1793, Anne, daughter of John Osborne, Esq. by whom he has one daughter, Eleonora-Elizabeth, and one son, Henry-Bourchier.

ARMS—Quarterly: 1, Wrey; sable, a fesse between three pole-axes, argent; helved, gules. 2, Bourchier; argent, a cross engrailed, gules; between four water-bougets, sable. 3, Plantagenet; quarterly, first and fourth azure, three fleurs-de-lis, or; second and third gules, three lions passant gardant, in pale, or. 4, Bohun; azure, on a bend argent, cottized or; between six lions, rampant, or.
CREST—An arm embowed, habited sable, the hand proper, holding a hatchet, argent; helved, gules:. but the present baronet uses a man's head in profile, couped below the shoulders; on the head a ducal coronet, therein a cap turned forwards, and tapelled of the second: thereon a catherine wheel of the same.
MOTTO—*Le bon temps viendra.*
SEAT—At Trebitch in Cornwall, and Tawstock House in Devonshire.*

---

56. TRELAWNY of TRELAWNY, CORNWALL.

Created Baronet July 1, 1628.

TRELAWNY, Trelany, Trelone, Trilone, and as in Doomsday Book, Treloen, a lordship situate in Alternon, in the county of Cornwall, gave denomination to this ancient family, that flourished in the said county before the conquest.

1. Eduni held the same in the time of the King Edward the confessor.
2. Hamelin, his son (as it is presumed) was likewise the possessor after the Norman invasion, by a tenure from the Earl of Mortain,† as found in that great assess-

---

* Tawstock House, the present seat of the family, came by the division of the Earl of Bath's estate, between the Earl of Stamford (whose mother was the other surviving co-heiress of the Earl of Bath) and Sir Bourchier Wrey, Bart.
I find that Tawstock was jointly possessed with the honours of Barnstaple, temp. Henry II. by William de Brewes aud Oliver de Tracy, and afterwards inhabited by Henry de Tracy; from whom the lords Martyn and Andelegh, of Hely, possessed it in hereditary succession, until in failure of issue male it came, by special intail, the property of Margaret, daughter and heir of the last Lord Audelegh; from whom, by marriage with Fulk lord Fitzwarren, afterwards Earl of Bath, Sir Chichester Wrey, by his marriage with Anne, co-heir of Edward earl of Bath, inherited, and whose issue made still enjoy it.
† Doomsday Book, sub. tit. Corn.

ment, made in the reign of King Wm. I. at which time it was rated at two carves and a half, two servants, and ten acres of wood, with ten of pasture, &c. A descendant of Hamelin was,

3. Richard de Trelony, who by deed without date,* gave to Pagan, son of Cleke, half an acre of land in Caron, parcel of the manor of South Caron.

4. William, his son, was seized in his demesne as of fee of a fourth part of a knight's fee in Tregenelek, as appears by a deed, whereby Reginald de Botrell confirmed the same to him and his heirs, to hold of John Osmer of Tregewe, and his heirs, witnessed by Sir William de Roscrowe, and Sir Ralph de Bovil, Knts.

5. John, his son and heir, married Joan, daughter of Reginald de Botrell.

6. William, his son and heir, married Joan, daughter of Stephen Trewynick.† He left issue,

7. John de Trelony, living 9 Edw. I. He married Lucy, daughter of Sir Richard Serjeaux, Knt. by whom he had a daughter Mary, the wife of Sir John Moeles, Knt. and

8. William, his son and heir, who was one of the burgesses for Launceston, 19 Edw. II. He married Margery, daughter to John de Rypariis or Rivers, testified by a release, dated 24 Edw. III. He, with Sir Reginald de Botreaux and Sir John Arundel, were commissioners to return the names of such who held 100*l*. yearly, in the county of Cornwall. His son and heir,

9. William, married Joan, sole sister and heir of John, and daughter of Richard Doyngell, by whom he had

10. John, his son and heir, who by gift of his father enjoyed, 40 Edw. III. lands in the ville of Trelawny, and in divers other places in Cornwall, and upon his father's death became possessed of the ancient patrimony, and had the honour of knighthood. He was living 8 Henry IV. at which time a fine was levied by him and his wife, Matilda, daughter to Robert Mynwenyke. He and his lady were both living 19 Richard II. (About this time, viz. 12 Henry VI. one Richard Trelenay was one of the members for Launceston). He had issue a son,

11. John, who received the honour of knighthood, was member for the county of Cornwall, and one of the coroners thereof; which office was conferred only upon the wisest knights of the county.‡

---

* Ex original. There are remaining in the custody of this ancient family, an immense quantity of deeds, from the time of this Richard, the abstracts whereof make two large volumes in Folio; so that only some few of them are referred to, to settle the descent, and the chronology.

† There was a fine levied by Stephen Trewynick and Isabel his wife, to this William Trelawny and Joan his wife, of lands in Trewynt, and other places in Mich. term, 3 Edw. I.

‡ He so eminently signalized himself in the wars of France, that King Henry V. at Gisors, in Normandy, (as a just recompence of his services) granted him 20*l*. yearly for life: and his successor, King Henry VI. was pleased to confirm it in the first year of his reign; and granted him (as it is said) in augmentation to his arms, the coat of the three oaken or laurel leaves, the symbols of conquest. Certain it is, that he was the first of this family who bore that addition. Under the picture of the former of these kings, which stood formerly over the great gate at Launceston was this obsolete rhyme:
        He that will doe ought for mee,
        Let hym love well Sir John Tirlawnee.

He married Agnes, daughter to Robert Trogodeck, by whom he had Joan, the wife of Thomas Upton of Treloish, and Isabel, of Stephen Trenewith, to whom, and their heirs, he gave lands in Trenthill, &c. and two sons, Sir Richard and John. Sir Richard, in the life-time of his father was one of the burgesses for Lyskeard, in the parliament 9 Henry V. and on July 1, 2 Henry VI. Sir John, the father, settled several lands in trustees, for the use of himself for life, then of Richard his son, the remainder to John, his second son, &c.

This Richard died without issue male in 1449, leaving by Agnes Henwood two daughters, from one of which descended Arundel of Talferne, by the match of Penpons; from the other daughter are descended, as heirs general, Wrey and Smith, of St. German's, who by virtue of a settlement, and an award after a long suit, had divers of the ancient manors belonging to this family.

12. John Trelawny, Esq. second son of Sir John, was burgess for Truro, in the parliament held Feb. 12, 27 Henry VI. and married Joan, daughter and heiress of Nicholas Helligan. This John, by the name of John Trelawny of Treserrett, had a general pardon granted him. In Sep. 1 Edw. IV. he was sheriff, and in 14 Edw. IV. had a quietus for collecting the tenths and fifteenths in Cornwall, granted by parliament. Thomas earl of Devon, in consideration of the annuity of ten marks yearly, granted him by this John Trelawny, covenants to be a firm and sure lord to him, in all things which appertain to his lands, as far as the law shall permit, 33 Henry VI. He is often stiled John Trelawny of Brightorre, and sometimes of Wolston, in St. Ive's parish.

13. John, his son, was a knight, temp. Henry VII. and augmented his patrimony by a double marriage: his first wife was Blanch (in the deeds often named Candida) daughter and co-heir to John Powna of Powna, the heir general of Noddetone; and Crooke, heir of Paderda, Pyncerna, and Devyoch. They were married in or before the 29th of Henry VI. as is manifest from a feoffment dated that year by the said Powna. His second wife was Jane, daughter and co-heir of Robert Holland (widow of John Kendall) by whom he had issue a daughter Jane, the wife of John Wideslade. By his first lady he had a daughter, the wife of Thomas Flammock, son and heir of Thomas Flammock of Bocara, in 4 Henry VII. and five sons; 1, John Trelawny; 2, another John Trelawny, of St. German's, who married first Joan, daughter and co-heir of Thomas Clemens of Lyskeard; and surviving her, without any issue, he married secondly Margaret, daughter to Richard Buckton of Buckton, whose posterity now remain at Coldrinnick, seized of a considerable estate: 3, Roger Trelawny of Brightorre, whose daughter and heir was the wife of —— Hawkins); 4, Richard Trelawny of Launceston, who had issue; and 5, Thomas, who died unmarried.

14. John, the eldest son and heir, succeeded his father: he was, with others, commissioned by King Henry VII. to hear the controversies between the prior of of Bodmyn and others; and having had in marriage Florence, fourth daughter of

He was living 12 Henry VI. as appears by an indenture made by Robert Whyttingham (receiver-general of the dutchy of Cornwall) and John Lower, of the profits of the said county, wherein mention is made of the payment, to the said Sir John, of the annuity aforesaid, for Mich. term that year.

Sir Hugh Courtenay of Boconnock, and sister to Edward earl of Devon, upon the extinction of which line, she, with her sisters, became co-heirs of that noble family; by her he had three sons; 1, Walter; 2, Alneth (to whom Catharine countess of Devon granted the bailiwick of Exitond, and the West gate of the city of Exeter, for his life, 3 Henry VIII.) He died at Tournay in 1515: 3, Edward: the two latter died without issue.

15. Walter, the eldest son, succeeded to the inheritance, and had a grant of the constableship and bailiwick of the honour and hundred of Plympton, during his life, by patent, dated Nov. 10, 1 Henry VIII. to whom, and Catharine, countess of Devon, daughter of King Edw. IV. he wrote several letters now remaining. By Isabel, his wife, daughter of John Towse of Taunton, in Somersetshire, by Jane his wife, afterwards the wife of Sir Thomas Grenville, he had two sons, John and Richard, who died without issue. This lady survived her husband, who died before 1518, as appears by letters, full of kind expressions, sent to her from Henry Courtenay, marquis of Exeter.

16. John, the eldest son, succeeded to the inheritance, and was burgess in parliament for Lyskeard in 6 Edw. VI. and had two wives; 1, Margery, daughter and heiress of Thomas Lamelion: by her he had John, his son and heir. His second wife was Lora, daughter and heir of Henry Trecarrel (who survived her husband): by her he had issue another John, who married Beatrice, daughter of Hugh Trevanion.*

17. John, his eldest son by his first wife, succeeded, being sometime denominated of Pool.† He was two years and six months old in the 28th of Henry VIII. at the death of his mother's father, Thomas Lamelion, Esq. to whom he is found, by an inquisition then taken, to be be heir, as son of John Trelawny, by Margery his wife, daughter and heiress of the said Thomas. In 1 Eliz. he was burgess for Lestwithiell, and was deputy lieutenant of Cornwall, under the earl of Bedford; and then paid 6l. for not taking the order of knighthood: 2 Eliz. he was high sheriff of Cornwall, and in the 5th year one of the knights of the shire for that county. In the 9th of the said Queen's reign he was again high sheriff of Cornwall. He married Anne, the fifth daughter and co-heir of William Reskymer, Esq. by whom he had a daughter Mary, first the wife of John Spring, Esq. son of Sir William, of Lavenham in Suffolk, Knt. and afterwards of Sir Robert Gardiner, Knt. and two sons, John and Jonathan. He departed this life in 1568, having made his will 10 Eliz. wherein he proposes an establishment of his inheritance on his name and family, leaving John, his eldest son, heir to his estate, who died an infant in 1570, whereupon

* He was found to be one of the heirs to the Earl of Devon, in the 4th and 5th of Philip and Mary, and his will bears date 5 Eliz. He obtained a confirmation of the liberties of Mynheniot, from Edw. VI. dated Feb. 8, 2do regni; and from Mary, dated Feb. 8, in the first of her reign; by whom he was appointed collector of the loans in Cornwall, 4th and 5th Philip and Mary; as also by Queen Eliz.

† Mr. Camden, in his Britannia, vol. I. p. 20, says, about two miles from the river Loo is the present seat of the ancient family of the Trelawnies; to which, by marriage with one of the daughters and co-heirs of Courtenay earl of Devonshire, a great part of the inheritance of that noble family came. They were possessed of this place only since the reign of Queen Elizabeth, having before been for many ages seated, first at Trelawny, and afterwards at Minhinnead (a town distant about six miles on the same river Loo) where they still have a large house (the place of their former residence) called Pool.

18. Jonathan, his brother, was the next heir, who was born Dec. 17, 1568, being eight weeks after the death of his father. His lady survived him, and was married to Sir William Mohun. This Jonathan was member of parliament for the borough of Lyskeard in 28, 31, and 35 Eliz. of which he was chosen recorder and had a quietus for collecting the queen's subsidies in Cornwall; in 37 Eliz. he was sheriff of that county; and knight of the shire for Cornwall in 39 Eliz. and chosen steward of the borough of Westlow in 1600. He was knighted in 1597, and was again chosen knight of the shire in the first of James I. in which year he made his will, and died during the session, June 21, 1604. He was a person of great honour and interest;* and married Elizabeth, second daughter of Sir Henry Killigrew, Knt. and had issue three daughters; Elizabeth, born in 1590; Anne in 1600, and Cordelia: and two sons, John, and Edward born in 1595.

I. JOHN TRELAWNY, Esq. the eldest son, was born April 27, 1592, and created baronet by King Charles I. He was high sheriff of Cornwall 6 Charles I. and married Elizabeth, daughter of Sir Reginald Mohun of Boconnock, in Cornwall, Bart. by whom he had five sons and eight daughters; 1, Sir Jonathan, his successor; 2, John; 3, Edward, who both died unmarried; 4, Francis, who married Margaret, daughter of Sir Edward Seymour of Bury Pomeroy, in Devonshire, Bart. and 5, Reginald, who died a batchelor. The daughters were 1, Eliz. the wife of Thomas Lower of Tremeer; 2, Anne, of John Vivian of Trewan, both in Cornwall, Esqrs. 3, Margaret, of Amos, younger son of Sir Francis Fulford of Fulford, in Devonshire, Knt. 4, Philippa, who died unmarried; 5, Bridget, the wife of —— Lee of Kent; 6, Mary, of the Rev. Mr. Greensworth; 7, Penelope, of Thomas Maynard, Esq. consul at Smyrna; and 8, Dorothy, of William Mohun of Trencreek, Esq.

II. Sir JONATHAN TRELAWNY, Bart. eldest son, who succeeded to the title and estate, married Mary, daughter of Sir Edward Seymour, Bart. (elder sister to his brother Francis's wife) by whom he had seven sons; 1, John, who died in his father's life-time, having married Catharine, third daughter and co-heir of James Jenkyn, Esq. by whom he had no issue; 2, Jonathan, who died an infant; 3, Sir Jonathan, of whom hereafter; 4, Major-general Charles Trelawny, who represented the town of Plymouth in several parliaments, in the reign of Queen Anne, who married first ——, and secondly Anne, daughter and co-heir of Richard Lower of. London, M.D. He died in Sep. 1731, aged 78, and was buried at Pelynt in Cornwall;† 5, William Trelawny, who died unmarried; 6, Chichester, who also died

---

* Carew's Survey of Cornwall, p. 63.

The house of commons, to shew their respect to him, attended his funeral, at St. Clement's Danes, where he was interred, as appears by what follows from their journal:—Die Ven. June 22, 1604. "It was informed, that Sir Jonathan Trelawny, one of the knights of the shire for Cornwall, died yesterday, being suddenly suffocated with a flux of blood, which came by breaking a vein with vehement coughing, and was said to be found sick, and dead in a quarter of an hour; and thereupon moved by Sir John Hollis, that the members of the house do attend his burial to-morrow in the afternoon, which was so ordered."

† A gentleman of an ancient and honourable family, which he also ennobled by his virtues. His first appearance in the field was about the year 1672, under the famous Turenne, a marshal of France;

unmarried, in 1694; 7, Henry, colonel of a regiment in the service of King William, who married Rebecca, daughter and co-heir of Matthew Hals, of Efford, in Devonshire, Esq. by Rebecca, his wife, daughter and co-heir of Charles Specott, of Thornbury, in Devonshire, Esq. by whom he had several children: what daughters Sir Jonathan had I do not find, but in Winchester cathedral is an inscription, as I take it, for one of them.*

III. Sir JONATHAN TRELAWNY, Bart. eldest surviving son and successor to his father, in title and estate,† was educated at Westminster School, entered into Christ Church College, Oxford, in 1668, aged 18 years; and in the year following was made student thereof. Though the title of baronet, and the paternal estate was to come to him after the death of his father, yet he continued in the church, and upon the translation of Dr. Lake to the see of Chichester, was nominated

---

and his gallantry and experience in military affairs spoke him worthy of so great a master. His public actions in several instances redound to his honour, but are not so particularly and perfectly known, as a relation of them may require; those who served with him can give the justest eulogium; his modesty was too delicate to recite his actions. He was so far from courting the applause which was due to his behaviour, that he very rarely made mention of the one, lest it should demand the other. He served in the troops which King Charles II. sent to the assistance of France, when they and their country gained the greatest reputation, by covering the retreat of the French, and repulsing the Germans; an action of that signal service, that it merited the public thanks of the King of France. This may be said to his and the nation's honour, that the armies of France have been protected, as well as conquered, by the English. Nor did he shine less in his private than in his active life: the reputation he acquired in public services he adorned with affability, tenderness, and charity to all about him: the bravery of the soldier was tempered with the politeness of the most accomplished gentleman. In short, so generous and noble a spirit attended his whole course of life, and so much patience and resignation his last most painful and lingering illness, that he appeared in both equally the hero, and died great as he had lived. He was very instrumental in bringing about the revolution, though he was sorry that his country required it; he loved his king, but his country more; interest would have inclined him to support the king and absolute power; his honour and the love of his country commanded his service for the constitution, the laws and liberty: he served then with reluctance as against the king, but he could not serve the king when against his country. In the great and famous battle of the Boyne he shared the glories of the field; and in confidence of his bravery and honour, the important city of Dublin was recommended to his care; an eminent sign of the high esteem he merited, when the metropolis of Ireland was thought safest under his government. As his arms were serviceable against the enemies of his majesty, so was his administration in protecting his subjects: he preserved the city from the violence of the soldiers, and generously despised the advantages of safeguards and contributions: when he left it, the sad effects of both broke in upon it. As he maintained his posts with honour, so he retired out of a point of honour; but his retirement was distinguished by particular marks of royal favour: King William sent a commission, appointing him governor of Plymouth. How his great qualities endeared him to the inhabitants of that place, their universal esteem, and public acknowledgments of his merits, abundantly testify.

* Here lieth the body of Madam Mary Davies, daughter of Sir Jonathan Trelawny, of Trelawny, in the county of Cornwall, Bart. A lady of excellent endowments, and exemplary virtue; of courage and resolution above her sex, and equal to the generous stock whence she sprang. She was maid of honour to Mary, Princess of Orange, and relict to lieutenant-colonel Davies, who at the seige of Namur, mounting the Trenches, at the head of the grenadiers of the first regiment of guards, was the first that threw the fascines (which others used to cover themselves with in their attack) over the ditch, and with his men passed it, beating the French out of their works, which was a gallant action, and greatly contributed towards the taking of the town; in performing of which he received the wound of which he died, and gained so just an esteem for the boldness and success of it with the king, that he designed him the great honour of a visit the morning on which he died; and being informed of his death, in kind and honourable terms expressed his concern and sorrow for the loss of so brave and deserving an officer. She died Sep. 24, 1707.   † Wood's Athen. Ox. vol. II. p. 1183.

by his majesty, King James II. to succeed him in Bristol, whereupon (after he had been diplomated doctor of divinity) being consecrated thereunto in the archbishop's palace at Lambeth, Nov. 8, 1685, he was introduced into the house of lords, with Bishop Ken, the 11th of the same month: on June 8, 1688 he was one of the six bishops, besides the Archbishop of Canterbury (Dr. Sancroft) that was committed to the Tower of London, for subscribing a petition to his majesty,* expressing their unwillingness *to the distributing and publishing in their churches his majesty's late declaration for liberty of conscience*, &c. where continuing till they were publicly tried in Westminster Hall for a libel, and acquitted, they were, to the great joy of the true sons of the church of England, released on the 15th of the same month. On the 13th of April, 1689, he was, by his majesty, King William III. as a reward for his services, translated to the see of Exeter, in the room of Dr. Lamplugh, translated to the archbishoprick of York; and from thence, 1707, was by her majesty, Queen Anne, translated to the see of Winchester, in the room of Bishop Mew, deceased, and dying July 19, 1721,† was buried at Pelynt, in Cornwall, with his ancestors. He married Rebecca, daughter and co-heir of Thomas Hele, of Bascomb, in Devonshire, Esq. by Elizabeth, his wife, daughter and co-heir of Matthew Hals, of Efford, in Devonshire, and Rebecca, his wife, daughter and coheir of Charles Specott of Thornbury, in the same county, Esqrs. by whom he left 1, Sir John, his successor; 2, Edward, who in the last parliament of King Georg I. was elected member of parliament for Westlow, in Cornwall, and appointed one of the commissioners of the Victualling Office, and in the first parliament of King George I. he was chosen again for the same place, and in the second parliament, which met in June, 1734, he was chosen for two places, Eastlow and Westlow, in Cornwall, but his seat was vacated, being then one of the commissioners of his majesty's customs; and afterwards governor of Jamaica. He married, in 1737, Mrs. Crawford, daughter of John Crawford, Esq. 3, Hele Trelawny, D.D. rector of the parishes of South Hill, and Lanreath, in Cornwall, and one of the proctors for the clergy of the diocese of Exeter, who died in June, 1740, leaving behind him a most amiable character both in public and private life, a zealous advocate for the Christian religion, and one who humbly followed the doctrines of it in his life and conversation; who lived beloved, and died lamented, leaving an example worthy of imitation. 4, Charles, prebendary of Winchester; and 5, Harry, who died at sea: 6, Charlotte, died unmarried; 7, Mary, the wife of the Rev. Mr. Allanson; 8, Rebecca, of John Buller, of Morval, Esq. 9, Letitia, of her first cousin, Harry Trelawny, Esq. afterwards Sir Harry; and 10, Anne, who died unmarried.

* The king, having read the petition, of the bishops, mentioned in his answer the word *rebellion*, on which Sir Jonathan says:—" Struck with that word rebellion, I fell on my knees, and in great heat and confusion spoke thus: 'Rebellion, Sir, I beseech your majesty do not say so hard a thing of us, for God's sake; do not believe we are, or can be guilty of rebellion. It is impossible for me, or my family, to be guilty of rebellion. Your majesty cannot but remember, that you sent me to quell Monmouth's rebellion, and I am as ready to do what I can to quell another. We will do our duty to your majesty, to the utmost, in every thing that does not interfere with our duty to God.'

† Willis's Survey of Cathedrals, vol. I. p. 782.

IV. Sir JOHN TRELAWNY, Bart. eldest son of the bishop, succeeded his father in title and estate: he was elected a representative in parliament for the borough of Lyskeard, in Cornwall, in the first parliament of King George I. and for Westlow, in the second; and in the first parliament of his late majesty, was elected again for the same place. Sir John lived a very retired life, and married Miss Blackwood, of Scotland, who died April 15, 1777, and whose memory is deservedly respected in the family. He died Feb. 1756, without issue; and his younger brother being dead before him, without issue, the title and estate descended to his first cousin,

V. Sir HARRY TRELAWNY, Bart. who was married, as before-mentioned, to Letitia, fourth daughter of the Bishop, who died May 28, 1775; by whom he had two daughters; Letitia, the wife of her first cousin, Sir William Trelawny, Bart. who died Aug. 24, 1772. Sir Harry had a brother William, a captain in the army, who had four sons; Charles, who died without issue; Sir William; Harry, a general, and governor of Landguard Fort, and died in Jan. 1800; and Thomas.

Sir Harry, in the beginning of his life, was aid-de-camp to the Duke of Marlborough, and was in parliament two or three sessions, but at last retired, and lived very privately, at Betshead, in Devonshire. He was a man of great learning, and dying in a very advanced age, in the beginning of the year 1762, was succeeded by his nephew,

VI. Sir WILLIAM TRELAWNY, Bart. late governor of Jamaica, and captain in the royal navy: he married Letitia, his cousin, daughter of the late baronet, by whom he had one son, Sir Harry, the present baronet, and one daughter, Letitia-Anne, the wife of Paul Treby Treby, of Plympton, in Devonshire, Esq. He died at Kingston, in Jamaica, in Dec. 1772; and was succeeded by his son,*

---

* *Extract of a letter from Kingston, in Jamaica, Dec.* 19, 1772.

It is with real concern we acquaint the public, that on Friday night, the 11th instant, his excellency, Sir William Trelawny, Bart. our very worthy and much-esteemed Governor, departed this life, after a long and tedious illness, which he bore with fortitude and magnanimity; and died with that firm hope of a happy immortality, after a virtuous and admirable uniformity and consistency of character, and the calm consciousness of a life well spent in the service of his country, at once inspired and justified. During four year's residence in the administration of this government, he so wisely guided, and steadily held the reins of power, and maintained such an inflexible integrity of conduct, altogether unbiassed by private attachments, or selfish considerations, that party herself forgot her resentments, and seemingly left no contest, but who should most promote the ease and happiness of an administration, which gave ease and happiness to all. The great and universal regret which the apprehension of this unhappy event has, for some time past, given to all ranks of people, is the surest proof of his Excellency's merit, as well as the strongest testimony, that a government conducted on the same principles, cannot fail of meeting the noblest reward, the general applause of a grateful and united people.

The next day, being Saturday, the 12th instant, the honourable the house of assembly came to the following resolution:—" *Resolved : In order to testify the grateful respect which this house entertained of his late Excellency's merit, the sense they have of the great and universal satisfaction, which his mild and equitable administration gave to all ranks of people, and the great regret which they feel at his loss, it be made the request of this house to Lady Trelawny, that her Ladyship consents, that his Excellency's funeral be conducted at the public expence.*"

In consequence of this vote, a joint committee of the honourable the council and assembly was appointed to conduct the funeral, which, notwithstanding the shortness of time, was managed with equal propriety and magnificence.

Accordingly, on Sunday evening, the 13th instant, the body, enclosed in a coffin of lead, placed in an outward shell, covered with crimson velvet, and richly furnished, lay in state, in the council chamber, which was hung with black, and illuminated with large tapers of wax; and to their great honour,

VII. The Rev. Sir HARRY TRELAWNY, Bart. who in 1778 married Miss Anne Brown; by whom he had a son, born June 20, 1780.

ARMS—Argent, a chevron, sable.
CREST—On a wreath, a wolf passant, proper.
MOTTO—*Sermoni consona facta.*
SEAT—At Trelawny, Cornwall.

---

the members of the legislature, the officers of the navy, army, and militia; the magistrates, and all ranks of people, seemed to vie with each other, in shewing the most grateful testimony of respect and regard to the Governor's memory.

About eleven o'clock the same evening the procession began from the king's house, in the following order, the artillery firing minute guns, viz. Spanish Town regiment of foot militia—the 36th regiment of foot, under the command of Col. Campbell, marching in form, with their arms reversed, preceded by a band of music, collected from the different regiments, and the battallion lately arrived, playing the dead march in Saul; eight mutes, the Governor's secretary and houshold, public officers, provost marshal-general, physicians, clergy, the body, supported by the hon. A. Sinclair, hon. W. Brown, hon. B. Edwards, hon. W. Harvie, hon. J. Scot, hon. T. Iredel, hon. J. Ellis, hon. T. Beach, and four aid-de-camps; chief mourners, hon. Mr. Harrison and hon. Mr. May; house of assembly, as mourners; Judges of the grand court and assize; colonel, provost, and officers of the fleet; barristers at law, masters in chancery, attendants, troops of horse.

The following address was presented by the council of Jamaica, to Lady Trelawny:

" The council of Jamaica being truly sensible of the great loss your ladyship has sustained, by the demise of our late worthy governor, beg leave to condole with you on that unhappy occasion. We have too great a share in the loss, not to participate with your ladyship in the affliction: yet we derive no small comfort from the consideration (and we earnestly hope your ladyship will join in the reflection) that the departure of great and good men, though a loss to us, is the consummation of perfect felicity to them. Your ladyship, too, has the satisfaction to reflect, that your worthy husband, even in this life, had the singular happiness of receiving that reward, which virtue too frequently fails of attaining. He died with the applause of all good men, and in the roll of honour is his memory recorded.

" We sincerely wish your ladyship a safe voyage to Great Britain, and that your future days may be brightened by happiness. On all occasions we beg leave to tender your ladyship our best services."
See also Long's Hist. Jamaica, vol. II. p. 263.

TRELAWNY, OF TRELAWNY, CORNWALL.

TABLE 57.

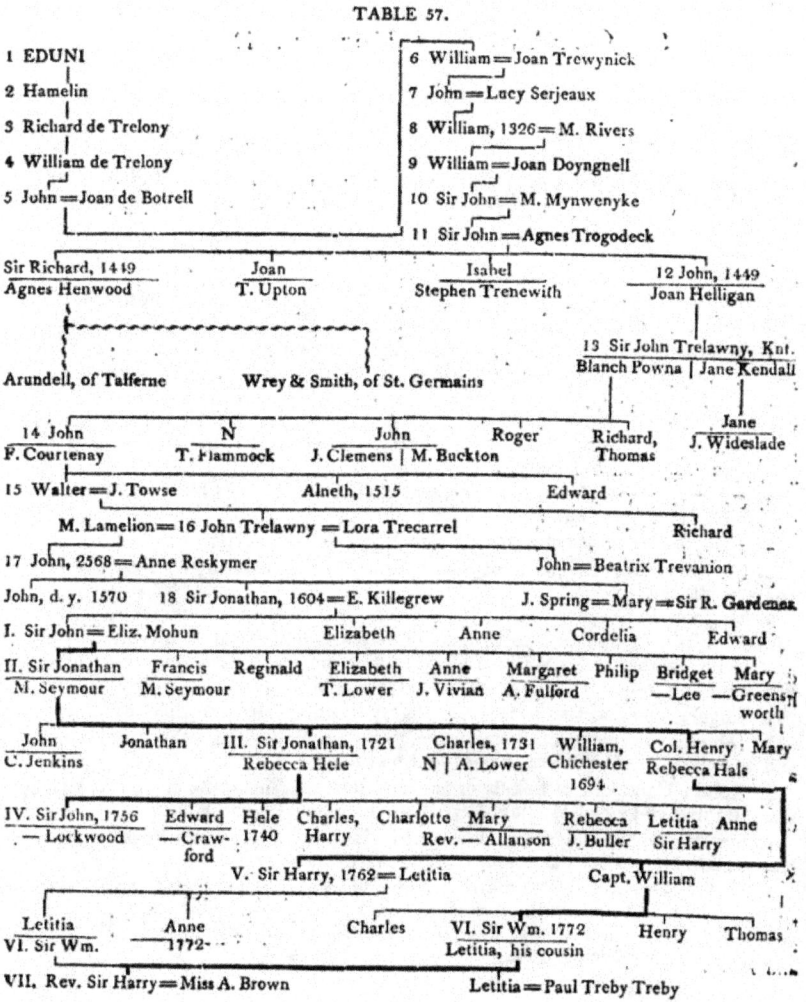

1 EDUNI
2 Hamelin
3 Richard de Trelony
4 William de Trelony
5 John = Joan de Botrell

6 William = Joan Trewynick
7 John = Lucy Serjeaux
8 William, 1326 = M. Rivers
9 William = Joan Doyngnell
10 Sir John = M. Mynwenyke
11 Sir John = Agnes Trogodeck

Sir Richard, 1449 — Agnes Henwood
Joan — T. Upton
Isabel — Stephen Trenewith
12 John, 1449 — Joan Helligan

Arundell, of Talferne
Wrey & Smith, of St. Germains

13 Sir John Trelawny, Knt.
Blanch Powna | Jane Kendall

14 John — F. Courtenay
N — T. Flammock
John — J. Clemens | M. Buckton
Roger
Richard, Thomas
Jane — J. Wideslade

15 Walter = J. Towse
Alneth, 1515
Edward

M. Lamelion = 16 John Trelawny = Lora Trecarrel
Richard

17 John, 2568 = Anne Reskymer
John = Beatrix Trevanion

John, d. y. 1570
18 Sir Jonathan, 1604 = E. Killegrew
J. Spring = Mary = Sir R. Gardener

I. Sir John = Eliz. Mohun
Elizabeth
Anne
Cordelia
Edward

II. Sir Jonathan — M. Seymour
Francis — M. Seymour
Reginald
Elizabeth — T. Lower
Anne — J. Vivian
Margaret — A. Fulford
Philip
Bridget — Lee
Mary — Greensworth

John — C. Jenkins
Jonathan
III. Sir Jonathan, 1721 — Rebecca Hele
Charles, 1731 — N | A. Lower
William, Chichester 1694
Col. Henry — Rebecca Hals
Mary

IV. Sir John, 1756 — Lockwood
Edward — Crawford
Hele 1740
Charles, Harry
Charlotte Rev. — Allanson
Mary J. Buller
Rebecca
Letitia Sir Harry
Anne

V. Sir Harry, 1762 = Letitia
Capt. William

Letitia
VI. Sir Wm.
Anne 1772
Charles
VI. Sir Wm. 1772 Letitia, his cousin
Henry
Thomas

VII. Rev. Sir Harry = Miss A. Brown
Letitia = Paul Treby Treby

57. CONYERS, of Horden, Durham.

Created Baronet July 14, 1628.

OF this ancient family, originally written Coigniers, denominated from a place of that name in France, was

1. Roger de Coigniers, that came into England about the end of the reign of William the Conqueror, to whom the Bishop of Durham, who died in 1095, gave the constableship of Durham.

2. Roger de Coigners, the second of that name, lord of Howton Coigniers, and of Sokebourne, by the gift of Ranulph, of Durham, who died in 1128.

3. Roger de Coigniers, the third, was of Howton Coigniers, in Yorkshire, and of Sokebourne, in Durham. He lived 24 Henry II.

4. Robert de Coigniers, of Howton Coigniers and of Sokebourne, lived temp. Rich. I. and King John: he had three sons, Thomas, Roger, and Geoffery.

5. Thomas de Coigniers, the eldest son, had issue, 1, Robert, who lived temp. Henry III. whose daughter and heir, Joan, was the wife of Sir Christopher Mallory, Knt. 2, Roger de Coigners, of Sokebourne, who had issue Robert, who alienated his inheritance to Geoffery, his uncle; 3,

6. Geoffery de Coigniers, of Sokebourne, after the death of his nephew, Robert: he lived 5 Henry III. and had issue,

7. John, father of three sons, the two eldest died issueless.

8. Sir Humphrey Coigners, of Sokebourne, Knt. third son, lived 55 Henry III. and was father of

9. Sir John de Coigners, Knt. (28 Edw. I.) who had issue two sons; 1,

10. John, who by his first wife, Elizabeth, had a daughter Isabel, the wife of Robert de Colvile, mother of Sir William Colvile, Knt. and by his second wife, Christian, had issue Petronilla, the wife of Robert Herle, and died without issue; and

11. Roger, who had two sons; 1, Geoffery (8 Edw. III.) who died issueless, and

12. John de Coigniers, of Sokebourne, who married Elizabeth, third daughter and co-heir of Sir William de Atton, and had issue,

13. Robert Coigniers, of Sokebourne, Esq. who died in 1433: he married Isabel, daughter and co-heir of William Pert, Esq. by whom he had issue,

14. Sir Christopher Coigniers, who by Mariora, daughter of Sir William de Eure, Knt. had issue four sons and four daughters: of the sons,

15. Sir William, the eldest, married Anne, daughter of Sir Ralph Bigott, of Setrington, Knt. but died without issue male, as did Robert and John, the second and fourth sons; and of the daughters, Maud was the wife of —— Wilberfoss, and Joan of —— Dymoke; but

16. Humphrey, the third son, had issue,

17. Sir John Coigniers, Knt. father of

18. Robert, whose younger son,

19. John, was one of the king's judges, and by his wife Margaret, the daughter and heir of Sir Anthony St. Quintin, had the castle and estate of Hornby, in Yorkshire, wherein he was succeeded by his son,

20. Sir Christopher Conyers, of Hornby, Knt. whose wife was Ellen, daughter and heir of —— Rylston, by whom he had issue,

21. Sir John Conyers, knight of the most noble order of the garter, who married Margaret, daughter and heir of Philip, lord Darcy, and had issue two sons, John, and Richard. John Conyers of Hornby, Esq. married Alice, or Anne, third daughter and co-heir of William de Nevil, lord Fawconbridge and earl of Kent; by whom he had two sons and two daughters; Sir William, John, Margery, the wife of Sir William Bulmer, of Wilton, and Anne, of Richard, lord Lumley.

Sir William, first lord Conyers, of Hornby, married Anne, daughter of Ralph Nevill, first earl of Westmorland; by whom he had one son and two daughters; Catharine, the wife of Francis Bygod, and Margaret, of Sir Richard Cholmondeley, of Rockesby, Knt. Sir William was succeeded by his son,

Christopher, second lord Conyers, of Hornby, who married Anne, daughter of Thomas, lord Dacres, of Gillesland; by whom he had two sons and two daughters; John, Leonard, Elizabeth, the wife of George Place, of Halnaby, and Jane, of Sir Marmaduke Constable, of Averingham, Knt. and was succeeded by his eldest son,

John, third lord Conyers, of Hornby, who married Matilda, daughter of Henry Clifford, earl of Cumberland, and had issue four daughters, his co-heirs; 1, Margaret, who died young; 2, Anne, the wife of Anthony Kemp, of Kent, Esq. 3, Elizabeth, of Thomas Darcy, second son to Sir Arthur Darcy, Knt. and 4, Catharine, of John Atherton, of Chowbent, in Lancashire, Esq. so that the elder branch becoming extinct, the family was continued by

22. Richard Conyers, of Horden, second son of Sir John Conyers, knight of the garter, who married Elizabeth, daughter and heir of Sir Robert Claxton, of Horden, Knt. and had issue three sons and three daughters; Richard, Robert, Percival, Catharine, Mary, and Anne.

23. Richard Conyers, the eldest son, was of Horden, in the bishoptick of Durham, and was succeeded by his son,

24. Christopher, who married Elizabeth, daughter of John Jackson, of Bedall, in Yorkshire, by whom he had two sons, Richard and George,

25. Richard, married Elizabeth, daughter of Roger Lumley, Esq. by whom he had two sons; Thomas, who died without issue, and

26. Christopher Conyers, of Horden, who was living in 1575, and married Elizabeth, daughter of Cuthbert Conyers, of Layton, Esq. but she dying without issue; he married secondly ——, second daughter of Sir Ralph Hedworth, of Harraton, in Durham, Knt. by whom he was father of

CONYERS, OF HORDEN, DURHAM.

I. Sir JOHN CONYERS, of Horden, the first baronet of this family, so created 4 Charles II. He married the daughter of —— Groves, of Yorkshire, Esq. and had issue,

II. Sir CHRISTOPHER CONYERS, Bart. his eldest son and successor, who married Elizabeth, daughter of William Langhorne, of London, Esq. sister of Sir William Langhorne, of Charlton, in Kent, Bart. and had issue Sir John, his successor. She died in child-bed, April 27, 1644 (before the title came to her husband) and lies buried at St. Giles's in the Fields, in the county of Middlesex. Sir Christopher married secondly Julia, daughter of Richard, lord viscount Lumley, and relict of Alexander Germyn, Esq. by whom he had issue a daughter, Julia, the wife of Sir William Blacket, of Newcastle, Bart. and after his decease of Sir William Thompson, Knt. recorder of the city of London, and one of the barons of the Exchequer. She died Aug. 16, 1722, and was buried at Hampsted in Middlesex.

III. Sir JOHN CONYERS, Bart. only son of Sir Christopher, and heir to Sir William Langhorne, Bart. whereby he became possessed of the seat and estate at Charlton, besides other considerable estates, which, by the death of Sir Baldwin, and his son, without issue male, went, according to the entail, first to William Langhorne Games, Esq. who dying without issue male, it then went to the Rev. Mr. Marrion, of Essex: which Sir John married Mrs. Mary Newman, with whom he had the estate of the Baldwins, at Great Stoughton, in Huntingdonshire, where the family chiefly resided. Of his six sons and two daughters, Mary was the wife of Edward Checkley, of Alwalton, in Huntingdonshire, Gent. Sir Baldwin was his successor; Christopher died young; and John, Edward, Christopher, and William, died without issue. Sir John died Sep. 14, 1719, aged 75, and lies buried in Great Stoughton church, in Huntingdonshire, with his lady, who died Oct. 24, 1714, aged 67.

IV. Sir BALDWIN CONYERS, Bart. his only surviving son and successor, married Sarah, only daughter and heir of Edward Conyers, of Blaston, in Leicestershire, Esq. (by which marriage he possessed the manor of Bradley, in Leicestershire) but had no issue. His second lady was Margaret, eldest daughter of Henry Nevil, of Holt, in Leicestershire, Esq. by whom he had two sons; Christopher, who died in his infancy; and John, who died Sep. 4, 1729, unmarried; also seven daughters, of which two were in a nunnery abroad; Elizabeth; Harriot, the wife of Thomas Wollascot, of Caversham, in Berkshire, Esq. Charlotte, of John Baptist Guastaldi, resident from Genoa to our court; Teresa, and one daughter died unmarried. Sir Baldwin dying April 17, 1731, was buried in Great Stoughton church, and was succeeded in the title by his cousin,

V. Sir RALPH, who is descended from a younger son of the first baronet: he married Jane, only daughter of Ralph Blackston, Esq. brother to Sir Nicholas Blackston, of Shieldsrow, in Durham, Bart. by whom he had five sons and three daughters; Blackston, John, Nicholas, Thomas, Mary, Jane, and Elizabeth. Of these, John, Nicholas, and Jane died in their infancy; Elizabeth died Nov. 22, 1767. Sir Ralph died Nov. 22, 1767, and was succeeded by his eldest son,

CONYERS, OF HORDEN, DURHAM.

TABLE 58.

```
1 ROGER DE COIGNIERS                          13 Robert, 1433 = Isabel Pert
  |                                              |
2 Roger de Coigniers                           14 Sir Christopher = Mariora de Eure
  |                                              |
3 Roger de Coigniers                           15 Sir Wm.   Rob.  16 Hump.  Maud   Joan
  |                                              A. Bigott  John            Wilbet- Dy-
4 Robert de Coigniers                                                        foss    moke
  |
5 Thomas        Roger        Geoffery          17 Sir John Cogniers, Knt.
                                                  |
   Robert       Roger      6 Geoffery          18 Robert Coigniers
                                                  |
Joan=Sir C. Mallory  Robert    7 Joan          19 John = Margaret St. Quintin
                                                  |
  2 sons      8 Sir Humphrey                   20 Sir Christopher = Ellen Rylston
                                                  |
9 Sir John Coigniers                           21 Sir John, K. G. = Marg. Darcy
  |                                               |
10 John Coigniers    11 Roger de Coigniers     Sir John Conyers              22 Rich. Conyers
Elizabeth | Christian                          Alice de Nevill                  Eliz. Claxton
  |
Isabel   Petronilla  Geoffery   12 John
Rob. de Colvile  Rob. Herle     Eliz. de Atton

Sir Wm. L. Conyers  John  Margery   Anne   23 Richard   Robert,   Catharine,  Anne
Anne Nevill         Sir Wm. Bulmer  Rich. L. Lumley     Percival  Mary

Christopher, L. Conyers  Catharine    Margaret        24 Christopher of Horden
Anne Dacres              F. Bigod     Sir R. Cholmondeley  Eliz. Bedall

John, L. Conyers   Leonard   Elizabeth    Jane    25 Richard Conyers        George
Maud Clifford                G. Halnaby   M. Constable  Eliz. Lumley        Conyers

Anne       Elizabeth   Catharine    Margaret    26 Christopher Conyers
A. Kemp    T. Darcy    J. Atherton                 E. Conyers | — Hedworth

              I. Sir John Conyers, Bart. = ——— Groves
Eliz. Langhorne, 1644 = II. Sir Christopher = Julia Lumley.

III. Sir John, 1719 = Mary Newman, 1714    Sir Wm. Blacket = Julia = Sir W. Thompson

IV. Sir Baldwin, 1731    Mary      Christopher,   Edward,      William
S. Conyers | M. Nevil    E. Checkey   John        Christopher

Christopher,  2 nuns    Elizabeth    Harriot      Charlotte    Teresa
John, 1729                           T. Wollascot J. Guastaldi

              V. Sir Ralph Conyers, 1767 = Jane Blackston

VI. Sir Blackston, 1791   John,     Thomas,    Mary,     Elizabeth
                          Nicholas  William    Jane      1767

VII. Sir Nicholas Conyers, Bart.
```

VI. Sir BLACKSTON CONYERS, who was appointed a captain in the marines, March 5, 1757, and died in Nov. 1791; and was succeeded by

VII. Sir NICHOLAS CONYERS, the present baronet.

ARMS—Azure, a maunch, or.
CREST—On a wreath, a trefoil erect, slipped proper.
SEAT—Chester le Street, Durham.

---

58. ASTON, of Aston, Cheshire.

Created Baronet July 25, 1628.

THE family of the Astons is of great antiquity, and have resided at Aston,[*] in Cheshire, from the time of Edward the Confessor; and from an ancient manuscript, now before me, it appears, they are descended from the Saxons.

1. Odard de Eston, lord of the manor of Eston,[†] held this town under William Fitznigell, baron of Halton in 1086; and had two sons; 1, Ernald, and 2, Odo, who had a son Robert, who lived in the time of Henry I.

2. Ernald de Eston, lived in the time of William the Conqueror, and married Emma, by whom he had

3. Thomas de Eston, who lived in the time of William Rufus, and Henry I. and was succeeded by his son,

4. Richard, lord of Aston, who married Sarah ———, by whom he had two sons; Juan, who was witness to a deed of Henry de Verdun, of Staffordshire; and

5. Gilbert de Aston, lord of Aston, and lived in the time of Henry II. Rich. I. and part of King John: he married Mary ———, by whom he had four sons; 1, Sir Richard; 2, William, who was witness to a deed of John Constable, of Chester, who died in 1183; 3, Gamwell; 4, Jeffery, all of whom had issue.

6. Sir Richard de Aston,[‡] by dame Joan, his wife, had two sons; 1, Richard, and 2, Robert; and a daughter, Hawis, the wife of John Lisnekarck.

7. Richard of Aston, lord of Aston, had two sons; 1, Hugh, and 2, Robert Capellanus, who lived in the time of Henry III.

8. Hugh Aston, lord of Aston, married Emelina, by whom he had

9. Edmund, lord of Aston, who was a ward in the beginning of Henry III. and had issue, Thomas and Hugh.

---

[*] Sir Peter Leycester's Cheshire, p. 208.   [†] Doomsday Book.
[‡] Richard de Aston, son of Gilbert, gave unto Hugh Dutton, of Dutton, *six bovatas terræ*, in Aston, about 1230. He also gave unto the priory of Norton, a place called Hendley, or Endley, now Endley Wood; and also one oxgang of land, in Aston, which John Lacy, constable of Cheshire, and baron of Halton, confirmed, as appears by Sir Willoughby Aston's deeds.

ASTON, OF ASTON, CHESHIRE.

10. Thomas de Aston, lord of Aston, by Rose, his wife, had several children; 1, Richard; 2, Lawrence Aston, of Halton; 3, William; 4, Simon, who married one of the co-heirs of Adam de Halton, juxta Darsbury; 5, Robert, to whom Richard, lord of Aston gave lands, as appears by deeds.

11. Richard, lord of Aston, lived in the time of Henry III. and married Maud, daughter and heir of William Walton; by whom he had 1, Sir Richard; 2, Adam, who had two sons, Robert and John; 3, Robert, the father of Adam, the father of Richard de Aston, temp. Richard II. 4, Margery, the wife of William, son of Hugh de Frodesham.

12. Sir Richard Aston, son and heir, gave to his brother Robert, two oxgangs of land, in Aston; one whereof *Domina Johanna quondam tenuit.* This deed was made *tempore Edwardi primi;* and this Joan seems to be the wife of Richard, son of Gilbert de Aston aforesaid. This Richard married Rose, youngest daughter and co-heir of Roger Throssel, of Maxfield, in Cheshire, in the reign of King Edward I. by whom he had 1, Richard Aston; 2, Hugh, prior of Birkenhed Abbey, in Wirral hundred. Rose was a widow, and living 18 Edw. III.*

13. Richard Aston, of Aston, son and heir, married Anabella, daughter of Eva, and sister of William de Rode, of Rode, in Cheshire, in the reign of Edw. II.† by whom he had 1, Sir Robert Aston, living 7 Edw. III. but then very young; 2, Thomas,‡ living also 7 Edw. III. and Margery, or Margaret, the wife of William, son of William Walensis de Halton, i. e. the son of William the Welchman, of Halton.

14. Sir Robert Aston, of Aston, Knt. son and heir of Richard, married Felice, daughter of John Hawarden, citizen of Chester, about 1338, by whom he had 1, Richard Aston; 2, Hugh; 3, Lawrence; and 4, James, living 49 Edw. III.§

15. Sir Richard Aston was treasurer to Queen Philippa, and steward of Hopesdale; and died, without issue, about 1369: he was succeeded by Sir Richard Aston, son of Robert Aston, of Ringey, in Aston, son of Hugh Aston, brother to Richard.‖

* Placita apud Cestriam, 18 Edw. III. in Vigilia Beatæ Mariæ.
† The Chartulary of Aston Deeds, p. 2.
‡ He lived near Aston Mondrem, which is now called Aston Green, and was the father of William Aston, of Aston Mondrem, the father of John, who married Agnes; by whom he had Peter, who married Margery; by whom he had Richard, the father of Hugh, the father of Hugh, who married Margery, the daughter of —— Harding; by whom he had Richard, and Anne, the wife of John Aldersay, of Spurstowe; from whence the Aldersays, now living, are descended. Richard, son of Hugh, married Mary Manning, of Cleveley, by whom he had John Aston, who married Margery Hough, by whom he had Richard, who married Dorothy Manwaring, by whom he had Thomas, who sold the estate at Aston Green.
§ By the French deed *(No. 57)* it appears, that Richard Aston, lord of Aston, covenanted with John Hawarden, citizen of Chester, that Robert, son of the said Richard, should take to wife Felice, daughter of the said John; and if Robert died before marriage, then Thomas, another son of the said Richard, should have her to wife.
‖ It appears by the testimony of Robin Hocan, 5 Henry V. then aged 70 years, that he knew Robin, of Aston, son and heir of Hugh, to be married by Hugh, his father, to Filot, daughter of Black John Hawarden, at that time steward of Hawarden; and that Robin and Filot were enfeoffed of a parcel of land, called Ringey, and had issue Sir Richard Aston, and other children; and afterwards Robin died in Spain, in the life-time of Hugh, his father.

15. Hugh, the second son of Sir Robert, married Sicilie (who after his death became the wife of —— Hocknull) by whom he had two sons; 1, Robert; 2, Sir William Aston, who was one of the witnesses in the great law suit, between Lord Scroope and Grosvenor, about a coat of arms, by the name of Monsieur William de Aston, in Villa de Aston Chevalier: this is recorded in the Tower.

16. Robert, the eldest son, married Filot, daughter of Black John, of Hawarden, who died of a pestilence, in Ringey; by whom he had,

17. Sir Richard Aston, of Aston, Knt. who married Jennet, daughter of John Hoknell, of Huxley, and had divers children by her, who, with their mother, died of the plague, at Ringey. Afterwards he married Ellen, daughter and heiress of Geoffery, third son of Sir Hugh Dutton, of Dutton; by whom he had 1, Robert; 2, Henry, living 10 Henry V. Eleanor, the wife of Richard Priestland of Priestland; Elizabeth, of Thomas, son of Thomas Boydell, of Caterich, in Gropenhall, in Bucklow hundred, 17 Rich. II. but had no issue; afterwards of Robert Massy, of Hale, 21 Rich. II. and lastly of Thomas Danyel, of Over Tabley: she died in 1410. Ellen, wife of Sir Richard, after his death was the wife of John Rycroft.

18. Sir Robert Aston, of Aston, Knt. married Isabel, daughter and heir of John Beeston, by whom he had 1, Richard; 2, David, living 23 Henry VI. and Alice, wife of John Massy, of Sale, 24 Henry VI. Sir Robert died in 1417; and Isabel, his widow, became the wife of John Carington, of Carington, in Bucklow hundred, in Cheshire, 9 Henry V. He was afterwards Sir John Carington, Knt.

19. Sir Richard Aston, of Aston, Knt. married Maud, daughter and heir of Peter Massy, of Horton, in Cheshire, by Margaret, his wife, daughter and heir of William de Horton, 9 Henry V. This Peter Massy was younger son of Richard Massy, of Rixton, in Lancashire; by whom he had 1, Thomas Aston; 2, John, living 7 Edw. IV. 3, Geoffery Aston, third son, living 19 Henry VII. 4, William, who died without issue, 20 Henry VII. Maud, the wife of John Done, of Flaxyoards, in Cheshire; Joan, of Roger Dutton, afterwards heir to all Dutton's lands; which Joan, after the death of Roger, became the wife of Sir Richard Strangeways; and Margery, of John Wood, of Sutton, 2 Henry VII. Sir Richard died in 1492.

20. Thomas Aston, of Aston, Esq. son and heir, married Margaret, daughter of Sir Thomas Dutton, of Dutton, 1467. She afterwards became a co-heir to Dutton lands, and had Kekwick, and Aston Mondrem, to her share. This Thomas died in the life-time of Sir Richard, his father, about 1484. Margaret, his widow, afterwards became the wife of Raufe Vernon, of Haslington, in Cheshire, Esq.

21. Richard Aston, of Aston, Esq. married Dowse, daughter of Peter Warburton, of Arley, Esq. 1 Richard III. and had issue 1, Thomas, son and heir; 2, Richard, a priest; 3, Robert, of Grange, in Staffordshire, who married Margaret, daughter of —— Dent; 4, John, who married Margaret, daughter of Ralph Thickness, and had one son, John, who died without issue: Catharine, the wife of Richard Broughton, of Broughton, in Staffordshire; Alice, of Randle, son and heir of Randle Manwaring, of Karincham, in Cheshire, Esq. 23 Henry VII. and Anne, of William Massy, of Rixton, in Lancashire, Esq. 10 Henry VIII. This Richard Aston died in 1529.

22. Thomas Aston, of Aston, Esq. son and heir, married Bridget, one of the daughters of John Harewell, and sister and co-heir of Thomas Harewell, of Shotery, in Warwickshire, who died in 1554; and had issue 1, John; 2, Richard; 3, Peter; 4, William, who married Anne, daughter of Thomas Ireland, of the Hutt, in Lancashire, Esq. and had issue; and 5, Francis. He had also a bastard son, Sir Roger Aston, gentleman of the bed-chamber to King James I. who married Mary Stewart, daughter to Alexander, lord Oghiltrey (Ochiltree) being lineally descended from Duncan, earl of Lennox, in Scotland; by whom he had issue Margaret, the wife of Sir Gilbert Houghton, of Houghton Tower, in Lancashire, Bart. Mary, of Sir Samuel Peyton, of Knowlton, in Kent. Bart. Elizabeth, of Sir Robert Winkfield, of Upton, in Northamptonshire; and Anne, of Sir Thomas Perient, of Colchester, in Essex, Knts. These were his four daughters and heirs. Afterwards Sir Roger Aston married Cordelia, sister to the Earl of Chesterfield, but had no issue by her. This Roger lies buried in Cranford church, in Middlesex. Thomas Aston, of Aston, before-mentioned, was sheriff of Cheshire in 1551, and died in 1553.

23. John Aston, of Aston, Esq. son and heir, married Margaret, daughter of Thomas Ireland, of the Hutt, in Lancashire, Esq. 1546, by Margaret, his wife, daughter of Sir Richard Bold, of Bold, in Lancashire, Knt. and had issue 1, Thomas; 2, John, a lawyer, who died without issue; 3, Edward, who also died without issue; 4, Bridget, the wife of Thomas Bunbury, of Stanney, in Cheshire, Esq. 5, Elizabeth, of John Massy, of Podington, Esq. 6, Margaret, wife first of Thomas Egerton, of Walgreve, and afterwards of Edward Tirrel, of Thornton, in Buckinghamshire; 7, Mary, died without issue; 8, Eleanor, the wife of James Whitlock; 9, Winifred, of Peter Derby, of Liverpool; 10, Ellen, of George Manwaring, of Ightfield, in Shropshire, a younger brother; 11, Ursula, of Geoffery Holcroft, of Hurst, in Lancashire: also Richard, a bastard son, who lived at Rock Savage, and died at Halton in 1616. This John died Aug. 5, 1573. Margaret, his widow, became the wife of Hugh Beeston, of Torperley, in Cheshire, Esq.

24. Sir Thomas Aston, of Aston, son and heir, was knighted in 1603, and married Elizabeth, daughter of Sir Arthur Manwaring, of Ightfield, in Shropshire, by whom he had 1, John; 2, Sir Arthur Aston, of Fulham, in Middlesex, who had two sons; 1, Richard, who married Susan, daughter of Sir William Berwick, of Thetford, in Norfolk; by whom he had one son, Robert; 2, Arthur, who commanded eight years in the wars in Russia; was captain of the guard, major and lieutenant-colonel ten years, under the king of Poland, made colonel by the King of Sweden, served seven years in the German wars; colonel-general of a brigade, and major-general of the trained bands of Yorkshire, appointed for the guard of the king's person against the Scots, 16 King Charles. He married Mary, daughter of Sir Samuel Bagnell, Knt. a famous soldier in the Irish wars; by whom he had 1, Isaac, a soldier in Germany; 2, William, a Turkey merchant; 3, Arthur; 4, Samuel; 5, Constantia, born in Polonia, and christened by the Queen of Poland; 6, Elizabeth, born in Russia, the wife of James Thompson, of Joyce Grove, in Berkshire. Sir Arthur was barbarously killed at Tredagh,* in Ireland, having sur-

* Lord Clarendon, in vol. II. p. 84, 8vo edit. says, "Sir Arthur Aston was commissary general of the horse, and governor of Reading;" and, p. 231, "at the beginning of the siege of Reading, in 1643,

rendered the town to the parliament rebels upon conditions, in 1655. 3, Sir Thomas, who was gentleman pensioner to Kings James and Charles; and was knighted at the coronation of King Charles: he married Elizabeth Stafford, widow, daughter of John Shuckborough, of Shuckborough, Esq. by whom he had Frances, the wife of Edward Mullins, of Westhall, in Dorsetshire, Esq. he married secondly Dowsabella Pawlet. 4, Frances, the wife of John Hocknell, of Hocknell, in Cheshire; secondly, of Richard Davis, of Croughton; and thirdly, of Owen Longford, of Burton, in Derbyshire: 5, Grace, who died without issue; 6, Margaret, the wife of Sir Thomas Ireland, vice chamberlain of Chester; 7, Elizabeth, of Richard Dod, of Cloverley, in Shropshire; 8, Mary, of Richard Brown, of Upton, near Chester, Gent. afterwards of Jaques Arnodio, a Frenchman; 9, Anne, of —— Greenhill, in Nether Witley, in Cheshire; 10, Catharine, of Peter Leigh, of Ridge, near Maxfield, Gent.

Sir Thomas had a second wife, Mary, daughter of William Unton, of Draiton, in Shropshire; but by her he had no issue: he was sheriff of Cheshire in 1601, and died in 1613. Mary, his widow, afterwards became the wife of Edw. Payler, of York, Esq.

25. John Aston, of Aston, Esq. son and heir, was sewer to Queen Anne, wife of King James I. and married Maud, daughter of Robert Nedham, of Shenton, in Shropshire, Esq. by whom he had 1, Thomas; 2, John Aston, who died unmarried, in 1648; 3, Robert, who died young; 4, Maud, the wife of Thomas Parsons, of Cubington, in Warwickshire, Esq. afterwards, of John Shuckburgh, of Upton, in Wirral hundred, 1666, a younger son of the Shuckburghs, in Warwickshire; 5, Anne, who died young; and 6, Elizabeth, who died unmarried, in 1628. This John died May 13, 1615, and was succeeded by

I. Sir THOMAS ASTON, who was entered a gentleman-commoner of Brazen Nose College, Oxford, in 1626-7; but was soon called home by his relations, and created a baronet in July, 1628. In 1635 he was high sheriff of Cheshire, being then esteemed a high flown monarchist. Upon the approach of the rebellion he wrote some pieces against the presbyterians, and was afterwards the chief man in his country that took part with the king. During the civil war he raised a party of horse, for his majesty's service, which was beaten by a party of rebels, under Sir William Beeston, of Honford, near Nantwich, in Cheshire, on the 28th of July, 1642; but Sir Thomas escaped with a slight wound. Some time after he

---

Sir Arthur Aston, the governor, being in a court of guard, near the line which was nearest to the enemies approaches, a cannon shot accidentally lighted upon the top of it, which was covered with bricktile, a piece whereof, the shot going through, hit the governor on the head, and made that impression upon him, that his senses shortly failed him, so that he was not only disabled afterwards from executing in his own person, but incompetent for counsel or direction; so that the command devolved to Col. Fielding, the eldest colonel of the garrison. This accident was then thought of great misfortune to the king, for there was not in his army an officer of greater reputation, and of whom the enemy had a greater dread." And vol. IV. p. 553, says, "Sir Arthur Aston, governor of Oxford, in the managing of his horse, caused him to fall, and had in the fall broken his own leg, and shortly after being compelled to cut it off; so that if he recovered at all, which was very doubtful, he could not be fit for any active service; and his majesty, with all the circumstances of grace and favour, sent him a warrant of 1000l. a year pension for his life, and then conferred that government on Col. Gage; yet he afterwards served at Tredagh, in Ireland, where the enemy put every man, governor, officer, and soldier, to the sword.' Vol. V. p. 341.

ASTON, OF ASTON, CHESHIRE.

was taken, in a skirmish in Staffordshire, and carried prisoner to Stafford; where, endeavouring to escape, a soldier spied him, and gave him a blow on the head, which, with other wounds he had a little before received, threw him into a fever, of which he died, March 24, 1645. His body was carried to Aston, and interred in the chapel belonging to his own house.*

He married Magdalene, daughter of Sir John Poultney, of Misterton, in Leicestershire, Knt. (by Margery, daughter of Sir John Fortescue, Knt.) and sister and co-heir to John Poultney, of Misterton, Esq. by whom he had issue Robert, who died young, 1634; Thomas, who died in 1637, at the age of six years; and two daughters, Jane and Elizabeth, who both died infants. Magdalene, his wife, dying June, 1635, he afterwards married Anne, daughter and sole heiress of Sir Wilughby, of Risley, in Derbyshire, Bart. 1639 (by Elizabeth, his first lady, one of the daughters and co-heirs of Henry Knollys, of Berks, Esq.) by whom he had one son and two daughters; Sir Wilughby, his successor; Magdalene, the wife of Sir Robert Burdet, of Bramcote, in Warwickshire, Bart. and Mary, of —— Biddulph, of Polesworth, in the same county, Esq. His lady surviving him, became the wife of the hon. Anchitel Grey, Esq. second son of Henry, earl of Stamford.

II. Sir WILUGHBY ASTON, Bart. only son and successor to his father, built a sumptuous house at Aston, a little distance from the old seat, and died Dec. 2, 1702. He married Mary, daughter of John Offley, of Madeley Manor, in Cheshire, Esq. by whom he had eight sons and thirteen daughters; 1, Sir Thomas; 2, John, a captain of a man of war, who died without issue; 3, Wilughby, who married ——, and left two daughters; 4, Arthur, who died at Constantinople, unmarried; 4, Gilbert, who died young; 6, Richard, who married Elizabeth, daughter of John Warren, of Oxfordshire, Esq. by whom he had 1, Sir Willoughby; 2, Richard, bred to the law, knighted, and sworn one of the judges of the court of King's Bench, in April, 1765. He married ——, daughter of —— Edred, and widow of Sir David Williams, Bart. 3, Robert, a merchant in London, who died without issue, Jan. 1741; 4, Elizabeth, living in 1797; and 5, Mary, the wife of —— Dawson, M. D. Of the daughters, Mary was the wife of Sir John Crew, of Utkington, in Cheshire, Knt. and afterwards of Dr. Chamberlayne; Magdalen, of Thomas Norris, of Speke, in Lancashire, Esq. Frances, Christian, Anne, and Bridget all died young; Elizabeth; Dorothy; Charlotte, the wife of John Pickering, of Thelwall, in Cheshire, Esq. Catharine died unmarried; Purefoy the wife of Henry Wright, of Mobberley, in Cheshire, Esq. Helena, of Capt. Penington, alias Leigh, of Booths, in Cheshire; and Letitia, of —— Jenks.

III. Sir THOMAS ASTON, Bart. succeeded his father in title and estate, and married Catharine, daughter of —— Withrington, Esq. and died Jan. 16, 1724-5, leaving only one son, Sir Thomas, his successor, and eight daughters; Catharine, the wife of the hon. Henry Hervey, Esq. fourth son of John, earl of Bristol; and Margaret, of Gilbert Walmesley, Esq. register of the diocese of Litchfield and Coventry.

* Wood's Ath. Oxon. vol. II. col. 88, 89.

ASTON, OF ASTON, CHESHIRE.

```
 1 ODARD DE ESTON                           11 Richard   Lawrence   Wm.   Simon   Robert
 2 Ernald═Emma              Robert             M. Walton
 3 Thomas de Eston                           12 Richard        Adam     Robert   Margery
 4 Richard═Sarah                                Rose Throssel                    W. de Fro-
 5 Gilbert═Mary              Juan                                                desham
 6 Sir Richard═Joan  Wm. Gamwell  Jeffery   13 Richard═Annabella de Rode    Hugh
 7 Richard   Robert  Hawise═J. Lisnekarck   14 Sir Robert Aston    Thomas,      Margery
 8 Hugh═Emelina                                Felice Hawarden    temp. Ed. III. W. Walensis
 9 Edmund                                    15 Sir Richard  15 Hugh═Sicilie Lawrence James
10 Thomas═Rose              Hugh            16 Robert═Filiot Hawarden       Sir William
                                               J. Hoknell═17 Sir Richard═E. Dutton═J. Rycroft

18 Sir Robert, 1417  Henry      Eleanor                    Elizabeth
   J. Beeston                   R. Priestland  T. Boydell | R. Massey | T. Danyel
19 Sir Richard, 1462═M. Massy   David    Alice═J. Massy   Margaret═R. Wolseley
20 Thomas═M. Dutton  John    Maud      Jeff.     Joan          Wm.        Margery
                             J. Done   R. Dutton | Sir R. Strangeways     John Wood
21 Richard, 1529 ═ Dowse Warburton
22 Thomas, 1553  Richard   Robert      John        Catharine    Alice       Anne
   B. Harewell             M. Dent  M. Thickness  R. Broughton  R. Manwaring  W. Massy
23 John         Richard,   William    Francis     Sir Roger Aston, Knt.
   M. Ireland   Peter      A. Ireland             M. Stewart | C. Stanhope
24 Sir Thomas, 1613  John,  Bridget  Eliza    Margaret    Mary    Eleanor  Winifred   Ellen   Ursula
   E. Manwaring | M. Unton  Edw. T. Bunbury J. Massy T. Egerton Sir Edw. J. Whitlock P. Derby G. Man-  G. Hol-
                                                              Tirrel                        waring  croft
25 John, 1615  Sir Arthur  Sir Thomas   Frances     Grace Margaret Eliza   Mary    Anne   Catharine
   M. Needham  2 wives  E. Staf- D. Paw- J. Hock- R. Da- O. Long- Sir T. Ire- R. Dod Rich. J. Ar- Rich.  P. Leigh
                        ford    let     nel      vis    ford    land      Brown       modia Allen

I. Sir Thomas, 1645    John,    Anne,    Maud                Richard      Sir Arthur
   M. Poulteney | A. Willoughby Robert   Eliz. T. Parsons | J. Shuckburgh S. Berwick   M. Bagnell
   1625
                                         II. Sir Willoughby, Bart. 1702   Magdalene    Mary
   Rob. & Thos.    Jane & Eliz.           Mary Offley                     Sir R. Burdet — Biddulph
III. Sir Thos. 1724 John, Arthur, Rich. 1741 Rob.  Mary    Magdalene 7 Charlotte Purefoy Helena Letitia
   C. Withrington Willoughby Gilbert E. Warren Edw. Sir J. D. Cham- Thos. drs. J. Pick- H. Wright Capt. Jenks
                                              Crew berlayne Norris            ering             Pennington
IV. Sir Thos. 1744  Cath.    Marg.    V. Sir Willoughby, 1772  Sir Rich. 1778  Robert    Mary
   — Sishe, 1737  H. Hervey G. Walmesley Eliz. Pye           — Williams     Eliz.   — Dawson
VI. Sir Willoughby      Elizabeth       Purefoy       Mary          Selina,    Sophia
   Jane Henley          A. Cotton       J. Preston   T. G. Gordon   Belinda
```

IV. Sir THOMAS ASTON, Bart. succeeded his father in title and estate, was elected member of parliament for Liverpool, 1 George II. and was afterwards chosen for the borough of St. Alban's, in Hertfordshire. He married in March, 1735-6, the daughter of —— Sishe, Esq. but she died in May, 1737, without issue. Sir Thomas dying in France, Feb. 17, 1744, without issue, bequeathed the family estate, of about 4000*l.* per annum, to his eldest sister, Catharine, the wife of the hon. and Rev. Henry Hervey, before-mentioned; who, by act of parliament, took the surname of this family: but the title descended to his cousin, the eldest son of his uncle, Richard Aston.

V. Sir WILLOUGHBY ASTON, Bart. who married Elizabeth, fourth daughter of Henry Pye, Esq. of Farringdon, in Berkshire, by Anne, sister of Lord Bathurst; by whom he had one son, Sir Willoughby, the present baronet, and six daughters; 1, Elizabeth, the wife of Admiral —— Cotton; 2, Purefoy, of the hon. James Preston, brother of Lord Gormonston; 3, Mary, of Capt. Francis Grant Gordon, of the navy; Selina, died at Paris, 1764; 5, Belinda; and 6, Sophia, both dead. Sir Willoughby died Aug. 24, 1762, and was succeeded by his only son,

VI. Sir WILLOUGHBY ASTON, Bart. who married Dec. 26, 1772, Jane, second daughter of Robert, earl of Northington.

ARMS—Party per chevron, sable and argent.
CREST—On a wreath, an ass's head, proper.
MOTTO—*Prêt d'accomplir.*
SEAT—At Farnham, Hants.

59. WISEMAN, of Canfield Hall, Essex.

Created Baronet Aug. 29, 1628.

IN the ordination made by King Edw. I. upon his establishing the kingdom of Scotland, in the 33d of his reign, towards its better government, William Wiseman was constituted Viscount, or sheriff of Elgin; and Alexander Wiseman, Viscount of Foreis and Innervan; and had other shires in their charge, with some English, some Scotch natives, under the king's lieutenant and chamberlain; so that the original extraction of the name remains uncertain. Not long after Simon Wiseman was found to be possessor of lands in Cotes, in Northamptonshire, as recited in a confirmation to a charter, 2 Edw. III. to the nuns of St. Mary de Pratis, in that county.* After that was

1. John Wiseman, who married Magdalen, daughter and heir of —— Rokell, by whom he had

2. Robert Wiseman, who married Mary, daughter of —— Hobart, of Norfolk, by whom he had

* Dugdale's Monasticon, vol. II. p. 1011.

3. George Wiseman, who married Margaret, daughter of —— Garnish, of Kenton, in Suffolk, by whom he had

4. John Wiseman, who married Anne, daughter of —— Windham, of Norfolk,* by whom he had

5. Simon, who by Margaret, his wife, daughter of —— Bokenham, had

6. William Wiseman, of Great Canfield, in the county of Essex, who married Mary, daughter of —— Glasscock, of Essex, by whom he had

7. John Wiseman, of Canfield, Esq. auditor of the Exchequer to King Henry VIII. who received the honour of knighthood at the battle of Spurs: he purchased Much Canfield Park,† consisting of a messuage, and 260 acres of land, by licence. He married Agnes, daughter of Ralph Joscelyn, lord-mayor of London, in 1464; by whom he had one son, John, and six daughters; 1, Philippa, the wife of William Glasscock, of Dunmow, in Essex; and secondly, of Andrew Pascall, of Essex; 2, Catharine, of Thomas Young, of Roxwell, in Essex, Gent. who died in 1598; 3, Margery, of John Pascall, and secondly of —— Reade; 4, Clement, of Riceard Everard, of Waltham, in Essex; 5, Margaret, of —— Everard; secondly, of —— Church; 6, Anne, of —— Lindhill; and secondly, of J. Glasscock, of Rockwell, in Essex. John died Aug. 17, 1558, and was succeeded by his only son,

8. John Wiseman,§ Esq. who married Margery, daughter of Sir William Waldegrave, of Smallbridge, in Suffolk, Knt. under treasurer of Calais, where he died, in 1602; by whom he had five sons and two daughters; 1, John, who married Anne, daughter of John Leventhorpe, and died in the life-time of his father, leaving a daughter, who died without issue, 2, Thomas, of whom hereafter; 3, William; 4, Robert; 5, Edmund, which three died without issue; 6, Agnes, the wife of Thomas Fitch, of Little Canfield, and secondly of George Wingate, of Sharpenhoe, in Essex; 7, Jane, of Nicholas Brocket, of Willingale, in Essex. John died Oct. 17, 1602, and was succeeded by his son,

9. Thomas Wiseman, of Canfield, Esq. who married Alice, daughter and heir of Robert Myles, of Sutton, in Suffolk, Esq. by whom he had five sons; 1, Robert, who married Anne, daughter of Sir Gamaliel Capel, Knt. by whom he had one son, John, who died in the life-time of his father; 2, Sir William; 3, Thomas; 4, Kenelme; 5, Edmund: and three daughters; 1, Mary, the wife of Thomes Bolton, of Woodbridge, in Suffolk; 2, Susan; 3, Parnell. The said Thomas died in 1624, and was succeeded by his second son,

I. Sir WILLIAM WISEMAN, who was created a baronet Aug. 29, 1628: he married Elizabeth, daughter of Sir Henry Capel, of Raynes, in Essex, Knt.‡ sister

---

* These three last matches are with three ancient families of Norfolk and Suffolk, it is therefore very probable, that a branch of the Wisemans might leave Northampton, and settle in Essex. John Wiseman, who flourished temp. Edw. IV. and purchased the capital messuage of Billocks, in the parish of North End, in Essex, I suppose to be son of the last John. He left two sons, John (ancestor to the Wisemans, of Rivenhall, in Essex, whose descendant, Sir William Wiseman, of Rivenhall, was created a baronet June 15, 1660, and dying in 1692, left only one daughter and heir, Elizabeth, the wife of John le Mott Honywood, of ——, in Essex, Esq. and afterwards of Sir Isaac Rebow, of Colchester, Knt. whereupon that title became extinct.

† Salmon's Essex, p. 217.   § Ibid, p. 218.   ‡ Collins's Peerage, vol. II. p. 86.

to that loyal Lord Capel, who lost his life for his sovereign, Charles I. (by Theodosia, sister to Edward, lord Montague, of Boughton, and to Henry, earl of Manchester); by whom he had 1, Sir William; 2, Sir Edward; 3, Capel, bishop of Dromore, in Ireland; 4, Robert; 5, Theodosia, the wife of Sir William Craven, of Speenholt, in Berks, Bart. 6, Elizabeth, of Robert Tyderleigh, Esq. She died April 26, 1654. Sir William died at Oxford in July, 1643, was buried there in the church of St. Peter's in the East, and was succeeded by his eldest son,

II. Sir WILLIAM WISEMAN, Bart. who was four years old in 1634: he married Anne, youngest daughter and co-heir of John Prescot, of Hoxne, in Suffolk, Knt. who died May 11, 1662, without issue. He married secondly Arabella, fifth daughter of Sir Thomas Hewet, of Pishiobury, in Hertfordshire, Bart. and sister to Lord Viscount Hewet, of Gowran, in Ireland,* by whom he had 1, Sir Thomas; 2, William, who died without issue, before 1700; 3, George, died without issue; 4, Sir Charles; 5, John Wiseman, of the Middle Temple, London, by his wife, Penelope, had one son, Sir William Wiseman, hereafter mentioned; 6, Anne, the wife of Henry Lumley, Esq. governor of the isle of Jersey, who died in 1722; she in 1736: 7, Margaret; 8, Arabella, the wife of Thomas Stisted, of Ipswich, in Suffolk, Esq. Sir William died Jan. 14, 1684, and was succeeded by his eldest son,

III. Sir THOMAS WISEMAN, Bart. who died unmarried. His will was proved in May, 1733, by his brother and executor,

IV. Sir CHARLES WISEMAN, Bart. who died unmarried, at Ipswich, in Suffolk. His will was proved by his nephews and executors, Charles and Thomas Stisted, July 3, 1751; and was succeeded by his nephew,

V. Sir WILLIAM WISEMAN, Bart. who was son of John Wiseman, beforementioned. He died without issue in 1784, and was succeeded by

Sir THOMAS WISEMAN, the present baronet, who is the great grandson of Sir Edmund Wiseman (second son of the first baronet): he was of the city of London, and was knighted at Hampton Court May 19, 1681. He married Elizabeth, daughter of Daniel Waldo, of the city of London, who died Dec. 8, 1694, aged 52; by whom he had one son, Edmund, and four daughters; Elizabeth, Mary, Sarah, and Arabella. He died May 8, 1704, aged 71, and was buried in St. Paul's cathedral; and was succeeded by his only son,

Edmund Wiseman, of London, afterwards of Tewksbury, in Gloucestershire, Esq. He died in Oct. 1741, and by his wife, Maria, third daughter of Edward Harnage, of Belserdine, in Salop, had three sons and one daughter; 1, Edmund; 2, John, of King's Street, Soho, in Middlesex, living in 1770, who had two sons, James Wiseman, Esq. ensign in the 30th regiment, 1764; lieutenant in the 50th regiment, 1770; captain in 1772; and major in 1790: Charles married, and had issue; and one daughter, Elizabeth, the wife of —— Addis, of Tooley Street, Southwark, London. 3, Edward, died young; Theophila-Mariana died unmarried, about 1770.

Edward Wiseman, Gent. the eldest son, was of Tewksbury; born Dec. 21, 1700; made a lieutenant in the 72d regiment of foot, in 1739; died at St. Helier, in the

* Her will was proved Aug. 14, 1705.

WISEMAN, OF CANFIELD HALL, ESSEX.

TABLE 60.

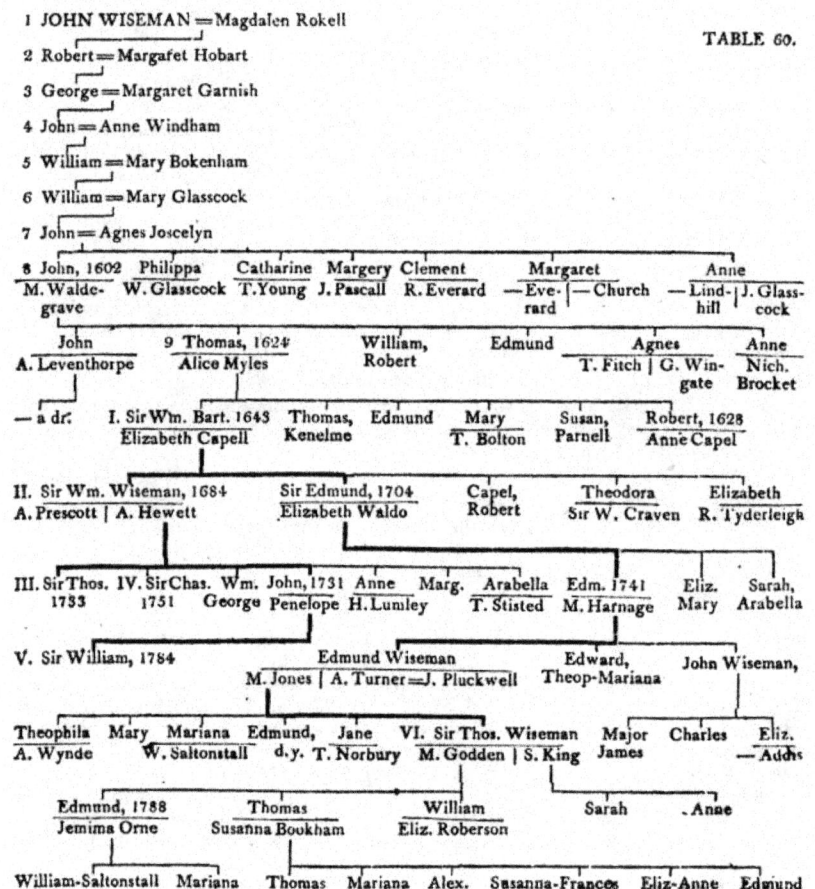

isle of Jersey, about 1767, and there buried. By his first wife, Mary, daughter of —— Jones, of Wales, who died in 1751, he had 1, Theophila, the wife of Arthur Wynde, of Tewksbury: she was living in 1793. 2, Mary died young; 3, Mariana, the wife of William Saltonstall, of Chatham; 4, Edmund died young; 5, Jane, the wife of Thomas Norbury, lieutenant in the royal navy: she died in 1788. 6, Sir Thomas. He married secondly Anne, daughter of Robert Turner, of Canterbury, living at Rochester in 1793. On the death of Sir William Wiseman, in 1784,

VI. Sir THOMAS WISEMAN, the only surviving son of Edmund, by Mary Jones, succeeded to the title: he married, Dec. 1, 1757, Mary, daughter of Michael Godden, Esq. master attendant of his majesty's dock yards at Chatham. She died June 11, 1766, leaving him three sons; 1, Edmund, who died suddenly, May 7, 1788, who by Jemima, his wife, daughter of Michael Arne, left one son, William-Saltonstall Wiseman, born March 5, 1784, a midshipman on board his majesty's ship the Warrior, Capt. Savage, 1798; and a daughter, Mariana, born in 1785; 2, Thomas, born in 1760, and married Susanna, daughter of Alexander Bookham, of Northfleet, by whom he has Thomas, Mariana, Alexander, Susanna-Frances, Elizabeth-Anne, and Edmund; 3, William, of Brompton, born in 1762, and married Elizabeth, daughter of John Roberson, of London; afterwards of Philadelphia, in America. Sir Thomas married secondly Sarah, daughter of Thomas King, of Gravesend, in Kent, who died in Dec. 1777, leaving him two daughters, Sarah and Anne.

ARMS—Sable, a chevron, ermine, between three cronels, argent.

CREST—On a wreath, a castle, triple towered, or; port open, argent; out of it a demi moor, issuant armed, proper; in his right hand a dart, argent; plumed and barbed, or; in his left a roman target, of the last.

RESIDENCE—Northfleet, Kent.

60. POLE, or POOLE, of Shute, Devonshire.

Created Baronet Sep. 12, 1628.

THIS is a younger branch of the family of the Pooles, of Poole Hall, in Wirrall, in the county of Chester. The first of the family who settled in Devonshire was

1. Arthur Pole, second son of Sir William Poole, of Wirral: he married Elizabeth, daughter and heir of John Pole, of Devonshire, Esq. the grandfather, and great-grandfather of which John, were returned members for the city of Exon, in a parliament, held at Westminster, 12 Edw. III. as was Thomas, another of the same family, for the borough of Barnstaple, in the 14th of the same reign. Arthur was succeeded by his son,

2. John, who married Alice, daughter of Robert Code, of Gidleigh, in Cornwall, Esq. and was succeeded by another

3. John, who married Edith, daughter of Robert Titherleigh, of Titherleigh, in Dorsetshire, Esq. He was succeeded by his second son,

4. William (his eldest son dying issueless before him): which William married Agnes, daughter of John Drake, of Ash, in Devonshire, Esq.

5. William, his eldest son, married Catharine, daughter of Alexander Popham, of Huntworth, in Somersetshire, Esq. and sister to Sir John Popham, Knt. lord chief justice of the King's Bench, by whom he left issue, Dorothy, first the wife of Thomas Erle, of Charmister, in Dorsetshire, Esq. and secondly of Sir Walter Vaughan, Knt. and one son,

6. Sir William Pole, Knt.* his heir, who married first Mary, the eldest daughter and one of the co-heirs of Sir William Peryam, Knt. lord chief baron of the

---

* This Sir William Pole was that famous antiquarian, whose manuscripts are so often quoted by our modern authors, and are justly esteemed as some of the most perfect pieces in their kind: valuable as they are, they are now irretrievably lost to his posterity; for the humanity of his successors was such, that they were never denied to any of the curious, who had an inclination to peruse them; the greater part of which have been so well approved by those gentlemen, that they never thought fit to return them.

Mr. Prince, in his Worthies of Devon, says, " He had the benefit of an academical education, in Exeter College, Oxford, and after that, an inclination to study the law, and removing to the inns of court, became a member of the Inner Temple, where he grew eminent for his skill and knowledge in that honourable profession. 3 Eliz. he was chosen *(Dugdale's Orig. Jurid. p.* 165) autumn reader, and the year following double reader; in which year there was a grand Christmas kept in the Inner Temple, at which the Lord Robert Dudley (afterwards Earl of Leicester) was the chief constable, or marshall, under the title of Palaphilos. This our Sir William was one of his great officers, being *(Ibid, p.* 150) chief justice of the common pleas, as divers persons of quality besides were others, as Mr. Onslow, lord chancellor; Mr. Stapleton, lord treasurer; Mr. Kelway, lord privy seal; Mr. Fuller, chief justice of the King's Bench, &c. which place, though personated only in shew and solemnity, if he had been called thereunto *(Prince's Worthies, p.* 505) he was highly qualified to have executed in truth and reality. 7 Eliz. he was chosen treasurer of the Inner Temple, a place then of trust and honour; but we are not to understand, that he spent his whole time in London, but as the terms and his occasions required: for he had his residence (during his father's life-time at least) at Colcomb, lying within both manors of Coliton and Whitford, in the parish of Coliton, in the south-east part of this county; it was some time the seat and dwelling, as well as inheritance, of the most noble family of the Courtenays, earls of Devon, from whose heirs general it was purchased by Sir William's father, and settled upon this his son, who new built it. Being thus settled here, he lived in great reputation, and became an ornament to, and a very useful person in his country, serving his prince in the quality of a justice of peace (then esteemed an honour) and high sheriff of this county, the last year of Queen Eliz. and 1 King James I, about four years after which he was advanced to the dignity of knighthood, by the said king, at Whitehall, Feb. 15, 1606. As to Sir William's personal qualifications," says the same author, " he was endowed with excellent parts, and adorned with great accomplishments; and, as what enamels and adds loveliness to all the other, beautified with a very civil, courteous, obliging carriage and disposition, which indeed is the true gentility. He was learned also, not only in the laws, but in other polite matters: he was very laborious in the study of antiquities, especially those of his own county, and a great lover of that venerable employment: a sufficient confirmation of which we have in those many volumes of manuscripts he left behind him: a few are yet in being, those which I have had the honour to peruse (says Mr. Prince) are,

1. The Description of Devonshire, in two vols. fol. manuscript: which contain an account of the several parishes in our county (beginning at the east, and coming round to the north), with the most eminent manors that are in them, whose originally they were, and whose since: the gentry therein, with an account of most of their matches and issue. In the beginning of the first volume we have the several ancient baronies of this county, whose they were, the particular barons of each,

Exchequer; secondly, Jane, daughter of William Symes, of Chard, Esq. and relict of Roger How, of London, merchant.* He rebuilt the mansion house at Colcum, once a castle belonging to the Courtenays, earls of Devonshire; which, with the house at Shute, was soon after burnt down by some troops of the parliament army, quartered at Lyme. By his first wife he had issue 1, Sir John, who succeeded him; 2, Peryam; 3, William; 4, Francis; and several daughters; Mary, the wife of —— Hurst, and afterwards of Francis, son and heir of William Courtenay, of Powderham, in Devon, Knt. ——, of —— Walrond, of Bovey, in Devonshire; Eleanor, of Anthony Floyer, of Floyer's Hayes, in Devonshire: most of the other daughters died young. Peryam, second son, was of Southcote Hayes, in the county of Devon, and had a son, Peryam Pole, of Ballyfin, of Queen's County, in Ireland, and possessed of great estates there, who married twice: 1, Penelope, daughter of Henry Walrond, of Devonshire, Esq. by whom he had no issue; secondly, Sarah, relict of John Blount, of Bolton Co, Kildare, by whom he

and their successers: together with a list of the knights of Devon, under the several king's reigns in which they lived; and of the most famous soldiers and statesmen: with a catalogue of the high sheriffs of this county; a very useful and elaborate work, from whose lamp our Risdon himself acknowledges, he received light in his Survey of Devon, written with great judgment and faithfulness, from the records of the Tower, the Herald's Office, original deeds and charters, &c.

2. He left behind him a vast manuscript volume in folio, as big as a church bible, containing copies of deeds, charters, and grants; out of which I suppose the former volumes were mostly composed; in which also the several seals, and coats of arms thereunto belonging, are finely drawn with a pen; with the pedigrees of divers gentlemen of this county, and some few of the neighbouring counties. In this volume also we have an account of the several knights' fees, and in whose hands they were; taken before Thomas de Ralegh and Nicholas de Kirkham, 31 Edw. I. at the end of which are these words:

"This was copied out of an old roll, and written all with mine own hand, in the month of April, in the year of our Lord God, 1616. WILLIAM POLE."

In this volume also are the charters of lands and privileges, granted by the founders of, and benefactors to, the abbey of Newenham, in the parish of Axminster; extracted out of the Leiger Book of that abbey, in the possession then of Robert Rolle, of Heanton Sackville, Esq. in 1606; wherein are many more deeds and charters than are found in Sir William Dugdale's Monasticon Anglicanum, belonging to that abbey.

3. He left a thin volume in folio, containing the coats of arms of the Devonshire gentry, drawn with a pen; wherein is the blazon of the coat, and the names of the persons by whom borne, in manuscript.

4. A pretty thick volume in folio, containing divers collections; as, the charters and grants to the abbey of Thorr, in this county; in the beginning whereof are these words:

"Here followeth a copy, briefly gathered out of the evidences and writings of the abbey of Thorr, in the county of Devon, collected into a leiger book, now in the custody of Mr. Ridgeway, now owner of the same place; and by him lent unto me, during my abode at Totnes, A. 1599, in manuscript."

In this volume is an abridgment also of the book called Doomsday; being a survey of the lands of England, and in whose hands they were; taken by command of King William the Conqueror, in 1086. Also an extract of Cheiverton's Book of Cornish Gentlemen's Obits and Burials. As likewise an inquisition of the fees of knighthood in Devon, with whose hands they were then in; taken according to the several hundreds thereof, at the command of King Edward II. A. Regni sui 8. Gratiæ 1314, pro Scutagio Scotiæ; with some other things.

There were several other volumes of manuscripts, written by this gentlemen, and his son, Sir John Pole, Bart. who made some additions to his father's Description of Devon, all of which were lost in the time of the civil wars in England; so that the very titles and arguments of them are perished.

He lies interred in the parish church of Colliton, under a flat stone, whose inscription is obliterated by time. *Thus far Prince's Worthies of Devon.*

* Seymour's Survey of London, vol. I. p. 540.

had a daughter, Sarah, the wife of Lieut. Col. Dudley Cosby, Knt. of the shire for Queen's County; and a son, William Pole, of Ballifin, Esq. who married Anne, sister of Richard Cowley Wellesley, Lord Mornington, in that kingdom, grandfather to the present Richard, Marquis Wellesley. By her he had two sons; 1, Peryam, who died in 1748, soon after his father; and 2, the right hon. William Pole, of Ballifin aforesaid, knight of the shire, and governor of Queen's County, and privy councellor in that kingdom, who married Lady Sarah Moore, eldest daughter of Edward, 5th Earl of Drogheda; but having no issue, and dying in Dec. 1782, he bequeathed his estates to his cousin, the hon. William Wellesley (next brother to the Marquis Wellesley) who has since taken the name of Pole; is a governor of Queen's County; and was, in 1784, member of parliament for Trim, in Ireland; and in 1790 for Eastloe, in the county of Cornwall. He was succeeded by his eldest son,

I. Sir JOHN POLE, raised to that dignity in the life-time of his father, 4 Charles I. was knight of the shire for the county of Devon, the same year, and married Elizabeth, daughter of Roger How, of London, merchant (the daughter of his father's second wife) by whom he had three sons; 1, Sir William Pole, Knt. 2, Sir Courtenay; and 3, John, who died young; and three daughters, Martha, the wife of —— Ivory, of Somersetshire; Jane, of —— Croker, of Lynham, in Devonshire, Esqrs. and Elizabeth, who died unmarried.

Sir William Pole, knighted by King Charles I. married Grace, daughter of Sir Thomas Trenchard, in Dorset, Knt. by whom he had no surviving issue; and secondly, Catharine, only daughter of Henry St. Barb, of Ashenton, in Somersetshire, and Broadlands, in the county of Southampton, Esq. by whom he had two sons, who died in their infancy, and four daughters; Catharine died unmarried, in 1668; Jane was the wife of Humphrey Sydenham, of Combe, in Dulverton, Somersetshire, Esq. Amy, of William Floyer, of Berne, in Dorsetshire, Esq. and Elizabeth, who died unmarried. This Sir William Pole died V. P. in 1648. Sir John Pole died April 16, 1658, and was succeeded in honour and estate by his second son,

II. Sir COURTENAY POLE, Bart. who was member of parliament for Honyton, 13 Charles II. and high sheriff of Devon in 1668. He married Urith, daughter of —— Shapcote, of Shapcote, Esq. by whom he had two sons, Sir John and Courtenay, and three daughters, Jane, Mary, and Penelope: Jane was the wife of Sir Copleston Bampfield, of Poltimore, in Devonshire, Bart. and secondly, of Edward Gibbons, of Whitechapel, in the same county, Esq. Penelope, of the hon. Francis Roberts, Esq. second son to the right hon. John, earl of Radnor, but died without issue: Mary and Courtenay died young. Sir Courtenay Pole died April 25, 1695, in the 78th year of his age, and was succeeded by his only surviving son,

III. Sir JOHN POLE, who in the year 1688 was a member of that parliament which settled the crown on King William and Queen Mary; as he was also of those parliaments which were summoned 1 and 10 Wm. III. and chosen knight of the shire for Devon, the 13th of the same reign; was elected again a burgess for Eastloe, in Cornwall, 1 Queen Anne; and for Newport, in the same county, the 4th of that reign. He died March 13, 1707, having married Anne, the youngest daughter of Sir William Morrice, of Werrington, in Devonshire, Knt. one of the principal secretaries of state to King Charles II. by whom he had four sons; 1, Sir William; 2, John, was a captain in the Earl of Barrimore's regiment, in the war in Spain, and died unmarried, in June, 1710; 3, Charles died in his infancy; 4, Carolus was rector of St. Breock, in Cornwall, and some time proctor in convocation for the clergy of the diocese of Exon. He married Sarah, eldest daughter of Jonathan Rashleigh, of Monabelly, in the county of Cornwall, Esq. by whom he had two sons; 1, Reginald, who married Anne, second daughter of John Francis Buller, of Mowal, in Cornwall, Esq. by whom he had five children; Anne, Reginald, Sarah, Charles, Morice, and Edward: all died in their minority. John, the second son, took holy orders, and died unmarried, in 1750, aged 29: and four daughters, Charlotte, Urith, Mary, and Anne, all of which died young, except Urith, who was the wife of Sir John Trevelyan, of Nettlecomb, in Somersetshire, Bart. Sir John Pole was succeeded by his eldest son,

IV. Sir WILLIAM POLE, of Shute, in Devonshire, Bart. He was elected member of parliament for the borough of Newport, in Cornwall, 13 Wm. III. and in every parliament summoned since that time to the year 1712, when he was chosen knight of the shire for Devon; and two years after constituted master of the household, by her majesty, Queen Anne; which place he held till the death of that princess. He married a daughter of Mr. Warren, by whom he left a son, Sir John, his successor, and a daughter, Elizabeth, the wife of John Anstis, clerk, second son of John Anstis, Esq. garter king at arms, and dying Dec. 31, 1741, of the gout in his stomach, was succeeded in dignity and estate by his only son,

V. Sir JOHN POLE, Bart. who married Elizabeth, daughter and co-heir of John Wills, of Woodford, in Essex, Esq. who died Aug. 10, 1758, aged 21: he married secondly ——, daughter of —— Palmer, and died Feb. 19, 1760, aged 27. His lady was afterwards the wife of George Clavering, Esq. and died in 1766. Sir John was succeeded by his son,

VI. Sir JOHN-WILLIAM POLE, Bart. who has taken the name of De la Pole, by his majesty's sign manual, and in Jan. 1779, married —— Templer, only daughter of James Templer, of Stover Lodge, Esq. by whom he has two sons, ——, born in Aug. 1782, and ——, Jan. 6, 1787.

ARMS—Azure, semee of fleur-de-lis, or; a lion, rampant, argent.
CREST—On a wreath, a lion's gambe, gules; armed, or.
SUPPORTERS—On the dexter side a stag, gules; attired and unguled, or: on the sinister a griffin, azure; gorged with a ducal crown, proper; armed and beaked, as the stag.
MOTTO—*Pollet virtus.*
SEATS—Shute, Tallaton, Collyton House, and Colcomb Castle, in Devonshire.

POLE, OF SHUTE, DEVONSHIRE.

TABLE 61.

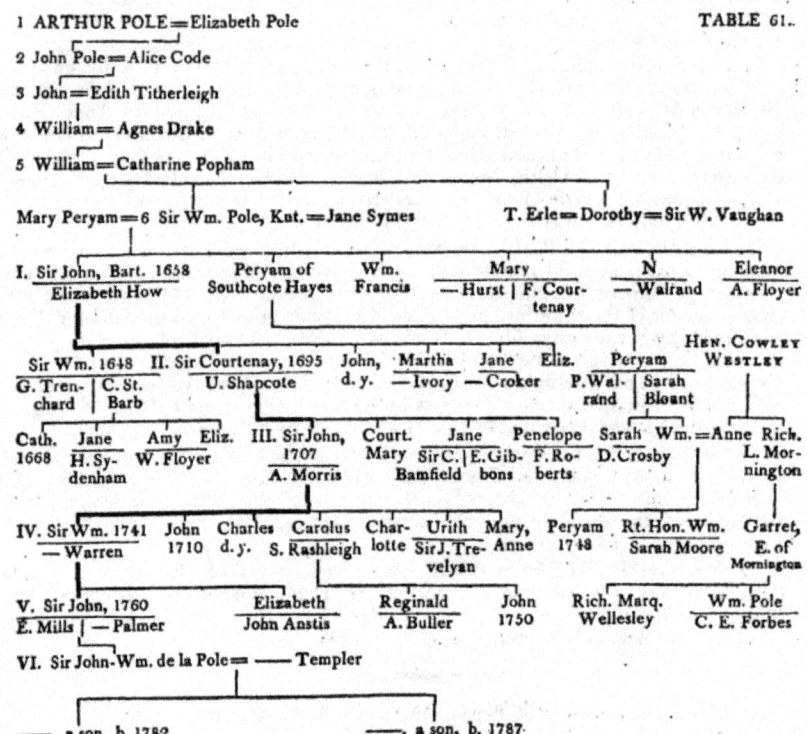

61. VAVASOR, of Haselwood, Yorkshire.

Created a Baronet Oct. 24, 1628.

THIS famous and very ancient family of Vavasor, or Valvasor (as Camden has it) have their name from their office, being formerly the king's valvasors (a degree then little inferior to a baron) and had anciently the addition of le to their names.†

1. Sir Mauger le Vavasor is mentioned in Doomsday Book, temp. Wm. I. He was the father of another

2. Sir Mauger, father of

3. Sir William Vavasor, lord of Haselwood, a judge in the reign of Henry II. and one of the witnesses to the charter of the abbey of Salley, in Yorkshire, re-founded by Matilda de Percy, countess of Warwick.

4. Robert, his son, in 21 Henry III. was high sheriff of Nottingham and Derby; and from the 31st of the same reign he served for eight years successively. He had the custody of the honour of Peverell committed to his charge, and died 38 Henry III. leaving by Julian,* daughter of Gilbert de Ross, of Steeton, in Yorkshire,

5. Sir John le Vavasor, Knt. lord of Haselwood,§ married Alice, daughter of Robert Rookfield,† by whom he had two sons, Sir William and Malgerius,‡ ancestor to the Vavasors, of Weston, Acaster, and Coppinthorp, in Yorkshire.

6. Sir William succeeded his father at Haselwood, which he had licence to castellate, from King Edw. I. in whose reign he was in the Gascoigne and Scotch wars, and was so esteemed, that he had summons to parliament among the barons from 28 Edw. I. to 6 Edw. II.|| and was a truly noble great man: he married Nichola, daughter of Sir Stephen, and sister of Sir Richard Wallis,¶ of Newton, by whom he had three sons; 1, Sir Robert,* who was likewise employed against the Scots, and had summons, as a baron, 7 Edw. II. but died without issue male, leaving two daughters, Elizabeth, the wife of Sir Robert Strelley, of Nottinghamshire, Knt. and Anne; 2, Sir Henry, of whom hereafter; 3, William, of Deneby, in Yorkshire, ancestor to those of that place.

7. Sir Henry le Vavasor, Knt. (second, but eldest surviving son of William, baron Vavasor) living 20 Edw. III. was buried in the abbey of Louth, in Lincolnshire. He had issue,

† Visit. York. 1612, No. 1487. Harl. MSS. in British Museum, p. 39.
* The Visit. of Yorkshire, 1612, calls her Maud. See Harl. MSS. prædict.
§ Haselwood has for many years been the chief seat of this family, from which place may be seen the two cathedrals of York and Lincoln, though 60 miles asunder. There is a famous quarry of stone here, from which the stately church of York was built, by the bounty of the Vavasors; and also the monasteries of Holden, Selby, and Beverley, with Thornton College, in Lincolnshire, and many others.
The arms and portraitures of this family, and that of the Percies, in the gate, the former with a stone, the latter with a piece of timber in their hands, are evident proofs of their being benefactors to that church, and also what materials each family contributed.
† Cockfield, of Cockfield, in the above MS. ‡ Malgerius is not mentioned in the Visitation.
|| In Visit. of York, 1612, temp. Hen. III. and Edw. I. ¶ Ibid. Wallies.
* Sir Robert is not mentioned as a baron, either in the abovementioned MS. or the Extinct Peerage

VAVASOR, OF HASELWOOD, YORKSHIRE.

8. Sir Henry, who by Amabilia,† daughter of Henry, lord Fitzhugh, had issue

9. William, who died in his father's life-time, leaving issue, by Elizabeth, daughter of William Stapleton, Sir William, who died without issue, 1387; and

10. Sir Henry le Vavasor, who by Margaret, daughter of Sir William Skipwith, Knt. had issue,

11. William le Vavasor, Esq. who died in 1452, leaving issue by Elizabeth, daughter of Sir John Langton, Knt. two sons; the younger was John le Vavasor, ancestor to those of Spalding Moor and Newton.

12. Sir Henry Vavasor, of Haselwood, Knt. the eldest son and heir, was high sheriff of Yorkshire, 10 Edw. IV. and died in 1460, leaving, by Joan, daughter of Sir William Gascoigne, Knt. four sons; 1, Henry, of whom hereafter; 2, John, who married Cicely, daughter of —— Langdale; 3, William; and 4, Leonard, a priest; and several daughters; Anne, the wife of Robert Maleverer, Esq. Catharine, of Sir Peter Middleton, of Stockheld, Knt. Mary, of Sir Thomas Gascoigne, Knt. Elizabeth, of Richard Goldsborough, of Goldsborough, Esq. and Matilda, of Sir Thomas Gilliot, of York, Knt.

13. Henry, the eldest son, succeeded his father, as lord of Haselwood, and died in 1515, leaving by Elizabeth, his wife, daughter of Sir John Everingham, Knt. three sons, John, William, and Christopher, who died under age; and five daughters; Elizabeth, the wife of Gilbert Topcliff, Esq. Agnes, who died an infant; Anne, the wife of Nicholas Cawnds, of London, merchant; Jennet, of Thomas Ogelthorpe, of Beal, Esq. and Dorothy, a nun.

14. John Vavasor, Esq. his son and heir, married Anne, daughter of Henry, baron Scrope, of Bolton, by whom he had three sons; Sir William, Christopher, living in 1594; and Leonard, married Mary, daughter of Sir John Hotham, Knt. and two daughters; Margaret, the wife of William Redman, of Twisleton; and Jane, of William Perchehay, of Ryton, in Yorkshire, Esqrs.

15. Sir William Vavasor, Knt. succeeded his father, 1548, and 6 Eliz. was high sheriff for the county of York. He married Elizabeth, daughter of Sir Anthony Cavalier, an Italian, and had issue by her five daughters; Mary, wife of William Plumpton, of Plumpton; Frances, of John Rider, of Rider; Anne, of Francis Gascoigne; Elizabeth, of Thomas Heyland; and Catharine, of Richard Pack, Esqrs. also six sons; 1, John; 2, Ralph, who married first Ursula, daughter of Sir William Fairfax, of Steton, Knt. by whom he had only one son, that died before baptism; 2, Elizabeth, daughter of Richard Peck, of Wakefield, Esq. by whom he had William, hereafter-mentioned, and a daughter Frances, the wife of William Percy, of Scotton. The other four sons of Sir William died S. P.

16. John Vavasor, of Haselwood, Esq. the eldest son, was living in 1598; but leaving no issue male, by Ellen, daughter of Sir Nicholas Fairfax, his nephew,

17. William,* son of his brother Ralph, became his heir, and married Anne, daughter of Sir Thomas Manners, Knt. son of Thomas, earl of Rutland; by whom

---

† Visitation calls her Constance.

* Vincent's Old Visit. of Yorkshire, No. 110, p. 122, called William, and said to be 15 years old in the year 1584.

he had five sons; 1, Thomas; 2, Henry, a secular priest; 3, John, a lay brother; 4, Francis, a franciscan; and 5, George, who died unmarried.

I. THOMAS, his eldest son and heir, was advanced to the degree of a baronet, 4 Charles I. For his recusancy he paid the composition of 150*l*. per annum to King Charles I. His lady was Ursula, daughter of Walter Giffard, of Chillington, in Staffordshire, Esq. by whom he had issue Sir Walter; William, a major, under his brother, in the service of King Charles I. who died unmarried; Thomas, slain at Marston Moor, in the same service, S. P. John, who died unmarried; and Peter, of York, M. D. who married Elizabeth, daughter of Philip Langdale, of Langthorp, in Yorkshire, Esq. also three daughters; Mary, who died in 1631;* Anne, a nun, and Frances, the wife of Alphonso Thwenge, of Kelton Castle, in Yorkshire, Esq.

II. Sir WALTER VAVASOR, of Haselwood, Bart. aged 58 in 1666, succeeded his father in dignity and estate. He stood firm in his allegiance in the grand rebellion, and raised a regiment of horse for the service of King Charles I. under William, marquis of Newcastle. He married Ursula, daughter of Thomas, viscount Fauconberg, and had issue four sons; 1, Thomas, who died an infant; 2, Sir Walter; 3, Henry, who died in his infancy; and 4, John, 13 years old in Aug. 1666, who died unmarried, at York; and a daughter, Ursula, that died in her infancy.

III. Sir WALTER VAVASOR, Bart. the eldest surviving son, successor to his father, married Jane, daughter of Sir Jordan Crossland, Knt. and died Feb. 16, 1712-13, leaving no issue; and was succeeded by his cousin,

IV. Sir WALTER VAVASOR, Bart. son of Peter Vavasor, Esq. doctor of physic, and Elizabeth, his wife, daughter of Philip Langdale, of Langthorpe, in Yorkshire, Esq. which Walter died in Lancashire, in May, 1740, aged 80, unmarried; and was succeeded by his nephew,

V. Sir WALTER, son of his brother Peter, who was another son of Dr. Peter Vavasor, and died Jan. 9, 1735, aged 68: which Sir Walter married Elizabeth, daughter of Peter Vavasor, of Willitoft, in the east riding of Yorkshire, Esq. by whom he had one daughter, who died young; and secondly in April, 1741, Dorothy, eldest daughter of the Lord Langdale, by whom he had three sons; 1, Sir Walter, born Jan. 16, 1744; 2, Thomas; 3, Peter. Sir Walter died April 13, 1766, and was succeeded by his eldest son,

VI. Sir WALTER VAVASOR, Bart. who in Sep. 1797, married Jane, daughter and heiress of William Langdale, of Langthorpe, Esq.

ARMS—Or, a fess, dancette, sable.
CREST—On a wreath (anciently) a cock, gules; crested, or.
SEAT—Haselwood, Yorkshire.

---

* In Trinity church, Coventry, on a brass plate.—Here lyeth the body of Mrs. Mary Vavasor, eldest daughter of Sir Thomas Vavasor, Knt. and Bart. late knight marshal of the king's household, who deceased this life the 24th of December, 1631. *Dugdale's Warw.* edit. 1730, *fo.* 176.

VAVASOR, OF HASELWOOD, YORKSHIRE.

TABLE 62.

1 Sir MAUGER LE VAVASOR
2 Sir Mauger le Vavasor
3 Sir William, L. of Haselwood
4 Robert = Julian de Ross
5 Sir John = Alice Rookfield
6 Sir William = Nichola Wallis

| Sir Robert | 7 Sir Henry | William |
| Elizabeth=Sir R. Strelley | 8 Sir Henry=A. Fitzhugh | Vavasors of Deneby |

9 William = Elizabeth Stapleton

| Sir Wm. Knt. 1387 | 10 Sir Henry = M. Skipwith |

11 William = Elizabeth Langton
12 Sir Henry, 1470 = Joan Gascoigne   John

13 Henry, 1515	John	William,	Anne	Catharine	Mary	Elizabeth	Matilda
E. Everingham	C. Langdale	Leonard	R. Maleverer	Sir P. Middleton	Sir T. Gascoigne	R. Goldsborough	Sir T. Gilliot
14 John, 1548	Wm.	Elizabeth	Agnes,	Anne,	Jennett		Dorothy,
Anne Scrope	Christ.	G. Topcliff	d. y.	N. Cawnds	T. Oglethorpe		a nun
15 Sir William, Knt.	Christopher		Leonard	Margaret	Jane		
Eliz. Cavalier			M. Hotham	Wm. Redman	W. Perchehay		
16 John	Ralph	Mary	Frances	Anne	Elizabeth	Catharine
E. Fairfax	U. Fair- fax	E. Peck	W. Plumpton	J. Rider	F. Gascoigne	T. Heyland	R. Peck
—, d. y.	17 William = A. Manners			Frances = Wm. Percy	

I. Sir Thomas, Bart. 1666 = U. Gifford   Henry   John   Francis   George

II. Sir Walter, Bart.	Wm. a major	Thomas,	Mary,	Peter, M.D.	Frances
U. Fauconberg		John	Anne	Eliz. Langdale	A. Thwenge
Thomas	III. Sir Walter, 1713	Henry,	Ursula	IV. Sir Walter	Peter Vavasor
	Jane Crossland	John		1740	N

Elizabeth Vavasor = V. Sir Walter Vavasor = Dorothy Langdale

—, a dr. d. v   VI. Sir Walter = Jane Langdale   Thomas   Peter

62. WOLSELEY, of WOLSELEY, STAFFORDSHIRE.

Created Baronet Nov. 24, 1628.

THIS is a family of great antiquity, and has been long seated in the county of Stafford: the first mentioned in the pedigree* is

1. Siwardus, lord of Wlselei, as appears by a deed without date: he was father of

2. William, who is thus mentioned in an old deed, also without date—*Sciant presentes et futuri, quod ego Willielmus, filius Siwardi Wlselia, dedi et concessi, et hac presenti carta mea confirmavi Stephano de Davenport, et heredibus suis, pro homagio et servitio suo, totam terram cum omnibus pertinentibus suis, quam Robertus Parvus, et Oddo Parvus, et Ranulphus, et Robertus Longus, et Faber, et Emach molendinarius tenuerent de me in villa de Wlselia, &c.*

3. Richard, his son, is also thus mentioned, in an old deed without date—*Sciant omnes presenti & futuri, quod ego Richardus, filius Wilielmi de Wlselia, dedi & concessi, & hac presenti carta mea confirmavi adi, Parsone de Colwiz, pro homagio & servitio suo, totam partem meam de Molendano de Wolseley, silicet tertiam partem de Cropsto predicto Molendino pertinent. sibi & cuicunq. assignare voluerit, tenend. & habend. de me, &c.* This Richard had two sons, Stephen and Ralph.

4. Stephen was the father of

5. Robert, lord of Wolseley, who by a deed in a very old hand, beginning thus: *Robertus, filius Stephani de Wlselseia, dedit & concessit Wilielmo, filio Ailwini, pro homagio & servitio suo, virgatam terræ in Walenton, quam Radulphus prius tenuit, cum omnibus, &c.* which deed also proves, that he was owner of Wlselia.

6. Robert, son of Robert, living in 1281, had issue

7. Robert, father of

8. William, lord of Wlselia, 30 Edw. I. and 11 Edw. II. He had issue

9. Richard, who had two sons, John and William.

10. John, lord of Wlselia, 11 Edw. III, by his wife Eleanor, had issue

11. Ralph de Wlselia, 15 and 20 Rich. II. who by his wife Maud, had issue

12. Thomas de Wlselia, 39 Henry VI. who by Margery, daughter of William Brocton, of Longdon, in Staffordshire, had issue

---

* Now in the custody of Sir William Wolseley, Bart. entitled, The Genealogie and Descent of the right worshipful family of the Wolseleys, ancient lords and owners of the manor of Wolseley aforesaid, in the county of Stafford, and of other great possessions, in the said county and other places, which family hath matched with the heirs of several worthy families, and hath been of ancient and long continuance at that place, as appears by their ancient evidences, without date, and other authentic matter, collected by the labour and industry of Sir Richard St. George, Knt. Clarencieux, king at arms, deduced down to Sir Robert Wolseley, of Wolseley, in the county of Stafford, Bart. 1635, and continued down to 1692, by Peers Mauduit, Esq. Windsor Herald.

13. Ralph Wlseley, one of the barons of the Exchequer, temp. Edw. IV. He married two wives; first, ———, daughter of the Lord Montjoy, by whom he had no issue; secondly, Margaret, daughter of Sir Robert Aston, of Heywood, Knt. and had one son,

14. John de Wolseley, who by Anne, daughter of George Stanley, of Bromwich, in Staffordshire, Esq. had issue three sons; 1, Anthony, who married Margaret, daughter of William Blith, of Norton, in Derbyshire, Esq. by whom he had two sons, Erasmus and Francis, who died without issue; and two daughters; Maud, the wife of Christopher Rolston; and Anne, of John Couney, of Weston Couney, in Staffordshire, Esqrs. Erasmus Wolseley, Esq. his eldest son, by Cassandra, daughter of Sir Thomas Gifford, of Chillington, in Staffordshire, Knt. had two daughters; Grisil, the wife of Ralph Fitzherbert; and Dorothy, of John Wolmer, of Kington, in Worcestershire, Esqrs. and several sons. Sir Thomas Wolseley, Knt. the eldest son, married first, Grace, daughter of Sir Thomas (or Sir William) Gresley, Knt. by whom he had no issue; secondly, Anne, daughter of Humphrey Moseley, Esq. by whom he had John, Humphrey, who died without issue, and Edward; and three daughters; Margaret, Mary, and Joan. The second son of John de Wolseley, was Ralph, of whom hereafter; 3, John, rector of Ecton Montgomery, in Northamptonshire. The daughters were, Helen, the wife of —— Westcote, of Handisacre, in Staffordshire; Isabel, of Geoffery Cawardyn; Joan, of —— Montgomery, of Ecton Montgomery; Margery, of John Barbor, of Glasburgh, in Staffordshire; Mary, a nun, and another daughter, the wife of —— Abney, of Willesley, in Derbyshire, Esq.

15. Ralph Wolseley, of Shugborough, Esq. second son of John de Wolseley, before-named, married Joyce, daughter and heir of John Salway, of Stanford, and widow of John Ashby, Esqrs. by whom he had two sons, John and George, who died without issue.

16. John Wolseley, of Stafford, Esq. eldest son, living in 1614, married Isabella, daughter of John Porter, of Chillington, in Staffordshire, Esq. by whom he had three sons and three daughters; 1, William, a captain in Ireland, aged 46, 1614. He married Eleanor, daughter and heir of Sir Marmaduke Whitchurch, of the kingdom of Ireland, Knt. but his issue failed; 2, Robert, hereafter-mentioned; 3, Richard, who died without issue. The daughters were, Mary, the wife of George Franke, Esq. Elizabeth, and Anne.

L ROBERT, the second son, was clerk of the king's letters patent, and advanced to the dignity of a baronet, 4 Charles I. He married Mary, second daughter of Sir George Wroughton, of Wilcot, in Wilts, Knt. by whom he had five sons and six daughters; 1, Sir Charles, his successor; 2, Robert; 3, Thomas; 4, Ralph; which three last all died unmarried: 5, Col. William Wolseley, who accompanied King William into Ireland, in the time of the troubles there, and commanded the Inniskillen men at the memorable battle of the Boyne: the success of that day was in a great measure owing to the gallant behaviour and bravery of those men, which King William acknowledged in a speech made to them on that occasion; whereupon Col. Wolseley was advanced to a brigadier on that establishment, and had the command of a regiment of horse, of twelve troops, consisting of a thousand men; and was made master of the ordnance, privy counsellor, and one of the lord's justices of Ireland. He died a batchelor, in the year 1697.

The daughters of Sir Robert were 1, Penelope, the wife of —— Fountaine, of Ireland; and afterwards of Richard Edwards of Old Church, in the county of Wicklow, in Ireland, Esqrs. by neither of whom she had any issue: 2, Mary, who died unmarried; 3, Frances, the wife of John Dives, Esq. third son of Sir Lewis Dives, of Bromham, in Bedfordshire, Knt. (she died in 1702) 4, Mary, of Thomas Nevil, of Holt, in Leicestershire, Esq. 5, Anne, of Copwood Hollins, of Ditton, in Staffordshire; 6, Dorothy, who died unmarried.

Sir Robert died Sep. 21, 1646, aged 59, and was succeeded by his eldest son,*

II. Sir CHARLES WOLSELEY, Bart. who represented the county of Stafford in parliament, in the reigns of King Charles I. and II. and was a very considerable man in those times. He married Anne, youngest daughter of William, lord viscount Say and Sele, by whom she had seven sons and ten daughters; 1, Robert, a zealous parliamentarian, who for his service was made one of Cromwell's lords; and being in favour with King William, was sent envoy to Brussels, March 3, 1691-2. He was very much the man of pleasure, and occasionally invoked the muse: he wrote the extraordinary Preface to Lord Rochester's Valentinian, a translation from the 6th book of Virgil, on Æneas meeting with Dido; not worth preserving; and some other little pieces: he died unmarried, 1697. 2, Charles, who married one of the daughters and co-heirs —— Beaumont, of Yorkshire, Esq. and relict of —— Tildsley, of the Lodge, in Lancashire, Esq. but had no issue; 3, Fiennes, who died young; 4, Sir William; 5, Sir Henry; 6, Capt. Richard Wolseley, who married Frances, daughter of Mr. Burneston, of Ireland, by whom he had four sons; Charles, who died young; Sir William, Robert, and Richard; 7, James, who married Christian, daughter of Mr Meritt, of Ireland, by whom he had only one daughter.

The daughters of Sir Charles were 1, Elizabeth, the wife of Robert Somervile, of Edstone, in Warwickshire, Esq. who left two sons; William Somervile, Esq. author of that excellent poem, called the *Chace*;† and Dr. Edward, rector of

---

* Sir Robert lies buried in Colwick church, in Staffordshire, in the north aisle, where is a monument of black and white marble, with his effigy, in full proportion, cumbent thereon; as also of one of his sons and a daughter, who are there buried: it is adorned with seven shields of arms; 1, Wolseley, argent, a talbot passant, gules, with a crescent for difference; 2, Washbourne, argent, on a fesse, between six martlets, gules, three caterfoils of the first; 3, Azure, a fesse, between three leopards' faces, or, a crescent for difference; 4, Umsard, gules, a lion rampant, argent; 5, as the second; 6, Or, a saltire engrailed, sable, Trumvin; 7, Wolseley, with the baronets' hand, impaling Wroughton, viz. argent, a chevron, between three boars' heads erased, sable; tusked and langued, gules.

† The following account, copied from the letters of his friend, Shenstone, will be read with pain by those whom his poems have delighted:—"Our old friend, Somervile, is dead! I did not imagine I could have been so sorry as I find myself on this occasion, '*Sublatum quærimus.*' I can now excuse all his foibles, impute them to age, and to distress of circumstances; the last of these considerations wrings my very soul to think on. For a man of high spirit, conscious of having (at least in one production) generally pleased the world, to be plagued and threatened by wretches that are low in every sense; to be forced to drink himself into pains of the body, in order to get rid of the pains of the mind, is a misery." He died July 14, 1743.

From Lady Luxborough's Letters, p. 211, we find, that Mr. Somervile translated, from Voltaire, the play of *Alzira*, which was then in manuscript, in her hands.

Adderbury, in Oxfordshire; 2, Mary, the wife of Richard Edwards, Esq. son of Richard, before-mentioned; 3, Anne, of John Berry, merchant in London; 4, Dorothy; 5, Bridget; 6, Penelope, who died young; 7, Susan, the wife of Charles Wegewood, at the Haracles, in Staffordshire, Esq. 8, Penelope; 9, Frances; and 10, Constance. Sir Charles died Oct. 9, 1714, aged 85, and lies buried in Colwick church, in Staffordshire; and was succeeded in dignity and estate by his fourth, but eldest surviving son,

III. Sir WILLIAM WOLSELEY, Bart. who was unfortunately drowned in his chariot and four, returning home from Litchfield, July 8, 1728, between seven and eight o'clock in the evening, passing a little brook, in a village called Long, in the high road. This accident happened by the sudden breaking down of a mill-dam at a small distance, occasioned by a violent thunder shower, which brought down such a vast body of water the very instant the chariot was passing the brook, that sunk it. The coachman was carried down the stream, by the torrent, into an orchard a hundred yards from the place, and saved himself by getting to the upper boughs of an apple tree.

Sir William died unmarried, in the 69th year of his age, and lies buried in Colwich church, near his father.

IV. Sir HENRY WOLSELEY, Bart. succeeded his brother in title and estate, and died in 1730, unmarried; whereupon the dignity and estate came to his nephew,

V. Sir WILLIAM WOLSELEY, Bart. eldest surviving son of Capt. Richard Wolseley, sixth son of Sir Charles Wolseley, Bart. before-mentioned. He married, and had a son William, born Aug. 24, 1740, the present baronet. Sir William died in 1779, and was succeeded by his son,

VI. Sir WILLIAM WOLSELEY, Bart. who married, July 2, 1765, Miss Chambers, of Wimbleton, in Surrey, by whom he has a son, Charles, who married Mary, eldest surviving daughter of the hon. Thomas Clifford; and a daughter, born in 1767.

ARMS—Argent, a talbot passant, gules.
CREST—Out of a ducal crown, or, a talbot's head, erased, proper.
SEAT—At Wolseley, in Staffordshire.

WOLSELEY, OF WOLSELEY, STAFFORDSHIRE.

TABLE 63.

1 SIWARDUS, L. of Wiselei
2 William
3 Richard
4 Stephen — Ralph
5 Robert
6 Robert, living in 1281
7 Robert
8 William

9 Richard
10 John, L. of Wiselei, temp. Edw. III. — Wm.
11 Ralph, temp. Rich. II. = Maud
12 Thomas = Margery Brockton
13 Ralph, B. of the Exchequer, temp. Edw. IV.
—, dr. of L. Montjoy | Margaret Aston

14 John de Wolseley = Anne Stanley

Anthony	15 Ralph	John	Helen	Isabel	Joan	Margery	Mary	N
M. Blith	J. Salway		— Westcote	G. Cawardyn	— Montgomery	J. Barber		— Abney

Erasmus	Francis	Maud	Anne	16 John Wolseley, living in 1614	George
G. Gifford		G. Ronston	J. Couney	Isabella Porter	

Sir Thomas	Grisel	Dorothy	Wm.	I. Sir Robert, 1646	Mary	Rich.
G. Gresley	A. Moseley	R. Fitzherbert	J. Wonner	E. Whitchurch	M. Wroughton	G. Frank	Eliz.

| John, Humph. Edw. | Marg. Mary, Joan | II. Sir Chas. 1714 Anne, dr. of Wm. V. Say & Sele | Rob. Thos. Ralph | Wm. 1697 | Penelope — Fountaine | Frances John R. Edwards | Mary Thos. Dives | Anne Copwood Nevil | Dorothy Hollens |

| Robert 1697 | Chas. — Beaumont | Fiennes d. y. | III. Sir Wm. Bt. 1728 | IV. Sir Hen. Bt. 1730 | Rich. r. Burnorton | James C. Meritt | Eliz. R. Somervile | Mary R. Edwards | Anne, &c. J. Berry |

| Charles d. y. | V. Sir William | Robert, Richard | William Somervile | Dr. Edward Somervile |

VI. Sir William Wolseley, b. 1740 = — Chambers

—, a dr. b. 1767   Charles = Mary Clifford

63. RUSSELL, of Chippenham, Cambridgeshire.

Created Baronet Jan. 19, 1628.

THE first we find mentioned of this family is Thomas Russell, of Yaverland, in the Isle of Wight, who held the manors and advowsons of Yaverland and Wathe, the manor of Rouburgh, in the Isle of Wight, and Carisbroke Castle, in capite; and died in 1438.

I. Sir WILLIAM RUSSELL, Knt. (son of William Russell, of Surrey, Esq. and grandson to Maurice Russell, of Yaverland, in the county of Southampton, Esq.) was many years treasurer of the royal navy. He was advanced to the dignity of a baronet Jan. 19, 1628; and died in 1653-4. By his first wife, Elizabeth, daughter of Sir Francis Cherry, Knt. he had no issue: by the second, Elizabeth, daughter of Thomas Gerard, of Burwell, in Cambridgeshire, Esq. a younger son of the Gerards, of Flamberds, of Harrow on the Hill, in Middlesex, he had 1, Sir Francis Russell, Bart. 2, Sir Sir William Russell, Knt. some time of St. Edmund's Bury, in Suffolk, commonly called black Sir William, and was stiled the cream of the Russells, on account of his loyalty; who married Anne, relict of —— Robinson, and daughter and heiress of —— Bendish, but left no issue;* 3, Gerard Russell, of Fordham, in the same county, Esq. (who married first Mary, daughter of —— Cherry, of Surrey, by whom he had three sons; 1, William Russell, of Fordham, who married Elizabeth, daughter of —— Cromwell, of Cambridgeshire, Esq. and left issue; 2, Gerard, and 3, John, who both died S. P. secondly, ——, daughter of —— Loyd, by whom he had one daughter, Mabel, the wife of Richard Russell, Esq. second son of Sir John, hereafter-mentioned; and died Dec. 1682, aged 65): 4, Edward Russell, buried at Chippenham July 10, 1647; 5, Robert Russell, buried there Feb. 17, 1640; 6, John Russell, who died an infant; and 7, John Russell, who died without issue. Sir William had also, by the said Elizabeth, three daughters; 1, Elizabeth, the eldest, was the wife of Edward Lewknor, of Denham, in Suffolk, Esq. by whom he had a daughter, Mary, the wife of Horatio, the first lord viscount Townshend; secondly, of John Gauden, D. D. afterwards bishop of Worcester. 2, Anne, the wife of John Bodvile, of Bodvile Castle, in Carnarvonshire, Esq. by whom he had a daughter, Sarah, the wife of John, lord viscount Bodmyn, son of the Earl of Radnor, who dying V. P.† his lady had a warrant for the same place, titles, precedence, &c. as if her husband had lived to be Earl of Radnor. 3, Sarah, was the wife of Sir Thomas Chichley, of Wimpole, in Cambridgeshire, Knt. Sir William's third wife was Elizabeth, daughter and co-heir of Michael Smallpage, of Chichester, in Sussex, Gent and Catharine, his wife, daughter and co-heir of William Devenish, of Hellingleigh, in Sussex, Esq. descended

---

* His daughter and only child died an infant, with whom he lies buried at Burwell aforesaid.
† Collins's Peerage, vol. II. p. 361.

from the Lord Hoo; which Elizabeth was the relict of John Wheatly, of Catesfield, in the same county, Esq. barrister of the Middle Temple; by whom he had issue two sons; William Russell, who died young, and Sir William Russell, of Langherne, in Carmarthenshire, Knt. created baronet Nov. 8, 1660, called white Sir William, who married Hesther, daughter of Sir Thomas Rouse, of Rouse Lench, in Worcestershire, Bart. and left only one daughter and heiress, Mary, the wife of Hugh Calveley Cotton, Esq. second son of Sir Robert Cotton, of Cumbermere, in Cheshire, Bart. and secondly, of the Lord Arthur, second surviving son of Henry, duke of Beaufort; whereupon this title of baronet became extinct.

II. Sir FRANCIS RUSSELL, Bart. son and heir to Sir William, married at Chippenham, Sep. 19, 1631, Catharine, daughter and sole heiress of John Wheatly, Esq. before-mentioned, by Elizabeth, his wife; by whom he had several children; 1, Elizabeth, born in 1634, the wife of Henry, younger son of Oliver Cromwell, lord protector; 2, William, born in 1635, and died unmarried; 3, Sarah; 4, Frances, both died young; 5, Sarah, born in 1639, the wife of —— Reynolds, of Cambridgeshire, Esq. afterwards of Henry O'Brian, earl of Thomund; 6, Sir John, of whom hereafter; 7, Catharine, born in 1641, the wife of —— Shairs, of Hertfordshire, and died in 1673; 8, Robert, born in 1644, who was some time of Freckenham, and afterwards of Mildenhall, in Suffolk: he married a widow, the daughter and co-heir of Thomas Soame, of Thurlow, in Suffolk, a captain of foot, in the service of King Charles I. 9, Gerard, born in 1645; he was a Hamburgh merchant, and married ——, daughter of —— Yonker, a merchant, at Hamburgh. 10, Killephet, born in 1647, and died young; 11, Frances, born in 1649, wife of John Hagar, of Bourn, in Cambridgeshire, Esq. 12, Anne, born in 1650, wife of Hugh Underwood, of Wittlesea, in the Isle of Ely, Esq. one of the deputy lieutenants of the said Isle; 13, Killephet, born in 1652; he was of Mildenhall, in Suffolk, and married Margaret Bullen, by whom he had a son, Francis, who died in 1680, and was buried at Isleham, in Cambridgeshire: 14, Edward, born in 1654; and 15, William, born in 1660.

III. Sir JOHN RUSSELL, Bart. son and heir to Sir Francis, was baptized at Chippenham, Oct. 6, 1640, and buried there, March 24, 1669. He married Frances, daughter of Oliver Cromwell, lord protector, and widow of Robert Rich, Esq. grandson to Robert Rich, earl of Warwick, and had issue by her; 1, Sir William Russell, his son and heir; 2, Rich Russell (so named from the Lord Rich) a captain of King William's guards, who married first Mabel, daughter of Gerard Russell, of Fordham, Esq. aforenamed; secondly, Catharine Burton: and another son, named John, first a factor for the East India Company at Bengal, and afterwards governor of Fort William there; and died at Bath, Dec. 5, 1735, aged 66. The aforesaid John had also, by the said Frances, two daughters; Christian, buried at Chippenham, Aug. 28, 1669; and Mary, wife of the late Sir Thomas Frankland, of Thirkelby, in Yorkshire, Bart.

IV. Sir WILLIAM RUSSELL, Bart. the eldest son, married ——, daughter of —— Gore, in Ireland; and having spent the remainder of a considerable fortune in raising troops at the revolution, sold his estate at Chippenham; and dying in 1707, left issue two sons and one daughter, Mary, who died Dec. 1735.

V. Sir WILLIAM RUSSELL, Bart. his eldest son and successor, died at Passage, near Waterford, in Ireland, in May, 1738, without issue; and was succeeded by his only brother,

VI. Sir FRANCIS RUSSELL, Bart. who was one of the council of Fort William, in Bengal, in the East Indies; and married in 1725 Anne, daughter of ——— Gee, merchant; and had by her one son,

VII. Sir WILLIAM RUSSELL, Bart. who was a lieutenant in the first regiment of guards, and died in 1735, unmarried.

The aforesaid John, third son of Sir John, and governor of Fort William, in Bengal, was born Oct. 14, 1670, and died at Bath Dec. 5, 1735, as before-mentioned. He first married Rebecca, sister of Sir Charles Eyre, of Kew, in Surrey, Knt. Dec. 17, 1697, by whom he had one son and three daughters; Frances, the wife of John Revett, of Checkers, in Bucks, Esq. and was bed-chamber woman to her royal highness the Princes Amelia: Mary, the wife of Mr. Holmes, in the East Indies, died without issue; and Elizabeth, of Samuel Greenhill, of Swencombe, in Oxfordshire, Esq. by whom she had two sons; the Rev. John Russell Greenhill, and Charles, who died young. Charles Russell, born Jan. 8, 1700, was appointed a major in the second regiment of guards, with the rank of colonel, in Nov. 1745; and colonel of the 34th regiment of foot, Dec. 17, 1751. He commanded (as appears by a memorial*) the first battalion of foot guards at the battle of Fontenoy; and when attending his regiment in the Isle of Minorca, contracted the distemper, of which he died in London, Nov. 20, 1754, and was buried at Kew. John Russell married secondly Johanna, widow of Col. Revett,† Sep. 7, 1715, by whom he had one daughter, who died young. His son Charles married, June 18, 1737, Mary-Johanna Cutts, daughter of the aforesaid Col. Revett (who was killed in the battle of Malplaquet, Sep. 11, 1709) by the aforesaid Johanna, sole daughter and heiress of Serjeant Thurbane, of Checkers, aforesaid; by whom he had issue Mary, born Dec. 13, 1739, now living unmarried: she was bed-chamber woman to her royal highness the Princess Amelia, at the time of her death, and

VIII. JOHN RUSSELL, Bart. born Oct. 31, 1741, who succeeded to the title on the death of Sir William, aforesaid, in 1757. He was a student of Christ Church, Oxford, and barrister at law. He married Catharine, daughter of the late General George Carey, second son of Viscount Falkland, by Isabella, only daughter and heiress of Arthur Ingram, Esq. of Baroley, in Yorkshire, and sister and co-heiress with the right hon. Lady Amherst. He left only two children, John, the present

---

* May it please your majesty:
The Memorial of Col. Charles Russell, first major to the Coldstream regiment of foot guards—that your memorialist has served 34 years in the foot guards, was at Gibraltar when last beseiged, was every year abroad, on service, during the late war, except the last campaign, and had the honour to command the first battalion of guards at the battle of Fontenoy. On presuming that the present vacancy of dragoons may occasion a vacancy of a regiment of foot, on the English establishment, humbly prays he may succeed to any such regiment as may become vacant.

† Checkers came into this family by Governor Russell's marrying the widow of Col. Revett, who was heir to Serjeant Thurbane (by Lord Cutt's sister) whose first wife, by whom he had no issue, was one of the three daughters and co-heiresses of Sir Robert Croke, of Checkers, to whom it had descended through the Hawtreys, from a Sir Ralph de Checkers.

RUSSELL, OF CHIPPENHAM, CAMBRIDGESHIRE.

baronet, and George Russell, Esq. of Leven Grove, in Yorkshire, now at Ch. Ch. Oxford. Sir John died in 1783, and was succeeded by his son,

IX. Sir JOHN RUSSELL, Bart.

ARMS—Argent, a lion rampant, gules; on a chief, sable, three roses of the first.
CREST—On a wreath, a goat, argent; attired and gorged with a crown mural, or.
SEAT—Checkers, Bucks.

TABLE 64.

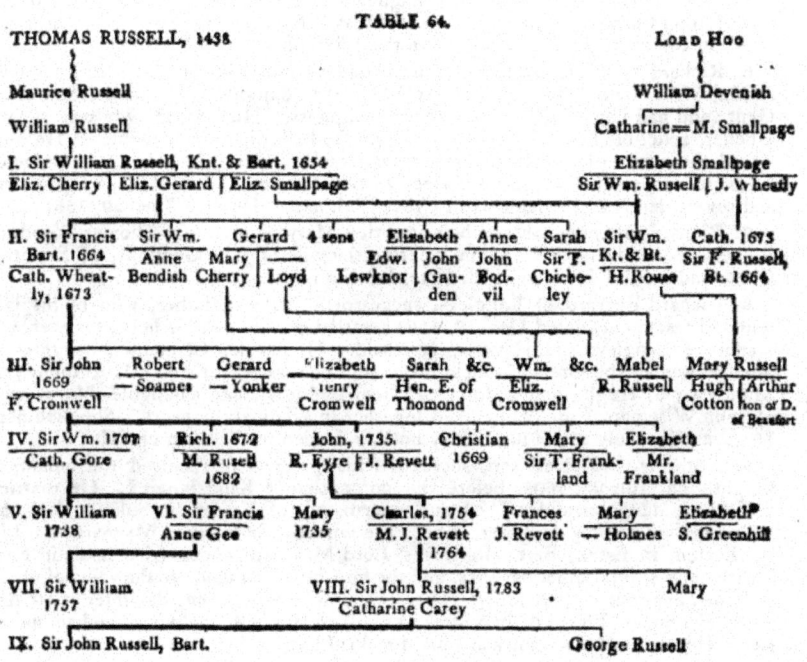

64. EVERARD, of Much Waltham, Essex.

Created Baronet Jan. 29, 1628.

1. RALPH EVERARD is the first of this ancient family, that we have an account of: he lived in the reign of Henry III. and Edw. I.

2. Walter Everard, his son, lived in the reign of Edw. II. and Edw. III.

3. William Everard, his son and heir, was of Marshbury, in Essex, and lived in the time of Richard II. and Henry IV. and left two sons of the name of John

4. John Everard, sen. of Newarks, in Good-Estre and Marshbury, in the said county, who had issue

5. Thomas Everard, of Waltham Magna, who married ———, daughter and co-heir of John Cornish, of Langleys, in Much Waltham, aforesaid; and had issue six sons and three daughters. He lived in the reign of Henry VII.

6. Richard Everard, fourth son, succeeded his father in the manor of Langleys, in Much Waltham. He married first Elizabeth, daughter of Richard Stephens, Gent. and had issue Richard, and three daughters. His second wife was Agnes Upcher, relict of Thomas Wood, by whom he had only one daughter. He possessed the manor of Langleys, and the manor of Havering, in Felsted, and several lands and tenements in Little Raine, Little Dunmow, Good-Estre, High-Estre, and several lands and tenements in Great Waltham. He died Dec. 29, 1561.

7. Richard, his only son and heir, married Mary, daughter of Thomas Wood, of Raine Parva, who surviving him, became the wife of John Goodday, of Braintre, Gent. and died in his father's life-time, leaving issue another

8. Richard Everard, of Langleys, successor to his grandfather, who by his last will and testament, dated Dec. 19, 1561, settled on him and his heirs, for ever, the manors of Langleys and Havering aforesaid. He married Clementia, daughter of John Wiseman, of Great Canfield, Esq. and had issue four sons; 1, Anthony; 2, Matthew; 3, Hugh; and 4, John, of Great Baddow; and a daughter Mary, wife of John Wiseman, Esq. They lived together in wedlock 53 years. She died Sep. 1611, and he July 25, 1617. They both lie buried in Waltham church.

9. Anthony, the eldest son, succeeded his father: he received the honour of knighthood, July 23, 1603, before the coronation of King James I. He married first Anne, daughter of Sir Thomas Bernardiston, of Ketton, in Suffolk, Knt. by whom he had an only daughter, Anne, the wife of Sir William Maynard, of Little Easton, in Essex, Bart. afterwards Lord Maynard, and carried lands in Fox-Heath, and several other parishes, and the lordship of Sandon, to the value of about 600l. per ann. out of the family. His second wife was Anne, daughter of Sir Anthony Felton, of Playford, in Suffolk, knight of the bath, by whom he had no issue. He died in 1614, and was buried at Waltham.

10. Hugh Everard, Esq. third son of Richard, succeeded to the estate at Waltham: he was high sheriff of Essex in 1626; and married Mary, daughter of Tho-

mas Brand, alias Bond, of Great Hormead, in Hertfordshire, Gent. and had issue Richard, his only son and heir. He and his wife both died in 1637, and are buried in Waltham church.

I. RICHARD EVERARD, Esq. his only son and heir, was advanced to the dignity of a baronet by King Charles I. He married Joan, daughter of Sir Thomas Barrington, Bart. by whom he had four sons; 1, Sir Richard Barrington; 2, Robert, who died without issue; 3, Hugh, fellow of Emmanuel college, Cambridge: and three daughters; Winifred, the youngest, was the wife of Sir William Luckyn, Bart. He married secondly Frances, daughter of Sir Robert Lee, of Bellisley, in Warwickshire, relict of Sir Gervase Elves, of Woodford, in Essex, Knt.

II. Sir RICHARD, his eldest son, succeeded him, and was sheriff 20 Charles I. for Essex. He married first Elizabeth, daughter of Sir Henry Gibbs, of Faulkland, in Scotland, knight of the bed-chamber to King James I. and had issue two sons; Richard, who died unmarried, and Sir Hugh; also a daughter, Jane, who died young. He married secondly Jane, daughter of Sir John Finnet, master of the ceremonies to King James I. and King Charles I. but had no issue by her. He died in Aug. 1694, aged 70.

III. Sir HUGH EVERARD, his second, but only surviving son, succeeded him, who, in his younger days, signalized himself in Flanders (his elder brother being then alive). He married Mary, daughter of John Brown, of Salisbury, M.D. by whom he had 1, Sir Richard; 2, Hugh,* drowned in the great storm in 1703, being lieutenant of the Restoration; and Morton, who was killed on board the Hampshire, commanded by Lord Maynard: also two daughters; Elizabeth, the wife of the Rev. —— Oburne, vicar of Thaxted, in Essex; and Frances, who died unmarried. He was receiver-general of the land-tax, and justice of the peace for the county of Essex, and died in Jan. 1705-6, aged 51, and lies buried at Waltham.

IV. Sir RICHARD EVERARD, his eldest son, succeeded him in dignity and estate, and married Susanna, one of the daughters and coheirs of Richard Kidder, D.D. lord bishop of Bath and Wells, who was killed at his palace in Wells, by the great storm in Nov. 1703, by the fall of a chimney; by whom he left issue two sons, Sir Richard and Hugh, who went to Georgia; and two daughters; Susanna, the wife of Mr. Mead, a considerable merchant and planter in Virginia; and Anne, the wife of George Lathbury, Gent. He was governor of North Carolina, under the lords proprietors; and died in Red Lion Street, Holborn, Feb. 17, 1732-3; and his lady in Sep. 12, 1739.

V. Sir RICHARD EVERARD, Bart. his eldest son and successor, died unmarried, March 7, 1741-2, and was succeeded by his brother,

VI. Sir HUGH EVERARD, Bart.

ARMS—Argent, a fesse wavy, between three estoils, gules.
CREST—On a wreath, a bust of a man in profile, habited in a long cap, checky.
SEAT—At Bromfield Green, Essex.

* Monumental Inscriptions for this family are in the History of Essex, pub. 1770, vol. I. p. 330, & seq.

EVERARD, OF MUCH WALTHAM, ESSEX.

TABLE 65.

1 RALPH EVERARD
2 Walter Everard
3 William, temp. Rich. II.
4 John — John, jun.
5 Thomas = —— Cornish
6 Richard, 1561 = E. Stephens = A. Upcher
7 Richard = Mary Wood
8 Richard, 1617 = Clementia Wiseman, 1617

9 Sir Anthony, Knt. 1614 — Matthew — 10 Hugh, 1637 — John — Mary
A. Barnardiston | A. Felton — Mary Brand — J. Wiseman
Anne = Sir Wm. Maynard — Joan Barrington = I. Sir Richard, Bart. = Frances Lee

II. Sir Richard Everard, 1694 — Barrington, — 2 drs — Winifred
Eliz. Gibbs | Jane Finnet — Robert, Hugh — Sir Wm. Luckyn, Bart.
Richard — III. Sir Hugh, 1706 = Mary Brown — Jane
IV. Sir Richard, 1733 = S. Kidder, 1739 — Hugh, 1703 — Morton — Eliz. = H. Oburne — Frances
V. Sir Richard, 1742 — VI. Sir Hugh — Susanna = —— Mead — Anne

---

65. EVERY, of Eggington, Derbyshire.

Created Baronet May 26, 1641.

THIS family was originally of Somersetshire, and

I. Sir SIMON EVERY, the first baronet, so created by King Charles I. was born at Chard, in that county, and a great sufferer for King Charles I. He married the eldest daughter and co-heir of Sir Henry Leigh, of Egginton, Knt. whereby he became possessed of that and other estates; by whom he had Sir Henry, his successor, and Capt. Every, who was seated at Burton upon Trent, and there died without issue; and left his Somersetshire estate to his nephew, Sir Simon Every, Bart.

II. Sir HENRY EVERY, Bart. the eldest son, who succeeded his father in title and estate, was a great sufferer for his loyalty in the reign of King Charles II. He married Vere, eldest daughter of Sir Henry Herbert, Knt. master of the revels to King Charles I. by whom he had six sons and five daughters; 1, Sir Henry; 2, Sir John; 3, Sir Simon; 4, William, killed at the siege of Cork, in Ireland, in the reign of King William; and two others, that died unmarried. Of the daughters, —— was the wife of Matthew Alured, of Burton upon Trent; ——, of Mr. Gayner; ——, of Mr. Cumming; and two died unmarried.

III. Sir HENRY, Bart. eldest son and successor, married first ——, daughter of the Lord Viscount Tracy, of Toddington, in Gloucestershire; secondly, Anne, daughter and co-heir of Sir Francis Russell, of Strensham, in Worcestershire, Bart. relict of Richard Lygon, of Madresford, in the same county, Esq. who surviving Sir Henry, married to her third husband, Sir John Guise, of Rendcomb, in Gloucestershire, Bart. but dying without issue male, was succeeded in dignity and estate by his brother,

IV. Sir JOHN EVERY, Bart. who was for some time captain of the Queen, a first-rate man of war, and did signal services for the government, in the reign of King Wm. III. He married first Martha, daughter of John, lord Haversham; secondly, Dorothy, daughter of Godfrey Meynell, of Bradley, in Derbyshire, Esq. and dying July 1, 1729, without issue, was succeeded in dignity and estate by his next brother,

V. Sir SIMON EVERY, Bart. who was rector of Naumby, in Lincolnshire, and married Mary, eldest daughter of the Rev. Joshua Clarke, rector of Somerby, in Lincolnshire, and one of the prebendaries of Lincoln (whose other daughter was the wife of Jacob Butler, of Barnwell, in Cambridgshire, Esq.) by whom he had issue five sons; 1, Henry, his successor; 2, John; 3, Simon; 4, Joshua-Clarke; and 5, Edward: and seven daughters; 1, Jane; 2, Anne; 3, Martha; 4, Susanna; 5, Mary; 6, Anne; and 7, Elizabeth, all of which died single, except Anne, who married, but had no issue. Sir Simon died Jan. 12, 1753, aged 93, and was succeeded by his eldest son,

VI. Sir HENRY EVERY, Bart. who was high sheriff of Derbyshire in 1749. He married, July 1, 1741, ——, daughter of Henry Ibbetson, of Yorkshire, Esq. and dying without issue, May 31, 1755, the title and estate descended to the next brother,

VII. Sir JOHN EVERY, Bart. who married ——, who died Sep. 11, 1769. He died in 1777, aged 71, and was succeeded by his next surviving brother,

VIII. Sir EDWARD EVERY, Bart. who was high sheriff for Derbyshire in 1782, and died Jan. 4, 1786; and was succeeded by

IX. Sir HENRY EVERY, Bart. late fellow commoner of Christ's College, Cambridge, who in 1798 married Penelope, daughter of Sir John Parker Mosley, Bart.

ARMS—Or, four chevronels, gules.
CREST—On a wreath, a unicorn's head, couped, proper.
SEAT—At Egginton, in Derbyshire,

EVERY, OF EGGINTON, DERBYSHIRE.

TABLE 66.

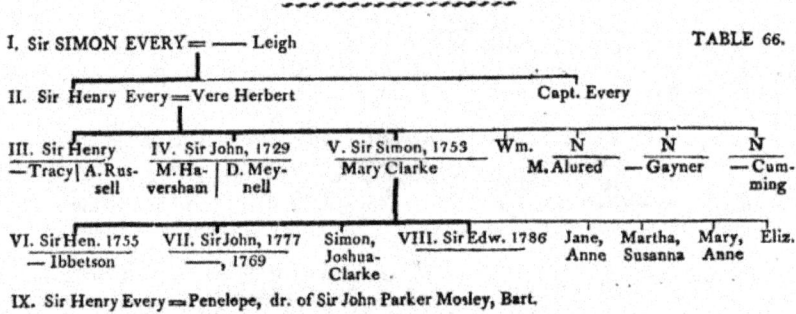

IX. Sir Henry Every═Penelope, dr. of Sir John Parker Mosley, Bart.

66. LANGLEY, of HIGHAM-GOBION, BEDFORDSHIRE.

Created Baronet May 29, 1641.

1. WILLIAM LANGLEY, of Langley,* in the bishopric of Durham, by Alice his wife, had issue,

2. Thomas Langley, father of two sons; 1, Henry, of whom hereafter; 2, Thomas Langley, lord chancellor of England, bishop of Durham, and a cardinal, 1417. Bishop Goodwin says,† he was consecrated bishop of Durham in 1406. June 6, 1411, he was made cardinal, together with Robert Halam, bishop of Salisbury, by pope John. He bestowed 499*l.* 6*s.* 7*d.* in repairing that gallery, in the west end of his church, which was first built by Hugh Pudsey, his predecessor: he also founded two schools in the Place Green, one for grammar, another for music. He died in 1437, and was buried (as I am informed) in the gallery; and lies entombed before the altar there, under the table of the consistory.

3. Henry Langley, Esq. before-mentioned, the eldest son, was of Dalton, in the west riding of Yorkshire; and married ——, the daughter of —— Kaye, of Woodsome, in Yorkshire, Esq. by whom he had two sons, Thomas and Robert; Thomas was of Rathorp Hall, in Dalton, Yorkshire, and ancestor to the Langleys of that place.

4. Robert Langley, of Langley, the second son, was the father of

---

* In Le Neve's MSS. vol. II. p. 111, is this entry:—"The following pedigree, as low as William Langley, was copied from a pedigree, 1694, in the hands of Sir Roger Langley, of Westminster, Bart. under the hand of Sir Richard St. George, Knt. Clarencieux king of arms, by me, Peter Le Neve; the rest I had from Sir Roger himself. Beatson Political Index.
† In his Catalogue of Bishops, p. 664.

LANGLEY, OF HIGHAM-GOBION, BEDFORDSHIRE.

5. George Langley, who had two sons; 1, Robert, whose daughter and heiress, Catharine, was the wife of Thomas Leigh, of Boothe, in Cheshire, Esq.

6. William Langley, Esq. second son, was the father of

7. George Langley, of Stainton, in Yorkshire, who by Jane, daughter of John Hall, of Sherbourn, in that county, had issue a daughter, ——, the wife of William Forster, of Erdswick, in Yorkshire, Esq. and three sons; Sir William, Matthew, who married, but left no issue, and John, who died S. P.

I. Sir WILLIAM LANGLEY, of Stainton, in Yorkshire, and of Higham-Gobion, in Bedfordshire, the first baronet of this family, advanced to that dignity 17 Charles I. married Elizabeth, daughter of Roger Lumley, Esq. (and sister of Richard, viscount Lumley, of Waterford, in Ireland, grandfather to Richard Lumley, earl of Scarborough); by whom he had issue William, who died unmarried, 1634, in his father's life-time; Sir Roger, and Dorothy, the wife of William Bristow, in Somersetshire, Esq. Sir William died in Holborn, and was buried at St. Andrew's church, 1651.

II. Sir ROGER LANGLEY, of Sheriff-Hutton Park, in Yorkshire, Bart. succeeded his father in title and estate. He was 38 years of age in 1665, and married first Mary, daughter of Thomas Keighley, of Hertingfordbury, in Hertfordshire, Esq. by whom he had 1, William; 2, Richard; 3, Roger; and 4, Thomas: the three last died without issue: also four daughters; Mary, the wife of Mr. Prescot, of Essex; Rose, of Peter Priaux, of London, merchant; Elizabeth and Frances both died unmarried. His second wife was Barbara, daughter and co-heir of —— Chapman, of Foxton, in Leicestetshire, Esq. serjeant at law, by whom he had no issue. His third lady was Sarah, daughter of John Neale, of Malden-Ash, in Essex, Esq. by whom he had three sons; 1, William, who died young; 2, John, a major in the army, who married a daughter of —— de la Hay, of Westminster, Esq. and 3, David, who was killed in an engagement in the West Indies, in 1708; also two daughters, Mary and Sarah, who died unmarried. Sir Roger was foreman of the jury on the trial of the seven bishops, and was a commissioner of the prize-office, in the reign of King William. He died in 1698.

William Langley, his eldest son, married Isabella, daughter of Sir John Griffith, of Erith, in Kent. (who surviving him, became the wife of Thomas Barnes, of East-Winch, in Norfolk, Esq.) He died in 1689, leaving six sons; 1, Sir Roger; 2, William Langley, who married Margaret, daughter of —— Sutton, of Barbadoes, Esq. and widow of Abraham Jaggard, and left one daughter, Isabella, the wife of William Ettrick, Esq. 3, Robert; 4, Samuel, who both died without issue; 5, Sir Thomas; and 6, Haldanby, who married Mary, daughter of Charles Peck, of Gildersley, in Derbyshire, Esq. and dying May 30, 1728, left three sons; Gilbert, who married ——, daughter of Mr. Brown, of Searle Street, near Lincoln's Inn Fields; Haldanby, and James.

III. Sir ROGER LANGLEY, Bart. succeeded his grandfather in title and estate, and married Mary, daughter of —— Browne, of Eastbourne, in Sussex, Esq. by whom he had only one son, Charles, who died an infant. He died in 1716, and was succeeded by his next surviving brother,

IV. Sir THOMAS LANGLEY, Bart. who married ——, second daughter of Capt. Robert Edgeworth, of Longwood, in the county of Meath, in Ireland; by

LANGLEY, OF HIGHAM-GOBION, BEDFORDSHIRE.

whom he had two sons, Tyrrell and John; and three daughters, all dead; one of them was the wife of Edward Johnson, of the Lottery Office, Esq. Sir Thomas died Dec. 1, 1762, aged 98, without issue, and was succeeded by his nephew,

V. Sir HALDANBY LANGLEY, Bart. who was succeeded by

VI. Sir HENRY LANGLEY, Bart.

ARMS—Paly of six, argent and vert.
CREST—Out of a ducal crown, or, a plume of five ostrich's feathers, three argent and two vert.
SEAT—At High-Gobion, Bedfordshire.

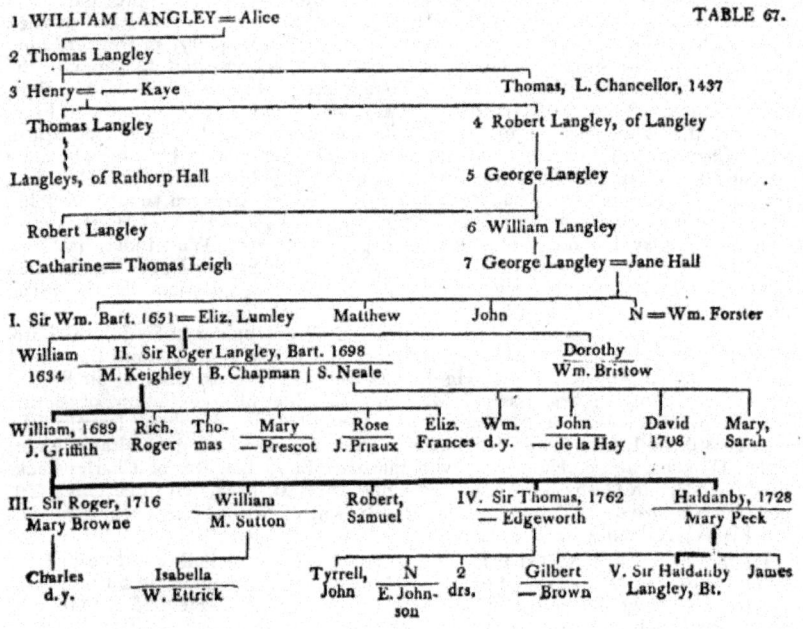

TABLE 67.

VI. Sir Henry Langley, Bart.

67. CAVE, of STANFORD, NORTHAMPTONSHIRE.

Created Baronet June 30, 1641.

WYAMARUS* and Jordayne, two brothers, were living at the time of the conquest: the first enjoyed, by the gift of William the Conqueror, in 1069, as marks of his royal favour and reward, the lordships of North and South Cave, Clyffe, Stanton, Haslosheſe, Newland, Skalby, and the manor of Waldingfene, cum membris, in Yorkshire, all which the said Wyamarus conveyed to his brother Jordayne, in the 7th year of William Rufus, in which reign Wyamarus died without issue.

1. Jordayne de Cave, heir to his brother, according to the custom of those times, was so surnamed from his lordship of Cave.

2. Bryan de Cave, his son and heir, had issue a daughter Joan, the wife of Nigell Fossard, lord of Ellaton, and one son.

3. Robert de Cave, who by a daughter of Thomas de Metham, had one son, Thomas, and three daughters; Isabella, the wife of Thomas de Redness, of Redness; Margaret, of Sir Gerard Furnivall, of Swanland, Knt. and Jane, of Sir John de Ufflet, Knt.

4. Thomas de Cave, son and heir, married Joyce, daughter of Sir William St. Quintin, lord of Braynsburton, in Yorkshire, Knt. by whom he had three sons; 1, Geoffery; 2, Robert, who married ——, the daughter of Robert de Haldanby; 3, John, who married ——, daughter of —— Estotes: also two daughters; Christian, the wife of Thomas Newbold, and Grace, of William Ayrmine, of Newland upon Ayre, Esq.

5. Geoffery de Cave, son and heir, married Mabel, daughter of Robert Saltmarsh, of Yorkshire, and had issue Peter, and Alexander de Cave, dean of Durham, and prebendary of Holden, where he lies interred.

6. Peter de Cave married a daughter and heir of Sir Thomas Bromflete, Knt. by whom he had two sons, Sir Alexander and Thomas, who married the daughter of Robert Cliffe, and was progenitor to the Caves, of Flinton, in Holderness, Yorkshire: also three daughters; Catharine, the wife of John Riplingham, of Riplingham; Beatrix, of Philip de Waldby; and Jane, of John Dawney, of Sesay, all in the county of York.

---

* From the pedigree in the family, thus entitled:—*Genealogia sive stemma gentilitium antiquissimæ familiæ De Cave omnia ex publiciis regni archivis, & privatis ejusdem familiæ archetypis Ecclesiis, Monumentis, Historiis Monasteriorum registris, & rotulis armorum, Vetustissimis Aliisque reverendæ Antiquitatis, & indubitatæ veritatis rebus maximo labore ac fide depromuntur; & ad perpetuam rei memoriam seriatim hoc ordine discribi curantur Aº Incarnationis Dominicæ* MDCXXXII, *Gulielmus Segar, garterus principalis rex armorum Anglicorum, ex Industriæ & Labore Hen. Lily Rouge Croix.*—Continued to 1737 by J. Pomfret Rouge Croix, and from that time by the present Sir Charles Cave, Bart.

7. Sir Alexander de Cave, Knt. eldest son and heir of Peter, and heir to his uncle Alexander,* married the daughter of Peter de Mawley, lord of Mulgrave, by whom he had one son, Peter, and four daughters; Margaret, the wife of Ralph Andlaby, of Andlaby; Joyce, of Sir Thomas Polington, of Polington, Knt. Jane, of —— Shelton, of Shelton; and Ursula, of Sir John Ella, of Kirk Ella, Knt.

8. Peter de Cave married Anne, daughter of Sir Simon Ward, Knt. and had issue Sir Alexander, and two daughters; Elizabeth, the wife of Sir John Middleton, of Middleton on the Woulds; but surviving him, she took the veil and ring; and Mary, who took upon her a religious life, and became prioress of Watton Abbey.

9. Sir Alexander Cave, Knt.† married Alice, daughter of Sir Geoffery Hotham, Knt. by whom he had one son, John, and two daughters; Margaret, the wife of Sir Anselme St. Quintin, Knt. and secondly of —— Moigne, of Hasell, in Yorkshire; and Jane, of Sir Roger Kelk, Knt.

10. John Cave, son and heir,‡ was a knight, and married Mary, daughter and coheir of Peter Genell, of Southcliffe, by his wife, the daughter and heir of —— Cliffe, of Southcliffe, whereby he much augmented his ancient patrimony, and had four sons, and two daughters; 1, Sir Alexander; 2, Thomas; 3, Peter; and 4, John, which three last died without issue. His daughters were Anne, the wife of Sir Marmaduke Grendall; and Mary, of Sir Peter de See, Knts.

11. Sir Alexander Cave, Knt. son and heir, married Catharine, daughter of Roger Somervile, of Grindall, by whom he had three sons and three daughters; 1, Sir Alexander; 2, Peter, of whom hereafter; and 3, John, who died without issue: Grace, a nun; Catharine, the wife of Sir John Markenfeild, Knt. and Anne, of Gilbert Stapleton, of Bayton.

12. Sir Alexander Cave, the eldest son, married Constance, daughter of Roger Leeds, and left only one daughter, Maud, the wife of Alexander Lownde, of Lownde Hall; the lordship of Cave, and other lands, went with her in marriage: and their daughter and heir, Janet, was the wife of Robert Sheffield, of Butterwick, in Lincolnshire, Esq. ancestor to the Duke of Buckingham, who thereupon quartered the arms of Cave.

12. Peter Cave, next brother to Sir Alexander, continued the line: he married Anne, daughter of Ralph Ingleby, by whom he had three sons; 1, Peter; 2, John, abbot of Selby, in Yorkshire (one of the parliamentary abbeys, who, according to Mr. Brown Willis, was chosen abbot in 1430, and died in 1436); 3, Alexander. John, the second son, lies buried in Stanford church, and on a flat stone is the figure of a religious in brass, whereon is cut, in old characters, this inscription:

* He had a grant from King Edw. I. of free warren in all his demesne lands of South Cave, Riplingham, Hamer, and Bemlingwell, in Yorkshire, dated in the second year of his reign, 1275. He had also a release of lands in South Cave, from Nicholas de Stuteville.

† He was living 4 Edw. II. 1320; for then Robert, son of Thomas Deacon, of South Cave, released to him the rent of 20s. by deed, stiling him, Dom. Alexander de Cave, Miles.

‡ He gave, by deed, to John de Bella Aqua, or Bellew, clerk, certain lands in South Cave, dated at South Cave, 14 Edw. II.

CAVE, OF STANFORD, NORTHAMPTONSHIRE.

Hic jacet Dominus Johannes Cave,
Primus Vicarius istius Ecclesiæ qui obiit penultimo die Mensis
*Februarii, Anno Dni. 1471.**

13. Peter Cave, the eldest son and heir of Peter, married Mary, daughter of —— Burdet, of Rothwell, in Northamptonshire, and had issue only one son,

14. Thomas Cave, Esq. who by Thomasine, daughter of —— Passemere, of Essex, had issue five sons; 1, Richard; 2, William, father of John and Peter Cave; 3, Christopher, who left a daughter, the wife of —— Noble, of Stowford, in Leicestershire; 4, John, father of Thomas, William, and Christopher Cave, of Stanford, and of Bartholomew and Edward Cave, of Welford; 5, Henry, who married first a daughter of —— Saunders, of Harrington, in Northamptonshire, Esq. secondly, a daughter of —— Belgrave, of Blaby, in Leicestershire, Esq. by the last he left issue. This Thomas died in 1495, and lies buried in Stanford church.

15. Richard Cave, Esq. son and heir, married two wives; first Elizabeth, daughter of —— Marvin, of Church Lawford, in Warwickshire, Esq. by whom he had one son, Edward, and a daughter, Margaret: Edward married Dorothy, daughter and co-heir of Nicholas Mallory, of Winwick, in Northamptonshire, and of Newbold Revell, in Warwickshire, Esq. but left only two daughters, his co-heirs; Catharine, the wife of Sir Thomas Andrews, of Charwelton, in Northamptonshire, Knt. and Margaret, of Thomas Boughton, of Lawford, in Warwickshire, Esq. who, surviving him, became the wife of George Ashby, Esq. Margaret was the wife of Thomas Saunders, of Harrington, in Northamptonshire, Esq. by whom she had Lawrence Saunders,† who was burnt for the testimony of the gospel, in the Little Park, within the city of Coventry, 2 and 3 Philip and Mary; Capt. Saunders, slain at Newbury; and Sir Edward Saunders, Knt. lord chief baron of the Exchequer; and other children. He married secondly Margaret, daughter of John Saxby, of Northampton, merchant of the staple, by whom he had eight sons and four daughters; 1, Sir Thomas; 2, Anthony, of Chichley, in Bucks, Esq. who married Elizabeth, daughter of Thomas Lovett, of Astwell, in Northamptonshire, Esq. she afterwards married to her second husband, John Newdigate, of Harfield, in Middlesex, Esq. and to her third husband, Richard Weston, Esq. one of the justices of the King's Bench. By her first husband she had only four daughters and co-heirs; 1, Judith, the wife of William Chester, Esq. son and heir of Sir William Chester, Knt. lord-mayor of London; 2, Anne, of Griffith Hampden, of Hampden, in Bucks,

---

* In South and North Cave churches, in Yorkshire, several of the ancestors of this family lie buried, as were evident by several of their remains in those churches; for in 1585, when Robert Glover, Somerset Herald, went his visitation, he found several of their arms painted on the glass in North Cave church; and several knights of this family, with their wives carved in stone, in kneeling postures, in South Cave church; with the Caves' arms, azure, frette of eight pieces, argent, on them; and particularly a very ancient tomb of an armed knight at full length, as large as life, with a helmet on his head, and thereon a ducal coronet, with a faulcon, and the arms of Cave round the tomb, but without any inscription. But at this time this tomb, and all the other remains, are gone to decay; nor are there any evidences remaining, that can determine when this family settled in the counties of Northampton and Leicester, though the monument of John Cave is the first we can find of this family in Stanford church, and probably he was presented to the vicarage by his father.

† Dugdale's Warw. vol. I. p. 149.

Esq. 3, Martha, of John Newdigate, of Arbury, in Warwickshire, Esq. and 4, Mary, of Sir Jerom Weston, Knt. son and heir of the judge, from whom the Westons, earls of Portland were descended. The third son was Clement Cave, who married Margery, daughter and co-heir of Nicholas Mallory, of Newbold Revell, in Warwickshire, Esq. and died without issue, 1538, and lies buried in Stanford church. His wife, surviving him, became the wife of John Cope, of Eydon, in Northamptonshire, Esq. 4, Sir Ambrose Cave, Knt. was high sheriff of Warwickshire and Leicestershire, 2 Edw. VI. and one of the knights of the shire for the county of Warwick, 4 and 5 Philip and Mary, and 5 Eliz. he was also chancellor of the dutchy of Lancaster, and one of the privy council to Queen Eliz. a gentleman in great esteem with that queen, and a most intimate friend of the lord treasurer Burleigh's. Attending at court, on a public night, her majesty's garter slipped off, as she was dancing; Sir Ambrose, taking it up, offered it to her, who, refusing it, he tied it on his left arm, and said he would wear it, for his mistress's sake, as long as he lived. In the possession of the family is an original picture of him, with the garter round his arm. He married Margaret, eldest daughter and co-heir of William Willington, of Barcheston, in Warwickshire, Esq. relict of Thomas Holte, of Aston, in Warwickshire, Esq. and left one daughter, Margaret, the wife of Henry Knollys, or Knowles, third son of Sir Francis Knollys, knight of the most noble order of the garter, by whom he had two daughters, his co-heirs; Elizabeth, the wife of Sir Henry Willoughby, of Risley, in Derbyshire, Knt. and Lætitia, of William, lord Paget, baron of Beaudesert, in Staffordshire, ancestor to the Earl of Uxbridge. This Sir Ambrose died April 2, 1568. A handsome monument is erected to his memory, in Stanford church, at the top of which is written*. 5, Francis Cave, who married Margaret, daughter of Thomas Lisle, of Surrey, LL.D. from whom the Caves, of Bargrave were descended. 6, Richard Cave, of Pickwell, in Leicestershire, Esq. who married Barbara, daughter of Sir William Fielding, of Newnham Padox, in Warwickshire, Knt. by whom he had John Cave, of Pickwell, Esq. high sheriff of the county of Leicester, 17 James I. who had several sons: His third son, John, was rector of Pickwell. of whose sufferings and ill-usage we have the following account, in Walker's Sufferings of the Clergy, p. 220. 221.†

---

* *Adsum Cave*; under it, *Tu Memor Esto dei, Semper Mortisque futuræ*; and under is this inscription:—Here lyeth the body of Sr. Ambrose Cave, Knt. sometime chancelor of the dutchy of Lancaster, & one of the most honble. privy council to our soveraigne lady Queen Elizabeth, who departed this life the 2. of April, A. Dni. 1568.

† He was born in the parish of Pickwell, and educated at Lincoln-College, in Oxford, where he was chamber-fellow with the famous Dr. Sanderson, for eight years. After he was settled here in his native parish, he attended his ministerial cure with great diligence, and lived in great esteem and respect with all his neighbours, till the breaking out of the great rebellion in the year 1642. The first attack that was made upon him, was when the parliament sent a regiment to be quartered about that place, where six troopers, with their horses, were quartered upon him, who continued off and on for a year or two. They first attempted him by way of dispute, concerning the liturgy and constitution of the church of England, which passed in writing, by way of objection and answer: but finding they were likely to do little good that way, they betook themselves to rougher methods: they ravaged his house, and abused his children and servants; demanded unreasonable provisions to be made for them; and would sometimes take up a good dish of meat from the table, and throw it upon the ground, because not cooked or dressed up to their humour and palate: they debauched some of the servants, and when complaint of it was

7 Bryan Cave, by Margaret Saxby, his second wife, before-mentioned, was sheriff of Leicestershire and Warwickshire, 6 Philip and Mary, and again temp. Eliz. He married Margaret, daughter of Sir George Throckmorton, Knt. by whom he had two sons; 1, Edward, who married Barbara, daughter and co-heir of Sir William Devereux, Knt. 2, Henry, of Ingarsby, in Leicestershire, who married the

made of it to some of the neighbouring justices, and to some of their superior officers, no remedy could be had. Not content with this, when three or four of their horses were stolen one night out of the stable, they accused him of the theft, carried him to their head quarters, and tried him at a council of war for his life, and were ready to pass sentence upon him, when Colonel Ireton, coming suddenly in, and examining into the matter, suspected there was some villainy in it, as indeed it afterwards appeared, that they were stolen by some of their own party; whereupon he put a stop to their proceedings, and dismissed him. When this would not do, they fell a tampering with the parishioners, to try if they could prefer, and bring articles against him; but at present they could find none for their purpose: and because he still persisted in a firm loyalty to the king, and unshaken zeal for the church of England, praying for the bishops, after they had been voted down by the parliament, they one time came into the church, and discharged a pistol at him, then in the pulpit; and at another time plucked him out of the pulpit, and pulled his gown over his ears. After several attempts to get false witnesses, they at last corrupted three or four, a taylor, a miller, a weaver, and one more; whereupon articles were drawn up, subscribed, and sworn to, before the committee of Leicester; though some of them afterwards, upon their death-beds, sent for him, and professed they could not die, till they had declared that they had been suborned to testify and swear against him. Some years matters hung in this way, he being banded from committee to committee, though the clearness of his case was such, that they could bring it to no conclusion. By this time one of the committee of Leicester had combined with one Wells, an independent preacher, who having a son brought up a silk weaver, in New England, sent for him over, to be married to the committee-man's daughter, and the rectory of Pickwell was pitched upon for the portion for his daughter: and now matters were pushed on with more vigour; but finding that little good would be done at country committees, the cause was removed to London, and brought before the committee of the house of commons; where Mr. Cave was advised to retain Bradshaw for his counsel, who at first told him, that his case was clear and good; but being tampered with the night before the trial, by the opposite party, he told him the next morning, he much feared how his case would go; and two of his near kinsmen, both members of the house, Sir William Armyn, and Sir Arthur Haslerigg (the only two he was related to of that party) firmly promised him to be at the committee, and to support his cause; but both of them thought fit to be absent. Accordingly the cause went against him, and an order was directed to the committee in the country, to dispossess him; who sent a file of musqueteers, and turned father, mother, and six children, out of doors at once, not suffering the neighbours to take them in, nor to have one bit of bread, nor draught of drink, out of their own house. And now, having made clean work of it, a parcel of itinerant preachers were sent to Pickwell, to mock God with a day of thanksgiving, that the people were delivered from such an ignorant, unlearned, and unskilful teacher. He and his family notwithstanding were entertained by the neighbours for the present, though they were not suffered long to continue there, nor he to keep a school there, or elsewhere: whereupon he took up his dwelling near Stamford; where, not being suffered to abide long, he removed to London; when being broken with age and sufferings, and worn out with long and tedious winter journeys, from committee to committee, he departed this life about the beginning of Nov. 1657.

Dr. William Cave, son of the said John, was born in 1637, and educated in St. John's college, at Cambridge. He was successively minister of Hasely, in Oxfordshire; Great Allhallows, and of Islington, near London. He became chaplain to Charles II. and in 1684 was installed dean of Windsor. He was the author of some large and learned works, relating to ecclesiastical antiquity. He composed a History of the Lives, Acts, Deaths, and Martyrdoms of those, who were contempary with the Apostles, and of the principal Fathers within the three first Centuries of the Church. In 1688 he published a work of a more extensive nature, called Historia Literaria, &c. in which he gives an exact account of all who had written upon Christianity, either for or against it, from Christ to the 14th century; mentions the times they lived in, the books they wrote, and the doctrines they maintained; and also enumerates the councils that were called in every age of the church. He died in 1713, and was buried at Islington.

daughter of Gregory Isham, of Pitchley, in Northamptonshire, Esq. 8, Austin Cave, who embraced a religious life.

The daughters were 1, Elizabeth, the wife of William Wirley, of Hamsted, in the parish of Houndesworth, in Staffordshire, Esq. 2, Dorothy, of William Smyth, alias Harris, of Witchcock, in Leicestershire, Esq. 3, Prudence, of John Crooke, alias Blunt, of Chilton, in Bucks, Esq. one of the six clerks in chancery, from whom descended the lord chief justice Crooke; 4, Bridget, of Francis Tanfield, of Gayton, in Northamptonshire, Esq. from whom descended Baron Tanfield.

Richard, the father of these sons and daughters, died April 20, 1528. Elizabeth, his first wife, Aug. 9, 1493; and Margaret, his second wife, March, 1530.

16. Sir Thomas Cave, Knt. his eldest son by the second venter, was lord of the whole manor of Stanford and Stormsmore, alias Stormsworth, and of Downe and Westerhill: he married Elizabeth, daughter and co-heir of Sir John Danvers, of Waterstock, in Oxfordshire, Knt. (and Margaret, his wife, daughter of — Hampden, of Hartwell, in Bucks, Esq. son and heir to William Danvers, Esq. lord chief justice of the common pleas, by Anne, his wife, daughter and heiress of John Purey, of Chamberhouse, in Thatcham, Berks, Esq. which William, the lord chief justice, was son and heir of John Danvers, of Colthorp, in Berks, Esq. and Jane, his second wife, daughter and heir of William Bruley, of Waterstock, Esq.) by whom he had six sons and eight daughters; 1, John, who died young; 2, Richard, of Little Oakley, in Northamptonshire, Esq. who married Elizabeth, eldest daughter of Sir Edward Montagu, Knt. lord chief justice of the common pleas, by whom he had two daughters; Elizabeth, the wife of Edward Gates, and Anne, who died young: his widow afterwards married William Markham, of Little Oakley, Esq. 3, Edward, who married Elizabeth, daughter of Sir John Conway, of Ragley, in Warwickshire, Knt. and left one son, John, who died young; 4, Roger, who continued the line; 5, Ambrose; and 6, Anthony, who both died young. The daughters were 1, Amy, the wife of John Hunt, of Lindon, in Rutlandshire, Esq. 2, Mary, of William Skevington, in Leicestershire, Esq. 3, Margaret, of Sir William Mering, of Mering, in Nottinghamshire, Knt. 4, Elizabeth, of Sir Humphrey Stafford, of Blotherwick, in Northamptonshire, Knt. 5, Margery, first of Francis Farnham, of Quarndon, in Leicestershire, and secondly of John Dasset, of Hill Morton, in Warwickshire, Esqrs. 6, Barbara, who died young; 7, Alice, the wife of John Skevington, of Fisherwick, in Staffordshire, Esq. 8, Susan of Sir John Bowes, of Elford, in Staffordshire, Knt. Sir Thomas, the father, died Sep. 4, 1558.*

17. Roger Cave, Esq. eldest surviving son, married Margaret, daughter of Richard Cecil, of Northamptonshire, Esq. sister to the famous William, lord Burleigh, lord high treasurer of England (ancestor to the Earls of Exeter and Salisbury)

---

* He lies buried, with his lady, in Stanford church, where, on a handsome monument, is both their effigies, at full length (he with a double gold chain about his neck) with their 14 children, kneeling under them, and this inscription round the monument:—

Orate pro animabus Thomas Cave, Militis Dni totius Manerii de Stanford, Down, Stormworth, et Bosworth, ac Rectoris et Patroni Ecclesia de Stanford.

On the side of this tomb are the arms of Cave, and wrote round it, Cave; and the arms of Cave, impaling Danvers, and his quarterings; and wrote round it, Danvers, Hampden, Purey, and Bruley.

by whom he had four sons and four daughters; 1, Sir Thomas, of whom hereafter; 2, Sir William Cave, Knt. who married first Eleanor, daughter of Thomas Grey, of Enfield, in Staffordshire, Esq. by whom he had several children; and secondly, Elizabeth, daughter of William Burnell, of Winckborne, in Nottinghamshire, Esq. by whom he had no issue; 3, Cecil, who married first Anne, daughter and sole heiress of Anthony Bennett, of Greenwich, in Kent, Esq. and left two daughters, his co-heirs; Abigail, the eldest, was the wife first of Henry Tresham, Esq. son and heir of Sir Thomas Tresham, of Newton, in Northamptonshire, Knt. and afterwards of Sir William Sherrard, of Stapleford, in Leicestershire, Knt. created Lord Sherrard, of Le Trim, in Ireland, ancestor to the Earl of Harborough: Anne, the youngest daughter and co-heir, was the wife of William Tufton, Esq. son and heir of Sir John Tufton, of Raynham, in Essex, Bart. By his second wife, Elizabeth, daughter of —— Markham, he had no issue. 4, John, who died a batchelor, May 3, 1639, and lies buried at St. Mary's, in Nottingham.

The daughters of Sir Roger were, Elizabeth, the wife of Walter Bagot, of Blithfield, in Staffordshire, Esq. Margaret, of Sir William Skipwith, of Cotes, in Leicestershire, Knt. Anne, of Sir Edmund Bussey, of Hather, in Lincolnshire, Knt. and Dorothy, of —— Hartop, of Leicestershire, Esq. This Roger Cave died at Stanford, July 26, 1586.

18. Sir Thomas Cave, Knt. eldest son of Roger, had, by Eleanor, daughter of Nicholas St. John, of Lydyard Tregoz, in Wilts, Esq. four sons and two daughters; 1, Richard, a young gentleman of great expectation, liberally educated at Oxford, and for farther improvement travelled into France, and intending for Italy, died at Padua, aged 19, July 26, 1606. Having, on his death-bed, refused extreme unction, and auricular confession, from the ecclesiastics there, they made a diligent search for the body, in order to burn his heretical remains, but it was preserved from their fury by his friends, who threw it into the Adriatic Gulph, esteeming the deep more merciful than a mistaken religious fury. In the chancel of Stanford church is an inscription to his memory, on a pyramidal monument, with his effigy, in a kneeling posture. 2, Sir Thomas, of whom hereafter; 3, Oliver Cave, of Swinford, in Leicestershire, who married Frances, daughter of Sherrington Talbot, of Ridge, in Salop, Esq. and died in Sep. 1660, aged 56; 4, St. John Cave, who married Bridget, daughter of ——, by whom he had Oliver Cave, of Clifton, in Warwickshire, Esq. and a daughter Eleanor, the wife of Edward Chamberlaine, of Princethorp, in Warwickshire, Esq. The two daughters of Sir Thomas were, Margaret, first the wife of Sir John Wynne, of Gwidder, in Carnarvonshire, Bart. and afterwards of the Lord Aungier, master of the rolls, in Ireland; and Eleanor, first the wife of Sir George Beeston, of Beeston Castle, in Cheshire, Knt. and afterwards of Sir Thomas Roe, of Bullwick, in Northamptonshire, Knt. chancellor of the most noble order of the garter, and ambassador to the Emperor, Ferdinand III. This Sir Thomas Cave lies buried under a most noble marble monument, in Stanford church, whereon are the effigies of a knight in armour, and his lady lying by him, in the dress of the times, both at full length, and their children kneeling, carved on the monument under them.

19. Sir Thomas Cave, the eldest surviving son and heir, married Elizabeth, daughter of Sir Herbert Croft, of Croft Castle, in Herefordshire, Knt. by whom he had

one son, Sir Thomas, and two daughters; Lucy, who died young; and Dorothy, the wife of Sir Rowland Berkley, of Cotheridge, in Worcestershire, Knt.

I. Sir THOMAS CAVE, his only son and successor, having received the honour of knighthood, was afterwards advanced to the dignity of an English baronet, 16 Charles I. He was one of the deputy lieutenants for the county of Northampton, and during the civil wars a strenuous asserter of his sovereign's cause, supplying him with arms, ammunition, &c.* Sir Thomas married Catharine, daughter of Sir Anthony Haslewood, of Maidwell, in Northamptonshire, Knt. by whom he had no issue; secondly, Penelope, daughter of the Lord Viscount Wenman, of Tuam, in the kingdom of Ireland, by whom he had Sir Roger, his successor; Thomas, who died a batchelor; Ambrose, a brigadier in the life-guards, who was unfortunately slain in 1690, as he was sitting peaceably in his chair, in public company, by one Biron, an officer, whose life he had frequently spared, though many provocations had caused frequent skirmishing between them, and in return for his generosity, Mr. Biron run his sword through his back, as he sat in his chair, of which wound he soon died: the sword was left in his body, but the offender fled, and no diligence could ever discover him. Sir Thomas had also a daughter Eleanor, who died unmarried, and Mary, the wife of Sir Orlando Bridgman, of Ridley, in Cheshire, Bart. second son of the lord keeper; and other sons and daughters, that died without issue.

II. Sir ROGER CAVE, Bart. the eldest son and heir represented the city of Coventry, in the Oxford parliament, 32 Charles II. and served again for the same city, in the parliament held at Westminster, 1 James II. He married first Martha, daughter and heir of John Brown, of Eydon, in Northamptonshire, Esq. clerk of the parliament; secondly, Mary, daughter of Sir William Bromley, of Bagington, in Warwickshire, knight of the bath, and sister of the right hon. William Bromley, Esq. late speaker of the house of commons, and principal secretary of State to

---

* The loyalty of both father and son appears by the following information made against them :—The information of Lieut. R. F. taken as aforesaid (supposed to be at Daventry) who informeth, that about Christmas last he went to Sir Thomas Cave's house, the elder, with Capt. Combes; and Sir Thomas Cave, the younger, had a fowling piece in his hand, upon the house; and there were with him, upon the house, about sixteen men, with muskets: and the arms being demanded, Sir Thomas Cave, the younger, said he would die before they should be delivered; and the bell upon the house rung, and the bells in the steeple, and there were divers men in the steeple; and there were centinels, with muskets at the doors, and many were gathered together in the yard, with forks and staves, and did oppose the execution of a warrant from the deputy lieutenant of the county of Northampton.

Sir Thomas Cave, the younger, his answer :—He confesses his father said, he would die in the house before he would deliver the arms (as well as himself); and that he would not have delivered them to any of either side, but the king himself; and he would have done as much if any other had come but his majesty.

April 11, 1648, an agreement was made with Sir Thomas Cave, the younger, for his release, if the parliament should consent; and Sir Thomas Cave undertakes to pay presently 200l. and Mr. Cotton, of Leicestershire is to be his security, to pay 200l. more at Michaelmas next, and 200l. more upon Lady-day in Lent next. Mr. Cotton undertakes the like; and that Sir Thomas should again render his person to the committee, if the parliament agrees not to this rule.

Sir Thomas Cave, senior, voluntarily left his house in Northamptonshire, to go and live within two or three miles of Worcester.

Sir Thomas Cave, junior, before the committee, affirmed, that his father, living so near Worcester, went two or three times a week to Worcester, to drink sack, and be merry; and Sir Anthony Haslewood confessed he went with him thither.

Queen Anne, who survived him, and died Nov. 22, 1721. By the first lady he had issue Sir Thomas, his successor, John, Charles, drowned at sea, in the great storm, in Nov. 1703, being on board one of her majesty's ships of war; another John, and Oliver: also two daughters; Elizabeth, first wife of Sir John Cheshire, Knt. serjeant at law, who died Aug. 16, 1705, and Penelope, the wife of John Creswell Wentworth, of Lillington Lovell, of Oxfordshire, Esq. who died June 4, 1726, having survived her said sister and brothers, who all, except Sir Thomas, died without issue. Sir Roger, by his second lady, before-mentioned, had issue Roger Cave, of Eydon, in Northamptonshire, and of Raunston, in Leicestershire, Esq. who married in 1721, Catharine, daughter of William Browne, of Derbyshire, Esq. and by her had several children: also two daughters; Mary, the wife of Sir William Dixwell, of Coton, in Warwickshire, Bart. who died without issue, in the first year after her marriage, Feb. 1712-13; and Eleanor, first the wife of Sir Holland Egerton, of Heaton, in Lancashire, Bart. and secondly of John Broke, Esq. son of Sir Thomas Broke, of Norton, in Cheshire, Bart, She died at Heaton, in Sep. 1734, leaving issue by both her husbands. Sir Roger died Oct. 11, 1703, aged 49.

III. Sir THOMAS CAVE, of Stanford, Bart. successor to his father, was in all the parliaments from 9 Anne till his death, April 21, 1719, representative for the county of Leicester. He married Margaret, youngest daughter of the right hon. Sir John Verney, viscount Fermannah, of the kingdom of Ireland, by whom he had two sons; Sir Verney, his successor; and Thomas Cave, of the Inner Temple, Esq. barrister at law: also two daughters; Elizabeth, the wife of Richard Pilsworth, Esq. of Oving, in Bucks, who died in 1748; she died in 1755: and Penelope, of Richard Thomson, of Lincoln's Inn, Esq. one of the prothonotaries of the court of common pleas, and of Ewell, in Surrey, who died in 1748: she died Oct. 1, 1786. Sir Thomas died April 21, 1719, and lies buried in Stanford church, under a handsome monument, erected by his lady.

IV. Sir VERNEY CAVE, Bart. his eldest son and successor, died Sep. 13, aged 29, unmarried, and is buried in Stanford church; whereupon the dignity and estate came to his only brother,

V. Sir THOMAS CAVE, Bart. who married in 1736, Elizabeth, sole daughter and heiress of Griffith Davies, of Birmingham, in Warwickshire, M. D. by Elizabeth, his wife, one of the daughters of Sir John Burgoyne, of Sutton, in Bedfordshire, Bart. who died at Stanford April 28, 1759, aged 42; by whom he had 1, Thomas; 2, Elizabeth, the wife of Bennet, earl of Harborough, of Stapleford, who died in 1770: she died March 5, 1797. 3, Penelope, died unmarried, April 28, 1771; 4, Margaret, first the wife of John Moses, of Kingston upon Hull, Esq. who died in 1773; secondly, of Thomas Robinson, of Kensington, Esq. 5, Maria-Constantia, of Sir Henry Etherington, Bart. 6, Rev. Sir Charles, the present baronet; 7, Anne, the wife of Thomas Marriott, D. D. prebendary of Westminster, rector of St. Michael, Basishaw, and chaplain in ordinary to his majesty: he died at Bristol in 1781. Sir Thomas represented the county of Leicester in four several parliaments, and died at Stanford Aug. 7, 1778, aged 67, and was succeeded by his son,*

---

* He was not only an able speaker in the house of commons, but his judgment and experience were often referred to in great questions. He had a love for his country; studied the history of Leicester-

CAVE, OF STANFORD, NORTHAMPTONSHIRE.

TABLE 62.

N
WYAMARUS, 1093 — 1 Jordayne de Cave
2 Bryan de Cave

3 Robert de Cave == Metham   Joan == N. Fossard
4 Thomas == J. St. Quintin   Isabella == T. de Redness   Marg. == Sir G. Furnivall   Jane == Sir J. de Ufflet
5 Geoffery de Cave   Robert   John   Christian   Grace
  Mabel Saltmarsh   — de Haldanby   — de Estotes   Thos. Newbolds   Wm. Ayrmine
6 Peter de Cave == — Bromflete   Alexander, dean of Durham
7 Sir Alexander   Thomas   Catharine   Beatrix   Jane
  — de Mawley   — Cliffe   J. Riplingham   P. de Waldby   J. Dawney
8 Peter   Margaret   Joyce   Jane   Ursula
  A. Ward   R. Anlaby   Sir T. Polington   — Shilton   Sir J. Elsu
9 Alexander == A. Hotham   Elizabeth == Sir J. Middleton   Mary, prioress of Walton Abbey
10 Sir John == M. Genell   Sir A. Quintin == Margaret == — Moigne   Jane == Sir R. Kelk
11 Sir Alexander == C. Somervile   Thomas   Peter   John   Anne == Sir M. Grindall   Mary == Sir P. de See
12 Sir Alexander   12 Peter   John,   Catharine   Anne
   Constance Leeds   A. Ingleby   Grace   Sir J. Markenfield   G. Stapleton
Maud == A. Lownde   13 Peter Cave == Mary Burdet   John, 1471   Alexander
Jane == R. Sheffield   14 Thomas, 1493 == Thomasine Passimere

   15 Richard, 1528   William,   John   Henry
Duke of Buck- E. Marvin | M. Saxby   Christopher   — Saunders | — Belgrave
ingham

Edward   Marg.   16 Sir THOMAS   Antony   Clement   Sir Ambrose   Francis   Richard   &c.
D. Mallory   T. Saun-   next page   E. Lovet   M. Mallo-   M. Welling-   M. Lisle   B. Fielding
            ders   ry   ton

Catharine   Marg.   Judith   Anne   Martha   Mary   Margaret   John Cave
Sir T. An- T. Bough- Wm. Griffith J. Newdi- Sir Jerom H. Knollys 1619
drews   ton   Chester Hambden gate   Weston

Elizabeth == Sir H. Willoughby   Letitia == Wm. L. Paget   John Cave,
                                                          rector of Pickwell
                                                          1657
              Henry Bayley, earl of Uxbridge   Dr. Wm. Cave
                                                          1713

shire, and made a considerable progress towards its completion; particularly respecting landed property. The warm attachment shewn to him by the freeholders, when he was a fourth time chosen to represent the county in parliament, evinces their judgment in the call, and his condescension, at an advanced period of life, in obeying it.

CAVE, OF STANFORD, NORTHAMPTONSHIRE.

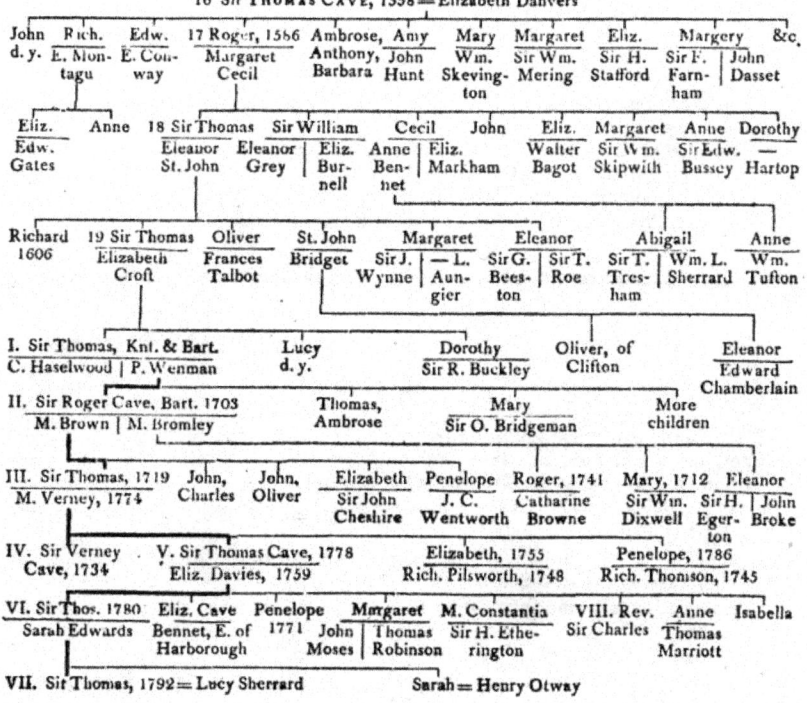

VI. Sir THOMAS CAVE, Bart. who married Sarah, daughter of John Edwards, of London, merchant, by whom he had one son, Sir Thomas, and a daughter Sarah, the wife of Henry Otway, Esq. of Ireland. Sir Thomas died May 31, 1780, aged 43, and was succeeded by his son,

VII. Sir THOMAS CAVE, Bart. who was elected one of the representatives in parliament for the county of Leicester, in 1790. June 2, 1791, he married Lucy, only daughter of the Rev. and right hon. Robert, earl of Harborough, of Stapleford, in Leicestershire. He died Jan. 15, 1792, aged 26; and was succeeded by his uncle,

VIII. Sir CHARLES CAVE, Bart. clerk, M. A. rector of Thingdon, Northamptonshire, and vicar of Thedingworth, in Leicestershire.

ARMS—Azure, frette of eight pieces, argent; four pieces one way, and four the other.
CREST—On a wreath, a greyhound currant, sable; to which, on an escroll, proceeeing from his mouth, for motto, Gardez (of the same signification with Cave, the imperative of Caveo) alluding to the name.
SEAT—At Stanford upon Avon, in Northamptonshire.

---

68. HATTON, of Long Stanton, Cambridgeshire.

Created Baronet July 5, 1641.

THIS family is of great antiquity in the county of Chester, Sir John, the present baronet, being the 25th, in a lineal descent from Wolfrid, brother of Nigel, baron of Halton, and constable of Chester, who were sons of

1. Yvon, vicecomes, or governor of Constantia,* in Normandy, by Eme, sister of Allan, earl of Britagne; which

2. Wolfrid, or Wolfaith, was lord of Hatton, by the gift of Hugh Lupus, earl of Chester, and was succeeded by

3. Robert, his son and heir, who, by Margaret, his wife, daughter of Gilbert Crispin, had

4. Sir Adam Hatton, of Hatton, Knt. whose son,

5. Sir Geoffery Hatton, Knt. married ——, daughter of Sir Adam Harthull, and had issue,

6. Sir Roger Hatton, who, by his wife, ——, daughter of Sir Peers Normanvile, Knt. left issue,

7. Ralph Hatton, Esq. the father of

8. Sir Hugh Hatton, who married Amy, daughter of Sir Randolph Venables, and was succeeded by,

9. Hugh, his son and heir, who married Mary, daughter of Sir John Ardern, Knt. and left two sons, John and Hugh.

10. John, the eldest, left an only daughter and heiress, Maud, the wife of Ralph Vernon, Esq. whose son, Robert Vernon, in right of his mother, inherited the manor of Hatton.

* Leycester's Cheshire, p. 263.

10. Hugh Hatton, the second son of Hugh Hatton, by Mary Ardern, married Margaret, the daughter and heir of Jeffery de Brayne, by whom he had

11. John Hatton, of Great Aldersey, Esq. living 30 Edw. III. who, by his wife, Joan, daughter and heir of Sir John Hallom, Knt. was father of

12. Adam Hatton, of Great Aldersey, 1 Rich. II. who, by Catharine, daughter of Sir William de Helesby, Knt. had

13. William Hatton, Esq. father of another

14. William Hatton, Esq. who had issue

15. Peter Hatton, Esq. who, by Margaret, his wife, daughter and co-heir of Sir George Bostock, of Mobberley, in Cheshire, Knt. had issue nine sons; 1, Richard, his son and heir, ancestor to those of Alderton, in Salop; 2, Peter, ancestor to those of Kirsty-Birches, in the same county; 3, Henry, to those of Holdenby and Kirby, in Northamptonshire; 4, Robert, to those of Norley, in Cheshire, and of London; 5, John, to those of Maxfield; 6, Ralph, to those of Weverham; 7, Adam, to those of Northwich, all in Cheshire, and to those of Sutton, near Nonsuch, in Surrey; 8, Simon, to those of Stocton-Yate, in Cheshire; and 9, Hugh, who died without issue.

16. Henry, the third son, married Elizabeth, daughter and heir of William Holdenby, of Holdenby, in Northamptonshire, Esq.* and had issue two sons, John and Richard.

17. John Hatton, the eldest son, married Joan, daughter of John Westby, of Kent, Esq. and had issue three sons, William, John, of whom hereafter, and Christopher.

18. William Hatton, of Holdenby, the eldest son, married Alice, daughter of Laurence Saunders, of Harringworth, in Northamptonshire, Esq. and had issue three sons; Francis, who died young; Thomas, who died without issue; and Sir Christopher Hatton, who, by his singular merit, first raised his family to the honour it now enjoys. He was chancellor in the reign of Elizabeth. It is singular of this personage, that altho' he had never followed the profession of the law, he was promoted to this high office. He was a great favourite with his mistress; and it is recorded of him, that notwithstanding the expectations of the lawyers, his decisions, as chancellor, were never found deficient, either in equity or judgment. It was the

---

* Mr. Camden, in his Britannia, vol. I. p. 517, speaking of Holdenby House, says, it was a stately and truly magnificent piece of building, erected by Sir Christopher Hatton, privy counsellor to Queen Elizabeth, lord chancellor of England, and knight of the garter, upon the lands and inheritance of his great grandmother, heir of the ancient family of the Holdenbies, for the greatest and last monument of his youth, as himself afterwards was wont to call it. A person, to say nothing of him, but what he truly deserved, eminent for his piety towards God, his fidelity to his country, his untainted integrity, and unparalleled charity: one also (which is not the least part of his character) who was always ready to support and encourage learning. Thus, as he lived piously, so he died, 1591, piously, in Christ; and the monument, which the learned, in their writings, have raised to him, shall render him more illustrious, than that noble and splendid tomb, in St. Paul's church, London, becoming so worthy and eminent a person, and erected at great charge, to his memory, by Sir William Hatton, Knt. his adopted son. But this once stately fabric (made more known since its founder's time, by the frequent mention of it in our histories, as the place of confinement to that virtuous and religious prince, King Charles I.) is now so ruinous, a very little of it excepted, that there is scarce one stone upon another.

artful eloquence of this man which prevailed on Mary, queen of Scots, to wave the claims of royal dignity, and submit to trial. He became first one of the queen's gentlemen-pensioners, then gentleman of the privy chamber, and next captain of the guard; from which office he was advanced to be vice-chamberlain, one of the privy council; and at length lord chancellor; being likewise made a knight of the garter, and installed May 23, 1588. His first preferment at court was to be one of the 50 pensioners; whence he was advanced to the privy chamber, captain of the guard, and vice-chamberlain; and his great improvement under Lord Burleigh, placed him in that grave assembly (the wisest convention in Europe at that time) the privy council; where he had not sate long before he was made chancellor, and knight of the garter.* None nobler, none less aspiring: none more busy, yet none more punctual in his hours and orders. Corpulent he was, but temperate; a batchelor, and the only one of the queen's favourites, yet chaste: quick were his dispatches, but weighty; many his orders, and consistent: numerous were the addresses to him, and easy the access. Seldom were his orders reversed in chancery, and seldomer his advice opposed in council. So just he was, that his sentence was law with the subject; so wise, that his opinion was oracle with his sovereign. So exact was Queen Elizabeth, that she called upon him for an old debt, though it broke his heart: so loving, that she carried him a cordial-broth with her own hand, though it could not revive him.†

He died a batchelor, Nov. 20, 1591, having adopted Sir William Newport, his nephew, son of Dorothy, his sister, by John Newport, of Harringham, in Warwickshire, Esq. for his heir, who changed his name to Sir William Hatton, and was then 26 years of age; but in default of issue male by him, he settled the

---

* Take his character from his own words, which prevailed with the Queen of Scots, to appear before the commissioners at Fotheringay, when neither Elizabeth's commission, nor the power of the kingdom could persuade her to it. The words are these:—

"You are accused, but not condemned. You say you are a queen, be it so: if you are innocent, you wrong your reputation in avoiding trial. You protest yourself innocent, the queen feareth the contrary, not without grief and shame. To examine your innocence are these honourable, prudent, and upright commissioners sent: glad will they be, with all their hearts, if they may return, and report you guiltless. Believe me, the queen herself will be much affected with joy, who affirmed to me, at my coming from her, that never any thing befel her more grievous, than that you were charged with such a crime: wherefore lay aside the bootless privilege of royal dignity, which here can be of no use to you; appear in judgment, and shew your innocence; lest, by avoiding trial, you draw upon yourself suspicion, and lay upon your reputation an eternal blot and aspersion."

Four thing I observe he did, that deserve a chronicle:—1, That he delayed the signing of Leicester's patent for the lieutenancy of England and Ireland, the preface to his kingdom, until that earl was sick.

2, That he reduced the chancery, and all other courts, to rules.

3, That he stood by the church against the enemies of both sides. Archbishop Whitgift, when checked by others for his due severity, writes to him thus:—"I think myself bound to you for your friendly message as long as I live: it hath not a little comforted me, having received unkind speeches not long since, &c." And therefore (after an expostulation about some states mens' proceedings against the law and state of the realm, and a declaration of his own resolution) says he' "Your honour, in offering that great courtesy, offered unto me as great a pleasure as I can desire. Her majesty must be my refuge, and I beseech you that I may use you as a means, when occasion shall serve; whereof I assure myself, and therein rest."

JOHN CANT.

4, That he promoted the proclamation for plain apparel, for free trade, for pure religion, and the laws against the papists. *Lloyd's Statesmen and Favourites,* p. 419, 420, 421.   † Ibid, 335.

greatest part of his estate on his godson, Christopher Hatton, son and heir of John Hatton, his nearest kinsman of the male line; being eldest son of John Hatton, second son of John Hatton, his father's brother, before-mentioned: which Sir William Newport, alias Hatton, leaving, by Elizabeth his wife, daughter and heir of Sir Francis Gawdy, Knt. lord chief justice of the common pleas, an only daughter Frances, the wife of Robert Rich, earl of Warwick, the said Christopher Hatton did accordingly enjoy the estate: which Christopher was made knight of the bath at the coronation of King James I. and was the ancestor to Lord Viscount Hatton, as is hereafter shewn.

18. John Hatton, Esq. second son of John, and Joan his wife, daughter of John Westby, before-mentioned, was of Gravesend, in Kent, and had by his wife, Dionis, daughter of —— War, or Ware, of Sussex, two sons; 1, William Hatton, of Gravesend; and 2, John: which

19. John was of Stanton, in Cambridgeshire, and living in 1579. He married Jane, daughter of Robert Shute, baron of the exchequer, and one of the justices of the common pleas; and by her had 1, Sir Christopher Hatton, of Kirby, in Northamptonshire, Knt. made knight of the bath at the coronation of King James I. from whom was descended the Lord Viscount Hatton, as before mentioned; 2, Robert; 3, Thomas.

I. Sir THOMAS HATTON, of Long Stanton, in Cambridgeshire, Knt. third son of the last-named John Hatton, Esq. was, by King Charles I. created a baronet of England. He married Mary, daughter of Sir Giles Allington, of Horseheath, in Cambridgeshire, Knt. and left three sons; 1, Thomas; 2, John, who died S. P. 3, Sir Christopher; and three daughters; Mary, Elizabeth, the wife of Sir William Boteler, of Kinton, in Bedfordshire, Knt. and Jane. He died Sep. 23, 1658, aged 75.

II. Sir THOMAS, his eldest son, succeeded him, who married Bridget, daughter of Sir William Goring, of Burton, in Sussex, Bart. and by her had two sons, Christopher and Thomas; and several daughters, of which Mary was the wife of John Pocklington, of Huntingdon; Elizabeth, of Thomas Day, of Qui, in Cambridgeshire, Esqrs. Rebecca, of —— Crayker, of London; and Dorothy, of Tirrel Dalton, of Fulborne, in Cambridgeshire, Esq. Sir Thomas was succeeded by his eldest son,

III. Sir CHRISTOPHER, who died young, and was succeeded by his brother,

IV. Sir THOMAS, who died soon after his brother.

V. Sir CHRISTOPHER HATTON, Bart. third son of Sir Thomas, the first baronet, John, the second son, dying without issue before his elder brother. This Sir Christopher married Elizabeth, daughter of Thomas Buck, of Westwick, in Cambridgeshire, Esq. and by her had several sons, and one daughter; 1, Sir Thomas; 2, Sir John; and 3, William, who married Susanna, daughter of Mr. Henton, by whom he had one son, Christopher, rector of Gorton, in Cambridgeshire. Sir Christopher died in Oct. 1720, and was succeeded in title and estate by his eldest surviving son,

VI. Sir THOMAS HATTON, Bart. who married first Elizabeth, daughter and heiress of Cooper Orlebar, of Henwick, in Bedfordshire, Esq. she dying May 5, 1732, aged 44, he soon after married to his second lady, Henrietta, daughter of Sir James Astry, of Woodend, in the parish of Harlington, in Bedfordshire, Knt. (by Anne, his wife, second daughter of Sir Thomas Penyston, of Cornwall, in Oxfordshire, Bart.) and dying at Woodend June 22, 1733, was buried in the chancel of Long Stanton. Leaving no issue the title and estate descended to his only surviving brother,

VII. Sir JOHN HATTON, Bart. who married Mary, daughter of Thomas Hawkes, Gent. and relict of Mr. William Hitch; by whom he left three daughters and one son, Sir Thomas; and dying in June, 1740, was succeeded by his son,

VIII. Sir THOMAS HATTON, Bart. born Sep. 14, 1728, who married ——, daughter of Dingley Ascham, of Connington, in Cambridgeshire, Esq. who died in 1795. Sir Thomas died Nov. 7, 1787, and was succeeded by his son,

IX. Sir JOHN HATTON, the present baronet, who married in 1798 ——, daughter of Mr. Bridgman, an American refugee.

ARMS—Azure, a chevron, between three garbs, or.
CREST—On a wreath, a hind, or.
SEAT—At Long Stanton, Cambridgeshire.

69. ABDY, of FELIX HALL, ESSEX.

Created Baronet July 7, 1641.

THIS family is descended from Abdy House, in the parish of Waith, in Yorkshire, from whence probably they took their name.*

1. Richard married Mrs. Joan Musgrave, and had issue

2. Robert Abdy, of Abdy, in the county of York, who married Mrs. Eleanor Metcalf. His son

3. Robert, married Mrs. Joan Norreys, and had issue

4. Thomas Abdy, of Abdy, who married Cecily, daughter of William Tijas, of Yorkshire, Esq. whose second son, Roger Abdy, of London, married Mary, daughter of Richard White, of Hutton Hall, in Essex, and died in 1595. His third son,

5. Anthony Abdy, Esq. alderman of London, died Sep.— 1640, having married Abigail, daughter of Sir Thomas Cambell, Knt. alderman of London, and by her had several children; and from him descended three baronets, Sir Thomas, of Fe-

* Attested by William Le Neeve, Clarencieux.

HATTON, OF LONG STANTON, CAMBRIDGESHIRE.

TABLE 69.

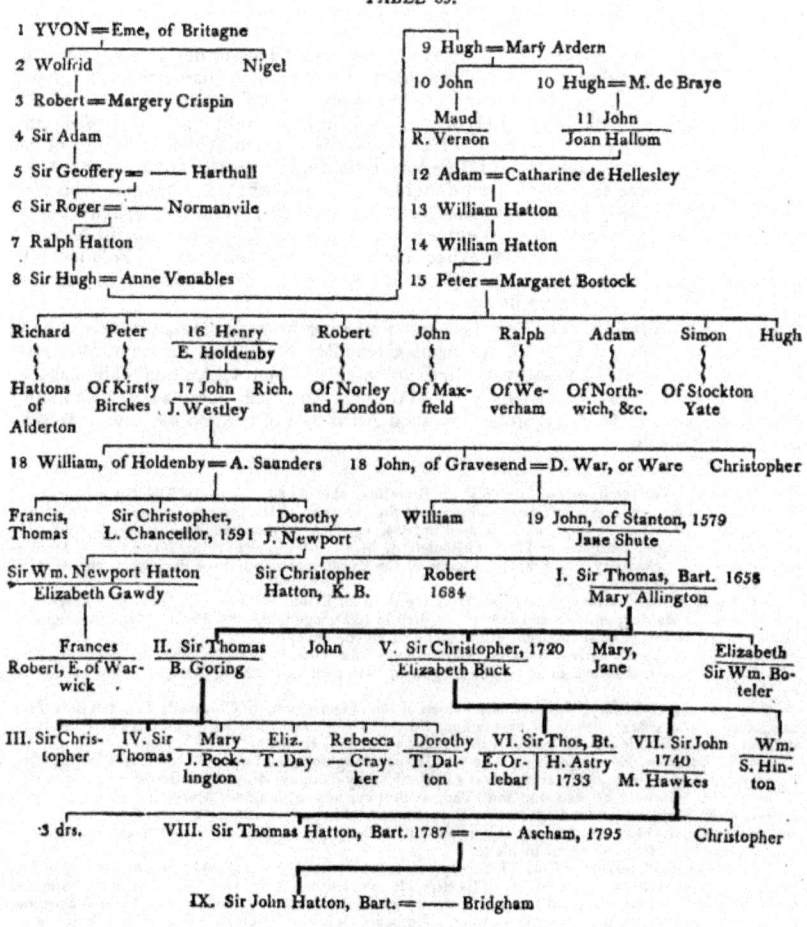

lix Hall, of whom hereafter; Sir Robert, of Albyns, in Essex, created a baronet June 9, 1660 (title extinct in 1759); and Sir John Abdy, of Moores, in Essex, created a baronet June 22, 1660, which title is also extinct. Alice, one of the daughters of this Anthony, was the wife of Sir John Bramston, knight of the bath.* His eldest son,

I. Sir THOMAS ABDY, of Felix Hall, was created a baronet July 7, 1641: he married Mary, daughter of Lucas Corsellis, of London, merchant, who died April 6, 1645, aged 27, by whom he had James, who died an infant, and two daughters; Rachael, the wife of Philip Gurdon, of Assington Hall, in Suffolk, Esq. and Abigail, of Sir Mark Guyon, Knt. He afterwards married Anne, daughter of Sir Thomas Soame, Knt. alderman of London, who died June 19, 1679, aged 57, by whom he had three sons and seven daughters; 1, Anthony; 2, Thomas, who died April 12, 1697; 3, William, who died in 1682, aged 25; 4, Sarah; 5, Anne, died in 1682; 6, Mary, the wife of Wentworth Garneys, of Boyland Hall, in Norfolk, Esq. 7, Joanna, died in 1710; 8, Alice, the wife of William Stane, of Folyots Hall, in High Ongar, Essex, Esq. 9, Judith; and 10, Sarah. Sir Thomas died Jan. 14, 1685, and was succeeded by his son,

II. Sir ANTHONY ABDY, Bart. who married Mary, sole daughter and heiress of Richard Milward, D. D. rector of Great Braxhead, and canon of Windsor, by whom he had 1, Thomas, who died an infant, 1684; 2, Anthony-Thomas; 3, William; 4, Charles; 5, Richard; 6, Mary; 7, Anne; 8, Joanna; 9, Elizabeth; 10, Rachael; and 11, Margaret. He died April 2, 1704, aged 49, and was succeeded by his son,

* This family derives its origin from William Bramston, sheriff of London, 18 Rich. II. whose direct descendant, John, was a man of great eminence in the law, and in 1635 was promoted to the high station of lord chief justice of England. He died in 1654, aged 78, having had issue by his first wife only, who was Bridget, daughter of Thomas Mondeford, M. D. three sons; 1, Sir John; 2, Sir Mondeford, a master in chancery; 3, Francis, a baron of the Exchequer; and three daughters, the wives of —— Palmer, —— Dyke, and —— Porter.

Sir John, K. B. the eldest son, was knight of the shire for Essex, in 1660 and 1661, and burgess in parliament, for Malden, in 1678 and 1685; and died in 1699, aged 89. By Alice Abdy, his wife, who died in 1647, he had several children, all which he survived, except

Anthony, who by Catharine, daughter and co-heir of Sir Thomas Nutt, of Mayes, in Sussex, Knt. who died in 1708, had two sons and eight daughters. He died in 1722, aged 83, and was succeeded by his eldest son,

John, who married Mary, daughter and heiress of John Pennington, of Chigwell, Esq. left only three daughters; Sarah; Mary, the wife of the hon. Edward Byng; and Elizabeth. On his death, in 1718, without issue male, his estates, came by the entail, to his only brother,

Thomas Bramston, Esq. whose first wife was Diana, daughter of Edmund Turner, of Lincoln, Esq. by whom he had no issue. His second was Elizabeth, only daughter of Richard Berney, Esq. recorder of Norwich; by whom he had one son, Thomas Berney, and a daughter Mary, the wife of William Dudes, of St. Stephen's, near Canterbury, Esq. He served in parliament, as knight of the shire for Essex, in 1734 and 1741; and before, as burgess for Malden, in five successive parliaments; and dying in 1765, aged 75, was succeeded by his son,

Thomas-Berney Bramston, Esq. of Screens, near Chelmsford, L. L. D. who is now, for the fifth time, knight of the shire for the county of Essex. He married in 1764, Mary, only daughter of Stephen Gardener, of Norwich, Esq. barrister at law, by whom he has issue, Thomas-Gardener Bramston, three other sons, and a daughter, Mary-Anne. He bears for his arms, or, on a fess, sable, three plates. *Hasted's Hist. Kent, vol. III. p. 510.*

ABDY, OF FELIX HALL, ESSEX.

III. Sir ANTHONY-THOMAS ABDY, Bart. who married first Mary, daughter and co-heir of Hope Gifford, of Colchester, Esq. who died in 1718; secondly, in 1729, Charlotte, daughter of Sir Thomas Barnardiston, of Kenton, in Suffolk, Bart. who died Feb. 19, 1731: thirdly, Anne, daughter of Thomas Williams, of Tendering Hall, in Stoke, Suffolk, Esq. who died Sep. 21, 1745. By the first and last he had no issue, but by the second he had two daughters; Charlotte, the wife of John, son of Sir John Williams, of Tendering Hall, Knt. and Elizabeth, the wife of Thomas Reeves, of Dorsetshire, Esq. Sir Anthony died in June, 1733, and was succeeded by his next brother,

IV. Sir WILLIAM ABDY, Bart. who married ———, daughter and sole heiress of Philip Stotherd, of Terlington, in Essex, Esq. by whom he had several daughters, and three sons; 1, Sir Anthony-Thomas; 2, the Rev. Stotherd, who married Theodosia, youngest daughter of Sir Robert Abdy, of Albyns, in Essex, Bart. secondly, Harriet, youngest daughter of Peyton Altham, of Markham Hall, in Essex, Esq. and died April 3, 1773, without issue; 3, William, the present baronet; and one daughter, the wife of the late Dr. Rutherforth, regius professor of divinity at Cambridge, and archdeacon of Essex, who died in 1771; by whom he had the Rev. Thomas Abdy, who on the death of his uncle, Sir Anthony-Thomas, in 1775, succeeded to his estate, and took his name. He married ———, daughter of James Hayes, Esq. of Holliport, bencher of the Middle Temple; by whom he has left issue: he died Oct. 14, 1798. Sir William died in Jan. 1750, and was succeeded by his eldest son,

V. Sir ANTHONY-THOMAS, Bart. who was king's council, and twice representative in parliament for the borough of Knaresborough, in Yorkshire: he married Catharine, youngest daughter and co-heir of ———— Hamilton, Esq. of Chancery Lane, London. He died April 7, 1775, without issue, and was succeeded in title and estate by his brother,

VI. Sir WILLIAM ABDY, the present baronet, a captain in the royal navy: he married Mary, the daughter of James Gordon, of More-Place, in Hertfordshire,

---

* 1. Sir Robert Abdy, Bart. the second son of Anthony (who died in 1640) was created a baronet, June 9, 1660: he married Catharine, daughter of Sir John Guyer, Knt. alderman of London, by whom he had seven sons and four daughters; and died in 1670. She died in 1672. He was succeeded by his eldest son,

2. Sir John Abdy, Bart. who married Jane, only daughter of George Nicholas, Esq. youngest son of the truly loyal and faithful servant of the crown, Sir Edward Nicholas, Knt. secretary of state to Charles I. and II. and was succeeded by his son,

3. Sir Robert Abdy, Bart. who was a man of deep knowledge in antiquity, and natural history; a great connoisseur in medals, of which he had a fine collection; and what is more valuable, a true patriot, and a person of unshaken integrity, and remarkable humanity; all which qualities gained him such universal love and esteem, that he was elected one of the knights of the shire for the county of Essex, in 1727; and continued to be chosen, in all succeeding parliaments, till his death, which happened Aug. 27, 1758. He married Theodosia, only daughter and heiress of George Bramston, LL.D. by whom he had four children; Jane, who died young; John; Robert, who died in 1735; and Theodosia, the wife of her relation, the Rev. Stotherd Abdy, rector of Theydon Gernon, &c. but she died Feb. 20, 1758. He was succeeded by his son,

4. Sir John Abdy, Bart. who was elected knight of the shire in his father's room; and dying in 1759, unmarried, settled, by will, his estates on his aunt, Mrs. Jane Crank, during her life; and after her decease, divided them to the posterity of his ancestor, Anthony Abdy, Esq. viz. to Sir Anthony Abdy, Bt. and then to his brother, the Rev. Stotherd Abdy, &c. *Morant's Essex, vol. I. p. 177.*

ABDY, OF FELIX HALL, ESSEX.

Esq. by whom he has William Abdy, Esq. and three daughters, Catharine-Mary, Charlotte-Anne, and Harriet.

ARMS—Or, two chevronels between three trefoils, slipped, sable.
CREST—On a wreath, an eagle's head, erased.
SEAT—Cobham Place, near Bagshot, Surrey.

TABLE 70.

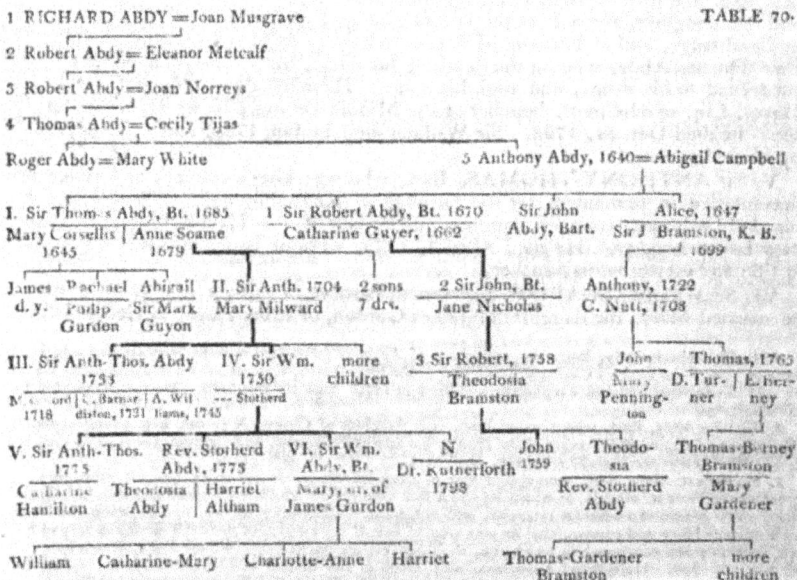

70. BAMPFYLDE, of POLTIMORE, DEVONSHIRE.

Created Baronet July 14, 1641.

THIS has been a family of consequence, in Devonshire, for many generations; but it is not certain when they first resided at Poltimore. They were sole lords of it in the reign of Edw. 1. having then presented to the living of Poltimore.* The first we find mentioned of this family is,

1. —— Baumfilde, who married a daughter of John Hastings, and had issue

2. —— Baumfilde, who married ——, daughter of —— Hockisham, by whom he had issue

3. John Baumfilde, Esq. who married Isabel, daughter and heiress of John Faber, and had issue

4. John Baumfilde, Esq. to whom the lands in Poltimore was given; who married Eleanor, daughter of Humphrey Beauchampe, of Kyme, and was father of

5. John Baumfilde, his son and heir, who by Joan, daughter of Sir Richard Morton, Knt. was father of

6. John Baumfilde, his son and heir, whose wife was Isabel, daughter of John de Cobham, of Blackbury Boiley; by whom he had

7. John Baumfilde, his son and heir, who married first Joan, daughter of Geoffery Gilbert, of Compton, Esq. secondly, Joan, daughter of —— Hastings. By his first wife he had issue John, who married the daughter and co-heir of Sir Richard Morton, Knt. but died without issue. Also

8. Thomas Baumfilde, of Poltimore, Esq. who married Agnes, daughter of Adam Coplestone; by whom he had two sons, John and Richard, who died young; also three daughters, Alice, Joanna, and Agnes.

9. John Baumfilde, of Poltimore, Esq. married Agnes, daughter and heir of John Pederton, of Hardington, in Somersetshire, Esq. by whom he had issue two sons, William and Peter Baumfilde, of Hardington (where that branch of the family continued about 250 years, when the last of that line, Warwick Baumfilde, Esq. set-

---

* The Hockisham estate lies contiguous to it, and is in the present baronet's possession, being brought into the family by the second match in this pedigree, who was a daughter of —— de Hockisham. Weston Bamfield, in Somersetshire, belongs now to Sir Charles, and has always been possessed by the heirs male, as far as there are any traces to be found of this family. A considerable estate at Hardington, in Somersetshire, was given to Sir Christoper Warwick Bampfylde, father of Sir Richard, by Warwick Bampfylde, a descendant from Peter Baumfilde, second son of John Baumfilde, by Agnes de Pederton; since which time the name of Warwick has been taken by the family. Margaret St. Maur was descended from the barons of that name, through the Loods, barons of Castle Cary; the Earls of Douglas, in Scotland; the Earls of Bretuiël, Pacey, and Ivery, in Normandy; also the Lords de la Zouche, of Ashby; Roger de Quinace, earl of Winchester, &c. &c. She was the heir of St. Maur, and Sir Charles appears to be entitled to that barony.

tled his lands upon his kinsman and godson, Sir Coplestone-Warwick Bampfylde, Bart. hereafter mentioned); also two daughters; Elizabeth, the wife of Henry Fraunceis, of Combflory, in Somersetshire, Esq. and Thomasine, of —— Paunsfoot, Esq. This John and his wife lie buried in Poltimore church.

10. Sir William Baumfilde, of Poltimore, his son and heir, married Margaret, daughter of Walter Paunsfoot, of Compton-Paunsfoot, Esq. by whom he had one son and two daughters, Agnes and Alice.

11. Walter Baumfilde, his son and heir, married Grace, daughter of Sir Ralph Pudsey, Knt. and afterwards Constance, daughter of Edward Longford, Esq. He died in 1479; and by his first wife left issue.

12. William Baumfilde, Esq. married first Margaret, daughter of John St. Maur, (and co-heir to Dame Mary Drewrie, and afterwards of John St. Maur); secondly, Margaret, daughter of Nicholas Kirkham, and relict of John Cheney, of Pinhoe, Esq. By his first wife he had issue one son and two daughters; Margaret, the wife of Richard Yarde, of Bradley, Esq. and Elizabeth, of —— Lye, Esq.

13. Edward Baumfilde, his only son and heir, married Elizabeth, daughter of Sir Nicholas Wadham, of Merrifield, Knt by whom he had one son, Richard, and five daughters; Laurentia, the wife of —— Bidwell, and afterwards of Robert Fulford, Esqrs. 2, Elizabeth, of George Percival,* from whom is descended the Earl of Egmont; 3, Mary, of William Warder, Esq. 4, Joanna, of Richard Pollard, Esq. 5, Catharine, of Erasmus Pym, of Somersetshire, Esq.

14. Richard, his son and heir, married Elizabeth, daughter of John Sydenham, of Brimpton, in Somersetshire, Esq. by whom he had three sons and nine daugh-

---

* This Elizabeth was considered as one of the greatest heiresses, both for family and fortune; as to the first, she was allied to many sovereign houses in Europe, besides other great families; and as to the second, her elder brother dying without issue, and another, named Richard, being reputed also dead for many years, she was thought to be a co-heir to the great estate of St. Maur and Bampfylde. The belief of this was so strong, that it prevailed every where; insomuch that in many contemporary pedigrees,* drawn by the greatest heralds of those times, this Elizabeth is insisted on as a co heir of that family. And the family of Percival did then, and since, continue to quarter all the arms of those great houses; from the heiresses of whicy they are derived in blood, through this of Bampfylde; among which those of the crown of Scotland, and of England, before the conquest, are not the least considerable.

It was consequently expected, that upon her husband's arrival at full age, he should have been admitted into the purparty of her estates, in right of his wife; when, on a sudden, appeared a man, who stiled himself Richard Bampfylde, the second son of the late Sir Edward Bampfylde, by Elizabeth Wadham. This man, gaining a woman, who pretended to have been the nurse, she swore positively, that she knew him to be the person he affirmed himself to be,† by certain marks upon his body, which tallied exactly with those of that Richard Bampfylde she had formerly nursed. And such was the weight of this evidence,‡ that however suspicious it might seem, the said Richard Bampfylde, who had been employed in the lowest offices in life, in the family of a private gentleman, and was at the time of this claim, no better than a husbandman in the same house, obtained possession of the estate; and from him descended the family Bampfylde, which still flourishes in the county of Devon.

* Lillie's Pedigrees of the English Nobility, penes Comit de Egmont. † Ibid. ‡ Prince's Worthies of Devon.
From Dr. Anderson's History of the Houses of Lovel, Yvery, &c. vol. II. p. 113, 114.

Wotton says, that in his memory he was taken into a distant country; that his quality and estate was concealed from him; but one of his tenants, being his nurse's husband, discovering where he was detained, convinced him, by a remarkable mole upon his back, who he was: that he brought him back privately to Brampton, the seat of John Sydenham, Esq. who assisted him in his return to Poltimore, and afterwards gave him his daughter in marriage.

ters; 1, Sir Amias; 2, Giles; and 3, Richard: the daughters were 1, Elizabeth, the wife of George Carey, of Calville, Esq. 2, Joanna; 3, Ursula, the wife of Thomas Fulford, of Fulford, Esq. 4, Susan, of John Hicks, of Witheredge, Esq. 5, Mary, of Humphry Moore, Esq. son of Sir John Moore, Knt. 6, Gertrude, of John Harding, of Dorset, Esq. 7, Anne, of Christopher Morgan, of Dorset, Esq. 8, Catharine; and 9, Margaret, the wife of W. Lucy, of Hartrowe, in Somersetshire, Esq. This Richard died May 29, 1594; she in 1599.

15. Sir Amias Baumfilde, his eldest son and heir, married Elizabeth, daughter of Sir John Clifton, of Barrington, in Somersetshire, Knt. by whom he had issue six sons and four daughters; 1, Richard, the eldest son, died without issue; 2, John, of whom hereafter; 3, William; 4, Amias; 5, Edward; and 6, James. Of the daughters, Dorothy was the wife of Edward Hancock, Esq. and afterwards of Sir John Dodridge, Knt. one of the justices of the King's Bench; Jane, of Sir Francis Drake, of Buckland, Knt. Anne and Elizabeth died unmarried. This Amias died at Cottonheath Feb. 9, 1625, aged 65, and lies buried in the church at North-Molton, in Devonshire.

16. John Baumfilde, of Poltimore, his eldest son, was member of parliament for Tiverton, in Devonshire, 1 James I. also for the county, 3 Charles I. and married Elizabeth, daughter of Thomas Drake, of Buckland-Monachorum, Esq. by whom he had eight sons and seven daughters; 1, Amias; 2, Arthur; 3, Sir John, of whom hereafter; 4, Richard; 5, Lewis; 6, Francis; 7, Alexander; and 8, Thomas. The daughters were 1, Elizabeth, the wife of —— Ashford, of Ashford, in Devonshire, Esq. 2, Dorothy, of Henry Worth, of Worth, in the same county; 3, Joan; 4, Anne; 5, Ursula; 6, Bridget, the wife of Henry Henley, of Lee, in Somersetshire, Esq. and 7, Mary, of James Rood, of Stoke, in Devonshire, Esq.

I. JOHN BAMPFYLDE, Esq. son and heir of John, was advanced to the dignity of a baronet 17 Charles I. being at that time member of parliament for Penryn, in Cornwall; and married Gertrude, daughter of Amias Coplestone, Esq. and co-heir of her brother John Coplestone, of Coplestone and Warleigh, in Devonshire, Esq. by whom he had five sons and eight daughters; 1, Sir Coplestone, his successor; 2, Amias, who married Arabella, daughter of Sir Hugh Wyndham, of Kentsford, in Somersetshire, knight banneret, and died, leaving two daughters, Gertrude and Mary; 3, Lewis, who married Elizabeth, daughter of —— Hull, of To-Puddle, in Dorsetshire; by whom he left two sons and two daughters; John, Edmund, Elizabeth, and Anne; 4, John; and 5, Richard, who both died unmarried. The daughters were 1, Elizabeth, the wife of Thomas Moore, of Hawchurch, in Devonshire, Esq. 2, Gertrude, of Sir William Maurice, of Werrington, in Devonshire, Bart. 3, Susanna, of John Gifford, of Brightly, Esq. 4, Grace, of Sir William Bastard, of Gorston; 5, Frances, of Sir John Ellwill, of Pinhoe; 6, Dorothy, of Sir Francis Drake, of Buckland, in Devonshire, Bart. 7, Ursula; and 8, Mary, who both died unmarried. Sir John was succeeded by his son,

II. Sir COPLESTONE BAMPFYLDE, Bart. who by his guardians was sent to Corpus Christi College, Oxford, where he became a member in the quality of a nobleman: how he answered that title appeared from his splendid mode of living, and the great quantity of plate which he left his college, which remained a monument of his munificence, till it was stolen. On his return to his native country he found it in anarchy and confusion; but his vigorous soul being actuated with principles of loyalty to his sovereign, though an exile, and of duty to the church, then under a cloud, he exerted himself with several other persons, for the restoration of both. His zeal at last rendered him suspected by those in power; so that he was obliged to conceal himself at Trill, one of the houses of his friend, John Drake, Esq. afterwards Sir John Drake, Knt. and Bart. by which means he escaped the hands of those messengers that were sent to apprehend him. However, at the general quarter sessions at Exeter, this gentleman, with several persons of rank, in the county of Devon, put themselves in arms, declaring for a free parliament; and agreed upon a remonstrance for that purpose, which was presented to the house by this gentleman's uncle, Thomas Bampfylde, Esq. then recorder of that city; which remonstrance became a precedent to many other towns and cities in England.

After this, when our most noble countryman, General Monk, was come into England, with his army, the county of Devon, together with the city of Exon, joined in a petition of right to his excellency; and it was agreed that it should be presented by the hands of Sir Coplestone Bampfylde, for which, what entertainment he met withal from the rump, you may take in my author's own words.*

---

* Sir Coplestone Bampfylde, presenting to General Monk an humble petition for right, in the name of the city and county of Exeter and Devon, without any respect to the counties whence he came, the message he carried, or the honourable person by whom employed, with another honourable gentleman that came on a like account, was confined to the tower by the rump. But his stay there was not long; for he at length came (by a miracle of providence) whose right it was, Charles II. of very gracious memory; and with him our religion and property, laws and liberties.

Hence this gentleman, having thus acted in conjunction with other worthy patriots, for restoring the public welfare, it may not be forgotten, what particular care and pains he took for the conserving thereof, beyond a possibility of an interruption: and this he did, by disarming disaffected and suspicious persons, whose disloyalty was now become not only their principle, but their interest, as being (some of them at least) in profitable offices and places of trust; others in the possession of the king's, or church's lands and houses, and they could now near as willingly have parted with their lives, as with them.

This gentleman, together with another very honourable person of our county (the hon. Sir William Courtenay, of Powderham Castle, Bart.) raising each a gallant troop of about 120 gentlemen (most of them persons of quality and estates) in the head of which they rode themselves, securing some, and disarming others, they brought all the disaffected in those parts, into a due subjection to the government, in a little time.

When these dangers now were so happily over, and the nation once more settled upon its ancient bottom, this honourable person had the whole *posse comitatus* of Devon put into his hands, by King Charles II. he being the first high sheriff of this county, which he made after his return to the throne; and this was in the year of our lord, 1661: which office Sir Coplestone executed with great splendor, in an extraordinary number of liveries and attendants. Nor was this the only place of trust and honour he was concerned in, for the service of his prince and country; but, besides his being constantly in commission of the peace, and deputy lieutenant of the county (a little while only excepted in the reign of King James II. when he, with a great many other loyal gentlemen, had the honour to be turned out) he was chosen (in despight of all the interest could be made to the contrary) knight of the shire, to serve as one of the representatives of this honourable county in parliament; so generally was he beloved.

Nor was this gentleman concerned only in the managery of the civil affairs of the county; but engaged in the military also, as being (what of long time was in his family) one of the colonels of the county militia, in which post he continued unto the time of the Monmouthian invasion; when somewhat decaying in his health, and his son being come of age, he was pleased to drop that honourable office into his hands.

He married first Margaret, daughter of —— Bulkeley, of Burgate, in Hampshire, Esq. by whom he had two sons, John Coplestone Bulkeley, who died without issue, and Hugh; also a daughter Margaret, who died an infant. His second wife was Jane, daughter of Sir Courtenay Pole, of Shute, in Devon, Bart. by whom he had no issue. Hugh Bampfylde, Esq. died in the life-time of his father; and by Mary, daughter of James Clifford, had two sons; 1, Sir Coplestone Warwick, the succeeding baronet, and 2, John, who represented first the county of Devon, and after his nephew, Sir Richard, came of age, he gave up the county of Devon to him, and represented the city of Exeter. He was born in 1691, and died Sep. 17; 1750. He married first Elizabeth, daughter of — Basset, of Yeanton Court, in Devon, Esq. by whom he had no issue; and secondly, Margaret, daughter and sole heir of Sir Francis Warre, of Hestercombe, in Somersetshire, Bart. by whom he had 1, Coplestone Warre, who married Mary, daughter of Edward Knight, of Wolverley, in Worcestershire, Esq. colonel of the Somersetshire militia, and sister of Lady Sebright; 2, Margaretta, the wife of George Tyndall, of Buthford, in Somersetshire, Esq. by whom he had two sons and three daughters; John, Thomas-Bampfylde, Margaretta, Elizabeth; and Charlotte-Maria: 3, Elizabeth; 4, Francis-Warre; 5, Margaret; 6, Frances; 7, Maria; 8, Anne; and 9, Charlotte: the five last died young. Hugh Bampfylde, Esq. aforesaid, had also one daughter, Margaret, who died an infant.

III. Sir COPLESTONE-WARWICK BAMPFYLDE, eldest son of Hugh, succeeded his grandfather in dignity and estate: he represented the city of Exeter in parliament 9 Queen Anne, and the county the 12th of that reign, and every succeeding parliament to his death; and by Gertrude, rector of Sir Godfrey Copley, Bart. daughter of Sir John Carew, of Anthony, in Cornwall, Bart. by his third wife, Mary, daughter of Sir William Morrice, of Werrington, in Devon, Bart. he had one son, Sir Richard Warwick, his successor, and one daughter, Mary, the wife of Coventry Carew, Esq. only son of Sir William Carew, of Anthony, in Cornwall, Bart. and after his death of —— Buller, Esq. member of parliament for Westlow: she died in Nov. 1762. Sir Coplestone Warwick dying Oct. 7, 1727, and his lady April 14, 1736: he was succeeded in dignity and estate by his only son,

Having thus accompanied this eminent person to the last scene of his life, we can do no less than observe, how he performed that part thereof, and so quitted this stage of mortality.

When the Prince of Orange first landed in Devon, and had marched with his army, so far as Exeter, Sir Coplestone, being ill himself, was yet pleased that his son, the colonel, should wait on his highness, and congratulate his arrival, as one come to preserve our laws and religion; and maintain the established government. But when at length he apprehended that matters were carried beyond all imaginations, fearing a change would be made in the fundamental constitution of the government, he so far declared against those proceedings, as to refuse payment of any new-made rates and taxes; and the collectors were enforced to levy them by distress upon his goods.

Not long after, going to visit his son's relict at Warleigh, the gout (with which, in his latter years, he had been greatly afflicted) returning upon him with violence, and, like an armed man, surprizing the castle of his heart, soon put a period to his days, in the five and fiftieth year of his life, A.D. 1691.

Before his decease (what is very remarkable) he called his family together, and left this in strict charge with them; that they should always continue faithful to the religion of the established church of England; and to be sure to pay their allegiance to the right heirs of the crown.

His remains being brought from Warleigh, lie entombed among his ancestors, in the parish church of Poltimore, without any funeral monument. *Thus far Prince's Worthies.*

BAMPFYLDE, OF POLTIMORE, DEVONSHIRE.

TABLE 71.

1. —— BAUMFILDE = ——, dr. of J. Hastings
2. —— Baumfilde = —— Hocrisham
3. John Baumpfilde = Isabella Faber
4. John = Eleanor Beauchampe
5. John = Joan Morton
6. John = Isabel Cobham
7. John = Joan Gilbert = J. Hastings

John = —— Morton	8 Thomas = A. Coplestone
9 John = A. Pederton	Richard	Alice	Joanna	Agnes
10 Sir William = M. Paunsfoot	Peter	Elizabeth = H. Fraunceis	Thomasine = —— Paunsfoot	Alice
C. Langford = 11 Walter, 1479 = Grace Pudsey	Agnes	Alice
Margaret St. Maur = 12 William = Margaret Kirkham
13 Edward = Elizabeth Wadham	Margaret = Richard Yarde	Elizabeth = —— Lye

Edward	14 Richard, 1594	Laurentia	Elizabeth	Mary	Joanna	Catharine
	Elizabeth Synenham 1599	— Bidwell	Robert Fulford	George Porcival	William Warder	Richard Pollard	Erasmus Pym

15 Sir Amias, 1625	2 sons	Elizabeth	Ursula	Susan	Mary	Gertrude	Anne	Margaret
Elizabeth Clifton	2 drs.	G. Carey	T. Fulford	J. Hicks	H. Moore	J. Harding	C. Morgan	W. Lucy

Richard	16 John	William,	Edward,	Dorothy	Jane	Anne,
	Elizabeth Drake	Anne	James	Edward Hancock	Sir John Dodridge	Sir Francis Drake	Elizabeth

I. Sir John	7 sons	Elizabeth	Dorothy	Bridget	Mary
G. Coplestone	3 drs.	—— Ashford	H. Worth	H. Henley	J. Rudd

II. Sir Coplestone, 1691	Amias	Lewis	John,	Elizabeth	Gertrude	Susanna	&c.
Margaret Bulkeley	Jane Pole	Arabella Wyndham	Eliz. Hull	Richard	T. Moore	Sir W. Morice	J. Gifford

John Coplestone Bulkeley	Hugh Bampfylde Mary Clifford	Margaret	Gertrude, Mary	John, Edmund	Elizabeth, Anne

III. Sir Coplestone-Warwick, 1727	John Bampfylde, 1755	Margaret
Gertrude, dr. of Sir J. Carew, 1736	Eliza. Basset	Marg. Warre	

IV. Sir Richard-Warwick, 1776	Mary, 1762	Copleston	Margaret
Jane Codrington	Sir C. Carew	—— Buller	M. Knight	G. Tyndall

V. Sir Charles-Warwick	John-Codrington-Warwick	Richard-Warwick d. y.	Amias-Warwick	Richard-Warwick	Gertrude O. Bowles	&c. &c.
—— Moore						

IV. Sir RICHARD-WARWICK BAMPFYLDE, Bart. who was knight of the shire for the county of Devon: he married Aug. 8, 1742, Jane, daughter and sole heiress of Col. John Codrington, of Wrexhall, in Somersetshire, who died Feb. 15, 1789; by whom he had issue six sons and seven daughters; 1, Charles-Warwick, who died young; 2, Sir Charles-Warwick, the present baronet, born Jan. 23, 1733; 3, John-Codrington-Warwick, born Aug. 24, 1754; 4, Richard-Warwick, who died an infant; 5, Amias-Warwick, born Nov. 24, 1757; 6, Richard-Warwick, born Feb. 5, 1759. The daughters were Gertrude, born May 12, 1743, the wife of Oldfield Bowles, of North-Ashton, in Oxfordshire, Esq. and died Sep. 28, 1769; 2, Elizabeth, born in April, 1745, the wife of Col. Gordon; 3, Jenny-Codrington; 4, Charlotte, the wife of Abel Moysey, Esq. member of parliament for Bath; 5, Harriot; 6, Mary-Frances; and 7, Georgiana-Sophia, born in 1764. Sir Richard-Warwick died Aug. 15, 1776, and was succeeded by his eldest surviving son,

V. Sir CHARLES-WARWICK BAMPFYLDE, Bart. who married in 1776, ———, eldest daughter of Sir John Moore, Bart. He is member of parliament for the county of Devon.

ARMS—Argent, on a bend, gules, three mullets, or.
CREST—On a wreath, a lion's head, erased, sable; ducally crowned, or.
MOTTO—*Delectare in Domino.*
SEATS—At Poltimore and North Molton, in Devonshire; and Hardington and Wrexhall in Somersetshire.

71. COTTON, of Landwade, Cambridgeshire.

Created Baronet July 14, 1641.

THIS family is said to be denominated from Cotton, a manor in Cambridgeshire, whereof was

1. Sir Henry Cotton, Knt.* lord of the manor of Cotton Hall, in Cambridgeshire: other authorities say, that Sir Henry lived in the seat of his ancestors,† at

---

* Visit. Com. Cantab. 1619.   † The manor of Cotton, in the parish of Stone, in Kent, was (as Mr. Philpot observes) as high as any private or public record can conduct us to a discovery, the possession of a family, who extracted their surname from hence, and had the appellation of Coton, or Cotton. John de Cotton held this manor in 20 Edw. III. and paid a respective supply for it at making the Black Prince, knight; and from their identity of armorials, this family, sealing with a chevron between three griffin's heads, erased, I guess it is probable, the noble family of Cotton, of Landwade, in Cambridgeshire, was originally extracted from hence. *See Philpot's Survey of Kent, p. 323.*

Cotton Hall, in Exning, Suffolk. All agree he married Anne, daughter and heir of Sir Henry le Fleming, Knt. and had issue

2. Thomas, his son and heir, father of

3. Humphrey, who by Anne, daughter of Sir Thomas Holbroke, Knt. had issue

4. Sir Thomas Cotton, who married Alice, daughter and heiress of John de Haistings, of Landwade, in Cambridgeshire, Esq. possessed that estate, and left issue

5. John Cotton, who was burgess in several parliaments for Cambridgeshire,* temp. Rich. II. and died in 1393. He married Bridget, daughter of Richard Grace, of Norfolk, by whom he had two sons, Thomas, and John. Thomas was lord of the manor of Trumpington, near Cambridge, and was returned among the gentry of Cambridge, by the commissioners, 2 Henry VI. he died without issue in 1434.

6. Walter Cotton, heir to his brother, who was also returned by the commissioners, among the gentry of Cambridgeshire; and by Joan, daughter of Sir Robert Read, of Oxfordshire, Knt. had four sons and two daughters; 1, William; 2, Walter, who bore the chevron in his arms, engrailed, and was progenitor to the Cottons, of Cotton Hall and Stersome; and by a younger son of that line, the Cottons of Swaffham Bulbeck, all in Cambridgeshire; 3, Thomas, who was knighted; and 4, Edmund. Walter, the father, departed this life May 14, 1445, and lies buried at Landwade.

7. William Cotton, of Landwade, Esq. eldest son, was vice-chamberlain to King Henry VI. from whom he had a grant of several privileges. He married Anne, daughter and co-heir of John Abbot, Esq. and had issue three daughters; 1, Catharine, the wife of Thomas Higham, of Higham, Esq. 2, Joan, of Sir Clement Higham, of Gilford, in Suffolk, Knt. and 3, Etheldred, who had three husbands; first Thomas Barton, Esq. secondly, Sir Richard Gardiner, Knt. lord-mayor of London; and thirdly, Sir Gilbert Talbot, Knt. also six sons; 1, Thomas; 2, William, from whom the Cottons, of Clavering, in Essex, are descended; 3, Andrew, who died S. P. 4, Edmund, of Redgrave, in Suffolk, who married Ela, daughter and heiress of —— Conyers, only son of Sir Robert Conyers, and of near alliance to the Lord Conyers, of Hornby Castle, in whose right he had the ancient seat called Conyers, alias Necton Hall, in Bramble Barton, alias Barton Magna, near Bury St. Edmund's, which was enjoyed by his posterity; 5, John, who died S. P. and 6 Robert. This William, the father, was slain at St. Alban's, May 22, 1455, fighting for King Henry VI. and lies buried at Landwade.

8. Sir Thomas Cotton, of Landwade, Knt. his son and heir, was sheriff of Cambridgeshire and Huntingdon, 16 Edw. IV. He married first Margaret, daughter of Sir Philip Wentworth, of Nettlested, in Essex, Knt. by whom he had only two daughters, one of which was Anne, the wife of Edward D'Oyley, and mother of Sir Henry D'Oyley, Knt. secondly, Joan, daughter and heiress of Nicholas Sharp, Esq. and by her had two daughters, Dorothy, and Andrea, the wife of John Bassingbourne, Esq. and five sons; 1, Robert; 2, John, who had issue; 3, William, who married Margaret, daughter and co-heir of — Colepeper, and was father of Sir Thomas Cotton, of Kent, Knt. 4, Leonard, and 5; Martin, both priests. He died July 30, 1499.

* Prynne's Parl. Regist. vol. IV. de iisd. an.

COTTON, OF LANDWADE, CAMBRIDGESHIRE.

9. Sir Robert, of Landwade, the eldest son, received the honour of knighthood from King Henry VII. in his chamber, at Baynard's Castle. He married first Dorothy, daughter of Sir Robert Clere, Knt. by whom he had Thomas, who died without issue, and Anne, heir to her brother, who being a nun, at Denny Abby, gave her estate to John Cotton, her half brother, son of Sir Robert Cotton, by his second wife, Alice, daughter of John Thornburgh, Esq. widow of Sir Nicholas Griffin, Knt. Sir Robert, by his second wife, had also a daughter Bridget, the wife of Sir John Huddleston, of Sarston, in Cambridgeshire, Knt. Sir Robert died July 18, 1519, and was succeeded by his son,

10. Sir John Cotton, who was sheriff for Cambridgeshire and Huntingdon 3 Edw. VI. likewise 4 and 5 Philip and Mary, being then a knight. He married Isabel, daughter of Sir William Spencer, of Althorpe, in Northamptonshire, Knt. and died April 21, 1593, aged 81: Isabel, his wife, died Nov. 2, 1578, aged 63. They had issue eight sons and five daughters, whereof five sons and two daughters died in their infancy; three sons, John, Robert, and Edmund were all knighted: Sir Robert, the second son, was seated at Wood-ditton, in Cambridgeshire, and married Elizabeth, daughter and heiress of John Dormer, Esq. and had posterity: Sir Edmund married Jane, daughter of —— Tanfield, but had no issue. Sir John had also three daughters; 1, Alice, the wife of Sir Thomas Revett, of Chippenham, in Cambridgeshire, Knt. 2, Anne, of Anthony Roper, of Farningham, in Kent; and 3, Frances, of Thomas Andrews, of Charwelton, in Northamptonshire, Esq.

11. Sir John Cotton, of Landwade, Knt. son and heir, married three wives; first, Elizabeth, daughter of Thomas Carryl, of Warnham, in Sussex, Esq. secondly, Elizabeth, daughter of Sir Humphrey Bradburne, of Bradburne, in Derbyshire, Knt. both which died without issue; and thirdly, Anne, daughter of Sir Richard Hoghton, of Hoghton Tower, in Lancashire, Bart. by whom he had issue James, John, and Catharine; James and Catharine died V. P. Sir John was custos rotulorum for Cambridgeshire, and served many years as knight of the shire for that county; and received the honour of knighthood, with several others, at Whitehall, July 23, 1603: he died in 1620, aged 77, and lies buried in a vault on the south aisle of Landwade church.

I. Sir JOHN COTTON, Knt. his only son, was created a baronet 17 Charles I. He was high sheriff of Cambridge when the unhappy rebellion broke out, and proclaimed the Earl of Essex a traitor, in every market town in the county: he immediately took up arms for his sovereign, and was entrusted to carry the plate of the university of Cambridge, to the king at Oxford, which he safely delivered, through many difficulties, being followed by a body of Cromwell's horse: he was soon after obliged, for his loyalty, to leave his own country, and lived some years abroad. He was born in Sep. 1615, and died about 1690, aged 74, having been many years deputy lieutenant and justice of the peace for this county. By his wife, Jane, daughter and sole heiress of Sir Edward Hinde, Esq. (grandson and heir of Sir Edward Hinde, of Maddingley, in Cambridgeshire, Knt. and co-heiress to her mother, the daughter and heiress of Sir Thomas Maples, of Stow, in Huntingdonshire, Bart.) He had issue two sons and two daughters; Sir John, and Thomas, who died young; and Jane and Catharine, who died unmarried.

II Sir JOHN COTTON, of Landwade and Maddingley Hall, Bart. succeeded his father: he was recorder of the town of Cambridge, and one of their representatives in parliament all King William's, and part of Queen Anne's reign. He died in Jan. 1712, and lies buried at Landwade. By Elizabeth, his wife, daughter and co-heir of Sir Joseph Sheldon, Knt. alderman, and some time lord-mayor of London, he had issue Sir John-Hinde Cotton, his successor in title and estate, and another son, who died young; also nine daughters; 1, Catharine; 2, Jane; 3, Jane; 4, Anne; 5, Catharine, the wife of William Sancroft, of Fressingfield, in Suffolk, Esq. nephew and heir to archbishop Sancroft, by whom he left two daughters, one of which was the wife of John Wogan, of Gawdy Hall, in Norfolk, Esq. she died in 1788, and was the last of the archbishop's family: her fortune, which was very considerable, devolved on Sir Charles, the present baronet. 6, Elizabeth; 7, Frances; 8, Dorothy; and 9, Agnes.

III. Sir JOHN-HINDE COTTON, only son and heir, succeeded his father in dignity and estate, in Jan. 1712-13. He was some time treasurer of the chamber to his majesty King George II. and in the reign of Queen Anne was one of the lords' commissioners of trade and plantations; also member, in several parliaments, for the town of Cambridge, in that reign, and in the first parliament of King George I. In the second he was chosen one of the knights for that county, and in the two first parliaments of King George II. was again chosen for the town of Cambridge; and afterwards for Marlborough, in the county of Wilts, which he represented to the time of his death, on Feb. 4, 1752, in the 64th year of his age; and was buried at Landwade, in a vault made by himself, between his two wives,* who were, first, Lettice, second daughter of Sir Ambrose Crowley, of Greenwich, in the county of Kent, Knt. who died in Aug. 1718, and left one son, John-Hinde Cotton, his successor, and one daughter, Mary, the wife of Jacob Houblon, of Hallingbury, in the county of Essex, Esq. (member in the second parliament of his late majesty, for the town of Colchester, and afterwards twice chosen representative for the county of Hereford; by whom he had two sons and one daughter. Sir John's second wife was Margaret, third daughter of James Craggs, Esq. one of the commissioners of the Post Office, sister and co-heiress of the right hon. James Craggs, Esq. some time one of the principal secretaries of state to King George I. and relict of Samuel Trefusis, of Trefusis, in the county of Cornwall, and of Hatley St. George, in the county of Cambridge, Esq. by whom he had one daughter, Margaret, who died at four years of age; and her mother died in Aug. 1734. Sir John was succeeded in dignity and estate by his only son,

---

* Attic Wit, British Spirit, Roman virtue, animated the bosom of that great man, whose remains are committed to this tomb.
Sir JOHN-HINDE COTTON, Baronet,
Whose lively genius, and solid understanding, were strictly devoted to the service of his country, as a British senator.
Without any views to venal reward; above the design of ill-got power; untainted with the itch of tinsel titles, he lived, he died, a Patriot.

COTTON, OF LANDWADE, CAMBRIDGESHIRE.

TABLE 72.

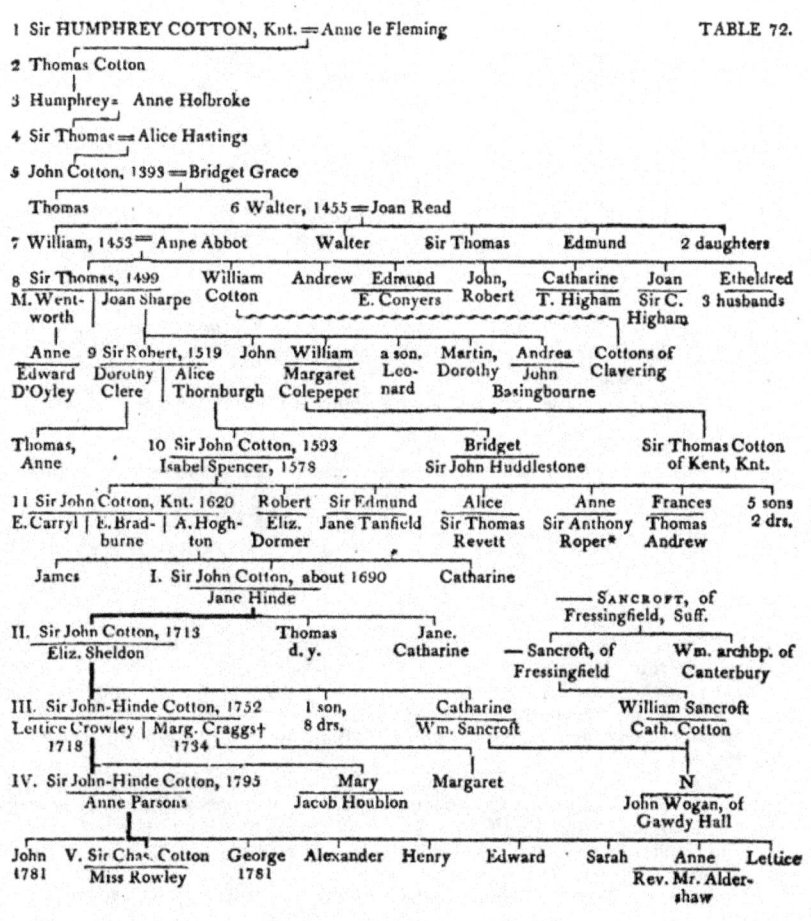

IV. Sir JOHN-HINDE COTTON, Bart. who in 1741 was chosen member of parliament for St. Germain's, in Cornwall, and for Marlborough on his father's death, in 1752; and again in 1754; and the county of Cambridge in 1765 and 1771. He married July 1, 1745, Anne, second daughter of Humphrey Parsons, Esq. of Rigate, twice lord-mayor of London, by his wife, Sarah, third daughter of Sir Ambrose Crowley, Knt. by whom he, Sir John, had six sons; 1, John, who died in 1781; 2, Sir Charles, the present baronet; 3, George, who died in 1781, and 4, Alexander, twins; 5, Henry, who died at his birth, and 6, Edward, twins: and three daughters; Sarah, Anne, the wife of the Rev. Mr. Oldershaw, and Lettice. Sir John-Hinde Cotton died Jan. 23, 1795, in his 78th year, and was succeeded by his son,

V. Sir CHARLES COTTON, Bart. rear-admiral of the red, who, Feb. 27, 1788, married ———, eldest daughter of Sir Joshua Rowley, Bart.

ARMS—Sable, a chevron between three griffin's heads, erased, argent.
CREST—On a wreath, a griffin's head, erased, as in the arms.
MOTTO—*Fidelitas Vincit.*
SEATS—At Landwade and Maddingley, both in Cambridgeshire.

---

72. BURGOYNE, of Sutton, Bedfordshire.

Created Baronet July 15, 1641.

THIS is certainly a family of great antiquity, and has been long seated in this county (according to tradition, ever since King John's time): whether they are the younger branch of the Burgoyne's that were anciently seated at Impington,* and Long Stanton, in the county of Cambridge, and were lords of Caxton, in that county, or whether those seated there were descended from this branch, we cannot determine.

1. Robert Burgoyne, Esq. was a person of considerable note temp. Henry VIII. and one of the auditors† of the Exchequer: he was also one of the commissioners appointed by King Henry VIII. to take the surrender of the monasteries‡ in Warwickshire and other counties, and to send an account of their state, the religion and virtue of the nuns, &c. His son,

2. Robert Burgoyne, of Sutton, in Bedfordshire, and of Wroxall, in Warwickshire, Esq. was high sheriff of the county of Warwick 39 Eliz. He married Judith,

* Weever's Fun. Mon. p. 325.   † Le Neeve's MSS. vol. II. p. 112.   ‡ Dug. Warw. vol. II. p. 1111.

daughter of —— Wroth: she died in March, 1606, and was buried at Wroxall; he was buried at Sutton, May 3, 1613. His son and heir,

3. Roger Burgoyne, of Sutton, in Bedfordshire, and Wroxall, in Warwickshire, Esq. was high sheriff of Bedfordshire 14 James I. and of Warwickshire 6 Charles I. and buried at Wroxall, June 28, 1636, having issue by his first wife, Margaret, daughter of Thomas Wendy, of Haslingfeild, in Cambridgeshire, Esq. (who was buried at Wroxall Aug. 19, 1629) a daughter Judith, the wife of Onslow Winch, Esq. son and heir of Sir Humphrey Winch, Knt. one of the justices of the common pleas, temp. James I. and Sir John, his successor. His second wife was Joyce, daughter of Roger Giffard, relict of —— Nichols; by whom he had no issue.

I. JOHN BURGOYNE, of Sutton, Esq. his only son, baptized at Haslingfeild Jan. 29, 1591, who was created a baronet 17 Charles I. married Jane, daughter and heiress of Jul. Kempe, of Spains Hall, in Finchingfield, in Essex, Esq. by whom he had four daughters; 1, Mary, the wife of Sir Edward Cater, of Kempston, in Bedfordshire, Knt. 2, Jane, of James Maine, of Bucks, Esq. 3, Judith, of Sir William Ascough, of Osgodby, in Lincolnshire, Knt. and 4, Elizabeth, of William Love, Esq. alderman of London: also three sons; 1, Sir Roger, his successor, who had the honour of knighthood conferred on him, Aug. 2, 1641; 2, John, of Woking, in Surrey, who, by Penelope, sister of Sir Thomas Darcy, of Essex, Knt. left issue; and 3, Robert, a merchant in London, who married Catharine, daughter of —— Heynon. This Sir John represented the county of Warwick in parliament 16 Charles I. and died about 1654.

II. Sir ROGER BURGOYNE, Knt. and Bart. eldest son and successor of his father, married first Anne, daughter and heiress of Charles Snelling, of London, merchant; by whom he had several children; 1, Jane, the wife of John Symmonds, of Yeldham, in Essex, Esq. barrister at law; 2, Sir John, his successor; 3, Anne, the wife of John Raymond, of Essex, Gent. 4, Mary, of William Guyon, of Essex, Gent. and 5, Judith, who died unmarried. This lady dying in 1656, Sir Roger married to his second lady, Anne, daughter of John Robinson, of Dighton, in Yorkshire, Esq. by whom he had several children, but only three daughters; Elizabeth, the wife of Matthew Hutton, S.T.P. rector of Aynho, in Northamptonshire; 2, Anne, born July 25, 1674, the wife of the right Rev. Dr. Charles Hickman, bishop of Londonderry, in Ireland; and 3, Philadelphia. This Sir Roger presented Mr. Edward Stillingfleet, the learned bishop of Worcester, to the rectory of Sutton, and there he wrote his *Origines Sacræ*, when he was very young. He died Sep. 16, 1677, aged 59; and lies buried in Sutton church.

His second lady lies buried at Wroxall, in Warwickshire, where, on a large marble monument, fixed to the east wall of the chancel, is a Latin inscription; below which, on a flat stone on the floor:—Here lieth the body of Anne, relict of Sir Roger Burgoyne, Knt. and Bart. who departed this life the 5th day of Feb. Anno Dom. 1694, according to the Julian account.

III. Sir JOHN BURGOYNE, Bart. only son and successor to his father, married Constance, daughter of Richard Lucy, of Cherlecote, in Warwickshire, Esq. by whom he had a numerous issue; but only four sons and three daughters survived him, viz. 1, Sir Roger, his successor; 2, John, who married ——, daughter of —— Burneston, and had issue; 3, Thomas, who married ——, daughter of Mr. Warren, and 4, Lucy, who married ——, daughter of —— Howell: she died in 1721. Of the daughters, one was the wife of Mr. Warren; ——, of Griffith Davis, M. D. of Birmingham, in Warwickshire; and the third died unmarried. This Sir John died April 9, 1709, and his lady April 22, 1711; and both lie buried in Sutton church, in Bedfordshire.

IV. Sir ROGER BURGOYNE, Bart. his eldest son and successor, married Constance, daughter of Sir Thomas Middleton, of Stansted Mount-Fichet, in Essex, Knt. (by Mary, his wife, daughter of Sir Stephen Langham, of Quentin, in Northamptonshire, Knt. third surviving son of John Langham, of Cottesbrook, Bart.) by whom he had two sons; Sir John, his successor, and Sir Roger; and one daughter, Constantia-Maria, born Nov. 3, 1705, the wife of Capt. John Pigott; and died July 26, 1739, leaving, by him, two daughters. Constance, relict of Sir Roger, was re-married in 1715, to Christopher Wren, Esq. son of Sir Christopher Wren, Knt. and died May 23, 1734.

V. Sir JOHN BURGOYNE, Bart. eldest son and successor to his father, in title and estate, survived him only six weeks, and dying unmarried, was succeeded in title and estate by his only brother,

VI. Sir ROGER BURGOYNE, Bart. who married in Jan. 1739, Frances Montagu, eldest daughter of George, earl of Halifax, who died July 24, 1788; by whom he had two sons, Sir John and Sir Montagu; and three daughters, Frances, Louisa, and Elizabeth. Sir Roger was succeeded by his eldest son,

VII. Sir JOHN BURGOYNE, Bart. he was a colonel in the 58th regiment of foot, and married ——, eldest daughter of General Johnston, of Overstone, near Northampton; and died, without issue male, in the East Indies, in 1786, and was succeeded by his brother,

VIII. Sir MONTAGU BURGOYNE, the present baronet, who, on Nov. 1, 1794, married Miss Burton. He married secondly ——, daughter of Eliab Harvey, Esq. by whom he had a son, born Oct. 16, 1796.

ARMS—Gules, a chevron, or, between three talbots, argent, on a chief crenelle of the last, as many martlets, azure.

CREST—On a wreath, a talbot, argent, sejant.

SEAT—At Sutton, in Bedfordshire.

BURGOYNE, OF SUTTON, BEDFORDSHIRE.

TABLE 72.

1 ROBERT BURGOYNE
|
2 Robert, 1613 = Judith Wroth, 1606
|
Margaret Wendy, 1629 = 3 Roger, 1636 = Joyce Giffard
|
Judith = Onslow Winch   I. Sir John, 1654 = Jane Kempe

II. Sir Roger, 1677	John	Robert	Mary	Jane	Judith	Elizabeth
A. Snelling | A. Robinson, 1694	Penelope Darcy	Catharine Heyden	Sir Edward Cater	James Maine	Sir Wm. Ascough	William Love

Jane	III. Sir John, 1709	Anne	Mary	Judith	Elizabeth	Anne	Philadelphia
John Symmonds	Constance Lucy 1711	John Paymond	William Guyon	.	Matthew Hutton	Bishop of Londonderry	

IV. Sir Roger	John	Thomas	Lucy	N	N	N
Constance Middleton, 1734	—Burneston	—Warren	—Howell	Mr. Warren	Griffith Davis	

V. Sir John   VI. Sir Roger = Frances Montagu   Constantia-Maria = Capt. John Pigott

VII. Sir John, 1786 = —Johnston   Miss Burton = VIII. Sir Montagu = —Harvey

---

73. NORTHCOTE, of HAYNE, DEVONSHIRE.

Created Baronet July 16, 1641.

CAMDEN, in his Remains, derives this, among other names, from their respective mansions. Originally there was an *at* or *de* set before them, and those distinctions were strictly observed till the time of King Edw. IV. Temp. Henry I. it is recorded, that

1. Galfridus Miles had his seat at Northcote, in the parish of East Down, in this county, and that

2. John Fitz-Gaulfrid held divers lands there, and in the hundreds of Witheridge, North Tawton, Black Torrington, &c.* He changed his name to Northcote. Gaulfrid de Northcote lived in 1188, and held lands in Colstan, in Witheridge hundred.

* Galfrid de Northcote, tenet dimidium fœdi in Woodham, de abbate de Tavistocke, per medium in hund. Witheridge et unum fœdum de abbate de Tavistock in manerio de Burrington, in hund. North Tawton, 1157.

3. William Northcote married Margarite, daughter of Robert de Afeton, 1190.

4. Andrew de Northcote, in 17 Edw. I. married Matilda, eldest daughter of Peter Faber.

5. William de Northcote, 1325, married the daughter and heir of —— Hillion.

6. John de Northcote, 16 Edw. III. married Johanna, daughter and co-heir of Roger Meoles (by a daughter of —— Prouze). John de Northcote was high sheriff of Devon 29 Edw. III. He wrote himself sometimes de Northcote, and sometimes de Newton: he married Margery, daughter of Thomas Buckington.

7. John de Northcote, 22 Rich. II. married Isolda, daughter of —— Sutton.

8. Walter de Northcote, 7 Henry IV. married the daughter and co-heir of Robert Hawkworthy.

9. John Northcote, of Widworthy, 5 Henry V. married ——, daughter of —— Medford: his son,

10. John Northcote, 23 Henry VI. married Johanna, daughter of John Lutterel, of Dunster Castle, in Somersetshire, Esq.

11. Walter Northcote, in 1457, married Alice, daughter and heiress of Guamed vel Mamhade.

12. John Northcote, his eldest son, married Joan, daughter and heiress of —— Passimere.

13. John Northcote, 12 Henry VIII. married Alice, daughter of John Durk.

14. Walter Northcote married ——, daughter of Richard Hill, of Shilston.

15. John Northcote, of Newton St. Cyress, in the reign of Philip and Mary, married Elizabeth, the daughter of Thomas Dowrish, of Sanford, in Devonshire, Esq. His eldest son,

16. Walter Northcote, married ——, daughter and heiress of Edmund Drew, of Hayne, in the parish of Newton St. Cyress, which place has ever since been the chief seat of the Northcotes. But Walter, dying without issue male, a considerable personal estate went to his daughters; but his lands came to

17. John, his second brother, who had two wives; first ——, daughter of Sir Anthony Rouse, of Haiton, in Cornwall, Knt. by whom he had one son, Anthony, who died an infant: his second wife was Susanna, daughter of Sir Hugh Pollard, of King's Nympton, in Devonshire, Knt. by whom he had twelve sons and six daughters, as appears by the inscription on his monument, in the church of Newton St. Cyress.

I. JOHN NORTHCOTE, his son, was the first baronet of this family, and was born in 1599. He married Grace, the daughter and heiress of Hugh Haswell, of Wells, in Somersetshire, Esq. was high sheriff of the county 2 Charles I. and knight of the shire in parliament 12 Charles II. He had issue five sons and three daughters; Sir Arthur, his successor; John, who married ——, daughter of —— Foljambe; Lewis, the daughter of —— Coplestone; Haswell, the daughter of —— Crook; and William, the daughter of —— Leigh. Of the daughters, Grace died in her minority; Susanna, was the second wife of Robert Fortescue, of Fillegh, in Devonshire, Esq. and Elizabeth, of Thomas Pointindon, Esq. barrister at law.

NORTHCOTE, OF HAYNE, DEVONSHIRE.

II. Sir ARTHUR, the eldest son and successor, married two wives; first Elizabeth, daughter and heir of James Welsh, of Alverdiscott, Esq. by whom he had large possessions, and two sons and one daughter; John, Arthur, and Elizabeth. John married ——, daughter of —— Leigh, Gent. by whom he had issue, but all died young: Arthur, second son, married ——, daughter of —— Gay, of Bristol, merchant, but left no issue. Sir Arthur married secondly Elizabeth, eldest daughter to the hon. Sir Francis Godolphin, of Godolphin, in Cornwall; by whom he had four sons and four daughters; Sir Francis, Sir Henry, William, who died in his minority; and Charles married to Sarah, daughter of John Northcote, Esq. his uncle, and left issue Arthur and Charles. Of the daughters; 1, Elizabeth died in an advanced age, unmarried; 2, Dorothy, the wife of Andrew, son of John Quick, of Newton St. Cyress, Esq. and had issue; 3, Penelope, of John Hesket, Esq. Lancaster herald, but had no issue; 4, Susanna died in her infancy. Sir Arthur was succeeded by his eldest son,

III. Sir FRANCIS NORTHCOTE, who married Anne, daughter of Sir Chichester Wrey, of Trebitch, in Cornwall, Bart. by the honourable Anne, countess of Middlesex, by whom he had no issue, whereupon the dignity and estate devolved upon,

IV. Sir Henry Northcote, Bart. his next brother, some time fellow of Exeter College, Oxford, and doctor of physic. He married Penelope, daughter of Edward Lovett, of Liscombe, in Bucks, and of Corfe, in Devonshire, Esq. (by Joan, his second wife, daughter and heir of James Hearle, of Tawstock, Gent.) by whom he left one son, Sir Henry, his successor, and two daughters; Elizabeth, the wife of John Incledon, of Buckland, in Devonshire, Esq. and Johanna, who died unmarried, in April 1739. Sir Henry, dying at his seat, at Corfe, in Feb. 1729-30, was succeeded in dignity and estate by his only son,

V. Sir HENRY NORTHCOTE, Bart. who was member of parliament for the city of Exeter; and married Jane, the only daughter and heiress of Hugh Stafford, of Pynes, in Devonshire, Esq. (she died in 1780, aged 94) by whom he had issue 1, Sir Stafford, born in May 1736; 2, Hugh, rector of Upton, in Devonshire; 3, Charles, who died an infant; and one daughter, ——, the wife of William Paynter, Esq. of the Navy Office. Sir Henry, dying in 1743, was succeeded by his eldest son,

VI. Sir STAFFORD NORTHCOTE, Bart. who, Oct. 17, 1751, married Catharine, daughter of the Rev. George Bradford, M. A. rector of Tallaton, in Devonshire; by whom he had a son, Stafford-Henry, the present baronet, born Oct. 6, 1762; and a daughter, Catharine-Jane, born Feb. 25, 1764. Sir Stafford died March 11, 1771, and was succeeded by his son,

VII. Sir STAFFORD-HENRY NORTHCOTE, Bart. who, May 6, 1791, married Jaquetta, daughter of Charles Baring, Esq. by whom he had a son and heir, born in 1792, and another son in 1793.

ARMS—Quarterly first and fourth, argent, a fesse between three crosses molines, sable; second and third, argent, three croslets in bend, sable.

NORTHCOTE, OF HAYNE, DEVONSHIRE.

CREST—Upon a cap of dignity, a stag trippant, argent.
MOTTO—*Christi crux est mea lux.*
SEAT—At Hayne, in Devonshire.

TABLE 74.

I. Sir JOHN NORTHCOTE = Grace Haswell

II. Sir Arthur Northcote — Elizabeth Welsh
John — Elizabeth Godolphin / Fol-jambe
Lewis — Cople-stone
Haswell — Crook
William — Leigh
Grace
Susanna — Robert Fortescue
Elizabeth — Thomas Pointindon

John — Leigh
Arthur — Gay
Eliz.
III. Sir Francis = Anne Wrey
IV. Sir Hen. 1730 = Penelope Lovett
Wm. Eliz.
Charles — Sarah Northcote
Dorothy — Andrew Quick
Penelope — John Hesket
Susanna

V. Sir Henry Northcote, 1743 = Jane Stafford, 1780
Elizabeth = John Incledon
Johanna

VI. Sir Stafford Northcote, 1771 = Catharine Bradford
Hugh
Charles
N = Wm. Paynter

VII. Sir Stafford-Henry Northcote = Jaquetta Baring

—, a son, b. 1792   —, a son, b. 1793

---

74. STRICKLAND, of BOYNTON, YORKSHIRE.

Created Baronet July 30, 1641.

THAT there have been several persons of this family of great eminence and reputation, and that their ancient seat was at Strickland Hall,* in the county of Westmoreland, appears from undoubted authorities.

Sir Walter de Stirkeland, Knt. (as the name was anciently written) was returned one of the knights for Westmoreland, in several parliaments, in the reign of King Edw. II. He was one of those to whom Sir William de Windsor, second son of Richard de Windsor, gave all his goods and chattels, &c. ordering them to pay his debts, and provide for his soul.†

Sir John Stirkeland, Knt. married Alice, cousin and heiress of Robert Banastre, of Hyndeley, in Lancashire, whom she survived; for in 12 Edw. II. she is called his widow.‡

---
* Burn's Westmoreland, p. 443.   † Coll. Parl. vol. IV. p. 68.   ‡ Ibid. vol. VII. p. 124.

John de Stirkeland, their son, was elected one of the knights of the shire for the county of Westmoreland in 1 Edw. III. and his son, Walter de Stirkeland, served in several parliaments in the same reign; as did also another Walter de Stirkeland, in the reign of King Richard II. In the reign of Henry IV. William Stirkeland was bishop of Carlisle,* and dying Aug. 30, 1419, was buried in the cathedral, under an arch, in the north aisle, on one side the choir, where is yet to be seen his effigies, elegantly cut in freestone, habited in his pontificalibus. And in the reign of Henry VI. Thomas Stirkeland, Esq. served in parliament for the county of Westmoreland; and John Stirkeland, Esq. for the same county, 12 Edw. IV.

I. Sir WILLIAM STRICKLAND, the first who was advanced to the dignity of a baronet, was son and heir of Walter Strickland, of Boynton, in Yorkshire, Esq. and of Frances, his wife, daughter of Peter Wentworth, of Lillingston Dayrel, in Bucks, Esq.) who was the son of William Strickland, Esq. which Sir William Strickland, Knt. and Bart. married first Margaret, eldest daughter of Sir Richard Cholmondeley, of Whitby, in Yorkshire, Knt. by whom he had four daughters; 1, Frances, the wife of Barington Bourchier, of Beningbrough, Esq.† 2, Margaret, of Sir John Cockeran, of Ocheltree, in Scotland, Knt. second son of William, lord Cockeran; 3, Milcha, of William Lawson, Esq. son and heir of Sir William Lawson, of Isell, in Cumberland, Knt. and 4, Elizabeth, of William, son and heir of Sir Henry St. Quintin, Bart. His second wife was Frances Finch, eldest daughter of Thomas, earl of Winchelsea,‡ by whom he had Sir Thomas, his son and heir. This Sir William was a considerable person in Oliver Cromwell's time, and one of those the protector summoned to take place as a lord,§ and to have that dignity in all commissions: he died about 1671, and was succeeded in dignity and estate by his only son,

II. Sir THOMAS STRICKLAND, Bart. who married Elizabeth, daughter and co-heiress of Sir Francis Pile, of Compton Beauchamp, in Berks, Bart. and had issue Sir William, his successor, and four other sons: also a daughter, ——, the wife of John Smith, Esq. speaker of the house of commons.

III. Sir WILLIAM STRICKLAND, Bart. successor to the title and estate, served in several parliaments in the reigns of King Wm. Queen Anne, and King George I. (who constituted him commissary-general of the musters) for Malton, in

---

* William Stirkeland, who had been before elected bishop of Carlisle, in 1395, but kept out of it till 1399, received the temporalities Nov. 15 that year, and became consecrated at Cawood, Aug. 15, 1400, by the archbishop of York, on the king's recommendation of him to the pope. He was a great benefactor to his cathedral, as his predecessor, Thomas Merks, alias de Newmarket, alias Somastro, monk of Westminster, had been to the bishoprick, by new building the belfry, and furnishing it with four bells; new roofing the choir, and making handsome stalls in it, as Leland informs us, in his *Collectanea*, in these words:—*Fecit Magnum Campanile a mediatate ad summum, una cum 4 magnis Campanis in eodem, & stalla perpulchra in choro, & co-operturam cancellæ ejusdem.* He likewise founded a chantry, in the church of St. Andrew's, at Peurith.

† By whom he left Sir Barington Bourchier, Knt. born in 1654. He was set down as possessing 1000*l*. a year, among such as were designed to have been knights of the royal oak [a strange circumstance, for the grandson of a regicide, to be so distinguished] and proves, that Charles II. who, with all his ill qualities, possessed mercy in an eminent degree, had reinstated the family in their personal estates, and perhaps very properly; for Sir Barington might be loyal, though descended from a traitor.

‡ Collins's Peerage, vol. III. p. 279.

§ See Catalogue of the Lords, &c. made by the Protector; printed in 1658, p. 3.

Yorkshire: he married Elizabeth, daughter of William Palmes, of Malton, in Yorkshire, Esq. who died in 1740: he died May 12, 1724, and was succeeded by his son,

IV. Sir WILLIAM STRICKLAND, Bart. who was elected member in the first parliament of King George I. for the city of Carlisle, in Cumberland; and in the first and second parliaments of King George II. for Scarborough, in Yorkshire; and was one of the right honourable the lords commissioners of the Treasury; afterwards treasurer to the queen's household, and secretary at war. He married Catharine, daughter of Sir Jeremy Sambrooke, of London, Knt. and died at Boynton, in Yorkshire, Sep. 1, 1735, leaving Sir George, his successor, and a daughter, the wife of —— Freeman, Esq. Sir William was succeeded by his son,

V. Sir GEORGE STRICKLAND, Bart. who married ————, by whom he has three sons; 1, William, who in 1778 married ————, daughter of Nathaniel Cholmley, of Howsham, Esq. 2, George, who in 1792 married ————, daughter of the late C. Craggs, Esq. 3, Charles, who was captain of the second battallion of the 82d regiment of foot; and died at Gibraltar Dec. 6, 1795.

ARMS—Gules, a chevron, or, between three crosses pattee, argent; on a canton, ermine, a buck's head, erased and attired, sable.

CREST—On a wreath, a turkey-cock in his pride, proper.

MOTTO—*A la Volonté de Dieu.*

SEAT—At Boynton, in Yorkshire.

WILLIAM STRICKLAND TABLE 75.

Walter = Frances Wentworth

Margaret Cholmondeley = I. Sir Wm. Strickland, Knt. & Bart. died about 1671 = Frances, dr. of Thomas E. of Winchelsea

Frances	Margaret	Milcha	Elizabeth	II. Sir Thomas, Bart.
Barington Bourchier	Sir John Cockeran	William Lawson	Wm. St. Quintin	Elizabeth Pile

III. Sir William Strickland, Bart. 1724 = Elizabeth Palmes N = John Smith 4 sons
1740

IV. Sir William, 1735 = Catharine Sambroke, 1767

V. Sir George Strickland N = —— Freeman

William = —— Cholmley George = —— Craggs Charles, 1795

75. BOUGHTON, of LAWFORD, WARWICKSHIRE.

Created Baronet Aug. 4, 1641.

OF this ancient family was Robert de Boveton, who had issue Richard, father of William, temp. Edw. III. His son William de Boveton, alias Boughton, was father of Richard, 2 Henry VI. His son Thomas is mentioned by Sir William Dugdale, in his Antiquities of the county of Warwick, to be possessed of the manor and seat at Lawford, by marriage, about the year 1440, with Elizabeth, daughter and heiress of Geoffery de Allesley, of that place, which he chose for his residence.* He was constituted a justice of peace in Warwickshire 21 Henry VI. and so continued till the end of that king's reign, as appears by several renewings of those commissions. In 31 Henry VI. he served in parliament, as one of the knights of the shire, for the county of Warwick, and in the 38th was appointed, with others, to array and arm all persons of body able, and estate sufficient, within that county, for the king's service.†

7. Richard, his son and heir, was constituted escheator for the counties of Warwick and Leicester, in 13 Edw. IV. and 1 Edw. V. and again sheriff of those

---

* We find that fines were levied in the 19th and 27th of Henry VI. of the manors of Little Lalleford, Little Herdeburgh, Newbold super Avon, and Long Lalleford, to the heirs of this marriage; in consequence whereof the descent of Boughton, from Sir William Allesley, of Grenburghe, Knt. Sir Gilbert de Sutton, Knt. John de Brailes, Francis de Dicheford, and William Harper de Rushall, by various alliances with the heiresses of those families, for about 200 years anterior to that date, is preserved amongst the Harleian Manuscripts, at the British Museum, No. 1196, fol. 20.

† A handsome monument to the memory of Geoffery Allesley, and Eleanor his wife, still remaining in the middle aisle of Newbold Church, in the county of Warwick, with this inscription round two recumbent figures:—Hic jacet Galfridus Allesley et uxor ejus, qui obiit xviii. die Augusti A° Dni. MCCCI. Quorum animabus propitietur Deus. Amen.

A similar monument, in the same church, of Thomas Boughton, and Elizabeth his wife, representing him in a suit of armour, with sword and spurs, a coronet on his head, and a bear at his feet, chained and muzzled, has the following inscription. *Dugd. Warw. p. 64.*

Quisquis eris, qui transieris, sta perlege, plora;
Sum quod eris, fueram que quod es; prome precor ora.

Orate pro bono statu Thomæ Boughton, & pro animâ Elizabet, ux. ejus, quæ obiit xx die. Mensis May, An. Dni. MCCCCLIIII. Lra Dnicalis A.

Sir William Dugdale says, the said Thomas Boughton was a Bedfordshire gentleman, as he had heard. However, there seems more reason to imagine the family came into Warwickshire out of the adjacent county of Northampton, since this Thomas is in a deed of 2 Henry VI. described as the son of Richard, the son of William Boughton, of Northampton, where the said William held certain messuages, by conveyance, from his father, Willielmus de Boveton, before date. From this circumstance, and from a benefaction in land, given to a monastery in that town, by Robert, son of Robert de Boveton, and confirmed by King Edw. III. in the second year of his reign, 1329, it is clear, that the family had possessions in the county of Northampton, as early as the 13th century. Moreover, it is stated, in Edmondton's Baronagium, that Sir Simon Monagu, ancestor to the Dukes of Manchester and Montagu, &c. *(circ. An. 1376)* married Elianor (in other places called Elizabeth) daughter and heir of William de Boughton, of Boughton, in the county of Northampton.

counties in 2 Rich. III. and lost his life in his service; but how is variously related. The tradition is, that he was killed in Bosworth field; but the inquisition taken after his death expresses, that he died Aug. 20, 3 Rich. III. which was two days before the battle; therefore it is probable, that raising forces in the county for the king, he was encountered by some of the Earl of Richmond's troops, in their passage towards Bosworth, and by that means lost his life. He married Agnes, daughter of —— Longvile, and had issue,

8. William Boughton, 12 years old at the death of his father, who was esquire of the body to King Henry VIII. which was, in those days, a post of high honour and distinction.* He married first ——, one of the daughters and co-heirs of John Danvers, of Waterstoke, in Oxfordshire, Esq. and by her had Edward Boughton, Esq. of whom hereafter; secondly, Elizabeth Barrington, of the Isle of Wight; from which match proceeded Thomas Boughton, Esq. who married Margaret, daughter and heiress of Edward Cave, Esq. and by grant, 37 Henry VIII. had possession of Causton, in the parish of Dunchurch. He was father of Edward Boughton, who, through the countenance of Robert, earl of Leicester (a potent man in Queen Elizabeth's time) bore a great sway in this county; and having got materials, by pulling down the White Friar's Church, in Coventry, raised here the most beautiful fabric that was then in all these parts. He married Susannah, daughter of Sir John Brocket, Knt. and died in 1589, leaving a daughter, Margaret, the wife of Thomas Trussell, of Billesley Colvar, Esq. and Henry, his son and heir; who, by his first wife, Howard, daughter of Edward Leigh, of Rushall, in Staffordshire, Esq. had issue Edward, who died in Oct. 1642, leaving a daughter, the wife first of Sir Richard Wortley, of Wortley, in Yorkshire, and secondly, of William Cavendish, first Earl of Devonshire; and by his second wife, Joyce, daughter of William Coombe, of Old Stratford, Esq. he had William and another son: William died without issue, and was buried, March 17, 1663; when the estate came to his nephew, Francis, which Francis Boughton, Esq. built and endowed a handsome free school at Dunchurch, in the county of Warwick, with a suitable establishment for a master and his family, in order that the children of the inhabitants of that parish might be instructed there gratis, for ever.† He married Frances, daughter of Sir Thomas Norton, of Coventry, Knt. and dying in the year 1709, without issue, he devised his estate to his kinsman, Edward Boughton, Esq. a younger branch of the Lawford family (son of Henry, and grandson of Sir William, the first baronet) who was high sheriff of Warwickshire in 1712; and married Jane, daughter and heiress of

* In the 8th year of that reign, he received a new grant of armorial bearings, an entire copy of which very curious record is now preserved in the Herald's College (*Vincent*, No. 88, fo. 2) under the double seals of the garter and Clarencieux, kings at arms. The grant bears strong testimony of the high reputation, virtue, and bravery of the said William Boughton. But the special occasion of this distinction does not appear; nor any cause for disusing the more simple coat of *sable*, three crescents, *or*, which seems to have been borne by his grandfather, Thomas, and was engraved upon his monument in six different places, as it is delineated by Sir William Dugdale.

† The estates he allotted by his will, for the maintenance of the master, were called Spittle Moor, near Coventry Walls, and another, near that city, known by the name of Ro Oakfield. He also left 30l. to buy plate for the communion table. *See Wotton and Kimber.*

Michael Tesmond, citizen of London, but left no issue; and in him ended the wealthy line of the Boughtons, of Causton. We return to

9. Edward Boughton, Esq. before-mentioned, son of Sir William (by his first wife, the daughter of John Danvers, Esq.) who, 33 Henry VIII. obtained a grant from the crown, of the lands called Newbold Grange; and married Elizabeth, daughter and co-heir of William Willington, of Barcheston, Esq. He died 1 Edw. VI. and was succeeded by his son and heir,*

10. William, who married Jane, sister of Sir Thomas Coningsby, of Hampton Court, in the county of Hereford, Knt. He was sheriff for the counties of Warwick and Leicester, 17 and 32 Queen Eliz. and in the commission of the peace during the greatest part of her reign. He died 38 Eliz. and was buried in the chancel of the church at Newbold.

11. Edward Boughton, Esq. his son and heir, was sheriff of the county of Warwick, 4 James, and in the commission of the peace. He improved his estate by adding to it the manor of Bilton, in Warwickshire, &c. and by Elizabeth, daughter and heir of Edward Catesby, of Lapworth Hall, in Warwickshire, Esq. a younger son of Sir Richard Catesby, of Ashby Legers, in Northamptonshire, Knt. he had issue William and Thomas, and a daughter, Catharine, the wife of William Combe, of Stratford upon Avon, in Warwickshire, Esq. On Thomas, his father settled the manor of Bilton; and he married Judith, one of the daughters and co-heirs of Henry Baker, of South Shobery, in Essex, Esq. by whom he had a son Thomas; who, by Mary, daughter of Sir Thomas Halford, of Leicestershire, Knt. was father of Edward Boughton, of Bilton, whom we shall have to mention in a future place; and of a daughter, Elizabeth, who died in 1702.†

I. WILLIAM BOUGHTON, Esq. of Lawford, his eldest son, was sheriff of Warwickshire, 8 Charles I. and having married Abigail, the eldest daughter of the aforesaid Henry Baker, Esq. was, by King Charles I. created a baronet, on the 4th of Aug. 1641. He left issue three sons, Sir Edward, Sir William, and Henry Boughton, who died July 17, 1668, leaving two sons, Humphrey and Edward, by his wife, Mary, daughter of Thomas Plant, of Shackerston, in Leicestershire, and widow of the Rev. Mr. Smith, of Stoke Goulding, in that county. Humphrey had a house and property at Allesley, in the county of Warwick, where he was buried in 1708, aged 46, with his wife, Dorothy, daughter of John Lacon, of West Coppice, in the county of Salop, Esq. and his daughters, Margaret and Bridget, born by a second wife. Edward afterwards inherited the magnificent house and estate of Caus-

---

* He lies buried in the church of Newbold super Avon, in Warwickshire, under a handsome monument, with this inscription:—Edwardus Boughton obiit mortem xxIII. die mensis Aprilis, A. D. 1548. Eliz. Boughton, uxor Edwardi, obiit mortem xxII. die mensis Aprilis, A. D. 1588, whose joy is in the Lord God. *Wotton, p. 222, vol. II.*

† Edward Boughton, of the elder branch, and his wife, both lie buried in the same church, with this inscription over them:—Here lieth the bodies of Edward Boughton, Esq. and Eliz. his wife, daughter of Edw. Catesby, of Lepworth Hall, in the county of Warwick, Esq. by whom he had issue two sons, William and Thomas; and one daughter, Catharine: which Thomas married Judith, one of the daughters and co-heirs of Henry Baker, of South Sowburie, in the county of Essex, Esq. and Catharine married William Combe, of Stratford upon Avon, in the county of Warwick, Esq. which Edward died the 9th of August, 1625; and Eliz. died the 12th of April, 1619.

ton, on the death of his kinsman, Francis Boughton, in 1709, whose ancestor, Thomas, had obtained a grant thereof from the crown, in 37 Henry VIII. Humphrey left five daughters and co-heiresses, one of whom, Judith, was the wife of Thomas Harris, Esq. of Rugby, who died in 1781.

II. Sir EDWARD, his eldest son, succeeded in honour and estate: he served in several parliaments as one of the knights of the shire for the county of Warwick, temp. Charles II. and sheriff of the county 13 Charles II. and married first.——, eldest daughter of Thomas Pope, earl of Down; secondly, Anne, daughter of Sir John Heyden, Knt. governor of Bermudas; but having no issue, the honour and estate devolved on his next brother,

III. Sir WILLIAM BOUGHTON, Bart. who was high sheriff of Warwickshire 1 Wm. and Mary, and married Mary, daughter of Hastings Ingram, Esq. of Little Woolford, in Warwickshire; by whom he had issue one son, Sir William, and three daughters; 1, Abigail, the wife of her second cousin, Edward Boughton, of Bilton, Esq. by whom she had two sons and four daughters; 1, William Boughton, of Bilton, Esq. who sold that lordship, in the year 1712, to Joseph Addison, Esq. and died in 1721; Elizabeth, who died in 1691; Anne in 1685; Mary, and Abigail, the wife of —— Barton. Edward, the second son, by his wife, Anne, left two daughters, Elizabeth and Catharine, the wife of Heward Oxburgh, and one son, William Boughton, of Rugby, who married Anna Deacon (afterwards the wife of William Caldecott) and died in 1746, leaving Anna, an only daughter and heiress to his manor of Rugby: she was the wife of the late Alexander Hume, of London, Esq. father of Abraham Hume, Esq. now of Bilton Grange, and Alexander; and two daughters, Anna-Hannah, the wife of Ambrose Proctor, and Harriott. Abraham, the elder son, married Sally, the daughter of Sir Charles Wheler, Bart. and has three sons.

The other daughter of Sir William, the third baronet, was Catharine the wife of William Smith, of Pelton, in Warwickshire, Esq. Sir William* died August 12, 1683: his lady, Feb. 24, 1693, and was succeeded by his son,

IV. Sir WILLIAM, who was (on the Earl of Northampton's being called up to the house of peers, as Lord Compton, in the reign of Queen Anne) unanimously chosen one of the knights of the shire for the county of Warwick; and in that station he honourably preferred the independence of a country gentleman, to the seductions of courtly favour, having declined the offer of peerage. He married first Mary, daughter of John Ramsey, Esq. an alderman of the city of London; by whom he had issue one son, Sir Edward, and two daughters; Mary, the wife of Sir Henry Hoghton, of Hoghton Tower, in Lancashire, Bart. and Anne. He married secondly, Catharine, daughter of Sir Charles Shuckburgh, Bart. who survived him; and by her he had five sons (of which William, Thomas, and Catharine died young) Shuckburgh, and Richard; with three daughters, Catharine, Meliza, and Elizabeth.

* This Sir William and his lady both lie buried in the chancel of Newbold church, where is thus inscribed, within the rails in the chancel, on a flat stone:—Hic situs est Gulielmus Boughton, Baronettus, obiit die duodecimo Augusti, Anno Ætatis suæ quinquagesimo tertio, 1683. And on another stone:—Hic jacet Maria, uxor Gulielmi Boughton, Baronetti, defuncti, obiit 24 Februarii, Anno Salutis 1693, Ætatis suæ 63. *Wotton, vol. II. p. 223.*

He died July 22, 1786, aged 53, and lies buried in Newbold upon Avon church, in Warwickshire.†

V. Sir EDWARD BOUGHTON, his only son by the first venter, succeeded to the title and estate: he was high sheriff of the county of Warwick 7 George I. and married Grace, eldest daughter of Sir John Shuckburgh, Bart. who survived her husband, and afterwards became the wife of —— Lister, Esq. son and heir of Matthew Lister, of Burwell, in Cambridgeshire. He, dying in Feb. 1721-2, at the age of 33, was succeeded by his son, and only child,

VI. Sir EDWARD BOUGHTON, Bart. who served the office of high sheriff for the county of Warwick, in 1748: he married first a daughter of —— Bridges, of the county of Somerset, Esq. by whom he had no issue; and secondly, Anna-Maria Beauchamp, who was an heiress of that ancient family. He died in 1772, leaving an only son, who succeeded to the title.

VII. Sir THEODOSIUS-EDWARD-ALLESLEY BOUGHTON, Bart. and one daughter, Theodosia, the wife of John Donellan, Esq. whose history has excited too much of the public attention to be passed over in this place ‡

We return now to the issue of Sir William, by his second marriage, with Catharine, daughter of Sir Charles Shuckburgh, Bart. by Catharine, daughter of Sir Hugh Stewkley, Bart. Shuckburgh Boughton, Esq. the eldest surviving son, was of Baliol College, in Oxford, and had for his inheritance an ancient family estate in the county of Leicester, under which they were arrayed for that county in the wars

---

† There is fixed to the south wall of the church a very handsome monument, with two statues of marble, in full proportion, erect, finely executed by Rysbrach, with the following inscription:—

Near this marble, in the vault of his ancestors, are deposited the sacred remains of Sir William Boughton, Bart. descended of an honourable and ancient family; but far greater in personal worth, than pedigree: for he has left to posterity an example of a tender and most endearing husband, a kind and prudent father, a generous neighbour, an hospitable entertainer of his friends at his table, and a constant receiver of the poor at his gates. These valuable qualities so effectually recommended him to the esteem and favour of his county, that he was unanimously elected their representative in the parliament of Queen Anne, renowned for peace; where his steady and untainted principles, loyalty to his sovereign, and zeal for the established church of England, eminently distinguished him. His mournful widow, Dame Catharine Boughton (the daughter of Sir Charles Shuckburgh, of Shuckburgh, Bart. and of Catharine Stewekeley, daughter to Sir Hugh Stewekeley, of Hinton, in Hampshire, Bart., Utroque Parente Augusta) in gratitude to his memory has erected this monument, not as a complete register of his well known merits, but as a sincere testimony of her conjugal affection. Ob. Jul. 22, Anno Dni. 1716, Ætat. 53. In this vault lie the bodies of William, Thomas, and Charles Boughton, sons of Sir William, and his wife, Dame Catharine Boughton, who died in their infancy.

‡ The sudden death of Sir Theodosius, at Lawford Hall, on the 29th of Aug. 1780, then in his 21st year, created such strong suspicions, and such as were pointed to Mr. Donellan, by various odd and questionable circumstances in his behaviour, that the body was taken up for examination, after it had been deposited in the family vault at Newbold; and in pursuance of the verdict of a coroner's inquest, Mr. Donellan was committed to prison at Warwick: where he was, on the 29th of March following, indicted for the supposed murder, before Mr. Justice Buller, at the joint prosecution of Sir Theodosius's mother, lady Boughton, and his successor, Sir Edward Boughton, of whom hereafter; was found guilty, after a trial which lasted 12 hours, and was executed at Warwick, April 2, 1781.

The poison by which this horrid act was perpetrated, was declared to be laurel water, and although to the last he made protestations of his innocence, little doubt has been entertained of his actual guilt. His widow, who inherited the greater part of the family fortune, became afterwards the wife of Sir Egerton Leigh, Bart.

of York and Lancaster; but he resided in the mansion and estate of Poston Court, in Herefordshire, which he purchased of Lord Arthur Somerset, second surviving son of Henry, first duke of Beaufort. He married in 1736, Mary, daughter of the hon. Algernon Greville, by Mary, daughter and co-heir of the said Lord Arthur Somerset, and had a numerous family.*

Richard Boughton, the next son, who was of All Soul's College, in Oxford, died a batchelor at Lyons, in France, where he went for the recovery of his health. Catharine was the wife of Sir George Walters, of Worcester Park, in Surrey, Knt. who walked as Duke of Aquitaine, at the coronation of George II. She died without issue in 1733, and lies buried at Malden, in Surrey. Meliza was the wife of the Rev. Henry Layng, of Baliol College, Oxford, afterwards a prebendary of Lincoln, and one of Mr. Pope's associates in his translation of Homer. She survived her husband, and died at the age of 83, in April, 1795, after having a son, who died at the university, a fellow of All Soul's College, and two daughters; one of whom was first the wife of Major Frankland, Bart. whose daughter was the wife of Penyston Portlock Powney, Esq. late member for Windsor; and secondly of Capt. Blomberg, father of the Rev. Mr. Blomberg, private secretary to the Prince of Wales, and now a prebendary of Bristol. Elizabeth, the youngest daughter, was the wife of Lieut. General Brudenell, and had sons, two of which are now living.

The said Shuckburgh died in the year 1763, about the age of 60. On the marriage of his present majesty, George III. in 1761, Mrs. Boughton was appointed one of the six bedchamber-women to the queen, in which station she continued till her death, March 1, 1786, aged 73, when she was buried by her husband, at St. Mary le Bone, in Middlesex. Their issue was 1, Arthur, who died in his infancy; 2, Sir Edward, the late baronet; 3, Mary, who became the second wife of Dr. John Egerton, first cousin of the Duke of Bridgewater, and bishop of Durham. She survived her husband five years, and died without issue, in 1792. 4, Anne, the wife of Capt. John Rutherford, who died without issue, by a fall from his horse, at the German Spa, in 1781: 5, Elizabeth, the wife of Clotworthy, lord Templetown, of Castle Upton, in the kingdom of Ireland, and a lady of the bed-chamber to her late royal highness the Princess Amelia, sister of King George II. He died in 1785, leaving three sons, viz. John-Henry, lord Templetown, who married Lady Mary Montagu, only daughter of the Earl of Sandwich; Fulke-Greville Upton, and Arthur-Percy Upton, officers in the guards; and three daughters, Eliza-Albana, the wife of John, lord Hervey, heir apparent to the Earl of Bristol; Caroline, and Sophia. 6, Sir Charles-William, the present baronet; 7, Lucy, the wife of Robert

---

* It was to this lady, that George, lord Littleton addressed, in the year 1735, his elegant little ode, on the occasion of Mr. Pope having lent his villa at Twickenham to the hon. Mrs. Greville.

Go Pope, and tell the busy town,	But now, sweet bard, thy heavenly song,
Not all its wealth or pride,	Enchant us here no more;
Could tempt me from the charms that crown	Their darling glory, lost too long,
Thy rural flowery side;	Thy once-loved shades deplore.
Thy flowery side, where Pope has placed	Yet still, for beauteous Greville's sake,
The Muse's green retreat;	The Muses here remain;
With every smile of nature graced,	Greville, whose eyes have power to make,
With every art complete.	A Pope of every swain.

Dodsley's Poems, vol. II. p. 56.

Wright, Esq. of the county of Suffolk, who has two daughters, Frances-Lucy, and Marianne. 8, William, who died in Bengal, under age, in the year 1773: 9, Jane, who died unmarried in 1781.

VIII. Sir EDWARD BOUGHTON, Bart. the eldest surviving son, was appointed a clerk in the Treasury, during his father's life. In 1780 he succeeded to the title, as above related, on the death of Sir Theodosius, with some part of the Warwickshire estates: but he pulled down the mansion house of Lawford Hall, and afterwards sold his estates in Warwickshire and Leicestershire, in order to enlarge those in Herefordshire, in which county he served the office of high sheriff, in 1786. He died unmarried, of a decline, in Jan. 1794, in the 53d year of his age; and was interred at Vow church, in Herefordshire; when the title devolved upon his only brother,

IX. Sir CHARLES-WILLIAM ROUSE BOUGHTON, Bart. In the year 1765, he went out to Bengal upon the civil establishment, where he distinguished himself by a knowledge of various languages used in that country, and discharged many respectable employments with ability and applause.* In the year 1768 he succeeded to a considerable estate in Rouse Lench, Hob Lench (or Abbot's Lench) Church Lench, and Westmancote, in the county of Worcester, and took the name and arms of Rouse, of Rouse Lench, from which family he was maternally descended, as will appear in a future part of this work, under the article of ROUSE, and in the genealogical tables: we shall then have to enter more particularly into the history of this ancient Norman family, which appears to have been settled in Warwickshire and Worcestershire soon after the Norman conquest, under the names of Rufus, Le Rous, Rouse, Rowse, and other modes of spelling.

* We find it stated by the Select Committee of the House of Commons (of which he was a member) appointed to consider the state of the administration of justice in Bengal, and how the British possessions in the East Indies might be best held and governed for the advantage of this country, and happiness of the natives, that during the period of near two years that he presided in a court, instituted for the decision of all causes of property amongst the natives in the city of Calcutta, between two and three thousand judgements were passed, from which there were no more than 25 appeals to the superior court, and no reversal in any one of them. His last station was that of Provincial Chief of Dacca, where it was said, by the Mahomedan and Hindoo inhabitants of that rich district, that his administration would be gratefully remembered as long as one stone remained of the ancient palace of the Mogul Viceroys: for he not only protected them in their heriditary property, and encouraged the freedom of trade, but guarded them against the violation of their civil and religious usages, which were infringed by the court of English law, established at Calcutta in 1773; and closed one of the remonstrances from him, and his provincial council, to the supreme government, with this humane and energetic appeal:—"As British-born subjects, we revere and glory in the sublime system of English penal law; but we should be wanting in the duty we owe to you, gentlemen, who are invested with the government of this territory, and to the inhabitants of the province we have the honour to superintend, if we were to refrain from remonstrance, when we see men, neither connected with Europeans, nor conversant in their customs, forced away to be tried as criminals, upon the solemn charge of life and death, at the distance of 500 miles from their friends and families, in a language, and mode of process, totally unknown to them; in the court of a British sovereign, who has never been announced to them; and by the test of laws, which have never been promulgated."

This subject was farther brought before parliament by him, in a speech of considerable length, in the sessions of 1781, and referred to a committee, who presented a very large report upon the alledged grievances; and after much discussion in both houses, an act was passed, to limit the jurisdiction of the English courts. *See Com. Reports, and Parliamentary Register,* 1781-2.

He returned from Bengal in 1778, and in the year 1780 was elected, after a sharp contest, member for the borough of Evesham, in Worcestershire, which had been represented in the last century by the Rouse Lench family. He was again chosen for the same place, without opposition, in the year 1784, and continued to represent that borough till the dissolution of parliament, in 1790. When a law was passed in 1784, under the administration of the right hon. William Pitt, for the better regulation of the affairs of India, which gave power to his majesty to constitute a board of commissioners, from the members of the privy council, for the general superintendance and controul of the British territorial possessions in the East Indies; Mr. Boughton Rouse was appointed chief secretary to that board, and on relinquishing the office in 1791, was, on the 21st of June, in that year, created a baronet, by his majesty, as a mark of public approbation, by the style of Sir Charles-William Boughton Rouse, of Rouse Lench, in the county of Worcester, and of Downton Hall, in the county of Salop: but on succeeding to his family baronetage, in Jan. 1794, by the death of his brother, Sir Edward, who died unmarried, he again altered his name, in conformity to the royal sign manual, which enables him and his male issue, entitled to the possession of the manor of Rouse Lench, to use and bear the name of Rouse either before or after that of Boughton; and his succession is accordingly so entered in the herald's college, by the style of Sir Charles William Rouse Boughton, Bart. pursuant to the regulations established for the order of baronets.*

Upon the general election, which took place in May 1796, he was returned member of parliament for the borough of Bramber, in Sussex, but vacated his seat in Dec. 1799, on being appointed, by patent under the great seal, one of the commissioners for auditing the public accounts of the kingdom, which office he now holds.

He married in 1782, Catharine, only daughter and heiress of William Pearce Hall, of Downton Hall, in the county of Salop, Esq. and thereby became possessed of the manors of Downton, Middleton, Bitterley, Ledwich, and Clee Staunton, and a moiety of Corpham and Culmington (which he has since sold) all in that county. His children are Catharine-Maria, who died in infancy; Louisa, Caroline, and William-Edward.

* Besides some smaller tracts and translations, from the Eastern languages, he published, in 1791, "*A Dissertation concerning the Landed Property of Bengal,*" dedicated to the right hon. Henry Dundas, then president of the board of controul for the affairs of India; in which he labours, in opposition to the notions of various European travellers, and even some of the servants of the East India Company, to establish, from histories written in the Persian language, and from official documents of the Indian government, the justice and policy of considering the lands of that extensive country, as hereditary property; which we understand has now been publicly confirmed to them.

In June, 1798, when the daring designs of the revolutionary government of France threatened, by a powerful invasion of Great Britain, the absolute destruction of the naval power, commerce, and free constitution of the country, and the utmost exertions of the nation were called forth by the government and the legislature, Sir Charles promoted an armed association amongst the inhabitants of Chiswick, in the county of Middlesex, whom he had before stimulated to unanimity and vigour, in a speech, which was published at their request, and passed through several editions. *(See British Critic, vol. XIII. p. 415).* He accordingly became their commander, under his majesty's commission, and as such, attended the volunteer reviews in Hyde Park, in honour of his majesty's birth-day, on the 4th of June, 1799 and 1800.

BOUUHTON, OF LAWFORD, WARWICKSHIRE.

ARMS.

Two Coats for Boughton of Lawford.

1. By grant of Henry VIII. Argent, on a chevron, between three crosslets botoné, fitchy; sable, three stags' head caboshed, or; on a chief, gules, a goat passant, of the field, for Boughton.
2. Ancient coat. Sable, three crescents, or, also for Boughton.
3. Sable, two bars, engrailed, argent, for Rous, or Rouse, of Rouse Lench.
4. Azure, fretty; argent, a chief of the last, for Allesley.
5. Gules, a chevron, between three mullets of six points, or, for Danvers.
6. Gules, a saltire, vair, for Willington.
7. Argent, two lions, passant gardant, sable; crowned, or, for Catesby.
8. Ermine, on a bar, engrailed; argent, three fleurs de lis, for Baker.

The Boughtons also quarter, by means of the several heiresses, with whose families they have intermarried, the arms of Sutton, Dicheford, Brailes, Harper, Aylesbury, Brandiston, Bishopsden, Pipard, Sheldon, Riviere, Coleshall, Dela Beech, Bracestre, Pusey, Craunford, Keynes, Arden, Trillow, Williamscote, Lodbroke Baresworth, &c.

Over the whole, on an escutcheon of pretence, for the arms of his lady, quarterly.

1. Sable, two bars, ermine, biletty of the first; in chief, a hound's head erased, between two chaplets, or, for Hall.
2. Argent, gutty, gules; a chief nebuleé of the last, for Pearce.
3. Azure, on a chevron, or, three estoiles, gules, between as many fleurs de lis, of the second, for Sheppard.
4. Or, a lion rampant, sable, for Wredenhall.

   CRESTS—On a wreath, or and sable, a stork's head erased, cheveronny of four pieces, sable and argent; in the beak a snake, proper, being the crest of Boughton.
2. On a wreath, sable and argent, a man's head, proper; beard, hair, and whiskers, sable: the head surrounded and crossed with a riband, knotted at the top, and flowing from the sides, argent, for Rous, or Rouse, of Rouse Lench.

MOTTO—*Ohne Bonum, Dei Donum.*

SEATS—At Rouse Lench, in Worcestershire; Downton Hall, in Shropshire; and Corney House, Chiswick, in the county of Middlesex.

TABLE 75.

BOUGHTON, OF LAWFORD, WARWICKSHIRE.

1 ROBERT DE BOVETON
2 Richard de Boveton
3 William de Boveton
4 William Boughton
   ├─ 5 Richard Boughton
   ├─ 6 Thomas = Elizabeth Allesley
   └─ 7 Richard = Agnes Longville

— Danvers = 8 William = Elizabeth Barington
9 Edward Boughton, 1547 = Elizabeth Willington
10 William Boughton, 1596 = Jane Coningsby
11 Edward Boughton, 1622 = Elizabeth Catesby, 1619

BILTON BRANCH.

CAUSTON BRANCH.

Thomas Boughton = Mary Cave
Edward Boughton, 1589 = S. Brocket
Margaret = T. Trussell │ H. Leigh = Henry = J. Combe
                                      Wm. Boughton, 1663 │ a son
                                      Francis, 1707 Fran. Norton

I. Sir Wm. Boughton │ Abigail Baker │ Catharine = Wm. Combe │ Thomas = Judith Baker │ Edw. Boughton, 1642
II. Sir Edward   Thomas │ Rich. Wm. Rumph. Mary │ Anne │ Judith │ Edward │ Abigail │ Eliz. │ Edward
   Pope │ A. Heydon   III. Sir William, 1683   M. Hatfield Sir R. Wortley │ Wm. E. of Devon St. John │ Thomas │ Howsley │ Boughton │ Barton │ Anne
                         Mary Ingram   co-heiresses   Taylor │ Harris │ Fowman   Mary
IV. Sir William, 1716 │ Catharine │ Humphrey, 1705 │ Edward
M. Kam- │ C. Shuck-   Abigail │ Wm.   Dorothy Lacon │ Jane Tesmond   5 drs.   William   Eliz.
sey   │ burgh   Edward │ Smith   1721   Anne   Wm. Catharine
                       Boughton   Jane Heward
V. Sir Edward │ Mary │ Anne │ Wm. Shuckburgh │ Rich.   Catharine │ Meliza   Eliz.   Elizabeth │ IX. Sir C.W. Lacy Wm. Anne
   1721   Sir Henry   1765   Sir George Rev. Hen.   Lord   R. Boughton Robert Jane Deacon
Grace Shuck- Hoghton   M. Greville   Walker Laying   Templetown Cath. Hall Wright
burgh
VI. Sir Edw. Bough- │ Arthur │ VIII. Sir Edw. │ Marg. Anne   Catie-Maria Louisa Caroline Wm-Edw.
    ton, 1772   Boughton   Dr. Eger- J. Ruther-
Brydges │ A. M. Beau-   1794   ton   ford
champ
VII. Sir Theodo-us-Edward-   Theodosia   Anne Boughton
Allesley Boughton, 1780   John │ Sir Edw.   Alex. Hume
                                              Donellan Leigh

76. CHICHESTER, of RALEIGH, DEVONSHIRE.

Created Baronet Aug. 4, 1641.

THIS family seems anciently to have borne the name of Cirencester, and was one of the most eminent in the county of Devon, for its antiquity, estate, employments, and alliances, having flourished for several generations at South Poole, not far from King's Bridge, where their most ancient habitation was: and a full representation of their dignity is manifested by that learned antiquary, Sir William Pole, in his MS. survey of Devonshire; who assures us, that they have a right to quarter the arms of the Raleighs, the Beaumonts, the Willington's, and many other noble families.

1. Walleran de Cirencester[*] (thought to be so denominated from Cirencester, in Gloucestershire) said to be descended from a brother of Robert de Cirencester, alias Chichester, dean of Salisbury, and consecrated, in 1128, bishop of Exeter.

2. John, his son, succeeded, and was the father of

3. Sir John de Cirencester, whose son,

4. Sir Thomas, was lord of the manor of St. Mary-Church (an eminent sea-mark on the east side of Torbay) by his marriage with Alicia de Rotomago, in the time of Henry III. from the beginning of whose reign, in 1216, he sustained many honourable employments: he had one son,

5. William, the father of

6. Sir John Cirencester, whose son,

7. Richard, leaving the name of Cirencester, fixed upon Chichester, which has continued the surname of the family.

8. John de Chichester, his son, in 34, 45, and 46 Edw. III.[†] was member of parliament for Melcomb Regis, in Dorsetshire, as he also was in 1381; and was succeeded by his son,

9. Sir John de Cirencester, who in 1433 was returned one of the principal gentry in the county of Devon, by the king's commissioners; and marrying Thomasine, daughter and heiress of Sir William Raleigh, of Raleigh, near Barnstaple, in Devonshire,[‡] acquired that inheritance; and was father of

10. John, of Raleigh, who was sheriff of the county 3 Edw. IV. and left issue,

11. Richard Chichester, Esq. who in the 8th and 14th of that reign served the same office; and marrying Alice, daughter and heiress of John Wotton, or Watton, of Widworthy, that estate accrued thereby to the family. By her, besides other children, he had John, his heir; and Richard, his third son, who married Thomasine, daughter and heiress of Simon Hall, of Hall, in Bishop's Tawton, became

---

[*] Prince's Worthies of Devon, p. 135, and Fuller.   [†] Ulster's Office.   [‡] Ibid.

seated there; and his posterity matched into the eminent houses of Gough of Aldercomb, in Cornwall; Ackland, of Ackland; Marwood, of Westcott; Bassett, of Umberleigh; Strode, of Newnham; Pollard, Carew, and others.

12. John Chichester, the eldest son, married Margaret, daughter and heiress of Hugh Beaumont, of Youlston, in Devonshire, Esq. with whom he had that seat; and by her he had Edward, his heir: and by his second wife, Joan, daughter of Robert Brett, of Whitstaunton, in Somersetshire; and of Pillond, in Devonshire, he had a son, John Chichester, of Widworthy, in the east; and Amias, of Arlinston, in the north parts of Devonshire, whose posterity flourished at both places.

13. Edward Chichester, Esq. (by the first wife) lived in the reign of Henry VIII. and married Elizabeth,¶ eldest daughter of John Bourcher, lord Fitz-Warine, and the first Earl of Bath (by Cecilia, his wife, daughter of Gyles, lord D'Aubeny, and sister and heir of Henry, lord D'Aubeny, earl of Bridgewater, who died April, 1547, without issue) by whom he was father of

14. Sir John Chichester, Knt.‖ who was, in 1552 and 1578, high sheriff for the county of Devon, which, in 1553 and 1562, he represented in parliament.* He married Gertrude,† daughter of Sir William Courtenay, of Powderham Castle, in Devonshire, Knt. ancestor to the Lord Viscount Courtenay, by whom he had five sons and eight daughters; 1, Sir John, of whom hereafter; 2, Arthur, whose abilities and services raised him to the peerage of Ireland.‡ He married Lettice, daughter of Sir John Perrot, lord deputy of Ireland; and having no issue by her, made his brother, 3, Sir Edward Chichester, Knt. his son and heir; whose son Arthur was created Earl of Donnegal, ancestor to the present marquis.§ 4, Sir

¶ Ulster's Office. ‖ Idem. * Fuller's Worthies. † Ulster.

‡ Santon, in Devonshire, was the seat of Thomas de Santon, whose son's daughter, Melior, was the wife of Robert de Stockey. Joan, the last of this family that lived here, carried these possessions, by marriage, to —— Crawthorne; and Joan, their only daughter, brought the same, by her marriage to Sir John Beaumont, Knt. She was, secondly, the wife of Sir William Esturmay, but these lands descended in the line of Beaumont to the family of Chichester, and was, by Sir John Chichester, Knt. given to Arthur, his second son, a man of excellent worth, lord deputy of Ireland, baron of Belfast, and viscount Carrickfergus, who sold it. *Risdon's Devonshire, p.* 111.

In the time of Edw. III. one Robert Chichester, a learned man, wrote a Chronicle, beginning it from the first coming of the Saxons into this land, in 449, and continued it to the year 1348. *Ibid* 420.

§ Dr. Leland gives a high character of Sir Arthur Chichester, as lord deputy of Ireland. He advanced the work of reformation farther than had been done by any preceding governor. By his wise conduct inferiors were emancipated from the tyranny of barbarous chieftains, and the whole body of old natives were brought to regard this system of English policy more favourably, when it was executed, not like the mockery of justice with which they had too often been insulted, but with general impartiality, without oppression or impunity. *Hist. of Ireland, vol. II. p.* 418.

With respect to the plantations of Ulster, Dr. Leland thus describes the superior abilities of the lord deputy, for carrying on that important undertaking: "The thoughts of Lord Bacon on this subject had been more precise and accurate, if his great genius had been assisted by a competent knowledge of the state of Ireland: but the man whose counsels were of the greatest service on this interesting occasion, was Sir Arthur Chichester, now lord deputy of the realm. He had capacity, judgment, firmness, and experience, and was already distinguished by his services, both in war and peace. What was of the greatest consequence, no man was better acquainted with the territories he planted, the state of the inhabitants, their characters, expectations, and pretensions; so that none could be better qualified to propose a scheme for the plantation, or to direct the execution of it. He caused surveys to be taken of the several counties where the new settlements were to be established, particularly the state of

John Chichester, the younger, who, while his brother Arthur was in France, sought glory in Ireland, where his services were rewarded with the post of serjeant major of the army, and the honour of knighthood; so that he came to be distinguished from his elder brother of the same name and degree, by the title of Sir John Chichester the younger. It was no unusual thing for parents, in former times, to give a favourite name to more of their children than one, living at the same time. He was governor of Carricfergus, and lost his life Nov. 4, 1597, in the following manner: James Mac Sorley Mac Donnell, afterwards Earl of Antrim, had a strong detachment of Highland foot, in a cave, about four miles distant from Carricfergus, whilst he advanced with a small body towards that place; and braving the garrison, Sir John Chichester made a sally, when Mac Donnell, seeming to fly, till he had brought Sir John to the place where he had formed his ambuscade, turned upon him and his party, who being instantly surrounded, were defeated. Sir John was taken prisoner, and beheaded upon a stone, at the head of the Glynn.* 5, Sir Thomas, to whom King James, in 1607, granted a lease for 21 years, of divers lands in the county of Wicklow; and in 1610 gave to him and his heirs the lands of Radonnell, containing 1000 acres, in the county of Donnegal.

Of the daughters, 1 Elizabeth, was the wife of Hugh Fortescue, of Philleigh, Esq. 2, Eleanor, of Sir Arthur Basset, of Umberleigh, Knt. 3, Mary, of Sir Richard Bluet, of Holcomb Regis, Knt. 4, Grace, of Robert Dillon; 5, Cecilia, of Thomas Hatch, of Aller, Esq. 6, Susannah, of John Fortescue, of Buckland Philleigh, Esq. 7, Dorothy, of Sir Hugh Pollard, of King's Nimpton, Knt. 8, Urith, of John Trevilian, of Nettlecombe, in Somersetshire, Esq. ancestor to Sir John Trevilian, Bart. and 9, Bridget, the first wife of Sir Edward Prideaux, of Farway, and of Netherton, in Devonshire.†

15. Sir John Chichester, the eldest son, married Anne, daughter of Sir Robert Dennis, of Holcomb, Knt. and being killed, with the judge of assize and others, by an infectious smell from the prisoners, at the Lent assizes, in Exeter Castle, 1585, left issue,

---

each; pointed out the situations for the erections of towns and castles, delineated the characters of the Irish chieftains, the manner in which they should be treated, the temper and circumstances of the old inhabitants, the rights of new purchasers, and the claims of both; the impediments which had obstructed former plantations, and the methods of removing them." The measures pursued by the lord deputy in this affair, are distinctly related by Dr. Leland, who afterwards observes, that Sir Arthur Chichester's administration was indeed active, vigilant, cautious, and firm, suited to a country scarcely emerging to tranquility and order; where disaffection was yet unextinguished, and discontents were publicly and boldly avowed. The chief governor's moderation, with regard to his treatment of the recusants, is likewise celebrated by the historian of Ireland. Sir Arthur's management, in this respect, was indeed highly displeasing to the puritans, and even occasioned complaints and murmurs to be whispered against him in the privy council: but Dr. Leland is of opinion, and we think, with good reason, that his conduct was dictated by the plainest rules of discretion, and that it was the only conduct which could be pursued with safety.

A few of Sir Arthur's state papers are preserved in the British Museum. Dr. Leland has made considerable use of a collection of his manuscript papers, now in the library of the university of Dublin.

* In King James's reign, Mac Donnell going one day to view the family monument, in St. Nicholas's church, at Carricfergus, and seeing Sir John's statue thereon, asked "*how the de'ell he came to get his head again, for he was sure he had once ta'en it frae him.*" ‡ Ulster's Office.

16. Sir Robert Chichester, of Raleigh, K. B. who married Frances, younger daughter of John, lord Harrington, of Exton, and co-heir to her brother John, lord Harrington (who died without issue, at Kew, in Surrey, Aug. 27, 1613, three days after his father had deceased, at Worms, in Germany, on his return from attending the Princess Elizabeth, King James's daughter, to the palatinate, after her marriage with Frederick Count Palatine of the Rhine, of which princess he had the tuition); and by her he had an only daughter, Anne, the wife of Thomas, lord Kinloffe; by whom she was mother of Robert, earl of Aylesbury. She died March 20, 1627, and was buried at Exon Church, in Rutlandshire, under a curious monument of marble, with a memorial on one side, in Latin, which is Englished on the other.*

Sir Robert married secondly Mary, daughter of —— Hill, of Shelson, Esq. and dying in 1626, had issue by her (who remarried with Sir Ralph Sydenham, Knt.)

I. JOHN CHICHESTER, of Raleigh, Esq. advanced to the dignity of a baronet by King Charles I. He married Elizabeth, eldest daughter of Sir John Rayney, of Wrotham, in Kent, Bart. by whom he had three sons, Sir John, Sir Arthur, and Henry, who married the widow of John Chichester, of Hall, Esq. and dying in 1667, was succeeded in dignity and estate by his eldest son,

II. Sir JOHN CHICHESTER, Bart. who in Nov. 1679, married ——, daughter of Sir Charles Bickerstaff, of Sele, in Kent, Knt. They both died in Sep. 1680, and were buried in Sele church, in Kent: he, aged 22 years 3 months; she 21 years 3 months; and having no issue male, the honour and estate came to his brother,

III. Sir ARTHUR CHICHESTER, Bart. who married Elizabeth, daughter of Thomas Drewe, of Grange, in Devonshire, Esq. by whom he had Sir John, his successor, and six daughters; 1, Florence, the wife of William Northmore, Esq. member of parliament for Oakhampton, and died Jan. 1, 1725-6, aged 27; 2, Mary, of —— Courtney, of Mullan, in Devonshire, and secondly of Mr. Cheney, of Launceston, in Cornwall; 3, Anne, of Francis Fulford, of Great Fulford, in Devonshire; 4, ——, of a clergyman, in the Isle of Wight; 5, ——, of Mr. Berry; and 6, Elizabeth. Sir Arthur was elected to parliament for Barnstaple, in the county of Devon, in the reigns of King James II. King Wm. III. Queen Anne, and King George I. but dying in 1717, was succeeded in dignity and estate by his son,

IV. Sir JOHN CHICHESTER, Bart. member for Barnstaple, in Devonshire; and married Anne, daughter of John Leigh, of Newport, in the Isle of Wight, Esq. by whom he left two sons, Sir John and William, rector of Ham, in Devonshire, who married Miss Bellamin, of Devonshire, deceased, and left sons and daughters. Sir John had also three daughters; 1, ——, the wife of —— Musgrave, of Somersetshire, and afterwards of the Rev. John Sandford, rector of Moniton, in Somersetshire [this lady is since dead] 2, ——, the wife of William Sandford, of Minehead, in Somersetshire; 3, Florence. Sir John died in Aug. 1740, and was succeeded in dignity and estate by his eldest son,

V. Sir JOHN CHICHESTER, Bart. who served high sheriff for the county of Devon in 1753. He married Frances, second daughter, and one of the four co-

---

* See Wright's Antiq. of Rutlandshire, p. 59: also Lodge's Peerage of Ireland, vol. I. p. 317.

CHICHESTER, OF RALEIGH, DEVONSHIRE.

heirs of Sir George Chudleigh, of Haldon, in Devonshire. He died Dec. 18, 1784, and was succeeded in title and estate by his only child,

VI. Sir JOHN CHICHESTER, Bart. who was high sheriff for Devonshire in 1788, and is unmarried.

ARMS—Chequy, or, and gules, a chief vaire.
CREST—On a wreath, a heron, rising with an eel in his beak, proper.
SEATS—At Youlston, near Barnstaple, and Sandford, near Crediton, Devon.

TABLE 77.

1 WALLERAN DE CIRENCESTER
2 John de Cirencester
3 Sir John de Cirencester
4 Sir Thomas = Alicia Rotemago
5 William de Cirencester
6 Sir John de Cirencester

7 Richard Chichester
8 John de Chichester
9 Sir John = Thomasine Raleigh
10 John, of Raleigh
11 Richard = Alice Wotton

Giles, L. D'Aubeny

12 John Chichester — Richard Chichester — Henry, F. of Bridgewater, 1547 — Cecilia John, E. of Bath
M. Beaumont | J. Brett — Thomasine Hall

13 Edward Chichester, bp. — John — Amias — Elizabeth
Elizabeth — Joan Gifford — Edw. Chichester

14 Sir John Chichester = Gertrude, dr. of Sir Wm. Courtenay

15 Sir John | Sir Arthur | Sir John | Edw. bp. | Sir | Elizabeth | Dorothy | Eleanor | Mary | Grace | Cecilia | Susanna | &c.
1585 | 1625 | Knt. | of Belfast | Thos. | Hugh | Sirutugh | Sir Arth. | Sir Rich. | Rob. | Thos. | John
A. Dennis | L. Pertot | | 1648 | | Fortescue | Pollard | Basset | Bluet | Dillon | Hatch | Fortescue

16 Sir Robert Chichester, K. B. 1626 — George Augustus, marquis of Donegall in Ireland
Frances Harrington | Mary Hill

Anne = Thomas, L. Bruce — I. Sir John Chichester, Bart. 1667 = Elizabeth Rayney

II. Sir John, 1680 = —— Bickerstaff, 1680 — III. Sir Arthur, 1717 = E. Drew — Henry = ——, widow of J. Chichester

IV. Sir John Chichester — Florence — Mary — Anne — 2 drs. — Elizabeth
1740 | 1726 | —Court- | —Che- | Francis
Anne Leigh | Wm. Northmore | ney | ney | Fulford

V Sir John, 1784 — William — N — N — Florence
Frances Chudleigh | Miss Bellamin | — Musgrave | J. Sandford | Wm. Sandford

VI. Sir John Chichester, Bart.

77. KNATCHBULL, of MERSHAM HATCH, KENT.

Created Baronet Aug. 4, 1641.

MERSHAM HATCH has been the principal seat of this family ever since the 2d year of Hen. VII. at which time it was purchased by Richard Knatchbull, of the executors of —— Edwards. The house is in that deed, and in several of much older date, called sometimes Mersham Hatch, and sometimes Mersham le Hatche.

Mr. Philipot, in his *Villare Cantianum*, has the following words concerning this family:* " Knatchbull, extracted originally from Limne, where I find the name by deeds very ancient, and owners of a plentiful patrimony." John Knatchbull held much land there in the reign of Edw. III. From him descended

1. Thomas Knatchbull, who was the father of Thomas and William, who married ——, daughter of John Brockman.

2. Thomas, the elder son, married Eleanor ——, and from him descended another

3. Thomas, who was the father of

4. Richard Knatchbull, who lived in the time of Henry VII. and married Catharine, daughter of Sir Thomas Lewknor, Knt. by whom he had

5. Richard Knatchbull, who married Agnes, daughter of Robert Brent; by whom he had one son, William; and died in 1523.

6. William was the father of 1, John; 2, Thomas, who died in 1523; and one daughter, Sibyll.

7. John married Alice, daughter of —— Fowle, of Tenterden: he died in 1540, and had issue, by the said Alice, 1, Richard; 2, John; 3, Reginald; and 4, William Knatchbull; and a daughter Mary, the wife of Thomas Finch. John, the second son, married ——, daughter of —— Sheaf (sister to his brother Richard's wife) by whom he had issue two sons and one daughter; 1, John, who married Jane, sister of Sir Thomas Honeywood, of Evington; and secondly, Mary, daughter of Sir Edward Filmer, of East Sutton, both in Kent, Knts. and Richard, who married Catharine, daughter of Thomas Boys, of Hythe, in Kent, and secondly Anne, daughter of William Gibbons: Mary, was the wife of Thomas Scot, of Egreston, son of Sir Reginald Scot, of Scot's Hall, in Kent, Knt. Reginald, the third son, married Anne, daughter of William Crispe, Esq. lieutenant of Dover Castle, and brother of Sir Henry Crispe, of Quekes, in the Isle of Thanet, a person very eminent in the reign of Hen. VIII. by whom he had issue another Reginald (who was father of Mary Knatchbull, who was lady abbess of the convent of Benedictine Nuns, at Ghent); and also one daughter, Anne, the wife of John Best, of Allington Castle. William, the fourth son, married Catharine, daughter of John Greene, by whom he had issue Richard, who married ——, daughter of George Goring; and also two daughters; Catharine, the wife of John Crispe, son and heir to the afore-

* Dr. Harris's History of Kent.

said William Crispe, Esq. lieutenant of Dover Castle; and Mary, of Timothy Johnson, of Fordwich.

8. Richard Knatchbull, Esq. eldest son and heir, married 1, Joan, daughter of —— Sheaf, and secondly Susan, daughter of Thomas Green, of Bobbing, in Essex: he had issue by the first wife two sons; 1, Richard, who married Anne, daughter of Sir Thomas Scot, of Scot's Hall, Knt. (who after his death was the wife of Sir Thomas Bromley, Knt.) by whom he had one son, Thomas, who died without issue; 2, John, who married Elizabeth, another daughter of the said Sir Thomas Scot, Knt. and died without issue (his relict was married again to Sir Richard Smythe, Knt.) and also four daughters, Alice, Anne, the wife of Sir Edward Boys, of Fredvile, Knt. Elizabeth, of Williams Gibbons, of Westcliff; and Catharine, of Alexander Hamon, of Acris. Richard had issue by his second wife, Susan, four sons; 1, Sir Norton; 2, Thomas, both of which we shall mention hereafter; 3, John, who died unmarried; and 4, George, who married Joan, daughter of Thomas Gilbert, of Sandwich, Esq. and died S. P. also two daughters; Ursula, the wife of Alexander Shepherd, of Peasemark, and Mary, of Paul Cleybrooke, of Nash Court, in the Isle of Thanet. This Richard died in 1582, aged 57, and lies buried, under a plain marble stone, at the entrance of the chancel of the parish church of Mersham. His son Richard died Jan. 20, 1590, aged 36, and was also buried in Mersham church.

9. Sir Norton Knatchbull, Knt. son and heir of the last Richard, was sheriff of Kent 5 James I. and served in parliament for the port of Hythe: he began the foundation of the free school at Ashford, in Kent, which was finished and endowed by his nephew, Sir Norton Knatchbull, Knt. and Bart. He had three wives; 1, Anne, daughter of Paul Wentworth, Esq. 2, Bridget, daughter of John Astley, of Maidstone, in Kent, Esq. who was master of the jewel office, and a gentleman of the privy chamber to Queen Elizabeth; and descended from the ancient Baron Astley, of Astley Castle, in Warwickshire, by his wife Margaret, daughter and heiress of Lord Thomas Grey, brother to Henry Grey, marquis of Dorset, and duke of Suffolk; sister and co-heir to Sir John Astley, of Allington, Knt. she died Nov. 4, 1625, in the 55th year of her age. 3, Mary Westrow, widow of Thomas Westrow, of London, Esq. and daughter of John Aldersea, of Spurgrove, Esq. in Cheshire (who after his death was remarried to Sir Edward Scot, K. B.) and died in 1678, aged 89.* He died in 1636, and lies buried in Mersham church.

Thomas Knatchbull, Esq. second son of Richard, and brother to Sir Norton, married Eleanor, another daughter and co-heir of the aforesaid John Astley, Esq. by his said wife, Margaret Grey, who died in 1638, aged 63; and by her had issue seven sons; 1, Richard, who died S. P. 2, Sir Norton, of whom hereafter; 3, Francis, who died S. P. 4, Thomas, who married Anne,† daughter of Edward Chute; 5, Astley; 6, John; and 7, George, which three last died S. P. he had also four daughters; 1, Bridget, the wife of George Curtis, of Tenterden; 2, Margaret,

---

* "This Sir Norton (Mr. Philipot says) was a person, who for his favour and love to learning and antiquities, in times when they are both fallen under such cheapness and contempt, cannot be mentioned without an epithet equivalent to so just a merit."

† Her will was proved in 1705, wherein she is stiled widow. She was buried at Mersham.

of Nicholas Toke, of Goddington, in Kent, Esqrs. 3, Susan; and 4, Alice. He died in 1623, aged 52, and lies buried at Maidstone, in Kent.*

I. NORTON KNATCHBULL, Esq. his son and heir, was knighted at Whitehall, and afterwards advanced to the dignity of a baronet, 17 Charles I. He served in parliament as knight of the shire for the county of Kent, temp Charles I. and for the port of New Romney in the reigns of King Charles I. and II. and was a person of great learning, of which his Annotations on the New Testament, will be a lasting monument. He married first Dorothy, daughter of the above-mentioned Mary Westrow, widow of Thomas Westrow, Esq. sheriff of London; by whom he had issue Sir John, his successor, Sir Thomas, successor to his brother, and Norton, who died unmarried: secondly, Dorothy, relict of Sir Edward Steward, Knt. and daughter of Sir Robert Honeywood, of Pett, in Charing, Kent, Knt. by whom he had no issue. He died Feb. 5, 1684, aged 83, and lies buried at Mersham.

II. Sir JOHN KNATCHBULL, Bart. son and heir of Sir Norton, married Jane, daughter and co-heir of Sir Edward Monins, of Waldershare, in Kent, Bart. by whom he had three sons, who died S. P. and nine daughters, three of which were married; viz. Eleanor, the wife of Roger West, of Marsworth, in Bucks, Esq. (the last heir male of that ancient family) Elizabeth, of —— Lely, and Jane, of Sir George Herbert, of Ireland, Bart. and secondly, of Richard Whitshed, Esq. brother to the late lord chief justice Whitshed, of the same kingdom. Sir John served for New Romney 12 Charles II. and as knight of the shire for Kent, temp. James II. and Wm. and Mary; and died Dec. 15, 1696, aged 60, without issue male: his lady died June 7, 1699; and both lie buried in the church at Mersham.

III. Sir THOMAS KNATCHBULL, Bart. brother and successor to Sir John, married Mary, daughter of Sir Edward Dering, of Surenden Dering, in Kent, Bart. by whom he had issue Sir Edward, his successor, Heneage, and Thomas, who both died unmarried; and one daughter, Catharine, the wife first of Sir George Rooke, Knt. vice admiral of England, and secondly, of the hon. Dr. Moore, rector of Malpas and Wilmslow, in Cheshire, uncle to the Earl of Drogheda: she died in London, Aug. 19, 1755, leaving three sons and one daughter; 1, Henry, born in 1709, who died in 1730; 2, Thomas, born in 1716, D. D. of Stow Hall, in Norfolk, and rector of Frampton Cotterell, in Gloucestershire, who, in 1653, married ——, daughter of William Lay, of Downham, in Norfolk, Esq. 3, John, who died in 1744; and Mary, the wife of the Rev. Poulter Forrester.

IV. Sir EDWARD KNATCHBULL, Bart. eldest son, and successor to his father, served as member for Rochester, in the first parliament of Queen Anne, and as knight of the shire for Kent in the 12th of the same reign; and served again for the same county in the second parliament of King George I. and for Lestwithiel, in Cornwall, in the first parliament of King George II. He married Alice, daughter of John Wyndham, of Nonington, in Wilts, Esq. (son of Sir Wadham Wyndham, Knt. one of the justices of the common pleas, ninth son of Sir John Wynd-

* His monument is remaining against the north wall of the chancel, being a most superb one, having his figure in white marble, in full proportion, lying at length on it; above which, under a canopy, is that of his lady, in a praying posture.

ham, of Orchard Wyndham, in Somersetshire, Bart. and sister to Thomas Wyndham, lord chancellor of Ireland; by whom he had five sons: 1, Sir Wyndham, his successor; 2, Thomas; 3, Edward; 4, Wadham, who was chancellor and prebendary of Durham, and vicar of Chillingham, in Kent; and died Dec. 1760, leaving, by Harriot, his wife, daughter of Charles Parry, Esq. three sons and one daughter; 1, Wadham Knatchbull, who died in 1773, aged 27; 2, Wyndham, of London; 3, Charles, an officer in the navy, who married Frances, his cousin, daughter and heiress of his uncle, Major Norton Knatchbull, of the county of Somerset; and Catharine, the wife of Thomas Knight, of Godmersham, Esq. 5, Major Norton. The daughters were, Mary, who died in 1729; Alice, the wife of Edward Hearst, of Salisbury, Esq. and Catharine, of Thomas Harris. Sir Edward died in Golden Square, April 3, 1730; and was succeeded by his eldest son,

V. Sir WYNDHAM KNATCHBULL, Bart. who married Catharine, daughter of James Harris, of Salisbury, Esq. who died Jan. 6, 1740-1; Sir Wyndham died July 3, 1749, leaving issue one son, Wyndham, and two daughters, Joan-Elizabeth and Catharine, who died unmarried. He was succeeded by his son,

VI. Sir WYNDHAM KNATCHBULL, Bart. he was created master of arts, at Oxford, July 6, 1758, and died Sep. 26, 1763, unmarried; and was succeeded by his uncle,

VII. Sir EDWARD KNATCHBULL, Bart. who married Grace, the second daughter of William Legg, of Salisbury, Esq. by whom he had issue, Anne-Elizabeth, Catharine-Maria, Sir Edward, the present baronet, now his only surviving son; Norton, who died unmarried; Alice, who also died unmarried, in 1779, aged 17; Grace, and Wyndham, who died infants; and Joan. He died Nov. 21, 1789, aged 86, and was succeeded by his only son,

VIII. Sir EDWARD KNATCHBULL, Bart. who served the office of high sheriff for the county of Kent, in 1785, and is now one of its members of parliament. He married first, in 1780, Mary, daughter and co-heir of William Western Hugessen, of Provenders, Esq. who died at Bristol in 1784; by whom he has two sons, Edward, born in 1782, and Norton; and secondly, in 1785, Frances, second daughter of Governor Graham, by whom he has a son, Wyndham.

ARMS—Azure, three cross crosslets fitchee, between two bendlets, or.
CREST—On a cap of dignity, Azure; turned up, ermine, a leopard, standing, argent; spotted, sable.
MOTTO—*In Crucifixa Gloria mea.*
SEAT—At Mersham Hatch, in the county of Kent.

There are pedigrees of this family in the Herald's Visitations, for the county of Kent, taken in 1574 and 1629. See also Hasted's History of Kent, vol. III. p. 287, &c. and Stemmata Chicheliana, No. 222.

KNATCHBULL, OF MERSHAM HATCH, KENT.

TABLE 78.

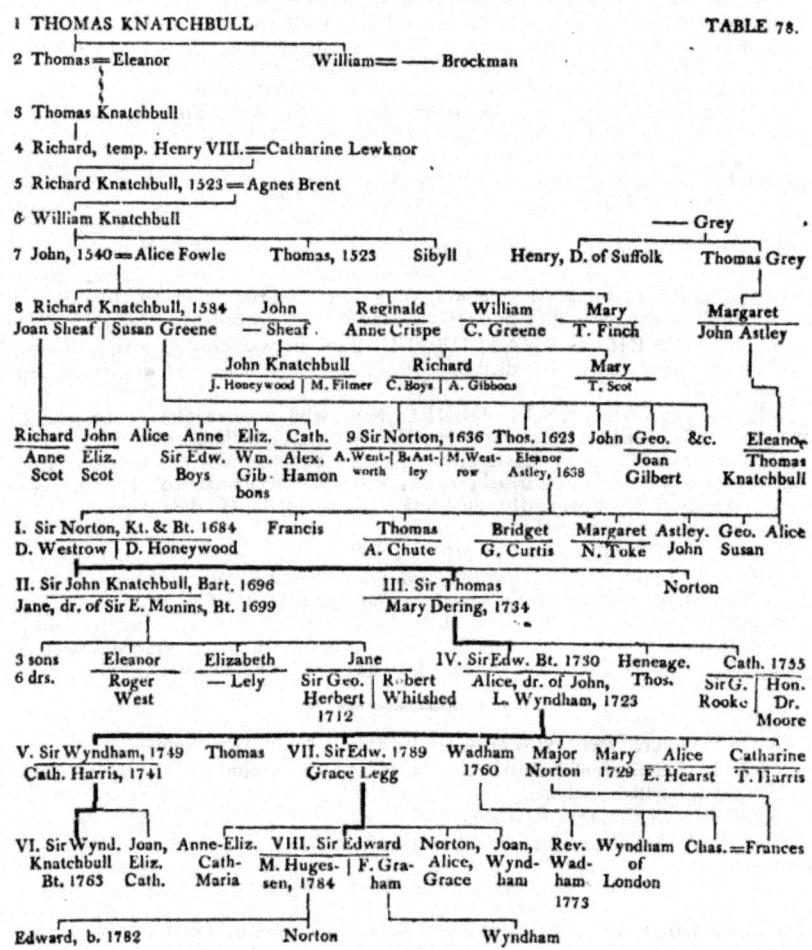

78. OWEN, of ORIELTON, PEMBROKESHIRE.

Created Baronet Aug. 11, 1641.

THIS family is descended from Hova, the son of Kundhelw, a nobleman of North Wales, who lived about the year of the incarnation, 1150, and was one of the 15 peers. He was of Cwmwd Lhivon, in the county of Carnarvon, and had issue,

3. Methusalem, the father of

4. Meredith ap Methusalem, of Cwmwd Lhivon, in Carnarvonshire; whose son,

5. Yorwerth, lord of Cwmwd Lhivon, had issue,

6. Griffith ap Yorwerth, of Cwmwd Lhivon, Esq. who married Gwenlean, daughter of Rhyvyd Vlaith, Esq. lord of Penlhyn, in North Wales; by whom he had

7. Yorwerth ap Griffith, lord of Cwmwd Menai, in Anglesea, Esq. who married Gladys, daughter of Howell Goeg, Esq. and was father of

8. Yorwerth Dha, Esq. (which signifies good) who married Gwenthlian, daughter and co-heir of Meredith Beukir, of Aberfraw, in Anglesea, Esq. and had issue

9. Howell ap Yorwerth, Esq. who married Angharad, daughter of Howell ap Kynvrig, of Ysdylais, in Denbigh, Esq. His son,

10. Halkin ap Howell, Esq. married Erdhylad, daughter and heiress of David ap Yorwerth, of Cwmwd Menai, in Anglesea, Esq. whose son,

11. Lewellin ap Halkin, married Maly, daughter of Jevan Lloyd ap Griffith, of Lechwedh, in Denbighshire, Esq. by whom he had issue,

12. Merik ap Llewellin, of Bodeon, alias Bodowen, in Anglesea; who, by Margaret, daughter to Jevan Vychan, of Weston, in Shropshire, Esq. had issue,

13. Owen ap Merick, of Bodowen, in Anglesea, Esq. This Owen lived in the time of King Henry VII. was a man of great note in this county, and his descendants ever after assumed the name of Owen. By his wife, Eleanor, daughter of Robert ap Meredith, of Glynlhyvon, in Carnarvonshire, Esq. he had issue

14. Hugh ap Owen, of Bodeon, Esq. who married Gwenlian, daughter of Maurice John, of Llanvroden, Merionethshire, Esq. and was father of

15. Owen ap Hugh, of Bodeon, Esq. who married Sibill, daughter of Sir William Griffith, of Penthryn, in Carnarvonshire, Knt. and was father of

16. Sir Hugh Owen, of Bodowen, Knt. barrister at law, and recorder of Carmarthen, who married Elizabeth, daughter and sole heiress of George Wyrryot, of Orielton, in Pembrokeshire, Esq. by whom he had two sons, John and William. To William he gave Bodowen, and his estate in North Wales: to

17. John, that in South Wales; both which are now joined, by the marriage of Sir Hugh Owen (father of Sir Arthur) to the heiress of the North Wales estate.

OWEN, OF ORIELTON, PEMBROKESHIRE.

I. Sir HUGH OWEN, Knt. of Orielton, son of John, and grandson of Sir Hugh, was the first baronet of this family: he married first Frances, daughter of Sir John Philipps, of Picton Castle, Pembrokeshire, Bart. by whom he had a son John, who married Anne, daughter and heiress of John Lewis, Esq. and died in his father's life-time, without issue [his widow afterwards was the wife of Col. Mark Trevor] and two daughters; Dorothy, who died unmarried, and ——, the wife of John Glynne, of North Wales, Esq. His second wife was Catharine, daughter of Evan Lloyd, of Yale, in Denbighshire, Esq. relict of John Lewis, of Prescood, Esq. by whom he had Sir Hugh, his successor, and Arthur, who married first ——, daughter of —— Horsey, and secondly ——, daughter of —— Powell, of Pembrokeshire, Esq. also a daughter, Mary, the wife of William Scurfeild, of the Mote, in Pembrokeshire, Esq. Sir Hugh died in 1670, and was succeeded by his eldest surviving son,

II. Sir HUGH OWEN, Bart. who also married two wives; first Anne, daughter and sole heiress of Henry Owen, of Bodowen, in Anglesea, Esq. by whom he had Sir Arthur, his successor, and two daughters; Catharine, the wife of John Williams, of Chester, Esq. second son of Sir William Williams, of Glascoed, in Denbighshire, Bart. and Elizabeth, wife of William Lewis Anwill, of Park, in Merionethshire, Esq. Sir Hugh's second lady was Catharine, daughter of William Griffith, of Len, Esq. relict of Lewis Anwill, of Park, Esq. by whom he had no issue. Sir Hugh died in 1698-9, and was succeeded by his only son,

III. Sir ARTHUR OWEN, Bart. lord lieutenant, custos rotulorum, and knight of the shire, in both the parliaments called by King George I. for the county of Pembroke, having before served for the town of Pembroke, in the reign of Queen Anne. He married Emma, daughter of Sir William Williams, of Glascoed, in Denbighshire, Bart. and had issue three sons and three daughters; 1, William, his successor; 2, John Owen, Esq. member of parliament for Beaumaris; and died Feb. 20, 1754. He married ——, sister of Wyrriot Owen, of Naish, Esq. by whom he had a son, who was in his father's regiment, and other children; and 3, Arthur. The daughters were Margaret, Emma, and Elizabeth, the wife first of William Owen, of Carnarvon, in North Wales, Esq. and secondly of Hugh Barlow, of Llawrenny, in Pembrokeshire, Esq. Sir Arthur died June 6, 1753, and was succeeded by his eldest son,

IV. Sir WILLIAM OWEN, Bart. who was elected knight of the shire for the county of Pembroke in 1747 (having represented the town of Pembroke in the five succeeding parliaments) for which place he was again chosen, and was also lord lieutenant and custos rotulorum of the said county. He resigned his seat in parliament, in favour of his son, in 1775. He married first Elizabeth, daughter and sole heiress of William Lloyd, of Grove, in the county of Pembroke, Esq. by whom he had one daughter; secondly, Elizabeth, daughter of John Williams, of Chester, Esq. who died Dec. 21, 1764, by whom he had four children. Sir William died May 7, 1781, and was succeeded by his son,

V. Sir HUGH OWEN, Bart. who was lord lieutenant, and member of parliament for Pembrokeshire: he married, June 9, 1789, ——, daughter of the late Sir Joseph Yates, Knt. and died Jan. 16, 1786; and was succeeded by his son,

OWEN, OF ORIELTON, PEMBROKESHIRE.

VI. Sir HUGH OWEN, Bart. born September 12, 1782.

ARMS—Gules, a chevron, between three lions rampant, or.
CREST—On a wreath, a lion rampant, or.
SUPPORTERS—Two savages, with each a holly-bush on his shoulder, proper; and wreathed about their heads and waists with holly leaves.
MOTTO—*Honestas optima Politia.*
SEATS—Orielton and Landshipping, both in Pembrokeshire; and Bodowen, near Aberfraw, in Anglesea.

TABLE 79.

1 KUNDHELW
2 Hova
3 Methusalem
4 Meredith ap Methusalem
5 Yorwerth, L. of Cwmwd Lhivon
6 Griffith = Gwenlean Vlaith
7 Yorwerth = Gladys Goeg
8 Yorwerth Dha = Gwenlean Beukir

9 Howell ap Yorwerth = Angharad Kynvrig
10 Halkin = Erdhylad ap Yorwerth
11 Lewellin = Maly ap Griffith
12 Merik = Margaret Vycham
13 Owen = Eleanor ap Meredith
14 Hugh = Gwenlean John
15 Owen = Sibill Griffith
16 Sir Hugh = Elizabeth Wyrryot

17 John Owen | William Owen
Frances Philipps = I. Sir Hugh Owen, Knt. & Bart, 1670 = Catharine Lloyd | Henry Owen

John | Dorothy | N | II. Sir Hugh Owen, Bart. 1699 | Arthur | Mary | Anne
A. Lewis | J. Glynne | A. Owen | C. Griffith — Hersey | — Powell | Wm. Scurfeild | Sir Hugh Owen

III. Sir Arthur, 1753 = Emma Williams | Catharine = John Williams | Elizabeth = Wm. Lewis

IV. Sir Wm. Owen, Bart. 1781 | John, 1754 | Arthur | Margaret | Emma | Elizabeth
E. Lloyd | E. Williams 1764 | — Owen | | | | Wm. Owen | Hugh Barlow

V. Sir Hugh Owen, Bart. 1786 = ——Yates

VI. Sir Hugh Owen, Bart.

79. BRIGGS, of Haughton, Shropshire.

Created Baronet August 12, 1641.

THIS family, before the time of Edw. I. assumed the surname of De Ponte or Pontibus, i. e. at Brigge, or at Brigges, as the ancient family of the Fountains of the same place assumed their's of De Fonte or Fontibus, i. e. at the fountain or fountains' heads; and the other by the bridge or bridges, over the currents that came from them. The eldest branches of both families continued at Salle, in Norfolk, till they united. The first of this family that we find on record was,

1. William Atte Brigge, of Salle, called in some deeds William de Ponte de Salle, and in others De Pontibus de Salle: he was living in 1334, and was succeeded by his second son,

2. John atte Brigge, of Salle, Esq. who, by deed, gave to his second son, Edmund, and his heirs, all his lands, tenements, and hereditaments at Crastfoot, in Westmoreland; which deed is without date, and must be full as old as Edw. II. and shews that the family was then considerable in the county of Norfolk. Simon, the fourth, in a lineal descent from the said Edmund, married Cicely, daughter of Oliver Gilpin, of Yorkshire; and Brian, his son, married also in Yorkshire.

Thomas, the fourth son of William, in 1392, went to the Holy Sepulchre, with Sir Thomas Swinburne, Knt. an account of which pilgrimage, written by himself, is still extant, in a MSS. in Caius College Library, at Cambridge.

William, the fifth son, had two sons, William and Sir John Brigge, chaplain, who in 1438 was presented to the rectory of St. Lawrence, in Norwich, by the abbot and convent of Bury: in 1446,* rector of Dickleburgh; in 1466, rector of Berford; and was buried in the chancel in 1481.†

3. John Brygges, Esq. his son and heir, was a man of good estate in the county of Norfolk, as appears by his will, dated 1454, in which he gave to Margaret, his second wife, who was daughter and co-heir of A. Rockwood, of Euston, in the county of Suffolk, all his lands, fald-courses, and water-mills, which of right was hers, in fee tail; and all his sheep there for life: she being to leave the manor and full stock to William, their son; who was mayor of Thetford in 1480, 1481, and divers other times. His manor of Lynford, which he purchased of the executors of Sir Constantine Clifton, of Buckenham Castle, Knt. his great friend, he ordered his executors to sell to the prior of St. Mary, at Thetford, for eight score marks, according to his agreement; out of which he assigned 40 marks to celebrate his anniversary in that monastery: every monk in priest's orders attending there, to have twelve-pence, and each other six-pence, as long as the money lasted.‡ Thomas, his younger son was to have the other six score marks; but William, his son, and Margaret, his wife, was to have the custody of him till

* Blomefield, vol. II. p. 128.   † Ibid, p. 711.   ‡ Ibid, p. 640.

he was of age to be a priest, or if not, till he was 24 years old. Margaret, his daughter, was to have Illington manor to her and her heirs, and if she died without heirs, it was to be sold and disposed of to pious uses. It appears, that on his second marriage he removed from Salle to Thetford; for he gave his house in Thetford, in which he dwelt, to his wife, having settled his paternal estate, at Salle, on his heirs male, by Eleanor, his first wife; and all his second wife's inheritance on her and her issue.* He was succeeded at Salle by his eldest son,

4. Thomas, who was a great friend of John Paston, Esq. by which he much advanced himself.†

5. Edward, his eldest son, by his wife Cicely Moore, had five sons; 1, John; 2, Thomas; 3, Henry; 4, William; and 5, Sir Thomas Briggs, clerk; who was rector of Brissingham in 1439, doctor of divinity in 1549, chaplain to Lady Mary (afterwards Queen Mary) vicar of Kenninghall and Windham.

6. John, the eldest son, married ——, daughter of —— Quaplode, by whom he had one son, James Briggs, of Salle, Esq. who married Mary, daughter of Thomas Estotevile, or Stutvile, of Suffolk, Esq. by whom he had a daughter Mary, who was the wife of John Fountain, of Salle, Esq. and their eldest son, at his baptism, had his mother's name given him.

6. Thomas, the second son of Edward, married Elizabeth, daughter of Richard Mounteyn, by whom he had

7. Augustine, of Norwich, who in 1626 gave ten pounds to the poor, and was a benefactor to South Conisford parishes, and St. Peter's Mancroft: he also left money to bind out twelve poor boys.‡

8. Augustine, his son, was born in 1617: being strenuous for his royal master in the rebellion, was turned out of the court of aldermen, by the rebels; but was§ restored again at the restoration, and elected sheriff that very year. He was one of those gentlemen who joined the Earl of Newcastle's forces, in the siege of Lynn, in 1643. The late recorder had a sword, with a label of Briggs's own hand-writing tied thereto—*This I won at the sige of Linn, in the servis of the royal martyr, K. Charles the first; A. Briggs.*∥

---

* Blomefield, vol. II. p. 640. He was baried at Salle church, with his effigy, in a winding sheet, on a brass plate; this under it:—
Here lyeth John Brigge under this marble ston,
Whos sowle our Lord Jesu have mercy apon,
For in this worlde, worthily he lived many a day,
And here hys bodi ys beried, and cowched under clay.
Lo! friends fre, whatever ye be, pray for me, I you pray,
As ye me see, in such degre, so shall ye be, another day.

† By will dated 1494, he founded a chantry priest to sing for his soul, for ten years after his decease, at the altar, by the image of the Virgin Mary, in the chapel of St. James's, on the south side of St. Peter and Paul's church, in Salle; which noble fabric was built in his time; and it appears, by the arms, carved on the south porch, south aisle and chapel aforesaid, that they were built at his expence.

‡ Blomefield, vol. II. p. 640. § Ibid. ∥ Ibid.

In 1660, at the restoration, he became alderman, and was very serviceable in composing the differences between the dean and chapter, and city; and in procuring a new charter for the city, in which he is named alderman; and had such great interest, as to be elected burgess in parliament for the city, in 1677, without opposition, having before refused it, in favour of the Paston family, which he much

Augustine, the eldest son, settled an estate in Norwich, on trustees, for the benefit of Southgate ward, according to his father's bequest of the 200*l*. He was one of the aldermen turned out by the mandate of James II. in 1687; but was restored in 1688: he was sheriff in 1685, mayor in 1695 and 1704.

9. William, the second son, was admitted when 13 years old at Bennet College, Cambridge, where he was educated under Dr. Thomas Tennison, afterwards archbishop of Canterbury; and being chosen fellow of the College, continued there several years, discharging the trust of a tutor with honour to the society. In 1671 he had a certificate under the university seal, that he had been regularly created master of arts; soon after which he was incorporated into the university of Oxford, and after he had improved himself by his travels in foreign countries, being well versed in most parts of learning, he settled in London; and on July 3, 1677, took his doctor's degree in physic, in the university of Cambridge; and soon after was chosen fellow of the college of physicians, in London, where, having gained the friendship of most of the learned men, by his remarkable skill in his profession, he was made physician in ordinary to King William III.* We now return to

7. Oliver, the second son of Thomas, by Elizabeth Mounteyn, who was the first of this family who settled in Shropshire,† at Ernestry Park, near Ludlow, in the beginning of Queen Elizabeth's reign. He married Anne, daughter of Humphrey Coningsby, of Nenesolers, Esq. by whom he had three sons; Humphrey, Oliver, and Brian; and died in 1596.

8. Humphrey succeeded his father, and lived at Ernestry Park: he was high sheriff for the county the year of gunpowder plot; and married Anne, eldest daughter and co-heir of Robert Moreton, of Haughton, Esq. by whom he had

valued and served: he was chosen no less than four times successively, a member for the city, having been mayor in 1670; and afterwards was major of the trained band, or city militia. He died Aug. 28, 1684, in the 67th year of his age.

By his will, dated Aug. 19, 1684, he gave all his estates, in Swerdestone, in Norfolk, unto Nicholas Bickerdike, alderman of Norwich, and other trustees; and to their heirs, in consideration, that they shall, without making any manner of benefit to their own use, always suffer the profits to be received by the mayor and aldermen, or their receivers, to be disposed of by them, after all necessary charges are defrayed, "the one half part yearly, and every year, to increase the maintenance and revenue of the Boys' Hospital, and the other half part to increase the revenue of the Girls' Hospital; to the intent, that the number of children in both the said hospitals to be placed, may be every year increased, so far forth as the same will extend." He also ordered his executors, within two years after his decease, to purchase, and settle on trustees, as much land, &c. in Norfolk or Norwich, being freehold, as they could purchase for 200*l*. for which they are to pay at the rate of 6*l*. per cent. till the purchase be made; the neat produce to be employed by the mayor and aldermen, or major part of them, "for the putting forth to convenient trades, yearly and every year, two such poor boys, of the ward of St. Peter of Southgate (whereof he was alderman) as can write and read, and have neither father nor mother able to put them forth to such trades": and if there be no such boys in the ward, then the money to be disposed of by the mayor and aldermen, for the relief only of the necessitous sick or impotent poor people of the ward aforesaid; and for no other purpose whatsoever."

Jan. 3, 1644, he had a grant of a crest to the ancient arms of his family, by Sir Edward Byshe, Knt. clarencieux, viz. On a helm and wreath of his colours, a pelican, sable, picking her breast, on the trunk of a tree, or; and was to bear them with the canton, or; mantled gules, doubled argent.

* See a farther account of this branch of the family in Blomefield's Norfolk, vol. II. p. 643.
† Wotton.

BRIGGS, OF HAUGHTON, SHROPSHIRE.

I. Sir MORETON BRIGGS, the first baronet, who married Cryzogan, daughter of Edward Grey, of Buildwas, in Salop, Esq. by whom he had three sons and six daughters; 1, Sir Humprey; 2, Moreton, who was killed in the civil wars at Sturton Castle, in Staffordshire, on the side of the king, S. P. 3, Robert, who married Sarah, daughter of Thomas Moreton, of Shiffnal, in Salop, Esq. and left one daughter, Martha, the wife first of Richard Spencer, of London, Turkey merchant, and secondly of Sir John Stonhouse, of Radley, in Berks, Bart. The daughters were 1, Priscilla, the wife of Robert Dod, of Petsey, Esq. 2, Anne, of Thomas Draper, of Walton, Esq. 3, Elizabeth, of Edmund Chapman, of Greenwich, Gent. 4, Frances, of Ferrers Fowke, of Brewood, Esq. 5, Martha, and 6, Sarah, who both died young.

II. Sir HUMPHREY, Bart. his eldest son, succeeded, who had been knighted in his father's life-time, and married four wives; first Elizabeth, daughter of Sir Philip Cary, of Marybone Park, in Middlesex, Knt. by whom he had two sons, Moreton and Edward, who both died young. His second wife was Elizabeth, youngest daughter of Sir Richard Wilbraham, of Woodhey, in Cheshire, Bart. by whom he left one son, Sir Humphrey, his successor. His third wife was Anne, widow of Richard Moreton, of Montgomeryshire, Esq. His fourth wife was Magdalen, daughter of Sir John Corbet, of Addesly, Bart. By the two last he had no issue.

III. Sir HUMPHREY BRIGGS, Bart. succeeded his father, and married Barbara, daughter of Sir Wadham Wyndham, of Nonyngton, in Wilts, Knt. one of the judges of the king's bench, by whom he had three sons; Sir Humphrey, Sir Hugh, and William: and five daughters; Barbara, the wife of Dr. Chandler, bishop of Durham; Elizabeth, of Leigh Brooke, of Staffordshire, Esq. Anne, Frances, the wife of Dr. Chetham, of Derbyshire; and Magdalen. He died in 1699, aged 49, and was succeeded by his eldest son,

IV. Sir HUMPHREY BRIGGS, Bart. he served for the county of Salop in that parliament when the succession was settled in the house of Hanover, and was member of parliament for Winlock, in the same county in the two parliaments of George I. and dying unmarried Dec. 8, 1734, was succeeded in dignity and estate by his brother,

V. Sir HUGH BRIGGS, Bart. who was sheriff for Shropshire in 1749.

VI. Sir JOHN BRIGGS, the present baronet.

ARMS—Gules, three bars gemell, or; a canton, ermine.
CREST—On a wreath, or and gules, on a stump of a tree, a pelican, or; vulning herself, proper.
MOTTO—*Virtus est Dei.*
SEAT—At Blackbrooke, in Monmonthshire.

BRIGGS, OF HAUGHTON, SHROPSHIRE.

TABLE 80.

1 WILLIAM ATTE BRIGGE, of Salle, temp. Edw. I. & II.

Walter — 2 John — Robert — Thomas — William

Eleanor=3 John Briggs=Marg. Rookwood — Edmund — William — Sir John Brigge

4 Thomas Briggs — Henry — George N — William / Margaret — Thomas — Marg.
M. Beau- | M. Rock-
pre | wood

5 Edw. Briggs=C. Moore — Thomas, S.T.P. 1550 — Wm. canon of the Holy Sepulchre — Agnes died about 1540

6 John Briggs — 6 Thomas — Henry — William — Sir Thomas, clerk
— Quaplode — Eliz. Mounteyn

James — 7 Augustine — 7 Oliver, 1596 — Samuel — Henry, geom. professor at Oxford
Mary Estoteville — of Norwich — Anne, dr. of Humphrey Coningsby — of Wakefield

Mary — 8 Augustine, 1684 — 8·Humphrey — Oliver, Brian — Joseph, A.M. Vicar of Kirkburton.&
John Fountain — Eliz. Aldred — Anne Moreton

Augustine, 1704 — 9 Wm. M.D. 1704 — I. Sir Moreton Briggs, Bart. — N, a dr.
Eliz. Cock — Hannah Hobart — Cryzogan, dr. of Edw. Grey, aged 97 — d. y.

Henry, D.D. — Mary — Hannah — II. Sir Humphrey Briggs, Knt. & Bart. &c.
Grace Briggs — T. Bromfield, M.D. — Denny Martin — Elizabeth Cary | Eliz. Wil-braham | Anne More-ton | Magdalen Corbet

Moreton d. y. — Edward d. y. — III. Sir Humphrey Briggs, Bart. 1699
Barbara Wyndham

IV. Sir Humph. Briggs, Bart. 1734 — V. Sir Hugh Briggs, Bart. — William — Barbara Dr. Chandler bp. of Durham — Elizabeth Leigh Brooke — Francis Dr. Cheat-ham — Anne, Mag-dalen

VI. Sir John Briggs, Bart.

* Blomefield, vol. II, p. 640.

---

80. HEYMAN, of SOMERFIELD, KENT.

Created Baronet Aug. 12, 1641.

THE honours, estates, and extensive charitable dispositions of the Heymans, in Kent, Essex, and the city of London, prove the family to be of considerable antiquity.*

* Tenterden free school, in Kent, was founded by them, about 350 years ago; and an estate of several hundred pounds a year, in divers parts of Kent, was left, by a branch of this family, for charitable uses, for ever.

HEYMAN, OF SOMERFIELD, KENT.

1. Ralph Heyman, Esq. was possessed of a good estate in the reign of King Henry VII. He purchased the manor of Harenge, in Kent, from Sir Francis Willoughby; which his son,

2. Peter, settled upon his second son, Peter. In 25 Henry VIII. Otterpole, in Kent, was purchased by Peter Heyman, Esq. from Thomas Wombwell, of Northfleet, Esq. Somerfield estate, in the parish of Sellinge, in Kent, belonged to William Tilde, Esq. who died, leaving one daughter, Elizabeth, who became the first wife of

3. Peter Heyman, Esq. about the middle of the reign of Henry VIII. by whom he had two sons, Ralph Heyman, Esq. of whom hereafter, and William, who married Elizabeth, daughter of Sir Reginald Scot, Knt. and six daughters; 1, Mary, the wife of Paul Johnson, of Fordwich; 2, Catharine, of William Hamon, of Acris; 3, Margaret, of John Poynet, and afterwards of John Hill; 4, Mildred, of Thomas Corbet, of London; 5, Anne, of Robert Cutts, of London; and 6, Emeline, who died unmarried. His second wife was Mary, daughter and heiress of William Tirrell, of Beeches, in Essex; by whom he left only one daughter, Jane, heiress to her mother, and the wife of John Honywood, of Elmsted, in Kent, Esq. by whom she had only one daughter, Catharine, the wife of Sir Edward Scot, of Scot's Hall, in Kent, Knt. This Peter Heyman, Esq. was one of the gentlemen of the bedchamber to King Edw. VI. and had a grant from that king, of Claverty, in Kent, and died in August, 1550.

4. Ralph Heyman, Esq. eldest son and heir, living in 1577, married Anne, daughter of William Naunton, of Suffolk, Esq. by whom he had two sons; Henry, of whom hereafter, and William, who gave a perpetual exhibition, for the education of youths, at the King's School, at Canterbury, and at Trinity College, Cambridge; and six daughters; 1, Elizabeth, the wife of Sir Thomas Scot, of Scot's Hall, Knt. 2, Mary, of John Boade, of Feversham; 3, Anne, of Adam Sprackling, Knt. 4, Elizabeth, of Thomas Tourney, of Salwood; 5, Margaret, of William Hales, of Hepington; and 6, Rebecca. He died in 1601.

5. Henry Heyman, Esq. his eldest son and heir, married Rebecca, daughter and co-heiress of the Right Rev. Robert Horne, bishop of Winchester; by whom he had Peter, Ralph, Betony, Robert, and Reginald; and three daughters, Elizabeth, the wife of Sir Peter Godfrey, of Lyd, in Kent, Knt. He died in 1613.

6. Sir Peter Heyman, Knt. his eldest son, married Sarah, daughter, and youngest co-heir of Peter Collett, of London, merchant; by whom he had one son, Henry, born at Selling, in Kent, Nov. 20, 1610; and a daughter, Sarah, the wife of Laurence Rooke, of Monksnorton, in Kent, Esq.* His second wife was Mary, daughter and co-heiress of Randolph Wolley, of London, merchant; by whom he had three sons and three daughters. On Peter, his second son, he settled Harenge, in Kent. Sir Peter was member of parliament for the port of Hythe, in Kent, in the reign of King James I. in the years 1620 and 1624; and in the reign of King Charles I. from 1625 to 1631.

* Hasted, in his History of Kent, says, she was the wife of Sir Peter Godfrey, vol. III. p. 419.

HEYMAN, OF SOMERFIELD, KENT.

I. HENRY HEYMAN, Esq. only son and heir, by the first venter, was styled of Somerfield, in Selling, and advanced to the dignity of a baronet. He served in parliament for the port of Hythe, after the death of his father, to the end of that reign, and also in the reign of King Charles II.* He married Mary, daughter and co-heiress of Daniel Holford, of Westurreck, in Essex, Esq. by whom he had three sons and two daughters; viz. Peter, born in Black Friers, London, July 10, 1642; Henry, born at Selling, March 24, 1646; Mary, born in Black Friers, April 28, 1643; and Anne, in the same place, May 19, 1644: two of the sons and one daughter died unmarried. Mary, the eldest daughter, was the wife of Richard Sandys, of Northbourn, in Kent, Esq. who was killed by his own gun, as he was getting over a hedge; by whom she had issue Richard Sandys, who was created a baronet Jan. 23, 1684; but the title is now extinct.† Sir Henry died at his seat, at Somerfield in 1658, and lies buried in the family vault, at Selling, in Kent.

II. Sir PETER HEYMAN, Bart. eldest son and successor, married Mary, daughter of — Rich, of Clapham, in Surrey, Gent. by whom he had three sons; Sir Bartholomew, the eldest, his successor; Peter, the youngest, who was rector of Headcorn, in Kent, and one of the ten vicars of the diocese of Canterbury, who married Catharine, daughter of Mr. Thomas Tilden, of Canterbury, a civilian ;. by whom he had several children; and Henry, of Stroud, who married Elizabeth, daughter of Hatch Underwood; by whom he had one son, the Rev. Sir Henry Pix Heyman, the present baronet, and one daughter. Sir Peter died at Canterbury, Oct. 5, 1723, and lies buried in the church of St. Alphage, in that city, together with his wife.

III. Sir BARTHOLOMEW HEYMAN, Bart. succeeded his father, and having had his sight injured by gunpowder, and the family estate being much diminished by the confusion of the times, in the reigns of King Charles I. and II. he was made one of the poor knights of Windsor. He married Elizabeth, daughter of Thomas Nelson, of Sandwich, in Kent, merchant (a relation of the late pious Robert Nelson) by whom he had one son Peter, his successor. He died June 9, 1742, and was succeeded by his son,‡

IV. Sir PETER HEYMAN, Bart. who was in the navy, and at the age of 17 married —— Kempe, daughter and sole heiress of —— Kempe, Esq. of Plymouth, by whom he had three children, who, as well as his lady, are long since dead. He died in July, 1790, aged 70, and was succeeded in title by the

V. Rev. Sir HENRY PIX HEYMAN, M. A. of Canterbury, Bart. rector, in 1797, of Fressingfield, in Suffolk. He is the son of Henry, who was son of Peter, brother of Sir Bartholomew.

ARMS—Argent, on a chevron engrailed, azure, three cinquefoils, or; between three martlets, sable.

---

* Mr. Philipot says, p. 140, "He was a person, to whom, if I should not affirm myself signally and extraordinarily engaged, I deserved to be represented to posterity under the darkest complexion of ingratitude"   † Collins's Peerage, vol. III. p. 375.

‡ On a gravestone in St. George's Chapel, Windsor—In memory of Sir Bartholomew Heyman, late of the county of Kent, Bart. who was one of his majesty's poor knights of this place, and died the 9th day of June, 1742, aged 52 years. *Pole's Hist. and Antiq. of Windsor, p. 401.*

HEYMAN, OF SOMERFIELD, KENT.

CREST—On a wreath, a demi blackmoor, full faced; wreathed about his temples, and holding a rose, slipped, proper.

RESIDENCE—At Canterbury, and Fressingfield, in Suffolk.

---

1 RALPH HEYMAN   TABLE 81.
|
2 Peter Heyman
|
Elizabeth Tilde══3 Peter Heyman, gent. of the bed-chamber to Edw. IV.══Mary Tirrel, 1601

4 Ralph, 1601	William	Mary	Catharine	Margaret	Mildred	Anne	Emilia	Jane
Anne Naunton	Elizabeth Scot	Paul Johnson	William Hamon	John Poynet	John Hill	Thos. Corbet	Robert Cutts	John Honeywood
5 Henry, 1613	Wm. 1627	Elizabeth Sir T. Scot	Mary J. Boade	Anne A. Sprackling	Elizabeth Thomas Tournay	Margaret William Hales	Rebecca	Catharine Sir E. Scot
R. Horne, 1629								

6 Sir Peter Heyman, 1623   Ralph,   Robert,   Elizabeth   2 drs.
Sarah Collet | Mary Wolley, 1615 Betony   Reginald   Sir P. Godfrey

I. Sir Henry Heyman, 1658   Sarah   Peter,   Robert,   Sir Peter Godfrey
Mary Hoslord, 1646   L. Rook | Sir P. Godfrey   William   Thomas   Sarah Heyman

II. Sir Peter, Bart. 1725══Mary Rich   Henry   Robert   Mary══Sir R. Sandys   Anne

III. Sir Bartholomew, 1742══E. Nelson   Peter, 1762══Cath. Tilden   Sir Richard Sandys

IV. Sir Peter, 1790══Miss Kempe   Henry Heyman══Elizabeth Underwood

V. Rev. Sir Henry Pix Heyman, Bart.

---

81. GOODRICKE, of RIBSTAN, YORKSHIRE.

Created Baronet Aug. 14, 1641.

GOODRICKE is a Saxon name, signifying God's jurisdiction. It is mentioned by Ingulphus, and other historians of the Saxon times, and is inscribed upon several old Saxon coins. It appears from the visitation of Robert Glover, Somerset herald, that this family flourished for several generations at Nortingley or Nortonlee, in Somersetshire, all whose names, marriages, and issue are specified in the family pedigree. At length Henry Goodricke, the third son of Robert Goodricke, of Nortingley, marrying an heiress, the daughter of Thomas Stickford, Esq. in Lincolnshire, the family flourished in that county, where, after six generations,

1. William Goodricke, of East Kirby, in Lincolnshire, Esq. married to his second wife, Jane, the heiress of Mr. Williamson, of Boston, by whom he had three sons and a daughter; 1, John; 2, Thomas; and 3, Henry, ancestor to the present baronet, of whom hereafter. John, the eldest, succeeded to his father's estate, and was denominated of Bullingbrook, in Lincolnshire; and married ———, daughter of Sir Lionel Dimock, of Maring, in that county, Knt. Thomas, the second son, was in great favour with King Henry VIII. and was employed by him in several negotiations with foreign princes. He was one of the 32 commissioners, impowered to reform the canon laws, in that king's reign; and when King Edw. VI. had reduced that number to eight, he was one of them. He was sent, with others, to reform the university of Cambridge, and was one of the compilers of the English liturgy. He was 20 years bishop of Ely, and by King Edw. VI. was joined in commission, with others, to carry the order of the garter to the French king, and made an oration at his being invested with it. The same king made him lord chancellor of England; from which office he was removed by Queen Mary, and died unmarried, May 10, 1554, nine months after King Edward.*

---

* The Rev. Mr. Downes, in his Lives of the Compilers of the English Liturgy, gives this account of him:—This worthy prelate was descended from an ancient and wealthy family, and was born at Kirby, in Lincolnshire, and educated at Corpus Christi College,* in Cambridge. He took his first degree in arts, in 1510, the same year with Cranmer and Latimer; commenced master in 1514; and in 1516 was proctor of the university. He applied himself to his studies with unwearied industry, and acquired a great reputation, for his uncommon proficience, not only in divinity, but in the knowledge of the civil and canon law. His great merit soon recommended him to the favour of King Henry, who sent for him to court, advised with him in the most difficult affairs of state, and employed him in frequent embassies to foreign princes. In his reign he commenced doctor of laws; and on April 19, 1534, was consecrated bishop of Ely, in archbishop Cranmer's chapel, at Croydon. He continued bishop of that diocese above 20 years, and finding the palace at Ely old and ruinous, at his own charge repaired and beautified it, and built a spacious and magnificent gallery on the north side of it. He was a great favourer of the reformation, and on account of his singular learning, was consulted with and employed in the most important affairs relating thereto. He had a great hand in drawing up the Institution of a Christian Man,† and was a sincere promoter of pure religion, and a patron to all learned men, who he thought might be of service, towards the abolition of the papal tyranny and superstitions, and the restitution of true primitive Christianity. Among these he had a particular esteem for Dr. Richard Cox, whom he made his chaplain; and by his interest at court, prevailed to have the education of the young Prince Edward, committed to his care.

After the death of King Henry he was found so serviceable in promoting the regular progress of the reformation, and so useful a counsellor in all difficult affairs both of church and state; that it was thought necessary to bestow a suitable reward on him, for his great services. Accordingly he was sworn into the privy council, and in 1551 was made lord chancellor of England. He is, on this occasion, much abused by Dr. Burnet, who not content with a large invective against him, for accepting a post so inconsistent with the function and duty of a clergyman, as he pretends, goes on to load his memory with a heavy accusation of inconstancy in religion, turning with every tide, and resolving not to suffer for the reformation in Queen Mary's reign: but this is a most malicious and groundless charge, a base and unworthy slander on a person, to whom our reformed church is so much indebted; and had Dr. Burnet been but as free from those crimes, as the worthy prelate, whom he so scurrilously reflects on, he had left a much fairer character behind him, and been in greater repute with impartial posterity, than he is now ever like to be.

* Dr. Ashton says of Jesus College, Cambridge; but Willis, of King's College, Cambridge. Willis's Cathedrals, p. 550.
† For a more particular account of which book see the Life of Archbishop Cranmer, p. 11, 12.

GOODRICKE, OF RIBSTAN, YORKSHIRE.

2. Henry Goodricke, Esq. the third brother, before-mentioned, purchased Ribstan and other lands, in Yorkshire, of Charles Brandon, duke of Suffolk, in 1542; and died in 1556. He married Margaret, daughter and co-heiress of Sir Christopher Rawson, of London, Knt. and had several children. He was succeeded by his son,

3. Richard, who was born in 1524; was high sheriff of Yorkshire in 1579, and died in 1581. He married Clare, daughter of Richard Norton, of Norton Coniers, in Yorkshire, Esq. and was succeeded in his estate by his son,

4. Richard, who was born in 1560, who was also high sheriff of Yorkshire in 1591, and died in 1601. He married Meriol, daughter of William, lord Evre, and by her had seven sons and several daughters. He was succeeded in his estate by his eldest son,

5. Sir Henry Goodricke, Knt. who was born in 1580, and died in July, 1641. He married Jane, the daughter of Sir John Savile,* of Methly, in Yorkshire, Knt. one of the barons of the Exchequer, who at length was heiress to her brother of the whole blood, Sir Henry Savile, Bart. There were twelve children by this marriage, of which were three daughters, Jane and Elizabeth, who died unmarried, and Mary, the wife of Richard Hawksworth, of Hawksworth, in Yorkshire, Esq. and nine sons, whereof only three survived their father, viz. Sir John, his eldest; 2, Savile Goodricke, Esq. who died at Vienna, aged 32; and 3, Sir Francis, who married Hester, daughter of Peter Warburton, of the Grange, in Cheshire, Esq. but died without issue, Aug. 1674, at Durham, where he was chancellor.

I. Sir JOHN GOODRICKE, Knt. the eldest son, was created a baronet by King Charles I. He was born April 20, 1617, and suffered very much in the civil wars, for his loyalty to the king; and had his estate sequestered, and paid 1343*l*. 10s. composition to the sequestrators. He was prisoner first at Manchester, and then in the Tower of London; from whence he made his escape into France, where he continued till the restoration, when he was chosen knight of the shire for

---

But to return to bishop Goodrich: While chancellor he was admired by all for his impartial distribution of justice; he had the blessings and prayers of the poor, and the favour and esteem of the rich: his greatest enemies could not but acknowledge him gentle, just, and gracious; and his most intimate friends, when they brought a bad cause before him, found him inflexible, severe, and unprejudiced. Having a great esteem of bishop Day's learning, he laboured earnestly to reduce him from his prejudices, and dispose him to a favourable opinion of the reformation; but could do no good on a man so wilful and obstinate. He was one of those who drew up that excellent book, the Reformation of the Ecclesiastical Laws; and at the request of King Edward, put the great seal to the instrument for the succession of the lady Jane Grey. This was the reason why, upon the fall of that lady, the great seal was taken from him, within two days after Queen Mary came to London: and though it was thought fit for the present, to let him enjoy the benefit of the general pardon, yet there is no question to be made, but that he would, amongst the rest of the martyrs, have been brought to the stake for his religion, had it not pleased God to prevent it, by taking him to himself, on the 10th of May, 1554.

He died at Somersham, of the stone, and lies buried in the middle of the presbytery. On his tomb is this inscription:—Thomas Goodrichus, annos plus minus 20 hujus Ecclesiæ Episcopus, hoc loco sepultus est. Duobus Angliæ illustrissimis Regibus, variis & Religionis & Rei-publicæ Muneribus, pergratus fuit: Foris enim apud exteros principes sæpe Legatus; domi quidem, cum Regi Edvardo, ejus nominis sexto, aliquandiu Consiliarius extitisset, magnus tandem factus Angliæ Cancellarius: Chariorne Principi propter singularem Prudentiam, an amabilior Populo propter Integritatem & Abstinentiam fuerit, ad judicandum est perquam difficile. Obiit X die Maii anno a Christo nato, milessimo quingentesimo quinquagesimo quarto. Si Deus nobiscum, quis contra? *Willis's Cathedrals, vol. III. p. 358.*

* Lodge's Peerage of Ireland, vol. III. p. 163.

Yorkshire, and died November, 1670. He married first Catharine, daughter and heiress of Stephen Norcliffe, Esq. by whom he had Sir Henry; and secondly, Elizabeth, daughter of Alexander Smith, Esq. of Suffolk, and widow of William, lord viscount Fairfax, of Gilling; and by her had one son, Sir John.

II. Sir HENRY GOODRICKE, Knt. and Bart. eldest son and successor to his father in title and estate, was born Oct. 24, 1642. He was envoy extraordinary from Charles II. king of England, to Charles II. king of Spain; and was lieutenant-general of the ordnance, and privy councellor to King William III. He married Mary, daughter of Col. William Legg, and sister to George, lord Dartmouth; but died without issue, after a long illness, at Brentford, in Middlesex, March 5, 1704-5; and was interred, with his ancestors, at Ribstan. He was succeeded by his brother,

III. Sir JOHN GOODRICKE, Bart. who was born Oct. 16, 1654, and died, Dec. 10, 1705. He married Sarah, daughter of Sir Richard Hopkins, of Coventry, Knt. serjeant at law; by whom he left five sons and five daughters; 1, Sir Henry, who succeeded him; 2, Francis, who married Mrs. Jane Prescott, and had only one daughter; 3, Richard, who took orders, but is since dead, unmarried; 4, John-Savile, who married Mrs. Adeliza Herbert, and had issue two daughters, Adeliza and Mary; and 5, William, who married Mrs. Mary Russel, by whom he had one son, Henry, and two daughters.

IV. Sir HENRY GOODRICKE, Bart. eldest son and successor to his father, was born Sep. 8, 1677; and married Mary, the only child of Tobias Jenkyns, of Grimston, in Yorkshire, Esq. by his first wife, Mary Paulet, second daughter of the first Duke of Bolton; and by her, who died March 14, 1767, had four sons; 1, Sir John, his successor; 2, Henry, dead; 3, Thomas, late lieutenant-colonel of the 25th regiment of foot; and 4, the Rev. Henry Goodricke, prebendary of York, &c. also four daughters; 1, Mary, dead; 2, Elizabeth, who died unmarried; 3, Sarah, the wife of Thomas Goodricke, Esq. in 1794; and 4, Jane, of the Rev Mr. Wanley, of Rippon. Sir Henry died July 21, 1738, and was succeeded in dignity and estate by his eldest son,

V. The Right Hon. Sir JOHN GOODRICKE, Bart. He resided some time at Stockholm, as envoy extraordinary from his majesty to that court, and was made a privy counsellor Sep. 1, 1773. He was member of parliament for Rippon, and died Aug. 3, 1789; and was succeeded by his son,

VI. Sir HENRY GOODRICKE, Bart. who married first ———, a foreign lady of family; and secondly, Charlotte Fortescue, niece to the Earl of Clermont, in 1796. He has two sons and one daughter.

ARMS—Argent, on a fesse, gules, between two lions, passant guardant, sable, a fleur de lis, or, between two crescents, argent.

CREST—A demi lion, ermines, armed and langued, gules, issuing out of a ducal coronet, or; holding in his paws a battle-axe, proper, helved, or.

GOODRICKE, OF RIBSTAN, YORKSHIRE.   449

SUPPORTERS—Two naked boys, which are on the monument of Richard Goodricke, Esq. who was high sheriff of Yorkshire in 1579.
SEAT—At Ribstan Hall, and Altofts, in Yorkshire.

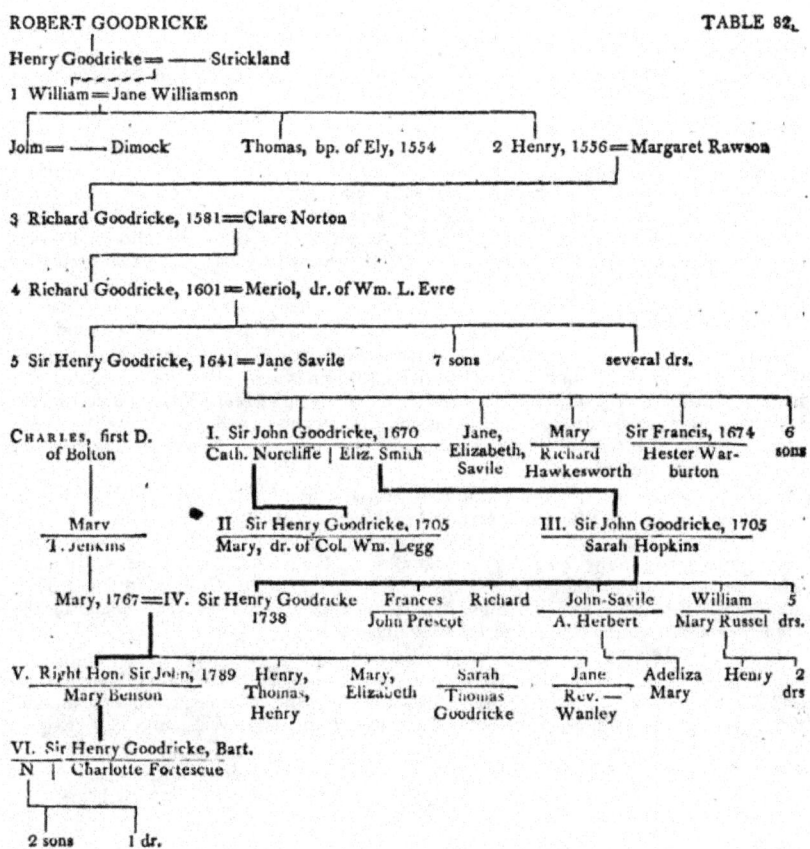

ROBERT GOODRICKE   TABLE 82.

Henry Goodricke = —— Strickland
1 William = Jane Williamson

John = —— Dimock   Thomas, bp. of Ely, 1554   2 Henry, 1556 = Margaret Rawson

3 Richard Goodricke, 1581 = Clare Norton

4 Richard Goodricke, 1601 = Meriol, dr. of Wm. L. Evre

5 Sir Henry Goodricke, 1641 = Jane Savile   7 sons   several drs.

CHARLES, first D. of Bolton | I. Sir John Goodricke, 1670 / Cath. Norcliffe | Elz. Smith | Jane, Elizabeth, Savile | Mary Richard Hawkesworth | Sir Francis, 1674 Hester Warburton | 6 sons

Mary / T. Jenkins | II Sir Henry Goodricke, 1705 / Mary, dr. of Col. Wm. Legg | III. Sir John Goodricke, 1705 / Sarah Hopkins

Mary, 1767 = IV. Sir Henry Goodricke 1738 | Frances John Prescot | Richard | John-Savile A. Herbert | William Mary Russel | 5 drs.

V. Right Hon. Sir John, 1789 / Mary Benson | Henry, Thomas, Henry | Mary, Elizabeth | Sarah Thomas Goodricke | Jane Rev. —— Wanley | Adeliza Mary | Henry | 2 drs

VI. Sir Henry Goodricke, Bart.
N | Charlotte Fortescue

2 sons   1 dr.

82. LAWLEY, of Spoonhill, Shropshire.

Created Baronet August 16, 1641.

IT appears by deeds in this family, that Thomas Lawley, Esq. was cousin and heir of John, lord Wenlock, privy counsellor to King Edw. IV. and knight of the garter; and succeeded to his lands in Wenlock, Calowton, &c. in the county of Salop, 17 Edw. IV.

2. Edward Lawley, of Wenlock, Esq. his son and heir, had issue

3. John, who married Mary, daughter of Thomas Cresset, of Upton, Esq. by whom he had two sons; 1, Thomas; 2, Richard, who married Beatrix, daughter and co-heiress of Griffin Hinton, Esq. and had issue Thomas, Robert, John, and George. Sir Thomas Lawley, of Wenlock, Knt. the eldest son, married Elizabeth, daughter of Sir Richard Newport, of High Arcall, in Salop, Knt. relict of Francis Lawley, of Spoonhill, Esq. He died Feb. 22, 1621, and had issue George, who died S. P. and Sir Edward Lawley, Knt. who by Susan, daughter of Sir Thomas Fisher, of Islington, in Middlesex, Bart. had issue only one daughter and heiress, Ursula,* the wife of Sir Roger Bertie, K. B. second son of Robert, earl of Lindsey.

4. Richard Lawley, of Spoonhill, Esq. before-mentioned, married Barbara, daughter and heiress of Edmund Rudgeley, Esq. (by Elizabeth, his wife, daughter and heiress of Robert Walsall, Esq.) by which marriage, 37 Henry VIII. he considerably augmented his estate, and had issue one son, Francis, and three daughters, Elizabeth, Alice, the wife of Thomas Salter, of Ricarden, and Mary, of Thomas Berisford, of Middlesex, Esq.

5. Francis Lawley, of Spoonhill, Esq. son and heir, married Elizabeth, daughter and heiress of Sir Richard Newport, of High Arcall, in Salop, Knt. (who surviving him was remarried to Sir Thomas Lawley, of Wenlock, Knt.) and left issue a daughter Jane, the wife of Stephen Smallman, Gent. and two sons; 1, Richard, who married Alice, daughter and heiress of John Caston, of Ceston, in Salop, Esq. and died S. P. 1623, and Thomas, heir to his brother, who was advanced to the dignity of a baronet by King Charles I. which

I. Sir THOMAS LAWLEY, Bart. married Anne, daughter and co-heiress of John Manning, of Hackney, in Middlesex, Esq. (remarried to Sir John Glynne, Knt.) and had issue two sons, Sir Francis, his successor, and Thomas, who died unmarried; also one daughter, Elizabeth, the wife of the hon. William Cecil, Esq. a younger son of William, earl of Salisbury.†

II. Sir FRANCIS LAWLEY, Bart. his eldest son and successor, married Anne, eldest daughter of Sir Thomas Whitmore, of Appley, in Salop, Bart. (by Elizabeth,

---

* Peerage of England, by Collins.
† Sir Thomas was buried, under a flat stone, in the north aisle of Twickenham church, Middlesex.

his wife, daughter and sole heiress of Sir William Acton, Knt. alderman of London) and left issue three sons; 1, Sir Thomas, his successor; 2, Francis, who died unmarried; and 3, Richard Lawley, of Ealing, in Middlesex, Esq. also three daughters; 1, Mary, the wife of John, second son of Sir Richard Verney, Bart. afterwards Lord Viscount Fermannagh, of the kingdom of Ireland; 2, Esther, of Robert Palmer, Esq. son of Sir Lewis Palmer, of Carlton, in Northamptonshire, Bart. and 3, Margaret, first of Leonard Powell, Esq. a younger son of Sir Nathaniel Powell, of Wyerton, in Kent, Bart. and secondly of Sir Nathan Wright, late of Southall, in Middlesex, Bart. by the last husband she had only two daughters. Sir Francis was master of the jewel office, and died in Oct. 1696; and was succeeded in dignity and estate by his eldest son,

III. Sir THOMAS LAWLEY, Bart. who married two wives, first Rebecca, second daughter and co-heiress of Sir Humphrey Winch, of Everton, in Bedfordshire, Bart. by whom he had nine sons and five daughters: eight of the sons died young, and Sir Robert was his successor: three of his daughters died also young; Anne was the wife of Sir John Cheshire, Knt. serjeant at law, who left her a widow, without issue, May 15, 1738; and Elizabeth, first the wife of Thomas Cotton, of Cotton-Bridge, in Warwickshire, Esq. who died June 10, 1710, aged 23, and was buried at Kingsbury church, Warwickshire, leaving an only son, Thomas;* and secondly of Sir Nicholas Lawes, Knt. governor of Jamaica: by the latter she had a daughter Maria, the wife of Simon Lutterel, Esq. created Lord Irnam in 1768, and Vis. Carhampton, of Castlehaven, in the county of Cork, Dec. 1780; by whom, among other children, she had Anne, first the wife of Chris. Horton, of Catton, in Derbyshire, and secondly of his royal highness Hen. Fred. duke of Cumberland, brother to his majesty, King George III. Sir Thomas married to his second lady, Mrs. Eliz. Perkins, widow (who surviving him, became the wife of Mr. Halfpenny) by whom he had issue one son, George Bateman Lawley, Esq. who married, June, 1738, Mary, daughter of —— Tomlinson, of Westminster, Esq. and one daughter, Judith, the wife of the hon. Richard Coningsby, Esq. who upon the death of the Earl Coningsby, his grandfather, succeeded him in the title of Lord Viscount Clanbrazil, of the kingdom of Ireland; but he dying, without issue, Dec. 18, 1729, she afterwards was the wife of Joseph Butler, of the Temple, Esq. who left her a second time a widow, Sep. 3, 1737. Sir Thomas dying Sep. 31, 1729, aged near 80 (and his second lady Jan. 28, 1739-40) was succeeded in dignity and estate by his only son by the first marriage,

IV. Sir ROBERT LAWLEY, Bart. who married, in 1726, Elizabeth, eldest daughter of Sir Lambert Blackwell, of Sprouston Hall, in Norfolk, Bart. by whom he had one son, Robert, and two daughters; Belina, the wife of Paul Orchard, of Stoke Abbey; and Jane, of the hon. Henry Willoughby, son of Lord Middleton. Sir Robert died in 1779, and was succeeded by his son,

V. Sir ROBERT LAWLEY, Bart. who was member of parliament for the county of Warwick; and in 1789 was made equerry to the Duke of Cumberland: he married Jane, only daughter of Beilby Thompson, Esq. and sister of Beilby Thomp. Esq. M.P. for Heydon. He died at his house in Holles Street, Cavendish Square, March 11, 1793, and was succeeded by his son,

* Dugdale's Warwickshire, vol. II. p. 1002.

LAWLEY, OF SPOONHILL, SHROPSHIRE.

VI. Sir ROBERT LAWLEY, Bart. who in Sep. 1793, married Maria, daughter of Joseph Denison, Esq. of London, banker.

ARMS—Argent, a cross formè, extended to the extremes of the shield, chequy, or and sable.
CREST—On a wreath, a wolf passant, sable.
SEATS—At Spoonhill, in Shropshire, and Canwall, in Staffordshire.

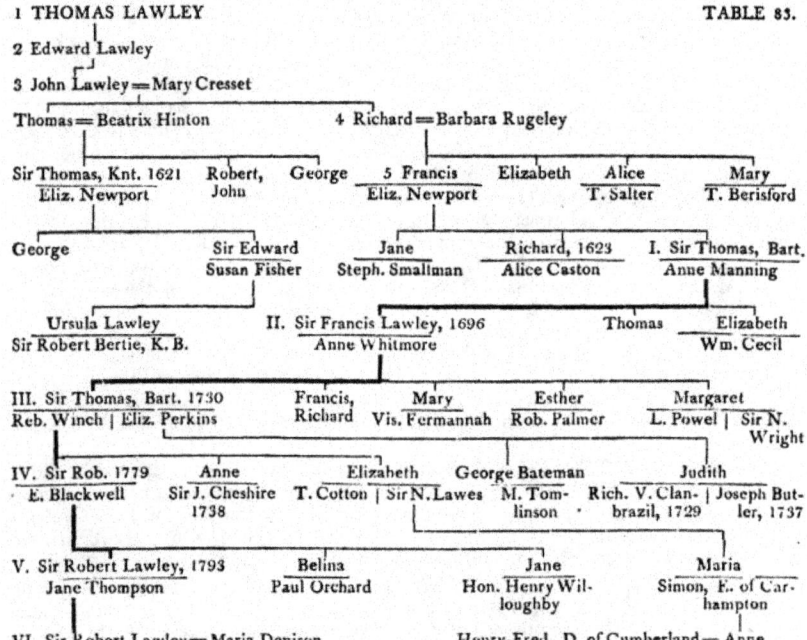

TABLE 83.

1 THOMAS LAWLEY
2 Edward Lawley
3 John Lawley = Mary Cresset

Thomas = Beatrix Hinton   4 Richard = Barbara Rugeley

Sir Thomas, Knt. 1621   Robert,   George   5 Francis   Elizabeth   Alice   Mary
Eliz. Newport   John   Eliz. Newport   T. Salter   T. Berisford

George   Sir Edward   Jane   Richard, 1623   I. Sir Thomas, Bart.
                    Susan Fisher   Steph. Smallman   Alice Caston   Anne Manning

Ursula Lawley   II. Sir Francis Lawley, 1696   Thomas   Elizabeth
Sir Robert Bertie, K. B. Anne Whitmore   Wm. Cecil

III. Sir Thomas, Bart. 1730   Francis,   Mary   Esther   Margaret
Reb. Winch | Eliz. Perkins   Richard   Vis. Fermannah Rob. Palmer   L. Powel | Sir N. Wright

IV. Sir Rob. 1779   Anne   Elizabeth   George Bateman   Judith
E. Blackwell   Sir J. Cheshire   T. Cotton | Sir N. Lawes   M. Tom-   Rich. V. Clan- | Joseph But-
                      1738   linson   brazil, 1729 ler, 1737

V. Sir Robert Lawley, 1793   Belina   Jane   Maria
Jane Thompson   Paul Orchard   Hon. Henry Wil-   Simon, E. of Car-
                                              loughby   hampton

VI. Sir Robert Lawley = Maria Denison   Henry-Fred. D. of Cumberland = Anne

83. DAVIE, of CREEDY, DEVONSHIRE.

Created Baronet Sep. 9, 1641.

THE name of this ancient family was originally local, and derived from the habitation of their progenitors, who (as appears by deeds, writings, and other records, in the Tower, and other places) were, among other lands, owners of an ancient mansion house and demesne lands, situate in the parish of Harwood, and anciently known by the name of the Wey, so called from the situation of it, being about the middle way, and almost equidistant from Barnstaple, Biddeford, and Torrington, three chief towns in the north part of Devon. The inhabitants of this seat, and ancestors of this family were first of all known by the name of De la Wey, and the first of them mentioned in their pedigree,* had coat armour, which has ever since continued the same to this family, although their names have diversly been written De la Wey,† then Dewy, De Vie, and afterwards contracted and softened into Davie; unto which variation it was the more subject, for that many hundred years since, one Walter Pollard, matching with the daughter and heiress-general of this family, became owner of the said ancient habitation, called Wey, which gave name to the family, as aforesaid, and which ever since the said marriage has continued with the Pollards, who in respect of that match do also, at this day, quarter the coat of the Davies. The first ancestor mentioned in the pedigree (which is a very fine one) is

1. William de-la-Wey, alias De-Wy, who came over with William the Conqueror: ‡ he left issue three sons; 1, Walter; 2, William; and 3, Henry, of Barling-

---

* Now in the possession of the family, drawn up by William Ryley, Norroy.

† Mr. Westcote's Survey of Devon, in Harw.

‡ And thus wrote at the bottom of it:—Whereas this descent or genealogy of Sir John Davy, of Creedy, in Crediton, in the county of Devon, Bart. is carefully compared with ancient deeds, evidences, and records, in the Tower of London and Office of Arms; and that the matches, quarterings, and alliances of this ancient family, are duly marshalled and delineated, which I have perused and examined, at the request of William Davy, aforesaid. Therefore I do approve thereof, and (as much as in me is) do allow and confirm the same. In testimony whereof I have hereunto subscribed my name, A. D. 1647.

WILLIAM RYLEY, Norroy.

His picture is painted on the side of the pedigree, in the armour of those times, with a helmet on his head, and a plume of feathers; and in his right hand a battle-axe, and his shield slung over his left arm; with his arms, argent, a chevron, sable, between three mullets, pierced, gules. On one side of him is wrote the following old lines, in English, being a translation of some old Latin verses, on the other side of him:

What profit pedigrees, or longe discents,	For keepinge up our fame, which else would fall,
From farre fetcht blood, or painted monuments.	If besides birth, theire bee noe worth at all;
Of our great grandsiers visage, 'tis most sad,	For who 'counts him a gentleman, whose grace
To trust unto the worth another had.	Is all in's name, but otherwise is base.

DAVIE, OF CREEDY, DEVONSHIRE.

ton Walter had one daughter, Elizabeth, his sole heiress, who was the wife of Walter Pollard.*

2. William Devie, alias Davy, the second son, was of Ebberleigh.†

3. William Devie, alias Dewey, his son and heir, had issue

4. David Devy, alias Dewy, whose son,

5. Thomas Dewye, alias Davy, died in 1303.

6. David Devye, alias Dewy, was his son and heir, aged 13 in 1303; whose son,

7. Robert Davye, alias Dewy, in an old deed, wrote Robertus De-Via, married Lettice, daughter and heiress of John De-Oulacombe, by whom he had issue

8. Roger Davy, who by Thomasine, daughter and heiress of John Fitzwalter, of Ebberleigh, had issue,

9. William, his son and heir, who married Alice, daughter of Richard Reyney, of Egsford, in Devonshire.‡ He served in parliament for Melcomb, in Dorsetshire, 4 Henry VI. and for Barnstaple 25 Henry VI.

10. Richard Davy, son and heir of William aforesaid, had two sons, William and Robert. This family, after having long flourished at Ebberleigh and Uppicot, in the parish of Benford, near Great Torrington, in Devonshire, which hereditarily descended to them from Gilbert Uppicot, who possessed it in the reign of Edw. II. now separated in these two brothers; William continued the line of Ebberleigh, and Robert, the second son, settled at Crediton; which

11. Robert married the daughter and heiress of John Thomas, alias Bardolph,§ of Titchfield, in Hants, by the daughter and heiress of William Bardolph, of Titchfield;

Or who will honour hime, that's honour's shame;
Noble in nothinge but a noble name.
Its better to be meanly borne, and good,
Then one unworthy of his noble blood.
Though all thy walls shine with thy pedigree,
Yet virtue only makes nobility.

Then that this pedigree may usefull bee,
Search out the vertues of your family;
And to be worthy of your fathers' name,
Learne out the good they did, and doe the same:
For if you beare their armes and not their fame,
Those ensignes of their worth will be your shame.

* Walterus de-la-Wey, filius & hæres Willimi De-la-Wey,* dedit & concessit Waltero Pollard totam terram De-la-Wey, habend. & tenend. sibi & heredibus impertuum, &c. Hys testibus, D.nus Henrico de Wolley, Thomæ de Martin, Millitibus, Willmo de Stapleton, Henrico de Winscott, Phillippo de Stafford, Rico Wittosley, Rogero Durant, & aliis. And sealed with the holy lamb.

† —— Willimus Davy modo de Ebberleigh, feofavit Henricum de Barlington fratrem de terris in Barlington, sans date; and a release per Nomen Will. de Vye, modo de Ebberleigh, to Henry, of Barlington, sans date; and both sealed with the chevron, between three mullets, pierced. Richard De-Wy, alias Devie, son and heir of William Devie, of Ebberleigh. Richardus Dewy, dedit Willmo primogenito suo, omnes terras in Ebberleigh. Teste Rado Monocke, Willo Stoford, Henrico de la Combe, & aliis; sans date.

‡ —— Rogerus Devy,† confirmavit Willo filio suo, & Aliciæ uxori suæ Terris in Ebberleigh, quæ ei descendebat per mortem Roberti Patris, & Leticiæ uxoris, Matris Dni Rogeri. Hys testibus, Richdo Barry, Johanne Pollard, Willo Wollacombe, & aliis. dat. 2 Henrici sexti. And we also find, that Johannes filius Walteri de Ebberleigh, dedit Willimo Davy, terram in Ebberleigh, per Cartam dat. 8vo Henrico 5ti. Hys testibus, Rico. Barry, Willimo Wollacombe, & aliis.

§ This Thomas, alias Bardolph, tooke a shippe in Ireland, of 400 tunne, with the ensigne of Burgundy, which was given unto him upon a canton, for an augmentation, and had also the armes of his

* From the pedigree.   † Ibid.

DAVIE, OF CREEDY, DEVONSHIRE.

by whom he had four sons; 1, John, the elder, of Crediton; 2, Gilbert, of Canon Teign; 3, Lawrance, of Medland; and 4, John,* the younger, of Creedy, in Samford, and Crediton; and they were the original of as many families of note, in the county of Devon.

12. John Davie, the younger, was thrice mayor of Exeter, a very hospitable person, and in his first mayoralty, 1584, when Don Antonio, king of Portugal, being driven out of his kingdom, by Philip, king of Spain, came to Plymouth, and from thence to Exeter, where he and his retinue were lodged by this mayor, in his own house, and by him very nobly entertained during his abode there, which was a considerable time.† He married Margaret, daughter of George Southcote, of Calverly, in Devon, Esq. by whom he left issue a daughter, Margaret, the wife of Gideon Heydon, of Farwood Epford, in Devon, Esq. and a son,

I. JOHN DAVIE, of Creedy, Esq. who on Sep. 9, 1641, was created a baronet by King Charles I. He married first Julian, daughter of Sir William Strode, of Newnham, by whom he had issue four daughters; 1, Mary, the wife of John Willoughby, of Payhembury, in Devon, Esq. 2, Elizabeth, of Arthur Copplestone, Esq. 3, Julian; and 4, Margaret, the wife of Thomas Bear, of Hunsome, in Devon, Esq. also four sons; 1, Sir John, his successor; 2, William, a counsellor at law, who married Margaret, daughter of Sir Francis Clark, of Putney, in Surrey, Knt. and had issue one son, Sir William, hereafter mentioned, and four daughters; 1, Margaret, the wife of Roger Tuckfield, of Raddon, in Devon, Esq. father of Roger Tuckfield, Esq. member for Ashburton; 2, ——, of Sir John Tremaine, Knt. serjeant at law; 3, Mary, who died Aug. 24, 1728, aged 71, and lies buried at Ealing, in Middlesex: she was the wife of Christopher Spicer, of London, Esq. father of the late William Spicer, Esq. master in chancery; and 4, Julian, who died unmarried. 3, Robert; and 4, Humphrey, a merchant, in London, both mentioned hereafter. The said Sir John married secondly Isabel, daughter of —— Hele, of Gnaton, in Devon, Esq. by whom he had issue only one daughter, Isabel, the wife of Sir Walter Yonge, of Culliton, in Devonshire, created a baronet in 1661,

---

mother, whoe was the daughter and heire of Bardolph, graunted him by Sir Gilbert Dethick, garter principall king of armes; which, together with the descent, were taken out of a record of the said Mr. Garter's owne writinge. *In the pedigree, signed Wm. Ryley, Norroy.*

* He founded an alms-house at Crediton, for the relief of two poor men and their wives, and two single persons: the couples are allowed 14*d.* a-piece, and the single people 18*d.* a-piece per week. He also founded another alms-house, for the like number, with the same allowance (both, in the whole 40*l.* per annum, for ever) within the parish of St. Mary Arches, Exeter. The inscription on his monument, in that church, to the honour of his memory, I here subjoin:*

This marble monument, this fading brass,	Whose bar was Faith, whose pillars Piety;
Might have beene spar'd, for neither needful was;	And whose engravings works of Charity.
To stand a register of Davie's name,	Then let the dead trust to a dying tomb;
Who, living, did erect a fairer frame;	But how can Death in Davie find a room?
And far more lasting; whose foundation,	Whose soul in Heaven alive doth aye remain,
Was firmly grounded on the Corner Stone;	Whose works on Earth so many lives maintain.

† This John Davie, the younger, affecting the coate of the noble familly of Bardolph, to which his mother was heire, had the said coate graunted him by Sir William Dethicke, garter principall king of armes, the 20th of Aprill, Anno 1594, and quartered his owne in the second place, as appears in this escocheon. *From the pedigree.*

* Prince's Worthies of Devon, p. 273.

DAVIE, OF CREEDY, DEVONSHIRE.

grandfather to the late Sir William Yonge, Bart. K. B. and secretary at war. He was succeeded in dignity and estate by his eldest son,

II. Sir JOHN DAVIE, Bart. who was high sheriff of Devon in 1671, and married three wives; first Eleanor, daughter of Sir John Ackland, of Columbe-John, in Devonshire, Bart. by whom he had no issue; secondly, Triphœna, daughter and co-heiress of Richard Reynel, of Creedy Wiger, alias Lower Creedy, in Devon, Esq. (by Mary, daughter and co-heiress of John Perryam, Esq.) by whom he became possessed of that estate; and by her he left issue Sir John, his successor; Richard, who died an infant; and Triphœna, who died unmarried. His third wife was Amy, daughter of Edmund Parker, of Burrington, in Devonshire, Esq. by whom he had no issue. He was succeeded in dignity and estate by his eldest son,

III. Sir JOHN DAVIE, Bart. who was high sheriff of Devon in 1689, and dying a bachelor, the dignity and estate descended to his cousin, Sir William, son of William, the counsellor, before-mentioned; which

IV. Sir WILLIAM DAVIE, Bart. successor to his cousin, married first Mary, daughter and heiress of —— Stedman, of Downside, in Somersetshire, Esq. by whom he left only one daughter, Mary, the wife of Nicholas Hooper, of Raleigh, in Devonshire, Esq. and secondly, Abigail, daughter of John Pollexfen, of Wembury, in Devonshire, Esq. by whom he left only three daughters; Margaret, the wife of Stephen Northleigh, of Paymor, Esq. Frances, of Sir George Chudleigh, of Ashton, Bart. and Triphœna, who died unmarried. This Sir William, leaving no issue male; and his uncle, Robert Davie, Esq. before-mentioned, having left only two sons, who both died bachelors, and a daughter, the wife of —— Fletcher, of London, he was succeeded in dignity and estate by his cousin, Sir John, the son of Humphrey, the merchant, before-mentioned, who had, about 1662, removed, with his family, to New England. He married ——, the sister of Edmund White, of Clapham, in Surrey, merchant, by whom he had issue the said Sir John, who was educated at the university of Cambridge, in New England, and there took his degree of bachelor of arts, and afterwards engaged and continued in his father's business, as a merchant, till he succeeded to the honour and estates of his ancestors. This

V. Sir JOHN DAVIE, Bart. while in New England, married Mrs. Elizabeth Richards, of that country, by whom he had three sons; 1, Sir John, his successor; 2, Humphrey, a bachelor; and 3, William, who married Ellen, daughter of Nicholas Jackson, of Bristol, merchant, who died Nov. 14, 1757, aged 51; and lies buried in the south aisle of Henbury church, in Gloucestershire: also three daughters; 1, Mary, the wife of the Rev. Thomas Bishop, of Barnstaple; 2, Sarah, of Christopher Savery, of Shilson, near Modbury, in Devonshire, Esq. and 3, Elizabeth, of Ebenezer Mussel, of London, Esq. Sir John was greatly esteemed for his piety, benevolence, and every virtue, religious and social. He was succeeded in honour and estate by his eldest son,

VI. Sir JOHN DAVIE, Bart. who by Elizabeth, daughter of John Acland, of Kelliton, in Devonshire, Esq. who died Jan. 7, 1777, left issue four children, all minors. Sir John, his successor; William, vicar of Exminster, in Devonshire, who died in 1778; and Anne, and Juliana.

DAVIE, OF CREEDY, DEVONSHIRE.

VII. Sir JOHN DAVIE, Bart. his eldest son and successor, married Catharine, daughter of John Stokes, of Rill, in Devonshire, Esq. who died in 1776; by whom he had five daughters; Susanna, Catharine, Juliana, Elizabeth, and Frances; one of which was the wife of the Rev. Mr. Hurrell, of Drewsteignton: and two sons; William, who died in Dec. 1769, and John, his successor. Sir John died at Creedy, Sep. 18, 1792, aged 62, and was succeeded by his only surviving son,

VIII. Sir JOHN DAVIE, Bart. who in Sep. 1796, married ———, eldest daughter of Sir William Lemon, Bart. by whom he has issue.

ARMS—Argent, sable, a chevron between three mullets, pierced, gules.
CREST—The holy lamb.
MOTTO—*Auspice Christo*.
SEAT—At Creedy, in Devonshire.

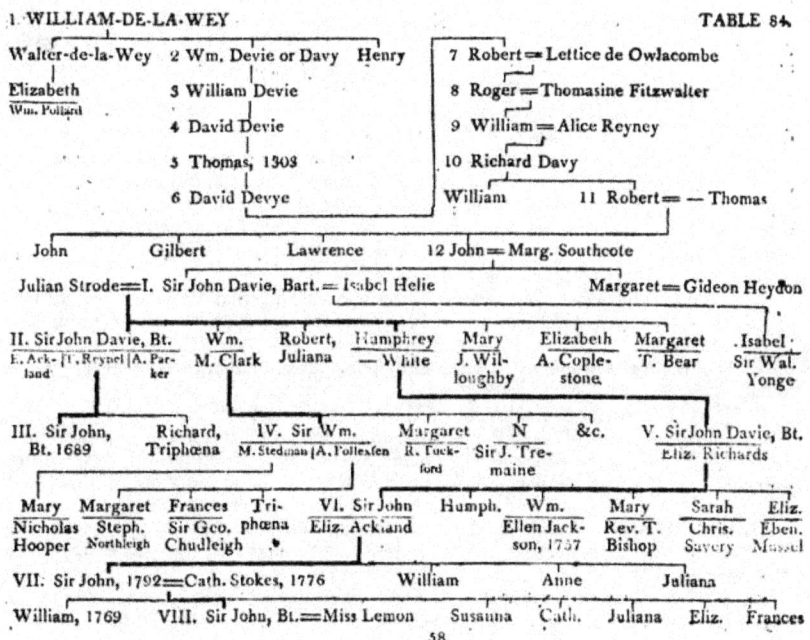

84. ANDREWS, of Denton, Northamptonshire.

Created Baronet Dec. 11, 1641.

1. SIR Robert Andrews, of Normandy, Knt. came into England with William the Conqueror, and married the daughter and heiress of Sir Robert Winwick, of Winwick, in the county of Northampton, a parish lying in the hundreds of Guilesburrow, on the skirts of that county, upon the borders of Warwickshire. On this match he settled there, and this place became the seat of his posterity for many ages. He was succeeded by his son and heir,

2. Sir Robert Andrews, of Winwick, Knt. who married the daughter of Sir Martin Brewer, and had issue

3. Sir John Andrews, of Winwick, Knt. who by the daughter of Sir John Norton, had issue

4. Sir Thomas Andrews, of Winwick, Knt. whose wife was the daughter of Sir John Cortney; by whom he had issue two sons, Sir Thomas and John, who settled at Mamwell, in Warwickshire, by marrying Mary, daughter and heiress of —— Mamuell, of Mamuell aforesaid, and left posterity.

5. Sir Thomas Andrews, of Winwick, Knt. eldest son and heir, married the daughter of the Lord Breasey, and had issue

6. George Andrews, of Winwick, Esq. who married the daughter and heiress of the Baron of Burford, and had issue two sons, George and Thomas. The posterity of George flourished at this place for several descents, and a branch of this family settled at Bolston, by marrying an heiress; from whom descended Richard Andrews, Esq. of Earlscoln, in Essex, and of Bromley, in Middlesex. This gentleman was of the 24th generation of this family.

7. Thomas Andrews, Esq. aforesaid, second son, married the daughter and heiress of —— Denton, in the county of Northampton (now called Doddington) and by her had issue

8. Thomas Andrews, Esq. his son and heir; from whom, after several generations, was

I. Sir WILLIAM ANDREWS, of Denton, the first baronet of this family, who married the daughter of —— Paris, of Linton, in Cambridgeshire, Esq. by whom he had five sons, three whereof were killed at the battle of Worcester, in the king's service. Sir William died of the gout, and was buried at Bury St. Edmund's, in Suffolk.

II. Sir JOHN ANDREWS, Bart. his eldest son, succeeded his father in title and estate; but leaving only a daughter, that died unmarried, was succeeded by his youngest brother,

III. Sir WILLIAM ANDREWS, Bart. who married Eleanor, daughter of Edward Atslow, of Downham Hall, in Essex, Esq. by whom he had two sons, Sir

ANDREWS, OF DENTON, NORTHAMPTONSHIRE.

Francis, his successor, and William, who died an infant: also six daughters; Mary, Anne, Frances, Eleanor, Magdalen, and Catharine, the wife of Joseph Petre, of Fidlers, in Essex, Esq. Sir William was succeeded in dignity and estate by his only son,

IV. Sir FRANCIS ANDREWS, Bart. who married Bridget, daughter of Sir Thomas Cliffton, of Lytham, in Lancashire, Knt. (by his second lady, Bridget, daughter of Sir Edward Hussey, of Hunnington, in Lincolnshire, Bart.) and has issue one son, William, and two daughters, Bridget and Eleanor. Sir Francis died April 3, 1759, and was succeeded by his only son,

V. Sir WILLIAM ANDREWS, the present baronet.

ARMS—Gules, a saltire, or; surmounted of another, vert.
CREST—On a wreath, a blackmoor's head in profile, couped at the shoulders, and wreathed about the temples.

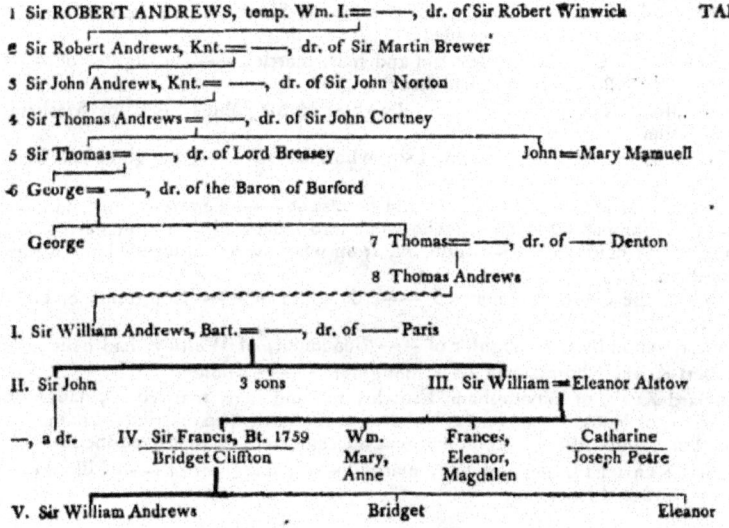

TABLE 85.

1 Sir ROBERT ANDREWS, temp. Wm. I.=——, dr. of Sir Robert Winwick
2 Sir Robert Andrews, Knt.=——, dr. of Sir Martin Brewer
3 Sir John Andrews, Knt.=——, dr. of Sir John Norton
4 Sir Thomas Andrews=——, dr. of Sir John Cortney
5 Sir Thomas=——, dr. of Lord Bressey   John=Mary Mamuell
6 George=——, dr. of the Baron of Burford

George   7 Thomas=——, dr. of —— Denton
                                8 Thomas Andrews

I. Sir William Andrews, Bart.=——, dr. of —— Paris

II. Sir John   3 sons   III. Sir William=Eleanor Alstow

——, a dr.   IV. Sir Francis, Bt. 1759   Wm.   Frances,   Catharine
            Bridget Cliffton   Mary, Eleanor,   Joseph Petre
                                         Anne   Magdalen

V. Sir William Andrews   Bridget   Eleanor

85. KAYE, of Woodesham, alias Woodsome.

Created Baronet Feb. 4, 1641.

THE family of Kaye is of great antiquity in the county of York, being descended from Sir Kaye,* one of the knights of the warlike table of Prince Arthur.

1. Sir John Kaye, in the reign of William the Conqueror, married ——, daughter and heiress of Sir John Woodesham, of Woodesham, Knt. an ancient Briton; by whom he had two sons; 1, Sir John; and 2, Robert, who went into Lancashire, and married the daughter and heiress of —— Cromton, of Cromton, from whom descended the Keays, of Lancashire.

2. Sir John Keay, of Woodesham, Knt. eldest son and heir, married ——, daughter and heiress of Sir John Copley, by whom he had

3. Sir Robert Keay, who married ——, daughter and heiress of —— Mallet, of Upton Mallet, and had issue

4. Sir Robert Keay, Knt. who married ——, daughter of the Lord Normanville, by whom he had two sons; 1, Sir Thomas; and 2, Ralph Keay, who married ——, daughter and heiress of —— Bendon, of Bendon, in Lincolnshire; from whom the Keays of Lincolnshire were descended.

5. Sir Thomas Keay, Knt. eldest son and heir, married ——, daughter of —— Bellingham, of Bellingham, and had issue

6. Sir William Keay, who by ——, daughter of Sir John Danby, of Masham, Knt. was father of

7. Thomas Keay, of Woodesham, Esq. who married ——, daughter and heiress of —— Bradfeld, whose son,

8. George, married ——, daughter and heiress of —— Tempest, and had issue two sons; 1, Thomas; 2, Robert, who went into Devonshire, and married ——, the daughter and heiress of —— Malbank, from whom were descended the Keays of Devonshire.

9. Thomas, the eldest son, married ——, daughter of —— Constable, of Cliff, and had issue,

10. Robert, who, by the daughter of —— Beaumont, of Whitley, had issue

11. Robert Keay, who married ——, daughter of —— Blundell.

12. Richard Keay, of Woodesham, Esq. his son and heir, married ——, daughter of —— Rookby, of Rookby, and had 1, Robert; 2, Richard, who married ——, daughter of —— Hanbury, and settled in Kent, and was ancestor to those that lived there.

13. Robert Keay, Esq. son and heir, married ——, daughter of —— Pilkington, of Bradley, and had issue

* Wotton, from the Inform. of the late Sir Ar. Kaye.

KAYE, OF WOODSOME, YORKSHIRE.

14. John Keay, Esq. who married ——, daughter and heiress of —— Gremston, of Gremston Garth, and had issue

15. Sir John Keay, of Woodesham, Knt. who by the daughter of —— Walcot, of Walcot, was father of

16. Sir Robert Keay, Knt. who married ——, daughter of Sir John Dabridgcourt, and had issue Sir William and Thomas, who went into Cumberland, and by ——, daughter of —— Walball, of Walball, was ancestor to the Keays of Carlisle.

17. Sir William Keay, Knt. married ——, daughter of Lord Darcye, whose son,

18. Sir Thomas, by ——, daughter of Sir John Deygton, Knt. had issue

19. Sir Roger Keay, Knt. who married ——, daughter of the Baron of Kinderton, and had issue

20. Sir George Keay, who married ——, daughter of Sir Robert Maleverer, Knt. and had issue Sir William Keay, Robert, ancestor to those of Oakenshaw, and John, ancestor to those of Thorpe.

21. Sir William Keay, Knt. eldest son and heir, married ——, daughter of —— Gaston, of Sedbuer, and had issue

22. John Keay, of Woodesham, Esq. who by ——, daughter of —— Harley, of Harley, had issue

23. Robert, who married ——, daughter of —— Plumpton, of Plumpton, and had issue

24. Arthur Keay, Esq. living temp. Henry VIII. who married Beatrice, daughter of Matthew Wentworth, of Bretton, in Yorkshire, Esq. by whom he had one son, John, and one daughter, Anne, the wife of William Aldbrough, of Aldbrough, Esq. who had a daughter, Dorothy, the wife of Francis Rawdon, Esq. ancestor to Francis, earl of Moira; and was succeeded by his son,[*]

25. John Keaye, Esq. living in 1585; who by Dorothy, daughter of Robert Maleverer, of Wothersome, in Yorkshire, Esq. son and heir of Sir William, had issue

26. Robert, living in 1612, who married Anne, daughter of John Flower, of Whitwell, in Rutlandshire, Esq. and had issue

27. John Kaye, of Woodsome, Esq. who married Anne, daughter of Sir John Ferne, Knt. secretary to the council in the North, temp. Charles I. and dying in 1641, left issue one son, John, and a daughter Elizabeth, the wife of Ralph Asheton, of Middleton, in Lancashire, Esq.

I. Sir JOHN KAYE, of Woodsome, Knt. the only son of John aforesaid, was advanced to the dignity of a baronet, by his majesty King Charles I. He was colonel of a regiment of horse, in that king's service, in the unfortunate civil war, and suffered very much, both in person and estate; but lived to see the happy restoration, and died July 25, 1662. He married first Margaret, daughter and coheiress of Thomas Moseley, Esq. lord-mayor of York, by Elizabeth, his wife, daughter and coheiress of Thomas Trigot, of South Kirby, in Yorkshire, Esq. by whom he had two sons, Sir John and Robert, who died unmarried; and one daughter,

[*] Irish Peerage, vol. III. p. 101.

Margaret, who also died unmarried. He married secondly Elizabeth, daughter of Sir Ferdinando Leigh, of Middleton, juxta Leeds, Knt. and relict of Francis Burdett, of Birthwaite, in Yorkshire, Esq. and by her had four sons; 1, George; 2, Arthur; 3, Matthew; and 4, another Arthur, who all died without issue; and five daughters; Anne, Grace, another Anne, Jane, and Elizabeth, who all died unmarried. His third lady was Catharine, daughter of Sir William St. Quintin, of Harpham, Bart. and relict of Michael, son and heir of Sir George Wentworth (who afterwards married first Henry Sandys, of Downe, in Kent, Esq. and to her fourth husband Hugh, earl of Eglington, in Scotland); but by her he had no issue. He was succeeded in title and estate by his eldest son by the first marriage,

II. Sir JOHN KAYE, Bart. who served several years as knight of the shire for the county of York, and married Anne, daughter of William Lister, of Thornton, in Craven, Esq. by whom he had five sons; John, and Robert, who both died young; Sir Arthur, his successor; George (who by Dorothy, daughter and heiress of Robert Savile, of Bryan Royd, near Eland, in Yorkshire, Esq. had issue Sir John, his successor; Robert, a merchant at Leeds, who died unmarried; George, who died young, and a daughter Catharine, the wife of Nicholas Roberts, of Hexham, in Northumberland, Esq.) and Thomas, who died without issue; also two daughters, Anne, the wife of Sir Bryan Stapylton, of Myton, in Yorkshire, Bart. and Catharine, who died young. Sir John died in 1706, and was succeeded in dignity and estate by his third, but eldest surviving son,

III. Sir ARTHUR KAYE, Bart. who served, for several years, as knight of the shire for the county of York, and married Anne, daughter and co-heiress of Sir Samuel Marrow, of Berkswell, in Warwickshire, Bart. by Mary, daughter and coheiress of Sir Arthur Gayley, of Newland, in Warwickshire, Knt.) by whom he had one daughter, Elizabeth, the wife first of George, lord Lewisham, eldest son of the right honourable the Earl of Dartmouth, who was member of parliament for Great Bedwin, in Wiltshire, and died of the small pox, at his house in Holles Street, Cavendish Square, London, Aug. 29, 1732. By her he had a son William, now Earl of Dartmouth. She was afterwards the wife of Francis, earl of Guildford, and died in 1745. Sir Arthur dying in 1726, without issue male, and his relict in Aug. 1740, the title descended to his nephew,

IV. Sir JOHN LISTER KAYE, Bart. son of George Kaye, Esq. younger brother to Sir Arthur: he was elected one of the representatives in parliament for the city of York, in June 1734; alderman of the said city, July 3, 1735, and lord-mayor thereof in 1737. He married first Ellen, daughter of John Wilkinson, of Greenhead, near Huthersfield, in Yorkshire, Esq. by whom he had one son, John, his successor, and one daughter, Ellen, who died young; secondly, Dorothy, daughter of Richard Richardson, of North Bierley, in the West Riding of the county of York, M. D. by whom he had Richard, who was elected by the university of Oxford, scholar of the laws of England, on the first establishment of the Vinerian Foundation, in 1758; and having made the tour of Europe, was on his return preferred to the rectory of Kirby, in Nottinghamshire, and elected fellow of the Royal Society, and of the Society of Antiquarians in 1765; appointed chaplain in ordinary to his majesty in 1766, and prebendary of York in 1768. Dorothy, the wife

KAYE, OF WOODSOME, YORKSHIRE.

TABLE 86.

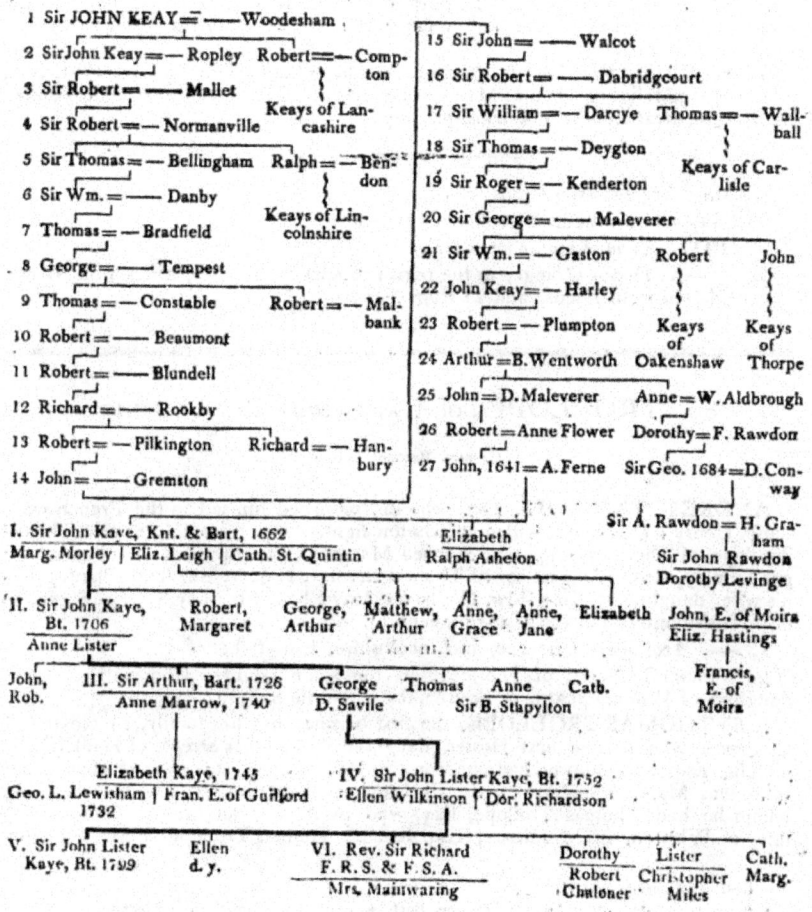

of Robert Chaloner, of Bishop of Auckland, Esq. and Lister, of Christopher Miles; Catharine and Margaret, since dead: one of his daughters was the wife of William Scott, of Leeds, Esq. Sir John died April 5, 1752; his lady Aug. 24, 1772; and was succeeded by his son,

V. Sir JOHN LISTER KAYE, Bart. he served the office of high sheriff for the county of York, in 1761, and died, unmarried, Dec. 27, 1789; and was succeeded by his half brother,

VI. Sir RICHARD KAYE, dean of Lincoln, who married Aug. 29, 1791, Mrs. Mainwaring, relict of Thomas Mainwaring, Esq. and daughter of William Fenton, of Glassho, near Leeds, in Yorkshire, Esq.

ARMS—Argent, two bends, sable.
CREST—On a wreath, a goldfinch, proper.
MOTTO—*Kynd Kynn Knawne Kepe.*
SEAT—At Denby Grange, in the parish of Kirkheaton, five Miles from Wakefield, ten from Leeds, and 27 from York.

86. TROLLOPE, of Casewick, Lincolnshire.

Created Baronet Feb. 5, 1641.

ANDREW TROLLOPE, Esq. who distinguished himself in the French wars, temp. Henry VI. and was killed at Towton fight, temp. Edw. IV. as also Thomas Trollope, of Thorleby, Esq. who married Margaret, daughter and co-heiress of Roger Lumley, Esq. youngest son of Thomas Lumley, Esq. by Elizabeth Plantagenet, his wife, daughter of King Edw. IV. by the lady Elizabeth Lucy,* are supposed to be of this family; but the first we meet with in a pedigree is

1. —— Trollope, of Bourne, in Lincolnshire, Esq. father of

2. William Trollope, of Thorleby, in the same county, who married Alice, daughter of William Sharp, of Bourne, by whom he had

I. Sir THOMAS TROLLOPE, the first baronet of this family, so created 17 Charles I. who married first Hester, daughter of Nicholas Street, of Hadleigh, in Suffolk, Esq. by whom he had one son, Sir William, his successor: † his second wife was Mary, daughter of Sir Christopher Clitherow, of London, Knt. by whom he had Thomas Trollope, Esq. who by Anne, daughter of Anthony Collins, of Whitton, in Middlesex, Esq. had Sir Thomas Trollope, Bart. hereafter-

* Collins's Peerage, vol. III. p. 445.
† Bridget, daughter of Sir Thomas Trollope, Bart. was married at Bowsley, in Lincolnshire, July 29, 1679, to Edward Mainwaring, of Whitmore, in Staffordshire. *From the Register of Whitmore parish.*

mentioned; Anthony, a barrister at law, who died unmarried, and other children.*
Sir Thomas dying in 1651, was succeeded in dignity and estate by his only son by the first venter,

II. Sir WILLIAM TROLLOPE, Bart. who married Elizabeth, daughter of Sir Robert Carr, of Sleaford, in Lincolnshire, Bart. (chancellor of the Exchequer, one of the privy council to King Charles II.) relict of William Thorold, Esq. eldest son of Sir William Thorold, of Marston, in Lincolnshire, Bart. by whom he had only one daughter, Elizabeth Carr, the wife of Charles Fox, Esq. eldest son of Sir Stephen Fox, Knt. who died without issue in 1702. Sir William dying in 1678, without issue male, was succeeded by his nephew,

III. Sir THOMAS TROLLOPE, Bart. son of Thomas, and grandson of Sir Thomas, the first baronet, who married Susannah, one of the daughters and co-heiresses of Sir John Clobery,† of Bradstone, in Devonshire, Knt. (niece and co-heiress of Sir

* Qu.—If this Thomas had not a second wife, the daughter of Thomas Burwell, of Dusby, in Lincolnshire, Esq. and if Thomas Trollope, of Oxford, Esq. did not descend from this second marriage; of this family also is Thomas Trollope, of Bourne, in Lincolnshire, Esq.

† As three baronets, Sir Lister Holte, Sir Thomas Trollope, and Sir Edward Noel, are descended from three daughters of this Sir John Clobery, it is thought proper to give the following authentic account of Sir John, as published in a note, by the editor of Dr. Barwick's Life, in English, p. 275.

Colonel Clobery was the younger son of an ancient family, in Devonshire, which had continued at Bradstone, their seat, above 500 years. They have had a plentiful estate in that county, and in Cornwall, and have frequently intermarried with the best families in both counties. He was born at Bradstone, in the year 1623 or 1624: his father, a royalist, gave him a good education, and sent him to the Temple, to study the law. His abilities were such, it is probable, he would have been very considerable in his profession, had he not quitted it, to serve under his countryman and kinsman, General Monk, who advanced him from one commission to another, till he gave him the command of a regiment. At the restoration, being presented by the General to the King, he was knighted, and had a pension of 600l. per annum granted to him, his heirs, and assigns, for ever, in consideration of his services at that time; but to cease and determine, upon his majesty's granting him lands of like value. The pension was afterwards surrendered, upon conveying to him certain fee farm rents, according to the terms of the grant of the pension. After disbanding the army, he had no command till 1667, when, upon the Dutch fleet coming up to Chatham, a commission was sent him, without his privity, with orders immediately to raise a troop of horse, and to march with them to Rye. He received his commission on a Sunday night, at Winchester, where he then lived, and where he was so much beloved, that the Wednesday morning following he marched at the head of more than 100 horse. When that danger was over, and the troops raised on that occasion disbanded, he returned to Winchester, for which city he served in parliament, with James, lord Annesly, the three last parliaments of King Charles II. In Monmouth's rebellion, at the request of the lords lieutenants of Hampshire and Wiltshire, who were commanded to raise the militia of those counties, and to march with them against the rebels (the militia being mutinous and unwilling to march) he was prevailed on to lead them to the king's camp, which, with great difficulty he performed: but upon their continuing mutinous and disorderly, he was forced to dismiss them, and served himself as a volunteer; and to his conduct, in a great measure, was owing the defeat of the rebels: for he marked out the ground for the camp at Sedgemore, and did the duty at first of the officers of horse, that were surprised, and not ready, when the rebels attacked them in the night. This the Earl of Feversham, who commanded the forces, and the officers under him, did Sir John the justice to acknowledge, and represented his services with such advantages to the king, that he was graciously pleased to send for him, to desire he would take the commission of lieutenant-colonel of the regiment of horse, then to be raised by the Lord Lumley, which he accepted: but the latter end of the year following he surrendered it, being disabled, by a dangerous fever, succeeded by a dropsy, of which he died at Winchester, in 1687, in the 63d or 64th year of his age, and was interred in that cathedral.

He was twice married, first to the widow of —— Erlisman, Esq. by whom he had no issue: his second wife was Anne, daughter of George Cranmer, of Canterbury, a descendant from Archbishop Cranmer.

TROLLOPE, OF CASEWICK, LINCOLNSHIRE.

William Cranmer, of London, Knt.) by whom he left four sons; 1, Sir Thomas, his successor: 2, John; 3, Henry, of London, wine merchant (who married Elizabeth, daughter of Mr. John Barne, an Italian merchant, and had four sons and three daughters, Thomas, Henry, John, ——, Sarah, Mary, and Diana); 4, William, fellow of Pembroke Hall, Cambridge: his daughters were, Mary, who died unmarried; Anne, the wife of Samuel Clarke, of West Bromwich, in Staffordshire, Esq. Elizabeth, of William Noel, Esq. brother of Sir Clobery Noel, of Kirkby Mallory, in Leicestershire, Bart. He was appointed one of his majesty's council, learned in the law, in 1738, being at that time (as he had been from the year 1722) member for Stamford, and was re-elected upon this promotion, and again to the next parliament. In 1747 he was elected for Westlow, and being, in 1749 made chief justice of Chester, a new writ was ordered, and he re-elected, as he was also at the next general election: in 1754 he was appointed one of the justices of the common pleas, and died in Dec. 1762. By his said wife, who died in 1767, he had four daughters; 1, Mary, the wife of Thomas Hill, of Tern, in Shropshire, and member of parliament for Shrewsbury, and died Feb. 14, 1760; 2, Anne, who died unmarried; 3, Frances, the wife of Bennet Sherrard, earl of Harborough, and died Dec. 13, 1760; and 4, Elizabeth.* Frances, who died unmarried; Catharine, and Cranmer. Sir Thomas died at Casewick, in Nov. 1729, and was succeeded in dignity and estate by his eldest son,

IV. Sir THOMAS TROLLOPE, Bart. who married Diana, daughter and coheiress of Thomas Middleton, of Stansted, in Essex, Esq. by whom he had six sons; 1, Thomas-Middleton, who married Isabella, eldest daughter of Sir John Thorold, of Syston, near Grantham, in Lincolnshire, Bart. who died in the life-time of his father, leaving Sir Thomas-William, successor to his grandfather, and John, successor to his brother; 2, Clobery, who died young; 3, John; 4, Arthur; 5, William; and 6, Anthony, who married, in 1767, ——, the second daughter of Adolphus Meetkirk, of the county of Hertford, Esq. by whom he had issue Diana, Elizabeth, Anne, Thomas, William, Isabella, John, and William: also one daughter, Susanna. Sir Thomas died October 7, 1784, aged 93, and was succeeded by his grandson,

V. Sir THOMAS-WILLIAM TROLLOPE, Bart. who died May 13, 1789, and was succeeded by his brother,

VI. Sir JOHN TROLLOPE, Bart. who married March 24, 1798, Miss Thorold, of Lincoln, by whom he has a son and heir, born May 8, 1800.

He had by her one son and two daughters, who died in their infancy, and four daughters that lived to be married: Anne was the wife of Sir Charles Holte, of Aston, in the county of Warwick, Bart. by whom she had a numerous issue (her eldest son was Sir Clobery Holte); Catharine, was the wife of William Bromley, of Bagington, in the same county, Esq. (speaker of the house of commons, and principal secretary of state) who had issue by her, only one son, Clobery Bromley, Esq. who died without issue, member of parliament for the city of Coventry: Susanna was the wife of Sir Thomas Trollope, of Casewick, in Lincolnshire, Bart. and Mary, of Sir John Noel, of Kirkby, in the county of Leicester, Bart. deceased, a branch of the Earl of Gainsborough's family: he left by her two sons and one daughter.

* Collins's Peerage, vol. VI. p. 215, 216.

TROLLOPE, OF CASEWICK, LINCOLNSHIRE.

ARMS—Vert, three bucks trippant, argent; armed, or; in a bordure, argent.

CREST—On a mount, proper, a buck trippant, as in the arms, holding an oak leaf in his mouth, proper.

SEAT—At Casewick, in Lincolnshire.

TABLE 87.

```
1 —— TROLLOPE, of Bourne, in Lincolnshire
 |
2 William Trollope = Alice Sharpe
 |
Hester Street = I. Sir Thomas Trollope, 1651 = Mary Clitherow
 |
II. Sir William, 1678 = Eliz. Carr    Thomas = Anne Collins    Bridget = E. Mainwaring
 |                                       |
Elizabeth Carr, 1702 = Charles Fox    III. Sir Thomas, Bt. 1729 = S. Clobery    More children
                                         |
IV. Sir Thomas, 1784   John,   Henry    Wm.    Anne      Eliz. 1767   Cath.
Diana Middleton       Frances E. Barnes Mary  S. Clarke  Wm. Noel   Cranmer
 |
Thos-Middleton  Clobery, John, William  Thos.  John,  Sarah,  Diana  Frances, 1780
J. Thorold      John    Susanna Meet-  Henry  ——     Mary          Bennet, E. of Har-
                1759           kirk                                 borough
 |
V. Sir Thomas-Wm.    VI. Sir John = Miss Thorold
   1789                        |
                        ——, a son, b. 1800
```

---

87. KEMP, of Gissing, Norfolk.

Created Baronet, March 14, 1641.

THE name Kemp* is derived from the Saxon word, to kemp or combat, which in Norfolk is retained to this day, a foot-ball match being called camping or kemping; and thus, in Saxon, a kemper signifies a combatant, a champion, a man of arms. This family has been of long continuance in this county. Galfrid Kemp lived at Norwich in 1272; Robert Kemp in 1306, and soon after, or about that time lived

1. Norman Kemp, whose son,
2. Roger, was father of

---

* Extracted chiefly from Blomefield's History of Norfolk, vol. I. p. 117.

3. Ralph, who married a daughter of —— De la Hants.

4. William Kemp, their son, married ——, daughter of —— Barnstaple, of Bainspath, whose son,

5. Alan Kemp, of Weston, in Suffolk, Esq. married Isabel, daughter of Sir Philip Hastyngs, of Gissing, in Norfolk, Knt. by whom he had John and Alexander, to which

6. John, Sir Philip Hastyngs, his grandfather, in 1324, gave the manor of Gissing: this John married Alice, daughter of Robert Duke, of Brampton, in Suffolk, Esq. by Julian, his wife, daughter of Sir Robert Buttevillain, of Gissing, and of Cottesbroke, in Northamptonshire, Knt. co-heir of Julian Buteveyleyn, and had for his share of her inheritance, the manors of Hastyngs and Dallings, in Gissing; and left issue 1, Robert; 2, Ralph; 3, John; 4, Alice; and 5, Anne: he is sometimes called, in evidences, John de Flordon, Esq.

7. Robert, the eldest son, married Mary, daughter of Bartholomew White, of Shottisham, in Norfolk, Esq. secondly Agnes ——; and thirdly Catharine, daughter of Roger Haukere, of Redenhall; and left issue by Mary, his first wife,

8. Jaffrey Kemp, of Weston, Esq. who married ——, daughter of —— Sharrington, of Cranworth, Esq. and left issue

9. Robert Kemp, of Gissing, Esq. who married Margaret, daughter of William Curson, of Sturston, in Suffolk, Esq. and by her had issue 1, Robert; 2, Edmund, who married Elizabeth, daughter of John Style, of London; 3, John; 4, William, who was rector of Sturston; 5, Ralph; 6, Cecily, the wife of John Melton, of Sturston aforesaid; and 7, Alice, a nun, at Barking.

10. Robert Kemp, of Gissing, Esq. the eldest son, had two wives; first Elizadeth, daughter of John Appleyard, of Braken-Ash, in Norfolk, Esq. by whom he had three daughters; 1, Mary, the wife of Thomas Jernegan, of Cove, Esq. 2, Elizabeth, lady of the bed-chamber to Queen Catharine, in 1523, and died unmarried; and 3, Anne, the wife of Richard Bacon, of Harleston, in Norfolk, Esq. His second wife was Anne, daughter of John Clifford, of Hornes Hall, in Bobbing, Esq. and by her he had issue 1, Bartholomew; 2, Margaret, the wife of Robert Blenerhasset, of Princethorp, in Warwickshire; 3, Lewes, who had a remainder in tail in these manors; and 4, Florence, the wife of Richard Woodhall, of Fraunston, in Suffolk.

11. Bartholomew, the eldest, kept his first court in 1527, and married Anne, daughter of John Alleyn, of Bury St. Edmunds, Esq. and Constance, his wife, daughter and heiress of William Gedding, Esq. by whom he had issue 1, Robert; 2, Bartholomew, who married Barbara Sharp, of Cambridgeshire; 3, Anthony; 4, Edward, who married Mary, daughter of Edmund de Grey, of Merton, in Norfolk, Esq. 5, John, who died unmarried; 6, William; 7, Francis; and 8, Elizabeth, the wife of Lionel Throckmorton, of Flixton. This Bartholomew died in 1554.

12. Robert Kemp, Esq. succeeded: he married first Elizabeth, daughter of John Smythwyne, of Buckinghamshire, Esq. by whom he had Richard and John, who first married Anne, daughter of C. Cuddon, of Weston, in Suffolk; and secondly

Anne, daughter of —— Calthorp, of Antingham, in Norfolk; Margaret, the wife of Thomas Rouse, of Cranford, in Suffolk; and Anne, of Anthony Drury, of Besthorp, in Norfolk: his second wife was Elizabeth, daughter of Thomas De Grey, of Merton, in Norfolk, Esq. by whom he had three sons and one daughter; 2, Thomas married Anne, one of the co-heiresses of John Moore; Robert married one of the co-heiresses of William Stanton, Esq. 3, William married Thomasine, daughter of William Waldegrave, Esq. 4, Elizabeth was the wife of John, son and heir of Robert Buxton, Esq. This Robert died April 27, 1596, aged 80.

13. Richard Kemp, Esq. his eldest son and heir, married Alice, daughter of Philip Cockerham, of Hampstead, in Middlesex, Esq. (relict of Edmund Poley, of Badley, in Suffolk, Esq.) being 55 years old at his father's death. He was a barrister at law, and left

14. Robert Kemp, Esq. his son and heir, who married Dorothy, daughter of Arthur Harris, of Crixeth, in Essex, Esq. and died April 23, 1612. His two daughters were Dorothy and Elizabeth, and his eldest son,

I. Sir ROBERT KEMP, of Gissing, Knt. one of the gentlemen of the privy chamber to King Charles I. by whom he was created a baronet, and as a signal instance of the said king's favour towards him, he forgave him all the fines and fees of passing the said patent, as therein specified. He married Jane, daughter of Sir Matthew Browne, of Beechworth Castle, in Surrey, Knt. and left 1, Robert; 2, Thomas; 3, Matthew, who married ——, daughter of —— Heyton, of Greenwich, in Kent, and had issue; 4, Richard; and 5, Jane, the wife of Thomas Waldegrave, of Smallbridge, Esq. He died Aug. 20, 1647, having suffered very much, both in his real and personal estate from the sequestrations of those times. He was succeeded by his eldest son,

II. Sir ROBERT KEMP, Bart. who first married Mary, daughter of John Kerridge, of Shelley Hall, in Suffolk, Esq. by whom he had four children, but all died in their minority; secondly, Mary, daughter and sole heiress of John Stone, of Ubbestone, in Suffolk, Gent. by whom he had 1, Sir Robert; 2, John, who died young; 3, William, who had Antingham, in Norfolk, given him by will: he married Elizabeth, only daughter of Alderman Shardelowe, who died July 14, 1726, aged 35, and was buried in St. Stephen's church,[*] in Norwich, having one son, Robert, ancestor to the present baronet. The daughters were Mary, the wife of Sir Charles Blois, of Cockfield, in Suffolk, Bart. and Jane, of Thomas Dade, M. D. of Tannington, in Suffolk. Sir Robert died Sep. 26, 1710, aged 83.

III. Sir ROBERT KEMP, of Ubbeston, in Suffolk, Bart. eldest son of the aforesaid Sir Robert, married Letitia, daughter of Robert King, of Great Thurlow, Esq. by Elizabeth, daughter of Thomas Steward, of Barton Mills, Esq. widow of Sir Robert Kemp, of Finchingfield, in Essex, Knt. by whom he had one daughter only that survived, viz. Mary, the wife of Sir Edmund Bacon, of Garboldisham, in Norfolk, Bart. secondly, Elizabeth, daughter and heiress of John Brand, of Edwardston, in Suffolk, Esq. by whom he had 1, Sir Robert, Bart. 2, Sir John, successor to his brother; Isaac, a barrister at law; 4, Thomas, rector of Gissing and Flordon,

---

[*] Blomefield's History of Norfolk, vol. II. p. 599.

KEMP, OF GISSING, NORFOLK.

TABLE 88.

1 NORMAN KEMP
2 Roger Kemp
3 Ralph Kemp === ——— De la Hants
4 William === ——— Barnstaple   Sir ROBERT BUTTEVYLEYN
5 Alan === Isabel Hastyngs   Robert Duke === Julian
6 John === Alice Duke   Alexander   Alice === John Kemp
7 Robert Kemp   Ralph   John   Alice   Anne
M. White | Agnes | C. Haukere
8 Jeffery === ——— Sharrington
9 Robert === Margaret Curzon

10 Robert Kemp   Edmund   John,   Ralph,   Cicely
E. Appleyard | A. Clifford   Eliz. Style   William   Alice   J. Mitton

Mary   Eliz.   Anne   11 Bartholomew, 1554   Margaret   Lewis   Florence
T. Jernegan   R. Bacon   Anne Alleyn   R. Blenerhasset   R. Woodhall

12 Robert Kemp, 1596   Bartholomew   Anthony   Edward   John,   Wm.   Elizabeth
E. Smyth — | E. Grey   Barbara Sharp   M. Grey   Frances   L. Throckmorton
wyne

13 Richard   John Kemp   Margaret   Anne   Thomas   Robert   William   Elizabeth
A. Cockerham | A. Cuddon | A. Calthorp   Thos. Rouse   A. Drury   A. Moore   — Stanton   T. Waldegrave   J. Buxton

14 Robert Kemp === Dorothy Harris

I. Sir Robert, Bart. 1647 === Jane Browne   Dorothy   Elizabeth

II. Sir Robert Kemp, Bart. 1710   Thomas,   Matthew   Jane
M. Kerridge | M. Stone, 1705   Richard   — Heyton   T. Waldegrave
1655

III. Sir Robert Kemp, Bt. 1734   John   William   Mary   Jane
L. King | E. Brand | M. Black | A. Philips   E. Shardelowe   Sir C. Blois   T. Dade

Mary   IV. Sir   V. Sir John   Isaac   Thomas   Benj.   Jane   Edw.   Martha   Marg.   Robert.
Sir E.   Robert   1761   P. Holden   Eliz.   Wm.   Lettice,   Wm.,   D. Short   Kemp
Bacon   1752   E. Brand   Blois   Anne
              Colt

VI. Sir John   VII. Sir Wm. Kemp, 1799
1771

VIII. Sir Wm. Kemp

who in May, 1753, married Priscilla, daughter of Thomas Holden, of Penryn, in Cornwall, Esq. by whom he had Sir John Kemp, Bart. of whom hereafter; 5, Benjamin, who married Mrs. Colt, of Tooting, in Surrey, and died in 1777; 6, Elizabeth; and 7, Jane, relict of William Blois, Esq. son of Sir Charles Blois, Bart. besides Edward, Letitia, and Anne, who died young. His third wife was Martha, daughter of William Blackwell, of Mortlock, in Surrey, Esq. by whom he had William, some time of Pembroke Hall, in Cambridge; and Martha, the wife of Darrel Short, of Wadhurst, in Sussex, Esq. besides a former daughter, Martha, who died an infant. His fourth wife was Amy, daughter of Richard Philips, of Edwardestone, in Suffolk, Esq. widow of John Burrough, of Ipswich, Esq. by her he had no issue. Sir Robert died Dec. 18, 1734, aged 68, having twice represented the county of Suffolk in parliament, and was succeeded in dignity and estate by his eldest son by the second venter,

IV. Sir ROBERT KEMP, Bart. who was representative in parliament for Orford, in Suffolk, in 1730. He died a bachelor, Feb. 15, 1752, and was succeeded by his next brother,

V. Sir JOHN KEMP, Bart. who married Elizabeth, widow of Isaac Brand Colt, of Brightlingsea, in Essex, Esq. by whom he had no issue. He died Nov. 25, 1761, and was succeeded by his nephew,

VI. Sir JOHN KEMP, Bart. who died a bachelor, aged 17, Jan. 16, 1771, and was succeeded by

VII. Sir WILLIAM KEMP, Bart. who was son of Captain Robert Kemp, of Antingham, who was son of William Kemp, of Antingham, son of Sir Robert, the second baronet. This Sir William died in Nov. 1799, and was succeeded by

VIII. Sir WILLIAM KEMP, the present baronet.

ARMS—Gules, three garbs, within a bordure engrailed, or.
CREST—On a wreath, a pelican vulning herself, proper, upon a garb, or.
MOTTO—*Lucem Spero*.   RESIDENCE—Briston, Norfolk.

88. WILLIAMSON, of EAST-MARKHAM, NOTTINGHAMSHIRE.

Created Baronet June 3, 1642.

THIS family is of considerable antiquity in Nottinghamshire. John Williamson, son and heir of William Williamson, of Horton Cockney, released to John Berry, lord of Teresholt, one messuage, in Dunsell, 13 Edw. IV.

1. John Williamson, of Walkeringham, in Nottinghamshire, Esq. a descendant of the said William, had issue two sons,* Giles and Richard, who married Margaret,† daughter of Sir Robert Thornhill, Knt.

2. Giles, the eldest son, married Catharine, daughter of Sir Robert Thornhill, Knt. (sister to his brother's wife) by whom he had two sons, Robert and John, of Gainsborough, in Lincolnshire, who by his second wife, Jane, daughter of Christopher Dobson, was father of Sir Richard Williamson, master of the requests in 1612, and the learned steward of the borough of Retford.‡

3. Robert, the eldest son, was living temp. Queen Eliz. high sheriff of Nottinghamshire 12 James I. § and married first Elizabeth, daughter of —— Rither, and secondly Anne, daughter of —— Stokeham. By the latter he had three sons; 1, Robert; 2, Barnabas, of Loundhall; and 3, Frances.

4. Robert, the eldest son, was of Great Markham, and temp. Eliz. married Faith, fifth daughter of Sir Edward Ayscough, of South Kelsey, in Lincolnshire, Knt. by whom he had issue Thomas, and Elizabeth, the wife of William Clarkson, of Kirketon and Willoughby, in Northamptonshire, Esq.

I. THOMAS WILLIAMSON, Esq. only son and heir of Robert, was high sheriff of the county of Nottingham 15 Charles I. and advanced by that king to the dignity of a baronet, in the 18th of his reign, by patent, dated at York. He suffered greatly for his loyalty in the civil wars, and paid 3400*l.* ‖ to the sequestrators, for his estate. He married first Jane, eldest daughter of Sir Edward Hussey, of Honington, in Lincolnshire, Bart. by whom he had several children, but all died young except three sons, Sir Thomas and Sir Robert, successively baronets, and John, who died unmarried: also a daughter Jane, the wife of John White, of Cotgrave, in Nottinghamshire, Esq. secondly, Dionysia, daughter of William, and granddaughter of Richard Hales, of Hale's Hall, in Norfolk, Esq. but by her he had no issue. This lady Dionysia Williamson, of Hale's Hall,¶ rebuilt the parish church of St. Dunstan's in the East, London, after the great fire, at the expence of 4000*l.* and in gratitude the parish set up a monument for her grandfather, Richard, who died in the year 1620.

II. Sir THOMAS WILLIAMSON, Bart. his eldest son, succeeded him, though the estate was encumbered with debts,* contracted in the service of King Charles I. and the family great sufferers also, by shutting up the Exchequer, temp. Charles II. He married Dorothy, youngest daughter and co-heiress of George Fenwick, of Brinkburne, in Northumberland, Esq. by whom he had no issue. The estate of Monkweremouth, which Sir Hedworth, the present baronet, possesses, was given to the family by this lady, who died Nov. 4 (her birth-day) 1699, and lies buried at Monkweremouth, near Sunderland, in the bishoprick of Durham.† Sir Thomas died April 23, 1703, and lies buried also in Monkweremouth church.‡

III. Sir ROBERT WILLIAMSON, Bart. second son of Sir Thomas, the first baronet, succeeded his brother, Sir Thomas: he married Rebecca, daughter of John

---

* Thoroton's Nott. p. 386. † Ibid. ‡ Ibid. § Ibid. ‖ See List of those that compounded for their Estates, in letter W. ¶ Stowe's Survey, vol. I. b. 2, p. 46. * Ibid. † Le Neve's Mon. Ang. vol. III. p. 203. ‡ Ibid, vol. IV. p. 56.

Burrows, merchant, by whom he had several children, and died in 1708. He was succeeded by his son,

IV. Sir WILLIAM WILLIAMSON, Bart. who was high sheriff for the county of Durham for 24 years successively: he married first Elizabeth, youngest daughter and co-heiress of John Hedworth, of Harraton, in the county of Durham, Esq. by whom he had several sons and daughters; 1, Fenwick was an ensign in the guards, and died several years before his father; 2, Sir Hedworth, the late baronet; 3, William, D. D. who died in possession of the living at Wickham, in Durham, 1763, leaving a son William, and a daughter Anne; 4, Henry married Sarah Crook, of London, by whom he had no issue; he was a lieutenant-colonel, and died suddenly: 5, Anne was the wife of William Wingfield, of Bridge End, in Cumberland, Esq. by whom he had two children; Elizabeth, the wife of Sir John St. Aubyn, of Clowance, in Cornwall, Bart. and George, who married Mary, daughter of George Sparrow, of Washington, in Durham, Esq. by whom he had two children; 6, Dorothy. Sir William married secondly Mary, daughter and heiress of William Fetherstonhaugh, of Stanley, near Stanhope Hall, in the county of Durham, Esq. by whom he had no issue. He died in April, 1747, and was succeeded by his son,

V. Sir HEDWORTH WILLIAMSON, Bart. who likewise succeeded his father, as high sheriff for the county of Durham, being appointed thereto by Bishop Chandler; and (I believe) continued in that office till his death, by the appointment of the succeeding bishops of Durham. In the year 1748 Sir Hedworth married Elizabeth, eldest daughter and heiress (by settlement) of William Huddleston, of Millam Castle, in Cumberland, Esq.* by whom he had three sons; 1, William Huddleston, who died April 12, 1782; 2, Sir Hedworth, the present baronet; 3, the Rev. Thomas, rector of Stoke Damorel, in Devonshire. Sir Edward died Jan. 13, 1789: his lady Oct. 10, 1793. He was succeeded by his eldest surviving son,

VI. Sir HEDWORTH WILLIAMSON, Bart. high sheriff for the county of Durham, in 1796. He married Oct. 10, 1794, Maria, daughter of Sir James Hamilton, of Monaghan, in the kingdom of Ireland, Knt.

---

* The HUDDLESTONS derive themselves for several generations before the conquest, but they came not to the seignory of Millam until the time of Henry III. by the marriage of Sir John Huddleston, Knt. with Joan, daughter and heiress of Adam de Boyvill: the said

1. Sir John Huddleston, Knt. at the time of his marriage with the lady Joan, was Baron de Anneys, in Millum. He was son of Adam, son of John, son of Richard, son of Reginald, son of Nigel, son of Richard, son of Richard, son of John, son of Adam, son of Adam de Huddlestone, in Yorkshire; which five last (according to the York manuscript) were before the conquest. In 20 Edw. I. before Hugh Cressingham, justice itinerant, it was proved, that he had *jura regalia*, within the seignory of Millum, and his plea was allowed. He sat as a peer of parliament, and signed, with the other peers of the realm, at the parliament held at Lincoln, 29 Edw. I. the famous letter to the pope.

2. John de Huddleston, son of Sir John and lady Joan, died unmarried, and was succeeded by

3. Sir Richard Huddleston, Knt. who married Alice, daughter of Richard Troughton, 13 Edw. II. and had issue,

4. Sir John Huddleston, Knt. who married Maud, daughter of Sir William Penington, Knt. and by her had issue,

5. John Huddleston, Esq. who married Catharine, daughter of Richard Tempest, of Bowling, in Yorkshire, 14 Rich. II. and had a son

6. Richard Huddleston, who married Anne, daughter and co heiress of —— Fenwick, of Fenwick, in Northumberland; by whom he had

WILLIAMSON, OF EAST MARKHAM, NOTTINGHAMSHIRE.

ARMS—Or, a chevron, gules, between three trefoils, slipped, sable.
CREST—On a mural crown, gules, a demi wyverne (or a dragon's head) or.
SEATS—At Monk-Weremouth, near Sunderland, and Millum Castle, in Cumberland.

---

7. Richard Huddleston, who married Margaret, sister of Sir William Harrington, K. G. He was made knight banneret, by Henry V. at the battle of Agincourt; and was succeeded by his son,

8. Sir John Huddleston, Knt. who married Jane, one of the co-heiresses of Sir Miles Stapleton, of Ingham, in Yorkshire. He was made bailiff and keeper of the king's woods and chaces in Barnoldwic, in the county of York; sheriff of the county of Cumberland, by the Duke of Gloucester, for his life; steward of Penrith, and warden of the marches; and in 7 Edw. IV. represented the county of Cumberland in parliament. He was succeeded by his son,

9. Sir Richard Huddleston, Knt. who married Margaret, daughter of Richard Neville, earl of Warwick.

10. Richard, his son, married Elizabeth, daughter of lady Mabel Dacre, and died without issue, in the reign of Henry VII. He had two sisters, but the estate being entailed passed to the next in the male line, namely, to his uncle John, brother to his father, Richard, son of the last Sir John. The two sisters were married, Johan to Hugh Fleming, of Rydal, Esq. and Margaret to Launcelot Salkeld, of Whitehall, Esq.

11. Sir John Huddleston, Knt. uncle to the last Richard, married Joan, daughter of Lord Fitz-Hugh.

12. John, his son, married Jane, daughter of Henry lord Clifford, K. G. and first Earl of Cumberland; by whom he had no issue. He married secondly Joan, sister of Sir John Seymour, Knt. father of the lady Jane Seymour, the wife of Henry VIII. thirdly, Joyce, daughter of — Richley, of Prickley, in the county of Worcester. By his second wife he had two sons; Anthony, who continued the family at Millum, and Andrew, who married one of the co-heiresses of Thomas Hutton, of Hutton-John, Esq. and was ancestor of the present family there.

13. Anthony Huddleston, Esq. son and heir of John, by his second wife, Joan Seymour, married Mary, daughter of Sir William Barrington, of the county of Oxford, Knt.

14. William, his son, married Mary Bridges, of the county of Gloucester. He served in parliament for the county of Cumberland, 43 Eliz. and was succeeded by his son,

15. Ferdinando Huddleston, who married Jane, daughter of Sir Ralph Grey, of Chillingham, in Northumberland, Knt. and had issue nine sons, every one of whom were officers in the service of Charles I. 1. William, the eldest, raised a regiment of foot for the king, at his own expence, and cloathed and paid them the whole war: he was made knight banneret, by the king, for his said services, but principally for retaking the royal standard, at the battle of Edge Hill; 2, John was colonel of dragoons; 3, Ferdinando, a major of foot; 4, Richard, a lieutenant-colonel of foot, who was slain in the Minster Yard, at York; 5, Ralph, a captain of foot; 6, Ingleby, a captain of foot; 7, Edward, a major of foot; 8, Robert, a captain of foot; and 9, Joseph, a captain of horse. Ferdinando, the father, was knight of the shire for the county of Cumberland, 21 James I.

16. Sir William Huddlestone, knight banneret, married Bridget, daughter of Joseph Pennington, of Muncaster, Esq.

17. Ferdinand, their son, married Dorothy, daughter of Peter Huxley, of London, merchant, and had an only daughter, Mary, the wife of Charles West, lord Delaware; and died without issue.

18. Joseph, brother to Ferdinand, married Bridget, daughter of Andrew Huddleston, of Hutton-John, Esq. and had issue Ferdinand, who died without issue, and was succeeded by

19. Richard, son of John, next brother to Sir William, who married Isabel, daughter of Thomas Huddleston, of Bainton, in the county of York, and had issue

20. Ferdinand, who married Elizabeth, daughter of Lyon Falconer, Esq. of Rutlandshire, son of Everard Falconer, by Elizabeth, daughter of Sir Maurice Tresham, Bart. and had issue

21. William Huddleston, Esq. who married Gertrude, daughter of Sir William Meredith, of Henbury, in Cheshire, and left two daughters, Elizabeth and Isabella.

22 Elizabeth was the wife of Sir Hedworth Williamson, of Monk Weremouth, in the county of Durham, Bart. who in the year 1774, sold the estate to Sir James Lowther (now Earl of Lonsdale) for above 20,000*l. Hist. and Antiq. of Cumberland, p.* 11.

The arms of Huddleston—Gules, a frette, argent.

WILLIAMSON, OF EAST MARKHAM, NOTTINGHAMSHIRE.

TABLE 89.

WILLIAM WILLIAMSON
|
John Williamson
|
1 John Williamson
|
2 Giles Williamson=C. Thornhill   Richard=M. Thornhill
|
3 Robert Williamson, 1614   John
Eliz. Rither | Anne Stokeham   J. Dobson
|
4 Robert= F. Ayscough   Barnabas   Francis
|
I. Sir Thomas, Bart.   Elizabeth
Jane Hussey | D. Hales   W. Clarkson
|
II. Sir Thomas, 1703   III. Sir Robert, 1708   John   Jane
Dor. Fenwick, 1699   Rebecca Burrows   J. White
|
E. Hedworth=IV. Sir Wm. Williamson, Bt.=M. Fetherstonhaugh
         1747
|
Fenwick   V. Sir Hedworth, 1789   Wm. 1763   Henry   Anne   Dorothy
     Eliz. Huddleston   N   S. Crook   Wm.
         1793   Wingfield
|
Wm. Huddleston-   VI. Sir Hedworth, Bart.   Rev. Thomas Williamson
Williamson, 1782   Maria Hamilton

---

11 Sir John Huddleston=Joan Fitz-Hugh
|
12 John Huddleston=Joan Seymour
|
13 Anthony=Mary Barrington
|
15 William Huddleston=Mary Bridges
|
15 Ferdinand Huddleston
     Jane Grey
|
16 Sir Wm. Huddleston=B. Pennington   John
|
17 Ferdinand   18 Joseph   19 Richard
— Huxley   B. Huddleston   I. Huddleston
|
20 Ferdinand Huddleston
     Eliz. Falconer
|
21 Wm. Huddleston=G. Meredith
|
Eliz. Huddleston
Sir Hedworth Williamson, Bart.

---

89. THOROLD, of Marston, Lincolnshire.

Created Baronet Aug. 24, 1642.

THIS family is of great antiquity, of Saxon extraction, and has been long seated in the county of Lincoln. They are descended from

1. Thoroldus, who was sheriff of Lincolnshire in 1052: he was father of
2. Sir Richard Thorold, of Selby, in Yorkshire, 42 Edw. III.* This Sir Richard, in an old parchment pedigree, drawn in or about 1622, and late in the custody of

---

* Certain evidences relating to the name and family of Thorold, which were in the custody of Sir William Thorold, of Marston, Knt. and Bart. 1654, are here inserted, to shew that the name and family of Thorold are of greater antiquity (and were possessors of estates in divers counties) than the time of 42 Edw. III.—*Ex regist. priorat. de Bingham, temp. Henry I. et circa an.* 1108. To the end of the deed of foundation of Bingham Abbey, founded by Peter de Valoines, with the consent of Albreda, his wife,

THOROLD, OF MARSTON, LINCOLNSHIRE.

Sir George Thorold, Knt. and Bart. is made to be the first who bore for his arms, sable, three goats, saliant, argent; the coat borne by this family before the said Sir Richard was, barry of six, argent and sable; on a canton, sable, a martlet, or. Sir Richard married Joan, daughter and heiress of Robert de Hogh, or Hough, of Marston, in Lincolnshire (son of Alexander de Hough, by Maud, daughter of Michael, sister and co-heiress of Robert de Marston) by whom he had issue

3. John Thorold, of Selby and of Marston, living 2 Rich. II. who married ———, the daughter of William Mirfield, and had issue

4. Richard Thorold, of Marston, living 16 Henry VI. who by Isabel, daughter of Ralph Birnaud, of Knaresborough, in Yorkshire, had issue

5. William, living 13 Edw. IV. who married Joan, daughter and heiress of William Brerehaugh, of Selby, in Yorkshire (remarried to Ralph Malhome, of Selby, 22 Edw. IV.) and had issue

6. John Thorold, of Marston, and of Westburgh, living 12 Henry VII. who married Alice, daughter of Thomas Staunton, of Staunton, in Nottinghamshire, Esq. and had issue William and Jane, the wife first of Robert Winter, of Swineshed, in Lincolnshire, and secondly of Richard Arnold, of Colby, in the same county.

7. William Thorold, lord of Marston and Blankney, in Lincolnshire, only son and heir, was high sheriff of Lincolnshire 5 and 6 Philip and Mary, and part of the first year of Queen Eliz. and died Nov. 24, 1569. He married first Dorothy, daughter of Thomas Leeke, of Hallom, in Nottinghamshire, Esq. and secondly, Margaret, daughter of Sir Robert Hussey, of Halton, in Lincolnshire, Knt. widow of

and Roger, his son, there are recited the manors and lands that he gave to the endowment of the said abbey; among which is the manor of Sanelingham, *quod tenet Thuroldus.—Int. chart. familiæ rot. claus. ann. 24 Hen. III. mandat. est vicecomiti Oxon qd. in man. recessit sine dilatione lib. Petro Thorold, &c.——Per inquit. anno 8 Edw. II. Henricus Thorold, tenet in Castor unum feodum militis, & dimid. feod. de abbate de Burgo. Ingulphus Thorold, vicecomes Lincoln. dedit monasterio de Crowland, maner. su de Buckenhall, cum pertinentiis, et manerium de Spalding.—Int. chart. familiæ de Ogle, anno 23 Edw. III. 1349. Maria, filia et una hæred. Thomæ Thorold, de Novo Castro sup. Tinam quiet. clamavit Roberto Ogle, totum jus, &c. in manerio de Twisell.*

Extracts of other deeds and evidences, relating to the name of Terold, Torold, Turold, Thurold, Thorald or Thorold, found among the fines of the county of Lincoln, &c. now remaining in the office of the chamberlains of the Exchequer, at Westminster, anno 1710.—*Rot. fin. anno primo Rs. Johis Int. Thoraldum, de Halketoft, petent. et Walterium Bearium, ten. un. mess. in Halketoft, jus Thoraldi.—Rot. fin. anno 10 Hen. III. inter Turoldum, de Horfington, Pet. et Johem. fil. Simonis de Edelington, terr. et ten. in Edelington, Turold concess. Johi et hæredib.—Rot. fin. anno 34 Hen. III. int. Galfrid. Magrum de Stykerwald, quer. et Thomam, fil. Thoraldi, et Hen. fil. Robti de hoc quod idem Thom. et Henric. acquiet. prior. de servitio qd. comes Derb. ab eo exigit in lib. tent. suo quod de præd. Thom. et Hen. ten. in Horsington.—Rot. fin. com. Bucks, anno 7 Edw. II. No. 142, int. Rad. fil. Willmi Falmwell, de Aston, quer. Ricum Thorold, de Parva Brykhull, et Joham Uxor. ejus, deforc. mess. terr. et reddit in Aston, jus Radulphi.*

These evidences, and the descent of this family, down to the father of the present baronet, are taken from the genealogy of the most ancient and knightly family of the Thorolds, which has flourished with honour and reputation, in the county of Lincoln, from the time of King Edw. III. in which is delineated the several branches of Thorold, of Marston and Blankney, Harmeston, Morton, and Claythorp, and of those of the High Hall and Low Hall, in Hough, all within the said county of Lincoln, faithfully collected from the books and records of the College of Arms and Inquisitions, monumental inscriptions, and other authentic testimonies; and deduced down to the person of the right worshipful Sir George Thorold, of Harmeston, Knt. and Bart. one of the aldermen of the city of London, and sheriff of the said city and county of Middlesex, 1710, *penes Dom. Nathan. Thorold, Bar.* This is a very fine pedigree, and takes in all the branches of the Thorolds, as well those that are extinct, as those that are existing, to that period.

Henry Sutton, of Wallenger, in the same county, Esq. By his first wife he had three sons and one daughter; 1, Sir Anthony Thorold, of Marston, Knt. 2, William Thorold, of Harmeston, who married Margaret, daughter and heiress of —— Baldock, of the city of London, and was ancestor to Sir George Thorold, Knt. and Bart. lord-mayor of London, and to Sir Samuel Thorold, of Harmeston, in Lincolnshire, Bart. which title is extinct; 3, Richard Thorold, of Morton, in Lincolnshire, ancestor to Sir Nathaniel Thorold, Bart. who was advanced to the dignity of a baronet 14 George II. and to the heirs male of his body, lawfully begotten; and in default of such issue, to his cousin, Charles Thorold, Esq. third son of Sir John Thorold, of Cranwell, in the county of Lincoln, Bart. and to the heirs male of his body, lawfully begotten. Sir Nathaniel Thorold (I believe) died unmarried; the title is now extinct. Alice, the daughter, was the wife first of Thomas Pell, of Barleston, and secondly of —— Porter, of Syston, in Lincolnshire. William, before-mentioned, had by his second wife two sons; 1, Sir Edmund Thorold, of the High Hall, in Hough, Knt. who married Eleanor, eldest daughter and co-heiress of William Audley, of Hough, in Lincolnshire, Gent. which line terminated in Sir William Thorold, of Hough, knighted by King Charles II. who married Anne, daughter of Sir Charles Dallison, Knt. serjeant at law, and died without issue, 1666; 2, Robert Thorold, of the Low Hall, in Hough, who married Agnes, second daughter and co-heiress of William Audley, of Hough, Gent. (remarried to Augustine Earle, of Straglethorp, in Lincolnshire, Esq.) and was father of Anthony Thorold, of the Haugh, Esq. who by Catharine, daughter of Edward Hasilwood, of Maidwell, in Northamptonshire, Esq. had issue Sir Robert Thorold, of the Haugh, created baronet June 14, 1644, who had two wives;* first Anne, daughter of Henry Carvil, of St. Mary's, in Marshland, in Norfolk, Knt. by whom he had no issue; but by his second wife, Catharine,† daughter of Christopher, lord Teynham, had issue Sir Robert Thorold, Bart. who married Catharine, daughter of Sir Henry Knollys, of Grove Place, in Hampshire, Knt. and had issue Sir Robert Thorold, Bart. who was a generous, compassionate, hospitable, well-bred man, without affectation or formality: he died in St. James's Place, Westminster, Nov. 30, 1706, without issue, and was buried in St. James's Church; whereupon that title became extinct.

8. Sir Anthony Thorold, of Marston, Knt. son and heir of William, before-mentioned, by the first venter, was sheriff of Lincolnshire 13 Eliz. and married first Margaret, daughter of Henry Sutton, of Wellingore, in Lincolnshire, Esq. (by Margaret, daughter of Sir Robert Hussey, Knt.) and by her had four sons and two daughters; 1, Thomas, who married Anne, daughter of Sir George Pierpoint, of Holme-Pierpoint, in Nottinghamshire, Knt. and by her left issue two daughters, Isabel and Anne, and died V. P. (his widow was afterwards the wife of Francis Beaumont, of Gracedieu, in Leicestershire, Esq. one of the justices of the common pleas, and died at Gracedieu April 22, 1598) 2, William, of whom hereafter; 3, Anthony, who died S. P. 4, Sir John Thorold, of Coringham, in Lincolnshire, and of Cawnton, in Nottinghamshire, Knt. who was sheriff of Lincolnshire 13 James I. and married Alice, daughter and co-heiress of Thomas Cranmer, of Aslacton, in

* Le Neve's MSS. ibid.   † Ibid.   ‡ Thoroton's Nott. p. 140.

Nottinghamshire, Esq ‡ relict of Thomas Molineux, of Teversal, Esq. and by her had issue Anthony, his son and heir, and Thomas. Mary, eldest daughter of Sir Anthony, was the wife of John Markham, of Sedgebroke, in Lincolnshire, Esq. and Martha of Sir Philip Tyrwhit, of Stainfield, in the same county, Knt.

Sir Anthony married secondly Anne, daughter and co-heiress of Sir John Constable, of Kinalton, in Nottinghamshire, Knt. (by Jane, his wife, daughter and co-heiress of Henry Sothel, of Ithel, in Yorkshire, Esq.) and widow of George Babington, of Kinalton, Esq. by whom he had issue Winifred, the wife first of George Clifton, of Clifton, in Nottinghamshire, Esq. father of Sir Gervase Clifton, the first baronet; secondly, of Henry Kervile, of Wigenhale, in Norfolk, Esq. and thirdly, of Sir Edward Gawsell, of Watlington, in Norfolk, Knt. This Sir Anthony died June 26, 1594.*

9. William Thorold, Esq. second son of Sir Anthony, married, as before-mentioned, Frances, daughter of Sir Robert Tyrwhit, of Ketleby, in Lincolnshire, Knt. and died before his father, leaving issue Sir Anthony and Sir William, and four daughters; 1, Anne, the wife of Christopher Colby, of Grantham, Esq. 2, Elizabeth, 3, Mary, who died without issue; and 4, Martha, the wife of Joshua Whichcote, of Haverholme, in Lincolnshire, Esq.

10. Sir Anthony Thorold, of Marston and Blankney, Knt. eldest son of William, and heir to his grandfather, married Elizabeth, daughter of Thomas Molineux, of

---

* It was customary, in former times, when persons of rank and distinction died, to make certificates of their funerals; accordingly we find the following one* for this gentleman:—

"Sr Anthonye Thorold of Marston in the Countye of Lyncolne Knight, maryed to hys first Wiffe Margarett doughter to Robert Sutton of the Cittye of Lyncolne Esquier, and by her had yssue Thomas Thorold hys Eldest Sone, who maried Anne Doughter to Sr Gorge Perpoynt of holme perpoynt in com. Nottingham Knight, and by her Leaft yssue, Isabell and Anne, hys doughters and Coeheires, and died before hys father; Wyllm Thorold second sone maried fraunces doughter to Sr Robert Tyrwhytt of Ketlebye in com. Lyncolne Knight, and by her Leaft yssue Anthonye hys Eldest Sone, Wyllm second Sone, Anne, Elizabeth, Marye, and Martha, and died before hys father: Johne Thorold 3. sone maried Alyce doughter and Coeheir to Thomas Cranmer of Oslackton in com. Nottingham Esquier, and by her hath issue, Anthonye his Eldest sone and heir apparent, and Thomas second sone, Marye Eldest Doughter of Sr Anthonye maried to John Markham of Sedgebroke in com. Lyncolne Esquier, Martha 2. doughter of Sr. Anthonye, maried to Phyllipe Tyrwhytt of Stanfelde in com. Lyncolne Esquier. After he said Sr Anthonye maried to hys second wiffe Anne doughter and one of the Coeheirs of Sr Johne Connstable of Kynelton in com. Nottingham, Knight, a fifte brother owt of the howse of Flamburough., and Wydowe to Gorge Babbington of Kynelton aforsaid, but he had no yssue; but Sr Anthonye had yssue by her one onlye doughter called Wynyfrid who was maryed to Gorge Clyfton sone & heir of Sr Gervys Clyfton of Clyfton in com. Nottingham Knight. and had yssue Gervys Clyfton hys onlye chyld & heire. The afore named Sr Anthonye departed thys Lyffe at Marston aforesaid the 26. June, 1594, and was worshipfullye accompanyed to the Churche of Marston and their buried the 23. of Julye in the yere afore-said he leaft executors of hys last Wyll and Testament, Phyllipe Tyrwhytt Richard Thorold Edmond Thorold Johne Thorold Richard Pell and Wyllm Ellys Esquiers. and hys said Funerall was ordered by Richard Lee Clarencieux Kinge of Armes and Rouge Croix, the daye and yere before mensioned. In Wytnes whearof we have sett hear unto our handes at the instant of the buryall.

"Be it feretlier remembred that Anthonye Thorold sone of Wyllm Thorold was at the makinge hearof of the age of sixe yeres at Mychelmas next followinge, and Wyllm hys brother of the age of thre years at hallontyd next or somewhat after."

* From the original, found in Mr. Clarencieux Lee's study, at his death.

Phillip Tyrwhitt   John Thorold
Richard Thorold   Richard Pell
Edmund Thorold   W: Ellis.

Houghton, in Nottinghamshire, Esq. but left only two daughters; Mary, the eldest, was the wife of William, lord Widrington, who was killed on the king's part, at Wigan, in Lancashire, 1651. The other daughter died unmarried.

I. Sir WILLIAM THOROLD, his next brother, was also knighted by King James I. when but 16 years old, and was afterwards created a baronet by King Charles I. He suffered greatly for his loyalty to that king, and paid to the sequestrators for his estate* 4160*l*. He married Anne, daughter of John Blythe, of Stroxton, near Grantham, in Lincolnshire, Esq. he was member in parliament for Grantham many years, and high sheriff of Lincolnshire in 1630. He had several sons; 1, William; 2, Anthony; 3, John, of whom hereafter; 4, Robert, who died in 1659; and 5, Thomas, who died Feb. 15, 1665-6, both without issue; and seven daughters; 1, Elizabeth. the wife of Sir Richard Wingfield, of Tickencote, in Rutlandshire, Knt. 2, Margaret, of William Beresford, of Ledenham, in Lincolnshire, Esq. 3, Anne, first of Robert Bateman, of London, and secondly of —— Cutts; 4, Catharine, who died unmarried; 5, Frances, the wife of Sir Francis Leeke, of Newark and Sandiacre, in Nottinghamshire, Knt. and Bart. 6, Mary, of Thomas Pechell, of Normanton, in Lincolnshire; and 7, Penelope, of George Lucas, of Fenton, in the same county, Esqrs. William, the eldest son, married Elizabeth, daughter of Sir Robert Carr, of Aswarby, in Lincolnshire, Bart. but died without issue before his father. His widow was afterwards the wife of Sir William Trollope, of Casewick, in Lincolnshire, Bart.† Anthony Thorold, Esq. second son, married Grisilla, daughter of Sir John Wray, of Glentworth, in Lincolnshire, Bart. and dying also before his father, left issue six sons; 1, Sir William; 2, Sir Anthony; 3, Sir John, successively baronets; 4, Thomas; 5, Robert; and 6, Robert: and seven daughters; 1, Elizabeth, who died young; 2, Anne, the wife of Sir Thomas Hodgson, of Branwith, in Yorkshire, Knt. 3, Mary; 4, Frances; 5, Elizabeth; 6, Theodosia; and 7, Catharine, most of whom, if not all, died unmarried.

II. Sir WILLIAM THOROLD, the eldest son, successor to his grandfather, married Mrs. Garret, of London.

III. Sir ANTHONY, the second, married ——, only daughter of Thomas Harrington, of Boothby, near Grantham, in Lincolnshire, Esq.

IV. Sir JOHN, the third son, married Margaret, relict of the hon. Francis Coventry, Esq. second son of the Lord Keeper Coventry; and served many years in parliament for the county of Lincoln, and for Grantham; but all three brothers died without issue. He was one of the most accomplished gentlemen of his time, had seen most of the cities in Europe, and was remarkable for his courage and bravery.‡

---

* See List of those that compounded for their estates, in letter T.

† He was buried in St. Giles's in the Fields (old) church, by the north door case, opening into the chancel, where was a very neat marble monument, inscribed thus, before the rebuilding the church:—Near this place interred lyes the body of the much lamented William Thorold, Esq. son and heir apparent of Sir William Thorold, of Marston, in the county of Lincoln, Baronet. The remainder of the inscription being eclipsed by the cornish of the door-case, could not be taken. The arms upon it were, sable, three goats, saliant, argent; impaled with gules, on a chevron, argent, three mullets, sable.
View of London, vol. I. p. 263.

‡ He lies buried in Syston Church, near Grantham, having this inscription, on black marble, in letters of gold:—Hic jacent Reliquiæ viri pii et integerrimi Johannis Thorold de Marston in com: Lincoln;

Thomas, Robert, and Bethel, the three youngest sons of Anthony, died unmarried, whereupon the title came to the heirs male of John, third son of Sir William, the first baronet: which John married first ——, daughter of Sir Robert Tredway, Knt. by whom he had issue one son, Sir William: his second wife was the relict of Thomas Saunderson, M.D. (eldest son of Bishop Saunderson) by whom he had another son, Sir John.

V. Sir WILLIAM THOROLD (the son by the first venter) succeeded his cousin, Sir John, in the title, in 1716, and had issue one son,

VI. Sir ANTHONY, who succeeded his father, but died in his 12th year at school, 1721, whereupon the title and estate fell to his uncle, Sir John, son of John, by the second venter; which

VII. Sir JOHN THOROLD, was high sheriff of the county of Lincoln, 1723, and married first Alice, the only daughter and heiress of Mr. William Sampson, of Gainsburgh, by whom he had issue two sons; 1, Sir John Thorold, the late baronet; 2, William: and one daughter, Elizabeth. Sir John married secondly ——, daughter of William Langley, by whom he had issue one son, Charles, and died in January, 1748, and was succeeded by his eldest son,

VIII. Sir JOHN THOROLD, Bart. who married Elizabeth, daughter and one of the co-heiresses of Samuel Ayton, of West Herrington, in Devonshire, Esq. by whom he had several children; John, George, and Samuel; Isabella, the wife of Thomas-Middleton Trollope, Esq. eldest son of Sir Thomas Trollope, of Casewick, in Lincolnshire, Bart. Elizabeth, of Willoughby Wood, of Thoresby, in the said county, Esq. Sir John died on his return from Bath, June 10, 1775, and was succeeded by his eldest son,

IX. Sir JOHN THOROLD, Bart. He married March 18, 1771, at Mary-le-bone church, Middlesex, ——, daughter and heiress of —— Hayford, of Cavendish Square, by whom he has several children.

ARMS—Sable, three goats saliant, argent.
CREST—On a wreath, a roebuck passant, argent; attired, or.
SEAT—At Syston, near Grantham, in Lincolnshire.

Bar^{ti}: Antonii Thorold Ar: Filii natu tertii qui per multos continua serie Annos in Inferiore Senatûs Domo non sine sua laude, et Publico Commodo versatus Antiquæ Patriæ Jura Summâ Fide Constantiâq; defendit et Ecclesiam Anglicanam tam puram credidit jam certo Apostolorum Fundamento innixam ut eam intaminatam Posteris tradendam esse strenue semper certaret a Reipublicæ Negotiis cum jam ante Mortem triennio recesserat libris se totum dedit. Authorumq; tam antiquorum quam recentium Principes utpote Linguam Latinam, Italicam, Gallicam apprime callens et judicio, Memoria, Ingenio vigens Multâ cum Voluptate, fructuq; perlegit. Hæredes instituit Johannem et Antonium Avunculi sui Filios. Obiit XIV, Cal: Jan: Anno D^{ni}. 1716. Æt. 54. In Memoriam Charissimi Mariti Pia, mœrensq; Vidua Dna Margaretta Thorold Hoc Monumentum posuit.

THOROLD, OF MARSTON, LINCOLNSHIRE.

TABLE 90.

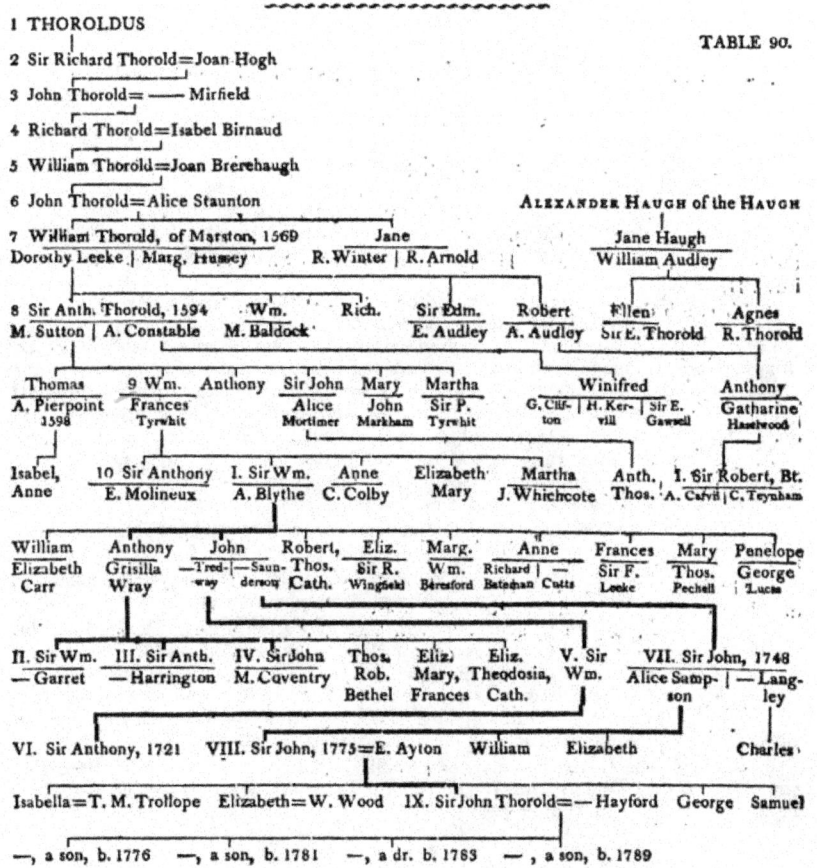

90. WROTTESLEY, of WROTTESLEY, STAFFORDSHIRE.

Created Baronet, August 30, 1642.

THE name of this family is local, being taken from the place of their habitation, which they are supposed to have been possessed of ever since, if not before, the Norman conquest; whereof —— de Wrottesley (so his name is written as a witness to two deeds in the Monasticon) lived temp. Henry II. Sir Hugh de Wrottesley was seated here temp. Henry III. as was also Sir William de Wrottesley, 9 Edw. II.

2. Sir Hugh de Wrottesley, son and heir of Sir William, in 21 Edw. III. had licence to make a park at Wrottesley, and in 23 of that king had the custody of the lands of William Pillatenhall, deceased; in which year he was made one of the knights companions of the most noble order of the garter, at the foundation of that order, and bore—Or, three piles, sable; a canton, ermine. In 24 Edw. III. he had a pension of 40l. granted him for his services. He married first Isabel, daughter of John Arderne, of Aldford, by whom he had lands at Budworth, in Cheshire, held under the king, as Earl of Chester, in capite, by knights service, 2 Henry IV. By her he had no issue; but by his second wife, Mabil, daughter of Rice Rees, he left issue John, and died in 1381.

3. John, his son and heir, held the lands of Isabel Arderne, in Cheshire abovementioned, and had issue

4. Hugh, who lived in 12 Henry VI. and 1 Edw. IV. He married Thomasine, daughter of Sir John Greisley, Knt. and was, by her, father of

5. Sir Walter Wrottesley, Knt. who was lord of Perton 9 Edw. IV. and was buried in the Grey Friers church, now Christ Church, in London, 1473. He married Jane, daughter and heiress of Hugh Barry, of Berks, Esq. and left issue Richard and Henry, who died fellow of a college in Oxford, 1486; and three daughters; Thomasine, the wife of William, lord Stourton; Alice, of Thomas, lord Scrope, of Upsale; and Anne, of Richard, lord St. Almand (or St. Amand).

6. Richard, the eldest son, married Dorothy,* daughter of Edmund Sutton, Esq. son of John, lord Dudley, K. G. and relict of Sir John Musgrave, Knt. by whom he had a son, named Walter.†

---

* Vide Dugdale's Baronage, under Sutton, lord Dudley.

† This couple was buried at Tetnal, and as their epitaph is in old English verse, made by a country poet, perhaps it may not be disagreeable to lovers of antiquity.

Here lies closed in cley,	The year MCCCCCVIII. of our lord
The body of Richard Wrott'sley,	Dorothy departed out of this word;*
And also Dorothy his wif,	And after within short space,
Which lyved togedir all their lif.	Richard was lay'd in this place.

* i. e. world; the poorer sort of people in this county pronounce this word so to this day.

7. Walter Wrottesley, Esq. son and heir, by Isabel, his wife, daughter of Sir Thomas Harcourt, Knt. had issue John and Elizabeth, first the wife of Sir John Talbot, of Albrighton, in Staffordshire; from whom the Talbots of Salwarp, Worvil, and also the present Earl Talbot lineally descend. He was sheriff of the county of Salop in the 9th, 29th, and 33d of Henry VIII. and died Sep. 10, 1549. She was afterwards the wife of Edward Littleton, Esq. nicknamed Long Edward.*

8. John, who succeeded his father, and married Elizabeth, daughter of Thomas Astley, of Pateshull, Esq. by whom he had four sons; 1, Walter; 2, Thomas; 3, Edward; and 4, John: and two daughters; Frances, the wife of —— Brooke, of Blackland, in Staffordshire, and Dorothy, of Richard White, of Sheppey, in Leicestershire, Esqrs. He died in 1578, and was buried at Tetnal, and was succeeded by his son,

9. Walter Wrottesley, Esq. eldest son and heir, married Mary, daughter and heiress of Hugh Lee, of Woodford, in Staffordshire, Esq. by whom he left issue Sir Hugh. His second wife was the daughter of Sir Edward Leighton, of Wattlesborough, in Salop, Knt. by whom he left two daughters; and died Dec. 10, 1630.

10. Sir Hugh Wrottesley, Knt. eldest son and heir, married Mary, daughter of Sir Edward Devereux, Knt. a younger son of Walter, lord viscount Hereford, by whom he had issue two sons and five daughters; 1, Walter; 2, William, who married Anne, daughter of —— Chamberlayne, Esq. Of the daughters; 1, Mary, first the wife of John Lengher, of Perton, in Staffordshire, and secondly, of Edward Williams, of Dudley, in Worcestershire; 2, Penelope; 3, Elizabeth, the wife of Walter Hopton, of Canon Frome, in Herefordshire; 4, Margaret, of Jonathan Langley, of Shropshire; and 5, Howard, of John Wingfield, of the same county, Esqrs.

I. Sir WALTER WROTTESLEY, the eldest son and heir, was advanced to the dignity of baronet, 18 Charles I. He suffered greatly for his loyalty to that king, and was fined† 1332*l*. 10*s*. 0*d*. by the sequestrators of those times, who obliged him also to settle 15*l*. per annum upon the minster of Tetnal. He married Mary, daughter of John Grey, of Envil, in Staffordshire, Esq. by whom he had issue 1, Sir Walter; 2, Edward, who married Martha, daughter of Sir Thomas Hewit, of Shire-Oakes, in Nottinghamshire, Knt. and 3, John, a merchant in Portugal; 4 and 5, Hugh and Richard, who died S. P. also five daughters; Elizabeth, the wife of Sir Francis Woolrich, of Dudmaston, in Salop, Bart. Mary, of Sir Edward Littleton, of Pillaton Hall, in Staffordshire, Bart. Dorothy, Anne, and Jane, the wife of Mr. Adams.

II. Sir WALTER WROTTESLEY, Bart. eldest son and successor to his father, married Elizabeth, daughter of Sir Thomas Woolrich, of Dudmaston, Bart. and had issue Sir Walter, Ursula, and Anne.

III. Sir WALTER WROTTESLEY, Bart. his son and heir, married first Eleanor, daughter of Sir John Archer, of Coopersale, in Theydon-Garnon, Essex, Knt.

| Here now our bodys do ly; | We desire now every Christian mon, |
| On our souls Jesus haf mercy. | To pray for our souls that be gon. |

* Collins's Peerage, vol. V. p. 399—vol. VII. p. 437.
† See List of those that compounded for their estates, letter W.

one of the justices of the common pleas, by whom he had three sons and four daughters; 1, Walter, who died unmarried; 2, Sir John, his successor; and 3, Hugh, who was of Lincoln's Inn, and died unmarried in 1725. The daughters were Eleanor, Henrietta,* Elizabeth, and Mary, who all died unmarried, except Elizabeth, who was the wife of Anthony Collins, of Baddow, in Essex, Esq. Sir Walter's second lady was Anne, daughter of —— Burton, Esq. by whom he had one son and two daughters, viz. Walter, who married ——, daughter of —— Craig, by whom he had one son, Thomas, who married Elizabeth, daughter of Sir John Wrottesley, Bart. Margaret, and Anne, the wife of — Hutchinson, of Nottinghamshire, Esq.

IV. Sir JOHN WROTTESLEY, Bart. eldest surviving son and successor to his father, married Frances, daughter of the hon. John Grey, of Envil, Esq. third son of the right hon. Henry, earl of Stamford (by Catharine, his second wife, daughter of Edward, lord Dudley and Ward) by whom he had five sons; John, who died in Nov. 1723, and Charles in 1724, both in their minority; Sir Hugh, Sir Walter, and Sir Richard, who were successively baronets: and five daughters; Frances, the wife of Heigham Bendish, of East Ham, in Essex, Esq. Elizabeth, of Thomas Wrottesley, of Wolverhampton, Esq. (who was only grandson of Sir Walter Wrottesley, Bart. by Anne Burton, his second wife) Henrietta, of Theodore-William Inge, of Thorp Constantine, in Staffordshire, Esq. Dorothy, and Mary. Sir John was a gentleman of strict honour and justice, was highly valued by the county where he lived, for which he was chosen a representative in 1708, and dying in Oct. 1726, was buried at Tetnal. He was succeeded in dignity and estate by his eldest surviving son,

V. Sir HUGH WROTTESLEY, Bart. who dying in his minority, Nov. 1729, aged 14 years, was succeeded by his next brother,

VI. Sir WALTER WROTTESLEY, Bart. who dying also in his minority, Feb. 1731, was succeeded in dignity and estate by his only brother,

VII. Sir RICHARD WROTTESLEY, Bart. who was born in 1711: he married Mary, second daughter of the right hon. John, lord Gower, by lady Evelyn Pierpoint, youngest daughter of Evelyn, duke of Kingston, his first lady, who died his widow, April 30, 1778;† by whom he had issue one son, Sir John, the present baronet, and four daughters; 1, Mary, born Nov. 1740, maid of honour to the queen: she was the wife of Col. Gardener, and died in 1769; 2, Elizabeth, married in 1769 to Henry Fitzroy, duke of Grafton; 3, ——, the wife of —— Pigott, Esq. brother of Lord Pigott; and 4, Frances. Sir Richard was elected member for Tavistock in 1747; appointed one of the principal clerks of the board of green cloth in June 1749, and re-elected for Tavistock. He afterwards went into orders, was appointed one of his majesty's chaplains in Dec. 1763, and promoted to the

---

* A neat monument in Worcester Cathedral, with the arms of Wrottesley, and this inscription:—To the memory of Henrietta Wrottesley, daughter of Sir Walter Wrottesley, in the county of Stafford, Bt. who died the 16th day of March, 1719, in the 30th year of her age. A lady, whose good nature, and good sense justly recommended her to the favour of the world; her exemplary piety and charity, to that of Heaven. *Non te facundia Non te Restituet Pietas—W. Davis grato anmino posuit.*
Dr. Thomas's Surv. Worc. Cath. p. 84.

† Collins's Peerage, vol. V. p. 144.

WROTTESLEY, OF WROTTESLEY, STAFFORDSHIRE.

TABLE 91.

1 Sir WILLIAM de WROTTESLEY

Isabel Arderne=2 Sir Hugh, 1381=Mabil Rees

3 John de Wrottesley

4 Hugh=Thomasine Greisley — JOHN, L. DUDLEY, K.G.

5 Sir William, 1473=Jane Barry — Edmund Sutton

6 Richard / Henry / Thomasine / Alice / Anne / Dorothy
D. Sutton / *1486 / Wm. L. Stourton / Thos. L. Scrope / Robert L. St. Almand / R. Wrottesley

7 Walter Wrottesley=Isabel Harcourt

8 John Wrottesley, 1578=Elizabeth Astley — Elizabeth=Sir J. Talbot, 1549

9 Walter Wrottesley, 1630 / Thomas / Edward / John / Frances—Brooke / Dorothy R. White
Mary Lee | ——Leighton

10 Sir Hugh Wrottesley, Knt.=Mary Devereux

EDWARD / I. Sir Walter / Wm. / Mary / Penelope / Elizabeth / Marg. / Howard
L. DUDLEY / Mary / Anne / John / Edward / Walter / Jonathan / John
and WARD / Grey / Chamber- / Leng- / Williams / Hopton / Langley / Wing-
/ / layn / her / / / / field

Catharine / II. Sir Walter / Edward / John, / Elizabeth / Mary / Dorothy, / Jane
Henry, E. of / Elizabeth / Martha / Hugh, / Sir Francis / Sir Edw. / Anne
Stamford / Woolrich / Hewet / Richard / Woolrich / Littleton / / Adams

EVELYN, D. / John / III. Sir Walter Wrottesley / Ursula / Anne
of Kingston / Grey / Eleanor Archer | Anne Burton

Mary / Frances / Walter / IV. Sir John, 1736 / Hugh, / Eliz. / Walter / Margaret / Anne
John, L. / Sir John / / Frances / Eleanor, / Anth. / Craig / / Hutchin-
Gower / Wrottesley / / / Henrietta, / Collins / / /
/ / / / Mary / / / /

Mary / John / V. Sir / VI. Sir / VII. Sir Rich. / Frances / Eliz. / Henrietta / Dorothy / Thos.
Sir Richard / 1723 / Hugh / Walter / 1769 / Higham / Thos. / T. Wm. / Mary / Eliz.
Wrottesley / Charles / 1729 / 1731 / M. Gower / Bendish / / Inge / / his cousin
/ / / / 1778

VIII. Sir John Wrottesley, 1787 / Mary / Elizabeth / N / Frances
Miss Courtenay / 1769 / Charles, D. of | ——, E. of Upper / Pigott
/ / Grafton / Ossory

IX. Sir John Wrottesley=Caroline, dr. of the Earl of Tankerville

deanery of Worcester in April 1765. He died July 29, 1769, and was succeeded by his son,

VIII. Sir JOHN WROTTESLEY, Bart. He was master of the horse to his late royal highness the Duke of York, and member of parliament for the county of Stafford. He married, June 7, 1770, at St. James's Church, Westminster, Miss Courtney, maid of honour to her majesty, by whom he had a son John, born Oct. 24, 1771. He died April 23, 1787, and was succeeded by his son,

IX. Sir JOHN WROTTESLEY, Bart. M. P. for the city of Litchfield: he married June 23, 1795, Caroline, daughter of the Earl of Tankerville.

ARMS—Or, three piles, sable, and a canton, ermine.

CREST—Out of a ducal coronet, a boar's head, ermine, sometimes azure, crined and tusked, or.

SUPPORTERS—As granted to Sir Hugh, knight of the garter, two unicorns.

SEAT—At Wrottesley, near Wolverhampton, in Staffordshire.

---

91. THROCKMORTON, of COUGHTON, WARWICKSHIRE.

Created Baronet Sep. 1, 1642.

THROCKEMERTONA, Throckmorton, or the Rockmoor-Town, from whence this family is denominated, is situated in the vale of Evesham, in the parish of Fladbury, anciently Flandenburgh, in Pershore hundred, in Warwickshire; a manor, containing two hamlets, Hull, alias Hill, and Moor.

1. John de Throckmorton, according to Sir William Dugdale, was lord of the manor of Throckmorton, in the vale of Evesham, about 60 years after the Norman conquest, 1130,* which leaves no room to doubt but that this family possessed it at the entrance of the Normans, or long before, the etymology of the name being either British, or Saxon. From this John descended

---

* Stemma. per Wm. Dugdale, Gart. The name of Throckmorton is not mentioned in Domesday; but in Lib. Aib. Episc. Wigorn. f. 57, is a deed, wherein John de Throckmorton demandeth of Maugerus, bishop of Worcester, who flourished about the year 1200 (2 John) half an hyde in Fladbury, with the apurtenances, and half an hyde, &c. in Hamlet de Hull, in the same manor; and one yard of land in Northwyke, in the manor of Blockley; and half an hyde in Upton, in the said manor.

Adam de Throckmorton released to bishop Blois, in the reign of Henry III. his right in a pasture near his parcary, or sheep-fold, at Throckmorton; for which the bishop gave him five marks of silver.

Nash's Worcest. p. 452.

2. Henry de Throckemerton, who made a grant of a yard of land in Hulla, temp. Henry III. 1220.*

3. Robert de Throckemerton, his son (I presume) 1252:† had issue

4. Simon de Throckmorton, who, with Isabel, his wife, 1266, paid half a mark to have a writ of oyer and terminer ad bancum; and a mandate thereupon was directed to the sheriff of Worcestershire.‡ He had issue two sons, John and Giles, which last had an annual revenue out of the manor of Throckmorton, 1330.

5. John, the eldest, was possessed of Throckmorton, 1339, and married Agnes, or Anne, daughter and heiress of Sir Richard Abberbury, of Adderbury, in Oxon, and was succeeded in the lordship of Throckmorton, &c. by

6. Thomas, his son and heir, who was of the retinue of Thomas Beauchamp, earl of Warwick, 20 Rich. II. as also escheator for the county of Worcester, in 3 Henry IV. (in those days an office of great trust): he was constable of Elmley Castle, 6 Henry IV. and by Agnes, his wife, daughter and heiress of —— Besford, was father of

7. Sir John Throckmorton,§ who was employed in the service of Earl Richard (son of Thomas, earl of Warwick) at Caen, in Normandy, 5 Henry V. and being brought up to the study of the law, was afterwards of his counsel.‖ He died April 12, 1445, leaving Eleanor, his wife, surviving, who was daughter and co-heiress of Sir Guy de la Spine, or Spineto (by the heir of Wyke) lord of Coughton, in Warwickshire, whose father, William, held notable employments in the said county, temp. Edw. II. and was grandson to another William de Spineto, by Johanna, his wife, daughter of Sir Simon de Cocton, Knt. the lineal heir male of Ralph, son of William de Cocton, lord of the manor of Coughton, before the reign of Henry II. John Throckmorton, left issue by Eleanor aforesaid, two sons and six daughters; 1, Thomas; 2, John, who married Isabel, daughter of Edward Bruges, of Lone,¶ in

---

* Charles Antiq. peoes Famil.
† He gave the king half a mark for a writ, &c. *brevi vi & armis habendo coram justic. ad primam assistam, &c.* (Rot. fin. ejusd. Ann. M. 7). and mandate thereupon was to the sheriff of Worcester, &c.
‡ Rot. fin. ejusd. An. M. 1.   § Dugdale's Warw. vol. II. p. 750.
‖ In 4 Henry VI. he was a commissioner, with sundry other persons of eminency, for proposing a loan of money from the king's subjects in Warwickshire, and in 9 Henry VI. one of the general attorneys, constituted by the said Earl, for managing all his affairs during his abode beyond sea; being the same year retained of his counsel for life, with an annuity of 20 marks per ann. In 12 Henry VI. he was constituted a commissioner for conservation of the peace in that county, and in 17 Henry VI. one of the executors to the before-specified Earl; upon whose death, which happened the same year, he was joined in authority with Richard, duke of York; Richard, earl of Salisbury, and sundry other persons of quality, for the custody of all the castles, lordships, &c. belonging to the said Earl, during the minority of Henry, his son and heir. In 17 Henry VI. he was again in commission of the peace, and having been one of the chamberlains of the Exchequer to the said king, for which respect he had the title of under-treasurer of England, by his testament, bearing date at London, April 12, 23 Henry VI. bequeathed his body to be buried in the parish church of St. John Baptist, at Fladbury: appointing, that his executors should provide a marble stone of such largeness, that it might cover the graves of his father, mother, and his own, with his wife's, in case she should determine to be there buried; and constituting Rauf Boteler, Lord Sudley, then treasurer of England, his overseer, departed this life the same year, as appears by the probate thereof.
¶ Collins's Peerage, vol. II. p. 126.

Gloucestershire, Esq. (from whom descended Sir William Throckmorton, of Tortworth, in Gloucestershire, created baronet, 9 James I. which title is extinct). Of the six daughters, Eleanor was the wife of Richard Knightly, of Fawsley, in Northamptonshire, Esq. Maud, of Sir Thomas Green, of Greens Norton, in Northamptonshire, Knt. Margaret, of John Rous; Agnes, of John Winslow; Elizabeth, of Robert Russel, and according to some pedigrees another Elizabeth, of Robert Gifford, and by others, of —— Seymour.

8. Thomas Throckmorton,* eldest son and heir, married Margaret, daughter and co-heiress of Sir Robert Olney, of Weston, in Bucks, Knt. (by Goditha, his wife, daughter and co-heiress of William Bosom, or Bosun) by whom he had four sons; 1, Robert; 2, John, who married Jane, daughter and co-heiress of Henry Baynard, of Spelshull, in Suffolk; and was ancestor to the Throckmortons, of Claxton, and Southelman, &c. in Norfolk and Suffolk; 3, Richard, ancestor to those of Great Stoughton, in Huntingdonshire; and 4, William, L L D. also four daughters; Goditha, the wife of Edward Peyto, of Chesterton, in Warwickshire; Mary, of Thomas Middlemore, of Edgbaston, in Warwickshire; Margaret, of William Tracy, of Tuddington, in Gloucestershire, Esqrs. and Elizabeth, the last abbess of Denny, who died Jan. 13, 1547, and lies buried at Coughton.

9. Robert Throckmorton, Esq. son and heir, 21 years old at his father's death,† was a justice of peace for Warwickshire, from 2 Rich. III. till towards his death. In 1 Henry VII. he was made of the king's privy council, and in 2 Henry VII. he made the park at Coughton,‡ inclosing therewith a certain common ground called Wikewood, whereunto he afterwards added Samburne Heath, and Spiney's Leys, lying within the said lordship of Samburne: and the same year was a commander in the king's army, at the battle of Stoke. In 10 Henry VII. he received summons, with divers other persons of quality, to appear before the king, in person, upon the feast day of All Saints, the same year, to receive the order of knight of the bath, upon advancement of Henry, the king's second son, to the dukedom of York.

* He, with his said mother, in 26 Henry VI. gave lands of six marks per ann. to the monks of Evesham, for the maintenance of a priest, to sing divine service perpetually at the altar of our Lady, in the church of Evesham, for the good estate of King Henry VI. Queen Margaret, his consort, and of the said Eleanor and Thomas, during this life; and for the health of their souls after their departure hence: as also for the souls of the said king's father and grandfather, late kings of England; of Catharine, late queen of England; and for the soul of John Throckmorton, before specified, Thomas his father, and Anne his mother, with their ancestors, and all the faithful deceased. Which king also, in consideration of the good service performed by the said John Throckmorton, to himself, and to Henry IV. and V. his father and grandfather, late kings of England, in the office of chamberlain of the Exchequer, gave farther licence to them, the said Thomas and Eleanor, that they or either of them, or the heirs of the longer liver of them, might found a chantry of one priest, to sing divine service every day during the world, at the altar of the Blessed Virgin, in the parish church of Fladbury, before specified, for the good estate of him the said king, and of all those above-mentioned; and to endow the same with lands to the value of 10l. per ann. Till the time of the said Thomas Throckmorton, it seems, that this family was not wholly possessed of Coughton, but then did John Tracy, son and heir of Alice, the other daughter and co-heir of Sir Guy Spine, by his deed, bearing date May 29, 27 Henry VI. grant unto him the said Thomas, and his heirs, that moiety thereof by inheritance belonging to him. Of which Thomas, all that I have seen farther memorable is, that in 5 Edw. IV. he underwent the office of sheriff of the counties of Warwick and Leicester, and that he departed this life in 1474.

† Dugdale's Warw. vol. II. p. 750. ‡ Ibid.

He was a man of singular piety; the sundry bequests contained in his testament do sufficiently manifest; and of no less devotion, as may seem by his pilgrimage to the Holy Land, which in 10 Henry VIII. (having settled his estate) he undertook; but died beyond sea in that journey.* He left issue by his first wife, Elizabeth, daughter of —— Baynham, only one daughter, Ursula, the wife of Sir Thomas Gifford, of Chillington, in Staffordshire, Knt. and by his second, Catharine, daughter of Sir William Marrow, Knt. alderman of London, he had four sons and seven daughters; 1, Sir George; 2, Anthony, killed in the battle of Pavia, in Italy; 3, Michael, who was of the retinue to Cardinal Pole, and died Nov. 1, 1558, and lies buried at Mantua; father to Francis Throckmorton, Esq. famous for his hospitality to the English travellers at Mantua, where he lived, notwithstanding his burial at Ullen Hall, 1617; 4, Richard, of Higham Ferrers, in Northamptonshire, who married Jane, daughter of Humphrey Beaufoe, of Edmundscot, in Warwickshire, and was ancestor to Sir George Throckmorton, serjeant of the hawks to Queen Elizabeth, and to those of Brampton and Ellington, in Huntingdonshire. Of the seven daughters of Sir Robert, Mary, was the wife of Thomas Burdet, of Bramcote, in Warwickshire; also of Richard Middlemore, of Edgbaston, in the same county, Esqrs. Elizabeth, of Sir Thomas Englefeild, Knt. Catharine, of ——. Boughton, of Lawford, in Warwickshire, Esq. Ursula, Bridget, and Alice, died unmarried, and Margaret, a nun.

10. Sir George, his eldest son, succeeded, and was one of those that attended in court at the coronation of Queen Anne: in 25 Henry VIII. and in 18 and 35

---

* By which testament, bearing date 1518, he bequeathed his body to be buried in the church at Coughton, in case he should die within this realm; appointing, that not above 6l. 13s. 4d. should be spent at his funeral; and farther directed, that after his burial, there should be said for his soul, in the monasteries of Studley and Evesham, 30 masses of Jesu; every priest to have 4d. for his labour: and willed, that the east window of the chancel at Coughton, should be glazed at the charge of his executors; as also, that 20s. should be given to the glazing of the east window of the north aisle there, with the representation of the seven sacraments; and as much for the east window of the south aisle, that to be of the seven works of mercy. He also willed, that the image of our lady should be set on the north side, at the end of the altar, in the said south aisle; and the image of the angel Gabriel on the same side of the aisle, at the pillar between the aisle and the chancel, with a roll in his hand, of greeting, looking towards our lady: and at the south end of the said altar, the image of St. Raphael, painted and gilded; and that in the north aisle, at the north end of the altar, the image of the Trinity; to be placed at the south end, the image of St. Michael; all which images to be richly painted and gilded.

And he farther willed, that certain lands to the value of 16l. per annum, should be put into the hands of feoffees, to the use of a priest to sing perpetually, in the north aisle of Coughton church, for his soul, and the souls of his ancestors; and that the said aisle should be called the Trinity chapel, and the priest, the Trinity priest; which priest was also, to teach a grammar-school freely, for all his tenants' children, and to have yearly thereof 8l. and his chamber; but the residue of the said 16l. to be paid monthly to five poor men dwelling in the alms-house, at Coughton, viz. every one 6d. a week, and his house-room for ever; the residue, viz. 8s. 8d. to go to the reparation of the alms-house: and that the said priest should, every Sunday, say a mass of the Trinity; Wednesday, mass of requiem; and Friday, mass of Jesu, in case he were disposed; and once in the week, dirige, for his soul, and all christian souls, except the days before rehearsed fell upon double festivals. Which poor men, so to be placed in the said alms-house, to be chosen out of those that had been his tenants, or serving men, at the discretion of his son and heir, and heirs successively; advertising his son and heir, that if he should so amortize this land for those uses, it would be a meritorious deed, and for which he should have God's blessing and his; and adjuring, that none should break his will, under pain of the church's curse; which will was dated August 10, 1518, and proved Nov. 9, 1520. *Dugdale, vol. II. p. 751.*

Henry VIII. executed the office of sheriff for the counties of Warwick and Leicester.* He married Catharine, daughter of Nicholas, lord Vaux, of Harrowden, by whom he had nine sons and ten daughters; 1, Sir Robert; 2, Deodatus; 3, Clement, of Haseley, in Warwickshire, sewer to the Queen, temp. Henry VIII. and afterwards a commander at the siege of Bologne, who, upon the dissolution of the abbies, had several ample grants from the king, and his successor, Edw. VI. and Queen Elizabeth. He married Catharine, daughter of Sir Edward Nevil, Knt. second son of the Lord Abergavenny, and from him descended those of Haseley and Ansley, in Warwickshire.† The fourth son of Sir George, before-mentioned, was Sir Nicholas, sewer to King Henry VIII. and a commander at Bologne; who, in the reign of Edw. VI. commanded at Musselburgh Field, and brought the news of the victory: he was in the highest favour and esteem with that king, who gave him Paulers Perry, in Northamptonshire, and several other lordships. In the reign of Queen Mary he was tried about Wyat's conspiracy; but there appearing no satisfactory evidence against him, he was able, by making an admirable defence, to obtain a verdict of the jury in his favour. The queen was so enraged at the disappointment, that instead of releasing him, as the law required, she re-committed him to the Tower, and kept him in close confinement during some time: but her resentment stopped not here; the jury, being summoned before the council, were all sent to prison, and afterwards fined; some of them a thousand pounds, others two thou-

---

* He built that stately castle-like gate-house, of free stone, at Coughton, intending to have made the rest of his house suitable thereto; but the Lord Cromwell, vicar general to the king, being lord of the manor of Oversley, in Warwickshire, and beholding with a rapacious eye this estate, lying in the vale below,* had him imprisoned in the Tower, for refusing the oath of supremacy, though he was ready to lay down his life for the same principles as bishop Fisher, and Sir Thomas More professed. But Queen Catharine Parr, neice to Sir George's lady, begged the life of her uncle, and was so great a friend to him, as to procure preferments for his sons, Clement, Nicholas, and George; and when the Lord Cromwell fell into disgrace, the king was pleased to advise with Sir George, amongst others, in what manner to proceed with that unfortunate statesman. Sir George afterwards† had the manor of Oversley granted to him, and his heirs, in exchange for lands in Bedfordshire, and the sum of 744*l*. 9*s*. 2*d*. which manor was forfeited by the attainder of the Lord Cromwell.

† His eldest son and heir, Job, was a considerable man, and the supposed author of Sir Martin Mar Prelate; and father of

Sir Clement Throckmorton, Knt. who was a gentleman not a little eminent for his learning and eloquence, having served in several parliaments, temp. Eliz. James I. and Charles I. as one of the knights of the shire for the county of Warwick.

Clement, his son, was lord of the manor of Haseley, 1610, and had three sons and five daughters.

Sir Clement, his eldest, knighted by King Charles II. sat in parliament, as one of the burgesses for Warwick, 1661. He died at Wolverhampton, before his father, without issue, whereupon his brother,

Francis, first son by his father's fourth wife, became heir to the estate, and enjoyed it about two years; and he dying also, without issue, his brother,

Robert, succeeded, who married into the Mordaunt family, and possessing it not much above two years, died, leaving his wife with child of a son, which was named Clement, who married Lucy, daughter of Capt. Thomas Lucy, of Cherlecote, and Catharine, his wife, daughter of Robert Wheatley, of Bracknel, in Berks, Esq. (who after his death married the Duke of Northumberland) but dying some time after, left his wife also with child of a daughter Lucy, the wife first of William Bromley, of Baginton, in Warwickshire, Esq. eldest son of the hon. William Bromley, Esq. secretary of state to Queen Anne; and secondly, of —— Chester, Esq. she died in Oct. 1771, in Conduit Street, London.

* Sir Nicholas's Life, written by himself, MS. in Weston library. † Dugdale's Warw. vol. II. p. 857.

sand 'a-piece.‡ This violence proved fatal to several; among others, to Sir John Throckmorton, brother to Sir Nicholas, who was condemned on no better evidence than had formerly been rejected. He was afterwards received into favour. In 1 Eliz. he was chief butler of England, and chamberlain of the Exchequer, and ambassador to Francis II. king of France, and Mary, queen of Scots, his consort, to expostulate with them for assuming the arms of England in their quarterings.

Much more might be said of his actions and negotiations, for he was a valiant soldier and commander, and a consummate statesman. He left his life in verse, written, as is supposed, in his imprisonment; and died Feb. 12, 1570, aged 57: and Fuller says,* " at supper, eating of sallad, not without suspicion of poison, the rather because happening in the house of one, no mean artist in that faculty, R. Earl of Leicester;" and lies buried on the south side of the chancel of St. Catharine Cree Church.† He married Anne, daughter of Sir Nicholas Carew, of Beddington, in Surrey; by whom he had two sons; 1, Sir Arthur Throckmorton, of Paulers Perry, in Northamptonshire, whose daughter Anne was the first wife of Richard, lord Dacre, of Chevening, in Kent.‡ From Sir Nicholas, a younger son, who had his mother's estate, and took the name of Carew, was the late Sir Nicholas-Hacket Carew, of Beddington, in Surrey, Bart. descended. The fifth son of Sir George was Kenelme; 6, Thomas, who died S. P. 7, Sir John, knighted by Queen Eliz. in the first year of her reign, at Kenillworth, and was master of the requests, and justice of Chester; and lies buried in the chancel at Coughton.§ He had issue Francis, attainted in 26 Eliz. for treason.‖ The eighth son of Sir George was George, who married Mary, daughter of John Bruges, the first Baron Chandos; and 9, Anthony, of Castleton, in Oxfordshire, who married Catharine, daughter and co-heiress of William Willington, of Barcheston, in Warwickshire, Esq. relict of William Catesby, of Ashby Legers, in Northamptonshire, Esq. and was ancestor to the Throckmortons

‡ Fox, vol. III. p. 99—Stowe, p. 624—Baker, p. 320—Hollingshed, p. 1104, 1121—Strype, vol. III. p. 120—Dep. de Noailles, vol. III. p. 173.

* Fuller, in his Worthies of Warwickshire, p. 123.

† On a monument of alabaster, where his statue in armour was cut, was this inscription:—Here lyeth the body of Sir Nicholas Throkmorton, Knt. the fourth son of Sir George Throkmorton, Knt. The which Sir Nicholas was chief butler of England, one of the chamberlains of the Exchequer, and ambassador leiger to the Queen's Majesty, Queen Elizabeth, in France; and after his return into England, he was sent ambassador again into France, and twice into Scotland. He married Anne Carew, daughter to Sir Nicholas Carew, Knt. and begat of her ten sons and three daughters. He died the 12th day of Feb. Anno Dom. 1570, aged 57 years. *Stowe's Survey, vol. I. b. 2, p. 63.*

‡ Collins's Peerage, vol. VI. p. 582.

§ Under a handsome monument, supported by pillars, with the image of himself and lady, in full proportion, was this inscription:—Here liethe interred the bodie of Syr John Throkmorton, Knyght, of Fekenham, the seventh sonne of Syr George Throkmorton, Knyght, of Coughton, sometime master of the requests unto Queen Marie, of happy memorie, who in respect of his faythful service, bestowed upon him the office of justice of Chester, and of her counsayle, in the Marches of Wales, in whiche roome hee continued xxiii years, and supplied, within the same time, the place of Mr. Vice President, the space of iii years. He had to wife Margerie Puttenham, daughter of Robert Puttenham, Esquier, by whom he had issewe v sons and iiii doughters. He departed this life the 22 of May A⁰ 1580. His wife survived, who lived and dyed his wydoe, a⁰......... and is here   o interred: on whose souls God have mercy. *Dugddle's Warw. vol. II. p. 754.*   ‖ Ibid, p. 752.

of Hertfordshire and Essex. Of the daughters of Sir George, Mary died S. P. Anne was the wife of John Digby, of Coleshill, in Warwickshire, Esq.* Elizabeth, first of Robert Winter, of Hodington, in Warwickshire, and secondly of Thomas Smith, of Cambden, in Gloucestershire, Esqrs. Margaret, first of —— Catesby, and afterwards of Brian Cave, Esqrs. Elizabeth, first of John Gifford, of Chillington, in Staffordshire; secondly of William Ligon, and thirdly of George Peyto, of Chesterton, in Warwickshire, Esqrs. Mary, of Sir John Huband,† of Ipsley, in Warwickshire, Knt. Elizabeth, Meriel, and Elizabeth, who died young, or unmarried.

Sir George, the father of these sons, lived to a very great age, and died in 1500: he had a more numerous posterity than perhaps any in England, at that time, having 112 grand-children.‡

11. Sir Robert Throckmorton, Knt. eldest son and heir of Sir George, beforementioned, was sheriff of the counties of Warwick and Leicester, 1 Queen Mary. He married first Mary, daughter of Thomas, lord Berkeley,§ by whom he had three sons; but only one son, Thomas, survived: and four daughters; Elizabeth, the wife of Sir John Goodwin, of Winchingdon, in Bucks, Knt. Catharine, of Henry Norwood; Anne, of Ralph Sheldon, of Besley, in Worcestershire, Esq. she was buried at Besley, Dec. 16, 1603;‖ and Mary, of Edward Arden, of Parkhall, in Warwickshire, Esqr. His second lady was Elizabeth, daughter of John, lord Hussey, relict of John, lord Hungerford; by whom he had two sons, who died unmarried, and five daughters; of which Meriel was the wife of Sir Thomas Tresham, of Rushton, in Northamptonshire; Anne, of Sir William Catesby, of Ashby Legers, in Northamptonshire; Elizabeth, of Sir Anthony Tyringham, of Tyringham, in Bucks; Temperance, of Sir Randal Brereton, of Cheshire, Knts. Sir Robert died 12 Eliz. and lies buried at Coughton.¶

12. Thomas Throckmorton, Esq. only surviving son of Sir Robert, succeeded him. His life was a continued scene of trouble, on account of his religion, his

---

* Collins's Peerage, vol. VIII. p. 249.
† See Huband's account, in the English Baronets, printed in 1727, vol. II. p. 198.
‡ He was buried under a very handsome monument, standing towards the north side of the chancel at Coughton, which he had caused to be erected in his life-time, having this inscription thereon: "+ Of your charitie praye for the soule of Syr George Throkmorton, Knyght; and Dame Katheryn, hys wyfe, one of the doughters of Sir Nicholas Vause, Knyght, Lord Harroden, wyche Syr George decessyd the — day of ——, in the yere of the incarnation of oure Lord God, a M CCCCC—and Dame Katheryn died the — day of ——, a Mv°—on whose soules Jhu have mercy, Amen.
§ Collins's Peerage, vol. IV. p. 20.   ‖ Dugdale's Warw. edit. 1730, p. 585.
¶ On his monument are these verses:

Conditur hoc tumulto generosæ gloria plebis,   Auxerunt famam neptes, clariq; nepotes,
Luget ut amissum patria chara patrem.   Undiq; Multiplici prole beatus erat.
Nam Plebs patronum, clari Sensere parentem: Erudienda bonos virtutis Semina Liquet,
Fautor erat miseris pauperibusq; pius: In cinerem rediit qui fuit ante cinis.
Religiosus, amans, observantissimus æqui,   Vita dedit mortem letam, mors ultima vita,
Sincerus cultor principis atq; Dei.   Vita fugax obiit, vita parennis adest.
Armatum Sensere hostes, Sensere togatum,   Magne Roberte vale, divæ virtutis alumne,
Pacificum cives, clarus utroq; fuit   Namq; tenes superas, non rediture, domos.

Circumscribed on the freze of this monument:—O Miser respice finem, qualis Sum in brevi eris; vigila ergo, quia nescis diem neq; horam.

estate being frequently under sequestration, and his person often imprisoned; but the severest hardship was the loss of the manor of Ravenston, which he held by lease from the crown, paying 63*l*. 13*s*. yearly, at Lady-day and Michaelmas, or within 40 days after, by equal portions: but advantage being taken many years after, for default of payment of the rent at the exact time (occasioned by a servant's losing part of the money at gaming, which he was sent to pay) he lost the same; and though the queen's receiver had afterwards received it, and gave an acquittance, as if paid at the proper time,* yet he never could recover it. He married Margaret, daughter and co-heiress of William Whorwood, Esq. attorney-general to King Henry VIII. (the other sister being the wife of Ambrose Dudley, earl of Warwick) by whom he had one son, John, and five daughters; Margaret, the wife of Sir Rice Griffin (or Griffith) of Brome Court, in Warwickshire; Elizabeth, of Sir Henry Griffith, of Whichnore, in Staffordshire, Knts. Eleanor, of Sir Henry Jerningham, of Cossey Hall, in Norfolk, Bart. and Meriel, of Henry Berkeley, Esq. son and heir of Sir Henry Berkeley, of Gloucestershire, Knt. and Mary, who died unmarried. This Thomas Throckmorton, Esq. died March 13, 1614, aged 81; and lies buried at Weston, in Bucks, with a short inscription over him.†

13. John Throckmorton, of Coughton, Esq. his only son, died in his father's lifetime: he married Agnes, daughter of Thomas, son of Sir James Wilford, of Newman Hall, in Quindon, Essex, Knt. by whom he had four sons; 1, Robert; 2, Ambrose; and 3, Thomas, who were both colonels in the army of King Charles I. and died unmarried; and 4, George, who died in Italy, unmarried: also five daughters; 1, Eleanor, the wife of Sir Edward Golding, of Colston Basset, in Nottinghamshire, Bart. 2, Winifrid, of John Powell, of Sandford, in Oxfordshire, Esq. 3, Margery, prioress of the English nunnery at Louvain; 4, Margaret; and 5, Mary.

I. ROBERT THROCKMORTON, of Coughton, Esq. eldest son and heir to his grandfather, was advanced to the dignity of a baronet 19 Charles I. He resided very little at Coughton, but kept a bountiful house at Weston for many years, till the breaking out of the civil wars, when his estate was sequestered, and his house at Coughton plundered and made a garrison of, by the parliament forces; whereupon he was forced to secure himself at Worcester, leaving his lady at Weston, and dying Jan. 16, 1650, was buried at Coughton.‡ He married first Dorothy, daughter of Sir John Fortescue, of Salden, in Bucks, K. B. by whom he had no issue: she died Nov. 4, 1617. Secondly, Mary, daughter of Sir Francis Smith, of Ashby Folvile, in Leicestershire, Knt. sister to Sir Charles, the first Baron Carrington, of Wotton, in Warwickshire, and of Sir John Smith, who with his own hands redeemed, in the battle of Edge Hill, the banner royal of King Charles I. for which signal valour he then received, in the field, the honour of knight banneret. By her Sir Robert had four sons,§ whereof only Sir Francis survived him, and one daugh-

---

* Lord Chief Justice Croke's Reports, vol. I. p. 220, 221.
† Hic jacet Thomas Throckmorton armiger qui obiit 13°. die Martii anno Dom. 1614, ætatis suæ 81.
‡ Dugdale's Warw. vol. II. p. 755.
§ In Weston church, Bucks:—Hic jacet Robert Throckmorton, filius natu maximus Roberti Throckmorton, Baronetti, qui obiit in prima infantia die Novembris, anno Dom. 1488. *Le Neve's Mon. Anglic.* vol. I. p. 45. Vide ibid, p. 106.

ter, Anne, the wife of Edward Guldeford, of Hempsted Place, in Kent, Esq. father of Sir Robert Guldeford, Bart.

II. Sir FRANCIS THROCKMORTON, Bart. his only surviving son and successor, in dignity and estate, rebuilt the mansion house at Coughton, and lived in great hospitality after the restoration. He married Anne, daughter and sole heiress of John Monson, of Kinnersley, in Surrey, Esq. son of Sir William Monson, Knt. vice-admiral of England, temp. James I. and had issue four sons and three daughters; 1, Francis, who died Sep. 10, 1676, at Bruges, in Flanders, aged 16; 2, Sir Robert, his successor; 3, John, who died at four years old; 4, George, who made such improvements by his travels into France and Italy, as to be esteemed one of the completest gentlemen of his time: he led a life, for some years before he died, with such devotion towards God, humility and charity towards his neighbours, and rigorous mortification against himself, that his life was printed. He died April 16, 1705, aged 34. The daughters were Anne, a nun of the order of St. Augustine, at Paris; Mary, the wife of Martin Wollascot, of Wollascot, in Salop, Esq. and Elizabeth. Sir Francis died Nov. 7, 1680, and lies buried at Weston.*

III. Sir ROBERT THROCKMORTON, Bart. eldest surviving son of Sir Francis, succeeded to the estates of his ancestors (being the heir general of Abberbury, Besford, Spiney, and Weston, heir of Bosum, or Bosun).† He married Mary, second daughter of Sir Charles Yate, of Buckland, in Berks, Bart. (sole surviving sister and heiress of Sir John Yate, of the same place, Bart.) and had issue three sons; Robert, who died an infant, Jan. 14, 1688, 15 days old; George, born Dec. 7, 1690, who died V. P. and Sir Robert, his successor: also eight daughters; Anne, the wife of John Petre, of Fidlers, in Essex, Esq. Mary, of James Fermor, of Tusmore, in Oxfordshire, Esq. Elizabeth and Catharine, nuns in St. Augustine's monastery, at Paris; Charlotte, the wife of Sir Thomas Windsor Hunloke, of Wingerworth, in Derbyshire, Bart. Appolonia, of Sir Edward Blount, of Soddington, in Worcestershire, Bart. and Barbara, of Peter Giffard, of Chillington, in Staffordshire, Esq. Sir Robert dying March 8, 1720, and his lady in 1728, the dignity and estate devolved upon his only son,

IV. Sir ROBERT THROCKMORTON, Bart. born Aug. 21, 1702: he married first Lady Teresa, daughter of William Herbert, marquis of Powis; by whom, who died at Weston June 17, 1723, he had two sons and one daughter; Robert, who

---

In Olney church, Bucks :—John Throckmorton, Gent. deceased the 29th day of Sep. anno Dom. 1695, aged — years, 11 months. *Le Neve's Mon. Ang. vol. I. p.* 142.
Francis Throckmorton, widow, deceased the — day of ——, 1696, in the 69th year of her age.

* Hic jacet Franciscus Throckmorton, Eques & Baronettus, qui obiit 7mo. die Novembris anno Dom. 1680. ætatis suæ 40.
Hic jacet Cor Francisci Throckmorton armigeri, filii. primogeniti Francis Throckmorton Equitis & Baronetti, qui obiit Brugis in Belgio 10°. die Septembris An. 1676. ætatis suæ 16.

† He was born Jan. 10, 1662, and in a manner new built his house at Weston, and gave a ring of six bells to the church: he also gave the like number of bells to Coughton church; and, in conjunction with some others, built a new school-house there, endowing the vicarage with the addition of 25l. per ann. for ever, provided the vicar teaches, in the said school-house, his tenants' children; and lastly, he gave lands for ever, for maintaining five poor decayed tenants.

died in France, unmarried; George, who married, in 1748, Anna-Maria, only daughter of William Paston, of Horton, in Gloucestershire, Esq. (by his wife, daughter and heiress of John Courtenay, of Molland, in Devonshire, Esq.) by whom he had nine children, six sons and three daughters; 1, Robert, born Aug. 23, 1750, died unmarried Nov. 11, 1779, at Bath, and is buried in the Abbey Church; 2, John-Courtenay; 3, George, born Sep. 15, 1754: he assumed, by letters patent, in 1792, the name and arms of Courtenay only, having inherited, from his mother, the estate of the Courtenays, of Molland, in Devonshire; he is also possessed, by deeds of settlement, made in 1782, of the estate at Weston, in the county of Bucks: he married June 29, 1792, Catharine, only daughter of Thomas Stapleton, of Carlton, in Yorkshire, Esq. 4, Charles, born Nov. 2, 1757, married Dec. 27, 1787, Mary, daughter of Edmund Plowden, of Plowden, in the county of Salop, Esq. 5, Francis, born Feb. 21, 1761, died at Lisbon, March 23, 1788, and is buried in the church of the English College, in that city: 6, William, born May 8, 1762. The daughters were, 1, Mary, born Aug. 29, 1749, and died at Paris, Sep. 30, 1763, unmarried; 2, Anne, born Nov. 21, 1751, died Nov. 6, 1783, at Caverleigh, in Devonshire, unmarried, and is buried there; 3, Teresa, born Feb. 28, 1759, and married Aug. 28, 1789, Thomas Metcalf, Esq. of Bath, by whom (who died Oct. 21, 1792, at Bath) she has two children; Teresa, born Feb. 6, 1791, and Thomas-Peter, born April 25, 1794. Mary-Teresa, daughter of Sir Robert Throckmorton, was the wife of Thomas Fitzherbert, of Swinnerton, in Staffordshire, Esq. and died at Bath Feb. 26, 1791, and is buried in the Abbey Church.

Sir Robert married secondly, in Jan. 1757-8, Catharine, daughter of George Collingwood, of Estlington, in the county of Northumberland, Esq. and by her (who was buried at Buckland, Aug. 3, 1761) he had two daughters, who died infants, and Barbara, the wife of Thomas Giffard, of Chillington, Esq. who died May 17, 1764, leaving one son, Thomas Giffard, Esq.

Sir Robert married thirdly, in 1763, Lucy, daughter of James Heywood, of Maristow, in Devonshire, Esq. by whom he had no children: she survived him, and died Nov. 20, 1795, at Richmond, and is there buried.

George Throckmorton, Esq. died at Bath, Dec. 30, 1762, and is buried in the Abbey Church. Anna-Maria, his widow, died at Abergavenny, Oct. 20, 1791, and is there buried.

Sir Robert Throckmorton, soon after the marriage of his son, settled at Buckland, in the county of Berks, which estate he inherited from his mother, as before-mentioned, where he built a handsome new house, and very much beautified the place; and where, after residing many years, he died Dec. 8, 1791; and was buried at Coughton, in Warwickshire, under the tomb erected in the church there, by his ancestor, Sir Robert Throckmorton, Knt. as before-mentioned; by whose death the dignity and estate devolved upon his eldest surviving grandson,

V. Sir JOHN-COURTENAY THROCKMORTON, Bart. born July 27, 1753, who married Aug. 19, 1782, Mary-Catharine, daughter of Thomas Giffard, of Chillington, Esq. by his first wife, Barbara, daughter of Robert, lord Petre.

ARMS—Gules, on a chevron, argent, three bars gemels, sable.

THROCKMORTON, OF COUGHTON, WARWICKSHIRE.

CREST now used by the family—On a wreath, an elephant's head.
MOTTO—*Virtus Sola Nobilitas*, or *Moribus Antiquis*.
SEATS—At Buckland, in Berkshire, and Coughton, in Warwickshire.

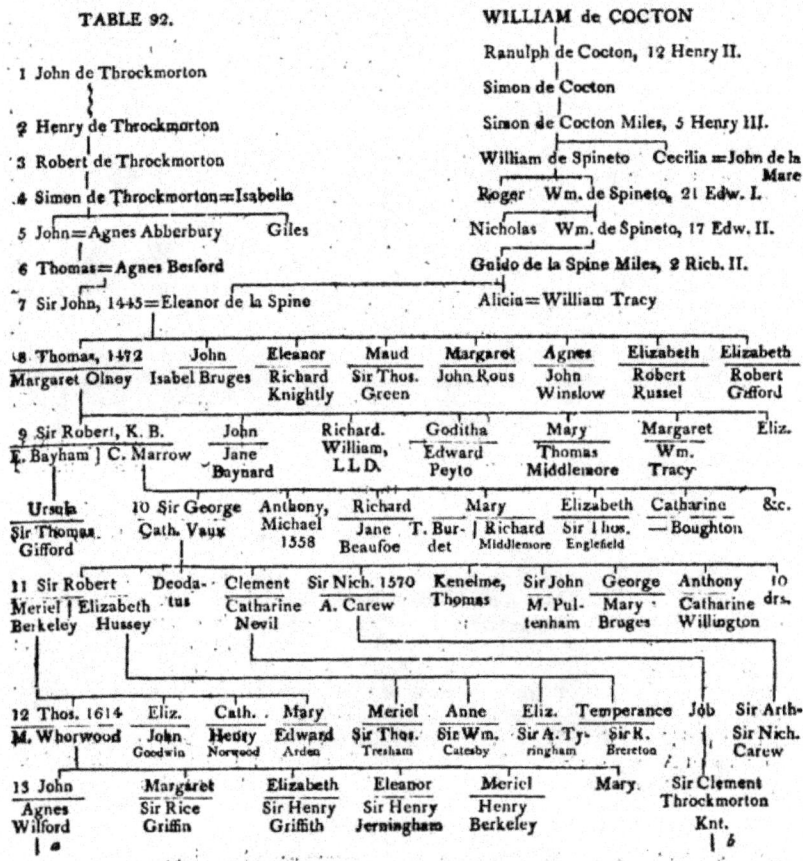

TABLE 92.

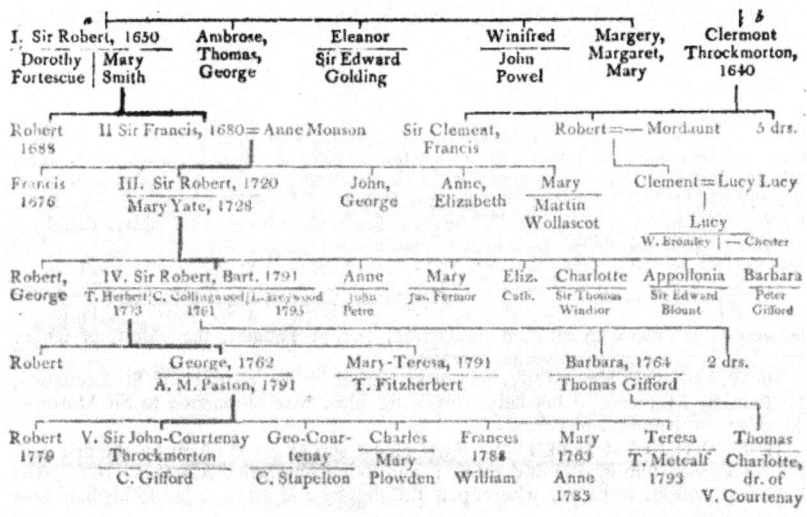

92. HALTON, of Samford, Essex.

Created Baronet Sep. 10, 1642.

1. JOHN HALTON,* of Swansea, a gentleman of Cambridgeshire, was living 12 Henry VI. 1433. His descendant, as is supposed, was

2. Robert Halton, Esq.† serjeant at law, who married Jane, daughter and heiress of —— Drayner, by whom he had three sons; 1, Roger; 2, Sir William Halton, of the Middle Temple, and of Great Abington, in Cambridgeshire, Knt. who died unmarried, and lies buried in Great Abington church.‡

3. Robert, of Sabridgeworth, in Hertfordshire, who married first Esther, daughter of William Booth, of Lincolnshire or Lancashire, by whom he had five sons; 1,

---

* Vide Visit. of Hert. 1634, and Salmon's Essex, p. 180, 181.   † Le Neve's MSS. vol. II. p. 203.

‡ There is a monument in the north chancel wall, whereon is a cumbent statue, in armour, and a lion at his feet, with this inscription:—Here, under this monument, lyeth interred, the body of Sir William Halton, Knight, who in faith and much patience changed this life for a better, upon the 20th of Nov. in the year of our Lord, 1639, being near upon the age of 70 years,

HALTON, OF SAMFORD, ESSEX.

Roger; 2, Thomas; 3, William; 4, Robert; and 5, John: secondly, ——, relict of Mr. Shute, by whom he had no issue.

I. WILLIAM HALTON, Esq. third son, executor and heir to his uncle, purchased the estate of Little Samford Halls, in Essex, of Sir Edward Green, Bart. and paid his ingress fine 16 Charles I. He married first Mary, daughter of Sir Edward Altham, of Marks Hall, in Latton, in Essex, Knt. by whom he had Sir William, his successor, and Mary, who died unmarried: she died Dec. 29, 1644, aged 26, and lies buried in the chancel of Little Samford church. Sir William married secondly Ursula, daughter of Sir Thomas Fisher, of Islington, in Middlesex, Bart. by whom he had two sons, Sir Thomas and Richard, who married Mary, daughter of George Johnson, Gent. by whom he had a son George, and two daughters, Ursula and Susan; and dying Sep. 14, 1703, was buried at St. Andrew's, Holborn.

George, his son and heir, married Hannah, eldest daughter of Mr. Fenwick Lambert, of London; and dying May 7, 1729, was buried at St. Andrew's, Holborn, leaving four sons, who all died unmarried, except Thomas, the eldest, of whom we shall have occasion to speak hereafter.

Sir William died about 1662, and was buried in the chancel of St. Leonard's, Shoreditch, Middlesex: his lady, surviving him, was re-married to Sir Matthew Meriton, of London, merchant.

II. Sir WILLIAM HALTON, Bart. eldest son of Sir William by the first venter, succeeded him in title and estate; and dying unmarried March 4, 1675, was buried at Latton, in Essex, whereupon the dignity and estate came to his half brother,

III. Sir THOMAS HALTON, Bart. who married Elizabeth, daughter of John Cressener, of London, Esq. she died Aug. 26, 1716, and was buried at Islington, in Middlesex; by whom he had several children, all of which died unmarried, except Sir William, his successor, and Mary, the wife of James Nicoll. of the Court Lodge, in Munfeild, near Robert's Bridge, in Sussex, Esq. she died May 29, 1739, and was buried at Munfeild. Sir Thomas died Sep. 6, 1726, and was buried at Islington; and was succeeded in dignity and estate by his eldest son,

IV. Sir WILLIAM HALTON, Bart. who married Frances, daughter of Sir George Dalston, Knt. eldest son and heir of Sir George Dalston, of Heath Hall, in Yorkshire, Bart. widow of John Jermy, of Sturton Hall, in Suffolk, Esq. Sir William died at his house, at Turnham Green, Feb. 12, 1754, without issue, and was succeeded by

V. Sir THOMAS, the eldest son of George (by Mrs. Fenwick) son of Richard, who was the youngest son of the first Sir William Halton, Bart. who went abroad about 40 years ago. He left one son,

VI. Sir WILLIAM, who married Mary, daughter of Michael Garner, of King Ripton, in Huntingdonshire, Esq. and is supposed to be the present baronet.

ARMS—Party per pale, azure and gules, a lion rampant, argent.
CREST—On a wreath, a lion seiant, argent, holding a broken lance, proper.
SEAT—At Reach, in Huntingdonshire.

HALTON, OF SAMFORD, ESSEX.

1 JOHN HALTON, of Swansea, living in 1433

TABLE 93.

2 Robert Halton=Jane Drayner

Roger — Sir William, Knt. — E. Booth=Robert=widow of —— Shute

Roger — Thomas — Mary Altham, 1644=I. Sir Wm. 1662=Ursula Fisher — John

II. Sir William, 1675 — Mary — III. Sir Thomas, 1726=E. Cressener 1716 — Richard, 1703=M. Johnson

IV. Sir William, 1754 F. Dalston — several children — Mary, 1759 James Nicoll — George Hannah Lambert — Ursula, Susan

V. Sir Thomas Halton.

VI. Sir William=Mary Garner

---

93. BLOUNT, of SODDINGTON, WORCESTERSHIRE.

Created Baronet Oct. 5, 1642.

THIS ancient family is said to take its rise from the Blondi, or Biondi, in Italy, whose historians derive them from the Roman Flavii.*

1. Blound, lord of Guisnes, in France, had three sons, who came into England with William the Conqueror: one returned into France; the other two, Sir Robert and Sir William Blound, gave a beginning to all the Blounts in this kingdom.

2. Sir Robert, created by the Conqueror, Baron of Ickworth, in Suffolk, married Gundred, daughter of the Earl Ferrers. He was *Dux Manuum Militarium*, Baron of Ickworth, lord of Orford Castle, Walsham, Stepworth, Ashfield, and Laningham, in Suffolk.†

3. Gilbert, his son (whom Camden calls *Magnæ Nobilitatis Vir;*) founded the priory at Ickworth, and endowed it with 280*l*. per ann. He married Alicia de Colekirk, and left issue,

4. William, baron of Ickworth, who married Sarah, daughter of Monchampes, or Monchensy, lord of Elwaiston, in Derbyshire, and had issue

5. Gilbert, by others called Hubert, baron of Ickworth; he married Agnes de Insula, or Lisle, and had issue two sons, William and Stephen.

* From the family, in 1727, from whom was the chief of this account.   † Vide Doomsday Book.

Sir William, the eldest, ~~married Cecilia de Vere, and~~ had issue one son, Sir William, who taking part with Mountford, earl of Leicester, was slain at the battle of Lewes, in Sussex; and attainted in parliament temp. Henry III. Here ended the Blounts, barons of Ickworth. But

6. Sir Stephen, second son of Gilbert, or Hubert, married Maria, sole daughter and heiress of Sir William le Blound, of Saxlingham, in Suffolk, the fourth in a right line from Sir William Blound, brother to the first Sir Robert, and general of foot to the Conqueror. From the families thus united, all the Blounts in England are descended.

7. Sir John Blount, their son and heir, married one of the sisters and co-heiresses of Richard de Wrotham; ~~and doing homage,~~ had livery of her purparty of lands in Somerset and Dorset, temp. Henry III. and had issue Peter, who died without issue, and

8. Sir William, who married Isabel, sole daughter and heiress to the Lord Beauchamp, of Hache, in Somersetshire, and relict of the Lord Lovet.* He had by her three sons; Sir Walter; Sir Thomas, from whom descended the Blounts of Maple Durham, Titenhanger, and others: of the third son there is no record.

* Mr. Abington, in his MS. of Worcestershire (in Jesus College Library, Oxford) in Hampton Lovet, mentions, that "It was the inheritance of the Blontes, who together with the Lovets, descended from one generall ancestor, Isabell, the wife fyrst of Henry Lovet, from whom isseued the Lovets, and after hys death, secondly, marryed Sir William Blont, Knight, from whom descended the Blonts of Sodington, whych eavery age synce produced knyghtes, the Barons Montjoye, and Earle of Devonshire, the knyghtly race of the Blontes of Kinlet, besides divers others of especiall estimation. The fyrst record concerning theyre estate in Hampton Lovet, is 2 Edw. III. shewinge, that William le Blont had charter warren in thys manor. The next 20 Edw. III. in the Book of Aids, in the Exchequer, where Johes le Blont, is specifyed to have landes in thys paryshe, and for evydences, Thomas de Hugford, parson of Hampton Lovet, conveygheth the manor of Hampton Lovet, with the advowson of the church, to Sir John le Blont, Knight, and Elizabeth hys wyfe, 19 Edw. III. and the same yeere Joane, late wyfe of Richard le Bosler, released to Sir John le Blont, Knight, lord of Hampton Lovet, in the manor of Thikenepeltre, which descended to Alice, syster of William le Blont, and wyfe of Sir Richard Stury, Knight, as appearethe by a petition in old French, Englished thus (by Abington) Humbly beeeechethe, your tenant, Alice, who was the wyfe of Sir Richard Stury, that whereas hee had towe messuages, towe plowlandes, five acres of modowe, &c. in Thikenpeltre, within the county of Worcester, which should descend to her, as her ryghtful inheritance, after the deathe of William le Blont, brother of your sayd suppliant, &c. Notwithstandinge, Hampton Lovet returned agayne to the Blountes; for 7 Henry VI. the record in the Exchekuer reportethe, that the heyre of John Blont, ten. landes in Hampton Lovet, which Sir John Blont, sometymes had. Theyse Blontes, of Hampton Lovet, spronge from Sir John le Blont, of Sodington, whose father, John le Blont, marryed Isolda Montjoy, the heyre of that familly. Their offspringe was advanced to greatness, which appearethe fyrst in St. Augustine's church, commonly called Dudurhull, neere which, wheare the armes of Blont, quartering (Furneux) gules, a bend between six crosse croslets or, is set out (amonge others of special accompt) next to the Earl of Warwicke. To showe the continewance of the Blontes, in Hampton Lovet, Sir Robert Hasyll, was admitted 5 die Novembris, An. Do. 1417 (*See the Leger of the priory of Worcester, sede vacante*) to the perpetuall chantry of St. Anne, in the churche of Hampton Lovet, beinge voyd after the resignation of Sir Henry Amys, the last chaplayne, by the presentation of Sir Thomas Blont, Knight, perpetuall patron of that chantry, after thys King Edward the fourth, raysed Sr. Walter Blount, Knight, to the dignity of a baron, with the tytell of the Lord Mountjoye, as descended from John le Blont, and Isulda, the heyre of Sir Rafe Montjoye. Hence issewed, after dyvers descents, Sr Charles Blont, Earl of Devonshire, Baron Montjoye, and Knight of the Garter: but longe before thys time hys ancestor, the Lord Montjoy, had sould Hampton Lovet to Sir John Pakington, Knight, who made thys hys seat.

BLOUNT, OF SODDINGTON, WORCESTERSHIRE.

9. Sir Walter, of Ockha, alias Rock, in Warwickshire (which estate is still in the possession of the Blounts of Soddington) son and heir, married Joan, daughter and heiress of Sir William de Soddington, whereby they possessed that estate, which has been the seat of the family to this day. He had issue Sir William Blount, who married Margaret, daughter and co-heiress of the Lord Verdun; but dying without issue, left many of his lands, temp. Edw. III. to his brother,

10. Sir John, who married Isolda, daughter and heiress of Thomas, lord Montjoye, and grand-daughter and heiress of the Lord Ralph Montjoye, whence that title was afterwards assumed, as a barony, in this family: Richard, their eldest son, died without issue.

11. Sir John, second son by his first wife, daughter of ———, was father of John. By his second wife, Isabella, daughter and heir, of Sir Bryan Cornwall, of Kinlet, descend the Blounts, of Kinlet, Eye, Kidderminster, Orlton, &c.

12. Sir John Blount, Knt. eldest son, married Isabel, daughter of Sir John Foulhurst; but dying before his father, left his son,

13. Sir John, who succeeded his grandfather, and married Catharine, daughter and heiress of Thomas Corbet, of Stanford, by whom he had divers children. His eldest surviving son,

14. Peter Blount, Esq. of Soddington, by Anne, daughter of Edward Cornwall, baron of Burford, had issue

15. Thomas Blount, of Soddington, Esq. who married first Catharine, daughter of Thomas Stanford, of Rowly, in Staffordshire, Esq. by whom he had two sons; 1, Walter Blount, Esq. who married first Margaret, daughter of Sir John Talbot, of Grafton, in Worcestershire, Knt. and secondly Catharine, daughter of Thomas Grey, of Enville, in Staffordshire, Esq. but had no issue by either of them; 2, Henry, who died S. P. but the said Thomas, by his second wife, Jocosa, daughter and heiress of Thomas Shirley, of Stockton, in Herefordshire, Esq. had two sons, Sir George and Peter, who died S. P.

16. Sir George Blount, Knt. eldest son by the second venter, and heir to his half brother, married Eleanor, daughter of William Norwood, of Leckhampton, in Gloucestershire, Esq. and left issue four sons and three daughters, viz. Elizabeth, the wife of William Walsh, of Aberly; Eleanor, of Henry Ingram, Esqrs. and Margaret, who died young. The younger sons served King Charles I. in England, Ireland, and Germany.

I. Sir WALTER BLOUNT, the oldest son, was advanced to the dignity of a baronet, 18 Charles I. and married very young to Elizabeth, daughter of George Wyld, of Droitwich, in Worcestershire, Esq. serjeant at law. This Sir Walter was a great sufferer for King Charles I. for whom he was long imprisoned, first at Oxford, then in the Tower of London: his brothers, and four sons were all in the same service. His second son, Col. John Blount, was lieutenant-colonel in King Charles the second's own regiment, when Prince of Wales. His third son, William, was major in the Queen's regiment. Peter, the fourth son, was a captain at Worcester fight, and married Frances, daughter of Sir John Pershall, of Horsley, in Staffordshire, Bart. relict of John Stanford, of Salford, Esq. Walter, Thomas, and Edward died young, or unmarried. His daughters were Eleanor, first the wife of Robert Knightly, of Offchurch, in Warwickshire, Esq. and secondly of the hon. Walter Aston, afterwards Lord Aston, of the kingdom of Scotland; Anne, the wife of James Anderton, of Birchley, in Lancashire, Esq. (who left only one daughter, by whose intermarriage that estate fell to Sir William Gerard, of Garswood, in that county, Bart.) Elizabeth, the wife of Henry Englefield, of Englefield, in Berks, Esq. and Francis, of Andrew, son of Sir Thomas Windsor. Of the younger sons, none left issue but Col. John Blount (who by his second wife, a daughter of —— Burgh, of Ireland, left a son George, who married ——, daughter of Mr. Bowyers, of Luntlow, in Herefordshire, and had many children). He was succeeded in dignity and estate by his eldest son,

II. Sir GEORGE BLOUNT, Bart. who married Mary, daughter and heiress of Richard Kirkham, of Blagdon, in Devonshire, Esq. son and heir of Sir William Kirkham, of Blagdon, Knt. (by his second wife, daughter of Sir Henry Tychburne, of Hampshire) by whom he had three sons and five daughters; 1, Walter-Kirkham, of whom hereafter; 2, George, who married first Mary, daughter of ——, earl of Thomond, and secondly Constantia, daughter of Sir George Cary, of Tor Abbey, in Devonshire, Knt. by whom he had three sons; George and Robert, both died young, and Edward, who succeeded; as also five daughters; Constantia, the wife of Sir John Smyth, of Acton Burnell, in Shropshire, Bart. Mary, of Edward Dickenson, Esq. Anne, living in 1768; Elizabeth, and Catharine, both died unmarried. His eldest son and successor was

III. Sir WALTER-KIRKHAM BLOUNT, Bart. who married first Alicia, daughter of Sir Thomas Strickland, of Thornton Brigg, in Yorkshire, Knt. by her he had two sons, who both died infants; and secondly, Mary, daughter of Sir Cæsar Cranmer, of Astwood Bury, in Bucks, Knt. He died, without issue, at Ghent, in Flanders, May 12, 1717. William, John, Charles, John, and Richard, all died young.

Edward Blount, of Blagdon, Esq. youngest son of Sir George, died in 1726, having married Anne, eldest daughter of Sir John Guise, of Rendcombe, in Gloucestershire, Bart. by whom he had four daughters; Elizabeth, the wife of the right hon. Hugh, lord Clifford, baron of Chudleigh; Mary, of his Grace, Edward, duke of Norfolk; Anne, and Henrietta, widow of the hon. Philip Howard, of Norfolk, Esq. Sir George had also five daughters; Mary, the wife of Henry Howard, of Clun, in Salop, Esq. and died May 5, 1732, aged about 80; Anne, of Sir Francis Jerningham, of Cossey Hall, in Norfolk, Bart. Elizabeth, of Beaumond Tasburgh, of Bodney, in Norfolk, Esq. Catharine, of Richard Minshall, of Bourton, in Bucks, Esq. she died March 1, 1739-40, aged about 83; and Lucy, who died young.

IV. Sir EDWARD BLOUNT, Bart. succeeded his uncle in dignity and estate.* He married Appollonia, daughter of Sir Robert Throckmorton, of Coughton, in Warwickshire, Bart. and had issue four sons; 1, Sir Edward; 2, Sir Walter, successively baronets; 3, Robert; and 4, George, who both died infants: also three daughters, Appollonia, Louisa, and Mary. He died in 1758, and was succeeded by his eldest son,

* From the family, in 1727.

BLOUNT; OF SODDINGTON, WORCESTERSHIRE.

TABLE 94.

1 BLOUND
2 Sir Robert, B. of Ickworth = Gundred Ferrers — Sir William, a general, temp. Wm. I.
3 Gilbert Blound = Alicia de Colekirk — Blound
4 William, B. of Ickworth = Sarah Monchampes — Blound
5 Gilbert, B. of Ickworth = Agnes de Insula — Sir William le Blound
Sir William = C. de Vere   6 Stephen = Maria le Blound
Sir William   7 Sir John Blount = — de Wrotham
Peter Blount   8 Sir William = Isabel, dr. of —, L. Beauchamp
9 Sir Walter = Joan de Soddington   Sir Thomas — a son
10 Sir William = M. Verdun   10 Sir John = Isolda Montjoye
Richard   11 Sir John Blount = Isabel Cornwall
12 Sir John Blount = Isabel Foulhurst
13 Sir John Blount = Catharine Corbet   Blounts of Maple Durham, &c.
14 Peter Blount = Anne Cornwall, dr. of Edw. B. of Burford
Catharine Stanford = 15 Thomas = Jocosa Shirley
Marg. Talbot = Walter = Cath. Grey   Henry   16 Sir George = L. Norwood   Peter
I. Sir Walter = Eliz. Wyld   Elizabeth = Wm. Walsh   Eleanor = H. Ingram   Margaret   3 sons
II. Sir George   John   Wm.   Peter   Walter,   Eleanor   Anne   Eliz.   Frances
Mary Kirkham   N | = Burgh   Francis   Thos.   Robert   Walter,   James   Henry   Andr.
            Pershall   Edw. Knightly   L. Anson   Anderton   Englefield   Windsor
III. Sir Walter, 1717   George   Wm.   John,   Edw. 1726   Mary   Anne   Eliz.   Cath. 1740   Geo.
Alice   Mary   M.dr.of E.   Const.   John,   Rich.   Anne   Henry   SirFras.   Beaumond   Richard
Strickland   Cranmer   Thornhill   Cary   Charles   Gage   Howard   Jerningham   Tasburgh   Mendhall   Bowyer
IV. Sir Edw. 1758   Constantia   Mary   Anne,   Elizabeth   Mary   Anne   Henrietta
Appollonia   Sir John   Edward   Eliz.   Hugh, B. of   Edw. D. of   Philip
Throckmorton   Smyth, Bt.   Dickenson   Cath.   Chudleigh   Norfolk   Howard
V. Sir Edward, 1765   VI. Sir Walter, 1785   Robert   Appollonia,   Mary
Frances Molineux   Mary, dr. of James L. Aston   George   Louisa
Edward   VII. Sir Walter Blount = Anne Riddel

LIDDELL, OF RAVENSWORTH CASTLE, DURHAM.

V. Sir EDWARD BLOUNT, Bart. who married in 1752, Frances, daughter and heiress of William Molineux, of Mosborough, in Lancashire, Esq. by whom he had one son, Edward, who died young: and Sir Edward dying in 1765, the title and estate descended to his brother,

VI. Sir WALTER BLOUNT, Bart. he married in 1766, Mary, eldest daughter of James, lord Aston, and baron of Forsar, in Scotland; by whom he had a son, born Sep. 30, 1767, who died the 4th of October following; and another son, Walter, born Sep. 3, 1768. Sir Walter died Oct. 5, 1785, at Lisle, in French Flanders, and was succeeded by his son,

VII. Sir WALTER BLOUNT, Bart. who married Nov. 25, 1792, Anne, youngest daughter of the late Thomas Riddell, of Swinburne Castle, in Northumberland. Esq.

ARMS—Barry nebule of six, or and sable.
CREST—An armed foot in the sun.
MOTTO—*Lux tua, Via mea.*
SEATS—At Soddington, in Worcestershire, and Mawly, in Shropshire.

The earls of Mountjoy, Devonshire, and Newport, that have been created out of the descendants of this noble family, are recorded by Dugdale, and the Peerage of England; and the three knights, who have been honoured with the most noble order of the garter, are inscribed in their stalls, that to mention them here, which are facts so well known, would swell this pedigree to a volume.

---

94. LIDDELL, of Ravensworth Castle, Durham.

Created Baronet Nov. 2, 1642.

THE Liddells were anciently lords of Liddell Castle,* and barony of Buff; and have been proprietors of considerable coal works in the counties of Durham and Northumberland. The first we find is

1. Thomas de Liddell,† who married Margaret, daughter of John de Laburne, by whom he had issue two sons, Thomas and George, who married Eleanor, daughter of John Burn, and had one son, George, who married ———, daughter of Robert Barker, Esq. and died without issue.

2. Thomas, the eldest son, married Barbara, daughter and coheiress of Richard Strangeways, by whom he had four sons and two daughters; 1, Francis; 2, Thomas; 3, Robert; and 4, Percival, who both died S. P. Alice, the wife of Oswald

* Ex Infor. Geo. Liddell, Arm. 1727.   † Ex Stem. Penes. Geo. Liddell, Arm. 1727.

Carr; Barbara died young. Francis, the eldest son married Anne, daughter of William de Segrave; but his line terminated in his son and heir, Bartrum, who married Barbara, daughter of Thomas Cramlington, and died without issue.

3. Thomas Liddell, Esq. (second son of Thomas) continued the line:[*] he purchased the manors of Ravensworth, Lamesly, and Eighton, of Sir William Gascoigne, in 1607. He married first Margaret, daughter of John Watson, Esq. by whom he had Thomas, his son and heir, and three daughters; Elizabeth, the wife of William Sherwood, of Middlesex; Alice, of Gawen Salkeld; and Eleanor, of Timothy Draper, of Newcastle, in Northumberland, Gent. His second wife was Jane, daughter of Henry Midford, Esq. by whom he had 1, Henry, who married Elizabeth, daughter of William Jennison, Esq. by whom he had a son Thomas, his heir; 2, Roger, who married Grace, daughter of James Clavering, Esq. 3, Barbara, the wife of Samuel Sanderson, Gent. they all had issue; and 4, Jane, of Robert Anderson, Esq.[†] he died in 1615, and was succeeded by his eldest son,

I. THOMAS LIDDELL, Esq. who was much esteemed, and had great interest in the county of Northumberland, which he exerted in support of King Charles I. defending Newcastle against the Scots; and his majesty, as a mark of his favour, conferred on him the dignity of a baronet, by letters patent, bearing date Nov. 2, 1642. In the time of the rebellion he was taken prisoner, as Whitlock relates; and that on Feb. 13, 1645, upon a petition of Sir Thomas Liddell, a prisoner, he was admitted to compound: it appears, that he paid 4000l.[‡] to the sequestrators for his estate. He was also so obnoxious to the then powers, that Sir Thomas Liddell, senior, is mentioned among those, in the propositions from the parliament, who were demanded to be removed from his majesty's councils, and to be restrained from coming within the verge of the court; and not, without advice or consent of both houses of parliament, to bear any office or employment. He survived those troublesome times, departing this life in 1650, and having married Isabel, daughter of Henry Anderson, Esq. (by a daughter and co-heir of —— Morland) by whom he had six sons, and three daughters, viz. 1, Sir Thomas Liddell, Knt. who died in 1627, leaving issue by Bridget (who was maid of honour to the Queen of Bohemia) daughter of Edward Woodward, of Lee, near Windsor, Esq. one son, Sir Thomas, hereafter-mentioned (she afterwards was the wife of Thomas Heneage, of Battersea, in Surrey, Esq. nephew of Sir Thomas Heneage, Bart.) 2, Francis,[§] married Elizabeth, daughter of Sir George Tonge, of Denton, in Durham, Knt. 3, William; 4, Robert; 5, George; and 6, Henry, who all died unmarried.

The daughters were 1, Elizabeth, the wife of George Baker, Esq. barrister at law, who afterwards was knighted; 2, Mary, of Nicholas Cole, of Brancepeth Castle, in Durham, Esq. (afterwards created a baronet) and 3, Isabel, who died unmarried.

---

[*] Ex stem. Penes. Geo. Liddell, Arm. 1727. [†] Ibid. [‡] See list of those that compounded, in letter L.

[§] Qu. If this Francis was not a knight, and if he had not two wives; for I find Sir Francis Liddell, of Redhaugh, in Northumberland, Knt. and said to be son of Thomas, who married Agnes, daughter and sole heiress of Sir William Chaytor, of Croft, in Yorkshire, Knt. relict first of Nicholas Forster, of Bamburgh, in Northumberland, and secondly of —— Dawson, near Ripon; and that he had a son Francis, married to Frances, daughter of Nicholas Forster, of Bamburgh. *Le Neve's MSS. vol. II. p.* 209, and *Dugdale's Northumb. b.* 14.

LIDDELL, OF RAVENSWORTH CASTLE, DURHAM.

II. Sir THOMAS LIDDELL, Bart. (only son of Sir Thomas, Knt.) succeeded his grandfather in dignity and estate, in 1650: he was knighted by King Charles I. and lived to be very aged, departing this life in 1697, having issue, by Anne, daughter of Sir Henry Vane, the elder, of Raby Castle, in Durham, Knt. five sons and three daughters; 1, Sir Henry, his successor; 2, Thomas, who died unmarried; 3, Edward, who died young; 4, Robert, who married Priscilla, daughter of William Kiffin, of London, merchant, who died March 15, 1679, aged 24, and is buried at Bunhill Fields: by her he had issue Thomas, who died May 14, 1718; and by Mary, daughter of —— Nelthorpe, had issue Henry Liddell, Esq. his only son and heir, and one daughter: 5, George, who died a batchelor.

The daughters were 1, Frances, the wife of Thomas Vane, of Raby Castle, in Durham, Esq. elder brother of the late Lord Barnard, and afterwards of Sir John Bright, Bart. 2, Elizabeth, of Christopher Stockdale, of Bilton Park, in the county of York, Esq. and had issue; and 3, Isabel, who died unmarried.

III. Sir HENRY LIDDELL, Bart. eldest son and successor to his father, married Catharine, daughter and heiress of Sir John Bright, of Carbrook, in Derbyshire, and Badsworth, in Yorkshire, Bart. (by Catharine his wife, daughter of Sir Richard Hawksworth, of Hawksworth, Knt. and relict of William Lister, of Thornton, Knt.) by whom he had issue five sons and one daughter; 1, Thomas; 2, John; 3, Henry; 4, George; and 5, Michael; and one daughter, Elizabeth. Thomas, the first son, married Jane, eldest daughter of James Clavering, of Greencroft, in the county Palatine of Durham, Esq. and died in the life-time of his father, 1715. He had issue four sons; 1, Henry, afterwards Lord Ravensworth; 2, James, died at the age of 14 years; 3, Thomas, died an infant; Catharine died at the age of 12 years; and Thomas, the fourth son, who married Margaret, daughter of Sir William Bowes, of Gibside.

IV. Sir HENRY LIDDELL, Bart. (afterwards Lord Ravensworth) grandson of Sir Henry Liddell, Bart. who died in 1723, succeeded his grandfather in dignity and estate; and in 1735 married Anne, only daughter of Sir Peter Delme, Knt. then deceased, by whom he had issue one son, who died an infant, very young, and one daughter, Anne, the wife of Lord Euston, now duke of Grafton.* He was created a peer, in the year 1747, by the name and title of Henry, Baron of Ravensworth, and died at Ravensworth Castle, in the county of Durham, Jan. 30, 1784.

Thomas Liddell, Esq. his lordship's brother, died in his lordship's life-time: he married Margaret, one of the daughters of Sir William Bowes, of Gibside, Knt. by whom he had two sons; Thomas, who died an infant, and Henry-George, who succeeded his uncle, Lord Ravensworth, in dignity of baronet and estate, in 1784.

V. Sir HENRY-GEORGE LIDDELL, Bart. married Elizabeth, the daughter of Thomas Steele, of Chichester, in the county of Sussex, Esq. by whom he had

---

* By the said Anne he had issue 1, Georgina, born May 8, 1757, the wife of John Smith, of Heath, Esq. in 1778; 2, George-Henry, earl of Euston, born Jan. 14, 1760, who married Anne-Horatia, daughter of the late earl of Waldegrave; 3, Charles, born July 17, 1764. His Grace obtained an act of parliament, which received the royal assent on March 23, 1769, whereby his grace's marriage with the said Anne Liddell was dissolved: in consequence whereof she was remarried to John, the present Earl of Upper Ossory, by whom he has two daughters, Anne and Gertrude; and his Grace, in May following, married Eliz. third daughter of the Rev. Sir Richard Wrottesley, Bt. by whom he has several children.

LIDDELL, OF RAVENSWORTH CASTLE, DURHAM.

issue three sons and three daughters; Thomas-Henry, Henry, who died an infant, very young; Henry-George; Elizabeth-Jane, Anna, and Charlotte-Amelia. He died Nov, 26, 1791,* and was succeeded in dignity and estate by

VI. Sir THOMAS-HENRY LIDDELL, his eldest son (the present baronet) who married Maria-Susanna, daughter of John Simpson, of Bradley, in the county of Durham, Esq.

ARMS—Argent, fretted gules; on a chief of the second, three leopards' faces, or.
CREST—On a wreath, a lion rampant, sable; crowned, or.
MOTTO—*Fama semper vivit.*
SEATS—Ravensworth Castle and Newton, both in the county of Durham; and Eslington, in the county of Northumberland.

TABLE 95.

1 THOMAS DE LIDDELL=Margaret de Laburne

2 Thomas=Marg. de Strangeways — George=Eleanor Burn

Francis / 3 Thomas / Robert, Percival / Alice O. Carr / Barbara / George—Barker
A. de Segrave / M. Watson | J. Midford

Bartrum / I. Sir Thos. 1650 / Eliz. Wm. Sherwood / Alice Gawen Salkeld / Eleanor Timothy Draper / Henry Elizabeth Jennison / Roger Grace Clavering / Jane Robert Anderson / Barbara Samuel Sanderson
B. Cramlington / J. Anderson

Sir Thomas, 1627 / Francis Eliz. Tonge / William, Robert / George, Henry / Elizabeth G. Baker / Mary N. Cole / Isabel
Bridget Woodward

II. Sir Thomas, 1697=Anne Vane

III. Sir Henry, 1723 / Thomas, Edward / Robert P. Kiffin, 1679 / George / Frances T. Vane | Sir J. Bright / Elizabeth C. Stockdale / Isabel
Catharine Bright

Thomas, 1715=Jane Clavering / John / Henry / George / Michael / Eliz.

IV. Sir Henry, 1784=A. Delme / James / Thomas / Catharine / Thomas=Marg. Bowes
Anne / Thomas / V. Sir Henry-George, 1791
Aug-Hen. D. of Grafton | John, E. of Upper Ossory / Elizabeth Steele

VI. Sir Thomas-Henry M. S. Simpson / Henry / Henry-George / Eliz-Jane / Anna / Charlotte-Amelia

* He was distinguished for a warm and generous spirit, which sometimes, however, carried him into romantic transactions. His excursion to Lapland, upon a wager, and his return with two Lapland girls, and some rein-deer, are well remembered. *See the Tour through Sweden, Swedish Lapland,* &c. &c. *by M. Consett, Esq.* The Lapland girls were returned safe to their native country, after an absence of several months, with 50*l.* and a cargo of trinkets; and the rein-deer have bred in England.

Gen. Mag.

95. HUNLOKE, of WINGERWORTH, DERBYSHIRE.

Created Baronet Feb. 28, 1642.

THAT this baronet is descended from an ancient family plainly appears, from a certificate given to Sir Henry Hunloke, Dec. 14, 1674, by James, earl of Suffolk, deputy to the right hon. Henry, earl of Norwich, earl-marshal of England, wherein he affirms, that his ancestors, for many descents, have borne and used for their arms, three tygers' heads, &c. as appears by old records remaining in the College of Arms, which leaves no room to doubt of their ancient extraction; and it is evident from the deeds and writings of this family, that

1. Nicholas Hunloke, in the reign of King Henry VIII. possessed a very considerable estate, not only at Hadley, in Middlesex, but likewise near Bramcot and Stapleford, in Nottinghamshire. He died at London, leaving issue two sons, Nicholas and Thomas.

2. Nicholas, the eldest son and heir, married Elizabeth, daughter of —— Barlow, of Barlow, and had issue Nicholas, Henry, Joan, Margaret, and Christopher. He not only enjoyed the paternal estate, but also the manor of Wingerworth, in Derbyshire, which he purchased from Richard Curson, Esq. and there the family has ever since resided, excepting a short space, during the time of Oliver Cromwell, who banished them (as known loyalists) from their house, which being a large stone building, he converted it into a garrison. But Lady Hunloke, relict of the first baronet, hereafter-mentioned, remarrying with Col. William Mitchell, one of Cromwell's officers, who was the happy instrument in preserving both the mansion and estate from any damage. She had one daughter by the colonel, who was the wife of Sir James Philyppes, of Stoke Charity, in Hampshire, Knt. but died without issue. This Nicholas died at Wingerworth, in 1551, and lies buried in that parish church. His eldest son, Nicholas, who married ——, daughter of —— Crashaw, dying without issue, his second son,

3. Henry, succeeded to the estate, and married Margaret, daughter of Nicholas Walker, by whom he had Henry, his only son and heir. He afterwards married Edith, daughter of William Reresby, of Thisburgh, in Yorkshire, Esq. widow of George Markham, of Idleston, alias Eaton, in the same county, Esq. He was interred at Wingerworth, Oct. 20, 1612, and was succeeded by his only son,

4. Henry Hunloke, Esq. who married first Anne, daughter of Henry Needham, of Kirklington, in Nottinghamshire, and relict of Lawrence Blundeston, of Hexgrove Park, in the same county; by whom he had no issue: secondly, Anne, daughter and heiress of Richard Alvey, of Corber, in Derbyshire, Gent. of the family of Alvey, in Nottinghamshire; by whom he had issue one son, Henry, and a daughter Anne, the wife of Henry Powtrell, of West Hallam, in the said county, Esq. after

which (the aforesaid Henry Hunloke, being a gentleman of great esteem and authority in his country, and sheriff for Derbyshire in 1624) to shew his affection to his prince, in a very advanced age,* took a journey to meet King James I. and attending him in his progress, with a fatigue above his strength, fell down dead in the presence of his majesty, at Ilkeston, in Devonshire, on the 17th of August, in the same year, acquiring as much renown by dying in his duty to his sovereign, as if he had lived to receive the honour of knighthood, which the king designed to confer upon him. He was succeeded by his only son,

I. HENRY, not only in estate, but also in loyalty, which he sufficiently testified, by lending to King Charles I. a considerable sum of money, in his most pressing necessity,† even at a time when there was little probability of ever being re-paid. This he did at the request of his majesty, who honoured him with a letter on this occasion, dated Sep. 14, 1642. But his support of the royal cause stopped not here; for he soon after (at his own expence) levied and accoutred a complete troop of horse, in the regiment of Col. John Frechevile, of Stavely, in Derbyshire, Esq. (afterwards Lord Frechevile) whereof he himself was lieutenant-colonel: and to the perpetual honour of his name and family, this young hero, not then 22 years of age, like a true patriot, at the memorable battle of Edge Hill, in Warwickshire, by an uncommon valour, conduct, and courage, so signalized himself, that King Charles, to publish the honour he had merited that day, knighted him in the field of battle, and soon after created him a baronet. Not long after, making a bold attempt upon the enemy, near Bestwood Park, in Nottinghamshire, in a skirmish with some of the adverse party that lay in ambush, he received a cut with a sword in his elbow, which so disabled his right hand, that it hung useless' in a scarf to his dying day; and for his loyalty to his sovereign, he was fined 1458l.‡ by the sequestrators.

He married Mariana, daughter of Dixey Hickman, of Kew, in the parish of Richmond, in Surrey, Esq. (by Elizabeth, his wife, daughter of Henry, lord Windsor, in whose right the barony of Windsor, with the estate, descended to her brother Thomas, lord Windsor, afterwards Earl of Plymouth). He left issue Henry, his son and heir, and a daughter Mariana, who became a benedictine nun, at Brussels, and a posthumous son, Thomas-Windsor, who died at Treves, in Germany, in Nov. 1672, being a volunteer in the French army against the Imperialists. This Sir Henry Hunloke died Jan. 13, 1648, was buried at Wingerworth; and was succeeded by his eldest son,

II. Sir HENRY HUNLOKE, Bart. who married Catharine, only daughter and heiress of Francis Tyrwhit, of Kettleby, in Lincolnshire, Esq. (son and heir of William Tyrwhit, Esq. who married Catharine, daughter of Anthony Brown, lord viscount Montague; which William was son and heir of Robert Tyrwhit, of Kettleby, Esq. by the lady Bridget Manners, his wife, eldest daughter of John, the fourth Earl of Rutland, lineally descended from Anne, dutchess of Exeter, and sister to King Edw. IV.) by whom he had seven sons and six daughters; 1, Henry, who died at Paris, in his travels through France; 2, Francis, who died young; 3, Sir Thomas-

---

* Ex. Inf. Dom. Tho. Windsor Hunloke, Bar.   † Ibid.   ‡ See list of those that comp. in letter H.

Windsor, his successor; 4, Robert; 5, Nicholas, who both died infants; 6, another Robert, who married Anne, daughter of Marmaduke Carver, of Chesterfield, Gent. but had no issue: she afterwards was the wife of John Salt, of Betley, in Staffordshire, Esq. but died without issue; 7, Francis, who died at Amsterdam.

Of his daughters, Elizabeth was the wife of George Heneage, of Hainton, in Lincolnshire, Esq. by whom he had six sons and two daughters: Catharine, Anne, and Teresa died unmarried; Mariana died an infant; and another Mariana, late lady abbess of the English Benedictine nuns, at Pontoise, in France.

It is remarkable, that Sir Henry Hunloke, above-mentioned, enjoyed the title and estate for the space of 67 years, in which time he very much improved it, having beautified his seat with a pleasant park, &c. He lived and died in the universal esteem of his country, and was interred at Wingerworth, Jan. 6, 1715.

III. Sir THOMAS-WINDSOR HUNLOKE, the third son, succeeded his father in title and estate, and married Charlotte, the sixth daughter of Sir Robert Throckmorton, of Coughton, in Warwickshire, Bart. by whom he had issue four sons and seven daughters; 1, Henry; 2, Thomas-Windsor; 3, Robert; and 4, James: Catharine, Charlotte, Anne, Mary, Mariana, Barbara, and Henrietta.

The said Sir Thomas-Windsor Hunloke, in 1726, took down the old seat, and erected a stately free-stone building, on a pleasant hill, adjoining his park. His lady died at Wingerworth Dec. 31, 1738, and Sir Thomas-Windsor, Jan. 30, 1752, and was succeeded by his eldest son,

IV. Sir HENRY HUNLOKE, the present baronet, who married Dec. 21, 1769, Margaret, eldest daughter of Wenman Coke, of Longford, in Derbyshire, Esq. (eldest son of Col. Philip Roberts, of Roxford, in Hertfordshire, Esq. by his wife Anne, youngest daughter of Edward Coke, of Holkham, in Norfolk, Esq. and youngest sister of Thomas Coke, lord Lovell, and earl of Leicester; and on the death of the said Thomas, and his son, lord Coke, he changed his name to Coke) by his wife Eliz. Denton, sole heiress of George Chamberlayne, of Wardington, in Bucks, Esq. who took the name of Denton, as nephew, and heir of the late Mr. Justice Denton; by whom he has had twelve children; 1, Charlotte-Constance, dead; 2, Margaret-Elizabeth; 3, Thomas-Windsor; 4, Charlotte-Susanna; 5, Henry-Edmund; 6, Mariana-Jane, dead; 7, Georgiana; 8, Anne-Sophia; 9, Henrietta-Frances; 10, James; 11, Louisa, dead; and 12, Marmaduke-Cuthbert.

ARMS—Azure, a fesse, between three tigers' heads, erased, or.

CREST—On a chapeau, azure; turned up, ermine, a cockatrice, with wings expanded, proper; comb, beak, and wattles, or.

SEAT—At Wingerworth, in Derbyshire.

HUNLOKE, OF WINGERWORTH, DERBYSHIRE.

TABLE 96.

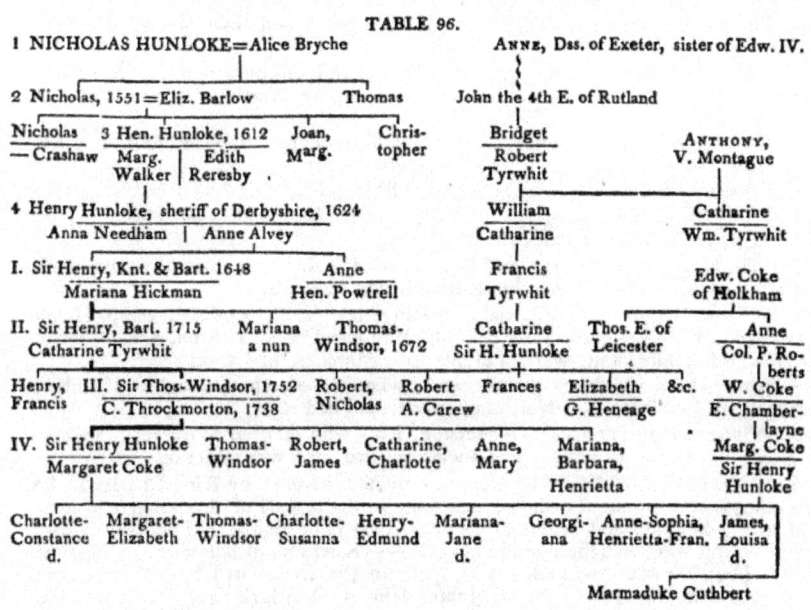

---

96. HAGGERSTON, of HAGGERSTON CASTLE, NORTHUMBERLAND.

Created Baronet Aug. 15, 1643.*

THE name of Haggerston is of great antiquity in Scotland, and local from Halkerston. William and Richard Haggerston are witnesses to a donation, in 1190. John de Haggerston was one of the Scots barons, who swore fealty to King Edward, 1296. Robert de Haggerston is a witness in a donation to the abbey of Cultre, 1468. Sir Thomas Haggerston was made travelling-governor to Alexander Stuart, son of James IV. 1506. Mr. Le Neeve, Norroy, begins the pedigree with

---

* Mr. Le Neve makes a quære to the date of the patent, and asks whether it should not be Aug. 15, 1642. MSS. vol. II. p. 217; but lower in the same page, he writes, "Sir Thomas Haggerston, in his letter to me, dated July 12, 1696, saith, his patent is dated Oct. 15, 1642." If so, his place is after Blount.

1. Thomas de Haggerston, who married Agnes, sister and co-heiress of Sir Gilbert Umfrevile, Knt. and had issue

2. Thomas Haggerston, of Haggerston Castle, in Northumberland, who married Mary, daughter of Alexander Selby, of Bildeston, in Northumberland, and was father of

3. William, who by Catharine, daughter of Miles Stapylton, of Wighill, in Yorkshire, had issue

4. Robert, who married Julian, daughter of Sir —— Umfrevile, Knt. and had issue

5. Henry, who married Margaret, daughter and heiress of —— Hesilrigge, of Hesilrigge, in Northumberland.

6. John Haggerston, his son and heir, married Isabel, daughter of George Collingwood, of Eslington, in Northumberland, and had issue

7. William Haggerston, Esq. slain at Panyerheugh, in Scotland, temp. Henry VIII. who by Margaret, daughter of Sir George Ratcliffe, of Dilston, Knt. sister to Sir George Ratcliffe, Knt. warden of the East Marches, had a son

8. Henry, born after his father's decease, who married Anne, daughter of Robert Beadnell, of Lemington, in Northumberland, and had issue

9. William Haggerston, of Haggerston, Esq. who married Margaret, daughter of Henry Butler, of Rawcliffe, in Lancashire, Esq. and was father of

I. THOMAS HAGGERSTON, Esq. created baronet by King Charles I. he was colonel of a regiment of horse and foot, in the service of that king, and married Alice, daughter and heiress of Henry Banaster, of Bank, in Lancashire, Esq. and ——, his wife, daughter and heiress of —— Kuerdon, of Kuerdon, in the same county (but her estate was all lost or spent in the civil wars) by whom he had three sons and four daughters; 1, John, slain at Ormskirk fight, in Lancashire, Oct. 1644; 2, Sir Thomas, successor to his father; 3, Henry, killed by a fall from his horse, at Lambton Gates, in Durham, 1684. He married at Liege, in Flanders, and left a daughter married abroad. The daughters were Ellen, the wife of William Selby, of Bidleston, in Northumberland; Anne, of William Blundel, of Crosby, in Lancashire; Margaret, of William Hodshon, of Hebbarne; in Durham, Esqrs. and Alice, who died unmarried. Sir Thomas died at a great age, and was succeeded in dignity and estate by his eldest surviving son,

II. Sir THOMAS HAGGERSTON, Bart. who married first Margaret, daughter of Sir Francis Howard, of Corby Castle, Knt.* and had issue nine sons and a daughter: this lady died in child-bed, of a daughter, who died almost as soon as born. Of the sons, Thomas, the eldest, was killed in Ireland, in the service of King James II. unmarried; 2, William, of whom hereafter; 3, Henry; 4, John; 5, Francis, who all embraced religious lives; 6, Edward, who married first Mary, daughter of Gerard Salvin, of Croxdale, in Durham, Esq. and secondly Mrs. Fitzharbe: the other sons (I suppose) died unmarried. Sir Thomas married secondly Jane, daughter and heiress of Sir William Carnaby, of Farnham, in Northumberland, Knt. by whom he had no issue. This Sir Thomas was governor of Berwick Castle, and his house there was burnt down, Feb. 19, 1687, when he lost most of

* Collins's Peerage, vol. III. p. 358.

HAGGERSTON, OF HAGGERSTON CASTLE, NORTHUMBERLAND.

his writings, and sustained above 6000*l.* damage; himself, wife, and family, narrowly escaping. William Haggerston, Esq. his eldest surviving son, married Anne, daughter of Sir Philip Constable, of Everingham, in Yorkshire, Bart. and died before his father, leaving three daughters; one the wife of —— Salvin, of Croxdale, in Durham, Esq. also his son and successor,

III. Sir CARNABY HAGGERSTON, Bart. who succeeded his grandfather in title and estate: he married Elizabeth Middleton, of Stockhill, in Yorkshire, who died at York, in Dec. 1769; by whom he had three sons; 1, Sir Thomas, his successor; 2, William-Constable, of Everingham, in Yorkshire; and 3, Edward, of Elingham, in Northumberland: also three daughters; ——, the wife of Thomas Clifton, of Lytham, in Lancashire, Esq. Sir Carnaby died in 1756, and was succeeded by his eldest son,

IV. Sir THOMAS HAGGERSTON, Bart. who in 1754 married Mary, daughter of George Silvertop, of Minsteracry, in Northumberland, Esq. she died on a journey from Bath to London, May 22, 1773. By her he had three sons; 1, Sir Carnaby; 2, Thomas; 3, Edward; and two daughters, Mary and Bridget. Sir Thomas died Nov. 1, 1777, and was succeeded by his eldest son,

V. Sir CARNABY HAGGERSTON, Bart. who married ——, daughter of —— Simpson, by whom he has issue

---

ARMS—Azure, on a bend cottized, argent, three billets, sable.
CREST—On a wreath, a lion rampant, argent.
SEAT—At Haggerston, in Northumberland.

TABLE 97.

1 THOMAS DE HAGGERSTON=A. Umfrevile 6 John=Isabel Collingwood
2 Thomas=Mary Selby   7 William, temp. Henry VIII.=M. Ratcliffe
3 William=Catharine Stapylton   8 Henry=Anne Beadnell
4 Robert=Julian Umfrevile   9 William=Margaret Butler
5 Henry=Margaret Hesilrigge   L. Sir Thomas, Bart.=Alice Banaster

John   II. Sir Thomas, Bt.   Henry, 1684   Ellen   Anne   Margaret   Alice
1644   M. Howard | J. Carnaby N. of Liege W. Selby W. Blundel W. Hodshon

Thomas   William=A. Constable Henry John Francis M. Salvin=Edw. Haggerston=Mrs. Fitzharbe
III. Sir Carnaby, Bart. 1756=Eliz. Middleton, 1769   ——, a dr.=T. Clifton   2 drs.

V. Sir Thomas=Mary Silvertop, 1773   William   Edward   ——=T. Clifton   2 drs.

V. Sir Carnaby=——Simpson   Thomas   Edward   Mary   Bridget

END OF THE FIRST VOLUME.

CONTENTS of VOL. I.

No.		Page.
1	Bacon, of Redgrave, Suffolk	1
2	Hoghton, of Hoghton Tower, Lancashire	34
3	Peyton, of Isleham, Cambridgeshire	42
4	Clifton, of Clifton, Nottinghamshire	49
5	Gerard, of Bryn, Lancashire	58
6	Shelley, of Michelgrove, Sussex	65
7	Barrington, of Barrington Hall, Essex	71
8	Musgrave, of Eden Hall, Cumberland	77
9	Cope, of Hanwell, Oxfordshire	87
10	Gresley, of Drakelow, Derbyshire	92
11	Molineux, of Teversal, Nottinghamshire	99
12	Harrington, of Redlington, Rutlandshire	106
13	Mordaunt, of Massingham, Norfolk	110
14	Worseley, of Apuldercombe, Hampshire	115
15	Fleetwood, of Calwiche, Staffordshire	120
16	Twysden, of Royden Hall, East Peckham, Kent	125
17	Hales, of Woodchurch, Kent	130
18	Temple, of Stowe, Buckinghamshire	136
20	Wray, of Glentworth, Lincolnshire	139
21	Englefield, of Wotton Basset, Wiltshire	145
22	Clarke, of Salford, Warwickshire	151
23	Boynton, of Bramston, Yorkshire	155
24	Burdet, of Bramcote, Warwickshire	160
25	Mackworth, of Normanton, Rutlandshire	167
26	Hicks, of Beverston, Gloucestershire	171
27	Mill, of Camois Court, Sussex	173
28	Foulis, of Ingleby, Yorkshire	177
29	Berney, of Parkhall, in Redham, Norfolk	181
30	Pakington, of Ailsbury, Buckinghamshire	185
31	Bishopp, of Parham, Sussex	194
32	Vincent, of Stoke D'Abernon, Surrey	198
33	Tichborne, of Tichborne, Hampshire	203
34	Palmer, of Wingham, Kent	211
35	Rivers Gay, of Chafford, Kent	217
36	Hewet, of Headley Hall, Yorkshire	220
37	Jerningham, of Cossey, Norfolk	223
38	Stepney, of Pendergast, Pembrokeshire	233
39	Wake, of Clevedon, Somersetshire	238
40	Hotham, of Scorbrough, Yorkshire	243
41	Mansel, of Muddlescombe, Cambridgeshire	248
42	Prideaux, of Netherton, Devonshire	254
43	Hesilrigge, of Noseley, Leicestershire	260
44	Burton, of Stockerston, Leicestershire	264
45	Drake, of Buckland, Devonshire	266
46	Skipwith, of Prestwould, Leicestershire	272
47	Harpur, of Calke, Derbyshire	277
48	Sebright, of Besford, Worcestershire	284
49	Dering of Surenden Dering, Kent	287
50	Style, of Wateringbury, Kent	294
51	Isham, of Lamport, Northamptonshire	298
52	Littleton, of Pileton Hall, Staffordshire	306
53	Goring, of Highden, Sussex	315
54	Stonhouse, of Radley, Berkshire	317
55	Wrey, of Trebitch, Cornwall	320
56	Trelawny, of Trelawny, Cornwall	323
57	Conyers, of Horden, Durham	334
58	Aston, of Aston, Cheshire	339
59	Wiseman, of Canfield Hall, Essex—see Addenda	345
60	Pole or Poole, of Shute, Devonshire	349
61	Vavasor, of Haselwood, Yorkshire	355
62	Wolseley, of Wolseley, Staffordshire	359
63	Russell, of Chippenham, Cambridgeshire	364
64	Everard, of Much Waltham, Essex	368
65	Every, of Eggington, Derbyshire	370
66	Langley, of Higham Gobion, Bedfordshire	372
67	Cave, of Stanford, Northamptonshire	375
68	Hatton, of Long Stanton, Cambridgeshire	386
69	Abdy, of Felix Hall, Essex	390
70	Bampfylde, of Poltimore, Devonshire	395
71	Cotton, of Landwade, Cambridgeshire	401
72	Burgoyne, of Sutton, Bedfordshire	406
73	Northcote, of Hayne, Devonshire	409
74	Strickland, of Boynton, Yorkshire	412
75	Boughton, of Lawford, Warwickshire	415
76	Chichester, of Raleigh, Devonshire	425
77	Knatchbull, of Mersham Hatch, Kent	430
78	Owen, of Orielton, Pembrokeshire	435
79	Briggs, of Haughton, Shropshire	438
80	Heyman, of Somerfield, Kent	442
81	Goodricke, of Ribstan, Yorkshire	445
82	Langley, of Spoonhill, Shropshire	450
83	Davie, of Creedy, Devonshire—see Add.	453
84	Andrews, of Denton, Northamptonshire	458
85	Kaye, of Woodesham, Yorkshire	460
86	Trollope, of Casewick, Lincolnshire	464
87	Kemp, of Gissing, Norfolk	467
88	Williamson, of East Markham, Nottinghamshire	471
89	Thorold, of Marston, Lincolnshire	475
90	Wrottesley, of Wrottesley, Staffordshire	482
91	Throckmorton, of Coughton, Warwick	486
92	Halton, of Samford, Essex	497
93	Blount, of Soddington, Worcestershire	499
94	Liddell, of Ravensworth Castle, Durham	504
95	Hunloke, of Wingerworth, Derbyshire	508
96	Haggerston, of Haggerston Castle, Northumberland	511

ADDENDA & CORRIGENDA.

Page	Line		
41	—	6, *bottom, read* Boughton.	*p.* 305.
53	—	22, *add*, one daughter, the wife of Sir Edw. Stanhope, Knt. who died in 1541. *Coll. Peer. vol. III.*	
57	—	24, *after* Frances *add*, who was the wife of George earl of Tyrconnel; by whom she had George, the present Earl. *Lodge's Peer. vol. III. p.* 94.	
62	—	1 & 2, *read* Sir William Dormer, and widow of Anthony Browne, Esq.	
64	—	*read* I. Sir Thomas.	
70	—	6, *bottom, read* George Matthew. in Gloucestershire, Esq.	
90	—	4, *after* Westmoreland *add* (who after his decease was the wife of William Cope, of Icombe,	
91	—	8, *read* Sir K. Digby.	
105	—	5, *read* A. Kyrton.	
125	—	17, *read* Robert Bathurst.	
128	—	7, *bottom, after* Ireland *add*, He left one daughter, Frances, his heiress, the wife of George Bussy, the sixth Viscount Grandison; by whom he has two sons and three daughters.	
142	—	25, *read* Cecil.	
198		title, *read* 32.	
222	—	2, *after* by, *read*, his brother, VIII. The Rev. Sir Thomas Hewet, Bart. who married Mary, daughter of —— Tebbut, of Sudborough, in Northamptonshire, Gent.	
225	—	2, *bottom, read* Henry Darell.	
226	—	13, *read* are extant.	
230	—	13, *read* Sodington.	
		14, *read* seven.	
248	—	16, *after* 1771 *add*, He married secondly Gertrude, eldest daughter of Philip, third Earl of Chesterfield, who died April 12, 1775.	
260	—	4, *add*—Supporters, Two knights templars, habited and attired, and holding in their right hands a staff, in the top of which is the cross of St. John of Jerusalem, all proper.	
264	—	*penult.* after died *add* 1553.	
265	—	*Arms, read* sable, on a chevron, a crescent, between	
287	—	14, *read* Battel.	
288	—	*penult.* after buried *add* in.	
300	—	6, *read* Bolesworth.	
316	—	*after* Seat *add*—Crest, on a wreath, a lion rampant, guardant.	
344	—	the black line should come from V. Sir Willoughby, and not from IV. Sir Thomas.	
347	—	16, *note to* Henry Lumley, *Esq.* ——They were buried under a neat marble monument, at Sabridgeworth, thus inscribed:—Here lieth the Hon. Henry Lumley, Esq. only brother to Richard, earl of Scarborough, who was in every battle, and every siege, as colonel, lieutenant-colonel, or general of the horse, with King William, or the Duke of Marlborough, in 20 campaigns in Ireland, Flanders, and Germany; where he was honoured, esteemed, and beloved by our own armies, by our allies, and even by the enemies, for his singular politeness and humanity, as well as for all his military virtues and capacity.	
		He sat long in parliament (for Arundel) always zealous for the honour of the crown, and for the good of his country; and knew no party, but that of truth, justice, and honour.	
		He died governor of the isle of Jersey, Oct. 18, 1722, in the 63d year of his age.	
		Here lieth also Dame Anne Lumley, daughter of Sir William Wiseman, Bart. of Canfield, in Essex, who set up this monument in 1723, in memory of the best of husbands, and her dear child, near whom she was deposited, anno 1736-7.	
		She died on the 4th of March, 1736-7, in an advanced age: she was a lady possessed of all those amiable qualifications which adorn her sex, and rendered her, whilst living, the delight of all those who had the happiness of her acquaintance, by whom her death was greatly lamented, as well by the poor, to whom she was, living and dying, a most bountiful benefactress.	
347	—	18, *after* Esq. *add*, by whom she had six children; 1, Thomas; 2, Joseph; 3, Charles, who in 1744, married ——, daughter of Henry Harcourt, of Pendley, near Tring, in Hertfordshire; by whom he had one son, Col. Charles Stisted, of Ipswich, in Suffolk, and two daughters, Arabella, who died young; and Louisa, the wife of Charles Squire, of Ipswich, Esq. 4, John; 5, William; and 6, Arabella.	
		18, *after* 1684 *add*, in the 55th year of his age.	

ADDENDA & CORRIGENDA.

Page. Line.

347 — 25, *after* mentioned *add*, was colonel in the Coldstream regiment of foot guards: he died May 25, 1774, and was buried in South Audley Chapel, London, June 3, and was succeeded by.

353 — — *read*, VI. Sir John-William Pole, Bart. who has taken the name of De la Pole, by his Majesty's sign manuel, and Jan. 9, 1779, married Anne, only daughter of James Templer, of Stover Lodge, in Devonshire, Esq. by whom he had issue William, born Aug. 2, 1782: Mariana, born Sep. 14, 1783; and John-George, born Dec. 5, 1787. Sir John was high sheriff for the county of Devon, and in 1790 was returned member of parliament for the borough of West Looe, in Cornwall; and died universally beloved and regretted, Nov. 30, 1799, in the 43d year of his age; and was succeeded by his eldest son,

VII. Sir William-Templer De la Pole, Bart. who is now pursuing his studies at Eton Coll.

406 — 9, *add the following as a note*——In memory of Lettice Cotton, youngest daughter of Sir John Hynde Cotton, Bart. of Maddingley and Landwade, in Cambridgeshire; who died justly and sincerely lamented by her numerous relations and friends, Oct. 18, 1798, aged 42.

415 — 7, *in note after* wife, *add* is.

15, *read* Sum quod eris, fueramque quod es, pro me, precor, ora.

416 — 3, *note*, Garter, not garter.

417 — 1, *after* London *cross out*, but left no issue, *and add*, by whom he had five daughters; Elizabeth, Mary, Judith, the wife of Thomas Harris; Jane, and Anne; and one son, Francis, who died S. P.

24, *after* 1702 *add*, and Judith, wife of Howsley Freeman, of Sutton, in Derbyshire; Anne, of Thomas Harris, of Leominster; Mary, of John Taylor, of Burgham, in Surrey.

418 — 26, *after* sons *add*, Abraham, Charles, and George.

424 — *penult.* Sir Egerton Leigh.

455 — 15, *read* Newingham, who was buried May 15, 1627.

penult. after Esq. *add*, who died in Oct. 1656.

456 — 1, *after* He *add*, was buried Oct. 13, 1654, and

9, *after* unmarried *add*, 1659.

11, *after* Esq. *add*, who was buried April 25, 1670.

12, *after* issue *add*, he died in 1678, and was succeeded.

6, *bottom, after* social *add*, he died Dec. 29, 1727.

3, *bottom, read*, who died in 1738, leaving.

penult. after who *add*, married Bridget, daughter of the Rev. Mr. Bertie, of Kenn, by whom he had two sons and two daughters: the eldest, John, was killed in an engagement on board the La Nymph, when she took the Cleopatra frigate; Thomas died of the yellow fever, in the West Indies. The eldest daughter, Frances-Mary, is the wife of Wm. Henry Beauchamp, Esq. Bridget is the wife of —— Beaumont, Esq.

456 — *last line, after* Juliana *add*, Sir John died in 1737, and was succeeded by his son.

457 — 3, *after* he had, *add*, 1, John died an infant, 1769; 2, Susanna Checke, died in 1771, aged six years; 3, Anne, in the same year; 4, Catharine, the wife of Joseph Hunt, Esq. 5, Juliana; 6, Elizabeth, died in 1792; 7, Frances; 8, John, the present baronet; 9, William, died in 1784, aged 10 years; 10, Humprey Phinehas, now a major in the 5th regiment of foot. Sir John died at Creedy, Sep. 18, 1792, and was succeeded by his eldest son,

VIII. Sir John Davie, Bart. who, Sep. 6, 1796, married Anne, daughter of Sir William Lemon, Bart. by whom he has three children; John and William, twins, born at Creedy, March 8, 1798; and Anne-Jane, born June 19, 1800.

Ipswich: printed by Burrell & Bransby.

APPENDIX
TO
VOLUME THE FIRST.

PREFACE, p. xiv. Instead of the three last lines, read,

GAZETTE.
SATURDAY, DEC. 6, 1783.   College of Arms.

His Majesty has been pleased, by warrant under his royal signet and sign manual, bearing date at St. James's the 3d inst. *To declare and ordain*, that for correcting divers abuses which have of late years crept into the order of Baronets, many persons having assumed the title without any just right, and for preventing the like in future, the title of Baronet should not, from the date thereof, be inserted in any commission, warrant, appointment, or other instrument thereafter to be issued, to any person claiming or using the said title from other of his Majesty's offices whatsoever, until such person, so claiming or using the said title, or some one on his behalf, should have proved his right thereto in his Majesty's College of Arms, and produced a certificate thereof from the said college, under the common seal of that corporation.

And, that his Majesty's secretaries of state for the time being should not, from thenceforth, prepare any warrant to pass under the royal signet and sign manual, for the purpose of advancing any person to the degree of a *Baronet of Great Britain*, until it should appear by a proper certificate that the family arms of the person so intended to be advanced, together with so much of the pedigree at least as may be necessary to ascertain the descent of the title, should have been duly registered in his Majesty's College of Arms; and that the clerk of the crown, for the time being, should transmit all patents of Baronets thereafter to be created, as soon as might be, after they should have passed the great seal, to the register of the College of Arms, for the purpose of an authentic copy thereof in the said college; which patent, so registered, should be returned to the clerk of the crown, for the use of the person to whom the same should be granted.

SURRY, D. E. M.

The following appeared in the Gentleman's Magazine:

MR. URBAN,   MAY 21,

In the minute books of the Scottish Corporation, in Crane-court, occurs the following entry, which I transcribe for you as an historical curiosity, wishing at the same time to know whether any, and what consequences arose from the grant:

"Monday, April 16, 1688, at a court of this corporation then held, ordered, that the Knights-Baronet's patent of England, granted by his Majesty in favour of the corporation, be exposed to sale at five hundred guineas, and not under, the corporation being at all reasonable charges; and that two Scotch patents, at three hundred guineas each, with full power to John Renny, John Alexander, John Hay, and Sir Andrew Forrester, any two of which, with the master, to be a quorum, and dispose of the same accordingly." Yours, &c.

EUGENIO.

In the account of Mr. Phineas Pett, one of the master-shipwrights to King James the First, drawn up by himself, is the following:

July 19, 1646. The great Duke of Buckingham, lately made lord-high-admiral of England, came to visit the navy then riding at Chatham, who, on his being here, used me with such extraordinary respect, &c.

Nov. 20. Attended at Theobald's, to deliver his Majesty a petition; but his Majesty, by means of the honourable old admiral, had, before my coming, bestowed on me, for the support of my present relief, the making of a knight-baronet, which I afterwards passed, under the broad seal of England, for one Francis Ratcliff, of Northumberland, a great recusant, for which I was to have seven hundred pounds; but, by reason of Sir Arnold Herbert, who brought him to me, played not fair with me, I lost some thirty pounds of my bargain—*MS. Life of Mr. Phineas Pett, in Vol. XII. of Archæologia for* 1796, *p.* 272. In the same volume of the Archæologia, p. 275, Mr. Phineas Pett says, "In the year 1627, his Majesty gave me a blank for making a Baronet, which was signed by his own hand about the beginning of June, 1629, by Captain Pennington's procurement, I passed the Baronet formerly given me by the king, for which the captain received for me two hundred pounds, which he sent to Woolwich.

P. 92, l. 16, after Durham, *add*, and senior prebendary of Westminster.

P. 118, *l.* 26, after Hamilton, *add*, who died Jan. 16, 1800.

l. 27, after Henrietta, *add*, wife of, June 3, 1784, the Hon. John Simpson, second son of Lord Bradford, and died Aug. 2, 1791.

Twysden, of Roydon-Hall.

P. 125. l. 26, after *Margaret*, add. This Robert Twysden, by his will, dated at Chart 1464, willed to be buried at the church of Great Chart, without the door of the chancel of the Sacred Trinity, on the west side near the tomb of Alice, his wife. He wills to Thomas, his son and heir, all his lands and tenements in Great Chart and elsewhere, in the county of Kent, after making provision for Agnes, his wife, mother of the said Thomas, directing certain lands to be sold, to pay Margaret, his daughter, her portion of twenty pounds; and he willed that a marble stone should be bought for his tomb in Great Chart church. Which Thomas, the son, likewise lies buried there with Bennet, his wife. He died Nov. 1539, and she Dec. 8, 1500. The inscription in brass is gone.—*Philipot, p.* 105.

P. 128, *l.* 29, after Ireland, *add*, who married ———, daughter of ———, by whom he had an only daughter, Frances, wife of (March 6, 1770) George Bussy Villiers, Earl of Jersey, by whom he has several children. The bishop's widow became the wife of General James Johnstone.

P. 128, *l.* 34, after Frances, *add*, wife (Aug. 15, 1783) of Archibald, Earl of Eglinton, who died Oct. 28, 1796; she was secondly the wife of ———, son of Dr. John Moore, author of Travels in France, Italy, &c.

Temple, of Stowe.

P. 139, *l.* 19, after *succeeded by*, read,

VIII. Sir JOHN TEMPLE, great-grandson of Sir Peter Temple, the second Baronet. He was born in 1730, and married Elizabeth, daughter of James Bowdoin, Esq. late governor of the commonwealth of Massachusetts, and had issue, 1, Grenville, born Oct. 16, 1768; 2, James-Bowdoin, born June 7, 1776, a captain in the army; 3, Elizabeth, wife of Thomas L. Winthrop, Esq.; 4, Augusta, of Captain Palmer, of the 18th light dragoons, in 1785. Sir John was appointed consul-general to the United States of North America, in which situation he died in 1798, and was succeeded by his son,

IX. Sir GRENVILLE TEMPLE, Bart. who married Elizabeth, daughter of George Watson, Esq. of the State of Massachusetts, and has had issue Augusta, born Jan. 1, 1798, and died the June following; Grenville, born July 20, 1779; and John, born June, 1801.

ARMS—First, and fourth, or, an eagle displayed, sable, second and third, argent, on two bars, sable, six martlets, or.
CREST—A martlet, or, couchant, on a ducal coronet.
RESIDENCE—Gloucester Place, London.

BOYNTON, of BARMSTON, Yorkshire.
Created Baronet, May 25, 1618.

Having been favoured by Lady Mary, widow of Sir Griffith, and mother of Sir Francis Boynton, the present Baronet, with a more correct account of the family than I have given in the first volume, p. 155, I think it a duty incumbent upon me to reprint the whole of it.

THIS is a family of very great antiquity, and was probably of note before the conquest, as we do not find it among those who attended the Duke in his invasion; and it is said, that Bartholomew de Boynton was lord of that manor in 1067. *

* This must be a mistake, as one Torchill possessed it at that period, as appears by Doomsday-Book. This Bartholomew had undoubtedly lands there (and probably previous to that time), being the residence of the Boyntons. It appears, from an old pedigree, that Sir William Boynton, Knt. 1165, 12 Hen. II. married Anne, daughter of Sir Ingram Monceaux, which evinceth the connection of these two families several years before the marriage of Sir Henry Boynton, Knt. with Margaret del See.

The barony of Somerville, and also of Merley (see the monumental inscriptions (a), are supposed to lie dormant in this family. The present Sir Francis is now investigating those claims: his lineal descent is certain. All *to be* proved *is,* Whether, *after* such summons (1 Edw. III.) *either* or *both* those persons sat. In Lord Botecourt's case, his ancestor's sitting was proved by his being present at a trial of one of the peers.

(a) Inscriptions on the monuments remaining in the north chapel, over the ancient family vault of the Somervile's and Griffiths, at Burton-Agnes, in the east-riding of the county of York.

Here lies Sir Roger Somervile,
Summoned to parliament among the barons of the realm,
The 1st of Edward III.
And died on February, 1336,
Leaving Sir Philip Somervile, his brother and heir,
Who departing this life the 23d of Jan. 1354, possessed
Of this and several other manors, was succeeded by his
Daughter and grand-daughter, viz. Joan, wife of
Sir Rees ap Griffith,
Who died Oct. 8, 1377, at Stockton, in Warwickshire,
And Maude, daughter of John Stafford, by Elizabeth,
2d daughter of the said Sir Philip Somervile.

APPENDIX.

Bovington is a small village, situated in the Woulds, in the east-riding of Yorkshire, and was the residence of the family many years: their arms are still preserved in the church, but only the slightest traces of the house are now remaining.

Sir William Dugdale says, " the town which is called Boynton, was formerly Bovington; cast out the superfluous *v* and *y* and it is Bointon, or Boynton, *i* and *y* being the same in signification.

1, Bartholomew de Boynton married, and had two sons, Walter, his successor, and John who married ———, daughter of Henry Powcher, and died without issue.

2, Walter de Boynton lived 1091, the 5th year of William Rufus, he married Anne, daughter of John Thwaytes, Esq. by whom he had two sons, 1, Sir Ingram; 2, Bartholomew, who married ———, daughter of Sir Anselme St. Quintin, but died without issue; and one daughter, Anne, wife of Sir William Inglebert, Knt.

3, Sir Ingram de Boynton, Knt. was seated at Acklam, in Yorkshire, and gave

On the window of painted glass in the said chapel.
(The figures in a devout kneeling posture.)
Sir Roger Somervile, and Maude, his wife,
Sir Rees ap Thomas, son of Thomas ap Griffith,
Knight of the Garter,
Married Catharine, daughter of Thomas Howard,
Duke of Norfolk;
Sir Walter Griffith, Knight of the Bath, married
Jane, daughter of Sir John Ferrers, of Tamworth,
And died Oct. 30, 1531.
Here lies the remains of Sir Walter Griffith, Knt.
Who departed this life on the 9th day of August, 1481;
And Jane, his first wife, daughter of Sir Ralph Nevill,
By Mary, grand-daughter of John of Gaunt, Duke of Lancaster.

In this chapel also lie the remains
Of Agnes, second wife of the said Sir Walter, daughter of
Sir Robert Constable, of Flamborough, and married secondly
To Sir Gervase Clifton, of Clifton, in the county of
Nottingham, Knt. of the Bath; she died Jan. 23, 1505,
Leaving issue by Sir Walter Griffith aforesaid, Walter,
His successor, made Knt. of the Bath on Allhallows Eve,
1494, at the creation of Henry, second son of Henry VII.
Duke of York; and Agnes, married to Sir Gervase Clifton,
Of Clifton, Nottinghamshire, Knt. of the Bath, son of
Sir Gervase abovementioned.

This Monument was erected
In memory of Sir Henry Griffith, Bart. and his two wives,
the one (as appears by the arms) a Willoughby, and the
other a Bellingham.

In memory of Sir Henry Griffith, Knt. and Bart. and Elizabeth, his wife, daughter of Thomas Throckmorton, of Coughton, in the county of Warwick, Esq. by Margaret, daughter and coheir of William Whorwood, Esq. attorney general to King Henry VIII. Sir Henry had issue, Walter, Ralph, Margaret, Henry, his successor, and Frances, married to Sir Matthew Boynton, of Barmston, in this county, Knt. and Bart.

to the priory of Grendal, or Handal, in that county, one oxgang of land, with two tofts, *cum pertinentibus, in campis et villa de marton**. He married Anne, daughter of Robert Craythorne, by whom he had two sons, 1, Thomas; 2, John, who married ———, daughter of —— Brigham, but died without issue; and two daughters, Isabel, wife of Sir Walter Grindall, Knt. and Mary, of William Twyer, or Tyer, Esq. 1112, 13 Hen. I. †

4, Sir Thomas Boynton, of Boynton, married Cicely, daughter of Humphrey Bradborne, by whom he had two sons, 1, Sir William; 2, Sir Robert, who married ———, daughter of Sir Gerard Salvin, or Salveyne, of Kilholme, Knt.; and Mary, wife of William Palsey, of Branby, 1141. This Sir Thomas lived also in the reign of Richard II. as appears from grant of lands in Rousby ‡.

5, Sir William Boynton, Knt. married Alice, daughter of Sir Ingram Monceaux, probably of Brampston, where that family resided, by whom he had, 1, Ingram; 2, Henry, who married ———, daughter of Adam Wasling, or Wasteneys; 3, Jane, wife of Sir Robert Octon; 4, Ursula, of Sir Roger Welwick, Knt. 1166, 12 Hen. II;

6, Sir Ingram de Boynton was seated at Acklam, and amerced fifty marks 30 Hen. III.; and 1248, granted a lease of lands to the miller of Scaling §. He married ———, daughter of Sir William St. Quintin, of Harpham, in Yorkshire, by whom he had, 1, Sir William; 2, Anne, wife of Sir John de Alta-rissa, alias, D'Aautry, Knt.; 3, Elizabeth, of Robert Eure.

7, Sir William Boynton, Knt. was seated at Sadbury, Yorkshire, 1213, and married Joan, daughter of John Wadsley, by whom he had 1, John; 2, Thomas, who married ———, daughter of William Constable, of Dormanby Esq.; 3, Jane, wife of Sir Pierce Fordingham, Knt. 4, Isabel, of John Thornholme, Esq.

8, John Boynton, Esq. married Albuda, daughter of Sir William Albimonastino, (Blanchminster or Albminster) by whom he had 1, Sir William; 2, John, who married ———, daughter of Robert Aske, of Aske; 3, Robert, who married —— daughter of —— Conyers, of Hooton-upon-Wiske, lived about 1237.

9, Sir William Boynton made a grant of lands in Sealing, 1277, obliging his tenants to grind all their corn at his mill ‖; and married ———, daughter of —— Brough, of Hackford, by whom he had Thomas, and John, who married Anne, daughter of Thomas Briggveild, of Yafforth, but died without issue.

10, Thomas Boynton, Esq. married ———, daughter of Henry Fitz Randolph, or Randall, by whom he had 1, William; 2, Barbara, wife of John Langton; 3, Thomasine, of John Vincent, or Vinson, of Smeaton, 1291, 20 Edw. I.

11, William Boynton received also the honour of knighthood, and is mentioned in a deed 1339. There is also a deed dated 1319, probably in his time, mentioning the soke and suit of Scaling mill ¶. He married ———, daughter of Ingram Covall, .

* Monast. Ang. Vol. I. p. 427.
† We now find a Bruis de Boynton witness, with the prior of Tinmouth and others, to a donation in *frankalmoigne*, made by Ranulph de Merley, 30 Hen. I. 1130, confirming to the monks of Durham, Morvic, with the appurtenances, which his father William de Merley had before granted them.—*Monast. Ang.* Vol. I. p. 49.
‡ Original in Sir F. Boynton's possession.
§ Ibid.
‖ Ibid.
¶ Both among the writings at Burton Agnes.

APPENDIX.

or Colville, by whom he had a son Sir Ingram, and three daughters; Anabella, wife of Nicholas Mennill; 2, Dionisia, first of ——— Pinkney, secondly of ——— Etherington; 3, Jane, 1350, of Thomas Lawson, of Fowlesgrave *.

12, Sir Ingram Boynton, of Boynton, Knt. married Isabel second daughter of Robert Nevile, of Hornby, &c. Esq. Knight of the shire for the county of York, 15 Richard II. 1390, and high sheriff of the same 1397†, by whom he had,

13, Sir Walter ‡ de Boynton who was knighted, and lord of the manor of Rousby, temp. Ed. I. § and 1356, being in the service of the Black Prince in Britanny, had the king's letters of protection, dated the 8th of Feb. that year ||, Walter married ———, daughter of William Avatton, or Atton, by whom he had one son,

14, Sir Thomas Boynton, Knt. 1377, the last of Edw. III. is stiled of Acklam, in Cleveland; and the same person who jointly with Thomas de Ingleby, had a grant from King Edw. III. in the 39th year of his reign, 1366, for free-warren in Aclam, Avesom, Rousby, Newton. Staynton, and Boynton, in Yorkshire ¶, and 1392 confirmed a gift of the fishery in the river Teyse, at Cattrick, by William de Aclam **. In his will July 28, 1402, he desires to be buried in the quire of the church at Aclam. This Sir Thomas married ———, daughter and heir of John Russell, or Rossell, of Newton, under Gainsborough, in Cleveland, and by whom he had,

15, Sir Thomas Boynton, Knt. †† who was lieutenant and constable of Carlisle, under Henry Percye, son of the Earl of Northumberland, 1383, 7 Richard II. and died before his father 1386, seized in right of his mother of the manors of Aclam, and Avesom, and of Roxby, (Rousby) Newton, and Staynton, and of the ancient demesnes, sixteen oxgangs of land in Boynton, as appears from the exchequer book 39 Edw. III. 1365. He married Margaret, daughter of Sir John Speton, by whom he had one son ‡‡,

---

* Thoresby's Antiquities of Leeds, and Lawson's pedigree.
† Thoresby's Leeds.
‡ Called William, Esch. 11 Hen. IV.
§ From a deed at Burton.
|| Rymer's Fœd. p. 344. Walter de Boynton is mentioned as witness to the grant of Handel, in Cleaveland; and also in a deed without date, concerning lands in Rousby, naming the yearly payment of a pair of spurs, a penny price.

At this time lived also Sir Roger Boynton, who enjoyed in Hunmanby, Risdeston, Thorp, and Bovington (a); and, according to a pedigree of the family by Sir John Boynton, of Rawcliff, Knt. serjeant at law, was son of Roger, son of John, son of Allan, son of Robert, son of Gerard, son of Walter, son of William, son of Walter, ut patet per chart, temp. Steph. and Hen. II. This Sir Roger was deputy to William de Ufford, Earl of Suffolk, lord-admiral in the north, 50 Edw. III. 1376, and in his time was the contention hereafter named.

¶ Ibid.
** Burton's Monast. Ebor.
†† Proved by inquisition after his mother's death, Le Neve, ibid.
‡‡ Contemporary with Sir Thomas was Sir Robert de Boynton, who received a grant of lands there in 1319 (b), and was witness, Oct. 14, 1339, with the earl-marshal of England, Peter Mawley, lord of the Luke (qu. Soc.), lord-chamberlain to Edward III. and Sir William Acton. to a deed, proving the right of Hammon Beckwith, Esq. to the coat armour of John, Lord Malebisse. He was also governor of Berwick-Castle, and a commissioner among others, 1 Ric. II. 1381, for receiving 4000 marks from Robert,

(a) Index to the Records of the Tower, p. 156. cart. 39, 40 Edw. III. No. 23, 24.
(b) The original at Burton Agnes.

APPENDIX. 7

16, Henry de Boynton, successor to his grandfather, was suspected to be n the interest of Henry Percy, Earl of Northumberland, and his son, who had taken arms against Hen. IV. for in the fourth year of his reign * when the battle of Shrewsbury was fought, John Wockerington, Gerald Heron, and John Mitford, were comissioned to tender an oath to this Henry de Boynton, and others, to be true to the king, and renounce Henry Earl of Northumberland, and his adherents; yet three years after † he was concerned with the said Earl, Thomas Mowbray, Earl Marshall, Richard Scroope, archbishop of Canterbury, &c. who had taken arms 7 Hen. IV. and flying to Berwick, was apprehended on the surrender thereof to the king, and with several others executed, being then a knight. He married Elizabeth, daughter of Sir John Conyers, of Sockburne, in the bishoprick of Durham, (afterwards wife of John Felton‡) by whom he had two sons William, and Thomas§, and two daughters; Elizabeth, wife of Thomas Marton, of Marton, in Cleveland; and Jennet, of John Widdesworth. Henry was succeeded by his son,

17, Sir Thomas Boynton, who was twelve years old at his father's decease ‖, and was of Sadbury; and desires to be interred in the church of Aclam, by will dated July 28, 1402, 3 Hen. IV. and proved Sept. 6, the next year. He married Margaret, daughter of Peter Mirfield, by whom he had Sir Robert, or Sir Henry, hearafter mentioned; and Sir Henry who received from his father, the lordship of Sadbury, Ravenshill, Castle-Stranton and Lemmorly, in the bishopric: Castle-

King of Scotland, in part of 56,000, which he had orders to pay to William de Melton, chevalier, mayor of York, and appears, from the following deed, to have burn *five bull's heads, argent, on a cross, sable,* which had some allusion to the name Bovington.

5 APRIL, 50 EDW. III. 1375.

Be it known unto all men, by this writing indented, made at Scimer the 5th day of April, in the year of grace 1375, how that Mr. William, of Atton, the father, in the presence of the Lord Piercie, challenged Mr. Robert Boynton of the arms that he bore : that is to know, gold, with a cross of sable, and five heads of bulls of silver on the cross; *the which, the aforesaid Mr. William, of Atton, and Mr. Robert, after long controversie, themselves put the dome of the Lord Piercie abovesaid. Lord Piercie; by good deliberation, awarded the arms abovesaid to Mr. William, of Atton, by this indenture, sealed with his seal, to the above-named Mr. Boynton, and to his heirs; that henceforth they shall have the arms of gold, with a cross sable, and five bull's heads silver on the cross without impeachment of him or his heirs for ever.*

In witness of which thing, to this part of these indentures remaining with the abovesaid Mr. Robert Boynton, Mr. William, of Atton, abovesaid, hath put his seal ; and to the part remaining with Mr. William abovesaid, the aforenamed Mr. Robert Boynton hath put his seal, the day, place, and year abovesaid.

This Sir Robert had a son and heir John, æt. 22, 1379, *(proved by inq. 2 Ric. II.)* by Isabel, his wife, whose daughter and heiress, Elizabeth, was wife of Thomas Newport, as appears from the following inscription on a flat stone, in old characters, in Boynton church:

Hic jacet Thomas Newport, et Elizabetha Uxor ejus, filia et heres Johannis Boynton, filii et heredis Dni. Roberti Boynton, Militis; qui Thos. obiit XV° die Novembris, A° Dni M°.CCCCXXIII° et illa obiit IIII° die Octobris A° Dni M.CCCCXXIII°. quorum animabus propitietur Deus, Amen.—*Dugdale's MS. Herald's Office.*

* Rymer, tom. 8, p. 322.
† Hollingshed's Chron.
‡ Esch. 10 Hen. IV. No. 28.
§ Ibid, 3 Hen. IV. Will. frater Thomæ, fil. Hen de Boynton, Mil, &c.
‖ There is a decree upon record in the court of York, concerning a cause between Sir Thomas Boynton, Knt. and others, 13 Edw. III. against John de Bruthwell, rector of Hilderwell, for not providing a resident minister within the chapelry of Rousby; which they obliged him to.

APPENDIX.

Lunpton, Cold-Ingleby, Houlden-field, the fourth part of Newam, and half of Rumpton; lands in Thornaby, Towlesby, Morton, Thesingby, Cottams, Skelton, Whitby-Strand, Stilton, Fauby, Potto, and the lordship of Holeyn, in Holderness; on his marriage with Isabel, only child of Bertram Lumley, who brought him an only child Isabel, wife of Henry, second son of Sir William Gascoigne, of Gawthorpe, Knt. * He bore in his arms a lion passant, and died at Sadbury. July 20, 1405. The aforesaid Margaret, survived her husband, and died in Oct. 1409 †.

18, Sir Henry Boynton‡, Knt. whose son Henry, hereafter mentioned, was created a knight banneret, by the Earl of Surry, in King Henry the Seventh's reign, increased his fortune very considerably by marrying Margaret, or Lucy, eldest of the two daughters, and coheirs of Martin del See, Esq. Lord of Barmston, in Yorkshire; the time of this marriage is not ascertained, but from a deed § dated Sept. 1, the 13th of Edw. IV. (1473,) it appears to have been before that period. Sir Henry had issue Isabel, wife of Bryan Tunstall, and four sons, 1, Thomas; 2, Cuthbert; 3, Henry; and 4, Martin, who, by will Sept. 2, 1507 ‖, leaves his mother, Dame Margaret, the guardianship of his son Henry, appointing her, his sister Dame Isabel Tunstall, and his son William Bulmer, supervisors. The above Martin del See was knighted, and died between Nov. 20 and Dec. 15, 1494, 10, Hen. VII. ¶ Cuthbert, their second son, died young; Henry was created a knight banneret in Henry the VIIth's time, by the Earl of Surry.

19, Thomas Boynton, Esq. married Cecilia, daughter of Sir James Strangeways, of Smeton, in Yorkshire, Knt. by whom he had Matthew; Jane, prioress of Nun Cotham, wife of Thomas Goldesburgh, of Goldesburgh, Esq.; and Anne, of Robert Haldenby, of Haldenby, Esq.**. He died March 29, 1523, and was

* Ex Stem. and Lodge's Peerage.
† Esch. p. 332.
‡ Some ancient pedigrees say, Sir Robert, but the deed hereafter alluded to, dated Sept. 1, 13th of Edw. IV. proves it to be Sir Henry. He was seated and possessed of Sadbury, now the inheritance of Sir Robert D'Arcy.
§ Amongst the family writings at Burton-Agnes.
‖ Registry of the archbishop's court of York.
¶ (a) There is an award, dated March 3, 1497, between Dame Margaret Boynton, widow, one of the daughters and coheirs of Sir Martin del See, deceased, and Peers Hildyard, and Jane his wife, another daughter of Sir Martin, granting themselves and their tenants free passage through the manors of Lysset, Willsthorp, and Gemlin. This Dame Margaret Boynton was a votary, and patroness to the priory of Nun Cotham (c). In a deed dated April 6, 15 Hen. VII. she mentions her sons Henry and Martin. Her will is dated Sept. 2, 1533, whereby she directs her son Thomas to enter upon Barmston at her decease, and appoints Cuthbert Tunstall, Bishop of Durham, one of her executors; which will was proved Nov. 21, 1536.
** In 1519, Thomas Boynton, Esq. petitioned the Cardinal of York, legate de lat. to Pope Leo X. to have the chapel of Rousby (d) consecrated de novo, and sacraments administered there. By his will, bearing date May 14, 12 Hen. VIII. he leaves his land in Langtofte to be distributed in alms, during the mino-

(a) Amongst the family writings at Burton-Agnes is a copy, the date and probate of his will; the latter from Torre's MSS. in the library of the cathedral church of York.
(c) See a MSS. belonging to the Holy Trinity at Kingston-upon-Hull.
(d) The petition and consecration deed are amongst the other evidences at Burton-Agnes.

APPENDIX.

buried in Rousby chapel *; near the high altar, in which his widow desired to be interred †.

20,¶ Mathew Boynton, Esq.; was deputed 1537, steward of the lordships belonging to St. Mary's Abbey, in York; and received a grant ‡ from King Henry VIII. dated at Westminster, May 5, 1539, of the highstewardship, for life, of all lands in the counties of York, and Lincoln, forfeited by the attainder of William Wood, prior of Bridlington. He married in his minority, Anne daughter of Sir John Bulmer §, of Wilton, Knt. by whom he had one son Thomas, and three daughters; 1, Anne, wife of William Norton, of Norton, in Yorkshire, Esq.; Cecilie, maid of honour to Queen Elizabeth, and wife of Edmund Norton, of Clowbeck, Esq.; who died about the year 1602, and Margaret, of William Forbisher, of Altofs, and Finningley, Esq. ∥ He died July 31, 1541, and was succeeded by his only son,

21, Thomas Boynton, Esq. a minor, aged 18 years and 44 days; whose custody was given to Sir Ralph Ebers, Knt. Jan. 28, 1542, with an order ¶ for the yearly payment of 25l. out of the manor of Barmston for the same. He was member of parliament for Boroughbridge**, 13 Eliz. and high sheriff of Yorkshire ††, the 18th,

rity of his son Matthew; to whom he gives, as heir looms, his chain of gold (a) (if it may be spared, and his debts paid), his harness, a chales, and agnus of gold, and his English books; also all his lands in Pocklington, Buttercram, and York, which he had by his mother's gift. His son, Thomas Goldesburgh, and Jane his wife, 20l. if she lives till her husband attains the age of twenty-one years, and they cohabit. His son Haldenby, and Anne, his wife, 6l. 13s. 4d. and all the feoffamentams to be reserved for their use. His sister Tunstall, a ring with a blue stone; also a legacy to his brother Bulmer; his land in Foxholes and Cowthorpe, to Sir William Pyndar, for life; and directs that such sums as shall be received of Sir William Bulmer, Knt. for the marriage of his son Matthew Boynton, be reserved to the performance of his last will, of which he appoints Sir William Bulmer, and his mother, Dame Margaret Boynton, supervisors.

* From the inscription on his grave-stone, remaining there, he appears to have been the first person buried.
† In her will, dated June 16, 1550.
‡ The original is preserved amongst the evidences at Burton-Agnes.
§ Confirmed by the Bulmer's pedigree.
∥ This Matthew Boynton dates his will Sept. 29, 1540, where he stiles himself of Barmston (formerly written Bermeson). desiring to be interred there, if he dies in Yorkshire, according to his degree, and leaves 20s. to the high altar in that church: his son and heir apparent, Thomas Boynton, the carved bed in the high gate-house, his black velvet gown, and all his silver plate, in recompence of a chain of gold which his father gave him as an heir-loom; to each of his daughters, Anne, Cecilie, and Margaret, 300 marks; to John Bertrome, during his life, the chapel of St. Oswalde, in Newton, and all the closing belonging to it. He was seized of the manors of Barmston, Grantlingham, Aclam, Bynpton, Rudstone, and Rykton; land in Salcote, Earthorpe, Bygton, Foston, Hollym, Fordon, Thorpe, Sigglethorne, Scaling, Greenholde, Great Driffield, and Laughbohm; and the advowson of Barmston rectory; also, after the decease of his mother Cecilie Boynton, several lands in Swayton and Boynton; and, on the decease of William Pyndar, Chaplin, land in Langtoste, Foxholes, and Cowthorpe; as appears by inquisition (b) taken at Malton, Sept. 16, 1541.
¶ This order by deed is also existing there.
** Willis's Notitia Parliament. Vol. II. p. 81.
†† List of high-sheriffs in Drake's Ebor. p. 354.

(a) A golden collar was then a badge of knighthood. In an act made for the reformation of appeal, 24 Hen. VIII. is a proviso, that knights may publicly wear a gold collar of SS.—*See Ashmole's Order of the Garter, p. 225.*
(b) The inquisition roll is preserved amongst the family writings at Burton-Agnes.

of that reign, knighted by her majesty at Hampton-Court, Jan. 1577, in which year he suffered a recovery of the manor of Barmston *, and advowson of the rectory. He was thrice married; first to Jane, daughter of Sir Nicholas Fairfax, of Gilling, Knt. who bore him no issue; secondly to Frances, daughter of Francis Forbisher, of Altofs, and Finningly, Esq. recorder of Doncaster, by her he had a son Francis; and one daughter Anne, wife of Sir Francis Vaughan, of Sutton upon Derwent, Knt. His third lady was Alice, daughter of Nicholas Tempest, of Stanley, or Holmside, Esq. widow of Walter Strickland, of Sizergh, in Westmoreland, Esq.†

22, Francis Boynton, Esq. his son and heir, July 2, 1590, had the assignment of a lease of the rectory and church of Rudstone, and tithes belonging to it. He was high sheriff of Yorkshire, 1596; on the 4th of Feb. 1602, he received a pardon under the great seal; and on the 19th, of Sept. following was appointed one of the northern council, knighted at York, April 17, 1603, as King James passed through that city in his way from Scotland; and had a deputation, dated ‡ at York, Mar. 11, 1615, for preserving the game in the north and east riding. He married Dorothy, daughter and coheiress of Christopher Place, of Halnaby Esq. by whom he had Alice, christened April 5, buried at Barmston, June 4, 1590; Mathew, christned there Jan. 26, 1591; Henry, who died young; and Dorothy, wife of Sir Henry Bellingham, of Levens, in Westmoreland, Knt. and Baronet, she had eight children; died in childbed, the 33d year of her age, Jan. 23, 1626, and was buried at Eversham, where a monument is erected for her §. Sir Francis desired to be interred at Barmston, wherever he deceases; left his sister Fairfax, his father's ring, and bequeathes legacies to his son and daughter Bellingham. He died April 9. 1617, seized of the manors of Barmston, cum Winton, Rousby, Acklam, Rudstone, a moiety of the manor of Middleton Tyas; lands in Boynton; and the rectories of Barmston, and Bridlington; he was buried at Barmston. An epitaph ‖ remains for him in latin verse, from which he appears to have been a man of learning; Dame Dorothy his widow was interred there, Feb. 12, 1632.

I. MATTHEW BOYNTON, Esq. succeeded his father, was knighted by King James, at White-Hall, May 9, 1618, and by letters patent, dated the 25th of that month, advanced to the dignity of a Baronet of great Britain. He was member for Heydon, in Yorkshire, the 3d parliament of James I. assembled at Westminster,

* As appears by the family writings.

† She afterwards married Sir Christopher Place, of Halnaby, Knt. and among other issue had Dorothy, heiress at length to that family, and mentioned hereafter.

This Sir Thomas Boynton made several purchases of lands, and appears to have incurred a considerable debt. He desires that his body may be privately buried among his ancestors at Barmston, where he was interred Jan. 5, 1581; the herald receiving twenty marks for setting out his funeral (a). He, by will, earnestly requests Henry, Earl of Huntingdom (stiling him that Man of God) to take upon him the guardianship of his only son.

‡ Among the writings at Burton-Agnes.

§ This monument was repaired and beautified in the year 1765, by Sir Griffith Boynton, Bart. the sixth baronet of his family.

‖ Preserved in Sir R. Dugdale's MS. Collections of Churches in Yorkshire, remaining in the College of Arms, London.

(a) College of Arms, London.

1620*; and received a pardon under the great seal, Feb. 10, 1625: in 1628, he was high sheriff of Yorkshire; and had a deputation dated at Westminster, April 5, 1631, for preserving the game in the north and east riding. He was again high sheriff of Yorkshire, in the 1643, and 1644, and was chosen a representative for Scarborough October 25, 1645; was in Charles the First's reign governor of that castle, and colonel of a troop of horse. Sir Mathew took an active part in the civil disorders of those times, (circumstantially related by Mr. Rushworth) He married 1614†, Frances, daughter of Sir Henry Griffith, Knt. and Baronet, of Wichnor, in the county of Stafford, and Burton Agnes, in Yorkshire, (and sole heiress to her brother Sir Henry) by his Lady Elizabeth, daughter of Thomas Throckmorton, Esq. of Coughton, in Warwickshire, and sister to Margaret, the wife of Sir Rice Griffith, of Brome-Court, in that county, lineally descended from the Kings of England, the Dukes of Normandy, the Princes of Wales, the Earls of Northumberland, before, and after the conquest; of the Earls of Marche, and Dunbar, in Scotland, &c. &c. ‡ Sir Mathew had issue by Dame Frances, his wife, eight sons and four daughters; 1, Francis; 2, Thomas, interred at Barmston, June 19, 1621; 3, Henry, christened there Nov. 30, 1620; 1, Elizabeth; Jan. 15, 1621, buried April 8, 1622; 2, Dorothy, baptized there Feb. 1623, wife of John Anlaby, of Etton, in Yorkshire, Esq.; 4, Cornelius, baptized March 1624; 5, John, July 27, 1626; 3, Elizabeth, Nov. 6, 1627, wife of John, son of Richard Heron, of Bockenfield, in Northumberland, Esq.; who died Aug. 18, 1678, and was buried in Beverly Minster §, and she also was interred there Jan. 28, 1691 ||, 4, Margaret, baptized at Barmston, April 7, 1629, and married there 1652, to John Robinson, of Ryther, in Yorkshire, Esq. whom she survived; 6, Chas, baptized at Barmston, Sept. 23, 1630, said to have died of a consumption, occasioned by grief ¶; 7, Marmaduke, baptized at Barmston, April 5, 1632, where he died, and was interred there Sept. 25, 1686**; and 8, Gustavus, baptized there 1633, of these sons, Matthew, married Isabel, daughter of Robert Stapilton, of Wighill, in Yorkshire, Esq.; and was lieut.-colonel††, he was slain at Wigan, in Lancashire, Aug. 26, 1651, in the advance of King Charles's army towards Worcester, leaving two daughters, Katherine, maid of honour to the Queen: Katherine, wife of Colonel Richard Talbot, afterwards Earl; and nominal Duke of Tyrconnel, captain-general of King James's forces, and lord-lieutenant of Ireland; and Isabella, Nov. 10, 1674, of the celebrated Wentworth, Earl of Roscommon‡‡; she was the second lady of this noble Earl; and remarried Aug. 2, 1702, Thomas

* See Willis's Notitia Parl. Vol. II. p. 179.
† The marriage settlement is dated Sept. 27.
‡ Griffith's pedigree, A. D. 1604, among the writings at Burton-Agnes, of immense extent, curiously emblazoned upon vellum, examined at the College of Arms, in London, and allowed to be accurately drawn up, and finely executed.
§ An escutcheon there remaining for him.
|| Register of St. John's Church, Beverley.
¶ By Crozier, an antiquary, living about his time in Holderness.
** June 28, 1625, was presented with his freedom of Aberdeen, and that of Dundee the fourth of July following.
†† Among the evidences at Burton-Agnes. He is stiled Colonel in the Barmston register.
‡‡ Lodge's Peerage, Vol. I. p. 162.

APPENDIX.

Carter, of Robert's Town, in the county of Meath, Esq.*; she died 1721: Sir Mathew Boynton's lady deceased, in the 36th year of her age, July 1634, and was buried at Rousby, where a tomb is erected for her, with an affectionate epitaph, (particularly expressive of her amiable conduct as a wife and a mother) written by her husband. He married secondly, Katherine, third daughter of Thomas Viscount Fairfax †, of Emely, (by Katherine his second wife, sister of Henry Viscount Dunbar) relict of Robert Stapilton, of Wighill, Esq.; and had several children, but none who lived long: Peregrine appears to have been their second son; he died at Beverly, in the sixth year of his age, Aug. 28, 1645, and was buried at Barmston, where his epitaph says ‡ " This child God gave unto them §, when they were strangers in a foreign land." He deceased at Highgate, in Middlesex, the latter end of April, or beginning of May, 1646. His widow married thirdly, Sir Arthur Ingram ‖, of Temple Newsam, in Yorkshire, Knt. who died July 4, 1655; and her ladyship Feb. 23, 1666, who was buried in Rousby chapel, where a tomb ¶ is standing to her memory, (it is not ascertained where Sir Matthew was interred, at Highgate, it is supposed).

II. Sir FRANCIS BOYNTON, Bart. eldest son and heir of Sir Matthew, married on Sunday, March 7**, 1637 ††, Constance, daughter of William Viscount Say and Sele, (and sister to Bridget who married Theophilus ‡‡, Earl of Lincoln) chamberlain of the household to King Charles II. and Lord privy-seal; (by Elizabeth, daughter of Thomas Temple, of Stowe, in the county of Buckingham, Esq. by whom he had 1, Mathion, born at Broughton Castle §§, July 28, 1639; —, a daughter born at Hanwell, Oxfordshire, June 9, 1640; 3, William born at Frankton, in Warwickshire, (a seat of Lord Say and Sele's) July 14, 1641; 4, Elizabeth, born there June 3, 1642, who died young; 4, Francis, born at Kingston-upon-Hull May 11, 1644, buried at Barmston August 28, 1679; 5, Henry, born at Burton-Agnes, May 6, 1646; 6, Alathea, born at Barmston, May 19, 1650, buried at Burton-Agnes ‖‖, April 30, 1656; and 7, Frances, born at Barmston, March 3, 1652.

* A gentleman, whose services to his country at the Revolution were very considerable: for he not only served King William at the seige of Londonderry and battle of the Boyne, but secured divers useful books and writings belonging to King James and his secretaries. He was father of the Right Hon. Thomas Carter, Esq. master of the rolls, member of parliament for Hillsborough, privy-counsellor, &c. &c.
† Lodge's Peerage, Vol. II. p. 414.
‡ Register of St. Mary's Church, Beverley.
§ There is a portrait at Burton-Agnes of Sir Matthew Boynton, Catharine, his wife, Benjamin, Peregrine, and Mary, by Vandyke.
‖ She is stiled Lady Ingram, in a release (a) dated Jan. 8, 1649, of the manor of Rousby, East and West Scaling, with divers property in Winton cum Barmston (which had been settled on her for life) to Sir Francis Boynton, Bart. in considertion of 12,000l.
¶ Whereon she is stiled Lady Ingram. This disproves Mr. Thoresby's account, in his Antiquities of Leeds, p. 231, of her marrying fourthly, William Wickham, Esq.
** Sir Francis's marriage, and births of his children, were transcribed from entries made of them in a family Bible.
†† From the family Bible.
‡‡ Biographical Dictionary, Vol. V. p. 93.
§§ Family Bible.
‖‖ Register of that church.

(a) Among the writings at Burton-Agnes.

The aforesaid Wm. was appointed capt. in his father's reg. of militia, Oct. 25, 1660; and afterwards lieut.-colonel; and married at Rise, in Yorkshire, Oct. 15, 1661, Elizabeth, daughter and coheiress of John Bernard, of Kingston-upon-Hull, Esq. by whom he had, 1, Margaret, born at Burton-Agnes, April 30, 1663; 2, Griffith, Dec. 8, 1664; and 3, Constance, born at Barmston, April 6, 1667; he was returned member of parliament for Heydon, Nov. 1680, and 1681, and buried at Burton-Agnes, Aug. 17, 1689, where his widow founded an hospital for the benefit of female servants of the family, when indisposed, or were in the decline of life, endowing it with an annual stipend, and an allowance for coals, &c. She died at Ripley, April 3, and was buried at Burton-Agnes on the 29th of the same month, 1708. Constance, his daughter, was wife in May 1702, of Richard Kirshaw, D.D. rector of Ripley, in Yorkshire, she died May 7, 1705, and was buried at Ripley, where an inscription remains for her; Henry, fifth son of Sir Francis Boynton, B. A. was of Merton College, Oxford, ordained at Bishopthorpe, May 29, 1670, and instituted the 13th of June following, to the rectory of Barmston, took also a M. A. degree, and married, at Tulford, near York, Sept. 21, 1675, Dorothea, daughter of Alexander Amcotts*, of Penshire, in the parish of Houghton-le-Spring, in the bishoprick of Durham, Esq. by whom he had, Francis†, hereafter mentioned; and Elizabeth, christened at Barmston, Nov. 29, 1678: their mother was interred there Oct. 17, 1680, and the said Elizabeth, March 26, 1683; Mr. Boynton, remarried at Paghill, or Paul, in Yorkshire, Oct. 15, 1685, Margaret, daughter of Leonard Robinson, of Newton-Garth, Esq. who bore him no issue: he died May 29, 1719, aged 73, in the parsonage-house at Barmston, of which he had been rector 49 years, and was interred there: his widow deceased at Bridlington, aged 67, and was buried by him Dec. 12, 1728; Frances, fourth daughter of Sir Francis Boynton, married at Barmston, Dec. 4, 1677, George Whichcote, of Harpswell, in Lincolnshire, Esq.; and died in child-bed of twins, at Barmston, where she was buried, May 7, 1682. Sir Francis succeeded to the inheritance of Burton-Agnes‡, Wichnor, &c. and received a pardon under the great-seal, April 8, 1661. Dame Constance, his wife, was interred at Barmston, Sept. 7, 1692. He died there aged 76, Sept. 9, where he was buried the 16, 1695.

III. Sir GRIFFITH BOYNTON, Bart. son of William Boynton, Esq. married 1712, Adriana, daughter and coheiress of John Sykes, sometime merchant at Dort, in Holland; and had a son still born, at Burton-Agnes. He improved his seat there, beautified the church, and built an hospital (for the men servants of his family) at Barmston. His lady deceased in Pall-Mall, Nov. 19, 1724, and was buried in the vault at Burton-Agnes. Sir Griffith, remarried in London, Nov. 1728, Rebeccah, daughter of John White, of Tunford, in Nottinghamshire, Esq. many years a representative of that county in parliament, had no issue by her; and dying in Ormond-street, aged 67, Dec. 22, 1731, was succeeded by his cousin, Francis Boynton, Esq.; son of the Rev. Henry Boynton, before-named. Sir Grif-

* Ancestor to the present lady of Sir John Ingleby, Bart. of Ripley, Yorkshire.
† From an injured part of the Barmston register, he appears to have been christened Nov. 17, 1677, which agrees exactly with his age.
‡ I believe, on the death of his uncle, Sir Henry Griffith, Bart. Feb. 20, 1654.

fith's, remains were interred at Burton-Agnes. His widow survived him till the 8th of Oct. following, when she died in London; and was also buried at Burton-Agnes.

IV. Sir FRANCIS BOYNTON, Bart. was of St. John's College, Cambridge, and studied the law. On the 15th of August, 1733, unanimously chosen recorder of Beverley, and was elected a representative for Heydon, at the general election 1734, was one of the members appointed by the house of commons, April 29, 1736, to address Queen Caroline, on the Prince of Wales's marriage; and also congratulated their Royal Hignesses, Feb. 3, 1739, on the birth of Prince Edward. He married at Beverly, April 8, 1703, Frances, daughter of * James Heblethwayte, of Norton-House, in Yorkshire, Esq. grand-daughter and sole heiress to Sir Wm Cobb, of Otteringham, Knt. and had the following issue, born at Beverly; Constance, Feb. 15, 1704; William, Sept. 2, 1705, who died the 6th of August following, and was buried in St. Mary's church there; Dorothy, born Feb. 16, 1708, buried by her brother Feb. 10, 1721; Adriana, born Jan. 24, 1709; Griffith, May 24, 1712; and Francis, Jan. 10, 1718: their mother died at Beverley, aged 43, April 1, 1720, and was interred in St. Mary's church, where a monument is erected to her memory. Sir Francis deceased after a short indisposition, in the 62d year of his age, Sept. 16, 1739, at Burton-Agnes, where he was buried. Constance, his eldest daughter, married April 28, 1741, Ralph Lutton, of Knapton, in Yorkshire, Esq.; whom she survived several years; and dying at York, 1785, was buried at Winteringham, in Yorkshire, by her husband. Francis, second surviving son of Sir Francis, was of Sidney College, Cambridge, and ensign of the guards; he received a considerable estate at Otteringham, from the bountiful generosity of his brother Sir Griffith; married July 26, 1762, Charlotte, daughter of Warton Warton, Esq. of Beverley, (who on the death of his brother, Sir William Pennyman, Bart. April 16, 1768, succeeded to the title) and had issue a son Francis, born April 27, 1764, who married in his minority at York, ———— and has now living a son ————, born ————, and a daughter ————, born ————; Adriana, the third daughter of Sir Francis, died at York, April 30, 1785, and was buried at Beverley, in St. Mary's church, by her mother.

V. Sir GRIFFITH BOYNTON, Bart. eldest surviving son, and heir of Sir Francis; was admitted of Gray's-Inn, April 23, 1730, and married in Audley chapel, April 5, 1742, Anne, daughter of Thomas White, of Walling-Wells, and Tuxford, in Nottinghamshire, Esq. clerk of the ordnance, and member of parliament for Retford, by whom he had one son Griffith, born at Walling-Wells, Feb. 22, 1744, her ladyship only survived her delivery till the 27th, aged 34 years, and was interred at Burton-Agnes. In 1751, Sir Griffith was high sheriff of Yorkshire, and died at Burton-Agnes, the 18th of October, 1761, where he was buried by his lady †.

* Eldest son of Sir Thomas Heblethwayte, Knt. by Barbara, his wife, daughter of Sir George Marwood, of Little Busby, in the north-riding, Knt.

† There is a monument erected for him (executed by Sir Henry Cheere, Bart.), with the following cha-

APPENDIX.

VI. Sir GRIFFITH BOYNTON, Bart. succeeded his father in the eighteenth year of his age, was then of Corpus Christi College, Cambridge; and married, in the cathedral of York, May 9, 1762, Charlotte, eldest daughter of Francis Topham, Esq. LL. D. master of the faculties, and judge of the prerogative courts of York: by her he had, a daughter still-born, Sept. 9, 1767; of whom she deceased, soon after her delivery, in the 29th year of her age, at York, and was buried in the vault at Burton-Agnes. Sir Griffith married secondly, at Burton-Agnes, Aug. 1, 1768, Mary, eldest daughter (born Jan. 5, 1749,) of James Hebelthwayte, Esq. of Norton, and Bridlington, in Yorkshire, and had issue, Griffith, born at Burton-Agnes, July 17, 1769; Francis, born in Berners-street, London, March 28, 1777, on Good-Friday, baptized there; and Henry, born March 22, 1778, (ten weeks and five days after his father's decease) in St. James's-street, London, where he was baptized. In 1771, Sir Griffith, was high sheriff of Yorkshire; that year chosen Fellow of the Antiquarian Society; and May 22, 1772, elected member of parliament for Beverly. He died of a violent fever at London, in St. James's-street, Jan. 6th 1778, and was interred at Burton-Agnes, on the 20th of that month, where a monument was erected for him by his affectionate, and afflicted widow, elegantly designed by (the celebrated poet) the Rev. William Mason; and executed by that late eminent artist, — Bacon, F.R.S. viz. a base of black marble, supporting a large medallion of pure white marble, representing the full length figure of his surviving lady, weeping over her second son Francis: now Sir Francis Boynton, Bart.

racter of him, written by the Rev. Dr. Green (a), Lord Bishop of Lincoln, and late master of Corpus Christi College, Cambridge:

In a vault, near this place, are deposited
The remains of Sir Griffith Boynton, Bart.
Who modestly chose to fill a private station,
With virtues, which would have adorned a public one;
Who, in the several relations of life in which he acted,
Supported in a becoming manner every character
Of a tender Husband, an affectionate Parent,
A generous Brother, a kind Master, a sincere Friend;
Was upright in his intentions, humane in his temper,
Gentle in his behaviour, and candid in his judgment;
Charitable without show, devout without affectation;
Who closed a truly christian and exemplary life,
With that calm resignation,
Which religion alone is capable of inspiring,
When it opens to a good man's view
The certain and joyful prospect of immortality.

(a) In the bishop's letter which accompanied the above, dated Sept. 9, 1762, addressed to Sir Griffith Boynton, Bart. I cannot forbear to transcribe, viz. " I have endeavoured, in the representation I have made, to exhibit, as well as I could, my own idea of my deceased friend. There are but few persons, of whose probity and good meaning so much can be justly said, and I would not have said what I did not think to be true. Inscriptions of this kind can be of no advantage to the dead, but they may be of some use to the living. We are all concerned, and may be all properly excited to imitation, example of so much worth and virtue. It is a particular credit to yourself to have had a father so deservedly esteemed for his many good qualities; and you do well to preserve, as far as monuments of this sort will do it, the remembrance of them."

an infant of nine months laying in her lap; and her eldest son Sir Griffith Boynton, Bart. clasping his mother's arm, his countenance sweetly expressive of filial affection, tenderness of heart, and poignant grief, entreating her to be comforted [*].

VII. Which Sir GRIFFITH BOYNTON, Bart. received the first rudiments of education at Cheam-school, in Surry, and was afterwards, for some years, under the immediate tuition of the Rev. Dr. Langford, at Eton, whose unremitting care and attention towards his pupil, deserve the highest praise and gratitude. Sir Griffith possessed an uncommon retention of memory, obtained a considerable degree of classical knowledge, and evinced an early taste for oratory, which he particularly displayed with much eclat in July 1787, when their Majesties honoured Eton with their presence at election holidays. He was from thence admitted of Trinity College, Cambridge, June 30, 1787, and took an honorary degree of Master of Arts, July —, 1789, on his leaving that seminary, ———— (and not that of LL. D. as recorded in some publications) His amiable disposition, and elegance of manners, (united with the most perfect symmetry of form and features) endeared him to his nearest relations and friends, and attracted universal admiration. At the age of ten years, he was complimented with a deputy-lieutenancy of the east riding of Yorkshire, by the Marquis of Carmarthen, (late Duke of Leeds) lord-lieutenant of that riding. Sir Griffith, married at Winchester, July 30, 1790) having attained his 21st year, on the 17th of that month. Anne[†] Parkhurst, (born Aug. 12, 1763) the sister of his father-in-law, John Parkhurst, Esq. and daughter of the late Capt. Robert Parkhurst, who was son of John Parkhurst, Esq. of Catesby Abby, Northamptonshire, by Ricarde his wife, daugter and coheiress of Rob. Dormer, Esq. a judge of his Majesty's court of common pleas, of Lea-Grange, in the county of Bucks, from which period, closed that perfect scene of harmony, replete with the tenderest affection, which had ever subsisted between mother and son, from the hour of his birth. Sir Griffith, totally secluded himself from society, and the world in general, several years preceding his dissolution, his indisposition was of a short duration; he deceased at Epsom,

---

[*] This inscription was left, with blanks to be filled up, by Sir Griffith Boynton, therefore his widow, Lady Mary Boynton, accordingly paid every due attention to it, otherwise Mr. Mason would have written an epitaph for Sir Griffith's monument.

Sir Griffith Boynton, Bart. born Feb. 22, 1744,
Succeeded his father, Oct. 18, 1761, was the sixth Baronet of
His family. He married, May 9, 1762, Charlotte, eldest
Daughter of Francis Topham, Esq. LL.D. had a daughter
Still born, who died aged 29, Sept. 9, 1767,
And was buried in a vault near this place.
He married secondly, Aug. 1, 1768, Mary, eldest
Daughter of James Heblethwayte, Esq. and had issue
Griffith, born July 17, 1769; Francis, March 28, 1777;
Henry, ten weeks and five days after his father's decease,
March 22, 1778. In 1771, Sir Griffith was high-sheriff of
Yorkshire; that year, chose Fellow of the Antiquarian
Society; and May 22, 1772, elected member of
Parliament for Beverley. He died of a fever at
London, Jan. 6, 1778, and was here interred.

[†] Taken from the parish register, Sheastone, Staffordshire. Baptized Sept. 25, 1763.

in Surry, on the 10th of July 1801, in consequence of the breaking of a blood-vessel in his head, as pronounced by those of the faculty who attended him. His remains were conveyed to Burton-Agnes, and interred in the family vault, on the 28th of that month; attended by his truly affectionate, and disconsolate mother, the Dowager Lady Boynton, with her surviving children. Sir Griffith, dying without issue; he was succeeded in title and estates by his next brother,

VIII. Sir FRANCIS BOYNTON, Bart. the eighth Bart. of his family, who was educated at Eton; and in June 17, 1794, was appointed ensign, in the North York regiment of militia, and is at present, first captain by seniority of rank. His brother Henry, was likewise educated at Eton; and on March 21, 1795, was admitted of Trinity College, Cambridge, and took a degree of Bachelor of Arts, July 6, 1799, he still remains a student of that college, with a view of entering holy orders. Their mother remarried at Burton-Agnes, (where she had resided the six years of her widowhood) to John Parkhurst, of Catesby Abbey, Esq. before mentioned, in the county of Northampton, and by him had issue, six children of whom within the course of three years, 1784, 1785, and 1786, two daughters and one son were still-born; Maria-Anne-Georgiana, born at Washingley-Hall, in the parish of Lutton, Huntingdonshire, Feb. 24, 1788; Lousia-Elizabeth, born there Aug. 6, 1789; George Dormer, born Sept. 3, 1792, at Hutton-Lodge, the seat of his father, in the parish of Hutton-Ambo, in north riding of Yorkshire, and was there baptized. He died of a fever, at Catesby Abbey*, the ancient seat of his father, July 24, 1798, and was interred in the family vault at Upper Catesby, on the 31st of that month, over which is a pyriamidical monument of stone, and on the west side, the following inscription and epitaph, written by his affectionate and distressed mother†.

* See Bridge's History of Northamptonshire.
†. The Poem, entitled, "The Sorrows of Adelina," was also written by her.

Here lieth the remains of George Dormer Parkhurst,
Only son and heir of John George Parkhurst, Esq. and
The dowager Mary Lady Boynton, his wife.
This sweet child was afflicted with a violent inflammatory fever,
Which terminated fatally on the 21st day,
To the inexpressible grief of his affectionate parents.
He was born Sept. 3, 1792, and died July 24, 1798, aged 5 years, 10 months, and 21 days.

To the memory of her beloved and departed child, his disconsolate mother
dedicates these lines:

His soul immortal, now to Heaven resign'd;
To sacred earth his angel form consign'd.
Oh! may that power of Providence divine,
Teach the fond parents at his hallowed shrine,
Calm resignation! soother of the mind,
Alone can plead the cause of human kind;
Give to each heart-felt pang benign relief,
And heal the wreck of agonizing grief.
M. B. July 31, 1798.

APPENDIX.

ARMS—Or, a fess between three cressents, gules*.
CREST—On a wreath, a goat passant, sable, guttee d'argent, beard, horns, and hoofs, or.
MOTTO—*Il tempo passa.*
SEAT—At Burton-Agnes, east riding of Yorkshire: the house circumstantially described by Sir William Dugdale.

* The Quarterings, Sir Francis has selected from those sketched out for him at the College of Arms, and which he at present bears, are: 1, Boynton; 2, Boynton, ancient; 3, Rosells; 4, Del See; 5, Monceaux; 6, Spencer; 7, Griffith; 8, Somervile; and 9, Merley.

TABLE OF BOYNTON.

1, BARTHOLOMEW DE BOYNTON
2, Walter=Anne Thwaytes   John=——Powcher
3, Sir Ingram=A. Craythorne   Bartholomew=——St. Quintin   Anne=Sir Wm. Inglebert
4, Thomas=C. Bradbourne John=——Brigham Isabel=Sir W. Grindall Mary=W. Twyer
5, Sir William=A. Monceaux   Sir Robert=——Salvayne   Mary=William Palsay
6, Sir Ingram=——St. Quintin   Henry=——Wastineys Jane=Sir R. Acton   Ursula=R. Welwick
7, Sir William=J. Wadsley   Anne=J. de Altaripa   Elizabeth=R. Eure
8, John=A. Albimonasterio Thomas=——Constable Jane=Sir F. Prodingham Isabel=J. Thurnholme
9, Sir William=——Brough   John=——Aske   Robert=——Conyers
10, Thomas=——Fitz Randolph   John=A. Brigveild
11, William=——Colvile   Barbara=J. Langton   Thomasine=J. Vincent
12, Sir Ingram   Anabel   Dionysia   Jane
    J. Nevile   N. Mennill   - Pinckney | - Etherington   T. Lawson
13, Sir Walter=——Avatton, or Atton
14, Sir Thomas=——Russell
15, Sir Thomas=M. Speton
16, Henry=Eliz. Conyers=J. Felton

William   17, Thomas   Elizabeth   Jennet
           M. Mirfield   T. Marton   J. Widdesworth
           |
           a Next Table.

APPENDIX.

TABLE OF BOYNTON *continued.*

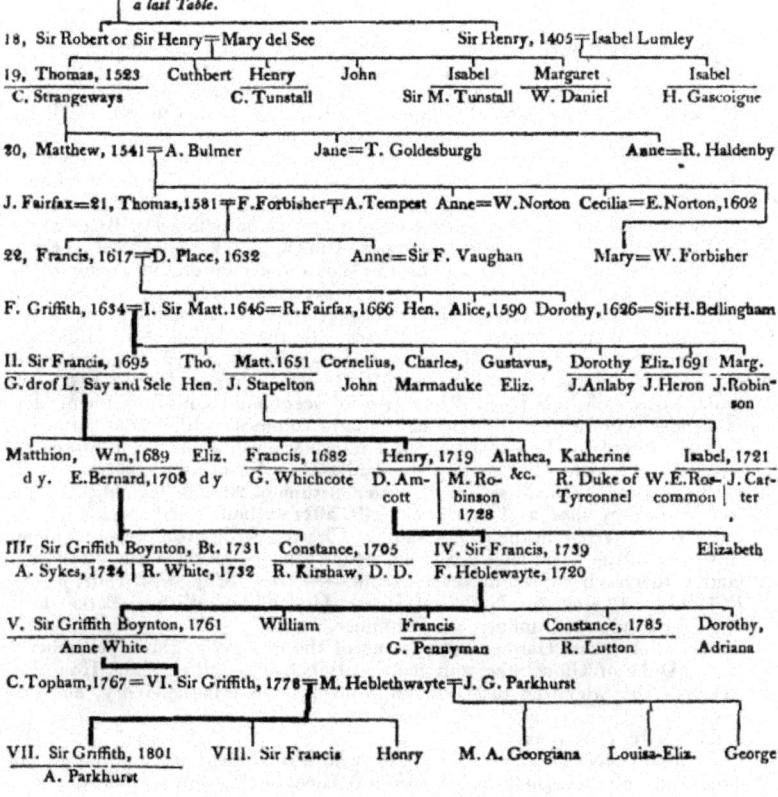

Burdet, of Bramcote,

P. 164, *l.* 1, after THOMAS BURDET, *add*, married first, Honora, daughter of Dr. Michael Boyle, archbishop of Armagh, and chancellor of Ireland, widow first, of Thomas Cromwell, the first Earl of Ardglass, and, secondly of Francis Cuff, Esq.——*Lodge, Vol. III. p.* 380.

APPENDIX.

P. 165, *l.* 26, after Baronet, *add*, and some daughters; Elizabeth was wife, in 1801, of James, brother of Sir William Langham, of Cottesbrooke, Bart.

P. 167. V. Sir FRANCIS BURDET, Bart. married ———, daughter of Thomas Coutts, Esq. and has issue.

Bishopp,

P. 195, *l.* 9, *bottom after* K. B. *add*, from whence she was separated, by a decision of the ecclesiastical court, in consequence of complaints against each other, for *incompatability of temper*, and personal habits, mutually repulsive. These mutual objections, were strongly stated in court, and seemed to indicate unappeasable antipathy; yet, after this public exposition of their grievances, resentments, and aversions, they came together again, and lived with each other, till death produced the final separation. The final pleadings, relative to the citation of Lady Warren, against Sir George, for cruelty, and thereby requiring a separate maintenance, and separation, *a mensa et thoro*, came on before Dr. Bettesworth, in the Prerogative Court, Doctors Commons, June 26, 1772; when after a hearing of eleven hours, the judge thought fit to dismiss the citation, in favour of Sir George Warren, the defendant. Sir George, represented the borough of Lancaster, in parliament, 1758, was K. B. 1761; and conceived he had a claim to the barony of the Earl of Warren, whose arms he bore with the addition of a canton, and accordingly employed the late Mr. Watson, (whom he presented to the rectory of Stockport) with the assistance of the late Mr. Brooke, Somerset Herald, to compile a regular history of those Earls, deducing his descent and claims from them. This work handsomely printed in two large quarto volumes, with costly plates, by Basire, was circulated for correction, and information, but on the death of the author, and ill health of the patron, was laid aside. Sir George, married to his first wife, in June, 1758, Miss Revell, with a fortune of 200,000*l.* she died Feb. 3, 1764: Sir George died at Tunbridge-Wells, after an hour's indisposition. His remains were interred in the family vault at Chester, with great personal pomp, except those of the royal family, the procession was one of the most costly, and attractive, that has been seen for several years.—— *Gent. Mag. Sept.* 1801, *p.* 861.

P. 195, *l.* 13, *read.* Sir Nathaniel Dance Holland, of Witten, Berks, Bart. her first husband was Dummer, *not* Drummer.

P. 201, *l.* 40, after Dormer, *add*, is one of the grooms of the bedchamber to William, Duke of Gloucester, and married Isabella, daughter of the Hon. Felton Harvey, by whom he had William, who died an infant, Henry, and Frederick.

P. 203, after *l.* 4, *read*,

VIII. Sir FRANCIS VINCENT, Bart. who was resident at Venice, and married Mary, only daughter and heiress of Richard Muilman Chiswell, Esq. M. P. for Essex, by whom he had one son, Sir Francis, and one daughter, Anna-Maria, born 1789. He died in 1791, and was succeeded by his son,

IX. Sir FRANCIS VINCENT, Bart. born July 23, 1780, and married, Jan. 16, 1802, Jane, daughter of the Hon. Edward Bouverie, uncle of the present Earl of Radnor.

P. 206, *l.* 2, bottom in note, instead of 1681, *r.* 1581.

APPENDIX.

P. 208, *l.* 7, bottom in note, instead of 1708, *r.* 1668.
P. 222. *l.* 2, after secondly *read*, his brother.
VIII. The Rev. Sir Thomas Hewet, who married Mary, daughter of — Tebbut, of Sudborough, in Northamptonshire, Gent.
P. 226, *l.* 13, instead of *extant are* read, are extant.
P. 230, *l.* 13, instead of *Toolington*, read, Sodington.
L. 14, instead of *veu*. read seven.
P. 241, *l.* 21, after *issue*, add, she was afterwards the wife of Sir Humphrey Monnoux, Bart. and died his widow, at her house, in Little Argyll-street, London, Sept. 1770.
P. 241, *l.* 6, bottom after 1770, add, wife of Col. Roberts, Oct. 15, 1801, of the Bengal establishment, and lieutenant of his Majesty's band of gentleman pensioners.
P. 248, *l.* 10, *read*, Sir Beaumont Hotham, Knt. one of the barons of the Court of Exchequer, who married Susan, daughter of Sir Thomas Hankey, of Clapham, Knt. by whom he has had one son, Beaumont, deceased, who married ———, daughter of Sir John Dyke, Bart. by whom he had two sons, and one daughter, Beaumont, Frances, and George-Frederick; and two daughters, Frances, wife of Captain John Sutton, of the royal navy; and Amelia, of John Woodcock, Esq.
P. 248, *l.* 12, after George, add, lieutenant-colonel, sub-governor to the Prince of Wales, June 8, 1776, treasurer and secretary to the Prince of Wales, 1780, in 1786, he was appointed one of the commissioners for executing the office and receiver general of his revenues. In 1787, secretary and keeper of his privy seal, and seal of his council.
P. 248, *l.* 12, after Beaumont, *read*, 5, Gen. George married Diana, daughter of Sir Warton Pennyman Warton, Bart. by whom he had three sons, and two daughters; 1, George, who married Caroline, daughter of the late Roger Gee, Esq. by whom he had, William, Sarah, George, Charles, and ———, a daughter; 2, William, a captain in the royal navy; 3, Montagu, in the army; 4, Diana; 5, Harriet.
P. 282, *l.* 21, *read*, Sir Henry Harpur, the sixth Baronet, married, July 17, 1754, Lady *Frances-Elizabeth* Greville, *second* daughter of Francis, Earl of Brooke and Warwick.
P. 296, *l.* 3, bottom, after issue, *add*, 1, Charles; 2, Robert; 3, Charlotte 4, Margaretta; 5, Henrietta; 6, William.
P. 303, *last line*, after 1770, *add*, rector of Polbrook, Northamptonshire, married, Sept. 10, 1801, Mrs. Bradford, of Stockton-upon-Tees.
P. 316, after *l.* 25, add, CREST—On a wreath, a lion rampant, guardant.

Stonhouse,

P. 318, *l.* 18, bottom instead of the five next paragraphs, read as follows:
5, Sir John Stonhouse, of Radley, Bart. comptroller of the household, and privy councellor to Queen Anne, and knight of the shire, in several parliaments, for the county of Berks. He married Penelope, daughter of Sir Rob. Dashwood, of Northbrook, in Oxfordshire, Bart. by whom he had three sons, 1, Sir John; 2,

Sir William; 3, Sir James: and six daughters, 1, Catharine, wife, in May, 1745, of Robert Lee, afterwards Earl of Litchfield, she died his widow, March 1, 1784; 2, ———, of the present Lord Rivers; 3, Anne, of Sir William Bowyer, Bart. by whom she had Sir William, an admiral, Sir George, major-general Henry, and Richard, and ———, wife of George Cooke, by whom she had several children; she is now the wife of General Smith; 4, Susanna, wife of Peter Serle, of Teswood, Hants, Esq. by whom she has one daughter, Sukey, wife of Sir William Oglander, of Nunwell, in the Isle of Wight, by whom she has five sons and two daughters; 5, Diana, of the Rev. ——— Bennet; 6, ———, of Arthur Vansittart, of Shotesbrook, in Berks, by whom she had Colonel Arthur, late member for the county; ——— Grosvenor, lost in going to Bengal; George, the present member for Berks; Henry, died at Calcutta, in Bengal, and two daughters, ———, wife of Sir Robert Palk, Bart. and the other was maid of honour to the late Princess Dowager of Wales. Sir John died Oct. 10, 1733, and was succeeded by his eldest son,

6, Sir John Stonhouse, who died unmarried, and was succeeded by his brother,

7, Sir William Stonhouse, Bart. who died unmarried, and was succeeded by his brother,

8, The Rev. Sir James Stonhouse, Bart. who died a bachelor, in 1792.

We now return to James, third son of Sir George, the third Baronet: he married ———, daughter of ———, by whom he had one son ———, who married ———, daughter of ———, by whom he had the Rev. Dr. Sir James, of whom hereafter; and Richard Stonhouse, of Tubney, Berks, who married Anne, daughter of John Saunders, of Uffington, Berks, Esq. by whom he had three daughters; 1, Caroline, wife of John Wattle, of Bengal, by whom she has a daughter, Anne, wife of Thomas Twisleton, son of the late Lord Say and Sele; 2, Sophia, of the Rev. William-Burrel Hayley, rector of Brightland, Sussex, by whom she has several children; 3, Charlotte, of Thomas Field, Esq. governor of Sandown Fort, in the Isle of Wight, descended from Margaret, Countess of Salisbury, daughter of George, Duke of Clarence, brother of King Edw. IV. * by whom she has three sons, 1, Ringsted-Plantagenet Field; 2, Henry-Edward-Plantagenet Field; 3, George-Bridges-Plantagenet Field; and one daughter, Anna-Maria-Plantagenet Field.

* Margaret, Countess of Salisbury, by Sir Richard Poole, of Wales, had four sons; Sir Geoffry, of Lordington, in Sussex, the second son, married Constance, daughter of Sir John Packenham, Knt. by whom, amongst others, he had two sons, Sir Geoffrey, who married Catharine Dutton, by whom he had one daughter, Catharine; and 2, Thomas, of whom hereafter; and one daughter, Margaret, wife of Walter Windsor, Esq. by whom she had one daughter, Winifred, wife of John Gosnold, of Otley, in Suffolk, Esq. who died Feb. 17, 1628, (*Kirby's Suff. Traveller*) by whom she had issue, Robert, the father of Anne, wife of ——— Hovell, by whom she had one daughter, Thomasine, wife of Jacob Chilton, rector of Kettleburgh, in Suffolk, by whom he had one son Jacob, rector of Ufford, rector of Eyke, vicar of Mendlesham, and chaplain to the Duke of Grafton. He left two sons, 1, Richard; 2, Thomas, rector of Eyke, father of Jacob Chilton, rector of Eyke; Richard, the elder son, was vicar of Mendlesham, and father of the Rev. Richard Corbould Chilton, vicar of Mendlesham. John Gosnold, by the said Winifred, had another son, ———, the father or grandfather of two daughters, 1, Mary, wife of John Shepherd, by whom she had Mary, wife of Thomas Peck, who left one son, Thomas Peck, of Mendlesham, Suffolk; 2, Elizabeth, was wife of John Fisk, Esq. who left one son, John Fisk, Esq. who had one daughter ———, the wife of Major J. H. Harrison, of Copford-Hall, Essex, by whom she has nine children.

3, Thomas, second son of Sir Geoffry Poole, married Anne Nevil, by whom he had one son,

The Rev. Sir James Stonhouse, Bart. died unmarried 1792, and was succeded by his cousin, above mentioned.

9, The Rev. Dr. Sir James Stonhouse, Bart. rector of Great and Little Cheveral Wilts. He married, first, —— Niel, daughter of —— Niel, maid of honour to the late Queen Caroline, by whom he had Sir Thomas, the present Baronet; and Sarah, wife of George Vansittart, Esq. the present member for Berks, by whom she has nine children, Sir James married, secondly, ——, daughter of —— Akins, by whom she had several children, two of which are now living, John, in Bengal, married ——, daughter of —— Stevens; and Timothy, married ——, daughter of —— Huntingford; and since the death of his late father, has taken the name of Vigor, for an estate left him by his late brother-in-law, Henry Vigor, Esq. The Rev. Dr. Sir James, died in 1795, aged 80, and was succeeded by his son*,

10, Sir Thomas Stonhouse, the present Baronet.

4, Ralph Poole, who purchased the estate of De Pickmeire, and others in the reign of James I. from George, Earl of Shrewsbury, which has continued ever since in the family, who married Catharine, daughter of his uncle, Sir Geoffery, by whom he had one son,

5, James Poole, who married, first, Catharine, daughter of John Talbot, of Longford, in the county of Shropshire, Esq. who died without issue; secondly, Catharine Peyshall, by whom he had one son,

6, Thomas Poole, Esq. who married Mary Barnett, of Northamptonshire, by whom he had one son,

7, John Poole, of De Picmeire, in Cheshire, Esq. who married Martha, daughter of William Anderton, of Aston, in Cheshire, Esq. by whom he had, four sons and five daughters, 1, John, of Kensington, in Middlesex, who married ——, daughter of Thomas Dutton, of Cheshire, Esq. by whom he had two daughters, Mary, the wife of —— Way, of Devonshire; and Elizabeth, of —— Mair, of Scotland; 2, Thomas, the second son, left a grandson, Thomas, who is a colonel in the East India Company's land service at Madras, and commands the 18th battallion of native infantry; 3, Joseph, married Mary, daughter of —— Jackson, of London, by whom he had, two sons and two daughters, Anderton; James; Margaret; and Susanna; 4, James, was of Teddington, in Middlesex; and married Lucy, daughter of Thomas Rolph, of Bedfordshire, by whom he had one son, John, of Emanuel College, Cambridge, and when he comes of age, will be reckoned amongst one of the richest commoners in England; and one daughter, Catharine, wife of —— Darrell, of Kent: the five daughters of John Poole, were 1, Margaret, wife of —— Burchall, who died without issue; 2, Anne, of —— Penlow, and left one daughter; 3, Katherine, of —— Peters, and died without issue; 4, Martha, of —— Painter, and died without issue; and 5, Mary, wife of Nicholas Field, by whom she has, now living, 1, Thomas; 2, Agustus-John, an officer in the marines, who distinguished himself in the late war, on board the Quebec, commanded by Captain Farmer, in the action with the French frigate, Le Surveillante. He married Anne, daughter of —— Sexton, of Berks, by whom he has three sons; 3, Margaret, wife of the late Charles Long, of Tubney, Berks, who was a lieutenant-colonel of foot, by whom she had one son and four daughters; 4, Mary, of James Anderson, of London, a gentleman of an independent fortune, by whom she has issue, one son John, and one daughter Charlotte. The family of Field, is recorded in the Heralds Office, in Dublin, and brought down to the issue of the late Nicholas Field, Esq. The first that went to Ireland, was John, in the thirteenth century, who was soon afterwards made bayliff of Dublin: he was second son of Nicholas De La Feld, as they then wrote it, who was custos of the Isle of Wight.

ARMS—Or, a lion rampant, gules, armed and azure, charged on the shoulder, with a trefoil, split with two tails, or, a crescent for difference.

CREST—Demy lion, charged on the shoulder, with a trefoil.

MOTTO—*God send grace.*

* The following inscription has been lately placed on a small plain oval monument in All Saints church, Northampton, immediately under that of the Baronet's first wife:

Sacred to the memory
Of her affectionate husband,

APPENDIX.

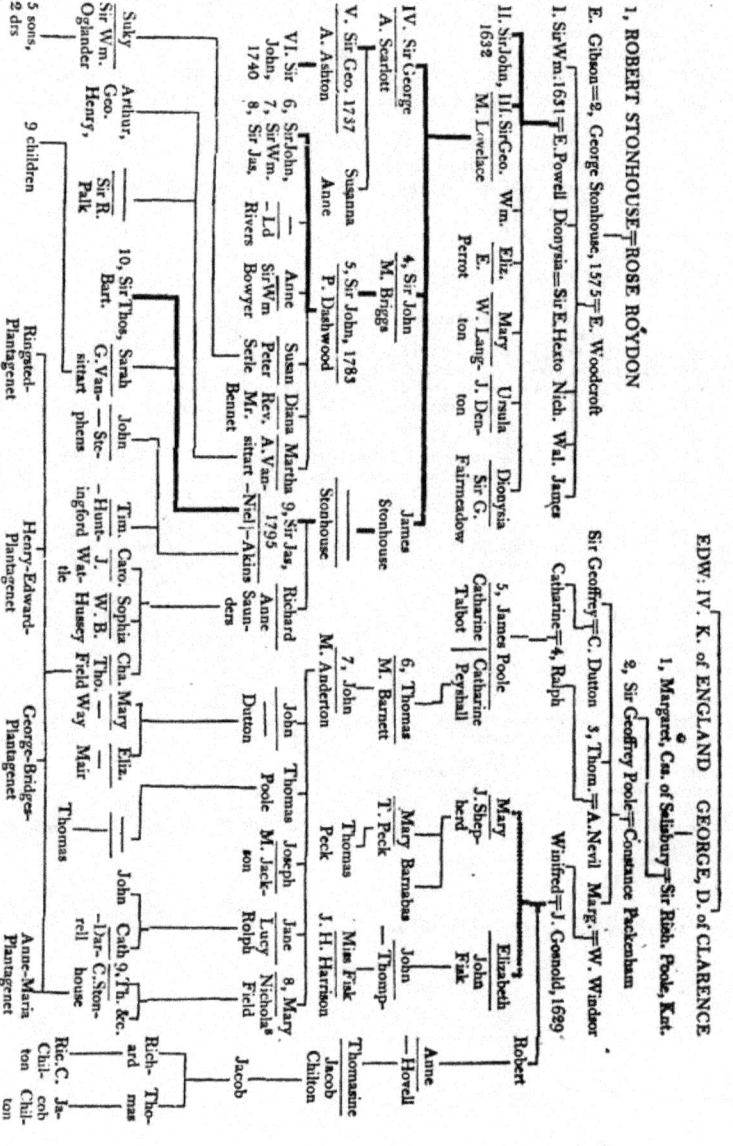

APPENDIX.

Sir James Stonhouse, Bart.
Doctor of Physic;
The projector, friend, and physician,
Of the County Infirmary,
Established in the year 1543;
Where the lame walk, and the sick are healed.
Afterwards,
He was, for many years,
Rector of Great and Little Cheverel, Wiltshire,
And exemplary as a minister.
But in that immortal state
In which he is now entered,
How dear is human excellence!
Reader,
It is his superior honour at this period,
That he was partaker with her
In the christian character,
In the conjugal relation.
He died the 8th day of December, 1795.
In the 80th year of his age

P. 331, *l.* 13, after 1800, *add*, he married ———, by whom he had Colonel Charles Trelawney, who, on the decease of Owen Salisbury Brereton, Esq. took the name of Brereton. He married Maria, sister of Sir Christopher Hawkins, Bart. of Trewithen, in Cornwall, M. P. by whom he has two sons and five daughters, 1, Heywood; 2, Harry-Brereton; 3, John; 4, Catharine; 5, Caroline; 6, Maria; and 7, Letitia. Sophia, second daughter of General Trelawney, was wife (June 10, 1801) of J. L. Freeman, Esq. of Crickmaillyn, Pembrokeshire.

P. 343, *l.* 2, bottom, after Bristol, *add*, by whom she had one son, ———, who married ———, daughter of ——— Dicconton, of Wrightington, in Lancashire, Esq. an old Roman Catholic family, by whom he had one son, the late Colonel Harvey Aston, who married ———, daughter of ———, the late Viscount Irwin. He was killed in a duel at the Cape of Good-Hope about 1798: his father's sister was wife of Mr. Plampin, of Suffolk.

P. 344, the last generation in the table are the children of V. Sir Willoughby Aston, and not of IV. Sir Thomas Aston.

P. 347, *l.* 17, after 1736, add, they lie buried in the family vault of Lord Viscount Hewet, of Gowran, under a neat marble monument thus inscribed:

Here lieth the Honourable Henry Lumley, Esq.
Only brother to Richard, Earl of Scarborough,
Who was in every battle, and at every siege,
As colonel, lieutenant-colonel, or general of the horse,
With King William, or the Duke of Marlborough,
In twenty campaigns in Ireland, Flanders, and
Germany, where he was honoured, esteemed, and
Beloved by our own armies, by our allies, and even
By the enemies, for his singular politeness and

APPENDIX.

Humanity, as well as for all his military virtues and capacity.
He sat long in parliament (for Arundel),
Always zealous for the honour of the crown, and
For the good of his country, and knew no party, but
That of truth, justice, and honour.
He died Governor of the Isle of Jersey, the
18th of October, 1722, in the 63d year of his age.

Here lieth also
Mrs. Frances Lumley, his only dear and beloved
Child, of great beauty and greater hopes, who
Died the 13th of October, 1719, in the 6th year of
Her age, sometime the joy, then the anguish, of
Her fond parents.

He lieth also
Dame Anne Lumley, daughter of Sir William
Wiseman, Bart. of Canfield, in Essex, who set
Up this Monument in 1723, in memory of the
Best of husbands, and her dear child, near whom
She was deposited, An? 1736-7.
She died on the 4th of March, 1736-7, in an
Advanced age. She was a lady possessed of all
Those amiable qualifications which adorn her
Sex, and rendered her, whilst living, the delight
Of all those who had the happiness of her
Acquaintance, by whom her death was greatly
Lamented, as well as by the poor, to whom she
Was, living and dying a most bountiful
Benefactress.

Lodge, Vol. IV. p. 265.

P. 347, *l.* 18, after Suffolk, Esq. *add,* by whom she had six children, 1, Thomas; 2, Joseph; 3, Charles, who in 1744, married ——, daughter of Henry Harcourt, of Pendley, near Tring, in Hertfordshire, Esq. by whom he had one son Colonel Charles Stisted, of Ipswich, Suffolk; and two daughters, Arabella, who died young, and Louisa, the wife of Charles Squire, of Ipswich, Esq.; 4, John; 5, William; and 6, Arabella.

P. 347, *l.* 18, after 1684, *add,* in the 55th year of his age.

l. 25, cross out the whole after *mentioned*, and *add,* was colonel in the Coldstream regiment of foot-guards, and died May 25, 1774, was buried in South Audley Chapel, London, June 3, and was succeeded by,

P. 348, V, Sir William died 1774, not 1784.

P. 353. Instead of the last paragraph before Arms, read as follows:
VI. Sir JOHN-WILLIAM POLE, Bart. who took the name of De la Pole

by his Majesty's sign-manual, and Jan. 9, 1779, married Anne, only daughter of James Templer, of Stover Lodge, in Devonshire, Esq. by whom he had two sons, and one daughter; William-Templer, born Aug. 2, 1782; Mariamne, born Sept. 14, 1783; and John-George, born Dec. 5, 1787. In 1782, Sir John was high-sheriff for the county of Devon, and in 1790, he was returned member of parliament for the borough of West Loo, in Cornwall, and died universally beloved and regretted on the 30th of November, 1799, in the 43d year of his age, and was succeeded in title and estate by his eldest son,

VII. Sir WILLIAM-TEMPLER DE LA POLE, Bart. who is now pursuing his studies at Eton College.

P. 383, last line, put the * after 67.

P. 385, last line, after Leicestershire, *add*, who, after his death, became the wife (Aug. 21, 1798) of the Hon. Philip Pusey, uncle to the Earl of Radnor, and has issue.

P. 401. *l.* 12, Harriet, wife of —— Daniel, M. D. of Exeter, and died in 1801, leaving issue.

   l. 15, read Catharine, eldest daughter.

   l. 8, bottom, after Devonshire, *add*, who died Jan. 1802.

P. 405, *l.* 9, after Lettice, *add*, who died Oct. 7, 1798. The following inscription is put up to her memory:

> In Memory of LETTICE COTTON, younger daughter of Sir
> John Hynde Cotton, Bart. of Maddingley, and Landwade,
> in the county of Cambridge, who died justly and sincerely lamented by her numerous relations and friends, Oct. 18, 1798,
> aged 42 years.

P. 408, *l.* 22, read, had two sons, Sir John, and Montague, who married ——, the only daughter and heiress of Eliab Harvey, of Mark-hall, in Essex, Esq.; and three daughters, Frances, Louisa, and Elizabeth. Sir Roger was succeeded by his eldest son,

VII. Sir JOHN BURGOYNE, Bart. who was a colonel in the 58th regiment of foot, and married Charlotte, eldest daughter of General Johnstone, of Overstone, near Northampton, by whom he had two sons, 1, Sir Montague; 2, Frederick, in the royal navy: and one daughter, Frances, wife (July 11, 1801) of Robert Henley, Lord Ongley: she was afterwards the wife of Hon. Major-General Eyre-Power French, son of Viscount Dunlo, of Ireland. Sir John died in 1786, and was succeeded by his son,

VIII. Sir MONTAGU BURGOYNE, Bart: who (in Nov. 1, 1794) married ——, daughter of —— Burton.

P. 433, *l.* 5, bottom, after Wyndham, *add*, she died Nov. 23, 1799, and he married, thirdly, (April 13, 1801), ——, second daughter of Thomas Hawkins, of Nash Court, in Kent, Esq.

P. 433, *l.* 8, bottom, after Norton-Joseph, *add*, a midshipman of his Majesty's ship Princess Royal, died at Plymouth March 19, 1801.

P. 433, *l.* 16, after Elizabeth, *add*, who died Nov. 10, 1801. Her amiable, benevolent temper, unaffected manners, and cheerful, entertaining conversation, enlivened by a natural turn of humour, and sprightly sallies of unoffending wit, rendered her company very desirable to society in general, and to her own neighbours in particular, who knew the value of her character, and how to estimate those virtues and abilities to which she only seemed unconscious.—*Gent. Mag.*

P. 448, *l.* 26, after York, *add*, rector of Hunsingrove, and vicar of Aldborough, both in that county, who died at Sutton-on-the-Forest, Nov. 1801, aged 82. He was a gentleman well known on the turf, and kept many fine race-horses, some of the best now existing; but, in respect for his clerical character, he always ran them in the names of some other gentlemen. He was reckoned the best whist player in the country.

P. 448, *l.* 5 from bottom, cross out what follows after 1773, and *add*, he married Mary, natural daughter of Robert Benson, Lord Bingley, chancellor of the exchequer in Queen Anne's reign. He left his fine seat of Bramham Park, laid out by the famous Le Notre, to his daughter, born in wedlock, wife of George-Fox Lane, created Lord Bingley 1763; but his only son, Mr. Fox Lane, dying without issue, after the death of Lady Bingley, this house came to Lady Goodricke, for her life only; and what is singular, Sir John Goodricke preferred residing at Bramham Park, and Lady Goodricke at her husband's seat of Ribstone-Hall. After her death, Bramham-hall went to Mr. Fox Lane, a relation of the last Lord Bingley. Sir John was member of parliament for Rippon, and had one son,

Henry Goodricke, Esq. who married a Dutch lady, by whom he had two sons, and three daughters, John; Sir Henry, the present Baronet; Harriet, wife of her cousin Thomas; Mary, of ―― Fairfax, of Gelling-Castle; and several other children. This Henry was a literary character, and was much esteemed by all men of science in or near York, where he lived. He was M. P. for Lymington in 1780, and died before his father. Sir John died Aug. 3, 1789, and was succeeded by his grandson,

VI. Sir HENRY GOODRICKE, Bart. who married ――――, by whom he has issue.

Davie, of Creedy.

P. 455, *l.* 15, for Newnham, *read* Newingham, who was buried May 15, 1627.

   line 2, bottom, after Esq. *add*, who died Oct. 1656.

P. 456, *l.* 1, after He, *add*, was buried Oct. 13, 1654, and
  l. 9, after unmarried, *add*, 1659.
 l. 10, after Esq, *add*, who was buried April 25, 1670.
 l. 11, after He, *add*, died 1678, and
 l. 15, after Esq. *add*, who died 1691.
 l. 18, after Esq. *add*, who was buried at Sandford, April 14, 1725.
 l. 20, after William, *add*, was buried at Sandford April 15, 1725.
 l. 32, after country, *add*, who died in 1713.
  l. 6, bottom, after social, *add*, died Dec. 29, 1727.

Cross out the account of the three last Baronets, and read,

APPENDIX.

VI. Sir JOHN DAVIE, Bart. who, by Elizabeth, daughter of John Acland, of Killiton, im Devonshire, Esq.—(*Hasted's Kent*, Vol. I. p. 269)—who, in 1738, left two sons and two daughters, all minors; 1, Sir John, his successor; 2, William, vicar of Exminster, in Devonshire, who died in 1778. By Bridget, daughter of the Rev —— Bertie, of Kerm, he had two sons and two daughters, John, killed in an engagement on board the Nymph, when she took the Cleopatra frigate; Thomas died of the yellow fever in the West Indies; Frances, the eldest daughter, is the wife of William Henry Beauchamp, Esq.; Bridget, the younger, of —— Beaumont, Esq. The two daughters of Sir John were Anne and Juliana. Sir John died in 1737, and was succeeded by his son,

VII. Sir JOHN DAVIE, Bart. who married Catharine, daughter of John Stokes, of Rill, in Devonshire, Esq. who died in 1776, by whom he had ten children, 1, John, who died young in 1769; 2, Susanna-Cheeke, died 1771, aged six years; 3, Anne, who died the same year, an infant; 4, Catharine, wife of Joseph Hunt, Esq.; 5, Juliana; 6, Elizabeth, died 1792; 7, Frances; 8, John, the present Baronet; 9, William, died 1784, aged ten years; 10, Humphrey-Phineas, now a major in the fifth regiment of foot. Sir John died at Creedy Sept. 18, 1792, aged sixty-two, and was succeeded by his son,

VIII. Sir JOHN DAVIE, Bart. who, on Sept. 6, 1796, married Anne, eldest daughter of Sir William Lemon, Bart. by whom he has three children, John and William, twins, born at Creedy March 8, 1798; and Anne-Jane, born in London, June 19, 1800.

TABLE OF DAVIE.

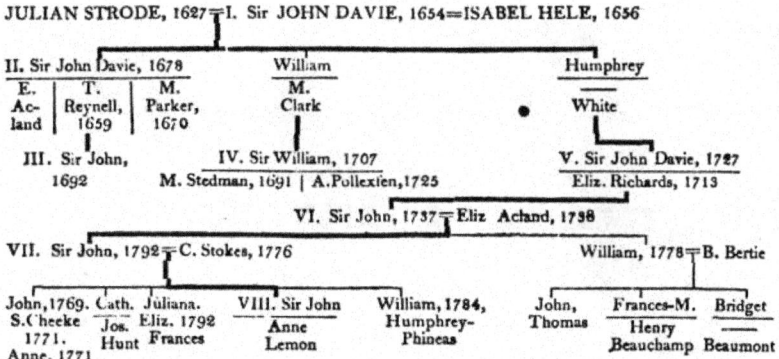

P. 484, the late Sir Wrottesley's eldest daughter, Mary, died unmarried in 1769; his youngest daughter, Harriet, who was also one of the maids of honour

APPENDIX.

to the Queen, was wife of Colonel William Gardener, brother to Viscount Mountjoy, of Ireland. Their sister, Frances, was the wife of the Baron Kutzleben, the minister from the court of Hesse-Cassel.

P. 486, *l.* 5, Frances, the present dowager Lady Wrottesley, was daughter of William Viscount Courtenay.

P. 510, *l.* 5, bottom, *add*, one of these daughters is the wife of John-Shelley Sydney, Esq. of Penhurst Place, Kent.

P. 513, read,

V. Sir CARNABY HAGGERSON, Bart. who married Frances, daughter of William, son of Walter Smythe, brother of Sir Edward Smythe, of Esh, in the county of Durham, Bart.

W: S. BETHAM, Printer, Furnival's-inn-Court, Holborn.

www.ingramcontent.com/pod-product-compliance
Lightning Source LLC
Chambersburg PA
CBHW062123160426
43191CB00013B/2175